COLLEGE & UNIVERSITY ALMANAC

5th Edition

THOMSON
★
PETERSON'S

Australia • Canada • Mexico • Singapore • Spain • United Kingdom • United States

About The Thomson Corporation and Peterson's

With revenues of US$7.2 billion, The Thomson Corporation (www.thomson.com) is a leading global provider of integrated information solutions for business, education, and professional customers. Its Learning businesses and brands (www.thomsonlearning.com) serve the needs of individuals, learning institutions, and corporations with products and services for both traditional and distributed learning.

Peterson's, part of The Thomson Corporation, is one of the nation's most respected providers of lifelong learning online resources, software, reference guides, and books. The Education Supersite^{SM} at www.petersons.com—the Internet's most heavily traveled education resource—has searchable databases and interactive tools for contacting U.S.-accredited institutions and programs. In addition, Peterson's serves more than 105 million education consumers annually.

For more information, contact Peterson's, 2000 Lenox Drive, Lawrenceville, NJ 08648; 800-338-3282; or find us on the World Wide Web at www.petersons.com/about.

COPYRIGHT © 2002 Peterson's, a division of Thomson Learning, Inc.
Thomson Learning™ is a trademark used herein under license.

Previous editions © 1998, 1999, 2000, 2001

Peterson's makes every reasonable effort to obtain accurate, complete, and timely data from reliable sources. Nevertheless, Peterson's and the third-party data suppliers make no representation or warranty, either expressed or implied, as to the accuracy, timeliness, or completeness of the data or the results to be obtained from using the data, including, but not limited to, its quality, performance, merchantability, or fitness for a particular purpose, non-infringement or otherwise.

Neither Peterson's nor the third-party data suppliers warrant, guarantee, or make any representations that the results from using the data will be successful or will satisfy users' requirements. The entire risk to the results and performance is assumed by the user.

ALL RIGHTS RESERVED. No part of this work covered by the copyright herein may be reproduced or used in any form or by any means—graphic, electronic, or mechanical, including photocopying, recording, taping, Web distribution, or information storage and retrieval systems—without the prior written permission of the publisher.

For permission to use material from this text or product, contact us by
Phone: 800-730-2214
Fax: 800-730-2215
Web: www.thomsonrights.com

ISSN 1523-9128
ISBN 0-7689-0834-5

Printed in Canada
10 9 8 7 6 5 4 3 2 1   04 03 02

Contents

A Guide to Good Four-Year Colleges   **1**
   by Ernest L. Boyer, edited by Paul Boyer

Financing a College Education   **7**
   by Don M. Betterton

Federal Financial Aid Programs   **15**

Returning to School: Advice for Adult Students   **19**
   by Sandra Cook, Ph.D.

Using This Book   **27**

Profiles   **33**

Descriptions   **389**

Index   **501**

A Guide to Good Four-Year Colleges

by Ernest L. Boyer, edited by Paul Boyer

When you think of college, you probably imagine the cliché or Hollywood image: a campus filled with ivy-covered buildings, students socializing in the academic quad, and the faint sounds of a professor's voice coming from an open window. Despite this stereotypical picture of what college might look like on the surface, there is no single model of a "good college." Missions and circumstances vary greatly from one campus to another. Each four-year college and university has something different to offer its students. And with increased college costs, you want to be assured that you will get the best value out of the college investment. This makes choosing the right college even more difficult. It may help to know that despite all of the differences among colleges, there are characteristics commonly shared by reputable schools that you should consider in your search.

Although these standards can be used to evaluate any college, you should narrow your list prior to the "test of quality" and put these questions to the schools on your final list. First, consider other facts that may be important to you, such as location or size. As you work through the list, you will find that a great deal of this information can be uncovered by reading material in print and online, as well as by reading literature from individual colleges. In order to come up with the most complete review of a particular school, though, you will need to discuss these items with your guidance counselor, representatives from the colleges, and other advisers.

Some Common Measures of Quality

Every college should be guided by a clear and vital mission. It should understand its unique role in higher education and present itself honestly to prospective students through its literature and other information outlets. An institution cannot be all things to all people, so choices must be made and priorities assigned. What shows the strength of an institution is whether it has clearly defined its focus and, beyond that, whether it has successfully turned those goals into a living purpose for the campus. Of course, you also need to determine if the college's mission matches up with your own goals and values. At the very least, you need to know that you will be comfortable at a college and that it will deliver the type of educational experience you are seeking.

The quality of the undergraduate college is measured largely by the extent of its cooperation with high schools and by its willingness to smooth the transition of students into college. The way you are recruited by a college helps to shape your expectations of that college. A good college conducts its recruitment and selection with the best interests of the student in mind and should, therefore, try to learn more about you than simply your test scores and class rank.

Beyond the admissions process, it is important for a college to continue to demonstrate commitment to you by taking steps to make you feel at home. The first few weeks on campus are a major rite of passage and may have a significant influence on your entire undergraduate experience. In short, you will want to determine whether the freshman year is viewed as something special and whether the college has a well-planned orientation program that addresses the particular concerns of the new student.

Since students need guidance throughout their entire education, a college of quality has a year-round program of academic advising and personal counseling, structured to serve all undergraduates, including part-time and commuting students. You will want to find out if faculty members are available to freshmen to talk about their disciplines and whether or not faculty members give guidance to young students who are considering career choices. A college worthy of commendation works as hard at holding students as it does at getting them to the campus in the first place. You may wish to investigate a college's retention rate over the past five years and find out whether or not it offers guidance programs for students who are having trouble. These are all measures of a college's dedication to its students.

A Planned, Yet Flexible, Curriculum

At a good college, the academic major will broaden rather than restrict the student's perspective, presenting, in effect, an enriched major. An enriched major will answer three essential questions: What are the history and traditions of the field to be examined? What are the social and economic implications to be pursued? What are the ethical and moral issues within the specialty that need to be confronted? Rather than dividing the undergraduate experience into separate camps—general versus specialized education—the curriculum at a college of high quality will bring the two together. Therefore, it is important to determine if the college has a coherent general education sequence—an integrated core—rather than a more loosely connected distribution arrangement. This core academic program should provide not only for an integration of the separate academic principles but also for their application and relationship to life. All colleges impose requirements for graduation, including a set number of credits and some predetermined courses within a major. But within this set of general expectations, there is also room for flexibility. Increasingly, innovative colleges are recognizing the needs and skills of older students, encouraging individual learning, giving credit for experience, and helping students craft their own unique majors. Students should not have to march on to graduation in four years if they have interests, skills, and needs that are not acknowledged by a traditional degree program. New types of students are enrolling, and the location of learning has moved beyond the campus—to the home, the workplace, and around the world. In recognition of this trend, an effective college designs programs that meet new patterns and creates ways to both extend and encourage diversity on the campus.

The Classroom Climate

The undergraduate experience, at its best, encourages students to be active rather than passive learners. In measuring the quality of a college, students should ask if the institution has a climate that encourages independent, self-directed study, where teaching is perceived as more than just lecturing. If a college encourages small discussion sessions in which students work together on group assignments, it may indicate dedication to the undergraduate curriculum. In addition, if undergraduate courses are taught by the most respected and most gifted teachers on campus, it speaks further to this commitment.

Indeed, the strength of the faculty plays a leading role in determining the quality of the undergraduate experience. Students and parents have become increasingly concerned with the balance of time that faculty members spend on research and publishing requirements versus lecturing or advising. To uncover how an institution views this balance, you should ask if good teaching is valued equally with research and if it is an important criterion for tenure and promotion. It is important to know if the college recognizes that some faculty members are great teachers, others great researchers, and still others a blend of both. The central qualities that make for successful teaching are the ones that can be simply stated: command of the material to be taught; a contagious enthusiasm for the play of ideas; optimism about the potential of one's students; and sensitivity, integrity, and warmth as a human being. At a good college, this combination is present in the classroom.

A GUIDE TO GOOD FOUR-YEAR COLLEGES

Devoting Resources to Learning

An institution of high quality is one that supports its mission of learning both financially and philosophically. In doing so, a college should allot ample funds to its library and other educational resources. In terms of its use, one should determine if the library is more than just a study hall and if students are encouraged to spend at least as much time with library resources as they spend in classes. These resources should primarily serve the interests of undergraduate research and not be dominated by narrow scholarly interests of faculty members or graduate students. In addition, computers offer great potential for learning on campus. Many colleges now require that you purchase a computer before coming to campus. Others make terminals available to all students in common areas. Particularly if you are looking to advance in computer-related fields, or if you are inclined toward furthering your computer skills, you will want to know if campus terminals are linked to the Internet and if the college connects technology, the library, and the classroom.

The Campus Culture

A college campus is also a community. A high-quality college will work to make the time spent outside of the classroom as meaningful as the time spent in class. The high-quality college sees academic and nonacademic functions as related and arranges events ranging from lecture series and concerts to sports and student organizations to reinforce the curriculum. These campuswide activities, intended for both faculty members and students, should encourage community, sustain college traditions, and stimulate both social and cultural interaction. Because much learning occurs outside the classroom, it is important to know how accessible faculty members are to their students—not only through office hours, but also elsewhere on the campus, at social or extracurricular functions. In this setting, the academic campus transcends the classroom and is viewed as a place for learning. Beyond the structured programs, the campus culture extends into the residence halls and other social areas on campus. Residential living can be one of the most chaotic parts of campus life, yet it has the potential of being one of the most rewarding. It is a good idea to find out if residence halls also promote a sense of community through organized activities and informal learning.

A Final Word of Advice

In the end, a high-quality college is concerned about outcomes. It asks questions about student development that go beyond the evaluation of skill. But a good college will avoid measuring that which matters least and will focus on the need for students to think clearly, to be well informed, to integrate their knowledge, and to apply what they have learned.

The impact of college extends beyond graduation, and a college of quality will provide placement guidance to its students and follow their careers. These students will be well equipped to put their work in context and adequately prepared to move from one intellectual challenge to another. The undergraduate experience will also have prepared students to see beyond the narrow boundaries of their own interests and discover global connections. The college succeeds as its graduates are inspired by a larger vision, using their newfound knowledge to form values and advance the common good.

When you make your college contacts and campus visits, you now know what questions to ask and what to look for in order to make an informed decision. In doing so, however, you should always take into account your specific goals. In the end, the important thing to remember is that a college of high quality is one that will prepare you for a productive career, but will also offer you values and principles that you can apply *beyond* graduation day.

Financing a College Education
by Don M. Betterton, Director of Undergraduate Aid,
Princeton University

Given the lifelong benefit of a college degree (college graduates are projected to earn in a lifetime an average of $800,000 to $1 million more than those with only a high school diploma), higher education is a very worthwhile investment. However, it is also an expensive one made even harder to manage by cost increases that have outpaced both inflation and gains in family income. This reality of higher education economics means that parental concern about how to pay college costs is a dilemma that shows no sign of getting easier.

Because of the high cost involved (even the most inexpensive four-year education at a public institution costs about $10,000 a year), good information about college budgets and strategies for reducing the "sticker price" is essential. Here you will learn valuable information about the four main sources of aid—federal, state, college, and private. Before you learn about the various programs, however, it will be helpful if you have an overview of how the college financial aid system operates and what long-range financing strategies are available.

Financial Aid
Financial aid refers to money that is awarded to a student, usually in a "package" that consists of gift aid (commonly called a scholarship or grant), a student loan, and a campus job.

College Costs and Qualifying for Need-Based Aid
The starting point for organizing a plan to pay for your college education is to make a good estimate of the yearly cost of attendance. The next step is to evaluate whether or not you are likely to qualify for financial aid based on need. This step is critical, since more than 90 percent of the yearly total of $74 billion in student aid is awarded only after a determination is made that the family lacks sufficient financial resources to pay the full cost of college on their own. To judge your chance of receiving need-based aid, it is necessary to estimate an Expected Family Contribution (EFC) according to a government formula known as the Federal Methodology.

Applying for Need-Based Aid

Because the federal government provides about 75 percent of all aid awarded, the application and need evaluation process is controlled by Congress and the U.S. Department of Education. The application used is called the Free Application for Federal Student Aid, or FAFSA. The FAFSA is your "passport" to receiving your share of the billions of dollars awarded annually in need-based aid. If you think you might qualify for aid, pick up a FAFSA from your high school guidance office after mid-November. The form will ask for the following year's financial data, and it should be filed after January 1, in time to meet the earliest college or state scholarship deadline. Within two to four weeks after you submit the form, you will receive a summary of the FAFSA information, called the Student Aid Report, or SAR. The SAR will give you the EFC and will also allow you to make corrections to the data you submitted.

Students can apply for federal student aid over the Internet using FAFSA on the Web. FAFSA on the Web can be accessed at http://www.fafsa.ed.gov. Both the student and at least one parent should apply for a federal Personal Identification Number (PIN) at http://www.pin.ed.gov. The PIN serves as your electronic signature when applying for aid on the Web.

Many colleges feel that the federal aid system (FAFSA) does not collect or evaluate information thoroughly enough to be used to award their institutional funds. These colleges have made an arrangement with the College Scholarship Service, a branch of the College Board, to establish a separate application system to meet their needs. The application is called PROFILE, and the need formula is the Institutional Methodology. (When used, PROFILE is always in addition to the FAFSA; it does not replace it.) If you apply for financial aid at one of the approximately 400 colleges that uses PROFILE, the admission material will state that PROFILE is required in addition to the FAFSA. You should read the information carefully and file PROFILE to meet the earliest college deadline. Before you can receive PROFILE, however, you must register, providing enough basic information so the PROFILE package can be designed specifically for you. The FAFSA is free, but there is a charge for PROFILE.

Many colleges provide the option to apply for early decision admission. If you apply for this before January 1, which is prior to when FAFSA can be used, follow the college's instructions. Many colleges use either PROFILE or their own application form for early decision candidates.

FINANCING A COLLEGE EDUCATION

Awarding Aid

About the same time you receive the SAR, the colleges you list will receive the FAFSA information so they can calculate a financial aid award in a package that typically includes aid from at least one of the major sources—federal, state, college, or private. In addition, the award will probably consist of a combination of a scholarship or grant, a loan, and a campus job. These last two pieces—loan and job—are called self-help aid because they require effort on the part of the student. Scholarships or grants are outright gifts that have no such obligation.

When you receive an award letter from a college, it is important that you understand each part of the package. For example: How much is gift aid? What are the interest rate and repayment terms of the student loan? How many hours per week does the campus job require? There should be an enclosure with the award letter that answers these kinds of questions. If not, make a list of your questions and call or visit the financial aid office.

Once you understand the terms of each item in the award letter, you should turn your attention to the "bottom line"—how much you will have to pay for each college to which you are admitted. In addition to understanding the aid award, you must have a good estimate of the college budget so that you can accurately calculate how much you and your family will have to contribute (often an aid package does not cover the entire need). If you think that what the college expects you and your family to pay is too high, you should contact the college's financial aid office and ask whether additional aid is available. Many colleges, private high-cost colleges in particular, are enrollment oriented—they are willing to work with families to help make attendance at their colleges possible. If there is still a gap between the expected contribution and what you feel you can pay from income and savings, you are left with two choices. One option is to attend a college where paying your share of the bill will not be a problem. (This assumes that an affordable option was included on the original list of colleges, a wise admission application strategy.) The second is to look into an alternate method of financing, including loans and tuition payment plans. A loan can bring the yearly cost down to a manageable level by spreading payments over a number of years. A tuition payment plan is essentially a short-term loan and allows you to pay the cost over ten to twelve months. It is an option for families who have the resources available but need help with managing their cash flow.

Aid Not Based on Need

Whether or not you qualify for a need-based award, it is always worthwhile to look into merit, or non-need, scholarships from sources

FINANCING A COLLEGE EDUCATION

such as foundations, agencies, religious groups, and service organizations. If you are not eligible for need-based aid, merit scholarships are the only form of gift aid available. If you later qualify for a need-based award, a merit scholarship can be quite helpful in providing additional resources when the aid does not fully cover the costs. Even if the college meets 100 percent of need, a merit scholarship can benefit the student by reducing the self-help (loan and job) portion of an award.

In searching for outside merit-based scholarships, keep in mind that there are relatively few awards (compared to those that are need-based), and most of them are highly competitive. Use the following checklist when investigating merit scholarships:

- Take advantage of any scholarships for which you are automatically eligible based on employer benefits, military service, association or church membership, other affiliations, or student or parent attributes (ethnic background, nationality, etc.). Company or union tuition remissions are the most common examples of these awards.
- Look for other awards for which you might be eligible based on the characteristics and affiliations indicated above, but where there is a selection process and an application required. Computerized searches are available on the Internet. Scholarship directories are useful resources and can be found in bookstores, high school guidance offices, and public libraries.
- Look into national scholarship competitions. High school guidance counselors usually know about these scholarships. Examples of these awards are the National Merit Scholarship, Coca Cola Scholarship, Aid Association for Lutherans, Westinghouse Science Talent Search, and the U.S. Senate Youth Program.
- ROTC (Reserve Officers' Training Corps) scholarships are offered by the Army, Navy, Air Force, and Marine Corps. A full ROTC scholarship covers tuition, fees, and textbook costs. Acceptance of an ROTC scholarship entails a commitment to take military science courses and to serve for a specific number of years as an officer in the sponsoring branch of the service. Competition is heavy, and preference may be given to students in certain fields of study such as engineering or science. Contact an armed services recruiter or a high school guidance counselor for further information.
- Investigate community scholarships. The high school guidance counselor usually has a list of these awards, and announcements are published in the town newspaper. Most common are awards given by such service organizations as the American Legion, Rotary International, and the local women's club.

FINANCING A COLLEGE EDUCATION

- If you are strong academically (for example, a National Merit Commended Scholar or better) or are very talented in fields such as athletics or performing/creative arts, you may want to consider colleges that offer their own merit awards to gifted students they wish to enroll.

In addition to merit scholarships, there are loan and job opportunities for students who do not qualify for need-based aid. Some of the organizations that sponsor scholarships—for example, the Air Force Aid Society—also provide loans.

Work opportunities during the academic year are another type of assistance that are not restricted to aid recipients. Many colleges, after assigning jobs to students on aid, will open campus positions to all students looking for work. In addition, there are usually off-campus employment opportunities available to everyone.

Tuition Tax Credits

Tuition tax credits allow families to reduce their tax bill by the amount of out-of-pocket college tuition expenses. Unlike a tax deduction, which is modified according to your tax bracket, a tax credit is a dollar-for-dollar reduction in taxes paid.

There are two programs: the HOPE Scholarship tax credit and the Lifetime Learning tax credit. As is true of many federal programs, there are many rules and restrictions that apply. You should check with your tax preparer or financial adviser for information about your own particular situation.

HOPE Scholarship

The HOPE Scholarship is a tax credit that applies for the first two years of college. A student must be a dependent and enrolled in at least a half-time program. The party paying the tuition may deduct the net tuition paid after January 1 from his or her federal income tax. The credit equals the first $1000 of qualifying expenses and 50 percent of the next $1000, to a limit of $1500 per eligible student. There is no restriction on how many family members may be eligible for the credit.

Lifetime Learning Tax Credit

The Lifetime Learning tax credit is similar to the HOPE Scholarship, except that it applies to postsecondary education after the first two years of college and to graduate school education as well as training to improve job skills. The maximum credit is 20 percent of the out-of-pocket tuition expense up to $5000. The Lifetime Learning tax credit is limited to one $1000 credit per tax return. (The HOPE Scholarship can be multiplied by the number of eligible students.)

Other Restrictions

There are income limitations for these credits. Joint filers with an Adjusted Gross Income (AGI) of $100,000 or more and single filers with an AGI of $50,000 or more may not claim either tax credit. The credits are scaled down for joint filers with an AGI of more than $80,000 and for single filers with an AGI of $40,000 or more. The credit may not exceed the tax amount. Colleges are responsible for notifying families of the yearly charges against which the tax credit may be applied.

Financing Your College Education

"Financing" means putting together resources to pay the balance due to the college over and above payments from the primary sources of aid—scholarships, student loans, and jobs. Financing strategies are important because the high cost of a college education today often requires you, whether you receive aid or not, to think about stretching the college payment beyond the four-year period of enrollment. For high-cost colleges, it is not unreasonable to think about a 10-4-10 plan: ten years of saving; four years of paying college bills out of current income, savings, and borrowing; and ten years to repay a loan.

Savings

Although saving for college is always a good idea, many families are unclear about its advantages. Families do not save for two reasons. First, after expenses have been covered, many families do not have much money to set aside. An affordable but regular savings plan through a payroll deduction is usually the answer to the problem of spending your entire paycheck every month.

The second reason that saving for college is not a high priority is the belief that the financial aid system penalizes a family by lowering aid eligibility. The Federal Methodology of need determination is very kind to savers. In fact, savings are ignored completely for those who earn less than $50,000.

A sensible savings plan is important because of the financial advantage of saving compared to borrowing. The amount of money students borrow for college is now greater than the amount they receive in grants and scholarships. With loans becoming so widespread, savings should be carefully considered as an alternative to borrowing. Your incentive for saving is that a dollar saved is a dollar not borrowed.

FINANCING A COLLEGE EDUCATION

Borrowing

Once you've calculated your "bottom-line" parental contribution and determined that the amount is not affordable out of your current income and assets, the most likely alternative is borrowing. First determine if you are eligible for a subsidized Stafford or Direct loan. Because no interest is due while a student attends college, these are the most favorable loans. If you are not eligible, look into the unsubsidized Stafford or Direct loan, which does not require a needs test but where the interest is due each year. The freshman year limit (either subsidized or unsubsidized) is $2625.

After you have taken out the maximum amount of student loans, the next step is to look into parental loans. The federal government's parent loan program is called PLUS and is the standard against which other loans should be judged. A local bank that participates in PLUS can give you a schedule of monthly repayments per $1000 borrowed. Use this repayment figure to compare other parental loans available through commercial lenders (including home equity loans), state programs, or colleges themselves. Choose the one that offers the best terms after all up-front costs, tax advantages, and the amount of monthly payments are considered.

Creditworthiness

If you will be borrowing to pay for your college education, making sure you qualify for a loan is critical. For the most part, that means your credit record must be free of default or delinquency. You can check your credit history with a credit bureau and clean up any adverse information that appears.

Making Financial Aid Work for You

This overview is intended to provide you with a road map to help you think about financing strategies and navigate through the complexities of the financial aid process. If there is any chance you will qualify for aid, complete the FAFSA (and PROFILE if required). At the same time, look into merit scholarships. Finally, check out the terms of PLUS and other parental loan options. The key is to understand the financial aid system and to follow the best path for you. The result of good information and good planning should be that you will receive your fair share of the billions of dollars of financial aid available each year and that the cost of college will not prevent you from attending.

Federal Financial Aid Programs

There are a number of sources of financial aid available to students: federal and state governments, private agencies, and colleges themselves. In addition, there are three different forms of aid: grants, work, and loans.

The federal government is the single largest source of financial aid for students. The U.S. Department of Education's student financial aid programs will make more than $61 billion available to about 8.1 million students. There are two federal grant programs—the Federal Pell Grant and the Federal Supplemental Educational Opportunity Grant (FSEOG); three loan programs—the Federal Perkins Loan and the Stafford and Direct loans; and a program that helps colleges provide jobs for students, Federal Work-Study (FWS).

The two grants, Federal Work-Study, Federal Perkins Loan, and two subsidized loan programs—Direct and Stafford—are awarded to students with demonstrated financial need. Interest on the loans is paid by the government during the time the student is in school. For the unsubsidized Direct loan and unsubsidized Stafford loan, the interest begins to accrue as soon as the money is received. There is also a parental loan (PLUS) available.

Federal Pell Grant

The Federal Pell Grant is the largest grant program; almost 4 million students receive awards annually. This grant is intended to be the starting point of assistance for lower-income families. Eligibility for a Federal Pell Grant depends on the Expected Family Contribution (EFC). The amount you receive will depend on your EFC and the cost of education at the college you will attend. The highest award depends on how much the program is funded. The current maximum is $4000.

Federal Supplemental Educational Opportunity Grant (FSEOG)

As its name implies, the Federal Supplemental Educational Opportunity Grant provides additional need-based federal grant money to supplement

FEDERAL FINANCIAL AID PROGRAMS

the Federal Pell Grant. Each participating college is given funds to award to especially needy students. The maximum award is $4000 per year, but the amount you receive depends on the college's policy, the availability of FSEOG funds, the total cost of education, and the amount of other aid awarded.

Federal Work-Study (FWS)

This program provides jobs for students who demonstrate need. Salaries are paid by funds from the federal government as well as the college. You work on an hourly basis in jobs on or off campus and must be paid at least the federal minimum wage. You may earn only up to the amount awarded in the financial aid package.

Federal Perkins Loan

This loan is a low-interest (5 percent) loan for students with exceptional financial need. Federal Perkins loans are made through the college's financial aid office with the college as the lender. Students may borrow a maximum of $4000 per year for up to five years of undergraduate study. They may take up to ten years to repay the loan, beginning nine months after they graduate, leave school, or drop below half-time status. No interest accrues while they are in school, and, under certain conditions (e.g., they teach in low-income areas, work in law enforcement, are full-time nurses or medical technicians, serve as Peace Corps or VISTA volunteers, etc.), some or all of the loan can be canceled or payments deferred.

Stafford/Direct Loans

Stafford and Direct loans have the same interest rates, loan maximums, deferments, and cancellation benefits. A Stafford loan may be borrowed from a commercial lender such as a bank or credit union. A Direct loan is borrowed directly from the U.S. Department of Education.

The interest rate varies annually (there is a maximum of 8.25 percent); the current rate is 5.99 percent during repayment and 5.39 percent while students attend college. If you qualify for a need-based subsidized Stafford loan, the interest is paid by the federal government while you are enrolled in college. There is also an unsubsidized Stafford loan that is not based on need for which you are eligible regardless of your family income.

FEDERAL FINANCIAL AID PROGRAMS

The maximum amount dependent students may borrow in any one year is $2625 for freshmen, $3500 for sophomores, and $5500 for juniors and seniors, with a maximum of $23,000 for the total undergraduate program. The maximum amount independent students can borrow is $6625 for freshmen (no more than $2625 can be in subsidized loans), $7500 for sophomores (no more than $3500 can be in subsidized loans), and $10,500 for juniors and seniors (no more than $5500 can be in subsidized loans). Borrowers must pay a 3 percent fee, which is deducted from the loan proceeds.

To apply for a Stafford loan, you must first complete a FAFSA to determine eligibility for a subsidized loan and then complete a separate loan application that is submitted to a lender. The financial aid office can help in selecting a lender. The lender will send a promissory note where you agree to repay the loan. The proceeds of the loan, less the origination fee, will be sent to your college to be either credited to your account or released to you.

If you qualify for a subsidized Stafford loan, you do not have to pay interest while in school. For an unsubsidized Stafford loan, you will be responsible for paying the interest from the time the loan is established. However, some lenders will permit borrowers to delay making payments and will add the interest to the loan. Once the repayment period starts, borrowers of both subsidized and unsubsidized Stafford loans will have to pay a combination of interest and principal monthly for up to a ten-year period.

PLUS Loans

PLUS is for parents of dependent students to help families who may not have cash readily available to pay their share of the charges. There is no needs test to qualify. The loan has a variable interest rate that cannot exceed 9 percent (the current rate is 6.79 percent). There is no yearly limit; parents can borrow up to the cost of their child's education, less other financial aid received. Repayment begins sixty days after the money is advanced. A 3 or 4 percent fee is subtracted from the proceeds. Parent borrowers must generally have a good credit record to qualify.

PLUS loans may be processed under either the Direct or Stafford system, depending on the type of loan program for which the college has contracted.

AmeriCorps

AmeriCorps is a program for students. Participants work in a public or private nonprofit agency providing service to the community in one of

FEDERAL FINANCIAL AID PROGRAMS

four priority areas: education, human services, the environment, or public safety. In exchange, they earn a stipend between $7400 and $14,800 a year for living expenses and $4725 per year for up to two years to apply toward college expenses. Students can work either before, during, or after they go to college and can use the funds to pay either current educational expenses or repay federal student loans. Speak to a college financial aid officer for more details about this program.

Returning to School:
Advice for Adult Students
by Sandra Cook, Ph.D., Director, University Advising Center, San Diego State University

Many adults think about returning to school for a long time without taking any action. One purpose of this article is to help the "thinkers" finally make some decisions by examining what is keeping them from action. Another purpose is to describe not only some of the difficulties and obstacles that adult students may face when returning to school but also tactics for coping with them.

If you have been thinking about going back to college, and believing that you are the only person your age contemplating college, you should know that approximately 7 million adult students are currently enrolled in higher education institutions. This number represents 50 percent of total higher education enrollments. The majority of adult students are enrolled at two-year colleges.

There are many reasons why adult students choose to attend a two-year college. Studies have shown that the three most important criteria that adult students consider when choosing a college are location, cost, and availability of the major or program desired. Most two-year colleges are public institutions that serve a geographic district, making them readily accessible to the community. Costs at most two-year colleges are far less than at other types of higher education institutions. For many students who plan to pursue a bachelor's degree, completing their first two years of college at a community college is an affordable means to that end. If you are interested in an academic program that will transfer to a four-year institution, most two-year colleges offer the "general education" courses that comprise most freshman and sophomore years. If you are interested in a vocational or technical program, two-year colleges excel in providing this type of training.

Uncertainty, Choice, and Support
There are three different "stages" in the process of adults returning to school. The first stage is uncertainty. Do I really want to go back to school? What will my friends or family think? Can I compete with those 18-year-old whiz kids? Am I too old? The second stage is choice. Once the decision to return has been made, you must choose where you will attend. There are many criteria to use in making this decision. The third stage is support. You have just added another role to your already-too-

RETURNING TO SCHOOL: ADVICE FOR ADULT STUDENTS

busy life. There are, however, strategies that will help you accomplish your goals—perhaps not without struggle, but with grace and humor. Let's look at each of these stages.

Uncertainty

Why are you thinking about returning to school? Is it to:
- fulfill a dream that had to be delayed?
- become more educationally well-rounded?
- fill an intellectual void in your life?

These reasons focus on *personal growth*.

If you are returning to school to:
- meet people and make friends
- attain and enjoy higher social status and prestige among friends, relatives, and associates
- understand/study a cultural heritage, or
- have a medium in which to exchange ideas,

you are interested in *social and cultural opportunities*.

If you are like most adult students, you want to:
- qualify for a new occupation
- enter or reenter the job market
- increase earnings potential, or
- qualify for a more challenging position in the same field of work.

You are seeking *career growth*.

Understanding the reasons why you want to go back to school is an important step in setting your educational goals and will help you to establish some criteria for selecting a college. However, don't delay your decision because you have not been able to clearly define your motives. Many times, these aren't clear until you have already begun the process, and they may change as you move through your college experience.

Assuming that you agree that additional education will be of benefit to you, what is it that keeps you from returning to school? You may have a litany of excuses running through your mind:
- I don't have time.
- I can't afford it.
- I'm too old to learn.
- My friends will think I'm crazy.

RETURNING TO SCHOOL: ADVICE FOR ADULT STUDENTS

- The teachers will be younger than me.
- My family can't survive without me to take care of them every minute.
- I'll be X years old when I finish.
- I'm afraid.
- I don't know what to expect.

And that is just what these are—excuses. You can make school, like anything else in your life, a priority or not. If you really want to return, you can. The more you understand your motivation for returning to school and the more you understand what excuses are keeping you from taking action, the easier your task will be.

If you think you don't have time: The best way to decide how attending class and studying can fit into your schedule is to keep track of what you do with your time each day for several weeks. Completing a standard time-management grid (each day is plotted out by the half hour) is helpful for visualizing how your time is spent. For each 3-credit-hour class you take, you will need to find 3 hours for class plus 6 to 9 hours for reading-studying-library time. This study time should be spaced evenly throughout the week, not loaded up on one day. It is not possible to learn or retain the material that way. When you examine your grid, see where there are activities that could be replaced with school and study time. You may decide to give up your bowling league or some time in front of the TV. Try not to give up sleeping, and don't cut out every moment of free time. There are also a number of smaller ways to divert time to school. Here are some suggestions that have come from adults who have returned to school:

- Enroll in a time-management workshop. It helps you rethink how you use your time.
- Don't think you have to take more than one course at a time. You may eventually want to work up to taking more, but consider starting with one. (It is more than you are taking now!)
- If you have a family, start assigning those household chores that you usually do to them—and don't redo what they do.
- Use your lunch hour or commuting time for reading.

If you think you can not afford it: As mentioned earlier, two-year colleges are extremely affordable. If you cannot afford the tuition, look into the various financial aid options. Most federal and state funds are available to full- and part-time students. Loans are also available. While many people prefer not to accumulate a debt for school, these same people will think nothing of taking out a loan to buy a car. After five or six years, which is the better investment? Adult students who

RETURNING TO SCHOOL: ADVICE FOR ADULT STUDENTS

work should look into whether their company has a tuition-reimbursement policy. There are also an increasing number of private scholarships, available through foundations, service organizations, and clubs, that are focused on adult learners. Your public library and a college financial aid adviser are two excellent sources for reference materials regarding financial aid.

If you think you are too old to learn: This is pure myth. A number of studies have shown that adult learners perform as well as or better than traditional-age students.

If you are afraid your friends will think you're crazy: Who cares? Maybe they will, maybe they won't. Usually, they will admire your courage and be just a little jealous of your ambition (although they'll never tell you that). Follow your dreams, not theirs.

If you are concerned because the teachers or students will be younger than you: Don't be. The age differences that may be apparent in other settings evaporate in the classroom. If anything, an adult in the classroom strikes fear into the hearts of some 18-year-olds because adults have been known to be prepared, ask questions, be truly motivated, and be there to learn!

If you think your family will have a difficult time surviving while you are in school: If you have done everything for them up to now, they might struggle. Consider this an opportunity to help them become independent and self-sufficient. Your family can only make you feel guilty if you let them. You are not abandoning them; you are becoming an educational role model. When you are happy and working toward your goals, everyone benefits. Admittedly, it sometimes takes time for them to realize this. For single parents, there are schools that have begun to offer support groups, child care, and cooperative babysitting.

If you're appalled at the thought of being X years old when you graduate in Y years: How old will you be in Y years if you don't go back to school?

If you are afraid or don't know what to expect: Know that these are natural feelings when one encounters any new situation. Adult students find that their fears usually dissipate once they begin classes. Fear of trying is usually the biggest roadblock to the reentry process.

No doubt you have dreamed up a few more reasons for not making the decision to return to school. Keep in mind that what you are doing is making up excuses, and you are using these excuses to release you from the obligation to make a decision about your life. The thought of returning to college can be scary. Anytime anyone ventures into unknown territory, there is a risk, but taking risks is a necessary component of personal and professional growth. It is your life, and you alone are responsible for making the decisions that determine its course. Education is an investment in your future.

Choice

Once you have decided to go back to school, your next task is to decide where to go. If your educational goals are well defined (e.g., you want to pursue a degree in order to change careers), then your task is a bit easier. But even if your educational goals are still evolving, do not deter your return. Many students who enter higher education with a specific major in mind change that major at least once.

Most students who attend a public two-year college choose the community college in the district in which they live. This is generally the closest and least expensive option if the school offers the programs you want. If you are planning to begin your education at a two-year college and then transfer to a four-year school, there are distinct advantages to choosing your four-year school early. Many community and four-year colleges have "articulation" agreements that designate what credits from the two-year school will transfer to the four-year college and how. Some four-year institutions accept an associate degree as equivalent to the freshman and sophomore years, regardless of the courses you have taken. Some four-year schools accept two-year college work only on a course-by-course basis. If you can identify which school you will transfer to, you can know in advance exactly how your two-year credits will apply, preventing an unexpected loss of credit or time.

Each institution of higher education is distinctive. Your goal in choosing a college is to come up with the best student-institution fit—matching your needs with the offerings and characteristics of the school. The first step in choosing a college is to determine what criteria are most important to you in attaining your educational goals. Location, cost, and program availability are the three main factors that influence an adult student's college choice. In considering location, don't forget that some colleges have conveniently located branch campuses. In considering cost, remember to explore your financial aid options before ruling out an institution because of its tuition. Program availability should include not only the major in which you are interested, but also whether or not classes in that major are available when you can take them.

Some additional considerations beyond location, cost, and programs are:

RETURNING TO SCHOOL: ADVICE FOR ADULT STUDENTS

- Does the school have a commitment to adult students and offer appropriate services, such as child care, tutoring, and advising?
- Are classes offered at times when you can take them?
- Are there academic options for adults, such as credit for life or work experience, credit by examination (including CLEP and PEP), credit for military service, or accelerated programs?
- Is the faculty sensitive to the needs of adult learners?

Once you determine which criteria are vital in your choice of an institution, you can begin to narrow your choices. There are myriad ways for you to locate the information you desire. Many urban newspapers publish a "School Guide" several times a year in which colleges and universities advertise to an adult student market. In addition, schools themselves publish catalogs, class schedules, and promotional materials that contain much of the information you need, and they are yours for the asking. Many colleges sponsor information sessions and open houses that allow you to visit the campus and ask questions. An appointment with an adviser is a good way to assess the fit between you and the institution. Be sure to bring your questions with you to your interview.

Support

Once you have made the decision to return to school and have chosen the institution that best meets your needs, take some additional steps to ensure your success during your crucial first semester. Take advantage of institutional support and build some social support systems of your own. Here are some ways of doing just that:

- Plan to participate in any orientation programs. These serve the threefold purpose of providing you with a great deal of important information, familiarizing you with the campus and its facilities, and giving you the opportunity to meet and begin networking with other students.
- Take steps to deal with any academic weaknesses. Take mathematics and writing placement tests if you have reason to believe you may need some extra help in these areas. It is not uncommon for adult students to need a math refresher course or a program to help alleviate math anxiety. Ignoring a weakness won't make it go away.
- Look into adult reentry programs. Many institutions offer adults workshops focusing on ways to improve study skills, textbook reading, test-taking, and time-management skills.
- Build new support networks by joining an adult student organization, making a point of meeting other adult students through workshops, or

RETURNING TO SCHOOL: ADVICE FOR ADULT STUDENTS

actively seeking out a "study buddy" in each class—that invaluable friend who shares and understands your experience.
- You can incorporate your new status as "student" into your family life. Doing your homework with your children at a designated "homework time" is a valuable family activity and reinforces the importance of education.
- Make sure you take a reasonable course load in your first semester. It is far better to have some extra time on your hands and to succeed magnificently than to spend the entire semester on the brink of a breakdown. Also, whenever possible, try to focus your first courses not only on requirements, but also in areas of personal interest.
- Faculty members, advisers, and student affairs personnel are there to help you during difficult times—let them assist you as often as necessary.

After completing your first semester, you will probably look back in wonder at why you thought going back to school was so imposing. Certainly, it's not without its occasional exasperations. But, as with life, keeping things in perspective and maintaining your sense of humor make the difference between just coping and succeeding brilliantly.

Using This Book

This guide's easy-to-use college profiles are designed to provide you with the data you will need to single out colleges for "the final list." In addition to using resources such as this one, do not underestimate the guidance of your parents, high school guidance counselor, friends, and alumni of the institutions you are considering. Be sure to carefully review the college's viewbook and recruiting literature and make use of the campus visit, especially as a screening tool for your narrowed list.

How to Create Your Final List

If you have a very specific idea of what you want out of a college education, you will have an easier time compiling your list of prospective colleges. By considering some of the following criteria, you will soon find that your initial list of perhaps fifty colleges has been narrowed to a more reasonable number.

1. **Location**. For some students, staying close to home might be a priority. Or, venturing all the way across the country might be something you have always wanted to do and college seems like the perfect time to do it. Likewise, you may know that city life is not for you; therefore, you will need to limit your search to suburban or even rural colleges. Whatever the reason, the location of a college often plays a key role in the college selection process.
2. **Entrance Difficulty**. Many students will look to a college's entrance difficulty as an indication of whether or not they will be admitted. For instance, if you have an excellent academic record, you might wish to primarily consider highly selective colleges. Although entrance difficulty does not necessarily translate into quality of education, it does often indicate whether a college is highly sought-after.
3. **Education Costs**. As the price tag for higher education continues to rise, cost becomes an increasingly important factor when selecting a college. Certainly it is necessary to consider your family's resources when choosing a list of schools to which you might apply. On the other hand, avoid eliminating colleges that you might otherwise consider based solely on cost. You may be able to obtain the necessary financial aid to allow you to enroll in your higher-priced college of choice.

4. **Most Frequently Chosen Baccalaureate Fields**. Despite all of the other factors that might influence your selection, one of the most important is whether a college offers a program in your academic area of interest. Or, conversely, if you have not selected a program at the onset, you will want to find a college with a broad enough selection to satisfy your eventual choice.

Beyond these major factors, you will undoubtedly uncover other criteria that will strongly influence your choice of where to attend college. Questions about a particular institution's size, the diversity of its student body, or special academic programs or services may weigh heavily in the decision process. The straightforward format of the College Profiles makes it easy to gather the facts on all of these points and more, providing you with the answers you need to make the most informed choice.

How Hard Is It to Get In?

The following five levels of entrance difficulty are based on the percentage of applicants who were accepted for fall 2001 freshman admission (or, in the case of upper-level schools, for entering-class admission) and on the high school class rank and standardized test scores of the accepted freshmen who actually enrolled in fall 2001. The colleges were asked to select the level that most closely corresponds to their entrance difficulty, according to these guidelines, to assist prospective students in assessing their chances for admission.

The five levels of entrance difficulty are as follows:

1. **Most difficult:** More than 75% of the freshmen were in the top 10% of their high school class and scored 1250 or higher on the SAT I (verbal and mathematical combined) or 29 or higher on the ACT (composite); about 30% or fewer of the applicants were accepted.
2. **Very difficult:** More than 50% of the freshmen were in the top 10% of their high school class and scored 1150 or higher on the SAT I or 26 or higher on the ACT; about 60% or fewer of the applicants were accepted.
3. **Moderately difficult:** More than 75% of the freshmen were in the top half of their high school class and scored 900 or higher on the SAT I or 18 or higher on the ACT; about 85% or fewer of the applicants were accepted.
4. **Minimally difficult:** Most freshmen were not in the top half of their high school class and scored somewhat below 900 on the SAT I or below 19 on the ACT; up to 95% of the applicants were accepted.

5. **Noncompetitive:** Virtually all applicants were accepted regardless of high school rank or test scores.

Profile Highlights

Setting: Designated as urban (located within a major city), suburban (a residential area within commuting distance of a major city), small town (a small but compactly settled area not within commuting distance of a major city), or rural (a remote and sparsely populated area).

Total enrollment: The number of matriculated undergraduate and (if applicable) graduate students, both full-time and part-time, as of fall 2001.

Student/faculty ratio: The school's estimate of the ratio of matriculated undergraduate students to faculty members teaching undergraduate courses.

Application Deadline: Deadlines and dates for notification of acceptance or rejection are given either as specific dates or as rolling and continuous. Rolling means that applications are processed as they are received, and qualified students are accepted as long as there are openings. Continuous notification means that applicants are notified of acceptance or rejection as applications are processed up until the date indicated or the actual beginning of classes.

Freshmen: Figures are given for the percentage of applicants who were accepted.

Housing: Indicates whether or not on-campus housing is available.

Expenses: *Tuition* is the average basic tuition for an academic year presented as a dollar amount. *Room & board* is the average yearly room and board cost presented as a dollar amount.

Undergraduates: Percentages of undergraduates who are women, part-time students, 25 years or older, Native American (Indian, Eskimo, Polynesian), Hispanic, African American, and Asian American are given.

Most frequently chosen baccalaureate fields: The most popular majors of the 2000 graduating class.

Average class size: The average class size for required undergraduate courses.

Advanced placement: Credit toward a degree awarded for acceptable scores on some or all College Board Advanced Placement tests.

Accelerated degree program: Students may earn a bachelor's degree in three academic years.

Self-designed majors: Students may design their own program of study based on individual interests.

Honors program: Unusually challenging academic program for superior students.

Summer session for credit: Summer courses through which students may make up degree work or accelerate their program.

Part-time degree programs: Students may earn a degree without having to attend classes full-time; part-time degree programs may be offered for students attending regular-session classes (daytime) or evening, weekend, or summer classes.

External degree programs: Students may earn a degree through a program that (1) requires no more than 25% of the degree credit to be earned through campus-located instruction, (2) grants credit for documented extra-institutional and experiential learning, and (3) emphasizes off-campus self-directed study.

Adult/continuing education programs: Courses offered for nontraditional students who are currently working or are returning to formal education.

Cooperative (co-op) education programs: Formal arrangement with off-campus employers allowing students to combine work and study in order to gain degree-related experience, usually extending the time required to complete a degree.

Internships: College-arranged work experience for which students earn academic credit.

Contact: The name, title, mailing address, and telephone number of the person to contact for further information are given at the end of the profile. Toll-free telephone numbers may also be included. The admission office fax number, e-mail address, and Web site may be provided.

The Colleges and Universities in This Guide

The profiles of the colleges and universities include all four-year colleges in the United States that appear in *Peterson's Four-Year Colleges 2003*. The term "four-year college" is the commonly used designation for institutions that grant the baccalaureate, since four years is the normal duration of the traditional undergraduate curriculum. However, some bachelor's programs may be completed in three years, others require five years, and, of course, part-time programs may take a considerably longer period. Also included are upper-level institutions that award the baccalaureate but require that entering students have at least two years of previous college-level credit and, thus, normally require an additional two years to complete a degree program.

Accreditation

To be included in this guide, an institution must have full accreditation or candidate-for-accreditation (preaccreditation) status granted by an institutional or specialized accrediting body recognized by the U.S. Department of Education or the Council on Postsecondary Accreditation. Recognized institutional accrediting bodies, which consider each institution as a whole, are the following: the six regional associations of schools and colleges (Middle States, New England, North Central, Northwest, Southern, and Western), each of which is responsible for a specified portion of the United States and its territories; the Accrediting Association of Bible Colleges (AABC); the Accrediting Council for Independent Colleges and Schools (ACICS); the Accrediting Commission of Career Schools/Colleges of Technology (ACCSCT); The Distance Education and Training Council (DETC); and the Transnational Association of Christian Schools (TRACS). Program registration by the New York State Board of Regents is considered to be the equivalent of institutional accreditation, since the Board requires that all programs offered by an institution meet its standards before recognition is granted. A Canadian institution must be chartered and authorized to grant degrees by the provincial government, affiliated with a chartered institution, or accredited by a recognized U.S. accrediting body. This guide also includes institutions outside the United States, the U.S. territories, and Canada that are accredited by recognized U.S. accrediting bodies. There are recognized specialized accrediting bodies in more than forty different fields, each of which is authorized to accredit specific programs in its particular field. This can serve as the equivalent of institutional accreditation for specialized institutions that offer programs in one field only (schools of art, music, optometry, theology, etc.).

Research Procedures

The data contained in the college indexes and college profiles was collected between fall 2001 and spring 2002 through Peterson's Annual Survey of Undergraduate Institutions. Surveys were sent to the colleges

USING THIS BOOK

and universities that meet the criteria for inclusion outlined above. All data that appears in this edition has been submitted by officials (usually admission and financial aid officers, registrars, or institutional research personnel) at the schools themselves. In addition, the great majority of institutions that submitted data were contacted directly by Peterson's research staff to verify unusual figures, resolve discrepancies, and obtain additional data. All usable information received in time for publication has been included. The omission of any particular item from an index or profile listing signifies that the item is either not applicable to that institution or that data was not available. Because of the comprehensive editorial review that takes place in our offices and because all material comes directly from college officials, we have every reason to believe that the information presented in this guide is accurate at the time of printing. However, students should check with a specific college or university at the time of application to verify such figures as tuition and fees, which may have changed since the publication of this volume.

PROFILES

This section contains quick-reference profiles of colleges and universities, covering such items as background information, entrance difficulty, academic programs, and contact information. The data in each of these profiles, collected from fall 2001 to spring 2002, comes solely from Peterson's Annual Survey of Undergraduate Institutions, which was sent to deans or admissions officers at each institution. The profiles are organized first by region and then by state and arranged alphabetically within those sections by the official names of the institutions.

ALABAMA

ALABAMA AGRICULTURAL AND MECHANICAL UNIVERSITY
NORMAL, ALABAMA

General State-supported, university, coed **Entrance** Minimally difficult **Setting** 2,001-acre suburban campus **Total enrollment** 5,523 **Student-faculty ratio** 21:1 **Application deadline** Rolling (freshmen), rolling (transfer) **Freshmen** 24% were admitted **Housing** Yes **Expenses** Tuition $2820; Room & Board $4500 **Undergraduates** 52% women, 8% part-time, 9% 25 or older, 0.3% Native American, 0.3% Hispanic American, 91% African American, 0.3% Asian American/Pacific Islander **The most frequently chosen baccalaureate fields are** business/marketing, biological/life sciences, education **Academic program** Advanced placement, honors program, summer session, adult/continuing education programs **Contact** Mr. Antonio Boyle, Director of Admissions, Alabama Agricultural and Mechanical University, PO Box 908, Normal, AL 35762. Telephone: 256-851-5245 or toll-free 800-553-0816. Fax: 256-851-9747. E-mail: aboyle@asnaam.aamu.edu. Web site: http://www.aamu.edu/.

ALABAMA STATE UNIVERSITY
MONTGOMERY, ALABAMA

General State-supported, comprehensive, coed **Entrance** Minimally difficult **Setting** 114-acre urban campus **Total enrollment** 5,590 **Student-faculty ratio** 18:1 **Application deadline** 7/30 (freshmen), 7/30 (transfer) **Freshmen** 64% were admitted **Housing** Yes **Expenses** Tuition $2904; Room & Board $3500 **Undergraduates** 58% women, 12% part-time, 15% 25 or older, 0.04% Native American, 0.2% Hispanic American, 93% African American, 0.2% Asian American/Pacific Islander **The most frequently chosen baccalaureate fields are** education, business/marketing, protective services/public administration **Academic program** Advanced placement, honors program, summer session, adult/continuing education programs, internships **Contact** Mrs. Danielle Kennedy-Lamar, Director of Admissions and Recruitment, Alabama State University, PO Box 271, Montgomery, AL 36101-0271. Telephone: 334-229-4291 or toll-free 800-253-5037. Fax: 334-229-4984. E-mail: dlamar@asunet.alasu.edu. Web site: http://www.alasu.edu/.

AMERICAN COLLEGE OF COMPUTER & INFORMATION SCIENCES
BIRMINGHAM, ALABAMA

General Proprietary, comprehensive, coed **Entrance** Moderately difficult **Total enrollment** 11,000 **Application deadline** Rolling (freshmen), rolling (transfer) **The most frequently chosen baccalaureate field is** computer/information sciences **Academic program** Advanced placement, accelerated degree program, honors program, adult/continuing education programs **Contact** Ms. Natalie Nixon, Director of Admissions, American College of Computer & Information Sciences, 2101 Magnolia Avenue, Birmingham, AL 35205. Telephone: 205-323-6191 or toll-free 800-767-AICS. Fax: 205-328-2229. E-mail: admiss@accis.edu. Web site: http://www.accis.edu/.

ANDREW JACKSON UNIVERSITY
BIRMINGHAM, ALABAMA

General Private, comprehensive, coed **Total enrollment** 463 **Student-faculty ratio** 6:1 **Undergraduates** 49% women, 100% part-time, 3% Native American, 3% Hispanic American, 16% African American, 3% Asian American/Pacific Islander **The most frequently chosen baccalaureate fields are** business/marketing, communications/communication technologies **Contact** Ms. Bell Woods, Director of Admissions, Andrew Jackson University, 10 Old Montgomery Highway, Birmingham, AL 35209. Telephone: 205-871-9288. Web site: http://www.aju.edu/.

ATHENS STATE UNIVERSITY
ATHENS, ALABAMA

General State-supported, upper-level, coed **Entrance** Noncompetitive **Setting** 45-acre small-town campus **Total enrollment** 2,573 **Student-faculty ratio** 22:1 **Application deadline** Rolling (transfer) **First-Year Students** 80% were admitted **Housing** Yes **Expenses** Tuition $2730; Room only $900 **Undergraduates** 66% women, 58% part-time, 62% 25 or older, 2% Native American, 0.4% Hispanic American, 11% African American, 0.5% Asian American/Pacific Islander **The most frequently chosen baccalaureate fields are** computer/information sciences, education, protective services/public administration **Academic program** Advanced placement, summer session, adult/continuing education programs, internships **Contact** Ms. Necedah Henderson, Coordinator of Admissions, Athens State University, 300 North Beaty Street, Athens, AL 35611-1902. Telephone: 256-233-8217 or toll-free 800-522-0272. Fax: 256-233-6565. E-mail: henden@athens.edu. Web site: http://www.athens.edu/.

AUBURN UNIVERSITY
AUBURN UNIVERSITY, ALABAMA

General State-supported, university, coed **Entrance** Moderately difficult **Setting** 1,875-acre small-town campus **Total enrollment** 22,469 **Student-faculty ratio** 16:1 **Application deadline** 8/1 (freshmen), rolling (transfer) **Freshmen** 76% were admitted **Housing** Yes **Expenses** Tuition $3380; Room only $2130 **Undergraduates** 48% women, 10% part-time, 6% 25 or older, 0.5% Native American, 1% Hispanic American, 7% African American, 1% Asian American/Pacific Islander **The most frequently chosen baccalaureate fields are** business/marketing, education, engineering/engineering technologies **Academic program** English as a second language, advanced placement, accelerated degree program, honors program, summer session, adult/continuing education pro-

ALABAMA

Auburn University *(continued)*
grams, internships **Contact** Dr. John Fletcher, Acting Assistant Vice President of Enrollment Management, Auburn University, 202 Mary Martin Hall, Auburn University, AL 36849-0001. Telephone: 334-844-4080 or toll-free 800-AUBURN9. E-mail: admissions@mail.auburn.edu. Web site: http://www.auburn.edu/.

AUBURN UNIVERSITY MONTGOMERY
MONTGOMERY, ALABAMA

General State-supported, comprehensive, coed **Entrance** Moderately difficult **Setting** 500-acre suburban campus **Total enrollment** 4,982 **Student-faculty ratio** 18:1 **Application deadline** Rolling (freshmen), rolling (transfer) **Housing** Yes **Expenses** Tuition $3440; Room & Board $4770 **Undergraduates** 64% women, 39% part-time, 26% 25 or older, 1% Native American, 1% Hispanic American, 34% African American, 2% Asian American/Pacific Islander **The most frequently chosen baccalaureate fields are** business/marketing, education, protective services/public administration **Academic program** English as a second language, advanced placement, accelerated degree program, self-designed majors, honors program, summer session, adult/continuing education programs, internships **Contact** Ms. Valerie Samuel, Assistant Director, Admissions, Auburn University Montgomery, PO Box 244023, Montgomery, AL 36124-4023. Telephone: 334-244-3667 or toll-free 800-227-2649 (in-state). Fax: 334-244-3795. E-mail: auminfo@mickey.aum.edu. Web site: http://www.aum.edu/.

BIRMINGHAM-SOUTHERN COLLEGE
BIRMINGHAM, ALABAMA

General Independent Methodist, comprehensive, coed **Entrance** Moderately difficult **Setting** 196-acre urban campus **Total enrollment** 1,424 **Student-faculty ratio** 12:1 **Application deadline** Rolling (freshmen), rolling (transfer) **Freshmen** 92% were admitted **Housing** Yes **Expenses** Tuition $17,185; Room & Board $5980 **Undergraduates** 60% women, 5% part-time, 6% 25 or older, 1% Native American, 1% Hispanic American, 7% African American, 3% Asian American/Pacific Islander **The most frequently chosen baccalaureate fields are** business/marketing, biological/life sciences, visual/performing arts **Academic program** Advanced placement, accelerated degree program, self-designed majors, honors program, summer session, adult/continuing education programs, internships **Contact** Ms. DeeDee Barnes Bruns, Vice President for Admission and Financial Aid, Birmingham-Southern College, Box 549008, Birmingham, AL 35254. Telephone: 205-226-4696 or toll-free 800-523-5793. Fax: 205-226-3074. E-mail: admissions@bsc.edu. Web site: http://www.bsc.edu/.

COLUMBIA SOUTHERN UNIVERSITY
ORANGE BEACH, ALABAMA

General Proprietary, comprehensive, coed **Entrance** Noncompetitive **Total enrollment** 2,200 **Application deadline** Rolling (freshmen), rolling (transfer) **Undergraduates** 98% 25 or older **The most frequently chosen baccalaureate fields are** business/marketing, health professions and related sciences, natural resources/environmental science **Academic program** Adult/continuing education programs **Contact** Mr. Poche Waguespack, Dean of Students, Columbia Southern University, 24847 Commercial Avenue, Orange Beach, AL 36561. Telephone: 334-981-3771 Ext. 110 or toll-free 800-977-8449. E-mail: tommy@columbiasouthern.edu. Web site: http://www.columbiasouthern.edu/.

CONCORDIA COLLEGE
SELMA, ALABAMA

Contact Ms. Gwendolyn Moore, Director of Admissions, Concordia College, 1804 Green Street, PO Box 1329, Selma, AL 36701. Telephone: 334-874-7143. Fax: 334-874-3728.

EDUCATION AMERICA, SOUTHEAST COLLEGE OF TECHNOLOGY, MOBILE CAMPUS
MOBILE, ALABAMA

General Independent, 4-year **Total enrollment** 631 **Student-faculty ratio** 16:1 **Freshmen** 100% were admitted **Housing** No **Expenses** Tuition $24,885 **Undergraduates** 37% women, 47% 25 or older, 0.3% Native American, 1% Hispanic American, 38% African American, 3% Asian American/Pacific Islander **The most frequently chosen baccalaureate field is** business/marketing **Contact** Mr. Randall Olson, Director of Recruitment, Education America, Southeast College of Technology, Mobile Campus, 828 Downtower Loop West, Mobile, AL 36609. Telephone: 251-343-8200 Ext. 221 or toll-free 251-343-8200 Ext. 201 (in-state); 800-866-0850 Ext. 201 (out-of-state). Fax: 251-343-0577. Web site: http://www.educationamerica.com.

FAULKNER UNIVERSITY
MONTGOMERY, ALABAMA

General Independent, comprehensive, coed, affiliated with Church of Christ **Entrance** Minimally difficult **Setting** 75-acre urban campus **Total enrollment** 2,640 **Student-faculty ratio** 19:1 **Application deadline** Rolling (freshmen), rolling (transfer) **Freshmen** 71% were admitted **Housing** Yes **Expenses** Tuition $8700; Room & Board $4300 **Undergraduates** 61% women, 27% part-time, 58% 25 or older, 1% Native American, 1% Hispanic American, 39% African American, 1% Asian American/Pacific Islander **The most frequently chosen baccalaureate fields are** business/marketing, education, law/legal studies **Academic program** Advanced placement, accelerated degree program, summer session, adult/continuing education programs, internships **Contact** Mr. Keith Mock, Director of Admissions, Faulkner University, 5345 Atlanta Highway, Montgomery, AL 36109. Telephone: 334-386-7200 or toll-free 800-879-

ALABAMA

9816. Fax: 334-386-7137. E-mail: admissions@faulkner.edu. Web site: http://www.faulkner.edu/.

HERITAGE CHRISTIAN UNIVERSITY
FLORENCE, ALABAMA

General Independent, comprehensive, coed, affiliated with Church of Christ **Entrance** Noncompetitive **Setting** 43-acre small-town campus **Total enrollment** 166 **Student-faculty ratio** 9:1 **Application deadline** Rolling (freshmen), rolling (transfer) **Freshmen** 100% were admitted **Housing** Yes **Expenses** Tuition $6024; Room only $1300 **Undergraduates** 21% women, 60% part-time, 70% 25 or older, 1% Hispanic American, 10% African American **The most frequently chosen baccalaureate fields are** philosophy, philosophy, religion, and theology **Academic program** Accelerated degree program, summer session, adult/continuing education programs, internships **Contact** Mr. Jim Collins, Director of Enrollment Services, Heritage Christian University, PO Box HCU, Florence, AL 35630-0050. Telephone: 256-766-6610 Ext. 48 or toll-free 800-367-3565. Web site: http://www.hcu.edu/.

HUNTINGDON COLLEGE
MONTGOMERY, ALABAMA

General Independent United Methodist, 4-year, coed **Entrance** Moderately difficult **Setting** 58-acre suburban campus **Total enrollment** 615 **Student-faculty ratio** 12:1 **Application deadline** Rolling (freshmen), rolling (transfer) **Freshmen** 82% were admitted **Housing** Yes **Expenses** Tuition $12,420; Room & Board $5750 **Undergraduates** 65% women, 6% part-time, 12% 25 or older, 1% Native American, 0.3% Hispanic American, 7% African American, 1% Asian American/Pacific Islander **The most frequently chosen baccalaureate fields are** business/marketing, parks and recreation, visual/performing arts **Academic program** Advanced placement, accelerated degree program, self-designed majors, honors program, summer session, adult/continuing education programs, internships **Contact** Mrs. Laura Huncan, Director of Admissions, Huntingdon College, 1500 East Fairview Avenue, Montgomery, AL 36106. Telephone: 334-833-4496 or toll-free 800-763-0313. Fax: 334-833-4347. E-mail: admiss@huntingdon.edu. Web site: http://www.huntingdon.edu/.

INTERNATIONAL BIBLE COLLEGE
See Heritage Christian University

JACKSONVILLE STATE UNIVERSITY
JACKSONVILLE, ALABAMA

General State-supported, comprehensive, coed **Entrance** Minimally difficult **Setting** 345-acre small-town campus **Total enrollment** 8,478 **Student-faculty ratio** 22:1 **Application deadline** Rolling (freshmen), rolling (transfer) **Freshmen** 47% were admitted **Housing** Yes **Expenses** Tuition $2940; Room & Board $3080 **Undergraduates** 58% women, 20% part-time, 25% 25 or older **The most fre-** quently chosen baccalaureate fields are business/marketing, education, protective services/public administration **Academic program** English as a second language, advanced placement, accelerated degree program, honors program, summer session, adult/continuing education programs, internships **Contact** Ms. Martha Mitchell, Freshman Admission and Recruiting, Jacksonville State University, 700 Pelham Road North, Jacksonville, AL 36265. Telephone: 256-782-5363 or toll-free 800-231-5291. Fax: 256-782-5291. E-mail: jsmith@jsucc.edu. Web site: http://www.jsu.edu/.

JUDSON COLLEGE
MARION, ALABAMA

General Independent Baptist, 4-year, women only **Entrance** Moderately difficult **Setting** 80-acre rural campus **Total enrollment** 345 **Student-faculty ratio** 10:1 **Application deadline** Rolling (freshmen), rolling (transfer) **Freshmen** 81% were admitted **Housing** Yes **Expenses** Tuition $8490; Room & Board $5300 **Undergraduates** 16% part-time, 14% 25 or older, 1% Native American, 0% Hispanic American, 11% African American, 1% Asian American/Pacific Islander **The most frequently chosen baccalaureate fields are** business/marketing, biological/life sciences, psychology **Academic program** Advanced placement, accelerated degree program, self-designed majors, honors program, summer session, adult/continuing education programs, internships **Contact** Mrs. Charlotte Clements, Director of Admissions, Judson College, PO Box 120, Marion, AL 36756. Telephone: 334-683-5110 Ext. 110 or toll-free 800-447-9472. Fax: 334-683-5158. E-mail: admissions@future.judson.edu. Web site: http://home.judson.edu/.

MILES COLLEGE
BIRMINGHAM, ALABAMA

Contact Mr. Cornell Howard, Interim Director of Admissions and Recruitment, Miles College, PO Box 3800, Birmingham, AL 35208. Telephone: 205-929-1657.

OAKWOOD COLLEGE
HUNTSVILLE, ALABAMA

General Independent Seventh-day Adventist, 4-year, coed **Entrance** Minimally difficult **Setting** 1,200-acre campus **Total enrollment** 1,778 **Student-faculty ratio** 14:1 **Application deadline** Rolling (freshmen), rolling (transfer) **Freshmen** 55% were admitted **Housing** Yes **Expenses** Tuition $9420; Room & Board $5484 **Undergraduates** 57% women, 11% part-time, 15% 25 or older, 0.3% Native American, 0.4% Hispanic American, 85% African American, 0.3% Asian American/Pacific Islander **The most frequently chosen baccalaureate fields are** biological/life sciences, business/marketing, education **Academic program** Advanced placement, honors program, internships **Contact** Mr. Fred Pullins, Director of Enrollment Management, Oakwood College, 7000 Adventist Boulevard, NW, Huntsville, AL 35896.

ALABAMA

Oakwood College *(continued)*
Telephone: 256-726-7354 or toll-free 800-358-3978 (in-state). Fax: 256-726-7154. E-mail: admission@oakwood.edu. Web site: http://www.oakwood.edu/.

SAMFORD UNIVERSITY
BIRMINGHAM, ALABAMA

General Independent Baptist, university, coed **Entrance** Moderately difficult **Setting** 180-acre suburban campus **Total enrollment** 4,377 **Student-faculty ratio** 13:1 **Application deadline** 8/1 (freshmen), rolling (transfer) **Freshmen** 88% were admitted **Housing** Yes **Expenses** Tuition $11,490; Room & Board $4850 **Undergraduates** 63% women, 7% part-time, 8% 25 or older, 0.5% Native American, 1% Hispanic American, 6% African American, 1% Asian American/Pacific Islander **The most frequently chosen baccalaureate fields are** business/marketing, education, social sciences and history **Academic program** Advanced placement, accelerated degree program, self-designed majors, honors program, summer session, adult/continuing education programs, internships **Contact** Dr. Phil Kimrey, Dean of Admissions and Financial Aid, Samford University, 800 Lakeshore Drive, Samford Hall, Birmingham, AL 35229-0002. Telephone: 205-726-3673 or toll-free 800-888-7218. Fax: 205-726-2171. E-mail: seberry@samford.edu. Web site: http://www.samford.edu/.

SOUTHEASTERN BIBLE COLLEGE
BIRMINGHAM, ALABAMA

General Independent nondenominational, 4-year, coed **Entrance** Moderately difficult **Setting** 10-acre suburban campus **Total enrollment** 202 **Student-faculty ratio** 13:1 **Application deadline** Rolling (freshmen), rolling (transfer) **Freshmen** 52% were admitted **Housing** Yes **Expenses** Tuition $6600; Room & Board $3440 **Undergraduates** 35% women, 24% part-time, 38% 25 or older, 1% Hispanic American, 9% African American **The most frequently chosen baccalaureate fields are** education, liberal arts/general studies, philosophy **Academic program** Advanced placement, summer session, adult/continuing education programs, internships **Contact** Mr. Adam McClendon, Admissions Director, Southeastern Bible College, 3001 Highway 280 East, Birmingham, AL 35243. Telephone: 205-970-9209 or toll-free 800-749-8878 (in-state). Fax: 205-970-9207. E-mail: amcclendon@sebc.edu. Web site: http://www.sebc.edu.

SOUTHERN CHRISTIAN UNIVERSITY
MONTGOMERY, ALABAMA

General Independent, comprehensive, coed, affiliated with Church of Christ **Entrance** Minimally difficult **Setting** 9-acre urban campus **Total enrollment** 420 **Student-faculty ratio** 14:1 **Application deadline** Rolling (freshmen), rolling (transfer) **Housing** No **Expenses** Tuition $8480 **Undergraduates** 32% women, 5% part-time, 87% 25 or older, 1% Native American, 7% Hispanic American, 29% African American, 0% Asian American/Pacific Islander **The most frequently chosen baccalaureate field is** philosophy **Academic program** Advanced placement, accelerated degree program, summer session, adult/continuing education programs, internships **Contact** Mr. Rick Johnson, Director of Enrollment Management, Southern Christian University, 1200 Taylor Road, Montgomery, AL 36117. Telephone: 334-387-3877 Ext. 213 or toll-free 800-351-4040 Ext. 213. E-mail: admissions@southernchristian.edu. Web site: http://www.southernchristian.edu/.

SPRING HILL COLLEGE
MOBILE, ALABAMA

General Independent Roman Catholic (Jesuit), comprehensive, coed **Entrance** Moderately difficult **Setting** 500-acre suburban campus **Total enrollment** 1,483 **Student-faculty ratio** 14:1 **Application deadline** 7/1 (freshmen), 8/10 (transfer) **Freshmen** 77% were admitted **Housing** Yes **Expenses** Tuition $17,230; Room & Board $6170 **Undergraduates** 62% women, 18% part-time, 18% 25 or older, 1% Native American, 4% Hispanic American, 14% African American, 1% Asian American/Pacific Islander **The most frequently chosen baccalaureate fields are** business/marketing, biological/life sciences, communications/communication technologies **Academic program** English as a second language, advanced placement, accelerated degree program, self-designed majors, honors program, summer session, adult/continuing education programs, internships **Contact** Ms. Florence W. Hines, Dean of Enrollment Management, Spring Hill College, 4000 Dauphin Street, Mobile, AL 36608-1791. Telephone: 251-380-3030 or toll-free 800-SHC-6704. Fax: 251-460-2186. E-mail: admit@shc.edu. Web site: http://www.shc.edu/.

STILLMAN COLLEGE
TUSCALOOSA, ALABAMA

Contact Mr. Mason Bonner, Director of Admissions, Stillman College, P.O. Box 1430, 3600 Stillman Boulevard, Tuscaloosa, AL 35403. Telephone: 205-366-8817 or toll-free 800-841-5722. Web site: http://www.stillman.edu/.

TALLADEGA COLLEGE
TALLADEGA, ALABAMA

General Independent, 4-year, coed **Entrance** Minimally difficult **Setting** 130-acre small-town campus **Total enrollment** 540 **Student-faculty ratio** 10:1 **Application deadline** 4/1 (freshmen), rolling (transfer) **Freshmen** 70% were admitted **Housing** Yes **Expenses** Tuition $6752; Room & Board $3395 **Undergraduates** 64% women, 6% part-time, 13% 25 or older, 0% Native American, 0.2% Hispanic American, 98% African American, 0% Asian American/Pacific Islander **The most frequently chosen baccalaureate fields are** biological/life sciences, psychology, social sciences and history **Academic program** Adult/continuing education programs, internships **Contact** Mr. Johnny Byrd, Enrollment Manager,

ALABAMA

Talladega College, 627 West Battle Street, Talladega, AL 35160. Telephone: 256-761-6235 or toll-free 800-762-2168 (in-state); 800-633-2440 (out-of-state). Fax: 256-362-2268. E-mail: be21long@talladega.edu. Web site: http://www.talladega.edu/.

TROY STATE UNIVERSITY
TROY, ALABAMA

General State-supported, comprehensive, coed **Entrance** Moderately difficult **Setting** 577-acre small-town campus **Total enrollment** 6,777 **Student-faculty ratio** 19:1 **Application deadline** Rolling (freshmen), rolling (transfer) **Freshmen** 72% were admitted **Housing** Yes **Expenses** Tuition $3296; Room & Board $4400 **Undergraduates** 60% women, 22% part-time, 23% 25 or older, 1% Native American, 1% Hispanic American, 23% African American, 1% Asian American/Pacific Islander **The most frequently chosen baccalaureate fields are** business/marketing, education, protective services/public administration **Academic program** English as a second language, advanced placement, accelerated degree program, self-designed majors, honors program, summer session, adult/continuing education programs, internships **Contact** Mr. Buddy Starling, Dean of Enrollment Services, Troy State University, Adams Administration Building, Room 134, Troy, AL 36082. Telephone: 334-670-3179 or toll-free 800-551-9716 (in-state). Fax: 334-670-3733. E-mail: bstar@trojan.troyst.edu. Web site: http://www.troyst.edu/.

TROY STATE UNIVERSITY DOTHAN
DOTHAN, ALABAMA

General State-supported, comprehensive, coed **Entrance** Minimally difficult **Setting** 250-acre small-town campus **Total enrollment** 1,855 **Student-faculty ratio** 21:1 **Application deadline** Rolling (freshmen), rolling (transfer) **Freshmen** 58% were admitted **Housing** No **Expenses** Tuition $3296 **Undergraduates** 64% women, 55% part-time, 62% 25 or older, 1% Native American, 2% Hispanic American, 20% African American, 2% Asian American/Pacific Islander **The most frequently chosen baccalaureate fields are** business/marketing, computer/information sciences, education **Academic program** Advanced placement, accelerated degree program, summer session, internships **Contact** Mr. Bob Willis, Director of Enrollment Services, Troy State University Dothan, PO Box 8368, Dothan, AL 36304-0368. Telephone: 334-983-6556 Ext. 205. Fax: 334-983-6322. E-mail: bwillis@tsud.edu. Web site: http://www.tsud.edu/.

TROY STATE UNIVERSITY MONTGOMERY
MONTGOMERY, ALABAMA

General State-supported, comprehensive, coed **Entrance** Noncompetitive **Setting** 6-acre urban campus **Student-faculty ratio** 20:1 **Application deadline** Rolling (freshmen), rolling (transfer) **Housing** No **Expenses** Tuition $3080 **Undergraduates** 59% 25 or older **The most frequently chosen baccalaureate fields are** business/marketing, psychology, social sciences and history **Academic program** Advanced placement, accelerated degree program, self-designed majors, honors program, summer session, adult/continuing education programs **Contact** Mr. Frank Hrabe, Director of Enrollment Management, Troy State University Montgomery, PO Drawer 4419, Montgomery, AL 36103-4419. Telephone: 334-241-9506 or toll-free 800-355-TSUM. E-mail: admit@tsum.edu. Web site: http://www.tsum.edu/.

TUSKEGEE UNIVERSITY
TUSKEGEE, ALABAMA

General Independent, comprehensive, coed **Entrance** Moderately difficult **Setting** 4,390-acre small-town campus **Total enrollment** 2,880 **Student-faculty ratio** 12:1 **Application deadline** 4/15 (freshmen), 4/15 (transfer) **Freshmen** 67% were admitted **Housing** Yes **Expenses** Tuition $10,496; Room & Board $5542 **Undergraduates** 58% women, 6% part-time, 13% 25 or older, 0% Native American, 0.1% Hispanic American, 98% African American, 0.04% Asian American/Pacific Islander **The most frequently chosen baccalaureate fields are** business/marketing, engineering/engineering technologies, social sciences and history **Academic program** English as a second language, honors program, summer session, internships **Contact** Ms. Iolantha E. Spencer, Admissions, Tuskegee University, 102 Old Administration Building, Tuskegee, AL 36088. Telephone: 334-727-8500 or toll-free 800-622-6531. Web site: http://www.tusk.edu/.

THE UNIVERSITY OF ALABAMA
TUSCALOOSA, ALABAMA

General State-supported, university, coed **Entrance** Moderately difficult **Setting** 1,000-acre suburban campus **Total enrollment** 19,130 **Student-faculty ratio** 19:1 **Application deadline** 7/1 (freshmen), rolling (transfer) **Freshmen** 79% were admitted **Housing** Yes **Expenses** Tuition $3292; Room & Board $4110 **Undergraduates** 53% women, 11% part-time, 12% 25 or older, 1% Native American, 1% Hispanic American, 15% African American, 1% Asian American/Pacific Islander **The most frequently chosen baccalaureate fields are** business/marketing, communications/communication technologies, education **Academic program** English as a second language, advanced placement, accelerated degree program, self-designed majors, honors program, summer session, adult/continuing education programs, internships **Contact** Dr. Lisa B. Harris, Assistant Vice President for Undergraduate Admissions and Financial Aid, The University of Alabama, Box 870132, Tuscaloosa, AL 35487-0132. Telephone: 205-348-5666 or toll-free 800-933-BAMA. Fax: 205-348-9046. E-mail: admissions@ua.edu. Web site: http://www.ua.edu/.

ALABAMA

THE UNIVERSITY OF ALABAMA AT BIRMINGHAM
BIRMINGHAM, ALABAMA

General State-supported, university, coed **Entrance** Moderately difficult **Setting** 265-acre urban campus **Total enrollment** 14,686 **Student-faculty ratio** 18:1 **Application deadline** 7/1 (freshmen), 7/15 (transfer) **Freshmen** 91% were admitted **Housing** Yes **Expenses** Tuition $3640; Room & Board $6471 **Undergraduates** 59% women, 32% part-time, 30% 25 or older, 0.3% Native American, 1% Hispanic American, 30% African American, 3% Asian American/Pacific Islander **The most frequently chosen baccalaureate fields are** business/marketing, education, health professions and related sciences **Academic program** Advanced placement, self-designed majors, honors program, summer session, adult/continuing education programs, internships **Contact** Ms. Chenise Ryan, Director of Undergraduate Admissions, The University of Alabama at Birmingham, Office of Undergraduate Admissions, 260 HUC, 1530 3rd Avenue south, Birmingham, AL 35294-1150. Telephone: 205-934-8221 or toll-free 800-421-8743 (in-state). Fax: 205-975-7114. E-mail: uabadmit@uabdpo.dpo.uab.edu. Web site: http://www.uab.edu/.

THE UNIVERSITY OF ALABAMA IN HUNTSVILLE
HUNTSVILLE, ALABAMA

General State-supported, university, coed **Entrance** Moderately difficult **Setting** 376-acre suburban campus **Total enrollment** 6,754 **Student-faculty ratio** 14:1 **Application deadline** 8/15 (freshmen), 8/15 (transfer) **Freshmen** 84% were admitted **Housing** Yes **Expenses** Tuition $3536; Room & Board $4380 **Undergraduates** 50% women, 38% part-time, 29% 25 or older, 2% Native American, 2% Hispanic American, 14% African American, 4% Asian American/Pacific Islander **The most frequently chosen baccalaureate fields are** business/marketing, engineering/engineering technologies, health professions and related sciences **Academic program** English as a second language, advanced placement, accelerated degree program, honors program, summer session, adult/continuing education programs, internships **Contact** Ms. Sabrina Williams, Associate Director of Admissions, The University of Alabama in Huntsville, 301 Sparkman Drive, Huntsville, AL 35899. Telephone: 256-824-6070 or toll-free 800-UAH-CALL. Fax: 256-824-6073. E-mail: admitme@email.uah.edu. Web site: http://www.uah.edu/.

UNIVERSITY OF MOBILE
MOBILE, ALABAMA

General Independent Southern Baptist, comprehensive, coed **Entrance** Moderately difficult **Setting** 830-acre suburban campus **Total enrollment** 1,987 **Student-faculty ratio** 17:1 **Application deadline** Rolling (freshmen), rolling (transfer) **Freshmen** 98% were admitted **Housing** Yes **Expenses** Tuition $8770; Room & Board $4850 **Undergraduates** 68% women, 23% part-time, 22% 25 or older, 2% Native American, 1% Hispanic American, 25% African American, 1% Asian American/Pacific Islander **The most frequently chosen baccalaureate fields are** education, health professions and related sciences, interdisciplinary studies **Academic program** English as a second language, advanced placement, accelerated degree program, honors program, summer session, adult/continuing education programs, internships **Contact** Mr. Brian Boyle, Director of Admissions, University of Mobile, PO Box 13220, Mobile, AL 36663-0220. Telephone: 251-442-2287 or toll-free 800-946-7267. Fax: 251-442-2498. E-mail: adminfo@umobile.edu. Web site: http://www.umobile.edu/.

UNIVERSITY OF MONTEVALLO
MONTEVALLO, ALABAMA

General State-supported, comprehensive, coed **Entrance** Moderately difficult **Setting** 106-acre small-town campus **Total enrollment** 2,935 **Student-faculty ratio** 16:1 **Application deadline** 8/1 (freshmen), rolling (transfer) **Freshmen** 73% were admitted **Housing** Yes **Expenses** Tuition $3974; Room & Board $3576 **Undergraduates** 68% women, 10% part-time, 10% 25 or older, 1% Native American, 1% Hispanic American, 14% African American, 0.5% Asian American/Pacific Islander **The most frequently chosen baccalaureate fields are** business/marketing, education, social sciences and history **Academic program** Advanced placement, accelerated degree program, honors program, summer session, internships **Contact** Mr. William C. Cannon, Director of Admissions, University of Montevallo, Station 66030, Montevallo, AL 35115-6030. Telephone: 205-665-6030 or toll-free 800-292-4349. Fax: 205-665-6032. E-mail: admissions@montevallo.edu. Web site: http://www.montevallo.edu/.

UNIVERSITY OF NORTH ALABAMA
FLORENCE, ALABAMA

General State-supported, comprehensive, coed **Entrance** Minimally difficult **Setting** 125-acre urban campus **Total enrollment** 5,522 **Student-faculty ratio** 21:1 **Application deadline** Rolling (freshmen), rolling (transfer) **Freshmen** 82% were admitted **Housing** Yes **Expenses** Tuition $3678; Room & Board $3662 **Undergraduates** 59% women, 16% part-time, 22% 25 or older, 2% Native American, 1% Hispanic American, 11% African American, 1% Asian American/Pacific Islander **The most frequently chosen baccalaureate fields are** business/marketing, education, social sciences and history **Academic program** English as a second language, advanced placement, accelerated degree program, summer session, adult/continuing education programs, internships **Contact** Mrs. Kim O. Mauldin, Director of Admissions, University of North Alabama, Office of Admissions, Box 5011, Florence, AL 35632-0001. Telephone: 256-765-4680 or toll-free 800-TALKUNA. Fax: 256-765-4329. E-mail: admis1@unanov.una.edu. Web site: http://www.una.edu/.

UNIVERSITY OF SOUTH ALABAMA
MOBILE, ALABAMA

General State-supported, university, coed **Entrance** Moderately difficult **Setting** 1,215-acre suburban campus **Total enrollment** 12,122 **Student-faculty ratio** 22:1 **Application deadline** 8/10 (freshmen), 8/10 (transfer) **Freshmen** 93% were admitted **Housing** Yes **Expenses** Tuition $3070; Room & Board $3746 **Undergraduates** 58% women, 38% part-time, 26% 25 or older, 1% Native American, 1% Hispanic American, 17% African American, 3% Asian American/Pacific Islander **The most frequently chosen baccalaureate fields are** business/marketing, education, health professions and related sciences **Academic program** English as a second language, advanced placement, accelerated degree program, self-designed majors, summer session, adult/continuing education programs, internships **Contact** Ms. Melissa Jones, Director, University of South Alabama, 307 University Boulevard, Mobile, AL 36688-0002. Telephone: 251-460-6141 or toll-free 800-872-5247. E-mail: admiss@jaguar1.usouthal.edu. Web site: http://www.southalabama.edu/.

THE UNIVERSITY OF WEST ALABAMA
LIVINGSTON, ALABAMA

General State-supported, comprehensive, coed **Entrance** Minimally difficult **Setting** 595-acre small-town campus **Total enrollment** 1,974 **Student-faculty ratio** 18:1 **Application deadline** Rolling (freshmen), rolling (transfer) **Freshmen** 69% were admitted **Housing** Yes **Expenses** Tuition $3174; Room & Board $2874 **Undergraduates** 54% women, 8% part-time, 12% 25 or older, 0.5% Native American, 0.4% Hispanic American, 41% African American, 0.1% Asian American/Pacific Islander **The most frequently chosen baccalaureate fields are** business/marketing, biological/life sciences, education **Academic program** Advanced placement, accelerated degree program, honors program, summer session, internships **Contact** Mr. Richard Hester, Vice President for Student Affairs, The University of West Alabama, Station 4, Livingston, AL 35470. Telephone: 205-652-3400 Ext. 3578 or toll-free 800-621-7742 (in-state); 800-621-8044 (out-of-state). Fax: 205-652-3522. E-mail: rhester@uwa.edu. Web site: http://www.uwa.edu/.

VIRGINIA COLLEGE AT BIRMINGHAM
BIRMINGHAM, ALABAMA

General Proprietary, 4-year, coed **Entrance** Moderately difficult **Setting** 1-acre urban campus **Total enrollment** 1,641 **Student-faculty ratio** 10:1 **Application deadline** Rolling (freshmen) **Freshmen** 77% were admitted **Housing** No **Expenses** Tuition $8100 **Undergraduates** 64% women, 75% 25 or older, 0.2% Native American, 1% Hispanic American, 53% African American, 1% Asian American/Pacific Islander **Contact** Ms. Bibbie J. McLaughlin, Director of Admissions, Virginia College at Birmingham, 65 Bagby Drive, PO Box 19249, Birmingham, AL 35209.

Telephone: 205-802-1200 Ext. 207. Fax: 205-802-7045. E-mail: bibbie@vc.edu. Web site: http://www.vc.edu/.

ALASKA

ALASKA BIBLE COLLEGE
GLENNALLEN, ALASKA

General Independent nondenominational, 4-year, coed **Entrance** Minimally difficult **Setting** 80-acre rural campus **Total enrollment** 44 **Student-faculty ratio** 6:1 **Application deadline** 7/1 (freshmen), 7/1 (transfer) **Freshmen** 77% were admitted **Housing** Yes **Expenses** Tuition $4975; Room & Board $4000 **Undergraduates** 34% women, 23% part-time, 30% 25 or older, 11% Native American, 0% Hispanic American, 0% African American, 3% Asian American/Pacific Islander **The most frequently chosen baccalaureate fields are** philosophy, philosophy, religion, and theology **Academic program** Advanced placement, self-designed majors, internships **Contact** Ms. Jackie Colwell, Admissions Officer, Alaska Bible College, Box 289, Glennallen, AK 99588-0289. Telephone: 907-822-3201 or toll-free 800-478-7884. Fax: 907-822-5027. E-mail: info@akbible.edu. Web site: http://www.akbible.edu/.

ALASKA PACIFIC UNIVERSITY
ANCHORAGE, ALASKA

General Independent, comprehensive, coed **Entrance** Moderately difficult **Setting** 170-acre suburban campus **Total enrollment** 632 **Student-faculty ratio** 7:1 **Application deadline** 2/1 (freshmen), 2/1 (transfer) **Freshmen** 96% were admitted **Housing** Yes **Expenses** Tuition $14,480; Room & Board $5647 **Undergraduates** 72% women, 35% part-time, 59% 25 or older, 17% Native American, 4% Hispanic American, 4% African American, 3% Asian American/Pacific Islander **The most frequently chosen baccalaureate fields are** business/marketing, liberal arts/general studies, natural resources/environmental science **Academic program** Advanced placement, accelerated degree program, self-designed majors, summer session, adult/continuing education programs, internships **Contact** Mr. Ernie Norton, Director of Admissions, Alaska Pacific University, 4101 University Drive, Anchorage, AK 99508-4672. Telephone: 907-564-8248 or toll-free 800-252-7528. Fax: 907-564-8317. E-mail: admissions@alaskapacific.edu. Web site: http://www.alaskapacific.edu/.

SHELDON JACKSON COLLEGE
SITKA, ALASKA

General Independent, 4-year, coed, affiliated with Presbyterian Church (U.S.A.) **Entrance** Noncompetitive **Setting** 320-acre small-town campus **Total enrollment** 251 **Student-faculty ratio** 14:1 **Application deadline** 7/15 (freshmen), 7/15 (transfer)

ALASKA

Sheldon Jackson College *(continued)*
Freshmen 66% were admitted **Housing** Yes **Expenses** Tuition $8020; Room & Board $6920 **Undergraduates** 55% women, 47% part-time, 68% 25 or older **Academic program** Advanced placement, self-designed majors, internships **Contact** Ms. Elizabeth Lower, Director of Admissions, Sheldon Jackson College, 801 Lincoln Street, Sitka, AK 99835. Telephone: 907-747-5208 or toll-free 800-478-4556. Fax: 907-747-6366. E-mail: elower@sj-alaska.edu. Web site: http://www.sj-alaska.edu/.

UNIVERSITY OF ALASKA ANCHORAGE
ANCHORAGE, ALASKA

General State-supported, comprehensive, coed **Entrance** Noncompetitive **Setting** 428-acre urban campus **Total enrollment** 15,040 **Student-faculty ratio** 13:1 **Application deadline** Rolling (freshmen), rolling (transfer) **Freshmen** 75% were admitted **Housing** Yes **Expenses** Tuition $2748; Room & Board $5780 **Undergraduates** 61% women, 59% part-time, 62% 25 or older, 10% Native American, 4% Hispanic American, 4% African American, 5% Asian American/Pacific Islander **The most frequently chosen baccalaureate fields are** business/marketing, education, protective services/public administration **Academic program** Advanced placement, self-designed majors, summer session, adult/continuing education programs, internships **Contact** Ms. Cecile Mitchell, Director of Enrollment Services, University of Alaska Anchorage, Administration Building, Room 176, Anchorage, AK 99508-8060. Telephone: 907-786-1558. Fax: 907-786-4888. Web site: http://www.uaa.alaska.edu/.

UNIVERSITY OF ALASKA FAIRBANKS
FAIRBANKS, ALASKA

General State-supported, university, coed **Entrance** Moderately difficult **Setting** 2,250-acre small-town campus **Total enrollment** 7,142 **Student-faculty ratio** 9:1 **Application deadline** 8/1 (freshmen), 8/1 (transfer) **Freshmen** 81% were admitted **Housing** Yes **Expenses** Tuition $3495; Room & Board $4770 **Undergraduates** 59% women, 49% part-time, 33% 25 or older, 16% Native American, 3% Hispanic American, 4% African American, 3% Asian American/Pacific Islander **The most frequently chosen baccalaureate fields are** business/marketing, engineering/engineering technologies, social sciences and history **Academic program** Advanced placement, accelerated degree program, self-designed majors, honors program, summer session, adult/continuing education programs, internships **Contact** Ms. Nancy Dix, Interim Director of Admissions and Enrollment Management, University of Alaska Fairbanks, PO Box 757480, Fairbanks, AK 99775-7480. Telephone: 907-474-7500 or toll-free 800-478-1823 (out-of-state). Fax: 907-474-5379. E-mail: fyapply@aurora.alaska.edu. Web site: http://www.uaf.edu/.

UNIVERSITY OF ALASKA SOUTHEAST
JUNEAU, ALASKA

General State-supported, comprehensive, coed **Entrance** Noncompetitive **Setting** 198-acre small-town campus **Total enrollment** 2,799 **Application deadline** Rolling (freshmen), rolling (transfer) **Housing** Yes **Expenses** Tuition $2062 **Undergraduates** 56% 25 or older **Academic program** Advanced placement, self-designed majors, summer session, adult/continuing education programs, internships **Contact** Mr. Greg Wagner, Director of Admissions, University of Alaska Southeast, 11120 Glacier Highway, Juneau, AK 99801. Telephone: 907-465-6239. Fax: 907-465-6365. E-mail: jyuas@acadi.alaska.edu. Web site: http://www.jun.alaska.edu/.

AL COLLINS GRAPHIC DESIGN SCHOOL
See Collins College: A School of Design and Technology

ARIZONA

AMERICAN INDIAN COLLEGE OF THE ASSEMBLIES OF GOD, INC.
PHOENIX, ARIZONA

General Independent, 4-year, coed, affiliated with Assemblies of God **Entrance** Minimally difficult **Setting** 10-acre urban campus **Total enrollment** 72 **Student-faculty ratio** 6:1 **Application deadline** 8/15 (freshmen), 8/15 (transfer) **Freshmen** 46% were admitted **Housing** Yes **Expenses** Tuition $4330; Room & Board $3480 **Undergraduates** 58% women, 18% part-time, 42% 25 or older, 74% Native American, 6% Hispanic American, 3% African American, 1% Asian American/Pacific Islander **The most frequently chosen baccalaureate fields are** business/marketing, philosophy, philosophy, religion, and theology **Academic program** Internships **Contact** Ms. Sandy Ticeahkie, Admissions Coordinator, American Indian College of the Assemblies of God, Inc., 10020 North 15th Avenue, Phoenix, AZ 85021. Telephone: 602-944-3335 Ext. 234 or toll-free 800-933-3828. Fax: 602-943-8299. E-mail: aicadm@juno.com. Web site: http://www.aicag.org/.

ARIZONA STATE UNIVERSITY
TEMPE, ARIZONA

General State-supported, university, coed **Entrance** Moderately difficult **Setting** 814-acre suburban campus **Total enrollment** 45,693 **Student-faculty ratio** 20:1 **Application deadline** Rolling (freshmen), rolling (transfer) **Freshmen** 87% were admitted **Housing** Yes **Expenses** Tuition $2488; Room & Board $5416 **Undergraduates** 52% women, 21% part-time, 18% 25 or older, 2% Native American, 11% Hispanic American, 3% African American, 5% Asian American/Pacific Islander **The most frequently cho-**

sen baccalaureate fields are business/marketing, communications/communication technologies, social sciences and history **Academic program** Advanced placement, accelerated degree program, honors program, summer session, adult/continuing education programs, internships **Contact** Mr. Timothy J. Desch, Director of Undergraduate Admissions, Arizona State University, Box 870112, Tempe, AZ 85287-0112. Telephone: 480-965-7788. Fax: 480-965-3610. E-mail: ugradinq@asu.edu. Web site: http://www.asu.edu/.

ARIZONA STATE UNIVERSITY EAST
MESA, ARIZONA

General State-supported, comprehensive, coed **Entrance** Moderately difficult **Setting** 600-acre suburban campus **Total enrollment** 2,403 **Student-faculty ratio** 16:1 **Application deadline** Rolling (freshmen), rolling (transfer) **Freshmen** 38% were admitted **Housing** Yes **Expenses** Tuition $2412; Room & Board $4740 **Undergraduates** 50% women, 66% part-time, 37% 25 or older, 2% Native American, 11% Hispanic American, 2% African American, 5% Asian American/Pacific Islander **The most frequently chosen baccalaureate fields are** engineering/engineering technologies, agriculture, home economics/vocational home economics **Academic program** Advanced placement, accelerated degree program, self-designed majors, honors program, summer session, internships **Contact** Ms. Carmen Newland, Program Coordinator (Enrollment), Arizona State University East, 7001 East Williams Field Road #20, Mesa, AZ 85212. Telephone: 480-727-1165 or toll-free 480-965-7788 (in-state). Fax: 480-727-1008. E-mail: carmen.newland@asu.edu. Web site: http://www.east.asu.edu/.

ARIZONA STATE UNIVERSITY WEST
PHOENIX, ARIZONA

General State-supported, upper-level, coed **Entrance** Moderately difficult **Setting** 300-acre urban campus **Total enrollment** 5,804 **Student-faculty ratio** 17:1 **Application deadline** Rolling (transfer) **First-Year Students** 98% were admitted **Housing** No **Expenses** Tuition $2488 **Undergraduates** 71% women, 45% part-time, 49% 25 or older, 2% Native American, 16% Hispanic American, 4% African American, 4% Asian American/Pacific Islander **The most frequently chosen baccalaureate fields are** business/marketing, education, protective services/public administration **Academic program** Self-designed majors, honors program, summer session, adult/continuing education programs, internships **Contact** Ms. B.J. Hart, Manager, Admission Services, Arizona State University West, 4701 West Thunderbird Road, PO Box 37100, Phoenix, AZ 85069-7100. Telephone: 602-543-8093. Fax: 602-543-8312. Web site: http://www.west.asu.edu/.

THE ART INSTITUTE OF PHOENIX
PHOENIX, ARIZONA

General Proprietary, 4-year, coed, primarily men **Entrance** Minimally difficult **Setting** suburban campus **Total enrollment** 1,122 **Student-faculty ratio** 20:1 **Application deadline** Rolling (freshmen), rolling (transfer) **Housing** Yes **Expenses** Tuition $14,304; Room only $5324 **Undergraduates** 36% women, 10% part-time, 25% 25 or older, 2% Native American, 9% Hispanic American, 2% African American, 1% Asian American/Pacific Islander **Academic program** Advanced placement, honors program, internships **Contact** Director of Admissions, The Art Institute of Phoenix, 2233 West Dunlap Avenue, Phoenix, AZ 85021-2859. Telephone: 602-678-4300 Ext. 102 or toll-free 800-474-2479. Fax: 602-216-0439. E-mail: udyavar@aii.edu. Web site: http://www.aipx.edu/.

▶ **For more information, see page 396.**

COLLINS COLLEGE: A SCHOOL OF DESIGN AND TECHNOLOGY
TEMPE, ARIZONA

General Proprietary, 4-year, coed **Setting** 3-acre urban campus **Total enrollment** 1,804 **Application deadline** Rolling (freshmen), rolling (transfer) **Freshmen** 65% were admitted **Housing** Yes **Expenses** Tuition $10,082 **Undergraduates** 32% women, 26% 25 or older, 5% Native American, 19% Hispanic American, 8% African American, 4% Asian American/Pacific Islander **The most frequently chosen baccalaureate field is** visual/performing arts **Contact** Ms. Patti Drace, Director of Admissions and Marketing, Collins College: A School of Design and Technology, 1140 South Priest, Tempe, AZ 85281. Telephone: 480-966-3000 Ext. 147 or toll-free 800-876-7070 (out-of-state). Fax: 480-966-2599. E-mail: jen@alcollins.com. Web site: http://www.collinscollege.edu/.

DEVRY UNIVERSITY
PHOENIX, ARIZONA

General Proprietary, 4-year, coed **Entrance** Minimally difficult **Setting** 18-acre urban campus **Total enrollment** 3,050 **Student-faculty ratio** 27:1 **Application deadline** Rolling (freshmen), rolling (transfer) **Freshmen** 90% were admitted **Housing** No **Expenses** Tuition $8805 **Undergraduates** 24% women, 23% part-time, 43% 25 or older, 5% Native American, 15% Hispanic American, 6% African American, 6% Asian American/Pacific Islander **The most frequently chosen baccalaureate fields are** business/marketing, computer/information sciences, engineering/engineering technologies **Academic program** Advanced placement, accelerated degree program, summer session, adult/continuing education programs **Contact** Mr. Raymond Toledo, Director of Admissions, DeVry University, 2149 West Dunlap, Phoenix, AZ 85021-2995. Telephone: 602-870-9201 Ext. 451 or toll-free 800-528-0250 (out-of-state). Fax: 602-331-1494. E-mail: webadmin@devry-phx.edu. Web site: http://www.devry-phx.edu/.

ARIZONA

EDUCATION AMERICA, TEMPE CAMPUS
TEMPE, ARIZONA

Contact Education America, Tempe Campus, 875 West Elliot Road, Suite 216, Tempe, AZ 85284. Telephone: or toll-free 800-395-4322. Web site: http://educationamerica.com/.

EMBRY-RIDDLE AERONAUTICAL UNIVERSITY
PRESCOTT, ARIZONA

General Independent, comprehensive, coed, primarily men **Entrance** Moderately difficult **Setting** 547-acre small-town campus **Total enrollment** 1,740 **Student-faculty ratio** 18:1 **Application deadline** Rolling (freshmen), rolling (transfer) **Freshmen** 79% were admitted **Housing** Yes **Expenses** Tuition $18,210; Room & Board $5040 **Undergraduates** 16% women, 9% part-time, 10% 25 or older, 1% Native American, 5% Hispanic American, 1% African American, 6% Asian American/Pacific Islander **The most frequently chosen baccalaureate fields are** engineering/engineering technologies, computer/information sciences, trade and industry **Academic program** English as a second language, advanced placement, summer session, adult/continuing education programs, internships **Contact** Bill Thompson, Director of Admissions, Embry-Riddle Aeronautical University, 3200 Willow Creek Road, Prescott, AZ 86301. Telephone: 928-777-6692 or toll-free 800-888-3728. Fax: 928-777-6606. E-mail: admit@pc.erau.edu. Web site: http://www.embryriddle.edu/.

GRAND CANYON UNIVERSITY
PHOENIX, ARIZONA

General Independent Southern Baptist, comprehensive, coed **Entrance** Moderately difficult **Setting** 90-acre suburban campus **Total enrollment** 4,113 **Student-faculty ratio** 16:1 **Application deadline** Rolling (freshmen), rolling (transfer) **Freshmen** 69% were admitted **Housing** Yes **Expenses** Tuition $10,500; Room & Board $4500 **Undergraduates** 64% women, 18% part-time, 30% 25 or older, 1% Native American, 7% Hispanic American, 3% African American, 2% Asian American/Pacific Islander **The most frequently chosen baccalaureate fields are** business/marketing, education, health professions and related sciences **Academic program** English as a second language, advanced placement, accelerated degree program, honors program, summer session, adult/continuing education programs, internships **Contact** Mrs. April Chapman, Director of Admissions, Grand Canyon University, 3300 West Camelback Road, PO Box 11097, Phoenix, AZ 86017-3030. Telephone: 602-589-2855 Ext. 2811 or toll-free 800-800-9776 (in-state). Fax: 602-589-2580. E-mail: admiss@grand-canyon.edu. Web site: http://www.grand-canyon.edu/.

INTERNATIONAL BAPTIST COLLEGE
TEMPE, ARIZONA

General Independent Baptist, comprehensive, coed **Entrance** Minimally difficult **Setting** 12-acre suburban campus **Total enrollment** 65 **Application deadline** Rolling (freshmen), rolling (transfer) **Housing** Yes **Expenses** Tuition $4350; Room & Board $3000 **Undergraduates** 0% Native American, 8% Hispanic American, 6% African American, 4% Asian American/Pacific Islander **Contact** Dr. Stanley Bushey, Administrative Services Director, International Baptist College, 2150 East Southern Avenue, Tempe, AZ 85282. Telephone: 480-838-7070 or toll-free 800-422-4858. Fax: 480-838-1533.

METROPOLITAN COLLEGE OF COURT REPORTING
PHOENIX, ARIZONA

General Proprietary, 4-year, coed, primarily women **Setting** 1-acre suburban campus **Total enrollment** 118 **Student-faculty ratio** 12:1 **Freshmen** 100% were admitted **Housing** No **Expenses** Tuition $5990 **Undergraduates** 97% women, 85% 25 or older **Academic program** Accelerated degree program, summer session, adult/continuing education programs, internships **Contact** Ms. Shannon Buchanan, Admissions, Metropolitan College of Court Reporting, 4640 East Elwood Street, Suite 12, Phoenix, AZ 85040. Telephone: 480-955-5900. Fax: 480-894-8999. Web site: http://www.metropolitancollege.edu/.

NORTHCENTRAL UNIVERSITY
PRESCOTT, ARIZONA

Contact Northcentral University, 600 East Gurley Street #E, Prescott, AZ 86301. Telephone: or toll-free 800-903-9381. Web site: http://www.ncu.edu/.

NORTHERN ARIZONA UNIVERSITY
FLAGSTAFF, ARIZONA

General State-supported, university, coed **Entrance** Moderately difficult **Setting** 730-acre small-town campus **Total enrollment** 19,728 **Student-faculty ratio** 17:1 **Application deadline** Rolling (freshmen), rolling (transfer) **Freshmen** 80% were admitted **Housing** Yes **Expenses** Tuition $2488; Room & Board $4910 **Undergraduates** 60% women, 16% part-time, 15% 25 or older, 7% Native American, 10% Hispanic American, 2% African American, 2% Asian American/Pacific Islander **The most frequently chosen baccalaureate fields are** business/marketing, education, liberal arts/general studies **Academic program** English as a second language, advanced placement, accelerated degree program, honors program, summer session, internships **Contact** Ms. Pamela Van Wyck, Assistant Director, Northern Arizona University, PO Box 4084, Flagstaff, AZ 86011. Telephone: 928-523-6008 or toll-free 888-MORE-NAU. Fax: 928-523-6023. E-mail: undergraduate.admissions@nau.edu. Web site: http://www.nau.edu/.

PRESCOTT COLLEGE
PRESCOTT, ARIZONA

General Independent, comprehensive, coed **Entrance** Moderately difficult **Setting** small-town campus **Total**

ARIZONA

enrollment 1,005 **Student-faculty ratio** 12:1 **Application deadline** 2/1 (freshmen), 2/1 (transfer) **Housing** No **Expenses Tuition** $14,055 **Undergraduates** 59% women, 11% part-time, 39% 25 or older, 5% Native American, 3% Hispanic American, 1% African American, 1% Asian American/Pacific Islander **The most frequently chosen baccalaureate fields are** education, parks and recreation, protective services/public administration **Academic program** Advanced placement, accelerated degree program, self-designed majors, summer session, adult/continuing education programs, internships **Contact** Ms. Shari Sterling, Director of Admissions, Prescott College, 220 Grove Avenue, Prescott, AZ 86301-2990. Telephone: 928-778-2090 Ext. 2101 or toll-free 800-628-6364 (out-of-state). Fax: 928-776-5137. E-mail: rdpadmissions@prescott.edu. Web site: http://www.prescott.edu/.

SOUTHWESTERN COLLEGE
PHOENIX, ARIZONA

General Independent Conservative Baptist, 4-year, coed **Entrance** Minimally difficult **Setting** 19-acre urban campus **Total enrollment** 309 **Student-faculty ratio** 24:1 **Application deadline** 8/15 (freshmen), 8/15 (transfer) **Freshmen** 66% were admitted **Housing** Yes **Expenses Tuition** $8850; Room & Board $3630 **Undergraduates** 55% women, 11% part-time, 17% 25 or older, 1% Native American, 5% Hispanic American, 4% African American, 2% Asian American/Pacific Islander **The most frequently chosen baccalaureate fields are** education, philosophy, psychology **Academic program** Advanced placement, accelerated degree program, summer session, adult/continuing education programs, internships **Contact** Mrs. Karen Lokken, Admissions Coordinator, Southwestern College, 2625 East Cactus Road, Phoenix, AZ 85032-7042. Telephone: 602-992-6101 Ext. 108 or toll-free 800-247-2697 (out-of-state). Fax: 602-404-2159. E-mail: admissions@southwesterncollege.edu. Web site: http://www.southwesterncollege.edu/.

UNIVERSITY OF ADVANCING COMPUTER TECHNOLOGY
TEMPE, ARIZONA

General Proprietary, comprehensive, coed **Setting** urban campus **Total enrollment** 729 **Student-faculty ratio** 15:1 **Application deadline** Rolling (freshmen) **Housing** No **Expenses Tuition** $11,844; Room & Board $4946 **Undergraduates** 18% women, 1% Native American, 11% Hispanic American, 6% African American, 3% Asian American/Pacific Islander **Academic program** Accelerated degree program **Contact** Mr. Dominic Pistillo, President, University of Advancing Computer Technology, 2625 West Baseline Road, Tempe, AZ 85283-1042. Telephone: 602-383-8228 or toll-free 602-383-8228 (in-state); 800-658-5744 (out-of-state). Fax: 602-383-8222. E-mail: admissions@uact.edu. Web site: http://www.uact.edu/.

THE UNIVERSITY OF ARIZONA
TUCSON, ARIZONA

General State-supported, university, coed **Entrance** Moderately difficult **Setting** 351-acre urban campus **Total enrollment** 35,747 **Student-faculty ratio** 18:1 **Application deadline** 4/1 (freshmen), 5/1 (transfer) **Freshmen** 84% were admitted **Housing** Yes **Expenses Tuition** $2490; Room & Board $6124 **Undergraduates** 53% women, 15% part-time, 16% 25 or older, 2% Native American, 14% Hispanic American, 3% African American, 6% Asian American/Pacific Islander **The most frequently chosen baccalaureate fields are** business/marketing, biological/life sciences, social sciences and history **Academic program** English as a second language, advanced placement, honors program, summer session, adult/continuing education programs, internships **Contact** Ms. Lori Goldman, Director of Admissions, The University of Arizona, PO Box 210040, Tucson, AZ 85721-0040. Telephone: 520-621-3237. Fax: 520-621-9799. E-mail: appinfo@arizona.edu. Web site: http://www.arizona.edu/.

UNIVERSITY OF PHOENIX–PHOENIX CAMPUS
PHOENIX, ARIZONA

General Proprietary, comprehensive, coed **Entrance** Noncompetitive **Setting** urban campus **Total enrollment** 88,730 **Student-faculty ratio** 14:1 **Application deadline** Rolling (freshmen), rolling (transfer) **Housing** No **Expenses Tuition** $8100 **Undergraduates** 54% women, 77% 25 or older **The most frequently chosen baccalaureate fields are** business/marketing, computer/information sciences, health professions and related sciences **Academic program** Advanced placement, accelerated degree program, adult/continuing education programs **Contact** Ms. Beth Barilla, Director of Admissions, University of Phoenix–Phoenix Campus, 4615 East Elwood Street, Phoenix, AZ 85040-1958. Telephone: 480-927-0099 Ext. 1216 or toll-free 800-776-4867 (in-state); 800-228-7240 (out-of-state). Fax: 480-894-1758. E-mail: babarill@apollogrp.edu. Web site: http://www.phoenix.edu/.

UNIVERSITY OF PHOENIX–SOUTHERN ARIZONA CAMPUS
TUCSON, ARIZONA

General Proprietary, comprehensive, coed **Entrance** Noncompetitive **Total enrollment** 88,730 **Student-faculty ratio** 14:1 **Application deadline** Rolling (freshmen), rolling (transfer) **Housing** No **Expenses Tuition** $7800 **Undergraduates** 57% women, 76% 25 or older **The most frequently chosen baccalaureate fields are** business/marketing, computer/information sciences, health professions and related sciences **Academic program** Advanced placement, accelerated degree program, adult/continuing education programs **Contact** Ms. Beth Barilla, Director of Admissions, University of Phoenix–Southern Arizona Campus, 4615 East Elwood Street, Phoenix, AZ 85040-1958. Telephone: 480-927-0099 Ext. 1218 or

ARIZONA

University of Phoenix–Southern Arizona Campus *(continued)*

toll-free 800-228-7240. Fax: 480-594-1758. E-mail: beth.barilla@apollogrp.edu. Web site: http://www.phoenix.edu/.

WESTERN INTERNATIONAL UNIVERSITY
PHOENIX, ARIZONA

General Proprietary, comprehensive, coed **Entrance** Moderately difficult **Setting** 4-acre urban campus **Total enrollment** 3,504 **Student-faculty ratio** 10:1 **Application deadline** Rolling (freshmen), rolling (transfer) **Housing** No **Expenses** Tuition $7680 **Undergraduates** 53% women, 90% 25 or older, 0.5% Native American, 5% Hispanic American, 3% African American, 2% Asian American/Pacific Islander **Academic program** English as a second language, advanced placement, accelerated degree program, honors program, summer session, adult/continuing education programs **Contact** Ms. Jo Arney, Director of Student Services, Western International University, 9215 North Black Canyon Highway, Phoenix, AZ 85021-2718. Telephone: 602-943-2311 Ext. 139. Web site: http://www.wintu.edu/.

ARKANSAS

ARKANSAS BAPTIST COLLEGE
LITTLE ROCK, ARKANSAS

General Independent Baptist, 4-year, coed **Entrance** Noncompetitive **Setting** urban campus **Total enrollment** 225 **Student-faculty ratio** 9:1 **Application deadline** Rolling (freshmen) **Freshmen** 100% were admitted **Housing** Yes **Expenses** Tuition $2520; Room & Board $3600 **Undergraduates** 98% African American **The most frequently chosen baccalaureate fields are** business/marketing, education, philosophy **Academic program** Accelerated degree program, summer session, adult/continuing education programs **Contact** Mrs. Annie A. Hightower, Registrar, Arkansas Baptist College, 1600 Bishop Street, Little Rock, AR 72202-6067. Telephone: 501-374-7856 Ext. 19. Web site: http://www.arbaptcoll.edu/.

ARKANSAS STATE UNIVERSITY
JONESBORO, ARKANSAS

General State-supported, comprehensive, coed **Entrance** Moderately difficult **Setting** 900-acre small-town campus **Total enrollment** 10,568 **Student-faculty ratio** 19:1 **Application deadline** Rolling (freshmen), rolling (transfer) **Freshmen** 82% were admitted **Housing** Yes **Expenses** Tuition $4270; Room & Board $3210 **Undergraduates** 58% women, 20% part-time, 22% 25 or older, 0.2% Native American, 1% Hispanic American, 13% African American, 1% Asian American/Pacific Islander **The most frequently chosen baccalaureate fields are** business/marketing, education, health professions and related sciences **Academic program** English as a second language, advanced placement, accelerated degree program, honors program, summer session, internships **Contact** Ms. Paula James Lynn, Director of Admissions, Arkansas State University, PO Box 1630, State University, AR 72467. Telephone: 870-972-3024 or toll-free 800-382-3030 (in-state). Fax: 870-910-8094. E-mail: admissions@astate.edu. Web site: http://www.astate.edu/.

ARKANSAS TECH UNIVERSITY
RUSSELLVILLE, ARKANSAS

General State-supported, comprehensive, coed **Entrance** Minimally difficult **Setting** 517-acre small-town campus **Total enrollment** 5,576 **Student-faculty ratio** 20:1 **Freshmen** 52% were admitted **Housing** Yes **Expenses** Tuition $2976; Room & Board $3280 **Undergraduates** 52% women, 16% part-time, 21% 25 or older, 1% Native American, 1% Hispanic American, 4% African American, 1% Asian American/Pacific Islander **The most frequently chosen baccalaureate fields are** business/marketing, computer/information sciences, education **Academic program** English as a second language, advanced placement, accelerated degree program, honors program, summer session, adult/continuing education programs, internships **Contact** Ms. Shauna Donnell, Director of Enrollment Management, Arkansas Tech University, L.L. "DOC" Bryan Student Services Building, Suite 141, Russellville, AR 72801-2222. Telephone: 501-968-0404 or toll-free 800-582-6953 (in-state). Fax: 501-964-0522. E-mail: tech.enroll@mail.atu.edu. Web site: http://www.atu.edu/.

CENTRAL BAPTIST COLLEGE
CONWAY, ARKANSAS

General Independent Baptist, 4-year, coed **Entrance** Minimally difficult **Setting** 11-acre small-town campus **Total enrollment** 358 **Student-faculty ratio** 16:1 **Application deadline** 8/15 (freshmen), 8/15 (transfer) **Freshmen** 86% were admitted **Housing** Yes **Expenses** Tuition $6384; Room & Board $3888 **Undergraduates** 46% women, 11% part-time, 20% 25 or older, 1% Native American, 1% Hispanic American, 8% African American, 1% Asian American/Pacific Islander **The most frequently chosen baccalaureate fields are** philosophy, philosophy, religion, and theology **Academic program** Advanced placement, summer session, adult/continuing education programs, internships **Contact** Mr. Cory Calhoun, Admissions Counselor, Central Baptist College, 1501 College Avenue, Conway, AR 72034. Telephone: 501-329-6872 Ext. 167 or toll-free 800-205-6872. Fax: 501-329-2941. E-mail: cjackson@cbc.edu. Web site: http://www.cbc.edu/.

HARDING UNIVERSITY
SEARCY, ARKANSAS

General Independent, comprehensive, coed, affiliated with Church of Christ **Entrance** Moderately difficult **Setting** 200-acre small-town campus **Total**

ARKANSAS

enrollment 4,677 **Student-faculty ratio** 16:1 **Application deadline** 7/1 (freshmen), 7/1 (transfer) **Freshmen** 70% were admitted **Housing** Yes **Expenses** Tuition $9030; Room & Board $4498 **Undergraduates** 54% women, 6% part-time, 8% 25 or older, 1% Native American, 1% Hispanic American, 4% African American, 0.5% Asian American/Pacific Islander **The most frequently chosen baccalaureate fields are** business/marketing, education, health professions and related sciences **Academic program** English as a second language, advanced placement, accelerated degree program, self-designed majors, honors program, summer session, adult/continuing education programs, internships **Contact** Mr. Mike Williams, Assistant Vice President of Admissions, Harding University, Box 11255, Searcy, AR 72149-0001. Telephone: 501-279-4407 or toll-free 800-477-4407. Fax: 501-279-4865. E-mail: admissions@harding.edu. Web site: http://www.harding.edu/.

HENDERSON STATE UNIVERSITY
ARKADELPHIA, ARKANSAS

General State-supported, comprehensive, coed **Entrance** Moderately difficult **Setting** 135-acre small-town campus **Total enrollment** 3,428 **Student-faculty ratio** 16:1 **Application deadline** 7/15 (freshmen), rolling (transfer) **Freshmen** 69% were admitted **Housing** Yes **Expenses** Tuition $2736 **Undergraduates** 57% women, 11% part-time, 18% 25 or older, 1% Native American, 1% Hispanic American, 15% African American, 0.4% Asian American/Pacific Islander **The most frequently chosen baccalaureate fields are** business/marketing, education, social sciences and history **Academic program** Advanced placement, honors program, summer session, internships **Contact** Ms. Vikita Hardwrick, Director of University Relations/Admissions, Henderson State University, 1100 Henderson Street, PO Box 7560, Arkadelphia, AR 71999-0001. Telephone: 870-230-5028 or toll-free 800-228-7333. Fax: 870-230-5066. E-mail: hardwrv@hsu.edu. Web site: http://www.hsu.edu/.

HENDRIX COLLEGE
CONWAY, ARKANSAS

General Independent United Methodist, comprehensive, coed **Entrance** Very difficult **Setting** 158-acre suburban campus **Total enrollment** 1,085 **Student-faculty ratio** 13:1 **Application deadline** Rolling (freshmen), rolling (transfer) **Freshmen** 82% were admitted **Housing** Yes **Expenses** Tuition $13,711; Room & Board $4752 **Undergraduates** 54% women, 1% part-time, 1% 25 or older, 1% Native American, 2% Hispanic American, 5% African American, 2% Asian American/Pacific Islander **The most frequently chosen baccalaureate fields are** biological/life sciences, psychology, social sciences and history **Academic program** Advanced placement, self-designed majors, internships **Contact** Mr. Art Weeden, Vice President for Enrollment, Hendrix College, 1600 Washington Avenue, Conway, AR 72032. Telephone: 501-450-1362 or toll-free 800-277-9017. Fax: 501-450-3843. E-mail: adm@hendrix.edu. Web site: http://www.hendrix.edu/.

JOHN BROWN UNIVERSITY
SILOAM SPRINGS, ARKANSAS

General Independent interdenominational, comprehensive, coed **Entrance** Moderately difficult **Setting** 200-acre small-town campus **Total enrollment** 1,675 **Student-faculty ratio** 16:1 **Application deadline** 3/1 (freshmen), 3/1 (transfer) **Freshmen** 84% were admitted **Housing** Yes **Expenses** Tuition $12,374; Room & Board $4658 **Undergraduates** 55% women, 6% part-time, 24% 25 or older, 1% Native American, 2% Hispanic American, 2% African American, 1% Asian American/Pacific Islander **The most frequently chosen baccalaureate fields are** communications/communication technologies, business/marketing, education **Academic program** English as a second language, advanced placement, honors program, adult/continuing education programs, internships **Contact** Ms. Karyn Byrne, Application Coordinator, John Brown University, 200 West University Street, Siloam Springs, AR 72761-2121. Telephone: 501-524-7454 or toll-free 877-JBU-INFO. Fax: 501-524-4196. E-mail: jbuinfo@acc.jbu.edu. Web site: http://www.jbu.edu/.

LYON COLLEGE
BATESVILLE, ARKANSAS

General Independent Presbyterian, 4-year, coed **Entrance** Very difficult **Setting** 136-acre small-town campus **Total enrollment** 526 **Student-faculty ratio** 11:1 **Application deadline** Rolling (freshmen), rolling (transfer) **Freshmen** 78% were admitted **Housing** Yes **Expenses** Tuition $11,375; Room & Board $5125 **Undergraduates** 57% women, 8% part-time, 8% 25 or older, 1% Native American, 2% Hispanic American, 3% African American, 1% Asian American/Pacific Islander **The most frequently chosen baccalaureate fields are** psychology, business/marketing, social sciences and history **Academic program** Advanced placement, self-designed majors, summer session, internships **Contact** Mr. David Wilkey, Vice President for Enrollment Services, Lyon College, PO Box 2317, Batesville, AR 72503-2317. Telephone: 870-698-4250 or toll-free 800-423-2542. Fax: 870-793-1791. E-mail: admissions@lyon.edu. Web site: http://www.lyon.edu/.

OUACHITA BAPTIST UNIVERSITY
ARKADELPHIA, ARKANSAS

General Independent Baptist, 4-year, coed **Entrance** Moderately difficult **Setting** 84-acre small-town campus **Total enrollment** 1,657 **Student-faculty ratio** 13:1 **Application deadline** 8/15 (freshmen), 8/15 (transfer) **Freshmen** 84% were admitted **Housing** Yes **Expenses** Tuition $12,010; Room & Board $4450 **Undergraduates** 53% women, 4% part-time, 3% 25 or older, 0.2% Native American, 1% Hispanic American, 4% African American, 0.4% Asian American/Pacific Islander **The most frequently chosen baccalaureate fields are** education, business/marketing, philosophy, religion, and theology **Academic program** English as a second language, advanced place-

ARKANSAS

Ouachita Baptist University *(continued)*
ment, accelerated degree program, honors program, summer session, internships **Contact** Mrs. Rebecca Jones, Director of Admissions Counseling, Ouachita Baptist University, 410 Ouachita Street, Arkadelphia, AR 71998-0001. Telephone: 870-245-5110 or toll-free 800-342-5628 (in-state). Fax: 870-245-5500. E-mail: jonesj@sigma.obu.edu. Web site: http://www.obu.edu/.

PHILANDER SMITH COLLEGE
LITTLE ROCK, ARKANSAS

General Independent United Methodist, 4-year, coed **Entrance** Noncompetitive **Setting** 25-acre urban campus **Total enrollment** 859 **Student-faculty ratio** 12:1 **Application deadline** Rolling (freshmen), rolling (transfer) **Freshmen** 73% were admitted **Housing** Yes **Expenses** Tuition $4320; Room & Board $3046 **Undergraduates** 64% women, 23% part-time, 32% 25 or older, 0% Native American, 1% Hispanic American, 97% African American, 0% Asian American/Pacific Islander **The most frequently chosen baccalaureate fields are** business/marketing, education, social sciences and history **Academic program** Summer session, adult/continuing education programs, internships **Contact** Ms. Arnella Hayes, Admission Officer, Philander Smith College, 812 West 13th Street, Little Rock, AR 72202-3718. Telephone: 501-370-5310 or toll-free 800-446-6772. Fax: 501-370-5225. E-mail: admvonda@philander.edu. Web site: http://www.philander.edu/.

SOUTHERN ARKANSAS UNIVERSITY–MAGNOLIA
MAGNOLIA, ARKANSAS

General State-supported, comprehensive, coed **Entrance** Moderately difficult **Setting** 781-acre small-town campus **Total enrollment** 3,127 **Student-faculty ratio** 20:1 **Application deadline** 8/15 (freshmen), 8/15 (transfer) **Freshmen** 82% were admitted **Housing** Yes **Expenses** Tuition $2716; Room & Board $3082 **Undergraduates** 56% women, 14% part-time, 18% 25 or older, 0.4% Native American, 2% Hispanic American, 24% African American, 0.2% Asian American/Pacific Islander **The most frequently chosen baccalaureate fields are** business/marketing, agriculture, education **Academic program** Advanced placement, accelerated degree program, summer session, adult/continuing education programs, internships **Contact** Ms. Sarah Jennings, Dean of Enrollment Services, Southern Arkansas University–Magnolia, PO Box 9382, 100 East University, Magnolia, AR 71754-9382. Telephone: 870-235-4040. Fax: 870-235-5005. E-mail: addanne@saumag.edu. Web site: http://www.saumag.edu/.

UNIVERSITY OF ARKANSAS
FAYETTEVILLE, ARKANSAS

General State-supported, university, coed **Entrance** Moderately difficult **Setting** 445-acre suburban campus **Total enrollment** 15,752 **Student-faculty ratio** 16:1 **Application deadline** 8/15 (freshmen), 8/15 (transfer) **Freshmen** 89% were admitted **Housing** Yes **Expenses** Tuition $3880; Room & Board $4454 **Undergraduates** 48% women, 16% part-time, 12% 25 or older, 2% Native American, 1% Hispanic American, 6% African American, 3% Asian American/Pacific Islander **The most frequently chosen baccalaureate fields are** business/marketing, education, engineering/engineering technologies **Academic program** English as a second language, advanced placement, honors program, summer session, internships **Contact** Ms. Maxine Jones, Interim Director, University of Arkansas, 200 Silas H. Hunt Hall, Fayetteville, AR 72701-1201. Telephone: 479-575-5346 or toll-free 800-377-8632. Fax: 479-575-7515. E-mail: uafadmis@uark.edu. Web site: http://www.uark.edu/.

UNIVERSITY OF ARKANSAS AT LITTLE ROCK
LITTLE ROCK, ARKANSAS

General State-supported, university, coed **Entrance** Minimally difficult **Setting** 150-acre urban campus **Total enrollment** 11,318 **Student-faculty ratio** 11:1 **Application deadline** Rolling (freshmen), rolling (transfer) **Freshmen** 97% were admitted **Housing** Yes **Expenses** Tuition $3138; Room only $2600 **Undergraduates** 62% women, 41% part-time, 35% 25 or older, 1% Native American, 2% Hispanic American, 32% African American, 2% Asian American/Pacific Islander **The most frequently chosen baccalaureate fields are** business/marketing, liberal arts/general studies, protective services/public administration **Academic program** English as a second language, advanced placement, accelerated degree program, self-designed majors, honors program, summer session, adult/continuing education programs, internships **Contact** John Noah, Director of Admissions, University of Arkansas at Little Rock, 2801 South University Avenue, Little Rock, AR 72204-1099. Telephone: 501-569-3127 or toll-free 800-482-8892 (in-state). Fax: 501-569-8915. Web site: http://www.ualr.edu/.

UNIVERSITY OF ARKANSAS AT MONTICELLO
MONTICELLO, ARKANSAS

General State-supported, comprehensive, coed **Entrance** Noncompetitive **Setting** 400-acre small-town campus **Total enrollment** 2,323 **Student-faculty ratio** 17:1 **Application deadline** 8/1 (freshmen), 8/1 (transfer) **Housing** Yes **Expenses** Tuition $2670; Room & Board $2780 **Undergraduates** 57% women, 13% part-time, 22% 25 or older, 1% Native American, 1% Hispanic American, 22% African American, 1% Asian American/Pacific Islander **The most frequently chosen baccalaureate fields are** business/marketing, agriculture, education **Academic program** Advanced placement, accelerated degree program, summer session **Contact** Mary Whiting, Director of Admissions, University of Arkansas at Monticello, PO Box 3600, Monticello, AR 71656. Telephone: 870-460-1026 or toll-free 800-844-1826 (in-state). Fax: 870-460-1321. E-mail: admissions@uamont.edu. Web site: http://www.uamont.edu/.

UNIVERSITY OF ARKANSAS AT PINE BLUFF
PINE BLUFF, ARKANSAS

General State-supported, comprehensive, coed **Entrance** Minimally difficult **Setting** 327-acre urban campus **Total enrollment** 3,144 **Student-faculty ratio** 16:1 **Application deadline** 8/1 (freshmen) **Freshmen** 72% were admitted **Housing** Yes **Expenses** Tuition $3209; Room & Board $4716 **Undergraduates** 56% women, 11% part-time, 16% 25 or older, 0.03% Native American, 0.2% Hispanic American, 96% African American, 0.1% Asian American/Pacific Islander **The most frequently chosen baccalaureate fields are** business/marketing, liberal arts/general studies, protective services/public administration **Academic program** Advanced placement, accelerated degree program, honors program, summer session, adult/continuing education programs, internships **Contact** Mrs. Erica W. Fulton, Director of Admissions and Academic Records, University of Arkansas at Pine Bluff, UAPB Box 17, 1200 University Drive, Pine Bluff, AR 71601-2799. Telephone: 870-575-8487 or toll-free 800-264-6585 (in-state). Fax: 870-543-2021.

UNIVERSITY OF ARKANSAS FOR MEDICAL SCIENCES
LITTLE ROCK, ARKANSAS

General State-supported, upper-level, coed **Entrance** Very difficult **Setting** 5-acre urban campus **Total enrollment** 1,936 **Housing** Yes **Undergraduates** 42% 25 or older, 1% Native American, 2% Hispanic American, 15% African American, 2% Asian American/Pacific Islander **The most frequently chosen baccalaureate field is** health professions and related sciences **Contact** University of Arkansas for Medical Sciences, 4301 West Markham-Slot 601, Little Rock, AR 72205-7199. Web site: http://www.uams.edu/.

UNIVERSITY OF CENTRAL ARKANSAS
CONWAY, ARKANSAS

General State-supported, comprehensive, coed **Entrance** Moderately difficult **Setting** 365-acre small-town campus **Total enrollment** 8,486 **Student-faculty ratio** 18:1 **Application deadline** Rolling (freshmen), rolling (transfer) **Freshmen** 73% were admitted **Housing** Yes **Expenses** Tuition $3738; Room & Board $3490 **Undergraduates** 60% women, 7% part-time, 12% 25 or older, 1% Native American, 1% Hispanic American, 15% African American, 1% Asian American/Pacific Islander **The most frequently chosen baccalaureate fields are** business/marketing, education, health professions and related sciences **Academic program** English as a second language, advanced placement, accelerated degree program, honors program, summer session, internships **Contact** Ms. Penny Hatfield, Director of Admissions, University of Central Arkansas, 201 Donaghey Avenue, Conway, AR 72035-0001. Telephone: 501-450-5145 or toll-free 800-243-8245 (in-state). Fax: 501-450-5228. E-mail: admisson@ecom.uca.edu. Web site: http://www.uca.edu/.

UNIVERSITY OF THE OZARKS
CLARKSVILLE, ARKANSAS

General Independent Presbyterian, 4-year, coed **Entrance** Moderately difficult **Setting** 56-acre small-town campus **Total enrollment** 654 **Student-faculty ratio** 11:1 **Application deadline** Rolling (freshmen), 8/15 (transfer) **Freshmen** 82% were admitted **Housing** Yes **Expenses** Tuition $9624; Room & Board $4280 **Undergraduates** 55% women, 4% part-time, 6% 25 or older, 2% Native American, 3% Hispanic American, 3% African American, 1% Asian American/Pacific Islander **The most frequently chosen baccalaureate fields are** business/marketing, communications/communication technologies, education **Academic program** English as a second language, advanced placement, summer session, internships **Contact** Mr. James D. Decker, Director of Admissions, University of the Ozarks, 415 North College Avenue, Clarksville, AR 72830-2880. Telephone: 501-979-1209 or toll-free 800-264-8636. Fax: 501-979-1355. E-mail: admiss@ozarks.edu. Web site: http://www.ozarks.edu/.

WILLIAMS BAPTIST COLLEGE
WALNUT RIDGE, ARKANSAS

General Independent Southern Baptist, 4-year, coed **Entrance** Minimally difficult **Setting** 186-acre rural campus **Total enrollment** 683 **Student-faculty ratio** 16:1 **Application deadline** Rolling (freshmen), rolling (transfer) **Freshmen** 75% were admitted **Housing** Yes **Expenses** Tuition $7250; Room & Board $3400 **Undergraduates** 58% women, 26% part-time, 13% 25 or older, 1% Native American, 1% Hispanic American, 3% African American, 0.2% Asian American/Pacific Islander **The most frequently chosen baccalaureate fields are** education, philosophy, religion, and theology, psychology **Academic program** Advanced placement, self-designed majors, honors program, summer session, adult/continuing education programs, internships **Contact** Ms. Angela Flippo, Director of Admissions, Williams Baptist College, PO Box 3665, Walnut Ridge, AR 72476. Telephone: 870-886-6741 Ext. 4117 or toll-free 800-722-4434. Fax: 870-886-3924. E-mail: admissions@wbcoll.edu. Web site: http://wbcoll.edu/.

CALIFORNIA

ACADEMY OF ART COLLEGE
SAN FRANCISCO, CALIFORNIA

General Proprietary, comprehensive, coed **Entrance** Noncompetitive **Setting** 3-acre urban campus **Total enrollment** 6,282 **Student-faculty ratio** 15:1 **Application deadline** Rolling (freshmen), rolling (trans-

CALIFORNIA

Academy of Art College *(continued)*
fer) **Freshmen** 63% were admitted **Housing** Yes **Expenses** Tuition $12,060; Room only $8000 **Undergraduates** 43% women, 37% part-time, 28% 25 or older, 1% Native American, 8% Hispanic American, 3% African American, 15% Asian American/Pacific Islander **The most frequently chosen baccalaureate field is** visual/performing arts **Academic program** English as a second language, summer session, adult/continuing education programs, internships **Contact** Ms. Eliza Alden, Vice President-Admissions, Academy of Art College, 79 New Montgomery Street, San Francisco, CA 94105. Telephone: 415-263-7757 Ext. 7757 or toll-free 800-544-ARTS. Fax: 415-263-4130. E-mail: info@academyart.edu. Web site: http://www.academyart.edu/.

ALLIANT INTERNATIONAL UNIVERSITY
SAN DIEGO, CALIFORNIA

General Independent, university, coed **Entrance** Moderately difficult **Setting** 200-acre suburban campus **Total enrollment** 1,926 **Student-faculty ratio** 16:1 **Application deadline** Rolling (freshmen), rolling (transfer) **Freshmen** 51% were admitted **Housing** Yes **Expenses** Tuition $14,340; Room & Board $6180 **Undergraduates** 58% women, 6% part-time, 19% 25 or older, 1% Native American, 19% Hispanic American, 12% African American, 9% Asian American/Pacific Islander **The most frequently chosen baccalaureate fields are** business/marketing, psychology, social sciences and history **Academic program** English as a second language, advanced placement, honors program, summer session, adult/continuing education programs, internships **Contact** Ms. Susan Topham, Director of Admissions, Alliant International University, 10455 Pomerado Road, San Diego, CA 92131-1799. Telephone: 858-635-4772. Fax: 858-635-4739. E-mail: admissions@alliant.edu. Web site: http://www.alliant.edu/.

AMERICAN INTERCONTINENTAL UNIVERSITY
LOS ANGELES, CALIFORNIA

General Proprietary, comprehensive, coed **Entrance** Noncompetitive **Setting** urban campus **Total enrollment** 1,188 **Student-faculty ratio** 24:1 **Application deadline** Rolling (freshmen), rolling (transfer) **Housing** Yes **Undergraduates** 3% 25 or older **Academic program** English as a second language, accelerated degree program, summer session, internships **Contact** Mr. Sam Hinojosa, Director of Admissions, American InterContinental University, 12655 West Jefferson Boulevard, Los Angeles, CA 90066. Telephone: 310-302-2423. Fax: 310-302-2001. Web site: http://www.aiula.edu/.

ANTIOCH UNIVERSITY LOS ANGELES
MARINA DEL REY, CALIFORNIA

General Independent, upper-level, coed **Entrance** Moderately difficult **Setting** 1-acre urban campus **Total enrollment** 499 **Student-faculty ratio** 21:1 **Application deadline** 8/1 (transfer) **Housing** No **Expenses** Tuition $13,600 **Undergraduates** 74% women, 70% part-time, 0% Native American, 8% Hispanic American, 21% African American, 3% Asian American/Pacific Islander **Academic program** Advanced placement, accelerated degree program, self-designed majors, summer session, adult/continuing education programs, internships **Contact** Ms. Chloe Reid, Executive Dean, Antioch University Los Angeles, 13274 Fiji Way, Marina del Rey, CA 90292-7090. Telephone: 310-578-1080 Ext. 244 or toll-free 800-7ANTIOCH. Fax: 310-822-4824. E-mail: admissions@antiochla.edu. Web site: http://www.antiochla.edu/.

ANTIOCH UNIVERSITY SANTA BARBARA
SANTA BARBARA, CALIFORNIA

General Independent, upper-level, coed **Entrance** Minimally difficult **Setting** small-town campus **Total enrollment** 296 **Student-faculty ratio** 15:1 **Application deadline** Rolling (transfer) **Housing** No **Expenses** Tuition $10,800 **Undergraduates** 82% women, 49% part-time, 1% Native American, 11% Hispanic American, 4% African American, 5% Asian American/Pacific Islander **The most frequently chosen baccalaureate field is** liberal arts/general studies **Academic program** Accelerated degree program, self-designed majors, summer session, adult/continuing education programs, internships **Contact** Mrs. Carol Flores, Director of Admissions, Antioch University Santa Barbara, 801 Garden Street, Santa Barbara, CA 93101-1580. Telephone: 805-962-8179 Ext. 113. Fax: 805-962-4786. E-mail: cflores@antiochsb.edu. Web site: http://www.antiochsb.edu/.

ARGOSY UNIVERSITY-ORANGE COUNTY
ORANGE, CALIFORNIA

Contact Argosy University-Orange County, 3745 Chapman Avenue, Suite 100, Orange, CA 92868. Telephone: or toll-free 800-716-9598. Web site: http://www.argosyu.edu/.

ARMSTRONG UNIVERSITY
OAKLAND, CALIFORNIA

General Independent, comprehensive, coed **Entrance** Moderately difficult **Setting** urban campus **Total enrollment** 103 **Application deadline** Rolling (freshmen), rolling (transfer) **Housing** No **Expenses** Tuition $6192 **Undergraduates** 45% 25 or older **Academic program** English as a second language, advanced placement, accelerated degree program, summer session **Contact** Ms. Sarah Hofberg, Director of Admission, Armstrong University, 1608 Webster Street, Oakland, CA 94612. Telephone: 510-835-7900 Ext. 10. Fax: 510-835-8935. E-mail: info@armstrong-u.edu. Web site: http://www.armstrong-u.edu/.

ART CENTER COLLEGE OF DESIGN
PASADENA, CALIFORNIA

General Independent, comprehensive, coed **Entrance** Very difficult **Setting** 175-acre suburban campus

CALIFORNIA

Total enrollment 1,465 Student-faculty ratio 12:1 Application deadline Rolling (freshmen), rolling (transfer) Freshmen 65% were admitted Housing No Expenses Tuition $21,110 Undergraduates 40% women, 47% 25 or older, 1% Native American, 10% Hispanic American, 2% African American, 32% Asian American/Pacific Islander The most frequently chosen baccalaureate field is visual/performing arts Academic program Advanced placement, accelerated degree program, summer session, adult/continuing education programs, internships Contact Ms. Kit Baron, Vice President of Student Services, Art Center College of Design, 1700 Lida Street, Pasadena, CA 91103-1999. Telephone: 626-396-2373. Fax: 626-795-0578. E-mail: admissions@artcenter.edu. Web site: http://www.artcenter.edu/.

THE ART INSTITUTE OF CALIFORNIA
SAN DIEGO, CALIFORNIA

General Proprietary, 4-year, coed Entrance Minimally difficult Setting urban campus Total enrollment 490 Student-faculty ratio 28:1 Application deadline Rolling (freshmen), rolling (transfer) Freshmen 85% were admitted Housing No Expenses Tuition $14,600 Undergraduates 37% women, 10% 25 or older, 0% Native American, 12% Hispanic American, 2% African American, 8% Asian American/Pacific Islander The most frequently chosen baccalaureate fields are communications/communication technologies, visual/performing arts Academic program Summer session, internships Contact Ms. Sandy Park, Director of Admissions, The Art Institute of California, 10025 Mesa Rum Road, San Diego, CA 92122. Telephone: 858-546-0602 Ext. 3117 or toll-free 866-275-2422 Ext. 3117 (in-state). Fax: 858-457-0903. E-mail: info@aii.edu. Web site: http://www.aica.artinstitutes.edu.

THE ART INSTITUTE OF CALIFORNIA-SAN FRANCISCO
SAN FRANCISCO, CALIFORNIA

General Independent, 4-year, coed Entrance Moderately difficult Setting urban campus Total enrollment 345 Student-faculty ratio 12:1 Application deadline Rolling (freshmen), rolling (transfer) Housing No Expenses Tuition $16,230 Undergraduates 43% women, 19% part-time, 1% Native American, 20% Hispanic American, 8% African American, 14% Asian American/Pacific Islander Academic program Accelerated degree program, summer session, internships Contact Mr. Doug Worsley, Director of Admissions, The Art Institute of California-San Francisco, 1170 Market Street, San Francisco, CA 94102-4908. Telephone: 415-865-0198 Ext. 2536 or toll-free 888-493-3261. Web site: http://www.aicasf.aii.edu/.

ART INSTITUTE OF SOUTHERN CALIFORNIA
LAGUNA BEACH, CALIFORNIA

General Independent, 4-year, coed Entrance Moderately difficult Setting 9-acre small-town campus Total enrollment 280 Student-faculty ratio 10:1 Application deadline 3/2 (freshmen), 4/2 (transfer) Freshmen 93% were admitted Housing No Expenses Tuition $14,285 Undergraduates 46% women, 26% 25 or older The most frequently chosen baccalaureate field is visual/performing arts Academic program English as a second language, advanced placement, summer session, adult/continuing education programs, internships Contact Mr. Anthony Padilla, Dean of Admissions, Art Institute of Southern California, 2222 Laguna Canyon Road, Laguna Beach, CA 92651-1136. Telephone: 949-376-6000 Ext. 232 or toll-free 800-255-0762. Fax: 949-376-6009. E-mail: admissions@aisc.edu. Web site: http://www.aisc.edu/.

ART INSTITUTES INTERNATIONAL AT SAN FRANCISCO
See The Art Institute of California-San Francisco

AZUSA PACIFIC UNIVERSITY
AZUSA, CALIFORNIA

General Independent nondenominational, comprehensive, coed Entrance Moderately difficult Setting 60-acre small-town campus Total enrollment 6,835 Student-faculty ratio 16:1 Application deadline 7/1 (freshmen), 7/1 (transfer) Freshmen 70% were admitted Housing Yes Expenses Tuition $17,495; Room & Board $6230 Undergraduates 64% women, 2% part-time, 12% 25 or older, 0.5% Native American, 12% Hispanic American, 3% African American, 5% Asian American/Pacific Islander The most frequently chosen baccalaureate fields are business/marketing, education, liberal arts/general studies Academic program English as a second language, advanced placement, accelerated degree program, honors program, summer session, adult/continuing education programs, internships Contact Mrs. Deana. Porterfield, Dean of Enrollment, Azusa Pacific University, 901 East Alosta Avenue, PO Box 7000, Azusa, CA 91720-7000. Telephone: 626-812-3016 or toll-free 800-TALK-APU. E-mail: admissions@apu.edu. Web site: http://www.apu.edu/.

BETHANY COLLEGE OF THE ASSEMBLIES OF GOD
SCOTTS VALLEY, CALIFORNIA

General Independent, comprehensive, coed, affiliated with Assemblies of God Entrance Minimally difficult Setting 40-acre small-town campus Total enrollment 568 Student-faculty ratio 11:1 Application deadline 7/1 (freshmen), 7/1 (transfer) Freshmen 74% were admitted Housing Yes Expenses Tuition $11,375; Room & Board $4928 Undergraduates 38% women, 26% part-time, 48% 25 or older, 0.4% Native American, 15% Hispanic American, 8% African American, 4% Asian American/Pacific Islander The most frequently chosen baccalaureate fields are philosophy, interdisciplinary studies, psychology Academic program Advanced placement, acceler-

CALIFORNIA

Bethany College of the Assemblies of God *(continued)*
ated degree program, summer session, adult/ continuing education programs, internships **Contact** Ms. Pam Smallwood, Director of Admissions, Bethany College of the Assemblies of God, 800 Bethany Drive, Scotts Valley, CA 95066-2820. Telephone: 831-438-3800 Ext. 1400 or toll-free 800-843-9410. Fax: 831-438-4517. E-mail: info@bethany.edu. Web site: http://www.bethany.edu/.

BETHESDA CHRISTIAN UNIVERSITY
ANAHEIM, CALIFORNIA

General Independent, comprehensive, affiliated with Full Gospel World Mission **Entrance** Moderately difficult **Total enrollment** 235 **Student-faculty ratio** 15:1 **Application deadline** 8/10 (freshmen), 8/10 (transfer) **Freshmen** 91% were admitted **Housing** No **Expenses** Tuition $3180 **Undergraduates** 70% women, 34% part-time, 70% 25 or older, 0% Native American, 0% Hispanic American, 0% African American, 30% Asian American/Pacific Islander **The most frequently chosen baccalaureate fields are** education, philosophy, religion, and theology **Academic program** English as a second language, accelerated degree program, summer session, adult/continuing education programs, internships **Contact** Ms. Haein Hong, Admissions & Registrar, Bethesda Christian University, 730 N. Euclid Street, Anaheim, CA 92801. Telephone: 714-517-1945. Fax: 714-517-1948. E-mail: admin@bcu.edu. Web site: http://www.bcu.edu/.

BIOLA UNIVERSITY
LA MIRADA, CALIFORNIA

General Independent interdenominational, university, coed **Entrance** Moderately difficult **Setting** 95-acre suburban campus **Total enrollment** 4,317 **Student-faculty ratio** 18:1 **Application deadline** 6/1 (freshmen), 6/1 (transfer) **Freshmen** 55% were admitted **Housing** Yes **Expenses** Tuition $17,410; Room & Board $5445 **Undergraduates** 61% women, 9% part-time, 19% 25 or older, 0.4% Native American, 8% Hispanic American, 4% African American, 8% Asian American/Pacific Islander **The most frequently chosen baccalaureate fields are** business/marketing, communications/communication technologies, philosophy **Academic program** English as a second language, advanced placement, accelerated degree program, honors program, summer session, adult/continuing education programs, internships **Contact** Mr. Greg Vaughan, Director of Enrollment Management, Biola University, 13800 Biola Avenue, La Mirada, CA 90639. Telephone: 562-903-4752 or toll-free 800-652-4652. Fax: 562-903-4709. E-mail: admissions@biola.edu. Web site: http://www.biola.edu/.

BROOKS INSTITUTE OF PHOTOGRAPHY
SANTA BARBARA, CALIFORNIA

Contact Ms. Inge B. Kautzmann, Director of Admissions, Brooks Institute of Photography, 801 Alston Road, Santa Barbara, CA 93108. Telephone: 805-966-3888 Ext. 4601 or toll-free 888-304-3456 (out-of-state). Fax: 805-564-1475. E-mail: admissions@brooks.edu. Web site: http://www.brooks.edu/.

CALIFORNIA BAPTIST UNIVERSITY
RIVERSIDE, CALIFORNIA

General Independent Southern Baptist, comprehensive, coed **Entrance** Minimally difficult **Setting** 75-acre suburban campus **Total enrollment** 2,090 **Student-faculty ratio** 19:1 **Application deadline** 8/18 (freshmen), 8/2 (transfer) **Freshmen** 79% were admitted **Housing** Yes **Expenses** Tuition $11,690; Room & Board $5046 **Undergraduates** 65% women, 20% part-time, 20% 25 or older, 1% Native American, 12% Hispanic American, 6% African American, 3% Asian American/Pacific Islander **The most frequently chosen baccalaureate fields are** business/marketing, liberal arts/general studies, psychology **Academic program** Advanced placement, accelerated degree program, summer session, adult/continuing education programs, internships **Contact** Mr. Allen Johnson, Director, Undergraduate Admissions, California Baptist University, 8432 Magnolia Avenue, Riverside, CA 92504-3297. Telephone: 909-343-4212 or toll-free 877-228-8866. Fax: 909-343-4525. E-mail: admissions@calbaptist.edu. Web site: http://www.calbaptist.edu/.

CALIFORNIA CHRISTIAN COLLEGE
FRESNO, CALIFORNIA

General Independent religious, 4-year, coed **Entrance** Noncompetitive **Total enrollment** 77 **Student-faculty ratio** 8:1 **Application deadline** Rolling (freshmen), rolling (transfer) **Freshmen** 100% were admitted **Housing** Yes **Expenses** Tuition $4425; Room & Board $3150 **Undergraduates** 31% women, 23% part-time, 55% 25 or older, 0% Native American, 3% Hispanic American, 19% African American, 3% Asian American/Pacific Islander **The most frequently chosen baccalaureate fields are** philosophy, philosophy, religion, and theology **Academic program** Accelerated degree program, summer session **Contact** Mrs. Marjorie James, Registrar, California Christian College, 4881 East University Avenue, Fresno, CA 93703. Telephone: 559-251-4215 Ext. 5565. Fax: 559-251-4231. E-mail: cccfresno@aol.com. Web site: http://www.calchristiancollege.org/.

CALIFORNIA COLLEGE FOR HEALTH SCIENCES
NATIONAL CITY, CALIFORNIA

General Proprietary, comprehensive, coed **Entrance** Noncompetitive **Setting** 2-acre urban campus **Total enrollment** 7,380 **Application deadline** Rolling (freshmen), rolling (transfer) **Housing** No **Undergraduates** 85% 25 or older **Contact** Ms. Marita Gubbe, Director of Student Affairs, California College for Health Sciences, 2423 Hoover Avenue, National City, CA 91950. Telephone: 619-477-4800 Ext. 320 or toll-free 800-221-7374 (out-of-state).

Fax: 619-477-4360. E-mail: admissions@cchs.edu. Web site: http://www.cchs.edu/.

CALIFORNIA COLLEGE OF ARTS AND CRAFTS
SAN FRANCISCO, CALIFORNIA

General Independent, comprehensive, coed **Entrance** Moderately difficult **Setting** 4-acre urban campus **Total enrollment** 1,291 **Student-faculty ratio** 10:1 **Application deadline** Rolling (freshmen), rolling (transfer) **Freshmen** 71% were admitted **Housing** Yes **Expenses** Tuition $20,690; Room & Board $6776 **Undergraduates** 60% women, 12% part-time, 38% 25 or older, 1% Native American, 6% Hispanic American, 2% African American, 12% Asian American/Pacific Islander **The most frequently chosen baccalaureate fields are** architecture, trade and industry, visual/performing arts **Academic program** Advanced placement, self-designed majors, summer session, internships **Contact** Molly Ryan, Director of Admissions, California College of Arts and Crafts, 1111 Eighth Street at 16th and Wisconsin, San Francisco, CA 94107. Telephone: 415-703-9523 Ext. 9532 or toll-free 800-447-1ART. Fax: 315-703-9539. E-mail: enroll@ccac-art.edu. Web site: http://www.ccac-art.edu/.

▶ For more information, see page 403.

CALIFORNIA INSTITUTE OF INTEGRAL STUDIES
SAN FRANCISCO, CALIFORNIA

General Independent, upper-level, coed **Student-faculty ratio** 19:1 **Expenses** Tuition $14,542 **Academic program** Adult/continuing education programs **Contact** Mr. Henry B. Villareal, Dean of Enrollment Management, California Institute of Integral Studies, 1453 Mission Street, San Francisco, CA 94103. Telephone: 415-575-6156. Fax: 415-575-1268. E-mail: info@ciis.edu. Web site: http://www.ciis.edu/.

CALIFORNIA INSTITUTE OF TECHNOLOGY
PASADENA, CALIFORNIA

General Independent, university, coed **Entrance** Most difficult **Setting** 124-acre suburban campus **Total enrollment** 2,058 **Student-faculty ratio** 3:1 **Application deadline** 1/1 (freshmen), 3/1 (transfer) **Freshmen** 15% were admitted **Housing** Yes **Expenses** Tuition $21,120; Room & Board $6543 **Undergraduates** 33% women, 1% 25 or older, 0.3% Native American, 7% Hispanic American, 2% African American, 25% Asian American/Pacific Islander **The most frequently chosen baccalaureate fields are** engineering/engineering technologies, biological/life sciences, physical sciences **Academic program** Self-designed majors, internships **Contact** Ms. Charlene Liebau, Director of Admissions, California Institute of Technology, 1200 East California Boulevard, Pasadena, CA 91125-0001. Telephone: 626-395-6341 or toll-free 800-568-8324. Fax: 626-683-3026. E-mail: ugadmissions@caltech.edu. Web site: http://www.caltech.edu/.

CALIFORNIA INSTITUTE OF THE ARTS
VALENCIA, CALIFORNIA

General Independent, comprehensive, coed **Entrance** Very difficult **Setting** 60-acre suburban campus **Total enrollment** 1,249 **Student-faculty ratio** 6:1 **Application deadline** Rolling (freshmen), rolling (transfer) **Freshmen** 36% were admitted **Housing** Yes **Expenses** Tuition $22,535; Room & Board $6000 **Undergraduates** 42% women, 1% part-time, 18% 25 or older, 2% Native American, 10% Hispanic American, 5% African American, 11% Asian American/Pacific Islander **The most frequently chosen baccalaureate field is** visual/performing arts **Academic program** Advanced placement, self-designed majors, internships **Contact** Ms. Carol Kim, Director of Enrollment Services, California Institute of the Arts, 24700 McBean Parkway, Valencia, CA 91355. Telephone: 661-255-1050. E-mail: admiss@calarts.edu. Web site: http://www.calarts.edu/.

CALIFORNIA LUTHERAN UNIVERSITY
THOUSAND OAKS, CALIFORNIA

General Independent Lutheran, comprehensive, coed **Entrance** Moderately difficult **Setting** 290-acre suburban campus **Total enrollment** 2,857 **Student-faculty ratio** 15:1 **Application deadline** 6/1 (freshmen), 6/1 (transfer) **Freshmen** 83% were admitted **Housing** Yes **Expenses** Tuition $18,800; Room & Board $6656 **Undergraduates** 57% women, 12% part-time, 5% 25 or older, 1% Native American, 12% Hispanic American, 2% African American, 5% Asian American/Pacific Islander **The most frequently chosen baccalaureate fields are** business/marketing, communications/communication technologies, liberal arts/general studies **Academic program** Advanced placement, accelerated degree program, self-designed majors, summer session, adult/continuing education programs, internships **Contact** Mr. Darryl Calkins, Dean of Undergraduate Enrollment, California Lutheran University, Office of Admission, #1350, Thousand Oaks, CA 91360. Telephone: 805-493-3135 or toll-free 877-258-3678. Fax: 805-493-3114. E-mail: cluadm@clunet.edu. Web site: http://www.clunet.edu/.

CALIFORNIA MARITIME ACADEMY
VALLEJO, CALIFORNIA

General State-supported, 4-year, coed, primarily men **Entrance** Moderately difficult **Setting** 67-acre suburban campus **Total enrollment** 653 **Student-faculty ratio** 15:1 **Application deadline** 4/1 (freshmen), 4/1 (transfer) **Freshmen** 58% were admitted **Housing** Yes **Expenses** Tuition $2206; Room & Board $5900 **Undergraduates** 20% women, 6% part-time, 19% 25 or older, 1% Native American, 6% Hispanic American, 3% African American, 11% Asian American/Pacific Islander **The most frequently chosen baccalaureate fields are** business/marketing, engineering/

CALIFORNIA

California Maritime Academy *(continued)*
engineering technologies **Academic program** Advanced placement, summer session, internships **Contact** Mr. Chris Krzak, Director of Admission and Outreach, California Maritime Academy, PO Box 1392, Vallejo, CA 94590-0644. Telephone: 707-654-1331 or toll-free 800-561-1945. Fax: 707-654-1336. E-mail: admission@csum.edu. Web site: http://www.csum.edu/.

CALIFORNIA NATIONAL UNIVERSITY FOR ADVANCED STUDIES
NORTH HILLS, CALIFORNIA

Contact California National University for Advanced Studies, 16909 Parthenia Street, North Hills, CA 91343. Web site: http://www.cnuas.edu/.

CALIFORNIA POLYTECHNIC STATE UNIVERSITY, SAN LUIS OBISPO
SAN LUIS OBISPO, CALIFORNIA

General State-supported, comprehensive, coed **Entrance** Moderately difficult **Setting** 6,000-acre small-town campus **Total enrollment** 18,079 **Student-faculty ratio** 20:1 **Application deadline** 11/30 (freshmen), 11/30 (transfer) **Freshmen** 47% were admitted **Housing** Yes **Expenses** Tuition $2153; Room & Board $6594 **Undergraduates** 45% women, 6% part-time, 6% 25 or older, 1% Native American, 10% Hispanic American, 1% African American, 11% Asian American/Pacific Islander **The most frequently chosen baccalaureate fields are** business/marketing, agriculture, engineering/engineering technologies **Academic program** English as a second language, advanced placement, honors program, summer session, internships **Contact** Mr. James Maraviglia, Director of Admissions and Evaluations, California Polytechnic State University, San Luis Obispo, San Luis Obispo, CA 93407. Telephone: 805-756-2311. Fax: 805-756-5400. E-mail: admprosp@calpoly.edu. Web site: http://www.calpoly.edu/.

CALIFORNIA SCHOOL OF PROFESSIONAL PSYCHOLOGY
See Alliant International University

CALIFORNIA STATE POLYTECHNIC UNIVERSITY, POMONA
POMONA, CALIFORNIA

General State-supported, comprehensive, coed **Entrance** Moderately difficult **Setting** 1,400-acre urban campus **Total enrollment** 19,041 **Student-faculty ratio** 20:1 **Application deadline** 4/1 (freshmen), 5/1 (transfer) **Freshmen** 67% were admitted **Housing** Yes **Expenses** Tuition $1772; Room & Board $6843 **Undergraduates** 43% women, 19% part-time, 20% 25 or older, 1% Native American, 23% Hispanic American, 3% African American, 34% Asian American/Pacific Islander **The most frequently chosen baccalaureate fields are** business/marketing, engineering/engineering technologies, liberal arts/general studies **Academic program** English as a second language, advanced placement, summer session, adult/continuing education programs, internships **Contact** Ms. Dena Bennett, Assistant Director of Admissions, California State Polytechnic University, Pomona, 3801 West Temple Avenue, Pomona, CA 91768. Telephone: 909-869-2991. Fax: 909-869-4529. E-mail: cppadmit@csupomona.edu. Web site: http://www.csupomona.edu/.

▶ For more information, see page 404.

CALIFORNIA STATE UNIVERSITY, BAKERSFIELD
BAKERSFIELD, CALIFORNIA

General State-supported, comprehensive, coed **Entrance** Moderately difficult **Setting** 575-acre urban campus **Total enrollment** 7,050 **Application deadline** 9/23 (freshmen), 9/23 (transfer) **Housing** Yes **Expenses** Tuition $1797; Room & Board $5400 **Undergraduates** 65% women, 21% part-time, 35% 25 or older, 1% Native American, 31% Hispanic American, 7% African American, 6% Asian American/Pacific Islander **The most frequently chosen baccalaureate fields are** business/marketing, liberal arts/general studies, social sciences and history **Academic program** English as a second language, advanced placement, accelerated degree program, self-designed majors, honors program, summer session, adult/continuing education programs, internships **Contact** Dr. Homer S. Montalvo, Associate Dean of Admissions and Records, California State University, Bakersfield, 9001 Stockdale Highway, Bakersfield, CA 93311-1099. Telephone: 805-664-2160 or toll-free 800-788-2782 (in-state). Web site: http://www.csubak.edu/.

CALIFORNIA STATE UNIVERSITY, CHICO
CHICO, CALIFORNIA

General State-supported, comprehensive, coed **Entrance** Moderately difficult **Setting** 119-acre small-town campus **Total enrollment** 16,704 **Student-faculty ratio** 20:1 **Application deadline** 11/30 (freshmen) **Freshmen** 90% were admitted **Housing** Yes **Expenses** Tuition $2070; Room & Board $6528 **Undergraduates** 53% women, 10% part-time, 17% 25 or older, 1% Native American, 10% Hispanic American, 2% African American, 5% Asian American/Pacific Islander **The most frequently chosen baccalaureate fields are** business/marketing, liberal arts/general studies, social sciences and history **Academic program** English as a second language, advanced placement, self-designed majors, honors program, summer session, adult/continuing education programs, internships **Contact** Mr. John F. Swiney, Director of Admissions, California State University, Chico, 400 West First Street, Chico, CA 95929-0722. Telephone: 530-898-4879 or toll-free 800-542-4426. Fax: 530-898-6456. E-mail: info@csuchico.edu. Web site: http://www.csuchico.edu/.

CALIFORNIA

CALIFORNIA STATE UNIVERSITY, DOMINGUEZ HILLS
CARSON, CALIFORNIA

General State-supported, comprehensive, coed **Entrance** Moderately difficult **Setting** 350-acre urban campus **Total enrollment** 12,871 **Student-faculty ratio** 21:1 **Application deadline** Rolling (freshmen), rolling (transfer) **Freshmen** 76% were admitted **Housing** Yes **Expenses** Tuition $1800; Room & Board $6156 **Undergraduates** 70% women, 41% part-time, 56% 25 or older, 1% Native American, 34% Hispanic American, 30% African American, 10% Asian American/Pacific Islander **The most frequently chosen baccalaureate field is** philosophy, religion, and theology **Academic program** English as a second language, advanced placement, self-designed majors, honors program, summer session, adult/continuing education programs, internships **Contact** Information Center, California State University, Dominguez Hills, 1000 East Victoria Street, Carson, CA 90747-0001. Telephone: 310-243-3696. Web site: http://www.csudh.edu/.

CALIFORNIA STATE UNIVERSITY, FRESNO
FRESNO, CALIFORNIA

General State-supported, comprehensive, coed **Entrance** Moderately difficult **Setting** 1,410-acre urban campus **Total enrollment** 20,007 **Student-faculty ratio** 13:1 **Application deadline** 7/28 (freshmen), 7/28 (transfer) **Freshmen** 66% were admitted **Housing** Yes **Expenses** Tuition $1762; Room & Board $6000 **Undergraduates** 58% women, 20% part-time, 22% 25 or older, 1% Native American, 28% Hispanic American, 5% African American, 12% Asian American/Pacific Islander **The most frequently chosen baccalaureate fields are** education, health professions and related sciences, social sciences and history **Academic program** English as a second language, advanced placement, accelerated degree program, self-designed majors, honors program, summer session, adult/continuing education programs, internships **Contact** Ms. Vivian Franco, Director, California State University, Fresno, 5150 North Maple Avenue, M/S JA 57, Fresno, CA 93740-8026. Telephone: 559-278-2261. Fax: 559-278-4812. E-mail: donna_mills@csufresno.edu. Web site: http://www.csufresno.edu/.

CALIFORNIA STATE UNIVERSITY, FULLERTON
FULLERTON, CALIFORNIA

General State-supported, comprehensive, coed **Entrance** Moderately difficult **Setting** 225-acre suburban campus **Total enrollment** 30,357 **Student-faculty ratio** 21:1 **Application deadline** Rolling (freshmen), rolling (transfer) **Freshmen** 69% were admitted **Housing** Yes **Expenses** Tuition $1849; Room only $3993 **Undergraduates** 60% women, 30% part-time, 25% 25 or older, 1% Native American, 25% Hispanic American, 3% African American, 24% Asian American/Pacific Islander **The most frequently chosen baccalaureate fields are** business/marketing, communications/communication technologies, education **Academic program** English as a second language, advanced placement, self-designed majors, honors program, summer session, adult/continuing education programs, internships **Contact** Ms. Nancy J. Dority, Admissions Director, California State University, Fullerton, Office of Admissions and Records, PO Box 6900, Fullerton, CA 92834-6900. Telephone: 714-278-2370. Web site: http://www.fullerton.edu/.

CALIFORNIA STATE UNIVERSITY, HAYWARD
HAYWARD, CALIFORNIA

General State-supported, comprehensive, coed **Entrance** Moderately difficult **Setting** 343-acre suburban campus **Total enrollment** 13,240 **Student-faculty ratio** 21:1 **Application deadline** 9/7 (freshmen), 9/7 (transfer) **Freshmen** 89% were admitted **Housing** Yes **Expenses** Tuition $1767; Room only $3200 **Undergraduates** 64% women, 25% part-time, 35% 25 or older, 1% Native American, 11% Hispanic American, 11% African American, 25% Asian American/Pacific Islander **The most frequently chosen baccalaureate fields are** business/marketing, liberal arts/general studies, social sciences and history **Academic program** English as a second language, advanced placement, accelerated degree program, self-designed majors, honors program, summer session, adult/continuing education programs, internships **Contact** Ms. Susan Lakis, Associate Director of Admissions, California State University, Hayward, 25800 Carlos Bee Boulevard, Hayward, CA 94542-3035. Telephone: 510-885-3248. Fax: 510-885-3816. E-mail: adminfo@csuhayward.edu. Web site: http://www.csuhayward.edu/.

CALIFORNIA STATE UNIVERSITY, LONG BEACH
LONG BEACH, CALIFORNIA

General State-supported, comprehensive, coed **Entrance** Moderately difficult **Setting** 320-acre suburban campus **Total enrollment** 33,259 **Student-faculty ratio** 20:1 **Application deadline** 11/30 (freshmen) **Freshmen** 85% were admitted **Housing** Yes **Expenses** Tuition $1744; Room & Board $5800 **Undergraduates** 59% women, 23% part-time, 24% 25 or older, 1% Native American, 23% Hispanic American, 7% African American, 21% Asian American/Pacific Islander **The most frequently chosen baccalaureate fields are** business/marketing, social sciences and history, visual/performing arts **Academic program** English as a second language, advanced placement, accelerated degree program, self-designed majors, honors program, summer session, adult/continuing education programs, internships **Contact** Mr. Thomas Enders, Director of Enrollment Services, California State University, Long Beach, Brotman Hall, 1250 Bellflower Boulevard, Long

CALIFORNIA

California State University, Long Beach *(continued)*
Beach, CA 90840. Telephone: 562-985-4641. Web site: http://www.csulb.edu/.

CALIFORNIA STATE UNIVERSITY, LOS ANGELES
LOS ANGELES, CALIFORNIA

General State-supported, comprehensive, coed **Entrance** Moderately difficult **Setting** 173-acre urban campus **Total enrollment** 20,675 **Student-faculty ratio** 21:1 **Application deadline** 6/15 (freshmen), 6/15 (transfer) **Freshmen** 53% were admitted **Housing** Yes **Expenses** Tuition $1782; Room & Board $6399 **Undergraduates** 61% women, 28% part-time, 0.4% Native American, 49% Hispanic American, 8% African American, 20% Asian American/Pacific Islander **The most frequently chosen baccalaureate fields are** business/marketing, home economics/vocational home economics, protective services/public administration **Academic program** English as a second language, advanced placement, accelerated degree program, self-designed majors, honors program, summer session, adult/continuing education programs, internships **Contact** Mr. Vince Lopez, Assistant Director of Outreach and Recruitment, California State University, Los Angeles, 5151 State University Drive, Los Angeles, CA 90032-8530. Telephone: 323-343-3839. E-mail: jslanin@calstatela.edu. Web site: http://www.calstatela.edu/.

CALIFORNIA STATE UNIVERSITY, MONTEREY BAY
SEASIDE, CALIFORNIA

General State-supported, comprehensive, coed **Entrance** Minimally difficult **Setting** 1,500-acre campus **Total enrollment** 3,020 **Student-faculty ratio** 20:1 **Application deadline** Rolling (freshmen), rolling (transfer) **Freshmen** 83% were admitted **Housing** Yes **Expenses** Tuition $928; Room & Board $4900 **Undergraduates** 58% women, 3% part-time, 29% 25 or older, 1% Native American, 27% Hispanic American, 4% African American, 6% Asian American/Pacific Islander **The most frequently chosen baccalaureate fields are** computer/information sciences, liberal arts/general studies, natural resources/environmental science **Academic program** Self-designed majors, internships **Contact** Ms. Valarie E. Brown, Director of Admissions and Records, California State University, Monterey Bay, 100 Campus Center, Building 47, Seaside, CA 93955. Telephone: 831-582-4093. Fax: 831-582-3087. E-mail: moreinfo-prospective@csumb.edu. Web site: http://www.csumb.edu/.

CALIFORNIA STATE UNIVERSITY, NORTHRIDGE
NORTHRIDGE, CALIFORNIA

General State-supported, comprehensive, coed **Entrance** Moderately difficult **Setting** 353-acre urban campus **Total enrollment** 31,448 **Application deadline** 11/30 (freshmen), rolling (transfer) **Freshmen** 83% were admitted **Housing** Yes **Expenses** Room & Board $6400 **Undergraduates** 59% women, 25% part-time, 1% Native American, 26% Hispanic American, 8% African American, 13% Asian American/Pacific Islander **Academic program** English as a second language, advanced placement, accelerated degree program, self-designed majors, honors program, summer session, adult/continuing education programs **Contact** Ms. Mary Baxton, Associate Director of Admissions and Records, California State University, Northridge, 18111 Nordhoff Street, Northridge, CA 91330-8207. Telephone: 818-677-3777. Fax: 818-677-3766. E-mail: outreach.recruitment@csun.edu. Web site: http://www.csun.edu/.

CALIFORNIA STATE UNIVERSITY, SACRAMENTO
SACRAMENTO, CALIFORNIA

General State-supported, comprehensive, coed **Entrance** Moderately difficult **Setting** 288-acre urban campus **Total enrollment** 26,923 **Student-faculty ratio** 21:1 **Application deadline** Rolling (freshmen), 8/1 (transfer) **Freshmen** 52% were admitted **Housing** Yes **Expenses** Tuition $1887; Room & Board $5601 **Undergraduates** 57% women, 25% part-time, 28% 25 or older, 1% Native American, 13% Hispanic American, 6% African American, 19% Asian American/Pacific Islander **The most frequently chosen baccalaureate fields are** business/marketing, protective services/public administration, social sciences and history **Academic program** English as a second language, advanced placement, self-designed majors, summer session, internships **Contact** Mr. Emiliano Diaz, Director of University Outreach Services, California State University, Sacramento, 6000 J Street, Lassen Hall, Sacramento, CA 95819-6048. Telephone: 916-278-7362. Fax: 916-278-5603. E-mail: glasmirel@csus.edu. Web site: http://www.csus.edu/.

CALIFORNIA STATE UNIVERSITY, SAN BERNARDINO
SAN BERNARDINO, CALIFORNIA

General State-supported, comprehensive, coed **Entrance** Moderately difficult **Setting** 430-acre suburban campus **Total enrollment** 15,985 **Student-faculty ratio** 19:1 **Application deadline** Rolling (freshmen), rolling (transfer) **Freshmen** 100% were admitted **Housing** Yes **Expenses** Room & Board $4783 **Undergraduates** 63% women, 17% part-time, 52% 25 or older, 1% Native American, 29% Hispanic American, 11% African American, 7% Asian American/Pacific Islander **The most frequently chosen baccalaureate fields are** business/marketing, liberal arts/general studies, social sciences and history **Academic program** English as a second language, advanced placement, self-designed majors, honors program, summer session, adult/continuing education programs **Contact** Ms. Cynthia Shum, Admissions Counselor, California State University, San Bernardino, 5500 University Parkway, San Bernardino, CA 92407-2397. Telephone: 909-880-5212

CALIFORNIA

or toll-free 909-880-5188. Fax: 909-880-7034. E-mail: moreinfo@mail.csusb.edu. Web site: http://www.csusb.edu/.

CALIFORNIA STATE UNIVERSITY, SAN MARCOS
SAN MARCOS, CALIFORNIA

General State-supported, comprehensive, coed **Entrance** Moderately difficult **Setting** 302-acre suburban campus **Total enrollment** 5,676 **Student-faculty ratio** 18:1 **Application deadline** Rolling (freshmen), rolling (transfer) **Freshmen** 62% were admitted **Housing** Yes **Expenses** Tuition $1706 **Undergraduates** 60% women, 35% part-time, 37% 25 or older, 1% Native American, 18% Hispanic American, 3% African American, 9% Asian American/Pacific Islander **The most frequently chosen baccalaureate fields are** liberal arts/general studies, business/marketing, social sciences and history **Academic program** English as a second language, advanced placement, self-designed majors, summer session, adult/continuing education programs, internships **Contact** Ms. Cherine Heckman, Director of Admissions, California State University, San Marcos, San Marcos, CA 92096-0001. Telephone: 760-750-4848. Fax: 760-750-3285. E-mail: apply@csusm.edu. Web site: http://ww2.csusm.edu/.

CALIFORNIA STATE UNIVERSITY, STANISLAUS
TURLOCK, CALIFORNIA

General State-supported, comprehensive, coed **Entrance** Moderately difficult **Setting** 220-acre small-town campus **Total enrollment** 7,534 **Student-faculty ratio** 18:1 **Application deadline** 5/31 (freshmen), 5/31 (transfer) **Freshmen** 68% were admitted **Housing** Yes **Expenses** Tuition $1875; Room & Board $7020 **Undergraduates** 67% women, 32% part-time, 34% 25 or older, 1% Native American, 25% Hispanic American, 3% African American, 9% Asian American/Pacific Islander **The most frequently chosen baccalaureate fields are** business/marketing, liberal arts/general studies, social sciences and history **Academic program** English as a second language, advanced placement, self-designed majors, honors program, summer session, adult/continuing education programs, internships **Contact** Admissions Office, California State University, Stanislaus, Enrollment Services, 801 West Monte Vista Avenue, Mary Stuart Rogers Gateway Center, Room 120, Turlock, CA 95382. Telephone: 209-667-3070 or toll-free 800-300-7420 (in-state). Fax: 209-667-3788. E-mail: outreach@toto.csustan.edu. Web site: http://www.csustan.edu/.

CHAPMAN UNIVERSITY
ORANGE, CALIFORNIA

General Independent, comprehensive, coed, affiliated with Christian Church (Disciples of Christ) **Entrance** Moderately difficult **Setting** 42-acre suburban campus **Total enrollment** 4,192 **Student-faculty ratio** 13:1 **Application deadline** 1/31 (freshmen), 3/15 (transfer) **Freshmen** 77% were admitted **Housing** Yes **Expenses** Tuition $22,256; Room & Board $7712 **Undergraduates** 56% women, 8% part-time, 17% 25 or older **The most frequently chosen baccalaureate fields are** business/marketing, social sciences and history, visual/performing arts **Academic program** English as a second language, advanced placement, accelerated degree program, honors program, summer session, adult/continuing education programs, internships **Contact** Mr. Michael O. Drummy, Associate Dean for Enrollment Services and Chief Admission Officer, Chapman University, One University Drive, Orange, CA 92866. Telephone: 714-997-6711 or toll-free 888-CUAPPLY. Fax: 714-997-6713. E-mail: admit@chapman.edu. Web site: http://www.chapman.edu/.

CHARLES R. DREW UNIVERSITY OF MEDICINE AND SCIENCE
LOS ANGELES, CALIFORNIA

General Independent, comprehensive, coed **Entrance** Moderately difficult **Total enrollment** 626 **Application deadline** 4/30 (freshmen), 4/30 (transfer) **Freshmen** 25% were admitted **Housing** No **Academic program** Internships **Contact** Ms. Mala Sharma, Director of Enrollment Services, Charles R. Drew University of Medicine and Science, 1731 East 120th Street, Los Angeles, CA 90059. Telephone: 323-563-4832. Web site: http://www.cdrewu.edu/.

CHRISTIAN HERITAGE COLLEGE
EL CAJON, CALIFORNIA

General Independent nondenominational, 4-year, coed **Entrance** Moderately difficult **Setting** 32-acre suburban campus **Total enrollment** 636 **Student-faculty ratio** 11:1 **Application deadline** 8/1 (freshmen), 8/1 (transfer) **Freshmen** 46% were admitted **Housing** Yes **Expenses** Tuition $12,550; Room & Board $5330 **Undergraduates** 58% women, 13% part-time, 27% 25 or older, 1% Native American, 10% Hispanic American, 7% African American, 4% Asian American/Pacific Islander **The most frequently chosen baccalaureate fields are** business/marketing, interdisciplinary studies, philosophy **Academic program** English as a second language, advanced placement, self-designed majors, summer session, adult/continuing education programs, internships **Contact** Ms. Jennifer Wiersma, Director of Admissions, Christian Heritage College, 2100 Greenfield Drive, El Cajon, CA 92019-1157. Telephone: 619-588-7747 or toll-free 800-676-2242. Fax: 619-440-0209. E-mail: chcadm@adm.christianheritage.edu. Web site: http://www.christianheritage.edu/.

CLAREMONT MCKENNA COLLEGE
CLAREMONT, CALIFORNIA

General Independent, 4-year, coed **Entrance** Very difficult **Setting** 50-acre small-town campus **Total enrollment** 1,044 **Student-faculty ratio** 7:1 **Application deadline** 1/1 (freshmen), 4/1 (transfer) **Freshmen** 29% were admitted **Housing** Yes **Expenses**

CALIFORNIA

Claremont McKenna College *(continued)*
Tuition $24,540; Room & Board $8160 **Undergraduates** 47% women, 1% 25 or older, 0.4% Native American, 9% Hispanic American, 4% African American, 15% Asian American/Pacific Islander **The most frequently chosen baccalaureate field is** philosophy, religion, and theology **Academic program** Advanced placement, accelerated degree program, self-designed majors, honors program, internships **Contact** Mr. Richard C. Vos, Vice President/Dean of Admission and Financial Aid, Claremont McKenna College, 890 Columbia Avenue, Claremont, CA 91711. Telephone: 909-621-8088. E-mail: admission@mckenna.edu. Web site: http://www.claremontmckenna.edu.

▶ For more information, see page 412.

CLEVELAND CHIROPRACTIC COLLEGE-LOS ANGELES CAMPUS
LOS ANGELES, CALIFORNIA

Contact Cleveland Chiropractic College-Los Angeles Campus, 590 North Vermont Avenue, Los Angeles, CA 90004-2196. Telephone: or toll-free 800-446-CCLA. Web site: http://www.clevelandchiropractic.edu/.

COGSWELL POLYTECHNICAL COLLEGE
SUNNYVALE, CALIFORNIA

General Independent, 4-year, coed, primarily men **Entrance** Moderately difficult **Setting** 2-acre suburban campus **Total enrollment** 413 **Student-faculty ratio** 15:1 **Application deadline** 6/1 (freshmen), 6/1 (transfer) **Freshmen** 100% were admitted **Housing** Yes **Expenses** Tuition $9600; Room only $6300 **Undergraduates** 12% women, 52% part-time, 50% 25 or older, 0.2% Native American, 7% Hispanic American, 2% African American, 15% Asian American/Pacific Islander **The most frequently chosen baccalaureate fields are** engineering/engineering technologies, visual/performing arts **Academic program** Advanced placement, summer session, adult/continuing education programs **Contact** Mr. Paul A. Schreivogel, Dean of Recruitment and Marketing, Cogswell Polytechnical College, 1175 Bordeaux Drive, Sunnyvale, CA 94089. Telephone: 408-541-0100 Ext. 112 or toll-free 800-264-7955. Fax: 408-747-0764. E-mail: admin@cogswell.edu. Web site: http://www.cogswell.edu/.

COLEMAN COLLEGE
LA MESA, CALIFORNIA

General Independent, comprehensive, coed **Entrance** Moderately difficult **Setting** suburban campus **Total enrollment** 1,022 **Application deadline** Rolling (freshmen), rolling (transfer) **Housing** No **Expenses** Tuition $6000 **Undergraduates** 68% 25 or older, 0% Native American, 12% Hispanic American, 5% African American, 15% Asian American/Pacific Islander **The most frequently chosen baccalaureate field is** computer/information sciences **Academic program** Accelerated degree program, summer session **Contact** Admissions Department, Coleman College, 7380 Parkway Drive, La Mesa, CA 91942-1532. Telephone: 619-465-3990. Fax: 619-465-0162. E-mail: jschafer@cts.com. Web site: http://www.coleman.edu/.

COLLEGE OF NOTRE DAME
See Notre Dame de Namur University

COLUMBIA COLLEGE–HOLLYWOOD
TARZANA, CALIFORNIA

General Independent, 4-year, coed **Entrance** Minimally difficult **Setting** 1-acre urban campus **Total enrollment** 109 **Student-faculty ratio** 5:1 **Application deadline** Rolling (freshmen) **Freshmen** 85% were admitted **Housing** No **Expenses** Tuition $10,725 **Undergraduates** 21% women, 21% 25 or older, 0% Native American, 7% Hispanic American, 4% African American, 5% Asian American/Pacific Islander **The most frequently chosen baccalaureate field is** communications/communication technologies **Academic program** Accelerated degree program, summer session, adult/continuing education programs **Contact** Amanda Kraus, Admissions Director, Columbia College–Hollywood, 18618 Oxnard Street, Tarzana, CA 91356. Telephone: 818-345-8414. Fax: 818-345-9053. E-mail: cchadfin@columbiacollege.edu. Web site: http://www.columbiacollege.edu/.

CONCORDIA UNIVERSITY
IRVINE, CALIFORNIA

General Independent, comprehensive, coed, affiliated with Lutheran Church–Missouri Synod **Entrance** Moderately difficult **Setting** 70-acre suburban campus **Total enrollment** 1,314 **Student-faculty ratio** 16:1 **Application deadline** Rolling (freshmen), rolling (transfer) **Freshmen** 28% were admitted **Housing** Yes **Expenses** Tuition $16,480; Room & Board $5810 **Undergraduates** 67% women, 9% part-time, 13% 25 or older, 1% Native American, 9% Hispanic American, 3% African American, 7% Asian American/Pacific Islander **The most frequently chosen baccalaureate fields are** business/marketing, philosophy, philosophy, religion, and theology **Academic program** English as a second language, advanced placement, self-designed majors, honors program, summer session, adult/continuing education programs, internships **Contact** Ms. Lori McDonald, Director of Enrollment Services, Concordia University, 1530 Concordia West, Irvine, CA 92612-3299. Telephone: 949-854-8002 Ext. 1170 or toll-free 800-229-1200. Fax: 949-854-6894. E-mail: admission@cui.edu. Web site: http://www.cui.edu/.

DESIGN INSTITUTE OF SAN DIEGO
SAN DIEGO, CALIFORNIA

General Proprietary, 4-year, coed **Entrance** Noncompetitive **Setting** urban campus **Total enrollment** 350 **Application deadline** Rolling (freshmen), rolling (transfer) **Housing** No **Expenses** Tuition $10,200 **Undergraduates** 70% 25 or older **Academic program** Internships **Contact** Ms. Paula Parrish, Director of Admissions, Design Institute of San Diego,

CALIFORNIA

8555 Commerce Avenue, San Diego, CA 92121-2685. Telephone: 619-566-1200 or toll-free 800-619-4DESIGN (out-of-state). Fax: 619-566-2711. E-mail: admissions@disd.edu. Web site: http://www.disd.edu/.

DEVRY UNIVERSITY
FREMONT, CALIFORNIA

General Proprietary, 4-year, coed **Entrance** Minimally difficult **Setting** 17-acre suburban campus **Total enrollment** 2,278 **Student-faculty ratio** 26:1 **Application deadline** Rolling (freshmen), rolling (transfer) **Freshmen** 84% were admitted **Housing** No **Expenses** Tuition $9800 **Undergraduates** 22% women, 18% part-time, 30% 25 or older, 6% Native American, 17% Hispanic American, 6% African American, 40% Asian American/Pacific Islander **The most frequently chosen baccalaureate fields are** business/marketing, computer/information sciences, engineering/engineering technologies **Academic program** Advanced placement, accelerated degree program, summer session, adult/continuing education programs **Contact** Mr. Bruce Williams, New Student Coordinator, DeVry University, 6600 Dumbarton Circle, Fremont, CA 94555. Telephone: 510-574-1111 or toll-free 888-393-3879. Web site: http://www.fre.devry.edu/.

DEVRY UNIVERSITY
LONG BEACH, CALIFORNIA

General Proprietary, 4-year, coed **Entrance** Minimally difficult **Setting** 23-acre urban campus **Total enrollment** 2,853 **Student-faculty ratio** 22:1 **Application deadline** Rolling (freshmen), rolling (transfer) **Freshmen** 81% were admitted **Housing** No **Expenses** Tuition $9205 **Undergraduates** 28% women, 29% part-time, 47% 25 or older, 1% Native American, 26% Hispanic American, 13% African American, 32% Asian American/Pacific Islander **The most frequently chosen baccalaureate fields are** business/marketing, computer/information sciences, engineering/engineering technologies **Academic program** Advanced placement, summer session, adult/continuing education programs **Contact** Ms. Lisa Flores, New Student Coordinator, DeVry University, 3880 Kilroy Airport, Long Beach, CA 90806. Telephone: 562-427-0861 or toll-free 800-597-0444 (out-of-state). Fax: 562-997-5371. Web site: http://www.lb.devry.edu/.

DEVRY UNIVERSITY
POMONA, CALIFORNIA

General Proprietary, 4-year, coed **Entrance** Minimally difficult **Setting** 15-acre urban campus **Total enrollment** 3,669 **Student-faculty ratio** 25:1 **Application deadline** Rolling (freshmen), rolling (transfer) **Freshmen** 85% were admitted **Housing** No **Expenses** Tuition $9205 **Undergraduates** 26% women, 30% part-time, 42% 25 or older, 1% Native American, 31% Hispanic American, 8% African American, 34% Asian American/Pacific Islander **The most frequently chosen baccalaureate fields are** business/marketing, computer/information sciences, engineering/engineering technologies **Academic program** Advanced placement, accelerated degree program, summer session, adult/continuing education programs **Contact** Ms. Melanie Guerra, New Student Coordinator, DeVry University, 901 Corporate Center Drive, Pomona, CA 91768-2642. Telephone: 909-622-8866 or toll-free 800-243-3660. Fax: 909-868-4165. Web site: http://www.pom.devry.edu/.

DEVRY UNIVERSITY
WEST HILLS, CALIFORNIA

General Proprietary, 4-year, coed **Entrance** Minimally difficult **Total enrollment** 1,351 **Student-faculty ratio** 16:1 **Application deadline** Rolling (freshmen), rolling (transfer) **Freshmen** 78% were admitted **Housing** No **Expenses** Tuition $9205 **Undergraduates** 24% women, 37% part-time, 40% 25 or older, 1% Native American, 26% Hispanic American, 6% African American, 31% Asian American/Pacific Islander **The most frequently chosen baccalaureate field is** business/marketing **Academic program** Advanced placement, summer session, adult/continuing education programs **Contact** Ms. Denise Barba, Acting Director of Admissions, DeVry University, 22801 Roscoe Boulevard, West Hills, CA 91304. Telephone: 818-932-3001. Fax: 818-713-8118. Web site: http://www.wh.devry.edu/.

DOMINICAN SCHOOL OF PHILOSOPHY AND THEOLOGY
BERKELEY, CALIFORNIA

General Independent Roman Catholic, upper-level, coed **Entrance** Moderately difficult **Setting** urban campus **Total enrollment** 118 **Student-faculty ratio** 6:1 **Application deadline** Rolling (transfer) **Housing** Yes **Expenses** Tuition $8618 **Undergraduates** 12% women, 65% 25 or older, 12% Hispanic American, 6% African American, 12% Asian American/Pacific Islander **The most frequently chosen baccalaureate field is** philosophy **Contact** Ms. Susan McGinnis Hardie, Admissions Director, Dominican School of Philosophy and Theology, 2401 Ridge Road, Berkeley, CA 94709-1295. Telephone: 510-883-2073. Fax: 510-849-1372. E-mail: smcginnishardie@dspt.edu. Web site: http://www.dspt.edu/.

DOMINICAN UNIVERSITY OF CALIFORNIA
SAN RAFAEL, CALIFORNIA

General Independent, comprehensive, coed, affiliated with Roman Catholic Church **Entrance** Moderately difficult **Setting** 80-acre suburban campus **Total enrollment** 1,436 **Student-faculty ratio** 12:1 **Application deadline** Rolling (freshmen), rolling (transfer) **Freshmen** 50% were admitted **Housing** Yes **Expenses** Tuition $17,606; Room & Board $8440 **Undergraduates** 77% women, 29% part-time, 42% 25 or older, 1% Native American, 10% Hispanic American, 7% African American, 12% Asian American/Pacific Islander **The most frequently chosen bacca-**

CALIFORNIA

Dominican University of California *(continued)*
laureate fields are business/marketing, health professions and related sciences, liberal arts/general studies **Academic program** English as a second language, advanced placement, self-designed majors, honors program, summer session, adult/continuing education programs, internships **Contact** Mr. Art Criss, Director of Admissions, Dominican University of California, 50 Acacia Avenue, San Rafael, CA 94901-2298. Telephone: 415-257-1376 or toll-free 888-323-6763. Fax: 415-385-3214. E-mail: enroll@dominican.edu. Web site: http://www.dominican.edu/.

EDUCATION AMERICA UNIVERSITY
SAN DIEGO, CALIFORNIA

Contact Education America University, 123 Camino de la Reina, North Building, Suite 100, San Diego, CA 92108. Telephone: or toll-free 800-214-7001.

EMMANUEL BIBLE COLLEGE
PASADENA, CALIFORNIA

General Independent, 4-year, affiliated with Church of the Nazarene **Total enrollment** 20 **Student-faculty ratio** 10:1 **Application deadline** 9/15 (freshmen) **Freshmen** 100% were admitted **Housing** No **Expenses** Tuition $48,000; Room & Board $4800 **Undergraduates** 20% women, 70% part-time, 100% 25 or older, 35% Hispanic American, 5% Asian American/Pacific Islander **The most frequently chosen baccalaureate field is** philosophy, religion, and theology **Academic program** Adult/continuing education programs, internships **Contact** Mr. Yeghia Babikian, President, Emmanuel Bible College, 1605 East Elizabeth Street, 1536 East Howard Street, Pasadena, CA 91104. Telephone: 626-791-2575. Fax: 626-398-2424. Web site: http://www.emmanuelbiblecollege.edu.

FRESNO PACIFIC UNIVERSITY
FRESNO, CALIFORNIA

General Independent, comprehensive, coed, affiliated with Mennonite Brethren Church **Entrance** Moderately difficult **Setting** 42-acre suburban campus **Total enrollment** 1,456 **Student-faculty ratio** 16:1 **Application deadline** Rolling (freshmen), rolling (transfer) **Freshmen** 73% were admitted **Housing** Yes **Expenses** Tuition $15,310; Room & Board $4430 **Undergraduates** 68% women, 9% part-time, 13% 25 or older, 1% Native American, 22% Hispanic American, 2% African American, 3% Asian American/Pacific Islander **The most frequently chosen baccalaureate fields are** business/marketing, education, philosophy **Academic program** English as a second language, advanced placement, accelerated degree program, self-designed majors, summer session, adult/continuing education programs, internships **Contact** Cary Templeton, Assistant Dean of Enrollment Services, Fresno Pacific University, 1717 South Chestnut Avenue, Fresno, CA 93702. Telephone: 559-453-2000 or toll-free 800-660-6089 (in-state). Fax: 559-453-2007. E-mail: ugadmis@fresno.edu. Web site: http://www.fresno.edu/.

GOLDEN GATE UNIVERSITY
SAN FRANCISCO, CALIFORNIA

General Independent, university, coed **Entrance** Moderately difficult **Setting** urban campus **Total enrollment** 5,322 **Student-faculty ratio** 17:1 **Application deadline** 6/1 (freshmen), 6/1 (transfer) **Freshmen** 100% were admitted **Housing** No **Expenses** Tuition $9192 **Undergraduates** 60% women, 73% part-time, 80% 25 or older, 0.4% Native American, 8% Hispanic American, 9% African American, 13% Asian American/Pacific Islander **The most frequently chosen baccalaureate fields are** business/marketing, computer/information sciences, psychology **Academic program** English as a second language, advanced placement, accelerated degree program, summer session, adult/continuing education programs, internships **Contact** Ms. Cherron Hoppes, Director of Admission, Golden Gate University, 536 Mission Street, San Francisco, CA 94105-2968. Telephone: 415-442-7800 or toll-free 800-448-4968. Fax: 415-442-7807. E-mail: info@ggu.edu. Web site: http://www.ggu.edu/.

HARVEY MUDD COLLEGE
CLAREMONT, CALIFORNIA

General Independent, comprehensive, coed **Entrance** Most difficult **Setting** 33-acre suburban campus **Total enrollment** 707 **Student-faculty ratio** 9:1 **Application deadline** 1/15 (freshmen), 4/1 (transfer) **Freshmen** 34% were admitted **Housing** Yes **Expenses** Tuition $25,506; Room & Board $8544 **Undergraduates** 32% women, 1% 25 or older, 1% Native American, 4% Hispanic American, 1% African American, 22% Asian American/Pacific Islander **The most frequently chosen baccalaureate fields are** engineering/engineering technologies, computer/information sciences, physical sciences **Academic program** Advanced placement, self-designed majors, internships **Contact** Mr. Deren Finks, Vice President and Dean of Admissions and Financial Aid, Harvey Mudd College, 301 East 12th Street, Claremont, CA 91711. Telephone: 909-621-8011. Fax: 909-607-7046. E-mail: admission@hmc.edu. Web site: http://www.hmc.edu/.

HOLY NAMES COLLEGE
OAKLAND, CALIFORNIA

General Independent Roman Catholic, comprehensive, coed, primarily women **Entrance** Moderately difficult **Setting** 60-acre urban campus **Total enrollment** 832 **Student-faculty ratio** 11:1 **Application deadline** 8/1 (freshmen), 8/1 (transfer) **Freshmen** 71% were admitted **Housing** Yes **Expenses** Tuition $16,620; Room & Board $6600 **Undergraduates** 78% women, 41% part-time, 59% 25 or older, 0.4% Native American, 14% Hispanic American, 33% African American, 8% Asian American/Pacific Islander **The most frequently chosen baccalaureate fields**

are business/marketing, health professions and related sciences, liberal arts/general studies **Academic program** English as a second language, advanced placement, accelerated degree program, self-designed majors, honors program, summer session, adult/continuing education programs, internships **Contact** Mr. Jeffrey D. Miller, Vice President for Enrollment Management, Holy Names College, Admission Office, Oakland, CA 94619. Telephone: 510-436-1351 or toll-free 800-430-1321. Fax: 510-436-1325. E-mail: admissions@admin.hnc.edu. Web site: http://www.hnc.edu/.

HOPE INTERNATIONAL UNIVERSITY
FULLERTON, CALIFORNIA

General Independent, comprehensive, coed, affiliated with Christian Churches and Churches of Christ **Entrance** Moderately difficult **Setting** 16-acre suburban campus **Total enrollment** 916 **Student-faculty ratio** 15:1 **Application deadline** 6/1 (freshmen), 5/1 (transfer) **Freshmen** 42% were admitted **Housing** Yes **Expenses** Tuition $12,140; Room & Board $4424 **Undergraduates** 53% women, 18% part-time, 37% 25 or older, 0.2% Native American, 14% Hispanic American, 4% African American, 4% Asian American/Pacific Islander **Academic program** English as a second language, advanced placement, accelerated degree program, self-designed majors, honors program, summer session, adult/continuing education programs, internships **Contact** Ms. Midge Madden, Office Manager, Hope International University, 2500 East Nutwood Avenue, Fullerton, CA 92831-3138. Telephone: 714-879-3901 Ext. 2235 or toll-free 800-762-1294 Ext. 2235. Fax: 714-526-0231 Ext. 2235. E-mail: mfmadden@hiu.edu. Web site: http://www.hiu.edu/.

HUMBOLDT STATE UNIVERSITY
ARCATA, CALIFORNIA

General State-supported, comprehensive, coed **Entrance** Moderately difficult **Setting** 161-acre rural campus **Total enrollment** 7,382 **Student-faculty ratio** 16:1 **Application deadline** Rolling (freshmen), 11/30 (transfer) **Freshmen** 74% were admitted **Housing** Yes **Expenses** Room & Board $6092 **Undergraduates** 55% women, 11% part-time, 25% 25 or older, 3% Native American, 8% Hispanic American, 3% African American, 3% Asian American/Pacific Islander **The most frequently chosen baccalaureate fields are** interdisciplinary studies, natural resources/environmental science, trade and industry **Academic program** English as a second language, advanced placement, self-designed majors, honors program, summer session, adult/continuing education programs, internships **Contact** Ms. Rebecca Kalal, Assistant Director of Admissions, Humboldt State University, 1 Harpst Street, Arcata, CA 95521-8299. Telephone: 707-826-4402. Fax: 707-826-6194. E-mail: hsuinfo@laurel.humboldt.edu. Web site: http://www.humboldt.edu/.

HUMPHREYS COLLEGE
STOCKTON, CALIFORNIA

Contact Ms. Wilma Okamoto Vaughn, Dean of Administration, Humphreys College, 6650 Inglewood Avenue, Stockton, CA 95207-3896. Telephone: 209-478-0800. Fax: 209-478-8721. Web site: http://www.humphreys.edu/.

INSTITUTE OF COMPUTER TECHNOLOGY
LOS ANGELES, CALIFORNIA

General Proprietary, 4-year, coed **Entrance** Noncompetitive **Setting** urban campus **Total enrollment** 286 **Student-faculty ratio** 21:1 **Freshmen** 30% were admitted **Housing** No **Expenses** Tuition $19,095 **Undergraduates** 27% women, 94% 25 or older, 0% Native American, 23% Hispanic American, 11% African American, 36% Asian American/Pacific Islander **The most frequently chosen baccalaureate fields are** business/marketing, computer/information sciences **Academic program** Advanced placement, internships **Contact** Mr. Phil Singer, Director of Admissions, Institute of Computer Technology, 3200 Wilshire Boulevard 4th Floor, Los Angeles, CA 90010. Telephone: 213-383-8300 Ext. 112. E-mail: psinger@ictcollege.edu. Web site: http://www.ictcollege.edu/.

INTERIOR DESIGNERS INSTITUTE
NEWPORT BEACH, CALIFORNIA

Contact Interior Designers Institute, 1061 Camelback Road, Newport Beach, CA 92660. Web site: http://www.idi.edu/main.html.

INTERNATIONAL TECHNOLOGICAL UNIVERSITY
SANTA CLARA, CALIFORNIA

Contact International Technological University, 1650 Warburton Avenue, Santa Clara, CA 95050. Web site: http://www.itu.edu/.

JOHN F. KENNEDY UNIVERSITY
ORINDA, CALIFORNIA

General Independent, comprehensive, coed **Entrance** Noncompetitive **Setting** 14-acre suburban campus **Total enrollment** 1,525 **Student-faculty ratio** 12:1 **Application deadline** Rolling (transfer) **Housing** No **Expenses** Tuition $11,646 **Undergraduates** 80% women, 90% part-time, 93% 25 or older **The most frequently chosen baccalaureate fields are** business/marketing, liberal arts/general studies, psychology **Academic program** Advanced placement, self-designed majors, summer session, adult/continuing education programs **Contact** Ms. Ellena Bloedorn, Director of Admissions and Records, John F. Kennedy University, 12 Altarinda Road, Orinda, CA 94563-2603. Telephone: 925-258-2213 or toll-free 800-696-JFKU. Fax: 925-254-6964. E-mail: proginfo@jfku.edu. Web site: http://www.jfku.edu/.

CALIFORNIA

LA SIERRA UNIVERSITY
RIVERSIDE, CALIFORNIA

Contact Dr. Tom Smith, Vice President for Enrollment Services, La Sierra University, 4700 Pierce Street, Riverside, CA 92515-8247. Telephone: 909-785-2432 or toll-free 800-874-5587. Fax: 909-785-2901. E-mail: ivy@polaris.lasierra.edu. Web site: http://www.lasierra.edu/.

LIFE BIBLE COLLEGE
SAN DIMAS, CALIFORNIA

General Independent, 4-year, coed, affiliated with International Church of the Foursquare Gospel **Entrance** Moderately difficult **Setting** 9-acre suburban campus **Total enrollment** 480 **Student-faculty ratio** 18:1 **Application deadline** 7/1 (freshmen), 7/1 (transfer) **Freshmen** 96% were admitted **Housing** Yes **Expenses** Tuition $6700; Room & Board $3600 **Undergraduates** 48% women, 26% part-time, 20% 25 or older, 2% Native American, 14% Hispanic American, 4% African American, 5% Asian American/Pacific Islander **The most frequently chosen baccalaureate fields are** philosophy, philosophy, religion, and theology **Academic program** Advanced placement, summer session, adult/continuing education programs, internships **Contact** Mrs. Linda Hibdon, Admissions Director, LIFE Bible College, 1100 Covina Boulevard, San Dimas, CA 91773-3298. Telephone: 909-599-5433 Ext. 343 or toll-free 877-886-5433. Fax: 909-599-6690. E-mail: adm@lifebible.edu. Web site: http://www.lifebible.edu/.

LINCOLN UNIVERSITY
OAKLAND, CALIFORNIA

General Independent, comprehensive, coed **Entrance** Minimally difficult **Setting** 2-acre urban campus **Total enrollment** 48 **Student-faculty ratio** 14:1 **Application deadline** 8/31 (freshmen), 8/31 (transfer) **Housing** No **Expenses** Tuition $7121 **Undergraduates** 40% women, 58% 25 or older **Academic program** English as a second language, advanced placement, summer session, internships **Contact** Ms. Vivian Xu, Admissions Officer, Lincoln University, 401 15th Street, Oakland, CA 94612. Telephone: 415-221-1212 Ext. 115. Fax: 415-387-9730. E-mail: admissions@lincolnuca.edu. Web site: http://www.lincolnuca.edu/.

LOMA LINDA UNIVERSITY
LOMA LINDA, CALIFORNIA

General Independent Seventh-day Adventist, university, coed **Setting** small-town campus **Total enrollment** 3,260 **Student-faculty ratio** 2:1 **Housing** Yes **Expenses** Tuition $15,600; Room only $2724 **Undergraduates** 75% women, 27% part-time, 25% 25 or older, 1% Native American, 18% Hispanic American, 7% African American, 21% Asian American/Pacific Islander **Academic program** English as a second language **Contact** Loma Linda University, Loma Linda, CA 92350. Web site: http://www.llu.edu/.

LOYOLA MARYMOUNT UNIVERSITY
LOS ANGELES, CALIFORNIA

General Independent Roman Catholic, comprehensive, coed **Entrance** Very difficult **Setting** 128-acre suburban campus **Total enrollment** 7,921 **Student-faculty ratio** 13:1 **Application deadline** 2/1 (freshmen), 6/1 (transfer) **Freshmen** 60% were admitted **Housing** Yes **Expenses** Tuition $20,954; Room & Board $7800 **Undergraduates** 57% women, 7% part-time, 4% 25 or older, 1% Native American, 19% Hispanic American, 6% African American, 11% Asian American/Pacific Islander **The most frequently chosen baccalaureate fields are** business/marketing, psychology, visual/performing arts **Academic program** Advanced placement, accelerated degree program, self-designed majors, honors program, summer session, adult/continuing education programs, internships **Contact** Mr. Matthew X. Fissinger, Director of Admissions, Loyola Marymount University, One LMU Drive, Xavier Hall, Los Angeles, CA 90045-2659. Telephone: 310-338-2750 or toll-free 800-LMU-INFO. E-mail: admissions@lmu.edu. Web site: http://www.lmu.edu/.

▶ **For more information, see page 447.**

THE MASTER'S COLLEGE AND SEMINARY
SANTA CLARITA, CALIFORNIA

General Independent nondenominational, comprehensive, coed **Entrance** Moderately difficult **Setting** 110-acre suburban campus **Total enrollment** 1,522 **Student-faculty ratio** 23:1 **Application deadline** 3/2 (freshmen), 3/2 (transfer) **Freshmen** 80% were admitted **Housing** Yes **Expenses** Tuition $16,620; Room & Board $5780 **Undergraduates** 51% women, 6% part-time, 15% 25 or older, 1% Native American, 5% Hispanic American, 2% African American, 3% Asian American/Pacific Islander **The most frequently chosen baccalaureate fields are** business/marketing, education, philosophy **Academic program** Advanced placement, accelerated degree program, summer session, adult/continuing education programs, internships **Contact** Mr. Yaphet Peterson, Director of Enrollment, The Master's College and Seminary, 21726 Placerita Canyon Road, Santa Clarita, CA 91321. Telephone: 661-259-3540 Ext. 3365 or toll-free 800-568-6248. Fax: 661-288-1037. E-mail: enrollment@masters.edu. Web site: http://www.masters.edu/.

MENLO COLLEGE
ATHERTON, CALIFORNIA

General Independent, 4-year, coed **Entrance** Minimally difficult **Setting** 45-acre small-town campus **Total enrollment** 668 **Student-faculty ratio** 17:1 **Application deadline** Rolling (freshmen), rolling (transfer) **Freshmen** 70% were admitted **Housing** Yes **Expenses** Tuition $19,800; Room & Board $8400 **Undergraduates** 43% women, 16% part-time, 22% 25 or older, 0.3% Native American, 10% Hispanic American, 7% African American, 15% Asian American/

CALIFORNIA

Pacific Islander **The most frequently chosen baccalaureate fields are** business/marketing, communications/communication technologies, liberal arts/general studies **Academic program** English as a second language, advanced placement, accelerated degree program, self-designed majors, honors program, summer session, adult/continuing education programs, internships **Contact** Dr. Greg Smith, Dean of Admission and Financial Aid, Menlo College, 1000 El Camino Real, Atherton, CA 94027. Telephone: 650-543-3910 or toll-free 800-556-3656. Fax: 650-617-2395. E-mail: admissions@menlo.edu. Web site: http://www.menlo.edu/.

MILLS COLLEGE
OAKLAND, CALIFORNIA

General Independent, comprehensive, women only **Entrance** Moderately difficult **Setting** 135-acre urban campus **Total enrollment** 1,176 **Student-faculty ratio** 10:1 **Application deadline** 2/1 (freshmen), 3/2 (transfer) **Freshmen** 74% were admitted **Housing** Yes **Expenses** Tuition $20,622; Room & Board $8000 **Undergraduates** 6% part-time, 25% 25 or older, 1% Native American, 9% Hispanic American, 9% African American, 9% Asian American/Pacific Islander **The most frequently chosen baccalaureate fields are** mathematics, social sciences and history, visual/performing arts **Academic program** Advanced placement, self-designed majors, adult/continuing education programs, internships **Contact** Avis Hinkson, Dean of Admission, Mills College, 5000 MacArthur Boulevard, Oakland, CA 94613-1000. Telephone: 510-430-2135 or toll-free 800-87-MILLS. Fax: 510-430-3314. E-mail: admission@mills.edu. Web site: http://www.mills.edu/.

▶ For more information, see page 457.

MOUNT ST. MARY'S COLLEGE
LOS ANGELES, CALIFORNIA

General Independent Roman Catholic, comprehensive, coed, primarily women **Entrance** Moderately difficult **Setting** 71-acre suburban campus **Total enrollment** 1,965 **Student-faculty ratio** 16:1 **Application deadline** Rolling (freshmen), 3/15 (transfer) **Housing** Yes **Expenses** Tuition $18,588; Room & Board $7459 **Undergraduates** 95% women, 23% part-time, 31% 25 or older, 0.3% Native American, 45% Hispanic American, 11% African American, 15% Asian American/Pacific Islander **The most frequently chosen baccalaureate field is** philosophy, religion, and theology **Academic program** Advanced placement, accelerated degree program, self-designed majors, honors program, summer session, adult/continuing education programs, internships **Contact** Ms. Katy Murphy, Executive Director of Admissions and Financial Aid, Mount St. Mary's College, 12001 Chalon Road, Los Angeles, CA 90049-1599. Telephone: 310-954-4252 or toll-free 800-999-9893. E-mail: admissions@msmc.la.edu. Web site: http://www.msmc.la.edu/.

MT. SIERRA COLLEGE
MONROVIA, CALIFORNIA

General Proprietary, 4-year, coed **Entrance** Moderately difficult **Total enrollment** 1,100 **Student-faculty ratio** 20:1 **Freshmen** 73% were admitted **Expenses** Tuition $9359 **Undergraduates** 30% women, 1% part-time, 60% 25 or older, 4% Native American, 26% Hispanic American, 5% African American, 26% Asian American/Pacific Islander **The most frequently chosen baccalaureate fields are** computer/information sciences, visual/performing arts **Academic program** Accelerated degree program, summer session, adult/continuing education programs, internships **Contact** Mr. Robert Gray, Director of Admissions, Mt. Sierra College, 101 E. Huntington Drive, Monrovia, CA 91016. Telephone: 626-873-2100 Ext. 213 or toll-free 888-MtSierra (in-state). Fax: 626-359-5528. Web site: http://www.mtsierra.edu/.

MUSICIANS INSTITUTE
HOLLYWOOD, CALIFORNIA

Contact Mr. Steve Lunn, Admissions Representative, Musicians Institute, 1655 North McCadden Place, Hollywood, CA 90028. Telephone: 323-462-1384 Ext. 156 or toll-free 800-255-PLAY. E-mail: admissions@mi.edu. Web site: http://www.mi.edu/.

THE NATIONAL HISPANIC UNIVERSITY
SAN JOSE, CALIFORNIA

General Independent, 4-year, coed **Entrance** Minimally difficult **Setting** 1-acre urban campus **Total enrollment** 450 **Student-faculty ratio** 14:1 **Application deadline** 8/15 (freshmen), 8/15 (transfer) **Freshmen** 82% were admitted **Housing** No **Expenses** Tuition $3100 **Undergraduates** 40% 25 or older **The most frequently chosen baccalaureate fields are** business/marketing, computer/information sciences, liberal arts/general studies **Academic program** English as a second language, advanced placement, accelerated degree program, summer session, adult/continuing education programs, internships **Contact** Office of Admissions, The National Hispanic University, 14271 Story Road, San Jose, CA 95127-3823. Telephone: 408-254-6900. Web site: http://www.nhu.edu/.

NATIONAL UNIVERSITY
LA JOLLA, CALIFORNIA

General Independent, comprehensive, coed **Entrance** Noncompetitive **Setting** 15-acre urban campus **Total enrollment** 18,267 **Student-faculty ratio** 16:1 **Application deadline** Rolling (freshmen), rolling (transfer) **Freshmen** 100% were admitted **Housing** No **Expenses** Tuition $8025 **Undergraduates** 57% women, 49% part-time, 82% 25 or older, 1% Native American, 19% Hispanic American, 13% African American, 10% Asian American/Pacific Islander **The most frequently chosen baccalaureate fields are** business/marketing, computer/information sciences,

CALIFORNIA

National University *(continued)*
psychology **Academic program** English as a second language, advanced placement, accelerated degree program, summer session, adult/continuing education programs, internships **Contact** Ms. Nancy Rohland, Associate Regional Dean, San Diego, National University, 11255 North Torrey Pines Road, La Jolla, CA 92037. Telephone: 858-541-7701 or toll-free 800-628-8648. Fax: 858-642-8710. E-mail: nrohland@nu.edu. Web site: http://www.nu.edu/.

NEW COLLEGE OF CALIFORNIA
SAN FRANCISCO, CALIFORNIA

General Independent, comprehensive, coed **Entrance** Noncompetitive **Setting** urban campus **Total enrollment** 1,088 **Student-faculty ratio** 15:1 **Application deadline** Rolling (freshmen), rolling (transfer) **Housing** No **Expenses** Tuition $9240 **Undergraduates** 50% 25 or older **Academic program** English as a second language, advanced placement, accelerated degree program, self-designed majors, internships **Contact** Ms. Jean Lee, Admissions Inquiry Office, New College of California, 50 Fell Street, San Francisco, CA 94102-5206. Telephone: 415-437-3429 or toll-free 888-437-3460. Fax: 415-865-2636. E-mail: jeanlee@ncgate.newcollege.edu. Web site: http://www.newcollege.edu/.

NEWSCHOOL OF ARCHITECTURE & DESIGN
SAN DIEGO, CALIFORNIA

General Proprietary, comprehensive, coed, primarily men **Entrance** Moderately difficult **Setting** urban campus **Total enrollment** 137 **Student-faculty ratio** 14:1 **Application deadline** 8/30 (freshmen), 8/30 (transfer) **Freshmen** 100% were admitted **Housing** Yes **Expenses** Tuition $17,514 **Undergraduates** 13% women, 13% part-time, 65% 25 or older, 0% Native American, 25% Hispanic American, 0% African American, 0% Asian American/Pacific Islander **Academic program** English as a second language, advanced placement, summer session, adult/continuing education programs, internships **Contact** Ms. Lexi Rogers, Director of Admissions, Newschool of Architecture & Design, 1249 F Street, San Diego, CA 92101-6634. Telephone: 619-235-4100 Ext. 106 or toll-free 619-235-4100 Ext. 106. E-mail: admissions@newschoolarch.edu. Web site: http://www.newschoolarch.edu/.

NORTHWESTERN POLYTECHNIC UNIVERSITY
FREMONT, CALIFORNIA

General Independent, comprehensive, coed **Setting** 2-acre urban campus **Total enrollment** 726 **Student-faculty ratio** 15:1 **Application deadline** 8/15 (freshmen), 8/15 (transfer) **Freshmen** 61% were admitted **Housing** Yes **Expenses** Tuition $9045 **Undergraduates** 37% women, 37% part-time, 48% 25 or older **Academic program** English as a second language, advanced placement, summer session, internships **Contact** Mr. Jack Xie, Director of Admission, Northwestern Polytechnic University, 117 Fourier Avenue, Fremont, CA 94539-7482. Telephone: 510-657-5913. Fax: 510-657-8975. E-mail: npuadm@npu.edu. Web site: http://www.npu.edu/.

NOTRE DAME DE NAMUR UNIVERSITY
BELMONT, CALIFORNIA

General Independent Roman Catholic, comprehensive, coed **Entrance** Moderately difficult **Setting** 80-acre suburban campus **Total enrollment** 1,712 **Student-faculty ratio** 13:1 **Application deadline** Rolling (freshmen), rolling (transfer) **Freshmen** 84% were admitted **Housing** Yes **Expenses** Tuition $18,446; Room & Board $8476 **Undergraduates** 72% women, 39% part-time, 41% 25 or older, 1% Native American, 16% Hispanic American, 7% African American, 12% Asian American/Pacific Islander **Academic program** English as a second language, advanced placement, accelerated degree program, summer session, adult/continuing education programs, internships **Contact** Ms. Melissa Garcia, Assistant Director for Undergraduate Admission, Notre Dame de Namur University, 1500 Ralston Avenue, Belmont, CA 94002-1997. Telephone: 650-508-3532 or toll-free 800-263-0545. Fax: 650-508-3426. E-mail: admiss@ndnu.edu. Web site: http://www.ndnu.edu/.

OCCIDENTAL COLLEGE
LOS ANGELES, CALIFORNIA

General Independent, comprehensive, coed **Entrance** Very difficult **Setting** 120-acre urban campus **Total enrollment** 1,796 **Student-faculty ratio** 12:1 **Application deadline** 1/15 (freshmen), 3/15 (transfer) **Freshmen** 48% were admitted **Housing** Yes **Expenses** Tuition $25,420; Room & Board $7100 **Undergraduates** 58% women, 2% 25 or older **The most frequently chosen baccalaureate fields are** philosophy, religion, and theology, visual/performing arts **Academic program** Advanced placement, accelerated degree program, self-designed majors, honors program, summer session, internships **Contact** Mr. Vince Cuseo, Director of Admission, Occidental College, 1600 Campus Road, Los Angeles, CA 90041-3314. Telephone: 323-259-2700 or toll-free 800-825-5262. Fax: 323-341-4875. E-mail: admission@oxy.edu. Web site: http://www.oxy.edu/.

OTIS COLLEGE OF ART AND DESIGN
LOS ANGELES, CALIFORNIA

General Independent, comprehensive, coed **Entrance** Moderately difficult **Setting** 5-acre urban campus **Total enrollment** 965 **Student-faculty ratio** 11:1 **Application deadline** Rolling (freshmen), rolling (transfer) **Freshmen** 64% were admitted **Housing** Yes **Expenses** Tuition $20,240 **Undergraduates** 20% 25 or older, 0.2% Native American, 11% Hispanic American, 2% African American, 28% Asian American/Pacific Islander **The most frequently chosen baccalaureate field is** visual/performing arts **Academic**

CALIFORNIA

program English as a second language, advanced placement, honors program, summer session, adult/continuing education programs, internships **Contact** Mr. Marc D. Meredith, Dean of Admissions, Otis College of Art and Design, 9045 Lincoln Boulevard, Los Angeles, CA 90045-9785. Telephone: 310-665-6820 or toll-free 800-527-OTIS. Fax: 310-665-6821. E-mail: otisart@otisart.edu. Web site: http://www.otis.edu/.

PACIFIC OAKS COLLEGE
PASADENA, CALIFORNIA

General Independent, upper-level, coed, primarily women **Setting** 2-acre small-town campus **Total enrollment** 798 **Student-faculty ratio** 9:1 **Application deadline** 6/1 (transfer) **First-Year Students** 86% were admitted **Housing** No **Expenses** Tuition $13,320 **Undergraduates** 93% women, 93% part-time, 90% 25 or older, 2% Native American, 29% Hispanic American, 12% African American, 4% Asian American/Pacific Islander **The most frequently chosen baccalaureate field is** social sciences and history **Academic program** Summer session, adult/continuing education programs, internships **Contact** Ms. Marsha Franker, Director of Admissions, Pacific Oaks College, Admissions Office, Pacific Oaks College, 5 Westmoreland Place, Pasadena, CA 91103. Telephone: 626-397-1349 or toll-free 800-684-0900. Fax: 626-577-6144. E-mail: admissions@pacificoaks.edu. Web site: http://www.pacificoaks.edu/.

PACIFIC STATES UNIVERSITY
LOS ANGELES, CALIFORNIA

General Independent, comprehensive, coed **Entrance** Minimally difficult **Setting** 1-acre urban campus **Total enrollment** 126 **Student-faculty ratio** 20:1 **Application deadline** 6/15 (freshmen) **Housing** No **Expenses** Tuition $8880 **Undergraduates** 42% women, 80% 25 or older, 100% Asian American/Pacific Islander **The most frequently chosen baccalaureate fields are** business/marketing, computer/information sciences **Academic program** English as a second language, accelerated degree program, self-designed majors, summer session, adult/continuing education programs **Contact** Mr. Seth Ozen, Admissions Officer, Pacific States University, 1516 South Western Avenue, Los Angeles, CA 90006. Telephone: 323-731-2383 or toll-free 888-200-0383. E-mail: admission@psuca.edu. Web site: http://www.psuca.edu/.

PACIFIC UNION COLLEGE
ANGWIN, CALIFORNIA

General Independent Seventh-day Adventist, comprehensive, coed **Entrance** Moderately difficult **Setting** 200-acre rural campus **Total enrollment** 1,422 **Student-faculty ratio** 12:1 **Application deadline** Rolling (freshmen), rolling (transfer) **Freshmen** 59% were admitted **Housing** Yes **Expenses** Tuition $15,075; Room & Board $4530 **Undergraduates** 56% women, 8% part-time, 0.4% Native American, 10% Hispanic American, 6% African American, 19% Asian American/Pacific Islander **The most frequently chosen baccalaureate fields are** business/marketing, biological/life sciences, health professions and related sciences **Academic program** English as a second language, advanced placement, accelerated degree program, self-designed majors, honors program, summer session, adult/continuing education programs, internships **Contact** Mr. Sean Kootsey, Director of Enrollment Services, Pacific Union College, Enrollment Services, Angwin, CA 94508-9707. Telephone: 707-965-6425 or toll-free 800-862-7080. Fax: 707-965-6432. E-mail: enroll@puc.edu. Web site: http://www.puc.edu/.

PATTEN COLLEGE
OAKLAND, CALIFORNIA

General Independent interdenominational, comprehensive, coed **Entrance** Noncompetitive **Setting** 5-acre urban campus **Total enrollment** 559 **Student-faculty ratio** 14:1 **Application deadline** 7/31 (freshmen), rolling (transfer) **Freshmen** 58% were admitted **Housing** Yes **Expenses** Tuition $8400; Room & Board $4800 **Undergraduates** 40% women, 54% part-time, 59% 25 or older **The most frequently chosen baccalaureate fields are** business/marketing, liberal arts/general studies, philosophy **Academic program** Advanced placement, accelerated degree program, honors program, summer session, adult/continuing education programs, internships **Contact** Ms. Inez Bailey, Director of Admissions, Patten College, 2433 Coolidge Avenue, Oakland, CA 94601. Telephone: 510-261-8500 Ext. 765. Fax: 510-534-4344. Web site: http://www.diac.com/~patten/.

PEPPERDINE UNIVERSITY
MALIBU, CALIFORNIA

General Independent, university, coed, affiliated with Church of Christ **Entrance** Very difficult **Setting** 830-acre small-town campus **Total enrollment** 7,383 **Student-faculty ratio** 12:1 **Application deadline** 1/15 (freshmen), 1/15 (transfer) **Freshmen** 28% were admitted **Housing** Yes **Expenses** Tuition $25,250; Room & Board $7580 **Undergraduates** 57% women, 16% part-time, 3% 25 or older, 1% Native American, 11% Hispanic American, 7% African American, 8% Asian American/Pacific Islander **The most frequently chosen baccalaureate fields are** business/marketing, communications/communication technologies, social sciences and history **Academic program** Advanced placement, accelerated degree program, self-designed majors, honors program, summer session, internships **Contact** Mr. Paul A. Long, Dean of Admission and Enrollment Management, Pepperdine University, 24255 Pacific Coast Highway, Malibu, CA 90263-4392. Telephone: 310-506-4392. Fax: 310-506-4861. E-mail: admission-seaver@pepperdine.edu. Web site: http://www.pepperdine.edu/.

PITZER COLLEGE
CLAREMONT, CALIFORNIA

General Independent, 4-year, coed **Entrance** Moderately difficult **Setting** 35-acre suburban campus

CALIFORNIA

Pitzer College *(continued)*
Total enrollment 921 **Student-faculty ratio** 12:1 **Application deadline** 1/15 (freshmen), 4/15 (transfer) **Freshmen** 54% were admitted **Housing** Yes **Expenses** Tuition $27,030; Room & Board $6900 **Undergraduates** 62% women, 6% part-time, 9% 25 or older, 1% Native American, 14% Hispanic American, 6% African American, 10% Asian American/Pacific Islander **The most frequently chosen baccalaureate fields are** psychology, social sciences and history, visual/performing arts **Academic program** English as a second language, advanced placement, self-designed majors, honors program, adult/continuing education programs, internships **Contact** Dr. Arnaldo Rodriguez, Vice President for Admission and Financial Aid, Pitzer College, 1050 North Mills Avenue, Claremont, CA 91711-6101. Telephone: 909-621-8129 or toll-free 800-748-9371. Fax: 909-621-8770. E-mail: admission@pitzer.edu. Web site: http://www.pitzer.edu/.

POINT LOMA NAZARENE UNIVERSITY
SAN DIEGO, CALIFORNIA

General Independent Nazarene, comprehensive, coed **Entrance** Moderately difficult **Setting** 88-acre suburban campus **Total enrollment** 2,881 **Student-faculty ratio** 16:1 **Application deadline** 3/1 (freshmen), rolling (transfer) **Freshmen** 76% were admitted **Housing** Yes **Expenses** Tuition $15,300; Room & Board $6320 **Undergraduates** 60% women, 3% part-time, 4% 25 or older, 1% Native American, 7% Hispanic American, 1% African American, 4% Asian American/Pacific Islander **The most frequently chosen baccalaureate fields are** business/marketing, health professions and related sciences, liberal arts/general studies **Academic program** English as a second language, advanced placement, summer session, internships **Contact** Mr. Scott Shoemaker, Director of Admissions, Point Loma Nazarene University, 3900 Lomaland Drive, San Diego, CA 92106-2899. Telephone: 619-849-2273 or toll-free 800-733-7770 (out-of-state). Fax: 619-849-2601. E-mail: admissions@ptloma.edu. Web site: http://www.ptloma.edu/.

POMONA COLLEGE
CLAREMONT, CALIFORNIA

General Independent, 4-year, coed **Entrance** Most difficult **Setting** 140-acre suburban campus **Total enrollment** 1,577 **Student-faculty ratio** 9:1 **Application deadline** 1/2 (freshmen), 3/15 (transfer) **Freshmen** 29% were admitted **Housing** Yes **Expenses** Tuition $25,010; Room & Board $8950 **Undergraduates** 49% women, 2% part-time, 1% 25 or older, 0.3% Native American, 9% Hispanic American, 6% African American, 16% Asian American/Pacific Islander **The most frequently chosen baccalaureate field is** philosophy, religion, and theology **Academic program** Advanced placement, self-designed majors, internships **Contact** Mr. Bruce Poch, Vice President and Dean of Admissions, Pomona College, 333 North College Way, Claremont, CA 91711. Telephone: 909-621-8134. Fax: 909-621-8952. E-mail: admissions@pomona.edu. Web site: http://www.pomona.edu/.

ST. JOHN'S SEMINARY COLLEGE
CAMARILLO, CALIFORNIA

General Independent Roman Catholic, 4-year, men only **Entrance** Moderately difficult **Setting** 100-acre suburban campus **Total enrollment** 103 **Student-faculty ratio** 5:1 **Application deadline** 6/21 (freshmen), 6/21 (transfer) **Freshmen** 100% were admitted **Housing** Yes **Expenses** Tuition $7855; Room & Board $5000 **Undergraduates** 8% part-time, 39% 25 or older **The most frequently chosen baccalaureate fields are** philosophy, foreign language/literature, philosophy, religion, and theology **Academic program** English as a second language, advanced placement, honors program, adult/continuing education programs **Contact** Ms. Kathryn Y. Musashi, Director of Admissions, St. John's Seminary College, 5118 Seminary Road, Camarillo, CA 93012-2599. Telephone: 805-482-2755 Ext. 2002. Fax: 805-987-5097. Web site: http://www.sjsc.edu/.

SAINT MARY'S COLLEGE OF CALIFORNIA
MORAGA, CALIFORNIA

General Independent Roman Catholic, comprehensive, coed **Entrance** Moderately difficult **Setting** 420-acre suburban campus **Total enrollment** 4,127 **Student-faculty ratio** 13:1 **Application deadline** 2/1 (freshmen), 7/1 (transfer) **Freshmen** 77% were admitted **Housing** Yes **Expenses** Tuition $19,525; Room & Board $8050 **Undergraduates** 62% women, 19% part-time, 2% 25 or older, 1% Native American, 14% Hispanic American, 6% African American, 8% Asian American/Pacific Islander **The most frequently chosen baccalaureate fields are** business/marketing, psychology, social sciences and history **Academic program** Advanced placement, self-designed majors, honors program, adult/continuing education programs, internships **Contact** Ms. Dorothy Benjamin, Dean of Admissions, Saint Mary's College of California, PO Box 4800, Moraga, CA 94556-4800. Telephone: 925-631-4224 or toll-free 800-800-4SMC. Fax: 925-376-7193. E-mail: smcadmit@stmarys-ca.edu. Web site: http://www.stmarys.edu/.

SAMUEL MERRITT COLLEGE
OAKLAND, CALIFORNIA

General Independent, comprehensive, coed, primarily women **Entrance** Moderately difficult **Setting** 1-acre urban campus **Total enrollment** 694 **Student-faculty ratio** 8:1 **Application deadline** 3/1 (freshmen), 3/1 (transfer) **Freshmen** 71% were admitted **Housing** Yes **Expenses** Tuition $18,350; Room only $3780 **Undergraduates** 56% 25 or older **The most frequently chosen baccalaureate field is** health professions and related sciences **Academic program** Advanced placement, summer session, internships **Contact** Mr. John Garten-Shuman, Director of Admis-

CALIFORNIA

sions, Samuel Merritt College, 370 Hawthorne Avenue, Oakland, CA 94609-3108. Telephone: 510-869-6727 or toll-free 800-607-MERRITT. Fax: 510-869-6525. E-mail: admission@samuelmerritt.edu. Web site: http://www.samuelmerritt.edu/.

SAN DIEGO STATE UNIVERSITY
SAN DIEGO, CALIFORNIA

General State-supported, university, coed Entrance Moderately difficult Setting 300-acre urban campus Total enrollment 34,171 Student-faculty ratio 17:1 Application deadline 11/30 (freshmen) Freshmen 63% were admitted Housing Yes Expenses Tuition $1776; Room & Board $7970 Undergraduates 57% women, 23% part-time, 19% 25 or older, 1% Native American, 21% Hispanic American, 4% African American, 15% Asian American/Pacific Islander The most frequently chosen baccalaureate fields are business/marketing, liberal arts/general studies, social sciences and history Academic program English as a second language, advanced placement, self-designed majors, honors program, summer session, internships Contact Prospective Student Center, San Diego State University, 5500 Campanile Drive, San Diego, CA 92182-7455. Telephone: 619-594-6886. Fax: 619-594-1250. E-mail: admissions@sdsu.edu. Web site: http://www.sdsu.edu/.

SAN FRANCISCO ART INSTITUTE
SAN FRANCISCO, CALIFORNIA

General Independent, comprehensive, coed Entrance Moderately difficult Setting 3-acre urban campus Total enrollment 637 Student-faculty ratio 8:1 Application deadline 8/27 (freshmen), rolling (transfer) Freshmen 82% were admitted Housing No Expenses Tuition $21,120 Undergraduates 56% women, 17% part-time, 44% 25 or older, 2% Native American, 8% Hispanic American, 2% African American, 6% Asian American/Pacific Islander The most frequently chosen baccalaureate field is visual/performing arts Academic program English as a second language, advanced placement, accelerated degree program, summer session, adult/continuing education programs, internships Contact Mark Takiguchi, Director of Admissions, San Francisco Art Institute, 800 Chestnut Street, San Francisco, CA 94133. Telephone: 415-749-4500 or toll-free 800-345-SFAI. E-mail: admissions@sfai.edu. Web site: http://www.sfai.edu/.

SAN FRANCISCO CONSERVATORY OF MUSIC
SAN FRANCISCO, CALIFORNIA

General Independent, comprehensive, coed Entrance Moderately difficult Setting 2-acre urban campus Total enrollment 275 Student-faculty ratio 6:1 Application deadline 2/1 (freshmen), 2/1 (transfer) Freshmen 63% were admitted Housing No Expenses Tuition $20,780 Undergraduates 56% women, 6% part-time, 11% 25 or older, 1% Native American, 7% Hispanic American, 3% African American, 12% Asian American/Pacific Islander The most frequently chosen baccalaureate field is visual/performing arts Academic program Advanced placement Contact Susan Dean, Director of Admissions, San Francisco Conservatory of Music, 1201 Ortega Street, San Francisco, CA 94122-4411. Telephone: 415-759-3431. Fax: 415-759-3499. E-mail: admit@sfcm.edu. Web site: http://www.sfcm.edu/.

SAN FRANCISCO STATE UNIVERSITY
SAN FRANCISCO, CALIFORNIA

General State-supported, comprehensive, coed Entrance Moderately difficult Setting 90-acre urban campus Total enrollment 26,862 Student-faculty ratio 20:1 Application deadline Rolling (freshmen) Freshmen 61% were admitted Housing Yes Expenses Room & Board $6930 Undergraduates 59% women, 28% part-time, 34% 25 or older, 1% Native American, 13% Hispanic American, 6% African American, 33% Asian American/Pacific Islander The most frequently chosen baccalaureate field is philosophy, religion, and theology Academic program English as a second language, advanced placement, accelerated degree program, self-designed majors, honors program, summer session, adult/continuing education programs, internships Contact Ms. Patricia Wade, Admissions Officer, San Francisco State University, 1600 Holloway Avenue, Administration 154, San Francisco, CA 94132. Telephone: 415-338-2037. Fax: 415-338-7196. E-mail: ugadmit@apollo.sfsu.edu. Web site: http://www.sfsu.edu/.

SAN JOSE CHRISTIAN COLLEGE
SAN JOSE, CALIFORNIA

General Independent nondenominational, 4-year, coed Entrance Noncompetitive Setting 9-acre urban campus Total enrollment 312 Student-faculty ratio 18:1 Application deadline 8/1 (freshmen), 8/1 (transfer) Freshmen 35% were admitted Housing Yes Expenses Tuition $10,986; Room & Board $5475 Undergraduates 63% 25 or older, 0.4% Native American, 9% Hispanic American, 7% African American, 14% Asian American/Pacific Islander The most frequently chosen baccalaureate fields are philosophy, philosophy, religion, and theology, protective services/public administration Academic program English as a second language, advanced placement, accelerated degree program, summer session, internships Contact Ms. Stephany Haskins, Admissions Counselor, San Jose Christian College, 790 South Twelfth Street, San Jose, CA 95112-2381. Telephone: 408-278-4333 or toll-free 800-355-7522. Fax: 408-293-7352. E-mail: rjones@sjchristian.edu. Web site: http://www.sjchristian.edu/.

SAN JOSE STATE UNIVERSITY
SAN JOSE, CALIFORNIA

General State-supported, comprehensive, coed Entrance Moderately difficult Setting 104-acre urban campus Total enrollment 28,007 Application deadline Rolling (freshmen), rolling (transfer) Freshmen

CALIFORNIA

San Jose State University *(continued)*
66% were admitted **Housing** Yes **Expenses** Tuition $1912; Room & Board $7220 **Undergraduates** 51% women, 30% part-time, 30% 25 or older, 1% Native American, 15% Hispanic American, 4% African American, 40% Asian American/Pacific Islander **Academic program** English as a second language, advanced placement, accelerated degree program, self-designed majors, honors program, summer session, adult/continuing education programs, internships **Contact** Mr. John Bradbury, Interim Director of Admissions, San Jose State University, One Washington Square, San Jose, CA 95192-0001. Telephone: 408-924-2000. Fax: 408-924-2050. E-mail: contact@sjsu.edu. Web site: http://www.sjsu.edu/.

SANTA CLARA UNIVERSITY
SANTA CLARA, CALIFORNIA

General Independent Roman Catholic (Jesuit), university, coed **Entrance** Moderately difficult **Setting** 104-acre suburban campus **Total enrollment** 7,368 **Student-faculty ratio** 12:1 **Application deadline** 1/15 (freshmen), 5/15 (transfer) **Freshmen** 63% were admitted **Housing** Yes **Expenses** Tuition $22,572; Room & Board $8436 **Undergraduates** 54% women, 3% part-time, 3% 25 or older, 0.4% Native American, 14% Hispanic American, 2% African American, 19% Asian American/Pacific Islander **The most frequently chosen baccalaureate fields are** business/marketing, engineering/engineering technologies, social sciences and history **Academic program** Advanced placement, self-designed majors, honors program, summer session, internships **Contact** Ms. Sandra Hayes, Dean of Undergraduate Admissions, Santa Clara University, 500 El Camino Real, Santa Clara, CA 95053. Telephone: 408-554-4700. Fax: 408-554-5255. E-mail: ugadmissions@scu.edu. Web site: http://www.scu.edu/.

SCRIPPS COLLEGE
CLAREMONT, CALIFORNIA

General Independent, 4-year, women only **Entrance** Very difficult **Setting** 30-acre suburban campus **Total enrollment** 816 **Student-faculty ratio** 11:1 **Application deadline** 2/1 (freshmen), 4/1 (transfer) **Freshmen** 64% were admitted **Housing** Yes **Expenses** Tuition $24,400; Room & Board $8100 **Undergraduates** 1% part-time, 1% 25 or older, 1% Native American, 6% Hispanic American, 3% African American, 13% Asian American/Pacific Islander **The most frequently chosen baccalaureate fields are** social sciences and history, biological/life sciences, visual/performing arts **Academic program** Advanced placement, accelerated degree program, self-designed majors, honors program, internships **Contact** Ms. Patricia F. Goldsmith, Dean of Admission and Financial Aid, Scripps College, 1030 Columbia Avenue, Claremont, CA 91711-3948. Telephone: 909-621-8149 or toll-free 800-770-1333. Fax: 909-607-7508. E-mail: admission@scrippscol.edu. Web site: http://www.scrippscol.edu/.

SHASTA BIBLE COLLEGE
REDDING, CALIFORNIA

General Independent nondenominational, comprehensive, coed **Entrance** Noncompetitive **Setting** 25-acre small-town campus **Total enrollment** 189 **Student-faculty ratio** 11:1 **Freshmen** 100% were admitted **Housing** Yes **Expenses** Tuition $5870; Room only $1575 **Undergraduates** 48% women, 36% part-time, 50% 25 or older **The most frequently chosen baccalaureate fields are** education, philosophy **Academic program** Adult/continuing education programs **Contact** Ms. Dawn Rodriguez, Registrar, Shasta Bible College, 2980 Hartnell Avenue, Redding, CA 96002. Telephone: 530-221-4275 or toll-free 800-800-45BC (in-state); 800-800-6929 (out-of-state). Fax: 530-221-6929. E-mail: ggunn@shasta.edu. Web site: http://www.shasta.edu/.

SIMPSON COLLEGE AND GRADUATE SCHOOL
REDDING, CALIFORNIA

General Independent, comprehensive, coed, affiliated with The Christian and Missionary Alliance **Entrance** Moderately difficult **Setting** 60-acre suburban campus **Total enrollment** 1,161 **Student-faculty ratio** 19:1 **Application deadline** Rolling (freshmen), rolling (transfer) **Freshmen** 63% were admitted **Housing** Yes **Expenses** Tuition $12,470; Room & Board $5410 **Undergraduates** 67% women, 2% part-time, 25% 25 or older, 1% Native American, 5% Hispanic American, 1% African American, 5% Asian American/Pacific Islander **The most frequently chosen baccalaureate fields are** business/marketing, liberal arts/general studies, psychology **Academic program** English as a second language, advanced placement, accelerated degree program, self-designed majors, summer session, adult/continuing education programs, internships **Contact** Mrs. Beth Spencer, Director of Enrollment Support, Simpson College and Graduate School, 2211 College View Drive, Redding, CA 96003. Telephone: 530-226-4606 Ext. 2602 or toll-free 800-598-2493. Fax: 530-226-4861. E-mail: admissions@simpsonca.edu. Web site: http://www.simpsonca.edu/.

SONOMA STATE UNIVERSITY
ROHNERT PARK, CALIFORNIA

General State-supported, comprehensive, coed **Entrance** Moderately difficult **Setting** 220-acre small-town campus **Total enrollment** 7,590 **Student-faculty ratio** 21:1 **Application deadline** 12/31 (freshmen), 1/31 (transfer) **Freshmen** 92% were admitted **Housing** Yes **Expenses** Tuition $2032; Room & Board $6921 **Undergraduates** 64% women, 15% part-time, 22% 25 or older, 1% Native American, 10% Hispanic American, 2% African American, 5% Asian American/Pacific Islander **The most frequently chosen baccalaureate fields are** business/marketing, liberal arts/general studies, social sciences and history **Academic program** English as a second language, advanced placement, accelerated degree

CALIFORNIA

program, self-designed majors, honors program, summer session, adult/continuing education programs, internships **Contact** Dr. Katharyn Crabbe, Vice Provost, Sonoma State University, 1801 East Cotati Avenue, Rohnert Park, CA 94928. Telephone: 707-664-2114. Fax: 707-664-2060. E-mail: csumentor@sonoma.edu. Web site: http://www.sonoma.edu/.

SOUTHERN CALIFORNIA BIBLE COLLEGE & SEMINARY
EL CAJON, CALIFORNIA

Contact Southern California Bible College & Seminary, 2075 East Madison Avenue, El Cajon, CA 92019. Web site: http://www.scbcs.edu/.

SOUTHERN CALIFORNIA INSTITUTE OF ARCHITECTURE
LOS ANGELES, CALIFORNIA

General Independent, comprehensive, coed **Entrance** Moderately difficult **Setting** urban campus **Total enrollment** 450 **Application deadline** Rolling (freshmen), rolling (transfer) **Housing** No **Expenses** Tuition $16,810 **Undergraduates** 42% 25 or older **The most frequently chosen baccalaureate field is** architecture **Academic program** English as a second language, advanced placement, summer session, internships **Contact** Ms. DebraAbel, Director of Admissions, Southern California Institute of Architecture, Freight Yard, 960 East 3rd Street, Los Angeles, CA 90013. Telephone: 213-613-2200 Ext. 320 or toll-free 800-774-7242. Fax: 213-613-2260. E-mail: admissions@sciarc.edu. Web site: http://www.sciarc.edu/.

STANFORD UNIVERSITY
STANFORD, CALIFORNIA

General Independent, university, coed **Entrance** Most difficult **Setting** 8,180-acre suburban campus **Total enrollment** 17,540 **Student-faculty ratio** 7:1 **Application deadline** 12/15 (freshmen), 3/15 (transfer) **Freshmen** 13% were admitted **Housing** Yes **Expenses** Tuition $25,917; Room & Board $8305 **Undergraduates** 51% women, 11% part-time, 1% 25 or older, 2% Native American, 11% Hispanic American, 9% African American, 25% Asian American/Pacific Islander **The most frequently chosen baccalaureate fields are** engineering/engineering technologies, interdisciplinary studies, social sciences and history **Academic program** Advanced placement, self-designed majors, honors program, summer session, internships **Contact** Ms. Robin G. Mamlet, Dean of Undergraduate Admissions and Financial Aid, Stanford University, Old Union 232, 520 Lasuen Mall, Stanford, CA 94305. Telephone: 650-723-2091. Fax: 650-723-6050. E-mail: undergrad.admissions@forsythe.stanford.edu. Web site: http://www.stanford.edu/.

THOMAS AQUINAS COLLEGE
SANTA PAULA, CALIFORNIA

General Independent Roman Catholic, 4-year, coed **Entrance** Very difficult **Setting** 170-acre rural campus **Total enrollment** 301 **Student-faculty ratio** 11:1 **Application deadline** Rolling (freshmen) **Freshmen** 87% were admitted **Housing** Yes **Expenses** Tuition $15,900; Room & Board $4600 **Undergraduates** 50% women, 4% 25 or older, 0.3% Native American, 8% Hispanic American, 1% African American, 3% Asian American/Pacific Islander **The most frequently chosen baccalaureate field is** liberal arts/general studies **Contact** Mr. Thomas J. Susanka Jr., Director of Admissions, Thomas Aquinas College, 10000 North Ojai Road, Santa Paula, CA 93060-9980. Telephone: 805-525-4417 Ext. 361 or toll-free 800-634-9797. Fax: 805-525-9342. E-mail: admissions@thomasaquinas.edu. Web site: http://www.thomasaquinas.edu/.

TOURO UNIVERSITY INTERNATIONAL
LOS ALAMITOS, CALIFORNIA

General Independent, comprehensive, coed **Entrance** Minimally difficult **Total enrollment** 1,357 **Student-faculty ratio** 7:1 **Application deadline** Rolling (freshmen) **Freshmen** 89% were admitted **Housing** No **Expenses** Tuition $5760 **Undergraduates** 35% women, 30% part-time, 75% 25 or older **The most frequently chosen baccalaureate fields are** business/marketing, health professions and related sciences **Academic program** Summer session, adult/continuing education programs **Contact** Wei Ren, Registrar, Touro University International, 10542 Calle Lee, Los Alamitos, CA 90720. Telephone: 714-816-0366 or toll-free 714-816-0366. Fax: 714-816-0367. E-mail: rkoester@tourou.edu. Web site: http://www.tourouniversity.edu/.

UNITED STATES INTERNATIONAL UNIVERSITY
See Alliant International University

UNIVERSITY OF CALIFORNIA, BERKELEY
BERKELEY, CALIFORNIA

General State-supported, university, coed **Entrance** Very difficult **Setting** 1,232-acre urban campus **Total enrollment** 31,276 **Student-faculty ratio** 17:1 **Application deadline** 11/30 (freshmen), 11/30 (transfer) **Freshmen** 26% were admitted **Housing** Yes **Expenses** Tuition $4122; Room & Board $10,047 **Undergraduates** 52% women, 7% part-time, 0% 25 or older, 1% Native American, 10% Hispanic American, 4% African American, 40% Asian American/Pacific Islander **The most frequently chosen baccalaureate fields are** biological/life sciences, engineering/engineering technologies, social sciences and history **Academic program** English as a second language, advanced placement, accelerated degree program, self-designed majors, honors program, summer session, adult/continuing education programs, internships **Contact** Pre-Admission Advising, Office of Undergraduate Admission and Relations With Schools, University of California, Berkeley, Berkeley, CA 94720. Telephone: 510-642-3175. Fax: 510-642-7333. E-mail: ouars@uclink.berkeley.edu. Web site: http://www.berkeley.edu/.

CALIFORNIA

UNIVERSITY OF CALIFORNIA, DAVIS
DAVIS, CALIFORNIA

General State-supported, university, coed **Entrance** Very difficult **Setting** 5,993-acre suburban campus **Total enrollment** 26,513 **Student-faculty ratio** 19:1 **Application deadline** 11/30 (freshmen), 11/30 (transfer) **Freshmen** 63% were admitted **Housing** Yes **Expenses** Tuition $4594; Room & Board $6982 **Undergraduates** 57% women, 12% part-time, 6% 25 or older, 1% Native American, 10% Hispanic American, 3% African American, 35% Asian American/Pacific Islander **The most frequently chosen baccalaureate fields are** biological/life sciences, engineering/engineering technologies, social sciences and history **Academic program** English as a second language, advanced placement, self-designed majors, honors program, summer session, adult/continuing education programs, internships **Contact** Dr. Gary Tudor, Director of Undergraduate Admissions, University of California, Davis, Undergraduate Admission and Outreach Services, 175 Mrak Hall, Davis, CA 95616. Telephone: 530-752-2971. Fax: 530-752-1280. E-mail: thinkucd@ucdavis.edu. Web site: http://www.ucdavis.edu/.

UNIVERSITY OF CALIFORNIA, IRVINE
IRVINE, CALIFORNIA

General State-supported, university, coed **Entrance** Moderately difficult **Setting** 1,489-acre suburban campus **Total enrollment** 21,885 **Student-faculty ratio** 18:1 **Application deadline** 11/30 (freshmen), 11/30 (transfer) **Freshmen** 59% were admitted **Housing** Yes **Expenses** Tuition $4556; Room & Board $7098 **Undergraduates** 52% women, 4% part-time, 5% 25 or older **The most frequently chosen baccalaureate field is** philosophy, religion, and theology **Academic program** English as a second language, advanced placement, honors program, summer session, adult/continuing education programs, internships **Contact** Dr. Susan Wilbur, Director of Admissions, University of California, Irvine, 204 Administration, Irvine, CA 92697-1075. Telephone: 949-824-6701. Web site: http://www.uci.edu/.

UNIVERSITY OF CALIFORNIA, LOS ANGELES
LOS ANGELES, CALIFORNIA

General State-supported, university, coed **Entrance** Very difficult **Setting** 419-acre urban campus **Total enrollment** 37,494 **Student-faculty ratio** 17:1 **Application deadline** 11/30 (freshmen), 11/30 (transfer) **Freshmen** 27% were admitted **Housing** Yes **Expenses** Tuition $4236; Room & Board $8991 **Undergraduates** 55% women, 5% part-time, 8% 25 or older, 0.5% Native American, 14% Hispanic American, 4% African American, 37% Asian American/Pacific Islander **The most frequently chosen baccalaureate fields are** psychology, biological/life sciences, social sciences and history **Academic program** English as a second language, advanced placement, self-designed majors, honors program, summer session, adult/continuing education programs, internships **Contact** Dr. Rae Lee Siporin, Director of Undergraduate Admissions, University of California, Los Angeles, 405 Hilgard Avenue, Los Angeles, CA 90095. Telephone: 310-825-3101. E-mail: ugadm@saonet.ucla.edu. Web site: http://www.ucla.edu/.

UNIVERSITY OF CALIFORNIA, RIVERSIDE
RIVERSIDE, CALIFORNIA

General State-supported, university, coed **Entrance** Very difficult **Setting** 1,200-acre urban campus **Total enrollment** 14,429 **Student-faculty ratio** 19:1 **Application deadline** 11/30 (freshmen), rolling (transfer) **Freshmen** 85% were admitted **Housing** Yes **Expenses** Tuition $4379; Room & Board $7200 **Undergraduates** 54% women, 4% part-time, 8% 25 or older, 0.5% Native American, 22% Hispanic American, 6% African American, 42% Asian American/Pacific Islander **The most frequently chosen baccalaureate fields are** business/marketing, biological/life sciences, social sciences and history **Academic program** Advanced placement, accelerated degree program, self-designed majors, honors program, summer session, adult/continuing education programs, internships **Contact** Ms. Laurie Nelson, Director of Undergraduate Admission, University of California, Riverside, 1138 Hinderaker Hall, Riverside, CA 92521. Telephone: 909-787-3411. Fax: 909-787-6344. E-mail: discover@pop.ucr.edu. Web site: http://www.ucr.edu/.

UNIVERSITY OF CALIFORNIA, SAN DIEGO
LA JOLLA, CALIFORNIA

General State-supported, university, coed **Entrance** Very difficult **Setting** 1,976-acre suburban campus **Total enrollment** 21,560 **Student-faculty ratio** 19:1 **Application deadline** 11/30 (freshmen), 11/30 (transfer) **Freshmen** 43% were admitted **Housing** Yes **Expenses** Tuition $3863; Room & Board $7510 **Undergraduates** 52% women, 1% part-time, 5% 25 or older, 0.5% Native American, 10% Hispanic American, 1% African American, 35% Asian American/Pacific Islander **Academic program** English as a second language, accelerated degree program, self-designed majors, honors program, summer session, internships **Contact** Associate Director of Admissions and Relations with Schools, University of California, San Diego, 9500 Gilman Drive, 0021, La Jolla, CA 92093-0021. Telephone: 858-534-4831. E-mail: admissionsinfo@ucsd.edu. Web site: http://www.ucsd.edu/.

UNIVERSITY OF CALIFORNIA, SANTA BARBARA
SANTA BARBARA, CALIFORNIA

General State-supported, university, coed **Entrance** Very difficult **Setting** 989-acre suburban campus **Total enrollment** 20,373 **Student-faculty ratio** 19:1 **Application deadline** 11/30 (freshmen), 11/30 (transfer) **Freshmen** 50% were admitted **Housing** Yes **Expenses** Tuition $3841; Room & Board $7891

CALIFORNIA

Undergraduates 54% women, 4% part-time, 4% 25 or older, 1% Native American, 15% Hispanic American, 3% African American, 14% Asian American/Pacific Islander **The most frequently chosen baccalaureate fields are** business/marketing, biological/life sciences, social sciences and history **Academic program** Advanced placement, accelerated degree program, self-designed majors, honors program, summer session, internships **Contact** Mr. William Villa, Director of Admissions/Relations with Schools, University of California, Santa Barbara, Santa Barbara, CA 93106. Telephone: 805-893-2485. Fax: 805-893-2676. E-mail: appinfo@sa.ucsb.edu. Web site: http://www.ucsb.edu/.

UNIVERSITY OF CALIFORNIA, SANTA CRUZ
SANTA CRUZ, CALIFORNIA

General State-supported, university, coed **Entrance** Very difficult **Setting** 2,000-acre small-town campus **Total enrollment** 13,170 **Student-faculty ratio** 19:1 **Application deadline** 11/30 (freshmen), 11/30 (transfer) **Freshmen** 81% were admitted **Housing** Yes **Expenses** Tuition $4300; Room & Board $8661 **Undergraduates** 57% women, 5% part-time, 6% 25 or older, 1% Native American, 13% Hispanic American, 2% African American, 16% Asian American/Pacific Islander **The most frequently chosen baccalaureate fields are** biological/life sciences, psychology, visual/performing arts **Academic program** English as a second language, advanced placement, self-designed majors, honors program, summer session, adult/continuing education programs, internships **Contact** Mr. Kevin M. Browne, Executive Director of Admissions and University Registrar, University of California, Santa Cruz, Admissions Office, Cook House, Santa Cruz, CA 95064. Telephone: 831-459-5779. Fax: 831-459-4452. E-mail: admissions@cats.ucsc.edu. Web site: http://www.ucsc.edu/.

UNIVERSITY OF JUDAISM
BEL AIR, CALIFORNIA

General Independent Jewish, comprehensive, coed **Entrance** Moderately difficult **Setting** 28-acre suburban campus **Total enrollment** 229 **Student-faculty ratio** 6:1 **Application deadline** 1/31 (freshmen), 4/15 (transfer) **Freshmen** 87% were admitted **Housing** Yes **Expenses** Tuition $15,530; Room & Board $8100 **Undergraduates** 57% women, 8% part-time, 14% 25 or older, 0% Native American, 10% Hispanic American, 3% African American, 0% Asian American/Pacific Islander **The most frequently chosen baccalaureate fields are** area/ethnic studies, English, psychology **Academic program** Advanced placement, accelerated degree program, self-designed majors, honors program, adult/continuing education programs, internships **Contact** Ms. Jillian Rothschild, Assistant Director of Undergraduate Admissions, University of Judaism, 15600 Mulholland Drive, Bel Air, CA 90077. Telephone: 310-476-9777 Ext. 299 or toll-free 888-853-6763. Fax: 310-471-3657. E-mail: admissions@uj.edu. Web site: http://www.uj.edu/.

UNIVERSITY OF LA VERNE
LA VERNE, CALIFORNIA

General Independent, university, coed **Entrance** Moderately difficult **Setting** 26-acre suburban campus **Total enrollment** 3,358 **Student-faculty ratio** 14:1 **Application deadline** Rolling (freshmen), rolling (transfer) **Freshmen** 72% were admitted **Housing** Yes **Expenses** Tuition $18,000; Room & Board $6280 **Undergraduates** 60% women, 6% part-time, 6% 25 or older, 1% Native American, 36% Hispanic American, 9% African American, 7% Asian American/Pacific Islander **The most frequently chosen baccalaureate fields are** business/marketing, liberal arts/general studies, social sciences and history **Academic program** English as a second language, advanced placement, accelerated degree program, self-designed majors, honors program, summer session, adult/continuing education programs, internships **Contact** Ms. Lisa Meyer, Dean of Admissions, University of La Verne, 1950 Third Street, La Verne, CA 91750-4443. Telephone: 800-876-4858 or toll-free 800-876-4858. Fax: 909-392-2714. E-mail: admissions@ulv.edu. Web site: http://www.ulv.edu/.

UNIVERSITY OF PHOENIX-NORTHERN CALIFORNIA CAMPUS
PLEASANTON, CALIFORNIA

General Proprietary, comprehensive, coed **Entrance** Noncompetitive **Total enrollment** 88,730 **Student-faculty ratio** 13:1 **Application deadline** Rolling (freshmen), rolling (transfer) **Housing** No **Expenses** Tuition $10,200 **Undergraduates** 59% women, 78% 25 or older **The most frequently chosen baccalaureate fields are** business/marketing, health professions and related sciences **Academic program** Advanced placement, accelerated degree program, adult/continuing education programs **Contact** Ms. Beth Barilla, Director of Admissions, University of Phoenix-Northern California Campus, 4615 East Elwood Street, Phoenix, AZ 85040-1958. Telephone: 480-927-0099 Ext. 1218 or toll-free 877-4-STUDENT. Fax: 480-594-1758. E-mail: beth.barilla@apollogrp.edu. Web site: http://www.phoenix.edu/.

UNIVERSITY OF PHOENIX-SACRAMENTO CAMPUS
SACRAMENTO, CALIFORNIA

General Proprietary, comprehensive, coed **Entrance** Noncompetitive **Total enrollment** 88,730 **Student-faculty ratio** 13:1 **Application deadline** Rolling (freshmen), rolling (transfer) **Housing** No **Expenses** Tuition $10,500 **Undergraduates** 58% women, 86% 25 or older **The most frequently chosen baccalaureate fields are** business/marketing, health professions and related sciences **Academic program** Advanced placement, accelerated degree program, adult/continuing education programs **Contact** Ms. Beth Barilla, Director of Admissions, University of Phoenix-Sacramento Campus, 4615 East Elwood Street, Phoenix, AZ 85040-1958. Telephone: 480-927-0099 Ext. 1218 or toll-free 800-266-2107. Fax: 480-

CALIFORNIA

University of Phoenix–Sacramento Campus *(continued)*
594-1758. E-mail: beth.barilla@apollo.grp.edu. Web site: http://www.phoenix.edu/.

UNIVERSITY OF PHOENIX–SAN DIEGO CAMPUS
SAN DIEGO, CALIFORNIA

General Proprietary, comprehensive, coed **Entrance** Noncompetitive **Total enrollment** 88,730 **Student-faculty ratio** 13:1 **Application deadline** Rolling (freshmen), rolling (transfer) **Housing** No **Expenses** Tuition $9750 **Undergraduates** 52% women, 77% 25 or older **The most frequently chosen baccalaureate fields are** business/marketing, health professions and related sciences **Academic program** Advanced placement, accelerated degree program, adult/continuing education programs **Contact** Ms. Beth Barilla, Director of Admissions, University of Phoenix–San Diego Campus, 4615 East Elwood Street, Phoenix, AZ 85040-1958. Telephone: 480-927-0099 Ext. 1218 or toll-free 888-UOP-INFO. Fax: 480-594-1758. E-mail: beth.barilla@apollogrp.edu. Web site: http://www.phoenix.edu/.

UNIVERSITY OF PHOENIX–SOUTHERN CALIFORNIA CAMPUS
FOUNTAIN VALLEY, CALIFORNIA

General Proprietary, comprehensive, coed **Entrance** Noncompetitive **Total enrollment** 88,730 **Student-faculty ratio** 13:1 **Application deadline** Rolling (freshmen), rolling (transfer) **Housing** No **Expenses** Tuition $10,470 **Undergraduates** 41% women, 86% 25 or older **The most frequently chosen baccalaureate fields are** business/marketing, health professions and related sciences **Academic program** Advanced placement, accelerated degree program, adult/continuing education programs **Contact** Ms. Beth B arilla, Director of Admissions, University of Phoenix–Southern California Campus, 4615 East Elwood Street, Phoenix, AZ 85040-1958. Telephone: 480-927-0099 Ext. 1218 or toll-free 800-228-7240. E-mail: beth.barilla@apollogrp.edu. Web site: http://www.phoenix.edu/.

UNIVERSITY OF REDLANDS
REDLANDS, CALIFORNIA

General Independent, comprehensive, coed **Entrance** Moderately difficult **Setting** 140-acre small-town campus **Total enrollment** 2,017 **Student-faculty ratio** 12:1 **Application deadline** 7/1 (freshmen), rolling (transfer) **Freshmen** 77% were admitted **Housing** Yes **Expenses** Tuition $21,406; Room & Board $7840 **Undergraduates** 58% women, 2% part-time, 2% 25 or older, 1% Native American, 11% Hispanic American, 3% African American, 6% Asian American/Pacific Islander **The most frequently chosen baccalaureate fields are** liberal arts/general studies, business/marketing, social sciences and history **Academic program** Advanced placement, self-designed majors, honors program, adult/continuing education programs, internships **Contact** Mr. Paul Driscoll, Dean of Admissions, University of Redlands, PO Box 3080, Redlands, CA 92373-0999. Telephone: 909-335-4074 or toll-free 800-455-5064. Fax: 909-335-4069. E-mail: admissions@uor.edu. Web site: http://www.redlands.edu/.

UNIVERSITY OF SAN DIEGO
SAN DIEGO, CALIFORNIA

General Independent Roman Catholic, university, coed **Entrance** Moderately difficult **Setting** 180-acre urban campus **Total enrollment** 7,062 **Student-faculty ratio** 16:1 **Application deadline** 1/5 (freshmen), 3/1 (transfer) **Freshmen** 50% were admitted **Housing** Yes **Expenses** Tuition $20,458; Room & Board $8440 **Undergraduates** 60% women, 4% part-time, 11% 25 or older, 1% Native American, 14% Hispanic American, 2% African American, 7% Asian American/Pacific Islander **The most frequently chosen baccalaureate fields are** business/marketing, communications/communication technologies, social sciences and history **Academic program** Advanced placement, honors program, summer session, adult/continuing education programs, internships **Contact** Mr. Stephen Pultz, Director of Undergraduate Admissions, University of San Diego, 5998 Alcala Park, San Diego, CA 92110. Telephone: 619-260-4506 or toll-free 800-248-4873. Fax: 619-260-6836. E-mail: admissions@sandiego.edu. Web site: http://www.sandiego.edu/.

▶ **For more information, see page 488.**

UNIVERSITY OF SAN FRANCISCO
SAN FRANCISCO, CALIFORNIA

General Independent Roman Catholic (Jesuit), university, coed **Entrance** Moderately difficult **Setting** 55-acre urban campus **Total enrollment** 8,063 **Student-faculty ratio** 13:1 **Application deadline** 2/1 (freshmen), rolling (transfer) **Freshmen** 79% were admitted **Housing** Yes **Expenses** Tuition $20,310; Room & Board $8800 **Undergraduates** 62% women, 6% part-time, 6% 25 or older, 1% Native American, 11% Hispanic American, 4% African American, 26% Asian American/Pacific Islander **The most frequently chosen baccalaureate fields are** business/marketing, health professions and related sciences, interdisciplinary studies **Academic program** English as a second language, advanced placement, accelerated degree program, self-designed majors, honors program, summer session, adult/continuing education programs, internships **Contact** Mr. William Henley, Director of Admissions, University of San Francisco, Office of Admissions, 2130 Fulton Street, San Francisco, CA 94117-1080. Telephone: 415-422-6563 or toll-free 800-CALL USF (out-of-state). Fax: 415-422-2217. E-mail: admissions@usfca.edu. Web site: http://www.usfca.edu/.

UNIVERSITY OF SARASOTA, CALIFORNIA CAMPUS
See Argosy University-Orange County

CALIFORNIA

UNIVERSITY OF SOUTHERN CALIFORNIA
LOS ANGELES, CALIFORNIA

General Independent, university, coed **Entrance** Very difficult **Setting** 155-acre urban campus **Total enrollment** 29,813 **Student-faculty ratio** 11:1 **Application deadline** 1/10 (freshmen), 3/1 (transfer) **Freshmen** 32% were admitted **Housing** Yes **Expenses** Tuition $25,533; Room & Board $8114 **Undergraduates** 50% women, 4% part-time, 6% 25 or older, 1% Native American, 14% Hispanic American, 6% African American, 22% Asian American/Pacific Islander **The most frequently chosen baccalaureate fields are** business/marketing, social sciences and history, visual/performing arts **Academic program** English as a second language, advanced placement, accelerated degree program, self-designed majors, honors program, summer session, internships **Contact** Ms. Laurel Baker-Tew, Director of Admission, University of Southern California, University Park Campus, Los Angeles, CA 90089. Telephone: 213-740-1111. Fax: 213-740-6364. E-mail: admapp@enroll1.usc.edu. Web site: http://www.usc.edu/.

UNIVERSITY OF THE PACIFIC
STOCKTON, CALIFORNIA

General Independent, university, coed **Entrance** Moderately difficult **Setting** 175-acre suburban campus **Total enrollment** 5,697 **Student-faculty ratio** 13:1 **Application deadline** 2/15 (freshmen), 2/15 (transfer) **Freshmen** 78% were admitted **Housing** Yes **Expenses** Tuition $21,525; Room & Board $6730 **Undergraduates** 58% women, 3% part-time, 7% 25 or older, 1% Native American, 10% Hispanic American, 3% African American, 26% Asian American/Pacific Islander **The most frequently chosen baccalaureate fields are** business/marketing, biological/life sciences, social sciences and history **Academic program** English as a second language, advanced placement, accelerated degree program, self-designed majors, honors program, summer session, adult/continuing education programs, internships **Contact** Mr. Marc McGee, Director of Admissions, University of the Pacific, 3601 Pacific Avenue, Stockton, CA 95211-0197. Telephone: 209-946-2211 or toll-free 800-959-2867. Fax: 209-946-2413. E-mail: admissions@uop.edu. Web site: http://www.uop.edu/.

UNIVERSITY OF WEST LOS ANGELES
INGLEWOOD, CALIFORNIA

General Independent, upper-level, coed **Entrance** Minimally difficult **Setting** 2-acre suburban campus **Total enrollment** 227 **Student-faculty ratio** 10:1 **Application deadline** Rolling (transfer) **Housing** No **Expenses** Tuition $6435 **Undergraduates** 72% women, 91% part-time, 90% 25 or older, 0% Native American, 23% Hispanic American, 45% African American, 7% Asian American/Pacific Islander **The most frequently chosen baccalaureate fields are** (pre)law, law/legal studies **Academic program** Adult/continuing education programs, internships **Contact** Ms. Yvonne Alwag, Admissions Counselor, University of West Los Angeles, School of Paralegal Studies, 1155 West Arbor Vitae Street, Inglewood, CA 90301-2902. Telephone: 310-342-5287. Fax: 310-342-5296. E-mail: aalwag@uwla.edu. Web site: http://www.uwla.edu/.

VANGUARD UNIVERSITY OF SOUTHERN CALIFORNIA
COSTA MESA, CALIFORNIA

General Independent, comprehensive, coed, affiliated with Assemblies of God **Entrance** Moderately difficult **Setting** 38-acre suburban campus **Total enrollment** 1,827 **Student-faculty ratio** 17:1 **Application deadline** Rolling (freshmen), rolling (transfer) **Freshmen** 87% were admitted **Housing** Yes **Expenses** Tuition $14,944; Room & Board $5268 **Undergraduates** 60% women, 24% part-time, 31% 25 or older, 1% Native American, 12% Hispanic American, 4% African American, 3% Asian American/Pacific Islander **The most frequently chosen baccalaureate fields are** business/marketing, philosophy, religion, and theology, psychology **Academic program** Advanced placement, accelerated degree program, summer session, adult/continuing education programs, internships **Contact** Ms. Jessica Mireles, Director of Admissions, Vanguard University of Southern California, 55 Fair Drive, Costa Mesa, CA 92626. Telephone: 714-556-3610 Ext. 327 or toll-free 800-722-6279. Fax: 714-966-5471. E-mail: admissions@vanguard.edu. Web site: http://www.vanguard.edu/.

WESTMONT COLLEGE
SANTA BARBARA, CALIFORNIA

General Independent nondenominational, 4-year, coed **Entrance** Moderately difficult **Setting** 133-acre suburban campus **Total enrollment** 1,374 **Student-faculty ratio** 13:1 **Application deadline** 2/15 (freshmen), 3/1 (transfer) **Freshmen** 75% were admitted **Housing** Yes **Expenses** Tuition $22,256; Room & Board $7492 **Undergraduates** 63% women, 1% part-time, 1% 25 or older, 2% Native American, 7% Hispanic American, 1% African American, 5% Asian American/Pacific Islander **The most frequently chosen baccalaureate fields are** communications/communication technologies, biological/life sciences, social sciences and history **Academic program** Advanced placement, accelerated degree program, self-designed majors, honors program, summer session, internships **Contact** Mrs. Joyce Luy, Director of Admissions, Westmont College, 955 La Paz Road, Santa Barbara, CA 93108. Telephone: 805-565-6200 Ext. 6005 or toll-free 800-777-9011. Fax: 805-565-6234. E-mail: admissions@westmont.edu. Web site: http://www.westmont.edu/.

WHITTIER COLLEGE
WHITTIER, CALIFORNIA

General Independent, comprehensive, coed **Entrance** Moderately difficult **Setting** 95-acre suburban campus **Total enrollment** 2,170 **Student-faculty ratio**

CALIFORNIA

Whittier College *(continued)*
12:1 **Application deadline** Rolling (freshmen), rolling (transfer) **Freshmen** 80% were admitted **Housing** Yes **Expenses** Tuition $21,336; Room & Board $7042 **Undergraduates** 58% women, 2% part-time, 7% 25 or older, 1% Native American, 26% Hispanic American, 5% African American, 8% Asian American/Pacific Islander **The most frequently chosen baccalaureate field is** philosophy, religion, and theology **Academic program** Advanced placement, accelerated degree program, self-designed majors, summer session, adult/continuing education programs, internships **Contact** Ms. Urmi Kar, Dean of Enrollment, Whittier College, 13406 E Philadelphia Street, PO Box 634, Whittier, CA 90608-0634. Telephone: 562-907-4238. Fax: 562-907-4870. E-mail: admission@whittier.edu. Web site: http://www.whittier.edu/.

WOODBURY UNIVERSITY
BURBANK, CALIFORNIA

General Independent, comprehensive, coed **Entrance** Moderately difficult **Setting** 23-acre suburban campus **Total enrollment** 1,404 **Student-faculty ratio** 11:1 **Application deadline** Rolling (freshmen), rolling (transfer) **Freshmen** 79% were admitted **Housing** Yes **Expenses** Tuition $18,344; Room & Board $6454 **Undergraduates** 56% women, 28% part-time, 37% 25 or older, 1% Native American, 30% Hispanic American, 7% African American, 15% Asian American/Pacific Islander **The most frequently chosen baccalaureate fields are** architecture, business/marketing, computer/information sciences **Academic program** Advanced placement, accelerated degree program, summer session, adult/continuing education programs, internships **Contact** Mr. Don St. Clair, Vice-President of Enrollment Planning, Woodbury University, 7500 Glenoaks Boulevard, Burbank, CA 91504-1099. Telephone: 818-767-0888 or toll-free 800-784-WOOD. Fax: 818-767-7520. E-mail: admissions@vaxb.woodbury.edu. Web site: http://www.woodbury.edu/.

YESHIVA OHR ELCHONON CHABAD/WEST COAST TALMUDICAL SEMINARY
LOS ANGELES, CALIFORNIA

General Independent Jewish, 4-year, men only **Entrance** Moderately difficult **Setting** 4-acre urban campus **Total enrollment** 62 **Application deadline** Rolling (freshmen), rolling (transfer) **Housing** Yes **Expenses** Tuition $7900; Room & Board $4500 **Undergraduates** 0% 25 or older, 0% Native American, 0% Hispanic American, 0% African American, 3% Asian American/Pacific Islander **The most frequently chosen baccalaureate field is** philosophy, religion, and theology **Academic program** Honors program, summer session, adult/continuing education programs, internships **Contact** Rabbi Ezra Binyomin Schochet, Dean, Yeshiva Ohr Elchonon Chabad/West Coast Talmudical Seminary, 7215 Waring Avenue, Los Angeles, CA 90046-7660. Telephone: 213-937-3763.

COLORADO

ADAMS STATE COLLEGE
ALAMOSA, COLORADO

General State-supported, comprehensive, coed **Entrance** Moderately difficult **Setting** 90-acre small-town campus **Total enrollment** 2,417 **Student-faculty ratio** 15:1 **Application deadline** 8/1 (freshmen), 8/1 (transfer) **Freshmen** 71% were admitted **Housing** Yes **Expenses** Tuition $2278; Room & Board $5392 **Undergraduates** 54% women, 14% part-time, 29% 25 or older, 2% Native American, 28% Hispanic American, 4% African American, 1% Asian American/Pacific Islander **The most frequently chosen baccalaureate fields are** business/marketing, biological/life sciences, liberal arts/general studies **Academic program** Advanced placement, accelerated degree program, self-designed majors, summer session, adult/continuing education programs, internships **Contact** Mr. Matt Gallegas, Director of Admissions, Adams State College, 208 Edgemont Boulevard, Alamosa, CO 81102. Telephone: 719-587-7712 or toll-free 800-824-6494. Fax: 719-587-7522. E-mail: ascadmit@adams.edu. Web site: http://www.adams.edu/.

THE ART INSTITUTE OF COLORADO
DENVER, COLORADO

General Proprietary, 4-year, coed **Entrance** Minimally difficult **Setting** urban campus **Total enrollment** 2,253 **Student-faculty ratio** 20:1 **Application deadline** Rolling (freshmen), rolling (transfer) **Freshmen** 74% were admitted **Housing** Yes **Expenses** Tuition $19,840; Room & Board $7400 **Undergraduates** 44% women, 22% part-time, 41% 25 or older, 1% Native American, 5% Hispanic American, 3% African American, 4% Asian American/Pacific Islander **Academic program** Advanced placement, adult/continuing education programs, internships **Contact** Barbara Browning, Vice President and Director of Admissions, The Art Institute of Colorado, 1200 Lincoln Street, Denver, CO 80203. Telephone: 303-837-0825 Ext. 4729 or toll-free 800-275-2420. Fax: 303-860-8520. E-mail: aicinfo@aii.edu. Web site: http://www.aic.artinstitutes.edu/.

COLORADO CHRISTIAN UNIVERSITY
LAKEWOOD, COLORADO

General Independent interdenominational, comprehensive, coed **Entrance** Moderately difficult **Setting** 26-acre suburban campus **Total enrollment** 1,849 **Student-faculty ratio** 11:1 **Application deadline** 8/1 (freshmen) **Freshmen** 75% were admitted **Housing** Yes **Expenses** Tuition $12,244; Room & Board $5470 **Undergraduates** 55% women, 28% part-time, 52% 25 or older, 1% Native American, 5% Hispanic American, 6% African American, 1% Asian American/Pacific Islander **The most frequently chosen baccalaureate fields are** business/marketing, computer/information sciences, liberal arts/general

COLORADO

studies **Academic program** Advanced placement, accelerated degree program, self-designed majors, honors program, summer session, adult/continuing education programs, internships **Contact** Ms. Kim Myrick, Director of Admissions, Colorado Christian University, 180 South Garrison Street, Lakewood, CO 80226-7499. Telephone: 303-963-3403 or toll-free 800-44-FAITH. Fax: 303-963-3201. E-mail: admission@ccu.edu. Web site: http://www.ccu.edu/.

THE COLORADO COLLEGE
COLORADO SPRINGS, COLORADO

General Independent, comprehensive, coed **Entrance** Very difficult **Setting** 90-acre urban campus **Total enrollment** 1,952 **Student-faculty ratio** 9:1 **Application deadline** 1/15 (freshmen), 4/1 (transfer) **Freshmen** 69% were admitted **Housing** Yes **Expenses** Tuition $24,893; Room & Board $6632 **Undergraduates** 55% women, 1% part-time, 1% 25 or older, 1% Native American, 6% Hispanic American, 2% African American, 4% Asian American/Pacific Islander **The most frequently chosen baccalaureate fields are** biological/life sciences, English, social sciences and history **Academic program** English as a second language, advanced placement, self-designed majors, honors program, summer session **Contact** Mr. Mark Hatch, Dean of Admission and Financial Aid, The Colorado College, 900 Block North Cascade, West, Colorado Springs, CO 80903-3294. Telephone: 719-389-6344 or toll-free 800-542-7214. Fax: 719-389-6816. E-mail: admission@coloradocollege.edu. Web site: http://www.coloradocollege.edu/.

COLORADO SCHOOL OF MINES
GOLDEN, COLORADO

General State-supported, university, coed **Entrance** Very difficult **Setting** 373-acre small-town campus **Total enrollment** 3,255 **Student-faculty ratio** 13:1 **Application deadline** 6/1 (freshmen), 6/1 (transfer) **Freshmen** 82% were admitted **Housing** Yes **Expenses** Tuition $5898; Room & Board $5680 **Undergraduates** 25% women, 4% part-time, 2% 25 or older, 1% Native American, 6% Hispanic American, 1% African American, 5% Asian American/Pacific Islander **The most frequently chosen baccalaureate fields are** engineering/engineering technologies, mathematics, physical sciences **Academic program** English as a second language, advanced placement, accelerated degree program, honors program, summer session, internships **Contact** Ms. Tricia Douthit, Assistant Director of Enrollment Management, Colorado School of Mines, 1600 Maple Street, Golden, CO 80401-1842. Telephone: 303-273-3224 or toll-free 800-446-9488 (out-of-state). Fax: 303-273-3509. E-mail: admit@mines.edu. Web site: http://www.mines.edu/.

COLORADO STATE UNIVERSITY
FORT COLLINS, COLORADO

General State-supported, university, coed **Entrance** Moderately difficult **Setting** 666-acre urban campus **Total enrollment** 23,934 **Student-faculty ratio** 18:1 **Application deadline** 7/1 (freshmen), 7/1 (transfer) **Freshmen** 78% were admitted **Housing** Yes **Expenses** Tuition $4252; Room & Board $5670 **Undergraduates** 52% women, 11% part-time, 12% 25 or older, 1% Native American, 6% Hispanic American, 2% African American, 3% Asian American/Pacific Islander **The most frequently chosen baccalaureate fields are** agriculture, business/marketing, engineering/engineering technologies **Academic program** English as a second language, advanced placement, accelerated degree program, self-designed majors, honors program, summer session, adult/continuing education programs, internships **Contact** Ms. Mary Ontiveros, Director of Admissions, Colorado State University, Spruce Hall, Fort Collins, CO 80523-0015. Telephone: 970-491-6909. Fax: 970-491-7799. E-mail: admissions@vines.colostate.edu. Web site: http://www.colostate.edu/.

COLORADO TECHNICAL UNIVERSITY
COLORADO SPRINGS, COLORADO

General Proprietary, comprehensive, coed **Entrance** Minimally difficult **Setting** 14-acre suburban campus **Total enrollment** 1,680 **Student-faculty ratio** 20:1 **Application deadline** Rolling (freshmen), rolling (transfer) **Freshmen** 93% were admitted **Housing** No **Expenses** Tuition $8532 **Undergraduates** 24% women, 76% part-time, 82% 25 or older, 0.4% Native American, 6% Hispanic American, 8% African American, 4% Asian American/Pacific Islander **The most frequently chosen baccalaureate fields are** computer/information sciences, engineering/engineering technologies **Academic program** Advanced placement, accelerated degree program, summer session, adult/continuing education programs, internships **Contact** Ms. Terri Johnson, Director of Admissions, Colorado Technical University, 4435 North Chestnut Street, Colorado Springs, CO 80907-3896. Telephone: 719-598-0200. Fax: 719-598-3740. E-mail: tjohnson@cos.coloradotech.edu. Web site: http://www.coloradotech.edu.

COLORADO TECHNICAL UNIVERSITY DENVER CAMPUS
GREENWOOD VILLAGE, COLORADO

General Proprietary, comprehensive, coed **Entrance** Minimally difficult **Setting** 1-acre urban campus **Total enrollment** 292 **Student-faculty ratio** 14:1 **Application deadline** Rolling (freshmen), rolling (transfer) **Freshmen** 67% were admitted **Housing** No **Expenses** Tuition $8532 **Undergraduates** 27% women, 80% part-time, 78% 25 or older, 1% Native American, 6% Hispanic American, 8% African American, 6% Asian American/Pacific Islander **The most frequently chosen baccalaureate fields are** computer/information sciences, engineering/engineering technologies **Academic program** Advanced placement, honors program, adult/continuing education programs **Contact** Ms. Terri Johnson, Director of Admissions, Colorado Technical University Denver Campus, 5775 DTC Boulevard, Suite 700, Greenwood Village, CO 80111. Telephone: 303-694-6600. Fax: 303-

COLORADO

Colorado Technical University Denver Campus *(continued)*
694-6673. E-mail: ctudenver@coloradotech.edu. Web site: http://www.coloradotech.edu/.

DENVER TECHNICAL COLLEGE
DENVER, COLORADO

General Proprietary, 4-year, coed, primarily men **Entrance** Moderately difficult **Setting** 1-acre urban campus **Total enrollment** 269 **Student-faculty ratio** 5:1 **Application deadline** Rolling (freshmen), rolling (transfer) **Freshmen** 89% were admitted **Housing** No **Expenses** Tuition $9300 **Undergraduates** 24% women, 36% part-time, 54% 25 or older, 1% Native American, 10% Hispanic American, 14% African American, 4% Asian American/Pacific Islander **Academic program** Accelerated degree program, honors program, summer session, adult/continuing education programs **Contact** Ms. Pam Smith, Directors of Admissions, Denver Technical College, 925 South Niagara Street, Denver, CO 80224. Telephone: 303-329-3340 or toll-free 303-329-3340 (out-of-state). Fax: 303-329-0955. Web site: http://www.den.devry.edu/.

DENVER TECHNICAL COLLEGE AT COLORADO SPRINGS
COLORADO SPRINGS, COLORADO

General Proprietary, 4-year, coed **Entrance** Noncompetitive **Setting** 3-acre urban campus **Total enrollment** 450 **Application deadline** 9/15 (freshmen), 9/15 (transfer) **Freshmen** 97% were admitted **Housing** No **Undergraduates** 74% 25 or older **Academic program** Summer session, adult/continuing education programs, internships **Contact** Mr. Rick Modman, Director of Admissions, Denver Technical College at Colorado Springs, 225 South Union Boulevard, Colorado Springs, CO 80910. Telephone: 719-632-3000 Ext. 8133. Fax: 719-632-1909. Web site: http://www.dtc.edu/.

DEVRY UNIVERSITY
COLORADO SPRINGS, COLORADO

General Proprietary, 4-year, coed **Total enrollment** 128 **Student-faculty ratio** 4:1 **Application deadline** Rolling (freshmen), rolling (transfer) **Freshmen** 87% were admitted **Housing** No **Expenses** Tuition $9400 **Undergraduates** 29% women, 30% part-time, 41% 25 or older, 2% Native American, 12% Hispanic American, 14% African American, 5% Asian American/Pacific Islander **Contact** Mr. Rick Rodman, Director of Admissions, DeVry University, 925 South Niagara Street, Denver, CO 80224. Telephone: 303-329-3340 Ext. 7121. Web site: http://www.cs.devry.edu/.

DEVRY UNIVERSITY
DENVER, COLORADO

Contact DeVry University, 925 South Niagara Street, Denver, CO 80224. Web site: http://www.den.devry.edu/.

EDUCATION AMERICA, COLORADO SPRINGS CAMPUS
COLORADO SPRINGS, COLORADO

Contact Education America, Colorado Springs Campus, 6050 Erin Park Drive, #250, Colorado Springs, CO 80918. Telephone: or toll-free 719-264-1234 (out-of-state).

EDUCATION AMERICA, DENVER CAMPUS
LAKEWOOD, COLORADO

Contact Admissions Office, Education America, Denver Campus, 11011 West 6th Avenue, Lakewood, CO 80215-0090. Telephone: 303-426-1000 or toll-free 800-999-5181.

FORT LEWIS COLLEGE
DURANGO, COLORADO

General State-supported, 4-year, coed **Entrance** Moderately difficult **Setting** 350-acre small-town campus **Total enrollment** 4,441 **Student-faculty ratio** 19:1 **Application deadline** 8/1 (freshmen), 7/15 (transfer) **Freshmen** 84% were admitted **Housing** Yes **Expenses** Tuition $2521; Room & Board $5424 **Undergraduates** 47% women, 9% part-time, 14% 25 or older, 16% Native American, 5% Hispanic American, 1% African American, 1% Asian American/Pacific Islander **The most frequently chosen baccalaureate fields are** business/marketing, interdisciplinary studies, social sciences and history **Academic program** English as a second language, advanced placement, accelerated degree program, self-designed majors, honors program, summer session, adult/continuing education programs, internships **Contact** Ms. Sheri Rochford, Dean of Admissions and Development, Fort Lewis College, 1000 Rim Drive, Durango, CO 81301. Telephone: 970-247-7184. Fax: 970-247-7179. E-mail: admission@fortlewis.edu. Web site: http://www.fortlewis.edu/.

JOHNSON & WALES UNIVERSITY
DENVER, COLORADO

General Independent, 4-year, coed **Entrance** Minimally difficult **Setting** small-town campus **Total enrollment** 646 **Student-faculty ratio** 18:1 **Application deadline** Rolling (freshmen), rolling (transfer) **Freshmen** 81% were admitted **Housing** Yes **Expenses** Tuition $16,893; Room & Board $7506 **Undergraduates** 43% women, 4% part-time, 1% Native American, 13% Hispanic American, 7% African American, 3% Asian American/Pacific Islander **Academic program** Summer session, adult/continuing education programs, internships **Contact** Mr. Dave McKlveen, Director of Admissions, Johnson & Wales University, 7150 Montview Boulevard, Denver, CO 80220. Telephone: 303-256-9300 or toll-free 877-598-3368. Fax: 303-256-9333. E-mail: admissions@jwu.edu. Web site: http://www.jwu.edu/.

COLORADO

JONES INTERNATIONAL UNIVERSITY
ENGLEWOOD, COLORADO

General Independent, upper-level, coed **Entrance** Noncompetitive **Total enrollment** 2,000 **Student-faculty ratio** 12:1 **Application deadline** Rolling (transfer) **Housing** No **Expenses** Tuition $4290 **Undergraduates** 90% 25 or older **Academic program** Accelerated degree program, summer session, adult/continuing education programs **Contact** Ms. Candice Morrissey, Associate Director of Admissions, Jones International University, 9697 East Mineral Avenue, Englewood, CO 80112. Telephone: 303-784-8247 or toll-free 800-811-5663 Ext. 8247. Fax: 303-784-8547. E-mail: admissions@international.edu. Web site: http://www.jonesinternational.edu/.

MESA STATE COLLEGE
GRAND JUNCTION, COLORADO

General State-supported, comprehensive, coed **Entrance** Minimally difficult **Setting** 42-acre small-town campus **Total enrollment** 5,346 **Student-faculty ratio** 18:1 **Application deadline** 8/15 (freshmen), 8/15 (transfer) **Freshmen** 99% were admitted **Housing** Yes **Expenses** Tuition $2288; Room & Board $5763 **Undergraduates** 58% women, 25% part-time, 38% 25 or older **The most frequently chosen baccalaureate fields are** business/marketing, biological/life sciences, social sciences and history **Academic program** Advanced placement, accelerated degree program, self-designed majors, honors program, summer session, adult/continuing education programs, internships **Contact** Mr. Mike Poll, Associate Director, Admissions and Recruitment, Mesa State College, PO Box 2647, Grand Junction, CO 81502-2647. Telephone: 970-248-1875 or toll-free 800-982-MESA. Fax: 970-248-1973. E-mail: pjones@mesa5.mesa.colorado.edu. Web site: http://www2.mesastate.edu/.

METROPOLITAN STATE COLLEGE OF DENVER
DENVER, COLORADO

General State-supported, 4-year, coed **Entrance** Minimally difficult **Setting** 175-acre urban campus **Total enrollment** 18,445 **Student-faculty ratio** 21:1 **Application deadline** 8/12 (freshmen), rolling (transfer) **Freshmen** 86% were admitted **Housing** No **Expenses** Tuition $2338 **Undergraduates** 57% women, 44% part-time, 40% 25 or older, 1% Native American, 13% Hispanic American, 6% African American, 4% Asian American/Pacific Islander **The most frequently chosen baccalaureate fields are** business/marketing, protective services/public administration, social sciences and history **Academic program** Advanced placement, accelerated degree program, self-designed majors, honors program, summer session, adult/continuing education programs, internships **Contact** Ms. Miriam Tapia, Associate Director, Metropolitan State College of Denver, PO Box 173362, Campus Box 16, Denver, CO 80217-3362.

Telephone: 303-556-2615. Fax: 303-556-6345. Web site: http://www.mscd.edu/.

NAROPA UNIVERSITY
BOULDER, COLORADO

General Independent, comprehensive, coed **Entrance** Moderately difficult **Setting** 4-acre urban campus **Total enrollment** 1,127 **Student-faculty ratio** 12:1 **Application deadline** Rolling (freshmen), rolling (transfer) **Freshmen** 97% were admitted **Housing** Yes **Expenses** Tuition $15,056; Room & Board $5810 **Undergraduates** 65% women, 24% part-time, 31% 25 or older, 1% Native American, 3% Hispanic American, 1% African American, 1% Asian American/Pacific Islander **The most frequently chosen baccalaureate fields are** psychology, English, visual/performing arts **Academic program** Advanced placement, self-designed majors, summer session, adult/continuing education programs, internships **Contact** Ms. Sally Forester, Admissions Counselor, Naropa University, 2130 Arapahoe Avenue, Boulder, CO 80302. Telephone: 303-546-5285 or toll-free 800-772-0410 (out-of-state). Fax: 303-546-3583. E-mail: tracy@naropa.edu. Web site: http://www.naropa.edu/.

NATIONAL AMERICAN UNIVERSITY
COLORADO SPRINGS, COLORADO

General Proprietary, 4-year, coed **Entrance** Noncompetitive **Setting** 1-acre suburban campus **Total enrollment** 325 **Application deadline** Rolling (freshmen), rolling (transfer) **Housing** No **Expenses** Tuition $9600 **Undergraduates** 98% 25 or older **Academic program** English as a second language, accelerated degree program, summer session, adult/continuing education programs, internships **Contact** Ms. Dawn Collins, Director of Admissions, National American University, 5125 North Academy Boulevard, Colorado Springs, CO 80918. Telephone: 719-277-0588 or toll-free 888-471-4781. Fax: 719-471-4751. E-mail: nau@clsp.uswest.net. Web site: http://www.national.edu/col_springs.html.

NATIONAL AMERICAN UNIVERSITY
DENVER, COLORADO

General Proprietary, 4-year, coed **Entrance** Noncompetitive **Setting** urban campus **Total enrollment** 380 **Application deadline** Rolling (freshmen), rolling (transfer) **Housing** No **Expenses** Tuition $9360 **Undergraduates** 85% 25 or older **Academic program** English as a second language, advanced placement, accelerated degree program, summer session, adult/continuing education programs **Contact** Mr. Tom De Felice, Director of Admissions, National American University, 1325 South Colorado Blvd, Suite 100, Denver, CO 80222. Telephone: 303-758-6700. Fax: 303-758-6810.

NAZARENE BIBLE COLLEGE
COLORADO SPRINGS, COLORADO

General Independent, 4-year, coed, affiliated with Church of the Nazarene **Entrance** Noncompetitive

COLORADO

Nazarene Bible College *(continued)*
Setting 64-acre urban campus **Total enrollment** 473 **Student-faculty ratio** 14:1 **Application deadline** 8/31 (freshmen), 8/31 (transfer) **Freshmen** 60% were admitted **Housing** No **Expenses** Tuition $9246 **Undergraduates** 30% women, 59% part-time, 89% 25 or older, 2% Native American, 1% Hispanic American, 3% African American, 2% Asian American/Pacific Islander **The most frequently chosen baccalaureate field is** philosophy, religion, and theology **Academic program** Summer session, internships **Contact** Dr. David Phillips, Director of Admissions/Public Relations, Nazarene Bible College, 1111 Academy Park Loop, Colorado Springs, CO 80910-3704. Telephone: 719-884-5031 or toll-free 800-873-3873. Fax: 719-884-5199. Web site: http://www.nbc.edu/.

REGIS UNIVERSITY
DENVER, COLORADO

General Independent Roman Catholic (Jesuit), comprehensive, coed **Entrance** Moderately difficult **Setting** 90-acre suburban campus **Total enrollment** 13,547 **Student-faculty ratio** 14:1 **Application deadline** 8/15 (freshmen), 8/15 (transfer) **Freshmen** 86% were admitted **Housing** Yes **Expenses** Tuition $18,570; Room & Board $7150 **Undergraduates** 7% 25 or older, 1% Native American, 8% Hispanic American, 4% African American, 2% Asian American/Pacific Islander **Academic program** Advanced placement, accelerated degree program, self-designed majors, honors program, summer session, adult/continuing education programs, internships **Contact** Mr. Vic Davolt, Director of Admissions, Regis University, 3333 Regis Boulevard, Denver, CO 80221-1099. Telephone: 303-458-4905 or toll-free 800-388-2366 Ext. 4900. Fax: 303-964-5534. E-mail: regisadm@regis.edu. Web site: http://www.regis.edu/.

ROCKY MOUNTAIN COLLEGE OF ART & DESIGN
DENVER, COLORADO

General Proprietary, 4-year, coed **Entrance** Moderately difficult **Setting** 1-acre urban campus **Total enrollment** 425 **Student-faculty ratio** 12:1 **Application deadline** Rolling (freshmen), rolling (transfer) **Freshmen** 74% were admitted **Housing** Yes **Expenses** Tuition $11,562; Room only $3000 **Undergraduates** 54% women, 21% part-time, 22% 25 or older, 0.2% Native American, 9% Hispanic American, 1% African American, 2% Asian American/Pacific Islander **The most frequently chosen baccalaureate field is** visual/performing arts **Academic program** Advanced placement, accelerated degree program, summer session, internships **Contact** Ms. Sandy Sprock, Assistant Admissions Coordinator, Rocky Mountain College of Art & Design, 6875 East Evans Avenue, Denver, CO 80224-2329. Telephone: 303-753-6046 or toll-free 800-888-ARTS. Fax: 303-759-4970. E-mail: admit@rmcad.edu. Web site: http://www.rmcad.info/.

TEIKYO LORETTO HEIGHTS UNIVERSITY
DENVER, COLORADO

Contact Teikyo Loretto Heights University, 3001 South Federal Boulevard, Denver, CO 80236-2711.

UNITED STATES AIR FORCE ACADEMY
COLORADO SPRINGS, COLORADO

General Federally supported, 4-year, coed, primarily men **Entrance** Most difficult **Setting** 18,000-acre suburban campus **Total enrollment** 4,365 **Student-faculty ratio** 8:1 **Application deadline** 1/31 (freshmen), 1/31 (transfer) **Freshmen** 17% were admitted **Housing** Yes **Undergraduates** 16% women, 0.4% 25 or older, 1% Native American, 6% Hispanic American, 6% African American, 4% Asian American/Pacific Islander **The most frequently chosen baccalaureate fields are** engineering/engineering technologies, business/marketing, social sciences and history **Academic program** English as a second language, advanced placement, self-designed majors, summer session, internships **Contact** Mr. Rolland Stoneman, Associate Director of Admissions/Selections, United States Air Force Academy, HQ USAFA/RR 2304 Cadet Drive, Suite 200, USAF Academy, CO 80840-5025. Telephone: 719-333-2520 or toll-free 800-443-9266. Fax: 719-333-3012. E-mail: wilsoncm.rr@usafa.af.mil. Web site: http://www.usafa.edu/rr.

UNIVERSITY OF COLORADO AT BOULDER
BOULDER, COLORADO

General State-supported, university, coed **Entrance** Moderately difficult **Setting** 600-acre suburban campus **Total enrollment** 29,609 **Student-faculty ratio** 15:1 **Application deadline** 2/15 (freshmen), 4/1 (transfer) **Freshmen** 79% were admitted **Housing** Yes **Expenses** Tuition $3357; Room & Board $5898 **Undergraduates** 48% women, 11% part-time, 8% 25 or older, 1% Native American, 6% Hispanic American, 2% African American, 6% Asian American/Pacific Islander **The most frequently chosen baccalaureate fields are** business/marketing, communications/communication technologies, social sciences and history **Academic program** English as a second language, advanced placement, accelerated degree program, self-designed majors, honors program, summer session, adult/continuing education programs, internships **Contact** Mr. Kevin MacLennan, Associate Director, University of Colorado at Boulder, 552 UCB, Boulder, CO 80309-0552. Telephone: 303-492-1394. Fax: 303-492-7115. E-mail: apply@colorado.edu. Web site: http://www.colorado.edu/.

UNIVERSITY OF COLORADO AT COLORADO SPRINGS
COLORADO SPRINGS, COLORADO

General State-supported, comprehensive, coed **Entrance** Moderately difficult **Setting** 400-acre suburban campus **Total enrollment** 6,835 **Student-

COLORADO

faculty ratio 16:1 **Application deadline** 7/1 (freshmen), 7/1 (transfer) **Freshmen** 74% were admitted **Housing** Yes **Expenses** Tuition $4250; Room & Board $5893 **Undergraduates** 61% women, 26% part-time, 1% Native American, 9% Hispanic American, 4% African American, 6% Asian American/Pacific Islander **The most frequently chosen baccalaureate fields are** business/marketing, psychology, social sciences and history **Academic program** Advanced placement, accelerated degree program, summer session, adult/continuing education programs, internships **Contact** Mr. James Tidwell, Assistant Admissions Director, University of Colorado at Colorado Springs, PO Box 7150, Colorado Springs, CO 80933-7150. Telephone: 719-262-3383 or toll-free 800-990-8227 Ext. 3383. E-mail: admrec@mail.uccs.edu. Web site: http://www.uccs.edu/.

UNIVERSITY OF COLORADO AT DENVER
DENVER, COLORADO

General State-supported, university, coed **Entrance** Moderately difficult **Setting** 171-acre urban campus **Total enrollment** 15,004 **Student-faculty ratio** 14:1 **Application deadline** 7/22 (freshmen), 7/22 (transfer) **Freshmen** 73% were admitted **Housing** No **Expenses** Tuition $2934 **Undergraduates** 57% women, 46% part-time, 34% 25 or older, 1% Native American, 10% Hispanic American, 4% African American, 10% Asian American/Pacific Islander **The most frequently chosen baccalaureate fields are** business/marketing, psychology, social sciences and history **Academic program** Advanced placement, self-designed majors, honors program, summer session, adult/continuing education programs, internships **Contact** Ms. Barbara Edwards, Director of Admissions, University of Colorado at Denver, 1250 14th Street, Denver, CO 80217-3364. Telephone: 303-556-3287. Fax: 303-556-4838. E-mail: admissions@castle.cudenver.edu. Web site: http://www.cudenver.edu/.

UNIVERSITY OF COLORADO HEALTH SCIENCES CENTER
DENVER, COLORADO

General State-supported, upper-level, coed **Entrance** Moderately difficult **Setting** 40-acre urban campus **Total enrollment** 2,165 **Application deadline** 10/1 (transfer) **First-Year Students** 55% were admitted **Housing** No **Expenses** Tuition $8980 **Undergraduates** 86% women, 1% Native American, 8% Hispanic American, 4% African American, 11% Asian American/Pacific Islander **The most frequently chosen baccalaureate field is** health professions and related sciences **Academic program** Advanced placement, summer session, adult/continuing education programs, internships **Contact** Dr. David P. Sorenson, Director of Admissions, University of Colorado Health Sciences Center, 4200 East Ninth Avenue, Denver, CO 80262. Telephone: 303-315-7676. Fax: 303-315-3358. E-mail: stuserv@mongo.uchsc.edu. Web site: http://www.uchsc.edu/.

UNIVERSITY OF DENVER
DENVER, COLORADO

General Independent, university, coed **Entrance** Moderately difficult **Setting** 125-acre suburban campus **Total enrollment** 9,385 **Student-faculty ratio** 9:1 **Application deadline** 2/1 (freshmen), 2/1 (transfer) **Freshmen** 72% were admitted **Housing** Yes **Expenses** Tuition $22,035; Room & Board $6747 **Undergraduates** 57% women, 11% part-time, 16% 25 or older, 1% Native American, 6% Hispanic American, 4% African American, 5% Asian American/Pacific Islander **The most frequently chosen baccalaureate fields are** business/marketing, communications/communication technologies, social sciences and history **Academic program** English as a second language, advanced placement, accelerated degree program, self-designed majors, honors program, summer session, adult/continuing education programs, internships **Contact** Ms. Colleen Hillmeyer, Director of New Student Programs, University of Denver, University Park, Denver, CO 80208. Telephone: 303-871-2782 or toll-free 800-525-9495 (out-of-state). Fax: 303-871-3301. E-mail: admission@du.edu. Web site: http://www.du.edu/.

UNIVERSITY OF NORTHERN COLORADO
GREELEY, COLORADO

General State-supported, university, coed **Entrance** Moderately difficult **Setting** 240-acre suburban campus **Total enrollment** 12,301 **Student-faculty ratio** 21:1 **Application deadline** Rolling (freshmen), rolling (transfer) **Freshmen** 78% were admitted **Housing** Yes **Expenses** Tuition $2842; Room & Board $5240 **Undergraduates** 61% women, 10% part-time, 8% 25 or older, 1% Native American, 7% Hispanic American, 2% African American, 4% Asian American/Pacific Islander **The most frequently chosen baccalaureate fields are** business/marketing, communications/communication technologies, social sciences and history **Academic program** English as a second language, advanced placement, self-designed majors, honors program, summer session, adult/continuing education programs, internships **Contact** Mr. Gary O. Gullickson, Director of Admissions, University of Northern Colorado, Greeley, CO 80639. Telephone: 970-351-2881 or toll-free 888-700-4UNC (in-state). Fax: 970-351-2984. E-mail: unc@mail.unco.edu. Web site: http://www.unco.edu/.

UNIVERSITY OF PHOENIX–COLORADO CAMPUS
LONE TREE, COLORADO

General Proprietary, comprehensive, coed **Entrance** Noncompetitive **Total enrollment** 88,730 **Student-faculty ratio** 13:1 **Application deadline** Rolling (freshmen), rolling (transfer) **Housing** No **Expenses** Tuition $7950 **Undergraduates** 54% women, 77% 25 or older **The most frequently chosen baccalaureate fields are** business/marketing, health professions and related sciences **Academic program** Advanced placement, accelerated degree program,

COLORADO

University of Phoenix–Colorado Campus *(continued)*

adult/continuing education programs **Contact** Ms. Beth Barilla, Director of Admissions, University of Phoenix–Colorado Campus, 4615 East Elwood Street, Phoenix, AZ 85040-1958. Telephone: 480-927-0099 Ext. 1218 or toll-free 800-228-7240. Fax: 480-594-1758. E-mail: beth.barilla@apollogrp.edu. Web site: http://www.phoenix.edu/.

UNIVERSITY OF PHOENIX–SOUTHERN COLORADO CAMPUS
COLORADO SPRINGS, COLORADO

General Proprietary, comprehensive, coed **Entrance** Noncompetitive **Total enrollment** 88,730 **Student-faculty ratio** 12:1 **Application deadline** Rolling (freshmen), rolling (transfer) **Housing** No **Expenses** Tuition $7950 **Undergraduates** 55% women, 84% 25 or older **Academic program** Advanced placement, accelerated degree program, adult/continuing education programs **Contact** Ms. Beth Barilla, Director of Admissions, University of Phoenix–Southern Colorado Campus, 4615 East Elwood Street, Phoenix, AZ 85040-1958. Telephone: 480-927-0099 Ext. 1218 or toll-free 800-228-7240. Fax: 480-894-1758. E-mail: beth.barilla@apollogrp.edu. Web site: http://www.phoenix.edu/.

UNIVERSITY OF SOUTHERN COLORADO
PUEBLO, COLORADO

General State-supported, comprehensive, coed **Entrance** Moderately difficult **Setting** 275-acre suburban campus **Total enrollment** 5,531 **Student-faculty ratio** 17:1 **Application deadline** Rolling (freshmen), rolling (transfer) **Freshmen** 83% were admitted **Housing** Yes **Expenses** Tuition $2449; Room & Board $5372 **Undergraduates** 57% women, 37% part-time, 35% 25 or older, 1% Native American, 25% Hispanic American, 4% African American, 2% Asian American/Pacific Islander **Academic program** English as a second language, advanced placement, accelerated degree program, honors program, summer session, adult/continuing education programs, internships **Contact** Ms. Pamela L. Anastassiou, Director of Admissions and Records, University of Southern Colorado, 2200 Bonforte Boulevard, Pueblo, CO 81001. Telephone: 719-549-2461 or toll-free 877-872-9653. Fax: 719-549-2419. E-mail: info@uscolo.edu. Web site: http://www.uscolo.edu/.

WESTERN STATE COLLEGE OF COLORADO
GUNNISON, COLORADO

General State-supported, 4-year, coed **Entrance** Moderately difficult **Setting** 381-acre small-town campus **Total enrollment** 2,302 **Student-faculty ratio** 20:1 **Application deadline** Rolling (freshmen), rolling (transfer) **Freshmen** 85% were admitted **Housing** Yes **Expenses** Tuition $2403; Room & Board $5690 **Undergraduates** 42% women, 9% part-time, 12% 25 or older, 1% Native American, 5% Hispanic American, 1% African American, 1% Asian American/Pacific Islander **The most frequently chosen baccalaureate fields are** business/marketing, parks and recreation, social sciences and history **Academic program** Advanced placement, accelerated degree program, self-designed majors, honors program, summer session, adult/continuing education programs, internships **Contact** Mr. Timothy L. Albers, Director of Admissions, Western State College of Colorado, 600 North Adams Street, Gunnison, CO 81231. Telephone: 970-943-2119 or toll-free 800-876-5309. Fax: 970-943-2212. E-mail: talbers@western.edu. Web site: http://www.western.edu/.

YESHIVA TORAS CHAIM TALMUDICAL SEMINARY
DENVER, COLORADO

Contact Rabbi Israel Kagan, Dean, Yeshiva Toras Chaim Talmudical Seminary, 1400 Quitman Street, Denver, CO 80204-1415. Telephone: 303-629-8200. Fax: 303-623-5949.

CONNECTICUT

ALBERTUS MAGNUS COLLEGE
NEW HAVEN, CONNECTICUT

General Independent Roman Catholic, comprehensive, coed **Entrance** Moderately difficult **Setting** 55-acre suburban campus **Total enrollment** 2,278 **Student-faculty ratio** 15:1 **Application deadline** Rolling (freshmen), rolling (transfer) **Freshmen** 98% were admitted **Housing** Yes **Expenses** Tuition $15,246; Room & Board $6908 **Undergraduates** 66% women, 8% part-time, 65% 25 or older, 1% Native American, 7% Hispanic American, 19% African American, 1% Asian American/Pacific Islander **The most frequently chosen baccalaureate fields are** business/marketing, psychology, social sciences and history **Academic program** English as a second language, advanced placement, accelerated degree program, self-designed majors, honors program, summer session, adult/continuing education programs, internships **Contact** Ms. Rebecca George, Associate Dean of Admissions, Albertus Magnus College, 700 Prospect Street, New Haven, CT 06511-1189. Telephone: 203-773-8501 or toll-free 800-578-9160. Fax: 203-773-5248. E-mail: admissions@albertus.edu. Web site: ..

BETH BENJAMIN ACADEMY OF CONNECTICUT
STAMFORD, CONNECTICUT

Contact Rabbi David Mayer, Director of Admissions, Beth Benjamin Academy of Connecticut, 132 Prospect Street, Stamford, CT 06901-1202. Telephone: 203-325-4351.

CONNECTICUT

CENTRAL CONNECTICUT STATE UNIVERSITY
NEW BRITAIN, CONNECTICUT

General State-supported, comprehensive, coed **Entrance** Moderately difficult **Setting** 294-acre suburban campus **Total enrollment** 12,368 **Student-faculty ratio** 17:1 **Application deadline** 5/1 (freshmen), 5/1 (transfer) **Freshmen** 65% were admitted **Housing** Yes **Expenses** Tuition $4374; Room & Board $6030 **Undergraduates** 52% women, 31% part-time, 24% 25 or older, 0.4% Native American, 5% Hispanic American, 7% African American, 3% Asian American/Pacific Islander **The most frequently chosen baccalaureate fields are** business/marketing, psychology, social sciences and history **Academic program** English as a second language, advanced placement, self-designed majors, honors program, summer session, adult/continuing education programs, internships **Contact** Ms. Myrna Garcia-Bowen, Director of Admissions, Central Connecticut State University, 1615 Stanley Street, New Britain, CT 06050-4010. Telephone: 860-832-2285 or toll-free 800-755-2278 (out-of-state). Fax: 860-832-2522. E-mail: admissions@ccsu.edu. Web site: http://www.ccsu.edu/.

CHARTER OAK STATE COLLEGE
NEW BRITAIN, CONNECTICUT

General State-supported, 4-year, coed **Entrance** Noncompetitive **Setting** small-town campus **Total enrollment** 1,496 **Application deadline** Rolling (transfer) **Housing** No **Undergraduates** 50% women, 100% part-time, 98% 25 or older, 1% Native American, 4% Hispanic American, 8% African American, 1% Asian American/Pacific Islander **The most frequently chosen baccalaureate field is** liberal arts/general studies **Academic program** Advanced placement, accelerated degree program, self-designed majors, adult/continuing education programs **Contact** Mr. Harry White, Dean of Enrollment Management, Charter Oak State College, 55 Paul Manafort Drive, New Britain, CT 06053-2142. Telephone: 860-832-3855. Fax: 860-832-3855. E-mail: info@charteroak.edu. Web site: http://www.charteroak.edu/.

CONNECTICUT COLLEGE
NEW LONDON, CONNECTICUT

General Independent, comprehensive, coed **Entrance** Very difficult **Setting** 702-acre suburban campus **Total enrollment** 1,879 **Student-faculty ratio** 11:1 **Application deadline** 1/1 (freshmen), 4/1 (transfer) **Freshmen** 34% were admitted **Housing** Yes **Expenses** Tuition $33,585 **Undergraduates** 59% women, 4% part-time, 1% 25 or older, 0.5% Native American, 3% Hispanic American, 3% African American, 3% Asian American/Pacific Islander **The most frequently chosen baccalaureate fields are** biological/life sciences, psychology, social sciences and history **Academic program** Advanced placement, accelerated degree program, self-designed majors, honors program, summer session, adult/continuing education programs, internships **Contact** Ms. Martha Merrill, Dean of Admissions and Financial Aid, Connecticut College, 270 Mohegan Avenue, New London, CT 06320-4196. Telephone: 860-439-2200. Fax: 860-439-4301. E-mail: admission@conncoll.edu. Web site: http://www.connecticutcollege.edu.

EASTERN CONNECTICUT STATE UNIVERSITY
WILLIMANTIC, CONNECTICUT

General State-supported, comprehensive, coed **Entrance** Moderately difficult **Setting** 178-acre small-town campus **Total enrollment** 5,313 **Student-faculty ratio** 16:1 **Application deadline** Rolling (transfer) **Freshmen** 64% were admitted **Housing** Yes **Expenses** Tuition $4146; Room & Board $5850 **Undergraduates** 58% women, 28% part-time, 27% 25 or older, 1% Native American, 3% Hispanic American, 7% African American, 2% Asian American/Pacific Islander **The most frequently chosen baccalaureate fields are** social sciences and history, business/marketing, trade and industry **Academic program** Advanced placement, self-designed majors, honors program, summer session, adult/continuing education programs, internships **Contact** Ms. Kimberly Crone, Director of Admissions and Enrollment Management, Eastern Connecticut State University, 83 Windham Street, Willimantic, CT 06336. Telephone: 860-465-5286 or toll-free 877-353-3278. Fax: 860-465-5544. E-mail: admissions@easternct.edu. Web site: http://www.easternct.edu/.

FAIRFIELD UNIVERSITY
FAIRFIELD, CONNECTICUT

General Independent Roman Catholic (Jesuit), comprehensive, coed **Entrance** Moderately difficult **Setting** 200-acre suburban campus **Total enrollment** 5,154 **Student-faculty ratio** 13:1 **Application deadline** 2/1 (freshmen), 6/1 (transfer) **Freshmen** 49% were admitted **Housing** Yes **Expenses** Tuition $22,885; Room & Board $8000 **Undergraduates** 55% women, 18% part-time, 0.2% Native American, 5% Hispanic American, 3% African American, 3% Asian American/Pacific Islander **The most frequently chosen baccalaureate fields are** business/marketing, English, trade and industry **Academic program** Advanced placement, honors program, summer session, adult/continuing education programs, internships **Contact** Ms. Judith M. Dobai, Director of Admission, Fairfield University, 1073 North Benson Road, Fairfield, CT 06430-5195. Telephone: 203-254-4100. Fax: 203-254-4199. E-mail: admis@mail.fairfield.edu. Web site: http://www.fairfield.edu/.

HARTFORD COLLEGE FOR WOMEN
HARTFORD, CONNECTICUT

General Independent, 4-year, women only **Entrance** Moderately difficult **Setting** 13-acre suburban campus **Total enrollment** 178 **Student-faculty ratio** 7:1 **Application deadline** Rolling (freshmen), rolling (transfer) **Freshmen** 50% were admitted **Under-

CONNECTICUT

Hartford College for Women *(continued)*
graduates 93% part-time, 89% 25 or older, 1% Native American, 6% Hispanic American, 18% African American, 1% Asian American/Pacific Islander **The most frequently chosen baccalaureate fields are** (pre)law, area/ethnic studies **Academic program** Advanced placement, accelerated degree program, summer session, adult/continuing education programs, internships **Contact** Ms. Annette Rogers, Admissions Director, Hartford College for Women, 1265 Asylum Avenue, Hartford, CT 06105-2299. Telephone: 860-768-5646 or toll-free 888-GO-TO-HCW. Fax: 860-768-5693. E-mail: arogers@mail.hartford.edu. Web site: http://www.hartford.edu/hcw.

HOLY APOSTLES COLLEGE AND SEMINARY
CROMWELL, CONNECTICUT

General Independent Roman Catholic, comprehensive, coed **Entrance** Noncompetitive **Setting** small-town campus **Total enrollment** 250 **Student-faculty ratio** 8:1 **Application deadline** Rolling (freshmen), rolling (transfer) **Housing** Yes **Expenses** Tuition $7920; Room & Board $6400 **Undergraduates** 45% women, 76% part-time, 95% 25 or older, 0% Native American, 0% Hispanic American, 0% African American, 13% Asian American/Pacific Islander **The most frequently chosen baccalaureate field is** philosophy **Academic program** English as a second language, accelerated degree program, adult/continuing education programs, internships **Contact** Very Rev. Douglas Mosey CSB, Director of Admissions, Holy Apostles College and Seminary, 33 Prospect Hill Road, Cromwell, CT 06416-2005. Telephone: 860-632-3010 or toll-free 800-330-7272. Fax: 860-632-3075. E-mail: holy_apostles@msn.com. Web site: http://www.holyapostles.edu/.

LYME ACADEMY COLLEGE OF FINE ARTS
OLD LYME, CONNECTICUT

General Independent, 4-year, coed **Entrance** Moderately difficult **Setting** 3-acre small-town campus **Total enrollment** 203 **Student-faculty ratio** 7:1 **Application deadline** Rolling (freshmen), rolling (transfer) **Freshmen** 48% were admitted **Housing** No **Expenses** Tuition $12,770 **Undergraduates** 66% women, 67% part-time, 57% 25 or older, 1% Native American, 8% Hispanic American, 1% African American, 2% Asian American/Pacific Islander **The most frequently chosen baccalaureate field is** visual/performing arts **Academic program** Summer session **Contact** Christopher Rose, Associate Dean of Enrollment Management, Lyme Academy College of Fine Arts, 84 Lyme Street, Old Lyme, CT 06371. Telephone: 860-434-5232 Ext. 122. Fax: 860-434-8725. E-mail: admissions@lymeacademy.edu. Web site: http://www.lymeacademy.edu/.

PAIER COLLEGE OF ART, INC.
HAMDEN, CONNECTICUT

General Proprietary, 4-year, coed **Entrance** Minimally difficult **Setting** 3-acre suburban campus **Total enrollment** 284 **Student-faculty ratio** 6:1 **Application deadline** Rolling (freshmen), rolling (transfer) **Freshmen** 73% were admitted **Housing** No **Expenses** Tuition $11,200 **Undergraduates** 55% women, 44% part-time, 18% 25 or older **The most frequently chosen baccalaureate field is** visual/performing arts **Academic program** Advanced placement, summer session **Contact** Ms. Lynn Pascale, Secretary to Admissions, Paier College of Art, Inc., 20 Gorham Avenue, Hamden, CT 06514-3902. Telephone: 203-287-3031. Fax: 203-287-3021. E-mail: info@paierart.com. Web site: http://www.paierart.com/.

QUINNIPIAC UNIVERSITY
HAMDEN, CONNECTICUT

General Independent, comprehensive, coed **Entrance** Moderately difficult **Setting** 300-acre suburban campus **Total enrollment** 6,675 **Student-faculty ratio** 16:1 **Application deadline** 2/15 (freshmen), 6/1 (transfer) **Freshmen** 74% were admitted **Housing** Yes **Expenses** Tuition $18,840; Room & Board $8530 **Undergraduates** 63% women, 9% part-time, 10% 25 or older, 0.3% Native American, 4% Hispanic American, 2% African American, 2% Asian American/Pacific Islander **The most frequently chosen baccalaureate fields are** business/marketing, health professions and related sciences, liberal arts/general studies **Academic program** Advanced placement, self-designed majors, honors program, summer session, adult/continuing education programs, internships **Contact** Ms. Joan Isaac Mohr, Vice President and Dean of Admissions, Quinnipiac University, 275 Mount Carmel Avenue, Hamden, CT 06518-1940. Telephone: 203-582-8600 or toll-free 800-462-1944 (out-of-state). Fax: 203-582-8706. E-mail: admissions@quinnipiac.edu. Web site: http://www.quinnipiac.edu/.

SACRED HEART UNIVERSITY
FAIRFIELD, CONNECTICUT

General Independent Roman Catholic, comprehensive, coed **Entrance** Moderately difficult **Setting** 56-acre suburban campus **Total enrollment** 5,959 **Student-faculty ratio** 12:1 **Application deadline** Rolling (freshmen), rolling (transfer) **Freshmen** 73% were admitted **Housing** Yes **Expenses** Tuition $17,060; Room & Board $7998 **Undergraduates** 63% women, 31% part-time, 1% 25 or older, 0.2% Native American, 6% Hispanic American, 7% African American, 2% Asian American/Pacific Islander **The most frequently chosen baccalaureate fields are** business/marketing, biological/life sciences, psychology **Academic program** English as a second language, advanced placement, accelerated degree program, self-designed majors, honors program, summer session, adult/continuing education programs, internships **Contact** Ms. Karen N. Guastelle, Dean of Undergraduate Admissions, Sacred Heart University,

CONNECTICUT

5151 Park Avenue, Fairfield, CT 06432-1000. Telephone: 203-371-7880. Fax: 203-365-7607. E-mail: enroll@sacredheart.edu. Web site: http://www.sacredheart.edu/.

SAINT JOSEPH COLLEGE
WEST HARTFORD, CONNECTICUT

General Independent Roman Catholic, comprehensive, women only **Entrance** Moderately difficult **Setting** 84-acre suburban campus **Total enrollment** 1,939 **Student-faculty ratio** 11:1 **Application deadline** 5/1 (freshmen), 7/1 (transfer) **Freshmen** 37% were admitted **Housing** Yes **Expenses** Tuition $18,360; Room & Board $7600 **Undergraduates** 45% part-time, 27% 25 or older, 0.2% Native American, 6% Hispanic American, 12% African American, 2% Asian American/Pacific Islander **The most frequently chosen baccalaureate fields are** health professions and related sciences, education, social sciences and history **Academic program** English as a second language, advanced placement, accelerated degree program, self-designed majors, honors program, summer session, adult/continuing education programs, internships **Contact** Ms. Mary Yuskis, Director of Admissions, Saint Joseph College, 1678 Asylum Avenue, West Hartford, CT 06117. Telephone: 860-231-5216 or toll-free 800-285-6565. Fax: 860-233-5695. E-mail: admissions@mercy.sjc.edu. Web site: http://www.sjc.edu/.

SOUTHERN CONNECTICUT STATE UNIVERSITY
NEW HAVEN, CONNECTICUT

General State-supported, comprehensive, coed **Entrance** Moderately difficult **Setting** 168-acre urban campus **Total enrollment** 12,254 **Student-faculty ratio** 15:1 **Application deadline** 7/1 (freshmen), 7/1 (transfer) **Freshmen** 69% were admitted **Housing** Yes **Expenses** Tuition $4026; Room & Board $6588 **Undergraduates** 64% women, 24% part-time, 23% 25 or older, 0.2% Native American, 5% Hispanic American, 13% African American, 2% Asian American/Pacific Islander **The most frequently chosen baccalaureate fields are** psychology, education, social sciences and history **Academic program** Advanced placement, accelerated degree program, self-designed majors, honors program, summer session, adult/continuing education programs, internships **Contact** Ms. Paula Kennedy, Associate Director of Admissions, Southern Connecticut State University, Admissions House, New Haven, CT 06515-1202. Telephone: 203-392-5651. Fax: 203-392-5727. E-mail: adminfo@scsu.ctstateu.edu. Web site: http://www.southernct.edu/.

▶ For more information, see page 477.

TEIKYO POST UNIVERSITY
WATERBURY, CONNECTICUT

General Independent, 4-year, coed **Entrance** Minimally difficult **Setting** 70-acre suburban campus **Total enrollment** 1,350 **Student-faculty ratio** 11:1 **Application deadline** Rolling (freshmen), rolling (transfer) **Freshmen** 78% were admitted **Housing** Yes **Expenses** Tuition $15,200; Room & Board $6600 **Undergraduates** 65% women, 55% part-time, 47% 25 or older, 0.3% Native American, 10% Hispanic American, 17% African American, 2% Asian American/Pacific Islander **The most frequently chosen baccalaureate fields are** business/marketing, liberal arts/general studies, psychology **Academic program** English as a second language, advanced placement, accelerated degree program, summer session, adult/continuing education programs, internships **Contact** Mr. William Johnson, Senior Assistant Director of Admissions, Teikyo Post University, PO Box 2540, Waterbury, CT 06723. Telephone: 203-596-4520 or toll-free 800-345-2562. Fax: 203-756-5810. E-mail: tpuadmiss@teikyopost.edu. Web site: http://teikyopost.edu/.

▶ For more information, see page 480.

TRINITY COLLEGE
HARTFORD, CONNECTICUT

General Independent, comprehensive, coed **Entrance** Very difficult **Setting** 100-acre urban campus **Total enrollment** 2,256 **Student-faculty ratio** 9:1 **Application deadline** 1/15 (freshmen), 4/1 (transfer) **Freshmen** 30% were admitted **Housing** Yes **Expenses** Tuition $26,786; Room & Board $7514 **Undergraduates** 51% women, 9% part-time, 0% 25 or older, 0.2% Native American, 5% Hispanic American, 6% African American, 5% Asian American/Pacific Islander **The most frequently chosen baccalaureate fields are** area/ethnic studies, English, social sciences and history **Academic program** Advanced placement, accelerated degree program, self-designed majors, honors program, summer session, adult/continuing education programs, internships **Contact** Mr. Larry Dow, Dean of Admissions and Financial Aid, Trinity College, 300 Summit Street, Hartford, CT 06106-3100. Telephone: 860-297-2180. Fax: 860-297-2287. E-mail: admissions.office@trincoll.edu. Web site: http://www.trincoll.edu/.

UNITED STATES COAST GUARD ACADEMY
NEW LONDON, CONNECTICUT

General Federally supported, 4-year, coed **Entrance** Very difficult **Setting** 110-acre suburban campus **Total enrollment** 917 **Student-faculty ratio** 8:1 **Application deadline** 12/15 (freshmen) **Freshmen** 7% were admitted **Housing** Yes **Undergraduates** 28% women, 0% 25 or older, 1% Native American, 6% Hispanic American, 5% African American, 5% Asian American/Pacific Islander **The most frequently chosen baccalaureate fields are** engineering/engineering technologies, law/legal studies, social sciences and history **Academic program** English as a second language, summer session, internships **Contact** Capt. Susan D. Bibeau, Director of Admissions, United States Coast Guard Academy, 31 Mohegan Avenue, New London, CT 06320-4195. Telephone: 860-444-8500 or toll-free 800-883-8724. Fax: 860-701-6700. E-mail: admissions@cga.uscg.mil. Web site: http://www.cga.edu/.

CONNECTICUT

UNIVERSITY OF BRIDGEPORT
BRIDGEPORT, CONNECTICUT

General Independent, comprehensive, coed **Entrance** Moderately difficult **Setting** 86-acre urban campus **Total enrollment** 3,162 **Student-faculty ratio** 12:1 **Application deadline** 4/1 (freshmen), rolling (transfer) **Freshmen** 83% were admitted **Housing** Yes **Expenses** Tuition $15,582; Room & Board $7500 **Undergraduates** 56% women, 26% part-time, 29% 25 or older, 0.3% Native American, 10% Hispanic American, 21% African American, 5% Asian American/Pacific Islander **The most frequently chosen baccalaureate fields are** business/marketing, engineering/engineering technologies, interdisciplinary studies **Academic program** English as a second language, advanced placement, accelerated degree program, self-designed majors, honors program, summer session, adult/continuing education programs, internships **Contact** Joseph Marrone, Director of Undergraduate Admissions, University of Bridgeport, 380 University Avenue, Bridgeport, CT 06601. Telephone: 203-576-4552 or toll-free 800-EXCEL-UB (in-state); 800-243-9496 (out-of-state). Fax: 203-576-4941. E-mail: admit@cse.bridgeport.edu. Web site: http://www.bridgeport.edu/.

UNIVERSITY OF CONNECTICUT
STORRS, CONNECTICUT

General State-supported, university, coed **Entrance** Moderately difficult **Setting** 4,178-acre rural campus **Total enrollment** 19,876 **Application deadline** 3/1 (freshmen), 5/1 (transfer) **Freshmen** 68% were admitted **Housing** Yes **Expenses** Tuition $5824; Room & Board $6298 **Undergraduates** 52% women, 7% part-time, 5% 25 or older, 0.2% Native American, 5% Hispanic American, 5% African American, 6% Asian American/Pacific Islander **The most frequently chosen baccalaureate fields are** business/marketing, liberal arts/general studies, social sciences and history **Academic program** English as a second language, advanced placement, accelerated degree program, self-designed majors, honors program, summer session, adult/continuing education programs, internships **Contact** Mr. Brian Usher, Associate Director of Admissions, University of Connecticut, 2131 Hillside Road, Unit 3088, Storrs, CT 06269-3088. Telephone: 860-486-3137. Fax: 860-486-1476. E-mail: beahusky@uconnvm.uconn.edu. Web site: http://www.uconn.edu/.

UNIVERSITY OF HARTFORD
WEST HARTFORD, CONNECTICUT

General Independent, comprehensive, coed **Entrance** Moderately difficult **Setting** 320-acre suburban campus **Total enrollment** 6,844 **Student-faculty ratio** 13:1 **Application deadline** Rolling (freshmen), rolling (transfer) **Freshmen** 72% were admitted **Housing** Yes **Expenses** Tuition $20,810; Room & Board $8074 **Undergraduates** 52% women, 21% part-time, 13% 25 or older, 0.2% Native American, 4% Hispanic American, 9% African American, 2% Asian American/Pacific Islander **The most frequently chosen baccalaureate fields are** health professions and related sciences, engineering/engineering technologies, visual/performing arts **Academic program** English as a second language, advanced placement, self-designed majors, honors program, summer session, adult/continuing education programs, internships **Contact** Mr. Richard Zeiser, Dean of Admissions, University of Hartford, 200 Bloomfield Avenue, West Hartford, CT 06117-1599. Telephone: 860-768-4296 or toll-free 800-947-4303. Fax: 860-768-4961. E-mail: admission@mail.hartford.edu. Web site: http://www.hartford.edu/.

UNIVERSITY OF NEW HAVEN
WEST HAVEN, CONNECTICUT

General Independent, comprehensive, coed **Entrance** Moderately difficult **Setting** 78-acre suburban campus **Total enrollment** 4,226 **Student-faculty ratio** 11:1 **Application deadline** Rolling (freshmen), rolling (transfer) **Freshmen** 76% were admitted **Housing** Yes **Expenses** Tuition $16,560; Room & Board $7300 **Undergraduates** 42% women, 33% part-time, 28% 25 or older, 0.3% Native American, 6% Hispanic American, 12% African American, 1% Asian American/Pacific Islander **The most frequently chosen baccalaureate fields are** business/marketing, engineering/engineering technologies, protective services/public administration **Academic program** English as a second language, advanced placement, accelerated degree program, self-designed majors, honors program, summer session, adult/continuing education programs, internships **Contact** Ms. Jane C. Sangeloty, Director of Undergraduate Admissions and Financial Aid, University of New Haven, Bayer Hall, 300 Orange Avenue, West Haven, CT 06516. Telephone: 203-932-7319 or toll-free 800-DIAL-UNH. Fax: 203-931-6093. E-mail: adminfo@charger.newhaven.edu. Web site: http://www.newhaven.edu/.

WESLEYAN UNIVERSITY
MIDDLETOWN, CONNECTICUT

General Independent, university, coed **Entrance** Most difficult **Setting** 120-acre small-town campus **Total enrollment** 3,237 **Student-faculty ratio** 9:1 **Application deadline** 1/1 (freshmen), 3/15 (transfer) **Freshmen** 26% were admitted **Housing** Yes **Expenses** Tuition $27,100; Room & Board $6950 **Undergraduates** 53% women, 1% part-time, 12% 25 or older, 0.3% Native American, 6% Hispanic American, 8% African American, 6% Asian American/Pacific Islander **The most frequently chosen baccalaureate fields are** social sciences and history, area/ethnic studies, visual/performing arts **Academic program** English as a second language, advanced placement, accelerated degree program, self-designed majors, summer session, adult/continuing education programs, internships **Contact** Mrs. Nancy Hargrave Meislahn, Dean of Admission and Financial Aid, Wesleyan University, Stewart M Reid House, 70 Wyllys Avenue, Middletown, CT 06459-0265. Telephone: 860-685-

3000. Fax: 860-685-3001. E-mail: admissions@wesleyan.edu. Web site: http://www.wesleyan.edu/.

WESTERN CONNECTICUT STATE UNIVERSITY
DANBURY, CONNECTICUT

General State-supported, comprehensive, coed **Entrance** Moderately difficult **Setting** 340-acre urban campus **Total enrollment** 5,918 **Student-faculty ratio** 17:1 **Application deadline** 5/1 (freshmen), 7/1 (transfer) **Freshmen** 67% were admitted **Housing** Yes **Expenses** Tuition $4116; Room & Board $5958 **Undergraduates** 53% women, 29% part-time, 19% 25 or older, 0.5% Native American, 6% Hispanic American, 7% African American, 3% Asian American/Pacific Islander **The most frequently chosen baccalaureate fields are** business/marketing, education, protective services/public administration **Academic program** English as a second language, advanced placement, accelerated degree program, self-designed majors, honors program, summer session, adult/continuing education programs, internships **Contact** Mr. William Hawkins, Enrollment Management Officer, Western Connecticut State University, 181 White Street, Danbury, CT 06810. Telephone: 203-837-9000 or toll-free 877-837-9278. Web site: http://www.wcsu.edu/.

YALE UNIVERSITY
NEW HAVEN, CONNECTICUT

General Independent, university, coed **Entrance** Most difficult **Setting** 200-acre urban campus **Total enrollment** 11,136 **Student-faculty ratio** 7:1 **Application deadline** 12/31 (freshmen), 3/1 (transfer) **Freshmen** 14% were admitted **Housing** Yes **Expenses** Tuition $26,100; Room & Board $7930 **Undergraduates** 49% women, 1% part-time, 1% 25 or older, 1% Native American, 6% Hispanic American, 8% African American, 14% Asian American/Pacific Islander **The most frequently chosen baccalaureate fields are** biological/life sciences, English, social sciences and history **Academic program** English as a second language, advanced placement, accelerated degree program, self-designed majors, honors program, summer session **Contact** Admissions Director, Yale University, PO Box 208234, New Haven, CT 06520-8324. Telephone: 203-432-9300. Fax: 203-432-9392. E-mail: undergraduate.admissions@yale.edu. Web site: http://www.yale.edu/.

DELAWARE

DELAWARE STATE UNIVERSITY
DOVER, DELAWARE

General State-supported, comprehensive, coed **Entrance** Moderately difficult **Setting** 400-acre small-town campus **Total enrollment** 3,343 **Student-faculty ratio** 15:1 **Application deadline** 4/1 (freshmen), 4/1 (transfer) **Freshmen** 68% were admitted **Housing** Yes **Expenses** Tuition $3682; Room & Board $5362 **Undergraduates** 57% women, 22% part-time, 17% 25 or older, 0.5% Native American, 2% Hispanic American, 79% African American, 1% Asian American/Pacific Islander **Academic program** English as a second language, advanced placement, accelerated degree program, self-designed majors, honors program, summer session, adult/continuing education programs, internships **Contact** Mr. Jethro C. Williams, Director of Admissions, Delaware State University, 1200 North Dupont Highway, Dover, DE 19901. Telephone: 302-857-6353. Fax: 302-857-6352. E-mail: dadmiss@dsc.edu. Web site: http://www.dsc.edu/.

GOLDEY-BEACOM COLLEGE
WILMINGTON, DELAWARE

General Independent, comprehensive, coed **Entrance** Moderately difficult **Setting** 27-acre suburban campus **Total enrollment** 1,400 **Student-faculty ratio** 28:1 **Application deadline** Rolling (freshmen), rolling (transfer) **Freshmen** 84% were admitted **Housing** Yes **Expenses** Tuition $9690; Room only $3760 **Undergraduates** 43% 25 or older **Academic program** Advanced placement, accelerated degree program, honors program, summer session, internships **Contact** Mr. Kevin M. McIntyre, Dean of Admissions, Goldey-Beacom College, 4701 Limestone Road, Wilmington, DE 19808-1999. Telephone: 302-998-8814 Ext. 266 or toll-free 800-833-4877. Fax: 302-996-5408. E-mail: mcintyrk@goldey.gbc.edu. Web site: http://www.gbc.edu/.

UNIVERSITY OF DELAWARE
NEWARK, DELAWARE

General State-related, university, coed **Entrance** Moderately difficult **Setting** 1,000-acre small-town campus **Total enrollment** 20,373 **Student-faculty ratio** 13:1 **Application deadline** 2/15 (freshmen), 5/1 (transfer) **Freshmen** 53% were admitted **Housing** Yes **Expenses** Tuition $5290; Room & Board $5534 **Undergraduates** 58% women, 16% part-time, 6% 25 or older, 0.2% Native American, 3% Hispanic American, 6% African American, 3% Asian American/Pacific Islander **The most frequently chosen baccalaureate fields are** business/marketing, education, social sciences and history **Academic program** English as a second language, advanced placement, accelerated degree program, self-designed majors, honors program, summer session, adult/continuing education programs, internships **Contact** Mr. Larry Griffith, Director of Admissions, University of Delaware, 116 Hullihen Hall, Newark, DE 19716. Telephone: 302-831-8123. Fax: 302-831-6905. E-mail: admissions@udel.edu. Web site: http://www.udel.edu/.

WESLEY COLLEGE
DOVER, DELAWARE

General Independent United Methodist, comprehensive, coed **Entrance** Moderately difficult **Setting**

DELAWARE

Wesley College *(continued)*
20-acre small-town campus **Total enrollment** 1,510 **Student-faculty ratio** 18:1 **Application deadline** Rolling (freshmen), rolling (transfer) **Freshmen** 77% were admitted **Housing** Yes **Expenses** Tuition $11,719; Room & Board $5266 **Undergraduates** 54% women, 22% part-time, 4% 25 or older, 0.4% Native American, 2% Hispanic American, 18% African American, 2% Asian American/Pacific Islander **The most frequently chosen baccalaureate fields are** business/marketing, education, psychology **Academic program** English as a second language, advanced placement, accelerated degree program, summer session, adult/continuing education programs, internships **Contact** Mr. Art Jacobs, Director of Admissions, Wesley College, 120 North State Street, Dover, DE 19901-3875. Telephone: 302-736-2400 or toll-free 800-937-5398 Ext. 2400 (out-of-state). Fax: 302-736-2301. E-mail: admissions@mail.wesley.edu. Web site: http://www.wesley.edu/.

WILMINGTON COLLEGE
NEW CASTLE, DELAWARE

General Independent, comprehensive, coed **Entrance** Noncompetitive **Setting** 17-acre suburban campus **Total enrollment** 5,051 **Student-faculty ratio** 18:1 **Application deadline** Rolling (freshmen), rolling (transfer) **Freshmen** 99% were admitted **Housing** No **Expenses** Tuition $6530 **Undergraduates** 69% women, 64% part-time, 51% 25 or older, 0.2% Native American, 2% Hispanic American, 12% African American, 1% Asian American/Pacific Islander **Academic program** Accelerated degree program, summer session, adult/continuing education programs, internships **Contact** Dr. JoAnn Ciuffetelli, Assistant Director of Admissions, Wilmington College, 320 DuPont Highway, New Castle, DE 19720-6491. Telephone: 302-328-9407 Ext. 104 or toll-free 877-967-5464. Fax: 302-328-5902. E-mail: jciuf@wilmcoll.edu. Web site: http://www.wilmcoll.edu/.

DISTRICT OF COLUMBIA

AMERICAN UNIVERSITY
WASHINGTON, DISTRICT OF COLUMBIA

General Independent Methodist, university, coed **Entrance** Moderately difficult **Setting** 77-acre suburban campus **Total enrollment** 10,693 **Student-faculty ratio** 14:1 **Application deadline** 2/1 (freshmen), 7/1 (transfer) **Freshmen** 68% were admitted **Housing** Yes **Expenses** Tuition $22,481; Room & Board $9063 **Undergraduates** 62% women, 9% part-time, 4% 25 or older, 0.2% Native American, 4% Hispanic American, 6% African American, 4% Asian American/Pacific Islander **The most frequently chosen baccalaureate fields are** business/marketing, communications/communication technologies, social sciences and history **Academic program** English as a second language, advanced placement, accelerated degree program, self-designed majors, honors program, summer session, adult/continuing education programs, internships **Contact** Dr. Sharon Alston, Director of Admissions, American University, 4400 Massachusetts Avenue, NW, Washington, DC 20016-8001. Telephone: 202-885-6000. Fax: 202-885-1025. E-mail: afa@american.edu. Web site: http://www.american.edu/.

THE CATHOLIC UNIVERSITY OF AMERICA
WASHINGTON, DISTRICT OF COLUMBIA

General Independent, university, coed, affiliated with Roman Catholic Church **Entrance** Moderately difficult **Setting** 144-acre urban campus **Total enrollment** 5,510 **Student-faculty ratio** 10:1 **Application deadline** 2/15 (freshmen), 8/1 (transfer) **Freshmen** 85% were admitted **Housing** Yes **Expenses** Tuition $20,950; Room & Board $8382 **Undergraduates** 54% women, 8% part-time, 8% 25 or older, 0.2% Native American, 4% Hispanic American, 7% African American, 3% Asian American/Pacific Islander **The most frequently chosen baccalaureate fields are** architecture, social sciences and history, visual/performing arts **Academic program** English as a second language, advanced placement, accelerated degree program, self-designed majors, honors program, summer session, adult/continuing education programs, internships **Contact** Ms. Michelle D. Petro-Siraj, Executive Director of Undergraduate Admission, The Catholic University of America, 102 McMahon Hall, Washington, DC 20064. Telephone: 202-319-5305 or toll-free 202-319-5305 (in-state); 800-673-2772 (out-of-state). Fax: 202-319-6533. E-mail: cua-admissions@cua.edu. Web site: http://www.cua.edu/.

▶ **For more information, see page 407.**

CORCORAN COLLEGE OF ART AND DESIGN
WASHINGTON, DISTRICT OF COLUMBIA

General Independent, 4-year, coed **Entrance** Moderately difficult **Setting** 7-acre urban campus **Total enrollment** 372 **Student-faculty ratio** 8:1 **Application deadline** Rolling (freshmen), rolling (transfer) **Freshmen** 62% were admitted **Housing** Yes **Expenses** Tuition $17,000; Room & Board $6800 **Undergraduates** 67% women, 10% part-time, 20% 25 or older, 0% Native American, 7% Hispanic American, 7% African American, 12% Asian American/Pacific Islander **The most frequently chosen baccalaureate field is** visual/performing arts **Academic program** English as a second language, advanced placement, summer session, adult/continuing education programs, internships **Contact** Ms. Anne E. Bowman, Director of Admissions, Corcoran College of Art and Design, 500 17th Street, NW, Washington, DC 20006-4804. Telephone: 202-639-1814 or toll-free 888-CORCORAN (out-of-state). Fax: 202-639-1830. E-mail: admofc@corcoran.org. Web site: http://www.corcoran.edu/.

DISTRICT OF COLUMBIA

GALLAUDET UNIVERSITY
WASHINGTON, DISTRICT OF COLUMBIA

General Independent, university, coed **Entrance** Moderately difficult **Setting** 99-acre urban campus **Total enrollment** 1,583 **Student-faculty ratio** 7:1 **Application deadline** 8/1 (freshmen), 8/1 (transfer) **Freshmen** 70% were admitted **Housing** Yes **Expenses** Tuition $8990; Room & Board $7564 **Undergraduates** 52% women, 6% part-time, 29% 25 or older, 0.4% Native American, 7% Hispanic American, 11% African American, 5% Asian American/Pacific Islander **The most frequently chosen baccalaureate fields are** education, protective services/public administration, psychology **Academic program** English as a second language, advanced placement, accelerated degree program, self-designed majors, honors program, summer session, adult/continuing education programs, internships **Contact** Ms. Deborah E. DeStefano, Director of Admissions, Gallaudet University, 800 Florida Avenue, NE, Washington, DC 20002-3625. Telephone: 202-651-5750 or toll-free 800-995-0550 (out-of-state). Fax: 202-651-5774. E-mail: admissions@gallua.gallaudet.edu. Web site: http://www.gallaudet.edu/.

GEORGETOWN UNIVERSITY
WASHINGTON, DISTRICT OF COLUMBIA

General Independent Roman Catholic (Jesuit), university, coed **Entrance** Most difficult **Setting** 110-acre urban campus **Total enrollment** 12,688 **Student-faculty ratio** 11:1 **Application deadline** 1/10 (freshmen), 3/1 (transfer) **Freshmen** 21% were admitted **Housing** Yes **Expenses** Tuition $25,425; Room & Board $9422 **Undergraduates** 53% women, 4% part-time, 4% 25 or older, 0.2% Native American, 5% Hispanic American, 6% African American, 10% Asian American/Pacific Islander **The most frequently chosen baccalaureate fields are** business/marketing, English, social sciences and history **Academic program** English as a second language, advanced placement, self-designed majors, honors program, summer session, adult/continuing education programs, internships **Contact** Mr. Charles A. Deacon, Dean of Undergraduate Admissions, Georgetown University, 37th and O Street, NW, Washington, DC 20057. Telephone: 202-687-3600. Fax: 202-687-6660. E-mail: guadmiss@gunet.georgetown.edu. Web site: http://www.georgetown.edu/.

THE GEORGE WASHINGTON UNIVERSITY
WASHINGTON, DISTRICT OF COLUMBIA

General Independent, university, coed **Entrance** Very difficult **Setting** 36-acre urban campus **Total enrollment** 22,184 **Student-faculty ratio** 14:1 **Application deadline** 1/15 (freshmen), 6/1 (transfer) **Freshmen** 48% were admitted **Housing** Yes **Expenses** Tuition $25,920; Room & Board $8830 **Undergraduates** 56% women, 13% part-time, 3% 25 or older, 0.3% Native American, 5% Hispanic American, 6% African American, 10% Asian American/Pacific Islander **The most frequently chosen baccalaureate fields are** business/marketing, psychology, social sciences and history **Academic program** English as a second language, advanced placement, accelerated degree program, self-designed majors, honors program, summer session, adult/continuing education programs, internships **Contact** Dr. Kathryn M. Napper, Director of Admission, The George Washington University, 2121 I Street, NW, Suite 201, Washington, DC 20052. Telephone: 202-994-6040 or toll-free 800-447-3765. Fax: 202-944-0325. E-mail: gwadm@gwu.edu. Web site: http://www.gwu.edu/.

HOWARD UNIVERSITY
WASHINGTON, DISTRICT OF COLUMBIA

General Independent, university, coed **Entrance** Moderately difficult **Setting** 242-acre urban campus **Total enrollment** 10,509 **Student-faculty ratio** 8:1 **Application deadline** 4/1 (freshmen), 4/1 (transfer) **Freshmen** 68% were admitted **Housing** Yes **Expenses** Tuition $10,070; Room & Board $5000 **Undergraduates** 65% women, 7% part-time, 33% 25 or older, 0.1% Native American, 1% Hispanic American, 87% African American, 1% Asian American/Pacific Islander **The most frequently chosen baccalaureate fields are** communications/communication technologies, biological/life sciences, health professions and related sciences **Academic program** Advanced placement, accelerated degree program, self-designed majors, honors program, summer session, adult/continuing education programs, internships **Contact** Ms. Linda Sanders-Hawkins, Interim Director of Admissions, Howard University, 2400 Sixth Street, NW, Washington, DC 20059-0002. Telephone: 202-806-2700 or toll-free 800-HOWARD-U (out-of-state). Fax: 202-806-4465. E-mail: admissions@howard.edu. Web site: http://www.howard.edu/.

POTOMAC COLLEGE
WASHINGTON, DISTRICT OF COLUMBIA

General Proprietary, 4-year, coed **Entrance** Noncompetitive **Setting** urban campus **Total enrollment** 511 **Student-faculty ratio** 11:1 **Application deadline** Rolling (freshmen), rolling (transfer) **Freshmen** 77% were admitted **Housing** No **Expenses** Tuition $10,728 **Undergraduates** 57% women, 98% 25 or older, 0% Native American, 3% Hispanic American, 68% African American, 2% Asian American/Pacific Islander **The most frequently chosen baccalaureate fields are** business/marketing, computer/information sciences **Academic program** Advanced placement, accelerated degree program, summer session, adult/continuing education programs, internships **Contact** Ms. Florence Tate, President, Potomac College, 4000 Chesapeake Street, NW, Washington, DC 20016. Telephone: 202-686-0876 or toll-free 888-686-0876. Fax: 202-686-0818. E-mail: cdresser@potomac.edu. Web site: http://www.potomac.edu/.

SOUTHEASTERN UNIVERSITY
WASHINGTON, DISTRICT OF COLUMBIA

General Independent, comprehensive, coed **Entrance** Noncompetitive **Setting** 1-acre urban campus **Total**

DISTRICT OF COLUMBIA

Southeastern University *(continued)*
enrollment 982 **Student-faculty ratio** 11:1 **Application deadline** Rolling (freshmen), rolling (transfer) **Freshmen** 29% were admitted **Housing** No **Expenses** Tuition $8505 **Undergraduates** 69% women, 75% part-time, 60% 25 or older, 0.2% Native American, 1% Hispanic American, 79% African American, 3% Asian American/Pacific Islander **The most frequently chosen baccalaureate fields are** computer/information sciences, liberal arts/general studies, protective services/public administration **Academic program** English as a second language, advanced placement, accelerated degree program, honors program, summer session, adult/continuing education programs, internships **Contact** Mr. Jack Flinter, Director of Admissions, Southeastern University, 501 I Street, SW, Washington, DC 20024-2788. Telephone: 202-265-5343 Ext. 211. Fax: 202-488-8162. E-mail: jackf@admin.seu.edu. Web site: http://www.seu.edu/.

STRAYER UNIVERSITY
WASHINGTON, DISTRICT OF COLUMBIA

General Proprietary, comprehensive, coed **Entrance** Minimally difficult **Setting** urban campus **Total enrollment** 14,009 **Student-faculty ratio** 22:1 **Application deadline** Rolling (freshmen), rolling (transfer) **Housing** No **Expenses** Tuition $8789 **Undergraduates** 57% women, 79% part-time, 90% 25 or older, 0.4% Native American, 4% Hispanic American, 43% African American, 5% Asian American/Pacific Islander **The most frequently chosen baccalaureate fields are** business/marketing, computer/information sciences, social sciences and history **Academic program** Advanced placement, accelerated degree program, summer session, adult/continuing education programs, internships **Contact** Mr. Michael Williams, Regional Director, Strayer University, 1025 Fifteenth Street, NW, Washington, DC 20005. Telephone: 703-339-2500 or toll-free 888-4-STRAYER. Fax: 202-289-1831. E-mail: info40@strayer.edu. Web site: http://www.strayer.edu/.

TRINITY COLLEGE
WASHINGTON, DISTRICT OF COLUMBIA

General Independent Roman Catholic, comprehensive, women only **Entrance** Moderately difficult **Setting** 26-acre urban campus **Total enrollment** 1,410 **Student-faculty ratio** 13:1 **Application deadline** 2/1 (freshmen), rolling (transfer) **Freshmen** 74% were admitted **Housing** Yes **Expenses** Tuition $14,440; Room & Board $6700 **Undergraduates** 39% part-time, 14% 25 or older, 0.1% Native American, 9% Hispanic American, 65% African American, 1% Asian American/Pacific Islander **The most frequently chosen baccalaureate fields are** business/marketing, psychology, social sciences and history **Academic program** English as a second language, advanced placement, accelerated degree program, self-designed majors, honors program, summer session, adult/continuing education programs, internships **Contact** Ms. Wendy Kares, Director of Admissions, Trinity College, 125 Michigan Avenue, NE, Washington, DC 20017-1094. Telephone: 202-884-9400. Fax: 202-884-9229. Web site: http://www.trinitydc.edu/.

UNIVERSITY OF THE DISTRICT OF COLUMBIA
WASHINGTON, DISTRICT OF COLUMBIA

General District-supported, comprehensive, coed **Entrance** Noncompetitive **Setting** 28-acre urban campus **Total enrollment** 5,456 **Student-faculty ratio** 13:1 **Application deadline** 8/1 (freshmen), 8/1 (transfer) **Freshmen** 90% were admitted **Housing** No **Expenses** Tuition $2070 **Undergraduates** 62% women, 66% part-time, 53% 25 or older, 0.1% Native American, 5% Hispanic American, 76% African American, 2% Asian American/Pacific Islander **The most frequently chosen baccalaureate fields are** computer/information sciences, biological/life sciences, education **Academic program** English as a second language, accelerated degree program, honors program, summer session, adult/continuing education programs, internships **Contact** Mr. LaHugh Bankston, Registrar, University of the District of Columbia, 4200 Connecticut Avenue NW, Building 39 - A-Level, Washington, DC 20008. Telephone: 202-274-6200. Fax: 202-274-6267. Web site: http://www.udc.edu/.

FLORIDA

AMERICAN COLLEGE OF PREHOSPITAL MEDICINE
NAVARRE, FLORIDA

General Proprietary, 4-year, coed **Entrance** Moderately difficult **Total enrollment** 240 **Application deadline** Rolling (freshmen), rolling (transfer) **Freshmen** 100% were admitted **Housing** No **Undergraduates** 90% 25 or older **The most frequently chosen baccalaureate field is** health professions and related sciences **Contact** Dr. Richard A. Clinchy, Chairman/CEO, American College of Prehospital Medicine, 7552 Navarre Parkway, Suite 1, Navarre, FL 32566-7312. Telephone: 850-939-0840 or toll-free 800-735-2276. Fax: 800-350-3870. E-mail: admit@acpm.edu. Web site: http://www.acpm.edu/.

AMERICAN INTERCONTINENTAL UNIVERSITY
PLANTATION, FLORIDA

General Proprietary, comprehensive, coed **Total enrollment** 894 **Student-faculty ratio** 24:1 **Undergraduates** 1% Native American, 33% Hispanic American, 43% African American, 4% Asian American/Pacific Islander **Contact** Joseph Rogalski, Director of Admissions, American InterContinental Univer-

FLORIDA

sity, 8151 West Peters Road, Suite 1000, Plantation, FL 33324. Telephone: 954-233-3990. Web site: http://www.aiufl.edu/.

ARGOSY UNIVERSITY-SARASOTA
SARASOTA, FLORIDA

Contact Argosy University-Sarasota, 5250 17th Street, Sarasota, FL 34235-8246. Telephone: or toll-free 800-331-5995 (in-state). Web site: http://www.argosyu.edu/.

THE ART INSTITUTE OF FORT LAUDERDALE
FORT LAUDERDALE, FLORIDA

General Proprietary, 4-year, coed **Entrance** Noncompetitive **Setting** urban campus **Total enrollment** 3,500 **Student-faculty ratio** 20:1 **Application deadline** Rolling (freshmen), rolling (transfer) **Freshmen** 72% were admitted **Housing** Yes **Expenses** Room & Board $4480 **Undergraduates** 12% 25 or older **Academic program** Advanced placement, accelerated degree program, summer session, adult/continuing education programs, internships **Contact** Ms. Eileen L. Northrop, Vice President and Director of Admissions, The Art Institute of Fort Lauderdale, 1799 Southeast 17th Street Causeway, Fort Lauderdale, FL 33316-3000. Telephone: 954-527-1799 Ext. 420 or toll-free 800-275-7603. Fax: 954-728-8637. Web site: http://www.aifl.edu/.

THE BAPTIST COLLEGE OF FLORIDA
GRACEVILLE, FLORIDA

General Independent Southern Baptist, 4-year, coed **Entrance** Noncompetitive **Setting** 165-acre small-town campus **Total enrollment** 575 **Student-faculty ratio** 19:1 **Application deadline** Rolling (freshmen), rolling (transfer) **Freshmen** 94% were admitted **Housing** Yes **Expenses** Tuition $4850; Room & Board $3150 **Undergraduates** 34% women, 21% part-time, 50% 25 or older, 1% Native American, 3% Hispanic American, 5% African American, 1% Asian American/Pacific Islander **The most frequently chosen baccalaureate fields are** philosophy, education, philosophy, religion, and theology **Academic program** Advanced placement, accelerated degree program, summer session, adult/continuing education programs, internships **Contact** Mr. Kyle S. Luke, Director of Admissions, The Baptist College of Florida, 5400 College Drive, Graceville, FL 32440-1898. Telephone: 850-263-3261 Ext. 460 or toll-free 800-328-2660 Ext. 460. Fax: 850-263-7506. E-mail: admissions@baptistcollege.edu. Web site: http://www.baptistcollege.edu/.

BARRY UNIVERSITY
MIAMI SHORES, FLORIDA

General Independent Roman Catholic, university, coed **Entrance** Moderately difficult **Setting** 122-acre suburban campus **Total enrollment** 8,691 **Student-faculty ratio** 13:1 **Application deadline** Rolling (freshmen), rolling (transfer) **Freshmen** 73% were admitted **Housing** Yes **Expenses** Tuition $17,500; Room & Board $6600 **Undergraduates** 65% women, 45% part-time, 32% 25 or older, 0.2% Native American, 32% Hispanic American, 20% African American, 1% Asian American/Pacific Islander **The most frequently chosen baccalaureate fields are** business/marketing, education, liberal arts/general studies **Academic program** English as a second language, advanced placement, accelerated degree program, honors program, summer session, adult/continuing education programs, internships **Contact** Ms. Tracey Fontaine, Director of Admissions, Barry University, Kelly House, 11300 Northeast Second Avenue, Miami Shores, FL 33161. Telephone: 308-699-3127 or toll-free 800-695-2279. Fax: 305-899-2971. E-mail: admissions@mail.barry.edu. Web site: http://www.barry.edu/.

BETHUNE-COOKMAN COLLEGE
DAYTONA BEACH, FLORIDA

General Independent Methodist, 4-year, coed **Entrance** Minimally difficult **Setting** 60-acre urban campus **Total enrollment** 2,724 **Student-faculty ratio** 18:1 **Application deadline** 7/30 (freshmen), 7/30 (transfer) **Freshmen** 56% were admitted **Housing** Yes **Expenses** Tuition $9617; Room & Board $6129 **Undergraduates** 58% women, 7% part-time, 10% 25 or older, 0% Native American, 1% Hispanic American, 89% African American, 0.3% Asian American/Pacific Islander **The most frequently chosen baccalaureate fields are** business/marketing, education, protective services/public administration **Academic program** Advanced placement, accelerated degree program, honors program, summer session, adult/continuing education programs, internships **Contact** Mr. Edwin Coffie, Director of Admissions, Bethune-Cookman College, 640 Dr. Mary McLeod Bethune Boulevard, Daytona Beach, FL 32114-3099. Telephone: 386-255-1401 Ext. 676 or toll-free 800-448-0228. Fax: 386-257-5338. E-mail: coffiee@cookman.edu. Web site: http://www.bethune.cookman.edu/.

CARLOS ALBIZU UNIVERSITY, MIAMI CAMPUS
MIAMI, FLORIDA

General Independent, upper-level, coed, primarily women **Setting** 2-acre urban campus **Total enrollment** 610 **Student-faculty ratio** 10:1 **Application deadline** Rolling (transfer) **First-Year Students** 77% were admitted **Housing** No **Expenses** Tuition $7869 **Undergraduates** 79% women, 50% part-time, 48% 25 or older, 0% Native American, 75% Hispanic American, 17% African American, 0% Asian American/Pacific Islander **The most frequently chosen baccalaureate field is** psychology **Academic program** Advanced placement, summer session, adult/continuing education programs, internships **Contact** Ms. Miriam Matos, Admissions Officer, Carlos Albizu University, Miami Campus, 2173 N.W. 99th Avenue, Miami, FL 33172. Telephone: 305-593-1223 Ext.

FLORIDA

Carlos Albizu University, Miami
Campus *(continued)*

134 or toll-free 800-672-3246. Fax: 305-593-1854. E-mail: msalva@albizu.edu. Web site: http://www.albizu.edu/.

CLEARWATER CHRISTIAN COLLEGE
CLEARWATER, FLORIDA

General Independent nondenominational, 4-year, coed **Entrance** Minimally difficult **Setting** 50-acre suburban campus **Total enrollment** 652 **Student-faculty ratio** 15:1 **Application deadline** Rolling (freshmen), rolling (transfer) **Freshmen** 86% were admitted **Housing** Yes **Expenses** Tuition $8950; Room & Board $4050 **Academic program** Advanced placement, summer session, internships **Contact** Mr. Benjamin J. Puckett, Dean of Enrollment Services, Clearwater Christian College, 3400 Gulf-to-Bay Boulevard, Clearwater, FL 33759-4595. Telephone: 727-726-1153 or toll-free 800-348-4463. Fax: 813-726-8597. E-mail: admissions@clearwater.edu. Web site: http://www.clearwater.edu/.

DEVRY UNIVERSITY
ORLANDO, FLORIDA

General Proprietary, 4-year, coed **Entrance** Minimally difficult **Total enrollment** 803 **Student-faculty ratio** 19:1 **Application deadline** Rolling (freshmen), rolling (transfer) **Freshmen** 77% were admitted **Housing** No **Expenses** Tuition $9865 **Undergraduates** 23% women, 24% part-time, 38% 25 or older, 1% Native American, 15% Hispanic American, 28% African American, 3% Asian American/Pacific Islander **Academic program** Advanced placement, accelerated degree program, summer session, adult/continuing education programs **Contact** Ms. Laura Dorsey, New Student Coordinator, DeVry University, 4000 Millenia Boulevard, Orlando, FL 32839. Telephone: 407-355-4833 or toll-free 866-fl-devry (in-state). Fax: 407-370-3198. Web site: http://www.orl.devry.edu/.

ECKERD COLLEGE
ST. PETERSBURG, FLORIDA

General Independent Presbyterian, 4-year, coed **Entrance** Moderately difficult **Setting** 267-acre suburban campus **Total enrollment** 1,582 **Student-faculty ratio** 14:1 **Application deadline** Rolling (freshmen), rolling (transfer) **Freshmen** 78% were admitted **Housing** Yes **Expenses** Tuition $20,085; Room & Board $5415 **Undergraduates** 56% women, 2% part-time, 3% 25 or older, 0% Native American, 4% Hispanic American, 2% African American, 2% Asian American/Pacific Islander **The most frequently chosen baccalaureate fields are** biological/life sciences, business/marketing, social sciences and history **Academic program** English as a second language, advanced placement, accelerated degree program, self-designed majors, honors program, summer session, adult/continuing education programs, internships **Contact** Dr. Richard R. Hallin, Dean of Admissions, Eckerd College, 4200 54th Avenue South, St. Petersburg, FL 33711. Telephone: 727-864-8331 or toll-free 800-456-9009. Fax: 727-866-2304. E-mail: admissions@eckerd.edu. Web site: http://www.eckerd.edu/.

EDWARD WATERS COLLEGE
JACKSONVILLE, FLORIDA

General Independent African Methodist Episcopal, 4-year, coed **Entrance** Noncompetitive **Setting** 20-acre urban campus **Total enrollment** 1,320 **Application deadline** Rolling (freshmen), rolling (transfer) **Housing** Yes **Expenses** Tuition $3695; Room & Board $2735 **Undergraduates** 49% women, 3% part-time, 1% Hispanic American, 91% African American **The most frequently chosen baccalaureate fields are** business/marketing, biological/life sciences, education **Academic program** Self-designed majors, honors program, summer session, adult/continuing education programs, internships **Contact** Ms. Sadie Milliner-Smith, Director of Admissions, Edward Waters College, 1658 Kings Road, Jacksonville, FL 32209-6199. Telephone: 904-366-2715. Web site: http://www.ewc.edu/.

EMBRY-RIDDLE AERONAUTICAL UNIVERSITY
DAYTONA BEACH, FLORIDA

General Independent, comprehensive, coed, primarily men **Entrance** Moderately difficult **Setting** 178-acre urban campus **Total enrollment** 4,921 **Student-faculty ratio** 20:1 **Application deadline** 7/1 (freshmen), 7/1 (transfer) **Freshmen** 81% were admitted **Housing** Yes **Expenses** Tuition $11,690; Room & Board $5390 **Undergraduates** 16% women, 10% part-time, 10% 25 or older, 1% Native American, 5% Hispanic American, 5% African American, 3% Asian American/Pacific Islander **The most frequently chosen baccalaureate fields are** education, business/marketing, trade and industry **Academic program** English as a second language, advanced placement, summer session, adult/continuing education programs, internships **Contact** Mr. Michael Novak, Director of Admissions, Embry-Riddle Aeronautical University, 600 South Clyde Morris Boulevard, Daytona Beach, FL 32114-3900. Telephone: 386-226-6112 or toll-free 800-862-2416. Fax: 386-226-7070. E-mail: admit@db.erau.edu. Web site: http://www.embryriddle.edu/.

EMBRY-RIDDLE AERONAUTICAL UNIVERSITY, EXTENDED CAMPUS
DAYTONA BEACH, FLORIDA

General Independent, comprehensive, coed, primarily men **Entrance** Minimally difficult **Total enrollment** 8,999 **Student-faculty ratio** 3:1 **Application deadline** Rolling (freshmen), rolling (transfer) **Housing** No **Expenses** Tuition $4152 **Undergraduates** 11% women, 97% part-time, 1% Native American, 7% Hispanic American, 8% African American, 3% Asian American/Pacific Islander **The most frequently chosen baccalaureate fields are** business/

FLORIDA

marketing, trade and industry **Academic program** Advanced placement, adult/continuing education programs **Contact** Mrs. Pam Thomas, Director of Admissions, Records and Registration, Embry-Riddle Aeronautical University, Extended Campus, 600 South Clyde Morris Boulevard, Daytona Beach, FL 32114-3900. Telephone: 386-226-7610 or toll-free 800-862-2416 (out-of-state). Fax: 386-226-6984. E-mail: ecinfo@ec.db.erau.edu. Web site: http://www.embryriddle.edu/.

EVERGLADES COLLEGE
FT. LAUDERDALE, FLORIDA

General Proprietary, 4-year, coed **Total enrollment** 175 **Student-faculty ratio** 15:1 **Freshmen** 76% were admitted **Expenses** Tuition $9000 **Undergraduates** 41% women **Contact** Ms. Susan Ziegelhoffer, Vice President of Enrollment Management, Everglades College, 1500 NW 49th Street, Suite 600, Ft. Lauderdale, FL 33309. Telephone: 954-772-2655. Web site: http://www.evergladescollege.edu/.

FLAGLER COLLEGE
ST. AUGUSTINE, FLORIDA

General Independent, 4-year, coed **Entrance** Moderately difficult **Setting** 36-acre small-town campus **Total enrollment** 1,852 **Student-faculty ratio** 19:1 **Application deadline** 3/1 (freshmen), 3/1 (transfer) **Freshmen** 28% were admitted **Housing** Yes **Expenses** Tuition $6550; Room & Board $4000 **Undergraduates** 63% women, 3% part-time, 5% 25 or older, 0.1% Native American, 2% Hispanic American, 1% African American, 1% Asian American/Pacific Islander **The most frequently chosen baccalaureate fields are** business/marketing, communications/communication technologies, education **Academic program** Advanced placement, summer session, internships **Contact** Mr. Marc G. Williar, Director of Admissions, Flagler College, PO Box 1027, St. Augustine, FL 32085-1027. Telephone: 904-829-6481 Ext. 220 or toll-free 800-304-4208. E-mail: admiss@flagler.edu. Web site: http://www.flagler.edu/.

FLORIDA AGRICULTURAL AND MECHANICAL UNIVERSITY
TALLAHASSEE, FLORIDA

General State-supported, university, coed **Entrance** Moderately difficult **Setting** 419-acre urban campus **Total enrollment** 12,316 **Application deadline** 5/1 (freshmen), 5/1 (transfer) **Freshmen** 71% were admitted **Housing** Yes **Expenses** Tuition $2691; Room & Board $4742 **Undergraduates** 56% women, 12% part-time, 20% 25 or older, 0.04% Native American, 1% Hispanic American, 95% African American, 0.5% Asian American/Pacific Islander **The most frequently chosen baccalaureate fields are** business/marketing, education, health professions and related sciences **Academic program** Advanced placement, accelerated degree program, honors program, summer session, adult/continuing education programs, internships **Contact** Ms. Barbara R. Cox, Director of Admissions, Florida Agricultural and Mechanical University, Office of Admissions, Tallahassee, FL 32307. Telephone: 850-599-3796. Fax: 850-599-3069. E-mail: bcox@ns1.famu.edu. Web site: http://www.famu.edu/.

FLORIDA ATLANTIC UNIVERSITY
BOCA RATON, FLORIDA

General State-supported, university, coed **Entrance** Moderately difficult **Setting** 850-acre suburban campus **Total enrollment** 23,537 **Student-faculty ratio** 15:1 **Application deadline** Rolling (freshmen), 6/1 (transfer) **Freshmen** 71% were admitted **Housing** Yes **Expenses** Tuition $2699; Room & Board $6134 **Undergraduates** 61% women, 48% part-time, 38% 25 or older, 0.4% Native American, 13% Hispanic American, 17% African American, 4% Asian American/Pacific Islander **The most frequently chosen baccalaureate fields are** business/marketing, education, English **Academic program** English as a second language, advanced placement, accelerated degree program, self-designed majors, honors program, summer session, adult/continuing education programs, internships **Contact** Coordinator, Freshmen Recruitment, Florida Atlantic University, 777 Glades Road, PO Box 3091, Boca Raton, FL 33431-0991. Telephone: 561-297-2458 or toll-free 800-299-4FAU. Fax: 561-297-2758. Web site: http://www.fau.edu/.

FLORIDA BAPTIST THEOLOGICAL COLLEGE
See The Baptist College of Florida

FLORIDA CHRISTIAN COLLEGE
KISSIMMEE, FLORIDA

General Independent, 4-year, coed, affiliated with Christian Churches and Churches of Christ **Entrance** Minimally difficult **Setting** 40-acre small-town campus **Total enrollment** 259 **Student-faculty ratio** 12:1 **Application deadline** 7/15 (freshmen), 7/15 (transfer) **Freshmen** 71% were admitted **Housing** Yes **Expenses** Tuition $6190; Room only $1680 **Undergraduates** 50% women, 9% part-time, 31% 25 or older, 0% Native American, 5% Hispanic American, 3% African American, 2% Asian American/Pacific Islander **The most frequently chosen baccalaureate fields are** education, business/marketing, philosophy **Academic program** Advanced placement, summer session, adult/continuing education programs, internships **Contact** Mr. Terry Davis, Admissions Director, Florida Christian College, 1011 Bill Beck Boulevard, Kissimmee, FL 34744-5301. Telephone: 407-847-8966 Ext. 305. Web site: http://www.fcc.edu/.

FLORIDA COLLEGE
TEMPLE TERRACE, FLORIDA

General Independent, 4-year, coed **Entrance** Moderately difficult **Setting** 95-acre small-town campus **Total enrollment** 560 **Student-faculty ratio** 16:1 **Application deadline** 8/1 (freshmen), 8/1 (transfer) **Housing** Yes **Expenses** Tuition $7900; Room &

FLORIDA

Florida College *(continued)*
Board $4700 **Undergraduates** 51% women, 4% part-time, 11% 25 or older, 0.2% Native American, 3% Hispanic American, 2% African American, 1% Asian American/Pacific Islander **The most frequently chosen baccalaureate fields are** education, philosophy, philosophy, religion, and theology **Academic program** Advanced placement **Contact** Mrs. Mari Smith, Assistant Director of Admissions, Florida College, 119 North Glen Arven Avenue, Temple Terrace, FL 33617. Telephone: 813-988-5131 Ext. 6716 or toll-free 800-326-7655. Fax: 813-899-6772. E-mail: admissions@flcoll.edu. Web site: http://www.flcoll.edu/.

FLORIDA GULF COAST UNIVERSITY
FORT MYERS, FLORIDA

General State-supported, comprehensive, coed **Entrance** Moderately difficult **Setting** 760-acre suburban campus **Total enrollment** 4,214 **Student-faculty ratio** 15:1 **Application deadline** 8/15 (freshmen), rolling (transfer) **Freshmen** 73% were admitted **Housing** Yes **Expenses** Tuition $2524; Room & Board $7000 **Undergraduates** 65% women, 40% part-time, 0.3% 25 or older, 0.5% Native American, 8% Hispanic American, 4% African American, 2% Asian American/Pacific Islander **The most frequently chosen baccalaureate fields are** education, liberal arts/general studies, protective services/public administration **Academic program** Advanced placement, accelerated degree program, honors program, summer session, internships **Contact** Ms. Michele Yovanovich, Director of Admissions, Florida Gulf Coast University, 10501 FGCU Boulevard South, Fort Myers, FL 33965-6565. Telephone: 941-590-7878 or toll-free 800-590-3428. Fax: 941-590-7894. E-mail: oar@fgcu.edu. Web site: http://www.fgcu.edu/.

FLORIDA INSTITUTE OF TECHNOLOGY
MELBOURNE, FLORIDA

General Independent, university, coed **Entrance** Moderately difficult **Setting** 130-acre small-town campus **Total enrollment** 4,409 **Student-faculty ratio** 12:1 **Application deadline** Rolling (freshmen), rolling (transfer) **Freshmen** 82% were admitted **Housing** Yes **Expenses** Tuition $19,700; Room & Board $5550 **Undergraduates** 30% women, 7% part-time, 7% 25 or older, 0.2% Native American, 5% Hispanic American, 4% African American, 2% Asian American/Pacific Islander **The most frequently chosen baccalaureate fields are** biological/life sciences, engineering/engineering technologies, trade and industry **Academic program** English as a second language, advanced placement, accelerated degree program, summer session, adult/continuing education programs, internships **Contact** Ms. Judith Marino, Director of Undergraduate Admissions, Florida Institute of Technology, 150 West University Boulevard, Melbourne, FL 32901-6975. Telephone: 321-674-8030 or toll-free 800-888-4348. Fax: 321-723-9468. E-mail: admissions@fit.edu. Web site: http://www.fit.edu/.

FLORIDA INTERNATIONAL UNIVERSITY
MIAMI, FLORIDA

General State-supported, university, coed **Entrance** Moderately difficult **Setting** 573-acre urban campus **Total enrollment** 31,727 **Student-faculty ratio** 14:1 **Application deadline** Rolling (freshmen), rolling (transfer) **Freshmen** 47% were admitted **Housing** Yes **Expenses** Tuition $2562; Room only $3504 **Undergraduates** 56% women, 42% part-time, 30% 25 or older, 0.2% Native American, 55% Hispanic American, 14% African American, 4% Asian American/Pacific Islander **The most frequently chosen baccalaureate fields are** business/marketing, education, health professions and related sciences **Academic program** English as a second language, advanced placement, accelerated degree program, honors program, summer session, adult/continuing education programs, internships **Contact** Ms. Carmen Brown, Director of Admissions, Florida International University, University Park, PC 140, 11200 SW 8 Street, PC140, Miami, FL 33199. Telephone: 305-348-3675. Fax: 305-348-3648. E-mail: admiss@fiu.edu. Web site: http://www.fiu.edu/.

FLORIDA MEMORIAL COLLEGE
MIAMI-DADE, FLORIDA

Contact Mrs. Peggy Murray Martin, Director of Admissions and International Student Advisor, Florida Memorial College, 15800 NW 42nd Avenue, Miami-Dade, FL 33054. Telephone: 305-626-3147 or toll-free 800-822-1362. Web site: http://www.fmc.edu/main.cfm.

FLORIDA METROPOLITAN UNIVERSITY– BRANDON CAMPUS
TAMPA, FLORIDA

General Proprietary, comprehensive, coed **Entrance** Minimally difficult **Setting** 5-acre urban campus **Total enrollment** 739 **Student-faculty ratio** 14:1 **Application deadline** Rolling (freshmen), rolling (transfer) **Housing** No **Expenses** Tuition $6735 **Undergraduates** 47% 25 or older, 1% Native American, 11% Hispanic American, 33% African American, 2% Asian American/Pacific Islander **The most frequently chosen baccalaureate fields are** business/marketing, computer/information sciences, protective services/public administration **Academic program** Accelerated degree program, honors program, summer session, adult/continuing education programs, internships **Contact** Mrs. Dee McKee, Director of Admissions, Florida Metropolitan University–Brandon Campus, 3924 Coconut Palm Drive, Tampa, FL 33619. Telephone: 813-621-0041 Ext. 45. Fax: 813-623-5769. E-mail: dpearson@cci.edu. Web site: http://www.fmu.edu/.

FLORIDA METROPOLITAN UNIVERSITY– FORT LAUDERDALE CAMPUS
FORT LAUDERDALE, FLORIDA

General Proprietary, comprehensive, coed **Entrance** Minimally difficult **Setting** suburban campus **Total**

enrollment 1,373 **Application deadline** Rolling (freshmen), rolling (transfer) **Housing** No **Expenses** Tuition $7638 **Undergraduates** 25% 25 or older **Academic program** English as a second language, advanced placement, accelerated degree program, summer session, adult/continuing education programs, internships **Contact** Mr. Tony Wallace, Director of Admissions, Florida Metropolitan University–Fort Lauderdale Campus, 1040 Bayview Drive, Fort Lauderdale, FL 33304-2522. Telephone: 954-568-1600 or toll-free 800-468-0168. Fax: 305-568-2008. Web site: http://www.fmu.edu/.

FLORIDA METROPOLITAN UNIVERSITY–JACKSONVILLE CAMPUS
JACKSONVILLE, FLORIDA

Contact Florida Metropolitan University–Jacksonville Campus, 8226 Phillips Highway, Jacksonville, FL 32256. Telephone: or toll-free 888-741-4271. Web site: http://www.cci.edu/.

FLORIDA METROPOLITAN UNIVERSITY–LAKELAND CAMPUS
LAKELAND, FLORIDA

General Proprietary, comprehensive, coed **Entrance** Minimally difficult **Setting** suburban campus **Total enrollment** 724 **Student-faculty ratio** 16:1 **Freshmen** 91% were admitted **Housing** No **Expenses** Tuition $8463 **Undergraduates** 56% 25 or older **Academic program** Advanced placement, summer session, adult/continuing education programs, internships **Contact** Joe Rostkowski, Director of Admissions, Florida Metropolitan University–Lakeland Campus, 995 East Memorial Boulevard, Suite 110, Lakeland, FL 33801. Telephone: 863-686-1444. Fax: 863-686-1727. E-mail: dsimmons@cci.edu. Web site: http://www.cci.edu/.

FLORIDA METROPOLITAN UNIVERSITY–MELBOURNE CAMPUS
MELBOURNE, FLORIDA

General Proprietary, comprehensive, coed **Entrance** Noncompetitive **Setting** 5-acre small-town campus **Total enrollment** 580 **Student-faculty ratio** 13:1 **Application deadline** Rolling (freshmen), rolling (transfer) **Freshmen** 68% were admitted **Housing** No **Expenses** Tuition $9942 **Undergraduates** 68% women, 1% Native American, 7% Hispanic American, 21% African American, 3% Asian American/Pacific Islander **Academic program** Advanced placement, accelerated degree program, summer session, internships **Contact** Ms. Teresa Stinson-Kumar, Director of Admissions, Florida Metropolitan University–Melbourne Campus, 2401 North Harbor City Boulevard, Melbourne, FL 32935-6657. Telephone: 407-253-2929 Ext. 11. Web site: http://www.fmu.edu/.

FLORIDA METROPOLITAN UNIVERSITY–NORTH ORLANDO CAMPUS
ORLANDO, FLORIDA

General Proprietary, comprehensive, coed **Entrance** Minimally difficult **Setting** 1-acre urban campus **Total enrollment** 867 **Student-faculty ratio** 15:1 **Application deadline** Rolling (freshmen), rolling (transfer) **Housing** No **Expenses** Tuition $7570 **Undergraduates** 66% women, 43% part-time, 32% 25 or older, 0.5% Native American, 18% Hispanic American, 32% African American, 4% Asian American/Pacific Islander **Academic program** Advanced placement, summer session, internships **Contact** Ms. Charlene Donnelly, Director of Admissions, Florida Metropolitan University–North Orlando Campus, 5421 Diplomat Circle, Orlando, FL 32810-5674. Telephone: 407-628-5870 Ext. 108 or toll-free 800-628-5870. Web site: http://www.fmu.edu/.

FLORIDA METROPOLITAN UNIVERSITY–PINELLAS CAMPUS
CLEARWATER, FLORIDA

Contact Mr. Wayne Childers, Director of Admissions, Florida Metropolitan University–Pinellas Campus, 2471 McMullen Booth Road, Suite 200, Clearwater, FL 33759. Telephone: 727-725-2688 Ext. 702 or toll-free 800-353-FMUS. Fax: 727-796-3722. E-mail: tcpinellas2@juno.com. Web site: http://www.fmu.edu/.

FLORIDA METROPOLITAN UNIVERSITY–SOUTH ORLANDO CAMPUS
ORLANDO, FLORIDA

General Proprietary, comprehensive, coed **Entrance** Minimally difficult **Total enrollment** 1,582 **Student-faculty ratio** 20:1 **Application deadline** Rolling (freshmen) **Housing** No **Expenses** Tuition $6806 **Undergraduates** 72% women, 10% part-time, 1% Native American, 28% Hispanic American, 32% African American, 2% Asian American/Pacific Islander **Academic program** Accelerated degree program, internships **Contact** Ms. Annette Cloin, Director of Admissions, Florida Metropolitan University–South Orlando Campus, 2411 Sand Lake Road, Orlando, FL 32809. Telephone: 407-851-2525 Ext. 111 or toll-free 407-851 Ext. 2525 (in-state); 866-508 Ext. 0007 (out-of-state). Fax: 407-851-1477. Web site: http://www.fmu.edu/.

FLORIDA METROPOLITAN UNIVERSITY–TAMPA CAMPUS
TAMPA, FLORIDA

General Proprietary, comprehensive, coed **Entrance** Minimally difficult **Setting** 4-acre urban campus **Total enrollment** 1,218 **Student-faculty ratio** 15:1 **Application deadline** Rolling (freshmen), rolling (transfer) **Housing** No **Expenses** Tuition $7638 **Undergraduates** 61% women, 38% part-time, 46% 25 or older **Academic program** English as a second

FLORIDA

Florida Metropolitan University–Tampa Campus *(continued)*
language, advanced placement, accelerated degree program, self-designed majors, summer session, adult/continuing education programs, internships **Contact** Mr. Donnie Broughton, Director of Admissions, Florida Metropolitan University–Tampa Campus, 3319 W. Hillsborough Avenue, Tampa, FL 33614. Telephone: 813-879-6000 Ext. 129. Fax: 813-871-2483. Web site: http://www.cci.edu/.

FLORIDA SOUTHERN COLLEGE
LAKELAND, FLORIDA

General Independent, comprehensive, coed, affiliated with United Methodist Church **Entrance** Moderately difficult **Setting** 100-acre suburban campus **Total enrollment** 1,875 **Student-faculty ratio** 16:1 **Application deadline** Rolling (transfer) **Freshmen** 77% were admitted **Housing** Yes **Expenses** Tuition $13,930; Room & Board $5500 **Undergraduates** 61% women, 4% part-time, 6% 25 or older, 0.3% Native American, 5% Hispanic American, 5% African American, 1% Asian American/Pacific Islander **The most frequently chosen baccalaureate fields are** business/marketing, education, health professions and related sciences **Academic program** Advanced placement, honors program, summer session, adult/continuing education programs, internships **Contact** Mr. Barry Conners, Director of Admissions, Florida Southern College, 111 Lake Hollingsworth Drive, Lakeland, FL 33801-5698. Telephone: 863-680-3909 or toll-free 800-274-4131. Fax: 863-680-4120. E-mail: fscadm@flsouthern.edu. Web site: http://www.flsouthern.edu/.

FLORIDA STATE UNIVERSITY
TALLAHASSEE, FLORIDA

General State-supported, university, coed **Entrance** Very difficult **Setting** 456-acre suburban campus **Total enrollment** 34,982 **Student-faculty ratio** 22:1 **Application deadline** 3/1 (freshmen), 7/1 (transfer) **Freshmen** 53% were admitted **Housing** Yes **Expenses** Tuition $2513; Room & Board $5322 **Undergraduates** 57% women, 15% part-time, 8% 25 or older, 0.5% Native American, 9% Hispanic American, 12% African American, 3% Asian American/Pacific Islander **The most frequently chosen baccalaureate fields are** business/marketing, protective services/public administration, social sciences and history **Academic program** English as a second language, advanced placement, accelerated degree program, honors program, summer session, adult/continuing education programs, internships **Contact** Office of Admissions, Florida State University, A2500 University Center, Tallahassee, FL 32306-2400. Telephone: 850-644-6200. Fax: 850-644-0197. E-mail: admissions@admin.fsu.edu. Web site: http://www.fsu.edu/.

HOBE SOUND BIBLE COLLEGE
HOBE SOUND, FLORIDA

General Independent nondenominational, 4-year, coed **Entrance** Noncompetitive **Setting** 84-acre small-town campus **Total enrollment** 146 **Student-faculty ratio** 8:1 **Application deadline** Rolling (freshmen), rolling (transfer) **Freshmen** 63% were admitted **Housing** Yes **Expenses** Tuition $4360; Room & Board $3375 **Undergraduates** 53% women, 30% part-time, 19% 25 or older, 0% Native American, 2% Hispanic American, 1% African American, 1% Asian American/Pacific Islander **The most frequently chosen baccalaureate fields are** education, philosophy **Academic program** English as a second language, advanced placement, summer session, internships **Contact** Mrs. Ann French, Director of Admissions, Hobe Sound Bible College, PO Box 1065, Hobe Sound, FL 33475-1065. Telephone: 561-546-5534 Ext. 415 or toll-free 800-881-5534. Fax: 561-545-1422. E-mail: hsbcuwin@aol.com.

INTERNATIONAL ACADEMY OF DESIGN & TECHNOLOGY
TAMPA, FLORIDA

General Proprietary, 4-year, coed **Entrance** Noncompetitive **Setting** 1-acre urban campus **Total enrollment** 1,688 **Student-faculty ratio** 14:1 **Application deadline** Rolling (freshmen), rolling (transfer) **Housing** No **Expenses** Tuition $10,260 **Undergraduates** 54% women, 29% part-time, 41% 25 or older, 1% Native American, 16% Hispanic American, 13% African American, 3% Asian American/Pacific Islander **The most frequently chosen baccalaureate fields are** computer/information sciences, visual/performing arts **Academic program** Advanced placement, accelerated degree program, summer session, adult/continuing education programs, internships **Contact** Ms. Kristine Fescina, Vice President of Admissions and Marketing, International Academy of Design & Technology, 5225 Memorial Highway, Tampa, FL 33634-7350. Telephone: 813-881-0007 Ext. 8095 or toll-free 800-ACADEMY. Fax: 813-881-0008. E-mail: mpage@academy.edu. Web site: http://www.academy.edu/.

INTERNATIONAL COLLEGE
NAPLES, FLORIDA

General Independent, comprehensive, coed **Entrance** Minimally difficult **Setting** suburban campus **Total enrollment** 1,227 **Student-faculty ratio** 19:1 **Application deadline** Rolling (freshmen), rolling (transfer) **Freshmen** 67% were admitted **Housing** No **Expenses** Tuition $7230 **Undergraduates** 60% women, 29% part-time, 79% 25 or older, 1% Native American, 12% Hispanic American, 9% African American, 2% Asian American/Pacific Islander **The most frequently chosen baccalaureate fields are** business/marketing, law/legal studies, protective services/public administration **Academic program** English as a second language, advanced placement, accelerated degree program, summer session, adult/continuing education programs, internships **Contact** Ms. Rita Lampus, Director of Admissions, International College, 2655 Northbrooke Drive, Naples, FL 34119. Telephone: 941-513-1122 Ext. 104 or toll-free 800-466-8017. E-mail: admit@

internationalcollege.edu. Web site: http://www.internationalcollege.edu/.

INTERNATIONAL FINE ARTS COLLEGE
MIAMI, FLORIDA

General Proprietary, comprehensive, coed **Entrance** Moderately difficult **Setting** 4-acre urban campus **Total enrollment** 1,100 **Student-faculty ratio** 18:1 **Application deadline** Rolling (freshmen), rolling (transfer) **Housing** Yes **Expenses** Tuition $13,025 **Undergraduates** 22% 25 or older **Academic program** English as a second language, summer session, internships **Contact** Ms. Elsia Suarez, Director of Admissions, International Fine Arts College, 1737 North Bayshore Drive, Miami, FL 33132-1121. Telephone: 305-373-4684 or toll-free 800-225-9023. Web site: http://www.ifac.edu/.

JACKSONVILLE UNIVERSITY
JACKSONVILLE, FLORIDA

General Independent, comprehensive, coed **Entrance** Moderately difficult **Setting** 260-acre suburban campus **Total enrollment** 2,346 **Student-faculty ratio** 14:1 **Application deadline** Rolling (freshmen), rolling (transfer) **Freshmen** 74% were admitted **Housing** Yes **Expenses** Tuition $15,990; Room & Board $5680 **Undergraduates** 50% women, 14% part-time, 15% 25 or older, 1% Native American, 4% Hispanic American, 15% African American, 2% Asian American/Pacific Islander **Academic program** English as a second language, advanced placement, accelerated degree program, self-designed majors, honors program, summer session, adult/continuing education programs, internships **Contact** Mr. Jeff Hammer, Director of Admissions, Jacksonville University, 2800 University Boulevard North, Jacksonville, FL 32211. Telephone: 904-745-7000 or toll-free 800-225-2027. Fax: 904-745-7012. E-mail: admissions@ju.edu. Web site: http://www.ju.edu/.

JOHNSON & WALES UNIVERSITY
NORTH MIAMI, FLORIDA

Contact Mr. Jeff Greenip, Director of Admissions, Johnson & Wales University, 1701 Northeast 127th Street, North Miami, FL 33181. Telephone: 305-892-7002 or toll-free 800-232-2433. Fax: 305-892-7020. E-mail: admissions@jwu.edu. Web site: http://www.jwu.edu/.

JONES COLLEGE
JACKSONVILLE, FLORIDA

General Independent, 4-year, coed **Entrance** Noncompetitive **Setting** 5-acre urban campus **Total enrollment** 585 **Student-faculty ratio** 14:1 **Application deadline** Rolling (freshmen), rolling (transfer) **Housing** No **Expenses** Tuition $4890 **Undergraduates** 76% women, 75% part-time, 78% 25 or older, 0% Native American, 2% Hispanic American, 53% African American, 2% Asian American/Pacific Islander **Academic program** Advanced placement, accelerated degree program, self-designed majors, summer session, adult/continuing education programs, internships **Contact** Mr. Barry Durden, Director of Admissions, Jones College, 5355 Arlington Expressway, Jacksonville, FL 32211. Telephone: 904-743-1122 Ext. 115. Fax: 904-743-4446. E-mail: bdurden@jones.edu. Web site: http://www.jones.edu/.

LYNN UNIVERSITY
BOCA RATON, FLORIDA

General Independent, comprehensive, coed **Entrance** Minimally difficult **Setting** 123-acre suburban campus **Total enrollment** 2,006 **Student-faculty ratio** 14:1 **Application deadline** Rolling (freshmen), rolling (transfer) **Freshmen** 74% were admitted **Housing** Yes **Expenses** Tuition $20,250; Room & Board $7200 **Undergraduates** 52% women, 16% part-time, 24% 25 or older, 0.2% Native American, 6% Hispanic American, 5% African American, 1% Asian American/Pacific Islander **Academic program** English as a second language, advanced placement, honors program, summer session, adult/continuing education programs, internships **Contact** Ms. Melanie Glines, Director of Admissions, Lynn University, 3601 North Military Trail, Boca Raton, FL 33431-5598. Telephone: 561-237-7900 or toll-free 800-888-LYNN (in-state); 800-544-8035 (out-of-state). Fax: 561-237-7100. E-mail: admission@lynn.edu. Web site: http://www.lynn.edu/.

▶ For more information, see page 451.

NEW COLLEGE OF FLORIDA
SARASOTA, FLORIDA

General State-supported, 4-year, coed **Entrance** Very difficult **Setting** 140-acre suburban campus **Total enrollment** 634 **Student-faculty ratio** 11:1 **Application deadline** 5/1 (freshmen), rolling (transfer) **Freshmen** 61% were admitted **Housing** Yes **Expenses** Tuition $2885; Room & Board $5120 **Undergraduates** 65% women, 4% 25 or older, 0.2% Native American, 6% Hispanic American, 2% African American, 3% Asian American/Pacific Islander **The most frequently chosen baccalaureate field is** liberal arts/general studies **Academic program** Accelerated degree program, self-designed majors, honors program, internships **Contact** Mr. Joel Bauman, Dean of Admissions and Financial Aid, New College of Florida, 5700 North Tamiami Trail, Sarasota, FL 34243-2197. Telephone: 941-359-4269. Fax: 941-359-4435. E-mail: admissions@ncf.edu. Web site: http://www.ncf.edu/.

NEW WORLD SCHOOL OF THE ARTS
MIAMI, FLORIDA

General State-supported, 4-year, coed **Entrance** Minimally difficult **Setting** 5-acre urban campus **Total enrollment** 370 **Student-faculty ratio** 4:1 **Freshmen** 50% were admitted **Housing** No **Expenses** Tuition $1542 **Undergraduates** 51% women, 10% 25 or older, 0% Native American, 49% Hispanic American, 12% African American, 4% Asian American/

FLORIDA

New World School of the Arts *(continued)*
Pacific Islander **The most frequently chosen baccalaureate field is** visual/performing arts **Academic program** English as a second language, advanced placement, honors program, summer session, internships **Contact** Ms. Pamela Neumann, Recruitment and Admissions Coordinator, New World School of the Arts, 300 NE Second Avenue, Miami, FL 33132. Telephone: 305-237-7007. Fax: 305-237-3794. E-mail: nwsapost.robs@mdcc.edu. Web site: http://www.mdcc.edu/nwsa/.

NORTHWOOD UNIVERSITY, FLORIDA CAMPUS
WEST PALM BEACH, FLORIDA

General Independent, 4-year, coed **Entrance** Moderately difficult **Setting** 90-acre suburban campus **Total enrollment** 963 **Student-faculty ratio** 15:1 **Application deadline** Rolling (freshmen), rolling (transfer) **Freshmen** 72% were admitted **Housing** Yes **Expenses** Tuition $12,531; Room & Board $6648 **Undergraduates** 48% women, 20% part-time, 3% 25 or older, 0% Native American, 9% Hispanic American, 14% African American, 1% Asian American/Pacific Islander **The most frequently chosen baccalaureate fields are** business/marketing, computer/information sciences **Academic program** English as a second language, advanced placement, accelerated degree program, honors program, summer session, adult/continuing education programs, internships **Contact** Mr. John M. Letvinchuck, Director of Admissions, Northwood University, Florida Campus, 2600 North Military Trail, West Palm Beach, FL 33409-2911. Telephone: 561-478-5500 or toll-free 800-458-8325. Fax: 561-640-3328. E-mail: fladmit@northwood.edu. Web site: http://www.northwood.edu/.

NOVA SOUTHEASTERN UNIVERSITY
FORT LAUDERDALE, FLORIDA

General Independent, university, coed **Entrance** Moderately difficult **Setting** 232-acre suburban campus **Total enrollment** 19,029 **Student-faculty ratio** 15:1 **Application deadline** 7/1 (freshmen), rolling (transfer) **Freshmen** 67% were admitted **Housing** Yes **Expenses** Tuition $12,180 **Undergraduates** 74% women, 41% part-time, 62% 25 or older, 0.4% Native American, 23% Hispanic American, 26% African American, 2% Asian American/Pacific Islander **The most frequently chosen baccalaureate fields are** business/marketing, education, health professions and related sciences **Academic program** Advanced placement, accelerated degree program, summer session, adult/continuing education programs, internships **Contact** Ms. Zeida Roderiguez, Acting Director of Undergraduate Admissions, Nova Southeastern University, 3301 College Avenue, Ft. Lauderdale, FL 33314. Telephone: 954-262-8000 or toll-free 800-541-6682 Ext. 8000. E-mail: ncsinfo@nova.edu. Web site: http://www.nova.edu/.

PALM BEACH ATLANTIC COLLEGE
WEST PALM BEACH, FLORIDA

General Independent nondenominational, comprehensive, coed **Entrance** Moderately difficult **Setting** 25-acre urban campus **Total enrollment** 2,584 **Student-faculty ratio** 17:1 **Application deadline** Rolling (freshmen), rolling (transfer) **Freshmen** 50% were admitted **Housing** Yes **Expenses** Tuition $13,170; Room & Board $5070 **Undergraduates** 64% women, 11% part-time, 24% 25 or older, 0.3% Native American, 7% Hispanic American, 11% African American, 1% Asian American/Pacific Islander **The most frequently chosen baccalaureate fields are** business/marketing, education, psychology **Academic program** English as a second language, advanced placement, self-designed majors, honors program, summer session, adult/continuing education programs, internships **Contact** Mr. Buck James, Vice President of Enrollment Services, Palm Beach Atlantic College, 901 South Flagler Dr, PO Box 24708, West Palm Beach, FL 33416-4708. Telephone: 561-803-2100 or toll-free 800-238-3998. Fax: 561-803-2115. E-mail: admit@pbac.edu. Web site: http://www.pbac.edu/.

RINGLING SCHOOL OF ART AND DESIGN
SARASOTA, FLORIDA

General Independent, 4-year, coed **Entrance** Moderately difficult **Setting** 35-acre urban campus **Total enrollment** 969 **Student-faculty ratio** 11:1 **Application deadline** Rolling (freshmen), rolling (transfer) **Freshmen** 44% were admitted **Housing** Yes **Expenses** Tuition $16,430; Room & Board $7920 **Undergraduates** 47% women, 2% part-time, 12% 25 or older, 0.4% Native American, 7% Hispanic American, 2% African American, 3% Asian American/Pacific Islander **The most frequently chosen baccalaureate field is** visual/performing arts **Academic program** Advanced placement, summer session, internships **Contact** Mr. James Dean, Dean of Admissions, Ringling School of Art and Design, 2700 North Tamiami Trail, Sarasota, FL 34234. Telephone: 937-351-5100 Ext. 7525 or toll-free 800-255-7695. Fax: 937-359-7517. E-mail: admissions@rsad.edu. Web site: http://www.rsad.edu/.

ROLLINS COLLEGE
WINTER PARK, FLORIDA

General Independent, comprehensive, coed **Entrance** Very difficult **Setting** 67-acre suburban campus **Total enrollment** 2,421 **Student-faculty ratio** 12:1 **Application deadline** 2/15 (freshmen), 4/15 (transfer) **Freshmen** 65% were admitted **Housing** Yes **Expenses** Tuition $23,882; Room & Board $7341 **Undergraduates** 61% women, 0.4% part-time, 2% 25 or older, 1% Native American, 7% Hispanic American, 3% African American, 3% Asian American/Pacific Islander **The most frequently chosen baccalaureate fields are** social sciences and history, psychology, visual/performing arts **Academic program** Advanced placement, accelerated degree program, self-designed

FLORIDA

majors, honors program, adult/continuing education programs, internships **Contact** Mr. David Erdmann, Dean of Admissions and Student Financial Planning, Rollins College, 1000 Holt Avenue, Winter Park, FL 32789-4499. Telephone: 407-646-2161. Fax: 407-646-1502. E-mail: admission@rollins.edu. Web site: http://www.rollins.edu/.

ST. JOHN VIANNEY COLLEGE SEMINARY
MIAMI, FLORIDA

Contact Br. Edward Van Merrienboer, Academic Dean, St. John Vianney College Seminary, 2900 Southwest 87th Avenue, Miami, FL 33165-3244. Telephone: 305-223-4561 Ext. 13. E-mail: academic@sjvcs.edu.

SAINT LEO UNIVERSITY
SAINT LEO, FLORIDA

General Independent Roman Catholic, comprehensive, coed **Entrance** Moderately difficult **Setting** 170-acre rural campus **Total enrollment** 1,159 **Student-faculty ratio** 15:1 **Application deadline** 8/1 (freshmen), 8/1 (transfer) **Freshmen** 81% were admitted **Housing** Yes **Expenses** Tuition $12,770; Room & Board $6480 **Undergraduates** 55% women, 6% part-time, 18% 25 or older, 1% Native American, 9% Hispanic American, 8% African American, 1% Asian American/Pacific Islander The most frequently chosen baccalaureate fields are business/marketing, education, social sciences and history **Academic program** English as a second language, advanced placement, accelerated degree program, honors program, summer session, adult/continuing education programs, internships **Contact** Mr. Gary Bracken, Vice President for Enrollment, Saint Leo University, MC 2008, PO Box 6665, Saint Leo, FL 33574-6665. Telephone: 352-588-8283 or toll-free 800-334-5532. Fax: 352-588-8257. E-mail: admission@saintleo.edu. Web site: http://www.saintleo.edu/.

ST. THOMAS UNIVERSITY
MIAMI, FLORIDA

General Independent Roman Catholic, comprehensive, coed **Entrance** Moderately difficult **Setting** 140-acre suburban campus **Total enrollment** 2,403 **Student-faculty ratio** 14:1 **Application deadline** Rolling (freshmen), rolling (transfer) **Freshmen** 65% were admitted **Housing** Yes **Expenses** Tuition $14,700; Room & Board $4800 **Undergraduates** 60% women, 15% part-time, 34% 25 or older, 0.1% Native American, 48% Hispanic American, 26% African American, 1% Asian American/Pacific Islander The most frequently chosen baccalaureate fields are business/marketing, communications/communication technologies, protective services/public administration **Academic program** English as a second language, advanced placement, honors program, summer session, adult/continuing education programs, internships **Contact** Mr. Andre Lightbourne, Associate Director of Admissions, St. Thomas University, 16400 Northwest 32nd Avenue, Miami, FL 33054-6459.

Telephone: 305-628-6546 or toll-free 800-367-9006 (in-state); 800-367-9010 (out-of-state). Fax: 305-628-6591. E-mail: signup@stu.edu. Web site: http://www.stu.edu/.

SCHILLER INTERNATIONAL UNIVERSITY
DUNEDIN, FLORIDA

General Independent, comprehensive, coed **Entrance** Noncompetitive **Setting** suburban campus **Total enrollment** 243 **Application deadline** Rolling (freshmen), rolling (transfer) **Housing** Yes **Expenses** Tuition $13,790; Room & Board $5700 **Undergraduates** 13% 25 or older **Academic program** English as a second language, advanced placement, accelerated degree program, self-designed majors, summer session, adult/continuing education programs, internships **Contact** Markus Leibrecht, Director of Admissions, Schiller International University, 453 Edgewater Drive, Dunedin, FL 34698-7532. Telephone: 727-736-5082 or toll-free 800-336-4133. Fax: 727-734-0359. E-mail: admissions@schiller.edu. Web site: http://www.schiller.edu/.

SOUTHEASTERN COLLEGE OF THE ASSEMBLIES OF GOD
LAKELAND, FLORIDA

General Independent, 4-year, coed, affiliated with Assemblies of God **Entrance** Minimally difficult **Setting** 62-acre small-town campus **Total enrollment** 1,363 **Student-faculty ratio** 21:1 **Application deadline** 8/1 (freshmen), 8/1 (transfer) **Freshmen** 64% were admitted **Housing** Yes **Expenses** Tuition $7542; Room & Board $4106 **Undergraduates** 53% women, 9% part-time, 15% 25 or older, 1% Native American, 10% Hispanic American, 7% African American, 1% Asian American/Pacific Islander The most frequently chosen baccalaureate field is philosophy, religion, and theology **Academic program** Advanced placement, summer session, internships **Contact** Mr. Omar Rashed, Director of Admission, Southeastern College of the Assemblies of God, 1000 Longfellow Boulevard, Lakeland, FL 33801-6099. Telephone: 863-667-5000 or toll-free 800-500-8760 (out-of-state). Fax: 863-667-5200. E-mail: rmshelto@secollege.edu. Web site: http://www.secollege.edu/.

STETSON UNIVERSITY
DELAND, FLORIDA

General Independent, comprehensive, coed **Entrance** Moderately difficult **Setting** 162-acre small-town campus **Total enrollment** 3,255 **Student-faculty ratio** 10:1 **Application deadline** 3/15 (freshmen), rolling (transfer) **Freshmen** 80% were admitted **Housing** Yes **Expenses** Tuition $19,310; Room & Board $6330 **Undergraduates** 57% women, 5% part-time, 7% 25 or older, 1% Native American, 6% Hispanic American, 4% African American, 2% Asian American/Pacific Islander The most frequently chosen baccalaureate fields are business/marketing, parks and recreation, social sciences and history **Academic program** Advanced placement, accelerated degree

FLORIDA

Stetson University *(continued)*
program, self-designed majors, honors program, summer session, adult/continuing education programs, internships **Contact** Ms. Deborah Thompson, Vice President for Admissions, Stetson University, Unit 8378, Griffith Hall, DeLand, FL 32723. Telephone: 386-822-7100 or toll-free 800-688-0101. Fax: 386-822-8832. E-mail: admissions@stetson.edu. Web site: http://www.stetson.edu/.

TALMUDIC COLLEGE OF FLORIDA
MIAMI BEACH, FLORIDA

Contact Ira Hill, Administrator, FAL, Talmudic College of Florida, 4014 Chase Avenue, Miami Beach, FL 33139. Telephone: 305-534-7050.

TRINITY BAPTIST COLLEGE
JACKSONVILLE, FLORIDA

General Independent Baptist, 4-year, coed **Entrance** Moderately difficult **Setting** 148-acre urban campus **Total enrollment** 400 **Student-faculty ratio** 10:1 **Application deadline** Rolling (freshmen), rolling (transfer) **Freshmen** 95% were admitted **Housing** Yes **Expenses** Tuition $4450; Room & Board $3400 **Undergraduates** 49% women, 14% part-time, 29% 25 or older, 0% Native American, 2% Hispanic American, 4% African American, 2% Asian American/Pacific Islander **The most frequently chosen baccalaureate fields are** philosophy, education, philosophy, religion, and theology **Academic program** Advanced placement, accelerated degree program, summer session, adult/continuing education programs, internships **Contact** Mr. Larry Appleby, Administrative Dean, Trinity Baptist College, 800 Hammond Boulevard, Jacksonville, FL 32221. Telephone: 904-596-2538 or toll-free 800-786-2206 (out-of-state). Fax: 904-596-2531. E-mail: trinity@tbc.edu. Web site: http://www.tbc.edu/.

TRINITY COLLEGE OF FLORIDA
NEW PORT RICHEY, FLORIDA

General Independent nondenominational, 4-year, coed **Entrance** Minimally difficult **Setting** 20-acre small-town campus **Total enrollment** 162 **Student-faculty ratio** 14:1 **Application deadline** Rolling (freshmen), rolling (transfer) **Freshmen** 57% were admitted **Housing** Yes **Expenses** Tuition $6252; Room & Board $3120 **Undergraduates** 44% women, 15% part-time, 54% 25 or older, 1% Native American, 4% Hispanic American, 6% African American, 2% Asian American/Pacific Islander **The most frequently chosen baccalaureate fields are** philosophy, philosophy, religion, and theology **Academic program** Advanced placement, summer session, adult/continuing education programs, internships **Contact** Mr. Paul Heier, Director of Admissions, Trinity College of Florida, 2430 Welbilt Boulevard, New Port Richey, FL 34655. Telephone: 727-376-6911 Ext. 1120 or toll-free 888-776-4999. Fax: 727-376-0781. E-mail: admissions@trinitycollege.edu. Web site: http://www.trinitycollege.edu/.

UNIVERSITY OF CENTRAL FLORIDA
ORLANDO, FLORIDA

General State-supported, university, coed **Entrance** Moderately difficult **Setting** 1,445-acre suburban campus **Total enrollment** 35,927 **Student-faculty ratio** 25:1 **Application deadline** 5/15 (freshmen), 5/15 (transfer) **Freshmen** 65% were admitted **Housing** Yes **Expenses** Tuition $2582; Room & Board $5670 **Undergraduates** 55% women, 27% part-time, 20% 25 or older, 1% Native American, 11% Hispanic American, 8% African American, 5% Asian American/Pacific Islander **The most frequently chosen baccalaureate fields are** business/marketing, education, health professions and related sciences **Academic program** English as a second language, advanced placement, accelerated degree program, honors program, summer session, adult/continuing education programs, internships **Contact** Undergraduate Admissions Office, University of Central Florida, PO Box 160111, Orlando, FL 32816. Telephone: 407-823-2000. Fax: 407-823-5625. E-mail: admission@mail.ucf.edu. Web site: http://www.ucf.edu/.

UNIVERSITY OF FLORIDA
GAINESVILLE, FLORIDA

General State-supported, university, coed **Entrance** Very difficult **Setting** 2,000-acre suburban campus **Total enrollment** 45,114 **Student-faculty ratio** 20:1 **Application deadline** 1/16 (freshmen), 1/30 (transfer) **Freshmen** 60% were admitted **Housing** Yes **Expenses** Tuition $2444; Room & Board $5430 **Undergraduates** 53% women, 10% part-time, 6% 25 or older, 1% Native American, 11% Hispanic American, 8% African American, 7% Asian American/Pacific Islander **The most frequently chosen baccalaureate fields are** business/marketing, engineering/engineering technologies, trade and industry **Academic program** English as a second language, advanced placement, accelerated degree program, self-designed majors, honors program, summer session, adult/continuing education programs, internships **Contact** Office of Admissions, University of Florida, PO Box 114000, Gainesville, FL 32611-4000. Telephone: 352-392-1365. E-mail: freshmen@ufl.edu. Web site: http://www.ufl.edu/.

UNIVERSITY OF MIAMI
CORAL GABLES, FLORIDA

General Independent, university, coed **Entrance** Moderately difficult **Setting** 260-acre suburban campus **Total enrollment** 14,436 **Student-faculty ratio** 13:1 **Application deadline** 2/15 (freshmen), 3/1 (transfer) **Freshmen** 46% were admitted **Housing** Yes **Expenses** Tuition $23,647; Room & Board $7948 **Undergraduates** 57% women, 8% part-time, 8% 25 or older, 0.3% Native American, 25% Hispanic American, 10% African American, 5% Asian American/Pacific Islander **The most frequently chosen baccalaureate fields are** business/marketing, engineering/engineering technologies, visual/performing arts **Academic program** English as a second language,

FLORIDA

advanced placement, accelerated degree program, self-designed majors, honors program, summer session, adult/continuing education programs, internships **Contact** Mr. Edward M. Gillis, Associate Dean of Enrollment and Director of Admission, University of Miami, PO Box 248025, Ashe Building Room 132, 1252 Memorial Drive, Coral Gables, FL 33146-4616. Telephone: 305-284-4323. Fax: 305-284-2507. E-mail: admission@admiss.msmail.miami.edu. Web site: http://www.miami.edu/.

UNIVERSITY OF NORTH FLORIDA
JACKSONVILLE, FLORIDA

General State-supported, comprehensive, coed **Entrance** Very difficult **Setting** 1,300-acre urban campus **Total enrollment** 12,992 **Student-faculty ratio** 21:1 **Application deadline** 7/2 (freshmen), 7/2 (transfer) **Freshmen** 71% were admitted **Housing** Yes **Expenses** Tuition $2669; Room & Board $5380 **Undergraduates** 59% women, 35% part-time, 27% 25 or older, 0.4% Native American, 5% Hispanic American, 10% African American, 6% Asian American/Pacific Islander **The most frequently chosen baccalaureate fields are** business/marketing, education, health professions and related sciences **Academic program** Advanced placement, accelerated degree program, honors program, summer session, adult/continuing education programs, internships **Contact** Ms. Sherry David, Director of Admissions, University of North Florida, 4567 St. Johns Bluff Road South, Jacksonville, FL 32224. Telephone: 904-620-2624. Fax: 904-620-2414. E-mail: osprey@unf.edu. Web site: http://www.unf.edu/.

UNIVERSITY OF PHOENIX–FORT LAUDERDALE CAMPUS
PLANTATION, FLORIDA

General Proprietary, comprehensive, coed **Entrance** Noncompetitive **Total enrollment** 88,730 **Student-faculty ratio** 13:1 **Application deadline** Rolling (freshmen), rolling (transfer) **Housing** No **Expenses** Tuition $8100 **Undergraduates** 63% women, 79% 25 or older **The most frequently chosen baccalaureate field is** business/marketing **Academic program** Advanced placement, accelerated degree program, adult/continuing education programs **Contact** Ms. Beth Barilla, Director of Admissions, University of Phoenix–Fort Lauderdale Campus, 4615 East Elwood Street, Phoenix, AZ 85040-1958. Telephone: 480-927-0099 Ext. 1218 or toll-free 800-228-7240. Fax: 480-594-1758. E-mail: beth.barilla@apollogrp.edu. Web site: http://www.phoenix.edu/.

UNIVERSITY OF PHOENIX–JACKSONVILLE CAMPUS
JACKSONVILLE, FLORIDA

General Proprietary, comprehensive, coed **Entrance** Noncompetitive **Total enrollment** 88,730 **Student-faculty ratio** 13:1 **Application deadline** Rolling (freshmen), rolling (transfer) **Housing** No **Expenses** Tuition $8100 **Undergraduates** 60% women, 100% 25 or older **The most frequently chosen baccalaureate fields are** business/marketing, health professions and related sciences **Academic program** Advanced placement, accelerated degree program, adult/continuing education programs **Contact** Ms. Beth Barilla, Director of Admissions, University of Phoenix–Jacksonville Campus, 4615 East Elwood Street, Phoenix, AZ 85040-1958. Telephone: 480-927-0099 Ext. 1218 or toll-free 800-228-7240. Fax: 480-594-1758. E-mail: beth.barilla@apollogrp.edu. Web site: http://www.phoenix.edu/.

UNIVERSITY OF PHOENIX–ORLANDO CAMPUS
MAITLAND, FLORIDA

General Proprietary, comprehensive, coed **Entrance** Noncompetitive **Total enrollment** 88,730 **Student-faculty ratio** 13:1 **Application deadline** Rolling (freshmen), rolling (transfer) **Housing** No **Expenses** Tuition $8100 **Undergraduates** 59% women, 81% 25 or older **The most frequently chosen baccalaureate fields are** business/marketing, health professions and related sciences **Academic program** Advanced placement, accelerated degree program, adult/continuing education programs **Contact** Ms. Beth Barilla, Director of Admissions, University of Phoenix–Orlando Campus, 4615 East Elwood Street, Phoenix, AZ 85040-1958. Telephone: 480-927-0099 Ext. 1218 or toll-free 800-228-7240. Fax: 480-594-1758. E-mail: beth.barilla@apollogrp.edu. Web site: http://www.phoenix.edu/.

UNIVERSITY OF PHOENIX–TAMPA CAMPUS
TAMPA, FLORIDA

General Proprietary, comprehensive, coed **Entrance** Noncompetitive **Total enrollment** 88,730 **Student-faculty ratio** 12:1 **Application deadline** Rolling (freshmen), rolling (transfer) **Housing** No **Expenses** Tuition $8100 **Undergraduates** 56% women, 80% 25 or older **The most frequently chosen baccalaureate fields are** business/marketing, health professions and related sciences **Academic program** Advanced placement, accelerated degree program, adult/continuing education programs **Contact** Ms. Beth Barilla, Director of Admissions, University of Phoenix–Tampa Campus, 4615 East Elwood Street, Phoenix, AZ 85040-1958. Telephone: 480-927-0099 Ext. 1218 or toll-free 800-228-7240. Fax: 480-594-1758. E-mail: beth.barilla@apollogrp.edu. Web site: http://www.phoenix.edu/.

UNIVERSITY OF SARASOTA
See Argosy University-Sarasota

UNIVERSITY OF SOUTH FLORIDA
TAMPA, FLORIDA

General State-supported, university, coed **Entrance** Moderately difficult **Setting** 1,913-acre urban campus **Total enrollment** 37,221 **Student-faculty ratio**

FLORIDA

University of South Florida *(continued)*
16:1 **Freshmen** 67% were admitted **Housing** Yes **Expenses** Tuition $2520; Room & Board $5600 **Undergraduates** 59% women, 37% part-time, 28% 25 or older, 0.4% Native American, 10% Hispanic American, 12% African American, 6% Asian American/Pacific Islander **The most frequently chosen baccalaureate fields are** business/marketing, education, social sciences and history **Academic program** Advanced placement, accelerated degree program, self-designed majors, honors program, summer session, adult/continuing education programs, internships **Contact** Mr. Dewey Holleman, Director of Admissions, University of South Florida, 4202 East Fowler Avenue, SVC 1036, Tampa, FL 33620-9951. Telephone: 813-974-3350. Fax: 813-974-9689. E-mail: bullseye@admin.usf.edu. Web site: http://www.usf.edu/.
▶ For more information, see page 489.

THE UNIVERSITY OF TAMPA
TAMPA, FLORIDA

General Independent, comprehensive, coed **Entrance** Moderately difficult **Setting** 75-acre urban campus **Total enrollment** 3,823 **Student-faculty ratio** 17:1 **Application deadline** Rolling (freshmen), rolling (transfer) **Freshmen** 81% were admitted **Housing** Yes **Expenses** Tuition $16,542; Room & Board $5890 **Undergraduates** 61% women, 14% part-time, 17% 25 or older, 1% Native American, 9% Hispanic American, 7% African American, 2% Asian American/Pacific Islander **The most frequently chosen baccalaureate fields are** business/marketing, education, social sciences and history **Academic program** English as a second language, advanced placement, honors program, summer session, adult/continuing education programs, internships **Contact** Ms. Barbara P. Strickler, Vice President for Enrollment, The University of Tampa, 401 West Kennedy Boulevard, Tampa, FL 33606-1480. Telephone: 813-253-6211 or toll-free 888-646-2438. Fax: 813-258-7398. E-mail: admissions@ut.edu. Web site: http://www.ut.edu/.

UNIVERSITY OF WEST FLORIDA
PENSACOLA, FLORIDA

General State-supported, comprehensive, coed **Entrance** Moderately difficult **Setting** 1,600-acre suburban campus **Total enrollment** 9,052 **Student-faculty ratio** 19:1 **Application deadline** 6/30 (freshmen), 6/30 (transfer) **Freshmen** 82% were admitted **Housing** Yes **Expenses** Tuition $2528; Room & Board $5440 **Undergraduates** 57% women, 33% part-time, 33% 25 or older, 1% Native American, 4% Hispanic American, 10% African American, 5% Asian American/Pacific Islander **The most frequently chosen baccalaureate fields are** business/marketing, communications/communication technologies, education **Academic program** English as a second language, advanced placement, honors program, summer session, internships **Contact** Ms. Susie Neeley, Director of Admissions, University of West Florida, 11000 University Parkway, Pensacola, FL 32514-5750. Telephone: 850-474-2230. E-mail: admissions@uwf.edu. Web site: http://uwf.edu/.

WARNER SOUTHERN COLLEGE
LAKE WALES, FLORIDA

General Independent, comprehensive, coed, affiliated with Church of God **Entrance** Minimally difficult **Setting** 320-acre rural campus **Total enrollment** 1,117 **Student-faculty ratio** 17:1 **Application deadline** Rolling (freshmen), rolling (transfer) **Freshmen** 67% were admitted **Housing** Yes **Expenses** Tuition $10,040; Room & Board $4820 **Undergraduates** 60% women, 11% part-time, 53% 25 or older, 1% Native American, 7% Hispanic American, 18% African American, 1% Asian American/Pacific Islander **The most frequently chosen baccalaureate fields are** business/marketing, education, philosophy, religion, and theology **Academic program** Advanced placement, summer session, adult/continuing education programs, internships **Contact** Mr. Jason Roe, Director of Admissions, Warner Southern College, Warner Southern Center, 13895 US 27, Lake Wales, FL 33859. Telephone: 863-638-7212 Ext. 7213 or toll-free 800-949-7248 (in-state). Fax: 863-638-1472. E-mail: admissions@warner.edu. Web site: http://www.warner.edu/.

WEBBER INTERNATIONAL UNIVERSITY
BABSON PARK, FLORIDA

General Independent, comprehensive, coed **Entrance** Moderately difficult **Setting** 110-acre small-town campus **Total enrollment** 498 **Student-faculty ratio** 20:1 **Application deadline** 8/1 (freshmen), 8/1 (transfer) **Freshmen** 71% were admitted **Housing** Yes **Expenses** Tuition $10,300; Room & Board $3734 **Undergraduates** 47% women, 14% part-time, 21% 25 or older, 0.2% Native American, 7% Hispanic American, 10% African American, 1% Asian American/Pacific Islander **The most frequently chosen baccalaureate fields are** business/marketing, (pre)law, parks and recreation **Academic program** Advanced placement, accelerated degree program, summer session, adult/continuing education programs, internships **Contact** Dr. Deborah Milliken, Executive Vice President, Webber International University, 1201 Scenic Highway, South, Babson Park, FL 33827. Telephone: 863-638-2910 or toll-free 800-741-1844. Fax: 863-638-1591. E-mail: admissions@webber.edu. Web site: http://www.webber.edu/.
▶ For more information, see page 495.

GEORGIA

AGNES SCOTT COLLEGE
DECATUR, GEORGIA

General Independent, comprehensive, women only, affiliated with Presbyterian Church (U.S.A.) **Entrance** Very difficult **Setting** 100-acre urban campus **Total enrollment** 885 **Student-faculty ratio** 10:1 **Application deadline** 3/1 (freshmen), 3/1 (transfer) **Freshmen** 74% were admitted **Housing** Yes **Expenses**

GEORGIA

Tuition $17,670; Room & Board $7280 **Undergraduates** 5% part-time, 6% 25 or older, 0.2% Native American, 4% Hispanic American, 22% African American, 5% Asian American/Pacific Islander **The most frequently chosen baccalaureate fields are** psychology, English, social sciences and history **Academic program** Advanced placement, accelerated degree program, self-designed majors, summer session, adult/continuing education programs, internships **Contact** Ms. Stephanie Balmer, Associate Vice President for Enrollment and Director of Admission, Agnes Scott College, 141 East College Avenue, Atlanta/Decatur, GA 30030-3797. Telephone: 404-471-6285 or toll-free 800-868-8602. Fax: 404-471-6414. E-mail: admission@agnesscott.edu. Web site: http://www.agnesscott.edu/.

ALBANY STATE UNIVERSITY
ALBANY, GEORGIA

General State-supported, comprehensive, coed **Entrance** Minimally difficult **Setting** 144-acre urban campus **Total enrollment** 3,456 **Student-faculty ratio** 20:1 **Application deadline** 7/1 (freshmen), 7/1 (transfer) **Freshmen** 36% were admitted **Housing** Yes **Expenses** Tuition $2476; Room & Board $3406 **Undergraduates** 67% women, 18% part-time **The most frequently chosen baccalaureate fields are** business/marketing, education, protective services/public administration **Academic program** Advanced placement, honors program, summer session, adult/continuing education programs, internships **Contact** Mrs. Patricia Price, Assistant Director of Recruitment and Admissions, Albany State University, 504 College Drive, Albany, GA 31705. Telephone: 229-430-4645 or toll-free 800-822-RAMS (in-state). Fax: 229-430-3936. E-mail: fsuttles@asurams.edu. Web site: http://asuweb.asurams.edu/asu/.

AMERICAN INTERCONTINENTAL UNIVERSITY
ATLANTA, GEORGIA

General Proprietary, 4-year, coed **Entrance** Noncompetitive **Setting** urban campus **Total enrollment** 1,292 **Student-faculty ratio** 14:1 **Application deadline** 10/15 (freshmen), rolling (transfer) **Freshmen** 53% were admitted **Housing** Yes **Expenses** Tuition $12,600; Room only $4835 **Undergraduates** 64% women, 35% part-time, 30% 25 or older, 0.5% Native American, 4% Hispanic American, 43% African American, 7% Asian American/Pacific Islander **The most frequently chosen baccalaureate fields are** business/marketing, visual/performing arts **Academic program** English as a second language, accelerated degree program, summer session, adult/continuing education programs, internships **Contact** Ms. Knitra Norwood, Director of Admissions, American InterContinental University, 3330 Peachtree Road, NE, Atlanta, GA 30326-1016. Telephone: 404-965-5700 or toll-free 888-999-4248 (out-of-state). Fax: 404-965-5701. E-mail: acatl@ix.netcom.com. Web site: http://www.aiuniv.edu/.

AMERICAN INTERCONTINENTAL UNIVERSITY
ATLANTA, GEORGIA

General Proprietary, comprehensive, coed **Total enrollment** 1,248 **Student-faculty ratio** 18:1 **Freshmen** 44% were admitted **Housing** No **Expenses** Tuition $22,050 **Contact** Mr. Jeff Bostick, Director of Admissions, American InterContinental University, 6600 Peachtree-Dunwoody Road, 500 Embassy Row, Atlanta, GA 30328. Telephone: 404-965-8050 or toll-free 800-255-6839. E-mail: info@aiuniv.edu. Web site: http://www.aiuniv.edu/.

ARMSTRONG ATLANTIC STATE UNIVERSITY
SAVANNAH, GEORGIA

General State-supported, comprehensive, coed **Entrance** Minimally difficult **Setting** 250-acre suburban campus **Total enrollment** 5,747 **Student-faculty ratio** 16:1 **Application deadline** 7/1 (freshmen), 7/1 (transfer) **Housing** Yes **Expenses** Tuition $2314; Room & Board $4770 **Undergraduates** 68% women, 42% part-time, 21% 25 or older **The most frequently chosen baccalaureate fields are** education, health professions and related sciences, liberal arts/general studies **Academic program** Advanced placement, honors program, summer session, adult/continuing education programs, internships **Contact** Ms. Melanie Mirande, Assistant Director of Recruitment, Armstrong Atlantic State University, 11935 Abercorn Street, Savannah, GA 31419. Telephone: 912-925-5275 or toll-free 800-633-2349. Fax: 912-921-5462. E-mail: cynthia_buskey@mailgate.armstrong.edu. Web site: http://www.armstrong.edu/.

ATLANTA CHRISTIAN COLLEGE
EAST POINT, GEORGIA

General Independent Christian, 4-year, coed **Entrance** Moderately difficult **Setting** 52-acre suburban campus **Total enrollment** 421 **Student-faculty ratio** 16:1 **Application deadline** Rolling (freshmen), rolling (transfer) **Freshmen** 77% were admitted **Housing** Yes **Expenses** Tuition $10,300; Room & Board $3950 **Undergraduates** 30% 25 or older **Academic program** Advanced placement, summer session, internships **Contact** Mr. Keith Wagner, Director of Admissions, Atlanta Christian College, 2605 Ben Hill Road, East Point, GA 30344-1999. Telephone: 404-761-8861 or toll-free 800-776-1ACC. Fax: 404-669-2024. E-mail: admissions@acc.edu. Web site: http://www.acc.edu/.

ATLANTA COLLEGE OF ART
ATLANTA, GEORGIA

General Independent, 4-year, coed **Entrance** Moderately difficult **Setting** 6-acre urban campus **Total enrollment** 388 **Student-faculty ratio** 12:1 **Application deadline** Rolling (freshmen), rolling (transfer) **Freshmen** 72% were admitted **Housing** Yes

GEORGIA

Atlanta College of Art *(continued)*
Expenses Tuition $15,000; Room only $4400 **Undergraduates** 53% women, 16% 25 or older, 0.3% Native American, 3% Hispanic American, 23% African American, 6% Asian American/Pacific Islander **The most frequently chosen baccalaureate field is** visual/performing arts **Academic program** Advanced placement, self-designed majors, summer session, internships **Contact** Ms. Lucy Leusch, Vice President of Enrollment Management, Atlanta College of Art, 1280 Peachtree Street, NE, Atlanta, GA 30309-3582. Telephone: 404-733-5101 or toll-free 800-832-2104. Fax: 404-733-5107. E-mail: acainfo@woodruff-arts.org. Web site: http://www.aca.edu/.

▶ For more information, see page 397.

AUGUSTA STATE UNIVERSITY
AUGUSTA, GEORGIA

General State-supported, comprehensive, coed **Entrance** Minimally difficult **Setting** 72-acre urban campus **Total enrollment** 5,407 **Student-faculty ratio** 17:1 **Application deadline** 7/21 (freshmen), rolling (transfer) **Freshmen** 68% were admitted **Housing** No **Expenses** Tuition $2282 **Undergraduates** 32% 25 or older **The most frequently chosen baccalaureate fields are** business/marketing, education, social sciences and history **Academic program** English as a second language, advanced placement, honors program, summer session, adult/continuing education programs, internships **Contact** Catherine R. Tuthill, Augusta State University, 2500 Walton Way, Augusta, GA 30904-2200. Telephone: 706-737-1400. Fax: 706-667-4355. E-mail: admissions@ac.edu. Web site: http://www.aug.edu/.

BEACON COLLEGE AND GRADUATE SCHOOL
COLUMBUS, GEORGIA

General Independent religious, comprehensive, coed **Total enrollment** 82 **Student-faculty ratio** 5:1 **Application deadline** Rolling (freshmen), rolling (transfer) **Freshmen** 89% were admitted **Housing** No **Expenses** Tuition $2535 **Undergraduates** 41% women, 33% part-time, 55% 25 or older, 3% Hispanic American, 44% African American **The most frequently chosen baccalaureate fields are** philosophy, philosophy, religion, and theology **Academic program** Advanced placement, accelerated degree program, summer session, adult/continuing education programs **Contact** Mrs. Paula Hardy, Director of Admissions and Student Records, Beacon College and Graduate School, 6003 Veterans Parkway, Columbus, GA 31909. Telephone: 706-323-5364 Ext. 254. Fax: 706-323-5891. E-mail: registrar@beacon.edu. Web site: http://www.beacon.edu/.

BERRY COLLEGE
MOUNT BERRY, GEORGIA

General Independent interdenominational, comprehensive, coed **Entrance** Moderately difficult **Setting** 28,000-acre small-town campus **Total enrollment** 2,038 **Student-faculty ratio** 12:1 **Application deadline** 7/28 (freshmen), 7/28 (transfer) **Freshmen** 82% were admitted **Housing** Yes **Expenses** Tuition $13,450; Room & Board $5730 **Undergraduates** 63% women, 2% part-time, 4% 25 or older, 0.1% Native American, 1% Hispanic American, 2% African American, 1% Asian American/Pacific Islander **The most frequently chosen baccalaureate fields are** business/marketing, education, social sciences and history **Academic program** Advanced placement, accelerated degree program, self-designed majors, honors program, summer session, adult/continuing education programs, internships **Contact** Mr. George Gaddie, Dean of Admissions, Berry College, PO Box 490159, 2277 Martha Berry Highway, Mount Berry, GA 30149-0159. Telephone: 706-236-2215 or toll-free 800-237-7942. Fax: 706-290-2178. E-mail: admissions@berry.edu. Web site: http://www.berry.edu/.

BEULAH HEIGHTS BIBLE COLLEGE
ATLANTA, GEORGIA

General Independent Pentecostal, 4-year, coed **Entrance** Noncompetitive **Setting** 10-acre urban campus **Total enrollment** 560 **Student-faculty ratio** 17:1 **Application deadline** Rolling (freshmen), rolling (transfer) **Freshmen** 46% were admitted **Housing** Yes **Expenses** Tuition $3680; Room only $3000 **Undergraduates** 56% women, 60% part-time, 90% 25 or older, 0.2% Native American, 5% Hispanic American, 72% African American, 0.4% Asian American/Pacific Islander **The most frequently chosen baccalaureate field is** philosophy, religion, and theology **Academic program** Advanced placement, accelerated degree program, summer session, adult/continuing education programs, internships **Contact** Ms. Dama Riles, Director of Admissions, Beulah Heights Bible College, 892 Berne Street, SE, PO Box 18145, Atlanta, GA 30316. Telephone: 404-627-2681 Ext. 114 or toll-free 888-777-BHBC. Fax: 404-627-0702. E-mail: cjkjr@aol.com. Web site: http://www.beulah.org/.

BRENAU UNIVERSITY
GAINESVILLE, GEORGIA

General Independent, comprehensive, women only **Entrance** Moderately difficult **Setting** 57-acre small-town campus **Total enrollment** 600 **Student-faculty ratio** 7:1 **Application deadline** Rolling (freshmen), rolling (transfer) **Freshmen** 81% were admitted **Housing** Yes **Expenses** Tuition $12,780; Room & Board $7320 **Undergraduates** 12% part-time, 17% 25 or older, 0.4% Native American, 2% Hispanic American, 9% African American, 2% Asian American/Pacific Islander **The most frequently chosen baccalaureate fields are** education, health professions and related sciences, visual/performing arts **Academic program** Advanced placement, honors program, summer session, internships **Contact** Ms. Christina Cochran, Coordinator of Women's College Admissions, Brenau University, Admissions, 1 Centennial Circle, Gainesville, GA 30501. Telephone:

GEORGIA

770-534-6100 or toll-free 800-252-5119. Fax: 770-538-4306. E-mail: wcadmissions@lib.brenau.edu. Web site: http://www.brenau.edu/.

BREWTON-PARKER COLLEGE
MT. VERNON, GEORGIA

General Independent Southern Baptist, 4-year, coed **Entrance** Minimally difficult **Setting** 280-acre rural campus **Total enrollment** 1,219 **Student-faculty ratio** 10:1 **Application deadline** Rolling (freshmen), rolling (transfer) **Freshmen** 98% were admitted **Housing** Yes **Expenses** Tuition $8000; Room & Board $3700 **Undergraduates** 63% women, 20% part-time, 37% 25 or older, 0.3% Native American, 2% Hispanic American, 19% African American, 1% Asian American/Pacific Islander **Academic program** English as a second language, advanced placement, honors program, summer session, adult/continuing education programs, internships **Contact** Mr. James E. Beall, Director of Admissions, Brewton-Parker College, Highway 280, Mt. Vernon, GA 30445-0197. Telephone: 912-583-3268 Ext. 268 or toll-free 800-342-1087. Fax: 912-583-4498. Web site: http://www.bpc.edu/.

CLARK ATLANTA UNIVERSITY
ATLANTA, GEORGIA

General Independent United Methodist, university, coed **Entrance** Moderately difficult **Setting** 113-acre urban campus **Total enrollment** 4,882 **Student-faculty ratio** 15:1 **Application deadline** 7/1 (freshmen), 7/1 (transfer) **Freshmen** 74% were admitted **Housing** Yes **Expenses** Tuition $12,538; Room & Board $6054 **Undergraduates** 71% women, 3% part-time, 5% 25 or older, 0% Native American, 0.1% Hispanic American, 93% African American, 0.03% Asian American/Pacific Islander **The most frequently chosen baccalaureate fields are** business/marketing, communications/communication technologies, education **Academic program** English as a second language, advanced placement, accelerated degree program, honors program, summer session, adult/continuing education programs, internships **Contact** Office of Admissions, Clark Atlanta University, 223 James P. Brawley Drive, SW, 101 Trevor Arnett Hall, Atlanta, GA 30314. Telephone: 404-880-8784 Ext. 6650 or toll-free 800-688-3228. Fax: 404-880-6174. Web site: http://www.cau.edu/.

CLAYTON COLLEGE & STATE UNIVERSITY
MORROW, GEORGIA

General State-supported, 4-year, coed **Entrance** Minimally difficult **Setting** 163-acre suburban campus **Total enrollment** 4,675 **Student-faculty ratio** 16:1 **Application deadline** 7/17 (freshmen) **Freshmen** 47% were admitted **Housing** No **Expenses** Tuition $2322 **Undergraduates** 65% women, 55% part-time, 52% 25 or older **The most frequently chosen baccalaureate fields are** business/marketing, computer/information sciences, health professions and related sciences **Academic program** Advanced placement, self-designed majors, honors program, summer session, adult/continuing education programs, internships **Contact** Ms. Carol S. Montgomery, Admissions, Clayton College & State University, 5900 North Lee Street, Morrow, GA 30260-0285. Telephone: 770-961-3500. Fax: 770-961-3752. E-mail: csc-info@ce.clayton.peachnet.edu. Web site: http://www.clayton.edu/.

COLUMBUS STATE UNIVERSITY
COLUMBUS, GEORGIA

General State-supported, comprehensive, coed **Entrance** Minimally difficult **Setting** 132-acre suburban campus **Total enrollment** 5,522 **Student-faculty ratio** 18:1 **Application deadline** 8/2 (freshmen), 8/2 (transfer) **Freshmen** 64% were admitted **Housing** Yes **Expenses** Tuition $2352; Room & Board $4876 **Undergraduates** 62% women, 35% part-time, 30% 25 or older, 0.5% Native American, 4% Hispanic American, 26% African American, 2% Asian American/Pacific Islander **Academic program** Advanced placement, honors program, summer session, adult/continuing education programs, internships **Contact** Ms. Susan Lovell, Associate Director of Admissions, Columbus State University, 4225 University Avenue, Columbus, GA 31907-5645. Telephone: 706-568-2035 Ext. 1681 or toll-free 866-264-2035. Fax: 706-568-2462. Web site: http://www.colstate.edu/.

COVENANT COLLEGE
LOOKOUT MOUNTAIN, GEORGIA

General Independent, comprehensive, coed, affiliated with Presbyterian Church in America **Entrance** Moderately difficult **Setting** 250-acre suburban campus **Total enrollment** 1,245 **Student-faculty ratio** 15:1 **Application deadline** Rolling (freshmen), rolling (transfer) **Freshmen** 96% were admitted **Housing** Yes **Expenses** Tuition $17,070; Room & Board $5000 **Undergraduates** 61% women, 3% part-time, 4% 25 or older, 0% Native American, 3% Hispanic American, 4% African American, 2% Asian American/Pacific Islander **The most frequently chosen baccalaureate fields are** education, biological/life sciences, social sciences and history **Academic program** Advanced placement, self-designed majors, summer session, adult/continuing education programs, internships **Contact** Ms. Leda Goodman, Regional Director, Covenant College, 14049 Scenic Highway, Lookout Mountain, GA 30750. Telephone: 706-419-1644 or toll-free 888-451-2683 (in-state). Fax: 706-820-0893. E-mail: admissions@covenant.edu. Web site: http://www.covenant.edu/.

DALTON STATE COLLEGE
DALTON, GEORGIA

General State-supported, 4-year, coed **Entrance** Noncompetitive **Setting** 141-acre small-town campus **Total enrollment** 3,647 **Student-faculty ratio** 25:1 **Application deadline** Rolling (freshmen), rolling

Dalton State College *(continued)*
(transfer) **Freshmen** 62% were admitted **Housing** No **Expenses** Tuition $2160 **Undergraduates** 63% women, 60% part-time, 43% 25 or older **Academic program** English as a second language, advanced placement, summer session, adult/continuing education programs, internships **Contact** Dr. Angela Harris, Assistant Director of Admissions, Dalton State College, 213 North College Drive, Dalton, GA 30720-3797. Telephone: 706-272-4476 or toll-free 800-829-4436. Fax: 706-272-2530. E-mail: aharris@em.daltonstate.edu. Web site: http://www.daltonstate.edu/.

DEVRY UNIVERSITY
ALPHARETTA, GEORGIA

General Proprietary, 4-year, coed **Entrance** Minimally difficult **Setting** 9-acre suburban campus **Total enrollment** 1,548 **Student-faculty ratio** 21:1 **Application deadline** Rolling (freshmen), rolling (transfer) **Freshmen** 83% were admitted **Housing** No **Expenses** Tuition $8740 **Undergraduates** 32% women, 24% part-time, 53% 25 or older, 0.3% Native American, 2% Hispanic American, 30% African American, 5% Asian American/Pacific Islander **The most frequently chosen baccalaureate fields are** business/marketing, computer/information sciences, engineering/engineering technologies **Academic program** Advanced placement, accelerated degree program, summer session, adult/continuing education programs **Contact** Ms. Kristi Franklin, New Student Coordinator, DeVry University, 2555 Northwinds Parkway, Alpharetta, GA 30004. Telephone: 770-521-4900. Fax: 770-664-8824. Web site: http://www.atl.devry.edu/alpharetta/.

DEVRY UNIVERSITY
DECATUR, GEORGIA

General Proprietary, 4-year, coed **Entrance** Minimally difficult **Setting** 21-acre suburban campus **Total enrollment** 2,925 **Student-faculty ratio** 13:1 **Application deadline** Rolling (freshmen), rolling (transfer) **Freshmen** 80% were admitted **Housing** No **Expenses** Tuition $8805 **Undergraduates** 41% women, 20% part-time, 47% 25 or older, 0.3% Native American, 1% Hispanic American, 80% African American, 2% Asian American/Pacific Islander **The most frequently chosen baccalaureate fields are** business/marketing, computer/information sciences, engineering/engineering technologies **Academic program** Advanced placement, accelerated degree program, summer session, adult/continuing education programs **Contact** Ms. Karen Krumenaker, New Student Coordinator, DeVry University, 250 North Arcadia Avenue, Decatur, GA 30030. Telephone: 404-292-2645 or toll-free 800-221-4771 (out-of-state). E-mail: dwalters@admin.atl.devry.edu. Web site: http://www.atl.devry.edu/.

EMMANUEL COLLEGE
FRANKLIN SPRINGS, GEORGIA

General Independent, 4-year, coed, affiliated with Pentecostal Holiness Church **Entrance** Minimally difficult **Setting** 90-acre rural campus **Total enrollment** 762 **Student-faculty ratio** 14:1 **Application deadline** 8/1 (freshmen), 8/1 (transfer) **Freshmen** 52% were admitted **Housing** Yes **Expenses** Tuition $8462; Room & Board $4154 **Undergraduates** 55% women, 7% part-time, 9% 25 or older, 0.4% Native American, 1% Hispanic American, 14% African American, 2% Asian American/Pacific Islander **The most frequently chosen baccalaureate fields are** education, philosophy, philosophy, religion, and theology **Academic program** English as a second language, advanced placement, summer session, internships **Contact** Ms. Donna Quick, Associate Director of Admissions, Emmanuel College, PO Box 129, 181 Spring Street, Franklin Springs, GA 30639-0129. Telephone: 706-245-7226 Ext. 2873 or toll-free 800-860-8800 (in-state). Fax: 706-245-4424. E-mail: admissions@emmanuel-college.edu. Web site: http://www.emmanuel-college.edu/.

EMORY UNIVERSITY
ATLANTA, GEORGIA

General Independent Methodist, university, coed **Entrance** Most difficult **Setting** 631-acre suburban campus **Total enrollment** 11,443 **Student-faculty ratio** 7:1 **Application deadline** 1/15 (freshmen), 6/1 (transfer) **Freshmen** 43% were admitted **Housing** Yes **Expenses** Tuition $25,552; Room & Board $8240 **Undergraduates** 55% women, 2% part-time, 2% 25 or older, 0.2% Native American, 3% Hispanic American, 10% African American, 15% Asian American/Pacific Islander **The most frequently chosen baccalaureate fields are** business/marketing, biological/life sciences, social sciences and history **Academic program** Advanced placement, accelerated degree program, honors program, summer session, internships **Contact** Mr. Daniel C. Walls, Dean of Admission, Emory University, Boisfeuillet Jones Center–Office of Admissions, Atlanta, GA 30322-1100. Telephone: 404-727-6036 or toll-free 800-727-6036. E-mail: admiss@unix.cc.emory.edu. Web site: http://www.emory.edu/.

FORT VALLEY STATE UNIVERSITY
FORT VALLEY, GEORGIA

General State-supported, comprehensive, coed **Entrance** Moderately difficult **Setting** 1,307-acre small-town campus **Total enrollment** 2,823 **Student-faculty ratio** 19:1 **Application deadline** 8/1 (freshmen), 8/1 (transfer) **Freshmen** 49% were admitted **Housing** Yes **Expenses** Tuition $1770; Room & Board $1915 **Academic program** Advanced placement, honors program, summer session, adult/continuing education programs, internships **Contact** Mrs. Debra McGhee, Dean of Admissions and Enrollment Management, Fort Valley State University, 1005 State University Drive, Fort Valley, GA 31030. Telephone: 478-825-6307 or toll-free 800-248-7343. Fax: 478-825-6169. E-mail: admissap@mail.fusu.edu. Web site: http://www.fvsu.edu/.

GEORGIA BAPTIST COLLEGE OF NURSING OF MERCER UNIVERSITY
ATLANTA, GEORGIA

General Independent Baptist, 4-year, coed, primarily women **Entrance** Moderately difficult **Setting** 20-acre urban campus **Total enrollment** 312 **Student-faculty ratio** 9:1 **Application deadline** 5/15 (freshmen), 5/15 (transfer) **Freshmen** 46% were admitted **Housing** Yes **Expenses** Tuition $10,589; Room only $940 **Undergraduates** 97% women, 20% part-time, 32% 25 or older, 0.4% Native American, 3% Hispanic American, 27% African American, 2% Asian American/Pacific Islander **The most frequently chosen baccalaureate field is** health professions and related sciences **Academic program** Advanced placement, summer session **Contact** Ms. Kim W. Hays, Associate Director of Admissions, Georgia Baptist College of Nursing of Mercer University, 274 Boulevard, NE, Atlanta, GA 30312. Telephone: 673-547-6702 or toll-free 800-551-8835. Fax: 673-547-6811. E-mail: gbcnadm@mindspring.com. Web site: http://www.nursing.mercer.edu/.

GEORGIA COLLEGE AND STATE UNIVERSITY
MILLEDGEVILLE, GEORGIA

General State-supported, comprehensive, coed **Entrance** Moderately difficult **Setting** 666-acre small-town campus **Total enrollment** 5,079 **Student-faculty ratio** 14:1 **Application deadline** 7/15 (freshmen), 7/15 (transfer) **Freshmen** 70% were admitted **Housing** Yes **Expenses** Tuition $3032; Room & Board $4962 **Undergraduates** 62% women, 18% part-time, 16% 25 or older, 0.1% Native American, 1% Hispanic American, 13% African American, 1% Asian American/Pacific Islander **The most frequently chosen baccalaureate fields are** business/marketing, education, health professions and related sciences **Academic program** Advanced placement, accelerated degree program, self-designed majors, honors program, summer session, internships **Contact** Ms. Maryllis Wolfgang, Director of Admissions, Georgia College and State University, CPO Box 023, Milledgeville, GA 31061. Telephone: 478-445-6285 or toll-free 800-342-0471 (in-state). Fax: 478-445-1914. E-mail: gcsu@mail.gac.peachnet.edu. Web site: http://www.gcsu.edu/.

GEORGIA INSTITUTE OF TECHNOLOGY
ATLANTA, GEORGIA

General State-supported, university, coed **Entrance** Very difficult **Setting** 360-acre urban campus **Total enrollment** 15,576 **Student-faculty ratio** 14:1 **Application deadline** 1/15 (freshmen), 5/1 (transfer) **Freshmen** 56% were admitted **Housing** Yes **Expenses** Tuition $3454; Room & Board $5574 **Undergraduates** 29% women, 8% part-time, 4% 25 or older, 0.1% Native American, 3% Hispanic American, 8% African American, 14% Asian American/Pacific Islander **The most frequently chosen baccalaureate fields are** business/marketing, computer/information sciences, engineering/engineering technologies **Academic program** English as a second language, advanced placement, accelerated degree program, self-designed majors, honors program, summer session, internships **Contact** Ms. Deborah Smith, Director of Admissions, Georgia Institute of Technology, 225 North Avenue, NW, Atlanta, GA 30332-0320. Telephone: 404-894-4154. Fax: 404-894-9511. E-mail: admissions@success.gatech.edu. Web site: http://www.gatech.edu/.

GEORGIA SOUTHERN UNIVERSITY
STATESBORO, GEORGIA

General State-supported, comprehensive, coed **Entrance** Moderately difficult **Setting** 601-acre small-town campus **Total enrollment** 14,371 **Student-faculty ratio** 18:1 **Application deadline** 8/1 (freshmen), rolling (transfer) **Freshmen** 61% were admitted **Housing** Yes **Expenses** Tuition $2596; Room & Board $4382 **Undergraduates** 52% women, 11% part-time, 7% 25 or older, 0.2% Native American, 1% Hispanic American, 26% African American, 1% Asian American/Pacific Islander **The most frequently chosen baccalaureate fields are** business/marketing, education, parks and recreation **Academic program** English as a second language, advanced placement, self-designed majors, honors program, summer session, adult/continuing education programs, internships **Contact** Dr. Teresa Thompson, Director of Admissions, Georgia Southern University, GSU PO Box 8024, Building #805, Forest Drive, Statesboro, GA 30460. Telephone: 912-681-5391. Fax: 912-486-7240. E-mail: admissions@gasou.edu. Web site: http://www.gasou.edu/.

GEORGIA SOUTHWESTERN STATE UNIVERSITY
AMERICUS, GEORGIA

General State-supported, comprehensive, coed **Entrance** Moderately difficult **Setting** 255-acre small-town campus **Total enrollment** 2,535 **Student-faculty ratio** 15:1 **Application deadline** Rolling (freshmen), rolling (transfer) **Freshmen** 69% were admitted **Housing** Yes **Expenses** Tuition $2500; Room & Board $3790 **Undergraduates** 63% women, 26% part-time, 5% 25 or older **The most frequently chosen baccalaureate fields are** business/marketing, education, psychology **Academic program** English as a second language, advanced placement, honors program, summer session, adult/continuing education programs, internships **Contact** Mr. Gary Fallis, Director of Admissions, Georgia Southwestern State University, 800 Wheatley Street, Americus, GA 31709-4693. Telephone: 229-928-1273 or toll-free 800-338-0082. Fax: 229-931-2983. E-mail: gswapps@canes.gsw.edu. Web site: http://www.gsw.edu/.

GEORGIA STATE UNIVERSITY
ATLANTA, GEORGIA

General State-supported, university, coed **Entrance** Moderately difficult **Setting** 24-acre urban campus

GEORGIA

Georgia State University *(continued)*
Total enrollment 25,745 **Student-faculty ratio** 14:1 **Application deadline** 6/1 (freshmen), 6/1 (transfer) **Freshmen** 53% were admitted **Housing** Yes **Expenses** Tuition $3292; Room only $4500 **Undergraduates** 61% women, 36% part-time, 32% 25 or older, 0.3% Native American, 3% Hispanic American, 32% African American, 10% Asian American/Pacific Islander **The most frequently chosen baccalaureate fields are** business/marketing, computer/information sciences, social sciences and history **Academic program** English as a second language, self-designed majors, honors program, summer session, adult/continuing education programs, internships **Contact** Mr. Rob Sheinkopf, Dean of Admissions and Acting Dean for Enrollment Services, Georgia State University, PO Box 4009, Atlanta, GA 30302-4009. Telephone: 404-651-2365 or toll-free 404-651-2365 (in-state). Fax: 404-651-4811. Web site: http://www.gsu.edu/.

KENNESAW STATE UNIVERSITY
KENNESAW, GEORGIA

General State-supported, comprehensive, coed **Entrance** Moderately difficult **Setting** 185-acre suburban campus **Total enrollment** 13,951 **Student-faculty ratio** 24:1 **Application deadline** 7/13 (freshmen), 7/13 (transfer) **Freshmen** 72% were admitted **Housing** No **Expenses** Tuition $2828 **Undergraduates** 37% 25 or older **The most frequently chosen baccalaureate fields are** business/marketing, computer/information sciences, education **Academic program** English as a second language, advanced placement, honors program, summer session, adult/continuing education programs, internships **Contact** Mr. Joe F. Head, Director of Admissions and Dean of Enrollment Services, Kennesaw State University, 1000 Chastain Road, Campus Box 0115, Kennesaw, GA 30144. Telephone: 770-423-6300. Fax: 770-420-4435. E-mail: ksuadmit@ksumail.kennesaw.edu. Web site: http://www.kennesaw.edu/.

LAGRANGE COLLEGE
LAGRANGE, GEORGIA

General Independent United Methodist, comprehensive, coed **Entrance** Moderately difficult **Setting** 120-acre small-town campus **Total enrollment** 942 **Student-faculty ratio** 11:1 **Application deadline** 8/15 (freshmen), 8/15 (transfer) **Freshmen** 79% were admitted **Housing** Yes **Expenses** Tuition $12,360; Room & Board $5136 **Undergraduates** 63% women, 16% part-time, 12% 25 or older, 1% Native American, 1% Hispanic American, 15% African American, 1% Asian American/Pacific Islander **The most frequently chosen baccalaureate fields are** business/marketing, computer/information sciences, education **Academic program** English as a second language, advanced placement, summer session, adult/continuing education programs, internships **Contact** Mr. Andy Geeter, Director of Admission, LaGrange College, 601 Broad Street, LaGrange, GA 30240-2999. Telephone: 706-880-8253 or toll-free 800-593-2885. Fax: 706-880-8010. E-mail: lgcadmis@lgc.edu. Web site: http://www.lgc.edu/.

▶ **For more information, see page 445.**

LIFE UNIVERSITY
MARIETTA, GEORGIA

Contact Office of Admissions, Life University, 1269 Barclay Circle, Marietta, GA 30060-2903. Telephone: 800-543-3202. Web site: http://www.life.edu/.

LUTHER RICE BIBLE COLLEGE AND SEMINARY
LITHONIA, GEORGIA

General Independent Baptist, comprehensive, coed **Entrance** Noncompetitive **Setting** 5-acre urban campus **Total enrollment** 1,600 **Application deadline** Rolling (freshmen), rolling (transfer) **Housing** No **Expenses** Tuition $2834 **Undergraduates** 19% women, 91% part-time, 88% 25 or older, 0.3% Native American, 5% Hispanic American, 16% African American, 10% Asian American/Pacific Islander **Academic program** Adult/continuing education programs **Contact** Dr. Dennis Dieringer, Director of Admissions and Records, Luther Rice Bible College and Seminary, 3038 Evans Mill Road, Lithonia, GA 30038-2454. Telephone: 770-484-1204 or toll-free 800-442-1577. E-mail: lrs@lrs.edu. Web site: http://www.lrs.edu/.

MACON STATE COLLEGE
MACON, GEORGIA

General State-supported, 4-year, coed **Entrance** Minimally difficult **Setting** 167-acre urban campus **Total enrollment** 4,482 **Student-faculty ratio** 20:1 **Application deadline** Rolling (freshmen), rolling (transfer) **Housing** No **Expenses** Tuition $1438 **Undergraduates** 64% women, 61% part-time, 49% 25 or older, 0.4% Native American, 1% Hispanic American, 32% African American, 2% Asian American/Pacific Islander **Academic program** Advanced placement, honors program, summer session, adult/continuing education programs, internships **Contact** Mr. Terrell Mitchell, Director of Admissions, Macon State College, 100 College Station Drive, Macon, GA 31206. Telephone: 912-471-2800 Ext. 2854 or toll-free 800-272-7619. E-mail: mcinfo@cennet.mc.peachnet.edu. Web site: http://www.maconstate.edu/.

MEDICAL COLLEGE OF GEORGIA
AUGUSTA, GEORGIA

General State-supported, upper-level, coed **Entrance** Moderately difficult **Setting** 100-acre urban campus **Total enrollment** 1,939 **Application deadline** Rolling (transfer) **Housing** Yes **Expenses** Tuition $3083; Room only $1302 **Undergraduates** 87% women, 8% part-time, 34% 25 or older, 1% Native American, 2% Hispanic American, 14% African American, 3% Asian American/Pacific Islander **The most frequently chosen baccalaureate field is** health profes-

GEORGIA

sions and related sciences **Academic program** Summer session **Contact** Ms. Carol S. Nobles, Director of Student Recruitment and Admissions, Medical College of Georgia, AA-170 Administration-Kelly Building, Augusta, GA 30912. Telephone: 706-721-2725. Fax: 706-721-7279. E-mail: underadm@mail.mcg.edu. Web site: http://www.mcg.edu/.

MERCER UNIVERSITY
MACON, GEORGIA

General Independent Baptist, comprehensive, coed **Entrance** Moderately difficult **Setting** 130-acre suburban campus **Total enrollment** 7,315 **Student-faculty ratio** 15:1 **Application deadline** 7/1 (freshmen), rolling (transfer) **Freshmen** 83% were admitted **Housing** Yes **Expenses** Tuition $18,290; Room & Board $5840 **Undergraduates** 67% women, 16% part-time, 7% 25 or older, 1% Native American, 1% Hispanic American, 28% African American, 3% Asian American/Pacific Islander **The most frequently chosen baccalaureate fields are** business/marketing, education, social sciences and history **Academic program** English as a second language, advanced placement, accelerated degree program, self-designed majors, honors program, summer session, adult/continuing education programs, internships **Contact** Mr. Allen S. London, Associate Vice President for Freshman Admissions, Mercer University, 1400 Coleman Avenue, Macon, GA 31207-0003. Telephone: 478-301-2650 or toll-free 800-840-8577. Fax: 478-301-2828. E-mail: admissions@mercer.edu. Web site: http://www.mercer.edu/.

MOREHOUSE COLLEGE
ATLANTA, GEORGIA

General Independent, 4-year, men only **Entrance** Moderately difficult **Setting** 61-acre urban campus **Total enrollment** 2,808 **Student-faculty ratio** 15:1 **Application deadline** 2/15 (freshmen), 2/15 (transfer) **Freshmen** 76% were admitted **Housing** Yes **Expenses** Tuition $12,432; Room & Board $7382 **Undergraduates** 5% part-time, 5% 25 or older, 0% Native American, 0.1% Hispanic American, 93% African American, 0.1% Asian American/Pacific Islander **The most frequently chosen baccalaureate fields are** business/marketing, biological/life sciences, foreign language/literature **Academic program** Advanced placement, honors program, summer session, internships **Contact** Mr. Terrance Dixon, Associate Dean for Admissions and Recruitment, Morehouse College, 830 Westview Drive, SW, Atlanta, GA 30314. Telephone: 404-215-2632 or toll-free 800-851-1254. Fax: 404-524-5635. E-mail: admissions@morehouse.edu. Web site: http://www.morehouse.edu/.

MORRIS BROWN COLLEGE
ATLANTA, GEORGIA

General Independent, 4-year, coed, affiliated with African Methodist Episcopal Church **Entrance** Minimally difficult **Setting** 21-acre urban campus **Total enrollment** 2,874 **Student-faculty ratio** 21:1 **Application deadline** Rolling (freshmen), rolling (transfer) **Freshmen** 67% were admitted **Housing** Yes **Expenses** Tuition $10,866; Room & Board $5870 **Undergraduates** 57% women, 3% part-time, 10% 25 or older, 0.03% Native American, 0.1% Hispanic American, 95% African American, 0.2% Asian American/Pacific Islander **The most frequently chosen baccalaureate fields are** business/marketing, psychology, social sciences and history **Academic program** English as a second language, accelerated degree program, honors program, adult/continuing education programs, internships **Contact** Ms. Karla Heyward, Interim Director, Morris Brown College, 643 Martin Luther King Jr. Drive, NW, Atlanta, GA 30314. Telephone: 404-739-1560. Fax: 404-739-1565. E-mail: admissions@morrisbrown.edu. Web site: http://www.morrisbrown.edu/.

NORTH GEORGIA COLLEGE & STATE UNIVERSITY
DAHLONEGA, GEORGIA

General State-supported, comprehensive, coed **Entrance** Moderately difficult **Setting** 140-acre small-town campus **Total enrollment** 3,864 **Student-faculty ratio** 13:1 **Application deadline** 7/1 (freshmen), rolling (transfer) **Freshmen** 59% were admitted **Housing** Yes **Expenses** Tuition $2496; Room & Board $3826 **Undergraduates** 65% women, 19% part-time, 6% 25 or older, 1% Native American, 1% Hispanic American, 3% African American, 1% Asian American/Pacific Islander **The most frequently chosen baccalaureate fields are** business/marketing, education, protective services/public administration **Academic program** Advanced placement, honors program, summer session, internships **Contact** Robert J. LaVerriere, Director of Admissions and Recruitment, North Georgia College & State University, Admissions Center, 32 College Circle, Dahlonega, GA 30597. Telephone: 706-864-1800 or toll-free 800-498-9581. Fax: 706-864-1478. E-mail: tdavis@nugget.ngc.peachnet.edu. Web site: http://www.ngcsu.edu/.

OGLETHORPE UNIVERSITY
ATLANTA, GEORGIA

General Independent, comprehensive, coed **Entrance** Very difficult **Setting** 118-acre suburban campus **Total enrollment** 1,267 **Student-faculty ratio** 13:1 **Application deadline** Rolling (freshmen), rolling (transfer) **Freshmen** 70% were admitted **Housing** Yes **Expenses** Tuition $19,100; Room & Board $6060 **Undergraduates** 67% women, 19% part-time, 5% 25 or older **The most frequently chosen baccalaureate field is** philosophy, religion, and theology **Academic program** Advanced placement, accelerated degree program, self-designed majors, honors program, summer session, adult/continuing education programs, internships **Contact** Mr. Dennis T. Matthews, Associate Dean for Enrollment Management, Oglethorpe University, 4484 Peachtree Road, NE, Atlanta, GA 30319-2797. Telephone: 404-364-8307 or toll-free 800-428-4484. Fax: 404-364-8500. E-mail: admission@oglethorpe.edu. Web site: http://www.oglethorpe.edu/.

GEORGIA

PAINE COLLEGE
AUGUSTA, GEORGIA

General Independent Methodist, 4-year, coed **Entrance** Minimally difficult **Setting** 54-acre urban campus **Total enrollment** 888 **Student-faculty ratio** 12:1 **Application deadline** 8/1 (freshmen), 8/1 (transfer) **Freshmen** 28% were admitted **Housing** Yes **Expenses** Tuition $8290; Room & Board $3606 **Undergraduates** 71% women, 16% part-time, 19% 25 or older, 0% Native American, 0.3% Hispanic American, 98% African American, 0.1% Asian American/Pacific Islander **The most frequently chosen baccalaureate fields are** business/marketing, psychology, social sciences and history **Academic program** Advanced placement, accelerated degree program, honors program, summer session, internships **Contact** Mr. Joseph Tinsley, Director of Admissions, Paine College, 1235 15th Street, Augusta, GA 30901-3182. Telephone: 706-821-8320 or toll-free 800-476-7703. Fax: 706-821-8691. E-mail: tinsleyj@mail.paine.edu. Web site: http://www.paine.edu/.

PIEDMONT COLLEGE
DEMOREST, GEORGIA

General Independent, comprehensive, coed, affiliated with Congregational Christian Church **Entrance** Moderately difficult **Setting** 115-acre rural campus **Total enrollment** 1,933 **Student-faculty ratio** 12:1 **Application deadline** Rolling (freshmen), rolling (transfer) **Freshmen** 67% were admitted **Housing** Yes **Expenses** Tuition $10,500; Room & Board $4400 **Undergraduates** 63% women, 15% part-time, 28% 25 or older, 0.2% Native American, 2% Hispanic American, 8% African American, 1% Asian American/Pacific Islander **The most frequently chosen baccalaureate fields are** business/marketing, education, social sciences and history **Academic program** Advanced placement, accelerated degree program, self-designed majors, honors program, summer session, adult/continuing education programs, internships **Contact** Ms. Kathy Edwards Rarey, Director of Undergraduate Admissions, Piedmont College, PO Box 10, Demorest, GA 30535-0010. Telephone: 706-776-0103 Ext. 1299 or toll-free 800-277-7020. Fax: 706-776-6635. E-mail: kedwards@piedmont.edu. Web site: http://www.piedmont.edu/.

REINHARDT COLLEGE
WALESKA, GEORGIA

General Independent, 4-year, coed, affiliated with United Methodist Church **Entrance** Moderately difficult **Setting** 600-acre rural campus **Total enrollment** 1,083 **Student-faculty ratio** 15:1 **Application deadline** Rolling (freshmen), rolling (transfer) **Freshmen** 85% were admitted **Housing** Yes **Expenses** Tuition $8700; Room & Board $4885 **Undergraduates** 59% women, 13% part-time, 32% 25 or older **The most frequently chosen baccalaureate fields are** business/marketing, communications/communication technologies, education **Academic program** Advanced placement, honors program, summer session, adult/continuing education programs, internships **Contact** Ms. Kathryn Smith, Director of Admissions, Reinhardt College, 7300 Reinhardt College Circle, Waleska, GA 30183-0128. Telephone: 770-720-5526 or toll-free 87-REINHARDT. Fax: 770-720-5602. E-mail: admissions@mail.reinhardt.edu. Web site: http://www.reinhardt.edu/.

SAVANNAH COLLEGE OF ART AND DESIGN
SAVANNAH, GEORGIA

General Independent, comprehensive, coed **Entrance** Moderately difficult **Setting** urban campus **Total enrollment** 5,338 **Student-faculty ratio** 18:1 **Application deadline** Rolling (freshmen), rolling (transfer) **Freshmen** 84% were admitted **Housing** Yes **Expenses** Tuition $17,325; Room & Board $7200 **Undergraduates** 46% women, 10% part-time, 9% 25 or older, 0.3% Native American, 3% Hispanic American, 5% African American, 2% Asian American/Pacific Islander **The most frequently chosen baccalaureate fields are** architecture, visual/performing arts **Academic program** English as a second language, advanced placement, summer session, internships **Contact** Ms. Pamela Afifi, Vice President for Admission, Savannah College of Art and Design, 342 Bull Street, PO Box 3146, Savannah, GA 31402-3146. Telephone: 912-525-5100 or toll-free 800-869-7223. Fax: 912-525-5983. E-mail: admission@scad.edu. Web site: http://www.scad.edu/.

▶ For more information, see page 473.

SAVANNAH STATE UNIVERSITY
SAVANNAH, GEORGIA

General State-supported, comprehensive, coed **Entrance** Minimally difficult **Setting** 165-acre suburban campus **Total enrollment** 2,360 **Student-faculty ratio** 16:1 **Application deadline** 6/1 (freshmen), 6/1 (transfer) **Freshmen** 27% were admitted **Housing** Yes **Expenses** Tuition $2550; Room & Board $4204 **Academic program** Advanced placement, accelerated degree program, summer session, adult/continuing education programs, internships **Contact** Mrs. Gwendolyn J. Moore, Associate Director of Admissions, Savannah State University, PO Box 20209, Savannah, GA 31404. Telephone: 912-356-2181 or toll-free 800-788-0478. Fax: 912-356-2566. Web site: http://www.savstate.edu/.

SHORTER COLLEGE
ROME, GEORGIA

General Independent Baptist, comprehensive, coed **Entrance** Moderately difficult **Setting** 155-acre small-town campus **Total enrollment** 970 **Student-faculty ratio** 12:1 **Application deadline** 8/25 (freshmen), 8/25 (transfer) **Freshmen** 86% were admitted **Housing** Yes **Expenses** Tuition $9920; Room & Board $5265 **Undergraduates** 67% women, 5% part-time, 7% 25 or older, 1% Native American, 1% Hispanic American, 4% African American, 1% Asian American/Pacific Islander **The most frequently cho-

GEORGIA

sen baccalaureate fields are biological/life sciences, education, philosophy **Academic program** Advanced placement, accelerated degree program, self-designed majors, honors program, summer session, adult/continuing education programs, internships **Contact** Ms. Wendy Sutton, Director of Admissions, Shorter College, 315 Shorter Avenue, Rome, GA 30165. Telephone: 706-233-7342 or toll-free 800-868-6980. Fax: 706-236-7224. E-mail: admissions@shorter.edu. Web site: http://www.shorter.edu/.

SOUTHERN POLYTECHNIC STATE UNIVERSITY
MARIETTA, GEORGIA

General State-supported, comprehensive, coed **Entrance** Moderately difficult **Setting** 200-acre suburban campus **Total enrollment** 3,397 **Student-faculty ratio** 17:1 **Application deadline** 8/1 (freshmen), 8/1 (transfer) **Freshmen** 61% were admitted **Housing** Yes **Expenses** Tuition $2354; Room & Board $4308 **Undergraduates** 17% women, 40% part-time, 37% 25 or older, 0.2% Native American, 3% Hispanic American, 19% African American, 6% Asian American/Pacific Islander **The most frequently chosen baccalaureate fields are** computer/information sciences, business/marketing, engineering/engineering technologies **Academic program** Advanced placement, summer session, adult/continuing education programs, internships **Contact** Ms. Virginia A. Head, Director of Admissions, Southern Polytechnic State University, 1100 South Marietta Parkway, Marietta, GA 30060-2896. Telephone: 770-528-7281 or toll-free 800-635-3204. Fax: 770-528-7292. E-mail: admissions@spsu.edu. Web site: http://www.spsu.edu/.

SOUTH UNIVERSITY
SAVANNAH, GEORGIA

General Proprietary, 4-year, coed **Entrance** Minimally difficult **Setting** 6-acre suburban campus **Total enrollment** 483 **Application deadline** Rolling (freshmen), rolling (transfer) **Housing** No **Expenses** Tuition $10,396 **Undergraduates** 75% women, 20% part-time, 53% 25 or older, 0% Native American, 3% Hispanic American, 33% African American, 1% Asian American/Pacific Islander **Academic program** Accelerated degree program, summer session, adult/continuing education programs, internships **Contact** Ms. Deborah Welsh, Director of Admissions, South University, 709 Mall Boulevard, Savannah, GA 31406-4881. Telephone: 912-691-6000. Fax: 912-691-6070. E-mail: southcollege@southcollege.edu. Web site: http://www.southuniversity.edu/.

SPELMAN COLLEGE
ATLANTA, GEORGIA

General Independent, 4-year, women only **Entrance** Very difficult **Setting** 32-acre urban campus **Total enrollment** 2,139 **Student-faculty ratio** 12:1 **Application deadline** 2/1 (freshmen), 2/1 (transfer) **Freshmen** 49% were admitted **Housing** Yes **Expenses** Tuition $11,880; Room & Board $7350 **Undergradu**ates 3% part-time, 3% 25 or older, 0% Native American, 0.2% Hispanic American, 97% African American, 0% Asian American/Pacific Islander **The most frequently chosen baccalaureate fields are** psychology, English, social sciences and history **Academic program** Advanced placement, self-designed majors, honors program, adult/continuing education programs, internships **Contact** Ms. Theodora Riley, Interim Director of Admissions and Orientation Services, Spelman College, 350 Spelman Lane, SW, Atlanta, GA 30314-4399. Telephone: 404-681-3643 Ext. 2585 or toll-free 800-982-2411 (out-of-state). Fax: 404-215-7788. E-mail: admiss@spelman.edu. Web site: http://www.spelman.edu/.

STATE UNIVERSITY OF WEST GEORGIA
CARROLLTON, GEORGIA

General State-supported, comprehensive, coed **Entrance** Minimally difficult **Setting** 400-acre small-town campus **Total enrollment** 9,040 **Student-faculty ratio** 19:1 **Application deadline** 7/31 (freshmen), 6/15 (transfer) **Freshmen** 60% were admitted **Housing** Yes **Expenses** Tuition $2468; Room & Board $4100 **Undergraduates** 61% women, 17% part-time, 14% 25 or older, 0.3% Native American, 1% Hispanic American, 22% African American, 1% Asian American/Pacific Islander **The most frequently chosen baccalaureate fields are** business/marketing, education, social sciences and history **Academic program** Advanced placement, accelerated degree program, honors program, summer session, adult/continuing education programs, internships **Contact** Dr. Robert Johnson, Director of Admissions, State University of West Georgia, 1600 Maple Street, Carrollton, GA 30118. Telephone: 770-836-6416. Fax: 770-836-4659. E-mail: rjohnson@westga.edu. Web site: http://www.westga.edu/.

THOMAS UNIVERSITY
THOMASVILLE, GEORGIA

General Independent, comprehensive, coed **Entrance** Noncompetitive **Setting** 24-acre small-town campus **Total enrollment** 642 **Student-faculty ratio** 10:1 **Application deadline** Rolling (freshmen), rolling (transfer) **Freshmen** 100% were admitted **Housing** Yes **Expenses** Tuition $7870; Room only $2400 **Undergraduates** 69% women, 25% part-time, 46% 25 or older, 0.2% Native American, 0% Hispanic American, 26% African American, 1% Asian American/Pacific Islander **The most frequently chosen baccalaureate fields are** health professions and related sciences, business/marketing, protective services/public administration **Academic program** Advanced placement, accelerated degree program, summer session, adult/continuing education programs, internships **Contact** Darla M. Glass, Director of Student Affairs, Thomas University, 1501 Millpond Road, Thomasville, GA 31792-7499. Telephone: 229-226-1621 Ext. 122 or toll-free 800-538-9784. Fax: 229-227-1653. Web site: http://www.thomasu.edu/.

GEORGIA

TOCCOA FALLS COLLEGE
TOCCOA FALLS, GEORGIA

General Independent interdenominational, 4-year, coed **Entrance** Moderately difficult **Setting** 1,100-acre small-town campus **Total enrollment** 916 **Student-faculty ratio** 14:1 **Application deadline** Rolling (freshmen), rolling (transfer) **Freshmen** 82% were admitted **Housing** Yes **Expenses** Tuition $9600; Room & Board $4170 **Undergraduates** 57% women, 8% part-time, 10% 25 or older, 0.1% Native American, 2% Hispanic American, 2% African American, 4% Asian American/Pacific Islander **The most frequently chosen baccalaureate fields are** philosophy, philosophy, religion, and theology, psychology **Academic program** Advanced placement, accelerated degree program, summer session, internships **Contact** Director of Admissions, Toccoa Falls College, Office of Admissions, PO Box 899, Toccoa Falls, GA 30598-1000. Telephone: 706-886-6831 or toll-free 800-868-3257. Fax: 706-282-6012. E-mail: admissions@toccoafalls.edu. Web site: http://www.toccoafalls.edu/.

UNIVERSITY OF GEORGIA
ATHENS, GEORGIA

General State-supported, university, coed **Entrance** Moderately difficult **Setting** 1,289-acre suburban campus **Total enrollment** 32,317 **Student-faculty ratio** 12:1 **Application deadline** 1/15 (freshmen), 6/1 (transfer) **Freshmen** 62% were admitted **Housing** Yes **Expenses** Tuition $3418; Room & Board $5388 **Undergraduates** 6% 25 or older, 0.2% Native American, 1% Hispanic American, 6% African American, 3% Asian American/Pacific Islander **The most frequently chosen baccalaureate fields are** business/marketing, education, social sciences and history **Academic program** English as a second language, advanced placement, accelerated degree program, self-designed majors, honors program, summer session, adult/continuing education programs, internships **Contact** Dr. John Albright, Associate Director of Admissions, University of Georgia, Athens, GA 30602. Telephone: 706-542-3000. E-mail: undergrad@admissions.uga.edu. Web site: http://www.uga.edu/.

UNIVERSITY OF PHOENIX-ATLANTA CAMPUS
ATLANTA, GEORGIA

General Proprietary, comprehensive, coed **Total enrollment** 88,730 **Housing** No **Expenses** Tuition $8550 **Contact** University of Phoenix-Atlanta Campus, 7000 Central Parkway, Suite 1700, Atlanta, GA 30328. Web site: http://www.phoenix.edu/.

VALDOSTA STATE UNIVERSITY
VALDOSTA, GEORGIA

General State-supported, university, coed **Entrance** Moderately difficult **Setting** 200-acre small-town campus **Total enrollment** 9,238 **Student-faculty ratio** 19:1 **Application deadline** 8/1 (freshmen), 8/1 (transfer) **Freshmen** 66% were admitted **Housing** Yes **Expenses** Tuition $2526; Room & Board $4462 **Undergraduates** 60% women, 22% part-time, 23% 25 or older, 0.2% Native American, 1% Hispanic American, 21% African American, 1% Asian American/Pacific Islander **The most frequently chosen baccalaureate fields are** education, health professions and related sciences, social sciences and history **Academic program** English as a second language, advanced placement, accelerated degree program, honors program, summer session, adult/continuing education programs, internships **Contact** Mr. Walter Peacock, Director of Admissions, Valdosta State University, 1500 North Patterson Street, Valdosta, GA 31698. Telephone: 229-333-5791 or toll-free 800-618-1878 Ext. 1. Fax: 229-333-5482. E-mail: admissions@valdosta.edu. Web site: http://www.valdosta.edu/.

WESLEYAN COLLEGE
MACON, GEORGIA

General Independent United Methodist, comprehensive, women only **Entrance** Moderately difficult **Setting** 200-acre suburban campus **Total enrollment** 721 **Student-faculty ratio** 11:1 **Application deadline** 6/1 (freshmen), rolling (transfer) **Freshmen** 74% were admitted **Housing** Yes **Expenses** Tuition $9800; Room & Board $7250 **Undergraduates** 22% part-time, 27% 25 or older, 0.3% Native American, 2% Hispanic American, 28% African American, 3% Asian American/Pacific Islander **The most frequently chosen baccalaureate fields are** business/marketing, communications/communication technologies, psychology **Academic program** Advanced placement, accelerated degree program, self-designed majors, honors program, summer session, adult/continuing education programs, internships **Contact** Mr. Jonathan Stroud, Vice President for Enrollment and Marketing, Wesleyan College, 4760 Forsyth Road, Macon, GA 31210-4462. Telephone: 478-757-5206 or toll-free 800-447-6610. Fax: 478-757-4030. E-mail: admissions@wesleyancollege.edu. Web site: http://www.wesleyancollege.edu/.

HAWAII

BRIGHAM YOUNG UNIVERSITY-HAWAII
LAIE, HAWAII

General Independent Latter-day Saints, 4-year, coed **Entrance** Moderately difficult **Setting** 60-acre small-town campus **Total enrollment** 2,278 **Student-faculty ratio** 21:1 **Application deadline** 2/15 (freshmen), 3/15 (transfer) **Freshmen** 10% were admitted **Housing** Yes **Expenses** Tuition $3113; Room & Board $5500 **Undergraduates** 57% women, 4% part-time, 23% 25 or older, 0.3% Native American, 2% Hispanic American, 0.4% African American, 16% Asian American/Pacific Islander **The most frequently chosen baccalaureate fields are** business/marketing, computer/information sciences, education

HAWAII

Academic program English as a second language, advanced placement, accelerated degree program, honors program, summer session, adult/continuing education programs, internships **Contact** Mr. Jeffrey N. Bunker, Dean for Admissions and Records, Brigham Young University–Hawaii, 55-220 Kulanui Street, Laie, Oahu, HI 96762. Telephone: 808-293-7010. Web site: http://www.byuh.edu/.

CHAMINADE UNIVERSITY OF HONOLULU
HONOLULU, HAWAII

General Independent Roman Catholic, comprehensive, coed **Entrance** Moderately difficult **Setting** 62-acre urban campus **Total enrollment** 2,547 **Student-faculty ratio** 16:1 **Application deadline** Rolling (freshmen), rolling (transfer) **Freshmen** 69% were admitted **Housing** Yes **Expenses** Tuition $12,705; Room & Board $5990 **Undergraduates** 60% women, 39% part-time, 40% 25 or older, 2% Native American, 8% Hispanic American, 12% African American, 37% Asian American/Pacific Islander **The most frequently chosen baccalaureate field is** philosophy, religion, and theology **Academic program** Advanced placement, accelerated degree program, self-designed majors, summer session, adult/continuing education programs, internships **Contact** Office of Admissions, Chaminade University of Honolulu, 3140 Waialae Avenue, Honolulu, HI 96816-1578. Telephone: 808-735-4735 or toll-free 800-735-3733 (out-of-state). Fax: 808-739-4647. E-mail: cuhadmin@lava.net. Web site: http://www.chaminade.edu/.

▶ For more information, see page 410.

EDUCATION AMERICA, HONOLULU CAMPUS
HONOLULU, HAWAII

Contact Education America, Honolulu Campus, 1111 Bishop Street, Suite 400, Honolulu, HI 96813.

HAWAI'I PACIFIC UNIVERSITY
HONOLULU, HAWAII

General Independent, comprehensive, coed **Entrance** Moderately difficult **Setting** 140-acre urban campus **Total enrollment** 8,033 **Student-faculty ratio** 17:1 **Application deadline** Rolling (freshmen), rolling (transfer) **Freshmen** 81% were admitted **Housing** Yes **Expenses** Tuition $9360; Room & Board $8430 **Undergraduates** 55% women, 37% part-time, 35% 25 or older, 1% Native American, 5% Hispanic American, 10% African American, 30% Asian American/Pacific Islander **The most frequently chosen baccalaureate fields are** business/marketing, health professions and related sciences, protective services/public administration **Academic program** English as a second language, advanced placement, accelerated degree program, self-designed majors, honors program, summer session, adult/continuing education programs, internships **Contact** Mr. Scott Stensrud, Associate Vice President Enrollment Management, Hawai'i Pacific University, 1164 Bishop Street, Honolulu, HI 96813-2785. Telephone: 808-544-0238 or toll-free 800-669-4724 (out-of-state). Fax: 808-544-1136. E-mail: admissions@hpu.edu. Web site: http://www.hpu.edu/.

▶ For more information, see page 438.

INTERNATIONAL COLLEGE AND GRADUATE SCHOOL
HONOLULU, HAWAII

General Independent interdenominational, upper-level, coed **Total enrollment** 43 **Student-faculty ratio** 12:1 **Application deadline** Rolling (transfer) **Housing** No **Expenses** Tuition $4360 **Undergraduates** 32% women, 79% part-time, 68% 25 or older, 0% Native American, 0% Hispanic American, 0% African American, 42% Asian American/Pacific Islander **Academic program** Advanced placement, summer session, adult/continuing education programs, internships **Contact** Mr. Jon Rawlings, Director of Admissions, International College and Graduate School, 20 Dowsett Avenue, Honolulu, HI 96817. Telephone: 808-595-4247. Fax: 808-595-4779. E-mail: icgs@pixi.com. Web site: http://www.icgshawaii.org/.

UNIVERSITY OF HAWAII AT HILO
HILO, HAWAII

General State-supported, comprehensive, coed **Entrance** Moderately difficult **Setting** 115-acre small-town campus **Total enrollment** 2,913 **Student-faculty ratio** 14:1 **Application deadline** 7/1 (freshmen), 7/1 (transfer) **Freshmen** 63% were admitted **Housing** Yes **Expenses** Tuition $1562; Room & Board $4839 **Undergraduates** 60% women, 20% part-time, 31% 25 or older, 1% Native American, 2% Hispanic American, 1% African American, 47% Asian American/Pacific Islander **The most frequently chosen baccalaureate fields are** physical sciences, psychology, social sciences and history **Academic program** English as a second language, advanced placement, self-designed majors, honors program, summer session, internships **Contact** Mr. James Cromwell, UH Student Services Specialist III/Director of Admissions, University of Hawaii at Hilo, 200 West Kawili Street, Hilo, HI 96720-4091. Telephone: 808-974-7414 or toll-free 808-974-7414 (in-state); 800-897-4456 (out-of-state). E-mail: uhhao@hawaii.edu. Web site: http://www.uhh.hawaii.edu/.

UNIVERSITY OF HAWAII AT MANOA
HONOLULU, HAWAII

General State-supported, university, coed **Entrance** Moderately difficult **Setting** 300-acre urban campus **Total enrollment** 17,532 **Student-faculty ratio** 12:1 **Application deadline** 6/1 (freshmen), 6/1 (transfer) **Freshmen** 71% were admitted **Housing** Yes **Expenses** Room & Board $5089 **Undergraduates** 56% women, 17% part-time, 19% 25 or older, 0.2% Native American, 2% Hispanic American, 1% African American, 72% Asian American/Pacific Islander **The most frequently chosen baccalaureate fields are** business/marketing, education, social sciences and history **Academic program** English as a second language,

HAWAII

University of Hawaii at Manoa *(continued)* advanced placement, accelerated degree program, self-designed majors, honors program, summer session, adult/continuing education programs, internships **Contact** Ms. Janice Heu, Interim Director of Admissions and Records, University of Hawaii at Manoa, 2600 Campus Road, Room 001, Honolulu, HI 96822. Telephone: 808-956-8975 or toll-free 800-823-9771. Fax: 808-956-4148. E-mail: ar-info@hawaii.edu. Web site: http://www.uhm.hawaii.edu/.

UNIVERSITY OF HAWAII–WEST OAHU
PEARL CITY, HAWAII

General State-supported, upper-level, coed **Entrance** Moderately difficult **Setting** small-town campus **Total enrollment** 740 **Student-faculty ratio** 13:1 **Application deadline** 8/1 (transfer) **First-Year Students** 77% were admitted **Housing** No **Expenses** Tuition $1978 **Undergraduates** 65% women, 58% part-time, 76% 25 or older, 0% Native American, 2% Hispanic American, 1% African American, 58% Asian American/Pacific Islander **Academic program** Summer session, internships **Contact** Jean M. Osumi, Dean of Student Services, University of Hawaii–West Oahu, 96-043 Ala Ike, Pearl City, HI 96782. Telephone: 808-453-4700. Fax: 805-453-6076. E-mail: jeano@uhwo.hawaii.edu.

UNIVERSITY OF PHOENIX–HAWAII CAMPUS
HONOLULU, HAWAII

General Proprietary, comprehensive, coed **Entrance** Noncompetitive **Total enrollment** 88,370 **Student-faculty ratio** 10:1 **Application deadline** Rolling (freshmen), rolling (transfer) **Housing** No **Expenses** Tuition $9360 **Undergraduates** 57% women, 75% 25 or older **The most frequently chosen baccalaureate fields are** business/marketing, health professions and related sciences **Academic program** Advanced placement, accelerated degree program, adult/continuing education programs **Contact** Ms. Beth Barilla, Director of Admissions, University of Phoenix–Hawaii Campus, 4615 East Elwood Street, Phoenix, AZ 85040-1958. Telephone: 480-927-0099 Ext. 1218 or toll-free 800-228-7240 (out-of-state). Fax: 480-594-1758. E-mail: beth.barilla@apollogrp.edu. Web site: http://www.phoenix.edu/.

IDAHO

ALBERTSON COLLEGE OF IDAHO
CALDWELL, IDAHO

General Independent, 4-year, coed **Entrance** Moderately difficult **Setting** 43-acre small-town campus **Total enrollment** 778 **Student-faculty ratio** 11:1 **Application deadline** 6/1 (freshmen), 8/1 (transfer) **Freshmen** 98% were admitted **Housing** Yes **Expenses** Tuition $17,040; Room & Board $4400 **Undergraduates** 54% women, 3% part-time, 3% 25 or older, 1% Native American, 4% Hispanic American, 1% African American, 4% Asian American/Pacific Islander **The most frequently chosen baccalaureate fields are** biological/life sciences, business/marketing, social sciences and history **Academic program** English as a second language, advanced placement, self-designed majors, honors program, internships **Contact** Brandie Allemand, Associate Dean of Admission, Albertson College of Idaho, 2112 Cleveland Boulevard, Caldwell, ID 83605-4494. Telephone: 208-459-5305 or toll-free 800-224-3246. Fax: 208-459-5757. E-mail: admission@albertson.edu. Web site: http://www.albertson.edu/.

BOISE BIBLE COLLEGE
BOISE, IDAHO

General Independent nondenominational, 4-year, coed **Entrance** Minimally difficult **Setting** 17-acre suburban campus **Total enrollment** 111 **Student-faculty ratio** 13:1 **Application deadline** Rolling (freshmen), rolling (transfer) **Freshmen** 94% were admitted **Housing** Yes **Expenses** Tuition $5470; Room & Board $4000 **Undergraduates** 44% women, 12% part-time, 24% 25 or older **The most frequently chosen baccalaureate fields are** philosophy, philosophy, religion, and theology **Academic program** Advanced placement, adult/continuing education programs, internships **Contact** Mr. Ross Knudsen, Director of Admissions, Boise Bible College, 8695 Marigold Street, Boise, ID 83704. Telephone: 208-376-7731 or toll-free 800-893-7755. Fax: 208-376-7743. E-mail: boibible@micron.net. Web site: http://www.boisebible.edu/.

BOISE STATE UNIVERSITY
BOISE, IDAHO

General State-supported, comprehensive, coed **Entrance** Minimally difficult **Setting** 130-acre urban campus **Total enrollment** 17,100 **Student-faculty ratio** 19:1 **Application deadline** 7/17 (freshmen), 7/17 (transfer) **Freshmen** 92% were admitted **Housing** Yes **Expenses** Tuition $2665; Room & Board $3869 **Undergraduates** 54% women, 40% part-time, 44% 25 or older, 1% Native American, 5% Hispanic American, 1% African American, 2% Asian American/Pacific Islander **The most frequently chosen baccalaureate fields are** business/marketing, education, social sciences and history **Academic program** English as a second language, advanced placement, self-designed majors, honors program, summer session, adult/continuing education programs, internships **Contact** Mr. Mark Wheeler, Dean of Enrollment Services, Boise State University, Enrollment Services, 1910 University Drive, Boise, ID 83725. Telephone: 208-426-1177 or toll-free 800-632-6586 (in-state); 800-824-7017 (out-of-state). E-mail: bsuinfo@boisestate.edu. Web site: http://www.boisestate.edu/.

ILLINOIS

IDAHO STATE UNIVERSITY
POCATELLO, IDAHO

General State-supported, university, coed **Entrance** Minimally difficult **Setting** 735-acre small-town campus **Total enrollment** 13,663 **Student-faculty ratio** 17:1 **Application deadline** 8/1 (freshmen), 8/1 (transfer) **Freshmen** 71% were admitted **Housing** Yes **Expenses** Room & Board $4230 **Undergraduates** 55% women, 33% part-time, 29% 25 or older, 2% Native American, 3% Hispanic American, 1% African American, 1% Asian American/Pacific Islander **The most frequently chosen baccalaureate fields are** business/marketing, education, health professions and related sciences **Academic program** English as a second language, advanced placement, self-designed majors, honors program, summer session, adult/continuing education programs, internships **Contact** Linda Ann Barnier, Director of Recruitment, Idaho State University, Campus Box 8270, Pocatello, ID 83209. Telephone: 208-282-3279. Fax: 208-282-4231. E-mail: echamike@isu.edu. Web site: http://www.isu.edu/.

▶ For more information, see page 441.

LEWIS-CLARK STATE COLLEGE
LEWISTON, IDAHO

General State-supported, 4-year, coed **Entrance** Minimally difficult **Setting** 44-acre small-town campus **Total enrollment** 2,953 **Student-faculty ratio** 17:1 **Application deadline** Rolling (freshmen), rolling (transfer) **Freshmen** 64% were admitted **Housing** Yes **Expenses** Tuition $5100; Room & Board $2970 **Undergraduates** 62% women, 26% part-time, 34% 25 or older, 5% Native American, 2% Hispanic American, 1% African American, 1% Asian American/Pacific Islander **The most frequently chosen baccalaureate fields are** business/marketing, education, protective services/public administration **Academic program** English as a second language, advanced placement, accelerated degree program, self-designed majors, honors program, summer session, adult/continuing education programs, internships **Contact** Ms. Rosanne English, Office Specialist II, Lewis-Clark State College, 500 8th Avenue, Lewiston, ID 83501. Telephone: 208-792-2210 or toll-free 800-933-LCSC Ext. 2210. Fax: 208-792-2876. E-mail: sbussoli@lcsc.edu. Web site: http://www.lcsc.edu/.

NORTHWEST NAZARENE UNIVERSITY
NAMPA, IDAHO

General Independent, comprehensive, coed, affiliated with Church of the Nazarene **Entrance** Moderately difficult **Setting** 85-acre small-town campus **Total enrollment** 1,316 **Student-faculty ratio** 12:1 **Application deadline** 8/27 (freshmen), 8/27 (transfer) **Freshmen** 77% were admitted **Housing** Yes **Expenses** Tuition $14,240; Room & Board $4140 **Undergraduates** 55% women, 9% part-time, 7% 25 or older, 1% Native American, 2% Hispanic American, 1% African American, 1% Asian American/ Pacific Islander **The most frequently chosen baccalaureate field is** philosophy, religion, and theology **Academic program** Advanced placement, accelerated degree program, self-designed majors, honors program, summer session, internships **Contact** Ms. Stacey Berggren, Director of Admissions, Northwest Nazarene University, 623 Holly Street, Nampa, ID 83686. Telephone: 208-467-8648 or toll-free 877-NNU-4YOU. Fax: 208-467-8645. E-mail: admissions@nnu.edu. Web site: http://www.nnu.edu/.

UNIVERSITY OF IDAHO
MOSCOW, IDAHO

General State-supported, university, coed **Entrance** Moderately difficult **Setting** 1,450-acre small-town campus **Total enrollment** 12,067 **Student-faculty ratio** 17:1 **Application deadline** 8/1 (freshmen), rolling (transfer) **Freshmen** 84% were admitted **Housing** Yes **Expenses** Tuition $2720; Room & Board $4306 **Undergraduates** 46% women, 13% part-time, 14% 25 or older, 1% Native American, 3% Hispanic American, 1% African American, 2% Asian American/Pacific Islander **The most frequently chosen baccalaureate fields are** business/marketing, education, engineering/engineering technologies **Academic program** Advanced placement, accelerated degree program, self-designed majors, honors program, summer session, adult/continuing education programs, internships **Contact** Mr. Dan Davenport, Director of Admissions, University of Idaho, Admissions Office, PO Box 444264, Moscow, ID 83844-4264. Telephone: 208-885-6326 or toll-free 888-884-3246 (out-of-state). Fax: 208-885-9119. E-mail: admappl@uidaho.edu. Web site: http://www.its.uidaho.edu/uihome/.

UNIVERSITY OF PHOENIX-IDAHO CAMPUS
BOISE, IDAHO

General Proprietary, comprehensive, coed **Total enrollment** 88,730 **Housing** No **Expenses** Tuition $7860 **Contact** University of Phoenix-Idaho Campus, 6148 North Discovery Way, Suite 120, Boise, ID 83713. Web site: http://www.phoenix.edu/.

ILLINOIS

AMERICAN ACADEMY OF ART
CHICAGO, ILLINOIS

General Proprietary, 4-year, coed **Entrance** Moderately difficult **Setting** urban campus **Total enrollment** 360 **Student-faculty ratio** 13:1 **Application deadline** Rolling (freshmen), rolling (transfer) **Freshmen** 100% were admitted **Housing** No **Expenses** Tuition $15,880 **Undergraduates** 34% women, 24% part-time, 13% 25 or older, 0% Native American, 24% Hispanic American, 9% African American, 3% Asian American/Pacific Islander **The most fre-

ILLINOIS

American Academy of Art *(continued)*
quently chosen baccalaureate field is visual/performing arts **Academic program** Accelerated degree program, summer session, adult/continuing education programs, internships **Contact** Ms. Ione Fitzgerald, Director of Admissions, American Academy of Art, 332 South Michigan Ave, Suite 300, Chicago, IL 60604-4302. Telephone: 312-461-0600 Ext. 143. Web site: http://www.aaart.edu/.

AMERICAN INTERCONTINENTAL UNIVERSITY ONLINE
HOFFMAN ESTATES, ILLINOIS

General Proprietary, comprehensive, coed **Total enrollment** 196 **Student-faculty ratio** 19:1 **Application deadline** Rolling (freshmen), rolling (transfer) **Expenses** Tuition $20,175 **Undergraduates** 39% women, 3% Native American, 6% Hispanic American, 24% African American, 6% Asian American/Pacific Islander **Contact** Mr. Steve Fireng, Vice President of Admissions, American InterContinental University Online, 2895 Greenspoint Parkway, Suite 400, Hoffman Estates, IL 60195. Telephone: 877-701-3800 or toll-free 877-221-5800 Ext. 2604 (in-state); 877-701-3800 (out-of-state). E-mail: info@aiu-online.com. Web site: http://www.aiu-online.com/.

AUGUSTANA COLLEGE
ROCK ISLAND, ILLINOIS

General Independent, 4-year, coed, affiliated with Evangelical Lutheran Church in America **Entrance** Moderately difficult **Setting** 115-acre suburban campus **Total enrollment** 2,232 **Student-faculty ratio** 12:1 **Application deadline** Rolling (freshmen), rolling (transfer) **Freshmen** 77% were admitted **Housing** Yes **Expenses** Tuition $18,720; Room & Board $5397 **Undergraduates** 57% women, 1% part-time, 2% 25 or older, 0.1% Native American, 3% Hispanic American, 2% African American, 2% Asian American/Pacific Islander **The most frequently chosen baccalaureate fields are** biological/life sciences, business/marketing, health professions and related sciences **Academic program** Advanced placement, accelerated degree program, honors program, summer session, internships **Contact** Mr. Martin Sauer, Director of Admissions, Augustana College, 639 38th Street, Rock Island, IL 61201-2296. Telephone: 309-794-7341 or toll-free 800-798-8100. Fax: 309-794-7422. E-mail: admissions@augustana.edu. Web site: http://www.augustana.edu/.

AURORA UNIVERSITY
AURORA, ILLINOIS

General Independent, comprehensive, coed **Entrance** Moderately difficult **Setting** 26-acre suburban campus **Total enrollment** 2,801 **Student-faculty ratio** 16:1 **Application deadline** Rolling (freshmen), rolling (transfer) **Freshmen** 62% were admitted **Housing** Yes **Expenses** Tuition $13,767; Room & Board $5133 **Undergraduates** 60% women, 22% part-time, 40% 25 or older, 0.3% Native American, 10% Hispanic American, 17% African American, 2% Asian American/Pacific Islander **The most frequently chosen baccalaureate fields are** business/marketing, education, protective services/public administration **Academic program** Advanced placement, self-designed majors, summer session, adult/continuing education programs, internships **Contact** Mr. James Lancaster, Freshman Recruitment Coordinator, Aurora University, 347 South Gladstone Avenue, Aurora, IL 60506-4892. Telephone: 630-844-5533 or toll-free 800-742-5281. Fax: 630-844-5535. E-mail: admissions@aurora.edu. Web site: http://www.aurora.edu/.

BARAT COLLEGE
See DePaul University

BENEDICTINE UNIVERSITY
LISLE, ILLINOIS

General Independent Roman Catholic, comprehensive, coed **Entrance** Moderately difficult **Setting** 108-acre suburban campus **Total enrollment** 2,700 **Student-faculty ratio** 14:1 **Application deadline** Rolling (freshmen), rolling (transfer) **Freshmen** 66% were admitted **Housing** Yes **Expenses** Tuition $15,630; Room & Board $5700 **Undergraduates** 62% women, 31% part-time, 29% 25 or older, 0.2% Native American, 8% Hispanic American, 9% African American, 14% Asian American/Pacific Islander **The most frequently chosen baccalaureate fields are** biological/life sciences, business/marketing, education **Academic program** English as a second language, advanced placement, accelerated degree program, honors program, summer session, adult/continuing education programs, internships **Contact** Dean of Undergraduate Admissions, Benedictine University, 5700 College Road, Lisle, IL 60532-0900. Telephone: 630-829-6306 or toll-free 888-829-6363 (out-of-state). Fax: 630-960-1126. E-mail: admissions@ben.edu. Web site: http://www.ben.edu/.

▶ For more information, see page 399.

BLACKBURN COLLEGE
CARLINVILLE, ILLINOIS

General Independent Presbyterian, 4-year, coed **Entrance** Moderately difficult **Setting** 80-acre small-town campus **Total enrollment** 571 **Student-faculty ratio** 15:1 **Application deadline** Rolling (freshmen), rolling (transfer) **Freshmen** 68% were admitted **Housing** Yes **Expenses** Tuition $8720; Room & Board $3990 **Undergraduates** 56% women, 3% part-time, 1% Native American, 1% Hispanic American, 11% African American, 1% Asian American/Pacific Islander **The most frequently chosen baccalaureate fields are** business/marketing, biological/life sciences, education **Academic program** Advanced placement, accelerated degree program, self-designed majors, honors program, internships **Contact** Mr. John Malin, Director of Admissions, Blackburn College, 700 College Avenue, Carlinville, IL 62626-1498. Telephone: 217-854-3231 Ext. 4252 or toll-free 800-233-3550. Fax: 217-854-3713. E-mail: admit@mail.blackburn.edu.

ILLINOIS

BLESSING-RIEMAN COLLEGE OF NURSING
QUINCY, ILLINOIS

General Independent, 4-year, coed, primarily women **Entrance** Moderately difficult **Setting** 1-acre small-town campus **Total enrollment** 153 **Student-faculty ratio** 10:1 **Application deadline** Rolling (freshmen), rolling (transfer) **Freshmen** 49% were admitted **Housing** Yes **Expenses** Tuition $11,500; Room & Board $4780 **Undergraduates** 92% women, 22% part-time, 26% 25 or older, 1% Native American, 2% Hispanic American, 3% African American, 0% Asian American/Pacific Islander **The most frequently chosen baccalaureate field is** health professions and related sciences **Academic program** Advanced placement, honors program, summer session, adult/continuing education programs, internships **Contact** Ms. Pam Brown, President/CEO, Blessing-Rieman College of Nursing, Broadway at 11th, Quincy, IL 62305-7005. Telephone: 217-228-5520 Ext. 6963 or toll-free 800-877-9140 Ext. 6964. Fax: 217-223-4661. E-mail: htourney@blessinghospital.com. Web site: http://www.brcn.edu/.

BRADLEY UNIVERSITY
PEORIA, ILLINOIS

General Independent, comprehensive, coed **Entrance** Moderately difficult **Setting** 65-acre urban campus **Total enrollment** 5,996 **Student-faculty ratio** 14:1 **Application deadline** Rolling (freshmen) **Freshmen** 76% were admitted **Housing** Yes **Expenses** Tuition $15,340; Room & Board $5630 **Undergraduates** 54% women, 8% part-time, 8% 25 or older, 0.3% Native American, 1% Hispanic American, 5% African American, 2% Asian American/Pacific Islander **The most frequently chosen baccalaureate fields are** business/marketing, communications/communication technologies, engineering/engineering technologies **Academic program** Advanced placement, accelerated degree program, self-designed majors, honors program, summer session, adult/continuing education programs, internships **Contact** Ms. Nickie Roberson, Director of Admissions, Bradley University, 1501 West Bradley Avenue, 100 Swords Hall, Peoria, IL 61625-0002. Telephone: 309-677-1000 or toll-free 800-447-6460. E-mail: admissions@bradley.edu. Web site: http://www.bradley.edu/.

CHICAGO STATE UNIVERSITY
CHICAGO, ILLINOIS

General State-supported, comprehensive, coed **Entrance** Moderately difficult **Setting** 161-acre urban campus **Total enrollment** 7,079 **Student-faculty ratio** 13:1 **Application deadline** 7/15 (freshmen), 7/15 (transfer) **Freshmen** 47% were admitted **Housing** Yes **Expenses** Tuition $3434; Room & Board $5825 **Undergraduates** 74% women, 39% part-time, 58% 25 or older, 0.2% Native American, 5% Hispanic American, 89% African American, 0.4% Asian American/Pacific Islander **The most frequently chosen baccalaureate fields are** business/marketing, education, liberal arts/general studies **Academic program** English as a second language, advanced placement, accelerated degree program, self-designed majors, honors program, summer session, adult/continuing education programs, internships **Contact** Ms. Addie Epps, Director of Admissions, Chicago State University, 95th Street at King Drive, ADM 200, Chicago, IL 60628. Telephone: 773-995-2513. E-mail: ug-admissions@csu.edu. Web site: http://www.csu.edu/.

CHRISTIAN LIFE COLLEGE
MOUNT PROSPECT, ILLINOIS

General Independent religious, 4-year, coed **Total enrollment** 80 **Student-faculty ratio** 10:1 **Freshmen** 57% were admitted **Expenses** Tuition $7600; Room only $3300 **Undergraduates** 44% women, 41% part-time, 0% Native American, 8% Hispanic American, 4% African American, 4% Asian American/Pacific Islander **The most frequently chosen baccalaureate field is** philosophy **Contact** Jim Spenner, Director of Admissions, Christian Life College, 400 East Gregory Street, Mount Prospect, IL 60056. Telephone: 847-259-1840 Ext. 17. E-mail: jspenner@christianlifecollege.edu. Web site: http://www.christianlifecollege.edu/.

COLUMBIA COLLEGE CHICAGO
CHICAGO, ILLINOIS

General Independent, comprehensive, coed **Entrance** Noncompetitive **Setting** urban campus **Total enrollment** 9,416 **Student-faculty ratio** 13:1 **Application deadline** 8/15 (freshmen), 8/15 (transfer) **Freshmen** 90% were admitted **Housing** Yes **Expenses** Tuition $12,844; Room only $5900 **Undergraduates** 51% women, 17% part-time, 21% 25 or older, 1% Native American, 11% Hispanic American, 18% African American, 4% Asian American/Pacific Islander **The most frequently chosen baccalaureate fields are** communications/communication technologies, liberal arts/general studies, visual/performing arts **Academic program** English as a second language, advanced placement, self-designed majors, summer session, internships **Contact** Ms. Susan Greenwald, Director of Admissions and Recruitment, Columbia College Chicago, 600 South Michigan Avenue, Chicago, IL 60605-1996. Telephone: 312-663-1600 Ext. 7133. E-mail: admissions@mail.colum.edu. Web site: http://www.colum.edu/.

CONCORDIA UNIVERSITY
RIVER FOREST, ILLINOIS

General Independent, comprehensive, coed, affiliated with Lutheran Church–Missouri Synod **Entrance** Moderately difficult **Setting** 40-acre suburban campus **Total enrollment** 1,947 **Student-faculty ratio** 9:1 **Application deadline** Rolling (freshmen), rolling (transfer) **Freshmen** 28% were admitted **Housing** Yes **Expenses** Tuition $15,000; Room & Board $4900 **Undergraduates** 68% women, 23% part-time, 22% 25 or older, 0.1% Native American, 4%

ILLINOIS

Concordia University *(continued)*
Hispanic American, 9% African American, 2% Asian American/Pacific Islander **The most frequently chosen baccalaureate fields are** business/marketing, education, health professions and related sciences **Academic program** Advanced placement, accelerated degree program, honors program, summer session, adult/continuing education programs, internships **Contact** Ms. Deborah A. Ness, Dean of Enrollment Services, Concordia University, 7400 Augusta Street, River Forest, IL 60305. Telephone: 708-209-3100 or toll-free 800-285-2668. Fax: 708-209-3473. E-mail: crfadmis@curf.edu. Web site: http://www.curf.edu/.

DEPAUL UNIVERSITY
CHICAGO, ILLINOIS

General Independent Roman Catholic, university, coed **Entrance** Moderately difficult **Setting** 36-acre urban campus **Total enrollment** 21,363 **Student-faculty ratio** 14:1 **Application deadline** Rolling (freshmen), rolling (transfer) **Freshmen** 72% were admitted **Housing** Yes **Expenses** Tuition $16,170; Room & Board $6960 **Undergraduates** 59% women, 27% part-time, 28% 25 or older, 0.3% Native American, 13% Hispanic American, 11% African American, 10% Asian American/Pacific Islander **The most frequently chosen baccalaureate fields are** business/marketing, computer/information sciences, liberal arts/general studies **Academic program** English as a second language, advanced placement, accelerated degree program, honors program, summer session, adult/continuing education programs, internships **Contact** Carlene Klaas, Undergraduate Admissions, DePaul University, 1 East Jackson Boulevard, Chicago, IL 60604. Telephone: 312-362-8300 or toll-free 800-4DE-PAUL (out-of-state). E-mail: admitdpu@wppost.depaul.edu. Web site: http://www.depaul.edu/.

DEVRY UNIVERSITY
ADDISON, ILLINOIS

General Proprietary, 4-year, coed **Entrance** Minimally difficult **Setting** 14-acre suburban campus **Total enrollment** 3,543 **Student-faculty ratio** 25:1 **Application deadline** Rolling (freshmen), rolling (transfer) **Freshmen** 88% were admitted **Housing** No **Expenses** Tuition $8740 **Undergraduates** 23% women, 35% part-time, 42% 25 or older, 0.5% Native American, 9% Hispanic American, 10% African American, 16% Asian American/Pacific Islander **The most frequently chosen baccalaureate fields are** business/marketing, computer/information sciences, engineering/engineering technologies **Academic program** Advanced placement, accelerated degree program, summer session, adult/continuing education programs **Contact** Ms. Jane Miritello, Assistant New Student Coordinator, DeVry University, 18624 W. Creek Drive, Tinley Park, IL 60477. Telephone: 708-342-3300 or toll-free 877-305-8184 (out-of-state). Fax: 708-342-3120. Web site: http://www.dpg.devry.edu/.

DEVRY UNIVERSITY
CHICAGO, ILLINOIS

General Proprietary, 4-year, coed **Entrance** Minimally difficult **Setting** 17-acre urban campus **Total enrollment** 4,011 **Student-faculty ratio** 21:1 **Application deadline** Rolling (freshmen), rolling (transfer) **Freshmen** 81% were admitted **Housing** No **Expenses** Tuition $8805 **Undergraduates** 36% women, 35% part-time, 44% 25 or older, 0.3% Native American, 25% Hispanic American, 33% African American, 14% Asian American/Pacific Islander **The most frequently chosen baccalaureate fields are** business/marketing, computer/information sciences, engineering/engineering technologies **Academic program** English as a second language, advanced placement, accelerated degree program, summer session, adult/continuing education programs **Contact** Ms. Christine Hierl, Director of Admissions, DeVry University, 3300 North Campbell Avenue, Chicago, IL 60618-5994. Telephone: 773-929-6550 or toll-free 800-383-3879 (out-of-state). Fax: 773-929-8093. E-mail: gkroepel@chi.devry.edu. Web site: http://www.chi.devry.edu/.

DEVRY UNIVERSITY
TINLEY PARK, ILLINOIS

General Proprietary, 4-year, coed **Entrance** Minimally difficult **Total enrollment** 1,662 **Student-faculty ratio** 20:1 **Application deadline** Rolling (freshmen), rolling (transfer) **Freshmen** 83% were admitted **Housing** No **Expenses** Tuition $8805 **Undergraduates** 27% women, 30% part-time, 36% 25 or older, 0.3% Native American, 8% Hispanic American, 32% African American, 2% Asian American/Pacific Islander **Academic program** Advanced placement, accelerated degree program, summer session, adult/continuing education programs **Contact** Ms. Jane Miritello, Assistant New Student Coordinator, DeVry University, 18624 W. Creek Drive, Tinley Park, IL 60477. Telephone: 708-342-3300 or toll-free 877-305-8184 (out-of-state). Web site: http://www.tp.devry.edu/.

DOMINICAN UNIVERSITY
RIVER FOREST, ILLINOIS

General Independent Roman Catholic, comprehensive, coed **Entrance** Moderately difficult **Setting** 30-acre suburban campus **Total enrollment** 2,533 **Student-faculty ratio** 12:1 **Application deadline** Rolling (freshmen), rolling (transfer) **Freshmen** 83% were admitted **Housing** Yes **Expenses** Tuition $15,700; Room & Board $5100 **Undergraduates** 68% women, 20% part-time, 23% 25 or older, 0.1% Native American, 15% Hispanic American, 5% African American, 2% Asian American/Pacific Islander **The most frequently chosen baccalaureate fields are** business/marketing, psychology, social sciences and history **Academic program** English as a second language, advanced placement, accelerated degree program, self-designed majors, honors program, summer session, adult/continuing education programs, internships **Contact** Ms. Hildegarde Schmidt, Dean of Admissions and Financial Aid, Dominican University, 7900 West Division Street, River Forest, IL 60305-1099. Telephone: 708-524-6800 or toll-free 800-828-8475. Fax: 708-366-5360. E-mail: domadmis@email.dom.edu. Web site: http://www.dom.edu/.

EASTERN ILLINOIS UNIVERSITY
CHARLESTON, ILLINOIS

General State-supported, comprehensive, coed **Entrance** Moderately difficult **Setting** 320-acre small-town campus **Total enrollment** 10,531 **Student-faculty ratio** 16:1 **Application deadline** Rolling (freshmen), rolling (transfer) **Freshmen** 70% were admitted **Housing** Yes **Expenses** Tuition $4300; Room & Board $5800 **Undergraduates** 57% women, 10% part-time, 11% 25 or older, 0.2% Native American, 2% Hispanic American, 7% African American, 1% Asian American/Pacific Islander **The most frequently chosen baccalaureate fields are** business/marketing, education, English **Academic program** English as a second language, advanced placement, honors program, summer session, adult/continuing education programs, internships **Contact** Mr. Dale W. Wolf, Director of Admissions, Eastern Illinois University, 600 Lincoln Avenue, Charleston, IL 61920-3099. Telephone: 217-581-2223 or toll-free 800-252-5711. Fax: 217-581-7060. E-mail: admissns@eiu.edu. Web site: http://www.eiu.edu/.

EAST-WEST UNIVERSITY
CHICAGO, ILLINOIS

General Independent, 4-year, coed **Entrance** Minimally difficult **Setting** urban campus **Total enrollment** 1,076 **Student-faculty ratio** 13:1 **Application deadline** Rolling (freshmen), rolling (transfer) **Freshmen** 82% were admitted **Housing** No **Expenses** Tuition $9570 **Undergraduates** 64% women, 1% part-time, 34% 25 or older **The most frequently chosen baccalaureate fields are** business/marketing, computer/information sciences, social sciences and history **Academic program** Summer session **Contact** Mr. William Link, Director of Admissions, East-West University, 816 South Michigan Avenue, Chicago, IL 60605-2103. Telephone: 312-939-0111 Ext. 1839. Fax: 312-939-0083.

ELMHURST COLLEGE
ELMHURST, ILLINOIS

General Independent, comprehensive, coed, affiliated with United Church of Christ **Entrance** Moderately difficult **Setting** 38-acre suburban campus **Total enrollment** 2,540 **Student-faculty ratio** 14:1 **Application deadline** 7/15 (freshmen), 8/1 (transfer) **Freshmen** 77% were admitted **Housing** Yes **Expenses** Tuition $16,200; Room & Board $5550 **Undergraduates** 64% women, 19% part-time, 36% 25 or older, 0.3% Native American, 5% Hispanic American, 7% African American, 2% Asian American/Pacific Islander **The most frequently chosen baccalaureate fields are** business/marketing, communications/communication

technologies, education **Academic program** Advanced placement, accelerated degree program, honors program, summer session, adult/continuing education programs, internships **Contact** Mr. Andrew B. Sison, Director of Admission, Elmhurst College, 190 Prospect Avenue, Elmhurst, IL 60126-3296. Telephone: 630-617-3400 Ext. 3068 or toll-free 800-697-1871 (out-of-state). Fax: 630-617-5501. E-mail: admit@elmhurst.edu. Web site: http://www.elmhurst.edu/.

EUREKA COLLEGE
EUREKA, ILLINOIS

General Independent, 4-year, coed, affiliated with Christian Church (Disciples of Christ) **Entrance** Moderately difficult **Setting** 112-acre small-town campus **Total enrollment** 544 **Student-faculty ratio** 13:1 **Application deadline** Rolling (freshmen), rolling (transfer) **Freshmen** 72% were admitted **Housing** Yes **Expenses** Tuition $16,900; Room & Board $5300 **Undergraduates** 59% women, 7% part-time, 5% 25 or older, 0% Native American, 1% Hispanic American, 6% African American, 1% Asian American/Pacific Islander **The most frequently chosen baccalaureate fields are** business/marketing, biological/life sciences, education **Academic program** Advanced placement, self-designed majors, honors program, internships **Contact** Mr. John R. Clayton, Dean of Admissions and Financial Aid, Eureka College, 300 East College Avenue, Eureka, IL 61530-1500. Telephone: 309-467-6350 or toll-free 888-4-EUREKA. Fax: 309-467-6576. E-mail: admissions@eureka.edu. Web site: http://www.eureka.edu/.

FINCH UNIVERSITY OF HEALTH SCIENCES/THE CHICAGO MEDICAL SCHOOL
NORTH CHICAGO, ILLINOIS

General Independent, upper-level, coed **Entrance** Minimally difficult **Setting** 50-acre suburban campus **Total enrollment** 1,372 **Application deadline** 8/15 (transfer) **Housing** No **Expenses** Tuition $34,533 **Undergraduates** 100% women, 18% part-time, 93% 25 or older, 0% Native American, 0% Hispanic American, 4% African American, 7% Asian American/Pacific Islander **The most frequently chosen baccalaureate field is** health professions and related sciences **Academic program** Advanced placement, summer session, adult/continuing education programs **Contact** Ms. Kristine A. Jones, Director of Admissions and Records, Finch University of Health Sciences/The Chicago Medical School, Undergraduate Admissions, 3333 Green Bay Road, North Chicago, IL 60064. Telephone: 847-578-3204. Fax: 847-578-3284. E-mail: admissions@finchcms.edu. Web site: http://www.finchcms.edu/.

GOVERNORS STATE UNIVERSITY
UNIVERSITY PARK, ILLINOIS

General State-supported, upper-level, coed **Entrance** Minimally difficult **Setting** 750-acre suburban campus **Total enrollment** 5,911 **Student-faculty ratio**

ILLINOIS

Governors State University *(continued)*
16:1 **Application deadline** 7/15 (transfer) **First-Year Students** 66% were admitted **Housing** No **Expenses** Tuition $2632 **Undergraduates** 69% women, 71% part-time, 56% 25 or older, 0.3% Native American, 6% Hispanic American, 29% African American, 1% Asian American/Pacific Islander **Academic program** Advanced placement, self-designed majors, honors program, summer session, adult/continuing education programs, internships **Contact** Mr. Larry Polselli, Executive Director of Enrollment Services, Governors State University, One University Parkway, University Park, IL 60466. Telephone: 708-534-3148. Fax: 708-534-1640. Web site: http://www.govst.edu/.

GREENVILLE COLLEGE
GREENVILLE, ILLINOIS

General Independent Free Methodist, comprehensive, coed **Entrance** Moderately difficult **Setting** 12-acre small-town campus **Total enrollment** 1,155 **Student-faculty ratio** 13:1 **Application deadline** Rolling (freshmen), rolling (transfer) **Freshmen** 73% were admitted **Housing** Yes **Expenses** Tuition $14,000; Room & Board $5186 **Undergraduates** 52% women, 4% part-time, 21% 25 or older, 0.5% Native American, 1% Hispanic American, 6% African American, 1% Asian American/Pacific Islander **The most frequently chosen baccalaureate fields are** business/marketing, biological/life sciences, education **Academic program** English as a second language, advanced placement, accelerated degree program, self-designed majors, honors program, summer session, adult/continuing education programs, internships **Contact** Mr. Randy Comfort, Dean of Admissions, Greenville College, 315 East College, PO Box 159, Greenville, IL 62246-0159. Telephone: 618-664-7100 or toll-free 800-248-2288 (in-state); 800-345-4440 (out-of-state). Fax: 618-664-9841. E-mail: admissions@greenville.edu. Web site: http://www.greenville.edu/.

HARRINGTON INSTITUTE OF INTERIOR DESIGN
CHICAGO, ILLINOIS

General Proprietary, 4-year, coed, primarily women **Entrance** Noncompetitive **Setting** urban campus **Total enrollment** 820 **Student-faculty ratio** 15:1 **Application deadline** Rolling (freshmen) **Freshmen** 73% were admitted **Housing** No **Undergraduates** 53% 25 or older **The most frequently chosen baccalaureate field is** visual/performing arts **Academic program** Adult/continuing education programs, internships **Contact** Ms. Wendi Franczyk, Director of Admissions, Harrington Institute of Interior Design, 410 South Michigan Avenue, Chicago, IL 60605-1496. Telephone: 877-939-4975 or toll-free 877-939-4975 (out-of-state). Fax: 312-939-8005. E-mail: harringtoninstitute@interiordesign.edu. Web site: http://www.interiordesign.edu/.

HEBREW THEOLOGICAL COLLEGE
SKOKIE, ILLINOIS

Contact Office of Admissions, Hebrew Theological College, 7135 North Carpenter Road, Skokie, IL 60077-3263. Telephone: 847-982-2500. Web site: http://www.htcnet.edu/.

ILLINOIS COLLEGE
JACKSONVILLE, ILLINOIS

General Independent interdenominational, 4-year, coed **Entrance** Moderately difficult **Setting** 62-acre small-town campus **Total enrollment** 874 **Student-faculty ratio** 14:1 **Application deadline** 8/15 (freshmen), 12/15 (transfer) **Freshmen** 67% were admitted **Housing** Yes **Expenses** Tuition $11,272; Room & Board $4962 **Undergraduates** 55% women, 2% part-time, 2% 25 or older, 0.2% Native American, 2% Hispanic American, 3% African American, 0.5% Asian American/Pacific Islander **The most frequently chosen baccalaureate fields are** business/marketing, education, social sciences and history **Academic program** Advanced placement, accelerated degree program, summer session, internships **Contact** Mr. Rick Bystry, Director of Admission, Illinois College, 1101 West College, Jacksonville, IL 62650. Telephone: 217-245-3030 or toll-free 866-464-5265. Fax: 217-245-3034. E-mail: admissions@ic.edu. Web site: http://www.ic.edu/.

THE ILLINOIS INSTITUTE OF ART
CHICAGO, ILLINOIS

General Proprietary, 4-year, coed **Entrance** Minimally difficult **Setting** urban campus **Total enrollment** 1,789 **Student-faculty ratio** 18:1 **Application deadline** Rolling (freshmen), rolling (transfer) **Freshmen** 93% were admitted **Housing** No **Expenses** Tuition $14,556 **Undergraduates** 30% 25 or older **Academic program** Advanced placement, accelerated degree program, summer session, adult/continuing education programs, internships **Contact** Ms. Janis Anton, Director of Admissions, The Illinois Institute of Art, 350 North Orleans, Chicago, IL 60654. Telephone: 312-280-3500 Ext. 132 or toll-free 800-351-3450. Fax: 312-280-8562. E-mail: antonj@aii.edu. Web site: http://www.ilia.aii.edu/.

THE ILLINOIS INSTITUTE OF ART-SCHAUMBURG
SCHAUMBURG, ILLINOIS

General Proprietary, 4-year, coed **Total enrollment** 850 **Student-faculty ratio** 16:1 **Freshmen** 75% were admitted **Housing** Yes **Expenses** Tuition $13,100 **Undergraduates** 28% 25 or older, 0% Native American, 7% Hispanic American, 3% African American, 9% Asian American/Pacific Islander **Contact** Ms. Stephanie Schweihofer, Director of Admissions, The Illinois Institute of Art-Schaumburg, 1000 Plaza Drive, Schaumburg, IL 60173. Telephone: 847-619-3450 Ext. 116 or toll-free 800-314-3450. Fax: 847-619-3064 Ext. 3064. Web site: http://www.ilis.artinstitutes.edu.

ILLINOIS

ILLINOIS INSTITUTE OF TECHNOLOGY
CHICAGO, ILLINOIS

General Independent, university, coed **Entrance** Very difficult **Setting** 128-acre urban campus **Total enrollment** 6,050 **Student-faculty ratio** 12:1 **Application deadline** Rolling (freshmen), 7/1 (transfer) **Freshmen** 62% were admitted **Housing** Yes **Expenses** Tuition $18,760; Room & Board $5624 **Undergraduates** 25% women, 20% part-time, 20% 25 or older, 0.4% Native American, 8% Hispanic American, 6% African American, 16% Asian American/Pacific Islander **The most frequently chosen baccalaureate fields are** architecture, computer/information sciences, engineering/engineering technologies **Academic program** English as a second language, advanced placement, accelerated degree program, summer session, internships **Contact** Mr. Terry Miller, Dean of Undergraduate Admission, Illinois Institute of Technology, 10 West 33rd Street PH101, Chicago, IL 60616-3793. Telephone: 312-567-3025 or toll-free 800-448-2329 (out-of-state). Fax: 312-567-6939. E-mail: admission@iit.edu. Web site: http://www.iit.edu/.

ILLINOIS STATE UNIVERSITY
NORMAL, ILLINOIS

General State-supported, university, coed **Entrance** Moderately difficult **Setting** 850-acre urban campus **Total enrollment** 21,240 **Student-faculty ratio** 19:1 **Application deadline** 3/1 (freshmen), rolling (transfer) **Freshmen** 77% were admitted **Housing** Yes **Expenses** Tuition $4478; Room & Board $4758 **Undergraduates** 58% women, 8% part-time, 8% 25 or older, 0.3% Native American, 2% Hispanic American, 6% African American, 2% Asian American/Pacific Islander **The most frequently chosen baccalaureate field is** philosophy, religion, and theology **Academic program** English as a second language, advanced placement, accelerated degree program, self-designed majors, honors program, summer session, adult/continuing education programs, internships **Contact** Mr. Steve Adams, Director of Admissions, Illinois State University, Campus Box 2200, Normal, IL 61790-2200. Telephone: 309-438-2181 or toll-free 800-366-2478 (in-state). Fax: 309-438-3932. E-mail: ugradadm@ilstu.edu. Web site: http://www.ilstu.edu/.

ILLINOIS WESLEYAN UNIVERSITY
BLOOMINGTON, ILLINOIS

General Independent, 4-year, coed **Entrance** Very difficult **Setting** 70-acre suburban campus **Total enrollment** 2,064 **Student-faculty ratio** 12:1 **Application deadline** 3/1 (freshmen), rolling (transfer) **Freshmen** 57% were admitted **Housing** Yes **Expenses** Tuition $21,640; Room & Board $5330 **Undergraduates** 56% women, 0.4% part-time, 0.05% Native American, 2% Hispanic American, 3% African American, 3% Asian American/Pacific Islander **The most frequently chosen baccalaureate fields are** business/marketing, social sciences and history, visual/performing arts **Academic program** Advanced placement, self-designed majors, honors program, summer session, internships **Contact** Mr. James R. Ruoti, Dean of Admissions, Illinois Wesleyan University, PO Box 2900, Bloomington, IL 61702-2900. Telephone: 309-556-3031 or toll-free 800-332-2498. Fax: 309-556-3411. E-mail: iwuadmit@titan.iwu.edu. Web site: http://www.iwu.edu/.

INTERNATIONAL ACADEMY OF DESIGN & TECHNOLOGY
CHICAGO, ILLINOIS

General Proprietary, 4-year, coed **Entrance** Minimally difficult **Setting** urban campus **Total enrollment** 2,063 **Student-faculty ratio** 16:1 **Application deadline** Rolling (freshmen), rolling (transfer) **Freshmen** 55% were admitted **Housing** No **Expenses** Tuition $12,300 **Undergraduates** 63% women, 17% part-time, 25% 25 or older, 0.05% Native American, 23% Hispanic American, 35% African American, 4% Asian American/Pacific Islander **The most frequently chosen baccalaureate fields are** business/marketing, visual/performing arts **Academic program** Advanced placement, summer session, adult/continuing education programs, internships **Contact** Ms. Andrea Schmoyer, Director of Student Management, International Academy of Design & Technology, One North State Street, Suite 400, Chicago, IL 60602. Telephone: 312-980-9200 or toll-free 877-ACADEMY (out-of-state). Fax: 312-541-3929. E-mail: academy@iadtchicago.com. Web site: http://www.iadtchicago.com/.

JUDSON COLLEGE
ELGIN, ILLINOIS

General Independent Baptist, 4-year, coed **Entrance** Moderately difficult **Setting** 80-acre suburban campus **Total enrollment** 1,089 **Student-faculty ratio** 15:1 **Application deadline** Rolling (freshmen), rolling (transfer) **Freshmen** 79% were admitted **Housing** Yes **Expenses** Tuition $14,422; Room & Board $5570 **Undergraduates** 57% women, 23% part-time, 28% 25 or older, 0% Native American, 3% Hispanic American, 5% African American, 1% Asian American/Pacific Islander **The most frequently chosen baccalaureate fields are** business/marketing, education, personal/miscellaneous services **Academic program** Advanced placement, accelerated degree program, self-designed majors, honors program, adult/continuing education programs, internships **Contact** Mr. Billy Dean, Director of Admissions, Judson College, 1151 North State Street, Elgin, IL 60123-1498. Telephone: 847-695-2500 Ext. 2322 or toll-free 800-879-5376. Fax: 847-695-0216. E-mail: admission@judson-il.edu. Web site: http://www.judson-il.edu/.

KENDALL COLLEGE
EVANSTON, ILLINOIS

General Independent United Methodist, 4-year, coed **Entrance** Minimally difficult **Setting** 1-acre subur-

Kendall College *(continued)*
ban campus **Total enrollment** 600 **Student-faculty ratio** 15:1 **Application deadline** Rolling (freshmen), rolling (transfer) **Freshmen** 83% were admitted **Housing** Yes **Expenses** Tuition $12,990; Room & Board $5529 **Undergraduates** 45% 25 or older, 0.2% Native American, 9% Hispanic American, 18% African American, 4% Asian American/Pacific Islander **Academic program** English as a second language, advanced placement, accelerated degree program, self-designed majors, summer session, adult/continuing education programs, internships **Contact** Carl Goodmonson, Assistant Director of Admissions, Kendall College, 2408 Orrington Avenue, Evanston, IL 60201-2899. Telephone: 847-866-1300 Ext. 1307 or toll-free 877-588-8860 (in-state). Fax: 847-866-1320. E-mail: admissions@kendall.edu. Web site: http://www.kendall.edu/.

KNOX COLLEGE
GALESBURG, ILLINOIS

General Independent, 4-year, coed **Entrance** Very difficult **Setting** 82-acre small-town campus **Total enrollment** 1,143 **Student-faculty ratio** 12:1 **Application deadline** 2/1 (freshmen), 4/1 (transfer) **Freshmen** 72% were admitted **Housing** Yes **Expenses** Tuition $22,620; Room & Board $5610 **Undergraduates** 56% women, 3% part-time, 2% 25 or older, 1% Native American, 4% Hispanic American, 4% African American, 4% Asian American/Pacific Islander **The most frequently chosen baccalaureate fields are** biological/life sciences, English, social sciences and history **Academic program** English as a second language, advanced placement, self-designed majors, honors program, internships **Contact** Paul Steenis, Director of Admissions, Knox College, Admission Office, Box K-148, Galesburg, IL 61401. Telephone: 309-341-7100 or toll-free 800-678-KNOX. Fax: 309-341-7070. E-mail: admission@knox.edu. Web site: http://www.knox.edu/.

LAKE FOREST COLLEGE
LAKE FOREST, ILLINOIS

General Independent, comprehensive, coed **Entrance** Very difficult **Setting** 110-acre suburban campus **Total enrollment** 1,277 **Student-faculty ratio** 12:1 **Application deadline** 3/1 (freshmen), rolling (transfer) **Freshmen** 69% were admitted **Housing** Yes **Expenses** Tuition $22,206; Room & Board $5254 **Undergraduates** 58% women, 1% part-time, 2% 25 or older, 0.4% Native American, 3% Hispanic American, 5% African American, 4% Asian American/Pacific Islander **The most frequently chosen baccalaureate fields are** business/marketing, psychology, social sciences and history **Academic program** Advanced placement, accelerated degree program, self-designed majors, honors program, summer session, adult/continuing education programs, internships **Contact** Mr. William D. Motzer Jr., Director of Admissions, Lake Forest College, 555 North Sheridan Road, Lake Forest, IL 60045-2399. Telephone: 847-735-5000 or toll-free 800-828-4751. Fax: 847-735-6271. E-mail: admissions@lakeforest.edu. Web site: http://www.lakeforest.edu/.

LAKEVIEW COLLEGE OF NURSING
DANVILLE, ILLINOIS

General Independent, upper-level, coed, primarily women **Entrance** Moderately difficult **Setting** small-town campus **Total enrollment** 56 **Student-faculty ratio** 4:1 **Application deadline** Rolling (transfer) **First-Year Students** 76% were admitted **Housing** No **Undergraduates** 93% women, 57% part-time, 75% 25 or older, 0% Native American, 4% Hispanic American, 7% African American, 2% Asian American/Pacific Islander **The most frequently chosen baccalaureate field is** health professions and related sciences **Academic program** Summer session **Contact** Ms. Kelly Holden, Registrar, Lakeview College of Nursing, 903 North Logan Avenue, Danville, IL 61832. Telephone: 217-443-5385 or toll-free 217-443-5238 Ext. 5454 (in-state); 217-443-5238 (out-of-state). Fax: 217-442-2279. E-mail: kholden@lakeviewcol.edu. Web site: http://www.lakeviewcol.edu/.

LEWIS UNIVERSITY
ROMEOVILLE, ILLINOIS

General Independent, comprehensive, coed, affiliated with Roman Catholic Church **Entrance** Moderately difficult **Setting** 600-acre small-town campus **Total enrollment** 4,407 **Student-faculty ratio** 15:1 **Application deadline** Rolling (freshmen), rolling (transfer) **Freshmen** 74% were admitted **Housing** Yes **Expenses** Tuition $14,040; Room & Board $6920 **Undergraduates** 58% women, 37% part-time, 13% 25 or older, 0.1% Native American, 7% Hispanic American, 16% African American, 3% Asian American/Pacific Islander **The most frequently chosen baccalaureate fields are** business/marketing, health professions and related sciences, protective services/public administration **Academic program** English as a second language, advanced placement, accelerated degree program, self-designed majors, honors program, summer session, adult/continuing education programs, internships **Contact** Ms. Arianne Martin, Assistant Director of Enrollment, Lewis University, Box 297, One University Parkway, Romeoville, IL 60446. Telephone: 815-838-0500 Ext. 5237 or toll-free 800-897-9000. Fax: 815-836-5002. E-mail: admissions@lewisu.edu. Web site: http://www.lewisu.edu/.

LINCOLN CHRISTIAN COLLEGE
LINCOLN, ILLINOIS

General Independent, 4-year, coed, affiliated with Christian Churches and Churches of Christ **Entrance** Moderately difficult **Setting** 227-acre small-town campus **Total enrollment** 670 **Student-faculty ratio** 13:1 **Application deadline** Rolling (freshmen), rolling (transfer) **Freshmen** 80% were admitted **Housing** Yes **Expenses** Tuition $8128; Room & Board $4100 **Undergraduates** 52% women, 18% part-time, 21% 25 or older, 1% Native American, 1% Hispanic American, 2% African American, 1% Asian

American/Pacific Islander **The most frequently chosen baccalaureate field is** philosophy **Academic program** English as a second language, advanced placement, summer session, adult/continuing education programs, internships **Contact** Mrs. Mary K. Davis, Assistant Director of Admissions, Lincoln Christian College, 100 Campus View Drive, Lincoln, IL 62656. Telephone: 217-732-3168 Ext. 2251 or toll-free 888-522-5228. Fax: 217-732-4199. E-mail: lccs-college@prairienet.org. Web site: http://www.lccs.edu/.

LOYOLA UNIVERSITY CHICAGO
CHICAGO, ILLINOIS

General Independent Roman Catholic (Jesuit), university, coed **Entrance** Moderately difficult **Setting** 105-acre urban campus **Total enrollment** 13,019 **Student-faculty ratio** 14:1 **Application deadline** 4/1 (freshmen), 7/9 (transfer) **Freshmen** 77% were admitted **Housing** Yes **Expenses** Tuition $19,274; Room & Board $7266 **Undergraduates** 65% women, 27% part-time, 4% 25 or older, 0.1% Native American, 10% Hispanic American, 9% African American, 12% Asian American/Pacific Islander **The most frequently chosen baccalaureate fields are** business/marketing, psychology, social sciences and history **Academic program** English as a second language, advanced placement, accelerated degree program, honors program, summer session, adult/continuing education programs, internships **Contact** Mr. Aaron Meis, Acting Director of Admissions, Loyola University Chicago, 820 North Michigan Avenue, Suite 613, Chicago, IL 60611. Telephone: 312-915-6500 or toll-free 800-262-2193. Fax: 312-915-7216. E-mail: admission@luc.edu. Web site: http://www.luc.edu/.

▶ **For more information, see page 448.**

MACMURRAY COLLEGE
JACKSONVILLE, ILLINOIS

General Independent United Methodist, 4-year, coed **Entrance** Moderately difficult **Setting** 60-acre small-town campus **Total enrollment** 655 **Student-faculty ratio** 12:1 **Application deadline** Rolling (freshmen), rolling (transfer) **Freshmen** 68% were admitted **Housing** Yes **Expenses** Tuition $14,000; Room & Board $5000 **Undergraduates** 53% women, 8% part-time, 11% 25 or older, 0.5% Native American, 5% Hispanic American, 12% African American, 1% Asian American/Pacific Islander **The most frequently chosen baccalaureate fields are** education, protective services/public administration, psychology **Academic program** Advanced placement, honors program, summer session, internships **Contact** Mr. Tom McGinnis, Dean of Enrollment, MacMurray College, 447 East College Avenue, Jacksonville, IL 62650. Telephone: 217-479-7056 or toll-free 800-252-7485 (in-state); 217-479-7056 (out-of-state). Fax: 217-291-0702. E-mail: admiss@mac.edu. Web site: http://www.mac.edu/.

MCKENDREE COLLEGE
LEBANON, ILLINOIS

General Independent, 4-year, coed, affiliated with United Methodist Church **Entrance** Moderately difficult **Setting** 80-acre small-town campus **Total enrollment** 2,107 **Student-faculty ratio** 17:1 **Application deadline** Rolling (freshmen), rolling (transfer) **Freshmen** 68% were admitted **Housing** Yes **Expenses** Tuition $13,350; Room & Board $4950 **Undergraduates** 62% women, 27% part-time, 38% 25 or older, 0.3% Native American, 1% Hispanic American, 10% African American, 1% Asian American/Pacific Islander **The most frequently chosen baccalaureate fields are** business/marketing, education, health professions and related sciences **Academic program** Advanced placement, accelerated degree program, self-designed majors, honors program, summer session, internships **Contact** Mr. Mark Campbell, Vice President for Admissions and Financial Aid, McKendree College, 701 College Road, Lebanon, IL 62254. Telephone: 618-537-4481 Ext. 6835 or toll-free 800-232-7228 Ext. 6835. Fax: 618-537-6496. E-mail: mecampbell@mckendree.edu. Web site: http://www.mckendree.edu/.

MILLIKIN UNIVERSITY
DECATUR, ILLINOIS

General Independent, 4-year, coed, affiliated with Presbyterian Church (U.S.A.) **Entrance** Moderately difficult **Setting** 70-acre suburban campus **Total enrollment** 2,389 **Student-faculty ratio** 13:1 **Application deadline** Rolling (freshmen), rolling (transfer) **Freshmen** 76% were admitted **Housing** Yes **Expenses** Tuition $17,359; Room & Board $5594 **Undergraduates** 58% women, 3% part-time, 5% 25 or older, 0.4% Native American, 2% Hispanic American, 7% African American, 1% Asian American/Pacific Islander **The most frequently chosen baccalaureate fields are** business/marketing, education, visual/performing arts **Academic program** Advanced placement, self-designed majors, honors program, summer session, internships **Contact** Mr. Lin Stoner, Dean of Admission, Millikin University, 1184 West Main Street, Decatur, IL 62522-2084. Telephone: 217-424-6210 or toll-free 800-373-7733 Ext. # 5. Fax: 217-425-4669. E-mail: admis@mail.millikin.edu. Web site: http://www.millikin.edu/.

MONMOUTH COLLEGE
MONMOUTH, ILLINOIS

General Independent, 4-year, coed, affiliated with Presbyterian Church **Entrance** Moderately difficult **Setting** 40-acre small-town campus **Total enrollment** 1,072 **Student-faculty ratio** 12:1 **Application deadline** Rolling (freshmen), rolling (transfer) **Freshmen** 79% were admitted **Housing** Yes **Expenses** Tuition $17,000; Room & Board $4550 **Undergraduates** 54% women, 2% part-time, 1% 25 or older, 0.2% Native American, 2% Hispanic American, 5% African American, 1% Asian American/Pacific Islander **The most frequently chosen baccalaureate fields**

ILLINOIS

Monmouth College *(continued)*
are business/marketing, education, social sciences and history **Academic program** Advanced placement, self-designed majors, honors program, internships **Contact** Mrs. Marybeth Kemp, Vice President for Admissions, Monmouth College, 700 East Broadway, Monmouth, IL 61462-1998. Telephone: 309-457-2131 or toll-free 800-747-2687. Fax: 309-457-2141. E-mail: admit@monm.edu. Web site: http://www.monm.edu/.

MOODY BIBLE INSTITUTE
CHICAGO, ILLINOIS

General Independent nondenominational, comprehensive, coed **Entrance** Moderately difficult **Setting** 25-acre urban campus **Total enrollment** 1,624 **Student-faculty ratio** 20:1 **Application deadline** 3/1 (freshmen), 3/1 (transfer) **Freshmen** 50% were admitted **Housing** Yes **Expenses** Tuition $1382; Room & Board $6020 **Undergraduates** 45% women, 7% part-time, 7% 25 or older, 0.4% Native American, 4% Hispanic American, 2% African American, 2% Asian American/Pacific Islander **The most frequently chosen baccalaureate fields are** philosophy, communications/communication technologies, philosophy, religion, and theology **Academic program** English as a second language, advanced placement, summer session, adult/continuing education programs, internships **Contact** Mrs. Marthe Campa, Application Coordinator, Moody Bible Institute, 820 North LaSalle Boulevard, Chicago, IL 60610. Telephone: 312-329-4266 or toll-free 800-967-4MBI. Fax: 312-329-8987. E-mail: admissions@moody.edu. Web site: http://www.moody.edu/.

NAES COLLEGE
CHICAGO, ILLINOIS

General Independent, 4-year, coed **Entrance** Noncompetitive **Total enrollment** 70 **Application deadline** Rolling (freshmen), rolling (transfer) **Freshmen** 100% were admitted **Housing** No **Undergraduates** 73% women, 34% part-time, 97% 25 or older, 89% Native American, 0% Hispanic American, 2% African American, 0% Asian American/Pacific Islander **The most frequently chosen baccalaureate field is** protective services/public administration **Academic program** Advanced placement, accelerated degree program, summer session **Contact** Ms. Christine Redcloud, Registrar, NAES College, 2838 West Peterson Avenue, Chicago, IL 60659-3813. Telephone: 773-761-5000. Fax: 773-761-3808.

NATIONAL-LOUIS UNIVERSITY
EVANSTON, ILLINOIS

General Independent, university, coed **Entrance** Minimally difficult **Setting** 12-acre campus **Total enrollment** 7,879 **Student-faculty ratio** 18:1 **Application deadline** Rolling (freshmen), rolling (transfer) **Freshmen** 77% were admitted **Housing** Yes **Expenses** Tuition $14,910; Room & Board $6013 **Undergraduates** 72% women, 19% part-time, 0.4% Native American, 7% Hispanic American, 22% African American, 2% Asian American/Pacific Islander **The most frequently chosen baccalaureate fields are** business/marketing, education, interdisciplinary studies **Academic program** English as a second language, advanced placement, accelerated degree program, honors program, summer session, adult/continuing education programs, internships **Contact** Ms. Pat Petillo, Director of Admissions, National-Louis University, 2840 Sheridan Road, Evanston, IL 60201-1796. Telephone: 888-NLU-TODAY or toll-free 888-NLU-TODAY Ext. 5151 (in-state); 800-443-5522 Ext. 5151 (out-of-state). Web site: http://www.nl.edu/.

NORTH CENTRAL COLLEGE
NAPERVILLE, ILLINOIS

General Independent United Methodist, comprehensive, coed **Entrance** Moderately difficult **Setting** 56-acre suburban campus **Total enrollment** 2,605 **Student-faculty ratio** 14:1 **Application deadline** Rolling (freshmen), rolling (transfer) **Freshmen** 78% were admitted **Housing** Yes **Expenses** Tuition $17,175; Room & Board $5724 **Undergraduates** 57% women, 16% part-time, 17% 25 or older, 0.2% Native American, 3% Hispanic American, 4% African American, 2% Asian American/Pacific Islander **The most frequently chosen baccalaureate fields are** business/marketing, education, social sciences and history **Academic program** English as a second language, advanced placement, accelerated degree program, self-designed majors, honors program, summer session, adult/continuing education programs, internships **Contact** Mr. Stephen Potts, Coordinator of Freshman Admission, North Central College, 30 North Brainard Street, PO Box 3063, Naperville, IL 60566-7063. Telephone: 630-637-5815 or toll-free 800-411-1861. Fax: 630-637-5819. E-mail: ncadm@noctrl.edu. Web site: http://www.noctrl.edu/.

NORTHEASTERN ILLINOIS UNIVERSITY
CHICAGO, ILLINOIS

General State-supported, comprehensive, coed **Entrance** Minimally difficult **Setting** 67-acre urban campus **Total enrollment** 10,999 **Student-faculty ratio** 18:1 **Application deadline** 7/1 (freshmen), 7/1 (transfer) **Freshmen** 72% were admitted **Housing** No **Expenses** Tuition $2898 **Undergraduates** 63% women, 43% part-time, 42% 25 or older, 0.3% Native American, 28% Hispanic American, 13% African American, 13% Asian American/Pacific Islander **The most frequently chosen baccalaureate fields are** education, business/marketing, liberal arts/general studies **Academic program** English as a second language, advanced placement, honors program, summer session, adult/continuing education programs, internships **Contact** Ms. Kay D. Gulli, Administrative Assistant, Northeastern Illinois University, 500 North St. Louis Avenue, Chicago, IL 60625. Telephone: 773-442-4000. Fax: 773-794-6243. E-mail: admrec@neiu.edu. Web site: http://www.neiu.edu/.

ILLINOIS

NORTHERN ILLINOIS UNIVERSITY
DE KALB, ILLINOIS

General State-supported, university, coed **Entrance** Moderately difficult **Setting** 589-acre small-town campus **Total enrollment** 23,783 **Student-faculty ratio** 17:1 **Application deadline** 8/1 (freshmen), 8/1 (transfer) **Freshmen** 64% were admitted **Housing** Yes **Expenses** Tuition $4475; Room & Board $5070 **Undergraduates** 53% women, 11% part-time, 13% 25 or older, 0.3% Native American, 6% Hispanic American, 13% African American, 6% Asian American/Pacific Islander **The most frequently chosen baccalaureate fields are** business/marketing, education, social sciences and history **Academic program** Advanced placement, accelerated degree program, self-designed majors, honors program, summer session, adult/continuing education programs, internships **Contact** Dr. Robert Burk, Director of Admissions, Northern Illinois University, DeKalb, IL 60113-2857. Telephone: 815-753-0446 or toll-free 800-892-3050 (in-state). E-mail: admission-info@niu.edu. Web site: http://www.niu.edu/.

NORTH PARK UNIVERSITY
CHICAGO, ILLINOIS

General Independent, comprehensive, coed, affiliated with Evangelical Covenant Church **Entrance** Moderately difficult **Setting** 30-acre urban campus **Total enrollment** 2,181 **Student-faculty ratio** 16:1 **Application deadline** Rolling (freshmen), rolling (transfer) **Freshmen** 74% were admitted **Housing** Yes **Expenses** Tuition $17,790; Room & Board $5830 **Undergraduates** 62% women, 20% part-time, 20% 25 or older, 0.4% Native American, 10% Hispanic American, 12% African American, 5% Asian American/Pacific Islander **The most frequently chosen baccalaureate fields are** education, biological/life sciences, philosophy **Academic program** English as a second language, advanced placement, accelerated degree program, self-designed majors, honors program, summer session, adult/continuing education programs, internships **Contact** Office of Admissions, North Park University, 3225 West Foster Avenue, Chicago, IL 60625-4895. Telephone: 773-244-5500 or toll-free 800-888-NPC8. Fax: 773-583-0858. E-mail: afao@northpark.edu. Web site: http://www.northpark.edu/.

NORTHWESTERN UNIVERSITY
EVANSTON, ILLINOIS

General Independent, university, coed **Entrance** Most difficult **Setting** 250-acre suburban campus **Total enrollment** 15,649 **Student-faculty ratio** 7:1 **Application deadline** 1/1 (freshmen), 6/1 (transfer) **Freshmen** 34% were admitted **Housing** Yes **Expenses** Tuition $25,839; Room & Board $7776 **Undergraduates** 53% women, 2% part-time, 1% 25 or older, 0.2% Native American, 4% Hispanic American, 6% African American, 17% Asian American/Pacific Islander **The most frequently chosen baccalaureate fields are** engineering/engineering technologies, communications/communication technologies, social sciences and history **Academic program** Advanced placement, accelerated degree program, self-designed majors, honors program, summer session, adult/continuing education programs, internships **Contact** Ms. Carol Lunkenheimer, Director of Admissions, Northwestern University, PO Box 3060, Evanston, IL 60204-3060. Telephone: 847-491-7271. E-mail: ug-admission@northwestern.edu. Web site: http://www.northwestern.edu/.

OLIVET NAZARENE UNIVERSITY
BOURBONNAIS, ILLINOIS

General Independent, comprehensive, coed, affiliated with Church of the Nazarene **Entrance** Moderately difficult **Setting** 168-acre small-town campus **Total enrollment** 3,350 **Student-faculty ratio** 20:1 **Application deadline** Rolling (freshmen), rolling (transfer) **Freshmen** 79% were admitted **Housing** Yes **Expenses** Tuition $13,464; Room & Board $4980 **Undergraduates** 57% women, 15% part-time, 17% 25 or older, 0.2% Native American, 2% Hispanic American, 7% African American, 1% Asian American/Pacific Islander **The most frequently chosen baccalaureate fields are** education, business/marketing, health professions and related sciences **Academic program** Advanced placement, summer session, adult/continuing education programs, internships **Contact** Mr. Brian Parker, Director of Admissions, Olivet Nazarene University, One University Avenue, Bourbonnais, IL 60914. Telephone: 815-939-5203 or toll-free 800-648-1463. Fax: 815-935-4998. E-mail: admissions@olivet.edu. Web site: http://www.olivet.edu/.

PRINCIPIA COLLEGE
ELSAH, ILLINOIS

General Independent Christian Science, 4-year, coed **Entrance** Moderately difficult **Setting** 2,600-acre rural campus **Total enrollment** 554 **Student-faculty ratio** 9:1 **Application deadline** 3/1 (freshmen), 3/1 (transfer) **Freshmen** 93% were admitted **Housing** Yes **Expenses** Tuition $16,840; Room & Board $5790 **Undergraduates** 56% women, 4% part-time, 3% 25 or older, 0% Native American, 2% Hispanic American, 1% African American, 1% Asian American/Pacific Islander **The most frequently chosen baccalaureate fields are** social sciences and history, biological/life sciences, visual/performing arts **Academic program** English as a second language, advanced placement, accelerated degree program, self-designed majors, honors program, adult/continuing education programs, internships **Contact** Martha Green Quirk, Dean of Admissions, Principia College, Office of Admissions and Enrollment, Elsah, IL 62028. Telephone: 618-374-5180 or toll-free 800-277-4648 Ext. 2802. Fax: 618-374-4000. E-mail: collegeadmissions@prin.edu. Web site: http://www.prin.edu/college.

QUINCY UNIVERSITY
QUINCY, ILLINOIS

General Independent Roman Catholic, comprehensive, coed **Entrance** Moderately difficult **Setting**

ILLINOIS

Quincy University *(continued)*
75-acre small-town campus **Total enrollment** 1,319 **Student-faculty ratio** 14:1 **Application deadline** Rolling (freshmen), rolling (transfer) **Freshmen** 96% were admitted **Housing** Yes **Expenses** Tuition $15,430; Room & Board $5020 **Undergraduates** 56% women, 13% part-time, 14% 25 or older, 0.2% Native American, 2% Hispanic American, 6% African American, 1% Asian American/Pacific Islander **The most frequently chosen baccalaureate fields are** business/marketing, education, protective services/public administration **Academic program** English as a second language, advanced placement, accelerated degree program, self-designed majors, honors program, summer session, adult/continuing education programs, internships **Contact** Mr. Kevin A. Brown, Director of Admissions, Quincy University, 1800 College Avenue, Quincy, IL 62301-2699. Telephone: 217-222-8020 Ext. 5215 or toll-free 800-688-4295. E-mail: admissions@quincy.edu. Web site: http://www.quincy.edu/.

ROBERT MORRIS COLLEGE
CHICAGO, ILLINOIS

General Independent, 4-year, coed **Entrance** Minimally difficult **Setting** urban campus **Total enrollment** 5,319 **Student-faculty ratio** 27:1 **Application deadline** Rolling (freshmen), rolling (transfer) **Freshmen** 69% were admitted **Housing** No **Expenses** Tuition $12,150 **Undergraduates** 68% women, 11% part-time, 39% 25 or older, 0.3% Native American, 24% Hispanic American, 41% African American, 3% Asian American/Pacific Islander **The most frequently chosen baccalaureate fields are** business/marketing, computer/information sciences, visual/performing arts **Academic program** Advanced placement, accelerated degree program, honors program, summer session, adult/continuing education programs, internships **Contact** Ms. Deb Dahlen, Senior Vice President for Institutional Advancement, Robert Morris College, 401 South State Street, Chicago, IL 60605. Telephone: 312-935-6600 or toll-free 800-225-1520. Fax: 312-935-6819. E-mail: enroll@rmcil.edu. Web site: http://www.rmcil.edu/.

ROCKFORD COLLEGE
ROCKFORD, ILLINOIS

General Independent, comprehensive, coed **Entrance** Moderately difficult **Setting** 130-acre suburban campus **Total enrollment** 1,359 **Student-faculty ratio** 10:1 **Application deadline** Rolling (freshmen), rolling (transfer) **Freshmen** 61% were admitted **Housing** Yes **Expenses** Tuition $17,450; Room & Board $5630 **Undergraduates** 63% women, 23% part-time, 16% 25 or older, 0.4% Native American, 5% Hispanic American, 8% African American, 2% Asian American/Pacific Islander **Academic program** English as a second language, advanced placement, self-designed majors, honors program, summer session, adult/continuing education programs, internships **Contact** Mr. William Laffey, Director of Admission, Rockford College, Nelson Hall, Rockford, IL 61108-2393. Telephone: 815-226-4050 Ext. 3330 or toll-free 800-892-2984. Fax: 815-226-2822. E-mail: admission@rockford.edu. Web site: http://www.rockford.edu/.

ROOSEVELT UNIVERSITY
CHICAGO, ILLINOIS

General Independent, comprehensive, coed **Entrance** Moderately difficult **Setting** urban campus **Total enrollment** 7,490 **Student-faculty ratio** 16:1 **Application deadline** 8/15 (freshmen), 8/15 (transfer) **Freshmen** 71% were admitted **Housing** Yes **Expenses** Tuition $13,970; Room & Board $6270 **Undergraduates** 64% women, 59% part-time, 63% 25 or older, 0.5% Native American, 12% Hispanic American, 27% African American, 4% Asian American/Pacific Islander **The most frequently chosen baccalaureate fields are** business/marketing, psychology, social sciences and history **Academic program** English as a second language, advanced placement, accelerated degree program, self-designed majors, honors program, summer session, adult/continuing education programs, internships **Contact** Mr. Brian Lynch, Director of Admission, Roosevelt University, Office of Admissions, 430 South Michigan Avenue, Room 576, Chicago, IL 60605-1394. Telephone: 312-341-2101 or toll-free 877-APPLYRU. Fax: 312-341-3523. E-mail: dessimm@admvsbk.roosevelt.edu. Web site: http://www.roosevelt.edu/.

RUSH UNIVERSITY
CHICAGO, ILLINOIS

General Independent, upper-level, coed **Entrance** Moderately difficult **Setting** 35-acre urban campus **Total enrollment** 1,268 **Student-faculty ratio** 8:1 **Application deadline** Rolling (transfer) **First-Year Students** 55% were admitted **Housing** Yes **Expenses** Tuition $14,175; Room only $7038 **Undergraduates** 88% women, 11% part-time, 43% 25 or older, 0% Native American, 16% Hispanic American, 8% African American, 16% Asian American/Pacific Islander **The most frequently chosen baccalaureate field is** biological/life sciences **Contact** Ms. Hicela Castruita Woods, Director of College Admission Services, Rush University, 600 S. Paulina - Suite 440, College Admissions Services, Chicago, IL 60612-3878. Telephone: 312-942-7100. Fax: 312-942-2219. E-mail: ruadmissions@rushu.rush.edu. Web site: http://www.rushu.rush.edu/.

SAINT ANTHONY COLLEGE OF NURSING
ROCKFORD, ILLINOIS

General Independent Roman Catholic, upper-level, coed, primarily women **Entrance** Moderately difficult **Setting** 17-acre urban campus **Total enrollment** 77 **Student-faculty ratio** 6:1 **Application deadline** Rolling (transfer) **First-Year Students** 61% were admitted **Housing** No **Expenses** Tuition $12,113 **Undergraduates** 95% women, 31% part-time, 50% 25 or older, 0% Native American, 3% Hispanic American, 3% African American, 3% Asian American/Pacific Islander **The most frequently chosen bacca-

ILLINOIS

laureate field is health professions and related sciences **Academic program** Advanced placement, summer session **Contact** Ms. Nancy Sanders, Director of Student Services, Saint Anthony College of Nursing, 5658 East State Street, Rockford, IL 61108-2468. Telephone: 815-395-5100. Fax: 815-395 Ext. 2275. E-mail: nancysanders@sacn.edu. Web site: http://www.sacn.edu/.

ST. AUGUSTINE COLLEGE
CHICAGO, ILLINOIS

General Independent, 4-year, coed **Entrance** Noncompetitive **Setting** 4-acre urban campus **Total enrollment** 1,814 **Student-faculty ratio** 13:1 **Application deadline** Rolling (freshmen), rolling (transfer) **Housing** No **Expenses** Tuition $7232 **Undergraduates** 78% women, 23% part-time, 60% 25 or older, 0.2% Native American, 86% Hispanic American, 8% African American, 3% Asian American/Pacific Islander **The most frequently chosen baccalaureate field is** social sciences and history **Academic program** English as a second language, summer session, internships **Contact** Ms. Soledad Ruiz, Director of Admissions, St. Augustine College, 1333-1345 West Argyle, Chicago, IL 60640-3501. Telephone: 773-878-8756 Ext. 243. Web site: http://www.staugustinecollege.edu/.

SAINT FRANCIS MEDICAL CENTER COLLEGE OF NURSING
PEORIA, ILLINOIS

General Independent Roman Catholic, upper-level, coed, primarily women **Entrance** Moderately difficult **Setting** urban campus **Total enrollment** 143 **Student-faculty ratio** 8:1 **Application deadline** Rolling (transfer) **First-Year Students** 80% were admitted **Housing** Yes **Expenses** Tuition $9372; Room only $1680 **Undergraduates** 94% women, 24% part-time, 45% 25 or older, 0% Native American, 1% Hispanic American, 1% African American, 3% Asian American/Pacific Islander **The most frequently chosen baccalaureate field is** health professions and related sciences **Academic program** Advanced placement, summer session **Contact** Mrs. Janice Farquharson, Director of Admissions and Registrar, Saint Francis Medical Center College of Nursing, 511 Greenleaf Street, Peoria, IL 61603-3783. Telephone: 309-655-2596. Fax: 309-624-8973. E-mail: janice.farquharson@osfhealthcare.org. Web site: http://www.sfmccon.edu/.

ST. JOHN'S COLLEGE
SPRINGFIELD, ILLINOIS

General Independent Roman Catholic, upper-level, coed, primarily women **Entrance** Moderately difficult **Setting** urban campus **Total enrollment** 58 **Student-faculty ratio** 4:1 **First-Year Students** 74% were admitted **Housing** No **Expenses** Tuition $8521 **Undergraduates** 95% women, 5% part-time, 28% 25 or older, 0% Native American, 5% Hispanic American, 3% African American, 0% Asian American/Pacific Islander **The most frequently chosen baccalaureate field is** health professions and related sciences **Contact** Ms. Beth Beasley, Student Development Officer, St. John's College, 421 North Ninth Street, Springfield, IL 62702-5317. Telephone: 217-525-5628 Ext. 45468. Web site: http://www.st-johns.org/collegeofnursing/.

SAINT XAVIER UNIVERSITY
CHICAGO, ILLINOIS

General Independent Roman Catholic, comprehensive, coed **Entrance** Moderately difficult **Setting** 55-acre urban campus **Total enrollment** 4,916 **Student-faculty ratio** 14:1 **Application deadline** 8/15 (freshmen), 8/15 (transfer) **Freshmen** 73% were admitted **Housing** Yes **Expenses** Tuition $15,130; Room & Board $5974 **Undergraduates** 71% women, 29% part-time, 28% 25 or older, 0.4% Native American, 12% Hispanic American, 16% African American, 2% Asian American/Pacific Islander **The most frequently chosen baccalaureate fields are** business/marketing, education, health professions and related sciences **Academic program** English as a second language, advanced placement, accelerated degree program, self-designed majors, honors program, summer session, adult/continuing education programs, internships **Contact** Elizabeth A. Gierach, Director of Enrollment Services, Saint Xavier University, 3700 West 103rd Street, Chicago, IL 60655-3105. Telephone: 773-298-3063 or toll-free 800-462-9288. Fax: 773-298-3076 Ext. 3050. E-mail: admissions@sxu.edu. Web site: http://www.sxu.edu/.

SCHOLL COLLEGE OF PODIATRIC MEDICINE AT FINCH UNIVERSITY OF HEALTH SCIENCES/THE CHICAGO MEDICAL SCHOOL
CHICAGO, ILLINOIS

General Independent, upper-level, coed **Entrance** Moderately difficult **Setting** urban campus **Total enrollment** 248 **Student-faculty ratio** 7:1 **Application deadline** 8/1 (transfer) **Housing** No **Expenses** Tuition $22,549 **Undergraduates** 62% 25 or older **The most frequently chosen baccalaureate field is** biological/life sciences **Academic program** Accelerated degree program, honors program, adult/continuing education programs **Contact** Mr. Thomas C. Taylor, Assistant Dean for Student Affairs, Scholl College of Podiatric Medicine at Finch University of Health Sciences/The Chicago Medical School, Office of Admissions, 3333 Green Bay Road, North Chicago, IL 60064-3095. Telephone: 312-280-2940 or toll-free 800-843-3059. Fax: 312-255-8169. E-mail: admiss@scholl.edu. Web site: http://www.finchcms.edu/scholl/.

SCHOOL OF THE ART INSTITUTE OF CHICAGO
CHICAGO, ILLINOIS

General Independent, comprehensive, coed **Entrance** Moderately difficult **Setting** 1-acre urban campus

School of the Art Institute of Chicago *(continued)*

Total enrollment 2,675 **Student-faculty ratio** 13:1 **Application deadline** 8/15 (freshmen), 8/15 (transfer) **Freshmen** 79% were admitted **Housing** Yes **Expenses** Tuition $21,300; Room only $6500 **Undergraduates** 64% women, 22% part-time, 16% 25 or older, 1% Native American, 5% Hispanic American, 3% African American, 10% Asian American/Pacific Islander **Academic program** English as a second language, advanced placement, self-designed majors, summer session, internships **Contact** Kendra E. Dane, Executive Director of Admissions and Marketing, School of the Art Institute of Chicago, 37 South Wabash, Chicago, IL 60603. Telephone: 312-899-5219 or toll-free 800-232-SAIC. E-mail: admiss@artic.edu. Web site: http://www.artic.edu/saic/.

SHIMER COLLEGE
WAUKEGAN, ILLINOIS

General Independent, 4-year, coed **Entrance** Moderately difficult **Setting** 3-acre suburban campus **Total enrollment** 106 **Student-faculty ratio** 10:1 **Application deadline** 8/30 (freshmen), 8/30 (transfer) **Freshmen** 94% were admitted **Housing** Yes **Expenses** Tuition $15,110; Room only $2300 **Undergraduates** 49% women, 7% part-time, 46% 25 or older, 1% Native American, 3% Hispanic American, 7% African American, 1% Asian American/Pacific Islander **Academic program** Accelerated degree program, self-designed majors, summer session, adult/continuing education programs **Contact** Mr. David Buchanan, Admissions Counselor, Shimer College, PO Box 500, Waukegan, IL 60079-0500. Telephone: 847-249-7174 or toll-free 800-215-7173. Fax: 847-249-7171. E-mail: admissions@shimer.edu. Web site: http://www.shimer.edu/.

SOUTHERN ILLINOIS UNIVERSITY CARBONDALE
CARBONDALE, ILLINOIS

General State-supported, university, coed **Entrance** Moderately difficult **Setting** 1,128-acre small-town campus **Total enrollment** 21,598 **Student-faculty ratio** 17:1 **Application deadline** Rolling (freshmen), rolling (transfer) **Freshmen** 69% were admitted **Housing** Yes **Expenses** Tuition $4254; Room & Board $4367 **Undergraduates** 44% women, 10% part-time, 24% 25 or older, 1% Native American, 3% Hispanic American, 13% African American, 1% Asian American/Pacific Islander **The most frequently chosen baccalaureate fields are** education, business/marketing, engineering/engineering technologies **Academic program** English as a second language, advanced placement, accelerated degree program, honors program, summer session, adult/continuing education programs, internships **Contact** Mr. Walker Allen, Director of Admissions, Southern Illinois University Carbondale, Mail Code 4710, Carbondale, IL 62901-4710. Telephone: 618-536-4405. Fax: 618-453-3250. E-mail: admrec@siu.edu. Web site: http://www.siuc.edu.

SOUTHERN ILLINOIS UNIVERSITY EDWARDSVILLE
EDWARDSVILLE, ILLINOIS

General State-supported, comprehensive, coed **Entrance** Moderately difficult **Setting** 2,660-acre suburban campus **Total enrollment** 12,442 **Student-faculty ratio** 17:1 **Application deadline** 5/31 (freshmen), 7/31 (transfer) **Freshmen** 87% were admitted **Housing** Yes **Expenses** Tuition $3,285; Room & Board $4870 **Undergraduates** 57% women, 18% part-time, 20% 25 or older, 0.4% Native American, 1% Hispanic American, 12% African American, 1% Asian American/Pacific Islander **The most frequently chosen baccalaureate fields are** business/marketing, education, social sciences and history **Academic program** English as a second language, advanced placement, accelerated degree program, self-designed majors, honors program, summer session, adult/continuing education programs, internships **Contact** Mr. Boyd Bradshaw, Director of Admissions, Southern Illinois University Edwardsville, Box 1600, Edwardsville, IL 62026-0001. Telephone: 618-650-3705 or toll-free 800-447-SIUE. Fax: 618-650-5013. E-mail: admis@siue.edu. Web site: http://www.siue.edu/.

TELSHE YESHIVA–CHICAGO
CHICAGO, ILLINOIS

Contact Rosh Hayeshiva, Telshe Yeshiva–Chicago, 3535 West Foster Avenue, Chicago, IL 60625-5598. Telephone: 773-463-7738.

TRINITY CHRISTIAN COLLEGE
PALOS HEIGHTS, ILLINOIS

General Independent interdenominational, 4-year, coed **Entrance** Moderately difficult **Setting** 53-acre suburban campus **Total enrollment** 973 **Student-faculty ratio** 13:1 **Application deadline** Rolling (freshmen), rolling (transfer) **Freshmen** 83% were admitted **Housing** Yes **Expenses** Tuition $13,970; Room & Board $5446 **Undergraduates** 63% women, 16% part-time, 6% 25 or older, 0.4% Native American, 2% Hispanic American, 7% African American, 2% Asian American/Pacific Islander **The most frequently chosen baccalaureate fields are** business/marketing, education, health professions and related sciences **Academic program** Advanced placement, honors program, adult/continuing education programs, internships **Contact** Mr. Pete Hamstra, Dean of Admissions, Trinity Christian College, 6601 West College Drive, Palos Heights, IL 60463. Telephone: 708-239-4709 or toll-free 800-748-0085. Fax: 708-239-4826. E-mail: admissions@trnty.edu. Web site: http://www.trnty.edu/.

TRINITY COLLEGE OF NURSING AND HEALTH SCIENCES SCHOOLS
MOLINE, ILLINOIS

General Independent, 4-year, coed **Entrance** Most difficult **Setting** 1-acre urban campus **Total enrollment 98 **Student-faculty ratio** 16:1 **Application deadline** 6/1 (freshmen), 6/1 (transfer) **Freshmen** 60% were admitted **Housing** Yes **Expenses** Tuition $8275 **Undergraduates** 98% women, 50% part-time, 35% 25 or older **The most frequently chosen baccalaureate field is** health professions and related sciences **Academic program** Honors program, summer session, adult/continuing education programs **Contact** Ms. Barbara Kimpe, Admissions Representative, Trinity College of Nursing and Health Sciences Schools, 555 6th Street, Moline, IL 61265-1216. Telephone: 309-779-7812. Fax: 309-757-2194. E-mail: con@trinityqc.com. Web site: http://www.trinitycollegeqc.edu/.

TRINITY INTERNATIONAL UNIVERSITY
DEERFIELD, ILLINOIS

General Independent, university, coed, affiliated with Evangelical Free Church of America **Entrance** Moderately difficult **Setting** 108-acre suburban campus **Total enrollment** 2,168 **Student-faculty ratio** 19:1 **Application deadline** Rolling (freshmen), rolling (transfer) **Freshmen** 82% were admitted **Housing** Yes **Expenses** Tuition $15,350; Room & Board $5290 **Undergraduates** 58% women, 8% part-time, 0.3% Native American, 4% Hispanic American, 10% African American, 3% Asian American/Pacific Islander **The most frequently chosen baccalaureate fields are** education, communications/communication technologies, philosophy **Academic program** Advanced placement, honors program, adult/continuing education programs, internships **Contact** Mr. Matt Yoder, Director of Undergraduate Admissions, Trinity International University, 2065 Half Day Road, Peterson Wing, McClennan Building, Deerfield, IL 60015-1284. Telephone: 847-317-7000 or toll-free 800-822-3225 (out-of-state). Fax: 847-317-7081. E-mail: tcdadm@tiu.edu. Web site: http://www.tiu.edu/.

UNIVERSITY OF CHICAGO
CHICAGO, ILLINOIS

General Independent, university, coed **Entrance** Most difficult **Setting** 203-acre urban campus **Total enrollment** 12,576 **Student-faculty ratio** 4:1 **Application deadline** 1/1 (freshmen), 4/11 (transfer) **Freshmen** 44% were admitted **Housing** Yes **Expenses** Tuition $26,475; Room & Board $8312 **Undergraduates** 51% women, 1% part-time, 1% 25 or older, 0.2% Native American, 7% Hispanic American, 4% African American, 16% Asian American/Pacific Islander **The most frequently chosen baccalaureate fields are** biological/life sciences, English, social sciences and history **Academic program** Advanced placement, accelerated degree program, self-designed majors, summer session, adult/continuing education programs, internships **Contact** Mr. Theodore O'Neill, Dean of Admissions, University of Chicago, 1116 East 59th Street, Chicago, IL 60637-1513. Telephone: 773-702-8650. Fax: 773-702-4199. E-mail: college-admissions@uchicago.edu. Web site: http://www.uchicago.edu/.

UNIVERSITY OF ILLINOIS AT CHICAGO
CHICAGO, ILLINOIS

General State-supported, university, coed **Entrance** Moderately difficult **Setting** 216-acre urban campus **Total enrollment** 24,955 **Student-faculty ratio** 14:1 **Application deadline** 2/28 (freshmen), 6/1 (transfer) **Freshmen** 64% were admitted **Housing** Yes **Expenses** Tuition $4944; Room & Board $6058 **Undergraduates** 55% women, 11% part-time, 14% 25 or older, 0.3% Native American, 17% Hispanic American, 9% African American, 24% Asian American/Pacific Islander **The most frequently chosen baccalaureate fields are** business/marketing, engineering/engineering technologies, psychology **Academic program** English as a second language, advanced placement, accelerated degree program, self-designed majors, honors program, summer session, internships **Contact** Mr. Rob Sheinkopf, Executive Director of Admissions, University of Illinois at Chicago, Box 5220, Chicago, IL 60680-5220. Telephone: 312-996-4350. Fax: 312-413-7628. E-mail: cqadmit@uicvmc.aiss.uic.edu. Web site: http://www.uic.edu/.

UNIVERSITY OF ILLINOIS AT SPRINGFIELD
SPRINGFIELD, ILLINOIS

General State-supported, upper-level, coed **Entrance** Minimally difficult **Setting** 746-acre suburban campus **Total enrollment** 4,288 **Student-faculty ratio** 15:1 **Application deadline** Rolling (transfer) **First-Year Students** 51% were admitted **Housing** Yes **Expenses** Tuition $3611; Room only $3060 **Undergraduates** 64% women, 47% part-time, 59% 25 or older, 0.1% Native American, 1% Hispanic American, 8% African American, 2% Asian American/Pacific Islander **The most frequently chosen baccalaureate fields are** business/marketing, communications/communication technologies, psychology **Academic program** Self-designed majors, summer session, adult/continuing education programs, internships **Contact** Office of Enrollment Services, University of Illinois at Springfield, Building SAB, Springfield, IL 62794-9243. Telephone: 217-206-6626 or toll-free 800-252-8533 (in-state). Fax: 217-206-6620. Web site: http://www.uis.edu/.

UNIVERSITY OF ILLINOIS AT URBANA–CHAMPAIGN
CHAMPAIGN, ILLINOIS

General State-supported, university, coed **Entrance** Very difficult **Setting** 1,470-acre small-town campus **Total enrollment** 38,759 **Student-faculty ratio** 15:1 **Application deadline** 1/1 (freshmen), 3/15 (transfer) **Freshmen** 62% were admitted **Housing** Yes **Expenses** Tuition $5794; Room & Board $6090 **Undergraduates** 48% women, 4% part-time, 2% 25 or older, 0.2% Native American, 6% Hispanic American, 7% African American, 13% Asian American/Pacific Islander **The most frequently chosen baccalaureate fields are** business/marketing, engineering/engineering technologies, social sciences and history

ILLINOIS

University of Illinois at Urbana–Champaign *(continued)*
Academic program Advanced placement, accelerated degree program, self-designed majors, honors program, summer session, internships **Contact** Mr. Abel Mandujano, Assistant Director of Admissions, University of Illinois at Urbana–Champaign, 901 West Illinois, Urbana, IL 61801. Telephone: 217-333-0302. E-mail: admssion@uiuc.edu. Web site: http://www.uiuc.edu/.

UNIVERSITY OF ST. FRANCIS
JOLIET, ILLINOIS

General Independent Roman Catholic, comprehensive, coed **Entrance** Moderately difficult **Setting** 16-acre suburban campus **Total enrollment** 2,630 **Student-faculty ratio** 11:1 **Application deadline** Rolling (freshmen), rolling (transfer) **Freshmen** 80% were admitted **Housing** Yes **Expenses** Tuition $14,990; Room & Board $5580 **Undergraduates** 67% women, 21% part-time, 28% 25 or older, 0.2% Native American, 6% Hispanic American, 7% African American, 2% Asian American/Pacific Islander **The most frequently chosen baccalaureate fields are** education, communications/communication technologies, health professions and related sciences **Academic program** Advanced placement, accelerated degree program, self-designed majors, summer session, adult/continuing education programs, internships **Contact** Mr. Mike Rodewald, Director of Freshman Admission, University of St. Francis, 500 North Wilcox Street, Joliet, IL 60435-6188. Telephone: 815-740-5037 or toll-free 800-735-7500. Fax: 815-740-5078. E-mail: admissions@stfrancis.edu. Web site: http://www.stfrancis.edu/.

VANDERCOOK COLLEGE OF MUSIC
CHICAGO, ILLINOIS

General Independent, comprehensive, coed **Entrance** Moderately difficult **Setting** 1-acre urban campus **Total enrollment** 230 **Student-faculty ratio** 7:1 **Application deadline** 5/1 (freshmen), 5/1 (transfer) **Housing** Yes **Expenses** Tuition $13,810; Room & Board $5600 **Undergraduates** 38% women, 49% part-time, 16% 25 or older, 0% Native American, 17% Hispanic American, 17% African American, 0% Asian American/Pacific Islander **The most frequently chosen baccalaureate field is** education **Academic program** Advanced placement, summer session, adult/continuing education programs, internships **Contact** Mr. James Malley, Director of Undergraduate Admission, VanderCook College of Music, 3140 South Federal Street, Chicago, IL 60616. Telephone: 800-448-2655 Ext. 241 or toll-free 800-448-2655. Fax: 312-225-5211. E-mail: admissions@vandercook.edu. Web site: http://www.vandercook.edu/.

WESTERN ILLINOIS UNIVERSITY
MACOMB, ILLINOIS

General State-supported, comprehensive, coed **Entrance** Moderately difficult **Setting** 1,050-acre small-town campus **Total enrollment** 13,206 **Student-faculty ratio** 17:1 **Application deadline** 8/1 (freshmen), rolling (transfer) **Freshmen** 61% were admitted **Housing** Yes **Expenses** Tuition $4206; Room & Board $4822 **Undergraduates** 51% women, 14% part-time, 16% 25 or older, 0.2% Native American, 3% Hispanic American, 7% African American, 1% Asian American/Pacific Islander **The most frequently chosen baccalaureate fields are** education, liberal arts/general studies, protective services/public administration **Academic program** English as a second language, advanced placement, self-designed majors, honors program, summer session, adult/continuing education programs, internships **Contact** Ms. Karen Helmers, Director of Admissions, Western Illinois University, 1 University Circle, 115 Sherman Hall, Macomb, IL 61455-1390. Telephone: 309-298-3157 or toll-free 877-742-5948. Fax: 309-298-3111. E-mail: karen_helmers@wiu.edu. Web site: http://www.wiu.edu/.

▶ For more information, see page 498.

WEST SUBURBAN COLLEGE OF NURSING
OAK PARK, ILLINOIS

General Independent, 4-year, coed **Entrance** Moderately difficult **Setting** 10-acre suburban campus **Total enrollment** 121 **Student-faculty ratio** 10:1 **Application deadline** Rolling (freshmen), rolling (transfer) **Freshmen** 35% were admitted **Housing** Yes **Expenses** Tuition $15,000; Room & Board $4900 **Undergraduates** 98% women, 0% Native American, 7% Hispanic American, 14% African American, 7% Asian American/Pacific Islander **The most frequently chosen baccalaureate field is** health professions and related sciences **Academic program** Advanced placement, summer session, adult/continuing education programs **Contact** Ms. Dara P. Lawyer, Interim Director of Admission, West Suburban College of Nursing, 3 Erie Court, Oak Park, IL 60302. Telephone: 708-763-6530. Fax: 708-763-1531. E-mail: wsadmis@crf.cuis.edu.

WHEATON COLLEGE
WHEATON, ILLINOIS

General Independent nondenominational, comprehensive, coed **Entrance** Very difficult **Setting** 80-acre suburban campus **Total enrollment** 2,844 **Student-faculty ratio** 11:1 **Application deadline** 1/15 (freshmen), 3/1 (transfer) **Freshmen** 57% were admitted **Housing** Yes **Expenses** Tuition $16,390; Room & Board $5544 **Undergraduates** 51% women, 2% part-time, 1% 25 or older, 0.3% Native American, 3% Hispanic American, 2% African American, 4% Asian American/Pacific Islander **The most frequently chosen baccalaureate fields are** English, philosophy, philosophy, religion, and theology **Academic program** Advanced placement, self-designed majors, summer session, internships **Contact** Ms. Shawn Leftwich, Director of Admissions, Wheaton College, 501 College Avenue, Wheaton, IL 60187-5593. Telephone: 630-752-5011 or toll-free 800-222-2419 (out-

INDIANA

of-state). Fax: 630-752-5285. E-mail: admissions@wheaton.edu. Web site: http://www.wheaton.edu/.

INDIANA

ANDERSON UNIVERSITY
ANDERSON, INDIANA

General Independent, comprehensive, coed, affiliated with Church of God **Entrance** Moderately difficult **Setting** 100-acre suburban campus **Total enrollment** 2,426 **Student-faculty ratio** 13:1 **Application deadline** 7/1 (freshmen), 8/25 (transfer) **Freshmen** 76% were admitted **Housing** Yes **Expenses** Tuition $15,380; Room & Board $5020 **Undergraduates** 58% women, 10% part-time, 9% 25 or older, 0.3% Native American, 1% Hispanic American, 5% African American, 1% Asian American/Pacific Islander **The most frequently chosen baccalaureate fields are** business/marketing, education, philosophy **Academic program** Advanced placement, accelerated degree program, self-designed majors, honors program, summer session, adult/continuing education programs, internships **Contact** Mr. Jim King, Director of Admissions, Anderson University, 1100 East 5th Street, Anderson, IN 46012-3495. Telephone: 765-641-4080 or toll-free 800-421-3014 (in-state); 800-428-6414 (out-of-state). Fax: 765-641-3851. E-mail: info@anderson.edu. Web site: http://www.anderson.edu/.

BALL STATE UNIVERSITY
MUNCIE, INDIANA

General State-supported, university, coed **Entrance** Moderately difficult **Setting** 955-acre suburban campus **Total enrollment** 19,408 **Student-faculty ratio** 14:1 **Application deadline** Rolling (freshmen), rolling (transfer) **Freshmen** 76% were admitted **Housing** Yes **Expenses** Tuition $4034; Room & Board $5100 **Undergraduates** 53% women, 8% part-time, 8% 25 or older, 0.3% Native American, 1% Hispanic American, 6% African American, 1% Asian American/Pacific Islander **The most frequently chosen baccalaureate fields are** business/marketing, education, liberal arts/general studies **Academic program** English as a second language, advanced placement, honors program, summer session, adult/continuing education programs, internships **Contact** Dr. Lawrence Waters, Dean of Admissions and Financial Aid, Ball State University, 2000 University Avenue, Muncie, IN 47306. Telephone: 765-285-8300 or toll-free 800-482-4BSU. Fax: 765-285-1632. E-mail: askus@wp.bsu.edu. Web site: http://www.bsu.edu/.

BETHEL COLLEGE
MISHAWAKA, INDIANA

General Independent, comprehensive, coed, affiliated with Missionary Church **Entrance** Moderately difficult **Setting** 70-acre suburban campus **Total enrollment** 1,660 **Student-faculty ratio** 18:1 **Application deadline** 8/1 (freshmen), 8/1 (transfer) **Freshmen** 69% were admitted **Housing** Yes **Expenses** Tuition $13,400; Room & Board $4350 **Undergraduates** 64% women, 27% part-time, 33% 25 or older, 0.4% Native American, 1% Hispanic American, 9% African American, 1% Asian American/Pacific Islander **The most frequently chosen baccalaureate fields are** business/marketing, education, health professions and related sciences **Academic program** Advanced placement, accelerated degree program, honors program, summer session, adult/continuing education programs, internships **Contact** Ms. Andrea M. Helmuth, Director of Admissions, Bethel College, 1001 West McKinley Avenue, Mishawaka, IN 46545-5591. Telephone: 574-257-3319 or toll-free 800-422-4101. Fax: 574-257-3335. E-mail: admissions@bethelcollege.edu. Web site: http://www.bethelcollege.edu.

BUTLER UNIVERSITY
INDIANAPOLIS, INDIANA

General Independent, comprehensive, coed **Entrance** Moderately difficult **Setting** 290-acre urban campus **Total enrollment** 4,264 **Student-faculty ratio** 13:1 **Application deadline** 8/15 (freshmen), 8/15 (transfer) **Freshmen** 85% were admitted **Housing** Yes **Expenses** Tuition $19,130; Room & Board $6450 **Undergraduates** 63% women, 3% part-time, 3% 25 or older, 0.1% Native American, 1% Hispanic American, 4% African American, 2% Asian American/Pacific Islander **The most frequently chosen baccalaureate fields are** business/marketing, education, health professions and related sciences **Academic program** English as a second language, advanced placement, accelerated degree program, honors program, summer session, adult/continuing education programs, internships **Contact** Mr. William Preble, Dean of Admissions, Butler University, 4600 Sunset Avenue, Indianapolis, IN 46208-3485. Telephone: 317-940-8100 Ext. 8124 or toll-free 888-940-8100. Fax: 317-940-8150. E-mail: admission@butler.edu. Web site: http://www.butler.edu/.

CALUMET COLLEGE OF SAINT JOSEPH
WHITING, INDIANA

Contact Mr. Thomas A. Clark, Vice President for Enrollment Management, Calumet College of Saint Joseph, 2400 New York Avenue, Whiting, IN 46394-2195. Telephone: 219-473-4215 or toll-free 877-700-9100. Fax: 219-473-4259. Web site: http://www.ccsj.edu/.

CROSSROADS BIBLE COLLEGE
INDIANAPOLIS, INDIANA

Contact Crossroads Bible College, 601 North Shortridge Road, Indianapolis, IN 46219. Telephone: or toll-free 800-273-2224.

DEPAUW UNIVERSITY
GREENCASTLE, INDIANA

General Independent, 4-year, coed, affiliated with United Methodist Church **Entrance** Moderately dif-

INDIANA

DePauw University *(continued)*
ficult **Setting** 175-acre small-town campus **Total enrollment** 2,219 **Student-faculty ratio** 10:1 **Application deadline** 2/1 (freshmen), 3/1 (transfer) **Freshmen** 53% were admitted **Housing** Yes **Expenses** Tuition $21,500; Room & Board $6500 **Undergraduates** 56% women, 2% part-time, 0.2% 25 or older, 0.4% Native American, 2% Hispanic American, 6% African American, 2% Asian American/Pacific Islander **The most frequently chosen baccalaureate fields are** communications/communication technologies, computer/information sciences, English **Academic program** Advanced placement, self-designed majors, honors program, internships **Contact** Director of Admission, DePauw University, 101 East Seminary Street, Greencastle, IN 46135-0037. Telephone: 765-658-4006 or toll-free 800-447-2495. Fax: 765-658-4007. E-mail: admission@depauw.edu. Web site: http://www.depauw.edu/.

EARLHAM COLLEGE
RICHMOND, INDIANA

General Independent, comprehensive, coed, affiliated with Society of Friends **Entrance** Moderately difficult **Setting** 800-acre small-town campus **Total enrollment** 1,098 **Student-faculty ratio** 11:1 **Application deadline** 2/15 (freshmen), 4/1 (transfer) **Freshmen** 80% were admitted **Housing** Yes **Expenses** Tuition $22,308; Room & Board $5138 **Undergraduates** 55% women, 2% part-time, 2% 25 or older, 0.1% Native American, 2% Hispanic American, 8% African American, 2% Asian American/Pacific Islander **The most frequently chosen baccalaureate fields are** psychology, biological/life sciences, social sciences and history **Academic program** Advanced placement, accelerated degree program, self-designed majors, internships **Contact** Director of Admissions, Earlham College, 801 National Road West, Richmond, IN 47374. Telephone: 765-983-1200 or toll-free 800-327-5426. Fax: 765-983-1560. E-mail: admission@earlham.edu. Web site: http://www.earlham.edu/.

▶ **For more information, see page 421.**

FRANKLIN COLLEGE OF INDIANA
FRANKLIN, INDIANA

General Independent, 4-year, coed, affiliated with American Baptist Churches in the U.S.A. **Entrance** Moderately difficult **Setting** 74-acre small-town campus **Total enrollment** 1,028 **Student-faculty ratio** 12:1 **Application deadline** 5/1 (freshmen) **Freshmen** 77% were admitted **Housing** Yes **Expenses** Tuition $14,245; Room & Board $4590 **Undergraduates** 55% women, 7% part-time, 0% Native American, 1% Hispanic American, 3% African American, 0.4% Asian American/Pacific Islander **The most frequently chosen baccalaureate fields are** education, communications/communication technologies, social sciences and history **Academic program** Advanced placement, summer session, internships **Contact** Alan Hill, Vice President for Enrollment Management, Franklin College of Indiana, 501 East Monroe Street, Franklin, IN 46131-2598. Telephone: 317-738-8062 or toll-free 800-852-0232. Fax: 317-738-8274. E-mail: admissions@franklincollege.edu. Web site: http://www.franklincoll.edu/.

GOSHEN COLLEGE
GOSHEN, INDIANA

General Independent Mennonite, 4-year, coed **Entrance** Moderately difficult **Setting** 135-acre small-town campus **Total enrollment** 986 **Student-faculty ratio** 11:1 **Application deadline** 8/15 (freshmen), 8/15 (transfer) **Freshmen** 68% were admitted **Housing** Yes **Expenses** Tuition $13,890; Room & Board $5060 **Undergraduates** 61% women, 14% part-time, 7% 25 or older, 0% Native American, 3% Hispanic American, 2% African American, 1% Asian American/Pacific Islander **The most frequently chosen baccalaureate fields are** business/marketing, education, health professions and related sciences **Academic program** English as a second language, advanced placement, accelerated degree program, self-designed majors, honors program, summer session, adult/continuing education programs, internships **Contact** Director of Admissions, Goshen College, 1700 South Main Street, Goshen, IN 46526-4794. Telephone: 574-535-7535 or toll-free 800-348-7422. Fax: 574-535-7609. E-mail: admissions@goshen.edu. Web site: http://www.goshen.edu/.

GRACE COLLEGE
WINONA LAKE, INDIANA

General Independent, comprehensive, coed, affiliated with Fellowship of Grace Brethren Churches **Entrance** Moderately difficult **Setting** 160-acre small-town campus **Total enrollment** 1,299 **Student-faculty ratio** 19:1 **Application deadline** 8/1 (freshmen), 8/1 (transfer) **Freshmen** 81% were admitted **Housing** Yes **Expenses** Tuition $11,720; Room & Board $5008 **Undergraduates** 52% women, 9% part-time, 19% 25 or older, 0.4% Native American, 1% Hispanic American, 5% African American, 0.4% Asian American/Pacific Islander **The most frequently chosen baccalaureate fields are** business/marketing, education, psychology **Academic program** Advanced placement, accelerated degree program, summer session, internships **Contact** Rebecca E. Gehrke, Administrative Assistant to Director of Admissions, Grace College, 200 Seminary Drive, Winona Lake, TX 46590. Telephone: 219-372-5100 Ext. 6008 or toll-free 800-54-GRACE (in-state); 800-54 GRACE (out-of-state). E-mail: enroll@grace.edu. Web site: http://www.grace.edu/.

▶ **For more information, see page 435.**

HANOVER COLLEGE
HANOVER, INDIANA

General Independent Presbyterian, 4-year, coed **Entrance** Moderately difficult **Setting** 630-acre rural campus **Total enrollment** 1,111 **Student-faculty ratio** 11:1 **Application deadline** 3/1 (freshmen), rolling (transfer) **Freshmen** 80% were admitted **Hous-

INDIANA

ing Yes **Expenses** Tuition $12,370; Room & Board $5190 **Undergraduates** 54% women, 1% part-time, 1% 25 or older, 0.4% Native American, 2% Hispanic American, 2% African American, 2% Asian American/Pacific Islander **The most frequently chosen baccalaureate fields are** business/marketing, education, social sciences and history **Academic program** Advanced placement, accelerated degree program, honors program, internships **Contact** Mr. Kenneth Moyer Jr., Dean of Admissions, Hanover College, Box 108, Hanover, IN 47243-0108. Telephone: 812-866-7021 or toll-free 800-213-2178. Fax: 812-866-7098. E-mail: admissions@hanover.edu. Web site: http://www.hanover.edu/.

HUNTINGTON COLLEGE
HUNTINGTON, INDIANA

General Independent, comprehensive, coed, affiliated with Church of the United Brethren in Christ **Entrance** Moderately difficult **Setting** 200-acre small-town campus **Total enrollment** 970 **Student-faculty ratio** 16:1 **Application deadline** 8/1 (freshmen), rolling (transfer) **Freshmen** 95% were admitted **Housing** Yes **Expenses** Tuition $15,030; Room & Board $5450 **Undergraduates** 59% women, 8% part-time, 10% 25 or older, 0.1% Native American, 1% Hispanic American, 1% African American, 0.4% Asian American/Pacific Islander **The most frequently chosen baccalaureate fields are** business/marketing, education, physical sciences **Academic program** English as a second language, advanced placement, summer session, adult/continuing education programs **Contact** Mr. Jeff Berggren, Dean of Enrollment, Huntington College, 2303 College Avenue, Huntington, IN 46750-1299. Telephone: 260-356-6000 Ext. 4016 or toll-free 800-642-6493. Fax: 260-356-9448. E-mail: admissions@huntington.edu. Web site: http://www.huntington.edu/.

INDIANA INSTITUTE OF TECHNOLOGY
FORT WAYNE, INDIANA

General Independent, comprehensive, coed **Entrance** Moderately difficult **Setting** 25-acre urban campus **Total enrollment** 2,756 **Student-faculty ratio** 22:1 **Application deadline** 9/1 (freshmen) **Freshmen** 15% were admitted **Housing** Yes **Expenses** Tuition $14,560; Room & Board $5246 **Undergraduates** 54% women, 53% part-time, 1% Native American, 2% Hispanic American, 22% African American, 2% Asian American/Pacific Islander **The most frequently chosen baccalaureate fields are** business/marketing, computer/information sciences, engineering/engineering technologies **Academic program** English as a second language, advanced placement, accelerated degree program, self-designed majors, summer session, adult/continuing education programs, internships **Contact** Mr. Thomas R. Filus, Director of Admissions, Indiana Institute of Technology, 1600 East Washington Boulevard, Fort Wayne, IN 46803. Telephone: 219-422-5561 Ext. 2251 or toll-free 800-937-2448 (in-state); 888-666-TECH (out-of-state). Fax: 219-422-7696. E-mail: filus@indtech.edu. Web site: http://www.indtech.edu/.

INDIANA STATE UNIVERSITY
TERRE HAUTE, INDIANA

General State-supported, university, coed **Entrance** Moderately difficult **Setting** 91-acre suburban campus **Total enrollment** 11,321 **Student-faculty ratio** 15:1 **Application deadline** 8/15 (freshmen), rolling (transfer) **Freshmen** 86% were admitted **Housing** Yes **Expenses** Tuition $3722; Room & Board $4789 **Undergraduates** 53% women, 14% part-time, 18% 25 or older, 0.3% Native American, 1% Hispanic American, 11% African American, 1% Asian American/Pacific Islander **The most frequently chosen baccalaureate fields are** business/marketing, education, social sciences and history **Academic program** English as a second language, advanced placement, accelerated degree program, honors program, summer session, adult/continuing education programs, internships **Contact** Mr. Ronald Brown, Director of Admissions, Indiana State University, Tirey Hall 134, 217 North 7th Street, Terre Haute, IN 47809. Telephone: 812-237-2121 or toll-free 800-742-0891. Fax: 812-237-8023. E-mail: admisu@amber.indstate.edu. Web site: http://web.indstate.edu/.

INDIANA UNIVERSITY BLOOMINGTON
BLOOMINGTON, INDIANA

General State-supported, university, coed **Entrance** Moderately difficult **Setting** 1,931-acre small-town campus **Total enrollment** 37,963 **Student-faculty ratio** 20:1 **Application deadline** 2/1 (freshmen), rolling (transfer) **Freshmen** 83% were admitted **Housing** Yes **Expenses** Tuition $4735; Room & Board $5978 **Undergraduates** 53% women, 8% part-time, 41% 25 or older, 0.2% Native American, 2% Hispanic American, 4% African American, 3% Asian American/Pacific Islander **The most frequently chosen baccalaureate fields are** business/marketing, education, protective services/public administration **Academic program** English as a second language, advanced placement, accelerated degree program, self-designed majors, honors program, summer session, adult/continuing education programs, internships **Contact** Mr. Don Hossler, Vice Chancellor for Enrollment Services, Indiana University Bloomington, 300 North Jordan Avenue, Bloomington, IN 47405-1106. Telephone: 812-855-0661 or toll-free 812-855-0661 (in-state). Fax: 812-855-5102. E-mail: iuadmit@indiana.edu.

INDIANA UNIVERSITY EAST
RICHMOND, INDIANA

General State-supported, 4-year, coed **Entrance** Moderately difficult **Setting** 194-acre small-town campus **Total enrollment** 2,469 **Student-faculty ratio** 15:1 **Application deadline** Rolling (freshmen), rolling (transfer) **Freshmen** 79% were admitted **Housing** No **Expenses** Tuition $3415 **Undergraduates** 71% women, 53% part-time, 48% 25 or older, 1% Native American, 1% Hispanic American, 4% African American, 1% Asian American/Pacific Islander **The most frequently chosen baccalaureate fields**

Indiana University East *(continued)*

are education, health professions and related sciences, liberal arts/general studies **Academic program** Advanced placement, summer session, adult/continuing education programs, internships **Contact** Ms. Susanna Tanner, Admissions Counselor, Indiana University East, 2325 Chester Boulevard, WZ 116, Richmond, IN 47374-1289. Telephone: 765-973-8415 or toll-free 800-959-EAST. Fax: 765-973-8288. E-mail: eaadmit@indiana.edu. Web site: http://www.indiana.edu/.

INDIANA UNIVERSITY KOKOMO
KOKOMO, INDIANA

General State-supported, comprehensive, coed **Entrance** Minimally difficult **Setting** 51-acre small-town campus **Total enrollment** 2,741 **Student-faculty ratio** 16:1 **Application deadline** 8/3 (freshmen), 8/3 (transfer) **Freshmen** 87% were admitted **Housing** No **Expenses** Tuition $3,421 **Undergraduates** 70% women, 53% part-time, 38% 25 or older, 0.4% Native American, 2% Hispanic American, 3% African American, 1% Asian American/Pacific Islander **The most frequently chosen baccalaureate fields are** education, business/marketing, liberal arts/general studies **Academic program** Advanced placement, honors program, summer session, adult/continuing education programs, internships **Contact** Ms. Patty Young, Admissions Director, Indiana University Kokomo, PO Box 9003, Kelley Student Center 230A, Kokomo, IN 46904-9003. Telephone: 765-455-9217 or toll-free 888-875-4485. Fax: 765-455-9537. E-mail: iuadmis@iuk.edu. Web site: http://www.indiana.edu.

INDIANA UNIVERSITY NORTHWEST
GARY, INDIANA

General State-supported, comprehensive, coed **Entrance** Minimally difficult **Setting** 38-acre urban campus **Total enrollment** 4,639 **Student-faculty ratio** 14:1 **Application deadline** 8/1 (freshmen) **Freshmen** 79% were admitted **Housing** No **Expenses** Tuition $3,446 **Undergraduates** 70% women, 49% part-time, 42% 25 or older, 0.4% Native American, 11% Hispanic American, 24% African American, 1% Asian American/Pacific Islander **The most frequently chosen baccalaureate fields are** business/marketing, health professions and related sciences, liberal arts/general studies **Academic program** Advanced placement, accelerated degree program, self-designed majors, honors program, summer session, adult/continuing education programs, internships **Contact** Charmaine Connelly, Assistant Director of Admissions, Indiana University Northwest, Hawthorne 100, 3400 Broadway, Gary, IN 46408-1197. Telephone: 219-980-6991 or toll-free 800-968-7486. Fax: 219-981-4219. E-mail: pkeshei@iun.edu. Web site: http://www.indiana.edu/.

INDIANA UNIVERSITY–PURDUE UNIVERSITY FORT WAYNE
FORT WAYNE, INDIANA

General State-supported, comprehensive, coed **Entrance** Minimally difficult **Setting** 565-acre urban campus **Total enrollment** 11,129 **Student-faculty ratio** 17:1 **Application deadline** 8/1 (freshmen), 8/1 (transfer) **Freshmen** 97% were admitted **Housing** No **Expenses** Tuition $3166 **Undergraduates** 57% women, 44% part-time, 38% 25 or older, 0.4% Native American, 2% Hispanic American, 5% African American, 2% Asian American/Pacific Islander **The most frequently chosen baccalaureate fields are** business/marketing, education, liberal arts/general studies **Academic program** English as a second language, advanced placement, accelerated degree program, self-designed majors, honors program, summer session, adult/continuing education programs, internships **Contact** Ms. Carol Isaacs, Director of Admissions, Indiana University–Purdue University Fort Wayne, Admissions Office, 2101 East Coliseum Boulevard, Fort Wayne, IN 46805-1499. Telephone: 219-481-6812 or toll-free 800-324-4739 (in-state). Fax: 219-481-6880. E-mail: ipfwadms@ipfw.edu. Web site: http://www.ipfw.edu/.

INDIANA UNIVERSITY–PURDUE UNIVERSITY INDIANAPOLIS
INDIANAPOLIS, INDIANA

General State-supported, university, coed **Entrance** Moderately difficult **Setting** 511-acre urban campus **Total enrollment** 28,339 **Student-faculty ratio** 19:1 **Application deadline** Rolling (freshmen), rolling (transfer) **Freshmen** 73% were admitted **Housing** Yes **Expenses** Tuition $4,172; Room & Board $5302 **Undergraduates** 59% women, 42% part-time, 39% 25 or older, 0.3% Native American, 2% Hispanic American, 11% African American, 2% Asian American/Pacific Islander **The most frequently chosen baccalaureate fields are** biological/life sciences, health professions and related sciences, liberal arts/general studies **Academic program** English as a second language, advanced placement, honors program, summer session, adult/continuing education programs, internships **Contact** Michael Donahue, Director of Admissions, Indiana University–Purdue University Indianapolis, 425 N. University Boulevard, Cavanaugh Hall Room 129, Indianapolis, IN 46202-5143. Telephone: 317-274-4591. Fax: 317-278-1862. E-mail: apply@iupui.edu. Web site: http://www.indiana.edu/.

INDIANA UNIVERSITY SOUTH BEND
SOUTH BEND, INDIANA

General State-supported, comprehensive, coed **Entrance** Moderately difficult **Setting** 73-acre suburban campus **Total enrollment** 7,417 **Student-faculty ratio** 14:1 **Application deadline** 7/1 (freshmen), 6/1 (transfer) **Freshmen** 88% were admitted **Housing** No **Expenses** Tuition $3515 **Undergraduates** 64% women, 48% part-time, 38% 25 or older, 1% Native American, 3% Hispanic American, 7%

INDIANA

African American, 1% Asian American/Pacific Islander **The most frequently chosen baccalaureate fields are** business/marketing, education, liberal arts/general studies **Academic program** English as a second language, accelerated degree program, honors program, summer session, adult/continuing education programs, internships **Contact** Jeff Johnston, Director of Recruitment/Admissions, Indiana University South Bend, 1700 Mishawaka Avenue, Administration Building, Room 169, PO Box 7111, South Bend, IN 46634-7111. Telephone: 219-237-4480. Fax: 219-237-4834. E-mail: admissions@iusb.edu. Web site: http://www.indiana.edu/.

INDIANA UNIVERSITY SOUTHEAST
NEW ALBANY, INDIANA

General State-supported, comprehensive, coed **Entrance** Minimally difficult **Setting** 177-acre suburban campus **Total enrollment** 6,557 **Student-faculty ratio** 17:1 **Application deadline** 7/15 (freshmen), 7/1 (transfer) **Freshmen** 87% were admitted **Housing** No **Expenses** Tuition $3460 **Undergraduates** 63% women, 46% part-time, 35% 25 or older, 0.2% Native American, 0.5% Hispanic American, 2% African American, 0.4% Asian American/Pacific Islander **The most frequently chosen baccalaureate fields are** business/marketing, (pre)law, education **Academic program** Advanced placement, accelerated degree program, summer session, adult/continuing education programs, internships **Contact** Mr. David B. Campbell, Director of Admissions, Indiana University Southeast, University Center Building, Room 100, 4201 Grant Line Road, New Albany, IN 47150. Telephone: 812-941-2212 or toll-free 800-852-8835 (in-state). Fax: 812-941-2595. E-mail: admissions@ius.edu. Web site: http://www.indiana.edu/.

INDIANA WESLEYAN UNIVERSITY
MARION, INDIANA

General Independent Wesleyan, comprehensive, coed **Entrance** Moderately difficult **Setting** 132-acre small-town campus **Total enrollment** 7,933 **Student-faculty ratio** 17:1 **Application deadline** Rolling (freshmen), rolling (transfer) **Freshmen** 79% were admitted **Housing** Yes **Expenses** Tuition $12,740; Room & Board $4940 **Undergraduates** 59% 25 or older, 1% Native American, 1% Hispanic American, 10% African American, 1% Asian American/Pacific Islander **The most frequently chosen baccalaureate fields are** business/marketing, education, health professions and related sciences **Academic program** Advanced placement, accelerated degree program, self-designed majors, honors program, summer session, adult/continuing education programs, internships **Contact** Ms. Gaytha Holloway, Director of Admissions, Indiana Wesleyan University, 4201 South Washington Street, Marion, IN 46953. Telephone: 765-677-2138 or toll-free 800-332-6901. Fax: 765-677-2333. E-mail: admissions@indwes.edu. Web site: http://www.indwes.edu/.

MANCHESTER COLLEGE
NORTH MANCHESTER, INDIANA

General Independent, comprehensive, coed, affiliated with Church of the Brethren **Entrance** Moderately difficult **Setting** 125-acre small-town campus **Total enrollment** 1,166 **Student-faculty ratio** 14:1 **Application deadline** Rolling (freshmen), rolling (transfer) **Freshmen** 81% were admitted **Housing** Yes **Expenses** Tuition $15,440; Room & Board $5630 **Undergraduates** 55% women, 3% part-time, 2% 25 or older **The most frequently chosen baccalaureate fields are** business/marketing, communications/communication technologies, education **Academic program** Advanced placement, self-designed majors, honors program, summer session, adult/continuing education programs, internships **Contact** Ms. Jolane Rohr, Director of Admissions, Manchester College, 604 East College Avenue, North Manchester, IN 46962-1225. Telephone: 219-982-5055 or toll-free 800-852-3648. Fax: 260-982-5239. E-mail: admitinfo@manchester.edu. Web site: http://www.manchester.edu/.

MARIAN COLLEGE
INDIANAPOLIS, INDIANA

General Independent Roman Catholic, comprehensive, coed **Entrance** Moderately difficult **Setting** 114-acre urban campus **Total enrollment** 1,260 **Student-faculty ratio** 12:1 **Application deadline** 8/15 (freshmen), 8/1 (transfer) **Freshmen** 79% were admitted **Housing** Yes **Expenses** Tuition $15,670; Room & Board $5390 **Undergraduates** 75% women, 31% part-time, 37% 25 or older, 0.5% Native American, 2% Hispanic American, 17% African American, 1% Asian American/Pacific Islander **The most frequently chosen baccalaureate fields are** business/marketing, education, health professions and related sciences **Academic program** Advanced placement, accelerated degree program, honors program, summer session, adult/continuing education programs, internships **Contact** Ms. Karen Kist, Director of Admission, Marian College, 3200 Cold Spring Road, Indianapolis, IN 46222-1997. Telephone: 317-955-6300 or toll-free 800-772-7264 (in-state). Web site: http://www.marian.edu/.

MARTIN UNIVERSITY
INDIANAPOLIS, INDIANA

General Independent, comprehensive, coed **Entrance** Noncompetitive **Setting** 5-acre urban campus **Total enrollment** 556 **Student-faculty ratio** 20:1 **Application deadline** Rolling (freshmen), rolling (transfer) **Housing** No **Undergraduates** 73% women, 46% part-time, 80% 25 or older **Academic program** Advanced placement, accelerated degree program, self-designed majors, honors program, summer session, adult/continuing education programs, internships **Contact** Ms. Brenda Shaheed, Director of Enrollment Management, Martin University, 2171 Avondale Place, PO Box 18567, Indianapolis, IN 46218-3867. Telephone: 317-543-3237. Fax: 317-543-4790.

INDIANA

OAKLAND CITY UNIVERSITY
OAKLAND CITY, INDIANA

General Independent General Baptist, comprehensive, coed **Entrance** Minimally difficult **Setting** 20-acre rural campus **Total enrollment** 1,800 **Student-faculty ratio** 15:1 **Application deadline** Rolling (freshmen) **Freshmen** 100% were admitted **Housing** Yes **Expenses** Tuition $11,286; Room & Board $4118 **Undergraduates** 54% women, 18% part-time, 40% 25 or older, 1% Native American, 2% Hispanic American, 11% African American, 0.4% Asian American/Pacific Islander **The most frequently chosen baccalaureate fields are** business/marketing, education, philosophy, religion, and theology **Academic program** Advanced placement, accelerated degree program, summer session, adult/continuing education programs **Contact** Jeff Main, Director of Admissions, Oakland City University, 143 North Lucretia Street, Oakland City, IN 47660-1099. Telephone: 812-749-1222 or toll-free 800-737-5125. Web site: http://www.oak.edu/.

PURDUE UNIVERSITY
WEST LAFAYETTE, INDIANA

General State-supported, university, coed **Entrance** Moderately difficult **Setting** 1,579-acre suburban campus **Total enrollment** 38,158 **Student-faculty ratio** 16:1 **Application deadline** Rolling (freshmen), rolling (transfer) **Freshmen** 77% were admitted **Housing** Yes **Expenses** Tuition $4164; Room & Board $6120 **Undergraduates** 42% women, 6% part-time, 5% 25 or older, 0.4% Native American, 2% Hispanic American, 3% African American, 4% Asian American/Pacific Islander **The most frequently chosen baccalaureate fields are** business/marketing, education, engineering/engineering technologies **Academic program** Advanced placement, accelerated degree program, self-designed majors, honors program, summer session, adult/continuing education programs, internships **Contact** Director of Admissions, Purdue University, Schleman Hall, West Lafayette, IN 47907-1080. Telephone: 765-494-4600. E-mail: admissions@adms.purdue.edu. Web site: http://www.purdue.edu/.

PURDUE UNIVERSITY CALUMET
HAMMOND, INDIANA

General State-supported, comprehensive, coed **Entrance** Minimally difficult **Setting** 167-acre urban campus **Application deadline** Rolling (freshmen), rolling (transfer) **Freshmen** 99% were admitted **Housing** No **Expenses** Tuition $3339 **Undergraduates** 47% 25 or older **Academic program** Advanced placement, honors program, summer session, adult/continuing education programs, internships **Contact** Mr. Paul McGuinness, Director of Admissions, Purdue University Calumet, 173rd and Woodmar Avenue, Hammond, IN 46323-2094. Telephone: 219-989-2213 or toll-free 800-447-8738 (in-state). E-mail: adms@calumet.purdue.edu. Web site: http://www.calumet.purdue.edu/.

PURDUE UNIVERSITY NORTH CENTRAL
WESTVILLE, INDIANA

General State-supported, comprehensive, coed **Entrance** Noncompetitive **Setting** 264-acre rural campus **Total enrollment** 3,492 **Student-faculty ratio** 17:1 **Application deadline** 8/6 (freshmen), 8/1 (transfer) **Freshmen** 100% were admitted **Housing** No **Expenses** Tuition $3589 **Undergraduates** 60% women, 45% part-time, 38% 25 or older, 1% Native American, 3% Hispanic American, 4% African American, 1% Asian American/Pacific Islander **The most frequently chosen baccalaureate fields are** education, liberal arts/general studies, trade and industry **Academic program** Advanced placement, self-designed majors, honors program, summer session, adult/continuing education programs, internships **Contact** Ms. Cathy Buckman, Director of Admissions, Purdue University North Central, 1401 South U.S. Highway 421, Westville, IN 46391. Telephone: 219-785-5458 or toll-free 800-872-1231 (in-state). E-mail: cbuckman@purduenc.edu. Web site: http://www.purduenc.edu/.

ROSE-HULMAN INSTITUTE OF TECHNOLOGY
TERRE HAUTE, INDIANA

General Independent, comprehensive, coed, primarily men **Entrance** Very difficult **Setting** 130-acre rural campus **Total enrollment** 1,749 **Student-faculty ratio** 13:1 **Application deadline** 3/1 (freshmen), 6/15 (transfer) **Freshmen** 67% were admitted **Housing** Yes **Expenses** Tuition $21,668; Room & Board $6039 **Undergraduates** 18% women, 2% part-time, 1% 25 or older, 0.1% Native American, 2% Hispanic American, 1% African American, 3% Asian American/Pacific Islander **The most frequently chosen baccalaureate fields are** computer/information sciences, engineering/engineering technologies, physical sciences **Academic program** Advanced placement, honors program, summer session, adult/continuing education programs, internships **Contact** Mr. Charles G. Howard, Dean of Admissions/Vice President, Rose-Hulman Institute of Technology, 5500 Wabash Avenue, Terre Haute, IN 47803-3920. Telephone: 812-877-8213 or toll-free 800-552-0725 (in-state); 800-248-7448 (out-of-state). Fax: 812-877-8941. E-mail: admis.ofc@rose-hulman.edu. Web site: http://www.rose-hulman.edu/.

SAINT JOSEPH'S COLLEGE
RENSSELAER, INDIANA

General Independent Roman Catholic, comprehensive, coed **Entrance** Moderately difficult **Setting** 340-acre small-town campus **Total enrollment** 914 **Student-faculty ratio** 14:1 **Application deadline** Rolling (freshmen), rolling (transfer) **Freshmen** 74% were admitted **Housing** Yes **Expenses** Tuition $16,040; Room & Board $5600 **Undergraduates** 56% women, 14% part-time, 10% 25 or older, 0.2% Native American, 3% Hispanic American, 4% African American, 0.4% Asian American/Pacific Islander **The most**

INDIANA

frequently chosen baccalaureate fields are business/ marketing, education, social sciences and history **Academic program** Advanced placement, accelerated degree program, self-designed majors, honors program, summer session, internships **Contact** Mr. Frank P. Bevec, Director of Admissions, Saint Joseph's College, PO Box 815, Rensselaer, IN 47978-0850. Telephone: 219-866-6170 or toll-free 800-447-8781 (out-of-state). Fax: 219-866-6122. E-mail: admissions@saintjoe.edu. Web site: http://www.saintjoe.edu/.

SAINT MARY-OF-THE-WOODS COLLEGE
SAINT MARY-OF-THE-WOODS, INDIANA

General Independent Roman Catholic, comprehensive, women only **Entrance** Moderately difficult **Setting** 67-acre rural campus **Total enrollment** 1,498 **Student-faculty ratio** 12:1 **Application deadline** 8/15 (freshmen), 8/15 (transfer) **Freshmen** 89% were admitted **Housing** Yes **Expenses** Tuition $15,560; Room & Board $5750 **Undergraduates** 72% part-time, 50% 25 or older, 1% Native American, 1% Hispanic American, 3% African American, 0.5% Asian American/Pacific Islander **The most frequently chosen baccalaureate fields are** business/marketing, education, liberal arts/general studies **Academic program** Advanced placement, accelerated degree program, self-designed majors, summer session, adult/continuing education programs, internships **Contact** Mr. Joel Wincowski, Director of Admission, Saint Mary-of-the-Woods College, Guerin Hall, Saint Mary-of-the-Woods, IN 47876. Telephone: 812-535-5106 or toll-free 800-926-SMWC. Fax: 812-535-4900. E-mail: smwcadms@smwc.edu. Web site: http://www.smwc.edu/.

SAINT MARY'S COLLEGE
NOTRE DAME, INDIANA

General Independent Roman Catholic, 4-year, women only **Entrance** Moderately difficult **Setting** 275-acre suburban campus **Total enrollment** 1,523 **Student-faculty ratio** 11:1 **Application deadline** 3/1 (freshmen), rolling (transfer) **Freshmen** 82% were admitted **Housing** Yes **Expenses** Tuition $19,390; Room & Board $6549 **Undergraduates** 2% part-time, 1% 25 or older, 0.3% Native American, 5% Hispanic American, 1% African American, 2% Asian American/Pacific Islander **The most frequently chosen baccalaureate fields are** business/marketing, education, social sciences and history **Academic program** Advanced placement, accelerated degree program, self-designed majors, internships **Contact** Ms. Mary Pat Nolan, Director of Admissions, Saint Mary's College, Notre Dame, IN 46556. Telephone: 574-284-4587 or toll-free 800-551-7621 (in-state); 574-284-4716 (out-of-state). E-mail: admission@saintmarys.edu. Web site: http://www.saintmarys.edu/.

TAYLOR UNIVERSITY
UPLAND, INDIANA

General Independent interdenominational, 4-year, coed **Entrance** Very difficult **Setting** 250-acre rural campus **Total enrollment** 1,861 **Student-faculty ratio** 15:1 **Application deadline** Rolling (freshmen), rolling (transfer) **Freshmen** 78% were admitted **Housing** Yes **Expenses** Tuition $16,572; Room & Board $4990 **Undergraduates** 52% women, 2% part-time, 2% 25 or older **The most frequently chosen baccalaureate fields are** business/marketing, education, philosophy **Academic program** Advanced placement, accelerated degree program, self-designed majors, honors program, summer session, internships **Contact** Mr. Stephen R. Mortland, Director of Admissions, Taylor University, 236 West Reade Avenue, Upland, IN 46989-1001. Telephone: 765-998-5134 or toll-free 800-882-3456. Fax: 765-998-4925. E-mail: admissions_u@tayloru.edu. Web site: http://www.tayloru.edu/.

TAYLOR UNIVERSITY, FORT WAYNE CAMPUS
FORT WAYNE, INDIANA

General Independent interdenominational, 4-year, coed **Entrance** Moderately difficult **Setting** 32-acre suburban campus **Total enrollment** 515 **Student-faculty ratio** 14:1 **Application deadline** Rolling (freshmen), rolling (transfer) **Freshmen** 76% were admitted **Housing** Yes **Expenses** Tuition $14,200; Room & Board $4490 **Undergraduates** 58% women, 27% part-time, 9% 25 or older, 0.2% Native American, 2% Hispanic American, 6% African American, 1% Asian American/Pacific Islander **The most frequently chosen baccalaureate fields are** philosophy, communications/communication technologies, philosophy, religion, and theology **Academic program** Advanced placement, accelerated degree program, self-designed majors, summer session, internships **Contact** Mr. Leo Gonot, Director of Admissions, Taylor University, Fort Wayne Campus, 1025 West Rudisill Boulevard, Fort Wayne, IN 46807-2197. Telephone: 219-744-8689 or toll-free 800-233-3922. Fax: 219-744-8660. E-mail: admissions_f@tayloru.edu. Web site: http://www.tayloru.edu/fw.

TRI-STATE UNIVERSITY
ANGOLA, INDIANA

General Independent, 4-year, coed **Entrance** Moderately difficult **Setting** 400-acre small-town campus **Total enrollment** 1,268 **Student-faculty ratio** 17:1 **Application deadline** 6/1 (freshmen), 8/15 (transfer) **Freshmen** 76% were admitted **Housing** Yes **Expenses** Tuition $15,950; Room & Board $5250 **Undergraduates** 34% women, 11% part-time, 5% 25 or older, 0.3% Native American, 0.2% Hispanic American, 2% African American, 1% Asian American/Pacific Islander **The most frequently chosen baccalaureate fields are** business/marketing, education, engineering/engineering technologies **Academic program** Advanced placement, summer session, adult/continuing education programs, internships **Contact** Ms. Sara Yarian, Admissions Officer, Tri-State University, 1 University Avenue, Angola, IN 46703. Telephone: 219-665-4365 or toll-free 800-347-4TSU. Fax: 219-665-4578. E-mail: admit@tristate.edu. Web site: http://www.tristate.edu/.

INDIANA

UNIVERSITY OF EVANSVILLE
EVANSVILLE, INDIANA

General Independent, comprehensive, coed, affiliated with United Methodist Church **Entrance** Moderately difficult **Setting** 75-acre suburban campus **Total enrollment** 2,687 **Student-faculty ratio** 13:1 **Application deadline** 2/15 (freshmen), 7/1 (transfer) **Freshmen** 91% were admitted **Housing** Yes **Expenses** Tuition $17,395; Room & Board $5470 **Undergraduates** 61% women, 14% part-time, 5% 25 or older, 0.2% Native American, 1% Hispanic American, 2% African American, 1% Asian American/Pacific Islander **The most frequently chosen baccalaureate fields are** business/marketing, education, health professions and related sciences **Academic program** English as a second language, advanced placement, honors program, summer session, adult/continuing education programs, internships **Contact** Mr. Tom Bear, Dean of Admission, University of Evansville, 1800 Lincoln Avenue, Evansville, IN 47722-0002. Telephone: 812-479-2468 or toll-free 800-992-5877 (in-state); 800-423-8633 (out-of-state). Fax: 812-474-4076. E-mail: admission@evansville.edu. Web site: http://www.evansville.edu/.

UNIVERSITY OF INDIANAPOLIS
INDIANAPOLIS, INDIANA

General Independent, comprehensive, coed, affiliated with United Methodist Church **Entrance** Moderately difficult **Setting** 60-acre suburban campus **Total enrollment** 3,701 **Student-faculty ratio** 14:1 **Application deadline** Rolling (freshmen), rolling (transfer) **Freshmen** 80% were admitted **Housing** Yes **Expenses** Tuition $15,350; Room & Board $5490 **Undergraduates** 66% women, 29% part-time, 28% 25 or older, 0.3% Native American, 1% Hispanic American, 8% African American, 1% Asian American/Pacific Islander **The most frequently chosen baccalaureate fields are** business/marketing, education, psychology **Academic program** English as a second language, advanced placement, accelerated degree program, self-designed majors, honors program, summer session, adult/continuing education programs, internships **Contact** Mr. Ronald Wilks, Director of Admissions, University of Indianapolis, 1400 East Hanna Avenue, Indianapolis, IN 46227-3697. Telephone: 317-788-3216 or toll-free 800-232-8634 Ext. 3216. Fax: 317-778-3300. E-mail: admissions@uindy.edu. Web site: http://www.uindy.edu/.

UNIVERSITY OF NOTRE DAME
NOTRE DAME, INDIANA

General Independent Roman Catholic, university, coed **Entrance** Most difficult **Setting** 1,250-acre suburban campus **Total enrollment** 11,054 **Application deadline** 1/9 (freshmen), 4/15 (transfer) **Freshmen** 36% were admitted **Housing** Yes **Expenses** Tuition $24,497; Room & Board $6210 **Undergraduates** 46% women, 0.2% part-time, 0% 25 or older, 0.5% Native American, 7% Hispanic American, 3% African American, 4% Asian American/Pacific Islander **The most frequently chosen baccalaureate fields are** business/marketing, health professions and related sciences, social sciences and history **Academic program** English as a second language, advanced placement, self-designed majors, honors program, summer session, internships **Contact** Mr. Daniel J. Saracino, Assistant Provost for Enrollment, University of Notre Dame, 220 Main Building, Notre Dame, IN 46556-5612. Telephone: 574-631-7505. Fax: 574-631-8865. E-mail: admissions.admissio.1@nd.edu. Web site: http://www.nd.edu/.

UNIVERSITY OF SAINT FRANCIS
FORT WAYNE, INDIANA

General Independent Roman Catholic, comprehensive, coed **Entrance** Moderately difficult **Setting** 73-acre suburban campus **Total enrollment** 1,683 **Student-faculty ratio** 11:1 **Application deadline** Rolling (freshmen), rolling (transfer) **Freshmen** 84% were admitted **Housing** Yes **Expenses** Tuition $13,640; Room & Board $5000 **Undergraduates** 68% women, 25% part-time, 34% 25 or older, 0.3% Native American, 2% Hispanic American, 6% African American, 0.5% Asian American/Pacific Islander **The most frequently chosen baccalaureate fields are** education, business/marketing, health professions and related sciences **Academic program** Advanced placement, honors program, summer session, adult/continuing education programs, internships **Contact** Mr. David McMahan, Director of Admissions, University of Saint Francis, 2701 Spring Street, Fort Wayne, IN 46808. Telephone: 219-434-3279 or toll-free 800-729-4732. E-mail: admiss@sfc.edu. Web site: http://www.sf.edu/.

UNIVERSITY OF SOUTHERN INDIANA
EVANSVILLE, INDIANA

General State-supported, comprehensive, coed **Entrance** Noncompetitive **Setting** 300-acre suburban campus **Total enrollment** 9,362 **Student-faculty ratio** 18:1 **Application deadline** 8/15 (freshmen), 8/15 (transfer) **Freshmen** 93% were admitted **Housing** Yes **Expenses** Tuition $3143; Room & Board $5512 **Undergraduates** 60% women, 23% part-time, 18% 25 or older, 0.2% Native American, 1% Hispanic American, 4% African American, 1% Asian American/Pacific Islander **The most frequently chosen baccalaureate fields are** business/marketing, education, health professions and related sciences **Academic program** Advanced placement, honors program, summer session, adult/continuing education programs, internships **Contact** Mr. Eric Otto, Director of Admission, University of Southern Indiana, 8600 University Boulevard, Evansville, IN 47712-3590. Telephone: 812-464-1765 or toll-free 800-467-1965. Fax: 812-465-7154. E-mail: enroll@usi.edu. Web site: http://www.usi.edu/.

VALPARAISO UNIVERSITY
VALPARAISO, INDIANA

General Independent, comprehensive, coed, affiliated with Lutheran Church **Entrance** Moderately difficult **Setting** 310-acre small-town campus **Total enrollment** 3,533 **Student-faculty ratio** 13:1 **Application deadline** 8/15 (freshmen), rolling (transfer) **Freshmen** 80% were admitted **Housing** Yes **Expenses** Tuition $18,700; Room & Board $4870 **Undergraduates** 53% women, 6% part-time, 6% 25 or older, 0.5% Native American, 3% Hispanic American, 3% African American, 2% Asian American/Pacific Islander **The most frequently chosen baccalaureate fields are** business/marketing, education, engineering/engineering technologies **Academic program** Advanced placement, accelerated degree program, self-designed majors, honors program, summer session, adult/continuing education programs, internships **Contact** Ms. Karen Foust, Director of Admissions, Valparaiso University, 651 South College Avenue, Valparaiso, IN 46383-6493. Telephone: 219-464-5011 or toll-free 888-GO-VALPO (out-of-state). Fax: 219-464-6898. E-mail: undergrad_admissions@valpo.edu. Web site: http://www.valpo.edu/.

▶ For more information, see page 491.

WABASH COLLEGE
CRAWFORDSVILLE, INDIANA

General Independent, 4-year, men only **Entrance** Moderately difficult **Setting** 50-acre small-town campus **Total enrollment** 849 **Student-faculty ratio** 11:1 **Application deadline** 3/15 (freshmen), 3/15 (transfer) **Freshmen** 55% were admitted **Housing** Yes **Expenses** Tuition $19,243; Room & Board $6092 **Undergraduates** 1% part-time, 0.01% 25 or older, 0.4% Native American, 5% Hispanic American, 7% African American, 3% Asian American/Pacific Islander **The most frequently chosen baccalaureate fields are** English, biological/life sciences, social sciences and history **Academic program** Advanced placement, accelerated degree program, internships **Contact** Mr. Steve Klein, Director of Admissions, Wabash College, PO Box 362, Crawfordsville, IN 47933-0352. Telephone: 765-361-6225 or toll-free 800-345-5385. Fax: 765-361-6437. E-mail: admissions@wabash.edu. Web site: http://www.wabash.edu/.

IOWA

ALLEN COLLEGE
WATERLOO, IOWA

General Independent, comprehensive, coed, primarily women **Entrance** Moderately difficult **Setting** 20-acre suburban campus **Total enrollment** 257 **Student-faculty ratio** 8:1 **Application deadline** 8/1 (freshmen), 8/1 (transfer) **Freshmen** 53% were admitted **Housing** Yes **Expenses** Tuition $8572; Room & Board $4410 **Undergraduates** 94% women, 22% part-time, 27% 25 or older, 1% Native American, 1% Hispanic American, 2% African American, 0% Asian American/Pacific Islander **The most frequently chosen baccalaureate field is** health professions and related sciences **Academic program** Advanced placement **Contact** Ms. Lois Hagedorn, Student Services Assistant, Allen College, Barrett Forum, 1825 Logan Avenue, Waterloo, IA 50703. Telephone: 319-226-2000. Fax: 319-226-2051. E-mail: hagedole@ihs.org. Web site: http://www.allencollege.edu/.

BRIAR CLIFF UNIVERSITY
SIOUX CITY, IOWA

General Independent Roman Catholic, comprehensive, coed **Entrance** Moderately difficult **Setting** 70-acre suburban campus **Total enrollment** 969 **Student-faculty ratio** 14:1 **Application deadline** Rolling (freshmen), rolling (transfer) **Freshmen** 73% were admitted **Housing** Yes **Expenses** Tuition $14,495; Room & Board $4911 **Undergraduates** 62% women, 25% part-time, 27% 25 or older, 1% Native American, 3% Hispanic American, 3% African American, 1% Asian American/Pacific Islander **The most frequently chosen baccalaureate fields are** business/marketing, health professions and related sciences, protective services/public administration **Academic program** English as a second language, advanced placement, accelerated degree program, self-designed majors, summer session, adult/continuing education programs, internships **Contact** Ms. Tammy Namminga, Applications Specialist, Briar Cliff University, 3303 Rebecca Street, Sioux City, IA 51106. Telephone: 712-279-5200 Ext. 5460 or toll-free 800-662-3303 Ext. 5200. Fax: 712-279-1632. E-mail: admissions@briarcliff.edu. Web site: http://www.briarcliff.edu/.

BUENA VISTA UNIVERSITY
STORM LAKE, IOWA

General Independent, comprehensive, coed, affiliated with Presbyterian Church (U.S.A.) **Entrance** Moderately difficult **Setting** 60-acre small-town campus **Total enrollment** 1,392 **Student-faculty ratio** 15:1 **Application deadline** 6/1 (freshmen), 6/1 (transfer) **Freshmen** 85% were admitted **Housing** Yes **Expenses** Tuition $17,846; Room & Board $4982 **Undergraduates** 51% women, 3% part-time, 2% 25 or older, 0.3% Native American, 1% Hispanic American, 1% African American, 2% Asian American/Pacific Islander **The most frequently chosen baccalaureate fields are** education, communications/communication technologies, social sciences and history **Academic program** English as a second language, advanced placement, self-designed majors, honors program, summer session, adult/continuing education programs, internships **Contact** Ms. Louise Cummings-Simmons, Director of Admissions, Buena Vista University, 610 West Fourth Street, Storm Lake, IA 50588. Telephone: 712-749-2351 or toll-free 800-383-9600. E-mail: admissions@bvu.edu. Web site: http://www.bvu.edu/.

CENTRAL COLLEGE
PELLA, IOWA

General Independent, 4-year, coed, affiliated with Reformed Church in America **Entrance** Moderately

IOWA

Central College *(continued)*

difficult **Setting** 133-acre small-town campus **Total enrollment** 1,425 **Student-faculty ratio** 13:1 **Application deadline** Rolling (freshmen), rolling (transfer) **Freshmen** 87% were admitted **Housing** Yes **Expenses** Tuition $15,714; Room & Board $5492 **Undergraduates** 58% women, 4% part-time, 3% 25 or older, 0.1% Native American, 1% Hispanic American, 0.4% African American, 1% Asian American/Pacific Islander **The most frequently chosen baccalaureate fields are** business/marketing, education, parks and recreation **Academic program** English as a second language, advanced placement, self-designed majors, honors program, summer session, internships **Contact** John Olsen, Vice President for Admission and Student Enrollment Services, Central College, 812 University Street, Pella, IA 50219-1999. Telephone: 641-628-7600 or toll-free 800-458-5503. Fax: 641-628-5316. E-mail: admissions@central.edu. Web site: http://www.central.edu/.

CLARKE COLLEGE
DUBUQUE, IOWA

General Independent Roman Catholic, comprehensive, coed **Entrance** Moderately difficult **Setting** 55-acre urban campus **Total enrollment** 1,201 **Student-faculty ratio** 9:1 **Application deadline** Rolling (freshmen), rolling (transfer) **Freshmen** 58% were admitted **Housing** Yes **Expenses** Tuition $15,120; Room & Board $5505 **Undergraduates** 67% women, 27% part-time, 31% 25 or older, 0.3% Native American, 2% Hispanic American, 1% African American, 0.3% Asian American/Pacific Islander **The most frequently chosen baccalaureate fields are** business/marketing, computer/information sciences, health professions and related sciences **Academic program** English as a second language, advanced placement, self-designed majors, honors program, summer session, adult/continuing education programs, internships **Contact** Mr. Omar G. Correa, Executive Director of Admissions and Financial Aid, Clarke College, 1550 Clarke Drive, Dubuque, IA 52001-3198. Telephone: 563-588-6316 or toll-free 800-383-2345. Fax: 319-588-6789. E-mail: admissions@keller.clarke.edu. Web site: http://www.clarke.edu/.

COE COLLEGE
CEDAR RAPIDS, IOWA

General Independent, comprehensive, coed, affiliated with Presbyterian Church **Entrance** Moderately difficult **Setting** 55-acre urban campus **Total enrollment** 1,311 **Student-faculty ratio** 12:1 **Application deadline** 3/1 (freshmen), rolling (transfer) **Freshmen** 77% were admitted **Housing** Yes **Expenses** Tuition $19,340; Room & Board $5410 **Undergraduates** 56% women, 11% part-time, 3% 25 or older, 0.1% Native American, 1% Hispanic American, 2% African American, 1% Asian American/Pacific Islander **The most frequently chosen baccalaureate fields are** business/marketing, psychology, social sciences and history **Academic program** English as a second language, advanced placement, accelerated degree program, self-designed majors, honors program, summer session, adult/continuing education programs, internships **Contact** Mr. Dennis Trotter, Vice President of Admission and Financial Aid, Coe College, 1220 1st Avenue, NE, Cedar Rapids, IA 52402-5070. Telephone: 319-399-8500 or toll-free 877-225-5263. Fax: 319-399-8816. E-mail: admission@coe.edu. Web site: http://www.coe.edu/.

CORNELL COLLEGE
MOUNT VERNON, IOWA

General Independent Methodist, 4-year, coed **Entrance** Moderately difficult **Setting** 129-acre small-town campus **Total enrollment** 986 **Student-faculty ratio** 11:1 **Application deadline** 2/1 (freshmen), 2/1 (transfer) **Freshmen** 70% were admitted **Housing** Yes **Expenses** Tuition $20,250; Room & Board $5600 **Undergraduates** 58% women, 1% part-time, 1% 25 or older, 0.4% Native American, 2% Hispanic American, 3% African American, 1% Asian American/Pacific Islander **The most frequently chosen baccalaureate fields are** biological/life sciences, education, social sciences and history **Academic program** English as a second language, advanced placement, self-designed majors, adult/continuing education programs, internships **Contact** Dean of Admissions and Financial Assistance, Cornell College, 600 First Street West, Mount Vernon, IA 52314-1098. Telephone: 319-895-4477 or toll-free 800-747-1112. Fax: 319-895-4451. E-mail: admissions@cornell-iowa.edu. Web site: http://www.cornellcollege.edu/.

DIVINE WORD COLLEGE
EPWORTH, IOWA

Contact Br. Dennis Newton SVD, Vice President of Recruitment/Director of Admissions, Divine Word College, 102 Jacoby Drive SW, Epworth, IA 52045-0380. Telephone: 319-876-3332 or toll-free 800-553-3321. Fax: 319-876-3407. Web site: http://www.dwci.edu/.

DORDT COLLEGE
SIOUX CENTER, IOWA

General Independent Christian Reformed, comprehensive, coed **Entrance** Moderately difficult **Setting** 65-acre small-town campus **Total enrollment** 1,396 **Student-faculty ratio** 15:1 **Application deadline** 8/1 (freshmen), 8/1 (transfer) **Freshmen** 94% were admitted **Housing** Yes **Expenses** Tuition $14,100; Room & Board $4000 **Undergraduates** 56% women, 5% part-time, 10% 25 or older, 0.4% Hispanic American, 1% African American, 1% Asian American/Pacific Islander **The most frequently chosen baccalaureate fields are** business/marketing, education, engineering/engineering technologies **Academic program** English as a second language, advanced placement, self-designed majors, internships **Contact** Mr. Quentin Van Essen, Executive Director of Admissions, Dordt College, 498 4th Avenue, NE, Sioux Center, IA 51250-1697. Telephone: 712-722-6080 or toll-free 800-343-6738. Fax: 712-722-1967. E-mail: admissions@dordt.edu. Web site: http://www.dordt.edu/.

DRAKE UNIVERSITY
DES MOINES, IOWA

General Independent, university, coed **Entrance** Moderately difficult **Setting** 120-acre suburban campus **Total enrollment** 5,150 **Student-faculty ratio** 13:1 **Application deadline** Rolling (freshmen), rolling (transfer) **Freshmen** 87% were admitted **Housing** Yes **Expenses** Tuition $17,790; Room & Board $5040 **Undergraduates** 61% women, 8% part-time, 4% 25 or older, 0.3% Native American, 2% Hispanic American, 3% African American, 5% Asian American/Pacific Islander **The most frequently chosen baccalaureate fields are** business/marketing, communications/communication technologies, education **Academic program** English as a second language, advanced placement, self-designed majors, honors program, summer session, internships **Contact** Mr. Thomas F. Willoughby, Dean of Admission and Financial Aid, Drake University, 2507 University Avenue, Des Moines, IA 50311. Telephone: 515-271-3181 or toll-free 800-44DRAKE. Fax: 515-271-2831. E-mail: admission@drake.edu. Web site: http://www.drake.edu/.

EMMAUS BIBLE COLLEGE
DUBUQUE, IOWA

General Independent nondenominational, 4-year, coed **Entrance** Noncompetitive **Setting** 22-acre small-town campus **Total enrollment** 284 **Student-faculty ratio** 14:1 **Application deadline** 8/1 (freshmen), 8/1 (transfer) **Housing** Yes **Expenses** Tuition $6026; Room & Board $3130 **Undergraduates** 50% women, 10% part-time, 14% 25 or older, 1% Native American, 2% Hispanic American, 1% African American, 2% Asian American/Pacific Islander **The most frequently chosen baccalaureate fields are** philosophy, education, philosophy, religion, and theology **Academic program** Advanced placement, internships **Contact** Mrs. Laurel Rasmussen, Enrollment Services Manager, Emmaus Bible College, 2570 Asbury Road, Dubuque, IA 52001-3097. Telephone: 563-588-8000 Ext. 1310 or toll-free 800-397-2425. Fax: 563-588-1216. E-mail: registrar@emmausl.edu. Web site: http://www.emmaus.edu/.

FAITH BAPTIST BIBLE COLLEGE AND THEOLOGICAL SEMINARY
ANKENY, IOWA

General Independent, comprehensive, coed, affiliated with General Association of Regular Baptist Churches **Entrance** Minimally difficult **Setting** 52-acre small-town campus **Total enrollment** 487 **Student-faculty ratio** 18:1 **Application deadline** 8/1 (freshmen), 8/1 (transfer) **Freshmen** 91% were admitted **Housing** Yes **Expenses** Tuition $9010; Room & Board $3466 **Undergraduates** 57% women, 9% part-time, 6% 25 or older, 0% Native American, 1% Hispanic American, 1% African American, 1% Asian American/Pacific Islander **The most frequently chosen baccalaureate fields are** philosophy, education, philosophy, religion, and theology **Academic program** Advanced placement, summer session, adult/continuing education programs, internships **Contact** Mrs. Sherie Bartlett, Admissions Office Secretary, Faith Baptist Bible College and Theological Seminary, 1900 NW 4th Street, Ankeny, IA 50021. Telephone: 515-964-0601 Ext. 233 or toll-free 888-FAITH 4U. Fax: 515-964-1638. E-mail: admissions@faith.edu. Web site: http://www.faith.edu/.

GRACELAND UNIVERSITY
LAMONI, IOWA

General Independent Reorganized Latter Day Saints, comprehensive, coed **Entrance** Moderately difficult **Setting** 169-acre small-town campus **Total enrollment** 2,523 **Student-faculty ratio** 16:1 **Application deadline** Rolling (freshmen), rolling (transfer) **Freshmen** 61% were admitted **Housing** Yes **Expenses** Tuition $13,145; Room & Board $4305 **Undergraduates** 69% women, 44% part-time, 8% 25 or older, 1% Native American, 3% Hispanic American, 3% African American, 2% Asian American/Pacific Islander **The most frequently chosen baccalaureate fields are** business/marketing, education, health professions and related sciences **Academic program** English as a second language, advanced placement, accelerated degree program, self-designed majors, honors program, summer session, adult/continuing education programs, internships **Contact** Ms. Bonita A. Booth, Vice Provost for Enrollment and Dean of Admissions, Graceland University, 1 University Place, Lamoni, IA 50140. Telephone: 641-784-5118 or toll-free 888-472-235263 (in-state); 800-472-235263 (out-of-state). Fax: 641-784-5480. E-mail: admissions@graceland.edu. Web site: http://www2.graceland.edu/.

GRAND VIEW COLLEGE
DES MOINES, IOWA

General Independent, 4-year, coed, affiliated with Evangelical Lutheran Church in America **Entrance** Noncompetitive **Setting** 25-acre urban campus **Total enrollment** 1,402 **Student-faculty ratio** 15:1 **Application deadline** 8/15 (freshmen), rolling (transfer) **Freshmen** 99% were admitted **Housing** Yes **Expenses** Tuition $13,430; Room & Board $4166 **Undergraduates** 67% women, 31% part-time, 36% 25 or older, 0.4% Native American, 1% Hispanic American, 3% African American, 2% Asian American/Pacific Islander **The most frequently chosen baccalaureate fields are** business/marketing, education, health professions and related sciences **Academic program** Advanced placement, accelerated degree program, self-designed majors, honors program, summer session, internships **Contact** Ms. Diane Johnson, Director of Admission, Grand View College, 1200 Grandview Avenue, Des Moines, IA 50316-1599. Telephone: 515-263-6149 or toll-free 800-444-6083. Fax: 515-263-2974. E-mail: admiss@gvc.edu. Web site: http://www.gvc.edu/.

IOWA

GRINNELL COLLEGE
GRINNELL, IOWA

General Independent, 4-year, coed **Entrance** Very difficult **Setting** 95-acre small-town campus **Total enrollment** 1,338 **Student-faculty ratio** 10:1 **Application deadline** 1/20 (freshmen), 5/1 (transfer) **Freshmen** 65% were admitted **Housing** Yes **Expenses** Tuition $22,250; Room & Board $6050 **Undergraduates** 54% women, 3% part-time, 1% 25 or older, 1% Native American, 4% Hispanic American, 4% African American, 4% Asian American/Pacific Islander **The most frequently chosen baccalaureate fields are** biological/life sciences, English, social sciences and history **Academic program** Advanced placement, accelerated degree program, self-designed majors, internships **Contact** Mr. James Sumner, Dean for Admission and Financial Aid, Grinnell College, 1103 Park Street, Grinnell, IA 50112-1690. Telephone: 641-269-3600 or toll-free 800-247-0113. Fax: 641-269-4800. E-mail: askgrin@grinnell.edu. Web site: http://www.grinnell.edu/.

HAMILTON TECHNICAL COLLEGE
DAVENPORT, IOWA

General Proprietary, 4-year, coed **Entrance** Noncompetitive **Setting** urban campus **Total enrollment** 420 **Student-faculty ratio** 20:1 **Application deadline** Rolling (freshmen), rolling (transfer) **Housing** No **Expenses** Tuition $6300 **Academic program** Accelerated degree program **Contact** Mr. Chad Nelson, Admissions, Hamilton Technical College, 1011 East 53rd Street, Davenport, IA 52807. Telephone: 563-386-3570. Fax: 319-386-6756. Web site: http://www.hamiltontechcollege.com.

IOWA STATE UNIVERSITY OF SCIENCE AND TECHNOLOGY
AMES, IOWA

General State-supported, university, coed **Entrance** Moderately difficult **Setting** 1,788-acre suburban campus **Total enrollment** 27,823 **Student-faculty ratio** 16:1 **Application deadline** 8/21 (freshmen), rolling (transfer) **Freshmen** 90% were admitted **Housing** Yes **Expenses** Tuition $3442; Room & Board $4666 **Undergraduates** 44% women, 8% part-time, 8% 25 or older, 0.3% Native American, 2% Hispanic American, 3% African American, 3% Asian American/Pacific Islander **The most frequently chosen baccalaureate fields are** business/marketing, agriculture, engineering/engineering technologies **Academic program** English as a second language, advanced placement, accelerated degree program, self-designed majors, honors program, summer session, adult/continuing education programs, internships **Contact** Mr. Phil Caffrey, Associate Director for Freshman Admissions, Iowa State University of Science and Technology, 100 Alumni Hall, Ames, IA 50011-2010. Telephone: 515-294-5836 or toll-free 800-262-3810. Fax: 515-294-2592. E-mail: admissions@iastate.edu. Web site: http://www.iastate.edu/.

IOWA WESLEYAN COLLEGE
MOUNT PLEASANT, IOWA

General Independent United Methodist, 4-year, coed **Entrance** Moderately difficult **Setting** 60-acre small-town campus **Total enrollment** 777 **Student-faculty ratio** 11:1 **Application deadline** 8/15 (freshmen), 8/15 (transfer) **Freshmen** 82% were admitted **Housing** Yes **Expenses** Tuition $13,200; Room & Board $4250 **Undergraduates** 60% women, 38% part-time, 40% 25 or older, 0.1% Native American, 4% Hispanic American, 9% African American, 1% Asian American/Pacific Islander **Academic program** English as a second language, advanced placement, self-designed majors, summer session, adult/continuing education programs, internships **Contact** Mr. David File, Associate Vice President and Dean, Iowa Wesleyan College, 601 North Main Street, Mount Pleasant, IA 52641-1398. Telephone: 319-385-6230 or toll-free 800-582-2383. Fax: 319-385-6296. E-mail: admitrwl@iwc.edu. Web site: http://www.iwc.edu/.

LORAS COLLEGE
DUBUQUE, IOWA

General Independent Roman Catholic, comprehensive, coed **Entrance** Moderately difficult **Setting** 60-acre suburban campus **Total enrollment** 1,758 **Student-faculty ratio** 12:1 **Application deadline** Rolling (freshmen), rolling (transfer) **Freshmen** 80% were admitted **Housing** Yes **Expenses** Tuition $17,069; Room & Board $5925 **Undergraduates** 51% women, 7% part-time, 7% 25 or older, 0.2% Native American, 2% Hispanic American, 1% African American, 0.3% Asian American/Pacific Islander **The most frequently chosen baccalaureate fields are** business/marketing, communications/communication technologies, education **Academic program** English as a second language, advanced placement, self-designed majors, honors program, summer session, adult/continuing education programs, internships **Contact** Mr. Tim Hauber, Director of Admissions, Loras College, 1450 Alta Vista, Dubuque, IA 52004-0178. Telephone: 563-588-7829 or toll-free 800-245-6727. Fax: 563-588-7119. E-mail: adms@loras.edu. Web site: http://www.loras.edu/.

LUTHER COLLEGE
DECORAH, IOWA

General Independent, 4-year, coed, affiliated with Evangelical Lutheran Church in America **Entrance** Moderately difficult **Setting** 800-acre small-town campus **Total enrollment** 2,575 **Student-faculty ratio** 13:1 **Freshmen** 83% were admitted **Housing** Yes **Expenses** Tuition $19,325; Room & Board $3975 **Undergraduates** 60% women, 3% part-time, 3% 25 or older, 0.2% Native American, 1% Hispanic American, 1% African American, 1% Asian American/Pacific Islander **The most frequently chosen baccalaureate fields are** biological/life sciences, business/marketing, education **Academic program** Advanced placement, self-designed majors, honors program, summer session, internships **Contact** Mr. Jon Lund,

IOWA

Vice President for Enrollment and Marketing, Luther College, 700 College Drive, Decorah, IA 52101. Telephone: 563-387-1287 or toll-free 800-458-8437. Fax: 563-387-2159. E-mail: admissions@luther.edu. Web site: http://www.luther.edu/.

▶ For more information, see page 450.

MAHARISHI UNIVERSITY OF MANAGEMENT
FAIRFIELD, IOWA

General Independent, university, coed **Entrance** Moderately difficult **Setting** 262-acre small-town campus **Total enrollment** 734 **Student-faculty ratio** 9:1 **Application deadline** 8/1 (freshmen), 8/1 (transfer) **Freshmen** 62% were admitted **Housing** Yes **Expenses** Tuition $16,390 **Undergraduates** 49% women, 6% part-time, 13% 25 or older, 0% Native American, 2% Hispanic American, 4% African American, 3% Asian American/Pacific Islander **The most frequently chosen baccalaureate fields are** business/marketing, biological/life sciences, visual/performing arts **Academic program** English as a second language, advanced placement, self-designed majors, honors program, adult/continuing education programs, internships **Contact** Mr. Brad Mylett, Director of Admissions, Maharishi University of Management, 1000 North 4th Street, Fairfield, IA 52557. Telephone: 641-472-1110. Fax: 641-472-1179. E-mail: admissions@mum.edu. Web site: http://www.mum.edu/.

MERCY COLLEGE OF HEALTH SCIENCES
DES MOINES, IOWA

General Independent, 4-year, coed, primarily women, affiliated with Roman Catholic Church **Total enrollment** 442 **Student-faculty ratio** 11:1 **Application deadline** Rolling (freshmen) **Freshmen** 52% were admitted **Expenses** Tuition $8925 **Undergraduates** 93% women, 44% part-time, 60% 25 or older, 0.5% Native American, 1% Hispanic American, 2% African American, 1% Asian American/Pacific Islander **The most frequently chosen baccalaureate field is** health professions and related sciences **Contact** Ms. Sandi Nagel, Admissions Representative, Mercy College of Health Sciences, 928 Sixth Avenue, Des Moines, IA 50309-1239. Telephone: 515-643-6605 or toll-free 800-637-2994. Web site: http://www.mchs.edu/.

MORNINGSIDE COLLEGE
SIOUX CITY, IOWA

General Independent United Methodist, comprehensive, coed **Entrance** Moderately difficult **Setting** 41-acre suburban campus **Total enrollment** 996 **Student-faculty ratio** 10:1 **Application deadline** Rolling (freshmen), rolling (transfer) **Freshmen** 73% were admitted **Housing** Yes **Expenses** Tuition $14,210; Room & Board $4914 **Undergraduates** 63% women, 12% part-time, 7% 25 or older, 0.5% Native American, 3% Hispanic American, 5% African American, 2% Asian American/Pacific Islander **The most frequently chosen baccalaureate fields are** business/marketing, education, health professions and related sciences **Academic program** English as a second language, advanced placement, accelerated degree program, self-designed majors, honors program, summer session, adult/continuing education programs, internships **Contact** Joel Weyand, Director of Admissions, Morningside College, 1501 Morningside Avenue, Sioux City, IA 51106-1751. Telephone: 712-274-5111 or toll-free 800-831-0806 Ext. 5111. Fax: 712-274-5101. E-mail: mscadm@morningside.edu. Web site: http://www.morningside.edu/.

MOUNT MERCY COLLEGE
CEDAR RAPIDS, IOWA

General Independent Roman Catholic, 4-year, coed **Entrance** Moderately difficult **Setting** 36-acre suburban campus **Total enrollment** 1,387 **Student-faculty ratio** 14:1 **Application deadline** 8/30 (freshmen), 8/30 (transfer) **Freshmen** 86% were admitted **Housing** Yes **Expenses** Tuition $14,560; Room & Board $4830 **Undergraduates** 68% women, 34% part-time, 8% 25 or older, 0.2% Native American, 1% Hispanic American, 1% African American, 1% Asian American/Pacific Islander **The most frequently chosen baccalaureate fields are** education, health professions and related sciences, protective services/public administration **Academic program** Advanced placement, accelerated degree program, self-designed majors, honors program, summer session, adult/continuing education programs, internships **Contact** Ms. Margaret M. Jackson, Dean of Admission, Mount Mercy College, 1330 Elmhurst Drive, NE, Cedar Rapids, IA 52402. Telephone: 319-368-6460 or toll-free 800-248-4504. Fax: 319-363-5270. E-mail: admission@mmc.mtmercy.edu. Web site: http://www.mtmercy.edu.

MOUNT ST. CLARE COLLEGE
CLINTON, IOWA

General Independent Roman Catholic, 4-year, coed **Entrance** Minimally difficult **Setting** 24-acre small-town campus **Total enrollment** 519 **Student-faculty ratio** 14:1 **Application deadline** 8/15 (freshmen), rolling (transfer) **Freshmen** 75% were admitted **Housing** Yes **Expenses** Tuition $14,300; Room & Board $5000 **Undergraduates** 56% women, 16% part-time, 28% 25 or older, 0% Native American, 2% Hispanic American, 7% African American, 1% Asian American/Pacific Islander **The most frequently chosen baccalaureate fields are** business/marketing, education, liberal arts/general studies **Academic program** English as a second language, advanced placement, self-designed majors, honors program, summer session, adult/continuing education programs, internships **Contact** Ms. Waunita M. Sullivan, Director of Enrollment, Mount St. Clare College, 400 North Bluff Boulevard, PO Box 2967, Clinton, IA 52733-2967. Telephone: 563-242-4023 Ext. 3401 or toll-free 800-242-4153 Ext. 3400. Fax: 563-243-6102. E-mail: admissns@clare.edu. Web site: http://www.clare.edu/.

IOWA

NORTHWESTERN COLLEGE
ORANGE CITY, IOWA

General Independent, 4-year, coed, affiliated with Reformed Church in America **Entrance** Moderately difficult **Setting** 45-acre rural campus **Total enrollment** 1,294 **Student-faculty ratio** 15:1 **Application deadline** Rolling (freshmen), rolling (transfer) **Freshmen** 86% were admitted **Housing** Yes **Expenses** Tuition $13,750; Room & Board $3880 **Undergraduates** 62% women, 4% part-time, 25% 25 or older, 0.2% Native American, 1% Hispanic American, 0.4% African American, 1% Asian American/Pacific Islander **The most frequently chosen baccalaureate fields are** business/marketing, biological/life sciences, education **Academic program** English as a second language, advanced placement, accelerated degree program, self-designed majors, honors program, summer session, internships **Contact** Mr. Ronald K. DeJong, Director of Admissions, Northwestern College, 101 College Lane, Orange City, IA 51041-1996. Telephone: 712-737-7130 or toll-free 800-747-4757. Fax: 712-707-7164. E-mail: markb@nwciowa.edu. Web site: http://www.nwciowa.edu/.

PALMER COLLEGE OF CHIROPRACTIC
DAVENPORT, IOWA

General Independent, comprehensive, coed **Entrance** Moderately difficult **Setting** 3-acre urban campus **Total enrollment** 1,721 **Student-faculty ratio** 17:1 **Application deadline** Rolling (freshmen) **Freshmen** 85% were admitted **Housing** No **Expenses** Tuition $17,550 **Undergraduates** 91% women, 13% part-time **The most frequently chosen baccalaureate field is** health professions and related sciences **Academic program** Summer session, internships **Contact** Dr. David Anderson, Director of Admissions, Palmer College of Chiropractic, 1000 Brady Street, Davenport, IA 52803-5287. Telephone: 563-884-5656 or toll-free 800-722-3648. Fax: 563-884-5414. E-mail: pcadmit@palmer.edu. Web site: http://www.palmer.edu/.

ST. AMBROSE UNIVERSITY
DAVENPORT, IOWA

General Independent Roman Catholic, comprehensive, coed **Entrance** Moderately difficult **Setting** 11-acre urban campus **Total enrollment** 3,291 **Student-faculty ratio** 16:1 **Application deadline** Rolling (freshmen), rolling (transfer) **Freshmen** 87% were admitted **Housing** Yes **Expenses** Tuition $14,654; Room & Board $5340 **Undergraduates** 59% women, 23% part-time, 28% 25 or older, 0.4% Native American, 4% Hispanic American, 3% African American, 1% Asian American/Pacific Islander **The most frequently chosen baccalaureate fields are** business/marketing, education, psychology **Academic program** Advanced placement, accelerated degree program, self-designed majors, summer session, adult/continuing education programs, internships **Contact** Ms. Meg Flaherty, Director of Admissions, St. Ambrose University, 518 West Locust, Davenport, IA 52803-2898. Telephone: 563-333-6300 Ext. 6311 or toll-free 800-383-2627. Fax: 563-333-6297. E-mail: mflahery@sau.edu. Web site: http://www.sau.edu/.

▶ For more information, see page 469.

SIMPSON COLLEGE
INDIANOLA, IOWA

General Independent United Methodist, 4-year, coed **Entrance** Moderately difficult **Setting** 68-acre small-town campus **Total enrollment** 1,816 **Student-faculty ratio** 14:1 **Application deadline** 8/15 (freshmen), 8/15 (transfer) **Freshmen** 86% were admitted **Housing** Yes **Expenses** Tuition $15,908; Room & Board $5292 **Undergraduates** 58% women, 28% part-time, 25% 25 or older, 1% Native American, 1% Hispanic American, 1% African American, 1% Asian American/Pacific Islander **The most frequently chosen baccalaureate fields are** business/marketing, communications/communication technologies, education **Academic program** Advanced placement, accelerated degree program, self-designed majors, honors program, summer session, adult/continuing education programs, internships **Contact** Ms. Deborah Tierney, Vice President for Enrollment, Simpson College, 701 North C Street, Indianola, IA 50125-1297. Telephone: 515-961-1624 or toll-free 800-362-2454. Fax: 515-961-1870. E-mail: admiss@simpson.edu. Web site: http://www.simpson.edu/.

▶ For more information, see page 476.

UNIVERSITY OF DUBUQUE
DUBUQUE, IOWA

General Independent Presbyterian, comprehensive, coed **Entrance** Moderately difficult **Setting** 56-acre suburban campus **Total enrollment** 1,036 **Student-faculty ratio** 14:1 **Application deadline** Rolling (freshmen), rolling (transfer) **Freshmen** 82% were admitted **Housing** Yes **Expenses** Tuition $14,910; Room & Board $5020 **Undergraduates** 37% women, 8% part-time, 8% 25 or older, 1% Native American, 3% Hispanic American, 11% African American, 1% Asian American/Pacific Islander **The most frequently chosen baccalaureate fields are** business/marketing, computer/information sciences, education **Academic program** English as a second language, advanced placement, accelerated degree program, self-designed majors, summer session, adult/continuing education programs, internships **Contact** Mr. Jesse James, Director of Admissions and Records, University of Dubuque, 2000 University Avenue, Dubuque, IA 52001-5099. Telephone: 319-589-3214 or toll-free 800-722-5583 (in-state). Fax: 319-589-3690. E-mail: admssns@dbq.edu. Web site: http://www.dbq.edu/.

THE UNIVERSITY OF IOWA
IOWA CITY, IOWA

General State-supported, university, coed **Entrance** Moderately difficult **Setting** 1,900-acre small-town campus **Total enrollment** 28,768 **Student-faculty ratio** 14:1 **Application deadline** 5/15 (freshmen),

IOWA

5/15 (transfer) **Freshmen** 85% were admitted **Housing** Yes **Expenses** Tuition $3522; Room & Board $4870 **Undergraduates** 55% women, 12% part-time, 10% 25 or older, 0.4% Native American, 2% Hispanic American, 2% African American, 3% Asian American/Pacific Islander **The most frequently chosen baccalaureate fields are** business/marketing, communications/communication technologies, social sciences and history **Academic program** English as a second language, advanced placement, accelerated degree program, self-designed majors, honors program, summer session, adult/continuing education programs, internships **Contact** Mr. Michael Barron, Director of Admissions, The University of Iowa, 107 Calvin Hall, Iowa City, IA 52242. Telephone: 319-335-3847 or toll-free 800-553-4692. Fax: 319-335-1535. E-mail: admissions@uiowa.edu. Web site: http://www.uiowa.edu/.

UNIVERSITY OF NORTHERN IOWA
CEDAR FALLS, IOWA

General State-supported, comprehensive, coed **Entrance** Moderately difficult **Setting** 940-acre small-town campus **Total enrollment** 14,410 **Student-faculty ratio** 16:1 **Application deadline** 8/15 (freshmen), 8/15 (transfer) **Freshmen** 81% were admitted **Housing** Yes **Expenses** Tuition $3440; Room & Board $4410 **Undergraduates** 58% women, 12% part-time, 8% 25 or older, 0.2% Native American, 1% Hispanic American, 2% African American, 1% Asian American/Pacific Islander **The most frequently chosen baccalaureate fields are** business/marketing, education, social sciences and history **Academic program** English as a second language, advanced placement, accelerated degree program, self-designed majors, honors program, summer session, adult/continuing education programs, internships **Contact** Mr. Clark Elmer, Director of Enrollment Management and Admissions, University of Northern Iowa, 120 Gilchrist Hall, Cedar Falls, IA 50614-0018. Telephone: 319-273-2281 or toll-free 800-772-2037. Fax: 319-273-2885. E-mail: admissions@uni.edu. Web site: http://www.uni.edu/.

UPPER IOWA UNIVERSITY
FAYETTE, IOWA

General Independent, comprehensive, coed **Entrance** Moderately difficult **Setting** 80-acre rural campus **Total enrollment** 718 **Student-faculty ratio** 16:1 **Application deadline** Rolling (freshmen), rolling (transfer) **Freshmen** 65% were admitted **Housing** Yes **Expenses** Tuition $12,856; Room & Board $4582 **Undergraduates** 39% women, 1% Native American, 5% Hispanic American, 12% African American, 8% Asian American/Pacific Islander **Academic program** Advanced placement, accelerated degree program, self-designed majors, summer session, adult/continuing education programs, internships **Contact** Mr. Kent McElvania, Director of Admissions, Upper Iowa University, Box 1859, Fayette, IA 52142-1857. Telephone: 563-425-5281 Ext. 5279 or toll-free 800-553-4150 Ext. 2. Fax: 563-425-5277. E-mail: admission@uiu.edu. Web site: http://www.uiu.edu/.

WALDORF COLLEGE
FOREST CITY, IOWA

General Independent Lutheran, 4-year, coed **Entrance** Moderately difficult **Setting** 29-acre small-town campus **Total enrollment** 642 **Student-faculty ratio** 13:1 **Application deadline** Rolling (freshmen), rolling (transfer) **Housing** Yes **Expenses** Tuition $14,328; Room & Board $5252 **Undergraduates** 46% women, 16% part-time, 2% 25 or older, 0.3% Native American, 1% Hispanic American, 3% African American, 1% Asian American/Pacific Islander **Academic program** English as a second language, advanced placement, accelerated degree program, honors program, summer session, adult/continuing education programs, internships **Contact** Mr. Steve Hall, Assistant Dean of Admission, Waldorf College, 106 South 6th Street, Forest City, IA 50436. Telephone: 641-585-8119 or toll-free 800-292-1903. Fax: 641-585-8194. E-mail: admissions@waldorf.edu. Web site: http://www.waldorf.edu/.

WARTBURG COLLEGE
WAVERLY, IOWA

General Independent Lutheran, 4-year, coed **Entrance** Moderately difficult **Setting** 118-acre small-town campus **Total enrollment** 1,649 **Student-faculty ratio** 14:1 **Freshmen** 88% were admitted **Housing** Yes **Expenses** Tuition $16,565; Room & Board $4600 **Undergraduates** 58% women, 5% part-time, 2% 25 or older, 0.1% Native American, 1% Hispanic American, 4% African American, 1% Asian American/Pacific Islander **The most frequently chosen baccalaureate fields are** business/marketing, biological/life sciences, education **Academic program** English as a second language, advanced placement, accelerated degree program, self-designed majors, honors program, summer session, internships **Contact** Doug Bowman, Dean of Admissions/Financial Aid, Wartburg College, 100 Wartburg Boulevard, PO Box 1003, Waverly, IA 50677-0903. Telephone: 319-352-8264 or toll-free 800-772-2085. Fax: 319-352-8579. E-mail: admissions@wartburg.edu. Web site: http://www.wartburg.edu/.

WILLIAM PENN UNIVERSITY
OSKALOOSA, IOWA

General Independent, 4-year, coed, affiliated with Society of Friends **Entrance** Moderately difficult **Setting** 40-acre rural campus **Total enrollment** 1,547 **Student-faculty ratio** 14:1 **Freshmen** 72% were admitted **Housing** Yes **Expenses** Tuition $13,270; Room & Board $4305 **Undergraduates** 48% women, 11% part-time, 30% 25 or older, 1% Native American, 3% Hispanic American, 9% African American, 0.4% Asian American/Pacific Islander **The most frequently chosen baccalaureate fields are** business/marketing, education, psychology **Academic program** English as a second language, advanced placement, accelerated degree program, self-designed majors, summer session, adult/continuing education programs, internships **Contact** Mrs. Mary Boyd,

IOWA

William Penn University *(continued)*
Director of Admissions, William Penn University, 201 Trueblood Avenue, Oskaloosa, IA 52577. Telephone: 641-673-1012 or toll-free 800-779-7366. Fax: 641-673-1396. E-mail: admissions@wmpenn.edu. Web site: http://www.wmpenn.edu/.

KANSAS

BAKER UNIVERSITY
BALDWIN CITY, KANSAS

General Independent United Methodist, comprehensive, coed **Entrance** Moderately difficult **Setting** 26-acre small-town campus **Total enrollment** 1,002 **Student-faculty ratio** 11:1 **Application deadline** Rolling (freshmen), rolling (transfer) **Freshmen** 88% were admitted **Housing** Yes **Expenses** Tuition $12,900; Room & Board $4880 **Undergraduates** 59% women, 6% part-time, 7% 25 or older, 1% Native American, 2% Hispanic American, 4% African American, 1% Asian American/Pacific Islander **The most frequently chosen baccalaureate fields are** business/marketing, education, health professions and related sciences **Academic program** English as a second language, advanced placement, self-designed majors, honors program, summer session, internships **Contact** Ms. Cheryl McCracy, Director of Admission, Baker University, PO Box 65, Baldwin City, KS 66006-0065. Telephone: 785-594-6451 Ext. 458 or toll-free 800-873-4282. Fax: 785-594-8372. E-mail: admission@bakeru.edu. Web site: http://www.bakeru.edu/.

BARCLAY COLLEGE
HAVILAND, KANSAS

General Independent, 4-year, coed, affiliated with Society of Friends **Entrance** Minimally difficult **Setting** 13-acre rural campus **Total enrollment** 196 **Student-faculty ratio** 7:1 **Application deadline** 9/1 (freshmen), 9/1 (transfer) **Freshmen** 30% were admitted **Housing** Yes **Expenses** Tuition $7450; Room & Board $3750 **Undergraduates** 59% women, 13% part-time, 51% 25 or older, 2% Native American, 2% Hispanic American, 6% African American, 1% Asian American/Pacific Islander **The most frequently chosen baccalaureate fields are** philosophy, business/marketing, philosophy, religion, and theology **Academic program** Advanced placement, accelerated degree program, self-designed majors, adult/continuing education programs, internships **Contact** Ryan Haase, Director of Admissions, Barclay College, 607 North Kingman, Haviland, KS 67059. Telephone: 620-862-5252 Ext. 41 or toll-free 800-862-0226. Fax: 620-862-5242. E-mail: admissions@barclaycollege.edu. Web site: http://www.barclaycollege.edu/.

BENEDICTINE COLLEGE
ATCHISON, KANSAS

General Independent Roman Catholic, comprehensive, coed **Entrance** Moderately difficult **Setting** 225-acre small-town campus **Total enrollment** 1,348 **Student-faculty ratio** 15:1 **Freshmen** 88% were admitted **Housing** Yes **Expenses** Tuition $13,265; Room & Board $5100 **Undergraduates** 52% women, 32% part-time, 4% 25 or older, 1% Native American, 7% Hispanic American, 5% African American, 0.5% Asian American/Pacific Islander **The most frequently chosen baccalaureate fields are** business/marketing, education, social sciences and history **Academic program** English as a second language, advanced placement, self-designed majors, summer session, internships **Contact** Ms. Kelly Vowels, Dean of Enrollment Management, Benedictine College, 1020 N. 2nd Street, Atchison, KS 66002. Telephone: 913-367-5340 Ext. 2476 or toll-free 800-467-5340. Fax: 913-367-5462. E-mail: bcadmiss@benedictine.edu. Web site: http://www.benedictine.edu/.

BETHANY COLLEGE
LINDSBORG, KANSAS

General Independent Lutheran, 4-year, coed **Entrance** Moderately difficult **Setting** 80-acre small-town campus **Total enrollment** 622 **Student-faculty ratio** 11:1 **Application deadline** 7/1 (freshmen), rolling (transfer) **Freshmen** 76% were admitted **Housing** Yes **Expenses** Tuition $12,943; Room & Board $3600 **Undergraduates** 47% women, 8% part-time, 8% 25 or older, 1% Native American, 4% Hispanic American, 6% African American, 2% Asian American/Pacific Islander **The most frequently chosen baccalaureate fields are** business/marketing, education, social sciences and history **Academic program** Advanced placement, accelerated degree program, self-designed majors, summer session, internships **Contact** Daniel McKinney, Dean of Admissions and Financial Aid, Bethany College, 421 North First Street, Lindsborg, KS 67456-1897. Telephone: 785-227-3311 Ext. 8108 or toll-free 800-826-2281. Fax: 785-227-2004. E-mail: admissions@bethanylb.edu. Web site: http://www.bethanylb.edu/.

BETHEL COLLEGE
NORTH NEWTON, KANSAS

General Independent, 4-year, coed, affiliated with General Conference Mennonite Church **Entrance** Moderately difficult **Setting** 60-acre small-town campus **Total enrollment** 525 **Student-faculty ratio** 11:1 **Application deadline** 8/1 (freshmen), 8/1 (transfer) **Freshmen** 75% were admitted **Housing** Yes **Expenses** Tuition $12,300; Room & Board $5150 **Undergraduates** 50% women, 8% part-time, 4% 25 or older, 1% Native American, 6% Hispanic American, 6% African American, 2% Asian American/Pacific Islander **The most frequently chosen baccalaureate fields are** education, business/marketing, health professions and related sciences **Academic program** Advanced placement, summer session,

KANSAS

internships **Contact** Dr. Shirley King, Dean of Enrollment Services, Bethel College, 300 East 27th Street, North Newton, KS 67117-0531. Telephone: 316-284-5230 or toll-free 800-522-1887 Ext. 230. Fax: 316-284-5870. E-mail: admissions@bethelks.edu. Web site: http://www.bethelks.edu/.

CENTRAL CHRISTIAN COLLEGE OF KANSAS
MCPHERSON, KANSAS

General Independent Free Methodist, 4-year, coed **Entrance** Moderately difficult **Setting** 16-acre small-town campus **Total enrollment** 314 **Student-faculty ratio** 15:1 **Application deadline** Rolling (freshmen), rolling (transfer) **Freshmen** 99% were admitted **Housing** Yes **Expenses** Tuition $11,100; Room & Board $4000 **Undergraduates** 52% women, 12% part-time, 11% 25 or older, 1% Native American, 7% Hispanic American, 9% African American, 5% Asian American/Pacific Islander **The most frequently chosen baccalaureate fields are** liberal arts/general studies, philosophy, philosophy, religion, and theology **Academic program** Advanced placement, self-designed majors, adult/continuing education programs, internships **Contact** Dr. David Ferrell, Dean of Admissions, Central Christian College of Kansas, PO Box 1403, McPherson, KS 67460. Telephone: 620-241-0723 Ext. 380 or toll-free 800-835-0078. Fax: 620-241-6032. E-mail: admissions@centralchristian.edu. Web site: http://www.centralchristian.edu/.

EMPORIA STATE UNIVERSITY
EMPORIA, KANSAS

General State-supported, comprehensive, coed **Entrance** Noncompetitive **Setting** 207-acre small-town campus **Total enrollment** 5,823 **Student-faculty ratio** 18:1 **Application deadline** Rolling (freshmen), rolling (transfer) **Freshmen** 90% were admitted **Housing** Yes **Expenses** Tuition $2284; Room & Board $3914 **Undergraduates** 61% women, 14% part-time, 10% 25 or older, 1% Native American, 4% Hispanic American, 4% African American, 1% Asian American/Pacific Islander **The most frequently chosen baccalaureate fields are** business/marketing, education, social sciences and history **Academic program** English as a second language, advanced placement, accelerated degree program, self-designed majors, honors program, summer session, adult/continuing education programs, internships **Contact** Ms. Susan Brinkman, Director of Admissions, Emporia State University, 1200 Commercial, Emporia, KS 66801-5087. Telephone: 620-341-5465 or toll-free 877-GOTOESU (in-state); 877-468-6378 (out-of-state). Fax: 620-341-5599. E-mail: go2esu@emporia.edu. Web site: http://www.emporia.edu/.

FORT HAYS STATE UNIVERSITY
HAYS, KANSAS

General State-supported, comprehensive, coed **Entrance** Noncompetitive **Setting** 200-acre small-town campus **Total enrollment** 5,626 **Student-faculty ratio** 17:1 **Application deadline** Rolling (freshmen), rolling (transfer) **Freshmen** 86% were admitted **Housing** Yes **Expenses** Tuition $2217; Room & Board $4077 **Undergraduates** 54% women, 19% part-time, 1% Native American, 2% Hispanic American, 1% African American, 0.5% Asian American/Pacific Islander **The most frequently chosen baccalaureate fields are** business/marketing, education, health professions and related sciences **Academic program** English as a second language, advanced placement, summer session, adult/continuing education programs, internships **Contact** Christy Befort, Senior Administrative Assistant, Office of Admissions, Fort Hays State University, 600 Park Street, Hays, KS 67601-4099. Telephone: 785-628-5830 or toll-free 800-628-FHSU. Fax: 785-628-4187. E-mail: tigers@fhsu.edu. Web site: http://www.fhsu.edu/.

FRIENDS UNIVERSITY
WICHITA, KANSAS

General Independent, comprehensive, coed **Entrance** Moderately difficult **Setting** 45-acre urban campus **Total enrollment** 3,190 **Application deadline** Rolling (freshmen), rolling (transfer) **Freshmen** 93% were admitted **Housing** Yes **Expenses** Tuition $11,740; Room & Board $3540 **Undergraduates** 0.3% 25 or older **Academic program** Advanced placement, accelerated degree program, self-designed majors, honors program, summer session, adult/continuing education programs, internships **Contact** Mr. Tony Myers, Director of Admissions, Friends University, 2100 West University Street, Wichita, KS 67213. Telephone: 316-295-5100 or toll-free 800-577-2233. Fax: 316-262-5027. E-mail: tmyers@friends.edu. Web site: http://www.friends.edu/.

HASKELL INDIAN NATIONS UNIVERSITY
LAWRENCE, KANSAS

General Federally supported, 4-year, coed **Entrance** Minimally difficult **Setting** 320-acre suburban campus **Total enrollment** 1,028 **Student-faculty ratio** 15:1 **Application deadline** 7/15 (freshmen), 7/15 (transfer) **Freshmen** 74% were admitted **Housing** Yes **Expenses** Tuition $210; Room & Board $70 **Undergraduates** 47% women, 10% part-time, 1% 25 or older, 100% Native American, 0% Hispanic American, 0% African American, 0% Asian American/Pacific Islander **Academic program** Advanced placement, self-designed majors, summer session **Contact** Ms. Patty Grant, Recruitment Officer, Haskell Indian Nations University, 155 Indian Avenue, #5031, Lawrence, KS 66046-4800. Telephone: 785-749-8437 Ext. 437. Fax: 785-749-8429.

KANSAS STATE UNIVERSITY
MANHATTAN, KANSAS

General State-supported, university, coed **Entrance** Noncompetitive **Setting** 668-acre suburban campus **Total enrollment** 22,396 **Student-faculty ratio** 15:1 **Application deadline** Rolling (freshmen), rolling

KANSAS

Kansas State University *(continued)*
(transfer) **Freshmen** 62% were admitted **Housing** Yes **Expenses** Tuition $2333; Room & Board $4662 **Undergraduates** 47% women, 14% part-time, 9% 25 or older, 1% Native American, 2% Hispanic American, 3% African American, 1% Asian American/Pacific Islander **The most frequently chosen baccalaureate fields are** agriculture, business/marketing, engineering/engineering technologies **Academic program** English as a second language, advanced placement, accelerated degree program, honors program, summer session, adult/continuing education programs, internships **Contact** Mr. Larry Moeder, Interim Director of Admissions, Kansas State University, 119 Anderson Hall, Manhattan, KS 66506. Telephone: 785-532-6250 or toll-free 800-432-8270 (in-state). Fax: 785-532-6393. E-mail: kstate@ksu.edu. Web site: http://www.ksu.edu/.

KANSAS WESLEYAN UNIVERSITY
SALINA, KANSAS

General Independent United Methodist, comprehensive, coed **Entrance** Moderately difficult **Setting** 28-acre urban campus **Total enrollment** 784 **Student-faculty ratio** 14:1 **Application deadline** Rolling (freshmen), rolling (transfer) **Freshmen** 68% were admitted **Housing** Yes **Expenses** Tuition $13,400; Room & Board $4600 **Undergraduates** 62% women, 32% part-time, 30% 25 or older **The most frequently chosen baccalaureate fields are** business/marketing, education, health professions and related sciences **Academic program** English as a second language, advanced placement, self-designed majors, summer session, adult/continuing education programs, internships **Contact** Ms. Tina Thayer, Director of Admissions, Kansas Wesleyan University, 100 East Claflin, Salina, KS 67401-6196. Telephone: 785-829-5541 Ext. 1283 or toll-free 800-874-1154 Ext. 1285. Fax: 785-827-0927. E-mail: admissions@diamond.kwu.edu. Web site: http://www.kwu.edu/.

MANHATTAN CHRISTIAN COLLEGE
MANHATTAN, KANSAS

General Independent, 4-year, coed, affiliated with Christian Churches and Churches of Christ **Entrance** Minimally difficult **Setting** 10-acre small-town campus **Total enrollment** 412 **Student-faculty ratio** 16:1 **Application deadline** 8/1 (freshmen), 8/1 (transfer) **Freshmen** 71% were admitted **Housing** Yes **Expenses** Tuition $6870; Room & Board $3610 **Undergraduates** 55% women, 30% part-time, 14% 25 or older, 0.3% Native American, 1% Hispanic American, 2% African American, 0.3% Asian American/Pacific Islander **The most frequently chosen baccalaureate fields are** business/marketing, philosophy, philosophy, religion, and theology **Academic program** Advanced placement, self-designed majors, summer session, internships **Contact** Mr. Scott Jenkins, Director of Admissions, Manhattan Christian College, 1415 Anderson, Manhattan, KS 66502-4081. Telephone: 785-539-3571 or toll-free 877-246-4622. Fax: 785-539-0832. E-mail: admit@mccks.edu. Web site: http://www.mccks.edu/.

MCPHERSON COLLEGE
MCPHERSON, KANSAS

General Independent, 4-year, coed, affiliated with Church of the Brethren **Entrance** Moderately difficult **Setting** 26-acre small-town campus **Total enrollment** 397 **Student-faculty ratio** 10:1 **Application deadline** Rolling (freshmen), rolling (transfer) **Freshmen** 78% were admitted **Housing** Yes **Expenses** Tuition $12,720; Room & Board $4990 **Undergraduates** 48% women, 9% part-time, 13% 25 or older, 1% Native American, 10% Hispanic American, 12% African American, 1% Asian American/Pacific Islander **The most frequently chosen baccalaureate fields are** business/marketing, education, social sciences and history **Academic program** English as a second language, advanced placement, self-designed majors, summer session, adult/continuing education programs, internships **Contact** Mr. Fred Schmidt, Dean of Enrollment, McPherson College, 1600 East Euclid, PO Box 1402, McPherson, KS 67460-1402. Telephone: 316-241-0731 Ext. 1270 or toll-free 800-365-7402 Ext. 1270. Fax: 316-241-8443 Ext. 1270. E-mail: admiss@mcpherson.edu. Web site: http://www.mcpherson.edu/.

MIDAMERICA NAZARENE UNIVERSITY
OLATHE, KANSAS

General Independent, comprehensive, coed, affiliated with Church of the Nazarene **Entrance** Minimally difficult **Setting** 112-acre suburban campus **Total enrollment** 1,684 **Student-faculty ratio** 18:1 **Application deadline** 8/1 (freshmen), 8/1 (transfer) **Freshmen** 51% were admitted **Housing** Yes **Expenses** Tuition $11,638; Room & Board $5322 **Undergraduates** 53% women, 11% part-time, 25% 25 or older, 1% Native American, 1% Hispanic American, 6% African American, 1% Asian American/Pacific Islander **The most frequently chosen baccalaureate fields are** business/marketing, education, health professions and related sciences **Academic program** Advanced placement, accelerated degree program, summer session, adult/continuing education programs, internships **Contact** Mr. Mike Redwine, Vice President for Enrollment Development, MidAmerica Nazarene University, 2030 East College Way, Olathe, KS 66062-1899. Telephone: 913-791-3380 Ext. 481 or toll-free 800-800-8887. Fax: 913-791-3481. E-mail: admissions@mnu.edu. Web site: http://www.mnu.edu/.

NEWMAN UNIVERSITY
WICHITA, KANSAS

General Independent Roman Catholic, comprehensive, coed **Entrance** Minimally difficult **Setting** 53-acre urban campus **Total enrollment** 2,071 **Student-faculty ratio** 14:1 **Application deadline** Rolling (freshmen), rolling (transfer) **Freshmen** 99% were admitted **Housing** Yes **Expenses** Tuition $11,210; Room & Board $4364 **Undergraduates** 66% women,

KANSAS

43% part-time, 46% 25 or older, 2% Native American, 5% Hispanic American, 8% African American, 2% Asian American/Pacific Islander **The most frequently chosen baccalaureate field is** philosophy, religion, and theology **Academic program** Advanced placement, accelerated degree program, summer session, adult/continuing education programs, internships **Contact** Mrs. Marla Sexson, Dean of Admissions, Newman University, 3100 McCormick Avenue, Wichita, KS 67213. Telephone: 316-942-4291 Ext. 144 or toll-free 877-NEWMANU Ext. 144. Fax: 316-942-4483. E-mail: admissions@newmanu.edu. Web site: http://www.newmanu.edu/.

OTTAWA UNIVERSITY
OTTAWA, KANSAS

General Independent American Baptist Churches in the USA, comprehensive, coed **Entrance** Moderately difficult **Setting** 60-acre small-town campus **Total enrollment** 433 **Student-faculty ratio** 14:1 **Application deadline** Rolling (freshmen), rolling (transfer) **Freshmen** 68% were admitted **Housing** Yes **Expenses** Tuition $11,800; Room & Board $5160 **Undergraduates** 45% women, 6% part-time, 9% 25 or older, 2% Native American, 4% Hispanic American, 11% African American, 0.5% Asian American/Pacific Islander **Academic program** English as a second language, advanced placement, self-designed majors, summer session, internships **Contact** Ms. Lanette Stineman, Director of Admissions, Ottawa University, 1001 South Cedar, Ottawa, KS 66067-3399. Telephone: 785-242-5200 Ext. 1051 or toll-free 800-755-5200. Fax: 785-242-7429. E-mail: wwwadmiss@ottawa.edu. Web site: http://www.ottawa.edu/.

PITTSBURG STATE UNIVERSITY
PITTSBURG, KANSAS

General State-supported, comprehensive, coed **Entrance** Noncompetitive **Setting** 233-acre small-town campus **Total enrollment** 6,723 **Student-faculty ratio** 23:1 **Application deadline** Rolling (freshmen), rolling (transfer) **Freshmen** 66% were admitted **Housing** Yes **Expenses** Tuition $2338; Room & Board $3890 **Undergraduates** 48% women, 11% part-time, 19% 25 or older **Academic program** English as a second language, advanced placement, self-designed majors, honors program, summer session, adult/continuing education programs, internships **Contact** Ms. Ange Peterson, Director of Admission and Retention, Pittsburg State University, 1701 South Broadway, Pittsburg, KS 66762. Telephone: 620-235-4251 or toll-free 800-854-7488 Ext. 1. Fax: 316-235-6003. E-mail: psuadmit@pittstate.edu. Web site: http://www.pittstate.edu/.

SAINT MARY COLLEGE
LEAVENWORTH, KANSAS

General Independent Roman Catholic, comprehensive, coed **Entrance** Moderately difficult **Setting** 240-acre small-town campus **Total enrollment** 772 **Student-faculty ratio** 12:1 **Application deadline** Rolling (freshmen), rolling (transfer) **Freshmen** 29% were admitted **Housing** Yes **Expenses** Tuition $12,312; Room & Board $4986 **Undergraduates** 62% women, 30% part-time, 11% 25 or older, 1% Native American, 4% Hispanic American, 8% African American, 2% Asian American/Pacific Islander **The most frequently chosen baccalaureate fields are** communications/communication technologies, engineering/engineering technologies, psychology **Academic program** Advanced placement, self-designed majors, honors program, summer session, adult/continuing education programs, internships **Contact** Mr. Todd Moore, Enrollment Services Director, Saint Mary College, 4100 South Fourth Street, Leavenworth, KS 66048. Telephone: 913-682-5151 Ext. 6118 or toll-free 800-758-6140 (out-of-state). E-mail: admis@hub.smcks.edu. Web site: http://www.smcks.edu/.

SOUTHWESTERN COLLEGE
WINFIELD, KANSAS

General Independent United Methodist, comprehensive, coed **Entrance** Moderately difficult **Setting** 70-acre small-town campus **Total enrollment** 1,276 **Student-faculty ratio** 13:1 **Application deadline** 8/1 (freshmen), 8/1 (transfer) **Freshmen** 72% were admitted **Housing** Yes **Expenses** Tuition $13,076; Room & Board $4580 **Undergraduates** 50% women, 50% part-time, 55% 25 or older **The most frequently chosen baccalaureate fields are** business/marketing, computer/information sciences, health professions and related sciences **Academic program** Advanced placement, self-designed majors, honors program, summer session, adult/continuing education programs, internships **Contact** Ms. Brenda D. Hicks, Director of Admission, Southwestern College, 100 College Street, Winfield, KS 67156-2499. Telephone: 620-229-6236 or toll-free 800-846-1543. Fax: 620-229-6344. E-mail: scadmit@sckans.edu. Web site: http://www.sckans.edu/.

STERLING COLLEGE
STERLING, KANSAS

General Independent Presbyterian, 4-year, coed **Entrance** Minimally difficult **Setting** 46-acre small-town campus **Total enrollment** 461 **Student-faculty ratio** 12:1 **Application deadline** Rolling (freshmen), rolling (transfer) **Freshmen** 59% were admitted **Housing** Yes **Expenses** Tuition $12,100; Room & Board $5020 **Undergraduates** 52% women, 5% part-time, 6% 25 or older, 1% Native American, 5% Hispanic American, 5% African American, 1% Asian American/Pacific Islander **The most frequently chosen baccalaureate fields are** business/marketing, biological/life sciences, education **Academic program** Advanced placement, self-designed majors, honors program, internships **Contact** Mr. Calvin White, Vice President for Enrollment Services, Sterling College, PO Box 98, Sterling, KS 67579-0098. Telephone: 620-278-4364 Ext. 364 or toll-free 800-346-1017. Fax: 620-278-4416. E-mail: admissions@sterling.edu. Web site: http://www.sterling.edu/.

KANSAS

TABOR COLLEGE
HILLSBORO, KANSAS

General Independent Mennonite Brethren, comprehensive, coed **Entrance** Moderately difficult **Setting** 26-acre small-town campus **Total enrollment** 593 **Student-faculty ratio** 13:1 **Application deadline** 8/1 (freshmen), 8/1 (transfer) **Freshmen** 35% were admitted **Housing** Yes **Expenses** Tuition $13,000; Room & Board $4900 **Undergraduates** 51% women, 29% part-time, 7% 25 or older, 1% Native American, 2% Hispanic American, 6% African American, 1% Asian American/Pacific Islander **The most frequently chosen baccalaureate fields are** business/marketing, education, philosophy **Academic program** Advanced placement, accelerated degree program, self-designed majors, honors program, summer session, adult/continuing education programs, internships **Contact** Glenn Lygrisse, Vice President for Enrollment Management, Tabor College, 400 South Jefferson, Hillsboro, KS 67063. Telephone: 620-947-3121 Ext. 1723 or toll-free 800-822-6799. Fax: 620-947-2607. E-mail: admissions@tabor.edu. Web site: http://www.tabor.edu/.

UNIVERSITY OF KANSAS
LAWRENCE, KANSAS

General State-supported, university, coed **Entrance** Moderately difficult **Setting** 1,000-acre suburban campus **Total enrollment** 28,190 **Student-faculty ratio** 15:1 **Application deadline** 4/1 (freshmen), rolling (transfer) **Freshmen** 69% were admitted **Housing** Yes **Expenses** Tuition $2884; Room & Board $4348 **Undergraduates** 53% women, 10% part-time, 8% 25 or older, 1% Native American, 3% Hispanic American, 3% African American, 3% Asian American/Pacific Islander **The most frequently chosen baccalaureate fields are** business/marketing, English, social sciences and history **Academic program** English as a second language, advanced placement, accelerated degree program, self-designed majors, honors program, summer session, adult/continuing education programs, internships **Contact** Mr. Alan Cerveny, Director of Admissions and Scholarships, University of Kansas, KU Visitor Center, 1502 Iowa Street, Lawrence, KS 66045-1910. Telephone: 785-864-3911 or toll-free 888-686-7323 (in-state). Fax: 785-864-5006. E-mail: adm@ku.edu. Web site: http://www.ku.edu/.

WASHBURN UNIVERSITY OF TOPEKA
TOPEKA, KANSAS

General City-supported, comprehensive, coed **Entrance** Noncompetitive **Setting** 160-acre urban campus **Total enrollment** 6,118 **Student-faculty ratio** 15:1 **Application deadline** Rolling (freshmen), 8/8 (transfer) **Freshmen** 100% were admitted **Housing** Yes **Expenses** Tuition $3356; Room & Board $4300 **Undergraduates** 62% women, 39% part-time, 35% 25 or older, 1% Native American, 4% Hispanic American, 6% African American, 2% Asian American/Pacific Islander **The most frequently chosen baccalaureate fields are** business/marketing, health professions and related sciences, protective services/public administration **Academic program** English as a second language, advanced placement, self-designed majors, honors program, summer session, adult/continuing education programs, internships **Contact** Ms. April Hansen, Director of Admission, Washburn University of Topeka, 1700 SW College Avenue, Topeka, KS 66621. Telephone: 785-231-1010 Ext. 1293 or toll-free 800-332-0291 (in-state). Fax: 785-231-1089. E-mail: zzgomez@acc.wacc.edu. Web site: http://www.washburn.edu/.

WICHITA STATE UNIVERSITY
WICHITA, KANSAS

General State-supported, university, coed **Entrance** Noncompetitive **Setting** 335-acre urban campus **Total enrollment** 14,854 **Student-faculty ratio** 17:1 **Application deadline** Rolling (transfer) **Freshmen** 73% were admitted **Housing** Yes **Expenses** Tuition $2857; Room & Board $4260 **Undergraduates** 56% women, 40% part-time, 32% 25 or older, 1% Native American, 5% Hispanic American, 7% African American, 8% Asian American/Pacific Islander **The most frequently chosen baccalaureate fields are** business/marketing, education, health professions and related sciences **Academic program** English as a second language, advanced placement, accelerated degree program, self-designed majors, honors program, summer session, internships **Contact** Ms. Christine Schneikart-Luebbe, Director of Admissions, Wichita State University, 1845 North Fairmount, Wichita, KS 67260. Telephone: 316-978-3085 or toll-free 800-362-2594. Fax: 316-978-3174. E-mail: admissions@wichita.edu. Web site: http://www.wichita.edu/.

KENTUCKY

ALICE LLOYD COLLEGE
PIPPA PASSES, KENTUCKY

General Independent, 4-year, coed **Entrance** Moderately difficult **Setting** 175-acre rural campus **Total enrollment** 565 **Student-faculty ratio** 19:1 **Application deadline** 8/1 (freshmen), rolling (transfer) **Freshmen** 58% were admitted **Housing** Yes **Expenses** Tuition $640; Room & Board $2810 **Undergraduates** 55% women, 5% part-time, 6% 25 or older, 0.4% Native American, 1% Hispanic American, 1% African American, 0.4% Asian American/Pacific Islander **The most frequently chosen baccalaureate fields are** biological/life sciences, business/marketing, education **Academic program** Advanced placement **Contact** Sean Damron, Director of Admissions, Alice Lloyd College, 100 Purpose Road, Pippa Passes, KY 41844. Telephone: 606-368-2101 Ext. 6134. Fax: 606-368-2125. E-mail: admissions@alc.edu. Web site: http://www.alc.edu/.

KENTUCKY

ASBURY COLLEGE
WILMORE, KENTUCKY

General Independent nondenominational, comprehensive, coed **Entrance** Moderately difficult **Setting** 400-acre small-town campus **Total enrollment** 1,352 **Student-faculty ratio** 12:1 **Application deadline** Rolling (freshmen), rolling (transfer) **Freshmen** 84% were admitted **Housing** Yes **Expenses** Tuition $14,764; Room & Board $3794 **Undergraduates** 59% women, 4% part-time, 4% 25 or older, 0.3% Native American, 1% Hispanic American, 1% African American, 1% Asian American/Pacific Islander **The most frequently chosen baccalaureate fields are** English, education, philosophy, religion, and theology **Academic program** Advanced placement, summer session, internships **Contact** Mr. Stan F. Wiggam, Dean of Admissions, Asbury College, 1 Macklem Drive, Wilmore, KY 40390. Telephone: 859-858-3511 Ext. 2142 or toll-free 800-888-1818. Fax: 859-858-3921. E-mail: admissions@asbury.edu. Web site: http://www.asbury.edu/.

BELLARMINE UNIVERSITY
LOUISVILLE, KENTUCKY

General Independent Roman Catholic, comprehensive, coed **Entrance** Moderately difficult **Setting** 120-acre suburban campus **Total enrollment** 2,248 **Student-faculty ratio** 14:1 **Application deadline** 8/15 (freshmen), 8/15 (transfer) **Freshmen** 84% were admitted **Housing** Yes **Expenses** Tuition $15,560; Room & Board $4880 **Undergraduates** 23% 25 or older, 0.3% Native American, 1% Hispanic American, 3% African American, 2% Asian American/Pacific Islander **The most frequently chosen baccalaureate fields are** business/marketing, education, health professions and related sciences **Academic program** Advanced placement, accelerated degree program, self-designed majors, honors program, summer session, adult/continuing education programs, internships **Contact** Mr. Timothy A. Sturgeon, Dean of Admission, Bellarmine University, 2001 Newburg Road, Louisville, KY 40205-0671. Telephone: 502-452-8131 or toll-free 800-274-4723 Ext. 8131. Fax: 502-452-8002. E-mail: admissions@bellarmine.edu. Web site: http://www.bellarmine.edu/.

BEREA COLLEGE
BEREA, KENTUCKY

General Independent, 4-year, coed **Entrance** Very difficult **Setting** 140-acre small-town campus **Total enrollment** 1,674 **Student-faculty ratio** 11:1 **Application deadline** Rolling (transfer) **Freshmen** 32% were admitted **Housing** Yes **Expenses** Tuition $205; Room & Board $4099 **Undergraduates** 56% women, 3% part-time, 5% 25 or older, 1% Native American, 1% Hispanic American, 15% African American, 1% Asian American/Pacific Islander **The most frequently chosen baccalaureate fields are** business/marketing, engineering/engineering technologies, home economics/vocational home economics **Academic program** Advanced placement, self-designed majors, honors program, summer session, internships **Contact** Mr. Joseph Bagnoli, Director of Admissions, Berea College, CPO 2220, Berea, KY 40404. Telephone: 859-985-3500 or toll-free 800-326-5948. Fax: 859-985-3512. E-mail: admissions@berea.edu. Web site: http://www.berea.edu/.

BRESCIA UNIVERSITY
OWENSBORO, KENTUCKY

General Independent Roman Catholic, comprehensive, coed **Entrance** Moderately difficult **Setting** 6-acre urban campus **Total enrollment** 791 **Student-faculty ratio** 14:1 **Application deadline** Rolling (freshmen), rolling (transfer) **Freshmen** 80% were admitted **Housing** Yes **Expenses** Tuition $9845; Room & Board $4380 **Undergraduates** 61% women, 29% part-time, 44% 25 or older, 0.3% Native American, 1% Hispanic American, 4% African American, 0.5% Asian American/Pacific Islander **The most frequently chosen baccalaureate fields are** business/marketing, education, protective services/public administration **Academic program** English as a second language, advanced placement, self-designed majors, honors program, summer session, adult/continuing education programs, internships **Contact** Sr. Mary Austin Blank, Director of Admissions, Brescia University, 717 Frederica Street, Owensboro, KY 42301-3023. Telephone: 270-686-4241 Ext. 241 or toll-free 877-BRESCIA. Fax: 270-686-4201. E-mail: admissions@brescia.edu. Web site: http://www.brescia.edu/.

CAMPBELLSVILLE UNIVERSITY
CAMPBELLSVILLE, KENTUCKY

General Independent, comprehensive, coed, affiliated with Kentucky Baptist Convention **Entrance** Moderately difficult **Setting** 70-acre small-town campus **Total enrollment** 1,777 **Student-faculty ratio** 16:1 **Application deadline** Rolling (freshmen), rolling (transfer) **Freshmen** 79% were admitted **Housing** Yes **Expenses** Tuition $10,070; Room & Board $4400 **Undergraduates** 58% women, 29% part-time, 18% 25 or older, 0.2% Native American, 1% Hispanic American, 5% African American, 0.2% Asian American/Pacific Islander **The most frequently chosen baccalaureate fields are** business/marketing, education, social sciences and history **Academic program** English as a second language, advanced placement, accelerated degree program, honors program, summer session, adult/continuing education programs, internships **Contact** Mr. R. Trent Argo, Director of Admissions, Campbellsville University, 1 University Drive, Campbellsville, KY 42718-2799. Telephone: 270-789-5552 or toll-free 800-264-6014. Fax: 270-789-5071. E-mail: admissions@campbellsvil.edu. Web site: http://www.campbellsvil.edu/.

CENTRE COLLEGE
DANVILLE, KENTUCKY

General Independent, 4-year, coed, affiliated with Presbyterian Church (U.S.A.) **Entrance** Very difficult **Setting** 100-acre small-town campus **Total**

KENTUCKY

Centre College *(continued)*
enrollment 1,070 **Student-faculty ratio** 11:1 **Application deadline** 2/1 (freshmen), 6/1 (transfer) **Freshmen** 82% were admitted **Housing** Yes **Expenses** Tuition $18,000; Room & Board $6000 **Undergraduates** 55% women, 1% part-time, 1% 25 or older, 0.3% Native American, 0.5% Hispanic American, 3% African American, 2% Asian American/Pacific Islander **The most frequently chosen baccalaureate fields are** biological/life sciences, English, social sciences and history **Academic program** Advanced placement, self-designed majors, internships **Contact** Mr. J. Carey Thompson, Dean of Admission and Financial Aid, Centre College, 600 West Walnut Street, Danville, KY 40422-1394. Telephone: 859-238-5350 or toll-free 800-423-6236. Fax: 859-238-5373. E-mail: admission@centre.edu. Web site: http://www.centre.edu/.

CLEAR CREEK BAPTIST BIBLE COLLEGE
PINEVILLE, KENTUCKY

General Independent Southern Baptist, 4-year, coed, primarily men **Entrance** Noncompetitive **Setting** 700-acre rural campus **Total enrollment** 198 **Student-faculty ratio** 13:1 **Application deadline** 7/15 (freshmen), 7/15 (transfer) **Freshmen** 90% were admitted **Housing** Yes **Expenses** Tuition $4396; Room & Board $3380 **Undergraduates** 12% women, 19% part-time, 90% 25 or older **Academic program** Summer session **Contact** Mr. Donnie Fox, Director of Admissions, Clear Creek Baptist Bible College, 300 Clear Creek Road, Pineville, KY 40977-9754. Telephone: 606-337-3196 Ext. 103. Fax: 606-337-2372. E-mail: ccbbc@ccbbc.edu. Web site: http://www.ccbbc.edu/.

CUMBERLAND COLLEGE
WILLIAMSBURG, KENTUCKY

General Independent Kentucky Baptist, comprehensive, coed **Entrance** Moderately difficult **Setting** 30-acre rural campus **Total enrollment** 1,707 **Student-faculty ratio** 17:1 **Application deadline** Rolling (freshmen), rolling (transfer) **Freshmen** 70% were admitted **Housing** Yes **Expenses** Tuition $10,388; Room & Board $4476 **Undergraduates** 53% women, 14% part-time, 4% 25 or older, 0.1% Native American, 1% Hispanic American, 5% African American, 0.3% Asian American/Pacific Islander **The most frequently chosen baccalaureate fields are** business/marketing, education, psychology **Academic program** English as a second language, advanced placement, accelerated degree program, self-designed majors, honors program, summer session, adult/continuing education programs, internships **Contact** Mrs. Erica Harris, Coordinator of Admissions, Cumberland College, 6178 College Station Drive, Williamsburg, KY 40769. Telephone: 606-539-4241 or toll-free 800-343-1609. Fax: 606-539-4303. E-mail: admiss@cc.cumber.edu. Web site: http://cc.cumber.edu/.

EASTERN KENTUCKY UNIVERSITY
RICHMOND, KENTUCKY

General State-supported, comprehensive, coed **Entrance** Noncompetitive **Setting** 500-acre small-town campus **Total enrollment** 14,697 **Student-faculty ratio** 16:1 **Application deadline** Rolling (freshmen), rolling (transfer) **Freshmen** 79% were admitted **Housing** Yes **Expenses** Tuition $2928; Room & Board $2924 **Undergraduates** 59% women, 25% part-time, 27% 25 or older, 0.2% Native American, 0.5% Hispanic American, 5% African American, 1% Asian American/Pacific Islander **The most frequently chosen baccalaureate fields are** education, health professions and related sciences, protective services/public administration **Academic program** English as a second language, advanced placement, accelerated degree program, self-designed majors, honors program, summer session, adult/continuing education programs, internships **Contact** Stephen A. Byrn, Director of Admissions, Eastern Kentucky University, Coates 2A, 521 Lancaster Avenue, Richmond, KY 40475-3102. Telephone: 859-622-2106 or toll-free 800-465-9191 (in-state). Web site: http://www.eku.edu/.

GEORGETOWN COLLEGE
GEORGETOWN, KENTUCKY

General Independent, comprehensive, coed, affiliated with Baptist Church **Entrance** Moderately difficult **Setting** 110-acre suburban campus **Total enrollment** 1,703 **Student-faculty ratio** 13:1 **Application deadline** 7/1 (freshmen), rolling (transfer) **Freshmen** 95% were admitted **Housing** Yes **Expenses** Tuition $13,580; Room & Board $4820 **Undergraduates** 57% women, 4% part-time, 2% 25 or older, 0.1% Native American, 0.2% Hispanic American, 2% African American, 0.3% Asian American/Pacific Islander **The most frequently chosen baccalaureate fields are** business/marketing, psychology, visual/performing arts **Academic program** Advanced placement, accelerated degree program, self-designed majors, summer session, internships **Contact** Mr. Brian Taylor, Director of Admissions, Georgetown College, 400 East College Street, Georgetown, KY 40324. Telephone: 502-863-8009 or toll-free 800-788-9985. Fax: 502-868-7733. E-mail: admissions@georgetowncollege.edu. Web site: http://www.georgetowncollege.edu/.

KENTUCKY CHRISTIAN COLLEGE
GRAYSON, KENTUCKY

General Independent, comprehensive, coed, affiliated with Christian Churches and Churches of Christ **Entrance** Moderately difficult **Setting** 124-acre rural campus **Total enrollment** 594 **Student-faculty ratio** 18:1 **Application deadline** Rolling (freshmen), rolling (transfer) **Freshmen** 83% were admitted **Housing** Yes **Expenses** Tuition $7942; Room & Board $4278 **Undergraduates** 52% women, 3% part-time, 8% 25 or older, 1% Native American, 0.3% Hispanic American, 2% African American, 0.2% Asian American/

KENTUCKY

Pacific Islander **The most frequently chosen baccalaureate fields are** philosophy, education, philosophy, religion, and theology **Academic program** Advanced placement, accelerated degree program, summer session, internships **Contact** Sandra Deakins, Director of Admissions, Kentucky Christian College, 100 Academic Parkway, Grayson, KY 41143-2205. Telephone: 606-474-3266 or toll-free 800-522-3181. Fax: 606-474-3155. E-mail: knights@email.kcc.edu. Web site: http://www.kcc.edu/.

KENTUCKY MOUNTAIN BIBLE COLLEGE
VANCLEVE, KENTUCKY

General Independent interdenominational, 4-year, coed **Entrance** Moderately difficult **Setting** 35-acre rural campus **Total enrollment** 82 **Student-faculty ratio** 6:1 **Application deadline** Rolling (freshmen), rolling (transfer) **Freshmen** 51% were admitted **Housing** Yes **Expenses** Tuition $4180; Room & Board $3000 **Undergraduates** 40% women, 22% part-time, 27% 25 or older, 0% Native American, 1% Hispanic American, 1% African American, 0% Asian American/Pacific Islander **The most frequently chosen baccalaureate fields are** philosophy, philosophy, religion, and theology **Academic program** Advanced placement, adult/continuing education programs, internships **Contact** Mr. James Nelson, Director of Recruiting, Kentucky Mountain Bible College, PO Box 10, Vancleve, KY 41385. Telephone: 606-666-5000 Ext. 130 or toll-free 800-879-KMBC Ext. 130. Fax: 606-666-7744. E-mail: jnelson@kmbc.edu. Web site: http://www.kmbc.edu/.

KENTUCKY STATE UNIVERSITY
FRANKFORT, KENTUCKY

General State-related, comprehensive, coed **Entrance** Minimally difficult **Setting** 485-acre small-town campus **Total enrollment** 2,254 **Student-faculty ratio** 15:1 **Application deadline** Rolling (freshmen), rolling (transfer) **Freshmen** 45% were admitted **Housing** Yes **Expenses** Tuition $2440; Room & Board $3740 **Undergraduates** 56% women, 29% part-time, 26% 25 or older **Academic program** English as a second language, advanced placement, accelerated degree program, self-designed majors, honors program, summer session, adult/continuing education programs, internships **Contact** Mr. Vory Billaps, Director of Records, Registration, and Admission, Kentucky State University, 400 East Main, Frankfort, KY 40601. Telephone: 502-597-6340 or toll-free 800-633-9415 (in-state); 800-325-1716 (out-of-state). Fax: 502-597-6239. E-mail: jburrell@qwmail.kysu.edu. Web site: http://www.kysu.edu/.

KENTUCKY WESLEYAN COLLEGE
OWENSBORO, KENTUCKY

General Independent Methodist, 4-year, coed **Entrance** Moderately difficult **Setting** 52-acre suburban campus **Total enrollment** 671 **Student-faculty ratio** 13:1 **Application deadline** 9/1 (freshmen), 9/1 (transfer) **Freshmen** 81% were admitted **Housing** Yes **Expenses** Tuition $10,920; Room & Board $4980 **Undergraduates** 46% women, 6% part-time, 62% 25 or older, 0% Native American, 0.3% Hispanic American, 7% African American, 0.5% Asian American/Pacific Islander **The most frequently chosen baccalaureate fields are** business/marketing, communications/communication technologies, education **Academic program** Advanced placement, self-designed majors, summer session, internships **Contact** Mr. Ken Rasp, Dean of Admission, Kentucky Wesleyan College, 3000 Frederica Street, PO Box 1039, Owensboro, KY 42302-1039. Telephone: 270-852-3120 or toll-free 800-999-0592 (in-state); 270-926-3111 (out-of-state). Fax: 270-926-3196. E-mail: admission@kwc.edu. Web site: http://www.kwc.edu/.

LINDSEY WILSON COLLEGE
COLUMBIA, KENTUCKY

General Independent United Methodist, comprehensive, coed **Entrance** Minimally difficult **Setting** 40-acre rural campus **Total enrollment** 1,303 **Student-faculty ratio** 20:1 **Application deadline** Rolling (freshmen), rolling (transfer) **Freshmen** 94% were admitted **Housing** Yes **Expenses** Tuition $11,592; Room & Board $5070 **Undergraduates** 61% women, 11% part-time, 29% 25 or older, 0.3% Native American, 2% Hispanic American, 7% African American, 0.2% Asian American/Pacific Islander **The most frequently chosen baccalaureate fields are** biological/life sciences, communications/communication technologies, education **Academic program** English as a second language, advanced placement, accelerated degree program, self-designed majors, summer session, adult/continuing education programs, internships **Contact** Mr. Claude Bacon, Director of Admissions, Lindsey Wilson College, 210 Lindsey Wilson Street, Columbia, KY 42728-1298. Telephone: 270-384-8100 Ext. 8008 or toll-free 800-264-0138. Fax: 270-384-8200. E-mail: baconc@lindsey.edu. Web site: http://www.lindsey.edu/.

MID-CONTINENT COLLEGE
MAYFIELD, KENTUCKY

General Independent Southern Baptist, 4-year, coed **Entrance** Minimally difficult **Setting** 60-acre small-town campus **Total enrollment** 265 **Student-faculty ratio** 14:1 **Application deadline** Rolling (freshmen), rolling (transfer) **Freshmen** 85% were admitted **Housing** Yes **Expenses** Tuition $6880; Room & Board $4800 **Undergraduates** 37% women, 15% part-time, 37% 25 or older **The most frequently chosen baccalaureate fields are** business/marketing, philosophy, philosophy, religion, and theology **Academic program** English as a second language, advanced placement, accelerated degree program, summer session **Contact** Mrs. Darla Zakowicz, Director of Enrollment and Retention Management, Mid-Continent College, 99 Powell Road East, Mayfield, KY 42068. Telephone: 270-247-8521 Ext. 311. E-mail: mcc@midcontinent.edu. Web site: http://www.midcontinent.edu.

KENTUCKY

MIDWAY COLLEGE
MIDWAY, KENTUCKY

General Independent, 4-year, women only, affiliated with Christian Church (Disciples of Christ) **Entrance** Minimally difficult **Setting** 105-acre small-town campus **Total enrollment** 874 **Student-faculty ratio** 15:1 **Application deadline** Rolling (freshmen), rolling (transfer) **Freshmen** 71% were admitted **Housing** Yes **Expenses** Tuition $10,175; Room & Board $5540 **Undergraduates** 27% part-time, 58% 25 or older, 1% Native American, 1% Hispanic American, 7% African American, 0% Asian American/Pacific Islander **The most frequently chosen baccalaureate fields are** agriculture, business/marketing, education **Academic program** Advanced placement, honors program, summer session, adult/continuing education programs, internships **Contact** Mr. K. Bryan, Director of Admissions, Midway College, 512 East Stephens Street, Pinkerton Building, Midway, KY 40347-1120. Telephone: 859-846-5346 or toll-free 800-755-0031. Fax: 859-846-5823. E-mail: admissions@midway.edu. Web site: http://www.midway.edu/.

MOREHEAD STATE UNIVERSITY
MOREHEAD, KENTUCKY

General State-supported, comprehensive, coed **Entrance** Minimally difficult **Setting** 809-acre small-town campus **Total enrollment** 9,027 **Student-faculty ratio** 18:1 **Application deadline** Rolling (freshmen), rolling (transfer) **Freshmen** 73% were admitted **Housing** Yes **Expenses** Tuition $2710; Room & Board $3800 **Undergraduates** 61% women, 15% part-time, 15% 25 or older, 0.4% Native American, 0.4% Hispanic American, 4% African American, 0.3% Asian American/Pacific Islander **The most frequently chosen baccalaureate fields are** business/marketing, education, social sciences and history **Academic program** English as a second language, advanced placement, accelerated degree program, self-designed majors, honors program, summer session, adult/continuing education programs, internships **Contact** Mr. Tim Rhodes, Assistant Vice President of Admissions, Financial Aid and Housing, Morehead State University, Howell McDowell 301, Morehead, KY 40351. Telephone: 606-783-2000 or toll-free 800-585-6781. Fax: 606-783-5038. E-mail: admissions@morehead-st.edu. Web site: http://www.moreheadstate.edu/.

MURRAY STATE UNIVERSITY
MURRAY, KENTUCKY

General State-supported, comprehensive, coed **Entrance** Moderately difficult **Setting** 238-acre small-town campus **Total enrollment** 9,635 **Student-faculty ratio** 17:1 **Application deadline** Rolling (freshmen), rolling (transfer) **Freshmen** 88% were admitted **Housing** Yes **Expenses** Tuition $2755; Room & Board $4150 **Undergraduates** 58% women, 15% part-time, 22% 25 or older, 0.3% Native American, 1% Hispanic American, 6% African American, 1% Asian American/Pacific Islander **The most frequently chosen baccalaureate fields are** business/marketing, communications/communication technologies, education **Academic program** English as a second language, advanced placement, accelerated degree program, honors program, summer session, adult/continuing education programs, internships **Contact** Mrs. Stacy Bell, Admission Clerk, Murray State University, PO Box 9, Murray, KY 42071-0009. Telephone: 270-762-3035 or toll-free 800-272-4678. Fax: 270-762-3050. E-mail: pbryan@msumusik.mursuky.edu. Web site: http://www.murraystate.edu/.

NORTHERN KENTUCKY UNIVERSITY
HIGHLAND HEIGHTS, KENTUCKY

General State-supported, comprehensive, coed **Entrance** Noncompetitive **Setting** 300-acre suburban campus **Total enrollment** 12,529 **Student-faculty ratio** 17:1 **Application deadline** 8/21 (freshmen), 8/1 (transfer) **Freshmen** 95% were admitted **Housing** Yes **Expenses** Tuition $2886; Room & Board $4460 **Undergraduates** 59% women, 28% part-time, 26% 25 or older, 0.3% Native American, 1% Hispanic American, 4% African American, 1% Asian American/Pacific Islander **The most frequently chosen baccalaureate fields are** business/marketing, education, social sciences and history **Academic program** Advanced placement, honors program, summer session, adult/continuing education programs, internships **Contact** Mrs. Debbie Poweleit, Associate Director of Admissions, Northern Kentucky University, Administrative Center 400, Highland Heights, KY 41099-7010. Telephone: 606-572-5220 Ext. 5154 or toll-free 800-637-9948 (out-of-state). Fax: 859-572-6665. E-mail: admitnku@nku.edu. Web site: http://www.nku.edu/.

PIKEVILLE COLLEGE
PIKEVILLE, KENTUCKY

General Independent, comprehensive, coed, affiliated with Presbyterian Church (U.S.A.) **Entrance** Noncompetitive **Setting** 25-acre small-town campus **Total enrollment** 1,194 **Student-faculty ratio** 15:1 **Application deadline** 8/24 (freshmen), 8/24 (transfer) **Freshmen** 100% were admitted **Housing** Yes **Expenses** Tuition $7800; Room & Board $3340 **Undergraduates** 59% women, 6% part-time, 16% 25 or older, 2% Native American, 2% Hispanic American, 9% African American, 1% Asian American/Pacific Islander **The most frequently chosen baccalaureate fields are** biological/life sciences, business/marketing, education **Academic program** Advanced placement, summer session, internships **Contact** Ms. Melinda Lynch, Director of Admissions, Pikeville College, 147 Sycamore Street, Pikeville, KY 41501. Telephone: 606-218-5251 or toll-free 866-232-7700. Fax: 606-218-5255. E-mail: wewantyou@pc.edu. Web site: http://www.pc.edu/.

KENTUCKY

SOUTHERN BAPTIST THEOLOGICAL SEMINARY
LOUISVILLE, KENTUCKY

Contact Southern Baptist Theological Seminary, 2825 Lexington Road, Louisville, KY 40280-0004. Web site: http://www.sbts.edu/.

SPALDING UNIVERSITY
LOUISVILLE, KENTUCKY

General Independent, comprehensive, coed, affiliated with Roman Catholic Church **Entrance** Moderately difficult **Setting** 5-acre urban campus **Total enrollment** 1,481 **Student-faculty ratio** 16:1 **Application deadline** 8/1 (freshmen), 8/1 (transfer) **Freshmen** 71% were admitted **Housing** Yes **Expenses** Tuition $11,496; Room & Board $2930 **Undergraduates** 77% women, 40% part-time, 53% 25 or older, 0.2% Native American, 1% Hispanic American, 15% African American, 1% Asian American/Pacific Islander **Academic program** Advanced placement, accelerated degree program, summer session, adult/continuing education programs, internships **Contact** Ms. Kathleen C. Hodapp, Director of Admission, Spalding University, 851 South Fourth Street, Louisville, KY 40203. Telephone: 502-585-7111 Ext. 2226 or toll-free 800-896-8941 Ext. 2111. Fax: 502-992-2148. E-mail: admissions@spalding.edu. Web site: http://www.spalding.edu/.

SULLIVAN UNIVERSITY
LOUISVILLE, KENTUCKY

General Proprietary, comprehensive, coed **Entrance** Minimally difficult **Setting** 10-acre suburban campus **Total enrollment** 4,422 **Student-faculty ratio** 18:1 **Application deadline** Rolling (freshmen), rolling (transfer) **Housing** Yes **Expenses** Tuition $11,135; Room only $3375 **Undergraduates** 61% women, 34% part-time, 50% 25 or older, 0.4% Native American, 2% Hispanic American, 17% African American, 0% Asian American/Pacific Islander **Academic program** Advanced placement, accelerated degree program, summer session, adult/continuing education programs **Contact** Mr. Greg Cawthon, Director of Admissions, Sullivan University, 3101 Bardstown Road, Louisville, KY 40205. Telephone: 502-456-6505 Ext. 370 or toll-free 800-844-1354 (in-state). Fax: 502-456-0040. E-mail: admissions@sullivan.edu. Web site: http://www.sullivan.edu/.

THOMAS MORE COLLEGE
CRESTVIEW HILLS, KENTUCKY

General Independent Roman Catholic, comprehensive, coed **Entrance** Moderately difficult **Setting** 100-acre suburban campus **Total enrollment** 1,555 **Student-faculty ratio** 12:1 **Application deadline** 8/15 (freshmen), 8/15 (transfer) **Freshmen** 76% were admitted **Housing** Yes **Expenses** Tuition $13,550; Room & Board $4150 **Undergraduates** 53% women, 30% part-time, 36% 25 or older **The most frequently chosen baccalaureate fields are** biological/life sciences, business/marketing, health professions and related sciences **Academic program** Advanced placement, accelerated degree program, self-designed majors, honors program, summer session, adult/continuing education programs, internships **Contact** Mr. Robert A. McDermott, Director of Admissions, Thomas More College, 333 Thomas More Parkway, Crestview Hills, KY 41017. Telephone: 606-344-3332 or toll-free 800-825-4557. Fax: 606-344-3444. E-mail: robert.mcdermott@thomasmore.edu. Web site: http://www.thomasmore.edu/.

TRANSYLVANIA UNIVERSITY
LEXINGTON, KENTUCKY

General Independent, 4-year, coed, affiliated with Christian Church (Disciples of Christ) **Entrance** Very difficult **Setting** 35-acre urban campus **Total enrollment** 1,052 **Student-faculty ratio** 13:1 **Application deadline** 2/1 (freshmen), rolling (transfer) **Freshmen** 88% were admitted **Housing** Yes **Expenses** Tuition $16,010; Room & Board $5770 **Undergraduates** 57% women, 1% part-time, 1% 25 or older, 0.3% Native American, 1% Hispanic American, 3% African American, 2% Asian American/Pacific Islander **The most frequently chosen baccalaureate fields are** biological/life sciences, business/marketing, psychology **Academic program** Advanced placement, self-designed majors, summer session, internships **Contact** Ms. Sarah Coen, Director of Admissions, Transylvania University, 300 North Broadway, Lexington, KY 40508-1797. Telephone: 859-233-8242 or toll-free 800-872-6798. Fax: 859-233-8797. E-mail: admissions@transy.edu. Web site: http://www.transy.edu/.

UNION COLLEGE
BARBOURVILLE, KENTUCKY

General Independent United Methodist, comprehensive, coed **Entrance** Moderately difficult **Setting** 110-acre small-town campus **Total enrollment** 837 **Student-faculty ratio** 11:1 **Application deadline** 8/1 (freshmen), 8/31 (transfer) **Freshmen** 75% were admitted **Housing** Yes **Expenses** Tuition $11,720; Room & Board $5650 **Undergraduates** 52% women, 9% part-time, 22% 25 or older **The most frequently chosen baccalaureate fields are** business/marketing, education, social sciences and history **Academic program** Advanced placement, accelerated degree program, honors program, summer session, internships **Contact** Joretta Nelson, Vice President for Enrollment and Recruitment, Union College, 310 College Street, Barbourville, KY 40906. Telephone: 606-546-1220 or toll-free 800-489-8646. Fax: 606-546-1667. E-mail: enroll@unionky.edu. Web site: http://www.unionky.edu/.

UNIVERSITY OF KENTUCKY
LEXINGTON, KENTUCKY

General State-supported, university, coed **Entrance** Moderately difficult **Setting** 685-acre urban campus **Total enrollment** 23,901 **Student-faculty ratio** 17:1 **Application deadline** 2/15 (freshmen), 8/1 (transfer)

KENTUCKY

University of Kentucky *(continued)*

Freshmen 82% were admitted **Housing** Yes **Expenses** Tuition $3734; Room & Board $3980 **Undergraduates** 52% women, 11% part-time, 13% 25 or older, 0.2% Native American, 1% Hispanic American, 6% African American, 2% Asian American/Pacific Islander **The most frequently chosen baccalaureate fields are** business/marketing, education, health professions and related sciences **Academic program** English as a second language, advanced placement, accelerated degree program, self-designed majors, honors program, summer session, adult/continuing education programs, internships **Contact** Ms. Michelle Nordin, Associate Director of Admissions, University of Kentucky, 100 W.D. Funkhouser Building, Lexington, KY 40506-0054. Telephone: 859-257-2000 or toll-free 800-432-0967 (in-state). E-mail: admissio@uky.edu. Web site: http://www.uky.edu/.

UNIVERSITY OF LOUISVILLE
LOUISVILLE, KENTUCKY

General State-supported, university, coed **Entrance** Moderately difficult **Setting** 169-acre urban campus **Total enrollment** 19,682 **Student-faculty ratio** 13:1 **Application deadline** Rolling (freshmen), rolling (transfer) **Freshmen** 68% were admitted **Housing** Yes **Expenses** Tuition $3794; Room & Board $3608 **Undergraduates** 54% women, 30% part-time, 32% 25 or older, 0.3% Native American, 1% Hispanic American, 13% African American, 3% Asian American/Pacific Islander **The most frequently chosen baccalaureate fields are** business/marketing, engineering/engineering technologies, social sciences and history **Academic program** English as a second language, advanced placement, accelerated degree program, self-designed majors, honors program, summer session, adult/continuing education programs, internships **Contact** Ms. Jenny Sawyer, Executive Director for Admissions, University of Louisville, 2211 South Brook, Louisville, KY 40292. Telephone: 502-852-6531 or toll-free 502-852-6531 (in-state); 800-334-8635 (out-of-state). Fax: 502-852-4776 Ext. 6531. E-mail: admitme@gwise.louisville.edu. Web site: http://www.louisville.edu/.

WESTERN KENTUCKY UNIVERSITY
BOWLING GREEN, KENTUCKY

General State-supported, comprehensive, coed **Entrance** Moderately difficult **Setting** 223-acre suburban campus **Total enrollment** 16,579 **Student-faculty ratio** 18:1 **Application deadline** 8/1 (freshmen), 8/1 (transfer) **Freshmen** 85% were admitted **Housing** Yes **Expenses** Tuition $2844; Room & Board $3990 **Undergraduates** 59% women, 24% part-time, 20% 25 or older, 0.3% Native American, 1% Hispanic American, 8% African American, 1% Asian American/Pacific Islander **The most frequently chosen baccalaureate fields are** business/marketing, education, social sciences and history **Academic program** English as a second language, advanced placement, accelerated degree program, self-designed majors, honors program, summer session, adult/continuing education programs, internships **Contact** Ms. Sharon Dyrsen, Director of Admissions and Academic Services, Western Kentucky University, Potter Hall 117, 1 Big Red Way, Bowling Green, KY 42101-3576. Telephone: 270-745-4241 or toll-free 800-495-8463 (in-state). Fax: 270-745-6133. E-mail: admission@wku.edu. Web site: http://www.wku.edu/.

LOUISIANA

CENTENARY COLLEGE OF LOUISIANA
SHREVEPORT, LOUISIANA

General Independent United Methodist, comprehensive, coed **Entrance** Moderately difficult **Setting** 65-acre suburban campus **Total enrollment** 1,049 **Student-faculty ratio** 12:1 **Application deadline** 2/15 (freshmen), 8/1 (transfer) **Freshmen** 86% were admitted **Housing** Yes **Expenses** Tuition $15,800; Room & Board $4800 **Undergraduates** 62% women, 2% part-time, 1% 25 or older, 1% Native American, 3% Hispanic American, 6% African American, 1% Asian American/Pacific Islander **The most frequently chosen baccalaureate fields are** business/marketing, biological/life sciences, visual/performing arts **Academic program** Advanced placement, self-designed majors, honors program, summer session, adult/continuing education programs, internships **Contact** Dr. Eugene Gregory, Vice President of College Relations, Centenary College of Louisiana, 2911 Centenary Blvd, PO Box 41188, Shreveport, LA 71134-1188. Telephone: 318-869-5131 or toll-free 800-234-4448. Fax: 318-869-5005. E-mail: jtmartin@centenary.edu. Web site: http://www.centenary.edu/.

DILLARD UNIVERSITY
NEW ORLEANS, LOUISIANA

General Independent interdenominational, 4-year, coed **Entrance** Moderately difficult **Setting** 46-acre urban campus **Total enrollment** 2,137 **Student-faculty ratio** 16:1 **Application deadline** 7/1 (freshmen), 7/1 (transfer) **Freshmen** 65% were admitted **Housing** Yes **Expenses** Tuition $10,030; Room & Board $6296 **Undergraduates** 77% women, 8% part-time, 10% 25 or older, 0% Native American, 0.1% Hispanic American, 99% African American, 0% Asian American/Pacific Islander **The most frequently chosen baccalaureate fields are** business/marketing, biological/life sciences, health professions and related sciences **Academic program** Advanced placement, honors program, summer session, internships **Contact** Mr. Darrin Q. Rankin, Assistant Vice President, Enrollment Management, Dillard University, 2601 Gentilly Boulevard, New Orleans, LA 70122. Telephone: 504-286-4670. Fax: 504-286-4895.

LOUISIANA

GRAMBLING STATE UNIVERSITY
GRAMBLING, LOUISIANA

General State-supported, comprehensive, coed **Entrance** Noncompetitive **Setting** 340-acre small-town campus **Total enrollment** 4,500 **Student-faculty ratio** 17:1 **Application deadline** 7/15 (freshmen), 7/15 (transfer) **Freshmen** 58% were admitted **Housing** Yes **Expenses** Tuition $2589; Room & Board $2712 **Undergraduates** 57% women, 8% part-time, 16% 25 or older, 0.02% Native American, 1% Hispanic American, 97% African American, 0.2% Asian American/Pacific Islander **The most frequently chosen baccalaureate fields are** business/marketing, computer/information sciences, protective services/public administration **Academic program** Advanced placement, honors program, summer session, adult/continuing education programs, internships **Contact** Mr. Martin Lemelle, Head Recruiter/Admission Officer, Grambling State University, PO Box 607, Grambling, LA 71245. Telephone: 318-274-3395. E-mail: bingamann@medgar.gram.edu. Web site: http://www.gram.edu/.

GRANTHAM COLLEGE OF ENGINEERING
SLIDELL, LOUISIANA

General Proprietary, 4-year, coed, primarily men **Entrance** Noncompetitive **Setting** small-town campus **Total enrollment** 967 **Application deadline** Rolling (freshmen), rolling (transfer) **Housing** No **Expenses** Tuition $5250 **Undergraduates** 96% 25 or older **Academic program** Advanced placement, accelerated degree program, honors program, adult/continuing education programs **Contact** Mrs. Maria Adcock, Student Services Manager, Grantham College of Engineering, PO Box 5700, Slidell, LA 70460-6815. Telephone: 504-649-4191 or toll-free 800-955-2527. Fax: 504-649-4183. E-mail: gce@grantham.edu. Web site: http://www.grantham.edu/.

LOUISIANA COLLEGE
PINEVILLE, LOUISIANA

General Independent Southern Baptist, 4-year, coed **Entrance** Moderately difficult **Setting** 81-acre small-town campus **Total enrollment** 1,204 **Student-faculty ratio** 16:1 **Application deadline** 8/1 (freshmen), 8/1 (transfer) **Freshmen** 70% were admitted **Housing** Yes **Undergraduates** 58% women, 12% part-time, 10% 25 or older, 1% Native American, 8% Hispanic American, 8% African American, 2% Asian American/Pacific Islander **The most frequently chosen baccalaureate fields are** biological/life sciences, business/marketing, health professions and related sciences **Academic program** Advanced placement, accelerated degree program, self-designed majors, honors program, summer session, adult/continuing education programs, internships **Contact** Mrs. Mary Wagner, Director of Admissions, Louisiana College, Box 560, Pineville, LA 71359-0001. Telephone: 318-487-7259 Ext. 7301 or toll-free 800-487-1906. Fax: 318-487-7550. E-mail: admissions@lacollege.edu. Web site: http://www.lacollege.edu/.

LOUISIANA STATE UNIVERSITY AND AGRICULTURAL AND MECHANICAL COLLEGE
BATON ROUGE, LOUISIANA

General State-supported, university, coed **Entrance** Moderately difficult **Setting** 2,000-acre urban campus **Total enrollment** 31,392 **Student-faculty ratio** 21:1 **Application deadline** 4/15 (freshmen), 4/15 (transfer) **Freshmen** 79% were admitted **Housing** Yes **Expenses** Tuition $3468; Room & Board $4546 **Undergraduates** 53% women, 10% part-time, 10% 25 or older, 0.3% Native American, 2% Hispanic American, 9% African American, 4% Asian American/Pacific Islander **The most frequently chosen baccalaureate fields are** business/marketing, education, engineering/engineering technologies **Academic program** English as a second language, advanced placement, accelerated degree program, self-designed majors, honors program, summer session, adult/continuing education programs, internships **Contact** Cleve Brooks, Director of Admissions, Louisiana State University and Agricultural and Mechanical College, 110 Thomas Boyd Hall, Baton Rouge, LA 70803. Telephone: 225-578-1175. Fax: 225-578-4433. E-mail: admissions@lsu.edu. Web site: http://www.lsu.edu/.

LOUISIANA STATE UNIVERSITY HEALTH SCIENCES CENTER
NEW ORLEANS, LOUISIANA

General State-supported, university, coed **Setting** urban campus **Total enrollment** 2,755 **Application deadline** 3/1 (transfer) **Housing** Yes **Expenses** Tuition $3875; Room only $1975 **Undergraduates** 21% 25 or older, 0.3% Native American, 2% Hispanic American, 9% African American, 5% Asian American/Pacific Islander **The most frequently chosen baccalaureate field is** health professions and related sciences **Academic program** Advanced placement, summer session, internships **Contact** Mr. Edmund A. Vidacovich, Registrar, Louisiana State University Health Sciences Center, 433 Bolivar Street, New Orleans, LA 70112-2223. Telephone: 504-568-4829. Web site: http://www.lsumc.edu/.

LOUISIANA STATE UNIVERSITY IN SHREVEPORT
SHREVEPORT, LOUISIANA

General State-supported, comprehensive, coed **Entrance** Noncompetitive **Setting** 200-acre urban campus **Total enrollment** 4,113 **Student-faculty ratio** 19:1 **Application deadline** 8/1 (freshmen), 8/1 (transfer) **Freshmen** 59% were admitted **Housing** Yes **Expenses** Tuition $2550 **Undergraduates** 62% women, 33% part-time, 34% 25 or older, 1% Native American, 2% Hispanic American, 20% African American, 2% Asian American/Pacific Islander **The most frequently chosen baccalaureate fields are** business/marketing, education, liberal arts/general studies **Academic program** Advanced placement,

LOUISIANA

Louisiana State University in Shreveport *(continued)*

accelerated degree program, self-designed majors, honors program, summer session, adult/continuing education programs, internships **Contact** Ms. Julie Wilkins, Assistant Director of Admissions and Records, Louisiana State University in Shreveport, One University Place, Shreveport, LA 71115-2399. Telephone: 318-797-5061 or toll-free 800-229-5957 (in-state). Fax: 318-797-5286. E-mail: admissions@pilot.lsus.edu. Web site: http://www.lsus.edu/.

LOUISIANA TECH UNIVERSITY
RUSTON, LOUISIANA

General State-supported, university, coed **Entrance** Moderately difficult **Setting** 247-acre small-town campus **Total enrollment** 10,694 **Student-faculty ratio** 24:1 **Application deadline** 7/3 (freshmen), rolling (transfer) **Freshmen** 93% were admitted **Housing** Yes **Expenses** Tuition $3041; Room & Board $3465 **Undergraduates** 48% women, 17% part-time, 19% 25 or older, 1% Native American, 1% Hispanic American, 15% African American, 1% Asian American/Pacific Islander **The most frequently chosen baccalaureate fields are** business/marketing, engineering/engineering technologies, liberal arts/general studies **Academic program** English as a second language, advanced placement, honors program, summer session, adult/continuing education programs, internships **Contact** Mrs. Jan B. Albritton, Director of Admissions, Louisiana Tech University, PO Box 3178, Ruston, LA 71272. Telephone: 318-257-3036 or toll-free 800-528-3241. Fax: 318-257-2499. E-mail: bulldog@latech.edu. Web site: http://www.latech.edu/.

LOYOLA UNIVERSITY NEW ORLEANS
NEW ORLEANS, LOUISIANA

General Independent Roman Catholic (Jesuit), comprehensive, coed **Entrance** Moderately difficult **Setting** 26-acre urban campus **Total enrollment** 5,509 **Student-faculty ratio** 14:1 **Application deadline** 1/15 (freshmen), rolling (transfer) **Freshmen** 69% were admitted **Housing** Yes **Expenses** Tuition $16,700; Room & Board $6806 **Undergraduates** 64% women, 15% part-time, 5% 25 or older, 0.5% Native American, 10% Hispanic American, 11% African American, 4% Asian American/Pacific Islander **The most frequently chosen baccalaureate fields are** business/marketing, communications/communication technologies, social sciences and history **Academic program** English as a second language, advanced placement, accelerated degree program, self-designed majors, honors program, summer session, adult/continuing education programs, internships **Contact** Ms. Deborah C. Stieffel, Dean of Admission and Enrollment Management, Loyola University New Orleans, 6363 Saint Charles Avenue, Box 18, New Orleans, LA 70118-6195. Telephone: 504-865-3240 or toll-free 800-4-LOYOLA. Fax: 504-865-3383. E-mail: admit@loyno.edu. Web site: http://www.loyno.edu/.

▶ For more information, see page 449.

MCNEESE STATE UNIVERSITY
LAKE CHARLES, LOUISIANA

General State-supported, comprehensive, coed **Entrance** Moderately difficult **Setting** 580-acre suburban campus **Total enrollment** 7,780 **Student-faculty ratio** 20:1 **Application deadline** Rolling (freshmen), rolling (transfer) **Freshmen** 86% were admitted **Housing** Yes **Expenses** Tuition $2511; Room & Board $2620 **Undergraduates** 59% women, 17% part-time, 22% 25 or older, 1% Native American, 1% Hispanic American, 1% African American, 1% Asian American/Pacific Islander **The most frequently chosen baccalaureate fields are** business/marketing, education, health professions and related sciences **Academic program** English as a second language, advanced placement, accelerated degree program, honors program, summer session, adult/continuing education programs, internships **Contact** Ms. Tammie Pettis, Director of Admissions, McNeese State University, PO Box 92495, Kaufman Hall, 4100 Ryan Street, Lake Charles, LA 70609-2495. Telephone: 337-475-5148 or toll-free 800-622-3352. Fax: 337-475-5189. E-mail: jmartin@mail.mcneese.edu. Web site: http://www.mcneese.edu/.

NEW ORLEANS BAPTIST THEOLOGICAL SEMINARY
NEW ORLEANS, LOUISIANA

General Independent Southern Baptist, comprehensive, coed, primarily men **Entrance** Minimally difficult **Setting** 81-acre suburban campus **Total enrollment** 2,712 **Application deadline** 8/9 (freshmen) **Freshmen** 82% were admitted **Housing** Yes **Expenses** Tuition $2700 **Undergraduates** 19% women, 70% part-time, 100% 25 or older, 0.2% Native American, 11% Hispanic American, 18% African American, 2% Asian American/Pacific Islander **The most frequently chosen baccalaureate field is** philosophy **Academic program** English as a second language, summer session, adult/continuing education programs, internships **Contact** Dr. Paul E. Gregoire Jr., Registrar/Director of Admissions, New Orleans Baptist Theological Seminary, 3939 Gentilly Boulevard, New Orleans, LA 70126-4858. Telephone: 504-282-4455 Ext. 3337 or toll-free 800-662-8701. Web site: http://www.nobts.edu/.

NICHOLLS STATE UNIVERSITY
THIBODAUX, LOUISIANA

General State-supported, comprehensive, coed **Entrance** Noncompetitive **Setting** 210-acre small-town campus **Total enrollment** 7,188 **Student-faculty ratio** 22:1 **Application deadline** Rolling (freshmen), rolling (transfer) **Freshmen** 99% were admitted **Housing** Yes **Expenses** Tuition $2440; Room & Board $3002 **Undergraduates** 63% women, 17% part-time, 22% 25 or older, 2% Native American, 1% Hispanic American, 16% African American, 1% Asian American/Pacific Islander **The most frequently chosen baccalaureate fields are** business/marketing, education, health professions and related

LOUISIANA

sciences **Academic program** English as a second language, advanced placement, accelerated degree program, honors program, summer session, adult/continuing education programs, internships **Contact** Mrs. Becky L. Durocher, Director of Admissions, Nicholls State University, PO Box 2004-NSU, Thibodaux, LA 70310. Telephone: 985-448-4507 or toll-free 877-NICHOLLS. Fax: 985-448-4929. E-mail: nicholls@nicholls.edu. Web site: http://www.nicholls.edu/.

NORTHWESTERN STATE UNIVERSITY OF LOUISIANA
NATCHITOCHES, LOUISIANA

General State-supported, comprehensive, coed **Entrance** Noncompetitive **Setting** 1,000-acre small-town campus **Total enrollment** 9,415 **Student-faculty ratio** 30:1 **Application deadline** Rolling (freshmen), rolling (transfer) **Freshmen** 100% were admitted **Housing** Yes **Expenses** Tuition $2429; Room & Board $3132 **Undergraduates** 65% women, 21% part-time, 25% 25 or older **Academic program** Advanced placement, honors program, summer session, adult/continuing education programs, internships **Contact** Ms. Jana Lucky, Director of Recruiting and Admissions, Northwestern State University of Louisiana, Roy Hall, Room 101, Natchitoches, LA 71497. Telephone: 318-357-4503 or toll-free 800-426-3754 (in-state); 800-327-1903 (out-of-state). E-mail: admissions@alpha.nsula.edu. Web site: http://www.nsula.edu/.

OUR LADY OF HOLY CROSS COLLEGE
NEW ORLEANS, LOUISIANA

General Independent Roman Catholic, comprehensive, coed **Entrance** Minimally difficult **Setting** 40-acre suburban campus **Total enrollment** 1,347 **Student-faculty ratio** 21:1 **Application deadline** Rolling (freshmen), rolling (transfer) **Freshmen** 37% were admitted **Housing** No **Expenses** Tuition $5620 **Undergraduates** 75% women, 43% part-time, 35% 25 or older, 1% Native American, 5% Hispanic American, 13% African American, 3% Asian American/Pacific Islander **The most frequently chosen baccalaureate fields are** education, business/marketing, health professions and related sciences **Academic program** Advanced placement, summer session, adult/continuing education programs, internships **Contact** Ms. Kristine Hatfield Kopecky, Vice President for Student Affairs and Admissions, Our Lady of Holy Cross College, 4123 Woodland Drive, New Orleans, LA 70131-7399. Telephone: 504-394-7744 Ext. 185 or toll-free 800-259-7744 Ext. 175. Fax: 504-391-2421. Web site: http://www.olhcc.edu/.

SAINT JOSEPH SEMINARY COLLEGE
SAINT BENEDICT, LOUISIANA

General Independent Roman Catholic, 4-year, coed, primarily men **Entrance** Minimally difficult **Setting** 1,300-acre rural campus **Total enrollment** 194 **Student-faculty ratio** 7:1 **Application deadline** Rolling (freshmen), rolling (transfer) **Freshmen** 100% were admitted **Housing** Yes **Expenses** Tuition $7450; Room & Board $5700 **Undergraduates** 27% women, 37% 25 or older **Academic program** English as a second language, advanced placement, adult/continuing education programs **Contact** Br. Bernard Boudreaux OSB, Academic Assistant, Saint Joseph Seminary College, 75376 River Road, St. Benedict, LA 70457. Telephone: 985-867-2248. E-mail: asec@stjosephabbey.org. Web site: http://www.stjosephabbey.org/.

SOUTHEASTERN LOUISIANA UNIVERSITY
HAMMOND, LOUISIANA

General State-supported, comprehensive, coed **Entrance** Minimally difficult **Setting** 375-acre small-town campus **Total enrollment** 14,522 **Student-faculty ratio** 25:1 **Application deadline** 7/15 (freshmen), rolling (transfer) **Freshmen** 87% were admitted **Housing** Yes **Expenses** Tuition $2607; Room & Board $3440 **Undergraduates** 63% women, 16% part-time, 22% 25 or older, 0.5% Native American, 2% Hispanic American, 14% African American, 0.4% Asian American/Pacific Islander **The most frequently chosen baccalaureate fields are** business/marketing, education, protective services/public administration **Academic program** Advanced placement, honors program, summer session, adult/continuing education programs, internships **Contact** Ms. Pat Duplessis, University Admissions Analyst, Southeastern Louisiana University, SLU 10752, North Campus-Basic Studies, Hammond, LA 70402. Telephone: 985-549-2066 or toll-free 800-222-7358. Fax: 985-549-5632. E-mail: ssoutullo@selu.edu. Web site: http://www.selu.edu/.

SOUTHERN UNIVERSITY AND AGRICULTURAL AND MECHANICAL COLLEGE
BATON ROUGE, LOUISIANA

General State-supported, comprehensive, coed **Entrance** Noncompetitive **Setting** 964-acre suburban campus **Total enrollment** 9,095 **Student-faculty ratio** 17:1 **Application deadline** 7/1 (freshmen), 7/1 (transfer) **Freshmen** 44% were admitted **Housing** Yes **Expenses** Tuition $2682; Room & Board $3683 **Undergraduates** 59% women, 10% part-time, 13% 25 or older, 0% Native American, 0.04% Hispanic American, 98% African American, 1% Asian American/Pacific Islander **The most frequently chosen baccalaureate fields are** education, business/marketing, health professions and related sciences **Academic program** Advanced placement, honors program, summer session, adult/continuing education programs, internships **Contact** Ms. Velva Thomas, Director of Admissions, Southern University and Agricultural and Mechanical College, PO Box 9901, Baton Rouge, LA 70813. Telephone: 225-771-2430 or toll-free 800-256-1531. Fax: 225-771-2500. E-mail: admit@subr.edu. Web site: http://www.subr.edu/.

LOUISIANA

SOUTHERN UNIVERSITY AT NEW ORLEANS
NEW ORLEANS, LOUISIANA

Contact Registrar/Director of Admissions, Southern University at New Orleans, 6400 Press Drive, New Orleans, LA 70126-1009. Telephone: 504-286-5314. Web site: http://www.suno.edu/.

TULANE UNIVERSITY
NEW ORLEANS, LOUISIANA

General Independent, university, coed **Entrance** Very difficult **Setting** 110-acre urban campus **Total enrollment** 12,373 **Student-faculty ratio** 12:1 **Application deadline** 1/15 (freshmen), 6/1 (transfer) **Freshmen** 61% were admitted **Housing** Yes **Expenses** Tuition $26,886; Room & Board $7128 **Undergraduates** 53% women, 24% part-time, 15% 25 or older, 0.3% Native American, 4% Hispanic American, 9% African American, 5% Asian American/Pacific Islander **The most frequently chosen baccalaureate fields are** business/marketing, engineering/engineering technologies, social sciences and history **Academic program** English as a second language, advanced placement, accelerated degree program, self-designed majors, honors program, summer session, adult/continuing education programs, internships **Contact** Mr. Richard Whiteside, Vice President of Enrollment Management and Institutional Research, Tulane University, 6823 St Charles Avenue, New Orleans, LA 70118-5669. Telephone: 504-865-5731 or toll-free 800-873-9283. Fax: 504-862-8715. E-mail: undergrad.admission@tulane.edu. Web site: http://www.tulane.edu/.

▶ For more information, see page 483.

UNIVERSITY OF LOUISIANA AT LAFAYETTE
LAFAYETTE, LOUISIANA

General State-supported, university, coed **Entrance** Minimally difficult **Setting** 1,375-acre urban campus **Total enrollment** 15,489 **Student-faculty ratio** 23:1 **Application deadline** Rolling (freshmen), rolling (transfer) **Freshmen** 82% were admitted **Housing** Yes **Expenses** Tuition $2316; Room & Board $2886 **Undergraduates** 57% women, 17% part-time, 22% 25 or older, 1% Native American, 2% Hispanic American, 18% African American, 2% Asian American/Pacific Islander **The most frequently chosen baccalaureate fields are** business/marketing, education, liberal arts/general studies **Academic program** Advanced placement, honors program, summer session, adult/continuing education programs, internships **Contact** Mr. Leroy Broussard Jr., Director of Admissions, University of Louisiana at Lafayette, PO Drawer 41210, Lafayette, LA 70504. Telephone: 337-482-6473 or toll-free 800-752-6553 (in-state). Fax: 337-482-6195. E-mail: admissions@louisiana.edu. Web site: http://www.louisiana.edu/.

UNIVERSITY OF LOUISIANA AT MONROE
MONROE, LOUISIANA

General State-supported, university, coed **Entrance** Noncompetitive **Setting** 238-acre urban campus **Total enrollment** 8,965 **Application deadline** Rolling (freshmen), rolling (transfer) **Housing** Yes **Expenses** Tuition $2307; Room & Board $5740 **Undergraduates** 63% women, 18% part-time, 28% 25 or older, 0.3% Native American, 1% Hispanic American, 27% African American, 2% Asian American/Pacific Islander **Academic program** English as a second language, advanced placement, accelerated degree program, honors program, summer session, internships **Contact** Ms. Carlette Browder, Associate Registrar, University of Louisiana at Monroe, 700 University Avenue, Monroe, LA 71209-1115. Telephone: 318-342-5252 or toll-free 800-372-5127. Fax: 318-342-5274. E-mail: rebrowder@ulm.edu. Web site: http://www.ulm.edu/.

UNIVERSITY OF NEW ORLEANS
NEW ORLEANS, LOUISIANA

General State-supported, university, coed **Entrance** Moderately difficult **Setting** 345-acre urban campus **Total enrollment** 17,014 **Student-faculty ratio** 24:1 **Application deadline** Rolling (freshmen), rolling (transfer) **Freshmen** 80% were admitted **Housing** Yes **Expenses** Tuition $3602; Room & Board $3900 **Undergraduates** 57% women, 28% part-time, 30% 25 or older, 0.5% Native American, 6% Hispanic American, 23% African American, 5% Asian American/Pacific Islander **The most frequently chosen baccalaureate fields are** business/marketing, education, liberal arts/general studies **Academic program** English as a second language, advanced placement, self-designed majors, honors program, summer session, adult/continuing education programs, internships **Contact** Ms. Roslyn S. Sheley, Director of Admissions, University of New Orleans, Lake Front, New Orleans, LA 70148. Telephone: 504-280-6595 or toll-free 888-514-4275. Fax: 504-280-5522. E-mail: admission@uno.edu. Web site: http://www.uno.edu/.

UNIVERSITY OF PHOENIX–LOUISIANA CAMPUS
METAIRIE, LOUISIANA

General Proprietary, comprehensive, coed **Entrance** Noncompetitive **Total enrollment** 88,730 **Student-faculty ratio** 13:1 **Application deadline** Rolling (freshmen), rolling (transfer) **Housing** No **Expenses** Tuition $7350 **Undergraduates** 63% women, 78% 25 or older **The most frequently chosen baccalaureate fields are** business/marketing, health professions and related sciences **Academic program** Advanced placement, accelerated degree program, adult/continuing education programs **Contact** Ms. Beth Barilla, Director of Admissions, University of Phoenix–Louisiana Campus, 4615 East Elwood Street, Phoenix, AZ 85040-1958. Telephone: 480-927-0099 Ext. 1218 or toll-free 800-228-7240. Fax: 480-594-1758. E-mail: beth.barilla@apollogrp.edu. Web site: http://www.phoenix.edu/.

XAVIER UNIVERSITY OF LOUISIANA
NEW ORLEANS, LOUISIANA

General Independent Roman Catholic, comprehensive, coed **Entrance** Moderately difficult **Setting** 23-acre urban campus **Total enrollment** 4,111 **Student-faculty ratio** 15:1 **Application deadline** 3/1 (freshmen), 6/1 (transfer) **Freshmen** 86% were admitted **Housing** Yes **Expenses** Tuition $10,500; Room & Board $5700 **Undergraduates** 74% women, 4% part-time, 20% 25 or older, 0% Native American, 0.3% Hispanic American, 92% African American, 2% Asian American/Pacific Islander **The most frequently chosen baccalaureate fields are** biological/life sciences, physical sciences, psychology **Academic program** Advanced placement, accelerated degree program, honors program, summer session, adult/continuing education programs, internships **Contact** Mr. Winston Brown, Dean of Admissions, Xavier University of Louisiana, 1 Drexel Drive, New Orleans, LA 70125. Telephone: 504-483-7388. E-mail: apply@xula.edu. Web site: http://www.xula.edu/.

MAINE

BATES COLLEGE
LEWISTON, MAINE

General Independent, 4-year, coed **Entrance** Most difficult **Setting** 109-acre suburban campus **Total enrollment** 1,767 **Student-faculty ratio** 10:1 **Application deadline** 1/15 (freshmen), 3/1 (transfer) **Freshmen** 33% were admitted **Housing** Yes **Expenses** Tuition $34,100 **Undergraduates** 51% women, 1% 25 or older, 0.2% Native American, 2% Hispanic American, 2% African American, 3% Asian American/Pacific Islander **The most frequently chosen baccalaureate fields are** English, physical sciences, social sciences and history **Academic program** Advanced placement, accelerated degree program, self-designed majors, honors program, internships **Contact** Mr. Wylie L. Mitchell, Dean of Admissions, Bates College, 23 Campus Avenue, Lewiston, ME 04240-6028. Telephone: 207-786-6000. Fax: 207-786-6025. E-mail: admissions@bates.edu. Web site: http://www.bates.edu/.

BOWDOIN COLLEGE
BRUNSWICK, MAINE

General Independent, 4-year, coed **Entrance** Most difficult **Setting** 110-acre small-town campus **Total enrollment** 1,635 **Student-faculty ratio** 10:1 **Application deadline** 1/1 (freshmen), 3/1 (transfer) **Freshmen** 24% were admitted **Housing** Yes **Expenses** Tuition $27,280; Room & Board $7000 **Undergraduates** 49% women, 1% part-time, 1% 25 or older, 1% Native American, 3% Hispanic American, 3% African American, 7% Asian American/Pacific Islander **The most frequently chosen baccalaureate fields are** business/marketing, foreign language/literature, social sciences and history **Academic program** Advanced placement, accelerated degree program, self-designed majors **Contact** Ms. Rose Woodd, Receptionist, Bowdoin College, 5000 College Station, Brunswick, ME 04011-8441. Telephone: 207-725-3958. Fax: 207-725-3101. E-mail: admissions@bowdoin.edu. Web site: http://www.bowdoin.edu/.

COLBY COLLEGE
WATERVILLE, MAINE

General Independent, 4-year, coed **Entrance** Most difficult **Setting** 714-acre small-town campus **Total enrollment** 1,809 **Student-faculty ratio** 11:1 **Application deadline** 1/1 (freshmen), 3/1 (transfer) **Freshmen** 34% were admitted **Housing** Yes **Expenses** Tuition $34,290 **Undergraduates** 52% women, 0.1% part-time, 0% 25 or older, 0.3% Native American, 2% Hispanic American, 2% African American, 4% Asian American/Pacific Islander **The most frequently chosen baccalaureate fields are** biological/life sciences, area/ethnic studies, social sciences and history **Academic program** English as a second language, advanced placement, self-designed majors, honors program, internships **Contact** Dean of Admissions and Financial Aid, Colby College, Office of Admissions and Financial Aid, 4800 Mayflower Hill, Waterville, ME 04901-8848. Telephone: 207-872-3168 or toll-free 800-723-3032. Fax: 207-872-3474. E-mail: admissions@colby.edu. Web site: http://www.colby.edu/.

COLLEGE OF THE ATLANTIC
BAR HARBOR, MAINE

General Independent, comprehensive, coed **Entrance** Very difficult **Setting** 25-acre small-town campus **Total enrollment** 271 **Student-faculty ratio** 10:1 **Application deadline** 3/1 (freshmen), 4/1 (transfer) **Freshmen** 75% were admitted **Housing** Yes **Expenses** Tuition $21,384; Room & Board $5610 **Undergraduates** 59% women, 3% part-time, 3% 25 or older, 0% Native American, 0% Hispanic American, 1% African American, 0.4% Asian American/Pacific Islander **Academic program** Advanced placement, accelerated degree program, self-designed majors, internships **Contact** Ms. Sarah G. Baker, Director of Admission, College of the Atlantic, 105 Eden Street, Bar Harbor, ME 04609-1198. Telephone: 207-288-5015 Ext. 233 or toll-free 800-528-0025. Fax: 207-288-4126. E-mail: inquiry@ecology.coa.edu. Web site: http://www.coa.edu/.

HUSSON COLLEGE
BANGOR, MAINE

General Independent, comprehensive, coed **Entrance** Moderately difficult **Setting** 170-acre suburban campus **Total enrollment** 1,797 **Student-faculty ratio** 19:1 **Application deadline** 9/1 (freshmen), 9/1 (transfer) **Freshmen** 98% were admitted **Housing** Yes **Expenses** Tuition $9990; Room & Board $5350 **Undergraduates** 66% women, 41% part-time, 18% 25 or older, 1% Native American, 1% Hispanic

MAINE

Husson College *(continued)*
American, 1% African American, 1% Asian American/ Pacific Islander **The most frequently chosen baccalaureate fields are** business/marketing, computer/ information sciences, health professions and related sciences **Academic program** English as a second language, advanced placement, self-designed majors, summer session, adult/continuing education programs, internships **Contact** Mrs. Jane Goodwin, Director of Admissions, Husson College, One College Circle, Bangor, ME 04401-2999. Telephone: 207-941-7100 or toll-free 800-4-HUSSON. Fax: 207-941-7935. E-mail: admit@husson.edu. Web site: http://www.husson.edu/.

MAINE COLLEGE OF ART
PORTLAND, MAINE

General Independent, comprehensive, coed **Entrance** Moderately difficult **Setting** urban campus **Total enrollment** 436 **Student-faculty ratio** 10:1 **Application deadline** Rolling (freshmen), rolling (transfer) **Freshmen** 90% were admitted **Housing** Yes **Expenses** Tuition $18,810; Room & Board $7542 **Undergraduates** 57% women, 8% part-time, 25% 25 or older, 0.5% Native American, 1% Hispanic American, 0.5% African American, 1% Asian American/ Pacific Islander **The most frequently chosen baccalaureate field is** visual/performing arts **Academic program** Advanced placement, self-designed majors, adult/continuing education programs, internships **Contact** Kathryn Quin-Easter, Admissions Assistant, Maine College of Art, 97 Spring Street, Portland, ME 04101-3987. Telephone: 207-775-3052 Ext. 226 or toll-free 800-639-4808. Fax: 207-772-5069. E-mail: admsns@meca.edu. Web site: http://www.meca.edu/.

MAINE MARITIME ACADEMY
CASTINE, MAINE

General State-supported, comprehensive, coed, primarily men **Entrance** Moderately difficult **Setting** 35-acre small-town campus **Total enrollment** 762 **Student-faculty ratio** 12:1 **Application deadline** 7/1 (freshmen), 7/1 (transfer) **Freshmen** 78% were admitted **Housing** Yes **Expenses** Tuition $5384; Room & Board $5327 **Undergraduates** 15% women, 2% part-time, 15% 25 or older, 1% Native American, 1% Hispanic American, 0.3% African American, 0.3% Asian American/Pacific Islander **The most frequently chosen baccalaureate fields are** engineering/ engineering technologies, business/marketing, trade and industry **Academic program** Advanced placement, adult/continuing education programs, internships **Contact** Jeffrey C. Wright, Director of Admissions, Maine Maritime Academy, Castine, ME 04420. Telephone: 207-326-2215 or toll-free 800-464-6565 (in-state); 800-227-8465 (out-of-state). Fax: 207-326-2515. E-mail: admissions@bell.mma.edu. Web site: http://www.mainemaritime.edu/.

NEW ENGLAND SCHOOL OF COMMUNICATIONS
BANGOR, MAINE

General Private, 4-year, coed **Entrance** Noncompetitive **Total enrollment** 168 **Student-faculty ratio** 12:1 **Application deadline** Rolling (freshmen) **Freshmen** 69% were admitted **Housing** Yes **Expenses** Tuition $8730; Room & Board $5390 **Undergraduates** 31% women, 4% part-time, 17% 25 or older, 1% Native American, 0% Hispanic American, 1% African American, 0% Asian American/Pacific Islander **The most frequently chosen baccalaureate field is** communications/communication technologies **Academic program** English as a second language, advanced placement, self-designed majors, adult/ continuing education programs, internships **Contact** Ms. Louise G. Grant, Director of Admissions, New England School of Communications, 1 College Circle, Bangor, ME 04401. Telephone: 207-941-7176 Ext. 1093 or toll-free 888-877-1876. Fax: 207-947-3987. E-mail: info@nescom.edu. Web site: http://www.nescom.org/.

SAINT JOSEPH'S COLLEGE
STANDISH, MAINE

General Independent, comprehensive, coed, affiliated with Roman Catholic Church **Entrance** Moderately difficult **Setting** 330-acre small-town campus **Total enrollment** 892 **Student-faculty ratio** 12:1 **Application deadline** Rolling (freshmen), rolling (transfer) **Freshmen** 87% were admitted **Housing** Yes **Expenses** Tuition $15,850; Room & Board $6650 **Undergraduates** 65% women, 4% part-time, 3% 25 or older, 0.3% Native American, 1% Hispanic American, 1% African American, 1% Asian American/ Pacific Islander **The most frequently chosen baccalaureate fields are** health professions and related sciences, education, liberal arts/general studies **Academic program** Advanced placement, accelerated degree program, honors program, summer session, adult/continuing education programs, internships **Contact** Mr. Alexander Popovics, Vice President for Enrollment and Dean of Admission and Financial Aid, Saint Joseph's College, 278 Whites Bridge Road, Standish, ME 04084-5263. Telephone: 207-893-7746 Ext. 7741 or toll-free 800-338-7057. Fax: 207-893-7862. E-mail: admissions@sjcme.edu. Web site: http://www.sjcme.edu/.

THOMAS COLLEGE
WATERVILLE, MAINE

General Independent, comprehensive, coed **Entrance** Minimally difficult **Setting** 70-acre small-town campus **Total enrollment** 802 **Student-faculty ratio** 17:1 **Application deadline** Rolling (freshmen), rolling (transfer) **Freshmen** 94% were admitted **Housing** Yes **Expenses** Tuition $13,290; Room & Board $5885 **Undergraduates** 55% women, 29% part-time, 43% 25 or older, 0.3% Native American, 0.5% Hispanic American, 0.3% African American, 0% Asian American/Pacific Islander **The most fre-**

quently chosen baccalaureate fields are business/ marketing, computer/information sciences, parks and recreation **Academic program** Advanced placement, summer session, adult/continuing education programs, internships **Contact** Ms. Jennifer Quinlan, Director of Admissions, Thomas College, 180 West River Road, Waterville, ME 04901. Telephone: 207-859-1101 or toll-free 800-339-7001. Fax: 207-859-1114. E-mail: admiss@thomas.edu. Web site: http://www.thomas.edu/.

UNITY COLLEGE
UNITY, MAINE

General Independent, 4-year, coed **Entrance** Moderately difficult **Setting** 205-acre rural campus **Total enrollment** 510 **Student-faculty ratio** 16:1 **Application deadline** Rolling (freshmen), rolling (transfer) **Freshmen** 69% were admitted **Housing** Yes **Expenses** Tuition $13,730; Room & Board $5500 **Undergraduates** 32% women, 5% part-time, 8% 25 or older, 0% Native American, 0.4% Hispanic American, 0.4% African American **The most frequently chosen baccalaureate fields are** natural resources/environmental science, liberal arts/general studies, parks and recreation **Academic program** English as a second language, advanced placement, accelerated degree program, self-designed majors, honors program, summer session, internships **Contact** Ms. Kay Fiedler, Director of Admissions, Unity College, PO Box 532, Unity, ME 04988-0532. Telephone: 800-624-1024. Fax: 207-948-6277. Web site: http://www.unity.edu/.

UNIVERSITY OF MAINE
ORONO, MAINE

General State-supported, university, coed **Entrance** Moderately difficult **Setting** 3,298-acre small-town campus **Total enrollment** 10,648 **Student-faculty ratio** 14:1 **Application deadline** Rolling (freshmen), rolling (transfer) **Freshmen** 80% were admitted **Housing** Yes **Expenses** Tuition $5070; Room & Board $5728 **Undergraduates** 53% women, 19% part-time, 15% 25 or older, 2% Native American, 1% Hispanic American, 1% African American, 1% Asian American/Pacific Islander **The most frequently chosen baccalaureate fields are** education, business/marketing, engineering/engineering technologies **Academic program** English as a second language, advanced placement, self-designed majors, honors program, summer session, adult/continuing education programs, internships **Contact** Mr. Jonathan H. Henry, Director, University of Maine, 5713 Chadbourne Hall, Orono, ME 04469-5713. Telephone: 207-581-1561 or toll-free 877-486-2364. Fax: 207-581-1213. E-mail: um-admit@maine.edu. Web site: http://www.umaine.edu/.

THE UNIVERSITY OF MAINE AT AUGUSTA
AUGUSTA, MAINE

General State-supported, 4-year, coed **Entrance** Noncompetitive **Setting** 165-acre small-town campus **Total enrollment** 5,575 **Student-faculty ratio** 20:1 **Application deadline** Rolling (freshmen), rolling (transfer) **Freshmen** 52% were admitted **Housing** No **Expenses** Tuition $3928 **Undergraduates** 75% women, 74% part-time, 67% 25 or older, 3% Native American, 0.5% Hispanic American, 1% African American, 0.4% Asian American/Pacific Islander **The most frequently chosen baccalaureate fields are** business/marketing, health professions and related sciences, social sciences and history **Academic program** Advanced placement, self-designed majors, honors program, summer session, adult/continuing education programs, internships **Contact** Mr. William Clark Ketcham, Director of Enrollment Services, The University of Maine at Augusta, 46 University Drive, Robinson Hall, Augusta, ME 04330. Telephone: 207-621-3185 or toll-free 800-696-6000 Ext. 3185 (in-state). Fax: 207-621-3116. E-mail: umaar@maine.maine.edu. Web site: http://www.uma.maine.edu/.

UNIVERSITY OF MAINE AT FARMINGTON
FARMINGTON, MAINE

General State-supported, 4-year, coed **Entrance** Moderately difficult **Setting** 50-acre small-town campus **Total enrollment** 2,435 **Student-faculty ratio** 16:1 **Freshmen** 68% were admitted **Housing** Yes **Expenses** Tuition $4317; Room & Board $4846 **Undergraduates** 67% women, 14% part-time, 10% 25 or older, 1% Native American, 0.4% Hispanic American, 0.4% African American, 0.5% Asian American/Pacific Islander **The most frequently chosen baccalaureate fields are** education, interdisciplinary studies, psychology **Academic program** Advanced placement, accelerated degree program, self-designed majors, honors program, summer session, internships **Contact** Mr. James G. Collins, Associate Director of Admissions, University of Maine at Farmington, 246 Main Street, Farmington, ME 04938-1994. Telephone: 207-778-7050. Fax: 207-778-8182. E-mail: umfadmit@maine.maine.edu. Web site: http://www.umf.maine.edu/.

UNIVERSITY OF MAINE AT FORT KENT
FORT KENT, MAINE

General State-supported, 4-year, coed **Entrance** Moderately difficult **Setting** 52-acre rural campus **Total enrollment** 897 **Student-faculty ratio** 14:1 **Application deadline** Rolling (freshmen), rolling (transfer) **Freshmen** 83% were admitted **Housing** Yes **Expenses** Tuition $3590; Room & Board $4224 **Undergraduates** 64% women, 34% part-time, 9% 25 or older, 1% Native American, 0.2% Hispanic American, 0.2% African American, 0.2% Asian American/Pacific Islander **Academic program** English as a second language, advanced placement, self-designed majors, honors program, summer session, internships **Contact** Mr. Melik Peter Khoury, Director of Admissions, University of Maine at Fort Kent, 23 University Drive, Fort Kent, ME 04743-1292. Telephone: 207-834-7600 Ext. 608 or toll-free 888-TRY-UMFK. Fax: 207-834-7609. E-mail: umfkadm@maine.maine.edu. Web site: http://www.umfk.maine.edu/.

MAINE

UNIVERSITY OF MAINE AT MACHIAS
MACHIAS, MAINE

General State-supported, 4-year, coed **Entrance** Moderately difficult **Setting** 42-acre rural campus **Total enrollment** 1,017 **Student-faculty ratio** 13:1 **Application deadline** Rolling (freshmen), rolling (transfer) **Freshmen** 81% were admitted **Housing** Yes **Expenses** Tuition $3755; Room & Board $4644 **Undergraduates** 69% women, 47% part-time, 31% 25 or older, 3% Native American, 0.4% Hispanic American, 1% African American, 1% Asian American/Pacific Islander **The most frequently chosen baccalaureate fields are** business/marketing, biological/life sciences, health professions and related sciences **Academic program** Advanced placement, accelerated degree program, self-designed majors, summer session, adult/continuing education programs, internships **Contact** Mr. David Baldwin, Director of Admissions, University of Maine at Machias, 9 O'Brien Avenue, Machias, ME 04654. Telephone: 207-255-1318 or toll-free 888-GOTOUMM. Fax: 207-255-1363. E-mail: admissions@acad.umm.maine.edu. Web site: http://www.umm.maine.edu/.

UNIVERSITY OF MAINE AT PRESQUE ISLE
PRESQUE ISLE, MAINE

General State-supported, 4-year, coed **Entrance** Minimally difficult **Setting** 150-acre small-town campus **Total enrollment** 1,367 **Student-faculty ratio** 14:1 **Application deadline** Rolling (freshmen), rolling (transfer) **Freshmen** 90% were admitted **Housing** Yes **Expenses** Tuition $3700; Room & Board $4264 **Undergraduates** 64% women, 30% part-time, 30% 25 or older, 3% Native American, 1% Hispanic American, 0.3% African American, 1% Asian American/Pacific Islander **The most frequently chosen baccalaureate fields are** education, interdisciplinary studies, liberal arts/general studies **Academic program** Advanced placement, accelerated degree program, self-designed majors, honors program, summer session, adult/continuing education programs, internships **Contact** Mr. Brian Manter, Director of Admissions, University of Maine at Presque Isle, 181 Main Street, Presque Isle, ME 04769. Telephone: 207-768-9536. Fax: 207-768-9608. E-mail: infoumpi@polaris.umpi.maine.edu. Web site: http://www.umpi.maine.edu/.

UNIVERSITY OF NEW ENGLAND
BIDDEFORD, MAINE

General Independent, comprehensive, coed **Entrance** Moderately difficult **Setting** 410-acre small-town campus **Total enrollment** 2,862 **Student-faculty ratio** 16:1 **Application deadline** Rolling (freshmen), rolling (transfer) **Freshmen** 76% were admitted **Housing** Yes **Expenses** Tuition $17,260; Room & Board $6770 **Undergraduates** 76% women, 21% part-time, 10% 25 or older, 0.1% Native American, 1% Hispanic American, 1% African American, 1% Asian American/Pacific Islander **The most frequently chosen baccalaureate fields are** business/marketing, biological/life sciences, health professions and related sciences **Academic program** English as a second language, advanced placement, accelerated degree program, self-designed majors, honors program, summer session, adult/continuing education programs, internships **Contact** Ms. Patricia Cribby, Dean of Admissions, University of New England, Hills Beach Road, Biddeford, ME 04005-9526. Telephone: 207-283-0170 Ext. 2240 or toll-free 800-477-4UNE. E-mail: jshae@mailbox.une.edu. Web site: http://www.une.edu/.

UNIVERSITY OF SOUTHERN MAINE
PORTLAND, MAINE

General State-supported, comprehensive, coed **Entrance** Moderately difficult **Setting** 144-acre suburban campus **Total enrollment** 10,966 **Student-faculty ratio** 13:1 **Application deadline** 2/1 (freshmen), 2/1 (transfer) **Freshmen** 75% were admitted **Housing** Yes **Expenses** Tuition $4696; Room & Board $5873 **Undergraduates** 61% women, 50% part-time, 33% 25 or older **The most frequently chosen baccalaureate fields are** business/marketing, health professions and related sciences, social sciences and history **Academic program** English as a second language, advanced placement, self-designed majors, honors program, summer session, adult/continuing education programs, internships **Contact** Mr. Jon Barker, Assistant Director, University of Southern Maine, 37 College Avenue, Gorham, ME 04038. Telephone: 207-780-5724 or toll-free 800-800-4USM Ext. 5670. Fax: 207-780-5640. E-mail: usmadm@usm.maine.edu. Web site: http://www.usm.maine.edu/.

MARYLAND

BALTIMORE HEBREW UNIVERSITY
BALTIMORE, MARYLAND

General Independent, comprehensive, coed **Entrance** Moderately difficult **Setting** 2-acre urban campus **Total enrollment** 163 **Student-faculty ratio** 4:1 **Application deadline** Rolling (freshmen), rolling (transfer) **Freshmen** 100% were admitted **Housing** No **Expenses** Tuition $6430 **Undergraduates** 71% women, 50% part-time, 90% 25 or older, 0% Native American, 0% Hispanic American, 3% African American, 0% Asian American/Pacific Islander **The most frequently chosen baccalaureate field is** area/ethnic studies **Academic program** English as a second language, advanced placement, accelerated degree program, honors program, summer session, adult/continuing education programs **Contact** Essie Keyser, Director of Admissions, Baltimore Hebrew University, 5800 Park Heights Avenue, Baltimore, MD 21215-3996. Telephone: 410-578-6967 or toll-free 888-248-7420. Fax: 410-578-6940. E-mail: bhu@bhu.edu. Web site: http://www.bhu.edu/.

MARYLAND

BALTIMORE INTERNATIONAL COLLEGE
BALTIMORE, MARYLAND

General Independent, 4-year, coed **Entrance** Minimally difficult **Setting** 6-acre urban campus **Total enrollment** 456 **Student-faculty ratio** 21:1 **Application deadline** Rolling (freshmen), rolling (transfer) **Freshmen** 49% were admitted **Housing** Yes **Expenses** Tuition $14,003; Room & Board $5182 **Undergraduates** 46% women, 5% part-time, 32% 25 or older, 0.2% Native American, 5% Hispanic American, 44% African American, 1% Asian American/Pacific Islander **Academic program** Advanced placement, accelerated degree program, honors program, adult/continuing education programs, internships **Contact** Ms. Lori Makowski, Director of Admissions, Baltimore International College, Commerce Exchange, 17 Commerce Street, Baltimore, MD 21202-3230. Telephone: 410-752-4710 Ext. 125 or toll-free 800-624-9926 Ext. 120 (out-of-state). Fax: 410-752-3730. E-mail: admissions@bic.edu. Web site: http://www.bic.edu/.

BOWIE STATE UNIVERSITY
BOWIE, MARYLAND

General State-supported, comprehensive, coed **Entrance** Minimally difficult **Setting** 312-acre small-town campus **Total enrollment** 5,181 **Student-faculty ratio** 18:1 **Application deadline** 4/1 (freshmen), 4/1 (transfer) **Freshmen** 53% were admitted **Housing** Yes **Expenses** Tuition $3782; Room & Board $5440 **Undergraduates** 62% women, 26% part-time, 31% 25 or older, 0.3% Native American, 1% Hispanic American, 89% African American, 1% Asian American/Pacific Islander **The most frequently chosen baccalaureate fields are** business/marketing, interdisciplinary studies, social sciences and history **Academic program** Advanced placement, accelerated degree program, honors program, summer session, adult/continuing education programs, internships **Contact** Shingiral Chanaiwa, Coordinator of Undergraduate Enrollment, Bowie State University, 14000 Jericho Park Road, Henry Building, Bowie, MD 20715-9465. Telephone: 301-860-3425 or toll-free 877-772-6943. Fax: 301-860-3438. E-mail: hope.ransome@bowiestate.edu. Web site: http://www.bowiestate.edu/.

▶ For more information, see page 401.

CAPITOL COLLEGE
LAUREL, MARYLAND

General Independent, comprehensive, coed **Entrance** Minimally difficult **Setting** 52-acre suburban campus **Total enrollment** 801 **Student-faculty ratio** 12:1 **Application deadline** Rolling (freshmen), rolling (transfer) **Freshmen** 90% were admitted **Housing** Yes **Expenses** Tuition $15,022; Room only $3440 **Undergraduates** 23% women, 49% part-time, 0.4% Native American, 2% Hispanic American, 37% African American, 7% Asian American/Pacific Islander **The most frequently chosen baccalaureate fields are** computer/information sciences, business/marketing, engineering/engineering technologies **Academic program** English as a second language, advanced placement, accelerated degree program, summer session, adult/continuing education programs **Contact** Director of Admissions, Capitol College, 11301 Springfield Road, Laurel, MD 20708-9759. Telephone: 301-953-3200 or toll-free 800-950-1992. E-mail: admissions@capitol-college.edu. Web site: http://www.capitol-college.edu/.

COLLEGE OF NOTRE DAME OF MARYLAND
BALTIMORE, MARYLAND

General Independent Roman Catholic, comprehensive, women only **Entrance** Moderately difficult **Setting** 58-acre suburban campus **Total enrollment** 3,187 **Student-faculty ratio** 12:1 **Application deadline** Rolling (freshmen), rolling (transfer) **Freshmen** 80% were admitted **Housing** Yes **Expenses** Tuition $17,925; Room & Board $7400 **Undergraduates** 0.3% Native American, 2% Hispanic American, 21% African American, 2% Asian American/Pacific Islander **Academic program** English as a second language, advanced placement, accelerated degree program, self-designed majors, honors program, summer session, adult/continuing education programs, internships **Contact** Mrs. Karen Stakem Hornig, Vice President for Enrollment Management, College of Notre Dame of Maryland, 4701 North Charles Street, Baltimore, MD 21210. Telephone: 410-532-5330 or toll-free 800-435-0200 (in-state); 800-435-0300 (out-of-state). Fax: 410-532-6287. E-mail: admiss@ndm.edu. Web site: http://www.ndm.edu/.

COLUMBIA UNION COLLEGE
TAKOMA PARK, MARYLAND

General Independent Seventh-day Adventist, comprehensive, coed **Entrance** Minimally difficult **Setting** 19-acre suburban campus **Total enrollment** 1,073 **Student-faculty ratio** 13:1 **Application deadline** Rolling (freshmen), rolling (transfer) **Freshmen** 46% were admitted **Housing** Yes **Expenses** Tuition $13,960; Room & Board $4849 **Undergraduates** 61% women, 40% part-time, 44% 25 or older, 0.2% Native American, 9% Hispanic American, 45% African American, 6% Asian American/Pacific Islander **The most frequently chosen baccalaureate fields are** business/marketing, computer/information sciences, psychology **Academic program** Advanced placement, accelerated degree program, self-designed majors, honors program, summer session, adult/continuing education programs, internships **Contact** Mr. Emil John, Director of Admissions, Columbia Union College, 7600 Flower Avenue, Takoma Park, MD 20912. Telephone: 301-891-4080 or toll-free 800-835-4212. Fax: 301-891-4230. E-mail: enroll@cuc.edu. Web site: http://www.cuc.edu/.

COPPIN STATE COLLEGE
BALTIMORE, MARYLAND

General State-supported, comprehensive, coed **Entrance** Moderately difficult **Setting** 33-acre urban

MARYLAND

Coppin State College *(continued)*
campus **Total enrollment** 4,003 **Student-faculty ratio** 17:1 **Application deadline** 7/15 (freshmen), 7/15 (transfer) **Freshmen** 47% were admitted **Housing** Yes **Expenses** Tuition $3477; Room & Board $5734 **Undergraduates** 50% 25 or older, 0.4% Native American, 1% Hispanic American, 95% African American, 0.2% Asian American/Pacific Islander **Academic program** English as a second language, advanced placement, honors program, summer session, adult/continuing education programs, internships **Contact** Ms. Michelle Gross, Director of Admissions, Coppin State College, 2500 W North Avenue, Baltimore, MD 21216. Telephone: 410-951-3600 or toll-free 800-635-3674. E-mail: mgross@coppin.edu. Web site: http://www.coppin.edu/.

FROSTBURG STATE UNIVERSITY
FROSTBURG, MARYLAND

General State-supported, comprehensive, coed **Entrance** Moderately difficult **Setting** 260-acre small-town campus **Total enrollment** 5,283 **Student-faculty ratio** 16:1 **Application deadline** Rolling (freshmen), rolling (transfer) **Freshmen** 75% were admitted **Housing** Yes **Expenses** Tuition $4256; Room & Board $5424 **Undergraduates** 52% women, 8% part-time, 9% 25 or older, 0.4% Native American, 2% Hispanic American, 13% African American, 2% Asian American/Pacific Islander **The most frequently chosen baccalaureate fields are** business/marketing, education, social sciences and history **Academic program** Advanced placement, honors program, summer session, adult/continuing education programs, internships **Contact** Ms. Trish Gregory, Associate Director for Admissions, Frostburg State University, 101 Braddock Road, Frostburg, MD 21532-1099. Telephone: 301-687-4201. Fax: 301-687-7074. E-mail: fsuadmissions@frostburg.edu. Web site: http://www.frostburg.edu/.

GOUCHER COLLEGE
BALTIMORE, MARYLAND

General Independent, comprehensive, coed **Entrance** Moderately difficult **Setting** 287-acre suburban campus **Total enrollment** 1,996 **Student-faculty ratio** 10:1 **Application deadline** 2/1 (freshmen), 4/1 (transfer) **Freshmen** 73% were admitted **Housing** Yes **Expenses** Tuition $22,300; Room & Board $7750 **Undergraduates** 72% women, 4% part-time, 3% 25 or older, 0.3% Native American, 3% Hispanic American, 7% African American, 3% Asian American/Pacific Islander **The most frequently chosen baccalaureate fields are** psychology, communications/communication technologies, visual/performing arts **Academic program** Advanced placement, accelerated degree program, adult/continuing education programs, internships **Contact** Mr. Carlton E. Surbeck III, Director of Admissions, Goucher College, 1021 Dulaney Valley Road, Baltimore, MD 21204-2794. Telephone: 410-337-6100 or toll-free 800-GOUCHER. Fax: 410-337-6354. E-mail: admission@goucher.edu. Web site: http://www.goucher.edu/.

▶ **For more information, see page 434.**

GRIGGS UNIVERSITY
SILVER SPRING, MARYLAND

General Independent Seventh-day Adventist, 4-year, coed, primarily men **Entrance** Minimally difficult **Setting** suburban campus **Total enrollment** 372 **Application deadline** Rolling (freshmen), rolling (transfer) **Housing** No **Expenses** Tuition $5760 **The most frequently chosen baccalaureate field is** philosophy, religion, and theology **Academic program** Advanced placement, accelerated degree program, summer session, adult/continuing education programs **Contact** Ms. Eva Michel, Enrollment Officer, Griggs University, PO Box 4437, Silver Spring, MD 20914-4437. Telephone: 301-680-6593 or toll-free 800-782-4769 (in-state). Fax: 301-680-6577. E-mail: 74617.74@compuserve.com. Web site: http://www.griggs.edu/.

HOOD COLLEGE
FREDERICK, MARYLAND

General Independent, comprehensive, women only **Entrance** Moderately difficult **Setting** 50-acre suburban campus **Total enrollment** 1,607 **Student-faculty ratio** 9:1 **Application deadline** 2/15 (freshmen), rolling (transfer) **Freshmen** 74% were admitted **Housing** Yes **Expenses** Tuition $19,120; Room & Board $6900 **Undergraduates** 24% part-time, 24% 25 or older, 0.3% Native American, 3% Hispanic American, 12% African American, 2% Asian American/Pacific Islander **The most frequently chosen baccalaureate fields are** biological/life sciences, business/marketing, education **Academic program** English as a second language, advanced placement, accelerated degree program, self-designed majors, honors program, summer session, adult/continuing education programs, internships **Contact** Dr. Susan Hallenbeck, Dean of Admissions, Hood College, 401 Rosemont Avenue, Frederick, MD 21701. Telephone: 301-696-3400 or toll-free 800-922-1599. Fax: 301-696-3819. E-mail: admissions@hood.edu. Web site: http://www.hood.edu/.

JOHNS HOPKINS UNIVERSITY
BALTIMORE, MARYLAND

General Independent, university, coed **Entrance** Most difficult **Setting** 140-acre urban campus **Total enrollment** 5,832 **Student-faculty ratio** 9:1 **Application deadline** 1/1 (freshmen), 3/15 (transfer) **Freshmen** 34% were admitted **Housing** Yes **Expenses** Tuition $26,710; Room & Board $8506 **Undergraduates** 41% women, 1% part-time, 0% 25 or older, 0.2% Native American, 2% Hispanic American, 4% African American, 19% Asian American/Pacific Islander **The most frequently chosen baccalaureate fields are** engineering/engineering technologies, health professions and related sciences, social sciences and

MARYLAND

history **Academic program** English as a second language, advanced placement, accelerated degree program, self-designed majors, honors program, summer session, adult/continuing education programs, internships **Contact** Mr. John Latting, Director of Undergraduate Admissions, Johns Hopkins University, 140 Garland Hall, 3400 North Charles Street, Baltimore, MD 21218-2699. Telephone: 410-516-8341. Fax: 410-516-6025. E-mail: gotojhu@jhu.edu. Web site: http://www.jhu.edu/.

LOYOLA COLLEGE IN MARYLAND
BALTIMORE, MARYLAND

General Independent Roman Catholic (Jesuit), comprehensive, coed **Entrance** Moderately difficult **Setting** 89-acre urban campus **Total enrollment** 6,144 **Student-faculty ratio** 13:1 **Application deadline** 1/15 (freshmen), 7/15 (transfer) **Freshmen** 61% were admitted **Housing** Yes **Expenses** Tuition $23,500; Room & Board $7400 **Undergraduates** 57% women, 2% part-time, 1% 25 or older, 0.03% Native American, 1% Hispanic American, 5% African American, 2% Asian American/Pacific Islander **The most frequently chosen baccalaureate fields are** business/marketing, communications/communication technologies, social sciences and history **Academic program** Advanced placement, accelerated degree program, honors program, summer session, internships **Contact** Mr. William Bossemeyer, Dean of Admissions, Loyola College in Maryland, 4501 North Charles Street, Baltimore, MD 21210. Telephone: 410-617-2000 Ext. 2252 or toll-free 800-221-9107 Ext. 2252 (in-state). Fax: 410-617-2176. Web site: http://www.loyola.edu/.

MAPLE SPRINGS BAPTIST BIBLE COLLEGE AND SEMINARY
CAPITOL HEIGHTS, MARYLAND

Contact Ms. Mazie Murphy, Assistant Director of Admissions and Records, Maple Springs Baptist Bible College and Seminary, 4130 Belt Road, Capitol Heights, MD 20743. Telephone: 301-736-3631. Fax: 301-735-6507.

MARYLAND INSTITUTE, COLLEGE OF ART
BALTIMORE, MARYLAND

General Independent, comprehensive, coed **Entrance** Very difficult **Setting** 12-acre urban campus **Total enrollment** 1,333 **Student-faculty ratio** 10:1 **Application deadline** 1/15 (freshmen), 3/15 (transfer) **Freshmen** 46% were admitted **Housing** Yes **Expenses** Tuition $21,080; Room & Board $6640 **Undergraduates** 61% women, 1% part-time, 3% 25 or older, 1% Native American, 4% Hispanic American, 4% African American, 6% Asian American/Pacific Islander **The most frequently chosen baccalaureate fields are** education, visual/performing arts **Academic program** Advanced placement, accelerated degree program, self-designed majors, summer session, adult/continuing education programs, internships **Contact** Mr. Hans Ever, Director of Undergraduate Admission, Maryland Institute, College of Art, 1300 Mount Royal Avenue, Baltimore, MD 21217-4191. Telephone: 410-225-2222. Fax: 410-225-2337. E-mail: admissions@mica.edu. Web site: http://www.mica.edu/.

MCDANIEL COLLEGE
WESTMINSTER, MARYLAND

General Independent, comprehensive, coed **Entrance** Moderately difficult **Setting** 160-acre small-town campus **Total enrollment** 3,124 **Student-faculty ratio** 12:1 **Application deadline** 3/15 (freshmen), 7/1 (transfer) **Freshmen** 77% were admitted **Housing** Yes **Expenses** Tuition $20,900; Room & Board $5450 **Undergraduates** 56% women, 4% part-time, 3% 25 or older, 0.1% Native American, 2% Hispanic American, 8% African American, 2% Asian American/Pacific Islander **The most frequently chosen baccalaureate fields are** business/marketing, communications/communication technologies, social sciences and history **Academic program** Advanced placement, self-designed majors, honors program, summer session, adult/continuing education programs, internships **Contact** Ms. M. Martha O'Connell, Dean of Admissions, McDaniel College, 2 College Hill, Westminster, MD 21157-4390. Telephone: 410-857-2230 or toll-free 800-638-5005. Fax: 410-857-2757. E-mail: admissio@wmdc.edu. Web site: http://www.wmdc.edu/.

▶ For more information, see page 455.

MORGAN STATE UNIVERSITY
BALTIMORE, MARYLAND

General State-supported, university, coed **Entrance** Moderately difficult **Setting** 140-acre urban campus **Total enrollment** 7,112 **Student-faculty ratio** 14:1 **Application deadline** Rolling (freshmen), rolling (transfer) **Freshmen** 35% were admitted **Housing** Yes **Expenses** Tuition $4508; Room & Board $5980 **Undergraduates** 57% women, 18% part-time, 27% 25 or older, 0.2% Native American, 0.5% Hispanic American, 92% African American, 0.3% Asian American/Pacific Islander **The most frequently chosen baccalaureate fields are** engineering/engineering technologies, computer/information sciences, trade and industry **Academic program** Advanced placement, accelerated degree program, honors program, summer session, adult/continuing education programs, internships **Contact** Mr. Edwin T. Johnson, Director of Admissions and Recruitment, Morgan State University, 1700 East Cold Spring Lane, Baltimore, MD 21251. Telephone: 443-885-3000 or toll-free 800-332-6674. E-mail: tjenness@moac.morgan.edu. Web site: http://www.morgan.edu/.

MOUNT SAINT MARY'S COLLEGE AND SEMINARY
EMMITSBURG, MARYLAND

General Independent Roman Catholic, comprehensive, coed **Entrance** Moderately difficult **Setting** 1,400-acre rural campus **Total enrollment** 1,969

MARYLAND

Mount Saint Mary's College and Seminary *(continued)*

Student-faculty ratio 14:1 **Application deadline** Rolling (freshmen), 6/1 (transfer) **Freshmen** 79% were admitted **Housing** Yes **Expenses** Tuition $18,680; Room & Board $7060 **Undergraduates** 59% women, 14% part-time, 13% 25 or older, 0.2% Native American, 3% Hispanic American, 5% African American, 2% Asian American/Pacific Islander **The most frequently chosen baccalaureate fields are** business/marketing, education, social sciences and history **Academic program** English as a second language, advanced placement, accelerated degree program, self-designed majors, honors program, summer session, adult/continuing education programs, internships **Contact** Mr. Stephen Neitz, Executive Director of Admissions and Financial Aid, Mount Saint Mary's College and Seminary, 16300 Old Emmitsburg Road, Emmitsburg, MD 21727. Telephone: 301-447-5214 or toll-free 800-448-4347. Fax: 301-447-5860. E-mail: admissions@msmary.edu. Web site: http://www.msmary.edu/.

NER ISRAEL RABBINICAL COLLEGE
BALTIMORE, MARYLAND

Contact Rabbi Berel Weisbord, Dean of Admissions, Ner Israel Rabbinical College, Mount Wilson Lane, Baltimore, MD 21208. Telephone: 410-484-7200.

PEABODY CONSERVATORY OF MUSIC OF THE JOHNS HOPKINS UNIVERSITY
BALTIMORE, MARYLAND

General Independent, comprehensive, coed **Entrance** Very difficult **Setting** urban campus **Total enrollment** 678 **Student-faculty ratio** 4:1 **Application deadline** 12/15 (freshmen), 12/15 (transfer) **Freshmen** 42% were admitted **Housing** Yes **Expenses** Tuition $23,975; Room & Board $8800 **Undergraduates** 49% women, 5% part-time, 4% 25 or older, 0% Native American, 4% Hispanic American, 4% African American, 11% Asian American/Pacific Islander **The most frequently chosen baccalaureate field is** visual/performing arts **Academic program** English as a second language, advanced placement, accelerated degree program, honors program, internships **Contact** Mr. David Lane, Director of Admissions, Peabody Conservatory of Music of The Johns Hopkins University, 1 East Mount Vernon Place, Baltimore, MD 21202-2397. Telephone: 410-659-8110 or toll-free 800-368-2521 (out-of-state). Web site: http://www.peabody.jhu.edu/.

ST. JOHN'S COLLEGE
ANNAPOLIS, MARYLAND

General Independent, comprehensive, coed **Entrance** Moderately difficult **Setting** 36-acre small-town campus **Total enrollment** 543 **Student-faculty ratio** 8:1 **Application deadline** Rolling (freshmen), rolling (transfer) **Freshmen** 78% were admitted **Housing** Yes **Expenses** Tuition $25,990; Room & Board $6770 **Undergraduates** 45% women, 1% part-time, 4% 25 or older, 0.4% Native American, 3% Hispanic American, 0.4% African American, 3% Asian American/Pacific Islander **The most frequently chosen baccalaureate field is** liberal arts/general studies **Academic program** Internships **Contact** Mr. John Christensen, Director of Admissions, St. John's College, PO Box 2800, 60 College Avenue, Annapolis, MD 21404. Telephone: 410-626-2522 or toll-free 800-727-9238. Fax: 410-269-7916. E-mail: admissions@sjca.edu. Web site: http://www.sjca.edu/.

ST. MARY'S COLLEGE OF MARYLAND
ST. MARY'S CITY, MARYLAND

General State-supported, 4-year, coed **Entrance** Moderately difficult **Setting** 275-acre rural campus **Total enrollment** 1,688 **Student-faculty ratio** 11:1 **Application deadline** 1/15 (freshmen), 3/15 (transfer) **Freshmen** 71% were admitted **Housing** Yes **Expenses** Tuition $7549; Room & Board $6555 **Undergraduates** 61% women, 10% part-time, 5% 25 or older, 1% Native American, 2% Hispanic American, 7% African American, 4% Asian American/Pacific Islander **The most frequently chosen baccalaureate fields are** biological/life sciences, psychology, social sciences and history **Academic program** Advanced placement, self-designed majors, honors program, summer session, adult/continuing education programs, internships **Contact** Mr. Richard J. Edgar, Director of Admissions, St. Mary's College of Maryland, 18952 East Fisher Road, St. Mary's City, MD 20686-3001. Telephone: 240-895-5000 or toll-free 800-492-7181. Fax: 240-895-5001. E-mail: admissions@smcm.edu. Web site: http://www.smcm.edu/.

▶ For more information, see page 471.

SALISBURY UNIVERSITY
SALISBURY, MARYLAND

General State-supported, comprehensive, coed **Entrance** Moderately difficult **Setting** 140-acre small-town campus **Total enrollment** 6,682 **Student-faculty ratio** 18:1 **Application deadline** 1/15 (freshmen), rolling (transfer) **Freshmen** 52% were admitted **Housing** Yes **Expenses** Tuition $4486; Room & Board $6090 **Undergraduates** 57% women, 13% part-time, 11% 25 or older, 0.3% Native American, 1% Hispanic American, 6% African American, 2% Asian American/Pacific Islander **The most frequently chosen baccalaureate fields are** business/marketing, communications/communication technologies, education **Academic program** English as a second language, advanced placement, self-designed majors, honors program, summer session, adult/continuing education programs, internships **Contact** Mrs. Jane H. Dané, Dean of Admissions, Salisbury University, Admissions House, 1101 Camden Avenue, Salisbury, MD 21801. Telephone: 410-543-6161 or toll-free 888-543-0148. Fax: 410-546-6016. E-mail: d3adadm@ssa.ssu.umd.edu. Web site: http://www.salisbury.edu/.

MARYLAND

SOJOURNER-DOUGLASS COLLEGE
BALTIMORE, MARYLAND

General Independent, comprehensive, coed, primarily women **Entrance** Noncompetitive **Setting** 15-acre urban campus **Total enrollment** 1,124 **Student-faculty ratio** 10:1 **Application deadline** Rolling (freshmen), rolling (transfer) **Housing** No **Expenses** Tuition $4984 **Undergraduates** 84% women, 33% part-time, 95% 25 or older, 0.1% Native American, 1% Hispanic American, 98% African American **Academic program** Accelerated degree program, self-designed majors, honors program, summer session, adult/continuing education programs, internships **Contact** Ms. Diana Samuels, Manager, Office of Admissions, Sojourner-Douglass College, 500 North Caroline Street, Baltimore, MD 21205-1814. Telephone: 410-276-0306 Ext. 251. Fax: 410-675-1810. Web site: http://sdc.edu/.

TOWSON UNIVERSITY
TOWSON, MARYLAND

General State-supported, comprehensive, coed **Entrance** Moderately difficult **Setting** 321-acre suburban campus **Total enrollment** 16,980 **Student-faculty ratio** 18:1 **Application deadline** 5/1 (freshmen), rolling (transfer) **Freshmen** 59% were admitted **Housing** Yes **Expenses** Tuition $4984; Room & Board $6030 **Undergraduates** 60% women, 16% part-time, 13% 25 or older, 0.3% Native American, 2% Hispanic American, 10% African American, 3% Asian American/Pacific Islander **The most frequently chosen baccalaureate fields are** business/marketing, communications/communication technologies, education **Academic program** English as a second language, advanced placement, self-designed majors, honors program, summer session, adult/continuing education programs, internships **Contact** Ms. Louise Shulack, Director of Admissions, Towson University, 8000 York Road, Towson, MD 21252. Telephone: 410-704-3687 or toll-free 888-4TOWSON. Fax: 410-830-3030. E-mail: admissions@towson.edu. Web site: http://www.towson.edu/.

▶ For more information, see page 482.

UNITED STATES NAVAL ACADEMY
ANNAPOLIS, MARYLAND

General Federally supported, 4-year, coed **Entrance** Very difficult **Setting** 329-acre small-town campus **Total enrollment** 4,297 **Student-faculty ratio** 7:1 **Application deadline** 2/15 (freshmen) **Freshmen** 13% were admitted **Housing** Yes **Undergraduates** 15% women, 1% 25 or older, 1% Native American, 8% Hispanic American, 6% African American, 4% Asian American/Pacific Islander **The most frequently chosen baccalaureate fields are** engineering/engineering technologies, physical sciences, social sciences and history **Academic program** English as a second language, advanced placement, honors program, summer session **Contact** Col. David A. Vetter, Dean of Admissions, United States Naval Academy, 117 Decatur Road, Annapolis, MD 21402-5000. Telephone: 410-293-4361. Fax: 410-293-4348. E-mail: webmail@gwmail.usna.edu. Web site: http://www.usna.edu/.

UNIVERSITY OF BALTIMORE
BALTIMORE, MARYLAND

General State-supported, upper-level, coed **Entrance** Noncompetitive **Setting** 49-acre urban campus **Total enrollment** 4,639 **Student-faculty ratio** 14:1 **Application deadline** Rolling (transfer) **First-Year Students** 88% were admitted **Housing** No **Expenses** Tuition $5324 **Undergraduates** 61% women, 55% part-time, 78% 25 or older, 1% Native American, 2% Hispanic American, 30% African American, 2% Asian American/Pacific Islander **The most frequently chosen baccalaureate field is** law/legal studies **Academic program** Advanced placement, accelerated degree program, self-designed majors, honors program, summer session, adult/continuing education programs, internships **Contact** Mr. Daryl Minus, Assistant Director of Admissions, University of Baltimore, 1420 North Charles St., Baltimore, MD 21201-5779. Telephone: 410-837-4777 or toll-free 877-APPLYUB (in-state). Fax: 410-837-4793. E-mail: admissions@ubmail.ubalt.edu. Web site: http://www.ubalt.edu/.

UNIVERSITY OF MARYLAND, BALTIMORE COUNTY
BALTIMORE, MARYLAND

General State-supported, university, coed **Entrance** Moderately difficult **Setting** 500-acre suburban campus **Total enrollment** 11,237 **Student-faculty ratio** 17:1 **Application deadline** 3/15 (freshmen), rolling (transfer) **Freshmen** 66% were admitted **Housing** Yes **Expenses** Tuition $5910; Room & Board $6280 **Undergraduates** 50% women, 19% part-time, 18% 25 or older, 1% Native American, 3% Hispanic American, 16% African American, 18% Asian American/Pacific Islander **The most frequently chosen baccalaureate fields are** computer/information sciences, social sciences and history, visual/performing arts **Academic program** English as a second language, advanced placement, self-designed majors, honors program, summer session, adult/continuing education programs, internships **Contact** Ms. Yvette Mozie-Ross, Director of Admissions, University of Maryland, Baltimore County, 1000 Hilltop Circle, Baltimore, MD 21250-5398. Telephone: 410-455-3799 or toll-free 800-UMBC-4U2 (in-state); 800-862-2402 (out-of-state). Fax: 410-455-1094. E-mail: admissions@umbc.edu. Web site: http://www.umbc.edu/.

UNIVERSITY OF MARYLAND, COLLEGE PARK
COLLEGE PARK, MARYLAND

General State-supported, university, coed **Entrance** Moderately difficult **Setting** 3,650-acre suburban campus **Total enrollment** 34,160 **Student-faculty ratio** 13:1 **Application deadline** 2/15 (freshmen), 7/1 (transfer) **Freshmen** 55% were admitted **Housing**

MARYLAND

University of Maryland, College Park *(continued)*

Yes **Expenses** Tuition $5341; Room & Board $6618 **Undergraduates** 49% women, 11% part-time, 9% 25 or older, 0.2% Native American, 5% Hispanic American, 13% African American, 14% Asian American/Pacific Islander **The most frequently chosen baccalaureate fields are** business/marketing, biological/life sciences, social sciences and history **Academic program** English as a second language, advanced placement, accelerated degree program, self-designed majors, honors program, summer session, adult/continuing education programs, internships **Contact** Barbara Gill, Director of Undergraduate Admissions, University of Maryland, College Park, Mitchell Building, College Park, MD 20742-5235. Telephone: 301-314-8385 or toll-free 800-422-5867. Fax: 301-314-9693. E-mail: um-admit@uga.umd.edu. Web site: http://www.maryland.edu/.

▶ For more information, see page 485.

UNIVERSITY OF MARYLAND EASTERN SHORE
PRINCESS ANNE, MARYLAND

General State-supported, university, coed **Entrance** Moderately difficult **Setting** 700-acre rural campus **Total enrollment** 3,426 **Student-faculty ratio** 20:1 **Application deadline** 7/15 (freshmen), rolling (transfer) **Freshmen** 66% were admitted **Housing** Yes **Expenses** Tuition $4128; Room & Board $5130 **Undergraduates** 58% women, 18% part-time, 13% 25 or older, 0.4% Native American, 1% Hispanic American, 75% African American, 1% Asian American/Pacific Islander **Academic program** Advanced placement, accelerated degree program, self-designed majors, honors program, summer session, adult/continuing education programs, internships **Contact** Ms. Cheryll Collier-Mills, Director of Admissions and Recruitment, University of Maryland Eastern Shore, Princess Anne, MD 21853-1299. Telephone: 410-651-8410. Fax: 410-651-7922. E-mail: umesadmissions@mail.umes.edu. Web site: http://www.umes.edu/.

UNIVERSITY OF MARYLAND UNIVERSITY COLLEGE
ADELPHI, MARYLAND

General State-supported, comprehensive, coed **Entrance** Noncompetitive **Setting** suburban campus **Total enrollment** 22,233 **Student-faculty ratio** 23:1 **Application deadline** Rolling (freshmen), rolling (transfer) **Freshmen** 100% were admitted **Housing** No **Expenses** Tuition $4728 **Undergraduates** 58% women, 86% part-time, 84% 25 or older, 1% Native American, 5% Hispanic American, 32% African American, 7% Asian American/Pacific Islander **The most frequently chosen baccalaureate field is** interdisciplinary studies **Academic program** Advanced placement, accelerated degree program, summer session, adult/continuing education programs **Contact** Ms. Anne Rahill, Technical Director, Admissions,

University of Maryland University College, 3501 University Boulevard, East, Adelphi, MD 20783. Telephone: 301-985-7000 or toll-free 800-888-UMUC (in-state). Fax: 301-985-7364. E-mail: umucinfo@nova.umuc.edu. Web site: http://www.umuc.edu/.

UNIVERSITY OF PHOENIX–MARYLAND CAMPUS
COLUMBIA, MARYLAND

General Proprietary, comprehensive, coed **Entrance** Noncompetitive **Total enrollment** 88,730 **Student-faculty ratio** 13:1 **Application deadline** Rolling (freshmen), rolling (transfer) **Housing** No **Expenses** Tuition $9000 **Undergraduates** 99.9% women **The most frequently chosen baccalaureate field is** business/marketing **Academic program** Advanced placement, accelerated degree program, adult/continuing education programs **Contact** Ms. Beth Barilla, Director of Admissions, University of Phoenix–Maryland Campus, 4615 East Elwood Street, Phoenix, AZ 85040-1958. Telephone: 480-927-0099 Ext. 1218 or toll-free 800-228-7240. Fax: 480-894-1758. E-mail: beth.barilla@apollogrp.edu. Web site: http://www.phoenix.edu/.

VILLA JULIE COLLEGE
STEVENSON, MARYLAND

General Independent, comprehensive, coed **Entrance** Moderately difficult **Setting** 60-acre suburban campus **Total enrollment** 2,447 **Student-faculty ratio** 12:1 **Application deadline** 7/15 (freshmen), 7/15 (transfer) **Freshmen** 84% were admitted **Housing** Yes **Expenses** Tuition $12,076; Room only $3950 **Undergraduates** 72% women, 25% part-time, 23% 25 or older, 0.2% Native American, 1% Hispanic American, 10% African American, 3% Asian American/Pacific Islander **The most frequently chosen baccalaureate fields are** computer/information sciences, health professions and related sciences, interdisciplinary studies **Academic program** English as a second language, advanced placement, accelerated degree program, self-designed majors, honors program, summer session, adult/continuing education programs, internships **Contact** Mr. Mark Hergan, Dean of Admissions, Villa Julie College, 125 Greenspring Valley Road, Stevenson, MD 21153. Telephone: 410-486-7001 or toll-free 877-468-6852 (in-state); 877-468-3852 (out-of-state). Fax: 410-602-6600. E-mail: admissions@vjc.edu. Web site: http://www.vjc.edu/.

WASHINGTON BIBLE COLLEGE
LANHAM, MARYLAND

General Independent nondenominational, 4-year, coed **Entrance** Moderately difficult **Setting** 63-acre suburban campus **Total enrollment** 331 **Student-faculty ratio** 13:1 **Application deadline** Rolling (freshmen), rolling (transfer) **Freshmen** 65% were admitted **Housing** Yes **Expenses** Tuition $6795; Room & Board $4690 **Undergraduates** 47% women, 44% part-time, 63% 25 or older, 0% Native American, 2% Hispanic American, 39% African American,

MASSACHUSETTS

8% Asian American/Pacific Islander **The most frequently chosen baccalaureate field is** philosophy, religion, and theology **Academic program** English as a second language, advanced placement, accelerated degree program, summer session, adult/continuing education programs, internships **Contact** Barbara Fox, Director of Enrollment Management, Washington Bible College, 6511 Princess Garden Parkway, Lanham, MD 20706. Telephone: 301-552-1400 Ext. 213 or toll-free 800-787-0256 Ext. 212. Fax: 301-552-2775 Ext. 212. E-mail: admissions@bible.edu. Web site: http://www.bible.edu/.

WASHINGTON COLLEGE
CHESTERTOWN, MARYLAND

General Independent, comprehensive, coed **Entrance** Moderately difficult **Setting** 120-acre small-town campus **Total enrollment** 1,509 **Student-faculty ratio** 12:1 **Application deadline** 2/15 (freshmen), rolling (transfer) **Freshmen** 73% were admitted **Housing** Yes **Expenses** Tuition $22,300; Room & Board $5740 **Undergraduates** 62% women, 5% part-time, 2% 25 or older, 0.3% Native American, 1% Hispanic American, 3% African American, 2% Asian American/Pacific Islander **The most frequently chosen baccalaureate fields are** biological/life sciences, psychology, social sciences and history **Academic program** English as a second language, advanced placement, self-designed majors, internships **Contact** Mr. Kevin Coveney, Vice President for Admissions, Washington College, 300 Washington Avenue, Chestertown, MD 21620-1197. Telephone: 410-778-7700 or toll-free 800-422-1782. E-mail: admissions_office@washcoll.edu. Web site: http://www.washcoll.edu/.

▶ For more information, see page 494.

WESTERN MARYLAND COLLEGE
See McDaniel College

MASSACHUSETTS

AMERICAN INTERNATIONAL COLLEGE
SPRINGFIELD, MASSACHUSETTS

General Independent, comprehensive, coed **Entrance** Moderately difficult **Setting** 58-acre urban campus **Total enrollment** 1,509 **Student-faculty ratio** 13:1 **Application deadline** Rolling (freshmen), rolling (transfer) **Freshmen** 77% were admitted **Housing** Yes **Expenses** Tuition $14,800; Room & Board $7468 **Undergraduates** 53% women, 17% part-time, 25% 25 or older, 0.3% Native American, 6% Hispanic American, 24% African American, 2% Asian American/Pacific Islander **Academic program** English as a second language, advanced placement, accelerated degree program, honors program, summer session, adult/continuing education programs, internships **Contact** Dean of Admissions, American International College, 1000 State Street, Springfield, MA 01109-3189. Telephone: 413-205-3201 or toll-free 800-242-3142. Fax: 413-205-3051. E-mail: inquiry@acad.aic.edu. Web site: http://www.aic.edu/.

AMHERST COLLEGE
AMHERST, MASSACHUSETTS

General Independent, 4-year, coed **Entrance** Most difficult **Setting** 964-acre small-town campus **Total enrollment** 1,631 **Student-faculty ratio** 9:1 **Application deadline** 12/31 (freshmen), 12/31 (transfer) **Freshmen** 19% were admitted **Housing** Yes **Expenses** Tuition $27,258; Room & Board $7100 **Undergraduates** 49% women, 1% 25 or older, 0% Native American, 8% Hispanic American, 9% African American, 11% Asian American/Pacific Islander **The most frequently chosen baccalaureate fields are** English, biological/life sciences, social sciences and history **Academic program** Self-designed majors, honors program **Contact** Mr. Thomas Parker, Dean of Admission and Financial Aid, Amherst College, PO Box 5000, Amherst, MA 01002. Telephone: 413-542-2328. Fax: 413-542-2040. E-mail: admission@amherst.edu. Web site: http://www.amherst.edu/.

ANNA MARIA COLLEGE
PAXTON, MASSACHUSETTS

General Independent Roman Catholic, comprehensive, coed **Entrance** Moderately difficult **Setting** 180-acre rural campus **Total enrollment** 1,264 **Student-faculty ratio** 11:1 **Application deadline** Rolling (freshmen), rolling (transfer) **Freshmen** 87% were admitted **Housing** Yes **Expenses** Tuition $16,500; Room & Board $6300 **Undergraduates** 63% women, 31% part-time, 31% 25 or older, 0.4% Native American, 3% Hispanic American, 3% African American, 1% Asian American/Pacific Islander **The most frequently chosen baccalaureate fields are** business/marketing, health professions and related sciences, protective services/public administration **Academic program** English as a second language, advanced placement, accelerated degree program, self-designed majors, summer session, adult/continuing education programs, internships **Contact** Ms. Jane Fidler, Director of Admissions, Anna Maria College, Box O, Sunset Lane, Paxton, MA 01612. Telephone: 508-849-3360 or toll-free 800-344-4586 Ext. 360. Fax: 508-849-3362. E-mail: admission@annamaria.edu. Web site: http://www.annamaria.edu/.

THE ART INSTITUTE OF BOSTON AT LESLEY UNIVERSITY
BOSTON, MASSACHUSETTS

General Independent, comprehensive, coed **Entrance** Moderately difficult **Setting** urban campus **Total enrollment** 588 **Student-faculty ratio** 11:1 **Application deadline** Rolling (freshmen), rolling (transfer) **Freshmen** 76% were admitted **Housing** Yes **Expenses** Tuition $14,090; Room & Board $7520 **Undergraduates** 56% women, 9% part-time, 7% 25 or older, 0% Native American, 5% Hispanic American, 3% African American, 3% Asian American/

MASSACHUSETTS

The Art Institute of Boston at Lesley University *(continued)*

Pacific Islander **The most frequently chosen baccalaureate field is** visual/performing arts **Academic program** English as a second language, advanced placement, self-designed majors, honors program, summer session, adult/continuing education programs, internships **Contact** Bradford White, Director of Admissions, The Art Institute of Boston at Lesley University, 700 Beacon Street, Boston, MA 02215-2598. Telephone: 617-585-6700 or toll-free 800-773-0494 (in-state). Fax: 617-437-1226. E-mail: admissions@aiboston.edu. Web site: http://www.aiboston.edu/.

ASSUMPTION COLLEGE
WORCESTER, MASSACHUSETTS

General Independent Roman Catholic, comprehensive, coed **Entrance** Moderately difficult **Setting** 145-acre urban campus **Total enrollment** 2,422 **Student-faculty ratio** 14:1 **Application deadline** 3/1 (freshmen), 5/1 (transfer) **Freshmen** 75% were admitted **Housing** Yes **Expenses** Tuition $18,945; Room & Board $7375 **Undergraduates** 61% women, 1% part-time, 1% 25 or older, 0% Native American, 2% Hispanic American, 1% African American, 1% Asian American/Pacific Islander **The most frequently chosen baccalaureate fields are** business/marketing, health professions and related sciences, social sciences and history **Academic program** Advanced placement, self-designed majors, honors program, summer session, adult/continuing education programs, internships **Contact** Ms. Mary Bresnahan, Dean of Admission, Assumption College, 500 Salisbury Street, Worcester, MA 01609-1296. Telephone: 508-767-7362 or toll-free 888-882-7786. Fax: 508-799-4412. E-mail: admiss@assumption.edu. Web site: http://www.assumption.edu/.

ATLANTIC UNION COLLEGE
SOUTH LANCASTER, MASSACHUSETTS

General Independent Seventh-day Adventist, comprehensive, coed **Entrance** Moderately difficult **Setting** 314-acre small-town campus **Total enrollment** 719 **Student-faculty ratio** 12:1 **Application deadline** 8/1 (freshmen), 8/1 (transfer) **Freshmen** 19% were admitted **Housing** Yes **Expenses** Tuition $13,580; Room & Board $4700 **Undergraduates** 59% women, 25% part-time, 0.4% Native American, 21% Hispanic American, 49% African American, 2% Asian American/Pacific Islander **The most frequently chosen baccalaureate fields are** business/marketing, health professions and related sciences, psychology **Academic program** English as a second language, advanced placement, honors program, summer session, adult/continuing education programs, internships **Contact** Mrs. Rosita Lashley, Associate Director for Admissions, Atlantic Union College, PO Box 1000, South Lancaster, MA 01561. Telephone: 978-368-2239 or toll-free 800-282-2030. Fax: 978-368-2015. E-mail: enroll@math.atlanticuc.edu. Web site: http://www.atlanticuc.edu/.

BABSON COLLEGE
WELLESLEY, MASSACHUSETTS

General Independent, comprehensive, coed **Entrance** Very difficult **Setting** 450-acre suburban campus **Total enrollment** 3,328 **Student-faculty ratio** 9:1 **Application deadline** 2/1 (freshmen), 4/1 (transfer) **Freshmen** 35% were admitted **Housing** Yes **Expenses** Tuition $24,544; Room & Board $8746 **Undergraduates** 37% women, 1% 25 or older, 0.3% Native American, 4% Hispanic American, 3% African American, 8% Asian American/Pacific Islander **Academic program** Advanced placement, self-designed majors, honors program, summer session, internships **Contact** Mrs. Monica Inzer, Dean of Undergraduate Admission and Student Financial Services, Babson College, Office of Undergraduate Admission, Mustard Hall, Babson Park, MA 02457-0310. Telephone: 800-488-3696 or toll-free 800-488-3696. Fax: 781-239-4006. E-mail: ugradadmission@babson.edu. Web site: http://www.babson.edu/.

BAY PATH COLLEGE
LONGMEADOW, MASSACHUSETTS

General Independent, comprehensive, women only **Entrance** Moderately difficult **Setting** 44-acre suburban campus **Total enrollment** 972 **Student-faculty ratio** 13:1 **Application deadline** Rolling (freshmen), rolling (transfer) **Freshmen** 72% were admitted **Housing** Yes **Expenses** Tuition $14,754; Room & Board $6867 **Undergraduates** 27% part-time, 37% 25 or older, 0.1% Native American, 5% Hispanic American, 11% African American, 2% Asian American/Pacific Islander **The most frequently chosen baccalaureate fields are** business/marketing, computer/information sciences, liberal arts/general studies **Academic program** English as a second language, advanced placement, self-designed majors, honors program, summer session, adult/continuing education programs, internships **Contact** Ms. Brenda Wishart, Director of Admissions, Bay Path College, 588 Longmeadow Street, Longmeadow, MA 01106-2292. Telephone: 413-565-1000 Ext. 229 or toll-free 800-782-7284 Ext. 331. Fax: 413-565-1105. E-mail: chobin@baypath.edu. Web site: http://www.baypath.edu/.

BECKER COLLEGE
WORCESTER, MASSACHUSETTS

General Independent, 4-year, coed **Entrance** Minimally difficult **Setting** urban campus **Total enrollment** 1,298 **Student-faculty ratio** 15:1 **Application deadline** Rolling (freshmen), rolling (transfer) **Freshmen** 90% were admitted **Housing** Yes **Expenses** Tuition $13,750; Room & Board $7180 **Undergraduates** 79% women, 43% part-time **The most frequently chosen baccalaureate field is** law/legal studies **Academic program** English as a second language, advanced placement, accelerated degree program, summer session, adult/continuing education programs, internships **Contact** Admissions Receptionist, Becker College, 61 Sever Street, Worcester, MA 01609. Telephone: 508-791-9241 Ext. 245 or toll-free 877-5BECKER Ext. 245. Fax: 508-890-1500. E-mail: admissions@go.becker.edu. Web site: http://www.beckercollege.edu/.

BENTLEY COLLEGE
WALTHAM, MASSACHUSETTS

General Independent, comprehensive, coed **Entrance** Moderately difficult **Setting** 143-acre suburban campus **Total enrollment** 5,587 **Student-faculty ratio** 14:1 **Application deadline** 2/1 (freshmen), 5/15 (transfer) **Freshmen** 38% were admitted **Housing** Yes **Expenses** Tuition $20,061; Room & Board $9010 **Undergraduates** 43% women, 13% part-time, 10% 25 or older, 0.1% Native American, 3% Hispanic American, 3% African American, 7% Asian American/Pacific Islander **The most frequently chosen baccalaureate fields are** business/marketing, computer/information sciences, interdisciplinary studies **Academic program** English as a second language, advanced placement, accelerated degree program, self-designed majors, honors program, summer session, adult/continuing education programs, internships **Contact** Ms. Judith A. Pearson, Director of Admission, Bentley College, 175 Forest Street, Waltham, MA 02452-4705. Telephone: 781-891-2244 or toll-free 800-523-2354 (out-of-state). Fax: 781-891-3414. E-mail: ugadmission@bentley.edu. Web site: http://www.bentley.edu/.

BERKLEE COLLEGE OF MUSIC
BOSTON, MASSACHUSETTS

General Independent, 4-year, coed **Entrance** Moderately difficult **Setting** urban campus **Total enrollment** 3,415 **Student-faculty ratio** 14:1 **Application deadline** Rolling (freshmen), rolling (transfer) **Freshmen** 35% were admitted **Housing** Yes **Expenses** Tuition $17,719; Room & Board $9290 **Undergraduates** 0.4% Native American, 3% Hispanic American, 4% African American, 3% Asian American/Pacific Islander **The most frequently chosen baccalaureate field is** visual/performing arts **Academic program** English as a second language, advanced placement, accelerated degree program, self-designed majors, summer session, internships **Contact** Ms. Marsha Ginn, Director of Admissions, Berklee College of Music, 1140 Boyleston Street, Boston, MA 02215-3693. Telephone: 617-747-2222 or toll-free 800-BERKLEE. Fax: 617-747-2047. E-mail: admissions@berklee.edu. Web site: http://www.berklee.edu/.

BOSTON ARCHITECTURAL CENTER
BOSTON, MASSACHUSETTS

General Independent, comprehensive, coed **Entrance** Noncompetitive **Setting** urban campus **Total enrollment** 677 **Student-faculty ratio** 10:1 **Application deadline** Rolling (freshmen), rolling (transfer) **Freshmen** 95% were admitted **Housing** No **Expenses** Tuition $7026 **Undergraduates** 25% women, 15% part-time, 67% 25 or older, 3% Native American, 5% Hispanic American, 2% African American, 2% Asian American/Pacific Islander **The most frequently chosen baccalaureate field is** architecture **Academic program** Advanced placement, summer session, adult/continuing education programs, internships **Contact** Mr. Will Dunfey, Director of Admissions, Boston Architectural Center, 320 Newbury Street, Boston, MA 02115-2795. Telephone: 617-585-0202 or toll-free 877-585-0100. Fax: 617-585-0121. E-mail: admissions@the-bac.edu. Web site: http://www.the-bac.edu/.

BOSTON COLLEGE
CHESTNUT HILL, MASSACHUSETTS

General Independent Roman Catholic (Jesuit), university, coed **Entrance** Very difficult **Setting** 240-acre suburban campus **Total enrollment** 13,510 **Student-faculty ratio** 13:1 **Application deadline** 1/2 (freshmen), 4/15 (transfer) **Freshmen** 34% were admitted **Housing** Yes **Expenses** Tuition $24,470; Room & Board $8860 **Undergraduates** 53% women, 0.3% Native American, 5% Hispanic American, 4% African American, 8% Asian American/Pacific Islander **The most frequently chosen baccalaureate fields are** business/marketing, communications/communication technologies, social sciences and history **Academic program** Advanced placement, accelerated degree program, self-designed majors, honors program, summer session, adult/continuing education programs, internships **Contact** Mr. John L. Mahoney Jr., Director of Undergraduate Admission, Boston College, 140 Commonwealth Avenue, Devlin Hall 208, 140 Commonwealth Avenue, Chestnut Hill, MA 02167-3809. Telephone: 617-552-3100 or toll-free 800-360-2522. Fax: 617-552-0798. E-mail: ugadmis@bc.edu. Web site: http://www.bc.edu/.

THE BOSTON CONSERVATORY
BOSTON, MASSACHUSETTS

General Independent, comprehensive, coed **Entrance** Moderately difficult **Setting** urban campus **Total enrollment** 510 **Student-faculty ratio** 6:1 **Application deadline** 3/1 (freshmen), rolling (transfer) **Freshmen** 16% were admitted **Housing** Yes **Expenses** Tuition $20,200; Room & Board $9280 **Undergraduates** 62% women, 1% part-time, 1% Native American, 5% Hispanic American, 5% African American, 5% Asian American/Pacific Islander **The most frequently chosen baccalaureate field is** visual/performing arts **Academic program** English as a second language, advanced placement, summer session, adult/continuing education programs **Contact** Ms. Halley Shefler, Dean of Enrollment, The Boston Conservatory, 8 The Fenway, Boston, MA 02215. Telephone: 617-912-9153. Fax: 617-536-3176. Web site: http://www.bostonconservatory.edu/.

BOSTON UNIVERSITY
BOSTON, MASSACHUSETTS

General Independent, university, coed **Entrance** Very difficult **Setting** 132-acre urban campus **Total enrollment** 27,756 **Student-faculty ratio** 12:1 **Application deadline** 1/1 (freshmen), 4/1 (transfer) **Freshmen**

MASSACHUSETTS

Boston University *(continued)*
48% were admitted **Housing** Yes **Expenses** Tuition $26,228; Room & Board $8750 **Undergraduates** 60% women, 11% part-time, 4% 25 or older, 0.3% Native American, 5% Hispanic American, 3% African American, 12% Asian American/Pacific Islander **The most frequently chosen baccalaureate fields are** communications/communication technologies, business/marketing, social sciences and history **Academic program** English as a second language, advanced placement, accelerated degree program, self-designed majors, honors program, summer session, adult/continuing education programs, internships **Contact** Ms. Kelly A. Walter, Director of Undergraduate Admissions, Boston University, 121 Bay State Road, Boston, MA 02215. Telephone: 617-353-2300. Fax: 617-353-9695. E-mail: admissions@bu.edu. Web site: http://www.bu.edu/.

BRANDEIS UNIVERSITY
WALTHAM, MASSACHUSETTS

General Independent, university, coed **Entrance** Most difficult **Setting** 235-acre suburban campus **Total enrollment** 4,882 **Student-faculty ratio** 8:1 **Application deadline** 1/31 (freshmen), 4/1 (transfer) **Freshmen** 41% were admitted **Housing** Yes **Expenses** Tuition $27,076; Room & Board $7405 **Undergraduates** 56% women, 1% part-time, 0% 25 or older, 0.2% Native American, 2% Hispanic American, 2% African American, 10% Asian American/Pacific Islander **The most frequently chosen baccalaureate fields are** biological/life sciences, psychology, social sciences and history **Academic program** English as a second language, advanced placement, self-designed majors, summer session, adult/continuing education programs, internships **Contact** Mr. Michael Kalafatas, Director of Admissions, Brandeis University, 415 South Street, Waltham, MA 02254-9110. Telephone: 781-736-3500 or toll-free 800-622-0622 (out-of-state). Fax: 781-736-3536. E-mail: sendinfo@brandeis.edu. Web site: http://www.brandeis.edu/.

BRIDGEWATER STATE COLLEGE
BRIDGEWATER, MASSACHUSETTS

General State-supported, comprehensive, coed **Entrance** Moderately difficult **Setting** 235-acre suburban campus **Total enrollment** 9,038 **Student-faculty ratio** 19:1 **Application deadline** 3/1 (freshmen), 4/1 (transfer) **Freshmen** 74% were admitted **Housing** Yes **Expenses** Tuition $2823; Room & Board $4996 **Undergraduates** 61% women, 22% part-time, 18% 25 or older, 0.3% Native American, 2% Hispanic American, 4% African American, 1% Asian American/Pacific Islander **The most frequently chosen baccalaureate fields are** education, psychology, social sciences and history **Academic program** English as a second language, advanced placement, self-designed majors, honors program, summer session, adult/continuing education programs, internships **Contact** Mr. Steve King, Director of Admissions, Bridgewater State College, Admission Office, Bridgewater, MA 02325-0001. Telephone: 508-531-1237. Fax: 508-531-1746. E-mail: admission@bridgew.edu. Web site: http://www.bridgew.edu/.

CAMBRIDGE COLLEGE
CAMBRIDGE, MASSACHUSETTS

General Independent, comprehensive, coed **Entrance** Minimally difficult **Setting** urban campus **Total enrollment** 2,700 **Student-faculty ratio** 18:1 **Application deadline** Rolling (freshmen), rolling (transfer) **Freshmen** 100% were admitted **Housing** No **Expenses** Tuition $9150 **Undergraduates** 95% 25 or older **Academic program** English as a second language, accelerated degree program, summer session, adult/continuing education programs, internships **Contact** Ms. Joy King, Undergraduate Enrollment Manager, Cambridge College, 1000 Massachusetts Avenue, Cambridge, MA 02138-5304. Telephone: 617-868-1000 or toll-free 800-877-4723. Fax: 617-349-3545. E-mail: enroll@idea.cambridge.edu. Web site: http://www.cambridge.edu/.

CLARK UNIVERSITY
WORCESTER, MASSACHUSETTS

General Independent, university, coed **Entrance** Moderately difficult **Setting** 50-acre urban campus **Total enrollment** 2,955 **Student-faculty ratio** 10:1 **Application deadline** 2/1 (freshmen), 4/15 (transfer) **Freshmen** 68% were admitted **Housing** Yes **Expenses** Tuition $24,620; Room & Board $4550 **Undergraduates** 60% women, 11% part-time, 1% 25 or older, 0.2% Native American, 3% Hispanic American, 3% African American, 4% Asian American/Pacific Islander **The most frequently chosen baccalaureate fields are** psychology, biological/life sciences, social sciences and history **Academic program** English as a second language, advanced placement, accelerated degree program, self-designed majors, honors program, summer session, adult/continuing education programs, internships **Contact** Mr. Harold M. Wingood, Dean of Admissions, Clark University, 950 Main Street, Worcester, MA 01610-1477. Telephone: 508-793-7431 or toll-free 800-GO-CLARK (out-of-state). E-mail: admissions@clarku.edu. Web site: http://www.clarku.edu/.

COLLEGE OF OUR LADY OF THE ELMS
See Elms College

COLLEGE OF THE HOLY CROSS
WORCESTER, MASSACHUSETTS

General Independent Roman Catholic (Jesuit), 4-year, coed **Entrance** Very difficult **Setting** 174-acre suburban campus **Total enrollment** 2,811 **Student-faculty ratio** 12:1 **Application deadline** 1/15 (freshmen), 5/1 (transfer) **Freshmen** 43% were admitted **Housing** Yes **Expenses** Tuition $25,020; Room & Board $7760 **Undergraduates** 52% women, 1% part-time, 0% 25 or older, 0.3% Native American, 5% Hispanic American, 3% African American, 4% Asian

MASSACHUSETTS

American/Pacific Islander **The most frequently chosen baccalaureate fields are** English, psychology, social sciences and history **Academic program** Advanced placement, accelerated degree program, self-designed majors, honors program, internships **Contact** Ms. Ann Bowe McDermott, Director of Admissions, College of the Holy Cross, 1 College Street, Worcester, MA 01610. Telephone: 508-793-2443 or toll-free 800-442-2421. E-mail: admissions@holycross.edu. Web site: http://www.holycross.edu/.

CURRY COLLEGE
MILTON, MASSACHUSETTS

General Independent, comprehensive, coed **Entrance** Moderately difficult **Setting** 131-acre suburban campus **Total enrollment** 2,399 **Student-faculty ratio** 12:1 **Application deadline** 4/1 (freshmen), 7/1 (transfer) **Freshmen** 79% were admitted **Housing** Yes **Expenses** Tuition $17,625 **Undergraduates** 50% women, 39% part-time, 43% 25 or older **The most frequently chosen baccalaureate field is** philosophy, religion, and theology **Academic program** Advanced placement, accelerated degree program, self-designed majors, honors program, summer session, adult/continuing education programs, internships **Contact** Mr. Michael Poll, Dean of Admission and Financial Aid, Curry College, 1071 Blue Hill Avenue, Milton, MA 02186. Telephone: 617-333-2210 or toll-free 800-669-0686. Fax: 617-333-2114. E-mail: curryadm@curry.edu. Web site: http://www.curry.edu/.

EASTERN NAZARENE COLLEGE
QUINCY, MASSACHUSETTS

General Independent, comprehensive, coed, affiliated with Church of the Nazarene **Entrance** Moderately difficult **Setting** 15-acre suburban campus **Total enrollment** 1,228 **Student-faculty ratio** 15:1 **Application deadline** Rolling (freshmen), rolling (transfer) **Freshmen** 61% were admitted **Housing** Yes **Expenses** Tuition $14,458; Room & Board $4925 **Undergraduates** 60% women, 2% part-time, 50% 25 or older **The most frequently chosen baccalaureate fields are** biological/life sciences, business/marketing, communications/communication technologies **Academic program** English as a second language, advanced placement, accelerated degree program, honors program, summer session, adult/continuing education programs, internships **Contact** Mr. James F. Heyward II, Director of Admissions, Eastern Nazarene College, 23 East Elm Avenue, Quincy, MA 02170. Telephone: 617-745-3868 or toll-free 800-88-ENC88. Fax: 617-745-3929. E-mail: admissions@enc.edu. Web site: http://www.enc.edu/.

ELMS COLLEGE
CHICOPEE, MASSACHUSETTS

General Independent Roman Catholic, comprehensive, coed, primarily women **Entrance** Moderately difficult **Setting** 32-acre suburban campus **Total enrollment** 719 **Student-faculty ratio** 11:1 **Application deadline** Rolling (freshmen), rolling (transfer) **Freshmen** 70% were admitted **Housing** Yes **Expenses** Tuition $14,720; Room & Board $5566 **Undergraduates** 86% women, 34% part-time, 34% 25 or older, 0% Native American, 4% Hispanic American, 4% African American, 2% Asian American/Pacific Islander **The most frequently chosen baccalaureate fields are** health professions and related sciences, psychology, social sciences and history **Academic program** English as a second language, advanced placement, accelerated degree program, self-designed majors, honors program, summer session, adult/continuing education programs, internships **Contact** Mr. Joseph P. Wagner, Director of Admissions, Elms College, 291 Springfield Street, Chicopee, MA 01013-2839. Telephone: 413-592-3189 Ext. 350 or toll-free 800-255-ELMS. Fax: 413-594-2781. E-mail: admissions@elms.edu. Web site: http://www.elms.edu/.

EMERSON COLLEGE
BOSTON, MASSACHUSETTS

General Independent, comprehensive, coed **Entrance** Very difficult **Setting** urban campus **Total enrollment** 4,339 **Student-faculty ratio** 15:1 **Application deadline** 2/1 (freshmen), 3/1 (transfer) **Freshmen** 47% were admitted **Housing** Yes **Expenses** Tuition $20,718; Room & Board $9290 **Undergraduates** 60% women, 16% part-time, 5% 25 or older, 0.3% Native American, 4% Hispanic American, 2% African American, 3% Asian American/Pacific Islander **The most frequently chosen baccalaureate fields are** communications/communication technologies, English, visual/performing arts **Academic program** Advanced placement, self-designed majors, honors program, summer session, adult/continuing education programs, internships **Contact** Ms. Sara Ramirez, Director of Admission, Emerson College, 120 Boylston Street, Boston, MA 02116-4624. Telephone: 617-824-8600. Fax: 617-824-8609. E-mail: admission@emerson.edu. Web site: http://www.emerson.edu/.

▶ For more information, see page 424.

EMMANUEL COLLEGE
BOSTON, MASSACHUSETTS

General Independent Roman Catholic, comprehensive, coed **Entrance** Moderately difficult **Setting** 16-acre urban campus **Total enrollment** 1,449 **Student-faculty ratio** 12:1 **Application deadline** Rolling (freshmen), rolling (transfer) **Freshmen** 19% were admitted **Housing** Yes **Expenses** Tuition $17,100; Room & Board $9615 **Undergraduates** 83% women, 33% part-time, 38% 25 or older, 0.3% Native American, 5% Hispanic American, 10% African American, 3% Asian American/Pacific Islander **The most frequently chosen baccalaureate fields are** business/marketing, English, health professions and related sciences **Academic program** English as a second language, advanced placement, accelerated degree program, self-designed majors, honors program, summer session, adult/continuing education programs, internships **Contact** Ms. Sandra Robbins, Dean of

MASSACHUSETTS

Emmanuel College *(continued)*
Admissions, Emmanuel College, 400 The Fenway, Boston, MA 02115. Telephone: 617-735-9715. Fax: 617-735-9801. E-mail: enroll@emmanuel.edu. Web site: http://www.emmanuel.edu/.

ENDICOTT COLLEGE
BEVERLY, MASSACHUSETTS

General Independent, comprehensive, coed **Entrance** Moderately difficult **Setting** 200-acre suburban campus **Total enrollment** 1,937 **Student-faculty ratio** 14:1 **Application deadline** Rolling (freshmen), rolling (transfer) **Freshmen** 61% were admitted **Housing** Yes **Expenses** Tuition $15,704; Room & Board $8000 **Undergraduates** 66% women, 11% part-time, 10% 25 or older, 0.4% Native American, 2% Hispanic American, 1% African American, 1% Asian American/Pacific Islander **The most frequently chosen baccalaureate fields are** business/marketing, parks and recreation, visual/performing arts **Academic program** English as a second language, advanced placement, accelerated degree program, honors program, summer session, adult/continuing education programs, internships **Contact** Mr. Thomas J. Redman, Vice President of Admissions and Financial Aid, Endicott College, 376 Hale Street, Beverly, MA 01915. Telephone: 978-921-1000 or toll-free 800-325-1114 (out-of-state). Fax: 978-232-2520. E-mail: admissio@endicott.edu. Web site: http://www.endicott.edu/.

FITCHBURG STATE COLLEGE
FITCHBURG, MASSACHUSETTS

General State-supported, comprehensive, coed **Entrance** Moderately difficult **Setting** 45-acre small-town campus **Total enrollment** 5,033 **Student-faculty ratio** 11:1 **Application deadline** 4/1 (freshmen), rolling (transfer) **Freshmen** 61% were admitted **Housing** Yes **Expenses** Tuition $2988; Room & Board $4838 **Undergraduates** 57% women, 30% part-time, 23% 25 or older, 0.1% Native American, 3% Hispanic American, 3% African American, 2% Asian American/Pacific Islander **The most frequently chosen baccalaureate fields are** business/marketing, communications/communication technologies, education **Academic program** Advanced placement, accelerated degree program, self-designed majors, honors program, summer session, adult/continuing education programs, internships **Contact** Mr. Robert McGann, Dean of Enrollment Management, Fitchburg State College, 160 Pearl Street, Fitchburg, MA 01420-2697. Telephone: 978-665-3144 or toll-free 800-705-9692. Fax: 978-665-4540. E-mail: admissions@fsc.edu. Web site: http://www.fsc.edu/.

▶ For more information, see page 429.

FRAMINGHAM STATE COLLEGE
FRAMINGHAM, MASSACHUSETTS

General State-supported, comprehensive, coed **Entrance** Moderately difficult **Setting** 73-acre suburban campus **Total enrollment** 5,912 **Student-faculty ratio** 15:1 **Application deadline** 3/1 (freshmen), 3/1 (transfer) **Freshmen** 60% were admitted **Housing** Yes **Expenses** Tuition $2770; Room & Board $4403 **Undergraduates** 64% women, 23% part-time, 0.5% Native American, 3% Hispanic American, 4% African American, 3% Asian American/Pacific Islander **The most frequently chosen baccalaureate fields are** business/marketing, psychology, social sciences and history **Academic program** English as a second language, advanced placement, honors program, summer session, adult/continuing education programs, internships **Contact** Dr. Philip Dooher, Vice President, Enrollment Management and Dean of Admissions, Framingham State College, P.O. Box 9101, Dwight Hall, Room 209, Framingham, MA 01701-9101. Telephone: 508-626-4500. E-mail: admiss@frc.mass.edu. Web site: http://www.framingham.edu/.

GORDON COLLEGE
WENHAM, MASSACHUSETTS

General Independent nondenominational, comprehensive, coed **Entrance** Moderately difficult **Setting** 500-acre small-town campus **Total enrollment** 1,694 **Student-faculty ratio** 15:1 **Application deadline** Rolling (freshmen), rolling (transfer) **Freshmen** 78% were admitted **Housing** Yes **Expenses** Tuition $18,134; Room & Board $5460 **Undergraduates** 66% women, 3% part-time, 3% 25 or older, 0.1% Native American, 2% Hispanic American, 1% African American, 1% Asian American/Pacific Islander **The most frequently chosen baccalaureate fields are** philosophy, education, philosophy, religion, and theology **Academic program** Advanced placement, self-designed majors, honors program, internships **Contact** Mr. Silvio E. Vazquez, Dean of Admissions, Gordon College, 255 Grapevine Road, Wenham, MA 01984-1899. Telephone: 978-927-2300 Ext. 4218 or toll-free 800-343-1379. Fax: 978-524-3722. E-mail: admissions@hope.gordon.edu. Web site: http://www.gordon.edu/.

HAMPSHIRE COLLEGE
AMHERST, MASSACHUSETTS

General Independent, 4-year, coed **Entrance** Moderately difficult **Setting** 800-acre rural campus **Total enrollment** 1,219 **Student-faculty ratio** 11:1 **Application deadline** 2/1 (freshmen), 3/1 (transfer) **Freshmen** 59% were admitted **Housing** Yes **Expenses** Tuition $26,871; Room & Board $7010 **Undergraduates** 58% women, 2% 25 or older, 0.4% Native American, 5% Hispanic American, 4% African American, 4% Asian American/Pacific Islander **Academic program** Advanced placement, accelerated degree program, self-designed majors, internships **Contact** Ms. Karen S. Parker, Director of Admissions, Hampshire College, 839 West Street, Amherst, MA 01002. Telephone: 413-559-5471 or toll-free 877-937-4267 (out-of-state). Fax: 413-559-5631. E-mail: admissions@hampshire.edu. Web site: http://www.hampshire.edu/.

MASSACHUSETTS

HARVARD UNIVERSITY
CAMBRIDGE, MASSACHUSETTS

General Independent, university, coed **Entrance** Most difficult **Setting** 380-acre urban campus **Total enrollment** 17,850 **Student-faculty ratio** 8:1 **Application deadline** 1/1 (freshmen), 2/1 (transfer) **Freshmen** 11% were admitted **Housing** Yes **Expenses** Tuition $26,019; Room & Board $8250 **Undergraduates** 1% 25 or older, 1% Native American, 8% Hispanic American, 8% African American, 17% Asian American/Pacific Islander **Academic program** English as a second language, advanced placement, accelerated degree program, self-designed majors, honors program, summer session, adult/continuing education programs, internships **Contact** Office of Admissions and Financial Aid, Harvard University, Byerly Hall, 8 Garden Street, Cambridge, MA 02138. Telephone: 617-495-1551. E-mail: college@harvard.edu. Web site: http://www.harvard.edu/.

HEBREW COLLEGE
NEWTON CENTRE, MASSACHUSETTS

General Independent Jewish, comprehensive, coed **Entrance** Minimally difficult **Setting** 3-acre suburban campus **Application deadline** 4/15 (freshmen), 4/15 (transfer) **Housing** No **Expenses** Tuition $14,940 **Academic program** Summer session, adult/continuing education programs, internships **Contact** Mrs. Norma Frankel, Registrar, Hebrew College, 160 Herrick Road, Newton Centre, MA 02459. Telephone: 617-278-4944 or toll-free 800-866-4814. Fax: 617-734-9769. E-mail: nfrankel@lynx.neu.edu. Web site: http://www.hebrewcollege.edu/.

HELLENIC COLLEGE
BROOKLINE, MASSACHUSETTS

General Independent Greek Orthodox, 4-year, coed **Entrance** Minimally difficult **Setting** 52-acre suburban campus **Total enrollment** 58 **Student-faculty ratio** 7:1 **Application deadline** Rolling (freshmen), rolling (transfer) **Freshmen** 60% were admitted **Housing** Yes **Expenses** Tuition $9665; Room & Board $7350 **Undergraduates** 34% women, 3% part-time, 10% 25 or older, 0% Native American, 0% Hispanic American, 0% African American, 0% Asian American/Pacific Islander **The most frequently chosen baccalaureate fields are** liberal arts/general studies, philosophy, religion, and theology **Academic program** Advanced placement, summer session, internships **Contact** Rev. James Katinas, Director of Admissions and Records, Hellenic College, 50 Goddard Avenue, Brookline, MA 02445-7496. Telephone: 617-731-3500 Ext. 1260. Fax: 617-850-1460. E-mail: admissions@hchc.edu. Web site: http://www.hchc.edu/.

LASELL COLLEGE
NEWTON, MASSACHUSETTS

General Independent, comprehensive, coed **Entrance** Moderately difficult **Setting** 50-acre suburban campus **Total enrollment** 894 **Student-faculty ratio** 10:1 **Application deadline** Rolling (freshmen), rolling (transfer) **Freshmen** 78% were admitted **Housing** Yes **Expenses** Tuition $16,100; Room & Board $8000 **Undergraduates** 74% women, 5% part-time, 5% 25 or older, 0% Native American, 6% Hispanic American, 10% African American, 5% Asian American/Pacific Islander **Academic program** English as a second language, advanced placement, honors program, internships **Contact** Mr. Darryl Tiggle, Director of Admission, Lasell College, 1844 Commonwealth Avenue, Newton, MA 02466. Telephone: 617-243-2225 or toll-free 888-LASELL-4. Fax: 617-796-4343. E-mail: info@lasell.edu. Web site: http://www.lasell.edu/.

LESLEY UNIVERSITY
CAMBRIDGE, MASSACHUSETTS

General Independent, comprehensive, coed, primarily women **Entrance** Moderately difficult **Setting** 5-acre urban campus **Total enrollment** 6,192 **Student-faculty ratio** 12:1 **Application deadline** 3/15 (freshmen), 6/1 (transfer) **Freshmen** 83% were admitted **Housing** Yes **Expenses** Tuition $16,475; Room & Board $7520 **Undergraduates** 78% women, 5% part-time, 7% 25 or older, 0.2% Native American, 7% Hispanic American, 9% African American, 5% Asian American/Pacific Islander **The most frequently chosen baccalaureate fields are** education, liberal arts/general studies, psychology **Academic program** English as a second language, advanced placement, summer session, adult/continuing education programs, internships **Contact** Jane A. Raley, Director of Women's College Admissions, Lesley University, 29 Everett Street, Cambridge, MA 02138-2790. Telephone: 617-349-8800 or toll-free 800-999-1959 Ext. 8800. Fax: 617-349-8810. E-mail: ugadm@mail.lesley.edu. Web site: http://www.lesley.edu/.

MASSACHUSETTS COLLEGE OF ART
BOSTON, MASSACHUSETTS

General State-supported, comprehensive, coed **Entrance** Very difficult **Setting** 5-acre urban campus **Total enrollment** 2,245 **Student-faculty ratio** 13:1 **Application deadline** 3/1 (freshmen), 4/1 (transfer) **Freshmen** 46% were admitted **Housing** Yes **Expenses** Tuition $4068; Room & Board $7742 **Undergraduates** 65% women, 41% part-time, 16% 25 or older, 0.1% Native American, 4% Hispanic American, 3% African American, 3% Asian American/Pacific Islander **The most frequently chosen baccalaureate fields are** education, visual/performing arts **Academic program** Self-designed majors, summer session, internships **Contact** Ms. Kay Ransdell, Dean of Admissions, Massachusetts College of Art, 621 Huntington Avenue, Boston, MA 02115-5882. Telephone: 617-232-1555 Ext. 235. Fax: 617-879-7250. E-mail: admissions@massart.edu. Web site: http://www.massart.edu/.

MASSACHUSETTS COLLEGE OF LIBERAL ARTS
NORTH ADAMS, MASSACHUSETTS

General State-supported, comprehensive, coed **Entrance** Moderately difficult **Setting** 80-acre small-

MASSACHUSETTS

Massachusetts College of Liberal Arts *(continued)*

town campus **Total enrollment** 1,613 **Student-faculty ratio** 13:1 **Application deadline** Rolling (freshmen), rolling (transfer) **Freshmen** 100% were admitted **Housing** Yes **Expenses** Tuition $3357; Room & Board $4290 **Undergraduates** 59% women, 21% part-time, 24% 25 or older, 0.3% Native American, 3% Hispanic American, 5% African American, 2% Asian American/Pacific Islander **The most frequently chosen baccalaureate fields are** business/marketing, English, social sciences and history **Academic program** Advanced placement, self-designed majors, honors program, summer session, internships **Contact** Ms. Denise Richardello, Dean of Enrollment Management, Massachusetts College of Liberal Arts, 375 Church Street, North Adams, MA 01247-4100. Telephone: 413-662-5410 Ext. 5416 or toll-free 800-292-6632 (in-state). Fax: 413-662-5179. E-mail: admissions@mcla.mass.edu. Web site: http://www.mcla.edu/.

MASSACHUSETTS COLLEGE OF PHARMACY AND HEALTH SCIENCES
BOSTON, MASSACHUSETTS

General Independent, university, coed **Entrance** Moderately difficult **Setting** 2-acre urban campus **Total enrollment** 1,907 **Student-faculty ratio** 14:1 **Application deadline** 2/1 (freshmen), 3/1 (transfer) **Freshmen** 33% were admitted **Housing** Yes **Expenses** Tuition $18,221; Room & Board $8910 **Undergraduates** 67% women, 11% part-time **The most frequently chosen baccalaureate fields are** health professions and related sciences, physical sciences **Academic program** English as a second language, advanced placement, summer session, adult/continuing education programs, internships **Contact** Jim Zarakas, Admissions Assistant, Massachusetts College of Pharmacy and Health Sciences, 179 Longwood Avenue, Boston, MA 02115. Telephone: 617-732-2846 or toll-free 617-732-2850 (in-state); 800-225-5506 (out-of-state). Fax: 617-732-2801. E-mail: admissions@mcp.edu. Web site: http://www.mcp.edu/.

MASSACHUSETTS INSTITUTE OF TECHNOLOGY
CAMBRIDGE, MASSACHUSETTS

General Independent, university, coed **Entrance** Most difficult **Setting** 154-acre urban campus **Total enrollment** 10,204 **Student-faculty ratio** 7:1 **Application deadline** 1/1 (freshmen), 3/15 (transfer) **Freshmen** 17% were admitted **Housing** Yes **Expenses** Tuition $26,960; Room & Board $7500 **Undergraduates** 42% women, 2% part-time, 1% 25 or older, 2% Native American, 11% Hispanic American, 6% African American, 28% Asian American/Pacific Islander **The most frequently chosen baccalaureate fields are** computer/information sciences, biological/life sciences, engineering/engineering technologies **Academic program** English as a second language, advanced placement, accelerated degree program, self-designed majors, summer session, internships **Contact** Ms. Marilee Jones, Dean of Admissions, Massachusetts Institute of Technology, 77 Massachusetts Avenue, Cambridge, MA 02139-4307. Telephone: 617-253-4791. E-mail: mitfrosh@mit.edu. Web site: http://web.mit.edu/.

MASSACHUSETTS MARITIME ACADEMY
BUZZARDS BAY, MASSACHUSETTS

General State-supported, 4-year, coed, primarily men **Entrance** Moderately difficult **Setting** 55-acre small-town campus **Total enrollment** 831 **Student-faculty ratio** 12:1 **Application deadline** Rolling (freshmen), rolling (transfer) **Freshmen** 72% were admitted **Housing** Yes **Expenses** Tuition $4206; Room & Board $5763 **Undergraduates** 13% women, 6% part-time, 6% 25 or older **Academic program** Advanced placement, summer session, adult/continuing education programs, internships **Contact** Roy Fulgueras, Director of Admissions, Massachusetts Maritime Academy, 101 Academy Drive, Buzzards Bay, MA 02532-1803. Telephone: 508-830-5031 or toll-free 800-544-3411. Fax: 508-830-5077. E-mail: mmadmit@bridge.mma.mass.edu. Web site: http://www.mma.mass.edu/.

MERRIMACK COLLEGE
NORTH ANDOVER, MASSACHUSETTS

General Independent Roman Catholic, comprehensive, coed **Entrance** Moderately difficult **Setting** 220-acre suburban campus **Total enrollment** 2,593 **Student-faculty ratio** 14:1 **Application deadline** 2/15 (freshmen), 6/1 (transfer) **Freshmen** 63% were admitted **Housing** Yes **Expenses** Tuition $17,645; Room & Board $8080 **Undergraduates** 53% women, 18% part-time, 16% 25 or older, 0.1% Native American, 2% Hispanic American, 1% African American, 1% Asian American/Pacific Islander **The most frequently chosen baccalaureate fields are** business/marketing, psychology, social sciences and history **Academic program** English as a second language, advanced placement, self-designed majors, honors program, summer session, adult/continuing education programs, internships **Contact** Ms. MaryLou Retelle, Dean of Admissions and Financial Aid, Merrimack College, Austin Hall, A22, North Andover, MA 01845. Telephone: 978-837-5100 Ext. 5120. Fax: 978-837-5133. E-mail: admission@merrimack.edu. Web site: http://www.merrimack.edu/.

MONTSERRAT COLLEGE OF ART
BEVERLY, MASSACHUSETTS

General Independent, 4-year, coed **Entrance** Moderately difficult **Setting** 10-acre suburban campus **Total enrollment** 392 **Student-faculty ratio** 11:1 **Application deadline** 8/1 (freshmen), 8/1 (transfer) **Freshmen** 84% were admitted **Housing** Yes **Expenses** Tuition $15,490; Room only $4258 **Undergraduates** 58% women, 7% part-time, 5% 25 or older, 1% Native American, 2% Hispanic American, 1% Afri-

MASSACHUSETTS

can American, 3% Asian American/Pacific Islander **The most frequently chosen baccalaureate field is** visual/performing arts **Academic program** English as a second language, advanced placement, self-designed majors, summer session, adult/continuing education programs, internships **Contact** Mr. Stephen M. Negron, Director of Admissions, Montserrat College of Art, 41 Essex Street, Beverly, MA 01945. Telephone: 978-921-4242 Ext. 1153 or toll-free 800-836-0487. Fax: 978-921-4241. E-mail: admiss@montserrat.edu. Web site: http://www.montserrat.edu/.

MOUNT HOLYOKE COLLEGE
SOUTH HADLEY, MASSACHUSETTS

General Independent, comprehensive, women only **Entrance** Very difficult **Setting** 800-acre small-town campus **Total enrollment** 2,038 **Student-faculty ratio** 10:1 **Application deadline** 1/15 (freshmen), 5/15 (transfer) **Freshmen** 49% were admitted **Housing** Yes **Expenses** Tuition $26,408; Room & Board $7720 **Undergraduates** 3% part-time, 8% 25 or older, 0.5% Native American, 4% Hispanic American, 5% African American, 10% Asian American/Pacific Islander **The most frequently chosen baccalaureate fields are** psychology, English, social sciences and history **Academic program** Advanced placement, self-designed majors, honors program, adult/continuing education programs, internships **Contact** Ms. Diane Anci, Dean of Admission, Mount Holyoke College, 50 College Street, South Hadley, MA 01075. Telephone: 413-538-2023. Fax: 413-538-2409. E-mail: admission@mtholyoke.edu. Web site: http://www.mtholyoke.edu/.

MOUNT IDA COLLEGE
NEWTON CENTER, MASSACHUSETTS

General Independent, 4-year, coed **Entrance** Minimally difficult **Setting** 85-acre suburban campus **Total enrollment** 1,165 **Student-faculty ratio** 15:1 **Application deadline** Rolling (freshmen), rolling (transfer) **Freshmen** 31% were admitted **Housing** Yes **Expenses** Tuition $15,830; Room & Board $8950 **Undergraduates** 61% women, 15% part-time, 6% 25 or older, 1% Native American, 6% Hispanic American, 18% African American, 5% Asian American/Pacific Islander **Academic program** English as a second language, accelerated degree program, self-designed majors, honors program, adult/continuing education programs, internships **Contact** Ms. Nancy Lemelman, Director of Admissions, Mount Ida College, 777 Dedham Street, Newton, MA 02459. Telephone: 617-928-4500 Ext. 4508. E-mail: admissions@mountida.edu. Web site: http://www.mountida.edu/.

NEW ENGLAND CONSERVATORY OF MUSIC
BOSTON, MASSACHUSETTS

General Independent, comprehensive, coed **Entrance** Very difficult **Setting** urban campus **Total enrollment** 772 **Student-faculty ratio** 7:1 **Application deadline** 12/3 (freshmen), 12/3 (transfer) **Freshmen** 56% were admitted **Housing** Yes **Expenses** Tuition $21,800; Room & Board $9400 **Undergraduates** 47% women, 7% part-time, 4% 25 or older, 1% Native American, 3% Hispanic American, 4% African American, 9% Asian American/Pacific Islander **The most frequently chosen baccalaureate field is** visual/performing arts **Academic program** English as a second language, advanced placement, summer session, adult/continuing education programs, internships **Contact** Dean of Enrollment Services, New England Conservatory of Music, 290 Huntington Avenue, Boston, MA 02115-5000. Telephone: 617-585-1101. Fax: 617-585-1115. E-mail: admissions@newenglandconservatory.edu. Web site: http://www.newenglandconservatory.edu/.

NICHOLS COLLEGE
DUDLEY, MASSACHUSETTS

General Independent, comprehensive, coed **Entrance** Moderately difficult **Setting** 210-acre rural campus **Total enrollment** 1,363 **Student-faculty ratio** 18:1 **Application deadline** Rolling (freshmen), rolling (transfer) **Freshmen** 85% were admitted **Housing** Yes **Expenses** Tuition $15,650; Room & Board $7810 **Undergraduates** 47% women, 42% part-time, 5% 25 or older **The most frequently chosen baccalaureate fields are** business/marketing, English, psychology **Academic program** Advanced placement, summer session, adult/continuing education programs, internships **Contact** Susan Montville, Admissions Assistant, Nichols College, P.O. Box 5000, Office of Admissions, Dudley, MA 01571. Telephone: 508-943-2055 or toll-free 800-470-3379. Fax: 508-943-9885. E-mail: sibolesl@nichols.edu. Web site: http://www.nichols.edu/.

NORTHEASTERN UNIVERSITY
BOSTON, MASSACHUSETTS

General Independent, university, coed **Entrance** Moderately difficult **Setting** 60-acre urban campus **Total enrollment** 18,180 **Student-faculty ratio** 16:1 **Application deadline** Rolling (freshmen), rolling (transfer) **Freshmen** 63% were admitted **Housing** Yes **Expenses** Tuition $20,733; Room & Board $9345 **Undergraduates** 49% women, 3% 25 or older, 0.3% Native American, 4% Hispanic American, 5% African American, 7% Asian American/Pacific Islander **The most frequently chosen baccalaureate fields are** business/marketing, engineering/engineering technologies, health professions and related sciences **Academic program** English as a second language, advanced placement, accelerated degree program, self-designed majors, honors program, summer session, adult/continuing education programs, internships **Contact** Ronne A. Patrick, Director of Admissions, Northeastern University, 150 Richards Hall, Boston, MA 02115. Telephone: 617-373-2200. Fax: 617-373-8780. E-mail: admissions@neu.edu. Web site: http://www.northeastern.edu/.

▶ For more information, see page 461.

MASSACHUSETTS

PINE MANOR COLLEGE
CHESTNUT HILL, MASSACHUSETTS

General Independent, 4-year, women only **Entrance** Moderately difficult **Setting** 65-acre suburban campus **Total enrollment** 406 **Student-faculty ratio** 13:1 **Application deadline** Rolling (freshmen), rolling (transfer) **Freshmen** 73% were admitted **Housing** Yes **Expenses** Tuition $12,370; Room & Board $7748 **Undergraduates** 4% part-time, 5% 25 or older, 1% Native American, 14% Hispanic American, 21% African American, 3% Asian American/Pacific Islander **The most frequently chosen baccalaureate fields are** business/marketing, biological/life sciences, education **Academic program** English as a second language, advanced placement, self-designed majors, honors program, summer session, adult/continuing education programs, internships **Contact** Mr. Bill Nichols, Dean of Admissions, Pine Manor College, 400 Heath Street, Chestnut Hill, MA 02167-2332. Telephone: 617-731-7104 or toll-free 800-762-1357. Fax: 617-731-7199. E-mail: admisson@pmc.edu. Web site: http://www.pmc.edu/.

REGIS COLLEGE
WESTON, MASSACHUSETTS

General Independent Roman Catholic, comprehensive, women only **Entrance** Moderately difficult **Setting** 168-acre small-town campus **Total enrollment** 1,081 **Student-faculty ratio** 10:1 **Application deadline** Rolling (freshmen), rolling (transfer) **Freshmen** 82% were admitted **Housing** Yes **Expenses** Tuition $18,400; Room & Board $8350 **Undergraduates** 24% part-time, 12% 25 or older, 0% Native American, 7% Hispanic American, 6% African American, 5% Asian American/Pacific Islander **The most frequently chosen baccalaureate fields are** health professions and related sciences, communications/communication technologies, social sciences and history **Academic program** English as a second language, advanced placement, self-designed majors, honors program, summer session, adult/continuing education programs, internships **Contact** Dr. Leona McCaughey-Oreszak, Director of Admission, Regis College, 235 Wellesley Street, Weston, MA 02493. Telephone: 781-768-7100 or toll-free 800-456-1820. Fax: 781-768-7071. E-mail: admission@regiscollege.edu. Web site: http://www.regiscollege.edu/.

SAINT JOHN'S SEMINARY COLLEGE OF LIBERAL ARTS
BRIGHTON, MASSACHUSETTS

General Independent Roman Catholic, 4-year, men only **Entrance** Minimally difficult **Setting** 70-acre urban campus **Total enrollment** 26 **Student-faculty ratio** 4:1 **Application deadline** 8/1 (freshmen), 8/1 (transfer) **Housing** Yes **Expenses** Tuition $10,000; Room & Board $4000 **Undergraduates** 50% 25 or older, 8% Hispanic American, 8% Asian American/Pacific Islander **The most frequently chosen baccalaureate fields are** philosophy, philosophy, religion, and theology **Academic program** English as a second language, self-designed majors **Contact** Rev. Robert W. Flagg, Dean of the College, Saint John's Seminary College of Liberal Arts, 127 Lake Street, Brighton, MA 02135. Telephone: 617-746-5460. Fax: 617-746-5499.

SALEM STATE COLLEGE
SALEM, MASSACHUSETTS

General State-supported, comprehensive, coed **Entrance** Minimally difficult **Setting** 62-acre small-town campus **Total enrollment** 8,349 **Student-faculty ratio** 16:1 **Application deadline** Rolling (freshmen), rolling (transfer) **Freshmen** 69% were admitted **Housing** Yes **Expenses** Tuition $3038; Room & Board $5034 **Undergraduates** 63% women, 32% part-time, 18% 25 or older, 1% Native American, 3% Hispanic American, 4% African American, 1% Asian American/Pacific Islander **The most frequently chosen baccalaureate fields are** business/marketing, education, protective services/public administration **Academic program** English as a second language, advanced placement, self-designed majors, honors program, summer session, adult/continuing education programs, internships **Contact** Mr. Nate Bryant, Director of Admissions, Salem State College, 352 Lafayette Street, Salem, MA 01970-5353. Telephone: 978-542-6200. Web site: http://www.salemstate.edu/.

SCHOOL OF THE MUSEUM OF FINE ARTS
BOSTON, MASSACHUSETTS

General Independent, comprehensive, coed **Entrance** Moderately difficult **Setting** 14-acre urban campus **Total enrollment** 1,085 **Application deadline** 3/1 (freshmen), rolling (transfer) **Housing** Yes **Expenses** Tuition $19,676; Room & Board $9240 **Undergraduates** 26% 25 or older, 0.4% Native American, 3% Hispanic American, 1% African American, 6% Asian American/Pacific Islander **The most frequently chosen baccalaureate field is** visual/performing arts **Academic program** Self-designed majors, summer session, adult/continuing education programs, internships **Contact** Mr. John A. Williamson, Director of Enrollment and Student Services, School of the Museum of Fine Arts, 230 The Fenway, Boston, MA 02115. Telephone: 617-369-3626 or toll-free 800-643-6078 (in-state). Fax: 617-369-3679. E-mail: admissions@smfa.edu. Web site: http://www.smfa.edu/.

SIMMONS COLLEGE
BOSTON, MASSACHUSETTS

General Independent, comprehensive, women only **Entrance** Moderately difficult **Setting** 12-acre urban campus **Total enrollment** 3,282 **Student-faculty ratio** 10:1 **Application deadline** 2/1 (freshmen), 4/1 (transfer) **Freshmen** 68% were admitted **Housing** Yes **Expenses** Tuition $21,668; Room & Board $8750 **Undergraduates** 12% part-time, 16% 25 or older, 0.2% Native American, 4% Hispanic American, 7% African American, 5% Asian American/Pacific Islander **The most frequently chosen baccalaureate fields**

MASSACHUSETTS

are health professions and related sciences, communications/ communication technologies, social sciences and history **Academic program** English as a second language, advanced placement, accelerated degree program, self-designed majors, honors program, summer session, adult/continuing education programs, internships **Contact** Ms. Jennifer O'Loughlin Hieber, Interim Director of Undergraduate Admissions, Simmons College, 300 The Fenway, Boston, MA 02115. Telephone: 617-521-2051 or toll-free 800-345-8468 (out-of-state). Fax: 617-521-3190. E-mail: ugadm@simmons.edu. Web site: http://www.simmons.edu/.

SIMON'S ROCK COLLEGE OF BARD
GREAT BARRINGTON, MASSACHUSETTS

General Independent, 4-year, coed **Entrance** Very difficult **Setting** 275-acre rural campus **Total enrollment** 414 **Student-faculty ratio** 9:1 **Application deadline** 6/15 (freshmen), 7/15 (transfer) **Freshmen** 42% were admitted **Housing** Yes **Expenses** Tuition $25,610; Room & Board $6840 **Undergraduates** 57% women, 4% part-time, 0.2% 25 or older, 1% Native American, 3% Hispanic American, 3% African American, 7% Asian American/Pacific Islander **The most frequently chosen baccalaureate fields are** English, social sciences and history, visual/performing arts **Academic program** Self-designed majors, adult/continuing education programs, internships **Contact** Ms. Mary King Austin, Director of Admissions, Simon's Rock College of Bard, 84 Alford Road, Great Barrington, MA 01230-9702. Telephone: 413-528-7317 or toll-free 800-235-7186. Fax: 413-528-7334. E-mail: admit@simons-rock.edu. Web site: http://www.simons-rock.edu/.

SMITH COLLEGE
NORTHAMPTON, MASSACHUSETTS

General Independent, comprehensive, women only **Entrance** Very difficult **Setting** 125-acre urban campus **Total enrollment** 3,113 **Student-faculty ratio** 9:1 **Application deadline** 1/15 (freshmen), 6/1 (transfer) **Freshmen** 54% were admitted **Housing** Yes **Expenses** Tuition $24,550; Room & Board $8560 **Undergraduates** 2% part-time, 8% 25 or older, 1% Native American, 5% Hispanic American, 5% African American, 9% Asian American/Pacific Islander **The most frequently chosen baccalaureate fields are** biological/life sciences, social sciences and history, visual/performing arts **Academic program** Advanced placement, accelerated degree program, self-designed majors, honors program, adult/continuing education programs, internships **Contact** Ms. Audrey Y. Smith, Director of Admissions, Smith College, 7 College Lane, Northampton, MA 01063. Telephone: 413-585-2500. Fax: 413-585-2527. E-mail: admission@smith.edu. Web site: http://www.smith.edu/.

SPRINGFIELD COLLEGE
SPRINGFIELD, MASSACHUSETTS

General Independent, comprehensive, coed **Entrance** Moderately difficult **Setting** 167-acre suburban campus **Total enrollment** 2,939 **Student-faculty ratio** 12:1 **Application deadline** 4/1 (freshmen), 5/1 (transfer) **Freshmen** 72% were admitted **Housing** Yes **Expenses** Tuition $18,000; Room & Board $6520 **Undergraduates** 0.4% Native American, 3% Hispanic American, 4% African American, 1% Asian American/Pacific Islander **The most frequently chosen baccalaureate fields are** education, business/marketing, health professions and related sciences **Academic program** English as a second language, advanced placement, accelerated degree program, honors program, summer session, adult/continuing education programs, internships **Contact** Mary N. DeAngelo, Director of Undergraduate Admissions, Springfield College, 263 Alden Street, Box M, Springfield, MA 01109. Telephone: 413-748-3136 or toll-free 800-343-1257 (out-of-state). Fax: 413-748-3694. E-mail: admissions@spfldcol.edu. Web site: http://www.springfieldcollege.edu.

▶ **For more information, see page 479.**

STONEHILL COLLEGE
EASTON, MASSACHUSETTS

General Independent Roman Catholic, comprehensive, coed **Entrance** Very difficult **Setting** 375-acre suburban campus **Total enrollment** 2,622 **Student-faculty ratio** 14:1 **Application deadline** 1/15 (freshmen), 4/1 (transfer) **Freshmen** 43% were admitted **Housing** Yes **Expenses** Tuition $18,360; Room & Board $8492 **Undergraduates** 60% women, 17% part-time, 1% 25 or older, 0.3% Native American, 2% Hispanic American, 2% African American, 2% Asian American/Pacific Islander **The most frequently chosen baccalaureate fields are** business/marketing, education, social sciences and history **Academic program** Advanced placement, self-designed majors, honors program, summer session, adult/continuing education programs, internships **Contact** Mr. Brian P. Murphy, Dean of Admissions and Enrollment, Stonehill College, 320 Washington Street, Easton, MA 02357-5610. Telephone: 508-565-1373. Fax: 508-565-1545. E-mail: admissions@stonehill.edu. Web site: http://www.stonehill.edu/.

SUFFOLK UNIVERSITY
BOSTON, MASSACHUSETTS

General Independent, comprehensive, coed **Entrance** Moderately difficult **Setting** 2-acre urban campus **Total enrollment** 6,897 **Student-faculty ratio** 12:1 **Application deadline** Rolling (freshmen), rolling (transfer) **Freshmen** 83% were admitted **Housing** Yes **Expenses** Tuition $16,616; Room & Board $9990 **Undergraduates** 57% women, 20% part-time, 14% 25 or older, 0.2% Native American, 5% Hispanic American, 4% African American, 6% Asian American/Pacific Islander **The most frequently chosen baccalaureate fields are** business/marketing, communications/communication technologies, social sciences and history **Academic program** English as a second language, advanced placement, accelerated degree program, honors program, summer session, adult/continuing education programs, internships **Contact**

MASSACHUSETTS

Suffolk University *(continued)*
Mr. Walter Caffey, Dean of Enrollment Management, Suffolk University, 8 Ashburton Place, Boston, MA 02108. Telephone: 617-573-8460 or toll-free 800-6-SUFFOLK. Fax: 617-742-4291. E-mail: admission@admin.suffolk.edu. Web site: http://www.suffolk.edu/.

TUFTS UNIVERSITY
MEDFORD, MASSACHUSETTS

General Independent, university, coed **Entrance** Most difficult **Setting** 150-acre suburban campus **Total enrollment** 9,031 **Student-faculty ratio** 9:1 **Application deadline** 1/1 (freshmen), 3/1 (transfer) **Freshmen** 23% were admitted **Housing** Yes **Expenses** Tuition $26,892; Room & Board $7987 **Undergraduates** 54% women, 2% part-time, 0.2% Native American, 6% Hispanic American, 7% African American, 13% Asian American/Pacific Islander **The most frequently chosen baccalaureate fields are** engineering/engineering technologies, social sciences and history, visual/performing arts **Academic program** Advanced placement, self-designed majors, honors program, summer session, adult/continuing education programs, internships **Contact** Mr. David D. Cuttino, Dean of Undergraduate Admissions, Tufts University, Bendetson Hall, Medford, MA 02155. Telephone: 617-627-3170. Fax: 617-627-3860. E-mail: admissions.inquiry@ase.tufts.edu. Web site: http://www.tufts.edu/.

UNIVERSITY OF MASSACHUSETTS AMHERST
AMHERST, MASSACHUSETTS

General State-supported, university, coed **Entrance** Moderately difficult **Setting** 1,463-acre small-town campus **Total enrollment** 24,678 **Student-faculty ratio** 18:1 **Application deadline** 2/1 (freshmen), 5/1 (transfer) **Freshmen** 73% were admitted **Housing** Yes **Expenses** Tuition $5880; Room & Board $5115 **Undergraduates** 51% women, 8% part-time, 6% 25 or older, 0.4% Native American, 3% Hispanic American, 4% African American, 6% Asian American/Pacific Islander **The most frequently chosen baccalaureate fields are** business/marketing, communications/communication technologies, social sciences and history **Academic program** English as a second language, advanced placement, self-designed majors, honors program, summer session, adult/continuing education programs, internships **Contact** Mr. Joseph Marshall, Assistant Dean for Enrollment Services, University of Massachusetts Amherst, 37 Mather Drive, Amherst, MA 01003-9291. Telephone: 413-545-0222. Fax: 413-545-4312. E-mail: mail@admissions.umass.edu. Web site: http://www.umass.edu/.

UNIVERSITY OF MASSACHUSETTS BOSTON
BOSTON, MASSACHUSETTS

General State-supported, university, coed **Entrance** Moderately difficult **Setting** 177-acre urban campus **Total enrollment** 13,348 **Student-faculty ratio** 15:1 **Application deadline** Rolling (freshmen), rolling (transfer) **Freshmen** 58% were admitted **Housing** No **Expenses** Tuition $4222 **Undergraduates** 56% women, 44% part-time, 52% 25 or older, 0.4% Native American, 6% Hispanic American, 14% African American, 11% Asian American/Pacific Islander **The most frequently chosen baccalaureate fields are** law/legal studies, philosophy, religion, and theology **Academic program** English as a second language, advanced placement, accelerated degree program, self-designed majors, honors program, summer session, adult/continuing education programs, internships **Contact** Office of Admissions Information Service, University of Massachusetts Boston, Office of Undergraduate Admissions, 100 Morrissey Boulevard, Boston, MA 02125-3393. Telephone: 617-287-6100. Fax: 617-287-6242. E-mail: bos.admiss@umassp.edu. Web site: http://www.umb.edu/.

UNIVERSITY OF MASSACHUSETTS DARTMOUTH
NORTH DARTMOUTH, MASSACHUSETTS

General State-supported, comprehensive, coed **Entrance** Moderately difficult **Setting** 710-acre suburban campus **Total enrollment** 7,460 **Student-faculty ratio** 13:1 **Application deadline** Rolling (freshmen), rolling (transfer) **Freshmen** 67% were admitted **Housing** Yes **Expenses** Tuition $4129; Room & Board $5723 **Undergraduates** 53% women, 19% part-time, 10% 25 or older, 1% Native American, 2% Hispanic American, 6% African American, 2% Asian American/Pacific Islander **The most frequently chosen baccalaureate fields are** business/marketing, social sciences and history, visual/performing arts **Academic program** Advanced placement, self-designed majors, honors program, summer session, adult/continuing education programs, internships **Contact** Mr. Steven Briggs, Director of Admissions, University of Massachusetts Dartmouth, 285 Old Westport Road, North Dartmouth, MA 02747-2300. Telephone: 508-999-8606. Fax: 508-999-8755. E-mail: admissions@umassd.edu. Web site: http://www.umassd.edu/.

▶ For more information, see page 486.

UNIVERSITY OF MASSACHUSETTS LOWELL
LOWELL, MASSACHUSETTS

General State-supported, university, coed **Entrance** Moderately difficult **Setting** 100-acre urban campus **Total enrollment** 12,397 **Student-faculty ratio** 15:1 **Application deadline** Rolling (freshmen), rolling (transfer) **Freshmen** 70% were admitted **Housing** Yes **Expenses** Tuition $4255; Room & Board $5095 **Undergraduates** 41% women, 33% part-time, 16% 25 or older, 0.1% Native American, 3% Hispanic American, 2% African American, 7% Asian American/Pacific Islander **The most frequently chosen baccalaureate fields are** business/marketing, engineering/engineering technologies, protective services/public administration **Academic program** Advanced place-

MASSACHUSETTS

ment, accelerated degree program, honors program, summer session, adult/continuing education programs, internships **Contact** Ms. Lisa Johnson, Assistant Vice Chancellor of Enrollment Management, University of Massachusetts Lowell, 883 Broadway Street, Room 110, Lowell, MA 01854-5104. Telephone: 978-934-3944 or toll-free 800-410-4607. Fax: 978-934-3086. E-mail: admissions@uml.edu. Web site: http://www.uml.edu/.

UNIVERSITY OF PHOENIX–BOSTON CAMPUS
BRAINTREE, MASSACHUSETTS

General Proprietary, comprehensive, coed **Total enrollment** 88,730 **Student-faculty ratio** 8:1 **Application deadline** Rolling (freshmen), rolling (transfer) **Housing** No **Expenses** Tuition $10,350 **Undergraduates** 75% women, 70% 25 or older **Contact** Ms. Beth Barilla, Director of Admissions, University of Phoenix–Boston Campus, 4615 East Elwood Street, Phoenix, AZ 85040-1958. Telephone: 480-927-0099 Ext. 1218 or toll-free 800-228-7240. Fax: 480-594-1758. E-mail: beth.barilla@apollogrp.edu. Web site: http://www.phoenix.edu/.

WELLESLEY COLLEGE
WELLESLEY, MASSACHUSETTS

General Independent, 4-year, women only **Entrance** Most difficult **Setting** 500-acre suburban campus **Total enrollment** 2,273 **Student-faculty ratio** 9:1 **Application deadline** 1/15 (freshmen), 2/10 (transfer) **Freshmen** 43% were admitted **Housing** Yes **Expenses** Tuition $25,504; Room & Board $7890 **Undergraduates** 3% part-time, 5% 25 or older, 0.4% Native American, 5% Hispanic American, 6% African American, 25% Asian American/Pacific Islander **The most frequently chosen baccalaureate fields are** psychology, English, social sciences and history **Academic program** Advanced placement, self-designed majors, summer session, adult/continuing education programs, internships **Contact** Ms. Janet Lavin Rapelye, Dean of Admission, Wellesley College, 106 Central Street, Wellesley, MA 02481-8203. Telephone: 781-283-2270. Fax: 781-283-3678. E-mail: admission@wellesley.edu. Web site: http://www.wellesley.edu/.

WENTWORTH INSTITUTE OF TECHNOLOGY
BOSTON, MASSACHUSETTS

General Independent, 4-year, coed **Entrance** Moderately difficult **Setting** 35-acre urban campus **Total enrollment** 3,273 **Student-faculty ratio** 24:1 **Application deadline** Rolling (freshmen), rolling (transfer) **Freshmen** 70% were admitted **Housing** Yes **Expenses** Tuition $13,650; Room & Board $7400 **Undergraduates** 18% women, 23% part-time, 0.3% Native American, 4% Hispanic American, 5% African American, 6% Asian American/Pacific Islander **The most frequently chosen baccalaureate fields are** computer/information sciences, engineering/ engineering technologies, visual/performing arts **Academic program** English as a second language, advanced placement, accelerated degree program, summer session, internships **Contact** Ms. Keiko S. Broomhead, Director of Admissions, Wentworth Institute of Technology, 550 Huntington Avenue, Boston, MA 02115-5998. Telephone: 617-989-4009 or toll-free 800-556-0610. Fax: 617-989-4010. E-mail: admissions@wit.edu. Web site: http://www.wit.edu/.

▶ **For more information, see page 497.**

WESTERN NEW ENGLAND COLLEGE
SPRINGFIELD, MASSACHUSETTS

General Independent, comprehensive, coed **Entrance** Moderately difficult **Setting** 185-acre suburban campus **Total enrollment** 4,540 **Student-faculty ratio** 17:1 **Application deadline** Rolling (freshmen), rolling (transfer) **Freshmen** 74% were admitted **Housing** Yes **Expenses** Tuition $16,494; Room & Board $7388 **Undergraduates** 36% women, 33% part-time **The most frequently chosen baccalaureate fields are** business/marketing, engineering/engineering technologies, protective services/public administration **Academic program** Advanced placement, self-designed majors, honors program, summer session, adult/continuing education programs, internships **Contact** Dr. Charles R. Pollock, Vice President of Enrollment Management, Western New England College, 1215 Wilbraham Road, Springfield, MA 01119. Telephone: 413-782-1321 or toll-free 800-325-1122 Ext. 1321. Fax: 413-782-1777. E-mail: ugradmis@wnec.edu. Web site: http://www.wnec.edu/.

WESTFIELD STATE COLLEGE
WESTFIELD, MASSACHUSETTS

General State-supported, comprehensive, coed **Entrance** Moderately difficult **Setting** 227-acre small-town campus **Total enrollment** 5,153 **Student-faculty ratio** 18:1 **Application deadline** 3/1 (freshmen), 4/1 (transfer) **Freshmen** 67% were admitted **Housing** Yes **Expenses** Tuition $2956; Room & Board $4789 **Undergraduates** 56% women, 17% part-time, 24% 25 or older, 0.2% Native American, 2% Hispanic American, 3% African American, 1% Asian American/Pacific Islander **The most frequently chosen baccalaureate fields are** education, business/marketing, protective services/public administration **Academic program** Advanced placement, accelerated degree program, self-designed majors, honors program, summer session, adult/continuing education programs, internships **Contact** Ms. Michelle Mattie, Director of Student Administrative Services, Westfield State College, 333 Western Avenue, Westfield, MA 01086. Telephone: 413-572-5218 or toll-free 800-322-8401 (in-state). Fax: 413-572-0520. E-mail: admission@wsc.mass.edu. Web site: http://www.wsc.ma.edu/.

WHEATON COLLEGE
NORTON, MASSACHUSETTS

General Independent, 4-year, coed **Entrance** Moderately difficult **Setting** 385-acre small-town campus

MASSACHUSETTS

Wheaton College (continued)
Total enrollment 1,551 **Student-faculty ratio** 12:1 **Application deadline** 1/15 (freshmen), 4/1 (transfer) **Freshmen** 61% were admitted **Housing** Yes **Expenses** Tuition $25,790; Room & Board $7150 **Undergraduates** 65% women, 1% part-time, 0% 25 or older, 0.3% Native American, 3% Hispanic American, 3% African American, 2% Asian American/Pacific Islander **The most frequently chosen baccalaureate fields are** psychology, English, social sciences and history **Academic program** Advanced placement, accelerated degree program, self-designed majors, honors program, adult/continuing education programs, internships **Contact** Ms. Lynne M. Stack, Director of Admission, Wheaton College, East Main Street, Norton, MA 02766. Telephone: 508-286-8251 or toll-free 800-394-6003. Fax: 508-286-8271. E-mail: admission@wheatonma.edu. Web site: http://www.wheatoncollege.edu/.

WHEELOCK COLLEGE
BOSTON, MASSACHUSETTS

General Independent, comprehensive, coed, primarily women **Entrance** Moderately difficult **Setting** 5-acre urban campus **Total enrollment** 1,090 **Student-faculty ratio** 11:1 **Application deadline** 3/1 (freshmen), 4/15 (transfer) **Freshmen** 81% were admitted **Housing** Yes **Expenses** Tuition $18,195; Room & Board $7325 **Undergraduates** 94% women, 1% part-time, 6% 25 or older, 1% Native American, 4% Hispanic American, 5% African American, 2% Asian American/Pacific Islander **The most frequently chosen baccalaureate fields are** education, health professions and related services, protective services/public administration **Academic program** Advanced placement, honors program, internships **Contact** Ms. Lynne E. Dailey, Dean of Admissions, Wheelock College, 200 The Riverway, Boston, MA 02215. Telephone: 617-879-2204 or toll-free 800-734-5212 (out-of-state). Fax: 617-566-4453. E-mail: undergrad@wheelock.edu. Web site: http://www.wheelock.edu/.

WILLIAMS COLLEGE
WILLIAMSTOWN, MASSACHUSETTS

General Independent, comprehensive, coed **Entrance** Most difficult **Setting** 450-acre small-town campus **Total enrollment** 2,048 **Student-faculty ratio** 9:1 **Application deadline** 1/1 (freshmen), 1/1 (transfer) **Freshmen** 24% were admitted **Housing** Yes **Expenses** Tuition $25,540; Room & Board $6930 **Undergraduates** 48% women, 2% part-time, 0% 25 or older, 0.4% Native American, 7% Hispanic American, 7% African American, 8% Asian American/Pacific Islander **The most frequently chosen baccalaureate fields are** psychology, English, social sciences and history **Academic program** Advanced placement, accelerated degree program, self-designed majors, honors program, internships **Contact** Mr. Richard L. Nesbitt, Director of Admission, Williams College, 988 Main Street, Williamstown, MA 01267. Telephone: 413-597-2211. Fax: 413-597-4052. E-mail: admission@williams.edu. Web site: http://www.williams.edu/.

WORCESTER POLYTECHNIC INSTITUTE
WORCESTER, MASSACHUSETTS

General Independent, university, coed **Entrance** Very difficult **Setting** 80-acre suburban campus **Total enrollment** 3,887 **Student-faculty ratio** 13:1 **Application deadline** 2/1 (freshmen), 4/15 (transfer) **Freshmen** 74% were admitted **Housing** Yes **Expenses** Tuition $24,890; Room & Board $7900 **Undergraduates** 23% women, 4% part-time, 3% 25 or older, 0.3% Native American, 3% Hispanic American, 1% African American, 7% Asian American/Pacific Islander **The most frequently chosen baccalaureate fields are** computer/information sciences, biological/life sciences, engineering/engineering technologies **Academic program** English as a second language, advanced placement, accelerated degree program, self-designed majors, summer session, adult/continuing education programs **Contact** Ms. Kristin Tichenor, Director of Admissions, Worcester Polytechnic Institute, 100 Institute Road, Worcester, MA 01609-2280. Telephone: 508-831-5286. Fax: 508-831-5875. E-mail: admissions@wpi.edu. Web site: http://www.wpi.edu/.

WORCESTER STATE COLLEGE
WORCESTER, MASSACHUSETTS

General State-supported, comprehensive, coed **Entrance** Moderately difficult **Setting** 53-acre urban campus **Total enrollment** 5,768 **Student-faculty ratio** 19:1 **Application deadline** 8/1 (freshmen), 8/1 (transfer) **Freshmen** 54% were admitted **Housing** Yes **Expenses** Tuition $2430; Room & Board $5186 **Undergraduates** 62% women, 37% part-time, 34% 25 or older **The most frequently chosen baccalaureate fields are** business/marketing, health professions and related sciences, psychology **Academic program** Advanced placement, accelerated degree program, honors program, summer session, adult/continuing education programs, internships **Contact** Ms. Elizabeth Axelson, Associate Director, Admissions, Worcester State College, 486 Chandler Street, Administration Building, Room 204, Worcester, MA 01602-2597. Telephone: 508-929-8040. Fax: 508-929-8131. E-mail: admissions@worcester.edu. Web site: http://www.worcester.edu/.

MICHIGAN

ADRIAN COLLEGE
ADRIAN, MICHIGAN

General Independent, 4-year, coed, affiliated with United Methodist Church **Entrance** Moderately difficult **Setting** 100-acre small-town campus **Total enrollment** 1,055 **Student-faculty ratio** 15:1 **Application deadline** 8/1 (freshmen), 8/1 (transfer) **Freshmen** 90% were admitted **Housing** Yes **Expenses** Tuition $14,850; Room & Board $4850 **Undergraduates** 57% women, 5% part-time, 1% 25 or older,

MICHIGAN

0.1% Native American, 1% Hispanic American, 5% African American, 1% Asian American/Pacific Islander **The most frequently chosen baccalaureate fields are** business/marketing, English, social sciences and history **Academic program** English as a second language, advanced placement, self-designed majors, honors program, summer session, adult/continuing education programs, internships **Contact** Ms. Janel Sutkus, Director of Admissions, Adrian College, 110 South Madison Street, Adrian, MI 49221. Telephone: 517-265-5161 Ext. 4326 or toll-free 800-877-2246. Fax: 517-264-3331. E-mail: admissions@adrian.edu. Web site: http://www.adrian.edu/.

ALBION COLLEGE
ALBION, MICHIGAN

General Independent Methodist, 4-year, coed **Entrance** Moderately difficult **Setting** 225-acre small-town campus **Total enrollment** 1,548 **Student-faculty ratio** 12:1 **Application deadline** 5/1 (freshmen), rolling (transfer) **Freshmen** 87% were admitted **Housing** Yes **Expenses** Tuition $19,620; Room & Board $5604 **Undergraduates** 56% women, 0.3% part-time, 2% 25 or older, 0.3% Native American, 1% Hispanic American, 2% African American, 2% Asian American/Pacific Islander **The most frequently chosen baccalaureate fields are** business/marketing, biological/life sciences, social sciences and history **Academic program** Advanced placement, self-designed majors, honors program, summer session, internships **Contact** Doug Kellar, Associate Vice President for Enrollment, Albion College, 611 East Porter Street, Albion, MI 49224. Telephone: 517-629-0600 or toll-free 800-858-6770. E-mail: admissions@albion.edu. Web site: http://www.albion.edu/.

ALMA COLLEGE
ALMA, MICHIGAN

General Independent Presbyterian, 4-year, coed **Entrance** Moderately difficult **Setting** 100-acre small-town campus **Total enrollment** 1,366 **Student-faculty ratio** 13:1 **Application deadline** Rolling (freshmen), rolling (transfer) **Freshmen** 82% were admitted **Housing** Yes **Expenses** Tuition $16,602; Room & Board $5984 **Undergraduates** 59% women, 3% part-time, 2% 25 or older, 1% Native American, 2% Hispanic American, 1% African American, 1% Asian American/Pacific Islander **The most frequently chosen baccalaureate fields are** business/marketing, education, social sciences and history **Academic program** English as a second language, advanced placement, accelerated degree program, self-designed majors, summer session, adult/continuing education programs, internships **Contact** Mr. Paul Pollatz, Director of Admissions, Alma College, Admissions Office, Alma, MI 48801-1599. Telephone: 989-463-7139 or toll-free 800-321-ALMA. Fax: 989-463-7057. E-mail: admissions@alma.edu. Web site: http://www.alma.edu/.

▶ For more information, see page 394.

ANDREWS UNIVERSITY
BERRIEN SPRINGS, MICHIGAN

General Independent Seventh-day Adventist, university, coed **Entrance** Moderately difficult **Setting** 1,650-acre small-town campus **Total enrollment** 2,721 **Student-faculty ratio** 10:1 **Application deadline** Rolling (freshmen), rolling (transfer) **Freshmen** 55% were admitted **Housing** Yes **Expenses** Tuition $13,676; Room & Board $4420 **Undergraduates** 56% women, 19% part-time, 17% 25 or older, 0.2% Native American, 11% Hispanic American, 21% African American, 8% Asian American/Pacific Islander **The most frequently chosen baccalaureate fields are** biological/life sciences, business/marketing, health professions and related sciences **Academic program** English as a second language, advanced placement, accelerated degree program, self-designed majors, honors program, summer session, adult/continuing education programs, internships **Contact** Ms. Charlotte Coy, Admissions Supervisor, Andrews University, Berrien Springs, MI 49104. Telephone: 616-471-7771 or toll-free 800-253-2874. Fax: 616-471-3228. E-mail: enroll@andrews.edu. Web site: http://www.andrews.edu/.

AQUINAS COLLEGE
GRAND RAPIDS, MICHIGAN

General Independent Roman Catholic, comprehensive, coed **Entrance** Moderately difficult **Setting** 107-acre suburban campus **Total enrollment** 2,571 **Student-faculty ratio** 16:1 **Application deadline** Rolling (freshmen), rolling (transfer) **Freshmen** 89% were admitted **Housing** Yes **Expenses** Tuition $14,876; Room & Board $5176 **Undergraduates** 68% women, 22% part-time, 1% 25 or older, 0.4% Native American, 3% Hispanic American, 4% African American, 1% Asian American/Pacific Islander **The most frequently chosen baccalaureate fields are** business/marketing, education, psychology **Academic program** Advanced placement, accelerated degree program, self-designed majors, honors program, summer session, adult/continuing education programs, internships **Contact** Ms. Amy Sprouse, Applications Specialist, Aquinas College, 1607 Robinson Road, SE, Grand Rapids, MI 49506-1799. Telephone: 616-732-4460 Ext. 5150 or toll-free 800-678-9593. Fax: 616-732-4469. E-mail: admissions@aquinas.edu. Web site: http://www.aquinas.edu/.

▶ For more information, see page 395.

AVE MARIA COLLEGE
YPSILANTI, MICHIGAN

General Independent Roman Catholic, 4-year, coed **Entrance** Very difficult **Total enrollment** 187 **Student-faculty ratio** 10:1 **Freshmen** 83% were admitted **Housing** Yes **Expenses** Tuition $7200; Room & Board $3200 **Undergraduates** 58% women, 16% part-time, 11% 25 or older, 0% Native American, 3% Hispanic American, 1% African American, 0% Asian American/Pacific Islander **Contact** Admissions Office Manager, Ave Maria College, 300 West

MICHIGAN

Ave Maria College *(continued)*
Forest, Ypsilanti, MI 48197. Telephone: 734-337-4545 or toll-free 866-866-3030 (out-of-state). Fax: 734-337-4140. E-mail: admissions@avemaria.edu. Web site: http://www.avemaria.edu/.

BAKER COLLEGE OF AUBURN HILLS
AUBURN HILLS, MICHIGAN

General Independent, 4-year, coed **Entrance** Noncompetitive **Setting** 7-acre urban campus **Total enrollment** 2,192 **Student-faculty ratio** 22:1 **Application deadline** Rolling (freshmen), rolling (transfer) **Freshmen** 100% were admitted **Housing** No **Expenses** Tuition $5580 **Undergraduates** 65% women, 46% part-time, 41% 25 or older **Academic program** Advanced placement, accelerated degree program, summer session, internships **Contact** Ms. Jan Bohlen, Vice President for Admissions, Baker College of Auburn Hills, 1500 University Drive, Auburn Hills, MI 48326-1586. Telephone: 248-340-0600 or toll-free 888-429-0410 (in-state). Fax: 248-340-0608. E-mail: bohlen_j@auburnhills.baker.edu. Web site: http://www.baker.edu/.

BAKER COLLEGE OF CADILLAC
CADILLAC, MICHIGAN

General Independent, 4-year, coed **Entrance** Noncompetitive **Setting** 40-acre small-town campus **Total enrollment** 1,021 **Student-faculty ratio** 16:1 **Application deadline** Rolling (freshmen), rolling (transfer) **Freshmen** 100% were admitted **Housing** No **Expenses** Tuition $5580 **Undergraduates** 72% women, 43% part-time, 56% 25 or older, 0.1% Native American, 0.4% Hispanic American, 0.1% African American, 0.1% Asian American/Pacific Islander **Academic program** Advanced placement, summer session, internships **Contact** Eric Runstrom, Vice President for Admissions, Baker College of Cadillac, 9600 East 13th Street, Cadillac, MI 49601. Telephone: 616-775-8458 or toll-free 888-313-3463 (in-state); 231-876-3100 (out-of-state). Fax: 231-775-8505. E-mail: runstr_e@cadillac.baker.edu. Web site: http://www.baker.edu/.

BAKER COLLEGE OF CLINTON TOWNSHIP
CLINTON TOWNSHIP, MICHIGAN

General Independent, 4-year, coed **Entrance** Noncompetitive **Setting** urban campus **Total enrollment** 3,091 **Student-faculty ratio** 19:1 **Application deadline** Rolling (freshmen), rolling (transfer) **Freshmen** 100% were admitted **Housing** No **Expenses** Tuition $5580 **Undergraduates** 77% women, 46% part-time, 42% 25 or older, 1% Native American, 1% Hispanic American, 16% African American, 2% Asian American/Pacific Islander **Academic program** Advanced placement, summer session, internships **Contact** Ms. Annette M. Looser, Vice President for Admissions, Baker College of Clinton Township, 34950 Little Mack Avenue, Clinton Township, MI 48035. Telephone: 810-791-6610 or toll-free 888-272-2842. Fax: 810-791-6611. E-mail: looser_a@mtclemens.baker.edu. Web site: http://www.baker.edu/.

BAKER COLLEGE OF FLINT
FLINT, MICHIGAN

General Independent, 4-year, coed **Entrance** Noncompetitive **Setting** 30-acre urban campus **Total enrollment** 4,399 **Student-faculty ratio** 37:1 **Application deadline** 9/20 (freshmen), 9/20 (transfer) **Freshmen** 100% were admitted **Housing** Yes **Expenses** Tuition $5580; Room only $1950 **Undergraduates** 1% Native American, 2% Hispanic American, 22% African American, 2% Asian American/Pacific Islander **Academic program** Advanced placement, accelerated degree program, summer session, internships **Contact** Mr. Mark Heaton, Vice President for Admissions, Baker College of Flint, 1050 West Bristol Road, Flint, MI 48507-5508. Telephone: 810-766-4015 or toll-free 800-964-4299. Fax: 810-766-4049. E-mail: heaton_m@fafl.baker.edu. Web site: http://www.baker.edu/.

BAKER COLLEGE OF JACKSON
JACKSON, MICHIGAN

General Independent, 4-year, coed **Entrance** Noncompetitive **Setting** 42-acre urban campus **Total enrollment** 1,238 **Student-faculty ratio** 13:1 **Application deadline** 9/19 (freshmen), rolling (transfer) **Freshmen** 100% were admitted **Housing** Yes **Expenses** Tuition $5580; Room only $1950 **Undergraduates** 56% 25 or older, 1% Native American, 2% Hispanic American, 7% African American, 1% Asian American/Pacific Islander **Academic program** Advanced placement, accelerated degree program, summer session, internships **Contact** Ms. Kelli Hoban, Director of Admissions, Baker College of Jackson, 2800 Springport Road, Jackson, MI 49202. Telephone: 517-788-7800 or toll-free 888-343-3683. Fax: 517-789-7331. E-mail: hoban_k@jackson.baker.edu. Web site: http://www.baker.edu/.

BAKER COLLEGE OF MUSKEGON
MUSKEGON, MICHIGAN

General Independent, 4-year, coed **Entrance** Noncompetitive **Setting** 40-acre suburban campus **Total enrollment** 2,924 **Student-faculty ratio** 30:1 **Application deadline** 9/24 (freshmen), rolling (transfer) **Freshmen** 100% were admitted **Housing** Yes **Expenses** Tuition $5580; Room only $1950 **Undergraduates** 45% 25 or older, 1% Native American, 4% Hispanic American, 13% African American, 1% Asian American/Pacific Islander **Academic program** Advanced placement, accelerated degree program, summer session, adult/continuing education programs, internships **Contact** Ms. Kathy Jacobson, Director of Admissions, Baker College of Muskegon, 1903 Marquette Avenue, Muskegon, MI 49442-3497. Telephone: 231-777-5207 or toll-free 800-937-0337 (in-state). Fax: 231-777-5201. E-mail: jacobs_k@muskegon.baker.edu. Web site: http://www.baker.edu/.

MICHIGAN

BAKER COLLEGE OF OWOSSO
OWOSSO, MICHIGAN

General Independent, 4-year, coed **Entrance** Noncompetitive **Setting** 32-acre small-town campus **Total enrollment** 2,062 **Student-faculty ratio** 38:1 **Application deadline** Rolling (freshmen), rolling (transfer) **Freshmen** 100% were admitted **Housing** Yes **Expenses** Tuition $5580 **Undergraduates** 66% women, 39% part-time, 41% 25 or older, 1% Native American, 2% Hispanic American, 1% African American, 0.2% Asian American/Pacific Islander **Academic program** Advanced placement, accelerated degree program, summer session, adult/continuing education programs, internships **Contact** Mr. Michael Konopacke, Director, Baker College of Owosso, 1020 South Washington Street, Owosso, MI 48867-4400. Telephone: 517-729-3353 or toll-free 800-879-3797. Fax: 517-729-3359. E-mail: konopa-_m@owosso.baker.edu. Web site: http://www.baker.edu/.

BAKER COLLEGE OF PORT HURON
PORT HURON, MICHIGAN

General Independent, 4-year, coed **Entrance** Noncompetitive **Setting** 10-acre urban campus **Total enrollment** 1,301 **Student-faculty ratio** 13:1 **Application deadline** 9/24 (freshmen), rolling (transfer) **Freshmen** 100% were admitted **Housing** No **Expenses** Tuition $5580 **Undergraduates** 77% women, 48% part-time, 51% 25 or older, 1% Native American, 2% Hispanic American, 4% African American, 0.5% Asian American/Pacific Islander **Academic program** Advanced placement, accelerated degree program, summer session, internships **Contact** Mr. Daniel Kenny, Director of Admissions, Baker College of Port Huron, 3403 Lapeer Road, Port Huron, MI 48060-2597. Telephone: 810-985-7000 or toll-free 888-262-2442. Fax: 810-985-7066. E-mail: kenny_d@porthuron.baker.edu. Web site: http://www.baker.edu/.

CALVIN COLLEGE
GRAND RAPIDS, MICHIGAN

General Independent, comprehensive, coed, affiliated with Christian Reformed Church **Entrance** Moderately difficult **Setting** 370-acre suburban campus **Total enrollment** 4,258 **Student-faculty ratio** 15:1 **Application deadline** 8/15 (freshmen), rolling (transfer) **Freshmen** 98% were admitted **Housing** Yes **Expenses** Tuition $14,870; Room & Board $5180 **Undergraduates** 56% women, 5% part-time, 2% 25 or older, 0.4% Native American, 1% Hispanic American, 1% African American, 2% Asian American/Pacific Islander **The most frequently chosen baccalaureate fields are** business/marketing, education, social sciences and history **Academic program** English as a second language, advanced placement, accelerated degree program, self-designed majors, honors program, summer session, adult/continuing education programs, internships **Contact** Mr. Dale D. Kuiper, Director of Admissions, Calvin College, 3201 Burton Street, SE, Grand Rapids, MI 49546-

4388. Telephone: 616-957-6106 or toll-free 800-688-0122. Fax: 616-957-6777. E-mail: admissions@calvin.edu. Web site: http://www.calvin.edu/.

▶ For more information, see page 405.

CENTER FOR CREATIVE STUDIES-COLLEGE OF ART AND DESIGN
See College for Creative Studies

CENTRAL MICHIGAN UNIVERSITY
MOUNT PLEASANT, MICHIGAN

General State-supported, university, coed **Entrance** Moderately difficult **Setting** 854-acre small-town campus **Total enrollment** 27,797 **Student-faculty ratio** 23:1 **Application deadline** Rolling (freshmen), rolling (transfer) **Freshmen** 83% were admitted **Housing** Yes **Expenses** Tuition $4366; Room & Board $5220 **Undergraduates** 60% women, 15% part-time, 6% 25 or older, 1% Native American, 2% Hispanic American, 6% African American, 1% Asian American/Pacific Islander **The most frequently chosen baccalaureate fields are** business/marketing, education, social sciences and history **Academic program** English as a second language, advanced placement, accelerated degree program, self-designed majors, honors program, summer session, adult/continuing education programs, internships **Contact** Mrs. Betty J. Wagner, Director of Admissions, Central Michigan University, Office of Admissions, 105 Warriner Hall, Mt. Pleasant, MI 48859. Telephone: 989-774-3076. Fax: 989-774-7267. E-mail: cmuadmit@cmich.edu. Web site: http://www.cmich.edu/.

CLEARY UNIVERSITY
ANN ARBOR, MICHIGAN

General Independent, comprehensive, coed **Entrance** Moderately difficult **Setting** 27-acre small-town campus **Total enrollment** 900 **Student-faculty ratio** 10:1 **Application deadline** Rolling (freshmen), rolling (transfer) **Housing** No **Expenses** Tuition $9230 **Undergraduates** 84% 25 or older, 1% Native American, 0.5% Hispanic American, 7% African American, 1% Asian American/Pacific Islander **Academic program** Advanced placement, accelerated degree program, summer session, adult/continuing education programs, internships **Contact** Ms. Mary Krowleski, Admissions Representative, Cleary University, 3750 Cleary College Drive, Howell, MI 48843. Telephone: 517-548-3670 Ext. 2215 or toll-free 888-5-CLEARY (in-state); 888-5-CLEARY Ext. 2249 (out-of-state). Fax: 517-552-7805. E-mail: admissions@cleary.edu. Web site: http://www.cleary.edu/.

▶ For more information, see page 414.

COLLEGE FOR CREATIVE STUDIES
DETROIT, MICHIGAN

General Independent, 4-year, coed **Entrance** Moderately difficult **Setting** 11-acre urban campus **Total enrollment** 1,152 **Student-faculty ratio** 9:1 **Application deadline** Rolling (freshmen), rolling (trans-

MICHIGAN

College for Creative Studies (continued)

fer) **Freshmen** 79% were admitted **Housing** Yes **Expenses** Tuition $17,638; Room only $3300 **Undergraduates** 41% women, 16% part-time, 22% 25 or older, 0.2% Native American, 3% Hispanic American, 7% African American, 5% Asian American/Pacific Islander **The most frequently chosen baccalaureate field is** visual/performing arts **Academic program** English as a second language, advanced placement, summer session, internships **Contact** Office of Admissions, College for Creative Studies, 201 East Kirby, Detroit, MI 48202-4034. Telephone: 313-664-7425 or toll-free 800-952-ARTS. Fax: 313-872-2739. E-mail: admissions@ccscad.org. Web site: http://www.ccscad.edu/.

CONCORDIA UNIVERSITY
ANN ARBOR, MICHIGAN

General Independent, comprehensive, coed, affiliated with Lutheran Church–Missouri Synod **Entrance** Moderately difficult **Setting** 234-acre suburban campus **Total enrollment** 568 **Student-faculty ratio** 11:1 **Application deadline** Rolling (freshmen), rolling (transfer) **Freshmen** 86% were admitted **Housing** Yes **Expenses** Tuition $14,700; Room & Board $5800 **Undergraduates** 56% women, 14% part-time, 21% 25 or older, 1% Native American, 2% Hispanic American, 9% African American, 0.4% Asian American/Pacific Islander **The most frequently chosen baccalaureate fields are** business/marketing, education, health professions and related sciences **Academic program** Advanced placement, accelerated degree program, self-designed majors, summer session, adult/continuing education programs, internships **Contact** Ms. Kathleen Rowe, Director of Admissions, Concordia University, 4090 Geddes Road, Ann Arbor, MI 48105. Telephone: 734-995-7322 Ext. 7211 or toll-free 800-253-0680. Fax: 734-995-7455. E-mail: admissions@cuaa.edu. Web site: http://www.cuaa.edu/.

CORNERSTONE UNIVERSITY
GRAND RAPIDS, MICHIGAN

General Independent nondenominational, 4-year, coed **Entrance** Moderately difficult **Setting** 132-acre suburban campus **Total enrollment** 1,937 **Student-faculty ratio** 16:1 **Application deadline** Rolling (freshmen), rolling (transfer) **Freshmen** 96% were admitted **Housing** Yes **Expenses** Tuition $12,005; Room & Board $4830 **Undergraduates** 61% women, 11% part-time, 5% 25 or older, 0.3% Native American, 2% Hispanic American, 7% African American, 0.4% Asian American/Pacific Islander **The most frequently chosen baccalaureate fields are** business/marketing, education, English **Academic program** Advanced placement, accelerated degree program, summer session, adult/continuing education programs, internships **Contact** Mr. Brent Rudin, Director of Admissions, Cornerstone University, 1001 East Beltline Avenue, NE, Grand Rapids, MI 49525. Telephone: 616-222-1426 or toll-free 800-787-9778. Fax: 616-222-1400. E-mail: admissions@cornerstone.edu. Web site: http://www.cornerstone.edu/.

DAVENPORT UNIVERSITY
DEARBORN, MICHIGAN

General Independent, comprehensive, coed **Entrance** Noncompetitive **Setting** 17-acre suburban campus **Total enrollment** 3,138 **Student-faculty ratio** 24:1 **Application deadline** Rolling (freshmen), rolling (transfer) **Freshmen** 100% were admitted **Housing** No **Expenses** Tuition $7449 **Undergraduates** 75% women, 46% part-time, 70% 25 or older, 1% Native American, 2% Hispanic American, 60% African American, 2% Asian American/Pacific Islander **The most frequently chosen baccalaureate fields are** business/marketing, health professions and related sciences **Academic program** Advanced placement, summer session, internships **Contact** Ms. Jennifer Salloum, Director of Admissions, Davenport University, 4801 Oakman Boulevard, Dearborn, MI 48126-3799. Telephone: 313-581-4400. Fax: 313-581-1985. E-mail: jennifer.salloum@davenport.edu. Web site: http://www.davenport.edu/.

DAVENPORT UNIVERSITY
GRAND RAPIDS, MICHIGAN

General Independent, comprehensive, coed **Entrance** Noncompetitive **Setting** 5-acre urban campus **Total enrollment** 1,743 **Student-faculty ratio** 19:1 **Application deadline** Rolling (freshmen), rolling (transfer) **Freshmen** 65% were admitted **Housing** Yes **Expenses** Tuition $8691; Room only $7335 **Undergraduates** 63% women, 57% part-time, 45% 25 or older, 1% Native American, 4% Hispanic American, 9% African American, 4% Asian American/Pacific Islander **The most frequently chosen baccalaureate field is** law/legal studies **Academic program** English as a second language, advanced placement, accelerated degree program, summer session, adult/continuing education programs, internships **Contact** Mr. Paul David, Director of Admissions, Davenport University, 415 East Fulton, Grand Rapids, MI 49503. Telephone: 616-732-1200 or toll-free 800-632-9569 (out-of-state). Web site: http://www.davenport.edu/.

DAVENPORT UNIVERSITY
KALAMAZOO, MICHIGAN

General Independent, 4-year, coed **Entrance** Noncompetitive **Setting** 5-acre suburban campus **Total enrollment** 1,063 **Student-faculty ratio** 13:1 **Application deadline** Rolling (freshmen), rolling (transfer) **Freshmen** 100% were admitted **Housing** No **Expenses** Tuition $9645 **Undergraduates** 75% women, 67% part-time, 71% 25 or older, 1% Native American, 1% Hispanic American, 16% African American, 2% Asian American/Pacific Islander **The most frequently chosen baccalaureate field is** law/legal studies **Academic program** English as a second language, summer session, adult/continuing education programs, internships **Contact** Ms. Gloria Stender, Admissions Director, Davenport University,

MICHIGAN

4123 West Main Street, Kalamazoo, MI 49006-2791. Telephone: 616-382-2835 Ext. 3309 or toll-free 800-632-8928 Ext. 3308 (in-state). Fax: 616-382-2661. Web site: http://www.davenport.edu/.

DAVENPORT UNIVERSITY
LANSING, MICHIGAN

General Independent, 4-year, coed **Entrance** Noncompetitive **Setting** 2-acre suburban campus **Total enrollment** 1,209 **Student-faculty ratio** 15:1 **Application deadline** 9/15 (freshmen), 9/15 (transfer) **Housing** No **Expenses** Tuition $8364 **Undergraduates** 72% women, 61% part-time, 83% 25 or older, 1% Native American, 5% Hispanic American, 18% African American, 2% Asian American/Pacific Islander **Academic program** Advanced placement, accelerated degree program, self-designed majors, summer session, adult/continuing education programs, internships **Contact** Mr. Tom Woods, Associate Dean of Enrollment, Davenport University, 220 East Kalamazoo, Lansing, MI 48933-2197. Telephone: 517-484-2600 Ext. 288 or toll-free 800-331-3306 (in-state). Fax: 517-484-9719. E-mail: laadmissions@davenport.edu. Web site: http://www.davenport.edu/.

DAVENPORT UNIVERSITY
WARREN, MICHIGAN

General Independent, comprehensive, coed **Entrance** Noncompetitive **Setting** 9-acre suburban campus **Total enrollment** 2,486 **Student-faculty ratio** 24:1 **Application deadline** Rolling (freshmen), rolling (transfer) **Freshmen** 100% were admitted **Housing** No **Expenses** Tuition $7449 **Undergraduates** 78% women, 45% part-time, 69% 25 or older, 0.5% Native American, 1% Hispanic American, 45% African American, 2% Asian American/Pacific Islander **The most frequently chosen baccalaureate fields are** business/marketing, health professions and related sciences **Academic program** Advanced placement, summer session, internships **Contact** Ms. Gerri Pavone, Director of Admissions, Davenport University, 27650 Dequindre Road, Warren, MI 48092-5209. Telephone: 586-558-8700. Fax: 810-558-7868. E-mail: gerripavone@davenport.edu. Web site: http://www.davenport.edu/.

EASTERN MICHIGAN UNIVERSITY
YPSILANTI, MICHIGAN

General State-supported, comprehensive, coed **Entrance** Moderately difficult **Setting** 460-acre suburban campus **Total enrollment** 23,798 **Student-faculty ratio** 19:1 **Application deadline** 6/30 (freshmen), 6/30 (transfer) **Freshmen** 75% were admitted **Housing** Yes **Expenses** Tuition $4603; Room & Board $5252 **Undergraduates** 61% women, 30% part-time, 23% 25 or older, 1% Native American, 2% Hispanic American, 17% African American, 2% Asian American/Pacific Islander **The most frequently chosen baccalaureate fields are** business/marketing, education, social sciences and history **Academic program** English as a second language, advanced placement, accelerated degree program, self-designed majors, honors program, summer session, adult/continuing education programs, internships **Contact** Ms. Judy Benfield-Tatum, Director of Admissions, Eastern Michigan University, Ypsilanti, MI 48197. Telephone: 734-487-3060 or toll-free 800-GO TO EMU. Fax: 734-487-1484. Web site: http://www.emich.edu/.

FERRIS STATE UNIVERSITY
BIG RAPIDS, MICHIGAN

General State-supported, comprehensive, coed **Entrance** Minimally difficult **Setting** 600-acre small-town campus **Total enrollment** 10,930 **Student-faculty ratio** 18:1 **Application deadline** Rolling (freshmen), rolling (transfer) **Freshmen** 51% were admitted **Housing** Yes **Expenses** Tuition $5070; Room & Board $5628 **Undergraduates** 46% women, 21% part-time, 22% 25 or older, 1% Native American, 2% Hispanic American, 9% African American, 2% Asian American/Pacific Islander **The most frequently chosen baccalaureate fields are** business/marketing, engineering/engineering technologies, health professions and related sciences **Academic program** English as a second language, advanced placement, accelerated degree program, honors program, summer session, adult/continuing education programs, internships **Contact** Mr. Ronnie Higgs, Assistant Vice President/Dean of Enrollment Services, Ferris State University, PRK 110, Big Rapids, MI 49307-2742. Telephone: 231-591-2100 or toll-free 800-433-7747. Fax: 616-592-2978. E-mail: admissions@ferris.edu. Web site: http://www.ferris.edu/.

▶ **For more information, see page 427.**

FINLANDIA UNIVERSITY
HANCOCK, MICHIGAN

General Independent, 4-year, coed, affiliated with Evangelical Lutheran Church in America **Entrance** Minimally difficult **Setting** 25-acre small-town campus **Total enrollment** 418 **Student-faculty ratio** 11:1 **Application deadline** 8/15 (freshmen), 8/15 (transfer) **Freshmen** 52% were admitted **Housing** Yes **Expenses** Tuition $12,150; Room & Board $4500 **Undergraduates** 66% women, 17% part-time, 29% 25 or older, 1% Native American, 0% Hispanic American, 1% African American, 0.2% Asian American/Pacific Islander **The most frequently chosen baccalaureate fields are** business/marketing, liberal arts/general studies, protective services/public administration **Academic program** English as a second language, advanced placement, accelerated degree program, summer session, adult/continuing education programs, internships **Contact** Mr. Ben Larson, Executive Director of Admissions, Finlandia University, 601 Quincy Street, Hancock, MI 49930. Telephone: 906-487-7311 Ext. 311 or toll-free 877-202-5491. Fax: 906-487-7383. E-mail: admissions@finlandia.edu. Web site: http://www.finlandia.edu.

MICHIGAN

GRACE BIBLE COLLEGE
GRAND RAPIDS, MICHIGAN

General Independent, 4-year, coed, affiliated with Grace Gospel Fellowship Entrance Minimally difficult Setting 16-acre suburban campus Total enrollment 149 Student-faculty ratio 11:1 Application deadline 7/15 (freshmen) Freshmen 51% were admitted Housing Yes Expenses Tuition $7950; Room & Board $4650 Undergraduates 48% women, 11% part-time, 11% 25 or older, 1% Native American, 1% Hispanic American, 2% African American, 2% Asian American/Pacific Islander The most frequently chosen baccalaureate fields are education, philosophy, visual/performing arts Academic program English as a second language, advanced placement, internships Contact Mr. Kevin Gilliam, Director of Enrollment, Grace Bible College, 1101 Aldon Street, SW, PO Box 910, Grand Rapids, MI 49509. Telephone: 616-538-2330 or toll-free 800-968-1887. Fax: 616-538-0599. E-mail: gbc@gbcol.edu. Web site: http://www.gbcol.edu/.

GRAND VALLEY STATE UNIVERSITY
ALLENDALE, MICHIGAN

General State-supported, comprehensive, coed Entrance Moderately difficult Setting 900-acre small-town campus Total enrollment 19,762 Student-faculty ratio 22:1 Application deadline 7/25 (freshmen), 7/25 (transfer) Freshmen 78% were admitted Housing Yes Expenses Tuition $4660; Room & Board $5380 Undergraduates 60% women, 18% part-time, 11% 25 or older, 1% Native American, 2% Hispanic American, 5% African American, 2% Asian American/Pacific Islander The most frequently chosen baccalaureate fields are business/marketing, health professions and related sciences, psychology Academic program English as a second language, advanced placement, accelerated degree program, honors program, summer session, adult/continuing education programs, internships Contact Ms. Jodi Chycinski, Director of Admissions, Grand Valley State University, 1 Campus Drive, Allendale, MI 49401. Telephone: 616-895-2025 or toll-free 800-748-0246. Fax: 616-895-2000. E-mail: go2gvsu@gvsu.edu. Web site: http://www.gvsu.edu/.

GREAT LAKES CHRISTIAN COLLEGE
LANSING, MICHIGAN

General Independent, 4-year, coed, affiliated with Christian Churches and Churches of Christ Entrance Moderately difficult Setting 50-acre suburban campus Total enrollment 220 Student-faculty ratio 17:1 Application deadline 8/1 (freshmen), 8/1 (transfer) Freshmen 64% were admitted Housing Yes Expenses Tuition $7490; Room & Board $3900 Undergraduates 36% 25 or older The most frequently chosen baccalaureate fields are education, philosophy, psychology Academic program Advanced placement, adult/continuing education programs, internships Contact Mr. Mike Klauka, Director of Admissions, Great Lakes Christian College, 6211 West Willow Highway, Lansing, MI 48917-1299. Telephone: 517-321-0242 Ext. 221 or toll-free 800-YES-GLCC. Fax: 517-321-5902. Web site: http://www.glcc.edu/.

HILLSDALE COLLEGE
HILLSDALE, MICHIGAN

General Independent, 4-year, coed Entrance Very difficult Setting 200-acre small-town campus Total enrollment 1,168 Student-faculty ratio 11:1 Application deadline Rolling (freshmen), rolling (transfer) Freshmen 85% were admitted Housing Yes Expenses Tuition $14,700; Room & Board $5886 Undergraduates 51% women, 3% part-time, 1% 25 or older The most frequently chosen baccalaureate fields are business/marketing, education, social sciences and history Academic program Advanced placement, accelerated degree program, honors program, summer session, internships Contact Mr. Jeffrey S. Lantis, Director of Admissions, Hillsdale College, 33 East College Street, Hillsdale, MI 49242-1298. Telephone: 517-607-2327 Ext. 2327. Fax: 517-607-2298. E-mail: admissions@hillsdale.edu. Web site: http://www.hillsdale.edu/.

HOPE COLLEGE
HOLLAND, MICHIGAN

General Independent, 4-year, coed, affiliated with Reformed Church in America Entrance Moderately difficult Setting 45-acre small-town campus Total enrollment 2,999 Student-faculty ratio 14:1 Application deadline Rolling (freshmen), rolling (transfer) Freshmen 89% were admitted Housing Yes Expenses Tuition $17,448; Room & Board $5474 Undergraduates 60% women, 4% part-time, 2% 25 or older, 0.2% Native American, 2% Hispanic American, 1% African American, 2% Asian American/Pacific Islander The most frequently chosen baccalaureate fields are business/marketing, English, social sciences and history Academic program English as a second language, advanced placement, self-designed majors, summer session, internships Contact Dr. James R. Bekkering, Vice President for Admissions, Hope College, 69 East 10th Street, PO Box 9000, Holland, MI 49422-9000. Telephone: 616-395-7955 or toll-free 800-968-7850. Fax: 616-395-7130. E-mail: admissions@hope.edu. Web site: http://www.hope.edu/.

KALAMAZOO COLLEGE
KALAMAZOO, MICHIGAN

General Independent, 4-year, coed, affiliated with American Baptist Churches in the U.S.A. Entrance Very difficult Setting 60-acre suburban campus Total enrollment 1,384 Student-faculty ratio 12:1 Application deadline 2/15 (freshmen), 2/15 (transfer) Freshmen 78% were admitted Housing Yes Expenses Tuition $20,652; Room & Board $6228 Undergraduates 56% women, 1% 25 or older, 0.1% Native American, 2% Hispanic American, 2% African American, 4% Asian American/Pacific Islander The most

MICHIGAN

frequently chosen baccalaureate fields are English, biological/life sciences, social sciences and history **Academic program** English as a second language, advanced placement, adult/continuing education programs, internships **Contact** Mrs. Linda Wirgau, Records Manager, Kalamazoo College, Mandelle Hall, 1200 Academy Street, Kalamazoo, MI 49006-3295. Telephone: 616-337-7166 or toll-free 800-253-3602. E-mail: admissions@kzoo.edu. Web site: http://www.kzoo.edu/.

KENDALL COLLEGE OF ART AND DESIGN OF FERRIS STATE UNIVERSITY
GRAND RAPIDS, MICHIGAN

General Independent, comprehensive, coed **Entrance** Minimally difficult **Setting** urban campus **Total enrollment** 744 **Student-faculty ratio** 13:1 **Application deadline** Rolling (freshmen), rolling (transfer) **Housing** No **Expenses** Tuition $8820 **Undergraduates** 57% women, 27% part-time, 28% 25 or older, 0.1% Native American, 2% Hispanic American, 4% African American, 2% Asian American/Pacific Islander **The most frequently chosen baccalaureate fields are** trade and industry, visual/performing arts **Academic program** Advanced placement, summer session, adult/continuing education programs, internships **Contact** Ms. Amy Packard, Director of Admissions, Kendall College of Art and Design of Ferris State University, 111 Division Avenue North, Grand Rapids, MI 49503-3194. Telephone: 616-451-2787 Ext. 109 or toll-free 800-676-2787. Fax: 616-831-9689. Web site: http://www.kcad.edu/.

KETTERING UNIVERSITY
FLINT, MICHIGAN

General Independent, comprehensive, coed **Entrance** Very difficult **Setting** 45-acre suburban campus **Total enrollment** 3,346 **Student-faculty ratio** 9:1 **Application deadline** Rolling (freshmen), rolling (transfer) **Freshmen** 71% were admitted **Housing** Yes **Expenses** Tuition $18,656; Room & Board $4600 **Undergraduates** 19% women, 3% 25 or older, 0.3% Native American, 2% Hispanic American, 7% African American, 4% Asian American/Pacific Islander **The most frequently chosen baccalaureate fields are** business/marketing, computer/information sciences, engineering/engineering technologies **Academic program** Advanced placement, accelerated degree program, internships **Contact** Mr. Rawlan Lillard II, Director of Admissions, Kettering University, 1700 West Third Avenue, Flint, MI 48504-4898. Telephone: 810-762-7865 or toll-free 800-955-4464 Ext. 7865 (in-state); 800-955-4464 (out-of-state). Fax: 810-762-9837. E-mail: admissions@kettering.edu. Web site: http://www.kettering.edu/.

▶ For more information, see page 444.

LAKE SUPERIOR STATE UNIVERSITY
SAULT SAINTE MARIE, MICHIGAN

General State-supported, 4-year, coed **Entrance** Moderately difficult **Setting** 121-acre small-town campus **Total enrollment** 3,219 **Student-faculty ratio** 18:1 **Application deadline** 8/15 (freshmen), rolling (transfer) **Freshmen** 66% were admitted **Housing** Yes **Expenses** Tuition $4334; Room & Board $5281 **Undergraduates** 52% women, 23% part-time, 24% 25 or older, 8% Native American, 1% Hispanic American, 1% African American, 1% Asian American/Pacific Islander **The most frequently chosen baccalaureate fields are** business/marketing, health professions and related sciences, protective services/public administration **Academic program** Advanced placement, self-designed majors, honors program, summer session, adult/continuing education programs, internships **Contact** Mr. Kevin Pollock, Director of Admissions, Lake Superior State University, 650 West Easterday Avenue, Sault Saint Marie, MI 49783-1699. Telephone: 906-635-2670 or toll-free 888-800-LSSU Ext. 2231. Fax: 906-635-6669. E-mail: admissions@gw.lssu.edu. Web site: http://www.lssu.edu/.

LAWRENCE TECHNOLOGICAL UNIVERSITY
SOUTHFIELD, MICHIGAN

General Independent, comprehensive, coed **Entrance** Moderately difficult **Setting** 110-acre suburban campus **Total enrollment** 4,117 **Student-faculty ratio** 12:1 **Application deadline** 4/15 (freshmen), 8/15 (transfer) **Freshmen** 78% were admitted **Housing** Yes **Expenses** Tuition $12,250; Room only $2475 **Academic program** Advanced placement, self-designed majors, honors program, summer session, adult/continuing education programs, internships **Contact** Mrs. Lisa Kujawa, Director of Admissions, Lawrence Technological University, 2100 West 10 Mile Road, Southfield, MI 48075. Telephone: 248-204-3180 or toll-free 800-225-5588. Fax: 248-204-3188. E-mail: admissions@ltu.edu. Web site: http://www.ltu.edu/.

MADONNA UNIVERSITY
LIVONIA, MICHIGAN

General Independent Roman Catholic, comprehensive, coed **Entrance** Moderately difficult **Setting** 49-acre suburban campus **Total enrollment** 3,819 **Student-faculty ratio** 17:1 **Application deadline** Rolling (freshmen), rolling (transfer) **Freshmen** 66% were admitted **Housing** Yes **Expenses** Tuition $7660; Room & Board $5054 **Undergraduates** 78% women, 55% part-time, 60% 25 or older, 0.4% Native American, 3% Hispanic American, 11% African American, 1% Asian American/Pacific Islander **The most frequently chosen baccalaureate fields are** health professions and related sciences, business/marketing, protective services/public administration **Academic program** English as a second language, advanced placement, accelerated degree program, summer session, adult/continuing education programs, internships **Contact** Mr. Frank J. Hribar, Director of Enrollment Management, Madonna University, 36600 Schoolcraft Road, Livonia, MI 48150-1173. Telephone: 734-432-5317 or toll-free 800-852-4951. Fax:

MICHIGAN

Madonna University *(continued)*
734-432-5393. E-mail: muinfo@smtp.munet.edu. Web site: http://www.munet.edu/.

MARYGROVE COLLEGE
DETROIT, MICHIGAN

General Independent Roman Catholic, comprehensive, coed, primarily women **Entrance** Moderately difficult **Setting** 50-acre urban campus **Total enrollment** 6,097 **Student-faculty ratio** 15:1 **Application deadline** 8/15 (freshmen), 8/15 (transfer) **Freshmen** 15% were admitted **Housing** Yes **Expenses** Tuition $10,750; Room & Board $5200 **Undergraduates** 81% women, 53% part-time, 70% 25 or older, 0.2% Native American, 1% Hispanic American, 75% African American, 0.2% Asian American/Pacific Islander **The most frequently chosen baccalaureate fields are** business/marketing, education, social sciences and history **Academic program** Advanced placement, self-designed majors, summer session, internships **Contact** Fred A. Schebor, Dean of Admissions, Marygrove College, Office of Admissions, Detroit, MI 48221-2599. Telephone: 313-927-1570 or toll-free 866-313-1297. Fax: 313-927-1345. E-mail: info@marygrove.edu. Web site: http://www.marygrove.edu/.

MICHIGAN STATE UNIVERSITY
EAST LANSING, MICHIGAN

General State-supported, university, coed **Entrance** Moderately difficult **Setting** suburban campus **Total enrollment** 44,227 **Student-faculty ratio** 18:1 **Application deadline** 7/30 (freshmen), 7/30 (transfer) **Freshmen** 65% were admitted **Housing** Yes **Expenses** Tuition $5627; Room & Board $4678 **Undergraduates** 53% women, 12% part-time, 6% 25 or older, 1% Native American, 3% Hispanic American, 9% African American, 5% Asian American/Pacific Islander **The most frequently chosen baccalaureate fields are** business/marketing, communications/communication technologies, social sciences and history **Academic program** English as a second language, advanced placement, accelerated degree program, self-designed majors, honors program, summer session, adult/continuing education programs, internships **Contact** Dr. Gordon Stanley, Assistant to the Provost for Enrollment and Director of Admissions, Michigan State University, 250 Administration Building, East Lansing, MI 48824. Telephone: 517-355-8332. Fax: 517-353-1647. E-mail: admis@msu.edu. Web site: http://www.msu.edu/.

MICHIGAN TECHNOLOGICAL UNIVERSITY
HOUGHTON, MICHIGAN

General State-supported, university, coed **Entrance** Moderately difficult **Setting** 240-acre small-town campus **Total enrollment** 6,336 **Student-faculty ratio** 12:1 **Application deadline** Rolling (freshmen), rolling (transfer) **Freshmen** 94% were admitted **Housing** Yes **Expenses** Tuition $5887; Room & Board $5181 **Undergraduates** 26% women, 13% part-time, 8% 25 or older, 1% Native American, 1% Hispanic American, 2% African American, 1% Asian American/Pacific Islander **Academic program** English as a second language, advanced placement, self-designed majors, summer session, internships **Contact** Ms. Nancy Rehling, Director of Undergraduate Admissions, Michigan Technological University, 1400 Townsend Drive, Houghton, MI 49931-1295. Telephone: 906-487-2335. Fax: 906-487-3343. E-mail: mtu4u@mtu.edu. Web site: http://www.mtu.edu/.

NORTHERN MICHIGAN UNIVERSITY
MARQUETTE, MICHIGAN

General State-supported, comprehensive, coed **Entrance** Minimally difficult **Setting** 300-acre small-town campus **Total enrollment** 8,577 **Student-faculty ratio** 20:1 **Application deadline** Rolling (freshmen), rolling (transfer) **Freshmen** 99% were admitted **Housing** Yes **Expenses** Tuition $4257; Room & Board $5436 **Undergraduates** 53% women, 13% part-time, 20% 25 or older, 2% Native American, 1% Hispanic American, 4% African American, 0.4% Asian American/Pacific Islander **The most frequently chosen baccalaureate fields are** business/marketing, education, health professions and related sciences **Academic program** Advanced placement, accelerated degree program, self-designed majors, summer session, adult/continuing education programs, internships **Contact** Ms. Gerri Daniels, Northern Michigan University, 1401 Presque Isle Avenue, Marquette, MI 49855. Telephone: 906-227-2650 or toll-free 800-682-9797 Ext. 1 (in-state); 800-682-9797 (out-of-state). Fax: 906-227-1747. E-mail: admiss@nmu.edu. Web site: http://www.nmu.edu/.

NORTHWOOD UNIVERSITY
MIDLAND, MICHIGAN

General Independent, comprehensive, coed **Entrance** Moderately difficult **Setting** 434-acre small-town campus **Total enrollment** 3,654 **Student-faculty ratio** 30:1 **Application deadline** Rolling (freshmen), rolling (transfer) **Freshmen** 88% were admitted **Housing** Yes **Expenses** Tuition $12,531; Room & Board $5829 **Undergraduates** 46% women, 34% part-time, 4% 25 or older, 0.1% Native American, 2% Hispanic American, 9% African American, 0.5% Asian American/Pacific Islander **The most frequently chosen baccalaureate fields are** business/marketing, computer/information sciences **Academic program** English as a second language, advanced placement, accelerated degree program, honors program, summer session, adult/continuing education programs, internships **Contact** Daniel F. Toland, Director of Admission, Northwood University, 4000 Whiting Drive, Midland, MI 48640. Telephone: 989-837-4273 or toll-free 800-457-7878. Fax: 989-837-4490. E-mail: admissions@northwood.edu. Web site: http://www.northwood.edu/.

▶ For more information, see page 462.

OAKLAND UNIVERSITY
ROCHESTER, MICHIGAN

General State-supported, university, coed **Entrance** Moderately difficult **Setting** 1,444-acre suburban cam-

MICHIGAN

pus **Total enrollment** 15,875 **Student-faculty ratio** 21:1 **Application deadline** Rolling (freshmen) **Freshmen** 77% were admitted **Housing** Yes **Expenses** Tuition $4638; Room & Board $4978 **Undergraduates** 63% women, 31% part-time, 25% 25 or older, 0.4% Native American, 2% Hispanic American, 8% African American, 3% Asian American/Pacific Islander **The most frequently chosen baccalaureate fields are** business/marketing, education, health professions and related sciences **Academic program** English as a second language, advanced placement, accelerated degree program, self-designed majors, honors program, summer session, internships **Contact** Mr. Robert E. Johnson, Associate Vice President for Enrollment Management, Oakland University, 101 North Foundation Hall, Rochester, MI 48309-4401. Telephone: 248-370-3360 or toll-free 800-OAK-UNIV. Fax: 248-370-4462. E-mail: ouinfo@oakland.edu. Web site: http://www.oakland.edu/.

OLIVET COLLEGE
OLIVET, MICHIGAN

General Independent, comprehensive, coed, affiliated with Congregational Christian Church **Entrance** Minimally difficult **Setting** 92-acre small-town campus **Total enrollment** 795 **Student-faculty ratio** 14:1 **Application deadline** Rolling (freshmen), rolling (transfer) **Freshmen** 93% were admitted **Housing** Yes **Expenses** Tuition $14,248; Room & Board $4802 **Undergraduates** 47% women, 8% part-time, 8% 25 or older, 1% Native American, 2% Hispanic American, 19% African American, 1% Asian American/Pacific Islander **The most frequently chosen baccalaureate fields** are biological/life sciences, business/marketing, education **Academic program** Advanced placement, accelerated degree program, self-designed majors, honors program, summer session, internships **Contact** Mr. Kevin Leonard, Director of Admissions, Olivet College, 320 South Main Street, Olivet, MI 49076. Telephone: 616-749-7635 or toll-free 800-456-7189. Fax: 616-749-3821. E-mail: admissions@olivetcollege.edu. Web site: http://www.olivetcollege.edu/.

REFORMED BIBLE COLLEGE
GRAND RAPIDS, MICHIGAN

General Independent religious, 4-year, coed **Entrance** Moderately difficult **Setting** 27-acre suburban campus **Total enrollment** 294 **Student-faculty ratio** 16:1 **Application deadline** Rolling (freshmen), rolling (transfer) **Freshmen** 59% were admitted **Housing** Yes **Expenses** Tuition $8825; Room & Board $4600 **Undergraduates** 48% women, 27% part-time, 10% 25 or older, 0.4% Native American, 1% Hispanic American, 4% African American, 0% Asian American/Pacific Islander **The most frequently chosen baccalaureate field is** philosophy, religion, and theology **Academic program** Advanced placement, summer session, adult/continuing education programs, internships **Contact** Ms. Jeanine Kopaska Brock, Assistant Director of Admissions, Reformed Bible College, 3333 East Beltline North East, Grand Rapids, MI 49525. Telephone: 616-222-3000 Ext.

631 or toll-free 800-511-3749. Fax: 616-222-3045. E-mail: admissions@reformed.edu. Web site: http://www.reformed.edu/.

ROCHESTER COLLEGE
ROCHESTER HILLS, MICHIGAN

General Independent, 4-year, coed, affiliated with Church of Christ **Entrance** Minimally difficult **Setting** 83-acre suburban campus **Total enrollment** 927 **Student-faculty ratio** 19:1 **Application deadline** Rolling (freshmen), rolling (transfer) **Freshmen** 83% were admitted **Housing** Yes **Expenses** Tuition $10,170; Room & Board $5184 **Undergraduates** 57% women, 32% part-time, 8% 25 or older, 1% Native American, 1% Hispanic American, 11% African American, 1% Asian American/Pacific Islander **The most frequently chosen baccalaureate fields are** business/marketing, education, philosophy **Academic program** Advanced placement, accelerated degree program, summer session, adult/continuing education programs, internships **Contact** Mr. Larry Norman, Vice President for Enrollment Management, Rochester College, 800 West Avon Road, Rochester Hills, MI 48307-2764. Telephone: 248-218-2032 or toll-free 800-521-6010. Fax: 248-218-2005. E-mail: admissions@rc.edu. Web site: http://www.rc.edu/.

SACRED HEART MAJOR SEMINARY
DETROIT, MICHIGAN

General Independent Roman Catholic, comprehensive, coed **Entrance** Moderately difficult **Setting** 24-acre urban campus **Total enrollment** 420 **Student-faculty ratio** 8:1 **Application deadline** 7/31 (freshmen), 7/31 (transfer) **Freshmen** 100% were admitted **Housing** Yes **Expenses** Tuition $6832; Room & Board $4658 **Undergraduates** 48% women, 89% part-time, 37% 25 or older, 0% Native American, 12% Hispanic American, 3% African American, 9% Asian American/Pacific Islander **The most frequently chosen baccalaureate fields are** liberal arts/general studies, philosophy, philosophy, religion, and theology **Academic program** Advanced placement, honors program **Contact** Fr. Patrick Halfpenny, Vice Rector, Sacred Heart Major Seminary, 2701 Chicago Boulevard, Detroit, MI 48206. Telephone: 313-883-8552.

SAGINAW VALLEY STATE UNIVERSITY
UNIVERSITY CENTER, MICHIGAN

General State-supported, comprehensive, coed **Entrance** Moderately difficult **Setting** 782-acre rural campus **Total enrollment** 8,900 **Student-faculty ratio** 24:1 **Application deadline** Rolling (freshmen), rolling (transfer) **Freshmen** 45% were admitted **Housing** Yes **Expenses** Tuition $4,340; Room & Board $5200 **Undergraduates** 60% women, 31% part-time, 29% 25 or older, 0.4% Native American, 3% Hispanic American, 6% African American, 1% Asian American/Pacific Islander **The most frequently chosen baccalaureate fields are** education, business/marketing, protective services/public administration

MICHIGAN

Saginaw Valley State University *(continued)*
Academic program English as a second language, advanced placement, accelerated degree program, self-designed majors, honors program, summer session, internships **Contact** Mr. James P. Dwyer, Director of Admissions, Saginaw Valley State University, 7400 Bay Road, University Center, HI 48710-0001. Telephone: 989-790-4200 or toll-free 800-968-9500. Fax: 517-790-0180. E-mail: admissions@svsu.edu. Web site: http://www.svsu.edu/.

SAINT MARY'S COLLEGE OF AVE MARIA UNIVERSITY
ORCHARD LAKE, MICHIGAN

General Independent Roman Catholic, 4-year, coed **Entrance** Moderately difficult **Setting** 120-acre suburban campus **Total enrollment** 513 **Student-faculty ratio** 12:1 **Application deadline** Rolling (freshmen), rolling (transfer) **Freshmen** 62% were admitted **Housing** Yes **Expenses** Tuition $6792; Room & Board $5140 **Undergraduates** 46% women, 50% part-time, 35% 25 or older, 0.2% Native American, 1% Hispanic American, 7% African American, 1% Asian American/Pacific Islander **The most frequently chosen baccalaureate fields are** biological/life sciences, business/marketing, communications/communication technologies **Academic program** English as a second language, advanced placement, accelerated degree program, internships **Contact** Mr. James Bass, Director of Admissions, Saint Mary's College of Ave Maria University, 3535 Indian Trail, Orchard Lake, MI 48324-1623. Telephone: 248-683-0523 or toll-free 877-252-3131 (in-state). Fax: 248-683-1756. E-mail: admissions@stmarys.avemaria.edu. Web site: http://www.stmarys.avemaria.edu/.

SIENA HEIGHTS UNIVERSITY
ADRIAN, MICHIGAN

General Independent Roman Catholic, comprehensive, coed **Entrance** Moderately difficult **Setting** 140-acre small-town campus **Total enrollment** 2,024 **Student-faculty ratio** 14:1 **Application deadline** Rolling (freshmen), rolling (transfer) **Freshmen** 78% were admitted **Housing** Yes **Expenses** Tuition $13,000; Room & Board $4750 **Undergraduates** 51% 25 or older **The most frequently chosen baccalaureate field is** philosophy, religion, and theology **Academic program** Advanced placement, accelerated degree program, self-designed majors, summer session, adult/continuing education programs, internships **Contact** Mr. Kevin Kucera, Dean of Admissions and Enrollment Services, Siena Heights University, 1247 East Siena Heights Drive, Adrian, MI 49221-1796. Telephone: 517-264-7180 or toll-free 800-521-0009. Fax: 517-264-7745. E-mail: admissions@sienahts.edu. Web site: http://www.sienahts.edu.

SPRING ARBOR UNIVERSITY
SPRING ARBOR, MICHIGAN

General Independent Free Methodist, comprehensive, coed **Entrance** Moderately difficult **Setting** 70-acre small-town campus **Total enrollment** 2,616 **Student-faculty ratio** 15:1 **Application deadline** Rolling (freshmen), rolling (transfer) **Freshmen** 86% were admitted **Housing** Yes **Expenses** Tuition $13,136; Room & Board $4840 **Undergraduates** 67% women, 17% part-time, 0.5% Native American, 1% Hispanic American, 11% African American, 1% Asian American/Pacific Islander **The most frequently chosen baccalaureate fields are** business/marketing, health professions and related sciences, home economics/vocational home economics **Academic program** English as a second language, advanced placement, accelerated degree program, self-designed majors, honors program, summer session, adult/continuing education programs, internships **Contact** Mr. Jim Weidman, Director of Admissions, Spring Arbor University, 106 East Main Street, Spring Arbor, MI 49283-9799. Telephone: 517-750-1200 Ext. 1475 or toll-free 800-968-0011. Fax: 517-750-6620. E-mail: shellya@admin.arbor.edu. Web site: http://www.arbor.edu/.

UNIVERSITY OF DETROIT MERCY
DETROIT, MICHIGAN

Contact Ms. Colleen Ezzeddine, Admissions Counselor, University of Detroit Mercy, PO Box 19900, Detroit, MI 48219-0900. Telephone: 313-993-1245 or toll-free 800-635-5020 (out-of-state). Fax: 313-993-3326. E-mail: admissions@udmercy.edu. Web site: http://www.udmercy.edu/.

UNIVERSITY OF MICHIGAN
ANN ARBOR, MICHIGAN

General State-supported, university, coed **Entrance** Very difficult **Setting** 2,861-acre suburban campus **Total enrollment** 38,248 **Student-faculty ratio** 16:1 **Application deadline** 2/1 (freshmen), 3/1 (transfer) **Freshmen** 52% were admitted **Housing** Yes **Expenses** Tuition $6935; Room & Board $6068 **Undergraduates** 50% women, 6% part-time, 4% 25 or older, 1% Native American, 4% Hispanic American, 8% African American, 12% Asian American/Pacific Islander **The most frequently chosen baccalaureate fields are** engineering/engineering technologies, psychology, social sciences and history **Academic program** English as a second language, advanced placement, accelerated degree program, self-designed majors, honors program, summer session, adult/continuing education programs, internships **Contact** Mr. Ted Spencer, Director of Undergraduate Admissions, University of Michigan, Ann Arbor, MI 48109-1316. Telephone: 734-764-7433. Fax: 734-936-0740. E-mail: ugadmiss@umich.edu. Web site: http://www.umich.edu/.

UNIVERSITY OF MICHIGAN–DEARBORN
DEARBORN, MICHIGAN

General State-supported, comprehensive, coed **Entrance** Moderately difficult **Setting** 210-acre suburban campus **Total enrollment** 8,049 **Student-faculty ratio** 15:1 **Application deadline** Rolling (freshmen), rolling (transfer) **Freshmen** 65% were admitted **Housing** No **Expenses** Tuition $5095

MICHIGAN

Undergraduates 54% women, 40% part-time, 31% 25 or older, 1% Native American, 2% Hispanic American, 7% African American, 6% Asian American/Pacific Islander **The most frequently chosen baccalaureate fields are** business/marketing, education, engineering/engineering technologies **Academic program** Accelerated degree program, self-designed majors, honors program, summer session, adult/continuing education programs, internships **Contact** Mr. David Placey, Director of Admissions, University of Michigan–Dearborn, 4901 Evergreen Road, Dearborn, MI 48128-1491. Telephone: 313-593-5100. E-mail: umdgoblu@umd.umich.edu. Web site: http://www.umd.umich.edu/.

UNIVERSITY OF MICHIGAN–FLINT
FLINT, MICHIGAN

General State-supported, comprehensive, coed **Entrance** Moderately difficult **Setting** 72-acre urban campus **Total enrollment** 6,397 **Student-faculty ratio** 17:1 **Application deadline** 9/2 (freshmen), 8/21 (transfer) **Freshmen** 81% were admitted **Housing** No **Expenses** Tuition $4328 **Undergraduates** 65% women, 42% part-time, 39% 25 or older, 1% Native American, 2% Hispanic American, 11% African American, 1% Asian American/Pacific Islander **The most frequently chosen baccalaureate fields are** business/marketing, education, health professions and related sciences **Academic program** Advanced placement, self-designed majors, honors program, summer session, adult/continuing education programs, internships **Contact** Dr. Virginia R. Allen, Vice Chancellor for Student Services and Enrollment, University of Michigan–Flint, 303 East Kearsley Street, Flint, MI 48502-1950. Telephone: 810-762-3434 or toll-free 800-942-5636 (in-state). Fax: 810-762-3272. E-mail: admissions@list.flint.umich.edu. Web site: http://www.flint.umich.edu/.

UNIVERSITY OF PHOENIX–METRO DETROIT CAMPUS
TROY, MICHIGAN

General Proprietary, comprehensive, coed **Entrance** Noncompetitive **Total enrollment** 88,730 **Student-faculty ratio** 13:1 **Application deadline** Rolling (freshmen), rolling (transfer) **Housing** No **Expenses** Tuition $8700 **Undergraduates** 57% women, 85% 25 or older **The most frequently chosen baccalaureate fields are** business/marketing, computer/information sciences, health professions and related sciences **Academic program** Advanced placement, accelerated degree program **Contact** Ms. Beth Barilla, Director of Admissions, University of Phoenix–Metro Detroit Campus, 4615 East Elwood Street, Phoenix, AZ 85040-1958. Telephone: 480-927-0099 Ext. 1218 or toll-free 800-834-2438. Fax: 480-594-1758. E-mail: beth.barilla@apollogrp.edu. Web site: http://www.phoenix.edu/.

UNIVERSITY OF PHOENIX–WEST MICHIGAN CAMPUS
GRAND RAPIDS, MICHIGAN

General Proprietary, comprehensive, coed **Entrance** Noncompetitive **Total enrollment** 88,730 **Student-faculty ratio** 11:1 **Application deadline** Rolling (freshmen), rolling (transfer) **Housing** No **Expenses** Tuition $8700 **Undergraduates** 50% women, 85% 25 or older **The most frequently chosen baccalaureate field is** business/marketing **Academic program** Advanced placement, accelerated degree program, adult/continuing education programs **Contact** Ms. Beth Barilla, Director of Admissions, University of Phoenix–West Michigan Campus, 4615 East Elwood Street, Phoenix, AZ 85040-1958. Telephone: 480-927-0099 Ext. 1218 or toll-free 800-228-7240. Fax: 480-594-1758. E-mail: beth.barilla@apollogrp.edu. Web site: http://www.phoenix.edu/.

WALSH COLLEGE OF ACCOUNTANCY AND BUSINESS ADMINISTRATION
TROY, MICHIGAN

General Independent, upper-level, coed **Entrance** Noncompetitive **Setting** 29-acre suburban campus **Total enrollment** 3,214 **Student-faculty ratio** 20:1 **Application deadline** Rolling (transfer) **First-Year Students** 65% were admitted **Housing** No **Expenses** Tuition $5452 **Undergraduates** 60% women, 83% part-time, 67% 25 or older, 0.3% Native American, 1% Hispanic American, 5% African American, 3% Asian American/Pacific Islander **The most frequently chosen baccalaureate field is** business/marketing **Academic program** Advanced placement, summer session, adult/continuing education programs, internships **Contact** Ms. Karen Mahaffy, Director of Admissions, Walsh College of Accountancy and Business Administration, 3838 Livernois, PO Box 7006, Troy, MI 48007-7006. Telephone: 248-823-1610 or toll-free 800-925-7401 (in-state). Fax: 248-524-2520. E-mail: admissions@walshcollege.edu. Web site: http://www.walshcollege.edu/.

WAYNE STATE UNIVERSITY
DETROIT, MICHIGAN

General State-supported, university, coed **Entrance** Moderately difficult **Setting** 203-acre urban campus **Total enrollment** 31,040 **Student-faculty ratio** 11:1 **Application deadline** 8/1 (freshmen), 8/1 (transfer) **Freshmen** 72% were admitted **Housing** Yes **Expenses** Tuition $4,330 **Undergraduates** 60% women, 50% part-time, 39% 25 or older, 0.4% Native American, 2% Hispanic American, 31% African American, 5% Asian American/Pacific Islander **The most frequently chosen baccalaureate fields are** business/marketing, education, health professions and related sciences **Academic program** English as a second language, advanced placement, accelerated degree program, self-designed majors, honors program, summer session, adult/continuing education programs, internships **Contact** Mr. Michael Wood, Interim Director of University Admissions, Wayne State Uni-

MICHIGAN

Wayne State University *(continued)*
versity, 3E HNJ, Detroit, MI 48202. Telephone: 313-577-3581. Fax: 313-577-7536. E-mail: admissions@wayne.edu. Web site: http://www.wayne.edu/.

WESTERN MICHIGAN UNIVERSITY
KALAMAZOO, MICHIGAN

General State-supported, university, coed **Entrance** Moderately difficult **Setting** 504-acre urban campus **Total enrollment** 28,931 **Student-faculty ratio** 16:1 **Application deadline** Rolling (freshmen), 8/1 (transfer) **Freshmen** 84% were admitted **Housing** Yes **Expenses** Tuition $4499; Room & Board $5517 **Undergraduates** 52% women, 14% part-time, 0.4% Native American, 2% Hispanic American, 5% African American, 1% Asian American/Pacific Islander **The most frequently chosen baccalaureate fields are** business/marketing, education, engineering/engineering technologies **Academic program** English as a second language, advanced placement, accelerated degree program, self-designed majors, honors program, summer session, adult/continuing education programs, internships **Contact** Mr. John Fraire, Dean, Office of Admissions and Orientation, Western Michigan University, 1903 West Michigan Avenue, Kalamazoo, MI 49008. Telephone: 616-387-2000 or toll-free 800-400-4968 (in-state). Fax: 616-387-2096. E-mail: ask-wmu@wmich.edu. Web site: http://www.wmich.edu/.

▶ For more information, see page 499.

WILLIAM TYNDALE COLLEGE
FARMINGTON HILLS, MICHIGAN

General Independent religious, 4-year, coed **Entrance** Minimally difficult **Setting** 28-acre suburban campus **Total enrollment** 608 **Student-faculty ratio** 7:1 **Application deadline** Rolling (freshmen), rolling (transfer) **Freshmen** 77% were admitted **Housing** Yes **Expenses** Tuition $7950; Room & Board $3200 **Undergraduates** 54% women, 48% part-time, 57% 25 or older, 0.5% Native American, 1% Hispanic American, 31% African American, 2% Asian American/Pacific Islander **The most frequently chosen baccalaureate fields are** business/marketing, philosophy, philosophy, religion, and theology **Academic program** Advanced placement, accelerated degree program, summer session, adult/continuing education programs, internships **Contact** Ms. Ann Corwell, Acting Director of Admissions, William Tyndale College, 37500 West Twelve Mile Road, Farmington Hills, MI 48331. Telephone: 248-553-7200 Ext. 204 or toll-free 800-483-0707. Fax: 248-553-5963. E-mail: admissions@williamtyndale.edu. Web site: http://www.williamtyndale.edu.

YESHIVA GEDDOLAH OF GREATER DETROIT RABBINICAL COLLEGE
OAK PARK, MICHIGAN

Contact Mr. Eric Krohner, Executive Director, Yeshiva Geddolah of Greater Detroit Rabbinical College, 24600 Greenfield, Oak Park, MI 48237-1544. Telephone: 810-968-3360.

MINNESOTA

AUGSBURG COLLEGE
MINNEAPOLIS, MINNESOTA

General Independent Lutheran, comprehensive, coed **Entrance** Moderately difficult **Setting** 23-acre urban campus **Total enrollment** 2,911 **Student-faculty ratio** 15:1 **Application deadline** 8/15 (freshmen), 8/10 (transfer) **Freshmen** 79% were admitted **Housing** Yes **Expenses** Tuition $17,438; Room & Board $5540 **Undergraduates** 58% women, 18% part-time, 37% 25 or older, 1% Native American, 1% Hispanic American, 5% African American, 3% Asian American/Pacific Islander **The most frequently chosen baccalaureate fields are** business/marketing, education, social sciences and history **Academic program** English as a second language, advanced placement, self-designed majors, honors program, summer session, adult/continuing education programs, internships **Contact** Ms. Sally Daniels, Director of Undergraduate Day Admissions, Augsburg College, 2211 Riverside Avenue, Minneapolis, MN 55454-1351. Telephone: 612-330-1001 or toll-free 800-788-5678. Fax: 612-330-1590. E-mail: admissions@augsburg.edu. Web site: http://www.augsburg.edu/.

BEMIDJI STATE UNIVERSITY
BEMIDJI, MINNESOTA

General State-supported, comprehensive, coed **Entrance** Moderately difficult **Setting** 89-acre small-town campus **Total enrollment** 4,660 **Student-faculty ratio** 20:1 **Application deadline** Rolling (freshmen), rolling (transfer) **Freshmen** 76% were admitted **Housing** Yes **Expenses** Tuition $4164; Room & Board $4158 **Undergraduates** 57% women, 23% part-time, 21% 25 or older, 3% Native American, 0.4% Hispanic American, 1% African American, 0.4% Asian American/Pacific Islander **The most frequently chosen baccalaureate fields are** business/marketing, education, protective services/public administration **Academic program** English as a second language, advanced placement, honors program, summer session, adult/continuing education programs, internships **Contact** Mr. Kevin Drexel, Director of Admissions, Bemidji State University, Deputy-102, Bemidji, MN 56601. Telephone: 218-755-2040 or toll-free 800-475-2001 (in-state); 800-652-9747 (out-of-state). Fax: 218-755-2074. E-mail: admissions@bemidjistate.edu. Web site: http://www.bemidjistate.edu/.

BETHEL COLLEGE
ST. PAUL, MINNESOTA

General Independent, comprehensive, coed, affiliated with Baptist General Conference **Entrance** Moderately difficult **Setting** 231-acre suburban campus

MINNESOTA

Total enrollment 2,991 **Student-faculty ratio** 16:1 **Application deadline** 3/1 (freshmen), 12/1 (transfer) **Freshmen** 67% were admitted **Housing** Yes **Expenses** Tuition $16,815; Room & Board $5960 **Undergraduates** 61% women, 10% part-time, 7% 25 or older, 0.3% Native American, 1% Hispanic American, 1% African American, 2% Asian American/Pacific Islander **The most frequently chosen baccalaureate fields are** business/marketing, education, health professions and related sciences **Academic program** English as a second language, advanced placement, accelerated degree program, self-designed majors, honors program, summer session, adult/continuing education programs, internships **Contact** Mr. Jay Fedje, Director of Admissions, Bethel College, 3900 Bethel Drive, St. Paul, MN 55112. Telephone: 651-638-6242 or toll-free 800-255-8706 Ext. 6242. Fax: 651-635-1490. E-mail: bcoll-admit@bethel.edu. Web site: http://www.bethel.edu/.

▶ For more information, see page 400.

CAPELLA UNIVERSITY
MINNEAPOLIS, MINNESOTA

General Proprietary, upper-level, coed **Total enrollment** 3,700 **Student-faculty ratio** 12:1 **First-Year Students** 48% were admitted **Expenses** Tuition $13,500 **The most frequently chosen baccalaureate field is** computer/information sciences **Academic program** Self-designed majors, summer session, adult/continuing education programs, internships **Contact** Ms. Liz Krumman, Associate Director, Enrollment Services, Capella University, 222 South 9th Street, 2nd Floor, Minneapolis, MN 55402. Telephone: 612-252-4286 or toll-free 888-CAPELLA. Fax: 612-339-8022. E-mail: info@capella.edu. Web site: http://www.capellauniversity.edu/.

CARLETON COLLEGE
NORTHFIELD, MINNESOTA

General Independent, 4-year, coed **Entrance** Very difficult **Setting** 955-acre small-town campus **Total enrollment** 1,948 **Student-faculty ratio** 10:1 **Application deadline** 1/15 (freshmen), 3/31 (transfer) **Freshmen** 37% were admitted **Housing** Yes **Expenses** Tuition $25,530; Room & Board $5250 **Undergraduates** 52% women, 1% part-time, 0% 25 or older, 0.4% Native American, 4% Hispanic American, 4% African American, 9% Asian American/Pacific Islander **The most frequently chosen baccalaureate fields are** physical sciences, biological/life sciences, social sciences and history **Academic program** Advanced placement, accelerated degree program, self-designed majors, internships **Contact** Mr. Paul Thiboutot, Dean of Admissions, Carleton College, 100 South College Street, Northfield, MN 55057. Telephone: 507-646-4190 or toll-free 800-995-2275. Fax: 507-646-4526. E-mail: admissions@acs.carleton.edu. Web site: http://www.carleton.edu/.

COLLEGE OF SAINT BENEDICT
SAINT JOSEPH, MINNESOTA

General Independent Roman Catholic, 4-year, coed, coordinate institution with Saint John's University (MN) **Entrance** Moderately difficult **Setting** 315-acre small-town campus **Total enrollment** 2,100 **Student-faculty ratio** 14:1 **Application deadline** Rolling (freshmen), rolling (transfer) **Freshmen** 82% were admitted **Housing** Yes **Expenses** Tuition $18,315; Room & Board $5606 **Undergraduates** 100% women, 3% part-time, 1% 25 or older, 0.2% Native American, 1% Hispanic American, 0.5% African American, 2% Asian American/Pacific Islander **The most frequently chosen baccalaureate fields are** business/marketing, English, health professions and related sciences **Academic program** English as a second language, advanced placement, accelerated degree program, self-designed majors, honors program, internships **Contact** Ms. Mary Milbert, Dean of Admissions, College of Saint Benedict, 37 South College Avenue, St. Joseph, MN 56374. Telephone: 320-363-5308 or toll-free 800-544-1489. Fax: 320-363-5010. E-mail: admissions@csbsju.edu. Web site: http://www.csbsju.edu/.

COLLEGE OF ST. CATHERINE
ST. PAUL, MINNESOTA

General Independent Roman Catholic, comprehensive, women only **Entrance** Moderately difficult **Setting** 110-acre urban campus **Total enrollment** 4,632 **Student-faculty ratio** 10:1 **Application deadline** 8/15 (freshmen), rolling (transfer) **Freshmen** 82% were admitted **Housing** Yes **Expenses** Tuition $17,402; Room & Board $4922 **Undergraduates** 36% part-time, 19% 25 or older, 1% Native American, 2% Hispanic American, 6% African American, 5% Asian American/Pacific Islander **The most frequently chosen baccalaureate fields are** education, business/marketing, health professions and related sciences **Academic program** English as a second language, advanced placement, self-designed majors, honors program, summer session, adult/continuing education programs, internships **Contact** Ms. Cory Piper-Hauswirth, Associate Director of Admission and Financial Aid, College of St. Catherine, 2004 Randolph Avenue, St. Paul, MN 55105-1789. Telephone: 651-690-6047 or toll-free 800-945-4599 (in-state). Fax: 651-690-8824. E-mail: stkate@stkate.edu. Web site: http://www.stkate.edu/.

THE COLLEGE OF ST. SCHOLASTICA
DULUTH, MINNESOTA

General Independent, comprehensive, coed, affiliated with Roman Catholic Church **Entrance** Moderately difficult **Setting** 160-acre suburban campus **Total enrollment** 2,231 **Student-faculty ratio** 12:1 **Application deadline** Rolling (freshmen), rolling (transfer) **Freshmen** 31% were admitted **Housing** Yes **Expenses** Tuition $17,180; Room & Board $5198 **Undergraduates** 70% women, 12% part-time, 26% 25 or older, 1% Native American, 1% Hispanic American, 1% African American, 1% Asian American/Pacific Islander **The most frequently chosen baccalaureate fields are** business/marketing, biological/life sciences, health professions and related sciences **Academic program** Advanced placement, acceler-

MINNESOTA

The College of St. Scholastica *(continued)*
ated degree program, self-designed majors, honors program, summer session, adult/continuing education programs, internships **Contact** Mr. Brian Dalton, Vice President for Enrollment Management, The College of St. Scholastica, 1200 Kenwood Avenue, Duluth, MN 55811-4199. Telephone: 218-723-6053 or toll-free 800-249-6412. Fax: 218-723-6290. E-mail: admissions@css.edu. Web site: http://www.css.edu/.

COLLEGE OF VISUAL ARTS
ST. PAUL, MINNESOTA

General Independent, 4-year, coed **Entrance** Minimally difficult **Setting** 2-acre urban campus **Total enrollment** 269 **Student-faculty ratio** 8:1 **Application deadline** Rolling (freshmen), rolling (transfer) **Freshmen** 84% were admitted **Housing** No **Expenses** Tuition $13,448 **Undergraduates** 58% women, 11% part-time, 15% 25 or older, 1% Native American, 2% Hispanic American, 1% African American, 4% Asian American/Pacific Islander **The most frequently chosen baccalaureate field is** visual/performing arts **Academic program** Advanced placement, summer session, internships **Contact** Ms. Lynn E. Tanaka, Director of Admissions, College of Visual Arts, 344 Summit Avenue, St. Paul, MN 55102-2124. Telephone: 651-224-3416 or toll-free 800-224-1536. Fax: 651-224-8854. E-mail: info@cva.edu. Web site: http://www.cva.edu/.

CONCORDIA COLLEGE
MOORHEAD, MINNESOTA

General Independent, 4-year, coed, affiliated with Evangelical Lutheran Church in America **Entrance** Moderately difficult **Setting** 120-acre suburban campus **Total enrollment** 2,766 **Student-faculty ratio** 14:1 **Application deadline** Rolling (freshmen), rolling (transfer) **Freshmen** 86% were admitted **Housing** Yes **Expenses** Tuition $14,847; Room & Board $4110 **Undergraduates** 62% women, 2% part-time, 3% 25 or older, 1% Native American, 1% Hispanic American, 1% African American, 1% Asian American/Pacific Islander **The most frequently chosen baccalaureate fields are** business/marketing, education, foreign language/literature **Academic program** English as a second language, advanced placement, honors program, summer session, adult/continuing education programs, internships **Contact** Mr. Scott E. Ellingson, Director of Admissions, Concordia College, 901 8th Street South, Moorhead, MN 56562. Telephone: 218-299-3004 or toll-free 800-699-9897. Fax: 218-299-3947. E-mail: admissions@gloria.cord.edu. Web site: http://www.concordiacollege.edu/.

CONCORDIA UNIVERSITY
ST. PAUL, MINNESOTA

General Independent, comprehensive, coed, affiliated with Lutheran Church–Missouri Synod **Entrance** Minimally difficult **Setting** 37-acre urban campus **Total enrollment** 1,773 **Student-faculty ratio** 12:1 **Application deadline** 8/15 (freshmen), 8/15 (transfer) **Freshmen** 54% were admitted **Housing** Yes **Expenses** Tuition $15,786; Room & Board $5266 **Undergraduates** 60% women, 9% part-time, 37% 25 or older, 0.4% Native American, 1% Hispanic American, 5% African American, 4% Asian American/Pacific Islander **The most frequently chosen baccalaureate fields are** business/marketing, education, philosophy, religion, and theology **Academic program** English as a second language, advanced placement, accelerated degree program, self-designed majors, summer session, adult/continuing education programs, internships **Contact** Ms. Rhonda Behm-Severeid, Director of Freshman Admissions, Concordia University, 275 Syndicate North, St. Paul, MN 55104-5494. Telephone: 651-641-8230 or toll-free 800-333-4705. Fax: 651-659-0207. E-mail: admiss@luther.csp.edu. Web site: http://www.csp.edu/.

CROWN COLLEGE
ST. BONIFACIUS, MINNESOTA

General Independent, comprehensive, coed, affiliated with The Christian and Missionary Alliance **Entrance** Minimally difficult **Setting** 193-acre suburban campus **Total enrollment** 877 **Student-faculty ratio** 14:1 **Application deadline** Rolling (freshmen), rolling (transfer) **Freshmen** 75% were admitted **Housing** Yes **Expenses** Tuition $11,346; Room & Board $4720 **Undergraduates** 55% women, 19% part-time, 31% 25 or older, 0.3% Native American, 2% Hispanic American, 2% African American, 3% Asian American/Pacific Islander **The most frequently chosen baccalaureate fields are** education, philosophy, philosophy, religion, and theology **Academic program** English as a second language, advanced placement, honors program, summer session, adult/continuing education programs, internships **Contact** Ms. Kimberely LaQuay, Application Coordinator/Office Systems Manager, Crown College, 6425 County Road 30, St. Bonifacius, MN 55375-9001. Telephone: 952-446-4143 or toll-free 800-68-CROWN. Fax: 952-446-4149. E-mail: pearsont@gw.crown.edu. Web site: http://www.crown.edu/.

GUSTAVUS ADOLPHUS COLLEGE
ST. PETER, MINNESOTA

General Independent, 4-year, coed, affiliated with Evangelical Lutheran Church in America **Entrance** Very difficult **Setting** 330-acre small-town campus **Total enrollment** 2,592 **Student-faculty ratio** 13:1 **Application deadline** 4/1 (freshmen), 4/1 (transfer) **Freshmen** 76% were admitted **Housing** Yes **Expenses** Tuition $19,355; Room & Board $4900 **Undergraduates** 58% women, 1% part-time, 0% 25 or older, 0.2% Native American, 1% Hispanic American, 1% African American, 3% Asian American/Pacific Islander **The most frequently chosen baccalaureate fields are** business/marketing, biological/life sciences, social sciences and history **Academic program** Advanced placement, accelerated degree program, self-designed majors, honors program, summer session, internships **Contact** Mr. Mark H. Anderson, Dean of Admission, Gustavus Adolphus College, 800 West College

MINNESOTA

Avenue, St. Peter, MN 56082-1498. Telephone: 507-933-7676 or toll-free 800-GUSTAVU(S). Fax: 507-933-7474. E-mail: admission@gac.edu. Web site: http://www.gustavus.edu/.

HAMLINE UNIVERSITY
ST. PAUL, MINNESOTA

General Independent, comprehensive, coed, affiliated with United Methodist Church **Entrance** Moderately difficult **Setting** 50-acre urban campus **Total enrollment** 4,123 **Student-faculty ratio** 13:1 **Application deadline** Rolling (freshmen), rolling (transfer) **Freshmen** 79% were admitted **Housing** Yes **Expenses** Tuition $17,602; Room & Board $5887 **Undergraduates** 64% women, 6% part-time, 9% 25 or older, 1% Native American, 1% Hispanic American, 4% African American, 4% Asian American/Pacific Islander **The most frequently chosen baccalaureate fields are** psychology, business/marketing, social sciences and history **Academic program** English as a second language, advanced placement, self-designed majors, honors program, summer session, adult/continuing education programs, internships **Contact** Mr. Steven Bjork, Director of Undergraduate Admission, Hamline University, 1536 Hewitt Avenue C1930, St. Paul, MN 55104-1284. Telephone: 651-523-2207 or toll-free 800-753-9753. Fax: 651-523-2458. E-mail: cla-admis@gw.hamline.edu. Web site: http://www.hamline.edu/.

MACALESTER COLLEGE
ST. PAUL, MINNESOTA

General Independent Presbyterian, 4-year, coed **Entrance** Very difficult **Setting** 53-acre urban campus **Total enrollment** 1,822 **Student-faculty ratio** 11:1 **Application deadline** 1/15 (freshmen), 4/1 (transfer) **Freshmen** 50% were admitted **Housing** Yes **Expenses** Tuition $22,608; Room & Board $6204 **Undergraduates** 58% women, 3% part-time, 0.2% 25 or older, 1% Native American, 3% Hispanic American, 3% African American, 5% Asian American/Pacific Islander **The most frequently chosen baccalaureate fields are** biological/life sciences, psychology, social sciences and history **Academic program** Self-designed majors, honors program, internships **Contact** Mr. Lorne T. Robinson, Dean of Admissions and Financial Aid, Macalester College, 1600 Grand Avenue, St. Paul, MN 55105-1899. Telephone: 651-696-6357 or toll-free 800-231-7974. Fax: 651-696-6724. E-mail: admissions@macalester.edu. Web site: http://www.macalester.edu/.

MARTIN LUTHER COLLEGE
NEW ULM, MINNESOTA

General Independent, 4-year, coed, affiliated with Wisconsin Evangelical Lutheran Synod **Entrance** Moderately difficult **Setting** 50-acre small-town campus **Total enrollment** 1,060 **Student-faculty ratio** 13:1 **Application deadline** 4/15 (freshmen), 5/1 (transfer) **Freshmen** 95% were admitted **Housing** Yes **Expenses** Tuition $5195; Room & Board $2340

Undergraduates 51% women, 2% part-time, 0.4% Native American, 1% Hispanic American, 1% African American, 1% Asian American/Pacific Islander **The most frequently chosen baccalaureate fields are** education, philosophy, philosophy, religion, and theology **Academic program** Advanced placement, summer session, internships **Contact** Prof. Ronald B. Brutlag, Associate Director of Admissions, Martin Luther College, 1995 Luther Court, New Ulm, MN 56073. Telephone: 507-354-8221 Ext. 280. Fax: 507-354-8225. E-mail: sebaldja-fac@mlc-wels.edu. Web site: http://www.mlc-wels.edu/.

MAYO SCHOOL OF HEALTH SCIENCES
ROCHESTER, MINNESOTA

General Independent, upper-level, coed **Entrance** Moderately difficult **Setting** urban campus **Total enrollment** 762 **Housing** No **Expenses** Tuition $13,500 **Undergraduates** 22% women **Academic program** Internships **Contact** Ms. Kate Ray, Enrollment and Student Services, Mayo School of Health Sciences, Siebins Building, 200 First Street, SW, Rochester, MN 55905. Telephone: 507-266-4077 or toll-free 800-626-9041. Fax: 507-284-0656. E-mail: kray@mayo.edu. Web site: http://www.mayo.edu/hrs/hrs.htm.

METROPOLITAN STATE UNIVERSITY
ST. PAUL, MINNESOTA

General State-supported, comprehensive, coed **Entrance** Minimally difficult **Setting** urban campus **Total enrollment** 6,010 **Student-faculty ratio** 12:1 **Application deadline** Rolling (freshmen), rolling (transfer) **Housing** No **Expenses** Tuition $3111 **Undergraduates** 61% women, 73% part-time, 76% 25 or older, 1% Native American, 1% Hispanic American, 7% African American, 5% Asian American/Pacific Islander **The most frequently chosen baccalaureate fields are** business/marketing, interdisciplinary studies, protective services/public administration **Academic program** English as a second language, self-designed majors, summer session, adult/continuing education programs, internships **Contact** Ms. Janice Harring Hendon, Director, Metropolitan State University, 700 East 7th Street, St. Paul, MN 55106-5000. Telephone: 651-772-7660. Fax: 651-772-7792. E-mail: admissionmetro@metrostate.edu. Web site: http://www.metrostate.edu.

MINNEAPOLIS COLLEGE OF ART AND DESIGN
MINNEAPOLIS, MINNESOTA

General Independent, comprehensive, coed **Entrance** Moderately difficult **Setting** 7-acre urban campus **Total enrollment** 632 **Student-faculty ratio** 15:1 **Application deadline** Rolling (freshmen), rolling (transfer) **Freshmen** 80% were admitted **Housing** Yes **Expenses** Tuition $20,490; Room only $3880 **Undergraduates** 43% women, 9% part-time, 17% 25 or older, 1% Native American, 2% Hispanic American, 2% African American, 4% Asian American/

MINNESOTA

Minneapolis College of Art and Design *(continued)*

Pacific Islander **The most frequently chosen baccalaureate field is** visual/performing arts **Academic program** Advanced placement, summer session, adult/continuing education programs, internships **Contact** Mr. Brad Nuorala, Director of Admissions, Minneapolis College of Art and Design, 2501 Stevens Avenue South, Minneapolis, MN 55404-4347. Telephone: 612-874-3762 or toll-free 800-874-6223. E-mail: admissions@mn.mcad.edu. Web site: http://www.mcad.edu/.

▶ For more information, see page 458.

MINNESOTA BIBLE COLLEGE
ROCHESTER, MINNESOTA

General Independent, 4-year, coed, affiliated with Christian Churches and Churches of Christ **Entrance** Noncompetitive **Setting** 40-acre urban campus **Total enrollment** 109 **Student-faculty ratio** 8:1 **Application deadline** 8/15 (freshmen), 8/15 (transfer) **Freshmen** 56% were admitted **Housing** Yes **Expenses** Tuition $5660; Room only $1900 **Undergraduates** 45% women, 17% part-time, 24% 25 or older, 0% Native American, 2% Hispanic American, 0% African American, 2% Asian American/Pacific Islander **The most frequently chosen baccalaureate fields are** liberal arts/general studies, philosophy, religion, and theology **Academic program** Advanced placement, self-designed majors, internships **Contact** Mr. Michael Golembiesky, Director of Admissions, Minnesota Bible College, 920 Mayowood Road, SW, Rochester, MN 55902-2382. Telephone: 507-288-4563 Ext. 313 or toll-free 800-456-7651. Fax: 507-288-9046. E-mail: admissions@mnbc.edu. Web site: http://www.mnbc.edu/.

MINNESOTA STATE UNIVERSITY, MANKATO
MANKATO, MINNESOTA

General State-supported, comprehensive, coed **Entrance** Moderately difficult **Setting** 303-acre small-town campus **Total enrollment** 13,242 **Student-faculty ratio** 23:1 **Application deadline** Rolling (freshmen), rolling (transfer) **Freshmen** 82% were admitted **Housing** Yes **Expenses** Tuition $3619; Room & Board $3677 **Undergraduates** 52% women, 11% part-time, 13% 25 or older, 0.2% Native American, 1% Hispanic American, 1% African American, 1% Asian American/Pacific Islander **The most frequently chosen baccalaureate fields are** business/marketing, education, protective services/public administration **Academic program** English as a second language, advanced placement, accelerated degree program, self-designed majors, honors program, summer session, adult/continuing education programs, internships **Contact** Mr. Walt Wolff, Director of Admissions, Minnesota State University, Mankato, 122 Taylor Center, Mankato, MN 56001. Telephone: 507-389-6670 or toll-free 800-722-0544. Fax: 507-389-1511. E-mail: admissions@mnsu.edu. Web site: http://www.mnsu.edu.

MINNESOTA STATE UNIVERSITY MOORHEAD
MOORHEAD, MINNESOTA

General State-supported, comprehensive, coed **Entrance** Moderately difficult **Setting** 118-acre urban campus **Total enrollment** 7,431 **Student-faculty ratio** 18:1 **Application deadline** 8/7 (freshmen), 8/7 (transfer) **Housing** Yes **Expenses** Tuition $3377; Room & Board $3706 **Undergraduates** 62% women, 18% part-time, 19% 25 or older, 1% Native American, 1% Hispanic American, 0.5% African American, 1% Asian American/Pacific Islander **The most frequently chosen baccalaureate fields are** law/legal studies, philosophy, religion, and theology **Academic program** Advanced placement, self-designed majors, honors program, summer session, adult/continuing education programs, internships **Contact** Ms. Gina Monson, Director of Admissions, Minnesota State University Moorhead, Owens Hall, Moorhead, MN 56563-0002. Telephone: 218-236-2161 or toll-free 800-593-7246. Fax: 218-236-2168. Web site: http://www.mnstate.edu/.

NATIONAL AMERICAN UNIVERSITY–ST. PAUL CAMPUS
ST. PAUL, MINNESOTA

General Proprietary, 4-year, coed **Entrance** Noncompetitive **Setting** 1-acre urban campus **Total enrollment** 446 **Student-faculty ratio** 10:1 **Application deadline** Rolling (freshmen), rolling (transfer) **Freshmen** 100% were admitted **Housing** No **Expenses** Tuition $8745 **Undergraduates** 48% women, 51% part-time, 50% 25 or older, 0.4% Native American, 3% Hispanic American, 18% African American, 16% Asian American/Pacific Islander **Academic program** Advanced placement, accelerated degree program, summer session, internships **Contact** Mr. Steve Grunlan, Director of Admissions, National American University–St. Paul Campus, 1500 West Highway 36, Roseville, MN 55108-9952. Telephone: 651-644-1265. E-mail: natcoll@iaxs.net. Web site: http://www.nationalcollege.edu/.

NORTH CENTRAL UNIVERSITY
MINNEAPOLIS, MINNESOTA

General Independent, 4-year, coed, affiliated with Assemblies of God **Entrance** Noncompetitive **Setting** 9-acre urban campus **Total enrollment** 1,163 **Student-faculty ratio** 18:1 **Application deadline** 6/1 (freshmen), 6/1 (transfer) **Freshmen** 77% were admitted **Housing** Yes **Expenses** Tuition $8554; Room & Board $2270 **Undergraduates** 16% 25 or older, 1% Native American, 3% Hispanic American, 5% African American, 1% Asian American/Pacific Islander **The most frequently chosen baccalaureate fields are** education, communications/communication technologies, philosophy, religion, and theology **Academic program** Advanced placement, self-designed majors, summer session, adult/continuing education programs, internships **Contact** Ms. Mary Jo Meier, Admissions Secretary, North Central University, 910

Elliot Avenue, Minneapolis, MN 55404. Telephone: 612-343-4401 or toll-free 800-289-6222. Fax: 612-343-4146. E-mail: akgoetz@topaz.ncbc.edu. Web site: http://www.northcentral.edu/.

NORTHWESTERN COLLEGE
ST. PAUL, MINNESOTA

General Independent nondenominational, 4-year, coed **Entrance** Moderately difficult **Setting** 100-acre suburban campus **Total enrollment** 2,278 **Student-faculty ratio** 15:1 **Application deadline** 8/1 (freshmen), 8/1 (transfer) **Freshmen** 99% were admitted **Housing** Yes **Expenses** Tuition $15,600; Room & Board $5050 **Undergraduates** 63% women, 21% part-time, 3% 25 or older, 0.2% Native American, 1% Hispanic American, 3% African American, 2% Asian American/Pacific Islander **The most frequently chosen baccalaureate fields are** education, philosophy, philosophy, religion, and theology **Academic program** English as a second language, advanced placement, summer session, adult/continuing education programs, internships **Contact** Mr. Kenneth K. Faffler, Director of Recruitment, Northwestern College, 3003 Snelling Avenue North, Nazareth Hall, Room 229, St. Paul, MN 55113-1598. Telephone: 651-631-5209 or toll-free 800-827-6827. Fax: 651-631-5680. E-mail: admissions@nwc.edu. Web site: http://www.nwc.edu/.

OAK HILLS CHRISTIAN COLLEGE
BEMIDJI, MINNESOTA

General Independent interdenominational, 4-year, coed **Entrance** Minimally difficult **Setting** 180-acre rural campus **Total enrollment** 178 **Student-faculty ratio** 8:1 **Application deadline** Rolling (freshmen), rolling (transfer) **Freshmen** 32% were admitted **Housing** Yes **Expenses** Tuition $9450; Room & Board $3410 **Undergraduates** 53% women, 15% part-time, 16% 25 or older, 2% Native American, 1% Hispanic American, 4% African American, 1% Asian American/Pacific Islander **The most frequently chosen baccalaureate fields are** philosophy, philosophy, religion, and theology **Academic program** Advanced placement, honors program, internships **Contact** Mr. Dan Hovestol, Admissions Director, Oak Hills Christian College, 1600 Oak Hills Road, SW, Bemidji, MN 56601. Telephone: 218-751-8670 Ext. 220 or toll-free 888-751-8670 Ext. 285. Fax: 218-751-8825. E-mail: admissions@oakhill.edu. Web site: http://www.oakhills.edu/.

PILLSBURY BAPTIST BIBLE COLLEGE
OWATONNA, MINNESOTA

General Independent Baptist, 4-year, coed **Entrance** Noncompetitive **Setting** 14-acre small-town campus **Total enrollment** 222 **Student-faculty ratio** 10:1 **Application deadline** 9/1 (freshmen), 9/1 (transfer) **Freshmen** 70% were admitted **Housing** Yes **Expenses** Tuition $7228; Room & Board $3340 **Undergraduates** 58% women, 10% part-time, 0.5% Native American, 1% Hispanic American, 1% African American, 0.5% Asian American/Pacific Islander **The most frequently chosen baccalaureate fields are** business/marketing, education, philosophy **Academic program** Advanced placement, accelerated degree program, self-designed majors, summer session, adult/continuing education programs, internships **Contact** Mr. Gene Young, Director of Admissions, Pillsbury Baptist Bible College, 315 South Grove, Owatonna, MN 55060-3097. Telephone: 507-451-2710 Ext. 279 or toll-free 800-747-4557. Fax: 507-451-6459. Web site: http://www.pillsbury.edu/.

ST. CLOUD STATE UNIVERSITY
ST. CLOUD, MINNESOTA

General State-supported, comprehensive, coed **Entrance** Moderately difficult **Setting** 108-acre suburban campus **Total enrollment** 15,961 **Student-faculty ratio** 20:1 **Application deadline** 7/31 (freshmen), 8/1 (transfer) **Freshmen** 84% were admitted **Housing** Yes **Expenses** Tuition $3883; Room & Board $3614 **Undergraduates** 54% women, 19% part-time, 14% 25 or older, 1% Native American, 1% Hispanic American, 1% African American, 1% Asian American/Pacific Islander **The most frequently chosen baccalaureate fields are** business/marketing, communications/communication technologies, social sciences and history **Academic program** English as a second language, advanced placement, accelerated degree program, self-designed majors, honors program, summer session, adult/continuing education programs, internships **Contact** Ms. Debbie Tamte-Horan, Director of Admissions, St. Cloud State University, 720 4th Avenue South, St. Cloud, MN 56301-4498. Telephone: 320-255-2286 or toll-free 877-654-7278. Fax: 320-255-2243. E-mail: scsu4u@stcloudstate.edu. Web site: http://www.stcloudstate.edu/.

SAINT JOHN'S UNIVERSITY
COLLEGEVILLE, MINNESOTA

General Independent Roman Catholic, comprehensive, coed, coordinate institution with College of Saint Benedict **Entrance** Moderately difficult **Setting** 2,400-acre rural campus **Total enrollment** 2,039 **Student-faculty ratio** 11:1 **Application deadline** Rolling (freshmen), rolling (transfer) **Freshmen** 85% were admitted **Housing** Yes **Expenses** Tuition $18,325; Room & Board $5606 **Undergraduates** 2% part-time, 1% 25 or older, 0.3% Native American, 1% Hispanic American, 0.2% African American, 2% Asian American/Pacific Islander **The most frequently chosen baccalaureate fields are** business/marketing, English, social sciences and history **Academic program** English as a second language, advanced placement, accelerated degree program, self-designed majors, honors program, internships **Contact** Ms. Mary Milbert, Dean of Admissions, Saint John's University, PO Box 7155, Collegeville, MN 56321-7155. Telephone: 320-363-2196 or toll-free 800-24JOHNS. Fax: 320-363-3206. E-mail: admissions@csbsju.edu. Web site: http://www.csbsju.edu/.

MINNESOTA

SAINT MARY'S UNIVERSITY OF MINNESOTA
WINONA, MINNESOTA

General Independent Roman Catholic, comprehensive, coed **Entrance** Moderately difficult **Setting** 350-acre small-town campus **Total enrollment** 5,008 **Student-faculty ratio** 14:1 **Application deadline** 5/1 (freshmen), rolling (transfer) **Freshmen** 86% were admitted **Housing** Yes **Expenses** Tuition $15,195; Room & Board $4780 **Undergraduates** 54% women, 18% part-time, 2% 25 or older, 0.2% Native American, 1% Hispanic American, 1% African American, 1% Asian American/Pacific Islander **The most frequently chosen baccalaureate fields are** business/marketing, communications/communication technologies, social sciences and history **Academic program** English as a second language, advanced placement, accelerated degree program, self-designed majors, honors program, summer session, adult/continuing education programs, internships **Contact** Mr. Anthony M. Piscitiello, Vice President for Admission, Saint Mary's University of Minnesota, 700 Terrace Heights, Winona, MN 55987-1399. Telephone: 507-457-1700 or toll-free 800-635-5987. Fax: 507-457-1722. E-mail: admissions@smumn.edu. Web site: http://www.smumn.edu/.

ST. OLAF COLLEGE
NORTHFIELD, MINNESOTA

General Independent Lutheran, 4-year, coed **Entrance** Very difficult **Setting** 350-acre small-town campus **Total enrollment** 3,011 **Student-faculty ratio** 13:1 **Application deadline** Rolling (freshmen), rolling (transfer) **Freshmen** 76% were admitted **Housing** Yes **Expenses** Tuition $21,280; Room & Board $4600 **Undergraduates** 58% women, 2% part-time, 0.3% 25 or older, 0.2% Native American, 1% Hispanic American, 1% African American, 3% Asian American/Pacific Islander **The most frequently chosen baccalaureate fields are** biological/life sciences, social sciences and history, visual/performing arts **Academic program** English as a second language, advanced placement, accelerated degree program, self-designed majors, summer session, adult/continuing education programs, internships **Contact** Jeff McLaughlin, Acting Director of Admissions, St. Olaf College, 1520 St. Olaf Avenue, Northfield, MN 55057. Telephone: 507-646-3025 or toll-free 800-800-3025. Fax: 507-646-3832. E-mail: admiss@stolaf.edu. Web site: http://www.stolaf.edu/.

SOUTHWEST STATE UNIVERSITY
MARSHALL, MINNESOTA

General State-supported, comprehensive, coed **Entrance** Minimally difficult **Setting** 216-acre small-town campus **Total enrollment** 5,056 **Student-faculty ratio** 18:1 **Application deadline** Rolling (freshmen), rolling (transfer) **Freshmen** 52% were admitted **Housing** Yes **Expenses** Tuition $3716; Room & Board $3934 **Undergraduates** 60% women, 50% part-time, 10% 25 or older, 0.2% Native American, 0.3% Hispanic American, 1% African American, 1% Asian American/Pacific Islander **Academic program** Advanced placement, accelerated degree program, self-designed majors, honors program, summer session, adult/continuing education programs, internships **Contact** Richard Shearer, Director of Enrollment Services, Southwest State University, 1501 State Street, Marshall, MN 56258-1598. Telephone: 507-537-6286 or toll-free 800-642-0684. Fax: 507-537-7154. E-mail: shearerr@southwest.msus.edu. Web site: http://www.southwest.msus.edu/.

UNIVERSITY OF MINNESOTA, CROOKSTON
CROOKSTON, MINNESOTA

General State-supported, 4-year, coed **Entrance** Moderately difficult **Setting** 95-acre rural campus **Total enrollment** 2,529 **Student-faculty ratio** 18:1 **Application deadline** 8/1 (freshmen), 8/1 (transfer) **Freshmen** 88% were admitted **Housing** Yes **Expenses** Tuition $5632; Room & Board $4337 **Undergraduates** 56% women, 56% part-time, 3% 25 or older **The most frequently chosen baccalaureate fields are** agriculture, business/marketing, computer/information sciences **Academic program** Advanced placement, summer session, adult/continuing education programs, internships **Contact** Mr. Russell L. Kreager, Director of Admissions, University of Minnesota, Crookston, 2900 University Avenue, 170 Owen Hall, Crookston, MN 56716-5001. Telephone: 218-281-8569 or toll-free 800-232-6466. Fax: 218-281-8575. E-mail: info@mail.crk.umn.edu. Web site: http://www.crk.umn.edu/.

▶ For more information, see page 487.

UNIVERSITY OF MINNESOTA, DULUTH
DULUTH, MINNESOTA

General State-supported, comprehensive, coed **Entrance** Moderately difficult **Setting** 250-acre suburban campus **Total enrollment** 9,374 **Student-faculty ratio** 20:1 **Application deadline** 2/1 (freshmen), 8/1 (transfer) **Freshmen** 79% were admitted **Housing** Yes **Expenses** Tuition $5844; Room & Board $4592 **Undergraduates** 51% women, 13% part-time, 11% 25 or older, 1% Native American, 1% Hispanic American, 1% African American, 2% Asian American/Pacific Islander **The most frequently chosen baccalaureate fields are** business/marketing, education, social sciences and history **Academic program** English as a second language, advanced placement, self-designed majors, honors program, summer session, adult/continuing education programs, internships **Contact** Ms. Beth Esselstrom, Director of Admissions, University of Minnesota, Duluth, 23 Solon Campus Center, 1117 University Drive, Duluth, MN 55812-3000. Telephone: 218-726-7171 or toll-free 800-232-1339. Fax: 218-726-6394. E-mail: umdadmis@d.umn.edu. Web site: http://www.d.umn.edu/.

MISSISSIPPI

UNIVERSITY OF MINNESOTA, MORRIS
MORRIS, MINNESOTA

General State-supported, 4-year, coed **Entrance** Moderately difficult **Setting** 130-acre small-town campus **Total enrollment** 1,924 **Student-faculty ratio** 14:1 **Application deadline** 3/15 (freshmen), 5/1 (transfer) **Freshmen** 84% were admitted **Housing** Yes **Expenses** Tuition $6246; Room & Board $4470 **Undergraduates** 59% women, 5% part-time, 5% 25 or older, 7% Native American, 2% Hispanic American, 5% African American, 3% Asian American/Pacific Islander **The most frequently chosen baccalaureate fields are** English, biological/life sciences, social sciences and history **Academic program** English as a second language, advanced placement, accelerated degree program, self-designed majors, honors program, summer session, adult/continuing education programs, internships **Contact** Mr. Scott K. Hagg, Acting Director of Admissions, University of Minnesota, Morris, 600 East 4th Street, Morris, MN 56267-2199. Telephone: 320-539-6035 or toll-free 800-992-8863. Fax: 320-589-1673. E-mail: admissions@mrs.umn.edu. Web site: http://www.mrs.umn.edu/.

UNIVERSITY OF MINNESOTA, TWIN CITIES CAMPUS
MINNEAPOLIS, MINNESOTA

General State-supported, university, coed **Entrance** Moderately difficult **Setting** 2,000-acre urban campus **Total enrollment** 46,597 **Application deadline** Rolling (freshmen), 3/1 (transfer) **Freshmen** 76% were admitted **Housing** Yes **Expenses** Tuition $5536; Room & Board $5582 **Undergraduates** 53% women, 25% part-time, 12% 25 or older, 1% Native American, 2% Hispanic American, 4% African American, 8% Asian American/Pacific Islander **The most frequently chosen baccalaureate fields are** engineering/engineering technologies, business/marketing, social sciences and history **Academic program** English as a second language, advanced placement, accelerated degree program, self-designed majors, honors program, summer session, adult/continuing education programs, internships **Contact** Ms. Patricia Jones Whyte, Associate Director of Admissions, University of Minnesota, Twin Cities Campus, 240 Williamson Hall, Minneapolis, MN 55455-0115. Telephone: 612-625-2008 or toll-free 800-752-1000. Fax: 612-626-1693. E-mail: admissions@tc.umn.edu. Web site: http://www.umn.edu/tc/.

UNIVERSITY OF ST. THOMAS
ST. PAUL, MINNESOTA

General Independent Roman Catholic, university, coed **Entrance** Moderately difficult **Setting** 78-acre urban campus **Total enrollment** 11,473 **Student-faculty ratio** 14:1 **Application deadline** Rolling (freshmen), 8/1 (transfer) **Freshmen** 81% were admitted **Housing** Yes **Expenses** Tuition $18,421; Room & Board $5623 **Undergraduates** 53% women, 13% part-time, 11% 25 or older, 1% Native American, 2% Hispanic American, 2% African American, 5% Asian American/Pacific Islander **The most frequently chosen baccalaureate fields are** business/marketing, communications/communication technologies, social sciences and history **Academic program** English as a second language, advanced placement, self-designed majors, honors program, summer session, adult/continuing education programs, internships **Contact** Ms. Marla Friederichs, Associate Vice President of Enrollment Management, University of St. Thomas, Mail #32F-1, 2115 Summit Avenue, St. Paul, MN 55105-1096. Telephone: 651-962-6150 or toll-free 800-328-6819 Ext. 26150. Fax: 651-962-6160. E-mail: admissions@stthomas.edu. Web site: http://www.stthomas.edu/.

WINONA STATE UNIVERSITY
WINONA, MINNESOTA

General State-supported, comprehensive, coed **Entrance** Moderately difficult **Setting** 40-acre small-town campus **Total enrollment** 9,345 **Student-faculty ratio** 19:1 **Application deadline** Rolling (freshmen), 8/1 (transfer) **Freshmen** 85% were admitted **Housing** Yes **Expenses** Tuition $3630; Room & Board $3940 **Undergraduates** 63% women, 12% part-time, 8% 25 or older, 0.2% Native American, 1% Hispanic American, 0.4% African American, 1% Asian American/Pacific Islander **The most frequently chosen baccalaureate field is** law/legal studies **Academic program** English as a second language, advanced placement, accelerated degree program, self-designed majors, honors program, summer session, adult/continuing education programs, internships **Contact** Mr. Douglas Schacke, Director of Admissions, Winona State University, PO Box 5838, Winona, MN 55987. Telephone: 507-457-5100 or toll-free 800-DIAL WSU. Fax: 507-457-5620. E-mail: admissions@vax2.winona.msus.edu. Web site: http://www.winona.edu/.

MISSISSIPPI

ALCORN STATE UNIVERSITY
ALCORN STATE, MISSISSIPPI

General State-supported, comprehensive, coed **Entrance** Minimally difficult **Setting** 1,756-acre rural campus **Total enrollment** 3,096 **Student-faculty ratio** 13:1 **Application deadline** Rolling (freshmen), rolling (transfer) **Freshmen** 40% were admitted **Housing** Yes **Expenses** Tuition $3203; Room & Board $3090 **Undergraduates** 60% women, 11% part-time, 18% 25 or older, 0.04% Native American, 0.2% Hispanic American, 93% African American, 0.1% Asian American/Pacific Islander **The most frequently chosen baccalaureate fields are** business/marketing, biological/life sciences, liberal arts/general studies **Academic program** Advanced placement, honors program, internships **Contact** Mr. Emanuel Barnes, Director of Admissions, Alcorn State Univer-

MISSISSIPPI

Alcorn State University *(continued)*
sity, 1000 ASU Drive, Alcorn State, MS 39096-7500. Telephone: 601-877-6147 or toll-free 800-222-6790. Fax: 601-877-6347. E-mail: ebarnes@loman.alcorn.edu. Web site: http://www.alcorn.edu/.

BELHAVEN COLLEGE
JACKSON, MISSISSIPPI

General Independent Presbyterian, comprehensive, coed **Entrance** Moderately difficult **Setting** 42-acre urban campus **Total enrollment** 1,883 **Student-faculty ratio** 15:1 **Application deadline** Rolling (freshmen), rolling (transfer) **Freshmen** 67% were admitted **Housing** Yes **Expenses** Tuition $11,460; Room & Board $4440 **Undergraduates** 63% women, 9% part-time, 54% 25 or older, 1% Native American, 1% Hispanic American, 34% African American, 1% Asian American/Pacific Islander **The most frequently chosen baccalaureate fields are** business/marketing, parks and recreation, psychology **Academic program** English as a second language, advanced placement, accelerated degree program, honors program, summer session, adult/continuing education programs, internships **Contact** Suzanne Teel, Director of Admissions, Belhaven College, 150 Peachtree Street, Jackson, MS 39202. Telephone: 601-968-5940 or toll-free 800-960-5940. Fax: 601-968-8946. E-mail: admissions@belhaven.edu. Web site: http://www.belhaven.edu/.

BLUE MOUNTAIN COLLEGE
BLUE MOUNTAIN, MISSISSIPPI

General Independent Southern Baptist, 4-year, women only **Entrance** Noncompetitive **Setting** 44-acre rural campus **Total enrollment** 395 **Student-faculty ratio** 14:1 **Application deadline** Rolling (freshmen), rolling (transfer) **Freshmen** 80% were admitted **Housing** Yes **Expenses** Tuition $6200; Room & Board $3120 **Undergraduates** 22% part-time, 40% 25 or older, 0.3% Native American, 0.3% Hispanic American, 11% African American, 0.3% Asian American/Pacific Islander **The most frequently chosen baccalaureate fields are** education, philosophy, religion, and theology, psychology **Academic program** Advanced placement, accelerated degree program, honors program, summer session, internships **Contact** Ms. Tina Barkley, Director of Admissions, Blue Mountain College, PO Box 160, Blue Mountain, MS 38610-0160. Telephone: 662-685-4161 Ext. 176 or toll-free 800-235-0136. E-mail: tbarkley@bmc.edu. Web site: http://www.bmc.edu/.

DELTA STATE UNIVERSITY
CLEVELAND, MISSISSIPPI

General State-supported, comprehensive, coed **Entrance** Minimally difficult **Setting** 332-acre small-town campus **Total enrollment** 3,746 **Student-faculty ratio** 14:1 **Application deadline** 8/1 (freshmen), rolling (transfer) **Housing** Yes **Expenses** Tuition $3100; Room & Board $2920 **Undergraduates** 60% women, 14% part-time, 32% 25 or older, 0.2% Native American, 0.4% Hispanic American, 30% African American, 0.3% Asian American/Pacific Islander **The most frequently chosen baccalaureate fields are** business/marketing, education, protective services/public administration **Academic program** Advanced placement, honors program, summer session, internships **Contact** Ms. Debbie Heslep, Director of Admissions, Delta State University, Highway 8 West, Cleveland, MS 38733. Telephone: 662-846-4018 or toll-free 800-468-6378. Fax: 662-846-4683. E-mail: dheslep@dsu.deltast.edu. Web site: http://www.deltast.edu/.

JACKSON STATE UNIVERSITY
JACKSON, MISSISSIPPI

General State-supported, university, coed **Entrance** Minimally difficult **Setting** 128-acre urban campus **Total enrollment** 7,098 **Student-faculty ratio** 16:1 **Application deadline** 8/1 (freshmen), 8/1 (transfer) **Housing** Yes **Expenses** Tuition $3206; Room & Board $4014 **Undergraduates** 61% women, 14% part-time, 18% 25 or older, 0.02% Native American, 0.1% Hispanic American, 97% African American, 0.2% Asian American/Pacific Islander **The most frequently chosen baccalaureate fields are** business/marketing, education, protective services/public administration **Academic program** English as a second language, advanced placement, accelerated degree program, honors program, summer session, adult/continuing education programs, internships **Contact** Mrs. Linda Rush, Admissions Counselor, Jackson State University, PO Box 17230, 1400 John R. Lynch Street, Jackson, MS 39217. Telephone: 601-968-2911 or toll-free 800-682-5390 (in-state); 800-848-6817 (out-of-state). E-mail: schatman@ccaix.jsums.edu. Web site: http://www.jsums.edu/.

MAGNOLIA BIBLE COLLEGE
KOSCIUSKO, MISSISSIPPI

General Independent, 4-year, coed, primarily men, affiliated with Church of Christ **Entrance** Noncompetitive **Setting** 5-acre small-town campus **Total enrollment** 37 **Student-faculty ratio** 6:1 **Application deadline** 8/31 (freshmen), 8/31 (transfer) **Freshmen** 100% were admitted **Housing** Yes **Expenses** Tuition $4590; Room only $1120 **Undergraduates** 35% women, 43% part-time, 51% 25 or older, 3% Hispanic American, 33% African American, 3% Asian American/Pacific Islander **The most frequently chosen baccalaureate fields are** philosophy, philosophy, religion, and theology **Academic program** Summer session, internships **Contact** Mr. Allen Coker, Director of Admissions, Magnolia Bible College, PO Box 1109, Kosciusko, MS 39090-1109. Telephone: 601-289-2896 Ext. 106 or toll-free 800-748-8655 (in-state). Fax: 601-289-1850. E-mail: mbcadmissions@hotmail.com.

MILLSAPS COLLEGE
JACKSON, MISSISSIPPI

General Independent United Methodist, comprehensive, coed **Entrance** Moderately difficult **Setting**

MISSISSIPPI

100-acre urban campus **Total enrollment** 1,330 **Student-faculty ratio** 13:1 **Application deadline** 2/1 (freshmen), rolling (transfer) **Freshmen** 86% were admitted **Housing** Yes **Expenses** Tuition $16,546; Room & Board $6062 **Undergraduates** 55% women, 5% part-time, 9% 25 or older, 0.3% Native American, 1% Hispanic American, 11% African American, 2% Asian American/Pacific Islander **The most frequently chosen baccalaureate fields are** business/marketing, psychology, social sciences and history **Academic program** English as a second language, advanced placement, honors program, summer session, adult/continuing education programs, internships **Contact** Mr. John Gaines, Director of Admissions, Millsaps College, 1701 North State Street, Jackson, MS 39210-0001. Telephone: 601-974-1050 or toll-free 800-352-1050. Fax: 601-974-1059. E-mail: admissions@millsaps.edu. Web site: http://www.millsaps.edu/.

MISSISSIPPI COLLEGE
CLINTON, MISSISSIPPI

General Independent Southern Baptist, comprehensive, coed **Entrance** Moderately difficult **Setting** 320-acre suburban campus **Total enrollment** 3,223 **Student-faculty ratio** 16:1 **Application deadline** Rolling (freshmen), rolling (transfer) **Freshmen** 87% were admitted **Housing** Yes **Expenses** Tuition $10,150; Room & Board $4424 **Undergraduates** 59% women, 12% part-time, 15% 25 or older, 0.2% Native American, 0.3% Hispanic American, 11% African American, 1% Asian American/Pacific Islander **The most frequently chosen baccalaureate fields are** business/marketing, biological/life sciences, education **Academic program** Advanced placement, honors program, summer session, adult/continuing education programs, internships **Contact** Mr. Chad Phillips, Director of Admissions, Mississippi College, PO Box 4026, South Capitol Street, Clinton, MS 39058. Telephone: 601-925-3800 or toll-free 800-738-1236. Fax: 601-925-3804. E-mail: enrollment-services@mc.edu.

MISSISSIPPI STATE UNIVERSITY
MISSISSIPPI STATE, MISSISSIPPI

General State-supported, university, coed **Entrance** Moderately difficult **Setting** 4,200-acre small-town campus **Total enrollment** 16,878 **Student-faculty ratio** 18:1 **Application deadline** 5/1 (freshmen), 8/1 (transfer) **Freshmen** 72% were admitted **Housing** Yes **Expenses** Tuition $3586; Room & Board $5704 **Undergraduates** 47% women, 12% part-time, 14% 25 or older, 0.4% Native American, 1% Hispanic American, 19% African American, 1% Asian American/Pacific Islander **The most frequently chosen baccalaureate fields are** business/marketing, engineering/engineering technologies **Academic program** English as a second language, advanced placement, accelerated degree program, self-designed majors, honors program, summer session, adult/continuing education programs, internships **Contact** Mr. Jerry Inmon, Director of Admissions, Mississippi State University, PO Box 6305, Mississippi State, MS 39762. Telephone: 662-325-2224. Fax: 662-325-7360. E-mail: admit@admissions.msstate.edu. Web site: http://www.msstate.edu/.

MISSISSIPPI UNIVERSITY FOR WOMEN
COLUMBUS, MISSISSIPPI

General State-supported, comprehensive, coed, primarily women **Entrance** Moderately difficult **Setting** 110-acre small-town campus **Total enrollment** 2,328 **Student-faculty ratio** 13:1 **Application deadline** 9/6 (freshmen), 9/6 (transfer) **Freshmen** 65% were admitted **Housing** Yes **Expenses** Tuition $3054; Room & Board $3030 **Undergraduates** 83% women, 32% part-time, 42% 25 or older, 0.4% Native American, 1% Hispanic American, 28% African American, 1% Asian American/Pacific Islander **The most frequently chosen baccalaureate fields are** business/marketing, education, health professions and related sciences **Academic program** English as a second language, advanced placement, accelerated degree program, honors program, summer session, adult/continuing education programs, internships **Contact** Ms. Terri Heath, Director of Admissions, Mississippi University for Women, PO Box 1613, Columbus, MS 39701-9998. Telephone: 601-329-7106 or toll-free 877-GO 2 THE W. Fax: 601-241-7481. E-mail: admissions@muw.edu. Web site: http://www.muw.edu/.

MISSISSIPPI VALLEY STATE UNIVERSITY
ITTA BENA, MISSISSIPPI

General State-supported, comprehensive, coed **Entrance** Minimally difficult **Setting** 450-acre small-town campus **Total enrollment** 3,081 **Student-faculty ratio** 19:1 **Application deadline** Rolling (freshmen), rolling (transfer) **Freshmen** 16% were admitted **Housing** Yes **Expenses** Tuition $3158; Room & Board $3187 **Undergraduates** 69% women, 19% part-time, 41% 25 or older, 0% Native American, 0.04% Hispanic American, 95% African American, 0.1% Asian American/Pacific Islander **The most frequently chosen baccalaureate fields are** education, protective services/public administration, social sciences and history **Academic program** Honors program, summer session, adult/continuing education programs, internships **Contact** Mr. Wilson Lee, Director of Admissions and Recruitment, Mississippi Valley State University, 14000 Highway 82 West, Itta Bena, MS 38941-1400. Telephone: 662-254-3344 or toll-free 800-844-6885 (in-state). Fax: 662-254-7900. Web site: http://www.mvsu.edu/.

RUST COLLEGE
HOLLY SPRINGS, MISSISSIPPI

General Independent United Methodist, 4-year, coed **Entrance** Moderately difficult **Setting** 126-acre rural campus **Total enrollment** 801 **Student-faculty ratio** 17:1 **Application deadline** 7/15 (freshmen), 7/15 (transfer) **Freshmen** 43% were admitted **Housing** Yes **Expenses** Tuition $5600; Room & Board $2400 **Undergraduates** 65% women, 26% part-time, 20% 25 or older, 93% African American **The most fre-**

MISSISSIPPI

Rust College *(continued)*
quently chosen baccalaureate fields are biological/life sciences, business/marketing, communications/communication technologies **Academic program** Accelerated degree program, honors program, summer session, adult/continuing education programs, internships **Contact** Mr. Johnny McDonald, Director of Enrollment Services, Rust College, 150 Rust Avenue, Holly Springs, MS 38635-2328. Telephone: 601-252-8000 Ext. 4065 or toll-free 888-886-8492 Ext. 4065. Fax: 662-252-8895. E-mail: admissions@rustcollege.edu. Web site: http://www.rustcollege.edu/.

SOUTHEASTERN BAPTIST COLLEGE
LAUREL, MISSISSIPPI

Contact Mrs. Emma Bond, Director of Admissions, Southeastern Baptist College, 4229 Highway 15 North, Laurel, MS 39440-1096. Telephone: 601-426-6346.

TOUGALOO COLLEGE
TOUGALOO, MISSISSIPPI

General Independent, 4-year, coed, affiliated with United Church of Christ **Entrance** Minimally difficult **Setting** 500-acre suburban campus **Total enrollment** 950 **Student-faculty ratio** 18:1 **Application deadline** Rolling (freshmen), rolling (transfer) **Freshmen** 99% were admitted **Housing** Yes **Expenses** Tuition $7325; Room & Board $3400 **Undergraduates** 71% women, 9% part-time, 10% 25 or older, 0% Native American, 0% Hispanic American, 99% African American, 0% Asian American/Pacific Islander **The most frequently chosen baccalaureate fields are** psychology, computer/information sciences, social sciences and history **Academic program** Accelerated degree program, self-designed majors, honors program, adult/continuing education programs, internships **Contact** Ms. Adriene W. Walls, Data Entry Specialist, Tougaloo College, Student Enrollment Management Center, 500 West County Line Road, Tougaloo, MS 39174. Telephone: 601-977-7768 or toll-free 888-42GALOO. E-mail: carolyn.evans@tougaloo.edu. Web site: http://www.tougaloo.edu/.

UNIVERSITY OF MISSISSIPPI
OXFORD, MISSISSIPPI

General State-supported, university, coed **Entrance** Moderately difficult **Setting** 2,500-acre small-town campus **Total enrollment** 11,879 **Student-faculty ratio** 19:1 **Application deadline** 7/20 (freshmen), 7/24 (transfer) **Freshmen** 80% were admitted **Housing** Yes **Expenses** Tuition $3626; Room & Board $4040 **Undergraduates** 52% women, 1% part-time, 10% 25 or older **The most frequently chosen baccalaureate field is** philosophy, religion, and theology **Academic program** English as a second language, advanced placement, accelerated degree program, honors program, summer session, adult/continuing education programs, internships **Contact** Mr. Beckett Howorth, Director of Admissions, University of Mississippi, Office of Admissions, 145 Martindale Student Services Center, University, MS 38677. Telephone: 662-915-7226 or toll-free 800-653-6477 (in-state). Fax: 662-915-5869. E-mail: admissions@olemiss.edu. Web site: http://www.olemiss.edu/.

UNIVERSITY OF MISSISSIPPI MEDICAL CENTER
JACKSON, MISSISSIPPI

General State-supported, upper-level, coed **Entrance** Moderately difficult **Setting** 164-acre urban campus **Total enrollment** 1,200 **Student-faculty ratio** 2:1 **Application deadline** 2/15 (transfer) **Housing** Yes **Expenses** Tuition $2850; Room only $1836 **Undergraduates** 85% women, 0% Native American, 1% Hispanic American, 22% African American, 2% Asian American/Pacific Islander **The most frequently chosen baccalaureate field is** health professions and related sciences **Academic program** Summer session, internships **Contact** Director of Student Services and Records, University of Mississippi Medical Center, 2500 North State Street, Jackson, MS 39216-4505. Telephone: 601-984-1080. Fax: 601-984-1079. Web site: http://umc.edu/.

UNIVERSITY OF SOUTHERN MISSISSIPPI
HATTIESBURG, MISSISSIPPI

General State-supported, university, coed **Entrance** Moderately difficult **Setting** 1,090-acre suburban campus **Total enrollment** 15,233 **Student-faculty ratio** 20:1 **Application deadline** Rolling (freshmen), rolling (transfer) **Freshmen** 51% were admitted **Housing** Yes **Expenses** Tuition $3416; Room & Board $4450 **Undergraduates** 61% women, 15% part-time, 24% 25 or older, 0.3% Native American, 1% Hispanic American, 24% African American, 1% Asian American/Pacific Islander **The most frequently chosen baccalaureate fields are** business/marketing, education, health professions and related sciences **Academic program** English as a second language, advanced placement, accelerated degree program, honors program, summer session, adult/continuing education programs **Contact** Dr. Homer Wesley, Dean of Admissions, University of Southern Mississippi, Box 5166, Hattiesburg, MS 39406-5166. Telephone: 601-266-5000. Fax: 601-266-5148. E-mail: admissions@usm.edu. Web site: http://www.usm.edu/.

WESLEY COLLEGE
FLORENCE, MISSISSIPPI

General Independent Congregational Methodist, 4-year, coed **Entrance** Noncompetitive **Setting** 40-acre small-town campus **Total enrollment** 101 **Student-faculty ratio** 5:1 **Application deadline** Rolling (freshmen), rolling (transfer) **Freshmen** 97% were admitted **Housing** Yes **Expenses** Tuition $3900; Room & Board $2700 **Undergraduates** 41% women, 30% part-time, 40% 25 or older **The most frequently chosen baccalaureate field is** philosophy, religion, and theology **Academic program** Advanced placement, adult/continuing education programs, internships **Contact** Rev. Chris Lohrstorfer, Director of

Admissions, Wesley College, PO Box 1070, Florence, MS 39073-1070. Telephone: 601-845-2265 Ext. 21 or toll-free 800-748-9972. Fax: 601-845-2266. E-mail: wcadmit@aol.com. Web site: http://www.wesleycollege.com/.

WILLIAM CAREY COLLEGE
HATTIESBURG, MISSISSIPPI

General Independent Southern Baptist, comprehensive, coed **Entrance** Moderately difficult **Setting** 64-acre small-town campus **Total enrollment** 2,318 **Application deadline** Rolling (freshmen), rolling (transfer) **Freshmen** 52% were admitted **Housing** Yes **Undergraduates** 68% women, 21% part-time, 0.4% Native American, 2% Hispanic American, 29% African American, 1% Asian American/Pacific Islander **The most frequently chosen baccalaureate fields are** education, health professions and related sciences, psychology **Academic program** Accelerated degree program, honors program, summer session, adult/continuing education programs **Contact** Mr. David Armstrong, Director of Admissions, William Carey College, 498 Tuscan Avenue, Hattiesburg, MS 39401-5499. Telephone: 601-318-5051 Ext. 103 or toll-free 800-962-5991 (in-state). E-mail: admiss@mail.wmcarey.edu. Web site: http://www.wmcarey.edu/.

MISSOURI

AVILA COLLEGE
KANSAS CITY, MISSOURI

General Independent Roman Catholic, comprehensive, coed **Entrance** Minimally difficult **Setting** 50-acre suburban campus **Total enrollment** 1,644 **Student-faculty ratio** 13:1 **Application deadline** Rolling (freshmen), rolling (transfer) **Freshmen** 60% were admitted **Housing** Yes **Expenses** Tuition $13,420; Room & Board $5150 **Undergraduates** 66% women, 36% part-time, 35% 25 or older, 1% Native American, 3% Hispanic American, 14% African American, 2% Asian American/Pacific Islander **The most frequently chosen baccalaureate fields are** business/marketing, education, health professions and related sciences **Academic program** English as a second language, advanced placement, accelerated degree program, summer session, adult/continuing education programs, internships **Contact** Ms. Paige Illum, Director of Admissions, Avila College, 11901 Wornall Rd, Kansas City, MO 64145. Telephone: 816-501-3773 or toll-free 800-GO-AVILA. Fax: 816-501-2453. E-mail: admissions@mail.avila.edu. Web site: http://www.avila.edu/.

BAPTIST BIBLE COLLEGE
SPRINGFIELD, MISSOURI

General Independent Baptist, comprehensive, coed **Entrance** Noncompetitive **Setting** 38-acre campus **Total enrollment** 821 **Application deadline** Rolling (freshmen), rolling (transfer) **Freshmen** 100% were admitted **Housing** Yes **Expenses** Tuition $3480; Room & Board $4250 **Undergraduates** 1% Native American, 4% Hispanic American, 1% African American, 0.3% Asian American/Pacific Islander **Academic program** Summer session, internships **Contact** Dr. Joseph Gleason, Director of Admissions, Baptist Bible College, 628 East Kearney, Springfield, MO 65803-3498. Telephone: 417-268-6000 Ext. 6013. Fax: 417-268-6694. Web site: http://www.bbcnet.edu/bbgst.html.

CALVARY BIBLE COLLEGE AND THEOLOGICAL SEMINARY
KANSAS CITY, MISSOURI

General Independent interdenominational, comprehensive, coed **Entrance** Minimally difficult **Setting** 55-acre suburban campus **Total enrollment** 265 **Student-faculty ratio** 7:1 **Application deadline** Rolling (freshmen), rolling (transfer) **Housing** Yes **Expenses** Tuition $5010; Room & Board $3040 **Undergraduates** 47% women, 35% part-time, 50% 25 or older, 0% Native American, 1% Hispanic American, 7% African American, 4% Asian American/Pacific Islander **Academic program** Advanced placement, accelerated degree program, summer session, adult/continuing education programs **Contact** Mr. Timothy Smith, Director of Admissions, Calvary Bible College and Theological Seminary, 15800 Calvary Road, Kansas City, MO 64147-1341. Telephone: 816-322-0110 Ext. 1326 or toll-free 800-326-3960. Fax: 816-331-4474. E-mail: admissions@calvary.edu. Web site: http://www.calvary.edu/.

CENTRAL BIBLE COLLEGE
SPRINGFIELD, MISSOURI

General Independent, 4-year, coed, affiliated with Assemblies of God **Entrance** Moderately difficult **Setting** 108-acre suburban campus **Total enrollment** 805 **Student-faculty ratio** 21:1 **Application deadline** Rolling (freshmen), rolling (transfer) **Freshmen** 65% were admitted **Housing** Yes **Expenses** Tuition $6430; Room & Board $3400 **Undergraduates** 41% women, 10% part-time, 17% 25 or older, 1% Native American, 3% Hispanic American, 2% African American, 2% Asian American/Pacific Islander **The most frequently chosen baccalaureate fields are** philosophy, philosophy, religion, and theology **Academic program** Advanced placement, summer session, internships **Contact** Mrs. Eunice A. Bruegman, Director of Admissions and Records, Central Bible College, 3000 North Grant Avenue, Springfield, MO 65801-1096. Telephone: 417-833-2551 Ext. 1184 or toll-free 800-831-4222 Ext. 1184. Fax: 417-833-5141. E-mail: info@cbcag.edu. Web site: http://www.cbcag.edu/.

CENTRAL CHRISTIAN COLLEGE OF THE BIBLE
MOBERLY, MISSOURI

General Independent, 4-year, coed, affiliated with Christian Churches and Churches of Christ **Entrance**

MISSOURI

Central Christian College of the Bible *(continued)*
Noncompetitive **Setting** 40-acre small-town campus **Total enrollment** 191 **Student-faculty ratio** 19:1 **Application deadline** Rolling (freshmen), rolling (transfer) **Housing** Yes **Expenses** Tuition $4700; Room & Board $3190 **Undergraduates** 42% women, 6% part-time, 20% 25 or older, 0% Native American, 1% Hispanic American, 1% African American, 1% Asian American/Pacific Islander **The most frequently chosen baccalaureate field is** philosophy **Academic program** Self-designed majors, internships **Contact** Ms. Misty Rodda, Director of Admissions, Central Christian College of the Bible, 911 Urbandale Drive East, Moberly, MO 65270-1997. Telephone: 660-263-3900 or toll-free 888-263-3900 (in-state). Fax: 660-263-3936. E-mail: iwant2be@cccb.edu. Web site: http://www.cccb.edu/.

CENTRAL METHODIST COLLEGE
FAYETTE, MISSOURI

General Independent Methodist, comprehensive, coed **Entrance** Moderately difficult **Setting** 52-acre small-town campus **Total enrollment** 1,281 **Student-faculty ratio** 14:1 **Application deadline** 8/1 (freshmen), rolling (transfer) **Freshmen** 83% were admitted **Housing** Yes **Expenses** Tuition $12,320; Room & Board $4470 **Undergraduates** 61% women, 12% part-time, 24% 25 or older, 1% Native American, 1% Hispanic American, 6% African American, 1% Asian American/Pacific Islander **The most frequently chosen baccalaureate fields are** business/marketing, education, health professions and related sciences **Academic program** Advanced placement, self-designed majors, honors program, summer session, internships **Contact** Mr. Don Hapward, Dean of Admissions and Financial Assistance, Central Methodist College, 411 Central Methodist Square, Fayette, MO 65248-1198. Telephone: 660-248-6247 or toll-free 888-262-1854 (in-state). Fax: 660-248-1872. E-mail: admissions@cmc.edu. Web site: http://www.cmc.edu/.

CENTRAL MISSOURI STATE UNIVERSITY
WARRENSBURG, MISSOURI

General State-supported, comprehensive, coed **Entrance** Moderately difficult **Setting** 1,240-acre small-town campus **Total enrollment** 10,822 **Student-faculty ratio** 17:1 **Application deadline** Rolling (freshmen), rolling (transfer) **Freshmen** 72% were admitted **Housing** Yes **Expenses** Tuition $3510; Room & Board $4410 **Undergraduates** 53% women, 19% part-time, 29% 25 or older, 1% Native American, 1% Hispanic American, 5% African American, 1% Asian American/Pacific Islander **The most frequently chosen baccalaureate fields are** business/marketing, education, protective services/public administration **Academic program** English as a second language, advanced placement, self-designed majors, honors program, summer session, adult/continuing education programs, internships **Contact** Ms. Susan Duggins, Director of Admissions, Central Missouri State University, Administration Building Room 104, Warrensburg, MO 64093. Telephone: 660-543-4290 or toll-free 800-729-2678 (in-state). Fax: 660-543-8517. E-mail: admit@cmsuvmb.cmsu.edu. Web site: http://www.cmsu.edu/.

CLEVELAND CHIROPRACTIC COLLEGE-KANSAS CITY CAMPUS
KANSAS CITY, MISSOURI

General Independent, upper-level, coed **Total enrollment** 570 **Student-faculty ratio** 15:1 **Expenses** Tuition $15,150 **Academic program** Accelerated degree program, summer session, internships **Contact** Ms. Melissa Denton, Director of Admissions, Cleveland Chiropractic College-Kansas City Campus, 6401 Rockhill Road, Kansas City, MO 64131. Telephone: 816-501-0100 or toll-free 800-467-2252. Fax: 816-501-0205. E-mail: kc.admissions@cleveland.edu. Web site: http://www.cleveland.edu/.

COLLEGE OF THE OZARKS
POINT LOOKOUT, MISSOURI

General Independent Presbyterian, 4-year, coed **Entrance** Moderately difficult **Setting** 1,000-acre small-town campus **Total enrollment** 1,395 **Student-faculty ratio** 14:1 **Application deadline** 2/15 (freshmen), 2/1 (transfer) **Freshmen** 15% were admitted **Housing** Yes **Expenses** Tuition $150; Room & Board $2500 **Undergraduates** 56% women, 8% part-time, 11% 25 or older, 1% Native American, 1% Hispanic American, 0.4% African American, 1% Asian American/Pacific Islander **The most frequently chosen baccalaureate fields are** business/marketing, education, protective services/public administration **Academic program** Advanced placement, accelerated degree program, self-designed majors, honors program, summer session, internships **Contact** Mrs. Gayle Groves, Admissions Secretary, College of the Ozarks, PO Box 17, Point Lookout, MO 65726. Telephone: 417-334-6411 Ext. 4217 or toll-free 800-222-0525. Fax: 417-335-2618. E-mail: admiss4@cofo.edu. Web site: http://www.cofo.edu/.

COLUMBIA COLLEGE
COLUMBIA, MISSOURI

General Independent, comprehensive, coed, affiliated with Christian Church (Disciples of Christ) **Entrance** Minimally difficult **Setting** 29-acre small-town campus **Total enrollment** 996 **Student-faculty ratio** 12:1 **Application deadline** Rolling (freshmen), rolling (transfer) **Freshmen** 56% were admitted **Housing** Yes **Expenses** Tuition $10,506; Room & Board $4576 **Undergraduates** 57% women, 22% part-time, 18% 25 or older, 1% Native American, 2% Hispanic American, 5% African American, 1% Asian American/Pacific Islander **The most frequently chosen baccalaureate fields are** business/marketing, education, liberal arts/general studies **Academic program** English as a second language, advanced placement, accelerated degree program, self-designed majors, honors program, summer session, adult/

MISSOURI

continuing education programs, internships **Contact** Ms. Regina Morin, Director of Admissions, Columbia College, 1001 Rogers Street, Columbia, MO 65216. Telephone: 573-875-7352 or toll-free 800-231-2391 Ext. 7366. Fax: 573-875-7506. E-mail: admissions@email.ccis.edu. Web site: http://www.ccis.edu/.

CONCEPTION SEMINARY COLLEGE
CONCEPTION, MISSOURI

General Independent Roman Catholic, 4-year, men only **Entrance** Noncompetitive **Setting** 30-acre rural campus **Total enrollment** 90 **Student-faculty ratio** 4:1 **Application deadline** 7/31 (freshmen), 7/31 (transfer) **Freshmen** 100% were admitted **Housing** Yes **Expenses** Tuition $9312; Room & Board $5374 **Undergraduates** 9% part-time, 39% 25 or older, 0% Native American, 6% Hispanic American, 1% African American, 16% Asian American/Pacific Islander **The most frequently chosen baccalaureate fields are** liberal arts/general studies, philosophy, religion, and theology **Academic program** English as a second language, advanced placement **Contact** Mr. Keith Jiron, Director of Recruitment and Admissions, Conception Seminary College, PO Box 502, Highway 136 & VV, 37174 State Highway VV, Conception, MO 64433. Telephone: 660-944-2886. E-mail: vocations@conception.edu. Web site: http://www.conceptionabbey.edu/.

CULVER-STOCKTON COLLEGE
CANTON, MISSOURI

General Independent, 4-year, coed, affiliated with Christian Church (Disciples of Christ) **Entrance** Moderately difficult **Setting** 143-acre rural campus **Total enrollment** 821 **Student-faculty ratio** 12:1 **Freshmen** 86% were admitted **Housing** Yes **Expenses** Tuition $11,200; Room & Board $4975 **Undergraduates** 55% women, 9% part-time, 8% 25 or older, 0.1% Native American, 3% Hispanic American, 6% African American, 0.5% Asian American/Pacific Islander **The most frequently chosen baccalaureate fields are** business/marketing, education, health professions and related sciences **Academic program** Advanced placement, accelerated degree program, self-designed majors, honors program, summer session, internships **Contact** Mr. Ron Cronacher, Director of Enrollment Services, Culver-Stockton College, One College Hill, Canton, MO 63435-1299. Telephone: 800-537-1883 or toll-free 800-537-1883 (out-of-state). Fax: 217-231-6618. E-mail: enrollment@culver.edu. Web site: http://www.culver.edu/.

DEACONESS COLLEGE OF NURSING
ST. LOUIS, MISSOURI

General Proprietary, 4-year, coed **Entrance** Moderately difficult **Setting** 15-acre urban campus **Total enrollment** 244 **Student-faculty ratio** 9:1 **Application deadline** Rolling (freshmen), rolling (transfer) **Freshmen** 92% were admitted **Housing** Yes **Expenses** Tuition $9410; Room & Board $3990 **Undergraduates** 96% women, 37% part-time, 32% 25 or older, 0% Native American, 2% Hispanic American, 30% African American, 1% Asian American/Pacific Islander **The most frequently chosen baccalaureate field is** health professions and related sciences **Academic program** English as a second language, advanced placement, summer session **Contact** Ms. Andrea Gordon, Admissions Coordinator, Deaconess College of Nursing, 6150 Oakland Avenue, St. Louis, MO 63139-3215. Telephone: 314-768-3044 or toll-free 800-942-4310. Fax: 314-768-5673. Web site: http://www.deaconess.edu.

DEVRY UNIVERSITY
KANSAS CITY, MISSOURI

General Proprietary, 4-year, coed **Entrance** Minimally difficult **Setting** 12-acre urban campus **Total enrollment** 2,620 **Student-faculty ratio** 20:1 **Application deadline** Rolling (freshmen), rolling (transfer) **Freshmen** 90% were admitted **Housing** No **Expenses** Tuition $8740 **Undergraduates** 25% women, 30% part-time, 49% 25 or older, 1% Native American, 3% Hispanic American, 14% African American, 3% Asian American/Pacific Islander **The most frequently chosen baccalaureate fields are** business/marketing, computer/information sciences, engineering/engineering technologies **Academic program** Advanced placement, accelerated degree program, summer session, adult/continuing education programs **Contact** Ms. Anna Diamond, New Student Coordinator, DeVry University, 11224 Holmes Street, Kansas City, MO 64131. Telephone: 816-941-0430 or toll-free 800-821-3766 (out-of-state). Web site: http://www.kc.devry.edu/.

DRURY UNIVERSITY
SPRINGFIELD, MISSOURI

General Independent, comprehensive, coed **Entrance** Moderately difficult **Setting** 60-acre urban campus **Total enrollment** 1,777 **Student-faculty ratio** 11:1 **Application deadline** 3/15 (freshmen), rolling (transfer) **Freshmen** 85% were admitted **Housing** Yes **Expenses** Tuition $11,960; Room & Board $4248 **Undergraduates** 56% women, 2% part-time, 3% 25 or older, 1% Native American, 1% Hispanic American, 1% African American, 1% Asian American/Pacific Islander **The most frequently chosen baccalaureate fields are** biological/life sciences, business/marketing, communications/communication technologies **Academic program** English as a second language, advanced placement, accelerated degree program, self-designed majors, honors program, summer session, adult/continuing education programs, internships **Contact** Mr. Michael Thomas, Director of Admission, Drury University, 900 North Benton, Bay Hall, Springfield, MO 65802. Telephone: 417-873-7205 or toll-free 800-922-2274 (in-state). Fax: 417-866-3873. E-mail: druryad@drury.edu. Web site: http://www.drury.edu/.

EVANGEL UNIVERSITY
SPRINGFIELD, MISSOURI

General Independent, comprehensive, coed, affiliated with Assemblies of God **Entrance** Moderately

MISSOURI

Evangel University *(continued)*
difficult **Setting** 80-acre urban campus **Total enrollment** 1,570 **Student-faculty ratio** 18:1 **Application deadline** 8/1 (freshmen), 8/1 (transfer) **Freshmen** 89% were admitted **Housing** Yes **Expenses** Tuition $10,280; Room & Board $3900 **Undergraduates** 56% women, 5% part-time, 3% 25 or older **The most frequently chosen baccalaureate fields are** business/marketing, education, philosophy **Academic program** Advanced placement, summer session **Contact** Andrew Denton, Director of Admissions, Evangel University, 1111 North Glenstone, Springfield, MO 65802-2191. Telephone: 417-865-2811 Ext. 7342 or toll-free 800-382-6435 (in-state). Fax: 417-865-9599. E-mail: admissions@mail4.evangel.edu. Web site: http://www.evangel.edu/.

FONTBONNE UNIVERSITY
ST. LOUIS, MISSOURI

General Independent Roman Catholic, comprehensive, coed **Entrance** Moderately difficult **Setting** 13-acre suburban campus **Total enrollment** 2,192 **Student-faculty ratio** 12:1 **Application deadline** 8/1 (freshmen), rolling (transfer) **Freshmen** 84% were admitted **Housing** Yes **Expenses** Tuition $12,896; Room & Board $5500 **Undergraduates** 73% women, 22% part-time, 35% 25 or older, 1% Native American, 1% Hispanic American, 23% African American, 1% Asian American/Pacific Islander **The most frequently chosen baccalaureate fields are** business/marketing, education, visual/performing arts **Academic program** English as a second language, advanced placement, accelerated degree program, self-designed majors, honors program, summer session, adult/continuing education programs, internships **Contact** Ms. Peggy Musen, Associate Dean for Enrollment Management, Fontbonne University, 6800 Wydown Boulevard, St. Louis, MO 63105-3098. Telephone: 314-889-1400. Fax: 314-719-8021. E-mail: pmusen@fontbonne.edu. Web site: http://www.fontbonne.edu/.

GLOBAL UNIVERSITY OF THE ASSEMBLIES OF GOD
SPRINGFIELD, MISSOURI

General Independent, comprehensive, coed, affiliated with Assemblies of God **Entrance** Noncompetitive **Total enrollment** 4,284 **Application deadline** Rolling (freshmen), rolling (transfer) **Housing** No **Expenses** Tuition $1800 **Undergraduates** 32% women, 93% part-time, 91% 25 or older **The most frequently chosen baccalaureate field is** philosophy, religion, and theology **Academic program** Advanced placement, accelerated degree program, honors program, adult/continuing education programs, internships **Contact** Odell Jones, Dean of Student Affairs, Global University of the Assemblies of God, 1211 South Glenstone Avenue, Springfield, MO 65804. Telephone: 800-443-1083 or toll-free 800-443-1083. E-mail: berean@ag.org. Web site: http://www.globaluniversity.edu/.

HANNIBAL-LAGRANGE COLLEGE
HANNIBAL, MISSOURI

General Independent Southern Baptist, 4-year, coed **Entrance** Moderately difficult **Setting** 110-acre small-town campus **Total enrollment** 1,099 **Student-faculty ratio** 13:1 **Application deadline** 8/26 (freshmen), rolling (transfer) **Freshmen** 38% were admitted **Housing** Yes **Expenses** Tuition $9130; Room & Board $3400 **Undergraduates** 63% women, 36% part-time, 20% 25 or older, 0.1% Native American, 1% Hispanic American, 2% African American, 1% Asian American/Pacific Islander **The most frequently chosen baccalaureate fields are** business/marketing, education, protective services/public administration **Academic program** Advanced placement, accelerated degree program, self-designed majors, honors program, summer session, adult/continuing education programs, internships **Contact** Mr. Raymond Carty, Dean of Enrollment Management, Hannibal-LaGrange College, 2800 Palmyra Road, Hannibal, MO 63401-1999. Telephone: 573-221-3113 or toll-free 800-HLG-1119. E-mail: admissio@hlg.edu. Web site: http://www.hlg.edu/.

HARRIS-STOWE STATE COLLEGE
ST. LOUIS, MISSOURI

General State-supported, 4-year, coed **Entrance** Moderately difficult **Setting** 22-acre urban campus **Total enrollment** 1,306 **Student-faculty ratio** 18:1 **Application deadline** Rolling (freshmen), rolling (transfer) **Freshmen** 61% were admitted **Housing** No **Expenses** Tuition $2310 **Undergraduates** 70% women, 58% part-time, 0% Native American, 2% Hispanic American, 70% African American, 1% Asian American/Pacific Islander **The most frequently chosen baccalaureate fields are** business/marketing, education, protective services/public administration **Academic program** Advanced placement, summer session, internships **Contact** Jo Henderson, Director of Admissions, Harris-Stowe State College, 3026 Laclede Avenue, St. Louis, MO 63103. Telephone: 314-340-3300. Fax: 314-340-3555. E-mail: currierd@mail1.hssc.edu. Web site: http://www.hssc.edu/.

JEWISH HOSPITAL COLLEGE OF NURSING AND ALLIED HEALTH
ST. LOUIS, MISSOURI

General Independent, comprehensive, coed, primarily women **Entrance** Moderately difficult **Setting** urban campus **Total enrollment** 471 **Student-faculty ratio** 10:1 **Application deadline** Rolling (freshmen), rolling (transfer) **Freshmen** 100% were admitted **Housing** Yes **Expenses** Tuition $11,090; Room only $2385 **Undergraduates** 89% women, 68% part-time, 60% 25 or older, 1% Native American, 1% Hispanic American, 19% African American, 2% Asian American/Pacific Islander **The most frequently chosen baccalaureate field is** health professions and related sciences **Academic program** Advanced placement, summer session **Contact** Ms. Christie Schneider, Chief Admissions Officer, Jewish Hospital College

MISSOURI

of Nursing and Allied Health, 306 South Kingshighway, St. Louis, MO 63110-1091. Telephone: 314-454-7538 or toll-free 800-832-9009 (in-state). Fax: 314-454-5239. E-mail: jxi4885@bjcmail.carenet.org. Web site: http://jhconah.edu.

KANSAS CITY ART INSTITUTE
KANSAS CITY, MISSOURI

General Independent, 4-year, coed **Entrance** Moderately difficult **Setting** 12-acre urban campus **Total enrollment** 537 **Student-faculty ratio** 10:1 **Application deadline** Rolling (freshmen); rolling (transfer) **Freshmen** 79% were admitted **Housing** Yes **Expenses** Tuition $18,218; Room & Board $5500 **Undergraduates** 53% women, 2% part-time, 12% 25 or older, 1% Native American, 6% Hispanic American, 3% African American, 2% Asian American/Pacific Islander **The most frequently chosen baccalaureate field is** visual/performing arts **Academic program** English as a second language, advanced placement, summer session, adult/continuing education programs, internships **Contact** Mr. Gerald Valet, Director of Admission Technology, Kansas City Art Institute, 4415 Warwick Boulevard, Kansas City, MO 64111-1874. Telephone: 816-474-5224 or toll-free 800-522-5224. Fax: 816-802-3309. E-mail: admiss@kcai.edu. Web site: http://www.kcai.edu/.

KANSAS CITY COLLEGE OF LEGAL STUDIES
KANSAS CITY, MISSOURI

General Proprietary, 4-year, coed **Total enrollment** 123 **Student-faculty ratio** 19:1 **Application deadline** 9/24 (freshmen) **Freshmen** 90% were admitted **Housing** No **Contact** Mrs. Rosemary Velez, Admissions Director, Kansas City College of Legal Studies, 402 East Bannister Road, Suite A, Kansas City, MO 64131. Telephone: 816-444-2232 or toll-free 816-444-2232 (in-state); 816-444-3142 (out-of-state). Web site: http://www.metropolitancollege.edu/.

LESTER L. COX COLLEGE OF NURSING AND HEALTH SCIENCES
SPRINGFIELD, MISSOURI

General Independent, 4-year, coed, primarily women **Total enrollment** 312 **Student-faculty ratio** 15:1 **Application deadline** 2/1 (freshmen) **Freshmen** 93% were admitted **Housing** Yes **Expenses** Tuition $3144; Room only $1925 **Undergraduates** 94% women, 44% part-time, 44% 25 or older, 1% Native American, 2% Hispanic American, 1% African American, 1% Asian American/Pacific Islander **The most frequently chosen baccalaureate field is** health professions and related sciences **Academic program** Adult/continuing education programs **Contact** Ms. Virginia Mace, Admission Counselor, Lester L. Cox College of Nursing and Health Sciences, 1423 North Jefferson, Springfield, MO 65802. Telephone: 417-269-3069. Fax: 417-269-3581. E-mail: vsmace@coxnet.org. Web site: http://www.coxcollege.edu.

LINCOLN UNIVERSITY
JEFFERSON CITY, MISSOURI

General State-supported, comprehensive, coed **Entrance** Noncompetitive **Setting** 152-acre small-town campus **Total enrollment** 3,332 **Student-faculty ratio** 15:1 **Application deadline** 7/15 (freshmen), 6/15 (transfer) **Freshmen** 99% were admitted **Housing** Yes **Expenses** Tuition $3638; Room & Board $3790 **Undergraduates** 59% women, 33% part-time, 27% 25 or older, 1% Native American, 1% Hispanic American, 35% African American, 1% Asian American/Pacific Islander **The most frequently chosen baccalaureate fields are** business/marketing, education, psychology **Academic program** Advanced placement, accelerated degree program, self-designed majors, honors program, summer session, adult/continuing education programs, internships **Contact** Executive Director of Enrollment Management, Lincoln University, 820 Chestnut, Jefferson City, MO 65102. Telephone: 573-681-5599 or toll-free 800-521-5052. Web site: http://www.lincolnu.edu/.

LINDENWOOD UNIVERSITY
ST. CHARLES, MISSOURI

General Independent Presbyterian, comprehensive, coed **Entrance** Moderately difficult **Setting** 358-acre suburban campus **Total enrollment** 6,446 **Student-faculty ratio** 17:1 **Application deadline** Rolling (freshmen), rolling (transfer) **Housing** Yes **Expenses** Tuition $11,650; Room & Board $5600 **Undergraduates** 57% women, 11% part-time, 30% 25 or older, 0.1% Native American, 1% Hispanic American, 9% African American, 1% Asian American/Pacific Islander **The most frequently chosen baccalaureate fields are** business/marketing, communications/communication technologies, education **Academic program** Advanced placement, accelerated degree program, self-designed majors, honors program, summer session, adult/continuing education programs, internships **Contact** John Guffey, Dean of Admissions, Lindenwood University, 209 South Kingshighway, St. Charles, MO 63301-1695. Telephone: 636-949-4933. Fax: 636-949-4910. Web site: http://www.lindenwood.edu/.

LOGAN UNIVERSITY-COLLEGE OF CHIROPRACTIC
CHESTERFIELD, MISSOURI

General Independent, upper-level, coed **Entrance** Moderately difficult **Setting** 100-acre suburban campus **Total enrollment** 852 **Application deadline** Rolling (freshmen), rolling (transfer) **Housing** No **Expenses** Tuition $9874 **Undergraduates** 44% women, 19% part-time, 44% 25 or older, 0% Native American, 3% Hispanic American, 6% African American, 3% Asian American/Pacific Islander **The most frequently chosen baccalaureate field is** biological/life sciences **Academic program** Advanced placement, adult/continuing education programs, internships **Contact** Dr. Patrick Browne, Dean of Admissions, Logan University-College of Chiropractic, 1851

MISSOURI

Logan University-College of Chiropractic *(continued)*
Schoettler Road, Box 1065, Chesterfield, MO 63006-1065. Telephone: 636-227-2100 Ext. 149 or toll-free 800-533-9210. E-mail: loganadm@logan.edu. Web site: http://www.logan.edu/.

MARYVILLE UNIVERSITY OF SAINT LOUIS
ST. LOUIS, MISSOURI

General Independent, comprehensive, coed **Entrance** Moderately difficult **Setting** 130-acre suburban campus **Total enrollment** 3,262 **Student-faculty ratio** 13:1 **Application deadline** 8/15 (freshmen), rolling (transfer) **Freshmen** 82% were admitted **Housing** Yes **Expenses** Tuition $13,770; Room & Board $6000 **Undergraduates** 74% women, 46% part-time, 47% 25 or older, 0.3% Native American, 1% Hispanic American, 5% African American, 1% Asian American/Pacific Islander **The most frequently chosen baccalaureate fields are** law/legal studies, philosophy, religion, and theology **Academic program** English as a second language, advanced placement, accelerated degree program, honors program, summer session, adult/continuing education programs, internships **Contact** Ms. Teresa Bont, Admissions Director, Maryville University of Saint Louis, 13550 Conway Road, St. Louis, MO 63141-7299. Telephone: 314-529-9350 or toll-free 800-627-9855. Fax: 314-529-9927. E-mail: admissions@maryville.edu. Web site: http://www.maryville.edu/.

MESSENGER COLLEGE
JOPLIN, MISSOURI

General Independent Pentecostal, 4-year, coed **Entrance** Moderately difficult **Setting** 16-acre small-town campus **Total enrollment** 90 **Application deadline** 9/1 (freshmen), 9/1 (transfer) **Freshmen** 100% were admitted **Housing** Yes **Expenses** Tuition $4170; Room & Board $3100 **Undergraduates** 46% women, 16% part-time, 20% 25 or older, 2% Native American, 1% Hispanic American, 3% African American, 1% Asian American/Pacific Islander **The most frequently chosen baccalaureate fields are** philosophy, religion, and theology, visual/performing arts **Academic program** Honors program, internships **Contact** Gwen Minor, Vice President of Academic Affairs, Messenger College, 300 East 50th, PO Box 4050, Joplin, MO 64803. Telephone: 417-624-7070 Ext. 102 or toll-free 800-385-8940 (in-state). Fax: 417-624-5070. E-mail: mc@pcg.org.

MISSOURI BAPTIST COLLEGE
ST. LOUIS, MISSOURI

General Independent Southern Baptist, comprehensive, coed **Entrance** Moderately difficult **Setting** 65-acre suburban campus **Total enrollment** 3,105 **Student-faculty ratio** 18:1 **Application deadline** Rolling (freshmen), rolling (transfer) **Freshmen** 77% were admitted **Housing** Yes **Expenses** Tuition $10,682; Room & Board $5080 **Undergraduates** 62% women, 65% part-time, 28% 25 or older, 0.3% Native American, 2% Hispanic American, 6% African American, 1% Asian American/Pacific Islander **The most frequently chosen baccalaureate fields are** business/marketing, education, philosophy **Academic program** Advanced placement, accelerated degree program, self-designed majors, summer session, adult/continuing education programs, internships **Contact** Mr. Robert Cornwell, Associate Director of Admissions, Missouri Baptist College, One College Park Drive, St. Louis, MO 63141-8660. Telephone: 314-392-2296 or toll-free 877-434-1115 Ext. 2290. Fax: 314-434-7596. E-mail: admissions@mobap.edu. Web site: http://www.mobap.edu/.

MISSOURI SOUTHERN STATE COLLEGE
JOPLIN, MISSOURI

General State-supported, 4-year, coed **Entrance** Moderately difficult **Setting** 350-acre small-town campus **Total enrollment** 5,899 **Student-faculty ratio** 19:1 **Application deadline** 8/1 (freshmen), 8/1 (transfer) **Freshmen** 79% were admitted **Housing** Yes **Expenses** Tuition $2866; Room & Board $3800 **Undergraduates** 57% women, 35% part-time, 34% 25 or older, 3% Native American, 2% Hispanic American, 2% African American, 1% Asian American/Pacific Islander **The most frequently chosen baccalaureate fields are** business/marketing, education, protective services/public administration **Academic program** English as a second language, advanced placement, accelerated degree program, honors program, summer session, adult/continuing education programs, internships **Contact** Mr. Derek Skaggs, Director of Enrollment Services, Missouri Southern State College, 3950 East Newman Road, Joplin, MO 64801-1595. Telephone: 417-625-9537 or toll-free 800-606-MSSC. Fax: 417-659-4429. E-mail: admissions@mail.mssc.edu. Web site: http://www.mssc.edu/.

MISSOURI TECH
ST. LOUIS, MISSOURI

General Proprietary, 4-year, coed, primarily men **Entrance** Moderately difficult **Setting** suburban campus **Total enrollment** 266 **Student-faculty ratio** 10:1 **Application deadline** Rolling (freshmen) **Housing** Yes **Expenses** Room only $375 **Undergraduates** 12% women, 77% part-time **The most frequently chosen baccalaureate field is** engineering/engineering technologies **Academic program** Advanced placement, accelerated degree program, summer session, adult/continuing education programs, internships **Contact** Mr. Phil Eberle, Director of Admissions, Missouri Tech, 1167 Corporate Lake Drive, St. Louis, MO 63132. Telephone: 314-569-3600 or toll-free 800-960-8324 (out-of-state). Fax: 314-569-1167. Web site: http://www.motech.edu/.

MISSOURI VALLEY COLLEGE
MARSHALL, MISSOURI

General Independent, 4-year, coed, affiliated with Presbyterian Church **Entrance** Moderately difficult

MISSOURI

Setting 140-acre small-town campus **Total enrollment** 1,577 **Student-faculty ratio** 22:1 **Application deadline** Rolling (freshmen), rolling (transfer) **Freshmen** 62% were admitted **Housing** Yes **Expenses** Tuition $12,450; Room & Board $5000 **Undergraduates** 42% women, 17% part-time, 10% 25 or older, 1% Native American, 4% Hispanic American, 13% African American, 4% Asian American/Pacific Islander **The most frequently chosen baccalaureate fields are** business/marketing, education, protective services/public administration **Academic program** English as a second language, advanced placement, summer session, adult/continuing education programs, internships **Contact** Ms. Debbie Bultman, Admissions, Missouri Valley College, 500 East College, Marshall, MO 65340-3197. Telephone: 660-831-4114. Fax: 660-831-4039. E-mail: mo-valley@juno.com. Web site: http://www.moval.edu/.

MISSOURI WESTERN STATE COLLEGE
ST. JOSEPH, MISSOURI

General State-supported, 4-year, coed **Entrance** Noncompetitive **Setting** 744-acre suburban campus **Total enrollment** 5,102 **Student-faculty ratio** 19:1 **Application deadline** 7/30 (freshmen), 7/30 (transfer) **Freshmen** 100% were admitted **Housing** Yes **Expenses** Tuition $3224; Room & Board $3636 **Undergraduates** 61% women, 23% part-time, 24% 25 or older, 1% Native American, 2% Hispanic American, 9% African American, 1% Asian American/Pacific Islander **The most frequently chosen baccalaureate fields are** business/marketing, education, protective services/public administration **Academic program** Advanced placement, accelerated degree program, honors program, summer session, adult/continuing education programs, internships **Contact** Mr. Howard McCauley, Director of Admissions, Missouri Western State College, 4525 Downs Drive, St. Joseph, MO 64507-2294. Telephone: 816-271-4267 or toll-free 800-662-7041 Ext. 60. Fax: 816-271-5833. E-mail: admissn@mwsc.edu. Web site: http://www.mwsc.edu/.

NATIONAL AMERICAN UNIVERSITY
KANSAS CITY, MISSOURI

General Proprietary, 4-year, coed **Entrance** Noncompetitive **Setting** 1-acre urban campus **Total enrollment** 380 **Student-faculty ratio** 12:1 **Application deadline** Rolling (freshmen) **Housing** No **Expenses** Tuition $9360 **Undergraduates** 97% 25 or older **Academic program** Summer session **Contact** Janet Miller, Director of Admissions, National American University, 4200 Blue Ridge Boulevard, Kansas City, MO 64133-1612. Telephone: 816-353-4554. Fax: 816-353-1176. Web site: http://www.national.edu/.

NORTHWEST MISSOURI STATE UNIVERSITY
MARYVILLE, MISSOURI

General State-supported, comprehensive, coed **Entrance** Moderately difficult **Setting** 240-acre small-town campus **Total enrollment** 6,925 **Student-faculty ratio** 24:1 **Application deadline** Rolling (freshmen), rolling (transfer) **Freshmen** 90% were admitted **Housing** Yes **Expenses** Tuition $3600; Room & Board $4322 **Undergraduates** 56% women, 16% part-time, 6% 25 or older **The most frequently chosen baccalaureate fields are** business/marketing, computer/information sciences, education **Academic program** English as a second language, advanced placement, accelerated degree program, summer session, internships **Contact** Ms. Beverly Schenkel, Associate Director of Admission, Northwest Missouri State University, 800 University Drive, Maryville, MO 64468-6001. Telephone: 660-562-1149 or toll-free 800-633-1175. Fax: 660-562-1121. E-mail: admissions@acad.nwmissouri.edu. Web site: http://www.nwmissouri.edu/.

OZARK CHRISTIAN COLLEGE
JOPLIN, MISSOURI

General Independent Christian, 4-year, coed **Entrance** Noncompetitive **Setting** 110-acre suburban campus **Total enrollment** 757 **Student-faculty ratio** 21:1 **Application deadline** 8/15 (freshmen), rolling (transfer) **Freshmen** 100% were admitted **Housing** Yes **Expenses** Tuition $5155; Room & Board $3830 **Undergraduates** 50% women, 17% part-time, 25% 25 or older, 2% Native American, 2% Hispanic American, 1% African American, 1% Asian American/Pacific Islander **The most frequently chosen baccalaureate fields are** philosophy, philosophy, religion, and theology **Academic program** English as a second language, summer session, adult/continuing education programs, internships **Contact** Jim Marcum, Executive Director of Admissions, Ozark Christian College, 1111 North Main Street, Joplin, MO 64801-4804. Telephone: 417-624-2518 Ext. 2021 or toll-free 800-299-4622. Fax: 417-624-0090. E-mail: occadmin@occ.edu. Web site: http://www.occ.edu/.

PARK UNIVERSITY
PARKVILLE, MISSOURI

General Independent, comprehensive, coed **Entrance** Moderately difficult **Setting** 800-acre suburban campus **Total enrollment** 9,482 **Student-faculty ratio** 14:1 **Application deadline** 8/1 (freshmen), 8/1 (transfer) **Freshmen** 68% were admitted **Housing** Yes **Expenses** Tuition $5160; Room & Board $5000 **Undergraduates** 48% women, 90% part-time, 81% 25 or older, 1% Native American, 14% Hispanic American, 21% African American, 2% Asian American/Pacific Islander **The most frequently chosen baccalaureate fields are** business/marketing, protective services/public administration, psychology **Academic program** English as a second language, advanced placement, self-designed majors, honors program, summer session, adult/continuing education programs, internships **Contact** Dr. Ron Carruth, Director of Student Recruiting and Marketing, Park University, 8700 NW River Park Drive, Campus Box 1, Parkville, MO 64152. Telephone: 816-584-6215 or

MISSOURI

Park University *(continued)*
toll-free 800-745-7275. Fax: 816-741-4462. E-mail: admissions@mail.park.edu. Web site: http://www.park.edu/.

RESEARCH COLLEGE OF NURSING
KANSAS CITY, MISSOURI

General Independent, comprehensive, coed, primarily women **Entrance** Moderately difficult **Setting** 66-acre urban campus **Total enrollment** 250 **Student-faculty ratio** 7:1 **Application deadline** 6/30 (freshmen), 1/31 (transfer) **Freshmen** 78% were admitted **Housing** Yes **Expenses** Tuition $15,250; Room & Board $4950 **Undergraduates** 94% women, 7% part-time, 30% 25 or older, 1% Native American, 7% Hispanic American, 14% African American, 3% Asian American/Pacific Islander **The most frequently chosen baccalaureate field is** health professions and related sciences **Academic program** Advanced placement, accelerated degree program, honors program, summer session **Contact** Ms. Marisa Ferrara, Rockhurst College Admission Office, Research College of Nursing, 1100 Rockhurst Road, Kansas City, MO 64110. Telephone: 816-501-4100 Ext. 4654 or toll-free 800-842-6776. Fax: 816-501-4588. E-mail: mendenhall@vax2.rockhurst.edu. Web site: http://www.researchcollege.edu/.

ROCKHURST UNIVERSITY
KANSAS CITY, MISSOURI

General Independent Roman Catholic (Jesuit), comprehensive, coed **Entrance** Moderately difficult **Setting** 35-acre urban campus **Total enrollment** 2,730 **Student-faculty ratio** 11:1 **Application deadline** 6/30 (freshmen), rolling (transfer) **Freshmen** 87% were admitted **Housing** Yes **Expenses** Tuition $15,140; Room & Board $4920 **Undergraduates** 56% women, 40% part-time, 15% 25 or older, 1% Native American, 5% Hispanic American, 9% African American, 2% Asian American/Pacific Islander **The most frequently chosen baccalaureate fields are** business/marketing, health professions and related sciences, psychology **Academic program** Advanced placement, accelerated degree program, honors program, summer session, adult/continuing education programs, internships **Contact** Mr. Phillip Gebauer, Director of Undergraduate Admissions, Rockhurst University, 1100 Rockhurst Road, Kansas City, MO 64110-2561. Telephone: 816-501-4100 or toll-free 800-842-6776. Fax: 816-501-4142. E-mail: admission@rockhurst.edu. Web site: http://www.rockhurst.edu/.

ST. LOUIS CHRISTIAN COLLEGE
FLORISSANT, MISSOURI

General Independent Christian, 4-year, coed **Entrance** Minimally difficult **Setting** 20-acre suburban campus **Total enrollment** 223 **Student-faculty ratio** 10:1 **Application deadline** 8/15 (freshmen), 8/15 (transfer) **Freshmen** 62% were admitted **Housing** Yes **Expenses** Tuition $5824; Room & Board $3780 **Undergraduates** 39% women, 43% part-time, 42% 25 or older, 0.4% Native American, 1% Hispanic American, 26% African American, 0.4% Asian American/Pacific Islander **The most frequently chosen baccalaureate fields are** philosophy, philosophy, religion, and theology **Academic program** Advanced placement, accelerated degree program, adult/continuing education programs, internships **Contact** Mr. Richard Fordyce, Registrar, St. Louis Christian College, 1360 Grandview Drive, Florissant, MO 63033-6499. Telephone: 314-837-6777 Ext. 1500 or toll-free 800-887-SLCC. Fax: 314-837-8291. E-mail: questions@slcc4ministry.edu. Web site: http://www.slcc4ministry.edu/.

ST. LOUIS COLLEGE OF PHARMACY
ST. LOUIS, MISSOURI

General Independent, comprehensive, coed **Entrance** Moderately difficult **Setting** 5-acre urban campus **Total enrollment** 885 **Student-faculty ratio** 13:1 **Application deadline** Rolling (freshmen), 2/1 (transfer) **Freshmen** 66% were admitted **Housing** Yes **Expenses** Tuition $13,775; Room & Board $5364 **Undergraduates** 66% women, 2% part-time, 15% 25 or older, 0% Native American, 1% Hispanic American, 5% African American, 13% Asian American/Pacific Islander **The most frequently chosen baccalaureate field is** health professions and related sciences **Academic program** Advanced placement, summer session, adult/continuing education programs, internships **Contact** Ms. Penny Bryant, Director of Admissions/Registrar, St. Louis College of Pharmacy, 4588 Parkview Place, St. Louis, MO 63110-1088. Telephone: 314-367-8700 Ext. 1067 or toll-free 800-278-5267 (in-state). Fax: 314-367-2784. E-mail: pbryant@stlcop.edu. Web site: http://www.stlcop.edu/.

SAINT LOUIS UNIVERSITY
ST. LOUIS, MISSOURI

General Independent Roman Catholic (Jesuit), university, coed **Entrance** Moderately difficult **Setting** 279-acre urban campus **Total enrollment** 11,145 **Student-faculty ratio** 12:1 **Application deadline** 8/1 (freshmen), 8/1 (transfer) **Freshmen** 69% were admitted **Housing** Yes **Expenses** Tuition $19,830; Room & Board $6760 **Undergraduates** 55% women, 9% part-time, 13% 25 or older, 0.3% Native American, 2% Hispanic American, 8% African American, 4% Asian American/Pacific Islander **The most frequently chosen baccalaureate fields are** business/marketing, communications/communication technologies, health professions and related sciences **Academic program** English as a second language, advanced placement, accelerated degree program, self-designed majors, honors program, summer session, adult/continuing education programs, internships **Contact** Dr. Edwin Harris, Associate Provost, Saint Louis University, 221 North Grand Boulevard, St. Louis, MO 63103-2097. Telephone: 314-977-2500 or toll-free 800-758-3678 (out-of-state). Fax: 314-977-7136. E-mail: admitme@sluvca.slu.edu. Web site: http://www.slu.edu/.

MISSOURI

SAINT LUKE'S COLLEGE
KANSAS CITY, MISSOURI

General Independent Episcopal, upper-level, coed, primarily women **Entrance** Very difficult **Setting** 3-acre urban campus **Total enrollment** 129 **Student-faculty ratio** 7:1 **Application deadline** 12/31 (transfer) **Housing** Yes **Expenses** Tuition $8700; Room only $1600 **Undergraduates** 95% women, 11% part-time, 80% 25 or older, 0% Native American, 2% Hispanic American, 4% African American, 1% Asian American/Pacific Islander **The most frequently chosen baccalaureate field is** health professions and related sciences **Academic program** Summer session **Contact** Ms. Marsha Thomas, Director of Admissions, Saint Luke's College, 4426 Wornall Road, Kansas City, MO 64111. Telephone: 816-932-2073. E-mail: mjthomas@saint-lukes.org. Web site: http://www.saint-lukes.org/.

SOUTHEAST MISSOURI STATE UNIVERSITY
CAPE GIRARDEAU, MISSOURI

General State-supported, comprehensive, coed **Entrance** Moderately difficult **Setting** 693-acre small-town campus **Total enrollment** 9,352 **Student-faculty ratio** 17:1 **Application deadline** 8/1 (freshmen) **Freshmen** 55% were admitted **Housing** Yes **Expenses** Tuition $3525; Room & Board $4842 **Undergraduates** 60% women, 24% part-time, 18% 25 or older, 0.4% Native American, 1% Hispanic American, 6% African American, 1% Asian American/Pacific Islander **The most frequently chosen baccalaureate fields are** business/marketing, education, protective services/public administration **Academic program** English as a second language, advanced placement, self-designed majors, honors program, summer session, adult/continuing education programs, internships **Contact** Deborah Below, Director of Admissions, Southeast Missouri State University, MS 3550, Cape Girardeau, MO 63701. Telephone: 573-651-2590. Fax: 573-651-5936. E-mail: admissions@semovm.semo.edu. Web site: http://www.semo.edu/.

SOUTHWEST BAPTIST UNIVERSITY
BOLIVAR, MISSOURI

General Independent Southern Baptist, comprehensive, coed **Entrance** Moderately difficult **Setting** 152-acre small-town campus **Total enrollment** 3,564 **Student-faculty ratio** 19:1 **Application deadline** Rolling (freshmen), rolling (transfer) **Freshmen** 70% were admitted **Housing** Yes **Expenses** Tuition $10,326; Room & Board $3100 **Undergraduates** 66% women, 31% part-time, 25% 25 or older **The most frequently chosen baccalaureate fields are** education, health professions and related sciences, psychology **Academic program** English as a second language, advanced placement, accelerated degree program, honors program, summer session, internships **Contact** Mr. Rob Harris, Director of Admissions, Southwest Baptist University, 1600 University Avenue, Bolivar, MO 65613-2597. Telephone: 417-328-1809 or toll-free 800-526-5859. Fax: 417-328-1514. E-mail: rharris@sbuniv.edu. Web site: http://www.sbuniv.edu/.

SOUTHWEST MISSOURI STATE UNIVERSITY
SPRINGFIELD, MISSOURI

General State-supported, comprehensive, coed **Entrance** Moderately difficult **Setting** 225-acre suburban campus **Total enrollment** 18,252 **Student-faculty ratio** 18:1 **Application deadline** 8/1 (freshmen), 8/1 (transfer) **Freshmen** 86% were admitted **Housing** Yes **Expenses** Tuition $3748; Room & Board $4284 **Undergraduates** 54% women, 20% part-time, 15% 25 or older, 1% Native American, 1% Hispanic American, 3% African American, 1% Asian American/Pacific Islander **The most frequently chosen baccalaureate fields are** business/marketing, communications/communication technologies, education **Academic program** English as a second language, advanced placement, accelerated degree program, self-designed majors, honors program, summer session, adult/continuing education programs, internships **Contact** Ms. Jill Duncan, Associate Director of Admissions, Southwest Missouri State University, 901 South National, Springfield, MO 65804-0094. Telephone: 417-836-5517 or toll-free 800-492-7900. Fax: 417-836-6334. E-mail: smsuinfo@vma.smsu.edu. Web site: http://www.smsu.edu/.

STEPHENS COLLEGE
COLUMBIA, MISSOURI

General Independent, comprehensive, women only **Entrance** Moderately difficult **Setting** 202-acre urban campus **Total enrollment** 669 **Student-faculty ratio** 10:1 **Application deadline** 7/31 (freshmen), 7/31 (transfer) **Freshmen** 85% were admitted **Housing** Yes **Expenses** Tuition $16,245; Room & Board $6050 **Undergraduates** 29% part-time, 28% 25 or older, 1% Native American, 2% Hispanic American, 8% African American, 1% Asian American/Pacific Islander **The most frequently chosen baccalaureate fields are** business/marketing, education, visual/performing arts **Academic program** English as a second language, advanced placement, accelerated degree program, self-designed majors, honors program, adult/continuing education programs, internships **Contact** Patricia M. Gibbs, Dean of Enrollment Services, Stephens College, Box 2121, Columbia, MO 65215-0002. Telephone: 573-876-7207 or toll-free 800-876-7207. Fax: 573-876-7237. E-mail: apply@stephens.edu. Web site: http://www.stephens.edu/.

TRUMAN STATE UNIVERSITY
KIRKSVILLE, MISSOURI

General State-supported, comprehensive, coed **Entrance** Moderately difficult **Setting** 140-acre small-town campus **Total enrollment** 5,919 **Student-faculty ratio** 15:1 **Application deadline** 3/1 (freshmen), 5/1 (transfer) **Freshmen** 82% were admitted **Housing** Yes **Expenses** Tuition $3832; Room & Board $4736 **Undergraduates** 58% women, 3%

MISSOURI

Truman State University *(continued)*
part-time, 2% 25 or older, 0.4% Native American, 2% Hispanic American, 3% African American, 2% Asian American/Pacific Islander **The most frequently chosen baccalaureate fields are** biological/life sciences, business/marketing, English **Academic program** English as a second language, advanced placement, accelerated degree program, honors program, summer session, internships **Contact** Mr. Brad Chambers, Co-Director of Admissions, Truman State University, 205 McClain Hall, Kirksville, MO 63501-4221. Telephone: 660-785-4114 or toll-free 800-892-7792 (in-state). Fax: 660-785-7456. E-mail: admissions@truman.edu. Web site: http://www.truman.edu/.

UNIVERSITY OF MISSOURI–COLUMBIA
COLUMBIA, MISSOURI

General State-supported, university, coed **Entrance** Moderately difficult **Setting** 1,348-acre small-town campus **Total enrollment** 23,667 **Student-faculty ratio** 18:1 **Application deadline** Rolling (freshmen), rolling (transfer) **Freshmen** 64% were admitted **Housing** Yes **Expenses** Tuition $3985; Room & Board $5043 **Undergraduates** 52% women, 6% part-time, 4% 25 or older, 1% Native American, 1% Hispanic American, 6% African American, 3% Asian American/Pacific Islander **The most frequently chosen baccalaureate fields are** business/marketing, communication technologies, engineering/engineering technologies **Academic program** English as a second language, advanced placement, accelerated degree program, self-designed majors, honors program, summer session, adult/continuing education programs, internships **Contact** Ms. Georgeanne Porter, Director of Admissions, University of Missouri–Columbia, 225 Jesse Hall, Columbia, MO 65211. Telephone: 573-882-7786 or toll-free 800-225-6075 (in-state). Fax: 573-882-7887. E-mail: mu4u@missouri.edu. Web site: http://www.missouri.edu/.

UNIVERSITY OF MISSOURI–KANSAS CITY
KANSAS CITY, MISSOURI

General State-supported, university, coed **Entrance** Moderately difficult **Setting** 191-acre urban campus **Total enrollment** 12,969 **Student-faculty ratio** 8:1 **Application deadline** Rolling (freshmen), rolling (transfer) **Freshmen** 73% were admitted **Housing** Yes **Expenses** Tuition $5050; Room & Board $4950 **Undergraduates** 58% women, 47% part-time, 24% 25 or older, 1% Native American, 4% Hispanic American, 13% African American, 6% Asian American/Pacific Islander **The most frequently chosen baccalaureate fields are** business/marketing, education, liberal arts/general studies **Academic program** English as a second language, advanced placement, accelerated degree program, self-designed majors, honors program, summer session, adult/continuing education programs, internships **Contact** Mr. Melvin F. Tyler, Director of Admissions, University of Missouri–Kansas City, 5100 Rockhill Road, Kansas City, MO 64110-2499. Telephone: 816-235-1111. Fax: 816-235-5544. E-mail: admit@umkc.edu. Web site: http://www.umkc.edu/.

UNIVERSITY OF MISSOURI–ROLLA
ROLLA, MISSOURI

General State-supported, university, coed **Entrance** Very difficult **Setting** 284-acre small-town campus **Total enrollment** 4,883 **Student-faculty ratio** 14:1 **Application deadline** 7/1 (freshmen), 7/1 (transfer) **Freshmen** 96% were admitted **Housing** Yes **Expenses** Tuition $4974; Room & Board $5060 **Undergraduates** 23% women, 11% part-time, 13% 25 or older, 1% Native American, 1% Hispanic American, 5% African American, 3% Asian American/Pacific Islander **The most frequently chosen baccalaureate fields are** computer/information sciences, engineering/engineering technologies, physical sciences **Academic program** English as a second language, advanced placement, accelerated degree program, honors program, summer session, adult/continuing education programs, internships **Contact** Mr. Jay W. Goff, Acting Director of Admission and Dean of Enrollment Management, University of Missouri–Rolla, 106 Parker Hall, Rolla, MO 65409. Telephone: 573-341-4164 or toll-free 800-522-0938. Fax: 573-341-4082. E-mail: umrolla@umr.edu. Web site: http://www.umr.edu/.

UNIVERSITY OF MISSOURI–ST. LOUIS
ST. LOUIS, MISSOURI

General State-supported, university, coed **Entrance** Moderately difficult **Setting** 250-acre suburban campus **Total enrollment** 14,993 **Student-faculty ratio** 22:1 **Application deadline** Rolling (freshmen), rolling (transfer) **Freshmen** 52% were admitted **Housing** Yes **Expenses** Tuition $5120; Room & Board $5220 **Undergraduates** 60% women, 55% part-time, 37% 25 or older, 0.3% Native American, 1% Hispanic American, 14% African American, 3% Asian American/Pacific Islander **The most frequently chosen baccalaureate fields are** business/marketing, education, social sciences and history **Academic program** English as a second language, advanced placement, accelerated degree program, self-designed majors, honors program, summer session, adult/continuing education programs, internships **Contact** Mr. Curtis C. Coonrod, Director of Admissions, University of Missouri–St. Louis, 351 Millennium Student Center, St. Louis, MO 63121-4499. Telephone: 314-516-5460 or toll-free 888-GO2-UMSL (in-state). Fax: 314-516-5310. E-mail: curt_coonrod@umsl.edu. Web site: http://www.umsl.edu/.

UNIVERSITY OF PHOENIX–ST. LOUIS CAMPUS
ST. LOUIS, MISSOURI

General Proprietary, comprehensive, coed **Entrance** Noncompetitive **Total enrollment** 88,730 **Student-faculty ratio** 11:1 **Application deadline** Rolling (freshmen), rolling (transfer) **Housing** No **Expenses**

MISSOURI

Tuition $9600 **Undergraduates** 63% women, 74% 25 or older **Academic program** Advanced placement, accelerated degree program, adult/continuing education programs **Contact** Ms. Beth Barilla, Director of Admissions, University of Phoenix–St. Louis Campus, 4615 East Elwood Street, Phoenix, AZ 85040-1958. Telephone: 480-927-0099 Ext. 1218 or toll-free 888-326-7737 (in-state); 800-228-7240 (out-of-state). Fax: 480-594-1758. E-mail: beth.barilla@apollogrp.edu. Web site: http://www.phoenix.edu/.

WASHINGTON UNIVERSITY IN ST. LOUIS
ST. LOUIS, MISSOURI

General Independent, university, coed **Entrance** Most difficult **Setting** 169-acre suburban campus **Total enrollment** 12,187 **Student-faculty ratio** 7:1 **Application deadline** 1/15 (freshmen), 4/15 (transfer) **Freshmen** 23% were admitted **Housing** Yes **Expenses** Tuition $26,327; Room & Board $8216 **Undergraduates** 51% women, 13% part-time, 1% 25 or older, 0.1% Native American, 3% Hispanic American, 8% African American, 10% Asian American/Pacific Islander **The most frequently chosen baccalaureate fields are** business/marketing, engineering/engineering technologies, social sciences and history **Academic program** English as a second language, advanced placement, accelerated degree program, self-designed majors, summer session, adult/continuing education programs, internships **Contact** Ms. Nanette Tarbouni, Director of Admissions, Washington University in St. Louis, Campus Box 1089, One Brookings Drive, St. Louis, MO 63130-4899. Telephone: 314-935-6000 or toll-free 800-638-0700. Fax: 314-935-4290. E-mail: admissions@wustl.edu. Web site: http://www.wustl.edu/.

WEBSTER UNIVERSITY
ST. LOUIS, MISSOURI

General Independent, comprehensive, coed **Entrance** Moderately difficult **Setting** 47-acre suburban campus **Total enrollment** 15,402 **Student-faculty ratio** 13:1 **Application deadline** 7/1 (freshmen), 8/1 (transfer) **Freshmen** 56% were admitted **Housing** Yes **Expenses** Tuition $13,920; Room & Board $5889 **Undergraduates** 63% women, 36% part-time, 40% 25 or older, 0.4% Native American, 2% Hispanic American, 10% African American, 2% Asian American/Pacific Islander **The most frequently chosen baccalaureate fields are** business/marketing, communications/communication technologies, computer/information sciences **Academic program** English as a second language, advanced placement, accelerated degree program, self-designed majors, summer session, adult/continuing education programs, internships **Contact** Mr. Andrew Laue, Associate Director of Undergraduate Admission, Webster University, 470 East Lockwood Avenue, St. Louis, MO 63119-3194. Telephone: 314-961-2660 Ext. 7712 or toll-free 800-75-ENROL. Fax: 314-968-7115. E-mail: admit@websteruniv.edu. Web site: http://www.webster.edu/.

WESTMINSTER COLLEGE
FULTON, MISSOURI

General Independent, 4-year, coed, affiliated with Presbyterian Church **Entrance** Moderately difficult **Setting** 65-acre small-town campus **Total enrollment** 768 **Student-faculty ratio** 11:1 **Application deadline** Rolling (freshmen), rolling (transfer) **Freshmen** 88% were admitted **Housing** Yes **Expenses** Tuition $14,870; Room & Board $5120 **Undergraduates** 42% women, 3% part-time, 2% 25 or older, 1% Native American, 1% Hispanic American, 2% African American, 1% Asian American/Pacific Islander **The most frequently chosen baccalaureate fields are** education, psychology, social sciences and history **Academic program** English as a second language, advanced placement, self-designed majors, summer session, internships **Contact** Dr. Patrick Kirby, Dean of Enrollment Services, Westminster College, 501 Westminster Avenue, Fulton, MO 65251-1299. Telephone: 573-592-5251 or toll-free 800-475-3361. Fax: 573-592-5255. E-mail: admissions@jaynet.wcmo.edu. Web site: http://www.westminster-mo.edu/.

WILLIAM JEWELL COLLEGE
LIBERTY, MISSOURI

General Independent Baptist, 4-year, coed **Entrance** Moderately difficult **Setting** 149-acre small-town campus **Total enrollment** 1,089 **Student-faculty ratio** 11:1 **Application deadline** Rolling (freshmen), rolling (transfer) **Freshmen** 80% were admitted **Housing** Yes **Expenses** Tuition $14,750; Room & Board $4390 **Undergraduates** 59% women, 3% part-time, 5% 25 or older, 0.5% Native American, 1% Hispanic American, 2% African American, 0.5% Asian American/Pacific Islander **The most frequently chosen baccalaureate fields are** business/marketing, education, psychology **Academic program** Advanced placement, self-designed majors, honors program, summer session, adult/continuing education programs, internships **Contact** Mr. Chad Jolly, Dean of Enrollment Development, William Jewell College, 500 College Hill, Liberty, MO 64068. Telephone: 816-781-7700 or toll-free 800-753-7009. Fax: 816-415-5027. E-mail: admission@william.jewell.edu. Web site: http://www.jewell.edu/.

WILLIAM WOODS UNIVERSITY
FULTON, MISSOURI

General Independent, comprehensive, coed, affiliated with Christian Church (Disciples of Christ) **Entrance** Moderately difficult **Setting** 170-acre small-town campus **Total enrollment** 1,659 **Student-faculty ratio** 10:1 **Application deadline** Rolling (freshmen), rolling (transfer) **Freshmen** 96% were admitted **Housing** Yes **Expenses** Tuition $13,790; Room & Board $5600 **Undergraduates** 71% women, 14% part-time, 1% Native American, 1% Hispanic American, 4% African American, 5% Asian American/Pacific Islander **The most frequently chosen baccalaureate fields are** business/marketing, computer/

William Woods University *(continued)* information sciences, visual/performing arts **Academic program** English as a second language, advanced placement, accelerated degree program, self-designed majors, honors program, summer session, adult/continuing education programs, internships **Contact** Ms. Laura Archuleta, Executive Director of Enrollment Services, William Woods University, One University Avenue, Fulton, MO 65251. Telephone: 573-592-4221 or toll-free 800-995-3159 Ext. 4221. Fax: 573-592-1146. E-mail: admissions@williamwoods.edu. Web site: http://www.williamwoods.edu/.

MONTANA

CARROLL COLLEGE
HELENA, MONTANA

General Independent Roman Catholic, 4-year, coed **Entrance** Moderately difficult **Setting** 64-acre small-town campus **Total enrollment** 1,347 **Student-faculty ratio** 14:1 **Application deadline** 6/1 (freshmen), 6/1 (transfer) **Freshmen** 89% were admitted **Housing** Yes **Expenses** Tuition $12,816; Room & Board $5168 **Undergraduates** 61% women, 15% part-time, 7% 25 or older, 1% Native American, 2% Hispanic American, 0.2% African American, 1% Asian American/Pacific Islander **The most frequently chosen baccalaureate fields are** biological/life sciences, business/marketing, education **Academic program** English as a second language, advanced placement, accelerated degree program, self-designed majors, honors program, summer session, adult/continuing education programs, internships **Contact** Ms. Candace A. Cain, Director of Admission, Carroll College, 1601 North Benton Avenue, Helena, MT 59625-0002. Telephone: 406-447-4384 or toll-free 800-992-3648. Fax: 406-447-4533. E-mail: enroll@carroll.edu. Web site: http://www.carroll.edu/.

MONTANA STATE UNIVERSITY–BILLINGS
BILLINGS, MONTANA

General State-supported, comprehensive, coed **Entrance** Moderately difficult **Setting** 92-acre urban campus **Total enrollment** 4,313 **Student-faculty ratio** 21:1 **Application deadline** 7/1 (freshmen), rolling (transfer) **Freshmen** 100% were admitted **Housing** Yes **Expenses** Tuition $3430; Room & Board $3000 **Undergraduates** 64% women, 22% part-time, 33% 25 or older, 7% Native American, 3% Hispanic American, 1% African American, 1% Asian American/Pacific Islander **The most frequently chosen baccalaureate fields are** business/marketing, education, liberal arts/general studies **Academic program** English as a second language, advanced placement, accelerated degree program, honors program, summer session, adult/continuing education programs, internships **Contact** Ms. Shelly Beatty, Associate Director of Admissions, Montana State University–Billings, 1500 North 30th Street, Billings, MT 59101. Telephone: 406-657-2158 or toll-free 800-565-6782. Fax: 406-657-2302. E-mail: keverett@msubillings.edu. Web site: http://www.msubillings.edu/.

MONTANA STATE UNIVERSITY–BOZEMAN
BOZEMAN, MONTANA

General State-supported, university, coed **Entrance** Moderately difficult **Setting** 1,170-acre small-town campus **Total enrollment** 11,670 **Student-faculty ratio** 20:1 **Application deadline** Rolling (freshmen), rolling (transfer) **Freshmen** 75% were admitted **Housing** Yes **Expenses** Tuition $3381; Room & Board $5050 **Undergraduates** 46% women, 13% part-time, 16% 25 or older, 2% Native American, 1% Hispanic American, 0.3% African American, 1% Asian American/Pacific Islander **The most frequently chosen baccalaureate fields are** business/marketing, biological/life sciences, engineering/engineering technologies **Academic program** English as a second language, advanced placement, self-designed majors, honors program, summer session, adult/continuing education programs, internships **Contact** Ms. Ronda Russell, Director of New Student Services, Montana State University–Bozeman, PO Box 172190, Bozeman, MT 59717-2190. Telephone: 406-994-2452 or toll-free 888-MSU-CATS. Fax: 406-994-1923. E-mail: zam1202@msu.oscs.montana.edu. Web site: http://www.montana.edu/.

MONTANA STATE UNIVERSITY–NORTHERN
HAVRE, MONTANA

General State-supported, comprehensive, coed **Entrance** Moderately difficult **Setting** 105-acre small-town campus **Total enrollment** 1,589 **Student-faculty ratio** 15:1 **Application deadline** Rolling (freshmen), rolling (transfer) **Freshmen** 82% were admitted **Housing** Yes **Expenses** Tuition $3214; Room & Board $4190 **Undergraduates** 53% women, 26% part-time, 65% 25 or older, 14% Native American, 1% Hispanic American, 1% African American, 1% Asian American/Pacific Islander **The most frequently chosen baccalaureate fields are** business/marketing, education, trade and industry **Academic program** English as a second language, advanced placement, honors program, summer session, adult/continuing education programs, internships **Contact** Ms. Rosalie Spinler, Director of Admissions, Montana State University–Northern, PO Box 7751, Havre, MT 59501-7751. Telephone: 406-265-3704 or toll-free 800-662-6132 (in-state). Fax: 406-265-3777. E-mail: msunadmit@nmc1.nmclites.edu. Web site: http://www.msun.edu/.

MONTANA TECH OF THE UNIVERSITY OF MONTANA
BUTTE, MONTANA

General State-supported, comprehensive, coed **Entrance** Moderately difficult **Setting** 56-acre small-

MONTANA

town campus **Total enrollment** 2,086 **Student-faculty ratio** 16:1 **Application deadline** Rolling (freshmen), rolling (transfer) **Freshmen** 96% were admitted **Housing** Yes **Expenses** Tuition $3404; Room & Board $4441 **Undergraduates** 45% women, 18% part-time, 30% 25 or older, 1% Native American, 2% Hispanic American, 0.3% African American, 1% Asian American/Pacific Islander **The most frequently chosen baccalaureate fields are** business/marketing, engineering/engineering technologies, health professions and related sciences **Academic program** Advanced placement, self-designed majors, summer session, adult/continuing education programs, internships **Contact** Tony Campeau, Associate Director of Admissions, Montana Tech of The University of Montana, 1300 West Park Street, Butte, MT 59701-8997. Telephone: 406-496-4178 Ext. 4632 or toll-free 800-445-TECH Ext. 1. Fax: 406-496-4170. E-mail: admissions@p01.mtech.edu. Web site: http://www.mtech.edu/.

ROCKY MOUNTAIN COLLEGE
BILLINGS, MONTANA

General Independent interdenominational, 4-year, coed **Entrance** Moderately difficult **Setting** 60-acre urban campus **Total enrollment** 777 **Student-faculty ratio** 13:1 **Application deadline** Rolling (freshmen), rolling (transfer) **Freshmen** 83% were admitted **Housing** Yes **Expenses** Tuition $12,835; Room & Board $5278 **Undergraduates** 53% women, 8% part-time, 25% 25 or older, 10% Native American, 2% Hispanic American, 1% African American, 1% Asian American/Pacific Islander **The most frequently chosen baccalaureate fields are** business/marketing, education, health professions and related sciences **Academic program** English as a second language, advanced placement, accelerated degree program, self-designed majors, honors program, summer session, adult/continuing education programs, internships **Contact** Ms. LynAnn Henderson, Director of Admissions, Rocky Mountain College, 1511 Poly Drive, Billings, MT 59102. Telephone: 406-657-1026 or toll-free 800-877-6259. Fax: 406-259-9751. E-mail: admissions@rocky.edu. Web site: http://www.rocky.edu/.

UNIVERSITY OF GREAT FALLS
GREAT FALLS, MONTANA

General Independent Roman Catholic, comprehensive, coed **Entrance** Noncompetitive **Setting** 40-acre urban campus **Total enrollment** 879 **Student-faculty ratio** 11:1 **Application deadline** 8/1 (freshmen), 8/1 (transfer) **Freshmen** 68% were admitted **Housing** Yes **Expenses** Tuition $10,260; Room & Board $5100 **Undergraduates** 69% women, 36% part-time, 96% 25 or older **The most frequently chosen baccalaureate fields are** education, business/marketing, protective services/public administration **Academic program** Advanced placement, accelerated degree program, summer session, adult/continuing education programs, internships **Contact** Mr. Michael Myers, Assistant Director of Admissions, University of Great Falls, 1301 Twentieth Street South, Great Falls, MT 59405. Telephone: 406-791-5200 or toll-free 800-856-9544. Fax: 406-791-5209. E-mail: adminrec@ugf.edu. Web site: http://www.ugf.edu/.

THE UNIVERSITY OF MONTANA–MISSOULA
MISSOULA, MONTANA

General State-supported, university, coed **Entrance** Moderately difficult **Setting** 220-acre urban campus **Total enrollment** 12,646 **Student-faculty ratio** 19:1 **Application deadline** 7/1 (freshmen), rolling (transfer) **Freshmen** 88% were admitted **Housing** Yes **Expenses** Tuition $3642; Room & Board $4890 **Undergraduates** 53% women, 13% part-time, 21% 25 or older, 3% Native American, 1% Hispanic American, 0.5% African American, 1% Asian American/Pacific Islander **The most frequently chosen baccalaureate fields are** business/marketing, English, social sciences and history **Academic program** English as a second language, advanced placement, honors program, summer session, adult/continuing education programs, internships **Contact** Office of New Student Services, The University of Montana–Missoula, Missoula, MT 59812-0002. Telephone: 406-243-6266 or toll-free 800-462-8636. Fax: 406-243-5711. E-mail: admiss@selway.umt.edu. Web site: http://www.umt.edu/.

THE UNIVERSITY OF MONTANA–WESTERN
DILLON, MONTANA

General State-supported, 4-year, coed **Entrance** Moderately difficult **Setting** 36-acre small-town campus **Total enrollment** 1,163 **Student-faculty ratio** 17:1 **Application deadline** 7/1 (freshmen), 7/1 (transfer) **Freshmen** 100% were admitted **Housing** Yes **Expenses** Tuition $3016; Room & Board $4220 **Undergraduates** 60% women, 23% part-time, 35% 25 or older, 3% Native American, 2% Hispanic American, 0.4% African American, 1% Asian American/Pacific Islander **The most frequently chosen baccalaureate fields are** business/marketing, education, natural resources/environmental science **Academic program** Advanced placement, accelerated degree program, self-designed majors, honors program, summer session, adult/continuing education programs, internships **Contact** Ms. Arlene Williams, Director of Admissions, The University of Montana–Western, 710 South Atlantic, Dillon, MT 59725. Telephone: 406-683-7331 or toll-free 866-UMW-M0NT (in-state); 866-UMW-MONT (out-of-state). Fax: 406-683-7493. E-mail: admissions@wmwestern.edu. Web site: http://www.umwesten.edu/.

WESTERN MONTANA COLLEGE
See The University of Montana–Western

NEBRASKA

BELLEVUE UNIVERSITY
BELLEVUE, NEBRASKA

General Independent, comprehensive, coed **Entrance** Noncompetitive **Setting** 19-acre suburban campus **Total enrollment** 3,925 **Student-faculty ratio** 17:1 **Application deadline** Rolling (freshmen), rolling (transfer) **Freshmen** 96% were admitted **Housing** No **Expenses** Tuition $4085 **Undergraduates** 50% women, 34% part-time, 80% 25 or older, 0.5% Native American, 3% Hispanic American, 6% African American, 1% Asian American/Pacific Islander **Academic program** English as a second language, advanced placement, accelerated degree program, summer session, adult/continuing education programs, internships **Contact** Kelley Dengel, Information Center Manager, Bellevue University, 1000 Galvin Road South, Bellevue, NE 68005-3098. Telephone: 402-293-3769 or toll-free 800-756-7920. Fax: 402-293-2020. E-mail: set@scholars.bellevue.edu. Web site: http://www.bellevue.edu/.

CHADRON STATE COLLEGE
CHADRON, NEBRASKA

General State-supported, comprehensive, coed **Entrance** Noncompetitive **Setting** 281-acre small-town campus **Total enrollment** 2,804 **Student-faculty ratio** 18:1 **Application deadline** Rolling (freshmen), rolling (transfer) **Freshmen** 100% were admitted **Housing** Yes **Expenses** Tuition $2481; Room & Board $3828 **Undergraduates** 59% women, 27% part-time, 76% 25 or older, 1% Native American, 2% Hispanic American, 1% African American, 0.4% Asian American/Pacific Islander **The most frequently chosen baccalaureate fields are** business/marketing, education, protective services/public administration **Academic program** Advanced placement, self-designed majors, honors program, summer session, adult/continuing education programs, internships **Contact** Ms. Tena Cook Gould, Director of Admissions, Chadron State College, 1000 Main Street, Chadron, NE 69337-2690. Telephone: 308-432-6263 or toll-free 800-242-3766 (in-state). Fax: 308-432-6229. E-mail: inquire@csc1.csc.edu. Web site: http://www.csc.edu/.

▶ For more information, see page 409.

CLARKSON COLLEGE
OMAHA, NEBRASKA

General Independent, comprehensive, coed, primarily women **Entrance** Moderately difficult **Setting** 3-acre urban campus **Total enrollment** 450 **Student-faculty ratio** 12:1 **Application deadline** Rolling (freshmen), rolling (transfer) **Freshmen** 82% were admitted **Housing** Yes **Expenses** Tuition $9378; Room only $2800 **Undergraduates** 92% women, 42% part-time, 41% 25 or older, 0.3% Native American, 3% Hispanic American, 6% African American, 0.3% Asian American/Pacific Islander **The most frequently chosen baccalaureate fields are** business/marketing, health professions and related sciences **Academic program** Advanced placement, accelerated degree program, summer session, adult/continuing education programs, internships **Contact** Mr. Tony Damewood, Dean of Enrollment Services, Clarkson College, 101 South 42nd Street, Omaha, NE 68131-2739. Telephone: 402-552-3100 or toll-free 800-647-5500. Fax: 402-552-6057. E-mail: admiss@clarksoncollege.edu. Web site: http://www.clarksoncollege.edu/.

▶ For more information, see page 413.

COLLEGE OF SAINT MARY
OMAHA, NEBRASKA

General Independent Roman Catholic, 4-year, women only **Entrance** Minimally difficult **Setting** 25-acre suburban campus **Total enrollment** 930 **Student-faculty ratio** 10:1 **Application deadline** Rolling (freshmen), rolling (transfer) **Freshmen** 68% were admitted **Housing** Yes **Expenses** Tuition $13,750; Room & Board $4976 **Undergraduates** 41% part-time, 52% 25 or older, 1% Native American, 3% Hispanic American, 6% African American, 1% Asian American/Pacific Islander **The most frequently chosen baccalaureate fields are** business/marketing, education, health professions and related sciences **Academic program** Advanced placement, accelerated degree program, summer session, adult/continuing education programs, internships **Contact** Natalie Vrbka, Senior Admissions Counselor, College of Saint Mary, 1901 South 72nd Street, Omaha, NE 68124-2377. Telephone: 402-399-2405 or toll-free 800-926-5534. Fax: 402-399-2412. E-mail: enroll@csm.edu. Web site: http://www.csm.edu/.

CONCORDIA UNIVERSITY
SEWARD, NEBRASKA

General Independent, comprehensive, coed, affiliated with Lutheran Church–Missouri Synod **Entrance** Moderately difficult **Setting** 120-acre small-town campus **Total enrollment** 1,369 **Student-faculty ratio** 14:1 **Application deadline** 8/1 (freshmen), 8/1 (transfer) **Freshmen** 93% were admitted **Housing** Yes **Expenses** Tuition $13,468; Room & Board $4302 **Undergraduates** 56% women, 5% part-time, 4% 25 or older, 0.2% Native American, 1% Hispanic American, 2% African American, 1% Asian American/Pacific Islander **Academic program** English as a second language, advanced placement, accelerated degree program, honors program, summer session, adult/continuing education programs, internships **Contact** Mr. Pete Kenow, Director of Admissions, Concordia University, 800 North Columbia Avenue, Seward, NE 68434-1599. Telephone: 402-643-7233 or toll-free 800-535-5494. Fax: 402-643-4073. E-mail: admiss@seward.ccsn.edu. Web site: http://www.cune.edu/.

CREIGHTON UNIVERSITY
OMAHA, NEBRASKA

General Independent Roman Catholic (Jesuit), university, coed **Entrance** Moderately difficult **Setting**

NEBRASKA

90-acre urban campus **Total enrollment** 6,297 **Student-faculty ratio** 14:1 **Application deadline** 8/1 (freshmen), rolling (transfer) **Freshmen** 90% were admitted **Housing** Yes **Expenses** Tuition $17,136; Room & Board $6190 **Undergraduates** 58% women, 11% part-time, 4% 25 or older, 1% Native American, 3% Hispanic American, 3% African American, 9% Asian American/Pacific Islander **The most frequently chosen baccalaureate fields are** business/marketing, biological/life sciences, health professions and related sciences **Academic program** English as a second language, advanced placement, accelerated degree program, honors program, summer session, adult/continuing education programs, internships **Contact** Mr. Dennis J. O'Driscoll, Director of Admissions, Creighton University, 2500 California Plaza, Omaha, NE 68178-0001. Telephone: 402-280-2703 or toll-free 800-282-5835. Fax: 402-280-2685. E-mail: admissions@creighton.edu. Web site: http://www.creighton.edu/.

DANA COLLEGE
BLAIR, NEBRASKA

General Independent, 4-year, coed, affiliated with Evangelical Lutheran Church in America **Entrance** Moderately difficult **Setting** 150-acre small-town campus **Total enrollment** 565 **Student-faculty ratio** 10:1 **Application deadline** Rolling (freshmen) **Freshmen** 89% were admitted **Housing** Yes **Expenses** Tuition $13,950; Room & Board $4412 **Undergraduates** 46% women, 2% part-time, 4% 25 or older, 1% Native American, 2% Hispanic American, 5% African American, 3% Asian American/Pacific Islander **The most frequently chosen baccalaureate fields are** business/marketing, education, protective services/public administration **Academic program** English as a second language, advanced placement, accelerated degree program, self-designed majors, honors program, summer session, adult/continuing education programs, internships **Contact** Ms. Judy Mathiesen, Office Manager, Dana College, 2848 College Drive, Blair, NE 68008-1099. Telephone: 402-426-7337 or toll-free 800-444-3262. Fax: 402-426-7386. E-mail: admissions@dana.edu. Web site: http://www.dana.edu/.

DOANE COLLEGE
CRETE, NEBRASKA

General Independent, comprehensive, coed, affiliated with United Church of Christ **Entrance** Moderately difficult **Setting** 300-acre small-town campus **Total enrollment** 1,597 **Student-faculty ratio** 12:1 **Application deadline** Rolling (freshmen), rolling (transfer) **Freshmen** 84% were admitted **Housing** Yes **Expenses** Tuition $13,470; Room & Board $4130 **Undergraduates** 50% women, 1% part-time **The most frequently chosen baccalaureate fields are** business/marketing, education, social sciences and history **Academic program** English as a second language, advanced placement, accelerated degree program, self-designed majors, honors program, summer session, adult/continuing education programs, internships **Contact** Mr. Dan Kunzman, Dean of Admissions, Doane College, 1014 Boswell Avenue, Crete, NE 68333. Telephone: 402-826-8222 or toll-free 800-333-6263. Fax: 402-826-8600. E-mail: admissions@doane.edu. Web site: http://www.doane.edu/.

GRACE UNIVERSITY
OMAHA, NEBRASKA

General Independent interdenominational, comprehensive, coed **Entrance** Moderately difficult **Setting** 15-acre urban campus **Total enrollment** 595 **Student-faculty ratio** 18:1 **Application deadline** Rolling (freshmen), rolling (transfer) **Freshmen** 50% were admitted **Housing** Yes **Expenses** Tuition $9175; Room & Board $4000 **Undergraduates** 55% women, 26% part-time, 20% 25 or older, 0% Native American, 1% Hispanic American, 4% African American, 0.2% Asian American/Pacific Islander **The most frequently chosen baccalaureate fields are** business/marketing, philosophy, social sciences and history **Academic program** Advanced placement, accelerated degree program, self-designed majors, summer session, adult/continuing education programs, internships **Contact** Mrs. Terri L. Dingfield, Director of Admissions, Grace University, 1311 South Ninth Street, Omaha, NE 68108. Telephone: 402-449-2831 or toll-free 800-383-1422. Fax: 402-341-9587. E-mail: admissions@graceuniversity.edu. Web site: http://www.graceuniversity.edu/.

HASTINGS COLLEGE
HASTINGS, NEBRASKA

General Independent Presbyterian, comprehensive, coed **Entrance** Moderately difficult **Setting** 88-acre small-town campus **Total enrollment** 1,108 **Student-faculty ratio** 13:1 **Application deadline** 8/1 (freshmen), rolling (transfer) **Freshmen** 90% were admitted **Housing** Yes **Expenses** Tuition $13,666; Room & Board $4188 **Undergraduates** 51% women, 3% part-time, 4% 25 or older, 1% Native American, 2% Hispanic American, 1% African American, 0.4% Asian American/Pacific Islander **The most frequently chosen baccalaureate fields are** business/marketing, communications/communication technologies, education **Academic program** Advanced placement, self-designed majors, summer session, adult/continuing education programs, internships **Contact** Mr. Michael Karloff, Director of Admissions, Hastings College, 800 North Turner Avenue, Hastings, NE 68901-7696. Telephone: 402-461-7316 or toll-free 800-532-7642. Fax: 402-461-7490. E-mail: admissions@hastings.edu. Web site: http://www.hastings.edu/.

MIDLAND LUTHERAN COLLEGE
FREMONT, NEBRASKA

General Independent Lutheran, 4-year, coed **Entrance** Moderately difficult **Setting** 27-acre small-town campus **Total enrollment** 991 **Student-faculty ratio** 15:1 **Application deadline** Rolling (freshmen), rolling (transfer) **Freshmen** 87% were admitted **Housing** Yes **Expenses** Tuition $14,600; Room & Board

NEBRASKA

Midland Lutheran College *(continued)*
$4080 **Undergraduates** 57% women, 5% part-time, 4% 25 or older, 0.1% Native American, 2% Hispanic American, 3% African American, 2% Asian American/Pacific Islander **The most frequently chosen baccalaureate fields are** business/marketing, education, social sciences and history **Academic program** English as a second language, advanced placement, accelerated degree program, self-designed majors, honors program, summer session, internships **Contact** Mr. John W. Klockentager, Vice President for Enrollment Management, Midland Lutheran College, Admissions Office, Fremont, NE 68025-4200. Telephone: 402-941-6508 or toll-free 800-642-8382 Ext. 6501. Fax: 402-941-6513. E-mail: admissions@admin.mlc.edu. Web site: http://www.mlc.edu/.

NEBRASKA CHRISTIAN COLLEGE
NORFOLK, NEBRASKA

General Independent, 4-year, coed, affiliated with Christian Churches and Churches of Christ **Entrance** Minimally difficult **Setting** 85-acre small-town campus **Total enrollment** 150 **Student-faculty ratio** 12:1 **Application deadline** Rolling (freshmen), rolling (transfer) **Freshmen** 57% were admitted **Housing** Yes **Expenses** Tuition $5400; Room & Board $3360 **Undergraduates** 50% women, 12% part-time, 12% 25 or older, 1% Native American, 2% Hispanic American, 1% African American, 2% Asian American/Pacific Islander **The most frequently chosen baccalaureate field is** philosophy, religion, and theology **Academic program** Internships **Contact** Mr. Jason Epperso, Associate Director of Admissions, Nebraska Christian College, 1800 Syracuse Avenue, Norfolk, NE 68701-2458. Telephone: 402-378-5000 Ext. 413. Fax: 402-379-5100. E-mail: admissions@nechristian.edu. Web site: http://www.nechristian.edu/.

NEBRASKA METHODIST COLLEGE
OMAHA, NEBRASKA

General Independent, comprehensive, coed, affiliated with United Methodist Church **Entrance** Moderately difficult **Setting** 5-acre urban campus **Total enrollment** 380 **Student-faculty ratio** 10:1 **Application deadline** 4/1 (freshmen), 4/1 (transfer) **Freshmen** 93% were admitted **Housing** Yes **Expenses** Tuition $9600; Room only $1560 **Undergraduates** 90% women, 38% part-time, 45% 25 or older, 0% Native American, 2% Hispanic American, 5% African American, 1% Asian American/Pacific Islander **The most frequently chosen baccalaureate field is** health professions and related sciences **Academic program** Advanced placement, accelerated degree program, summer session, internships **Contact** Ms. Deann Sterner, Director of Admissions, Nebraska Methodist College, 8501 West Dodge Road, Omaha, NE 68114. Telephone: 402-354-4922 or toll-free 800-335-5510. Fax: 402-354-8875. E-mail: dsterne@methodistcollege.edu. Web site: http://www.methodistcollege.edu/.

NEBRASKA WESLEYAN UNIVERSITY
LINCOLN, NEBRASKA

General Independent United Methodist, comprehensive, coed **Entrance** Moderately difficult **Setting** 50-acre suburban campus **Total enrollment** 1,719 **Student-faculty ratio** 13:1 **Application deadline** 5/1 (freshmen), rolling (transfer) **Freshmen** 93% were admitted **Housing** Yes **Expenses** Tuition $14,641; Room & Board $4126 **Undergraduates** 57% women, 9% part-time, 6% 25 or older, 0.1% Native American, 1% Hispanic American, 1% African American, 2% Asian American/Pacific Islander **The most frequently chosen baccalaureate fields are** business/marketing, parks and recreation, psychology **Academic program** Advanced placement, summer session, adult/continuing education programs, internships **Contact** Mr. Kendal E. Sieg, Director of Admissions, Nebraska Wesleyan University, 5000 Saint Paul Avenue, Lincoln, NE 68504. Telephone: 402-465-2218 or toll-free 800-541-3818. Fax: 402-465-2179. E-mail: admissions@nebrwesleyan.edu. Web site: http://www.nebrwesleyan.edu/.

PERU STATE COLLEGE
PERU, NEBRASKA

General State-supported, comprehensive, coed **Entrance** Noncompetitive **Setting** 103-acre rural campus **Total enrollment** 1,629 **Student-faculty ratio** 16:1 **Application deadline** Rolling (freshmen), rolling (transfer) **Freshmen** 73% were admitted **Housing** Yes **Expenses** Tuition $2546; Room & Board $3796 **Undergraduates** 54% women, 39% part-time, 5% 25 or older, 0.3% Native American, 2% Hispanic American, 2% African American, 1% Asian American/Pacific Islander **Academic program** Advanced placement, honors program, adult/continuing education programs, internships **Contact** Ms. Janelle Moran, Director of Recruitment and Admissions, Peru State College, PO Box 10, Peru, NE 68421. Telephone: 402-872-2221 or toll-free 800-742-4412 (in-state). Fax: 402-872-2296. E-mail: jmoran@oakmail.peru.edu. Web site: http://www.peru.edu/.

UNION COLLEGE
LINCOLN, NEBRASKA

General Independent Seventh-day Adventist, 4-year, coed **Entrance** Moderately difficult **Setting** 26-acre suburban campus **Total enrollment** 992 **Student-faculty ratio** 14:1 **Application deadline** Rolling (freshmen), rolling (transfer) **Freshmen** 58% were admitted **Housing** Yes **Expenses** Tuition $11,504; Room & Board $3260 **Undergraduates** 55% women, 22% part-time, 15% 25 or older, 1% Native American, 4% Hispanic American, 2% African American, 2% Asian American/Pacific Islander **The most frequently chosen baccalaureate fields are** education, business/marketing, health professions and related sciences **Academic program** English as a second language, advanced placement, accelerated degree program, self-designed majors, honors program, summer session, adult/continuing education programs, internships **Contact** Huda McClelland, Director of Admissions, Union College, 3800 South 48th Street, Lincoln, NE 68516. Telephone: 402-486-2504 or toll-free 800-228-4600 (out-of-state). Fax: 402-486-2895. E-mail: ucenrol@ucollege.edu. Web site: http://www.ucollege.edu/.

UNIVERSITY OF NEBRASKA AT KEARNEY
KEARNEY, NEBRASKA

General State-supported, comprehensive, coed **Entrance** Moderately difficult **Setting** 235-acre small-town campus **Total enrollment** 6,426 **Student-faculty ratio** 16:1 **Application deadline** 8/1 (freshmen), 8/1 (transfer) **Freshmen** 96% were admitted **Housing** Yes **Expenses** Tuition $3106; Room & Board $3902 **Undergraduates** 55% women, 12% part-time, 11% 25 or older, 0.3% Native American, 2% Hispanic American, 1% African American, 0.3% Asian American/Pacific Islander **The most frequently chosen baccalaureate fields are** business/marketing, education, protective services/public administration **Academic program** English as a second language, advanced placement, honors program, summer session, internships **Contact** Mr. John Kundel, Director of Admissions, University of Nebraska at Kearney, 905 West 25th Street, Kearney, NE 68849-0001. Telephone: 308-865-8702 or toll-free 800-532-7639. Fax: 308-865-8987. E-mail: admissionsug@unk.edu. Web site: http://www.unk.edu/.

UNIVERSITY OF NEBRASKA AT OMAHA
OMAHA, NEBRASKA

General State-supported, university, coed **Entrance** Minimally difficult **Setting** 88-acre urban campus **Total enrollment** 14,143 **Student-faculty ratio** 17:1 **Application deadline** Rolling (freshmen), rolling (transfer) **Freshmen** 86% were admitted **Housing** Yes **Expenses** Tuition $2638; Room only $2439 **Undergraduates** 54% women, 29% part-time, 25% 25 or older, 0.4% Native American, 3% Hispanic American, 6% African American, 2% Asian American/Pacific Islander **The most frequently chosen baccalaureate fields are** business/marketing, education, protective services/public administration **Academic program** English as a second language, advanced placement, self-designed majors, honors program, summer session, adult/continuing education programs, internships **Contact** Ms. Jolene Adams, Associate Director of Admissions, University of Nebraska at Omaha, 6001 Dodge Street, Omaha, NE 68182. Telephone: 402-554-2416 or toll-free 800-858-8648 (in-state). Fax: 402-554-3472. Web site: http://www.unomaha.edu/.

UNIVERSITY OF NEBRASKA–LINCOLN
LINCOLN, NEBRASKA

General State-supported, university, coed **Entrance** Moderately difficult **Setting** 623-acre urban campus **Total enrollment** 22,764 **Student-faculty ratio** 15:1 **Application deadline** 6/30 (freshmen), 6/30 (transfer) **Freshmen** 91% were admitted **Housing** Yes **Expenses** Tuition $3759; Room & Board $4565 **Undergraduates** 47% women, 10% part-time, 9% 25 or older, 0.5% Native American, 2% Hispanic American, 2% African American, 2% Asian American/Pacific Islander **The most frequently chosen baccalaureate fields are** business/marketing, communications/communication technologies, engineering/engineering technologies **Academic program** English as a second language, advanced placement, accelerated degree program, self-designed majors, honors program, summer session, adult/continuing education programs, internships **Contact** Patrick McBride, Interim Director of Admissions, University of Nebraska–Lincoln, 1410 Q Street, Lincoln, NE 68588-0417. Telephone: 402-472-2030 or toll-free 800-742-8800. Fax: 402-472-0670. E-mail: nuhusker@unl.edu. Web site: http://www.unl.edu/.

UNIVERSITY OF NEBRASKA MEDICAL CENTER
OMAHA, NEBRASKA

General State-supported, upper-level, coed **Entrance** Moderately difficult **Setting** 51-acre urban campus **Total enrollment** 2,724 **Application deadline** Rolling (transfer) **First-Year Students** 33% were admitted **Housing** No **Expenses** Tuition $4,115 **Undergraduates** 92% women, 14% part-time, 0% Native American, 3% Hispanic American, 1% African American, 1% Asian American/Pacific Islander **The most frequently chosen baccalaureate field is** health professions and related sciences **Academic program** Honors program, summer session, internships **Contact** Ms. Jo Wagner, Assistant Director of Academic Records, University of Nebraska Medical Center, 984280 Nebraska Medical Center, Omaha, NE 68198-4230. Telephone: 402-559-6468 or toll-free 800-626-8431. Fax: 402-559-6796. Web site: http://www.unmc.edu/.

WAYNE STATE COLLEGE
WAYNE, NEBRASKA

General State-supported, comprehensive, coed **Entrance** Noncompetitive **Setting** 128-acre small-town campus **Total enrollment** 3,311 **Student-faculty ratio** 19:1 **Application deadline** Rolling (freshmen), rolling (transfer) **Freshmen** 100% were admitted **Housing** Yes **Expenses** Tuition $2735; Room & Board $3590 **Undergraduates** 58% women, 9% part-time, 12% 25 or older, 1% Native American, 2% Hispanic American, 3% African American, 0.5% Asian American/Pacific Islander **The most frequently chosen baccalaureate fields are** business/marketing, education, psychology **Academic program** Self-designed majors, honors program, summer session, adult/continuing education programs, internships **Contact** Ms. Teresa Moore, Director of Admissions, Wayne State College, 1111 Main Street, Wayne, NE 68787. Telephone: 402-375-7234 or toll-free 800-228-9972 (in-state). Fax: 402-375-7204. E-mail: wscadmit@wscgate.wsc.edu. Web site: http://www.wsc.edu/.

NEBRASKA

YORK COLLEGE
YORK, NEBRASKA

General Independent, 4-year, coed, affiliated with Church of Christ **Entrance** Moderately difficult **Setting** 44-acre small-town campus **Total enrollment** 455 **Student-faculty ratio** 12:1 **Application deadline** Rolling (freshmen), rolling (transfer) **Freshmen** 61% were admitted **Housing** Yes **Expenses** Tuition $10,300; Room & Board $3200 **Undergraduates** 57% women, 6% part-time, 5% 25 or older, 0% Native American, 0.2% Hispanic American, 4% African American, 2% Asian American/Pacific Islander **The most frequently chosen baccalaureate fields are** business/marketing, education, psychology **Academic program** Advanced placement, honors program, summer session, adult/continuing education programs, internships **Contact** Kristin Mathews, Admissions Counselor, York College, 1125 East 8th Street, York, NE 68467-2699. Telephone: 402-363-5629 or toll-free 800-950-9675. Fax: 402-363-5623. E-mail: enroll@york.edu. Web site: http://www.york.edu/.

NEVADA

MORRISON UNIVERSITY
RENO, NEVADA

Contact Ms. Teresa Sanders, Director of Admissions, Morrison University, 140 Washington Street, Reno, NV 89503-5600. Telephone: 775-323-4145 or toll-free 800-369-6144. Web site: http://www.morrison.edu/.

SIERRA NEVADA COLLEGE
INCLINE VILLAGE, NEVADA

General Independent, comprehensive, coed **Entrance** Moderately difficult **Setting** 20-acre small-town campus **Total enrollment** 345 **Student-faculty ratio** 11:1 **Application deadline** Rolling (freshmen), rolling (transfer) **Freshmen** 89% were admitted **Housing** Yes **Expenses** Tuition $15,060; Room & Board $6060 **Undergraduates** 44% women, 7% part-time, 22% 25 or older, 1% Native American, 1% Hispanic American, 1% African American, 0.3% Asian American/Pacific Islander **Academic program** Advanced placement, accelerated degree program, honors program, summer session, adult/continuing education programs, internships **Contact** Mr. Brett Schraeder, Dean of Admission, Sierra Nevada College, 999 Tahoe Boulevard, David Hall II, Incline Village, NV 89451. Telephone: 775-831-1314 Ext. 4047 or toll-free 800-332-8666 Ext. 4046 (out-of-state). Fax: 775-831-1347. E-mail: admissions@sierranevada.edu. Web site: http://www.sierranevada.edu/.

UNIVERSITY OF NEVADA, LAS VEGAS
LAS VEGAS, NEVADA

General State-supported, university, coed **Entrance** Moderately difficult **Setting** 335-acre urban campus **Total enrollment** 23,314 **Student-faculty ratio** 20:1 **Application deadline** 7/15 (freshmen), 7/15 (transfer) **Freshmen** 80% were admitted **Housing** Yes **Expenses** Tuition $2481; Room & Board $5800 **Undergraduates** 55% women, 34% part-time, 31% 25 or older, 1% Native American, 10% Hispanic American, 7% African American, 12% Asian American/Pacific Islander **The most frequently chosen baccalaureate fields are** business/marketing, education, health professions and related sciences **Academic program** English as a second language, advanced placement, self-designed majors, honors program, summer session, adult/continuing education programs, internships **Contact** Mrs. Susan Bozarth, Associate Director of Admissions, University of Nevada, Las Vegas, 4505 Maryland Parkway, Box 451021, Las Vegas, NV 89154-1021. Telephone: 702-895-3443. Fax: 702-895-1118. E-mail: gounlv@ccmail.nevada.edu. Web site: http://www.unlv.edu/.

UNIVERSITY OF NEVADA, RENO
RENO, NEVADA

General State-supported, university, coed **Entrance** Moderately difficult **Setting** 200-acre urban campus **Total enrollment** 14,316 **Student-faculty ratio** 18:1 **Application deadline** 3/1 (freshmen), rolling (transfer) **Freshmen** 95% were admitted **Housing** Yes **Expenses** Tuition $2454; Room & Board $5650 **Undergraduates** 55% women, 25% part-time, 19% 25 or older, 1% Native American, 6% Hispanic American, 3% African American, 7% Asian American/Pacific Islander **The most frequently chosen baccalaureate fields are** business/marketing, education, health professions and related sciences **Academic program** English as a second language, advanced placement, honors program, summer session, adult/continuing education programs, internships **Contact** Dr. Melissa N. Choroszy, Associate Dean of Records and Enrollment Services, University of Nevada, Reno, Mail Stop 120, Reno, NV 89557. Telephone: 775-784-6865. Fax: 775-784-4283. E-mail: asknevada@unr.edu. Web site: http://www.unr.edu/.

UNIVERSITY OF PHOENIX–NEVADA CAMPUS
LAS VEGAS, NEVADA

General Proprietary, comprehensive, coed **Entrance** Noncompetitive **Total enrollment** 88,730 **Student-faculty ratio** 16:1 **Application deadline** Rolling (freshmen), rolling (transfer) **Housing** No **Expenses** Tuition $8160 **Undergraduates** 57% women, 79% 25 or older **The most frequently chosen baccalaureate field is** business/marketing **Academic program** Advanced placement, accelerated degree program, adult/continuing education programs **Contact** Ms. Beth Barilla, Director of Admissions, University of Phoenix–Nevada Campus, 4615 East Elwood Street, Phoenix, AZ 85040-1958. Telephone: 480-927-0099 Ext. 1218 or toll-free 800-228-7240. Fax: 480-594-1758. E-mail: beth.barilla@apollogrp.edu. Web site: http://www.phoenix.edu/.

NEW HAMPSHIRE

COLBY-SAWYER COLLEGE
NEW LONDON, NEW HAMPSHIRE

General Independent, 4-year, coed **Entrance** Moderately difficult **Setting** 190-acre small-town campus **Total enrollment** 901 **Student-faculty ratio** 12:1 **Application deadline** Rolling (freshmen), rolling (transfer) **Freshmen** 87% were admitted **Housing** Yes **Expenses** Tuition $20,130; Room & Board $7720 **Undergraduates** 64% women, 3% part-time, 3% 25 or older, 0.3% Native American, 0.4% Hispanic American, 0.2% African American, 0.4% Asian American/Pacific Islander **The most frequently chosen baccalaureate fields are** parks and recreation, psychology, visual/performing arts **Academic program** English as a second language, advanced placement, accelerated degree program, self-designed majors, honors program, internships **Contact** Ms. Wendy Beckemeyer, Vice President for Enrollment Management and Dean of Admissions, Colby-Sawyer College, 100 Main Street, New London, NH 03257. Telephone: 603-526-3700 or toll-free 800-272-1015. Fax: 603-526-3452. E-mail: csadmiss@colby-sawyer.edu. Web site: http://www.colby-sawyer.edu/.

DANIEL WEBSTER COLLEGE
NASHUA, NEW HAMPSHIRE

General Independent, 4-year, coed **Entrance** Moderately difficult **Setting** 50-acre suburban campus **Total enrollment** 1,055 **Student-faculty ratio** 13:1 **Application deadline** Rolling (freshmen), rolling (transfer) **Freshmen** 71% were admitted **Housing** Yes **Expenses** Tuition $17,870; Room & Board $7000 **Undergraduates** 28% women, 26% part-time, 8% 25 or older, 0.1% Native American, 2% Hispanic American, 2% African American, 1% Asian American/Pacific Islander **The most frequently chosen baccalaureate fields are** business/marketing, computer/information sciences, trade and industry **Academic program** Advanced placement, summer session, adult/continuing education programs, internships **Contact** Mr. James Thatcher, Director of Enrollment Services, Daniel Webster College, 20 University Drive, Nashua, NH 03063. Telephone: 603-577-6664 or toll-free 800-325-6876. Fax: 603-577-6001. E-mail: admissions@dwc.edu. Web site: http://www.dwc.edu/.

DARTMOUTH COLLEGE
HANOVER, NEW HAMPSHIRE

General Independent, university, coed **Entrance** Most difficult **Setting** 265-acre rural campus **Total enrollment** 5,495 **Student-faculty ratio** 9:1 **Application deadline** 1/1 (freshmen), 3/1 (transfer) **Freshmen** 23% were admitted **Housing** Yes **Expenses** Tuition $26,562; Room & Board $7896 **Undergraduates** 49% women, 1% part-time, 3% Native American, 6% Hispanic American, 6% African American, 11% Asian American/Pacific Islander **The most frequently chosen baccalaureate fields are** English, biological/life sciences, social sciences and history **Academic program** Advanced placement, accelerated degree program, self-designed majors, honors program, summer session, internships **Contact** Mr. Karl M. Furstenberg, Dean of Admissions and Financial Aid, Dartmouth College, 6016 McNutt Hall, Hanover, NH 03755. Telephone: 603-646-2875. E-mail: admissions.office@dartmouth.edu. Web site: http://www.dartmouth.edu/.

FRANKLIN PIERCE COLLEGE
RINDGE, NEW HAMPSHIRE

General Independent, comprehensive, coed **Entrance** Moderately difficult **Setting** 1,000-acre rural campus **Total enrollment** 1,548 **Student-faculty ratio** 19:1 **Application deadline** Rolling (freshmen), rolling (transfer) **Freshmen** 81% were admitted **Housing** Yes **Expenses** Tuition $19,775; Room & Board $6600 **Undergraduates** 52% women, 5% part-time, 3% 25 or older, 0.3% Native American, 3% Hispanic American, 4% African American, 1% Asian American/Pacific Islander **The most frequently chosen baccalaureate fields are** business/marketing, protective services/public administration, visual/performing arts **Academic program** English as a second language, advanced placement, self-designed majors, honors program, summer session, adult/continuing education programs, internships **Contact** Ms. Lucy C. Shonk, Dean of Admissions, Franklin Pierce College, 20 College Road, Franklin Pierce College, Rindge, NH 03461-0060. Telephone: 603-899-4050 or toll-free 800-437-0048. Fax: 603-899-4394. E-mail: admissions@fpc.edu. Web site: http://www.fpc.edu/.

KEENE STATE COLLEGE
KEENE, NEW HAMPSHIRE

General State-supported, comprehensive, coed **Entrance** Moderately difficult **Setting** 160-acre small-town campus **Total enrollment** 4,633 **Student-faculty ratio** 17:1 **Application deadline** 4/1 (freshmen), 5/1 (transfer) **Freshmen** 78% were admitted **Housing** Yes **Expenses** Tuition $5554; Room & Board $5256 **Undergraduates** 58% women, 14% part-time, 8% 25 or older, 0.3% Native American, 1% Hispanic American, 0.3% African American, 1% Asian American/Pacific Islander **The most frequently chosen baccalaureate fields are** education, engineering/engineering technologies, visual/performing arts **Academic program** English as a second language, advanced placement, self-designed majors, honors program, summer session, internships **Contact** Ms. Margaret Richmond, Director of Admissions, Keene State College, 229 Main Street, Keene, NH 03435-2604. Telephone: 603-358-2273 or toll-free 800-572-1909. Fax: 603-358-2767. E-mail: admissions@keene.edu. Web site: http://www.keene.edu/.

MAGDALEN COLLEGE
WARNER, NEW HAMPSHIRE

General Independent Roman Catholic, 4-year, coed **Entrance** Moderately difficult **Total enrollment** 85 **Student-faculty ratio** 9:1 **Application deadline** 5/1

NEW HAMPSHIRE

Magdalen College *(continued)*
(freshmen) **Freshmen** 66% were admitted **Housing** Yes **Expenses** Tuition $7500; Room & Board $5250 **Undergraduates** 47% women, 3% 25 or older **The most frequently chosen baccalaureate field is** liberal arts/general studies **Academic program** Summer session **Contact** Paul V. Sullivan, Director of Admissions, Magdalen College, 511 Kearsarge Mountain Road, Warner, NH 03278. Telephone: 603-456-2656 Ext. 11 or toll-free 877-498-1723 (out-of-state). Fax: 603-456-2660. E-mail: admissions@magdalen.edu. Web site: http://www.magdalen.edu/.

NEW ENGLAND COLLEGE
HENNIKER, NEW HAMPSHIRE

General Independent, comprehensive, coed **Entrance** Moderately difficult **Setting** 225-acre small-town campus **Total enrollment** 887 **Student-faculty ratio** 13:1 **Application deadline** Rolling (freshmen), rolling (transfer) **Freshmen** 93% were admitted **Housing** Yes **Expenses** Tuition $19,590; Room & Board $7116 **Undergraduates** 49% women, 9% part-time, 9% 25 or older, 0% Native American, 1% Hispanic American, 2% African American, 0.3% Asian American/Pacific Islander **The most frequently chosen baccalaureate fields are** business/marketing, psychology, social sciences and history **Academic program** English as a second language, advanced placement, self-designed majors, honors program, summer session, adult/continuing education programs, internships **Contact** Ms. Lisa M. Partridge, Director of Admission, New England College, 26 Bridge Street, Henniker, NH 03242. Telephone: 603-428-2223 or toll-free 800-521-7642 (out-of-state). Fax: 603-428-3155. E-mail: admission@nec.edu. Web site: http://www.nec.edu/.

NEW HAMPSHIRE INSTITUTE OF ART
MANCHESTER, NEW HAMPSHIRE

Contact Ms. Felicia Menard, Admissions Office, New Hampshire Institute of Art, 148 Concord Street, Manchester, NH 03104-4858. Telephone: 603-623-0313 Ext. 576 or toll-free 866-241-4918 (in-state). E-mail: fmenard@nhia.edu. Web site: http://www.nhia.edu/.

PLYMOUTH STATE COLLEGE
PLYMOUTH, NEW HAMPSHIRE

General State-supported, comprehensive, coed **Entrance** Moderately difficult **Setting** 170-acre small-town campus **Total enrollment** 4,418 **Student-faculty ratio** 16:1 **Application deadline** 4/1 (freshmen), 4/1 (transfer) **Freshmen** 77% were admitted **Housing** Yes **Expenses** Tuition $5550; Room & Board $5474 **Undergraduates** 52% women, 7% part-time, 5% 25 or older, 0.4% Native American, 1% Hispanic American, 1% African American, 1% Asian American/Pacific Islander **The most frequently chosen baccalaureate fields are** business/marketing, education, visual/performing arts **Academic program** Advanced placement, accelerated degree program, self-designed majors, honors program, summer session, internships **Contact** Mr. Eugene Fahey, Senior Associate Director of Admission, Plymouth State College, 17 High Street, MSC #52, Plymouth, NH 03264-1595. Telephone: 800-842-6900 or toll-free 800-842-6900. Fax: 603-535-2714. E-mail: pscadmit@mail.plymouth.edu. Web site: http://www.plymouth.edu/.

RIVIER COLLEGE
NASHUA, NEW HAMPSHIRE

General Independent Roman Catholic, comprehensive, coed **Entrance** Moderately difficult **Setting** 64-acre suburban campus **Total enrollment** 2,375 **Student-faculty ratio** 13:1 **Application deadline** Rolling (freshmen), rolling (transfer) **Freshmen** 70% were admitted **Housing** Yes **Expenses** Tuition $15,520; Room & Board $6100 **Undergraduates** 47% 25 or older, 0.3% Native American, 2% Hispanic American, 1% African American, 3% Asian American/Pacific Islander **The most frequently chosen baccalaureate field is** law/legal studies **Academic program** English as a second language, advanced placement, honors program, summer session, adult/continuing education programs, internships **Contact** Mr. David Boisvert, (Interim Director of Undergraduate Admissions) Executive Assistant to President for Enrollment Management, Rivier College, 420 Main Street, Nashua, NH 03060. Telephone: 603-897-8502 or toll-free 800-44RIVIER. Fax: 603-891-1799. E-mail: rivadmit@rivier.edu. Web site: http://www.rivier.edu/.

SAINT ANSELM COLLEGE
MANCHESTER, NEW HAMPSHIRE

General Independent Roman Catholic, 4-year, coed **Entrance** Moderately difficult **Setting** 450-acre suburban campus **Total enrollment** 1,964 **Student-faculty ratio** 14:1 **Application deadline** Rolling (freshmen), rolling (transfer) **Freshmen** 75% were admitted **Housing** Yes **Expenses** Tuition $20,125; Room & Board $7350 **Undergraduates** 55% women, 4% part-time, 1% 25 or older, 0.2% Native American, 1% Hispanic American, 0.3% African American, 1% Asian American/Pacific Islander **The most frequently chosen baccalaureate fields are** business/marketing, psychology, social sciences and history **Academic program** Advanced placement, honors program, summer session, internships **Contact** Ms. Alice Dunfey, Associate Director of Admissions, Saint Anselm College, 100 Saint Anselm Drive, Manchester, NH 03102-1310. Telephone: 603-641-7500 Ext. 7171 or toll-free 888-4ANSELM. Fax: 603-641-7550. E-mail: admissions@anselm.edu. Web site: http://www.anselm.edu/.

SOUTHERN NEW HAMPSHIRE UNIVERSITY
MANCHESTER, NEW HAMPSHIRE

General Independent, comprehensive, coed **Entrance** Moderately difficult **Setting** 280-acre suburban campus **Total enrollment** 5,611 **Student-faculty ratio** 18:1 **Application deadline** Rolling (freshmen), rolling (transfer) **Freshmen** 80% were admitted **Housing** Yes **Expenses** Tuition $16,786; Room & Board $7066 **Undergraduates** 55% women, 38% part-time, 42% 25 or older, 0.1% Native American, 2% Hispanic American, 2% African American, 1% Asian American/Pacific Islander **Academic program** English as a second language, advanced placement, accelerated degree program, honors program, summer session, adult/continuing education programs, internships **Contact** Mr. Brad Poznanski, Director of Admission and Enrollment Planning, Southern New Hampshire University, 2500 North River Road, Belknap Hall, Manchester, NH 03106-1045. Telephone: 603-645-9611 Ext. 9633 or toll-free 800-642-4968. Fax: 603-645-9693. E-mail: admission@snhu.edu. Web site: http://www.snhu.edu/.

THOMAS MORE COLLEGE OF LIBERAL ARTS
MERRIMACK, NEW HAMPSHIRE

General Independent, 4-year, coed, affiliated with Roman Catholic Church **Entrance** Moderately difficult **Setting** 14-acre small-town campus **Total enrollment** 69 **Student-faculty ratio** 9:1 **Application deadline** Rolling (freshmen), rolling (transfer) **Freshmen** 97% were admitted **Housing** Yes **Expenses** Tuition $10,000; Room & Board $7700 **Undergraduates** 46% women, 2% 25 or older, 3% Native American, 4% Hispanic American, 0% African American, 0% Asian American/Pacific Islander **The most frequently chosen baccalaureate fields are** philosophy, English, social sciences and history **Contact** Ms. Catherine M. Alcarez, Director of Admissions, Thomas More College of Liberal Arts, 6 Manchester Street, Merrimack, NH 03054-4818. Telephone: 603-880-8308 or toll-free 800-880-8308. Fax: 603-880-9280. E-mail: admissions@thomasmorecollege.edu. Web site: http://www.thomasmorecollege.edu/.

UNIVERSITY OF NEW HAMPSHIRE
DURHAM, NEW HAMPSHIRE

General State-supported, university, coed **Entrance** Moderately difficult **Setting** 200-acre small-town campus **Total enrollment** 13,650 **Student-faculty ratio** 14:1 **Application deadline** 2/1 (freshmen), 3/1 (transfer) **Freshmen** 76% were admitted **Housing** Yes **Expenses** Tuition $7693; Room & Board $5514 **Undergraduates** 57% women, 8% part-time, 5% 25 or older, 0.2% Native American, 1% Hispanic American, 1% African American, 2% Asian American/Pacific Islander **The most frequently chosen baccalaureate fields are** business/marketing, health professions and related sciences, social sciences and history **Academic program** English as a second language, advanced placement, accelerated degree program, self-designed majors, honors program, summer session, adult/continuing education programs, internships **Contact** Mr. Gary Cilley, Acting Co-Director of Admissions, University of New Hampshire, Grant House, 4 Garrison Avenue, Durham, NH 03824.

Telephone: 603-862-1360. Fax: 603-862-0077. E-mail: admissions@unh.edu. Web site: http://www.unh.edu/.

UNIVERSITY OF NEW HAMPSHIRE AT MANCHESTER
MANCHESTER, NEW HAMPSHIRE

General State-supported, comprehensive, coed **Entrance** Moderately difficult **Setting** 800-acre urban campus **Total enrollment** 1,086 **Student-faculty ratio** 13:1 **Application deadline** 6/15 (freshmen), 6/15 (transfer) **Freshmen** 73% were admitted **Housing** No **Expenses** Tuition $5064 **Undergraduates** 62% women, 60% part-time, 0.3% Native American, 1% Hispanic American, 2% African American, 1% Asian American/Pacific Islander **The most frequently chosen baccalaureate fields are** foreign language/literature, communications/communication technologies, psychology **Academic program** Advanced placement, self-designed majors, summer session, adult/continuing education programs, internships **Contact** Ms. Susan Miller, Administrative Assistant, University of New Hampshire at Manchester, 400 Commercial Street, Manchester, NH 03101. Telephone: 603-641-4150 or toll-free 800-735-2964 (out-of-state). Fax: 603-641-4125. E-mail: unhm@unh.edu. Web site: http://www.unh.edu/unhm/.

UNIVERSITY SYSTEM COLLEGE FOR LIFELONG LEARNING
CONCORD, NEW HAMPSHIRE

General State and locally supported, 4-year, coed **Entrance** Noncompetitive **Setting** rural campus **Total enrollment** 2,095 **Student-faculty ratio** 10:1 **Application deadline** Rolling (freshmen), rolling (transfer) **Housing** No **Expenses** Tuition $4302 **Undergraduates** 80% women, 96% part-time **Academic program** Advanced placement, accelerated degree program, self-designed majors, summer session, adult/continuing education programs, internships **Contact** Ms. Teresa McDonnell, Associate Dean of Learner Services, University System College for Lifelong Learning, 125 North State Street, Concord, NH 03301. Telephone: 603-228-3000 Ext. 308 or toll-free 800-582-7248 Ext. 313 (in-state). Fax: 603-229-0964. E-mail: n_dumont@unhf.unh.edu. Web site: http://www.cll.edu/.

WHITE PINES COLLEGE
CHESTER, NEW HAMPSHIRE

General Independent, 4-year, coed **Entrance** Moderately difficult **Setting** 83-acre rural campus **Total enrollment** 140 **Student-faculty ratio** 10:1 **Application deadline** Rolling (freshmen), rolling (transfer) **Freshmen** 85% were admitted **Housing** Yes **Expenses** Tuition $12,100; Room & Board $6050 **Undergraduates** 62% women, 26% part-time, 4% 25 or older, 1% Native American, 1% Hispanic American, 2% African American, 2% Asian American/Pacific Islander **The most frequently chosen baccalaureate field is** visual/performing arts **Academic program** English as a second language, advanced

White Pines College *(continued)*
placement, self-designed majors, honors program, summer session, adult/continuing education programs, internships **Contact** Ms. Jessie Girvin, Director of Admissions, White Pines College, 40 Chester Street, Chester, NH 03036. Telephone: 603-887-7400 or toll-free 877-818-0492. Fax: 603-887-1777. E-mail: admissions@whitepines.edu. Web site: http://www.whitepines.edu/.

NEW JERSEY

BETH MEDRASH GOVOHA
LAKEWOOD, NEW JERSEY

Contact Rabbi Yehuda Jacobs, Director of Admissions, Beth Medrash Govoha, 617 Sixth Street, Lakewood, NJ 08701-2797. Telephone: 908-367-1060.

BLOOMFIELD COLLEGE
BLOOMFIELD, NEW JERSEY

General Independent, 4-year, coed, affiliated with Presbyterian Church (U.S.A.) **Entrance** Minimally difficult **Setting** 12-acre suburban campus **Total enrollment** 1,785 **Student-faculty ratio** 14:1 **Application deadline** 8/1 (freshmen), rolling (transfer) **Freshmen** 40% were admitted **Housing** Yes **Expenses** Tuition $11,450; Room & Board $5550 **Undergraduates** 69% women, 29% part-time, 45% 25 or older, 0.2% Native American, 17% Hispanic American, 49% African American, 4% Asian American/Pacific Islander **The most frequently chosen baccalaureate fields are** business/marketing, health professions and related sciences, social sciences and history **Academic program** English as a second language, advanced placement, accelerated degree program, self-designed majors, honors program, summer session, internships **Contact** Mr. Michael Szarek, Associate Dean of Admission, Bloomfield College, 467 Franklin Street, Bloomfield, NJ 07003-9981. Telephone: 973-748-9000 Ext. 390 or toll-free 800-848-4555. Fax: 973-748-0916. E-mail: admission@bloomfield.edu. Web site: http://www.bloomfield.edu/.

CALDWELL COLLEGE
CALDWELL, NEW JERSEY

General Independent Roman Catholic, comprehensive, coed **Entrance** Moderately difficult **Setting** 100-acre suburban campus **Total enrollment** 2,238 **Student-faculty ratio** 13:1 **Application deadline** Rolling (transfer) **Freshmen** 77% were admitted **Housing** Yes **Expenses** Tuition $14,190; Room & Board $6600 **Undergraduates** 68% women, 48% part-time, 45% 25 or older, 0.2% Native American, 9% Hispanic American, 14% African American, 3% Asian American/Pacific Islander **The most frequently chosen baccalaureate fields are** business/marketing, education, psychology **Academic program** English as a second language, advanced placement, accelerated degree program, self-designed majors, honors program, summer session, adult/continuing education programs, internships **Contact** Mr. Richard Ott, Vice President for Enrollment Management, Caldwell College, 9 Ryerson Avenue, Caldwell, NJ 07006. Telephone: 973-618-3224 or toll-free 888-864-9516 (out-of-state). Fax: 973-618-3600. E-mail: admissions@caldwell.edu. Web site: http://www.caldwell.edu/.

CENTENARY COLLEGE
HACKETTSTOWN, NEW JERSEY

General Independent, comprehensive, coed, affiliated with United Methodist Church **Entrance** Moderately difficult **Setting** 42-acre suburban campus **Total enrollment** 1,645 **Student-faculty ratio** 15:1 **Application deadline** Rolling (freshmen), rolling (transfer) **Freshmen** 83% were admitted **Housing** Yes **Expenses** Tuition $16,030; Room & Board $6400 **Undergraduates** 72% women, 50% part-time, 26% 25 or older, 0.3% Native American, 2% Hispanic American, 3% African American, 0.1% Asian American/Pacific Islander **The most frequently chosen baccalaureate fields are** business/marketing, psychology, social sciences and history **Academic program** English as a second language, advanced placement, accelerated degree program, self-designed majors, honors program, summer session, internships **Contact** Ms. Diane Finnan, Vice President for Enrollment Management, Centenary College, 400 Jefferson Street, Hackettstown, NJ 07840-2100. Telephone: 908-852-1400 Ext. 2217 or toll-free 800-236-8679. Fax: 908-852-3454. E-mail: admissions@centenarycollege.edu. Web site: http://www.centenarycollege.edu/.

THE COLLEGE OF NEW JERSEY
EWING, NEW JERSEY

General State-supported, comprehensive, coed **Entrance** Very difficult **Setting** 255-acre suburban campus **Total enrollment** 6,847 **Student-faculty ratio** 12:1 **Application deadline** 2/15 (freshmen), 2/15 (transfer) **Freshmen** 51% were admitted **Housing** Yes **Expenses** Tuition $6661; Room & Board $6764 **Undergraduates** 59% women, 6% part-time, 6% 25 or older, 0.1% Native American, 5% Hispanic American, 6% African American, 5% Asian American/Pacific Islander **The most frequently chosen baccalaureate fields are** business/marketing, education, social sciences and history **Academic program** Advanced placement, honors program, summer session, internships **Contact** Ms. Lisa Angeloni, Dean of Admissions, The College of New Jersey, PO Box 7718, Ewing, NJ 08628. Telephone: 609-771-2131 or toll-free 800-624-0967. Fax: 609-637-5174. E-mail: admiss@tcnj.edu. Web site: http://www.tcnj.edu/.

COLLEGE OF SAINT ELIZABETH
MORRISTOWN, NEW JERSEY

General Independent Roman Catholic, comprehensive, women only **Entrance** Moderately difficult **Setting** 188-acre suburban campus **Total enrollment**

1,741 **Student-faculty ratio** 10:1 **Application deadline** 8/15 (freshmen), rolling (transfer) **Freshmen** 80% were admitted **Housing** Yes **Expenses** Tuition $15,310; Room & Board $7200 **Undergraduates** 52% part-time, 38% 25 or older, 0.3% Native American, 12% Hispanic American, 13% African American, 4% Asian American/Pacific Islander **The most frequently chosen baccalaureate fields are** business/marketing, education, psychology **Academic program** English as a second language, advanced placement, accelerated degree program, self-designed majors, honors program, summer session, internships **Contact** Ms. Donna Tatarka, Dean of Admissions and Financial Aid, College of Saint Elizabeth, 2 Convent Road, Morristown, NJ 07960-6989. Telephone: 973-290-4700 or toll-free 800-210-7900. Fax: 973-290-4710. E-mail: apply@liza.st-elizabeth.edu. Web site: http://www.cse.edu/.

DEVRY COLLEGE OF TECHNOLOGY
NORTH BRUNSWICK, NEW JERSEY

General Proprietary, 4-year, coed **Entrance** Minimally difficult **Setting** 10-acre urban campus **Total enrollment** 3,912 **Student-faculty ratio** 20:1 **Application deadline** Rolling (freshmen), rolling (transfer) **Freshmen** 82% were admitted **Housing** No **Expenses** Tuition $8805 **Undergraduates** 23% women, 39% part-time, 43% 25 or older, 0.3% Native American, 17% Hispanic American, 24% African American, 9% Asian American/Pacific Islander **The most frequently chosen baccalaureate fields are** communications/communication technologies, engineering/engineering technologies **Academic program** Advanced placement, summer session, adult/continuing education programs **Contact** Ms. Norma Houze, New Student Coordinator, DeVry College of Technology, 630 US Highway One, North Brunswick, NJ 08902-3362. Telephone: 732-435-4880 or toll-free 800-333-3879. Web site: http://www.nj.devry.edu/.

DREW UNIVERSITY
MADISON, NEW JERSEY

General Independent, university, coed, affiliated with United Methodist Church **Entrance** Very difficult **Setting** 186-acre suburban campus **Total enrollment** 2,418 **Student-faculty ratio** 11:1 **Application deadline** 2/15 (freshmen), 8/1 (transfer) **Freshmen** 72% were admitted **Housing** Yes **Expenses** Tuition $25,122; Room & Board $7030 **Undergraduates** 61% women, 3% part-time, 3% 25 or older, 0.4% Native American, 4% Hispanic American, 4% African American, 6% Asian American/Pacific Islander **The most frequently chosen baccalaureate fields are** psychology, biological/life sciences, social sciences and history **Academic program** Advanced placement, accelerated degree program, self-designed majors, summer session, adult/continuing education programs, internships **Contact** Mr. Roberto Noya, Dean of Admissions and Financial Aid, Drew University, 36 Madison Avenue, Madison, NJ 07940. Telephone: 973-408-3739. Fax: 973-408-3036. E-mail: cadm@drew.edu. Web site: http://www.drew.edu/.

FAIRLEIGH DICKINSON UNIVERSITY, COLLEGE AT FLORHAM
MADISON, NEW JERSEY

General Independent, comprehensive, coed **Entrance** Moderately difficult **Setting** 178-acre suburban campus **Total enrollment** 3,460 **Student-faculty ratio** 17:1 **Application deadline** 3/1 (freshmen), 8/1 (transfer) **Freshmen** 69% were admitted **Housing** Yes **Expenses** Tuition $16,346; Room & Board $6842 **Undergraduates** 53% women, 18% part-time, 14% 25 or older, 0.1% Native American, 7% Hispanic American, 6% African American, 3% Asian American/Pacific Islander **The most frequently chosen baccalaureate fields are** business/marketing, liberal arts/general studies, psychology **Academic program** English as a second language, advanced placement, accelerated degree program, honors program, summer session, adult/continuing education programs, internships **Contact** Mr. Gary Hamme, Vice President for Enrollment Services, Fairleigh Dickinson University, College at Florham, 285 Madison Avenue, M-MS1-03, Madison, NJ 07940. Telephone: 201-692-7304 or toll-free 800-338-8803. Fax: 973-443-8088. E-mail: globaleducation@fdu.edu. Web site: http://www.fdu.edu/.

FAIRLEIGH DICKINSON UNIVERSITY, METROPOLITAN CAMPUS
TEANECK, NEW JERSEY

General Independent, comprehensive, coed **Entrance** Moderately difficult **Setting** 125-acre suburban campus **Total enrollment** 6,092 **Student-faculty ratio** 15:1 **Application deadline** 3/1 (freshmen), 8/1 (transfer) **Freshmen** 70% were admitted **Housing** Yes **Expenses** Tuition $16,346; Room & Board $6842 **Undergraduates** 58% women, 55% part-time, 30% 25 or older, 0.4% Native American, 14% Hispanic American, 21% African American, 6% Asian American/Pacific Islander **The most frequently chosen baccalaureate fields are** business/marketing, liberal arts/general studies, psychology **Academic program** English as a second language, advanced placement, accelerated degree program, honors program, summer session, adult/continuing education programs, internships **Contact** Mr. Gary Hamme, Vice President of Enrollment Services, Fairleigh Dickinson University, Metropolitan Campus, 1000 River Road, Teaneck, NJ 07666. Telephone: 201-692-7304 or toll-free 800-338-8803. Fax: 201-692-2560. E-mail: globaleducation@fdu.edu. Web site: http://www.fdu.edu/.

FELICIAN COLLEGE
LODI, NEW JERSEY

General Independent Roman Catholic, comprehensive, coed **Entrance** Moderately difficult **Setting** 37-acre suburban campus **Total enrollment** 1,717 **Student-faculty ratio** 15:1 **Application deadline** Rolling (freshmen), rolling (transfer) **Freshmen** 63% were admitted **Housing** Yes **Expenses** Tuition $12,410; Room & Board $6250 **Undergraduates** 76% women, 41% part-time, 32% 25 or older, 0.1% Native Ameri-

NEW JERSEY

Felician College *(continued)*
can, 15% Hispanic American, 13% African American, 4% Asian American/Pacific Islander **The most frequently chosen baccalaureate fields are** education, English, psychology **Academic program** English as a second language, advanced placement, accelerated degree program, self-designed majors, honors program, summer session, adult/continuing education programs, internships **Contact** College Admissions Office, Felician College, 262 South Main Street, Lodi, NJ 07644. Telephone: 201-559-6131. Fax: 201-559-6188. E-mail: admissions@inet.felician.edu. Web site: http://www.felician.edu/.

GEORGIAN COURT COLLEGE
LAKEWOOD, NEW JERSEY

General Independent Roman Catholic, comprehensive, women only **Entrance** Moderately difficult **Setting** 150-acre suburban campus **Total enrollment** 2,708 **Student-faculty ratio** 15:1 **Application deadline** 8/1 (freshmen), 8/1 (transfer) **Freshmen** 85% were admitted **Housing** Yes **Expenses** Tuition $13,264; Room & Board $5200 **Undergraduates** 33% part-time, 37% 25 or older, 0.1% Native American, 5% Hispanic American, 7% African American, 2% Asian American/Pacific Islander **The most frequently chosen baccalaureate fields are** business/marketing, education, psychology **Academic program** Advanced placement, honors program, summer session, adult/continuing education programs, internships **Contact** Mr. Michael Backes, Vice President for Enrollment, Georgian Court College, Office of Admissions, 900 Lakewood Avenue, Lakewood, NJ 08701-2697. Telephone: 732-364-2200 Ext. 760 or toll-free 800-458-8422. Fax: 732-364-4442. E-mail: admissions@georgian.edu. Web site: http://www.georgian.edu/.

KEAN UNIVERSITY
UNION, NEW JERSEY

General State-supported, comprehensive, coed **Entrance** Moderately difficult **Setting** 151-acre urban campus **Total enrollment** 12,094 **Student-faculty ratio** 20:1 **Application deadline** 5/31 (freshmen), 7/15 (transfer) **Freshmen** 51% were admitted **Housing** Yes **Expenses** Tuition $5121; Room only $4840 **Undergraduates** 65% women, 29% part-time, 66% 25 or older, 0.1% Native American, 18% Hispanic American, 20% African American, 6% Asian American/Pacific Islander **The most frequently chosen baccalaureate fields are** business/marketing, education, social sciences and history **Academic program** English as a second language, accelerated degree program, honors program, summer session, adult/continuing education programs, internships **Contact** Mr. Audley Bridges, Director of Admissions, Kean University, PO Box 411, Union, NJ 07083. Telephone: 908-527-2195. E-mail: admitme@kean.edu. Web site: http://www.kean.edu/.

MONMOUTH UNIVERSITY
WEST LONG BRANCH, NEW JERSEY

General Independent, comprehensive, coed **Entrance** Moderately difficult **Setting** 147-acre suburban campus **Total enrollment** 5,753 **Student-faculty ratio** 18:1 **Application deadline** 3/1 (freshmen), 1/1 (transfer) **Freshmen** 82% were admitted **Housing** Yes **Expenses** Tuition $17,074; Room & Board $7076 **Undergraduates** 58% women, 13% part-time, 15% 25 or older, 0.3% Native American, 4% Hispanic American, 6% African American, 2% Asian American/Pacific Islander **Academic program** Advanced placement, accelerated degree program, self-designed majors, honors program, summer session, adult/continuing education programs, internships **Contact** Ms. Christine Benol, Director of Undergraduate Admission, Monmouth University, 400 Cedar Avenue, West Long Branch, NJ 07764-1898. Telephone: 732-571-3456 or toll-free 800-543-9671 (out-of-state). Fax: 732-263-5166. E-mail: barson@mondec.monmouth.edu. Web site: http://www.monmouth.edu/.

MONTCLAIR STATE UNIVERSITY
UPPER MONTCLAIR, NEW JERSEY

General State-supported, comprehensive, coed **Entrance** Moderately difficult **Setting** 200-acre suburban campus **Total enrollment** 13,855 **Student-faculty ratio** 14:1 **Application deadline** 3/1 (freshmen), 5/1 (transfer) **Freshmen** 23% were admitted **Housing** Yes **Expenses** Tuition $4986; Room & Board $6754 **Undergraduates** 61% women, 23% part-time, 26% 25 or older, 0.2% Native American, 15% Hispanic American, 11% African American, 5% Asian American/Pacific Islander **The most frequently chosen baccalaureate fields are** business/marketing, psychology, social sciences and history **Academic program** English as a second language, advanced placement, accelerated degree program, honors program, summer session, adult/continuing education programs, internships **Contact** Mr. Dennis Craig, Director of Admissions, Montclair State University, One Normal Avenue, Upper Montclair, NJ 07043-1624. Telephone: 973-655-5116 or toll-free 800-331-9205. Fax: 973-893-5455. E-mail: undergraduate.admissions@montclair.edu. Web site: http://www.montclair.edu/.

NEW JERSEY CITY UNIVERSITY
JERSEY CITY, NEW JERSEY

General State-supported, comprehensive, coed **Entrance** Moderately difficult **Setting** 46-acre urban campus **Total enrollment** 8,824 **Student-faculty ratio** 15:1 **Application deadline** 4/1 (freshmen), rolling (transfer) **Freshmen** 70% were admitted **Housing** Yes **Expenses** Tuition $5063; Room & Board $5800 **Undergraduates** 61% women, 36% part-time, 36% 25 or older, 0.3% Native American, 32% Hispanic American, 20% African American, 10% Asian American/Pacific Islander **The most frequently chosen baccalaureate fields are** business/

NEW JERSEY

marketing, protective services/public administration, social sciences and history **Academic program** English as a second language, advanced placement, accelerated degree program, honors program, summer session, adult/continuing education programs, internships **Contact** Ms. Drusilla Blackman, Director of Admissions, New Jersey City University, 2039 Kennedy Boulevard, Jersey City, NJ 07305-1597. Telephone: 201-200-3234 or toll-free 800-441-NJCU. E-mail: admissions@njcu.edu. Web site: http://www.njcu.edu/core.htm.

NEW JERSEY INSTITUTE OF TECHNOLOGY
NEWARK, NEW JERSEY

General State-supported, university, coed **Entrance** Moderately difficult **Setting** 45-acre urban campus **Total enrollment** 8,862 **Student-faculty ratio** 14:1 **Application deadline** 4/1 (freshmen), 6/1 (transfer) **Freshmen** 65% were admitted **Housing** Yes **Expenses** Tuition $7200; Room & Board $7490 **Undergraduates** 22% women, 28% part-time, 24% 25 or older, 0.2% Native American, 11% Hispanic American, 11% African American, 23% Asian American/Pacific Islander **The most frequently chosen baccalaureate fields are** computer/information sciences, business/marketing, engineering/engineering technologies **Academic program** English as a second language, advanced placement, accelerated degree program, honors program, summer session, adult/continuing education programs, internships **Contact** Ms. Kathy Kelly, Director of Admissions, New Jersey Institute of Technology, University Heights, Newark, NJ 07102-1982. Telephone: 973-596-3300 or toll-free 800-925-NJIT. Fax: 973-596-3461. E-mail: admissions@njit.edu. Web site: http://www.njit.edu/.

PRINCETON UNIVERSITY
PRINCETON, NEW JERSEY

General Independent, university, coed **Entrance** Most difficult **Setting** 600-acre suburban campus **Total enrollment** 6,668 **Student-faculty ratio** 6:1 **Application deadline** 1/1 (freshmen) **Freshmen** 12% were admitted **Housing** Yes **Expenses** Tuition $26,160; Room & Board $7453 **Undergraduates** 48% women, 3% part-time, 0% 25 or older, 1% Native American, 6% Hispanic American, 8% African American, 12% Asian American/Pacific Islander **The most frequently chosen baccalaureate fields are** engineering/engineering technologies, biological/life sciences, social sciences and history **Academic program** Advanced placement, accelerated degree program, self-designed majors, honors program, adult/continuing education programs, internships **Contact** Mr. Fred A. Hargadon, Dean of Admission, Princeton University, PO Box 430, Princeton, NJ 08544. Telephone: 609-258-3062. Fax: 609-258-6743. E-mail: g3516@princeton.edu. Web site: http://www.princeton.edu/.

RABBINICAL COLLEGE OF AMERICA
MORRISTOWN, NEW JERSEY

General Independent Jewish, 4-year, men only **Entrance** Minimally difficult **Setting** 81-acre small-town campus **Total enrollment** 259 **Application deadline** Rolling (freshmen) **Freshmen** 100% were admitted **Housing** Yes **Expenses** Tuition $7000 **Academic program** Accelerated degree program, summer session, internships **Contact** Rabbi Israel Teitelbaum, Registrar, Rabbinical College of America, Box 1996, Morristown, NJ 07962. Telephone: 973-267-9404.

RAMAPO COLLEGE OF NEW JERSEY
MAHWAH, NEW JERSEY

General State-supported, comprehensive, coed **Entrance** Moderately difficult **Setting** 315-acre suburban campus **Total enrollment** 5,199 **Student-faculty ratio** 16:1 **Application deadline** 3/15 (freshmen), 5/1 (transfer) **Freshmen** 42% were admitted **Housing** Yes **Expenses** Tuition $6178; Room & Board $7372 **Undergraduates** 60% women, 28% part-time, 25% 25 or older, 0.3% Native American, 8% Hispanic American, 7% African American, 4% Asian American/Pacific Islander **The most frequently chosen baccalaureate fields are** business/marketing, communications/communication technologies, psychology **Academic program** English as a second language, advanced placement, accelerated degree program, self-designed majors, honors program, summer session, adult/continuing education programs, internships **Contact** Mr. Peter Goetz, Director of Recruitment and Retention, Ramapo College of New Jersey, Office of Admissions, 505 Ramapo Valley Road, Mahwah, NJ 07430-1680. Telephone: 201-684-7307 Ext. 7307 or toll-free 800-9RAMAPO (in-state). Fax: 201-684-7964. E-mail: admissions@ramapo.edu. Web site: http://www.ramapo.edu/.

THE RICHARD STOCKTON COLLEGE OF NEW JERSEY
POMONA, NEW JERSEY

General State-supported, comprehensive, coed **Entrance** Very difficult **Setting** 1,600-acre suburban campus **Total enrollment** 6,457 **Student-faculty ratio** 20:1 **Application deadline** 5/1 (freshmen), 6/1 (transfer) **Freshmen** 45% were admitted **Housing** Yes **Expenses** Tuition $5136; Room & Board $5845 **Undergraduates** 58% women, 18% part-time, 23% 25 or older, 0.3% Native American, 5% Hispanic American, 8% African American, 4% Asian American/Pacific Islander **The most frequently chosen baccalaureate fields are** business/marketing, biological/life sciences, social sciences and history **Academic program** Advanced placement, accelerated degree program, self-designed majors, honors program, summer session, adult/continuing education programs, internships **Contact** Mr. Salvatore Catalfamo, Dean of Enrollment Management, The Richard Stockton College of New Jersey, PO Box 195, F-101, Pomona, NJ 08240. Telephone: 609-652-4261. Fax: 609-748-5541. E-mail: admissions@pollux.stockton.edu. Web site: http://www.stockton.edu/.

▶ For more information, see page 466.

NEW JERSEY

RIDER UNIVERSITY
LAWRENCEVILLE, NEW JERSEY

General Independent, comprehensive, coed **Entrance** Moderately difficult **Setting** 340-acre suburban campus **Total enrollment** 5,456 **Student-faculty ratio** 13:1 **Application deadline** Rolling (freshmen), rolling (transfer) **Freshmen** 74% were admitted **Housing** Yes **Expenses** Tuition $18,320; Room & Board $7380 **Undergraduates** 58% women, 20% part-time, 13% 25 or older, 0.5% Native American, 4% Hispanic American, 8% African American, 3% Asian American/Pacific Islander The most frequently chosen baccalaureate fields are business/marketing, communications/communication technologies, education **Academic program** English as a second language, advanced placement, honors program, summer session, adult/continuing education programs, internships **Contact** Mrs. Susan C. Christian, Director, Office of Admissions, Rider University, 2083 Lawrenceville Road, Lawrenceville, NJ 08648-3099. Telephone: 609-895-5768 or toll-free 800-257-9026. Fax: 609-895-6645. E-mail: admissions@rider.edu. Web site: http://www.rider.edu/.

▶ For more information, see page 467.

ROWAN UNIVERSITY
GLASSBORO, NEW JERSEY

General State-supported, comprehensive, coed **Entrance** Moderately difficult **Setting** 200-acre small-town campus **Total enrollment** 9,790 **Student-faculty ratio** 14:1 **Application deadline** 3/15 (freshmen), 3/15 (transfer) **Freshmen** 52% were admitted **Housing** Yes **Expenses** Tuition $5779; Room & Board $6586 **Undergraduates** 58% women, 21% part-time, 32% 25 or older, 0.4% Native American, 6% Hispanic American, 9% African American, 4% Asian American/Pacific Islander The most frequently chosen baccalaureate fields are communications/communication technologies, business/marketing, education **Academic program** English as a second language, advanced placement, accelerated degree program, honors program, summer session, adult/continuing education programs, internships **Contact** Mr. Marvin G. Sills, Director of Admissions, Rowan University, 201 Mullica Hill Road, Glassboro, NJ 08028. Telephone: 856-256-4200 or toll-free 800-447-1165 (in-state). Fax: 856-256-4430. E-mail: admissions@rowan.edu. Web site: http://www.rowan.edu/.

RUTGERS, THE STATE UNIVERSITY OF NEW JERSEY, CAMDEN
CAMDEN, NEW JERSEY

General State-supported, university, coed **Total enrollment** 5,097 **Student-faculty ratio** 11:1 **Application deadline** Rolling (freshmen) **Freshmen** 59% were admitted **Expenses** Tuition $6484; Room & Board $6776 **Undergraduates** 60% women, 26% part-time, 32% 25 or older, 0.3% Native American, 6% Hispanic American, 15% African American, 7% Asian American/Pacific Islander The most frequently chosen baccalaureate fields are business/marketing, psychology, social sciences and history **Academic program** English as a second language, advanced placement, self-designed majors, honors program, summer session, internships **Contact** Ms. Diane Williams Harris, Associate Director of University Undergraduate Admissions, Rutgers, The State University of New Jersey, Camden, 65 Davidson Road, Piscataway, NJ 08854-8097. Telephone: 732-932-4636. Fax: 732-353-1440. Web site: http://camden-www.rutgers.edu/.

RUTGERS, THE STATE UNIVERSITY OF NEW JERSEY, NEWARK
NEWARK, NEW JERSEY

General State-supported, university, coed **Entrance** Moderately difficult **Total enrollment** 9,592 **Student-faculty ratio** 10:1 **Application deadline** Rolling (freshmen) **Freshmen** 52% were admitted **Expenses** Tuition $6376; Room & Board $7208 **Undergraduates** 58% women, 28% part-time, 27% 25 or older, 0.2% Native American, 18% Hispanic American, 20% African American, 20% Asian American/Pacific Islander The most frequently chosen baccalaureate fields are business/marketing, health professions and related sciences, protective services/public administration **Academic program** English as a second language, advanced placement, accelerated degree program, self-designed majors, honors program, summer session, adult/continuing education programs, internships **Contact** Ms. Diane William Harris, Associate Director of University Undergraduate Admissions, Rutgers, The State University of New Jersey, Newark, 65 Davidson Road, Piscataway, NJ 08854-8097. Telephone: 732-932-4636. Fax: 732-353-1440. Web site: http://info.rutgers.edu/newark/.

RUTGERS, THE STATE UNIVERSITY OF NEW JERSEY, NEW BRUNSWICK
NEW BRUNSWICK, NEW JERSEY

General State-supported, university, coed **Entrance** Moderately difficult **Total enrollment** 35,652 **Student-faculty ratio** 15:1 **Application deadline** Rolling (freshmen) **Freshmen** 60% were admitted **Housing** Yes **Expenses** Tuition $6620; Room & Board $6676 **Undergraduates** 53% women, 9% part-time, 10% 25 or older, 0.2% Native American, 8% Hispanic American, 8% African American, 19% Asian American/Pacific Islander The most frequently chosen baccalaureate fields are psychology, biological/life sciences, social sciences and history **Academic program** English as a second language, advanced placement, accelerated degree program, self-designed majors, honors program **Contact** Ms. Diane Williams Harris, Associate Director of University Undergraduate Admissions, Rutgers, The State University of New Jersey, New Brunswick, 65 Davidson Road, Piscataway, NJ 08854-8097. Telephone: 732-932-4636. Fax: 732-445-0237. Web site: http://www.rutgers.edu/.

NEW JERSEY

SAINT PETER'S COLLEGE
JERSEY CITY, NEW JERSEY

General Independent Roman Catholic (Jesuit), comprehensive, coed **Entrance** Moderately difficult **Setting** 15-acre urban campus **Total enrollment** 3,225 **Student-faculty ratio** 20:1 **Application deadline** Rolling (freshmen), 6/1 (transfer) **Freshmen** 73% were admitted **Housing** Yes **Expenses** Tuition $16,552; Room & Board $7053 **Undergraduates** 57% women, 19% part-time, 19% 25 or older, 0.5% Native American, 27% Hispanic American, 19% African American, 7% Asian American/Pacific Islander **The most frequently chosen baccalaureate fields are** business/marketing, computer/information sciences, social sciences and history **Academic program** Advanced placement, accelerated degree program, self-designed majors, honors program, summer session, adult/continuing education programs, internships **Contact** Stephanie Decker, Director of Recruitment, Saint Peter's College, 2627 Kennedy Blvd., Jersey City, NJ 07306. Telephone: 201-915-9213 or toll-free 888-SPC-9933. Fax: 201-432-5860. E-mail: admissions@spcvxa.spc.edu. Web site: http://www.spc.edu/.

SETON HALL UNIVERSITY
SOUTH ORANGE, NEW JERSEY

General Independent Roman Catholic, university, coed **Entrance** Moderately difficult **Setting** 58-acre suburban campus **Total enrollment** 9,604 **Student-faculty ratio** 14:1 **Application deadline** 3/1 (freshmen), 6/1 (transfer) **Freshmen** 88% were admitted **Housing** Yes **Expenses** Tuition $19,400; Room & Board $8060 **Undergraduates** 52% women, 12% part-time, 7% 25 or older, 0.1% Native American, 9% Hispanic American, 11% African American, 8% Asian American/Pacific Islander **The most frequently chosen baccalaureate fields are** business/marketing, communications/communication technologies, protective services/public administration **Academic program** English as a second language, advanced placement, accelerated degree program, honors program, summer session, internships **Contact** Ms. Alyssa McCloud, Acting Director of Admissions, Seton Hall University, Enrollment Services, Bayley Hall, South Orange, NJ 07079-2697. Telephone: 973-275-2576 or toll-free 800-THE HALL (out-of-state). Fax: 973-275-2040. E-mail: thehall@lanmail.shu.edu. Web site: http://www.shu.edu/.

STEVENS INSTITUTE OF TECHNOLOGY
HOBOKEN, NEW JERSEY

General Independent, university, coed **Entrance** Very difficult **Setting** 55-acre urban campus **Total enrollment** 4,263 **Student-faculty ratio** 9:1 **Application deadline** 2/15 (freshmen), 7/1 (transfer) **Freshmen** 49% were admitted **Housing** Yes **Expenses** Tuition $23,150; Room & Board $7730 **Undergraduates** 3% 25 or older **The most frequently chosen baccalaureate fields are** computer/information sciences, business/marketing, engineering/engineering technologies **Academic program** Advanced placement, accelerated degree program, honors program, summer session, internships **Contact** Mr. Daniel Gallagher, Dean of Undergraduate Admissions, Stevens Institute of Technology, Castle Point on Hudson, Hoboken, NJ 07030. Telephone: 201-216-5197 or toll-free 800-458-5323. Fax: 201-216-8348. E-mail: admissions@stevens-tech.edu. Web site: http://www.stevens-tech.edu/.

TALMUDICAL ACADEMY OF NEW JERSEY
ADELPHIA, NEW JERSEY

Contact Rabbi G. Finkel, Director of Admissions, Talmudical Academy of New Jersey, Route 524, Adelphia, NJ 07710. Telephone: 201-431-1600.

THOMAS EDISON STATE COLLEGE
TRENTON, NEW JERSEY

General State-supported, comprehensive, coed **Entrance** Noncompetitive **Total enrollment** 8,335 **Application deadline** Rolling (transfer) **Housing** No **Undergraduates** 47% women, 100% part-time, 91% 25 or older, 1% Native American, 4% Hispanic American, 10% African American, 2% Asian American/Pacific Islander **The most frequently chosen baccalaureate fields are** liberal arts/general studies, business/marketing, physical sciences **Academic program** Advanced placement, accelerated degree program, self-designed majors, summer session, adult/continuing education programs **Contact** Mr. Gordon Holly, Director of Admissions Services, Thomas Edison State College, 101 West State Street, Trenton, NJ 08608-1176. Telephone: 609-984-1150 or toll-free 888-442-8372. Fax: 609-984-8447. E-mail: info@tesc.edu. Web site: http://www.tesc.edu/.

WESTMINSTER CHOIR COLLEGE OF RIDER UNIVERSITY
PRINCETON, NEW JERSEY

General Independent, comprehensive, coed **Entrance** Moderately difficult **Setting** 23-acre small-town campus **Total enrollment** 446 **Student-faculty ratio** 7:1 **Application deadline** Rolling (freshmen), rolling (transfer) **Freshmen** 67% were admitted **Housing** Yes **Expenses** Tuition $18,230; Room & Board $7670 **Undergraduates** 60% women, 2% part-time **The most frequently chosen baccalaureate field is** visual/performing arts **Academic program** English as a second language, advanced placement, honors program, summer session, adult/continuing education programs, internships **Contact** Elizabeth S. Rush, Assistant Director of Admissions, Westminster Choir College of Rider University, 101 Walnut Lane, Princeton, NJ 08540-3899. Telephone: 609-921-7144 Ext. 221 or toll-free 800-96-CHOIR. Fax: 609-921-2538. E-mail: wccadmission@rider.edu. Web site: http://westminster.rider.edu/.

NEW JERSEY

WILLIAM PATERSON UNIVERSITY OF NEW JERSEY
WAYNE, NEW JERSEY

General State-supported, comprehensive, coed **Entrance** Moderately difficult **Setting** 300-acre suburban campus **Total enrollment** 10,466 **Student-faculty ratio** 12:1 **Application deadline** 5/1 (freshmen), 5/1 (transfer) **Freshmen** 67% were admitted **Housing** Yes **Expenses** Tuition $5700; Room & Board $6680 **Undergraduates** 59% women, 23% part-time, 22% 25 or older, 0.2% Native American, 14% Hispanic American, 12% African American, 3% Asian American/Pacific Islander **The most frequently chosen baccalaureate fields are** business/marketing, communications/communication technologies, social sciences and history **Academic program** English as a second language, advanced placement, accelerated degree program, honors program, summer session, adult/continuing education programs, internships **Contact** Mr. Jonathan McCoy, Director of Admissions, William Paterson University of New Jersey, 300 Pompton Road, Wayne, NJ 07470. Telephone: 973-720-2906 or toll-free 877-WPU-EXCEL (in-state). Fax: 973-720-2910. E-mail: admissions@wpunj.edu. Web site: http://www.wpunj.edu/.

▶ For more information, see page 500.

NEW MEXICO

COLLEGE OF SANTA FE
SANTA FE, NEW MEXICO

General Independent, comprehensive, coed **Entrance** Moderately difficult **Setting** 100-acre suburban campus **Total enrollment** 1,588 **Student-faculty ratio** 8:1 **Application deadline** Rolling (freshmen), rolling (transfer) **Freshmen** 76% were admitted **Housing** Yes **Expenses** Tuition $17,154; Room & Board $5464 **Undergraduates** 62% women, 49% part-time, 13% 25 or older, 2% Native American, 21% Hispanic American, 3% African American, 1% Asian American/Pacific Islander **The most frequently chosen baccalaureate fields are** business/marketing, education, visual/performing arts **Academic program** Advanced placement, accelerated degree program, self-designed majors, summer session, adult/continuing education programs, internships **Contact** Mr. Dale H. Reinhart, Director of Admissions and Enrollment Management, College of Santa Fe, Admissions Office, 1600 St. Michael's Drive, Santa Fe, NM 87505-7634. Telephone: 505-473-6133 or toll-free 800-456-2673. Fax: 505-473-6129. E-mail: admissions@csf.edu. Web site: http://www.csf.edu.

COLLEGE OF THE SOUTHWEST
HOBBS, NEW MEXICO

General Independent, comprehensive, coed **Entrance** Moderately difficult **Setting** 162-acre small-town campus **Total enrollment** 847 **Student-faculty ratio** 12:1 **Application deadline** Rolling (freshmen), rolling (transfer) **Freshmen** 64% were admitted **Housing** Yes **Expenses** Tuition $4990; Room & Board $3766 **Undergraduates** 66% women, 35% part-time, 61% 25 or older, 0.3% Native American, 22% Hispanic American, 3% African American, 0.5% Asian American/Pacific Islander **The most frequently chosen baccalaureate fields are** business/marketing, education, psychology **Academic program** Advanced placement, accelerated degree program, summer session, adult/continuing education programs, internships **Contact** Charlotte Smith, Director of Admissions, College of the Southwest, 6610 Lovington Highway, Hobbs, NM 88240. Telephone: 505-392-6561 Ext. 1012 or toll-free 800-530-4400 Ext. 1004. Fax: 505-392-6006. E-mail: csmith@csw.edu. Web site: http://www.csw.edu/.

EASTERN NEW MEXICO UNIVERSITY
PORTALES, NEW MEXICO

General State-supported, comprehensive, coed **Entrance** Minimally difficult **Setting** 240-acre rural campus **Total enrollment** 3,556 **Student-faculty ratio** 19:1 **Application deadline** Rolling (freshmen), rolling (transfer) **Freshmen** 93% were admitted **Housing** Yes **Expenses** Tuition $2088; Room & Board $4160 **Undergraduates** 59% women, 16% part-time, 27% 25 or older, 3% Native American, 30% Hispanic American, 5% African American, 1% Asian American/Pacific Islander **The most frequently chosen baccalaureate fields are** business/marketing, education, social sciences and history **Academic program** English as a second language, advanced placement, accelerated degree program, self-designed majors, honors program, summer session, adult/continuing education programs, internships **Contact** Dr. Karyl C. Lyne, Assistant Vice President for Student Affairs, Eastern New Mexico University, Station #7 ENMU, Portales, NM 88130. Telephone: 505-562-2178 or toll-free 800-367-3668. Fax: 505-562-2118. E-mail: karyl.lyne@enmu.edu. Web site: http://www.enmu.edu/.

METROPOLITAN COLLEGE OF COURT REPORTING
ALBUQUERQUE, NEW MEXICO

Contact Metropolitan College of Court Reporting, 1717 Louisiana Boulevard NE, Suite 207, Albuquerque, NM 87110-7027. Web site: http://www.metropolitancollege.edu/.

NATIONAL AMERICAN UNIVERSITY
ALBUQUERQUE, NEW MEXICO

General Proprietary, 4-year, coed **Entrance** Noncompetitive **Setting** suburban campus **Total enrollment** 625 **Student-faculty ratio** 12:1 **Application deadline** Rolling (freshmen), rolling (transfer) **Housing** No **Expenses** Tuition $9435 **Undergraduates** 49% women, 92% 25 or older **The most frequently chosen baccalaureate fields are** business/marketing, computer/information sciences **Academic program**

NEW MEXICO

Accelerated degree program, summer session, adult/continuing education programs, internships **Contact** Ms. Karina Elliott-Long, Executive Admissions Representative, National American University, 4775 Indian School, NE, Albuquerque, NM 87110. Telephone: 505-265-7517 or toll-free 800-843-8892. Fax: 505-265-7542.

NEW MEXICO HIGHLANDS UNIVERSITY
LAS VEGAS, NEW MEXICO

General State-supported, comprehensive, coed **Entrance** Minimally difficult **Setting** 120-acre small-town campus **Total enrollment** 3,284 **Application deadline** Rolling (freshmen), rolling (transfer) **Freshmen** 85% were admitted **Housing** Yes **Expenses** Tuition $2094; Room & Board $3998 **Undergraduates** 61% women, 32% part-time, 37% 25 or older, 8% Native American, 63% Hispanic American, 2% African American, 2% Asian American/Pacific Islander **The most frequently chosen baccalaureate fields are** business/marketing, education, health professions and related sciences **Academic program** Advanced placement, accelerated degree program, honors program, summer session, internships **Contact** Dr. Dianne Brimmer, Vice President/Dean of Students, New Mexico Highlands University, Box 9000, Las Vegas, NM 87701. Telephone: 505-454-3020 or toll-free 800-338-6648. Fax: 505-454-3311. E-mail: admission@venus.nmnu.edu. Web site: http://www.nmhu.edu/.

NEW MEXICO INSTITUTE OF MINING AND TECHNOLOGY
SOCORRO, NEW MEXICO

General State-supported, university, coed **Entrance** Moderately difficult **Setting** 320-acre small-town campus **Total enrollment** 1,588 **Student-faculty ratio** 12:1 **Application deadline** 8/1 (freshmen), 8/1 (transfer) **Freshmen** 84% were admitted **Housing** Yes **Expenses** Tuition $2722; Room & Board $4430 **Undergraduates** 38% women, 25% part-time, 10% 25 or older, 4% Native American, 20% Hispanic American, 1% African American, 3% Asian American/Pacific Islander **The most frequently chosen baccalaureate fields are** engineering/engineering technologies, computer/information sciences, physical sciences **Academic program** Advanced placement, accelerated degree program, self-designed majors, summer session, adult/continuing education programs, internships **Contact** Ms. Melissa Jaramillo-Fleming, Director of Admissions, New Mexico Institute of Mining and Technology, 801 Leroy Place, Socorro, NM 87801. Telephone: 505-835-5424 or toll-free 800-428-TECH. Fax: 505-835-5989. E-mail: admission@admin.nmt.edu. Web site: http://www.nmt.edu/.

NEW MEXICO STATE UNIVERSITY
LAS CRUCES, NEW MEXICO

General State-supported, university, coed **Entrance** Moderately difficult **Setting** 900-acre suburban campus **Total enrollment** 15,224 **Student-faculty ratio** 19:1 **Application deadline** 8/14 (freshmen), 8/14 (transfer) **Freshmen** 62% were admitted **Housing** Yes **Expenses** Tuition $3006; Room & Board $4296 **Undergraduates** 54% women, 16% part-time, 20% 25 or older, 3% Native American, 43% Hispanic American, 3% African American, 2% Asian American/Pacific Islander **The most frequently chosen baccalaureate fields are** business/marketing, education, engineering/engineering technologies **Academic program** Advanced placement, accelerated degree program, self-designed majors, honors program, summer session, adult/continuing education programs, internships **Contact** Ms. Angela Mora-Riley, Director of Admissions, New Mexico State University, Box 30001, MSC, Las Cruces, NM 88003-8001. Telephone: 505-646-3121 or toll-free 800-662-6678. Fax: 505-646-6330. E-mail: admssions@nmsu.edu. Web site: http://www.nmsu.edu/.

ST. JOHN'S COLLEGE
SANTA FE, NEW MEXICO

General Independent, comprehensive, coed **Entrance** Very difficult **Setting** 250-acre small-town campus **Total enrollment** 528 **Student-faculty ratio** 8:1 **Application deadline** Rolling (freshmen), rolling (transfer) **Freshmen** 86% were admitted **Housing** Yes **Expenses** Tuition $25,990; Room & Board $6770 **Undergraduates** 6% 25 or older, 1% Native American, 5% Hispanic American, 0.2% African American, 3% Asian American/Pacific Islander **Academic program** Summer session **Contact** Mr. Larry Clendenin, Director of Admissions, St. John's College, 1160 Camino Cruz Blanca, Santa Fe, NM 87501. Telephone: 505-984-6060 or toll-free 800-331-5232. Fax: 505-984-6162. E-mail: admissions@mail.sjcsf.edu. Web site: http://www.sjcsf.edu/.

UNIVERSITY OF NEW MEXICO
ALBUQUERQUE, NEW MEXICO

General State-supported, university, coed **Entrance** Moderately difficult **Setting** 625-acre urban campus **Total enrollment** 23,753 **Student-faculty ratio** 16:1 **Application deadline** 6/15 (freshmen) **Freshmen** 75% were admitted **Housing** Yes **Expenses** Tuition $3326; Room & Board $5217 **Undergraduates** 57% women, 23% part-time, 25% 25 or older, 6% Native American, 33% Hispanic American, 3% African American, 3% Asian American/Pacific Islander **The most frequently chosen baccalaureate fields are** business/marketing, education, health professions and related sciences **Academic program** English as a second language, advanced placement, accelerated degree program, self-designed majors, honors program, summer session, adult/continuing education programs, internships **Contact** Ms. Robin Ryan, Associate Director of Admissions, University of New Mexico, Office of Admissions, Student Service Center Room 140, Albuquerque, NM 87131-2046. Telephone: 505-277-2446 or toll-free 800-CALLUNM (in-state). Fax: 505-277-6686. E-mail: apply@unm.edu. Web site: http://www.unm.edu/.

NEW MEXICO

UNIVERSITY OF PHOENIX–NEW MEXICO CAMPUS
ALBUQUERQUE, NEW MEXICO

General Proprietary, comprehensive, coed **Entrance** Noncompetitive **Total enrollment** 88,730 **Student-faculty ratio** 15:1 **Application deadline** Rolling (freshmen), rolling (transfer) **Housing** No **Expenses** Tuition $7860 **Undergraduates** 56% women, 78% 25 or older **The most frequently chosen baccalaureate fields are** business/marketing, computer/information sciences, health professions and related sciences **Academic program** Advanced placement, accelerated degree program, adult/continuing education programs **Contact** Ms. Beth Barilla, Director of Admissions, University of Phoenix–New Mexico Campus, 4615 East Elwood Street, Phoenix, AZ 85040-1958. Telephone: 480-927-0099 Ext. 1218 or toll-free 800-228-7240. Fax: 480-594-1758. E-mail: beth.barilla@apollogrp.edu. Web site: http://www.phoenix.edu/.

WESTERN NEW MEXICO UNIVERSITY
SILVER CITY, NEW MEXICO

Contact Mr. Michael Alecksen, Director of Admissions, Western New Mexico University, College Avenue, Silver City, NM 88062-0680. Telephone: 505-538-6106 or toll-free 800-872-WNMU (in-state). Fax: 505-538-6155. Web site: http://www.wnmu.edu/.

NEW YORK

ADELPHI UNIVERSITY
GARDEN CITY, NEW YORK

General Independent, university, coed **Entrance** Moderately difficult **Setting** 75-acre suburban campus **Total enrollment** 6,291 **Student-faculty ratio** 14:1 **Application deadline** Rolling (freshmen), rolling (transfer) **Freshmen** 68% were admitted **Housing** Yes **Expenses** Tuition $16,270; Room & Board $7050 **Undergraduates** 71% women, 20% part-time, 28% 25 or older, 0.1% Native American, 7% Hispanic American, 11% African American, 4% Asian American/Pacific Islander **The most frequently chosen baccalaureate fields are** business/marketing, education, social sciences and history **Academic program** Advanced placement, honors program, summer session, internships **Contact** Ms. Rory Shaffer-Walsh, Director of Admissions, Adelphi University, South Avenue, Garden City, NY 11530. Telephone: 516-877-3056 or toll-free 800-ADELPHI. Fax: 516-877-3039. E-mail: admissions@adelphi.edu. Web site: http://www.adelphi.edu/.

ALBANY COLLEGE OF PHARMACY OF UNION UNIVERSITY
ALBANY, NEW YORK

General Independent, comprehensive, coed **Entrance** Moderately difficult **Setting** 1-acre urban campus **Total enrollment** 964 **Student-faculty ratio** 15:1 **Application deadline** 2/1 (freshmen), 2/1 (transfer) **Freshmen** 67% were admitted **Housing** Yes **Expenses** Tuition $14,373; Room & Board $5100 **Undergraduates** 56% women, 4% 25 or older **The most frequently chosen baccalaureate field is** health professions and related sciences **Academic program** Advanced placement, accelerated degree program, summer session, internships **Contact** Mr. Robert Gould, Director of Admissions, Albany College of Pharmacy of Union University, 106 New Scotland Avenue, Albany, NY 12208-3425. Telephone: 518-445-7221 or toll-free 888-203-8010. Fax: 518-445-7202. E-mail: admissions@acp.edu. Web site: http://www.acp.edu/.

ALFRED UNIVERSITY
ALFRED, NEW YORK

General Independent, university, coed **Entrance** Moderately difficult **Setting** 232-acre rural campus **Total enrollment** 2,443 **Student-faculty ratio** 12:1 **Application deadline** 2/1 (freshmen), 8/1 (transfer) **Freshmen** 75% were admitted **Housing** Yes **Expenses** Tuition $19,196; Room & Board $8016 **Undergraduates** 53% women, 5% part-time, 5% 25 or older, 0.5% Native American, 4% Hispanic American, 4% African American, 2% Asian American/Pacific Islander **The most frequently chosen baccalaureate fields are** engineering/engineering technologies, business/marketing, visual/performing arts **Academic program** Advanced placement, accelerated degree program, self-designed majors, honors program, summer session, adult/continuing education programs, internships **Contact** Mr. Scott Hooker, Director of Admissions, Alfred University, Alumni Hall, Alfred, NY 14802-1205. Telephone: 607-871-2115 or toll-free 800-541-9229. Fax: 607-871-2198. E-mail: adm@alfred.edu. Web site: http://www.alfred.edu/.

▶ For more information, see page 392.

AUDREY COHEN COLLEGE
NEW YORK, NEW YORK

General Independent, comprehensive, coed, primarily women **Entrance** Moderately difficult **Setting** urban campus **Total enrollment** 1,519 **Student-faculty ratio** 20:1 **Application deadline** 8/15 (freshmen), 8/15 (transfer) **Freshmen** 38% were admitted **Housing** No **Expenses** Tuition $14,505 **Undergraduates** 82% women, 65% 25 or older, 1% Native American, 18% Hispanic American, 60% African American, 3% Asian American/Pacific Islander **The most frequently chosen baccalaureate fields are** business/marketing, home economics/vocational home economics **Academic program** English as a second language, accelerated degree program, summer session, adult/continuing education programs, internships **Contact** Ms. Jennifer Gass, Admissions Counselor, Audrey Cohen College, 75 Varick Street, 12th Floor, New York, NY 10013. Telephone: 212-343-1234 Ext. 2704 or toll-free 800-33-THINK Ext. 5001 (in-state). Fax: 212-343-8470. Web site: http://www.audreycohen.edu/.

BARD COLLEGE
ANNANDALE-ON-HUDSON, NEW YORK

General Independent, comprehensive, coed **Entrance** Very difficult **Setting** 600-acre rural campus **Total enrollment** 1,515 **Student-faculty ratio** 9:1 **Application deadline** 1/15 (freshmen), 1/15 (transfer) **Freshmen** 44% were admitted **Housing** Yes **Expenses** Tuition $26,170; Room & Board $7742 **Undergraduates** 56% women, 4% part-time, 1% 25 or older, 0.4% Native American, 5% Hispanic American, 3% African American, 3% Asian American/Pacific Islander **The most frequently chosen baccalaureate field is** philosophy, religion, and theology **Academic program** English as a second language, advanced placement, accelerated degree program, self-designed majors, adult/continuing education programs, internships **Contact** Ms. Mary Inga Backlund, Director of Admissions, Bard College, Ravine Road, PO Box 5000, Annandale-on-Hudson, NY 12504. Telephone: 845-758-7472. Fax: 845-758-5208. E-mail: admission@bard.edu. Web site: http://www.bard.edu/.

BARNARD COLLEGE
NEW YORK, NEW YORK

General Independent, 4-year, women only **Entrance** Most difficult **Setting** 4-acre urban campus **Total enrollment** 2,261 **Student-faculty ratio** 10:1 **Application deadline** 1/1 (freshmen), 4/1 (transfer) **Freshmen** 33% were admitted **Housing** Yes **Expenses** Tuition $24,036; Room & Board $9658 **Undergraduates** 2% part-time, 1% 25 or older, 1% Native American, 6% Hispanic American, 5% African American, 21% Asian American/Pacific Islander **The most frequently chosen baccalaureate fields are** English, psychology, social sciences and history **Academic program** Advanced placement, accelerated degree program, self-designed majors, honors program, internships **Contact** Ms. Jennifer Gill Fondiller, Dean of Admissions, Barnard College, 3009 Broadway, New York, NY 10027. Telephone: 212-854-2014. Fax: 212-854-6220. E-mail: admissions@barnard.edu. Web site: http://www.barnard.edu/.

BERNARD M. BARUCH COLLEGE OF THE CITY UNIVERSITY OF NEW YORK
NEW YORK, NEW YORK

General State and locally supported, comprehensive, coed **Entrance** Very difficult **Setting** urban campus **Total enrollment** 15,821 **Student-faculty ratio** 22:1 **Application deadline** 4/1 (freshmen), 5/1 (transfer) **Freshmen** 33% were admitted **Housing** No **Expenses** Tuition $3350 **Undergraduates** 57% women, 32% part-time, 28% 25 or older, 0.1% Native American, 19% Hispanic American, 19% African American, 25% Asian American/Pacific Islander **The most frequently chosen baccalaureate fields are** business/marketing, psychology, social sciences and history **Academic program** English as a second language, advanced placement, self-designed majors, honors program, summer session, adult/continuing education programs, internships **Contact** Mr. James F. Murphy, Director of Undergraduate Admissions and Financial Aid, Bernard M. Baruch College of the City University of New York, Box H-0720, New York, NY 10010-5585. Telephone: 212-802-2300. E-mail: admissions@baruch.cuny.edu. Web site: http://www.baruch.cuny.edu/.

BETH HAMEDRASH SHAAREI YOSHER INSTITUTE
BROOKLYN, NEW YORK

Contact Mr. Menachem Steinberg, Director of Admissions, Beth HaMedrash Shaarei Yosher Institute, 4102-10 Sixteenth Avenue, Brooklyn, NY 11204. Telephone: 718-854-2290.

BETH HATALMUD RABBINICAL COLLEGE
BROOKLYN, NEW YORK

Contact Rabbi Osina, Director of Admissions, Beth Hatalmud Rabbinical College, 2127 Eighty-second Street, Brooklyn, NY 11214. Telephone: 718-259-2525.

BORICUA COLLEGE
NEW YORK, NEW YORK

General Independent, comprehensive, coed **Entrance** Moderately difficult **Setting** urban campus **Total enrollment** 1,520 **Student-faculty ratio** 20:1 **Application deadline** Rolling (freshmen), rolling (transfer) **Freshmen** 47% were admitted **Housing** No **Expenses** Tuition $7350 **Undergraduates** 89% 25 or older **Academic program** Accelerated degree program, honors program, summer session, adult/continuing education programs, internships **Contact** Dr. Alicea Mercedes, Director of Registration and Assessment, Boricua College, 3755 Broadway, New York, NY 10032-1560. Telephone: 212-694-1000 Ext. 525. Web site: www.boricua.edu.

BRIARCLIFFE COLLEGE
BETHPAGE, NEW YORK

General Proprietary, 4-year, coed **Entrance** Moderately difficult **Setting** 18-acre suburban campus **Total enrollment** 2,608 **Student-faculty ratio** 14:1 **Application deadline** Rolling (freshmen), rolling (transfer) **Freshmen** 65% were admitted **Housing** No **Expenses** Tuition $11,400 **Undergraduates** 53% women, 19% part-time, 42% 25 or older, 1% Native American, 7% Hispanic American, 6% African American, 1% Asian American/Pacific Islander **The most frequently chosen baccalaureate field is** business/marketing **Academic program** Advanced placement, accelerated degree program, summer session, adult/continuing education programs, internships **Contact** Ms. Theresa Donohue, Dean of Marketing and Admissions, Briarcliffe College, 1055 Stewart Avenue, Bethpage, NY 11714. Telephone: 516-918-3705 or toll-free 888-333-1150 (in-state). Fax: 516-470-6020. E-mail: donohuet@bcl.edu. Web site: http://www.briarcliffe.edu.

NEW YORK

BROOKLYN COLLEGE OF THE CITY UNIVERSITY OF NEW YORK
BROOKLYN, NEW YORK

General State and locally supported, comprehensive, coed **Entrance** Moderately difficult **Setting** 26-acre urban campus **Total enrollment** 15,137 **Student-faculty ratio** 13:1 **Application deadline** Rolling (freshmen), rolling (transfer) **Freshmen** 49% were admitted **Housing** No **Expenses** Tuition $3393 **Undergraduates** 62% women, 34% part-time, 35% 25 or older, 0.01% Native American, 10% Hispanic American, 29% African American, 9% Asian American/Pacific Islander **The most frequently chosen baccalaureate fields are** business/marketing, education, psychology **Academic program** English as a second language, advanced placement, honors program, summer session, adult/continuing education programs, internships **Contact** Ms. Celia Adams, Admissions Counselor/Recruiter, Brooklyn College of the City University of New York, 2900 Bedford Avenue, 1203 Plaza, Brooklyn, NY 11210-2889. Telephone: 718-951-5001. Fax: 718-951-4506. E-mail: admissions@brooklyn.cuny.edu. Web site: http://www.brooklyn.cuny.edu/.

CANISIUS COLLEGE
BUFFALO, NEW YORK

General Independent Roman Catholic (Jesuit), comprehensive, coed **Entrance** Moderately difficult **Setting** 26-acre urban campus **Total enrollment** 4,870 **Student-faculty ratio** 16:1 **Application deadline** Rolling (freshmen), rolling (transfer) **Freshmen** 81% were admitted **Housing** Yes **Expenses** Tuition $17,536; Room & Board $7160 **Undergraduates** 53% women, 12% part-time, 8% 25 or older **The most frequently chosen baccalaureate fields are** education, business/marketing, social sciences and history **Academic program** English as a second language, advanced placement, self-designed majors, honors program, summer session, internships **Contact** Miss Penelope H. Lips, Director of Admissions, Canisius College, 2001 Main Street, Buffalo, NY 14208-1098. Telephone: 716-888-2200 or toll-free 800-843-1517. Fax: 716-888-3230. E-mail: inquiry@canisius.edu. Web site: http://www.canisius.edu/.

CAZENOVIA COLLEGE
CAZENOVIA, NEW YORK

General Independent, 4-year, coed **Entrance** Minimally difficult **Setting** 40-acre small-town campus **Total enrollment** 913 **Student-faculty ratio** 15:1 **Application deadline** Rolling (freshmen), rolling (transfer) **Freshmen** 86% were admitted **Housing** Yes **Expenses** Tuition $13,395; Room & Board $6500 **Undergraduates** 71% women, 19% part-time, 5% 25 or older, 1% Native American, 4% Hispanic American, 6% African American, 0.5% Asian American/Pacific Islander **The most frequently chosen baccalaureate fields are** business/marketing, protective services/public administration, visual/performing arts **Academic program** Advanced placement, self-designed majors, honors program, summer session, adult/continuing education programs, internships **Contact** Mr. Robert A. Croot, Dean for Enrollment Management, Cazenovia College, 22 Sullivan Street, Cazenovia, NY 13035. Telephone: 315-655-7208 or toll-free 800-654-3210. Fax: 315-655-4860. E-mail: admission@cazcollege.edu. Web site: http://www.cazcollege.edu/.

CENTRAL YESHIVA TOMCHEI TMIMIM-LUBAVITCH
BROOKLYN, NEW YORK

Contact Moses Gluckowsky, Director of Admissions, Central Yeshiva Tomchei Tmimim-Lubavitch, 841-853 Ocean Parkway, Brooklyn, NY 11230. Telephone: 718-859-7600.

CITY COLLEGE OF THE CITY UNIVERSITY OF NEW YORK
NEW YORK, NEW YORK

General State and locally supported, university, coed **Entrance** Moderately difficult **Setting** 35-acre urban campus **Total enrollment** 10,824 **Student-faculty ratio** 15:1 **Application deadline** Rolling (freshmen), rolling (transfer) **Freshmen** 42% were admitted **Housing** No **Expenses** Tuition $3200 **Undergraduates** 52% women, 40% part-time, 39% 25 or older, 0.3% Native American, 26% Hispanic American, 28% African American, 12% Asian American/Pacific Islander **Academic program** English as a second language, advanced placement, accelerated degree program, self-designed majors, honors program, summer session, adult/continuing education programs, internships **Contact** Mr. Thomas F. Sabia, Acting Director of Admissions, City College of the City University of New York, Convent Avenue at 138th Street, New York, NY 10031-9198. Telephone: 212-650-6977. Fax: 212-650-6417. E-mail: admissions@ccny.cuny.edu. Web site: http://www.ccny.cuny.edu/.

CLARKSON UNIVERSITY
POTSDAM, NEW YORK

General Independent, university, coed **Entrance** Very difficult **Setting** 640-acre small-town campus **Total enrollment** 2,949 **Student-faculty ratio** 17:1 **Application deadline** 3/15 (freshmen), rolling (transfer) **Freshmen** 81% were admitted **Housing** Yes **Expenses** Tuition $21,800; Room & Board $8084 **Undergraduates** 25% women, 1% part-time, 3% 25 or older, 1% Native American, 1% Hispanic American, 2% African American, 3% Asian American/Pacific Islander **The most frequently chosen baccalaureate fields are** engineering/engineering technologies, business/marketing, interdisciplinary studies **Academic program** English as a second language, advanced placement, accelerated degree program, self-designed majors, honors program, summer session, internships **Contact** Mr. Brian T. Grant, Director of Enrollment Operations, Clarkson University, Holcroft House, Potsdam, NY 13699. Telephone: 315-268-6479 or

NEW YORK

toll-free 800-527-6577. Fax: 315-268-7647. E-mail: fradmis@agent.clarkson.edu. Web site: http://www.clarkson.edu/.

COLGATE UNIVERSITY
HAMILTON, NEW YORK

General Independent, comprehensive, coed **Entrance** Very difficult **Setting** 515-acre rural campus **Total enrollment** 2,785 **Student-faculty ratio** 11:1 **Application deadline** 1/15 (freshmen), 3/1 (transfer) **Freshmen** 37% were admitted **Housing** Yes **Expenses** Tuition $27,025; Room & Board $6455 **Undergraduates** 51% women, 0.3% part-time, 0% 25 or older **The most frequently chosen baccalaureate field is** philosophy, religion, and theology **Academic program** Advanced placement, self-designed majors, honors program **Contact** Mr. Gary L. Ross, Dean of Admission, Colgate University, 13 Oak Drive, Hamilton, NY 13346-1383. Telephone: 315-228-7401. Fax: 315-228-7544. E-mail: admission@mail.colgate.edu. Web site: http://www.colgate.edu/.

COLLEGE OF AERONAUTICS
FLUSHING, NEW YORK

General Independent, 4-year, coed, primarily men **Entrance** Minimally difficult **Setting** 6-acre urban campus **Total enrollment** 1,384 **Student-faculty ratio** 11:1 **Application deadline** Rolling (freshmen), rolling (transfer) **Freshmen** 57% were admitted **Expenses** Tuition $10,550 **Undergraduates** 9% women, 25% part-time, 35% 25 or older, 0% Native American, 36% Hispanic American, 20% African American, 13% Asian American/Pacific Islander **Academic program** Advanced placement, summer session, adult/continuing education programs, internships **Contact** Thomas Bracken, Associate Director, Admissions, College of Aeronautics, La Guardia Airport, 86-01 23rd Avenue, Flushing, NY 11369. Telephone: 718-429-6600 Ext. 167 or toll-free 800-776-2376 (in-state). Fax: 718-429-0256. E-mail: pro@aero.edu. Web site: http://www.aero.edu/.

COLLEGE OF MOUNT SAINT VINCENT
RIVERDALE, NEW YORK

General Independent, comprehensive, coed **Entrance** Moderately difficult **Setting** 70-acre suburban campus **Total enrollment** 1,379 **Student-faculty ratio** 12:1 **Application deadline** Rolling (freshmen), rolling (transfer) **Freshmen** 70% were admitted **Housing** Yes **Expenses** Tuition $17,030; Room & Board $7300 **Undergraduates** 78% women, 20% part-time, 23% 25 or older, 0% Native American, 33% Hispanic American, 17% African American, 9% Asian American/Pacific Islander **The most frequently chosen baccalaureate fields are** business/marketing, education, health professions and related sciences **Academic program** English as a second language, advanced placement, accelerated degree program, self-designed majors, honors program, summer session, adult/continuing education programs, internships **Contact** Mr. Timothy Nash, Dean of Admissions and Financial Aid, College of Mount Saint Vincent, 6301 Riverdale Avenue, Riverdale, NY 10471-1093. Telephone: 718-405-3268 or toll-free 800-665-CMSV. Fax: 718-549-7945. E-mail: admissns@cmsv.edu. Web site: http://www.cmsv.edu/.

THE COLLEGE OF NEW ROCHELLE
NEW ROCHELLE, NEW YORK

General Independent, comprehensive, women only **Entrance** Moderately difficult **Setting** 20-acre suburban campus **Total enrollment** 2,506 **Student-faculty ratio** 8:1 **Application deadline** Rolling (freshmen), rolling (transfer) **Freshmen** 60% were admitted **Housing** Yes **Expenses** Tuition $12,470; Room & Board $6550 **Undergraduates** 36% part-time, 7% 25 or older, 0.2% Native American, 12% Hispanic American, 27% African American, 3% Asian American/Pacific Islander **The most frequently chosen baccalaureate fields are** health professions and related sciences, communications/communication technologies, psychology **Academic program** English as a second language, advanced placement, accelerated degree program, self-designed majors, honors program, summer session, adult/continuing education programs, internships **Contact** Ms. Stephany Decker, Director of Admission, The College of New Rochelle, 29 Castle Place, New Rochelle, NY 10805-2339. Telephone: 914-654-5452 or toll-free 800-933-5923. Fax: 914-654-5486. Web site: http://cnr.edu/.

THE COLLEGE OF SAINT ROSE
ALBANY, NEW YORK

General Independent, comprehensive, coed **Entrance** Moderately difficult **Setting** 22-acre urban campus **Total enrollment** 4,411 **Student-faculty ratio** 14:1 **Application deadline** 2/1 (freshmen), 2/1 (transfer) **Freshmen** 77% were admitted **Housing** Yes **Expenses** Tuition $13,918; Room & Board $6746 **Undergraduates** 72% women, 20% part-time, 34% 25 or older, 0.4% Native American, 2% Hispanic American, 3% African American, 1% Asian American/Pacific Islander **The most frequently chosen baccalaureate fields are** business/marketing, education, social sciences and history **Academic program** Advanced placement, accelerated degree program, self-designed majors, summer session, adult/continuing education programs, internships **Contact** Ms. Mary Elizabeth Amico, Associate Dean of Admissions and Enrollment Services, The College of Saint Rose, 432 Western Avenue, Albany, NY 12203-1419. Telephone: 518-454-5150 or toll-free 800-637-8556. Fax: 518-454-2013. E-mail: admit@rosnet.strose.edu. Web site: http://www.strose.edu/.

COLLEGE OF STATEN ISLAND OF THE CITY UNIVERSITY OF NEW YORK
STATEN ISLAND, NEW YORK

General State and locally supported, comprehensive, coed **Entrance** Noncompetitive **Setting** 204-acre urban campus **Total enrollment** 11,284 **Student-faculty ratio** 17:1 **Application deadline** Rolling

NEW YORK

College of Staten Island of the City University of New York *(continued)*
(freshmen), rolling (transfer) **Freshmen** 100% were admitted **Housing** No **Expenses** Tuition $3358 **Undergraduates** 59% women, 37% part-time, 34% 25 or older, 0.2% Native American, 8% Hispanic American, 9% African American, 7% Asian American/Pacific Islander **The most frequently chosen baccalaureate fields are** business/marketing, liberal arts/general studies, social sciences and history **Academic program** English as a second language, advanced placement, accelerated degree program, honors program, summer session, adult/continuing education programs, internships **Contact** Ms. Mary-Beth Riley, Director of Admissions and Recruitment, College of Staten Island of the City University of New York, 2800 Victory Boulevard, Staten Island, NY 10314-6600. Telephone: 718-982-2011. Fax: 718-982-2500. Web site: http://www.csi.cuny.edu/.

COLUMBIA COLLEGE
NEW YORK, NEW YORK

General Independent, 4-year, coed **Entrance** Most difficult **Setting** 35-acre urban campus **Total enrollment** 4,092 **Student-faculty ratio** 7:1 **Application deadline** 1/2 (freshmen), 3/15 (transfer) **Freshmen** 12% were admitted **Housing** Yes **Expenses** Tuition $26,908; Room & Board $8280 **Undergraduates** 51% women, 0% 25 or older, 0.2% Native American, 8% Hispanic American, 9% African American, 13% Asian American/Pacific Islander **Academic program** English as a second language, advanced placement, self-designed majors, honors program, summer session, internships **Contact** Mr. Eric Furda, Director of Undergraduate Admissions, Columbia College, 1130 Amsterdam Avenue MC 2807, New York, NY 10027. Telephone: 212-854-2522. Fax: 212-854-1209. E-mail: ugrad-admiss@columbia.edu. Web site: http://www.columbia.edu/.

COLUMBIA UNIVERSITY, SCHOOL OF GENERAL STUDIES
NEW YORK, NEW YORK

General Independent, 4-year, coed **Entrance** Most difficult **Setting** 36-acre urban campus **Total enrollment** 1,167 **Student-faculty ratio** 7:1 **Application deadline** 7/1 (freshmen), 7/1 (transfer) **Freshmen** 45% were admitted **Housing** Yes **Expenses** Tuition $21,655; Room only $7980 **Undergraduates** 75% 25 or older, 0.3% Native American, 10% Hispanic American, 8% African American, 10% Asian American/Pacific Islander **Academic program** English as a second language, advanced placement, accelerated degree program, self-designed majors, honors program, summer session, adult/continuing education programs, internships **Contact** Mr. Carlos A. Porro, Director of Admissions, Columbia University, School of General Studies, Mail Code 4101, Lewisohn Hall, 2970 Broadway, New York, NY 10027-9829. Telephone: 212-854-2772 or toll-free 800-895-1169 (out-of-state). Fax: 212-854-6316. E-mail: gs-admit@columbia.edu. Web site: http://www.gs.columbia.edu/.

▶ For more information, see page 416.

COLUMBIA UNIVERSITY, THE FU FOUNDATION SCHOOL OF ENGINEERING AND APPLIED SCIENCE
NEW YORK, NEW YORK

General Independent, university, coed **Entrance** Most difficult **Setting** urban campus **Total enrollment** 21,000 **Student-faculty ratio** 7:1 **Application deadline** 1/1 (freshmen), 3/15 (transfer) **Freshmen** 26% were admitted **Housing** Yes **Expenses** Tuition $26,908; Room & Board $8280 **Undergraduates** 27% women, 0% 25 or older, 6% Hispanic American, 5% African American, 34% Asian American/Pacific Islander **The most frequently chosen baccalaureate fields are** engineering/engineering technologies, computer/information sciences, social sciences and history **Academic program** English as a second language, advanced placement, accelerated degree program, honors program, summer session, adult/continuing education programs, internships **Contact** Mr. Eric J. Furda, Director of Undergraduate Admissions, Columbia University, The Fu Foundation School of Engineering and Applied Science, 1130 Amsterdam Avenue MC 2807, New York, NY 10027. Telephone: 212-854-2522. Fax: 212-854-1209. E-mail: ugrad-admiss@columbia.edu. Web site: http://www.columbia.edu/.

CONCORDIA COLLEGE
BRONXVILLE, NEW YORK

General Independent Lutheran, 4-year, coed **Entrance** Moderately difficult **Setting** 33-acre suburban campus **Total enrollment** 662 **Student-faculty ratio** 12:1 **Application deadline** 3/15 (freshmen), 7/15 (transfer) **Freshmen** 72% were admitted **Housing** Yes **Expenses** Tuition $15,550; Room & Board $6850 **Undergraduates** 61% women, 18% part-time, 18% 25 or older **The most frequently chosen baccalaureate fields are** business/marketing, education, liberal arts/general studies **Academic program** English as a second language, advanced placement, accelerated degree program, self-designed majors, honors program, adult/continuing education programs, internships **Contact** Rebecca Hendricks, Director of Admission, Concordia College, 171 White Plains Road, Bronxville, NY 10708. Telephone: 914-337-9300 Ext. 2149 or toll-free 800-YES-COLLEGE. Fax: 914-395-4636. E-mail: admission@concordia-ny.edu. Web site: http://www.concordia-ny.edu/.

COOPER UNION FOR THE ADVANCEMENT OF SCIENCE AND ART
NEW YORK, NEW YORK

General Independent, 4-year, coed **Entrance** Most difficult **Setting** urban campus **Total enrollment** 906 **Student-faculty ratio** 7:1 **Application deadline** 1/1 (freshmen), 1/1 (transfer) **Freshmen** 13% were admitted **Housing** Yes **Expenses** Tuition $600; Room & Board $11,400 **Undergraduates** 36% women, 2% part-time, 2% 25 or older, 0.5% Native American, 7% Hispanic American, 5% African American, 28% Asian American/Pacific Islander **Academic program** Advanced

NEW YORK

placement, self-designed majors, honors program, summer session, internships **Contact** Mr. Richard Bory, Dean of Admissions and Records and Registrar, Cooper Union for the Advancement of Science and Art, 30 Cooper Square, New York, NY 10003. Telephone: 212-353-4120. Fax: 212-353-4342. E-mail: admission@cooper.edu. Web site: http://www.cooper.edu/.

CORNELL UNIVERSITY
ITHACA, NEW YORK

General Independent, university, coed **Entrance** Most difficult **Setting** 745-acre small-town campus **Total enrollment** 19,420 **Student-faculty ratio** 13:1 **Application deadline** 1/1 (freshmen), 3/15 (transfer) **Freshmen** 27% were admitted **Housing** Yes **Expenses** Tuition $26,062; Room & Board $8552 **Undergraduates** 48% women, 1% 25 or older, 1% Native American, 5% Hispanic American, 5% African American, 16% Asian American/Pacific Islander **The most frequently chosen baccalaureate fields are** agriculture, business/marketing, engineering/engineering technologies **Academic program** English as a second language, advanced placement, accelerated degree program, self-designed majors, honors program, summer session, internships **Contact** Ms. Wendy Schaerer, Director of Undergraduate Admissions, Cornell University, 410 Thurston Avenue, Ithaca, NY 14850. Telephone: 607-255-5241. Fax: 607-255-0659. E-mail: admissions@cornell.edu. Web site: http://www.cornell.edu/.

THE CULINARY INSTITUTE OF AMERICA
HYDE PARK, NEW YORK

General Independent, 4-year, coed **Entrance** Moderately difficult **Setting** 150-acre small-town campus **Total enrollment** 2,012 **Student-faculty ratio** 18:1 **Application deadline** Rolling (freshmen), rolling (transfer) **Freshmen** 54% were admitted **Housing** Yes **Expenses** Tuition $19,035; Room only $3780 **Undergraduates** 32% women, 25% 25 or older, 0.2% Native American, 5% Hispanic American, 2% African American, 3% Asian American/Pacific Islander **The most frequently chosen baccalaureate field is** personal/miscellaneous services **Academic program** Adult/continuing education programs, internships **Contact** Mr. Larry Lopez, Interim Director of Admissions, The Culinary Institute of America, 1946 Campus Drive, Hyde Park, NY 12538. Telephone: 845-451-1534 or toll-free 800-CULINARY. Fax: 845-451-1068. E-mail: admissions@culinary.edu. Web site: http://www.ciachef.edu/.

DAEMEN COLLEGE
AMHERST, NEW YORK

General Independent, comprehensive, coed **Entrance** Moderately difficult **Setting** 35-acre suburban campus **Total enrollment** 1,984 **Student-faculty ratio** 14:1 **Application deadline** Rolling (freshmen), rolling (transfer) **Freshmen** 77% were admitted **Housing** Yes **Expenses** Tuition $13,620; Room & Board $7000 **Undergraduates** 77% women, 24% part-time, 25% 25 or older, 1% Native American, 2% Hispanic American, 13% African American, 2% Asian American/Pacific Islander **The most frequently chosen baccalaureate fields are** business/marketing, education, health professions and related sciences **Academic program** Advanced placement, self-designed majors, summer session, adult/continuing education programs, internships **Contact** Ms. Kimberly Pagano, Interim Director of Admissions, Daemen College, 4380 Main Street, Amherst, NY 14226-3592. Telephone: 716-839-8225 or toll-free 800-462-7652. Fax: 716-839-8370. E-mail: admissions@daemen.edu. Web site: http://www.daemen.edu/.

DARKEI NOAM RABBINICAL COLLEGE
BROOKLYN, NEW YORK

Contact Rabbi Pinchas Horowitz, Director of Admissions, Darkei Noam Rabbinical College, 2822 Avenue J, Brooklyn, NY 11210. Telephone: 718-338-6464.

DEVRY INSTITUTE OF TECHNOLOGY
LONG ISLAND CITY, NEW YORK

General Proprietary, 4-year, coed **Entrance** Minimally difficult **Setting** urban campus **Total enrollment** 2,036 **Student-faculty ratio** 20:1 **Application deadline** Rolling (freshmen), rolling (transfer) **Freshmen** 67% were admitted **Housing** No **Expenses** Tuition $9800 **Undergraduates** 21% women, 25% part-time, 40% 25 or older, 1% Native American, 16% Hispanic American, 22% African American, 5% Asian American/Pacific Islander **The most frequently chosen baccalaureate fields are** business/marketing, engineering/engineering technologies **Academic program** Advanced placement, accelerated degree program, summer session, adult/continuing education programs **Contact** Ms. Edith Bolanos, New Student Coordinator, DeVry Institute of Technology, 30-20 Thomson Avenue, Long Island City, NY 11101. Telephone: 718-472-2728 or toll-free 888-71-Devry (out-of-state). Fax: 718-269-4288. Web site: http://www.ny.devry.edu/.

DOMINICAN COLLEGE
ORANGEBURG, NEW YORK

General Independent, comprehensive, coed **Entrance** Moderately difficult **Setting** 14-acre suburban campus **Total enrollment** 1,618 **Student-faculty ratio** 12:1 **Application deadline** Rolling (freshmen), rolling (transfer) **Freshmen** 67% were admitted **Housing** Yes **Expenses** Tuition $13,910; Room & Board $7400 **Undergraduates** 69% women, 50% part-time, 51% 25 or older, 12% Hispanic American, 18% African American, 5% Asian American/Pacific Islander **The most frequently chosen baccalaureate fields are** business/marketing, health professions and related sciences, social sciences and history **Academic program** English as a second language, advanced placement, accelerated degree program, honors program, summer session, adult/continuing education programs, internships **Contact** Joyce Elbe, Director of Admissions, Dominican College, 470 Western Highway, Orangeburg, NY 10962-1210. Telephone: 914-

NEW YORK

Dominican College *(continued)*
359-7800 Ext. 271. Fax: 914-365-3150. E-mail: admissions@dc.edu. Web site: http://www.dc.edu.

DOWLING COLLEGE
OAKDALE, NEW YORK

General Independent, comprehensive, coed **Entrance** Moderately difficult **Setting** 156-acre suburban campus **Total enrollment** 5,580 **Student-faculty ratio** 17:1 **Application deadline** Rolling (freshmen), rolling (transfer) **Freshmen** 86% were admitted **Housing** Yes **Expenses** Tuition $14,090; Room only $4800 **Undergraduates** 61% women, 33% part-time, 54% 25 or older, 0.3% Native American, 9% Hispanic American, 10% African American, 3% Asian American/Pacific Islander **The most frequently chosen baccalaureate fields are** computer/information sciences, education, liberal arts/general studies **Academic program** English as a second language, advanced placement, accelerated degree program, self-designed majors, honors program, summer session, internships **Contact** Ms. Nancy Brewer, Director of Enrollment Services and Financial Aid, Dowling College, 150 Idle Hour Boulevard, Oakdale, NY 11769. Telephone: 631-244-3385 or toll-free 800-DOWLING. Fax: 631-563-3827. E-mail: brewern@dowling.edu. Web site: http://www.dowling.edu/.

D'YOUVILLE COLLEGE
BUFFALO, NEW YORK

General Independent, comprehensive, coed **Entrance** Moderately difficult **Setting** 7-acre urban campus **Total enrollment** 2,486 **Student-faculty ratio** 12:1 **Application deadline** Rolling (freshmen), rolling (transfer) **Freshmen** 71% were admitted **Housing** Yes **Expenses** Tuition $12,550; Room & Board $6154 **Undergraduates** 75% women, 23% part-time, 40% 25 or older, 1% Native American, 4% Hispanic American, 10% African American, 3% Asian American/Pacific Islander **The most frequently chosen baccalaureate fields are** business/marketing, health professions and related sciences, home economics/vocational home economics **Academic program** Accelerated degree program, summer session, adult/continuing education programs, internships **Contact** Mr. Ron Dannecker, Director of Admissions and Financial Aid, D'Youville College, 320 Porter Avenue, Buffalo, NY 14201-1084. Telephone: 716-881-7600 or toll-free 800-777-3921. Fax: 716-881-7790. E-mail: admiss@dyc.edu. Web site: http://www.dyc.edu/.

ELMIRA COLLEGE
ELMIRA, NEW YORK

General Independent, 4-year, coed **Entrance** Moderately difficult **Setting** 42-acre small-town campus **Total enrollment** 1,941 **Student-faculty ratio** 12:1 **Application deadline** 5/15 (freshmen), 8/1 (transfer) **Freshmen** 80% were admitted **Housing** Yes **Expenses** Tuition $23,540; Room & Board $7530 **Undergraduates** 69% women, 22% part-time, 4% 25 or older, 0.2% Native American, 2% Hispanic American, 2% African American, 1% Asian American/Pacific Islander **The most frequently chosen baccalaureate fields are** education, business/marketing, psychology **Academic program** English as a second language, advanced placement, accelerated degree program, self-designed majors, summer session, adult/continuing education programs, internships **Contact** Mr. William S. Neal, Dean of Admissions, Elmira College, Office of Admissions, Elmira, NY 14901. Telephone: 607-735-1724 or toll-free 800-935-6472. Fax: 607-735-1718. E-mail: admissions@elmira.edu. Web site: http://www.elmira.edu/.

▶ For more information, see page 423.

EUGENE LANG COLLEGE, NEW SCHOOL UNIVERSITY
NEW YORK, NEW YORK

General Independent, 4-year, coed **Entrance** Moderately difficult **Setting** 5-acre urban campus **Total enrollment** 595 **Student-faculty ratio** 10:1 **Application deadline** 2/1 (freshmen), 5/1 (transfer) **Freshmen** 65% were admitted **Housing** Yes **Expenses** Tuition $21,980; Room & Board $9612 **Undergraduates** 68% women, 5% part-time, 5% 25 or older, 0.3% Native American, 9% Hispanic American, 6% African American, 5% Asian American/Pacific Islander **The most frequently chosen baccalaureate field is** liberal arts/general studies **Academic program** Accelerated degree program, summer session, adult/continuing education programs, internships **Contact** Mr. Terence Peavy, Director of Admissions, Eugene Lang College, New School University, 65 West 11th Street, New York, NY 10011-8601. Telephone: 212-229-5665. E-mail: lang@newschool.edu. Web site: http://www.newschool.edu/.

EXCELSIOR COLLEGE
ALBANY, NEW YORK

General Independent, comprehensive, coed **Entrance** Noncompetitive **Setting** urban campus **Total enrollment** 19,131 **Application deadline** Rolling (freshmen), rolling (transfer) **Housing** No **Undergraduates** 62% women, 100% part-time, 98% 25 or older, 1% Native American, 5% Hispanic American, 12% African American, 6% Asian American/Pacific Islander **The most frequently chosen baccalaureate fields are** business/marketing, health professions and related sciences, liberal arts/general studies **Academic program** Advanced placement, accelerated degree program, self-designed majors, adult/continuing education programs **Contact** Ms. Chari Leader, Vice President for Enrollment Management, Excelsior College, 7 Columbia Circle, Albany, NY 12203-5159. Telephone: 518-464-8500 or toll-free 888-647-2388. Fax: 518-464-8777. E-mail: info@excelsior.edu. Web site: http://www.excelsior.edu/.

FASHION INSTITUTE OF TECHNOLOGY
NEW YORK, NEW YORK

General State and locally supported, comprehensive, coed **Entrance** Moderately difficult **Setting** 5-acre

NEW YORK

urban campus **Total enrollment** 10,786 **Student-faculty ratio** 13:1 **Application deadline** 1/1 (freshmen), 1/1 (transfer) **Freshmen** 36% were admitted **Housing** Yes **Expenses** Tuition $3366; Room & Board $7535 **Undergraduates** 82% women, 40% part-time, 35% 25 or older, 0.2% Native American, 10% Hispanic American, 7% African American, 11% Asian American/Pacific Islander **The most frequently chosen baccalaureate fields are** business/marketing, engineering/engineering technologies, visual/performing arts **Academic program** English as a second language, advanced placement, honors program, summer session, adult/continuing education programs, internships **Contact** Mr. Jim Pidgeon, Director of Admissions, Fashion Institute of Technology, Seventh Avenue at 27th Street, New York, NY 10001-5992. Telephone: 212-217-7675 or toll-free 800-GOTOFIT (out-of-state). Fax: 212-217-7481. E-mail: fitinfo@sfitva.cc.fitsuny.edu. Web site: http://www.fitnyc.suny.edu/.

FIVE TOWNS COLLEGE
DIX HILLS, NEW YORK

General Independent, comprehensive, coed **Setting** 40-acre suburban campus **Total enrollment** 1,081 **Student-faculty ratio** 13:1 **Application deadline** Rolling (freshmen), rolling (transfer) **Freshmen** 70% were admitted **Housing** Yes **Expenses** Tuition $11,000; Room & Board $7800 **Undergraduates** 33% women, 3% part-time, 0.1% Native American, 14% Hispanic American, 20% African American, 2% Asian American/Pacific Islander **The most frequently chosen baccalaureate field is** visual/performing arts **Academic program** Advanced placement, summer session, internships **Contact** Mr. Jerry Cohen, Enrollment Services, Five Towns College, 305 North Service Road, Dix Hills, NY 11746-6055. Telephone: 631-424-7000 Ext. 2110. Fax: 631-424-7008. Web site: http://www.fivetowns.edu/.

▶ **For more information, see page 430.**

FORDHAM UNIVERSITY
NEW YORK, NEW YORK

General Independent Roman Catholic (Jesuit), university, coed **Entrance** Very difficult **Setting** 85-acre urban campus **Total enrollment** 13,843 **Student-faculty ratio** 10:1 **Application deadline** 2/1 (freshmen), 7/1 (transfer) **Freshmen** 55% were admitted **Housing** Yes **Expenses** Tuition $22,460; Room & Board $8745 **Undergraduates** 60% women, 11% part-time, 10% 25 or older, 0.2% Native American, 11% Hispanic American, 5% African American, 5% Asian American/Pacific Islander **The most frequently chosen baccalaureate fields are** business/marketing, communications/communication technologies, social sciences and history **Academic program** English as a second language, advanced placement, accelerated degree program, self-designed majors, honors program, summer session, adult/continuing education programs, internships **Contact** Mr. John W. Buckley, Dean of Admission, Fordham University, Theband Hall, 441 East Fordham Road, New York, NY 10458. Telephone: 718-817-4000 or toll-free 800-FORDHAM. Fax: 718-367-9404. E-mail: enroll@fordham.edu. Web site: http://www.fordham.edu/.

▶ **For more information, see page 431.**

GLOBE INSTITUTE OF TECHNOLOGY
NEW YORK, NEW YORK

General Proprietary, 4-year, coed **Total enrollment** 620 **Student-faculty ratio** 18:1 **Freshmen** 80% were admitted **Expenses** Tuition $8620 **Undergraduates** 45% women, 15% part-time, 8% Hispanic American, 17% African American, 18% Asian American/Pacific Islander **The most frequently chosen baccalaureate field is** computer/information sciences **Academic program** English as a second language, internships **Contact** Mr. Leon Rabinovich, President, Globe Institute of Technology, 291 Boradway, New York, NY 10007. Telephone: 212-349-4330 Ext. 102. Fax: 212-227-5920. Web site: http://www.globe.edu/.

HAMILTON COLLEGE
CLINTON, NEW YORK

General Independent, 4-year, coed **Entrance** Very difficult **Setting** 1,200-acre rural campus **Total enrollment** 1,770 **Student-faculty ratio** 9:1 **Application deadline** 1/15 (freshmen), 3/15 (transfer) **Freshmen** 35% were admitted **Housing** Yes **Expenses** Tuition $27,350; Room & Board $6800 **Undergraduates** 51% women, 2% part-time, 0% 25 or older, 0.2% Native American, 4% Hispanic American, 4% African American, 4% Asian American/Pacific Islander **The most frequently chosen baccalaureate fields are** psychology, English, social sciences and history **Academic program** English as a second language, advanced placement, accelerated degree program, self-designed majors, adult/continuing education programs, internships **Contact** Mr. Richard M. Fuller, Dean of Admission and Financial Aid, Hamilton College, 198 College Hill Road, Clinton, NY 13323-1296. Telephone: 315-859-4421 or toll-free 800-843-2655. Fax: 315-859-4457. E-mail: admission@hamilton.edu. Web site: http://www.hamilton.edu/.

HARTWICK COLLEGE
ONEONTA, NEW YORK

General Independent, 4-year, coed **Entrance** Moderately difficult **Setting** 425-acre small-town campus **Total enrollment** 1,446 **Student-faculty ratio** 11:1 **Application deadline** 2/15 (freshmen), 8/1 (transfer) **Freshmen** 89% were admitted **Housing** Yes **Expenses** Tuition $26,040; Room & Board $7050 **Undergraduates** 56% women, 9% part-time, 12% 25 or older, 1% Native American, 2% Hispanic American, 4% African American, 1% Asian American/Pacific Islander **The most frequently chosen baccalaureate fields are** business/marketing, social sciences and history, visual/performing arts **Academic program** Advanced placement, accelerated degree program, self-designed majors, honors program, internships **Contact** Ms. Susan Dileno, Dean of Admissions, Hartwick College, One Hartwick Drive, P.O. Box 4022, Oneonta,

Hartwick College *(continued)*
NY 13820-4022. Telephone: 607-431-4150 or toll-free 888-HARTWICK (out-of-state). Fax: 607-431-4138. E-mail: admissions@hartwick.edu. Web site: http://www.hartwick.edu/.

HILBERT COLLEGE
HAMBURG, NEW YORK

General Independent, 4-year, coed **Entrance** Minimally difficult **Setting** 40-acre small-town campus **Total enrollment** 964 **Student-faculty ratio** 16:1 **Application deadline** 9/1 (freshmen), 8/1 (transfer) **Freshmen** 86% were admitted **Housing** Yes **Expenses** Tuition $12,600; Room & Board $4855 **Undergraduates** 63% women, 32% part-time, 36% 25 or older, 1% Native American, 1% Hispanic American, 4% African American, 0.3% Asian American/Pacific Islander **The most frequently chosen baccalaureate fields are** business/marketing, (pre)law, protective services/public administration **Academic program** Advanced placement, honors program, summer session, internships **Contact** Admissions Counselor, Hilbert College, 5200 South Park Avenue, Hamburg, NY 14075-1597. Telephone: 716-649-7900 Ext. 211. Fax: 716-649-0702. Web site: http://www.hilbert.edu/.

HOBART AND WILLIAM SMITH COLLEGES
GENEVA, NEW YORK

General Independent, 4-year, coed **Entrance** Very difficult **Setting** 200-acre small-town campus **Total enrollment** 1,892 **Student-faculty ratio** 12:1 **Application deadline** 2/1 (freshmen), rolling (transfer) **Freshmen** 69% were admitted **Housing** Yes **Expenses** Tuition $26,177; Room & Board $7018 **Undergraduates** 56% women, 1% part-time, 0% 25 or older, 0.3% Native American, 4% Hispanic American, 4% African American, 2% Asian American/Pacific Islander **The most frequently chosen baccalaureate fields are** English, psychology, social sciences and history **Academic program** English as a second language, advanced placement, accelerated degree program, self-designed majors, honors program, adult/continuing education programs, internships **Contact** Ms. Mara O'Laughlin, Director of Admissions, Hobart and William Smith Colleges, 629 South Main Street, Geneva, NY 14456-3397. Telephone: 315-781-3472 or toll-free 800-245-0100. Fax: 315-781-5471. E-mail: admissions@hws.edu. Web site: http://www.hws.edu/.

HOFSTRA UNIVERSITY
HEMPSTEAD, NEW YORK

General Independent, university, coed **Entrance** Moderately difficult **Setting** 240-acre suburban campus **Total enrollment** 13,428 **Student-faculty ratio** 16:1 **Application deadline** Rolling (freshmen), rolling (transfer) **Freshmen** 77% were admitted **Housing** Yes **Expenses** Tuition $15,722; Room & Board $7530 **Undergraduates** 53% women, 13% part-time, 10% 25 or older, 0.1% Native American, 7% Hispanic American, 8% African American, 4% Asian American/Pacific Islander **The most frequently chosen baccalaureate fields are** business/marketing, communications/communication technologies, psychology **Academic program** English as a second language, advanced placement, accelerated degree program, self-designed majors, honors program, summer session, adult/continuing education programs, internships **Contact** Ms. Mary Beth Carey, Vice President for Enrollment Services, Hofstra University, 100 Hofstra University, Hempstead, NY 11549. Telephone: 516-463-6700 or toll-free 800-HOFSTRA. Fax: 516-560-7660. E-mail: hofstra@hofstra.edu. Web site: http://www.hofstra.edu/.

▶ **For more information, see page 440.**

HOLY TRINITY ORTHODOX SEMINARY
JORDANVILLE, NEW YORK

General Independent Russian Orthodox, 5-year, men only **Entrance** Noncompetitive **Setting** 900-acre rural campus **Total enrollment** 41 **Student-faculty ratio** 4:1 **Application deadline** 5/1 (freshmen), 5/1 (transfer) **Freshmen** 55% were admitted **Housing** Yes **Expenses** Tuition $2000; Room & Board $2000 **Undergraduates** 15% part-time, 30% 25 or older **The most frequently chosen baccalaureate field is** philosophy **Academic program** English as a second language, accelerated degree program **Contact** Fr. Vladimir Tsurikov, Assistant Dean, Holy Trinity Orthodox Seminary, PO Box 36, Jordanville, NY 13361. Telephone: 315-858-0945. Fax: 315-858-0945. E-mail: info@hts.edu. Web site: http://www.hts.edu/.

HOUGHTON COLLEGE
HOUGHTON, NEW YORK

General Independent Wesleyan, 4-year, coed **Entrance** Moderately difficult **Setting** 1,300-acre rural campus **Total enrollment** 1,422 **Student-faculty ratio** 15:1 **Application deadline** Rolling (freshmen), rolling (transfer) **Freshmen** 91% were admitted **Housing** Yes **Expenses** Tuition $16,290; Room & Board $5520 **Undergraduates** 64% women, 5% part-time, 9% 25 or older, 0.4% Native American, 1% Hispanic American, 2% African American, 1% Asian American/Pacific Islander **The most frequently chosen baccalaureate fields are** business/marketing, education, visual/performing arts **Academic program** Advanced placement, honors program, summer session, adult/continuing education programs, internships **Contact** Mr. Bruce Campbell, Director of Admission, Houghton College, PO Box 128, Houghton, NY 14744. Telephone: 585-567-9353 or toll-free 800-777-2556. Fax: 585-567-9522. E-mail: admission@houghton.edu. Web site: http://www.houghton.edu/.

HUNTER COLLEGE OF THE CITY UNIVERSITY OF NEW YORK
NEW YORK, NEW YORK

General State and locally supported, comprehensive, coed **Entrance** Moderately difficult **Setting** urban campus **Total enrollment** 20,398 **Student-faculty ratio** 18:1 **Application deadline** 1/15 (freshmen), 3/1 (transfer) **Freshmen** 47% were admitted **Housing** Yes **Expenses** Tuition $3343; Room only $1890 **Undergraduates** 70% women, 36% part-time, 40% 25 or older, 0.2% Native American, 24% Hispanic American, 21% African American, 15% Asian American/Pacific Islander **Academic program** English as a second language, advanced placement, self-designed majors, honors program, summer session, internships **Contact** Office of Admissions, Hunter College of the City University of New York, 695 Park Avenue, New York, NY 10021-5085. Telephone: 212-772-4490. Web site: http://www.hunter.cuny.edu/.

IONA COLLEGE
NEW ROCHELLE, NEW YORK

General Independent, comprehensive, coed, affiliated with Roman Catholic Church **Entrance** Moderately difficult **Setting** 35-acre suburban campus **Total enrollment** 4,388 **Student-faculty ratio** 15:1 **Application deadline** 3/15 (freshmen), 8/15 (transfer) **Freshmen** 80% were admitted **Housing** Yes **Expenses** Tuition $17,040; Room & Board $9416 **Undergraduates** 51% women, 15% part-time, 15% 25 or older, 0.2% Native American, 11% Hispanic American, 9% African American, 2% Asian American/Pacific Islander **The most frequently chosen baccalaureate fields are** business/marketing, communications/communication technologies, health professions and related sciences **Academic program** Advanced placement, accelerated degree program, honors program, summer session, adult/continuing education programs, internships **Contact** Mr. Thomas Weede, Director of Undergraduate Admissions, Iona College, Admissions, 715 North Avenue, New Rochelle, NY 10801. Telephone: 914-633-2502 or toll-free 800-231-IONA (in-state); 914-633-2502 (out-of-state). Fax: 914-637-2778. E-mail: icad@iona.edu. Web site: http://www.iona.edu/.

▶ For more information, see page 442.

ITHACA COLLEGE
ITHACA, NEW YORK

General Independent, comprehensive, coed **Entrance** Moderately difficult **Setting** 757-acre small-town campus **Total enrollment** 6,483 **Student-faculty ratio** 13:1 **Application deadline** 3/1 (freshmen), 7/15 (transfer) **Freshmen** 66% were admitted **Housing** Yes **Expenses** Tuition $20,104; Room & Board $8615 **Undergraduates** 55% women, 2% part-time, 1% 25 or older, 0.2% Native American, 3% Hispanic American, 2% African American, 3% Asian American/Pacific Islander **The most frequently chosen baccalaureate fields are** communications/communication technologies, health professions and related sciences, visual/performing arts **Academic program** Advanced placement, accelerated degree program, self-designed majors, honors program, summer session, adult/continuing education programs, internships **Contact** Ms. Paula J. Mitchell, Director of Admission, Ithaca College, 100 Job Hall, Ithaca, NY 14850-7020. Telephone: 607-274-3124 or toll-free 800-429-4274. Fax: 607-274-1900. E-mail: admission@ithaca.edu. Web site: http://www.ithaca.edu/.

▶ For more information, see page 443.

JEWISH THEOLOGICAL SEMINARY OF AMERICA
NEW YORK, NEW YORK

General Independent Jewish, university, coed **Entrance** Very difficult **Setting** 1-acre urban campus **Total enrollment** 585 **Student-faculty ratio** 5:1 **Application deadline** 2/15 (freshmen), 5/1 (transfer) **Freshmen** 59% were admitted **Housing** Yes **Expenses** Tuition $9940; Room only $6470 **Undergraduates** 50% women, 9% part-time, 1% 25 or older **The most frequently chosen baccalaureate fields are** philosophy, philosophy, religion, and theology **Academic program** Advanced placement, self-designed majors, honors program, summer session, adult/continuing education programs, internships **Contact** Ms. Reena Kamins, Assistant Director of Admissions, Jewish Theological Seminary of America, Room 614 Schiff, 3080 Broadway, New York, NY 10027-4649. Telephone: 212-678-8832. Fax: 212-678-8947. E-mail: rekamins@jtsa.edu. Web site: http://www.jtsa.edu/.

JOHN JAY COLLEGE OF CRIMINAL JUSTICE OF THE CITY UNIVERSITY OF NEW YORK
NEW YORK, NEW YORK

General State and locally supported, comprehensive, coed **Entrance** Moderately difficult **Setting** urban campus **Total enrollment** 11,209 **Student-faculty ratio** 20:1 **Application deadline** Rolling (freshmen), rolling (transfer) **Freshmen** 73% were admitted **Housing** No **Expenses** Tuition $3310 **Undergraduates** 60% women, 35% 25 or older **The most frequently chosen baccalaureate field is** law/legal studies **Academic program** English as a second language, advanced placement, honors program, summer session, internships **Contact** Mr. Richard Saulnier, Acting Dean for Admissions and Registration, John Jay College of Criminal Justice of the City University of New York, 899 Tenth Avenue, New York, NY 10019-1093. Telephone: 212-237-8878. Web site: http://www.jjay.cuny.edu/.

THE JUILLIARD SCHOOL
NEW YORK, NEW YORK

General Independent, comprehensive, coed **Entrance** Most difficult **Setting** urban campus **Total enrollment** 813 **Application ratio** 4:1 **Application deadline** 12/1 (freshmen), 12/1 (transfer) **Freshmen** 9% were admitted **Housing** Yes **Expenses** Tuition $19,000; Room & Board $7500 **Undergraduates** 51% women, 0.2% part-time, 5% 25 or older, 5% Hispanic American, 10% African American, 14% Asian American/Pacific Islander **Academic program** English as a second language, accelerated degree program, self-designed majors, adult/continuing education programs **Contact** Ms. Mary

NEW YORK

The Juilliard School *(continued)*
K. Gray, Associate Dean for Admissions, The Juilliard School, 60 Lincoln Center Plaza, New York, NY 10023-6588. Telephone: 212-799-5000 Ext. 527. Fax: 212-724-0263. E-mail: webmaster@juilliard.edu. Web site: http://www.juilliard.edu/.

KEHILATH YAKOV RABBINICAL SEMINARY
BROOKLYN, NEW YORK

Contact Rabbi Zalman Gombo, Admissions Officer, Kehilath Yakov Rabbinical Seminary, 206 Wilson Street, Brooklyn, NY 11211-7207. Telephone: 718-963-1212.

KEUKA COLLEGE
KEUKA PARK, NEW YORK

General Independent, comprehensive, coed, affiliated with American Baptist Churches in the U.S.A. **Entrance** Moderately difficult **Setting** 173-acre rural campus **Total enrollment** 1,063 **Student-faculty ratio** 15:1 **Application deadline** Rolling (freshmen), rolling (transfer) **Freshmen** 96% were admitted **Housing** Yes **Expenses** Tuition $14,290; Room & Board $6880 **Undergraduates** 73% women, 3% part-time, 15% 25 or older **The most frequently chosen baccalaureate fields are** education, business/marketing, health professions and related sciences **Academic program** Advanced placement, accelerated degree program, self-designed majors, summer session, adult/continuing education programs, internships **Contact** Mr. Robert Callahan, Dean of Enrollment Management, Keuka College, Office of Admissions, Keuka Park, NY 14478-0098. Telephone: 315-279-4411 Ext. 5254 or toll-free 800-33-KEUKA. Fax: 315-279-5386. E-mail: admissions@mail.keuka.edu. Web site: http://www.keuka.edu/.

KOL YAAKOV TORAH CENTER
MONSEY, NEW YORK

Contact Assistant Director of Admissions, Kol Yaakov Torah Center, 29 West Maple Avenue, Monsey, NY 10952-2954. Telephone: 914-425-3871. E-mail: horizonss@aol.com. Web site: http://horizons.edu/.

LABORATORY INSTITUTE OF MERCHANDISING
NEW YORK, NEW YORK

General Proprietary, 4-year, coed, primarily women **Entrance** Moderately difficult **Setting** urban campus **Total enrollment** 340 **Student-faculty ratio** 8:1 **Application deadline** Rolling (freshmen), rolling (transfer) **Freshmen** 74% were admitted **Housing** No **Expenses** Tuition $13,750 **Undergraduates** 95% women, 1% part-time, 1% 25 or older, 1% Native American, 17% Hispanic American, 9% African American, 7% Asian American/Pacific Islander **Academic program** Advanced placement, summer session, internships **Contact** Ms. Karen Hammil Iglio, Director of Admissions, Laboratory Institute of Merchandising, 12 East 53rd Street, New York, NY 10022-5268. Telephone: 212-752-1530 Ext. 17 or toll-free 800-677-1323. Fax: 212-421-4341. E-mail: admissions@limcollege.edu. Web site: http://www.limcollege.edu/.

LEHMAN COLLEGE OF THE CITY UNIVERSITY OF NEW YORK
BRONX, NEW YORK

General State and locally supported, comprehensive, coed **Entrance** Moderately difficult **Setting** 37-acre urban campus **Total enrollment** 9,027 **Student-faculty ratio** 23:1 **Application deadline** Rolling (freshmen), rolling (transfer) **Freshmen** 48% were admitted **Housing** No **Expenses** Tuition $1710 **Undergraduates** 72% women, 45% part-time, 54% 25 or older, 0.1% Native American, 36% Hispanic American, 26% African American, 3% Asian American/Pacific Islander **The most frequently chosen baccalaureate fields are** health professions and related sciences, computer/information sciences, social sciences and history **Academic program** English as a second language, advanced placement, self-designed majors, honors program, summer session, adult/continuing education programs, internships **Contact** Ms. Gloria Ortiz, Assistant Director of Undergraduate Admissions, Lehman College of the City University of New York, 250 Bedford Park Boulevard West, Bronx, NY 10468. Telephone: 718-960-8096 or toll-free 877-Lehman1 (out-of-state). Fax: 718-960-8712. E-mail: cawic@cunyum.cunx.edu. Web site: http://www.lehman.cuny.edu/.

LE MOYNE COLLEGE
SYRACUSE, NEW YORK

General Independent Roman Catholic (Jesuit), comprehensive, coed **Entrance** Moderately difficult **Setting** 151-acre suburban campus **Total enrollment** 3,166 **Student-faculty ratio** 13:1 **Application deadline** 3/1 (freshmen), 6/1 (transfer) **Freshmen** 77% were admitted **Housing** Yes **Expenses** Tuition $16,850; Room & Board $6990 **Undergraduates** 59% women, 12% part-time, 10% 25 or older, 1% Native American, 3% Hispanic American, 4% African American, 1% Asian American/Pacific Islander **The most frequently chosen baccalaureate fields are** business/marketing, psychology, social sciences and history **Academic program** Advanced placement, accelerated degree program, honors program, summer session, adult/continuing education programs, internships **Contact** Mr. Dennis J. Nicholson, Director of Admission, Le Moyne College, 1419 Salt Spring Road, Syracuse, NY 13214-1399. Telephone: 315-445-4300 or toll-free 800-333-4733. Fax: 315-445-4711. E-mail: admission@lemoyne.edu. Web site: http://www.lemoyne.edu/.

▶ For more information, see page 446.

NEW YORK

LONG ISLAND UNIVERSITY, BRENTWOOD CAMPUS
BRENTWOOD, NEW YORK

General Independent, upper-level, coed **Total enrollment** 901 **Student-faculty ratio** 7:1 **Application deadline** 9/14 (transfer) **First-Year Students** 100% were admitted **Expenses** Tuition $17,960 **Undergraduates** 66% women, 68% part-time, 95% 25 or older, 1% Native American, 11% Hispanic American, 6% African American, 1% Asian American/Pacific Islander **Contact** Mr. John P. Metcalfe, Director of Admissions, Long Island University, Brentwood Campus, 100 Second Avenue, Brentwood, NY 11717. Telephone: 631-273-5112 Ext. 26. E-mail: brentwd@raptor.liu.edu. Web site: http://www.liunet.edu/cwis/brent/brent.htm.

LONG ISLAND UNIVERSITY, BROOKLYN CAMPUS
BROOKLYN, NEW YORK

General Independent, university, coed **Entrance** Minimally difficult **Setting** 10-acre urban campus **Total enrollment** 8,051 **Student-faculty ratio** 19:1 **Application deadline** Rolling (freshmen), rolling (transfer) **Freshmen** 74% were admitted **Housing** Yes **Expenses** Tuition $15,036 **Undergraduates** 71% women, 20% part-time, 34% 25 or older, 0.2% Native American, 16% Hispanic American, 48% African American, 11% Asian American/Pacific Islander **The most frequently chosen baccalaureate fields are** business/marketing, education, health professions and related sciences **Academic program** English as a second language, advanced placement, self-designed majors, honors program, summer session, adult/continuing education programs, internships **Contact** Mr. Alan B. Chaves, Dean of Admissions, Long Island University, Brooklyn Campus, One University Plaza, Brooklyn, NY 11201-8423. Telephone: 718-488-1011 or toll-free 800-LIU-PLAN (in-state). Fax: 718-797-2399. E-mail: admissions@brooklyn.liu.edu. Web site: http://www.liu.edu/.

LONG ISLAND UNIVERSITY, C.W. POST CAMPUS
BROOKVILLE, NEW YORK

General Independent, comprehensive, coed **Entrance** Moderately difficult **Setting** 308-acre suburban campus **Total enrollment** 10,133 **Student-faculty ratio** 15:1 **Application deadline** Rolling (freshmen), rolling (transfer) **Freshmen** 84% were admitted **Housing** Yes **Expenses** Tuition $18,090; Room & Board $7290 **Undergraduates** 58% women, 40% part-time, 14% 25 or older **The most frequently chosen baccalaureate fields are** education, communications/communication technologies, visual/performing arts **Academic program** English as a second language, advanced placement, accelerated degree program, self-designed majors, honors program, summer session, adult/continuing education programs, internships **Contact** Ms. Jacqueline Reyes, Associate Director of Admissions, Long Island University, C.W. Post Campus, 720 Northern Boulevard, Brookville, NY 11548-1300. Telephone: 516-299-2900 or toll-free 800-LIU-PLAN. Fax: 516-299-2137. E-mail: admissions@collegehall.liunet.edu. Web site: http://www.liuedu/cwpost.

LONG ISLAND UNIVERSITY, SOUTHAMPTON COLLEGE
SOUTHAMPTON, NEW YORK

General Independent, comprehensive, coed **Entrance** Moderately difficult **Setting** 110-acre rural campus **Total enrollment** 1,531 **Student-faculty ratio** 17:1 **Application deadline** Rolling (freshmen), rolling (transfer) **Freshmen** 67% were admitted **Housing** Yes **Expenses** Tuition $18,120; Room & Board $8150 **Undergraduates** 70% women, 9% part-time, 13% 25 or older, 1% Native American, 4% Hispanic American, 5% African American, 2% Asian American/Pacific Islander **The most frequently chosen baccalaureate fields are** biological/life sciences, interdisciplinary studies, liberal arts/general studies **Academic program** English as a second language, advanced placement, self-designed majors, honors program, summer session, adult/continuing education programs, internships **Contact** Bernetta McCall, Director of Admissions, Long Island University, Southampton College, 239 Montauk Highway, Southampton, NY 11968-9822. Telephone: 631-287-8200 Ext. 8342 or toll-free 800-LIU PLAN Ext. 2. Fax: 631-287-8130. E-mail: admissions@southampton.liu.edu. Web site: http://www.southampton.liu.edu/.

LONG ISLAND UNIVERSITY, SOUTHAMPTON COLLEGE, FRIENDS WORLD PROGRAM
SOUTHAMPTON, NEW YORK

General Independent, 4-year, coed **Entrance** Noncompetitive **Setting** 110-acre rural campus **Total enrollment** 192 **Student-faculty ratio** 9:1 **Application deadline** Rolling (freshmen), rolling (transfer) **Freshmen** 85% were admitted **Housing** Yes **Expenses** Tuition $17,960; Room & Board $8280 **Undergraduates** 72% women, 10% part-time **The most frequently chosen baccalaureate field is** interdisciplinary studies **Academic program** Advanced placement, self-designed majors, internships **Contact** Trish Maginsky, Admissions Secretary, Long Island University, Southampton College, Friends World Program, 239 Montauk Highway, Southampton, NY 11968. Telephone: 631-287-8474 or toll-free 800-LIU PLAN (out-of-state). Fax: 631-287-8463. E-mail: fw@southampton.liu.edu. Web site: http://www.southampton.liu.edu/fw/.

MACHZIKEI HADATH RABBINICAL COLLEGE
BROOKLYN, NEW YORK

Contact Rabbi Abraham M. Lezerowitz, Director of Admissions, Machzikei Hadath Rabbinical College,

Machzikei Hadath Rabbinical College *(continued)*
5407 Sixteenth Avenue, Brooklyn, NY 11204-1805. Telephone: 718-854-8777.

MANHATTAN COLLEGE
RIVERDALE, NEW YORK

General Independent, comprehensive, coed, affiliated with Roman Catholic Church **Entrance** Moderately difficult **Setting** 31-acre urban campus **Total enrollment** 2,946 **Student-faculty ratio** 13:1 **Application deadline** 3/1 (freshmen), 7/1 (transfer) **Freshmen** 63% were admitted **Housing** Yes **Expenses** Tuition $19,200; Room & Board $7700 **Undergraduates** 48% women, 6% part-time, 3% 25 or older, 0.1% Native American, 14% Hispanic American, 6% African American, 6% Asian American/Pacific Islander The most frequently chosen baccalaureate fields are business/marketing, education, engineering/engineering technologies **Academic program** English as a second language, advanced placement, accelerated degree program, honors program, summer session, adult/continuing education programs, internships **Contact** Mr. William J. Bisset Jr., Assistant Vice President for Enrollment Management, Manhattan College, 4513 Manhattan College Parkway, Riverdale, NY 10471. Telephone: 718-862-7200 or toll-free 800-622-9235 (in-state). Fax: 718-862-8019. E-mail: admit@manhattan.edu. Web site: http://www.manhattan.edu/.

MANHATTAN SCHOOL OF MUSIC
NEW YORK, NEW YORK

General Independent, comprehensive, coed **Entrance** Very difficult **Setting** 1-acre urban campus **Total enrollment** 831 **Student-faculty ratio** 8:1 **Application deadline** 12/1 (freshmen), 12/1 (transfer) **Freshmen** 40% were admitted **Housing** Yes **Expenses** Tuition $21,500; Room only $7200 **Undergraduates** 52% women, 6% part-time, 8% 25 or older, 1% Native American, 6% Hispanic American, 4% African American, 10% Asian American/Pacific Islander The most frequently chosen baccalaureate field is visual/performing arts **Academic program** English as a second language, advanced placement **Contact** Mrs. Amy Anderson, Director of Admission, Manhattan School of Music, 120 Claremont Avenue, New York, NY 10027. Telephone: 212-749-2802 Ext. 4449. Fax: 212-749-3025. E-mail: admission@msmnyc.edu. Web site: http://www.msmnyc.edu/.

MANHATTANVILLE COLLEGE
PURCHASE, NEW YORK

General Independent, comprehensive, coed **Entrance** Moderately difficult **Setting** 100-acre suburban campus **Total enrollment** 2,468 **Student-faculty ratio** 13:1 **Application deadline** 3/1 (freshmen), 3/1 (transfer) **Freshmen** 58% were admitted **Housing** Yes **Expenses** Tuition $20,410; Room & Board $8320 **Undergraduates** 69% women, 11% part-time, 2% 25 or older, 0.1% Native American, 13% Hispanic American, 6% African American, 2% Asian American/Pacific Islander The most frequently chosen baccalaureate fields are business/marketing, social sciences and history, visual/performing arts **Academic program** English as a second language, advanced placement, accelerated degree program, self-designed majors, honors program, summer session, adult/continuing education programs, internships **Contact** Mr. Jose Flores, Director of Admissions, Manhattanville College, 2900 Purchase Street, Purchase, NY 10577-2132. Telephone: 914-323-5124 or toll-free 800-328-4553. Fax: 914-694-1732. E-mail: admissions@mville.edu. Web site: http://www.mville.edu/.

MANNES COLLEGE OF MUSIC, NEW SCHOOL UNIVERSITY
NEW YORK, NEW YORK

General Independent, comprehensive, coed **Entrance** Very difficult **Setting** urban campus **Total enrollment** 278 **Student-faculty ratio** 2:1 **Application deadline** 12/15 (freshmen), rolling (transfer) **Freshmen** 37% were admitted **Housing** Yes **Expenses** Tuition $20,246; Room & Board $9612 **Undergraduates** 65% women, 13% 25 or older, 0% Native American, 4% Hispanic American, 4% African American, 7% Asian American/Pacific Islander The most frequently chosen baccalaureate field is visual/performing arts **Academic program** English as a second language, advanced placement, accelerated degree program, summer session, adult/continuing education programs **Contact** Ms. Allison Scola, Director of Enrollment, Mannes College of Music, New School University, 150 West 85th Street, New York, NY 10024-4402. Telephone: 212-580-0210 Ext. 247 or toll-free 800-292-3040 (out-of-state). Fax: 212-580-1738. E-mail: mannasadmissions@newschool.edu. Web site: http://www.mannes.edu/.

MARIST COLLEGE
POUGHKEEPSIE, NEW YORK

General Independent, comprehensive, coed **Entrance** Moderately difficult **Setting** 135-acre small-town campus **Total enrollment** 5,553 **Student-faculty ratio** 14:1 **Application deadline** 2/15 (freshmen), 6/1 (transfer) **Freshmen** 52% were admitted **Housing** Yes **Expenses** Tuition $16,792; Room & Board $7964 **Undergraduates** 57% women, 13% part-time, 16% 25 or older, 0.1% Native American, 4% Hispanic American, 3% African American, 1% Asian American/Pacific Islander The most frequently chosen baccalaureate fields are business/marketing, communications/communication technologies, protective services/public administration **Academic program** English as a second language, advanced placement, accelerated degree program, honors program, summer session, adult/continuing education programs, internships **Contact** Mr. Jay Murray, Director of Admissions, Marist College, 3399 North Road, Poughkeepsie, NY 12601-1387. Telephone: 845-575-3226 Ext. 2190 or toll-free 800-436-5483. E-mail: admissions@marist.edu. Web site: http://www.marist.edu/.

NEW YORK

MARYMOUNT COLLEGE OF FORDHAM UNIVERSITY
TARRYTOWN, NEW YORK

General Independent, 4-year, women only **Entrance** Moderately difficult **Setting** 25-acre suburban campus **Total enrollment** 1,001 **Student-faculty ratio** 9:1 **Application deadline** Rolling (transfer) **Freshmen** 81% were admitted **Housing** Yes **Expenses** Tuition $15,750; Room & Board $8100 **Undergraduates** 17% part-time, 29% 25 or older, 0.1% Native American, 15% Hispanic American, 15% African American, 5% Asian American/Pacific Islander **The most frequently chosen baccalaureate fields are** education, business/marketing, visual/performing arts **Academic program** English as a second language, advanced placement, self-designed majors, honors program, summer session, adult/continuing education programs, internships **Contact** Daniela Esposito, Director of Admissions, Marymount College of Fordham University, 100 Marymount Avenue, Tarrytown, NY 10591-3796. Telephone: 914-332-8295 or toll-free 800-724-4312. Fax: 914-332-7442. E-mail: admiss@mmc.marymt.edu. Web site: http://www.marymt.edu/.

▶ For more information, see page 453.

MARYMOUNT MANHATTAN COLLEGE
NEW YORK, NEW YORK

General Independent, 4-year, coed **Entrance** Moderately difficult **Setting** 1-acre urban campus **Total enrollment** 2,707 **Student-faculty ratio** 20:1 **Application deadline** Rolling (freshmen), rolling (transfer) **Freshmen** 57% were admitted **Housing** Yes **Expenses** Tuition $14,695; Room only $8500 **Undergraduates** 79% women, 32% part-time, 39% 25 or older, 0.3% Native American, 16% Hispanic American, 20% African American, 4% Asian American/Pacific Islander **Academic program** English as a second language, advanced placement, accelerated degree program, honors program, summer session, adult/continuing education programs, internships **Contact** Mr. Thomas Friebel, Associate Vice President for Enrollment Services, Marymount Manhattan College, 221 East 71st Street, New York, NY 10021. Telephone: 212-517-0430 or toll-free 800-MARYMOUNT (out-of-state). Fax: 212-517-0448. E-mail: admissions@mmm.edu. Web site: http://marymount.mmm.edu/.

MEDAILLE COLLEGE
BUFFALO, NEW YORK

General Independent, comprehensive, coed **Entrance** Moderately difficult **Setting** 13-acre urban campus **Total enrollment** 1,788 **Student-faculty ratio** 19:1 **Application deadline** 8/1 (freshmen), rolling (transfer) **Freshmen** 63% were admitted **Housing** Yes **Expenses** Tuition $12,520; Room & Board $5800 **Undergraduates** 71% women, 14% part-time, 51% 25 or older, 1% Native American, 3% Hispanic American, 13% African American, 1% Asian American/Pacific Islander **The most frequently chosen baccalaureate fields are** business/marketing, education, liberal arts/general studies **Academic program** Advanced placement, accelerated degree program, self-designed majors, summer session, adult/continuing education programs, internships **Contact** Mrs. Jacqueline S. Matheny, Director of Enrollment Management, Medaille College, Medaille College, Office of Admissions, Buffalo, NY 14214. Telephone: 716-884-3281 Ext. 203 or toll-free 800-292-1582 (in-state). Fax: 716-884-0291. E-mail: jmatheny@medaille.edu. Web site: http://www.medaille.edu/.

MEDGAR EVERS COLLEGE OF THE CITY UNIVERSITY OF NEW YORK
BROOKLYN, NEW YORK

General State and locally supported, 4-year, coed **Entrance** Noncompetitive **Setting** 1-acre urban campus **Total enrollment** 4,716 **Student-faculty ratio** 18:1 **Application deadline** Rolling (freshmen), rolling (transfer) **Housing** No **Expenses** Tuition $3282 **Undergraduates** 78% women, 45% part-time, 70% 25 or older, 0.2% Native American, 4% Hispanic American, 87% African American, 1% Asian American/Pacific Islander **The most frequently chosen baccalaureate fields are** education, business/marketing, health professions and related sciences **Academic program** English as a second language, advanced placement, honors program, summer session, adult/continuing education programs, internships **Contact** Mr. Gregory Thomas, Acting Director of Admissions, Medgar Evers College of the City University of New York, 1650 Bedford Avenue, Brooklyn, NY 11225. Telephone: 718-270-6025. Fax: 718-270-6198. Web site: http://www.mec.cuny.edu/.

MERCY COLLEGE
DOBBS FERRY, NEW YORK

General Independent, comprehensive, coed **Entrance** Noncompetitive **Setting** 60-acre suburban campus **Total enrollment** 9,752 **Student-faculty ratio** 13:1 **Application deadline** Rolling (freshmen), rolling (transfer) **Housing** Yes **Expenses** Tuition $8500; Room & Board $7700 **Undergraduates** 71% women, 36% part-time, 58% 25 or older **Academic program** English as a second language, advanced placement, accelerated degree program, self-designed majors, honors program, summer session, adult/continuing education programs, internships **Contact** Mrs. Sharon Handelson, Director of Admissions and Recruitment, Mercy College, 555 Broadway, Dobbs Ferry, NY 10522-1189. Telephone: 800-Mercy-NY Ext. 7499 or toll-free 800-MERCY-NY. Fax: 914-674-7382. E-mail: admissions@mercy.edu. Web site: http://www.mercy.edu/.

MESIVTA OF EASTERN PARKWAY RABBINICAL SEMINARY
BROOKLYN, NEW YORK

Contact Rabbi Joseph Halberstadt, Dean, Mesivta of Eastern Parkway Rabbinical Seminary, 510 Dahill Road, Brooklyn, NY 11218-5559. Telephone: 718-438-1002.

NEW YORK

MESIVTA TIFERETH JERUSALEM OF AMERICA
NEW YORK, NEW YORK

Contact Rabbi Fishellis, Director of Admissions, Mesivta Tifereth Jerusalem of America, 141 East Broadway, New York, NY 10002-6301. Telephone: 212-964-2830.

MESIVTA TORAH VODAATH RABBINICAL SEMINARY
BROOKLYN, NEW YORK

Contact Rabbi Issac Braun, Administrator, Mesivta Torah Vodaath Rabbinical Seminary, 425 East Ninth Street, Brooklyn, NY 11218-5209. Telephone: 718-941-8000. Fax: 718-941-8032.

MIRRER YESHIVA
BROOKLYN, NEW YORK

Contact Director of Admissions, Mirrer Yeshiva, 1795 Ocean Parkway, Brooklyn, NY 11223-2010. Telephone: 718-645-0536.

MOLLOY COLLEGE
ROCKVILLE CENTRE, NEW YORK

General Independent, comprehensive, coed **Entrance** Moderately difficult **Setting** 25-acre suburban campus **Total enrollment** 2,538 **Student-faculty ratio** 9:1 **Application deadline** Rolling (freshmen), rolling (transfer) **Freshmen** 86% were admitted **Housing** No **Expenses** Tuition $13,940 **Undergraduates** 77% women, 28% part-time, 36% 25 or older, 0.2% Native American, 7% Hispanic American, 17% African American, 3% Asian American/Pacific Islander **Academic program** English as a second language, advanced placement, self-designed majors, honors program, summer session, adult/continuing education programs, internships **Contact** Ms. Marguerite Lane, Director of Admissions, Molloy College, 1000 Hempstead Avenue, PO Box 5002, Rockville Centre, NY 11571-5002. Telephone: 516-678-5000 Ext. 6240 or toll-free 888-4MOLLOY. Fax: 516-256-2247. E-mail: lucieline@molloy.edu.

MOUNT SAINT MARY COLLEGE
NEWBURGH, NEW YORK

General Independent, comprehensive, coed **Entrance** Moderately difficult **Setting** 72-acre suburban campus **Total enrollment** 2,366 **Student-faculty ratio** 17:1 **Application deadline** Rolling (freshmen), rolling (transfer) **Freshmen** 82% were admitted **Housing** Yes **Expenses** Tuition $12,675; Room & Board $6020 **Undergraduates** 70% women, 24% part-time, 31% 25 or older, 0% Native American, 7% Hispanic American, 10% African American, 2% Asian American/Pacific Islander **The most frequently chosen baccalaureate fields are** business/marketing, health professions and related sciences, social sciences and history **Academic program** Advanced placement, accelerated degree program, honors program, summer session, adult/continuing education programs, internships **Contact** Mr. J. Randall Ognibene, Director of Admissions, Mount Saint Mary College, 330 Powell Avenue, Newburgh, NY 12550. Telephone: 845-569-3248 or toll-free 888-937-6762. Fax: 845-562-6762. E-mail: admissions@msmc.edu. Web site: http://www.msmc.edu/.

NAZARETH COLLEGE OF ROCHESTER
ROCHESTER, NEW YORK

General Independent, comprehensive, coed **Entrance** Moderately difficult **Setting** 75-acre suburban campus **Total enrollment** 3,107 **Student-faculty ratio** 12:1 **Application deadline** 2/15 (freshmen), 3/15 (transfer) **Freshmen** 76% were admitted **Housing** Yes **Expenses** Tuition $15,384; Room & Board $6660 **Undergraduates** 76% women, 14% part-time, 13% 25 or older, 0.2% Native American, 2% Hispanic American, 3% African American, 2% Asian American/Pacific Islander **The most frequently chosen baccalaureate fields are** education, business/marketing, health professions and related sciences **Academic program** Advanced placement, honors program, summer session, adult/continuing education programs, internships **Contact** Mr. Thomas K. DaRin, Vice President for Enrollment Management, Nazareth College of Rochester, 4245 East Avenue, Rochester, NY 14618-3790. Telephone: 585-389-2860 or toll-free 800-462-3944 (in-state). Fax: 585-389-2826. E-mail: admissions@naz.edu. Web site: http://www.naz.edu/.

NEW SCHOOL BACHELOR OF ARTS, NEW SCHOOL UNIVERSITY
NEW YORK, NEW YORK

General Independent, upper-level, coed **Entrance** Moderately difficult **Setting** urban campus **Total enrollment** 1,154 **Student-faculty ratio** 11:1 **Application deadline** 8/1 (transfer) **Housing** Yes **Expenses** Tuition $14,558; Room & Board $9612 **Undergraduates** 65% women, 53% part-time, 72% 25 or older, 0.2% Native American, 7% Hispanic American, 11% African American, 2% Asian American/Pacific Islander **The most frequently chosen baccalaureate field is** liberal arts/general studies **Academic program** English as a second language, advanced placement, accelerated degree program, self-designed majors, summer session, adult/continuing education programs, internships **Contact** Ms. Gerianne Brusati, Director of Educational Advising and Admissions, New School Bachelor of Arts, New School University, 66 West 12th Street, New York, NY 10011-8603. Telephone: 212-229-5630. E-mail: admissions@dialnsa.edu. Web site: http://www.newschool.edu/.

NEW YORK INSTITUTE OF TECHNOLOGY
OLD WESTBURY, NEW YORK

General Independent, comprehensive, coed **Entrance** Moderately difficult **Setting** 1,050-acre suburban campus **Total enrollment** 8,934 **Student-faculty ratio** 16:1 **Application deadline** Rolling (freshmen), rolling (transfer) **Freshmen** 79% were admitted **Housing** Yes **Expenses** Tuition $14,876; Room & Board $7580 **Undergraduates** 38% women, 29% part-time, 26% 25 or older, 0.4% Native American, 10% Hispanic American, 13% African American, 11% Asian American/Pacific Islander **The most frequently chosen baccalaureate fields are** business/marketing, architecture, health professions and related sciences **Academic program** English as a second language, advanced placement, accelerated degree program, self-designed majors, honors program, summer session, adult/continuing education programs, internships **Contact** Mr. James Newell, Director of Financial Aid, New York Institute of Technology, PO Box 8000, Old Westbury, NY 11568. Telephone: 516-686-7680 or toll-free 800-345-NYIT. Fax: 516-686-7613. E-mail: admissions@aol.nuit.edu. Web site: http://www.nyit.edu/.

NEW YORK SCHOOL OF INTERIOR DESIGN
NEW YORK, NEW YORK

General Independent, comprehensive, coed **Entrance** Moderately difficult **Setting** urban campus **Total enrollment** 640 **Student-faculty ratio** 8:1 **Application deadline** Rolling (freshmen), rolling (transfer) **Freshmen** 81% were admitted **Housing** No **Expenses** Tuition $16,940 **Undergraduates** 87% women, 71% part-time, 73% 25 or older **The most frequently chosen baccalaureate field is** visual/performing arts **Academic program** English as a second language, advanced placement, summer session, internships **Contact** Mr. Douglas Robbins, Admissions Associate, New York School of Interior Design, 170 East 70th Street, New York, NY 10021-5110. Telephone: 212-472-1500 Ext. 204 or toll-free 800-336-9743. Fax: 212-472-1867. E-mail: admissions@nysid.edu. Web site: http://www.nysid.edu/.

NEW YORK UNIVERSITY
NEW YORK, NEW YORK

General Independent, university, coed **Entrance** Most difficult **Setting** 28-acre urban campus **Total enrollment** 37,134 **Student-faculty ratio** 12:1 **Application deadline** 1/15 (freshmen), 4/1 (transfer) **Freshmen** 28% were admitted **Housing** Yes **Expenses** Tuition $25,380; Room & Board $9820 **Undergraduates** 60% women, 11% part-time, 11% 25 or older, 0.1% Native American, 7% Hispanic American, 6% African American, 14% Asian American/Pacific Islander **The most frequently chosen baccalaureate field is** philosophy, religion, and theology **Academic program** English as a second language, advanced placement, accelerated degree program, self-designed majors, honors program, summer session, adult/continuing education programs, internships **Contact** Mr. Richard A. Avisable, Assistant Vice President for Enrollment Services, New York University, 22 Washington Square North, New York, NY 10011. Telephone: 212-998-4500. Fax: 212-995-4902. E-mail: nyuadmit@uccvm.nyu.edu. Web site: http://www.nyu.edu/.

▶ **For more information, see page 460.**

NIAGARA UNIVERSITY
NIAGARA FALLS, NEW YORK

General Independent, comprehensive, coed, affiliated with Roman Catholic Church **Entrance** Moderately difficult **Setting** 160-acre suburban campus **Total enrollment** 3,278 **Student-faculty ratio** 16:1 **Application deadline** 8/1 (freshmen), 8/15 (transfer) **Freshmen** 83% were admitted **Housing** Yes **Expenses** Tuition $15,300; Room & Board $6950 **Undergraduates** 60% women, 8% part-time, 9% 25 or older, 1% Native American, 2% Hispanic American, 4% African American, 1% Asian American/Pacific Islander **The most frequently chosen baccalaureate fields are** business/marketing, education, social sciences and history **Academic program** English as a second language, advanced placement, accelerated degree program, honors program, summer session, adult/continuing education programs, internships **Contact** Ms. Christine M. McDermott, Associate Director of Admissions, Niagara University, Office of Admissions, Niagara, NY 14109. Telephone: 716-286-8700 Ext. 8715 or toll-free 800-462-2111. Fax: 716-286-8733. E-mail: admissions@niagara.edu. Web site: http://www.niagara.edu/.

NYACK COLLEGE
NYACK, NEW YORK

General Independent, 4-year, coed, affiliated with The Christian and Missionary Alliance **Entrance** Moderately difficult **Setting** 102-acre suburban campus **Total enrollment** 1,897 **Student-faculty ratio** 16:1 **Application deadline** Rolling (freshmen), rolling (transfer) **Freshmen** 67% were admitted **Housing** Yes **Expenses** Tuition $13,280; Room & Board $6200 **Undergraduates** 60% women, 9% part-time, 39% 25 or older, 0.1% Native American, 23% Hispanic American, 27% African American, 7% Asian American/Pacific Islander **The most frequently chosen baccalaureate fields are** business/marketing, philosophy, philosophy, religion, and theology **Academic program** English as a second language, advanced placement, accelerated degree program, honors program, summer session, adult/continuing education programs, internships **Contact** Mr. Miguel Sanchez, Director of Admissions, Nyack College, 1 South Boulevard, Nyack, NY 10960-3698. Telephone: 845-358-1710 Ext. 350 or toll-free 800-33-NYACK. Fax: 845-358-3047. E-mail: enroll@nyack.edu. Web site: http://www.nyackcollege.edu/.

OHR HAMEIR THEOLOGICAL SEMINARY
PEEKSKILL, NEW YORK

Contact Rabbi M. Z. Weisverg, Director of Admissions, Ohr Hameir Theological Seminary, Furnace Woods Road, Peekskill, NY 10566. Telephone: 914-736-1500.

OHR SOMAYACH/JOSEPH TANENBAUM EDUCATIONAL CENTER
MONSEY, NEW YORK

Contact Rabbi Avrohom Braun, Dean of Students, Ohr Somayach/Joseph Tanenbaum Educational Cen-

NEW YORK

Ohr Somayach/Joseph Tanenbaum Educational Center *(continued)*

ter, PO Box 334, Monsey, NY 10952-0334. Telephone: 914-425-1370 Ext. 22.

PACE UNIVERSITY
NEW YORK, NEW YORK

General Independent, university, coed **Entrance** Moderately difficult **Total enrollment** 13,498 **Student-faculty ratio** 15:1 **Application deadline** Rolling (freshmen), rolling (transfer) **Freshmen** 76% were admitted **Housing** Yes **Expenses** Tuition $17,030; Room & Board $7170 **Undergraduates** 60% women, 23% part-time, 16% 25 or older The most frequently chosen baccalaureate fields are business/marketing, computer/information sciences, health professions and related sciences **Academic program** English as a second language, advanced placement, accelerated degree program, honors program, summer session, adult/continuing education programs, internships **Contact** Ms. Joanna Broda, Director of Admission, NY and Westchester, Pace University, One Pace Plaza, New York, NY 10038. Telephone: 212-346-1323 or toll-free 800-874-7223. Fax: 212-346-1040. E-mail: infoctr@ny027.wan.pace.edu. Web site: http://www.pace.edu/.

PARSONS SCHOOL OF DESIGN, NEW SCHOOL UNIVERSITY
NEW YORK, NEW YORK

General Independent, comprehensive, coed **Entrance** Very difficult **Setting** 2-acre urban campus **Total enrollment** 2,733 **Student-faculty ratio** 11:1 **Application deadline** Rolling (freshmen), rolling (transfer) **Freshmen** 44% were admitted **Housing** Yes **Expenses** Tuition $23,126; Room & Board $9212 **Undergraduates** 75% women, 8% part-time, 22% 25 or older, 0.2% Native American, 7% Hispanic American, 4% African American, 20% Asian American/Pacific Islander The most frequently chosen baccalaureate fields are architecture, visual/performing arts **Academic program** English as a second language, advanced placement, accelerated degree program, honors program, summer session, adult/continuing education programs, internships **Contact** Ms. Nadine M. Bourgeois, Director of Admissions and Associate Dean of Enrollment Management, Parsons School of Design, New School University, 66 Fifth Avenue, New York, NY 10011-8878. Telephone: 212-229-8910 or toll-free 800-252-0852. E-mail: parsadm@newschool.edu. Web site: http://www.parsons.edu/.

PAUL SMITH'S COLLEGE OF ARTS AND SCIENCES
PAUL SMITHS, NEW YORK

General Independent, 4-year, coed **Entrance** Minimally difficult **Setting** 14,200-acre rural campus **Total enrollment** 817 **Student-faculty ratio** 13:1 **Application deadline** Rolling (freshmen), rolling (transfer) **Freshmen** 80% were admitted **Housing** Yes **Expenses** Tuition $14,300; Room & Board $6000 **Undergraduates** 30% women, 3% part-time, 7% 25 or older, 1% Native American, 2% Hispanic American, 4% African American, 1% Asian American/Pacific Islander The most frequently chosen baccalaureate fields are natural resources/environmental science, business/marketing, personal/miscellaneous services **Academic program** English as a second language, advanced placement, self-designed majors, honors program, summer session, adult/continuing education programs, internships **Contact** Mr. Douglas Zander, Vice President for Enrollment and Campus Life, Paul Smith's College of Arts and Sciences, PO Box 265, Paul Smiths, NY 12970-0265. Telephone: 518-327-6227 Ext. 6230 or toll-free 800-421-2605. Fax: 518-327-6016. Web site: http://www.paulsmiths.edu/.

PLATTSBURGH STATE UNIVERSITY OF NEW YORK
PLATTSBURGH, NEW YORK

General State-supported, comprehensive, coed **Entrance** Moderately difficult **Setting** 265-acre small-town campus **Total enrollment** 6,236 **Student-faculty ratio** 17:1 **Application deadline** Rolling (freshmen), rolling (transfer) **Freshmen** 63% were admitted **Housing** Yes **Expenses** Tuition $4149; Room & Board $5580 **Undergraduates** 57% women, 7% part-time, 11% 25 or older, 0.4% Native American, 3% Hispanic American, 3% African American, 2% Asian American/Pacific Islander The most frequently chosen baccalaureate fields are business/marketing, education, social sciences and history **Academic program** English as a second language, advanced placement, accelerated degree program, self-designed majors, honors program, summer session, adult/continuing education programs, internships **Contact** Mr. Richard Higgins, Director of Admissions, Plattsburgh State University of New York, 101 Broad Street, Plattsburgh, NY 12901-2681. Telephone: 518-564-2040 or toll-free 888-673-0012 (in-state). Fax: 518-564-2045. E-mail: admissions@plattsburgh.edu. Web site: http://www.plattsburgh.edu/.

POLYTECHNIC UNIVERSITY, BROOKLYN CAMPUS
BROOKLYN, NEW YORK

General Independent, university, coed **Entrance** Very difficult **Setting** 3-acre urban campus **Total enrollment** 3,051 **Student-faculty ratio** 12:1 **Application deadline** Rolling (freshmen), rolling (transfer) **Freshmen** 69% were admitted **Housing** Yes **Expenses** Tuition $22,940; Room & Board $5250 **Undergraduates** 20% women, 7% part-time, 7% 25 or older, 0.2% Native American, 6% Hispanic American, 10% African American, 40% Asian American/Pacific Islander The most frequently chosen baccalaureate fields are computer/information sciences, engineering/engineering technologies, liberal arts/general studies **Academic program** English as a second language, advanced placement, accelerated degree program, honors program, summer session, internships **Con-**

NEW YORK

tact Mr. John S. Kerge, Dean of Admissions, Polytechnic University, Brooklyn Campus, Six Metrotech Center, Brooklyn, NY 11201-2990. Telephone: 718-260-3100 or toll-free 800-POLYTECH. Fax: 718-260-3446. E-mail: admitme@poly.edu. Web site: http://www.poly.edu/.

PRACTICAL BIBLE COLLEGE
BIBLE SCHOOL PARK, NEW YORK

General Independent nondenominational, 4-year, coed **Entrance** Minimally difficult **Setting** 22-acre suburban campus **Total enrollment** 245 **Student-faculty ratio** 17:1 **Application deadline** Rolling (freshmen), rolling (transfer) **Freshmen** 53% were admitted **Housing** Yes **Expenses** Tuition $7025; Room & Board $4420 **Undergraduates** 44% women, 14% part-time, 22% 25 or older, 0% Native American, 2% Hispanic American, 2% African American, 0.4% Asian American/Pacific Islander **The most frequently chosen baccalaureate fields are** philosophy, philosophy, religion, and theology **Academic program** English as a second language, advanced placement, summer session, adult/continuing education programs, internships **Contact** Mr. Brian J. Murphy, Director of Admissions, Practical Bible College, PO Box 601, Bible School Park, NY 13737-0601. Telephone: 607-729-1581 Ext. 406 or toll-free 800-331-4137 Ext. 406. Fax: 607-729-2962. E-mail: pettyjohn1@juno.com. Web site: http://www.practical.edu/.

PRATT INSTITUTE
BROOKLYN, NEW YORK

General Independent, comprehensive, coed **Entrance** Very difficult **Setting** 25-acre urban campus **Total enrollment** 4,199 **Student-faculty ratio** 9:1 **Application deadline** 2/1 (freshmen), 2/11 (transfer) **Freshmen** 43% were admitted **Housing** Yes **Expenses** Tuition $21,354; Room & Board $7940 **Undergraduates** 51% women, 12% part-time, 27% 25 or older, 0.1% Native American, 8% Hispanic American, 7% African American, 10% Asian American/Pacific Islander **The most frequently chosen baccalaureate fields are** architecture, education, visual/performing arts **Academic program** English as a second language, advanced placement, summer session, internships **Contact** Ms. Erica Wilson, Visit Coordinator, Pratt Institute, DeKalb Hall, 200 Willoughby Avenue, Brooklyn, NY 11205-3899. Telephone: 718-636-3669 Ext. 3779 or toll-free 800-331-0834 (out-of-state). Fax: 718-636-3670. E-mail: admissions@pratt.edu. Web site: http://www.pratt.edu/.

▶ For more information, see page 464.

PURCHASE COLLEGE, STATE UNIVERSITY OF NEW YORK
PURCHASE, NEW YORK

General State-supported, comprehensive, coed **Entrance** Moderately difficult **Setting** 500-acre small-town campus **Total enrollment** 4,018 **Student-faculty ratio** 14:1 **Application deadline** 7/1 (freshmen), rolling (transfer) **Freshmen** 33% were admitted **Housing** Yes **Expenses** Tuition $4200; Room & Board $6500 **Undergraduates** 57% women, 21% part-time, 13% 25 or older, 0.3% Native American, 9% Hispanic American, 9% African American, 4% Asian American/Pacific Islander **The most frequently chosen baccalaureate fields are** liberal arts/general studies, social sciences and history, visual/performing arts **Academic program** English as a second language, advanced placement, self-designed majors, summer session, adult/continuing education programs, internships **Contact** Ms. Betsy Immergut, Director of Admissions, Purchase College, State University of New York, 735 Anderson Hill Road, Purchase, NY 10577-1400. Telephone: 914-251-6300. Fax: 914-251-6314. E-mail: admissn@purchase.edu. Web site: http://www.purchase.edu/.

QUEENS COLLEGE OF THE CITY UNIVERSITY OF NEW YORK
FLUSHING, NEW YORK

General State and locally supported, comprehensive, coed **Entrance** Very difficult **Setting** 76-acre urban campus **Total enrollment** 15,391 **Student-faculty ratio** 17:1 **Application deadline** Rolling (freshmen), rolling (transfer) **Freshmen** 46% were admitted **Housing** No **Expenses** Tuition $3403 **Undergraduates** 63% women, 36% part-time, 37% 25 or older, 0.1% Native American, 15% Hispanic American, 10% African American, 19% Asian American/Pacific Islander **The most frequently chosen baccalaureate fields are** business/marketing, psychology, social sciences and history **Academic program** English as a second language, advanced placement, accelerated degree program, self-designed majors, honors program, summer session, adult/continuing education programs, internships **Contact** Undergraduate Admissions Office, Queens College of the City University of New York, Undergraduate Admissions, Kiely Hall 217, 65-30 Kissena Boulevard, Flushing, NY 11367. Telephone: 718-997-5600. Fax: 718-997-5617. E-mail: admissions@qc.edu. Web site: http://www.qc.edu/.

RABBINICAL ACADEMY MESIVTA RABBI CHAIM BERLIN
BROOKLYN, NEW YORK

Contact Mr. Mayer Weinberger, Executive Administrator, Office of Admissions, Rabbinical Academy Mesivta Rabbi Chaim Berlin, 1605 Coney Island Avenue, Brooklyn, NY 11230-4715. Telephone: 718-377-0777. Fax: 718-338-5578.

RABBINICAL COLLEGE BETH SHRAGA
MONSEY, NEW YORK

Contact Rabbi Schiff, Director of Admissions, Rabbinical College Beth Shraga, 28 Saddle River Road, Monsey, NY 10952-3035. Telephone: 914-356-1980.

NEW YORK

RABBINICAL COLLEGE BOBOVER YESHIVA B'NEI ZION
BROOKLYN, NEW YORK

Contact Mr. Israel Licht, Director of Admissions, Rabbinical College Bobover Yeshiva B'nei Zion, 1577 Forty-eighth Street, Brooklyn, NY 11219. Telephone: 718-438-2018.

RABBINICAL COLLEGE CH'SAN SOFER
BROOKLYN, NEW YORK

Contact Director of Admissions, Rabbinical College Ch'san Sofer, 1876 Fiftieth Street, Brooklyn, NY 11204. Telephone: 718-236-1171.

RABBINICAL COLLEGE OF LONG ISLAND
LONG BEACH, NEW YORK

Contact Director of Admissions, Rabbinical College of Long Island, 201 Magnolia Boulevard, Long Beach, NY 11561-3305. Telephone: 516-431-7414.

RABBINICAL SEMINARY ADAS YEREIM
BROOKLYN, NEW YORK

Contact Mr. Hersch Greenschweig, Director of Admissions, Rabbinical Seminary Adas Yereim, 185 Wilson Street, Brooklyn, NY 11211-7206. Telephone: 718-388-1751.

RABBINICAL SEMINARY M'KOR CHAIM
BROOKLYN, NEW YORK

Contact Rabbi Benjamin Paler, Director of Admissions, Rabbinical Seminary M'kor Chaim, 1571 Fifty-fifth Street, Brooklyn, NY 11219. Telephone: 718-851-0183.

RABBINICAL SEMINARY OF AMERICA
FOREST HILLS, NEW YORK

Contact Rabbi Abraham Semmel, Director of Admissions, Rabbinical Seminary of America, 92-15 Sixty-ninth Avenue, Forest Hills, NY 11375. Telephone: 718-268-4700.

RENSSELAER POLYTECHNIC INSTITUTE
TROY, NEW YORK

General Independent, university, coed **Entrance** Very difficult **Setting** 260-acre suburban campus **Total enrollment** 8,106 **Student-faculty ratio** 16:1 **Application deadline** 1/1 (freshmen), 7/1 (transfer) **Freshmen** 68% were admitted **Housing** Yes **Expenses** Tuition $25,555; Room & Board $8308 **Undergraduates** 24% women, 2% part-time, 3% 25 or older, 0.4% Native American, 5% Hispanic American, 4% African American, 12% Asian American/Pacific Islander **The most frequently chosen baccalaureate fields are** business/marketing, computer/information sciences, engineering/engineering technologies **Academic program** English as a second language, advanced placement, accelerated degree program, self-designed majors, honors program, summer session, adult/continuing education programs, internships **Contact** Ms. Teresa Duffy, Dean of Enrollment Management, Rensselaer Polytechnic Institute, 110 8th Street, Troy, NY 12180-3590. Telephone: 518-276-6216 or toll-free 800-448-6562. Fax: 518-276-4072. E-mail: admissions@rpi.edu. Web site: http://www.rpi.edu/.

▶ For more information, see page 465.

ROBERTS WESLEYAN COLLEGE
ROCHESTER, NEW YORK

General Independent, comprehensive, coed, affiliated with Free Methodist Church of North America **Entrance** Moderately difficult **Setting** 75-acre suburban campus **Total enrollment** 1,697 **Student-faculty ratio** 14:1 **Application deadline** 2/1 (freshmen), rolling (transfer) **Freshmen** 84% were admitted **Housing** Yes **Expenses** Tuition $14,916; Room & Board $5244 **Undergraduates** 66% women, 9% part-time, 25% 25 or older, 0.5% Native American, 3% Hispanic American, 5% African American, 1% Asian American/Pacific Islander **The most frequently chosen baccalaureate fields are** business/marketing, education, health professions and related sciences **Academic program** English as a second language, advanced placement, honors program, summer session, adult/continuing education programs, internships **Contact** Ms. Linda Kurtz, Dean of Admissions, Roberts Wesleyan College, 2301 Westside Drive, Rochester, NY 14624. Telephone: 585-594-6400 or toll-free 800-777-4RWC. Fax: 585-594-6371. E-mail: admissions@roberts.edu. Web site: http://www.roberts.edu/.

ROCHESTER INSTITUTE OF TECHNOLOGY
ROCHESTER, NEW YORK

General Independent, comprehensive, coed **Entrance** Moderately difficult **Setting** 1,300-acre suburban campus **Total enrollment** 14,430 **Student-faculty ratio** 14:1 **Application deadline** 3/15 (freshmen), rolling (transfer) **Freshmen** 70% were admitted **Housing** Yes **Expenses** Tuition $18,966; Room & Board $7266 **Undergraduates** 32% women, 17% part-time, 19% 25 or older, 0.4% Native American, 3% Hispanic American, 5% African American, 6% Asian American/Pacific Islander **The most frequently chosen baccalaureate fields are** engineering/engineering technologies, computer/information sciences, visual/performing arts **Academic program** English as a second language, advanced placement, accelerated degree program, self-designed majors, honors program, summer session, adult/continuing education programs, internships **Contact** Mr. Daniel Shelley, Director of Admissions, Rochester Institute of Technology, 60 Lomb Memorial Drive, Rochester, NY 14623-5604. Telephone: 585-475-6631. Fax: 585-475-7424. E-mail: admissons@rit.edu. Web site: http://www.rit.edu/.

NEW YORK

RUSSELL SAGE COLLEGE
TROY, NEW YORK

General Independent, 4-year, women only **Entrance** Moderately difficult **Setting** 8-acre urban campus **Total enrollment** 797 **Student-faculty ratio** 11:1 **Application deadline** 8/1 (freshmen), rolling (transfer) **Freshmen** 90% were admitted **Housing** Yes **Expenses** Tuition $17,750; Room & Board $6164 **Undergraduates** 7% part-time, 20% 25 or older, 1% Native American, 3% Hispanic American, 6% African American, 3% Asian American/Pacific Islander **The most frequently chosen baccalaureate fields are** education, biological/life sciences, health professions and related sciences **Academic program** English as a second language, advanced placement, accelerated degree program, self-designed majors, honors program, summer session, adult/continuing education programs, internships **Contact** Ms. Beth Robertson, Senior Associate Director of Admissions, Russell Sage College, 45 Ferry Street, Troy, NY 12180. Telephone: 518-244-2217 or toll-free 888-VERY-SAGE (in-state); 888-VERY SAGE (out-of-state). Fax: 518-244-6880. E-mail: rscadmin@sage.edu. Web site: http://www.sage.edu/html/rsc/welcome.html.

SAGE COLLEGE OF ALBANY
ALBANY, NEW YORK

General Independent, 4-year, coed **Entrance** Minimally difficult **Setting** 15-acre urban campus **Total enrollment** 1,271 **Student-faculty ratio** 11:1 **Application deadline** 8/1 (freshmen), 8/1 (transfer) **Freshmen** 70% were admitted **Housing** Yes **Expenses** Tuition $10,200; Room & Board $6164 **Undergraduates** 71% women, 49% part-time, 45% 25 or older, 0.4% Native American, 3% Hispanic American, 12% African American, 1% Asian American/Pacific Islander **The most frequently chosen baccalaureate fields are** business/marketing, protective services/public administration, psychology **Academic program** English as a second language, advanced placement, self-designed majors, honors program, summer session, adult/continuing education programs, internships **Contact** Mr. Rob Janeski, Director of Admission, Sage College of Albany, 140 New Scotland Avenue, Albany, NY 12208. Telephone: 518-292-1730 or toll-free 888-VERY-SAGE. Fax: 518-292-1912. E-mail: scaadm@sage.edu. Web site: http://www.sage.edu/SCA/.

ST. BONAVENTURE UNIVERSITY
ST. BONAVENTURE, NEW YORK

General Independent, comprehensive, coed, affiliated with Roman Catholic Church **Entrance** Moderately difficult **Setting** 600-acre small-town campus **Total enrollment** 2,710 **Student-faculty ratio** 15:1 **Application deadline** 4/15 (freshmen), 8/15 (transfer) **Freshmen** 94% were admitted **Housing** Yes **Expenses** Tuition $16,156; Room & Board $5950 **Undergraduates** 53% women, 4% part-time, 3% 25 or older, 0.1% Native American, 1% Hispanic American, 1% African American, 0.3% Asian American/Pacific Islander **The most frequently chosen baccalaureate fields are** business/marketing, communications/communication technologies, education **Academic program** Advanced placement, self-designed majors, honors program, summer session, internships **Contact** Mr. James Dirisio, Director of Admissions, St. Bonaventure University, PO Box D, St. Bonaventure, NY 14778-2284. Telephone: 716-375-2400 or toll-free 800-462-5050. Fax: 716-375-4005. E-mail: admissions@sbu.edu. Web site: http://www.sbu.edu/.

ST. FRANCIS COLLEGE
BROOKLYN HEIGHTS, NEW YORK

General Independent Roman Catholic, 4-year, coed **Entrance** Moderately difficult **Setting** 1-acre urban campus **Total enrollment** 2,451 **Student-faculty ratio** 20:1 **Application deadline** Rolling (freshmen), rolling (transfer) **Freshmen** 81% were admitted **Housing** No **Expenses** Tuition $9550 **Undergraduates** 58% women, 18% part-time, 20% 25 or older, 0.2% Native American, 14% Hispanic American, 17% African American, 2% Asian American/Pacific Islander **Academic program** English as a second language, advanced placement, accelerated degree program, honors program, summer session, adult/continuing education programs, internships **Contact** Br. George Larkin OSF, Dean of Admissions, St. Francis College, 180 Remsen Street, Brooklyn Heights, NY 11201-4398. Telephone: 718-489-5200. Fax: 718-522-1274. Web site: http://www.stfranciscollege.edu/.

▶ For more information, see page 470.

ST. JOHN FISHER COLLEGE
ROCHESTER, NEW YORK

General Independent, comprehensive, coed, affiliated with Roman Catholic Church **Entrance** Moderately difficult **Setting** 136-acre suburban campus **Total enrollment** 2,968 **Student-faculty ratio** 16:1 **Application deadline** Rolling (freshmen), rolling (transfer) **Freshmen** 72% were admitted **Housing** Yes **Expenses** Tuition $15,550; Room & Board $6600 **Undergraduates** 60% women, 18% part-time, 17% 25 or older, 1% Native American, 2% Hispanic American, 5% African American, 1% Asian American/Pacific Islander **The most frequently chosen baccalaureate fields are** business/marketing, psychology, social sciences and history **Academic program** Advanced placement, accelerated degree program, self-designed majors, honors program, summer session, adult/continuing education programs, internships **Contact** Ms. Stacy A. Ledermann, Director of Freshmen Admissions, St. John Fisher College, 3690 East Avenue, Rochester, NY 14610. Telephone: 585-385-8064 or toll-free 800-444-4640. Fax: 585-385-8386. E-mail: admissions@sjfc.edu. Web site: http://www.sjfc.edu/.

ST. JOHN'S UNIVERSITY
JAMAICA, NEW YORK

General Independent, university, coed, affiliated with Roman Catholic Church **Entrance** Moderately diffi-

NEW YORK

St. John's University *(continued)*
cult **Setting** 95-acre urban campus **Total enrollment** 18,623 **Student-faculty ratio** 18:1 **Application deadline** Rolling (freshmen), rolling (transfer) **Freshmen** 80% were admitted **Housing** Yes **Expenses** Tuition $17,330; Room & Board $9330 **Undergraduates** 57% women, 20% part-time, 9% 25 or older, 0.2% Native American, 15% Hispanic American, 14% African American, 13% Asian American/Pacific Islander **The most frequently chosen baccalaureate fields are** business/marketing, education, health professions and related sciences **Academic program** English as a second language, advanced placement, accelerated degree program, honors program, summer session, adult/continuing education programs, internships **Contact** Mr. Glenn Sklarin, Vice President, Enrollment Management, St. John's University, 8000 Utopia Parkway, Jamaica, NY 11439. Telephone: 718-990-2000 or toll-free 888-9STJOHNS (in-state); 888-9ST JOHNS (out-of-state). Fax: 718-990-1677. E-mail: admissions@stjohns.edu. Web site: http://www.stjohns.edu/.

ST. JOSEPH'S COLLEGE, NEW YORK
BROOKLYN, NEW YORK

General Independent, 4-year, coed **Entrance** Moderately difficult **Setting** urban campus **Total enrollment** 1,189 **Student-faculty ratio** 16:1 **Application deadline** 8/15 (freshmen), 8/15 (transfer) **Freshmen** 51% were admitted **Housing** No **Expenses** Tuition $9802 **Undergraduates** 78% women, 54% part-time, 66% 25 or older, 0% Native American, 9% Hispanic American, 42% African American, 4% Asian American/Pacific Islander **The most frequently chosen baccalaureate fields are** education, business/marketing, health professions and related sciences **Academic program** Advanced placement, honors program, summer session, adult/continuing education programs, internships **Contact** Mr. Michael Learmond, Director of Admissions, St. Joseph's College, New York, 245 Clinton Avenue, Brooklyn, NY 11205-3688. Telephone: 718-636-6868. E-mail: asinfob@sjcny.edu. Web site: http://www.sjcny.edu/.

ST. JOSEPH'S COLLEGE, SUFFOLK CAMPUS
PATCHOGUE, NEW YORK

General Independent, comprehensive, coed **Entrance** Moderately difficult **Setting** 28-acre small-town campus **Total enrollment** 3,444 **Student-faculty ratio** 15:1 **Application deadline** Rolling (freshmen), rolling (transfer) **Freshmen** 74% were admitted **Housing** No **Expenses** Tuition $10,082 **Undergraduates** 78% women, 30% part-time, 45% 25 or older, 0.2% Native American, 4% Hispanic American, 3% African American, 2% Asian American/Pacific Islander **The most frequently chosen baccalaureate fields are** business/marketing, education, health professions and related sciences **Academic program** Advanced placement, summer session, adult/continuing education programs **Contact** Mrs. Marion E. Salgado, Director of Admissions, St. Joseph's

College, Suffolk Campus, 155 West Roe Boulevard, Patchogue, NY 11772. Telephone: 631-447-3219 or toll-free 866-AT ST JOE (in-state). Fax: 631-447-1734. E-mail: admissions_patchogue@sjcny.edu. Web site: http://www.sjcny.edu/.

ST. LAWRENCE UNIVERSITY
CANTON, NEW YORK

General Independent, comprehensive, coed **Entrance** Very difficult **Setting** 1,000-acre small-town campus **Total enrollment** 2,097 **Student-faculty ratio** 11:1 **Application deadline** 2/15 (freshmen), 4/1 (transfer) **Freshmen** 61% were admitted **Housing** Yes **Expenses** Tuition $24,850; Room & Board $7755 **Undergraduates** 53% women, 1% part-time, 0% 25 or older, 0.4% Native American, 2% Hispanic American, 2% African American, 1% Asian American/Pacific Islander **The most frequently chosen baccalaureate fields are** biological/life sciences, psychology, social sciences and history **Academic program** Advanced placement, self-designed majors, summer session, internships **Contact** Ms. Terry Cowdrey, Dean of Admissions and Financial Aid, St. Lawrence University, Canton, NY 13617-1455. Telephone: 315-229-5261 or toll-free 800-285-1856. Fax: 315-229-5818. E-mail: admissions@stlawu.edu. Web site: http://www.stlawu.edu/.

ST. THOMAS AQUINAS COLLEGE
SPARKILL, NEW YORK

General Independent, comprehensive, coed **Entrance** Moderately difficult **Setting** 46-acre suburban campus **Total enrollment** 2,140 **Student-faculty ratio** 17:1 **Application deadline** Rolling (freshmen), rolling (transfer) **Freshmen** 75% were admitted **Housing** Yes **Expenses** Tuition $13,440 **Undergraduates** 55% women, 35% part-time, 21% 25 or older, 0.1% Native American, 11% Hispanic American, 6% African American, 3% Asian American/Pacific Islander **Academic program** English as a second language, advanced placement, accelerated degree program, honors program, summer session, adult/continuing education programs, internships **Contact** Mr. John Edel, Dean of Enrollment Management, St. Thomas Aquinas College, 125 Route 340, Sparkill, NY 10976. Telephone: 914-398-4100 or toll-free 800-999-STAC. E-mail: joestacenroll@rockland.net. Web site: http://www.stac.edu/.

SARAH LAWRENCE COLLEGE
BRONXVILLE, NEW YORK

General Independent, comprehensive, coed **Entrance** Very difficult **Setting** 40-acre suburban campus **Total enrollment** 1,553 **Student-faculty ratio** 6:1 **Application deadline** 1/15 (freshmen), 3/1 (transfer) **Freshmen** 37% were admitted **Housing** Yes **Expenses** Tuition $27,982; Room & Board $9534 **Undergraduates** 73% women, 6% part-time, 5% 25 or older, 0.4% Native American, 4% Hispanic American, 5% African American, 5% Asian American/Pacific Islander **The most frequently chosen baccalaureate field is**

liberal arts/general studies **Academic program** Advanced placement, self-designed majors, adult/continuing education programs, internships **Contact** Ms. Thyra L. Briggs, Dean of Admission, Sarah Lawrence College, 1 Mead Way, Bronxville, NY 10708-5999. Telephone: 914-395-2510 or toll-free 800-888-2858. Fax: 914-395-2515. E-mail: slcadmit@slc.edu. Web site: http://www.slc.edu/.

SCHOOL OF VISUAL ARTS
NEW YORK, NEW YORK

General Proprietary, comprehensive, coed **Entrance** Moderately difficult **Setting** 1-acre urban campus **Total enrollment** 5,186 **Student-faculty ratio** 8:1 **Application deadline** Rolling (freshmen), rolling (transfer) **Freshmen** 62% were admitted **Housing** Yes **Expenses** Tuition $17,000; Room only $6700 **Undergraduates** 52% women, 38% part-time, 16% 25 or older, 0.4% Native American, 9% Hispanic American, 4% African American, 11% Asian American/ Pacific Islander **The most frequently chosen baccalaureate field is** visual/performing arts **Academic program** English as a second language, summer session, adult/continuing education programs, internships **Contact** Mr. Richard M. Longo, Executive Director of Admissions, School of Visual Arts, 209 East 23rd Street, New York, NY 10010-3994. Telephone: 212-592-2100 or toll-free 800-436-4204. Fax: 212-592-2116. E-mail: admissions@adm.schoolofvisualarts.edu. Web site: http://www.schoolofvisualarts.edu/.

SH'OR YOSHUV RABBINICAL COLLEGE
FAR ROCKAWAY, NEW YORK

Contact Rabbi Avrohom Halpern, Executive Director, Sh'or Yoshuv Rabbinical College, 1284 Central Avenue, Far Rockaway, NY 11691-4002. Telephone: 718-327-7244.

SIENA COLLEGE
LOUDONVILLE, NEW YORK

General Independent Roman Catholic, 4-year, coed **Entrance** Moderately difficult **Setting** 155-acre suburban campus **Total enrollment** 3,384 **Student-faculty ratio** 14:1 **Application deadline** 3/1 (freshmen), 6/1 (transfer) **Freshmen** 69% were admitted **Housing** Yes **Expenses** Tuition $15,870; Room & Board $6815 **Undergraduates** 54% women, 14% part-time, 8% 25 or older, 0.2% Native American, 2% Hispanic American, 2% African American, 2% Asian American/Pacific Islander **The most frequently chosen baccalaureate fields are** business/marketing, psychology, social sciences and history **Academic program** Advanced placement, honors program, summer session, adult/continuing education programs, internships **Contact** Mr. Edward Jones, Director of Admissions, Siena College, 515 Loudon Road, Loudonville, NY 12211-1462. Telephone: 518-783-2423 or toll-free 888-ATSIENA. Fax: 518-783-2436. E-mail: admit@siena.edu. Web site: http://www.siena.edu/.

SKIDMORE COLLEGE
SARATOGA SPRINGS, NEW YORK

General Independent, comprehensive, coed **Entrance** Very difficult **Setting** 800-acre small-town campus **Total enrollment** 2,544 **Student-faculty ratio** 11:1 **Application deadline** 1/15 (freshmen), 4/1 (transfer) **Freshmen** 42% were admitted **Housing** Yes **Expenses** Tuition $26,676; Room & Board $7525 **Undergraduates** 60% women, 10% part-time, 0% 25 or older, 0.4% Native American, 5% Hispanic American, 5% African American, 4% Asian American/Pacific Islander **The most frequently chosen baccalaureate fields are** business/marketing, social sciences and history, visual/performing arts **Academic program** Advanced placement, accelerated degree program, self-designed majors, honors program, summer session, adult/continuing education programs, internships **Contact** Ms. Mary Lou W. Bates, Director of Admissions, Skidmore College, 815 North Broadway, Saratoga Springs, NY 12866-1632. Telephone: 518-580-5570 or toll-free 800-867-6007. Fax: 518-580-5584. E-mail: admissions@scott.skidmore.edu. Web site: http://www.skidmore.edu/.

STATE UNIVERSITY OF NEW YORK AT ALBANY
ALBANY, NEW YORK

General State-supported, university, coed **Entrance** Moderately difficult **Setting** 560-acre suburban campus **Total enrollment** 16,831 **Student-faculty ratio** 19:1 **Application deadline** 3/1 (freshmen), 4/1 (transfer) **Freshmen** 58% were admitted **Housing** Yes **Expenses** Tuition $4720; Room & Board $6635 **Undergraduates** 49% women, 9% part-time, 10% 25 or older, 0.2% Native American, 7% Hispanic American, 9% African American, 7% Asian American/Pacific Islander **The most frequently chosen baccalaureate fields are** mathematics, health professions and related sciences, protective services/public administration **Academic program** English as a second language, advanced placement, self-designed majors, honors program, summer session, internships **Contact** Mr. Harry Wood, Director of Undergraduate Admissions, State University of New York at Albany, 1400 Washington Avenue, University Administration Building 101, Albany, NY 12222. Telephone: 518-442-5435 or toll-free 800-293-7869 (in-state). E-mail: ugadmissions@albany.edu. Web site: http://www.albany.edu/.

STATE UNIVERSITY OF NEW YORK AT BINGHAMTON
BINGHAMTON, NEW YORK

General State-supported, university, coed **Entrance** Very difficult **Setting** 606-acre suburban campus **Total enrollment** 12,820 **Student-faculty ratio** 19:1 **Application deadline** Rolling (freshmen), rolling (transfer) **Freshmen** 45% were admitted **Housing** Yes **Expenses** Tuition $4551; Room & Board $6102 **Undergraduates** 54% women, 3% part-time, 4% 25 or older, 0.3% Native American, 5% Hispanic Ameri-

NEW YORK

State University of New York at Binghamton *(continued)*

can, 6% African American, 17% Asian American/Pacific Islander **The most frequently chosen baccalaureate fields are** business/marketing, psychology, social sciences and history **Academic program** English as a second language, advanced placement, accelerated degree program, self-designed majors, honors program, summer session, adult/continuing education programs, internships **Contact** Cheryl S. Brown, Acting Director of Admissions, State University of New York at Binghamton, PO Box 6001, Binghamton, NY 13902-6001. Telephone: 607-777-2000. Fax: 607-777-4445. E-mail: admit@binghamton.edu. Web site: http://www.binghamton.edu/.

STATE UNIVERSITY OF NEW YORK AT BUFFALO
See University at Buffalo, The State University of New York

STATE UNIVERSITY OF NEW YORK AT FARMINGDALE
FARMINGDALE, NEW YORK

General State-supported, 4-year, coed **Entrance** Moderately difficult **Setting** 380-acre small-town campus **Total enrollment** 5,449 **Student-faculty ratio** 20:1 **Application deadline** Rolling (freshmen), rolling (transfer) **Freshmen** 70% were admitted **Housing** Yes **Expenses** Tuition $4139; Room & Board $7130 **Undergraduates** 44% women, 39% part-time, 33% 25 or older, 0.1% Native American, 10% Hispanic American, 14% African American, 4% Asian American/Pacific Islander **The most frequently chosen baccalaureate fields are** engineering/engineering technologies, communications/communication technologies, trade and industry **Academic program** Advanced placement, summer session, internships **Contact** Ms. Kathleen Fitzwilliam, Assistant Dean for Enrollment Services, State University of New York at Farmingdale, Route 110, Farmingdale, NY 11735-1021. Telephone: 631-420-2457 or toll-free 877-4-FARMINGDALE. Fax: 631-420-2633. E-mail: admissions@farmingdale.edu. Web site: http://www.farmingdale.edu/.

STATE UNIVERSITY OF NEW YORK AT NEW PALTZ
NEW PALTZ, NEW YORK

General State-supported, comprehensive, coed **Entrance** Moderately difficult **Setting** 216-acre small-town campus **Total enrollment** 7,868 **Student-faculty ratio** 17:1 **Application deadline** 3/30 (freshmen), 6/1 (transfer) **Freshmen** 35% were admitted **Housing** Yes **Expenses** Tuition $4000; Room & Board $5600 **Undergraduates** 63% women, 15% part-time, 18% 25 or older, 0.2% Native American, 9% Hispanic American, 8% African American, 4% Asian American/Pacific Islander **The most frequently chosen baccalaureate fields are** education, business/marketing, social sciences and history **Academic program** English as a second language, advanced placement, honors program, summer session, adult/continuing education programs, internships **Contact** Ms. Kimberly A. Lavoie, Director of Freshmen and International Admissions, State University of New York at New Paltz, 75 South Manheim Boulevard, Suite 1, New Paltz, NY 12561-2499. Telephone: 845-257-3200 or toll-free 888-639-7589 (in-state). Fax: 845-257-3209. E-mail: admissions@newpaltz.edu. Web site: http://www.newpaltz.edu/.

STATE UNIVERSITY OF NEW YORK AT OSWEGO
OSWEGO, NEW YORK

General State-supported, comprehensive, coed **Entrance** Moderately difficult **Setting** 696-acre small-town campus **Total enrollment** 8,407 **Student-faculty ratio** 20:1 **Application deadline** Rolling (freshmen), rolling (transfer) **Freshmen** 58% were admitted **Housing** Yes **Expenses** Tuition $4160; Room & Board $6696 **Undergraduates** 54% women, 10% part-time, 16% 25 or older, 0.5% Native American, 3% Hispanic American, 4% African American, 2% Asian American/Pacific Islander **The most frequently chosen baccalaureate fields are** business/marketing, communications/communication technologies, education **Academic program** English as a second language, advanced placement, accelerated degree program, self-designed majors, honors program, summer session, adult/continuing education programs, internships **Contact** Dr. Joseph F. Grant Jr., Vice President for Development, Enrollment, and Marketing, State University of New York at Oswego, 7060 State Route 104, Oswego, NY 13126. Telephone: 315-312-2250. Fax: 315-312-3260. E-mail: admiss@oswego.edu. Web site: http://www.oswego.edu/.

STATE UNIVERSITY OF NEW YORK AT STONY BROOK
See Stony Brook University, State University of New York

STATE UNIVERSITY OF NEW YORK COLLEGE AT BROCKPORT
BROCKPORT, NEW YORK

General State-supported, comprehensive, coed **Entrance** Moderately difficult **Setting** 435-acre small-town campus **Total enrollment** 8,634 **Student-faculty ratio** 19:1 **Application deadline** Rolling (freshmen), rolling (transfer) **Freshmen** 54% were admitted **Housing** Yes **Expenses** Tuition $4127; Room & Board $6140 **Undergraduates** 58% women, 15% part-time, 20% 25 or older, 0.4% Native American, 2% Hispanic American, 6% African American, 1% Asian American/Pacific Islander **The most frequently chosen baccalaureate fields are** business/marketing, health professions and related sciences, protective services/public administration **Academic program** Advanced placement, accelerated degree program, self-designed majors, honors program, sum-

NEW YORK

mer session, internships **Contact** Mr. Bernard S. Valento, Associate Director of Undergraduate Admissions, State University of New York College at Brockport, 350 New Campus Drive, Brockport, NY 14420-2997. Telephone: 585-395-5059 Ext. 5059 or toll-free 800-382-8447 (in-state). Fax: 585-395-5452. E-mail: ccasalin@brockuma.cc.brockport.edu. Web site: http://www.brockport.edu/.

STATE UNIVERSITY OF NEW YORK COLLEGE AT BUFFALO
BUFFALO, NEW YORK

General State-supported, comprehensive, coed **Entrance** Moderately difficult **Setting** 115-acre urban campus **Total enrollment** 11,743 **Student-faculty ratio** 18:1 **Application deadline** Rolling (freshmen), rolling (transfer) **Freshmen** 57% were admitted **Housing** Yes **Expenses** Tuition $4029; Room & Board $5484 **Undergraduates** 60% women, 18% part-time, 27% 25 or older, 1% Native American, 4% Hispanic American, 11% African American, 1% Asian American/Pacific Islander **The most frequently chosen baccalaureate fields are** business/marketing, education, social sciences and history **Academic program** English as a second language, advanced placement, honors program, summer session, adult/continuing education programs, internships **Contact** Ms. Lesa Loritts, Director of Admissions, State University of New York College at Buffalo, 1300 Elmwood Avenue, Buffalo, NY 14222-1095. Telephone: 716-878-5519. Fax: 716-878-6100. E-mail: admissio@buffalostate.edu. Web site: http://www.buffalostate.edu/.

STATE UNIVERSITY OF NEW YORK COLLEGE AT CORTLAND
CORTLAND, NEW YORK

General State-supported, comprehensive, coed **Entrance** Moderately difficult **Setting** 191-acre small-town campus **Total enrollment** 7,705 **Student-faculty ratio** 16:1 **Freshmen** 55% were admitted **Housing** Yes **Expenses** Tuition $4174; Room & Board $6390 **Undergraduates** 59% women, 5% part-time, 8% 25 or older, 0.3% Native American, 3% Hispanic American, 2% African American, 1% Asian American/Pacific Islander **The most frequently chosen baccalaureate fields are** education, health professions and related sciences, social sciences and history **Academic program** Advanced placement, self-designed majors, honors program, summer session, adult/continuing education programs, internships **Contact** Mr. Gradon Avery, Director of Admission, State University of New York College at Cortland, PO Box 2000, Cortland, NY 13045. Telephone: 607-753-4711. Fax: 607-753-5998. E-mail: admssn_info@snycorva.cortland.edu. Web site: http://www.cortland.edu/.

STATE UNIVERSITY OF NEW YORK COLLEGE AT FREDONIA
FREDONIA, NEW YORK

General State-supported, comprehensive, coed **Entrance** Moderately difficult **Setting** 266-acre small-town campus **Total enrollment** 5,305 **Student-faculty ratio** 19:1 **Application deadline** Rolling (freshmen), rolling (transfer) **Freshmen** 60% were admitted **Housing** Yes **Expenses** Tuition $4275; Room & Board $5600 **Undergraduates** 59% women, 6% part-time, 7% 25 or older, 1% Native American, 2% Hispanic American, 1% African American, 1% Asian American/Pacific Islander **The most frequently chosen baccalaureate fields are** business/marketing, communications/communication technologies, education **Academic program** Advanced placement, accelerated degree program, self-designed majors, honors program, summer session, adult/continuing education programs, internships **Contact** Mr. J. Denis Bolton, Director of Admissions, State University of New York College at Fredonia, Fredonia, NY 14063-1136. Telephone: 716-673-3251 or toll-free 800-252-1212. Fax: 716-673-3249. E-mail: admissionsinq@fredonia.edu. Web site: http://www.fredonia.edu/.

STATE UNIVERSITY OF NEW YORK COLLEGE AT GENESEO
GENESEO, NEW YORK

General State-supported, comprehensive, coed **Entrance** Very difficult **Setting** 220-acre small-town campus **Total enrollment** 5,649 **Student-faculty ratio** 19:1 **Application deadline** 2/15 (freshmen), 1/15 (transfer) **Freshmen** 52% were admitted **Housing** Yes **Expenses** Tuition $4310; Room & Board $5660 **Undergraduates** 65% women, 2% part-time, 3% 25 or older, 0.2% Native American, 3% Hispanic American, 2% African American, 5% Asian American/Pacific Islander **The most frequently chosen baccalaureate fields are** education, business/marketing, social sciences and history **Academic program** English as a second language, advanced placement, honors program, summer session, internships **Contact** Kris Shay, Associate Director of Admissions, State University of New York College at Geneseo, 1 College Circle, Geneseo, NY 14454-1401. Telephone: 585-245-5571 or toll-free 866-245-5211 (in-state). Fax: 585-245-5550. E-mail: admissions@geneseo.edu. Web site: http://www.geneseo.edu/.

STATE UNIVERSITY OF NEW YORK COLLEGE AT OLD WESTBURY
OLD WESTBURY, NEW YORK

General State-supported, comprehensive, coed **Entrance** Minimally difficult **Setting** 605-acre suburban campus **Total enrollment** 3,076 **Student-faculty ratio** 22:1 **Application deadline** Rolling (freshmen), 12/15 (transfer) **Freshmen** 50% were admitted **Housing** Yes **Expenses** Tuition $3985; Room & Board $5769 **Undergraduates** 60% women, 24% part-time, 37% 25 or older, 0.2% Native American, 15% Hispanic American, 30% African Ameri-

NEW YORK

State University of New York College at Old Westbury *(continued)*
can, 8% Asian American/Pacific Islander **The most frequently chosen baccalaureate fields are** business/marketing, education, social sciences and history **Academic program** English as a second language, advanced placement, summer session, internships **Contact** Ms. Mary Marquez Bell, Vice President, State University of New York College at Old Westbury, PO Box 307, Old Westbury, NY 11568. Telephone: 516-876-3073. Fax: 516-876-3307. Web site: http://www.oldwestbury.edu/.

STATE UNIVERSITY OF NEW YORK COLLEGE AT ONEONTA
ONEONTA, NEW YORK

General State-supported, comprehensive, coed **Entrance** Moderately difficult **Setting** 250-acre small-town campus **Total enrollment** 5,740 **Student-faculty ratio** 18:1 **Application deadline** Rolling (freshmen), rolling (transfer) **Freshmen** 52% were admitted **Housing** Yes **Expenses** Tuition $4231; Room & Board $5750 **Undergraduates** 60% women, 4% part-time, 9% 25 or older, 0.2% Native American, 4% Hispanic American, 3% African American, 2% Asian American/Pacific Islander **The most frequently chosen baccalaureate fields are** business/marketing, education, home economics/vocational home economics **Academic program** English as a second language, advanced placement, honors program, summer session, adult/continuing education programs, internships **Contact** Ms. Karen A. Brown, Director of Admissions, State University of New York College at Oneonta, Alumni Hall 116, Oneonta, NY 13820-4015. Telephone: 607-436-2524 or toll-free 800-SUNY-123. Fax: 607-436-3074. E-mail: admissions@oneonta.edu. Web site: http://www.oneonta.edu/.

STATE UNIVERSITY OF NEW YORK COLLEGE AT POTSDAM
POTSDAM, NEW YORK

General State-supported, comprehensive, coed **Entrance** Moderately difficult **Setting** 240-acre small-town campus **Total enrollment** 4,325 **Student-faculty ratio** 18:1 **Application deadline** Rolling (freshmen), rolling (transfer) **Freshmen** 67% were admitted **Housing** Yes **Expenses** Tuition $4129; Room & Board $6390 **Undergraduates** 59% women, 5% part-time, 14% 25 or older, 2% Native American, 2% Hispanic American, 2% African American, 1% Asian American/Pacific Islander **The most frequently chosen baccalaureate fields are** psychology, education, social sciences and history **Academic program** Advanced placement, self-designed majors, honors program, summer session, adult/continuing education programs, internships **Contact** Mr. Thomas Nesbitt, Director of Admissions, State University of New York College at Potsdam, 44 Pierrepont Avenue, Potsdam, NY 13676. Telephone: 315-267-2180 or toll-free 877-POTSDAM. Fax: 315-267-2163. E-mail: admissions@potsdam.edu. Web site: http://www.potsdam.edu/.

STATE UNIVERSITY OF NEW YORK COLLEGE OF AGRICULTURE AND TECHNOLOGY AT COBLESKILL
COBLESKILL, NEW YORK

General State-supported, 4-year, coed **Entrance** Moderately difficult **Setting** 750-acre rural campus **Total enrollment** 2,450 **Student-faculty ratio** 17:1 **Application deadline** Rolling (freshmen), rolling (transfer) **Freshmen** 84% were admitted **Housing** Yes **Expenses** Tuition $4740; Room & Board $6460 **Undergraduates** 44% women, 7% part-time, 11% 25 or older, 0.4% Native American, 4% Hispanic American, 6% African American, 1% Asian American/Pacific Islander **The most frequently chosen baccalaureate fields are** agriculture, computer/information sciences **Academic program** Advanced placement, honors program, summer session, adult/continuing education programs, internships **Contact** Mr. Clayton Smith, Director of Admissions, State University of New York College of Agriculture and Technology at Cobleskill, Cobleskill, NY 12043. Telephone: 518-255-5525 or toll-free 800-295-8988. Fax: 518-255-6769. E-mail: admwpc@cobleskill.edu. Web site: http://www.cobleskill.edu/.

STATE UNIVERSITY OF NEW YORK COLLEGE OF ENVIRONMENTAL SCIENCE AND FORESTRY
SYRACUSE, NEW YORK

General State-supported, university, coed **Entrance** Very difficult **Setting** 12-acre urban campus **Total enrollment** 1,971 **Student-faculty ratio** 12:1 **Application deadline** Rolling (freshmen), rolling (transfer) **Freshmen** 57% were admitted **Housing** Yes **Expenses** Tuition $3776; Room & Board $8670 **Undergraduates** 39% women, 12% part-time, 12% 25 or older, 0.4% Native American, 3% Hispanic American, 3% African American, 2% Asian American/Pacific Islander **The most frequently chosen baccalaureate fields are** biological/life sciences, architecture, natural resources/environmental science **Academic program** English as a second language, advanced placement, accelerated degree program, honors program, adult/continuing education programs, internships **Contact** Ms. Susan Sanford, Director of Admissions, State University of New York College of Environmental Science and Forestry, 1 Forestry Drive, Syracuse, NY 13210-2779. Telephone: 315-470-6600 or toll-free 800-777-7373. Fax: 315-470-6933. E-mail: esfinfo@lmailbox.syr.edu. Web site: http://www.esf.edu/.

STATE UNIVERSITY OF NEW YORK EMPIRE STATE COLLEGE
SARATOGA SPRINGS, NEW YORK

General State-supported, comprehensive, coed **Entrance** Minimally difficult **Setting** small-town campus **Total enrollment** 8,395 **Student-faculty ratio** 30:1 **Application deadline** Rolling (freshmen), rolling (transfer) **Freshmen** 43% were admitted **Hous-**

ing No **Expenses** Tuition $3555 **Undergraduates** 55% women, 72% part-time, 85% 25 or older, 1% Native American, 7% Hispanic American, 13% African American, 1% Asian American/Pacific Islander **The most frequently chosen baccalaureate fields are** business/marketing, interdisciplinary studies, protective services/public administration **Academic program** Advanced placement, self-designed majors, adult/continuing education programs **Contact** Ms. Jennifer Riley, Assistant Director of Admissions, State University of New York Empire State College, 2 Union Avenue, Saratoga Springs, NY 12866-4397. Telephone: 518-587-2100 Ext. 214 or toll-free 800-847-3000 (out-of-state). Fax: 518-580-0105. Web site: http://www.esc.edu/.

STATE UNIVERSITY OF NEW YORK HEALTH SCIENCE CENTER AT BROOKLYN
BROOKLYN, NEW YORK

General State-supported, upper-level, coed **Entrance** Moderately difficult **Setting** urban campus **Total enrollment** 1,451 **Application deadline** 5/1 (transfer) **Housing** Yes **Expenses** Tuition $4,002; Room & Board $9041 **Undergraduates** 87% women, 50% part-time, 7% Hispanic American, 47% African American, 6% Asian American/Pacific Islander **The most frequently chosen baccalaureate field is** health professions and related sciences **Academic program** Advanced placement, accelerated degree program, summer session, adult/continuing education programs, internships **Contact** Ms. Lorraine Terracina, Associate Vice President of Student Affairs and Dean of Students, State University of New York Health Science Center at Brooklyn, 450 Clarkson Avenue, Box 60, Brooklyn, NY 11203. Telephone: 718-270-2446 or toll-free 718-270-2446 (in-state). Fax: 718-270-7592. Web site: http://www.downstate.edu/.

STATE UNIVERSITY OF NEW YORK INSTITUTE OF TECHNOLOGY AT UTICA/ROME
UTICA, NEW YORK

General State-supported, upper-level, coed **Setting** 800-acre suburban campus **Total enrollment** 2,537 **Student-faculty ratio** 19:1 **Application deadline** Rolling (transfer) **Housing** Yes **Expenses** Tuition $4055; Room & Board $6240 **Undergraduates** 49% women, 42% part-time, 56% 25 or older, 1% Native American, 3% Hispanic American, 6% African American, 4% Asian American/Pacific Islander **The most frequently chosen baccalaureate fields are** business/marketing, computer/information sciences, engineering/engineering technologies **Academic program** English as a second language, advanced placement, accelerated degree program, summer session, adult/continuing education programs, internships **Contact** Ms. Marybeth Lyons, Director of Admissions, State University of New York Institute of Technology at Utica/Rome, PO Box 3050, Utica, NY 13504-3050. Telephone: 315-792-7500 or toll-free 800-SUNYTEC. Fax: 315-792-7837. E-mail: admissions@sunyit.edu. Web site: http://www.sunyit.edu/.

STATE UNIVERSITY OF NEW YORK MARITIME COLLEGE
THROGGS NECK, NEW YORK

General State-supported, comprehensive, coed, primarily men **Entrance** Moderately difficult **Setting** 56-acre suburban campus **Total enrollment** 764 **Student-faculty ratio** 8:1 **Application deadline** Rolling (freshmen), rolling (transfer) **Freshmen** 84% were admitted **Housing** Yes **Expenses** Tuition $5900; Room & Board $5900 **Undergraduates** 13% women, 8% part-time, 7% 25 or older, 0.2% Native American, 8% Hispanic American, 6% African American, 4% Asian American/Pacific Islander **The most frequently chosen baccalaureate fields are** business/marketing, engineering/engineering technologies, natural resources/environmental science **Academic program** Advanced placement, self-designed majors, summer session, adult/continuing education programs, internships **Contact** Ms. Deirdre Whitman, Vice President of Enrollment and Campus Life, State University of New York Maritime College, 6 Pennyfield Avenue, Throggs Neck, NY 10465-4198. Telephone: 718-409-7220 Ext. 7222 or toll-free 800-654-1874 (in-state); 800-642-1874 (out-of-state). Fax: 718-409-7465. E-mail: admissions@sunymaritime.edu. Web site: http://www.sunymaritime.edu/.

STATE UNIVERSITY OF NEW YORK UPSTATE MEDICAL UNIVERSITY
SYRACUSE, NEW YORK

General State-supported, upper-level, coed **Entrance** Moderately difficult **Setting** 25-acre urban campus **Total enrollment** 1,155 **Student-faculty ratio** 10:1 **Application deadline** Rolling (transfer) **First-Year Students** 49% were admitted **Housing** Yes **Expenses** Tuition $3860; Room & Board $6665 **Undergraduates** 80% women, 50% part-time, 63% 25 or older, 1% Native American, 0.4% Hispanic American, 4% African American, 4% Asian American/Pacific Islander **The most frequently chosen baccalaureate field is** health professions and related sciences **Academic program** Advanced placement, summer session, internships **Contact** Ms. Donna L. Vavonese, Associate Director of Admissions, State University of New York Upstate Medical University, Weiskotten Hall, 766 Irving Avenue, Syracuse, NY 13210. Telephone: 315-464-4570 or toll-free 800-736-2171. Fax: 315-464-8867. E-mail: stuadmis@upstate.edu. Web site: http://www.upstate.edu/.

STONY BROOK UNIVERSITY, STATE UNIVERSITY OF NEW YORK
STONY BROOK, NEW YORK

General State-supported, university, coed **Entrance** Very difficult **Setting** 1,100-acre small-town campus **Total enrollment** 20,855 **Student-faculty ratio** 18:1 **Application deadline** Rolling (freshmen), rolling

NEW YORK

Stony Brook University, State University of New York *(continued)*

(transfer) **Freshmen** 50% were admitted **Housing** Yes **Expenses** Tuition $4268; Room & Board $6730 **Undergraduates** 48% women, 10% part-time, 13% 25 or older, 0.1% Native American, 8% Hispanic American, 10% African American, 23% Asian American/Pacific Islander **The most frequently chosen baccalaureate fields are** psychology, biological/life sciences, social sciences and history **Academic program** English as a second language, advanced placement, self-designed majors, honors program, summer session, adult/continuing education programs, internships **Contact** Ms. Gigi Lamens, Director of Admissions and Enrollment Planning, Stony Brook University, State University of New York, Nicolls Road, Stony Brook, NY 11794. Telephone: 631-632-6868 or toll-free 800-USB-SUNY (out-of-state). E-mail: admiss@mail.upsa.sunysb.edu. Web site: http://www.stonybrook.edu/.

SYRACUSE UNIVERSITY
SYRACUSE, NEW YORK

General Independent, university, coed **Entrance** Very difficult **Setting** 200-acre urban campus **Total enrollment** 14,421 **Student-faculty ratio** 12:1 **Application deadline** 1/1 (freshmen), 1/1 (transfer) **Freshmen** 64% were admitted **Housing** Yes **Expenses** Tuition $21,960; Room & Board $8750 **Undergraduates** 55% women, 1% part-time, 2% 25 or older, 0.2% Native American, 4% Hispanic American, 7% African American, 5% Asian American/Pacific Islander **The most frequently chosen baccalaureate fields are** business/marketing, communications/communication technologies, social sciences and history **Academic program** English as a second language, advanced placement, accelerated degree program, self-designed majors, honors program, summer session, adult/continuing education programs, internships **Contact** Office of Admissions, Syracuse University, 201 Tolley Administration Building, Syracuse, NY 13244-1100. Telephone: 315-443-3611. E-mail: orange@suadmin.syr.edu. Web site: http://www.syracuse.edu/.

TALMUDICAL INSTITUTE OF UPSTATE NEW YORK
ROCHESTER, NEW YORK

General Independent Jewish, 5-year, men only **Entrance** Noncompetitive **Setting** 1-acre urban campus **Total enrollment** 30 **Application deadline** Rolling (freshmen), rolling (transfer) **Freshmen** 100% were admitted **Housing** Yes **Undergraduates** 0% 25 or older **Academic program** Self-designed majors **Contact** Director of Admissions, Talmudical Institute of Upstate New York, 769 Park Avenue, Rochester, NY 14607-3046. Telephone: 716-473-2810.

TALMUDICAL SEMINARY OHOLEI TORAH
BROOKLYN, NEW YORK

Contact Rabbi E. Piekarski, Director of Academic Affairs, Talmudical Seminary Oholei Torah, 667 Eastern Parkway, Brooklyn, NY 11213-3310. Telephone: 718-363-2034.

TORAH TEMIMAH TALMUDICAL SEMINARY
BROOKLYN, NEW YORK

Contact Rabbi I. Hisiger, Principal, Torah Temimah Talmudical Seminary, 555 Ocean Parkway, Brooklyn, NY 11218-5913. Telephone: 718-853-8500.

TOURO COLLEGE
NEW YORK, NEW YORK

General Independent, comprehensive, coed **Entrance** Moderately difficult **Setting** urban campus **Total enrollment** 7,791 **Student-faculty ratio** 21:1 **Application deadline** Rolling (freshmen), rolling (transfer) **Freshmen** 69% were admitted **Housing** Yes **Expenses** Tuition $10,250; Room only $4700 **Undergraduates** 69% women, 12% part-time, 51% 25 or older **The most frequently chosen baccalaureate fields are** business/marketing, health professions and related sciences, liberal arts/general studies **Academic program** English as a second language, advanced placement, accelerated degree program, self-designed majors, honors program, summer session, internships **Contact** Mr. Andre Baron, Director of Admissions, Touro College, 27-33 West 23rd Street, New York, NY 10010. Telephone: 212-463-0400 Ext. 665. Web site: http://www.touro.edu/.

UNION COLLEGE
SCHENECTADY, NEW YORK

General Independent, comprehensive, coed **Entrance** Very difficult **Setting** 100-acre suburban campus **Total enrollment** 2,427 **Student-faculty ratio** 11:1 **Application deadline** 1/15 (freshmen), 6/1 (transfer) **Freshmen** 41% were admitted **Housing** Yes **Expenses** Tuition $26,007; Room & Board $6639 **Undergraduates** 48% women, 2% part-time, 0% 25 or older, 0.1% Native American, 4% Hispanic American, 4% African American, 5% Asian American/Pacific Islander **The most frequently chosen baccalaureate fields are** business/marketing, engineering/engineering technologies, social sciences and history **Academic program** English as a second language, advanced placement, accelerated degree program, self-designed majors, honors program, summer session, internships **Contact** Mr. Daniel Lundquist, Vice President for Admissions and Financial Aid, Union College, Grant Hall, Schenectady, NY 12308. Telephone: 518-388-6112 or toll-free 888-843-6688 (in-state). Fax: 518-388-6986. E-mail: admissions@union.edu. Web site: http://www.union.edu/.

NEW YORK

UNITED STATES MERCHANT MARINE ACADEMY
KINGS POINT, NEW YORK

General Federally supported, 4-year, coed **Entrance** Very difficult **Setting** 80-acre suburban campus **Total enrollment** 931 **Student-faculty ratio** 12:1 **Application deadline** 3/1 (freshmen), 3/1 (transfer) **Freshmen** 18% were admitted **Housing** Yes **Undergraduates** 10% women, 0% 25 or older **The most frequently chosen baccalaureate field is** engineering/engineering technologies **Academic program** Honors program, internships **Contact** Capt. James M. Skinner, Director of Admissions, United States Merchant Marine Academy, 300 Steamboat Road, Wiley Hall, Kings Point, NY 11024-1699. Telephone: 516-773-5391 or toll-free 800-732-6267 (out-of-state). Fax: 516-773-5390. E-mail: admissions@usmma.edu. Web site: http://www.usmma.edu/.

UNITED STATES MILITARY ACADEMY
WEST POINT, NEW YORK

General Federally supported, 4-year, coed, primarily men **Entrance** Most difficult **Setting** 16,080-acre small-town campus **Total enrollment** 4,394 **Student-faculty ratio** 7:1 **Application deadline** 3/21 (freshmen), 3/21 (transfer) **Freshmen** 15% were admitted **Housing** Yes **Undergraduates** 20% women, 0% 25 or older, 1% Native American, 6% Hispanic American, 8% African American, 6% Asian American/Pacific Islander **The most frequently chosen baccalaureate fields are** engineering/engineering technologies, physical sciences, social sciences and history **Academic program** Advanced placement, summer session **Contact** Col. Michael C. Jones, Director of Admissions, United States Military Academy, United States Military Academy, West Point, NY 10996. Telephone: 845-938-4041. E-mail: 8dad@sunams.usma.army.mil. Web site: http://www.usma.edu/.

▶ For more information, see page 484.

UNITED TALMUDICAL SEMINARY
BROOKLYN, NEW YORK

Contact Director of Admissions, United Talmudical Seminary, 82 Lee Avenue, Brooklyn, NY 11211-7900. Telephone: 719-963-9770.

UNIVERSITY AT BUFFALO, THE STATE UNIVERSITY OF NEW YORK
BUFFALO, NEW YORK

General State-supported, university, coed **Entrance** Moderately difficult **Setting** 1,350-acre suburban campus **Total enrollment** 25,838 **Student-faculty ratio** 14:1 **Application deadline** Rolling (freshmen), rolling (transfer) **Freshmen** 63% were admitted **Housing** Yes **Expenses** Tuition $4790; Room & Board $6318 **Undergraduates** 46% women, 11% part-time, 13% 25 or older, 0.4% Native American, 4% Hispanic American, 8% African American, 9% Asian American/Pacific Islander **The most frequently chosen baccalaureate fields are** business/marketing, engineering/engineering technologies, social sciences and history **Academic program** English as a second language, advanced placement, self-designed majors, honors program, summer session, adult/continuing education programs, internships **Contact** Ms. Regina Toomey, Director of Admissions, University at Buffalo, The State University of New York, Capen Hall, Room 17, North Campus, Buffalo, NY 14260-1660. Telephone: 716-645-6900 or toll-free 888-UB-ADMIT. Fax: 716-645-6411. E-mail: ubadmissions@admissions.buffalo.edu. Web site: http://www.buffalo.edu/.

UNIVERSITY OF ROCHESTER
ROCHESTER, NEW YORK

General Independent, university, coed **Entrance** Very difficult **Setting** 534-acre suburban campus **Total enrollment** 7,355 **Student-faculty ratio** 12:1 **Application deadline** 1/15 (freshmen), rolling (transfer) **Freshmen** 50% were admitted **Housing** Yes **Expenses** Tuition $24,754; Room & Board $8585 **The most frequently chosen baccalaureate fields are** law/legal studies, philosophy, religion, and theology **Academic program** English as a second language, advanced placement, self-designed majors, summer session, internships **Contact** Mr. Jamie Hobba, Director of Admissions, University of Rochester, PO Box 270251, Rochester, NY 14627. Telephone: 585-275-3221 or toll-free 888-822-2256. Fax: 585-461-4595. E-mail: admit@admissions.rochester.edu. Web site: http://www.rochester.edu/.

UTICA COLLEGE OF SYRACUSE UNIVERSITY
UTICA, NEW YORK

General Independent, comprehensive, coed **Entrance** Moderately difficult **Setting** 138-acre suburban campus **Total enrollment** 2,286 **Student-faculty ratio** 17:1 **Application deadline** Rolling (freshmen), rolling (transfer) **Freshmen** 77% were admitted **Housing** Yes **Expenses** Tuition $18,050; Room & Board $7070 **Undergraduates** 60% women, 15% part-time, 18% 25 or older, 1% Native American, 4% Hispanic American, 8% African American, 2% Asian American/Pacific Islander **The most frequently chosen baccalaureate fields are** business/marketing, health professions and related sciences, protective services/public administration **Academic program** English as a second language, advanced placement, accelerated degree program, honors program, summer session, adult/continuing education programs, internships **Contact** Mr. Patrick Quinn, Vice President for Enrollment Management, Utica College of Syracuse University, 160 Burrstone Road, Utica, NY 13502. Telephone: 315-792-3006 or toll-free 800-782-8884. Fax: 315-792-3003. E-mail: admiss@utica.ucsu.edu. Web site: http://www.utica.edu/.

VASSAR COLLEGE
POUGHKEEPSIE, NEW YORK

General Independent, comprehensive, coed **Entrance** Very difficult **Setting** 1,000-acre suburban campus

NEW YORK

Vassar College *(continued)*
Total enrollment 2,439 Student-faculty ratio 9:1 Application deadline 1/1 (freshmen), 4/1 (transfer) Freshmen 34% were admitted Housing Yes Expenses Tuition $26,290; Room & Board $7160 Undergraduates 61% women, 3% part-time, 2% 25 or older, 0.4% Native American, 5% Hispanic American, 5% African American, 9% Asian American/Pacific Islander The most frequently chosen baccalaureate fields are social sciences and history, English, visual/performing arts Academic program Advanced placement, self-designed majors, internships Contact Dr. David M. Borus, Dean of Admission and Financial Aid, Vassar College, 124 Raymond Avenue, Poughkeepsie, NY 12604. Telephone: 845-437-7300 or toll-free 800-827-7270. Fax: 914-437-7063. E-mail: admissions@vassar.edu. Web site: http://www.vassar.edu/.

WADHAMS HALL SEMINARY-COLLEGE
OGDENSBURG, NEW YORK

General Independent Roman Catholic, 4-year, men only Entrance Moderately difficult Setting 208-acre rural campus Total enrollment 21 Student-faculty ratio 2:1 Application deadline 8/15 (freshmen), 8/15 (transfer) Freshmen 100% were admitted Housing Yes Expenses Tuition $6445; Room & Board $6000 Undergraduates 28% 25 or older, 0% Native American, 0% Hispanic American, 0% African American, 11% Asian American/Pacific Islander The most frequently chosen baccalaureate fields are liberal arts/general studies, philosophy, religion, and theology Academic program Advanced placement, adult/continuing education programs Contact Rev. Edward J. Sheedy, Director of Admissions, Wadhams Hall Seminary-College, 6866 State Highway 37, Ogdensburg, NY 13669. Telephone: 315-393-4231 Ext. 224. Fax: 315-393-4249. E-mail: admissions@wadhams.edu. Web site: http://www.wadhams.edu/.

WAGNER COLLEGE
STATEN ISLAND, NEW YORK

General Independent, comprehensive, coed Entrance Moderately difficult Setting 105-acre urban campus Total enrollment 2,124 Student-faculty ratio 16:1 Application deadline 2/15 (freshmen), rolling (transfer) Freshmen 67% were admitted Housing Yes Expenses Tuition $20,500; Room & Board $7000 Undergraduates 61% women, 4% part-time, 6% 25 or older, 0.2% Native American, 5% Hispanic American, 5% African American, 3% Asian American/Pacific Islander The most frequently chosen baccalaureate fields are biological/life sciences, business/marketing, education Academic program English as a second language, advanced placement, accelerated degree program, self-designed majors, honors program, summer session, internships Contact Mr. Angelo Araimo, Dean of Admissions, Wagner College, One Campus Road, Staten Island, NY 10301. Telephone: 718-390-3411 or toll-free 800-221-1010 (out-of-state). Fax: 718-390-3105. E-mail: admissions@wagner.edu. Web site: http://www.wagner.edu/.

WEBB INSTITUTE
GLEN COVE, NEW YORK

General Independent, 4-year, coed Entrance Most difficult Setting 26-acre suburban campus Total enrollment 73 Student-faculty ratio 5:1 Application deadline 2/15 (freshmen), 2/15 (transfer) Freshmen 42% were admitted Housing Yes Expenses Tuition $0; Room & Board $6250 Undergraduates 22% women, 1% 25 or older, 0% Native American, 0% Hispanic American, 0% African American, 3% Asian American/Pacific Islander The most frequently chosen baccalaureate field is engineering/engineering technologies Academic program Internships Contact Mr. William G. Murray, Executive Director of Student Administrative Services, Webb Institute, Crescent Beach Road, Glen Cove, NY 11542-1398. Telephone: 516-671-2213. Fax: 516-674-9838. E-mail: admissions@webb-institute.edu. Web site: http://www.webb-institute.edu/.

WELLS COLLEGE
AURORA, NEW YORK

General Independent, 4-year, women only Entrance Moderately difficult Setting 365-acre rural campus Total enrollment 443 Student-faculty ratio 9:1 Application deadline 3/1 (freshmen), rolling (transfer) Freshmen 88% were admitted Housing Yes Expenses Tuition $13,050; Room & Board $6300 Undergraduates 4% part-time, 9% 25 or older, 0.2% Native American, 4% Hispanic American, 5% African American, 4% Asian American/Pacific Islander The most frequently chosen baccalaureate fields are psychology, social sciences and history, visual/performing arts Academic program Advanced placement, accelerated degree program, self-designed majors, adult/continuing education programs, internships Contact Ms. Susan Raith Sloan, Director of Admissions, Wells College, MacMillan Hall, Aurora, NY 13026. Telephone: 315-364-3264 or toll-free 800-952-9355. Fax: 315-364-3227. E-mail: admissions@wells.edu. Web site: http://www.wells.edu/.

▶ For more information, see page 496.

YESHIVA DERECH CHAIM
BROOKLYN, NEW YORK

Contact Mr. Y. Borchardt, Administrator, Yeshiva Derech Chaim, 4907 18th Avenue, Brooklyn, NY 11218. Telephone: 718-438-5476.

YESHIVA KARLIN STOLIN RABBINICAL INSTITUTE
BROOKLYN, NEW YORK

General Independent Jewish, comprehensive, men only Entrance Very difficult Setting urban campus Total enrollment 53 Application deadline Rolling (freshmen), rolling (transfer) Housing Yes Expenses Tuition $5200; Room & Board $3200 Contact Mr. Aryeh L. Wolpin, Director of Admissions, Yeshiva Karlin Stolin Rabbinical Institute, 1818 Fifty-fourth

Street, Brooklyn, NY 11204. Telephone: 718-232-7800 Ext. 26. Fax: 718-331-4833.

YESHIVA OF NITRA RABBINICAL COLLEGE
MOUNT KISCO, NEW YORK

Contact Mr. Ernest Schwartz, Administrator, Yeshiva of Nitra Rabbinical College, Pines Bridge Road, Mount Kisco, NY 10549. Telephone: 718-384-5460. Fax: 718-387-9400.

YESHIVA SHAAR HATORAH TALMUDIC RESEARCH INSTITUTE
KEW GARDENS, NEW YORK

Contact Rabbi Kalman Epstein, Assistant Dean, Yeshiva Shaar Hatorah Talmudic Research Institute, 83-96 117th Street, Kew Gardens, NY 11418-1469. Telephone: 718-846-1940.

YESHIVATH VIZNITZ
MONSEY, NEW YORK

Contact Rabbi Bernard Rosenfeld, Registrar, Yeshivath Viznitz, Phyllis Terrace, PO Box 446, Monsey, NY 10952. Telephone: 914-356-1010.

YESHIVATH ZICHRON MOSHE
SOUTH FALLSBURG, NEW YORK

Contact Rabbi Abba Gorelick, Dean, Yeshivath Zichron Moshe, Laurel Park Road, South Fallsburg, NY 12779. Telephone: 914-434-5240.

YESHIVAT MIKDASH MELECH
BROOKLYN, NEW YORK

Contact Rabbi S. Churba, Director of Admissions, Yeshivat Mikdash Melech, 1326 Ocean Parkway, Brooklyn, NY 11230-5601. Telephone: 718-339-1090.

YESHIVA UNIVERSITY
NEW YORK, NEW YORK

General Independent, university, coed Entrance Moderately difficult Setting urban campus Total enrollment 5,998 Application deadline 2/15 (freshmen), 2/15 (transfer) Freshmen 78% were admitted Housing Yes Expenses Tuition $19,045; Room & Board $5950 Undergraduates 44% women, 1% part-time, 1% 25 or older Academic program English as a second language, advanced placement, self-designed majors, honors program, summer session, internships Contact Mr. Michael Kranzler, Director of Undergraduate Admissions, Yeshiva University, 500 West 185th Street, New York, NY 10033-3201. Telephone: 212-960-5277. Fax: 212-960-0086. E-mail: yuadmit@ymail.yu.edu. Web site: http://www.yu.edu/.

YORK COLLEGE OF THE CITY UNIVERSITY OF NEW YORK
JAMAICA, NEW YORK

General State and locally supported, 4-year, coed Entrance Noncompetitive Setting 50-acre urban campus Total enrollment 5,253 Application deadline Rolling (freshmen), rolling (transfer) Housing No Expenses Tuition $3290 Undergraduates 71% women, 46% part-time, 49% 25 or older, 0.2% Native American, 15% Hispanic American, 44% African American, 7% Asian American/Pacific Islander The most frequently chosen baccalaureate fields are business/marketing, education, psychology Academic program English as a second language, advanced placement, self-designed majors, honors program, summer session, adult/continuing education programs, internships Contact Ms. Sally Nelson, Director of Admissions, York College of the City University of New York, 94-20 Guy R. Brewer Boulevard, Jamaica, NY 11451. Telephone: 718-262-2165. Fax: 718-262-2601. Web site: http://www.york.cuny.edu/.

NORTH CAROLINA

APPALACHIAN STATE UNIVERSITY
BOONE, NORTH CAROLINA

General State-supported, comprehensive, coed Entrance Moderately difficult Setting 255-acre small-town campus Total enrollment 13,762 Student-faculty ratio 17:1 Application deadline Rolling (freshmen), rolling (transfer) Freshmen 65% were admitted Housing Yes Expenses Tuition $2308; Room & Board $4045 Undergraduates 51% women, 10% part-time, 10% 25 or older, 0.4% Native American, 1% Hispanic American, 3% African American, 1% Asian American/Pacific Islander The most frequently chosen baccalaureate fields are business/marketing, communications/communication technologies, education Academic program English as a second language, advanced placement, accelerated degree program, self-designed majors, honors program, summer session, adult/continuing education programs, internships Contact Mr. Joe Watts, Associate Vice Chancellor, Appalachian State University, John Thomas Hall, Boone, NC 28608. Telephone: 828-262-2120. Fax: 828-262-3296. E-mail: admissions@appstate.edu. Web site: http://www.appstate.edu/.

BARBER-SCOTIA COLLEGE
CONCORD, NORTH CAROLINA

General Independent, 4-year, coed, affiliated with Presbyterian Church (U.S.A.) Entrance Minimally difficult Setting 23-acre small-town campus Total enrollment 566 Student-faculty ratio 18:1 Application deadline Rolling (freshmen), rolling (transfer) Freshmen 69% were admitted Housing Yes Expenses Tuition $9048; Room & Board $3952 Undergraduates 49% women, 2% part-time, 20%

NORTH CAROLINA

Barber-Scotia College *(continued)*
25 or older, 1% Hispanic American, 97% African American, 0.2% Asian American/Pacific Islander **The most frequently chosen baccalaureate fields are** business/marketing, parks and recreation, social sciences and history **Academic program** Advanced placement, honors program, summer session, internships **Contact** Dr. Alexander Erwin, Academic Dean, Barber-Scotia College, 145 Cabarrus Avenue, West, Concord, NC 28025-5187. Telephone: 704-789-2948 or toll-free 800-610-0778. Fax: 704-784-3817. Web site: http://www.barber-scotia.edu/.

BARTON COLLEGE
WILSON, NORTH CAROLINA

General Independent, 4-year, coed, affiliated with Christian Church (Disciples of Christ) **Entrance** Minimally difficult **Setting** 62-acre small-town campus **Total enrollment** 1,229 **Student-faculty ratio** 13:1 **Application deadline** Rolling (freshmen), rolling (transfer) **Freshmen** 87% were admitted **Housing** Yes **Expenses** Tuition $12,264; Room & Board $4570 **Undergraduates** 69% women, 22% part-time, 25% 25 or older, 0.3% Native American, 2% Hispanic American, 19% African American, 0.4% Asian American/Pacific Islander **The most frequently chosen baccalaureate fields are** business/marketing, health professions and related sciences, social sciences and history **Academic program** Advanced placement, summer session, adult/continuing education programs, internships **Contact** Ms. Amy Denton, Director of In-State Admissions, Barton College, Box 500, College Station, Hardy Center, Wilson, NC 27893. Telephone: 252-399-6314 or toll-free 800-345-4973. Fax: 252-399-6652. E-mail: enroll@barton.edu. Web site: http://www.barton.edu.

BELMONT ABBEY COLLEGE
BELMONT, NORTH CAROLINA

General Independent Roman Catholic, 4-year, coed **Entrance** Moderately difficult **Setting** 650-acre small-town campus **Total enrollment** 873 **Student-faculty ratio** 15:1 **Application deadline** 8/1 (freshmen), 8/15 (transfer) **Freshmen** 79% were admitted **Housing** Yes **Expenses** Tuition $13,976; Room & Board $6856 **Undergraduates** 56% women, 14% part-time, 24% 25 or older, 0.4% Native American, 3% Hispanic American, 9% African American, 1% Asian American/Pacific Islander **The most frequently chosen baccalaureate fields are** business/marketing, biological/life sciences, education **Academic program** Advanced placement, accelerated degree program, honors program, summer session, adult/continuing education programs, internships **Contact** Mr. R. Lawton Blandford, Director of Administration, Belmont Abbey College, 100 Belmont-Mt. Holly Road, Belmont, NC 28012-1802. Telephone: 704-825-6665 or toll-free 888-BAC-0110. Fax: 704-825-6220. E-mail: admissions@bac.edu. Web site: http://www.belmontabbeycollege.edu/.

BENNETT COLLEGE
GREENSBORO, NORTH CAROLINA

General Independent United Methodist, 4-year, women only **Entrance** Moderately difficult **Setting** 55-acre urban campus **Total enrollment** 521 **Student-faculty ratio** 8:1 **Application deadline** Rolling (freshmen), rolling (transfer) **Freshmen** 62% were admitted **Housing** Yes **Expenses** Tuition $10,006; Room & Board $4291 **Undergraduates** 2% part-time, 3% 25 or older, 98% African American **The most frequently chosen baccalaureate fields are** biological/life sciences, business/marketing, psychology **Academic program** Self-designed majors, honors program, summer session, adult/continuing education programs, internships **Contact** Ms. Linda K. Torrence, Director of Admissions, Bennett College, Campus Box H, Greensboro, NC 27401. Telephone: 336-517-2167. E-mail: admiss@bennett.edu. Web site: http://www.bennett.edu/.

BREVARD COLLEGE
BREVARD, NORTH CAROLINA

General Independent United Methodist, 4-year, coed **Entrance** Minimally difficult **Setting** 120-acre small-town campus **Total enrollment** 701 **Student-faculty ratio** 9:1 **Application deadline** Rolling (freshmen), rolling (transfer) **Freshmen** 89% were admitted **Housing** Yes **Expenses** Tuition $12,170; Room & Board $5060 **Undergraduates** 47% women, 7% part-time, 10% 25 or older, 0.4% Native American, 2% Hispanic American, 8% African American, 0.3% Asian American/Pacific Islander **The most frequently chosen baccalaureate fields are** business/marketing, parks and recreation, visual/performing arts **Academic program** English as a second language, advanced placement, self-designed majors, honors program, adult/continuing education programs, internships **Contact** Ms. Bridgett N. Golman, Dean of Admissions and Financial Aid, Brevard College, 400 North Broad Street, Brevard, NC 28712-3306. Telephone: 828-884-8300 or toll-free 800-527-9090. Fax: 828-884-3790. E-mail: admissions@brevard.edu. Web site: http://www.brevard.edu/.

▶ For more information, see page 402.

CAMPBELL UNIVERSITY
BUIES CREEK, NORTH CAROLINA

General Independent Baptist, university, coed **Entrance** Moderately difficult **Setting** 850-acre rural campus **Total enrollment** 3,862 **Student-faculty ratio** 13:1 **Application deadline** Rolling (freshmen), rolling (transfer) **Freshmen** 70% were admitted **Housing** Yes **Expenses** Tuition $12,269; Room & Board $4330 **Undergraduates** 54% women, 3% part-time, 12% 25 or older, 1% Native American, 2% Hispanic American, 10% African American, 0% Asian American/Pacific Islander **The most frequently chosen baccalaureate fields are** business/marketing, health professions and related sciences, social sciences and history **Academic program** Advanced placement, accelerated degree program, honors program, summer session, adult/continuing education programs, internships **Contact** Ms. Peggy Mason, Director of Admissions, Campbell University, PO Box 546, Buies Creek, NC 27506. Telephone: 910-893-1300 or toll-free 800-334-4111. Fax: 910-893-1288. E-mail: adm@mailcenter.campbell.edu. Web site: http://www.campbell.edu/.

▶ For more information, see page 406.

CATAWBA COLLEGE
SALISBURY, NORTH CAROLINA

General Independent, comprehensive, coed, affiliated with United Church of Christ **Entrance** Moderately difficult **Setting** 210-acre small-town campus **Total enrollment** 1,453 **Student-faculty ratio** 17:1 **Application deadline** Rolling (freshmen), rolling (transfer) **Freshmen** 82% were admitted **Housing** Yes **Expenses** Tuition $14,540; Room & Board $5080 **Undergraduates** 51% women, 4% part-time, 25% 25 or older, 0.3% Native American, 2% Hispanic American, 16% African American, 1% Asian American/Pacific Islander **The most frequently chosen baccalaureate fields are** business/marketing, communications/communication technologies, computer/information sciences **Academic program** Advanced placement, self-designed majors, honors program, summer session, adult/continuing education programs, internships **Contact** Mr. Brian Best, Chief Enrollment Officer, Catawba College, 2300 West Innes Street, Salisbury, NC 28144-2488. Telephone: 800-CATAWBA or toll-free 800-CATAWBA. Fax: 704-637-4222. E-mail: bdbest@catawba.edu. Web site: http://www.catawba.edu/.

CHOWAN COLLEGE
MURFREESBORO, NORTH CAROLINA

General Independent Baptist, 4-year, coed **Entrance** Minimally difficult **Setting** 300-acre rural campus **Total enrollment** 795 **Student-faculty ratio** 10:1 **Application deadline** Rolling (freshmen), rolling (transfer) **Freshmen** 82% were admitted **Housing** Yes **Expenses** Tuition $12,500; Room & Board $5040 **Undergraduates** 47% women, 3% part-time, 2% 25 or older, 1% Native American, 2% Hispanic American, 26% African American, 2% Asian American/Pacific Islander **The most frequently chosen baccalaureate fields are** business/marketing, computer/information sciences, education **Academic program** Advanced placement, self-designed majors, summer session, internships **Contact** Mr. Don Williams, Associate Vice President for Enrollment Management, Chowan College, 200 Jones Drive, Murfreesboro, NC 27855. Telephone: 252-398-6314 or toll-free 800-488-4101. Fax: 252-398-1190. E-mail: admissions@chowan.edu. Web site: http://www.chowan.edu/.

DAVIDSON COLLEGE
DAVIDSON, NORTH CAROLINA

General Independent Presbyterian, 4-year, coed **Entrance** Very difficult **Setting** 464-acre small-town campus **Total enrollment** 1,673 **Student-faculty ratio** 11:1 **Application deadline** 1/2 (freshmen), 3/15 (transfer) **Freshmen** 35% were admitted **Housing** Yes **Expenses** Tuition $23,995; Room & Board $6828 **Undergraduates** 51% women, 0.1% part-time, 0.01% 25 or older, 0.4% Native American, 3% Hispanic American, 5% African American, 3% Asian American/Pacific Islander **The most frequently chosen baccalaureate fields are** English, biological/life sciences, social sciences and history **Academic program** Advanced placement, accelerated degree program, self-designed majors, honors program **Contact** Dr. Nancy J. Cable, Dean of Admission and Financial Aid, Davidson College, Box 7156, Davidson, NC 28035-7156. Telephone: 704-894-2230 or toll-free 800-768-0380. Fax: 704-894-2016. E-mail: admission@davidson.edu. Web site: http://www.davidson.edu/.

▶ For more information, see page 419.

DUKE UNIVERSITY
DURHAM, NORTH CAROLINA

General Independent, university, coed, affiliated with United Methodist Church **Entrance** Most difficult **Setting** 8,500-acre suburban campus **Total enrollment** 11,794 **Student-faculty ratio** 11:1 **Application deadline** 1/2 (freshmen), 3/15 (transfer) **Freshmen** 26% were admitted **Housing** Yes **Expenses** Tuition $26,768; Room & Board $7628 **Undergraduates** 48% women, 0.5% part-time, 1% 25 or older, 0.4% Native American, 6% Hispanic American, 10% African American, 12% Asian American/Pacific Islander **The most frequently chosen baccalaureate fields are** biological/life sciences, engineering/engineering technologies, social sciences and history **Academic program** English as a second language, advanced placement, accelerated degree program, self-designed majors, honors program, summer session, adult/continuing education programs, internships **Contact** Mr. Christoph Guttentag, Director of Admissions, Duke University, 2138 Campus Drive, Durham, NC 27708. Telephone: 919-684-3214. Fax: 919-684-8941. E-mail: askduke@admiss.duke.edu. Web site: http://www.duke.edu/.

EAST CAROLINA UNIVERSITY
GREENVILLE, NORTH CAROLINA

General State-supported, university, coed **Entrance** Moderately difficult **Setting** 465-acre urban campus **Total enrollment** 19,412 **Application deadline** 3/15 (freshmen), 4/15 (transfer) **Freshmen** 78% were admitted **Housing** Yes **Expenses** Tuition $2566; Room & Board $5200 **Undergraduates** 58% women, 8% part-time, 12% 25 or older, 1% Native American, 2% Hispanic American, 14% African American, 2% Asian American/Pacific Islander **The most frequently chosen baccalaureate fields are** business/marketing, education, health professions and related sciences **Academic program** Advanced placement, accelerated degree program, honors program, summer session, adult/continuing education programs, internships **Contact** Dr. Thomas Powell Jr., Director of Admissions, East Carolina University, East Fifth Street, Whichard Building 106, Greenville, NC 27858-

NORTH CAROLINA

East Carolina University *(continued)*
4353. Telephone: 252-328-6640. Fax: 252-328-6945. E-mail: admis@mail.ecu.edu. Web site: http://www.ecu.edu/.

ELIZABETH CITY STATE UNIVERSITY
ELIZABETH CITY, NORTH CAROLINA

General State-supported, comprehensive, coed **Entrance** Moderately difficult **Setting** 125-acre small-town campus **Total enrollment** 2,004 **Application deadline** Rolling (freshmen), rolling (transfer) **Freshmen** 71% were admitted **Housing** Yes **Expenses** Tuition $1840; Room & Board $4172 **Undergraduates** 25% 25 or older, 0.3% Native American, 1% Hispanic American, 78% African American, 0.4% Asian American/Pacific Islander **Academic program** Advanced placement, honors program, summer session, adult/continuing education programs, internships **Contact** Mr. Grady Deese, Director of Admissions, Elizabeth City State University, Campus Box 901, Elizabeth City, NC 27909-7806. Telephone: 252-335-3305 or toll-free 800-347-3278. Fax: 252-335-3537. E-mail: admissions@mail.ecsu.edu. Web site: http://www.ecsu.edu/.

ELON UNIVERSITY
ELON, NORTH CAROLINA

General Independent, comprehensive, coed, affiliated with United Church of Christ **Entrance** Moderately difficult **Setting** 500-acre suburban campus **Total enrollment** 4,341 **Student-faculty ratio** 16:1 **Application deadline** Rolling (freshmen), rolling (transfer) **Freshmen** 65% were admitted **Housing** Yes **Expenses** Tuition $14,560; Room & Board $4432 **Undergraduates** 61% women, 2% part-time, 2% 25 or older, 0.2% Native American, 1% Hispanic American, 6% African American, 1% Asian American/Pacific Islander **The most frequently chosen baccalaureate fields are** business/marketing, communications/communication technologies, education **Academic program** English as a second language, advanced placement, accelerated degree program, self-designed majors, honors program, summer session, internships **Contact** Director of Admissions Records, Elon University, 2700 Campus Box, Elon, NC 27244. Telephone: 336-278-3566 or toll-free 800-334-8448. Fax: 336-278-7699. E-mail: admissions@elon.edu. Web site: http://www.elon.edu/.

FAYETTEVILLE STATE UNIVERSITY
FAYETTEVILLE, NORTH CAROLINA

General State-supported, comprehensive, coed **Entrance** Minimally difficult **Setting** 156-acre urban campus **Total enrollment** 5,010 **Student-faculty ratio** 20:1 **Application deadline** Rolling (freshmen), rolling (transfer) **Freshmen** 85% were admitted **Housing** Yes **Expenses** Tuition $1770; Room & Board $3820 **Undergraduates** 63% women, 22% part-time, 35% 25 or older, 1% Native American, 4% Hispanic American, 77% African American, 1% Asian American/Pacific Islander **The most frequently chosen baccalaureate fields are** business/marketing, protective services/public administration, social sciences and history **Academic program** Accelerated degree program, honors program, summer session, adult/continuing education programs **Contact** Mr. Charles Darlington, Director of Enrollment Management and Admissions, Fayetteville State University, 1200 Murchison Road, Fayetteville, NC 28301-4298. Telephone: 910-486-1371 or toll-free 800-222-2594. Fax: 910-437-2512. Web site: http://www.uncfsu.edu/.

GARDNER-WEBB UNIVERSITY
BOILING SPRINGS, NORTH CAROLINA

General Independent Baptist, comprehensive, coed **Entrance** Moderately difficult **Setting** 200-acre small-town campus **Total enrollment** 3,564 **Student-faculty ratio** 16:1 **Application deadline** Rolling (freshmen), rolling (transfer) **Freshmen** 73% were admitted **Housing** Yes **Expenses** Tuition $12,870; Room & Board $4880 **Undergraduates** 65% women, 18% part-time, 34% 25 or older, 0.2% Native American, 1% Hispanic American, 13% African American, 1% Asian American/Pacific Islander **The most frequently chosen baccalaureate field is** philosophy, religion, and theology **Academic program** English as a second language, advanced placement, accelerated degree program, honors program, summer session, adult/continuing education programs, internships **Contact** Mr. Nathan Alexander, Director of Admissions and Enrollment Management, Gardner-Webb University, PO Box 817, Boiling Springs, NC 28017. Telephone: 704-406-4491 or toll-free 800-253-6472. Fax: 810-253-6477. E-mail: admissions@gardner-webb.edu. Web site: http://www.gardner-webb.edu/.

▶ For more information, see page 432.

GREENSBORO COLLEGE
GREENSBORO, NORTH CAROLINA

General Independent United Methodist, 4-year, coed **Entrance** Moderately difficult **Setting** 40-acre urban campus **Total enrollment** 1,139 **Student-faculty ratio** 13:1 **Application deadline** Rolling (freshmen), rolling (transfer) **Freshmen** 78% were admitted **Housing** Yes **Expenses** Tuition $13,700; Room & Board $5380 **Undergraduates** 54% women, 22% part-time, 25% 25 or older, 2% Native American, 2% Hispanic American, 16% African American, 1% Asian American/Pacific Islander **The most frequently chosen baccalaureate fields are** business/marketing, education, parks and recreation **Academic program** Advanced placement, accelerated degree program, self-designed majors, honors program, summer session, adult/continuing education programs, internships **Contact** Mr. Timothy L. Jackson, Director of Admissions, Greensboro College, 815 West Market Street, Greensboro, NC 27401-1875. Telephone: 336-272-7102 Ext. 211 or toll-free 800-346-8226. Fax: 336-378-0154. E-mail: admissions@gborocollege.edu. Web site: http://www.gborocollege.edu/.

NORTH CAROLINA

GUILFORD COLLEGE
GREENSBORO, NORTH CAROLINA

General Independent, 4-year, coed, affiliated with Society of Friends **Entrance** Moderately difficult **Setting** 340-acre suburban campus **Total enrollment** 1,490 **Student-faculty ratio** 15:1 **Application deadline** 2/15 (freshmen), 4/1 (transfer) **Freshmen** 79% were admitted **Housing** Yes **Expenses** Tuition $17,645; Room & Board $5610 **Undergraduates** 53% women, 12% part-time, 27% 25 or older, 1% Native American, 2% Hispanic American, 11% African American, 1% Asian American/Pacific Islander **The most frequently chosen baccalaureate fields are** business/marketing, English, social sciences and history **Academic program** English as a second language, advanced placement, accelerated degree program, self-designed majors, honors program, summer session, adult/continuing education programs, internships **Contact** Mr. Randy Doss, Vice President of Enrollment, Guilford College, 5800 West Friendly Avenue, Greensboro, NC 27410. Telephone: 336-316-2100 or toll-free 800-992-7759. Fax: 336-316-2954. E-mail: admission@guilford.edu. Web site: http://www.guilford.edu/.

HERITAGE BIBLE COLLEGE
DUNN, NORTH CAROLINA

General Independent Pentecostal Free Will Baptist, 4-year, coed **Entrance** Minimally difficult **Setting** 82-acre small-town campus **Total enrollment** 50 **Student-faculty ratio** 3:1 **Application deadline** Rolling (freshmen), rolling (transfer) **Freshmen** 100% were admitted **Housing** Yes **Expenses** Tuition $4200; Room & Board $2400 **Undergraduates** 26% women, 26% part-time, 66% 25 or older, 0% Native American, 6% Hispanic American, 34% African American **The most frequently chosen baccalaureate field is** philosophy **Academic program** Summer session, adult/continuing education programs, internships **Contact** Ms. Janice M. Guldan, Director of Admissions and Registrar, Heritage Bible College, PO Box 1628, Dunn, NC 28335. Telephone: 910-892-3178. Fax: 910-892-1809. E-mail: hbchead@intrstar.net. Web site: http://www.pfwb.org/non-frames/hbc/index.htm.

HIGH POINT UNIVERSITY
HIGH POINT, NORTH CAROLINA

General Independent United Methodist, comprehensive, coed **Entrance** Moderately difficult **Setting** 77-acre suburban campus **Total enrollment** 2,752 **Student-faculty ratio** 16:1 **Application deadline** 8/15 (freshmen), 8/15 (transfer) **Freshmen** 88% were admitted **Housing** Yes **Expenses** Tuition $13,900; Room & Board $6320 **Undergraduates** 63% women, 11% part-time, 8% 25 or older, 0.2% Native American, 1% Hispanic American, 18% African American, 1% Asian American/Pacific Islander **The most frequently chosen baccalaureate fields are** business/marketing, computer/information sciences, education **Academic program** English as a second language, advanced placement, accelerated degree program, self-designed majors, honors program, summer session, adult/continuing education programs, internships **Contact** Mr. James L. Schlimmer, Dean of Enrollment Management, High Point University, University Station 3188, 833 Montlieu Avenue, High Point, NC 27262-3598. Telephone: 336-841-9216 or toll-free 800-345-6993. Fax: 336-841-5123. E-mail: admiss@highpoint.edu. Web site: http://www.highpoint.edu/.

JOHNSON C. SMITH UNIVERSITY
CHARLOTTE, NORTH CAROLINA

General Independent, 4-year, coed **Entrance** Minimally difficult **Setting** 105-acre urban campus **Total enrollment** 1,595 **Student-faculty ratio** 16:1 **Application deadline** 8/1 (freshmen), 8/1 (transfer) **Freshmen** 44% were admitted **Housing** Yes **Expenses** Tuition $11,971; Room & Board $4589 **Undergraduates** 58% women, 6% part-time, 6% 25 or older, 0% Hispanic American, 99% African American, 0.1% Asian American/Pacific Islander **Academic program** Advanced placement, accelerated degree program, honors program, summer session, adult/continuing education programs, internships **Contact** Mr. Jeffrey Smith, Director of Admissions, Johnson C. Smith University, 100 Beatties Ford Road, Charlotte, NC 28216. Telephone: 704-378-1010 or toll-free 800-782-7303. Web site: http://www.jcsu.edu/.

JOHN WESLEY COLLEGE
HIGH POINT, NORTH CAROLINA

General Independent interdenominational, 4-year, coed **Entrance** Minimally difficult **Setting** 24-acre urban campus **Total enrollment** 179 **Student-faculty ratio** 12:1 **Application deadline** 8/1 (freshmen), 8/1 (transfer) **Freshmen** 79% were admitted **Housing** Yes **Expenses** Tuition $6712; Room only $1990 **Undergraduates** 43% women, 22% part-time, 64% 25 or older, 1% Native American, 1% Hispanic American, 23% African American, 1% Asian American/Pacific Islander **The most frequently chosen baccalaureate fields are** business/marketing, philosophy, philosophy, religion, and theology **Academic program** Advanced placement, summer session, adult/continuing education programs, internships **Contact** Mr. Greg Workman, Admissions Officer, John Wesley College, 2314 North Centennial Street, High Point, NC 27265-3197. Telephone: 336-889-2262 Ext. 127. Fax: 336-889-2261. E-mail: gworkman@johnwesley.edu. Web site: http://www.johnwesley.edu/.

LEES-MCRAE COLLEGE
BANNER ELK, NORTH CAROLINA

General Independent, 4-year, coed, affiliated with Presbyterian Church (U.S.A.) **Entrance** Minimally difficult **Setting** 400-acre rural campus **Total enrollment** 792 **Student-faculty ratio** 14:1 **Application deadline** 8/15 (freshmen), 8/15 (transfer) **Freshmen** 95% were admitted **Housing** Yes **Expenses** Tuition $12,442; Room & Board $4664 **Undergraduates**

NORTH CAROLINA

Lees-McRae College *(continued)*
57% women, 4% part-time, 18% 25 or older, 0.4% Native American, 1% Hispanic American, 6% African American, 1% Asian American/Pacific Islander **The most frequently chosen baccalaureate fields are** business/marketing, biological/life sciences, education **Academic program** Advanced placement, self-designed majors, honors program, summer session, adult/continuing education programs, internships **Contact** Mr. Bart Walker, Director of Admissions, Lees-McRae College, PO Box 128, Banner Elk, NC 28604-0128. Telephone: 828-898-8702 or toll-free 800-280-4562. Fax: 828-898-8707. E-mail: admissions@lmc.edu. Web site: http://www.lmc.edu/.

LENOIR-RHYNE COLLEGE
HICKORY, NORTH CAROLINA

General Independent Lutheran, comprehensive, coed **Entrance** Moderately difficult **Setting** 100-acre small-town campus **Total enrollment** 1,456 **Student-faculty ratio** 11:1 **Application deadline** Rolling (freshmen), rolling (transfer) **Freshmen** 85% were admitted **Housing** Yes **Expenses** Tuition $14,086; Room & Board $5100 **Undergraduates** 64% women, 12% part-time, 22% 25 or older, 0.3% Native American, 1% Hispanic American, 8% African American, 2% Asian American/Pacific Islander **The most frequently chosen baccalaureate fields are** business/marketing, education, psychology **Academic program** English as a second language, advanced placement, accelerated degree program, self-designed majors, honors program, summer session, adult/continuing education programs, internships **Contact** Mrs. Rachel Nichols, Director of Admissions and Financial Aid, Lenoir-Rhyne College, PO Box 7227, Hickory, NC 28603. Telephone: 828-328-7300 or toll-free 800-277-5721. Fax: 828-328-7338. E-mail: admission@lrc.edu. Web site: http://www.lrc.edu/.

LIVINGSTONE COLLEGE
SALISBURY, NORTH CAROLINA

General Independent, 4-year, coed, affiliated with African Methodist Episcopal Zion Church **Entrance** Minimally difficult **Setting** 272-acre small-town campus **Total enrollment** 917 **Student-faculty ratio** 17:1 **Application deadline** Rolling (freshmen), rolling (transfer) **Freshmen** 71% were admitted **Housing** Yes **Expenses** Tuition $8820; Room & Board $3700 **Undergraduates** 48% women, 5% part-time, 18% 25 or older, 0.4% Hispanic American, 94% African American, 0.2% Asian American/Pacific Islander **Academic program** Advanced placement, honors program, summer session, adult/continuing education programs, internships **Contact** Ms. Marjorie Kinard, Director of Enrollment Management, Livingstone College, 701 West Monroe Street, Salisbury, NC 28144. Telephone: 704-216-6183 or toll-free 800-835-3435. Fax: 704-216-6215. E-mail: admissions@livingstone.edu. Web site: http://www.livingstone.edu/.

MARS HILL COLLEGE
MARS HILL, NORTH CAROLINA

General Independent Baptist, 4-year, coed **Entrance** Moderately difficult **Setting** 194-acre small-town campus **Total enrollment** 1,242 **Student-faculty ratio** 12:1 **Application deadline** Rolling (freshmen), rolling (transfer) **Freshmen** 85% were admitted **Housing** Yes **Expenses** Tuition $13,800; Room & Board $4800 **Undergraduates** 57% women, 11% part-time, 20% 25 or older, 1% Native American, 1% Hispanic American, 11% African American, 0.4% Asian American/Pacific Islander **The most frequently chosen baccalaureate fields are** business/marketing, education, social sciences and history **Academic program** English as a second language, advanced placement, accelerated degree program, self-designed majors, honors program, summer session, adult/continuing education programs, internships **Contact** Ms. Ophelia H. DeGroot, Dean of Enrollment Services, Mars Hill College, PO Box 370, Mars Hill, NC 28754. Telephone: 828-689-1201 or toll-free 800-543-1514. Fax: 828-689-1473. E-mail: admissions@mhc.edu. Web site: http://www.mhc.edu/.

MEREDITH COLLEGE
RALEIGH, NORTH CAROLINA

General Independent, comprehensive, women only **Entrance** Moderately difficult **Setting** 225-acre urban campus **Total enrollment** 2,466 **Student-faculty ratio** 10:1 **Application deadline** 2/15 (freshmen), 2/15 (transfer) **Freshmen** 83% were admitted **Housing** Yes **Expenses** Tuition $12,300; Room & Board $4400 **Undergraduates** 22% part-time, 18% 25 or older, 0.2% Native American, 2% Hispanic American, 6% African American, 1% Asian American/Pacific Islander **The most frequently chosen baccalaureate fields are** business/marketing, psychology, visual/performing arts **Academic program** Advanced placement, accelerated degree program, self-designed majors, honors program, summer session, adult/continuing education programs, internships **Contact** Ms. Carol R. Kercheval, Director of Admissions, Meredith College, 3800 Hillsborough Street, Raleigh, NC 27607-5298. Telephone: 919-760-8581 or toll-free 800-MEREDITH. Fax: 919-760-2348. E-mail: admissions@meredith.edu. Web site: http://www.meredith.edu/.

METHODIST COLLEGE
FAYETTEVILLE, NORTH CAROLINA

General Independent United Methodist, comprehensive, coed **Entrance** Moderately difficult **Setting** 600-acre suburban campus **Total enrollment** 2,143 **Student-faculty ratio** 14:1 **Application deadline** Rolling (freshmen), rolling (transfer) **Freshmen** 73% were admitted **Housing** Yes **Expenses** Tuition $14,196; Room & Board $5330 **Undergraduates** 43% women, 23% part-time, 26% 25 or older, 1% Native American, 5% Hispanic American, 22% African American, 1% Asian American/Pacific Islander **The most frequently chosen baccalaureate fields are** business/

marketing, parks and recreation, social sciences and history **Academic program** English as a second language, advanced placement, accelerated degree program, honors program, summer session, adult/continuing education programs, internships **Contact** Ms. Jamie Legg, Director of Admissions, Methodist College, Admissions Office, 5400 Ramsey Street, Fayetteville, NC 28311. Telephone: 910-630-7027 or toll-free 800-488-7110 Ext. 7027. Fax: 910-630-7285. E-mail: admissions@methodist.edu. Web site: http://www.methodist.edu/.

MONTREAT COLLEGE
MONTREAT, NORTH CAROLINA

General Independent Presbyterian, comprehensive, coed **Entrance** Moderately difficult **Setting** 100-acre small-town campus **Total enrollment** 1,109 **Application deadline** 8/15 (freshmen), 8/15 (transfer) **Freshmen** 86% were admitted **Housing** Yes **Expenses** Tuition $12,318; Room & Board $4846 **Undergraduates** 61% women, 2% part-time, 58% 25 or older **The most frequently chosen baccalaureate fields are** business/marketing, parks and recreation, philosophy **Academic program** Advanced placement, adult/continuing education programs, internships **Contact** Ms. Anita Darby, Director of Admissions, Montreat College, PO Box 1267, 310 Gaither Circle, Montreat, NC 28757-1267. Telephone: 828-669-8012 Ext. 3784 or toll-free 800-622-6968 (in-state). Fax: 828-669-0120. E-mail: admissions@montreat.edu. Web site: http://www.montreat.edu/.

MOUNT OLIVE COLLEGE
MOUNT OLIVE, NORTH CAROLINA

General Independent Free Will Baptist, 4-year, coed **Entrance** Minimally difficult **Setting** 123-acre small-town campus **Total enrollment** 1,775 **Student-faculty ratio** 18:1 **Application deadline** Rolling (freshmen), rolling (transfer) **Freshmen** 89% were admitted **Housing** Yes **Expenses** Tuition $9660; Room & Board $4250 **Undergraduates** 55% women, 19% part-time, 49% 25 or older, 0% Native American, 2% Hispanic American, 25% African American, 0.2% Asian American/Pacific Islander **The most frequently chosen baccalaureate fields are** business/marketing, parks and recreation, protective services/public administration **Academic program** Advanced placement, accelerated degree program, honors program, summer session, adult/continuing education programs, internships **Contact** Mr. Tim Woodard, Director of Admissions, Mount Olive College, 634 Henderson Street, Mount Olive, NC 28365. Telephone: 919-658-2502 Ext. 3009 or toll-free 800-653-0854 (in-state). Fax: 919-658-8934. E-mail: twppdard@moc.edu. Web site: http://www.mountolivecollege.edu/.

NORTH CAROLINA AGRICULTURAL AND TECHNICAL STATE UNIVERSITY
GREENSBORO, NORTH CAROLINA

General State-supported, university, coed **Entrance** Moderately difficult **Setting** 191-acre urban campus **Total enrollment** 7,748 **Student-faculty ratio** 17:1 **Application deadline** 6/1 (freshmen), 6/1 (transfer) **Freshmen** 93% were admitted **Housing** Yes **Undergraduates** 53% women, 11% part-time, 21% 25 or older, 0.3% Native American, 0.4% Hispanic American, 93% African American, 1% Asian American/Pacific Islander **Academic program** Advanced placement, honors program, summer session, adult/continuing education programs, internships **Contact** Mr. John Smith, Director of Admissions, North Carolina Agricultural and Technical State University, 1601 East Market Street, Webb Hall, Greensboro, NC 27411. Telephone: 336-334-7946 or toll-free 800-443-8964 (in-state). Fax: 336-334-7478. Web site: http://www.ncat.edu/.

NORTH CAROLINA CENTRAL UNIVERSITY
DURHAM, NORTH CAROLINA

General State-supported, comprehensive, coed **Entrance** Minimally difficult **Setting** 103-acre urban campus **Total enrollment** 5,753 **Student-faculty ratio** 13:1 **Application deadline** 7/1 (freshmen), 7/1 (transfer) **Freshmen** 77% were admitted **Housing** Yes **Expenses** Tuition $2350; Room & Board $3284 **Undergraduates** 64% women, 20% part-time, 25% 25 or older, 0.3% Native American, 1% Hispanic American, 90% African American, 1% Asian American/Pacific Islander **The most frequently chosen baccalaureate fields are** business/marketing, education, social sciences and history **Academic program** Advanced placement, honors program, summer session, adult/continuing education programs, internships **Contact** Ms. Jocelyn L. Foy, Undergraduate Director of Admissions, North Carolina Central University, 1801 Fayetteville Street, Durham, NC 27707-3129. Telephone: 919-560-6298. Fax: 919-530-7625. E-mail: ebridges@wpo.nccu.edu. Web site: http://www.nccu.edu/.

NORTH CAROLINA SCHOOL OF THE ARTS
WINSTON-SALEM, NORTH CAROLINA

General State-supported, comprehensive, coed **Entrance** Very difficult **Setting** 57-acre urban campus **Total enrollment** 789 **Student-faculty ratio** 8:1 **Application deadline** Rolling (freshmen), rolling (transfer) **Freshmen** 45% were admitted **Housing** Yes **Expenses** Tuition $2877; Room & Board $4920 **Undergraduates** 43% women, 3% part-time, 5% 25 or older, 0.4% Native American, 2% Hispanic American, 10% African American, 2% Asian American/Pacific Islander **The most frequently chosen baccalaureate field is** visual/performing arts **Contact** Ms. Sheeler Lawson, Director of Admissions, North Carolina School of the Arts, 1533 South Main Street, PO Box 12189, Winston-Salem, NC 27127-2188. Telephone: 336-770-3290. Fax: 336-770-3370. E-mail: admissions@ncarts.edu. Web site: http://www.ncarts.edu/.

NORTH CAROLINA

NORTH CAROLINA STATE UNIVERSITY
RALEIGH, NORTH CAROLINA

General State-supported, university, coed **Entrance** Very difficult **Setting** 1,623-acre suburban campus **Total enrollment** 29,266 **Student-faculty ratio** 13:1 **Application deadline** 2/1 (freshmen), 4/1 (transfer) **Freshmen** 66% were admitted **Housing** Yes **Expenses** Tuition $2746; Room & Board $5274 **Undergraduates** 42% women, 18% part-time, 8% 25 or older, 1% Native American, 2% Hispanic American, 10% African American, 5% Asian American/Pacific Islander **The most frequently chosen baccalaureate fields are** business/marketing, biological/life sciences, engineering/engineering technologies **Academic program** Advanced placement, accelerated degree program, self-designed majors, honors program, summer session, adult/continuing education programs, internships **Contact** Dr. George R. Dixon, Vice Provost and Director of Admissions, North Carolina State University, Box 7103, 112 Peele Hall, Raleigh, NC 27695. Telephone: 919-515-2434. E-mail: undergrad_admissions@ncsu.edu. Web site: http://www.ncsu.edu/.

NORTH CAROLINA WESLEYAN COLLEGE
ROCKY MOUNT, NORTH CAROLINA

General Independent, 4-year, coed, affiliated with United Methodist Church **Entrance** Moderately difficult **Setting** 200-acre suburban campus **Total enrollment** 1,886 **Student-faculty ratio** 16:1 **Application deadline** 7/15 (freshmen), 7/15 (transfer) **Freshmen** 69% were admitted **Housing** Yes **Undergraduates** 58% women, 50% part-time, 64% 25 or older, 0.4% Native American, 2% Hispanic American, 35% African American, 1% Asian American/Pacific Islander **The most frequently chosen baccalaureate fields are** business/marketing, (pre)law, computer/information sciences **Academic program** Advanced placement, honors program, summer session, adult/continuing education programs, internships **Contact** Cecelia Summers, Associate Director of Admissions, North Carolina Wesleyan College, 3400 N Wesleyan Boulevard, Rocky Mount, NC 27804. Telephone: 800-488-6292 Ext. 5202 or toll-free 800-488-6292. Fax: 252-985-5295. E-mail: adm@ncwc.edu. Web site: http://www.ncwc.edu/.

PEACE COLLEGE
RALEIGH, NORTH CAROLINA

General Independent, 4-year, women only, affiliated with Presbyterian Church (U.S.A.) **Entrance** Moderately difficult **Setting** 16-acre urban campus **Total enrollment** 634 **Student-faculty ratio** 14:1 **Application deadline** Rolling (freshmen), rolling (transfer) **Freshmen** 87% were admitted **Housing** Yes **Expenses** Tuition $10,890; Room & Board $5200 **Undergraduates** 7% part-time, 83% 25 or older, 1% Native American, 1% Hispanic American, 8% African American, 2% Asian American/Pacific Islander **The most frequently chosen baccalaureate fields are** business/marketing, English, psychology **Academic program** English as a second language, advanced placement, honors program, adult/continuing education programs, internships **Contact** Dr. E. Carole Tyler, Dean of Admissions and Financial Aid, Peace College, Admissions and Financial Aid, Raleigh, NC 27604. Telephone: 919-508-2000 Ext. 2202 or toll-free 800-PEACE-47. Fax: 919-508-2306. E-mail: chill@peace.edu. Web site: http://www.peace.edu/.

PFEIFFER UNIVERSITY
MISENHEIMER, NORTH CAROLINA

General Independent United Methodist, comprehensive, coed **Entrance** Moderately difficult **Setting** 300-acre rural campus **Total enrollment** 1,671 **Student-faculty ratio** 13:1 **Application deadline** Rolling (freshmen), rolling (transfer) **Freshmen** 72% were admitted **Housing** Yes **Expenses** Tuition $12,066; Room & Board $3874 **Undergraduates** 58% women, 17% part-time, 0.1% Native American, 2% Hispanic American, 20% African American, 1% Asian American/Pacific Islander **The most frequently chosen baccalaureate fields are** business/marketing, education, protective services/public administration **Academic program** English as a second language, advanced placement, accelerated degree program, honors program, summer session, internships **Contact** Mr. Steve Cumming, Director of Admissions, Pfeiffer University, PO Box 960, Highway 52 North, Misenheimer, NC 28109. Telephone: 704-463-1360 Ext. 2079 or toll-free 800-338-2060. Fax: 704-463-1363. E-mail: admiss@pfeiffer.edu. Web site: http://www.pfeiffer.edu/.

PIEDMONT BAPTIST COLLEGE
WINSTON-SALEM, NORTH CAROLINA

General Independent Baptist, comprehensive, coed **Entrance** Noncompetitive **Setting** 12-acre urban campus **Total enrollment** 320 **Student-faculty ratio** 11:1 **Application deadline** Rolling (freshmen), rolling (transfer) **Freshmen** 59% were admitted **Housing** Yes **Expenses** Tuition $5970; Room & Board $3700 **Undergraduates** 40% women, 26% part-time, 32% 25 or older, 0.3% Native American, 0% Hispanic American, 4% African American, 8% Asian American/Pacific Islander **Academic program** Advanced placement, summer session, adult/continuing education programs, internships **Contact** Mrs. Carole Beverly, Director of Admissions, Piedmont Baptist College, 716 Franklin Street, Winston-Salem, NC 27101-5197. Telephone: 336-725-8344 Ext. 2327 or toll-free 800-937-5097. Fax: 336-725-5522. E-mail: admissions@pbc.edu. Web site: http://www.pbc.edu/.

QUEENS UNIVERSITY OF CHARLOTTE
CHARLOTTE, NORTH CAROLINA

General Independent Presbyterian, comprehensive, coed **Entrance** Moderately difficult **Setting** 25-acre suburban campus **Total enrollment** 1,704 **Student-faculty ratio** 12:1 **Application deadline** Rolling (freshmen), rolling (transfer) **Freshmen** 79% were admitted **Housing** Yes **Expenses** Tuition $11,360;

NORTH CAROLINA

Room & Board $5890 **Undergraduates** 78% women, 38% part-time, 1% Native American, 2% Hispanic American, 17% African American, 2% Asian American/Pacific Islander **The most frequently chosen baccalaureate fields are** business/marketing, communications/communication technologies, health professions and related sciences **Academic program** Advanced placement, self-designed majors, honors program, summer session, adult/continuing education programs, internships **Contact** Ms. Eileen T. Dills, Dean of Admissions and Financial Aid, Queens University of Charlotte, 1900 Selwyn Avenue, Charlotte, NC 28274. Telephone: 704-337-2212 or toll-free 800-849-0202. Fax: 704-337-2403. E-mail: case@rex.queens.edu. Web site: http://www.queens.edu/.

ROANOKE BIBLE COLLEGE
ELIZABETH CITY, NORTH CAROLINA

General Independent Christian, 4-year, coed **Entrance** Minimally difficult **Setting** 19-acre small-town campus **Total enrollment** 170 **Student-faculty ratio** 13:1 **Application deadline** 8/1 (freshmen), 8/1 (transfer) **Freshmen** 39% were admitted **Housing** Yes **Expenses** Tuition $5918; Room & Board $4265 **Undergraduates** 48% women, 15% part-time, 1% Native American, 1% Hispanic American, 6% African American, 6% Asian American/Pacific Islander **The most frequently chosen baccalaureate field is** philosophy **Academic program** Advanced placement, internships **Contact** Mrs. Deborah T. Roach, Director of Admissions, Roanoke Bible College, 715 North Poindexter Street, Elizabeth City, NC 27909-4054. Telephone: 252-334-2019 or toll-free 800-RBC-8980. Fax: 252-334-2071. E-mail: admissions@roanokebible.edu. Web site: http://www.roanokebible.edu/.

ST. ANDREWS PRESBYTERIAN COLLEGE
LAURINBURG, NORTH CAROLINA

General Independent Presbyterian, 4-year, coed **Entrance** Moderately difficult **Setting** 600-acre small-town campus **Total enrollment** 704 **Student-faculty ratio** 10:1 **Application deadline** Rolling (freshmen), rolling (transfer) **Freshmen** 87% were admitted **Housing** Yes **Expenses** Tuition $14,310; Room & Board $5410 **Undergraduates** 60% women, 14% part-time, 19% 25 or older, 1% Native American, 2% Hispanic American, 10% African American, 3% Asian American/Pacific Islander **The most frequently chosen baccalaureate fields are** business/marketing, computer/information sciences, social sciences and history **Academic program** Advanced placement, accelerated degree program, self-designed majors, honors program, summer session, adult/continuing education programs, internships **Contact** Rev. Glenn Batten, Dean for Student Affairs and Enrollment, St. Andrews Presbyterian College, 1700 Dogwood Mile, Laurinburg, NC 28352. Telephone: 910-277-5555 or toll-free 800-763-0198. Fax: 910-277-5087. E-mail: admission@sapc.edu. Web site: http://www.sapc.edu/.

SAINT AUGUSTINE'S COLLEGE
RALEIGH, NORTH CAROLINA

General Independent Episcopal, 4-year, coed **Entrance** Minimally difficult **Setting** 110-acre urban campus **Total enrollment** 1,360 **Student-faculty ratio** 13:1 **Application deadline** 7/1 (freshmen), rolling (transfer) **Freshmen** 24% were admitted **Housing** Yes **Expenses** Tuition $8030; Room & Board $4960 **Undergraduates** 59% women, 9% part-time, 21% 25 or older **The most frequently chosen baccalaureate fields are** business/marketing, computer/information sciences, social sciences and history **Academic program** Accelerated degree program, honors program, summer session, adult/continuing education programs, internships **Contact** Mr. Tim Chapman, Interim Director of Admissions, Saint Augustine's College, 1315 Oakwood Avenue, Raleigh, NC 27610-2298. Telephone: 919-516-4011 or toll-free 800-948-1126. Fax: 919-516-4415. E-mail: admissions@es.st-aug.edu. Web site: http://www.st-aug.edu/.

SALEM COLLEGE
WINSTON-SALEM, NORTH CAROLINA

General Independent Moravian, comprehensive, women only **Entrance** Moderately difficult **Setting** 57-acre urban campus **Total enrollment** 1,074 **Student-faculty ratio** 13:1 **Application deadline** Rolling (freshmen), rolling (transfer) **Freshmen** 76% were admitted **Housing** Yes **Expenses** Tuition $14,495; Room & Board $8570 **Undergraduates** 29% part-time, 39% 25 or older, 1% Native American, 2% Hispanic American, 18% African American, 2% Asian American/Pacific Islander **The most frequently chosen baccalaureate fields are** English, business/marketing, social sciences and history **Academic program** Advanced placement, self-designed majors, honors program, summer session, adult/continuing education programs, internships **Contact** Ms. Dana E. Evans, Dean of Admissions and Financial Aid, Salem College, PO Box 10548, Shober House, Winston-Salem, NC 27108. Telephone: 336-721-2621 or toll-free 800-327-2536. Fax: 336-724-7102. E-mail: admissions@salem.edu. Web site: http://www.salem.edu/.

SHAW UNIVERSITY
RALEIGH, NORTH CAROLINA

General Independent Baptist, comprehensive, coed **Entrance** Minimally difficult **Setting** 18-acre urban campus **Total enrollment** 2,523 **Student-faculty ratio** 15:1 **Application deadline** 7/30 (freshmen), 7/30 (transfer) **Freshmen** 64% were admitted **Housing** Yes **Expenses** Tuition $7930; Room & Board $4880 **Undergraduates** 67% women, 18% part-time, 50% 25 or older, 0.3% Native American, 0.4% Hispanic American, 85% African American, 0.04% Asian American/Pacific Islander **The most frequently chosen baccalaureate fields are** business/marketing, protective services/public administration, social sciences and history **Academic program**

NORTH CAROLINA

Shaw University *(continued)*
English as a second language, advanced placement, accelerated degree program, self-designed majors, honors program, summer session, adult/continuing education programs, internships **Contact** Mr. Paul Vandergrift, Director of Admissions and Recruitment, Shaw University, 118 East South Street, Raleigh, NC 27601-2399. Telephone: 919-546-8275 or toll-free 800-214-6683. Fax: 919-546-8271. E-mail: paulv@shawu.edu. Web site: http://www.shawuniversity.edu/.

THE UNIVERSITY OF NORTH CAROLINA AT ASHEVILLE
ASHEVILLE, NORTH CAROLINA

General State-supported, comprehensive, coed **Entrance** Moderately difficult **Setting** 265-acre suburban campus **Total enrollment** 3,247 **Student-faculty ratio** 13:1 **Application deadline** 3/15 (freshmen), 6/1 (transfer) **Freshmen** 59% were admitted **Housing** Yes **Expenses** Tuition $2496; Room & Board $4400 **Undergraduates** 58% women, 23% part-time, 21% 25 or older, 0.5% Native American, 1% Hispanic American, 3% African American, 1% Asian American/Pacific Islander The most frequently chosen baccalaureate fields are business/marketing, psychology, social sciences and history **Academic program** Advanced placement, self-designed majors, honors program, summer session, adult/continuing education programs, internships **Contact** Ms. Fran Barrett, Director of Admissions, The University of North Carolina at Asheville, 117 Lipinsky Hall, CPO 2210, One University Heights, Asheville, NC 28804-8510. Telephone: 828-251-6481 or toll-free 800-531-9842. Fax: 828-251-6482. E-mail: admissions@unca.edu. Web site: http://www.unca.edu/.

THE UNIVERSITY OF NORTH CAROLINA AT CHAPEL HILL
CHAPEL HILL, NORTH CAROLINA

General State-supported, university, coed **Entrance** Very difficult **Setting** 789-acre suburban campus **Total enrollment** 25,494 **Student-faculty ratio** 14:1 **Application deadline** 1/15 (freshmen), 3/1 (transfer) **Freshmen** 40% were admitted **Housing** Yes **Expenses** Tuition $3277; Room & Board $5570 **Undergraduates** 60% women, 5% part-time, 5% 25 or older, 1% Native American, 2% Hispanic American, 11% African American, 5% Asian American/Pacific Islander The most frequently chosen baccalaureate fields are communications/communication technologies, business/marketing, social sciences and history **Academic program** Advanced placement, self-designed majors, honors program, summer session, internships **Contact** Mr. Jerome A. Lucido, Vice Provost and Director of Undergraduate Admissions, The University of North Carolina at Chapel Hill, Office of Undergraduate Admissions, Jackson Hall 153A, Campus Box 2200, Chapel Hill, NC 27599-2200. Telephone: 919-966-3621. Fax: 919-962-3045. E-mail: uadm@email.unc.edu. Web site: http://www.unc.edu/.

THE UNIVERSITY OF NORTH CAROLINA AT CHARLOTTE
CHARLOTTE, NORTH CAROLINA

General State-supported, university, coed **Entrance** Moderately difficult **Setting** 1,000-acre suburban campus **Total enrollment** 18,308 **Student-faculty ratio** 16:1 **Application deadline** 7/1 (freshmen), 7/1 (transfer) **Freshmen** 73% were admitted **Housing** Yes **Expenses** Tuition $2460; Room & Board $4798 **Undergraduates** 54% women, 25% part-time, 22% 25 or older, 0.4% Native American, 2% Hispanic American, 17% African American, 5% Asian American/Pacific Islander The most frequently chosen baccalaureate fields are business/marketing, engineering/engineering technologies, social sciences and history **Academic program** English as a second language, advanced placement, honors program, summer session, adult/continuing education programs, internships **Contact** Mr. Craig Fulton, Director of Admissions, The University of North Carolina at Charlotte, 9201 University City Boulevard, Charlotte, NC 28223-0001. Telephone: 704-687-2213. Fax: 704-687-6483. E-mail: unccadm@email.uncc.edu. Web site: http://www.uncc.edu/.

THE UNIVERSITY OF NORTH CAROLINA AT GREENSBORO
GREENSBORO, NORTH CAROLINA

General State-supported, university, coed **Entrance** Moderately difficult **Setting** 200-acre urban campus **Total enrollment** 13,343 **Student-faculty ratio** 15:1 **Application deadline** 8/1 (freshmen), 8/1 (transfer) **Freshmen** 75% were admitted **Housing** Yes **Expenses** Tuition $2545; Room & Board $4313 **Undergraduates** 68% women, 16% part-time, 19% 25 or older, 0.4% Native American, 2% Hispanic American, 20% African American, 3% Asian American/Pacific Islander The most frequently chosen baccalaureate fields are business/marketing, education, health professions and related sciences **Academic program** English as a second language, advanced placement, accelerated degree program, self-designed majors, honors program, summer session, adult/continuing education programs, internships **Contact** Mr. Jerry Harrelson, Associate Director of Admissions, The University of North Carolina at Greensboro, 1000 Spring Garden Street, Greensboro, NC 27412-5001. Telephone: 336-334-5243. Fax: 336-334-4180. E-mail: undergrad_admissions@uncg.edu. Web site: http://www.uncg.edu/.

THE UNIVERSITY OF NORTH CAROLINA AT PEMBROKE
PEMBROKE, NORTH CAROLINA

General State-supported, comprehensive, coed **Entrance** Moderately difficult **Setting** 126-acre rural campus **Total enrollment** 3,933 **Student-faculty ratio** 17:1 **Application deadline** Rolling (freshmen), rolling (transfer) **Freshmen** 51% were admitted **Housing** Yes **Expenses** Tuition $2069; Room & Board $3845 **Undergraduates** 62% women, 23% part-time, 35% 25 or older, 22% Native American, 2% Hispanic American, 21% African American, 1% Asian American/Pacific Islander **The most frequently chosen baccalaureate fields are** business/marketing, protective services/public administration, social sciences and history **Academic program** English as a second language, advanced placement, accelerated degree program, honors program, summer session, adult/continuing education programs, internships **Contact** John Kelly Brookins III, Associate Director of Admissions, The University of North Carolina at Pembroke, PO Box 1510, Pembroke, NC 28372-1510. Telephone: 910-521-6262 or toll-free 800-949-UNCP (in-state); 800-949-uncp (out-of-state). Fax: 910-521-6497. Web site: http://www.uncp.edu/.

THE UNIVERSITY OF NORTH CAROLINA AT WILMINGTON
WILMINGTON, NORTH CAROLINA

General State-supported, comprehensive, coed **Entrance** Moderately difficult **Setting** 650-acre urban campus **Total enrollment** 10,599 **Student-faculty ratio** 16:1 **Application deadline** 2/1 (freshmen), rolling (transfer) **Freshmen** 80% were admitted **Housing** Yes **Expenses** Tuition $2627; Room & Board $5142 **Undergraduates** 60% women, 11% part-time, 15% 25 or older, 1% Native American, 1% Hispanic American, 4% African American, 1% Asian American/Pacific Islander **The most frequently chosen baccalaureate fields are** business/marketing, education, English **Academic program** English as a second language, advanced placement, accelerated degree program, honors program, summer session, adult/continuing education programs, internships **Contact** Dr. Roxie Shabazz, Assistant Vice Chancellor for Admissions, The University of North Carolina at Wilmington, 601 South College Road, Wilmington, NC 28403-3297. Telephone: 910-962-4198 or toll-free 800-228-5571 (out-of-state). Fax: 910-962-3038. E-mail: admissions@uncwil.edu. Web site: http://www.uncwil.edu/.

WAKE FOREST UNIVERSITY
WINSTON-SALEM, NORTH CAROLINA

General Independent, university, coed, affiliated with North Carolina Baptist State Convention **Entrance** Very difficult **Setting** 340-acre suburban campus **Total enrollment** 6,216 **Student-faculty ratio** 10:1 **Application deadline** 1/15 (freshmen), 2/15 (transfer) **Freshmen** 46% were admitted **Housing** Yes **Expenses** Tuition $23,530; Room & Board $6760 **Undergraduates** 51% women, 6% part-time, 3% 25 or older, 0.2% Native American, 1% Hispanic American, 7% African American, 3% Asian American/Pacific Islander **The most frequently chosen baccalaureate fields are** business/marketing, communications/communication technologies, social sciences and history **Academic program** Advanced placement, accelerated degree program, self-designed majors, honors program, summer session, internships **Contact** Martha Allman, Director of Admissions, Wake Forest University, PO Box 7305, Winston-Salem, NC 27109. Telephone: 336-758-5201. Fax: 336-758-6074. E-mail: admissions@wfu.edu. Web site: http://www.wfu.edu/.

WARREN WILSON COLLEGE
ASHEVILLE, NORTH CAROLINA

General Independent, comprehensive, coed, affiliated with Presbyterian Church (U.S.A.) **Entrance** Moderately difficult **Setting** 1,100-acre small-town campus **Total enrollment** 853 **Student-faculty ratio** 11:1 **Application deadline** 3/15 (freshmen), 3/15 (transfer) **Freshmen** 82% were admitted **Housing** Yes **Expenses** Tuition $15,094; Room & Board $4874 **Undergraduates** 61% women, 1% part-time, 4% 25 or older, 0.3% Native American, 2% Hispanic American, 1% African American, 1% Asian American/Pacific Islander **The most frequently chosen baccalaureate fields are** natural resources/environmental science, English, social sciences and history **Academic program** English as a second language, advanced placement, self-designed majors, honors program, internships **Contact** Mr. Richard Blomgren, Dean of Admission, Warren Wilson College, PO Box 9000, Asheville, NC 28815-9000. Telephone: 828-771-2073 or toll-free 800-934-3536. Fax: 828-298-1440. E-mail: admit@warren-wilson.edu. Web site: http://www.warren-wilson.edu/.

▶ **For more information, see page 493.**

WESTERN CAROLINA UNIVERSITY
CULLOWHEE, NORTH CAROLINA

General State-supported, comprehensive, coed **Entrance** Moderately difficult **Setting** 260-acre rural campus **Total enrollment** 6,863 **Student-faculty ratio** 15:1 **Application deadline** 8/1 (freshmen), 7/1 (transfer) **Freshmen** 73% were admitted **Housing** Yes **Expenses** Tuition $2243; Room & Board $3424 **Undergraduates** 52% women, 14% part-time, 16% 25 or older, 2% Native American, 1% Hispanic American, 5% African American, 1% Asian American/Pacific Islander **The most frequently chosen baccalaureate fields are** business/marketing, education, health professions and related sciences **Academic program** English as a second language, advanced placement, accelerated degree program, self-designed majors, honors program, summer session, adult/continuing education programs, internships **Contact** Mr. Philip Cauley, Director of Admissions, Western Carolina University, Cullowhee, NC 28723. Telephone: 828-227-7317 or toll-free 877-WCU4YOU. Fax: 828-277-7319. E-mail: admiss@email.wcu.edu. Web site: http://www.wcu.edu/.

WINGATE UNIVERSITY
WINGATE, NORTH CAROLINA

General Independent Baptist, comprehensive, coed **Entrance** Moderately difficult **Setting** 330-acre small-town campus **Total enrollment** 1,357 **Student-faculty ratio** 13:1 **Application deadline** Rolling (freshmen), rolling (transfer) **Freshmen** 80% were admitted **Housing** Yes **Expenses** Tuition $13,680;

NORTH CAROLINA

Wingate University *(continued)*
Room & Board $5460 **Undergraduates** 53% women, 3% part-time, 6% 25 or older, 0.4% Native American, 2% Hispanic American, 11% African American, 1% Asian American/Pacific Islander **The most frequently chosen baccalaureate fields are** business/marketing, liberal arts/general studies, parks and recreation **Academic program** Advanced placement, accelerated degree program, honors program, summer session, adult/continuing education programs, internships **Contact** Mr. Walter P. Crutchfield III, Dean of Admissions, Wingate University, PO Box 159, Wingate, NC 28174. Telephone: 704-233-8000 or toll-free 800-755-5550. Fax: 704-233-8110. E-mail: admit@wingate.edu. Web site: http://www.wingate.edu/.

WINSTON-SALEM STATE UNIVERSITY
WINSTON-SALEM, NORTH CAROLINA

General State-supported, comprehensive, coed **Entrance** Minimally difficult **Setting** 94-acre urban campus **Total enrollment** 2,992 **Student-faculty ratio** 15:1 **Application deadline** Rolling (freshmen), rolling (transfer) **Freshmen** 76% were admitted **Housing** Yes **Expenses** Tuition $2063; Room & Board $3864 **Undergraduates** 68% women, 18% part-time, 25% 25 or older, 0.2% Native American, 0.5% Hispanic American, 85% African American, 1% Asian American/Pacific Islander **The most frequently chosen baccalaureate fields are** business/marketing, health professions and related sciences, social sciences and history **Academic program** Advanced placement, accelerated degree program, honors program, summer session, adult/continuing education programs, internships **Contact** Mr. Van C. Wilson, Director of Admissions, Winston-Salem State University, 601 Martin Luther King Jr Drive, Winston-Salem, NC 27110-0003. Telephone: 336-750-2070 or toll-free 800-257-4052. Fax: 336-750-2079. E-mail: wilsonv@wssu1adp.wssu.edu. Web site: http://www.wssu.edu/.

NORTH DAKOTA

DICKINSON STATE UNIVERSITY
DICKINSON, NORTH DAKOTA

General State-supported, 4-year, coed **Entrance** Noncompetitive **Setting** 100-acre small-town campus **Total enrollment** 2,101 **Student-faculty ratio** 19:1 **Application deadline** Rolling (freshmen), rolling (transfer) **Freshmen** 100% were admitted **Housing** Yes **Expenses** Tuition $2463; Room & Board $3032 **Undergraduates** 57% women, 28% part-time, 19% 25 or older, 2% Native American, 1% Hispanic American, 0.5% African American, 0.1% Asian American/Pacific Islander **The most frequently chosen baccalaureate fields are** business/marketing, education, health professions and related sciences **Academic program** Advanced placement, acceler- ated degree program, self-designed majors, summer session, adult/continuing education programs, internships **Contact** Deb Dazell, Director of Student Recruitment, Dickinson State University, 8th Avenue West and 3rd Street West, Dickinson, ND 58601. Telephone: 701-483-2175 or toll-free 800-279-4295. Fax: 701-483-2409. E-mail: dsuhawk@eagle.dsu.nodak.edu. Web site: http://www.dsu.nodak.edu/.

JAMESTOWN COLLEGE
JAMESTOWN, NORTH DAKOTA

General Independent Presbyterian, 4-year, coed **Entrance** Minimally difficult **Setting** 107-acre small-town campus **Total enrollment** 1,136 **Student-faculty ratio** 18:1 **Application deadline** Rolling (freshmen), rolling (transfer) **Freshmen** 99% were admitted **Housing** Yes **Expenses** Tuition $7925; Room & Board $3385 **Undergraduates** 56% women, 7% part-time, 5% 25 or older, 1% Native American, 1% Hispanic American, 1% African American, 0.2% Asian American/Pacific Islander **The most frequently chosen baccalaureate fields are** business/marketing, education, health professions and related sciences **Academic program** Advanced placement, self-designed majors, honors program, summer session, internships **Contact** Judy Erickson, Director of Admissions, Jamestown College, 6081 College Lane, Jamestown, ND 58405. Telephone: 701-252-3467 Ext. 2548 or toll-free 800-336-2554. Fax: 701-253-4318. E-mail: admissions@jc.edu. Web site: http://www.jc.edu/.

MAYVILLE STATE UNIVERSITY
MAYVILLE, NORTH DAKOTA

General State-supported, 4-year, coed **Entrance** Noncompetitive **Setting** 60-acre rural campus **Total enrollment** 755 **Student-faculty ratio** 15:1 **Application deadline** Rolling (freshmen), rolling (transfer) **Freshmen** 100% were admitted **Housing** Yes **Expenses** Tuition $3314; Room & Board $3126 **Undergraduates** 54% women, 23% part-time, 29% 25 or older, 1% Native American, 1% Hispanic American, 2% African American, 0.3% Asian American/Pacific Islander **The most frequently chosen baccalaureate fields are** business/marketing, computer/information sciences, education **Academic program** Advanced placement, accelerated degree program, self-designed majors, summer session, adult/continuing education programs, internships **Contact** Brian Larson, Director of Enrollment Services, Mayville State University, 330 3rd Street, NE, Mayville, ND 58257-1299. Telephone: 701-786-4768 Ext. 34768 or toll-free 800-437-4104. Fax: 701-786-4748. E-mail: mvadmiss@plains.nodak.edu. Web site: http://www.masu.nodak.edu/.

MEDCENTER ONE COLLEGE OF NURSING
BISMARCK, NORTH DAKOTA

General Independent, upper-level, coed, primarily women **Entrance** Moderately difficult **Setting** 15-acre small-town campus **Total enrollment** 91 **Student-

NORTH DAKOTA

faculty ratio 9:1 **Application deadline** 11/7 (transfer) **First-Year Students** 48% were admitted **Housing** Yes **Expenses** Tuition $3578; Room only $900 **Undergraduates** 91% women, 11% part-time, 34% 25 or older, 1% Native American, 1% Hispanic American, 1% Asian American/Pacific Islander **The most frequently chosen baccalaureate field is** health professions and related sciences **Academic program** Honors program, summer session, internships **Contact** Mary Smith, Director of Student Services, Medcenter One College of Nursing, 512 North 7th Street, Bismarck, ND 58501-4494. Telephone: 701-323-6271. Fax: 701-323-6767. E-mail: msmith@mohs.org. Web site: http://www.medcenterone.com/nursing/nursing.htm/.

MINOT STATE UNIVERSITY
MINOT, NORTH DAKOTA

General State-supported, comprehensive, coed **Entrance** Minimally difficult **Setting** 103-acre small-town campus **Total enrollment** 3,515 **Student-faculty ratio** 15:1 **Application deadline** Rolling (freshmen), rolling (transfer) **Freshmen** 97% were admitted **Housing** Yes **Expenses** Tuition $2554; Room & Board $3100 **Undergraduates** 62% women, 25% part-time, 17% 25 or older, 4% Native American, 1% Hispanic American, 3% African American, 1% Asian American/Pacific Islander **The most frequently chosen baccalaureate fields are** business/marketing, education, protective services/public administration **Academic program** Advanced placement, accelerated degree program, self-designed majors, honors program, summer session, adult/continuing education programs, internships **Contact** Ms. Ann Hendrick, Admissions Specialist, Minot State University, 500 University Avenue West, Minot, ND 58707-0002. Telephone: 701-858-3346 or toll-free 800-777-0750 Ext. 3350. Fax: 701-839-6933. E-mail: beltz@warp6.cs.misu.nodak.edu. Web site: http://www.minotstateu.edu/.

NORTH DAKOTA STATE UNIVERSITY
FARGO, NORTH DAKOTA

General State-supported, university, coed **Entrance** Moderately difficult **Setting** 2,100-acre urban campus **Total enrollment** 10,538 **Student-faculty ratio** 19:1 **Application deadline** 8/15 (freshmen), 8/15 (transfer) **Freshmen** 66% were admitted **Housing** Yes **Expenses** Tuition $3272; Room & Board $3732 **Undergraduates** 42% women, 10% part-time, 10% 25 or older, 1% Native American, 0.4% Hispanic American, 1% African American, 1% Asian American/Pacific Islander **The most frequently chosen baccalaureate fields are** business/marketing, engineering/engineering technologies, health professions and related sciences **Academic program** English as a second language, advanced placement, accelerated degree program, self-designed majors, honors program, summer session, internships **Contact** Dr. Kate Haugen, Director of Admission, North Dakota State University, PO Box 5454, Fargo, ND 58105-5454. Telephone: 701-231-8643 or toll-free 800-488-NDSU.

Fax: 701-231-8802. E-mail: ndsu.admission@ndsu.nodak.edu. Web site: http://www.ndsu.edu/.

TRINITY BIBLE COLLEGE
ELLENDALE, NORTH DAKOTA

General Independent, 4-year, coed, affiliated with Assemblies of God **Entrance** Noncompetitive **Setting** 28-acre rural campus **Total enrollment** 272 **Student-faculty ratio** 11:1 **Application deadline** Rolling (freshmen), rolling (transfer) **Freshmen** 46% were admitted **Housing** Yes **Expenses** Tuition $7000; Room & Board $3640 **Undergraduates** 50% women, 6% part-time, 18% 25 or older, 2% Native American, 2% Hispanic American, 1% African American, 0% Asian American/Pacific Islander **The most frequently chosen baccalaureate fields are** education, philosophy **Academic program** Advanced placement, accelerated degree program, summer session, internships **Contact** Rev. Steve Tvedt, Vice President of College Relations, Trinity Bible College, 50 South Sixth Avenue, Ellendale, ND 58436. Telephone: 701-349-3621 Ext. 2045 or toll-free 800-TBC-2DAY. Fax: 701-349-5443. E-mail: TBC@DAY.edu.

UNIVERSITY OF MARY
BISMARCK, NORTH DAKOTA

General Independent Roman Catholic, comprehensive, coed **Entrance** Moderately difficult **Setting** 107-acre suburban campus **Total enrollment** 2,444 **Student-faculty ratio** 16:1 **Application deadline** Rolling (freshmen), rolling (transfer) **Freshmen** 83% were admitted **Housing** Yes **Expenses** Tuition $9000; Room & Board $3700 **Undergraduates** 61% women, 4% part-time, 30% 25 or older, 4% Native American, 1% Hispanic American, 1% African American, 1% Asian American/Pacific Islander **The most frequently chosen baccalaureate fields are** business/marketing, education, health professions and related sciences **Academic program** Advanced placement, accelerated degree program, summer session, adult/continuing education programs, internships **Contact** Dr. Dave Hebinger, Vice President for Enrollment Services, University of Mary, 7500 University Drive, Bismarck, ND 58504-9652. Telephone: 701-255-7500 Ext. 598 or toll-free 800-288-6279. Fax: 701-255-7687. E-mail: marauder@umary.edu. Web site: http://www.umary.edu/.

UNIVERSITY OF NORTH DAKOTA
GRAND FORKS, NORTH DAKOTA

General State-supported, university, coed **Entrance** Minimally difficult **Setting** 570-acre small-town campus **Total enrollment** 11,764 **Student-faculty ratio** 18:1 **Application deadline** 7/1 (freshmen), rolling (transfer) **Freshmen** 68% were admitted **Housing** Yes **Expenses** Tuition $3770; Room & Board $3805 **Undergraduates** 47% women, 10% part-time, 14% 25 or older, 3% Native American, 1% Hispanic American, 1% African American, 1% Asian American/Pacific Islander **The most frequently chosen baccalaureate fields are** business/marketing, health pro-

NORTH DAKOTA

University of North Dakota *(continued)*
fessions and related sciences, trade and industry **Academic program** Advanced placement, accelerated degree program, self-designed majors, honors program, summer session, adult/continuing education programs, internships **Contact** Ms. Heidi Kippenhan, Assistant Director of Admissions, University of North Dakota, Box 8382, Grand Forks, ND 58202. Telephone: 701-777-3821 or toll-free 800-CALL UND. Fax: 701-777-2696. E-mail: rob_carolin@mail.und.nodak.edu. Web site: http://www.und.edu/.

VALLEY CITY STATE UNIVERSITY
VALLEY CITY, NORTH DAKOTA

General State-supported, 4-year, coed **Entrance** Noncompetitive **Setting** 55-acre small-town campus **Total enrollment** 1,005 **Student-faculty ratio** 15:1 **Application deadline** Rolling (freshmen), rolling (transfer) **Freshmen** 95% were admitted **Housing** Yes **Expenses** Tuition $3306; Room & Board $3010 **Undergraduates** 57% women, 26% part-time, 22% 25 or older, 2% Native American, 1% Hispanic American, 1% African American, 0.3% Asian American/Pacific Islander **The most frequently chosen baccalaureate fields are** business/marketing, education, liberal arts/general studies **Academic program** English as a second language, self-designed majors, summer session, internships **Contact** Mr. Monte Johnson, Director of Admissions, Valley City State University, 101 College Street Southwest, Valley City, ND 58072. Telephone: 701-845-7101 Ext. 37297 or toll-free 800-532-8641 Ext. 37101. Fax: 701-845-7299. E-mail: enrollment_services@mail.vcsu.nodak.edu. Web site: http://www.vcsu.edu/.

OHIO

ANTIOCH COLLEGE
YELLOW SPRINGS, OHIO

General Independent, 4-year, coed **Entrance** Moderately difficult **Setting** 100-acre small-town campus **Total enrollment** 628 **Student-faculty ratio** 9:1 **Application deadline** 2/1 (freshmen), rolling (transfer) **Freshmen** 80% were admitted **Housing** Yes **Expenses** Tuition $25,072 **Undergraduates** 66% women, 4% part-time, 4% 25 or older, 1% Native American, 3% Hispanic American, 6% African American, 1% Asian American/Pacific Islander **Academic program** Advanced placement, self-designed majors, summer session, internships **Contact** Ms. Cathy Paige, Information Manager, Antioch College, 795 Livermore Street, Yellow Springs, OH 45387-1697. Telephone: 937-767-6400 Ext. 6559 or toll-free 800-543-9436 (out-of-state). Fax: 937-767-6473. E-mail: admissions@college.antioch.edu. Web site: http://www.antioch-college.edu/.

ANTIOCH UNIVERSITY MCGREGOR
YELLOW SPRINGS, OHIO

General Independent, upper-level, coed **Entrance** Noncompetitive **Setting** 100-acre small-town campus **Total enrollment** 626 **Student-faculty ratio** 7:1 **Application deadline** Rolling (transfer) **Housing** No **Expenses** Tuition $8325 **Undergraduates** 74% women, 63% part-time, 99% 25 or older, 0% Native American, 0% Hispanic American, 17% African American, 0% Asian American/Pacific Islander **The most frequently chosen baccalaureate fields are** business/marketing, liberal arts/general studies, psychology **Academic program** Advanced placement, accelerated degree program, summer session, adult/continuing education programs, internships **Contact** Oscar Robinson, Enrollment Services Manager, Antioch University McGregor, Student and Alumni Services Division, Enrollment Services, 800 Livermore Street, Yellow Springs, OH 45387. Telephone: 937-769-1823 or toll-free 937-769-1818. Fax: 937-769-1805. E-mail: sas@mcgregor.edu. Web site: http://www.mcgregor.edu/.

ART ACADEMY OF CINCINNATI
CINCINNATI, OHIO

General Independent, comprehensive, coed **Entrance** Moderately difficult **Setting** 184-acre urban campus **Total enrollment** 237 **Student-faculty ratio** 12:1 **Application deadline** 6/30 (freshmen), 6/30 (transfer) **Freshmen** 73% were admitted **Housing** No **Expenses** Tuition $13,000 **Undergraduates** 54% women, 2% part-time, 14% 25 or older, 0% Native American, 0% Hispanic American, 1% African American, 1% Asian American/Pacific Islander **The most frequently chosen baccalaureate field is** visual/performing arts **Academic program** Advanced placement, self-designed majors, summer session, adult/continuing education programs, internships **Contact** Ms. Mary Jane Zumwalde, Director of Admissions, Art Academy of Cincinnati, 1125 Saint Gregory Street, Cincinnati, OH 45202. Telephone: 513-562-8744 or toll-free 800-323-5692 (in-state). Fax: 513-562-8778. E-mail: admissions@artacademy.edu. Web site: http://www.artacademy.edu/.

ASHLAND UNIVERSITY
ASHLAND, OHIO

General Independent, comprehensive, coed, affiliated with Brethren Church **Entrance** Moderately difficult **Setting** 98-acre small-town campus **Total enrollment** 6,359 **Student-faculty ratio** 16:1 **Application deadline** 8/30 (freshmen), rolling (transfer) **Freshmen** 87% were admitted **Housing** Yes **Expenses** Tuition $16,320; Room & Board $5862 **Undergraduates** 56% women, 21% part-time, 30% 25 or older, 0.2% Native American, 1% Hispanic American, 9% African American, 0.4% Asian American/Pacific Islander **The most frequently chosen baccalaureate fields are** business/marketing, communications/communication technologies, education **Academic program** English as a second language, advanced placement, accelerated degree program, honors program, summer session, adult/continuing education programs, internships **Contact** Carolyn O'Lenic, Admission Representative, Ashland University, 401 College Avenue, Ashland, OH 44805. Telephone: 419-289-5943 or toll-free 800-882-1548. Fax: 419-289-5999. E-mail: auadmsn@ashland.edu. Web site: http://www.ashland.edu/.

BALDWIN-WALLACE COLLEGE
BEREA, OHIO

General Independent Methodist, comprehensive, coed **Entrance** Moderately difficult **Setting** 92-acre suburban campus **Total enrollment** 4,884 **Student-faculty ratio** 15:1 **Application deadline** Rolling (freshmen), rolling (transfer) **Freshmen** 85% were admitted **Housing** Yes **Expenses** Tuition $16,330; Room & Board $5680 **Undergraduates** 62% women, 24% part-time, 3% 25 or older, 0.2% Native American, 1% Hispanic American, 4% African American, 1% Asian American/Pacific Islander **The most frequently chosen baccalaureate fields are** business/marketing, education, social sciences and history **Academic program** English as a second language, advanced placement, accelerated degree program, self-designed majors, honors program, summer session, adult/continuing education programs, internships **Contact** Mrs. Julie Baker, Director of Undergraduate Admission, Baldwin-Wallace College, 275 Eastland Road, Berea, OH 44017-2088. Telephone: 440-826-2222 or toll-free 877-BWAPPLY (in-state). Fax: 440-826-3830. E-mail: admission@baldwinw.edu. Web site: http://www.bw.edu/.

BLUFFTON COLLEGE
BLUFFTON, OHIO

General Independent Mennonite, comprehensive, coed **Entrance** Moderately difficult **Setting** 65-acre small-town campus **Total enrollment** 1,020 **Student-faculty ratio** 14:1 **Application deadline** 5/31 (freshmen), rolling (transfer) **Freshmen** 75% were admitted **Housing** Yes **Expenses** Tuition $15,076 **Undergraduates** 58% women, 7% part-time, 9% 25 or older, 0.2% Native American, 1% Hispanic American, 2% African American, 1% Asian American/Pacific Islander **The most frequently chosen baccalaureate fields are** business/marketing, education, protective services/public administration **Academic program** English as a second language, advanced placement, accelerated degree program, self-designed majors, honors program, summer session, adult/continuing education programs, internships **Contact** Mr. Eric Fulcomer, Director of Admissions, Associate Dean for Enrollment Management, Bluffton College, 280 West College Avenue, Bluffton, OH 45817. Telephone: 419-358-3254 or toll-free 800-488-3257. Fax: 419-358-3232. E-mail: admissions@bluffton.edu. Web site: http://www.bluffton.edu/.

BOWLING GREEN STATE UNIVERSITY
BOWLING GREEN, OHIO

General State-supported, university, coed **Entrance** Moderately difficult **Setting** 1,230-acre small-town campus **Total enrollment** 18,739 **Student-faculty ratio** 19:1 **Application deadline** 7/15 (freshmen), 7/15 (transfer) **Freshmen** 92% were admitted **Housing** Yes **Expenses** Tuition $5604; Room & Board $5190 **Undergraduates** 56% women, 7% part-time, 6% 25 or older, 0.3% Native American, 2% Hispanic American, 5% African American, 1% Asian American/Pacific Islander **The most frequently chosen baccalaureate fields are** business/marketing, education, English **Academic program** English as a second language, advanced placement, accelerated degree program, self-designed majors, honors program, summer session, adult/continuing education programs, internships **Contact** Mr. Gary Swegan, Director of Admissions, Bowling Green State University, 110 McFall, Bowling Green, OH 43403. Telephone: 419-372-2086. Fax: 419-372-6955. E-mail: admissions@bgnet.bgsu.edu. Web site: http://www.bgsu.edu/.

BRYANT AND STRATTON COLLEGE
CLEVELAND, OHIO

General Proprietary, 4-year, coed **Entrance** Minimally difficult **Setting** urban campus **Total enrollment** 205 **Student-faculty ratio** 10:1 **Application deadline** Rolling (freshmen), rolling (transfer) **Freshmen** 93% were admitted **Housing** Yes **Expenses** Tuition $9472; Room only $4200 **Undergraduates** 40% women, 46% part-time, 59% 25 or older, 0% Native American, 4% Hispanic American, 50% African American, 0% Asian American/Pacific Islander **The most frequently chosen baccalaureate field is** engineering/engineering technologies **Academic program** Summer session, adult/continuing education programs, internships **Contact** Kerry Burton, Director of Admissions, Bryant and Stratton College, 1700 East 13th Street, Cleveland, OH 44114-3203. Telephone: 216-771-1700. Fax: 216-771-7787. Web site: http://www.bryantstratton.com/.

CAPITAL UNIVERSITY
COLUMBUS, OHIO

General Independent, comprehensive, coed, affiliated with Evangelical Lutheran Church in America **Entrance** Moderately difficult **Setting** 48-acre suburban campus **Total enrollment** 3,843 **Student-faculty ratio** 11:1 **Application deadline** 4/15 (freshmen), rolling (transfer) **Freshmen** 81% were admitted **Housing** Yes **Expenses** Tuition $17,990; Room & Board $5640 **Undergraduates** 64% women, 27% part-time, 2% 25 or older, 0.4% Native American, 2% Hispanic American, 16% African American, 1% Asian American/Pacific Islander **The most frequently chosen baccalaureate fields are** business/marketing, interdisciplinary studies, social sciences and history **Academic program** English as a second language, advanced placement, self-designed majors, summer session, adult/continuing education programs, internships **Contact** Mrs. Kimberly V. Ebbrecht, Director of Admission, Capital University, 2199 East Main Street, Columbus, OH 43209. Telephone: 614-236-6101 or toll-free 800-289-6289. Fax: 614-236-6926. E-mail: admissions@capital.edu. Web site: http://www.capital.edu/.

OHIO

CASE WESTERN RESERVE UNIVERSITY
CLEVELAND, OHIO

General Independent, university, coed **Entrance** Very difficult **Setting** 128-acre urban campus **Total enrollment** 9,216 **Student-faculty ratio** 8:1 **Application deadline** 2/1 (freshmen), 6/30 (transfer) **Freshmen** 74% were admitted **Housing** Yes **Expenses** Tuition $21,168; Room & Board $6250 **Undergraduates** 39% women, 8% part-time, 4% 25 or older, 0.2% Native American, 2% Hispanic American, 4% African American, 14% Asian American/Pacific Islander **The most frequently chosen baccalaureate fields are** biological/life sciences, business/marketing, engineering/engineering technologies **Academic program** English as a second language, advanced placement, accelerated degree program, self-designed majors, honors program, summer session, adult/continuing education programs, internships **Contact** Mr. William T. Conley, Dean of Undergraduate Admission, Case Western Reserve University, 10900 Euclid Avenue, Cleveland, OH 44106. Telephone: 216-368-4450. E-mail: admission@po.cwru.edu. Web site: http://www.cwru.edu/.

CEDARVILLE UNIVERSITY
CEDARVILLE, OHIO

General Independent Baptist, comprehensive, coed **Entrance** Moderately difficult **Setting** 300-acre rural campus **Total enrollment** 2,951 **Student-faculty ratio** 16:1 **Application deadline** Rolling (freshmen), rolling (transfer) **Freshmen** 73% were admitted **Housing** Yes **Expenses** Tuition $12,624; Room & Board $4929 **Undergraduates** 54% women, 4% part-time, 1% 25 or older, 0.2% Native American, 1% Hispanic American, 1% African American, 1% Asian American/Pacific Islander **The most frequently chosen baccalaureate fields are** education, business/marketing, philosophy, religion, and theology **Academic program** Advanced placement, accelerated degree program, honors program, summer session, internships **Contact** Mr. Roscoe Smith, Director of Admissions, Cedarville University, 251 North Main Street, Cedarville, OH 45314-0601. Telephone: 937-766-7700 or toll-free 800-CEDARVILLE. Fax: 937-766-7575. E-mail: admiss@cedarville.edu. Web site: http://www.cedarville.edu/.

CENTRAL STATE UNIVERSITY
WILBERFORCE, OHIO

General State-supported, comprehensive, coed **Entrance** Minimally difficult **Setting** 60-acre rural campus **Total enrollment** 1,400 **Student-faculty ratio** 13:1 **Application deadline** 6/15 (freshmen), 6/15 (transfer) **Freshmen** 49% were admitted **Housing** Yes **Expenses** Tuition $3714; Room & Board $5208 **Undergraduates** 54% women, 9% part-time, 16% 25 or older, 0.2% Native American, 0% Hispanic American, 89% African American, 0.2% Asian American/Pacific Islander **The most frequently chosen baccalaureate fields are** business/marketing, education, social sciences and history **Academic program** Honors program, summer session, adult/continuing education programs, internships **Contact** Mr. Thandabantu Maceo, Director, Admissions, Central State University, PO Box 1004, 1400 Blush Row Road, Wilberforce, OH 45384. Telephone: 937-376-6348 or toll-free 800-388-CSU1 (in-state). Fax: 937-376-6648. E-mail: admissions@csu.ces.edu. Web site: http://www.centralstate.edu/.

CINCINNATI BIBLE COLLEGE AND SEMINARY
CINCINNATI, OHIO

General Independent, comprehensive, coed, affiliated with Church of Christ **Entrance** Minimally difficult **Setting** 40-acre urban campus **Total enrollment** 968 **Student-faculty ratio** 16:1 **Application deadline** 8/10 (freshmen), 8/10 (transfer) **Freshmen** 99% were admitted **Housing** Yes **Expenses** Tuition $7500; Room & Board $4340 **Undergraduates** 20% 25 or older **Academic program** Advanced placement, summer session, adult/continuing education programs, internships **Contact** Mr. Alex Eady, Director of Undergraduate Admissions, Cincinnati Bible College and Seminary, 2700 Glenway Avenue, Cincinnati, OH 45204-1799. Telephone: 800-949-4222 Ext. 8610 or toll-free 800-949-4CBC. Fax: 513-244-8140. E-mail: admissions@cincybible.edu. Web site: http://www.cincybible.edu/.

CIRCLEVILLE BIBLE COLLEGE
CIRCLEVILLE, OHIO

General Independent, 4-year, coed, affiliated with Churches of Christ in Christian Union **Entrance** Minimally difficult **Setting** 40-acre small-town campus **Total enrollment** 308 **Student-faculty ratio** 13:1 **Application deadline** Rolling (freshmen), rolling (transfer) **Freshmen** 61% were admitted **Housing** Yes **Expenses** Tuition $7414; Room & Board $4931 **Undergraduates** 46% women, 10% part-time, 42% 25 or older, 1% Native American, 1% Hispanic American, 7% African American, 1% Asian American/Pacific Islander **The most frequently chosen baccalaureate field is** philosophy, religion, and theology **Academic program** Advanced placement, self-designed majors, honors program, summer session, adult/continuing education programs, internships **Contact** Rev. Matt Taylor, Director of Enrollment, Circleville Bible College, PO Box 458, Circleville, OH 43113-9487. Telephone: 740-477-7701 or toll-free 800-701-0222. Fax: 740-477-7755. E-mail: enroll@biblecollege.edu. Web site: http://www.biblecollege.edu/.

CLEVELAND COLLEGE OF JEWISH STUDIES
See Laura and Alvin Siegal College of Judaic Studies

THE CLEVELAND INSTITUTE OF ART
CLEVELAND, OHIO

General Independent, comprehensive, coed **Entrance** Moderately difficult **Setting** 488-acre urban campus

OHIO

Total enrollment 615 **Student-faculty ratio** 10:1 **Application deadline** Rolling (freshmen), rolling (transfer) **Freshmen** 91% were admitted **Housing** Yes **Expenses** Tuition $17,598; Room & Board $5596 **Undergraduates** 52% women, 7% part-time, 13% 25 or older, 0.3% Native American, 2% Hispanic American, 4% African American, 2% Asian American/Pacific Islander **The most frequently chosen baccalaureate field is** visual/performing arts **Academic program** Advanced placement, internships **Contact** Office of Admissions, The Cleveland Institute of Art, 11141 East Boulevard, Cleveland, OH 44106. Telephone: 216-421-7418 or toll-free 800-223-4700. Fax: 216-754-3634. E-mail: 74527.17@compuserve.com. Web site: http://www.cia.edu/.

CLEVELAND INSTITUTE OF MUSIC
CLEVELAND, OHIO

General Independent, comprehensive, coed **Entrance** Very difficult **Setting** 488-acre urban campus **Total enrollment** 382 **Student-faculty ratio** 7:1 **Application deadline** 12/1 (freshmen), 12/1 (transfer) **Freshmen** 29% were admitted **Housing** Yes **Expenses** Tuition $20,312; Room & Board $6200 **Undergraduates** 3% 25 or older, 0% Native American, 3% Hispanic American, 1% African American, 12% Asian American/Pacific Islander **Academic program** English as a second language, advanced placement, accelerated degree program, summer session, internships **Contact** Mr. William Fay, Director of Admission, Cleveland Institute of Music, 11021 East Boulevard, Cleveland, OH 44106-1776. Telephone: 216-795-3107. Fax: 216-791-1530. E-mail: cimadmission@po.cwru.edu. Web site: http://www.cim.edu/.

CLEVELAND STATE UNIVERSITY
CLEVELAND, OHIO

General State-supported, university, coed **Entrance** Noncompetitive **Setting** 70-acre urban campus **Total enrollment** 15,703 **Student-faculty ratio** 15:1 **Application deadline** 7/15 (freshmen), 7/15 (transfer) **Freshmen** 86% were admitted **Housing** Yes **Expenses** Tuition $4728; Room & Board $5550 **Undergraduates** 55% women, 35% part-time, 40% 25 or older, 0.3% Native American, 3% Hispanic American, 20% African American, 3% Asian American/Pacific Islander **The most frequently chosen baccalaureate fields are** business/marketing, education, social sciences and history **Academic program** English as a second language, advanced placement, accelerated degree program, self-designed majors, summer session, adult/continuing education programs, internships **Contact** Office of Admissions, Cleveland State University, 1983 East 24th Street, Rhodes Tower West, Room 204, Cleveland, OH 44115. Telephone: 216-687-3754 or toll-free 800-CSU-OHIO (in-state). Fax: 216-687-9210. E-mail: d.norris@csuohio.edu. Web site: http://www.csuohio.edu/.

COLLEGE OF MOUNT ST. JOSEPH
CINCINNATI, OHIO

General Independent Roman Catholic, comprehensive, coed **Entrance** Moderately difficult **Setting** 75-acre suburban campus **Total enrollment** 2,273 **Student-faculty ratio** 15:1 **Application deadline** 8/15 (freshmen), 8/15 (transfer) **Freshmen** 81% were admitted **Housing** Yes **Expenses** Tuition $15,040; Room & Board $5520 **Undergraduates** 71% women, 38% part-time, 36% 25 or older, 0.2% Native American, 0.5% Hispanic American, 8% African American, 1% Asian American/Pacific Islander **The most frequently chosen baccalaureate fields are** business/marketing, education, health professions and related sciences **Academic program** English as a second language, advanced placement, accelerated degree program, honors program, summer session, adult/continuing education programs, internships **Contact** Ms. Peggy Minnich, Director of Admission, College of Mount St. Joseph, 5701 Delhi Road, Cincinnati, OH 45233-1672. Telephone: 513-244-4814 or toll-free 800-654-9314. Fax: 513-244-4629. E-mail: peggy_minnich@mail.msj.edu. Web site: http://www.msj.edu/.

THE COLLEGE OF WOOSTER
WOOSTER, OHIO

General Independent, 4-year, coed, affiliated with Presbyterian Church (U.S.A.) **Entrance** Moderately difficult **Setting** 320-acre small-town campus **Total enrollment** 1,823 **Student-faculty ratio** 12:1 **Application deadline** 2/15 (freshmen), 6/1 (transfer) **Freshmen** 72% were admitted **Housing** Yes **Expenses** Tuition $22,430; Room & Board $5920 **Undergraduates** 53% women, 2% part-time, 0% 25 or older, 0.2% Native American, 1% Hispanic American, 5% African American, 1% Asian American/Pacific Islander **The most frequently chosen baccalaureate fields are** English, biological/life sciences, social sciences and history **Academic program** Advanced placement, self-designed majors, summer session, internships **Contact** Ms. Carol D. Wheatley, Director of Admissions, The College of Wooster, 1189 Beall Avenue, Wooster, OH 44691. Telephone: 330-263-2270 Ext. 2118 or toll-free 800-877-9905. Fax: 330-263-2621. E-mail: admissions@wooster.edu. Web site: http://www.wooster.edu/.

▶ For more information, see page 415.

COLUMBUS COLLEGE OF ART AND DESIGN
COLUMBUS, OHIO

General Independent, 4-year, coed **Entrance** Moderately difficult **Setting** 7-acre urban campus **Total enrollment** 1,737 **Student-faculty ratio** 11:1 **Application deadline** Rolling (freshmen), rolling (transfer) **Freshmen** 79% were admitted **Housing** Yes **Expenses** Tuition $16,330; Room & Board $6200 **Undergraduates** 51% women, 23% part-time, 16% 25 or older, 0.5% Native American, 2% Hispanic American, 6% African American, 6% Asian American/Pacific Islander **Academic program** English as a second language, advanced placement, summer session, internships **Contact** Mr. Thomas E. Green, Director of Admissions, Columbus College of Art and Design, 107 North Ninth Street, Columbus, OH

Columbus College of Art and Design *(continued)*
43215-1758. Telephone: 614-224-9101. Fax: 614-232-8344. E-mail: brooke@ccad.edu. Web site: http://www.ccad.edu/.

DAVID N. MYERS UNIVERSITY
CLEVELAND, OHIO

General Independent, comprehensive, coed **Entrance** Minimally difficult **Setting** 1-acre urban campus **Total enrollment** 1,177 **Student-faculty ratio** 12:1 **Application deadline** Rolling (freshmen), rolling (transfer) **Freshmen** 65% were admitted **Housing** No **Expenses** Tuition $9450 **Undergraduates** 71% women, 48% part-time, 50% 25 or older, 0% Native American, 3% Hispanic American, 45% African American, 0.3% Asian American/Pacific Islander **The most frequently chosen baccalaureate field is** law/legal studies **Academic program** Advanced placement, accelerated degree program, self-designed majors, summer session, adult/continuing education programs, internships **Contact** Ms. Tiffiney Payton, Interim Director of Admissions, David N. Myers University, 112 Prospect Avenue, Cleveland, OH 44115. Telephone: 216-523-3806 Ext. 805 or toll-free 800-424-3953. Fax: 216-696-6430. E-mail: tpayton@dnmyers.edu. Web site: http://www.dnmyers.edu/.

DEFIANCE COLLEGE
DEFIANCE, OHIO

General Independent, comprehensive, coed, affiliated with United Church of Christ **Entrance** Moderately difficult **Setting** 150-acre small-town campus **Total enrollment** 1,000 **Student-faculty ratio** 14:1 **Application deadline** 8/15 (freshmen), 8/15 (transfer) **Freshmen** 79% were admitted **Housing** Yes **Expenses** Tuition $15,855; Room & Board $4700 **Undergraduates** 56% women, 23% part-time, 29% 25 or older, 0.3% Native American, 3% Hispanic American, 4% African American, 0.3% Asian American/Pacific Islander **The most frequently chosen baccalaureate fields are** business/marketing, (pre)law, education **Academic program** Advanced placement, self-designed majors, honors program, summer session, adult/continuing education programs, internships **Contact** Mr. Brad M. Harsha, Acting Director of Admissions, Defiance College, 701 North Clinton Street, Defiance, OH 43512-1610. Telephone: 419-783-2365 or toll-free 800-520-4632 Ext. 2359. Fax: 419-783-2468. E-mail: admissions@defiance.edu. Web site: http://www.defiance.edu/.

DENISON UNIVERSITY
GRANVILLE, OHIO

General Independent, 4-year, coed **Entrance** Moderately difficult **Setting** 1,200-acre small-town campus **Total enrollment** 2,107 **Student-faculty ratio** 11:1 **Application deadline** 2/1 (freshmen), 5/1 (transfer) **Freshmen** 58% were admitted **Housing** Yes **Expenses** Tuition $23,090; Room & Board $6550 **Undergraduates** 57% women, 1% part-time, 1% 25 or older, 0.1% Native American, 2% Hispanic American, 5% African American, 3% Asian American/Pacific Islander **The most frequently chosen baccalaureate fields are** communications/communication technologies, biological/life sciences, social sciences and history **Academic program** Advanced placement, self-designed majors, honors program, internships **Contact** Ms. Mollie Rodenbeck, Campus Visit Coordinator, Denison University, Box H, Granville, OH 43023. Telephone: 740-587-6276 or toll-free 800-DENISON. E-mail: admissions@denison.edu. Web site: http://www.denison.edu/.

DEVRY UNIVERSITY
COLUMBUS, OHIO

General Proprietary, 4-year, coed **Entrance** Minimally difficult **Setting** 21-acre urban campus **Total enrollment** 3,793 **Student-faculty ratio** 24:1 **Application deadline** Rolling (freshmen), rolling (transfer) **Freshmen** 88% were admitted **Housing** No **Expenses** Tuition $8805 **Undergraduates** 24% women, 24% part-time, 39% 25 or older, 0.2% Native American, 1% Hispanic American, 19% African American, 3% Asian American/Pacific Islander **The most frequently chosen baccalaureate fields are** business/marketing, computer/information sciences, engineering/engineering technologies **Academic program** Advanced placement, accelerated degree program, summer session, adult/continuing education programs **Contact** Ms. Shelia Brown, New Student Coordinator, DeVry University, 1350 Alum Creek Drive, Columbus, OH 43209-2705. Telephone: 614-253-1850 or toll-free 800-426-3916 (in-state); 800-426-3090 (out-of-state). E-mail: admissions@devrycol5.edu. Web site: http://www.devrycols.edu/.

FRANCISCAN UNIVERSITY OF STEUBENVILLE
STEUBENVILLE, OHIO

General Independent Roman Catholic, comprehensive, coed **Entrance** Moderately difficult **Setting** 116-acre suburban campus **Total enrollment** 2,208 **Student-faculty ratio** 17:1 **Application deadline** 5/1 (freshmen), 5/1 (transfer) **Freshmen** 90% were admitted **Housing** Yes **Expenses** Tuition $13,900; Room & Board $5200 **Undergraduates** 59% women, 8% part-time, 12% 25 or older, 0.2% Native American, 4% Hispanic American, 1% African American, 1% Asian American/Pacific Islander **The most frequently chosen baccalaureate fields are** philosophy, business/marketing, philosophy, religion, and theology **Academic program** Advanced placement, accelerated degree program, honors program, summer session, adult/continuing education programs, internships **Contact** Mrs. Margaret Weber, Director of Admissions, Franciscan University of Steubenville, 1235 University Boulevard, Steubenville, OH 43952-1763. Telephone: 740-283-6226 or toll-free 800-783-6220. Fax: 740-284-5456. E-mail: admissions@franuniv.edu. Web site: http://www.franuniv.edu/.

OHIO

FRANKLIN UNIVERSITY
COLUMBUS, OHIO

General Independent, comprehensive, coed **Entrance** Noncompetitive **Setting** 14-acre urban campus **Total enrollment** 5,537 **Student-faculty ratio** 15:1 **Application deadline** Rolling (freshmen), rolling (transfer) **Freshmen** 100% were admitted **Housing** No **Expenses** Tuition $6324 **Undergraduates** 57% women, 69% part-time, 72% 25 or older, 0.3% Native American, 1% Hispanic American, 15% African American, 3% Asian American/Pacific Islander **The most frequently chosen baccalaureate fields are** business/marketing, computer/information sciences, health professions and related sciences **Academic program** English as a second language, advanced placement, accelerated degree program, self-designed majors, summer session, adult/continuing education programs, internships **Contact** Ms. Evelyn Levino, Vice President for Students, Franklin University, 201 South Grant Avenue, Columbus, OH 43215. Telephone: 614-341-6256 or toll-free 877-341-6300. Fax: 614-224-8027. E-mail: info@franklin.edu. Web site: http://www.franklin.edu/.

GOD'S BIBLE SCHOOL AND COLLEGE
CINCINNATI, OHIO

General Independent interdenominational, 4-year, coed **Entrance** Minimally difficult **Setting** 14-acre urban campus **Total enrollment** 259 **Student-faculty ratio** 15:1 **Application deadline** Rolling (freshmen), rolling (transfer) **Freshmen** 74% were admitted **Housing** Yes **Expenses** Tuition $4260; Room & Board $2800 **Undergraduates** 45% women, 15% part-time, 18% 25 or older, 0% Native American, 0% Hispanic American, 3% African American, 0% Asian American/Pacific Islander **Academic program** Advanced placement, summer session, internships **Contact** Ms. Laura Ellison, Director of Admissions, God's Bible School and College, 1810 Young Street, Cincinnati, OH 45210-1599. Telephone: 513-721-7944 Ext. 204 or toll-free 800-486-4637. Fax: 513-721-3971. E-mail: admissions@gbs.edu. Web site: http://www.gbs.edu/.

HEIDELBERG COLLEGE
TIFFIN, OHIO

General Independent, comprehensive, coed, affiliated with United Church of Christ **Entrance** Moderately difficult **Setting** 110-acre small-town campus **Total enrollment** 1,517 **Student-faculty ratio** 13:1 **Application deadline** 8/1 (freshmen), 8/1 (transfer) **Freshmen** 89% were admitted **Housing** Yes **Expenses** Tuition $18,130; Room & Board $5747 **Undergraduates** 54% women, 23% part-time, 4% 25 or older, 0.5% Native American, 1% Hispanic American, 3% African American, 0.5% Asian American/Pacific Islander **The most frequently chosen baccalaureate fields are** business/marketing, education, parks and recreation **Academic program** English as a second language, advanced placement, accelerated degree program, honors program, summer session, adult/continuing education programs, internships

Contact Ms. Sharon Pugh, Director of Admission, Heidelberg College, 310 East Market Street, Tiffin, OH 44883. Telephone: 419-448-2330 or toll-free 800-434-3352. Fax: 419-448-2334. E-mail: adminfo@nike.heidelberg.edu. Web site: http://www.heidelberg.edu/.

HIRAM COLLEGE
HIRAM, OHIO

General Independent, 4-year, coed, affiliated with Christian Church (Disciples of Christ) **Entrance** Very difficult **Setting** 110-acre rural campus **Total enrollment** 1,190 **Student-faculty ratio** 11:1 **Application deadline** 2/1 (freshmen), 7/15 (transfer) **Freshmen** 79% were admitted **Housing** Yes **Expenses** Tuition $19,392; Room & Board $6514 **Undergraduates** 57% women, 19% part-time, 26% 25 or older, 0.3% Native American, 1% Hispanic American, 8% African American, 1% Asian American/Pacific Islander **The most frequently chosen baccalaureate fields are** biological/life sciences, business/marketing, social sciences and history **Academic program** English as a second language, advanced placement, accelerated degree program, self-designed majors, summer session, adult/continuing education programs, internships **Contact** Mr. Ed Frato Sweeney, Director of Admission, Hiram College, Box 96, Hiram, OH 44234-0067. Telephone: 330-569-5169 or toll-free 800-362-5280. Fax: 330-569-5944. E-mail: admission@hiram.edu. Web site: http://www.hiram.edu/.

▶ For more information, see page 439.

JOHN CARROLL UNIVERSITY
UNIVERSITY HEIGHTS, OHIO

General Independent Roman Catholic (Jesuit), comprehensive, coed **Entrance** Moderately difficult **Setting** 60-acre suburban campus **Total enrollment** 4,301 **Student-faculty ratio** 15:1 **Application deadline** 2/1 (freshmen), rolling (transfer) **Freshmen** 86% were admitted **Housing** Yes **Expenses** Tuition $17,837; Room & Board $6312 **Undergraduates** 55% women, 5% part-time, 4% 25 or older, 0.2% Native American, 2% Hispanic American, 4% African American, 3% Asian American/Pacific Islander **The most frequently chosen baccalaureate fields are** business/marketing, communications/communication technologies, social sciences and history **Academic program** Advanced placement, accelerated degree program, self-designed majors, honors program, summer session, adult/continuing education programs, internships **Contact** Mr. Thomas P. Fanning, Director of Admission, John Carroll University, 20700 North Park Boulevard, University Heights, OH 44118-4581. Telephone: 216-397-4294. Fax: 216-397-4981. E-mail: admission@jcu.edu. Web site: http://www.jcu.edu/.

KENT STATE UNIVERSITY
KENT, OHIO

General State-supported, university, coed **Entrance** Moderately difficult **Setting** 1,200-acre small-town campus **Total enrollment** 22,828 **Student-faculty**

Kent State University *(continued)*
ratio 20:1 **Application deadline** 6/1 (freshmen), 10/1 (transfer) **Freshmen** 90% were admitted **Housing** Yes **Expenses** Tuition $5954; Room & Board $5150 **Undergraduates** 60% women, 16% part-time, 15% 25 or older **The most frequently chosen baccalaureate fields are** business/marketing, education, health professions and related sciences **Academic program** English as a second language, advanced placement, self-designed majors, honors program, summer session, adult/continuing education programs, internships **Contact** Mr. Christopher Buttenschon, Assistant Director of Admissions, Kent State University, 161 Michael Schwartz Center, Kent, OH 44242-0001. Telephone: 330-672-2444 or toll-free 800-988-KENT. Fax: 330-672-2499. E-mail: kentadm@admissions.kent.edu. Web site: http://www.kent.edu/.

KENYON COLLEGE
GAMBIER, OHIO

General Independent, 4-year, coed **Entrance** Very difficult **Setting** 800-acre rural campus **Total enrollment** 1,587 **Student-faculty ratio** 10:1 **Application deadline** 1/15 (freshmen), 4/1 (transfer) **Freshmen** 66% were admitted **Housing** Yes **Expenses** Tuition $27,550; Room & Board $4580 **Undergraduates** 55% women, 2% part-time, 0% 25 or older, 0% Native American, 3% Hispanic American, 4% African American, 2% Asian American/Pacific Islander **The most frequently chosen baccalaureate fields are** English, social sciences and history, visual/performing arts **Academic program** Advanced placement, accelerated degree program, self-designed majors, honors program, internships **Contact** Mr. John W. Anderson, Dean of Admissions, Kenyon College, Office of Admissions, Gambier, OH 43022-9623. Telephone: 740-427-5776 or toll-free 800-848-2468. Fax: 740-427-5770. E-mail: admissions@kenyon.edu. Web site: http://www.kenyon.edu/.

LAKE ERIE COLLEGE
PAINESVILLE, OHIO

General Independent, comprehensive, coed **Entrance** Minimally difficult **Setting** 57-acre small-town campus **Total enrollment** 848 **Student-faculty ratio** 13:1 **Freshmen** 83% were admitted **Housing** Yes **Expenses** Tuition $17,210; Room & Board $5700 **Undergraduates** 78% women, 17% part-time, 23% 25 or older, 0.4% Native American, 2% Hispanic American, 5% African American, 1% Asian American/Pacific Islander **The most frequently chosen baccalaureate fields are** business/marketing, agriculture, computer/information sciences **Academic program** Advanced placement, accelerated degree program, self-designed majors, summer session, adult/continuing education programs, internships **Contact** Kevin Coughlin, Dean of Admissions and Financial Aid, Lake Erie College, 391 West Washington Street, Painesville, OH 44077-3389. Telephone: 440-639-7879 or toll-free 800-916-0904. Fax: 440-352-3533. E-mail: lecadmit@lakeerie.edu. Web site: http://www.lec.edu/.

LAURA AND ALVIN SIEGAL COLLEGE OF JUDAIC STUDIES
BEACHWOOD, OHIO

General Independent, comprehensive, coed **Entrance** Noncompetitive **Setting** 2-acre suburban campus **Total enrollment** 134 **Student-faculty ratio** 8:1 **Application deadline** Rolling (freshmen), rolling (transfer) **Freshmen** 71% were admitted **Housing** No **Expenses** Tuition $6775 **Undergraduates** 88% women, 88% part-time, 100% 25 or older, 0% Native American, 0% Hispanic American, 0% African American, 0% Asian American/Pacific Islander **The most frequently chosen baccalaureate fields are** philosophy, philosophy, religion, and theology **Academic program** Summer session, adult/continuing education programs, internships **Contact** Ms. Linda L. Rosen, Director of Student Services, Laura and Alvin Siegal College of Judaic Studies, 26500 Shaker Boulevard, Beachwood, OH 44122-7116. Telephone: 216-464-4050 Ext. 101 or toll-free 888-336-2257. Fax: 216-464-5827. E-mail: admissions@ccjs.edu. Web site: http://www.siegalcollege.edu/.

LOURDES COLLEGE
SYLVANIA, OHIO

General Independent Roman Catholic, 4-year, coed **Entrance** Moderately difficult **Setting** 90-acre suburban campus **Total enrollment** 1,219 **Student-faculty ratio** 12:1 **Application deadline** Rolling (freshmen), rolling (transfer) **Freshmen** 49% were admitted **Housing** No **Expenses** Tuition $13,100 **Undergraduates** 81% women, 63% part-time, 61% 25 or older, 0.3% Native American, 2% Hispanic American, 10% African American, 0.3% Asian American/Pacific Islander **The most frequently chosen baccalaureate fields are** business/marketing, health professions and related sciences, protective services/public administration **Academic program** Advanced placement, accelerated degree program, self-designed majors, summer session, adult/continuing education programs, internships **Contact** Office of Admissions, Lourdes College, 6832 Convent Boulevard, Sylvania, OH 43560. Telephone: 419-885-5291 or toll-free 800-878-3210 Ext. 1299. Fax: 419-882-3987. E-mail: lcadmits@lourdes.edu. Web site: http://www.lourdes.edu/.

MALONE COLLEGE
CANTON, OHIO

General Independent, comprehensive, coed, affiliated with Evangelical Friends Church–Eastern Region **Entrance** Moderately difficult **Setting** 78-acre suburban campus **Total enrollment** 2,139 **Student-faculty ratio** 14:1 **Application deadline** 7/1 (freshmen), 7/1 (transfer) **Freshmen** 86% were admitted **Housing** Yes **Expenses** Tuition $13,550; Room & Board $5640 **Undergraduates** 60% women, 11% part-time, 23% 25 or older, 0.2% Native American, 1% Hispanic American, 5% African American, 0.3% Asian American/Pacific Islander **The most frequently chosen baccalaureate fields are** business/

marketing, education, health professions and related sciences **Academic program** Advanced placement, accelerated degree program, self-designed majors, honors program, summer session, adult/continuing education programs, internships **Contact** Mr. John Chopka, Vice President of Enrollment Management, Malone College, 515 25th Street, NW, Canton, OH 44709-3897. Telephone: 330-471-8145 or toll-free 800-521-1146. Fax: 330-471-8149. E-mail: admissions@malone.edu. Web site: http://www.malone.edu/.

MARIETTA COLLEGE
MARIETTA, OHIO

General Independent, comprehensive, coed **Entrance** Moderately difficult **Setting** 120-acre small-town campus **Total enrollment** 1,278 **Student-faculty ratio** 12:1 **Application deadline** 4/15 (freshmen), rolling (transfer) **Freshmen** 94% were admitted **Housing** Yes **Expenses** Tuition $19,076; Room & Board $5504 **Undergraduates** 50% women, 7% part-time, 2% 25 or older, 0.3% Native American, 1% Hispanic American, 2% African American, 1% Asian American/Pacific Islander **The most frequently chosen baccalaureate fields are** business/marketing, education, parks and recreation **Academic program** English as a second language, advanced placement, accelerated degree program, self-designed majors, honors program, summer session, adult/continuing education programs, internships **Contact** Ms. Marke Vickers, Director of Admission, Marietta College, 215 Fifth Street, Marietta, OH 45750-4000. Telephone: 740-376-4600 or toll-free 800-331-7896. Fax: 740-376-8888. E-mail: admit@marietta.edu. Web site: http://www.marietta.edu/.

MIAMI UNIVERSITY
OXFORD, OHIO

General State-related, university, coed **Entrance** Moderately difficult **Setting** 2,000-acre small-town campus **Total enrollment** 16,946 **Student-faculty ratio** 17:1 **Application deadline** 1/31 (freshmen), 5/1 (transfer) **Freshmen** 74% were admitted **Housing** Yes **Expenses** Tuition $6915; Room & Board $5970 **Undergraduates** 55% women, 3% part-time, 3% 25 or older, 1% Native American, 2% Hispanic American, 4% African American, 2% Asian American/Pacific Islander **The most frequently chosen baccalaureate fields are** business/marketing, education, social sciences and history **Academic program** Advanced placement, self-designed majors, honors program, summer session, adult/continuing education programs, internships **Contact** Miami University, 301 South Campus Avenue, Campus Avenue Building, Oxford, OH 45056. Fax: 513-529-1550. E-mail: admission@muohio.edu. Web site: http://www.muohio.edu/.

MOUNT CARMEL COLLEGE OF NURSING
COLUMBUS, OHIO

General Independent, 4-year **Total enrollment** 375 **Student-faculty ratio** 8:1 **Freshmen** 50% were admitted **Expenses** Tuition $9200; Room only $2592 **Undergraduates** 0% Native American, 1% Hispanic American, 7% African American, 1% Asian American/Pacific Islander **The most frequently chosen baccalaureate field is** health professions and related sciences **Contact** Ms. Merschel Menefield, Director of Admissions, Mount Carmel College of Nursing, 127 South Davis Avenue, Columbus, OH 43222. Telephone: 614-234-5800. Web site: http://www.mccn.edu/.

MOUNT UNION COLLEGE
ALLIANCE, OHIO

General Independent United Methodist, 4-year, coed **Entrance** Moderately difficult **Setting** 105-acre suburban campus **Total enrollment** 2,368 **Student-faculty ratio** 14:1 **Application deadline** Rolling (freshmen), rolling (transfer) **Freshmen** 81% were admitted **Housing** Yes **Expenses** Tuition $16,310; Room & Board $4810 **Undergraduates** 58% women, 13% part-time, 3% 25 or older, 0.3% Native American, 1% Hispanic American, 4% African American, 0.3% Asian American/Pacific Islander **The most frequently chosen baccalaureate fields are** business/marketing, education, parks and recreation **Academic program** English as a second language, advanced placement, accelerated degree program, self-designed majors, honors program, summer session, adult/continuing education programs, internships **Contact** Ms. Amy Tomko, Vice President of Enrollment Services, Mount Union College, 1972 Clark Avenue, Alliance, OH 44601. Telephone: 330-823-2590 or toll-free 800-334-6682 (in-state); 800-992-6682 (out-of-state). Fax: 330-823-3487. E-mail: admissn@muc.edu. Web site: http://www.muc.edu/.

MOUNT VERNON NAZARENE UNIVERSITY
MOUNT VERNON, OHIO

General Independent Nazarene, comprehensive, coed **Entrance** Moderately difficult **Setting** 210-acre small-town campus **Total enrollment** 2,232 **Student-faculty ratio** 18:1 **Application deadline** 5/31 (freshmen), 5/31 (transfer) **Freshmen** 83% were admitted **Housing** Yes **Expenses** Tuition $12,590; Room & Board $4437 **Undergraduates** 56% women, 9% part-time, 28% 25 or older, 0.3% Native American, 1% Hispanic American, 2% African American, 1% Asian American/Pacific Islander **The most frequently chosen baccalaureate fields are** business/marketing, education, philosophy **Academic program** Advanced placement, honors program, summer session, adult/continuing education programs, internships **Contact** Mrs. Doris Webb, Director of Admissions and Student Recruitment, Mount Vernon Nazarene University, 800 Martinsburg Road, Mount Vernon, OH 43050-9500. Telephone: 740-397-6862 Ext. 4510 or toll-free 800-782-2435. Fax: 740-393-0511. E-mail: admissions@mvnc.edu. Web site: http://www.mvnc.edu/.

OHIO

MUSKINGUM COLLEGE
NEW CONCORD, OHIO

General Independent, comprehensive, coed, affiliated with Presbyterian Church (U.S.A.) **Entrance** Moderately difficult **Setting** 215-acre small-town campus **Total enrollment** 2,022 **Student-faculty ratio** 16:1 **Application deadline** 6/1 (freshmen), 8/1 (transfer) **Freshmen** 86% were admitted **Housing** Yes **Expenses** Tuition $12,665; Room & Board $5100 **Undergraduates** 51% women, 5% part-time **Academic program** English as a second language, advanced placement, accelerated degree program, self-designed majors, summer session, internships **Contact** Mrs. Beth DaLonzo, Director of Admission, Muskingum College, 163 Stormont Street, New Concord, OH 43762. Telephone: 740-826-8137 or toll-free 800-752-6082. Fax: 740-826-8100. E-mail: adminfo@muskingum.edu. Web site: http://www.muskingum.edu/.

NOTRE DAME COLLEGE
SOUTH EUCLID, OHIO

General Independent Roman Catholic, comprehensive, coed **Entrance** Moderately difficult **Setting** 53-acre suburban campus **Total enrollment** 923 **Student-faculty ratio** 12:1 **Application deadline** Rolling (freshmen), rolling (transfer) **Freshmen** 37% were admitted **Housing** Yes **Expenses** Tuition $14,800; Room & Board $5625 **Undergraduates** 90% women, 62% part-time, 75% 25 or older, 0.2% Native American, 1% Hispanic American, 30% African American, 1% Asian American/Pacific Islander **The most frequently chosen baccalaureate fields are** business/marketing, computer/information sciences, education **Academic program** Advanced placement, accelerated degree program, self-designed majors, summer session, adult/continuing education programs, internships **Contact** Director of Admissions, Notre Dame College, 4545 College Road, South Euclid, OH 44121-4293. Telephone: 216-381-1680 Ext. 355 or toll-free 800-NDC-1680. Fax: 216-381-3802. E-mail: admissions@ndc.edu. Web site: http://www.ndc.edu/.

OBERLIN COLLEGE
OBERLIN, OHIO

General Independent, comprehensive, coed **Entrance** Very difficult **Setting** 440-acre small-town campus **Total enrollment** 2,863 **Student-faculty ratio** 10:1 **Application deadline** 1/15 (freshmen), 5/1 (transfer) **Freshmen** 36% were admitted **Housing** Yes **Expenses** Tuition $26,580; Room & Board $6560 **Undergraduates** 57% women, 3% part-time, 1% 25 or older, 1% Native American, 4% Hispanic American, 8% African American, 6% Asian American/Pacific Islander **The most frequently chosen baccalaureate fields are** social sciences and history, biological/life sciences, visual/performing arts **Academic program** English as a second language, advanced placement, accelerated degree program, self-designed majors, honors program, internships **Contact** Ms. Debra Chermonte, Dean of Admissions and Financial Aid, Oberlin College, Admissions Office, Carnegie Building, Oberlin, OH 44074-1090. Telephone: 440-775-8411 or toll-free 800-622-OBIE. Fax: 440-775-6905. E-mail: ad_mail@oberlin.edu. Web site: http://www.oberlin.edu/.

OHIO DOMINICAN COLLEGE
COLUMBUS, OHIO

General Independent Roman Catholic, 4-year, coed **Entrance** Moderately difficult **Setting** 62-acre urban campus **Total enrollment** 2,197 **Student-faculty ratio** 18:1 **Application deadline** Rolling (freshmen), rolling (transfer) **Freshmen** 60% were admitted **Housing** Yes **Expenses** Tuition $12,730; Room & Board $5370 **Undergraduates** 69% women, 30% part-time, 52% 25 or older, 0.3% Native American, 2% Hispanic American, 26% African American, 2% Asian American/Pacific Islander **The most frequently chosen baccalaureate fields are** business/marketing, education, social sciences and history **Academic program** English as a second language, advanced placement, self-designed majors, honors program, summer session, adult/continuing education programs, internships **Contact** Ms. Vicki Thompson-Campbell, Director of Admissions, Ohio Dominican College, 1216 Sunbury Road, Columbus, OH 43219-2099. Telephone: 614-251-4500 or toll-free 800-854-2670. Fax: 614-251-0156. E-mail: admissions@odc.edu. Web site: http://www.odc.edu/.

OHIO NORTHERN UNIVERSITY
ADA, OHIO

General Independent United Methodist, comprehensive, coed **Entrance** Moderately difficult **Setting** 260-acre small-town campus **Total enrollment** 3,345 **Student-faculty ratio** 13:1 **Application deadline** 8/15 (freshmen), 8/15 (transfer) **Freshmen** 91% were admitted **Housing** Yes **Expenses** Tuition $22,275; Room & Board $5490 **Undergraduates** 47% women, 5% part-time, 3% 25 or older **The most frequently chosen baccalaureate fields are** business/marketing, engineering/engineering technologies, health professions and related sciences **Academic program** Advanced placement, honors program, summer session, internships **Contact** Ms. Karen Condeni, Vice President of Admissions and Financial Aid, Ohio Northern University, 525 South Main, Ada, OH 45810-1599. Telephone: 419-772-2260 or toll-free 888-408-4ONU. Fax: 419-772-2313. E-mail: admissions-ug@onu.edu. Web site: http://www.onu.edu/.

THE OHIO STATE UNIVERSITY
COLUMBUS, OHIO

General State-supported, university, coed **Entrance** Moderately difficult **Setting** urban campus **Total enrollment** 48,477 **Student-faculty ratio** 13:1 **Application deadline** 2/15 (freshmen), 6/25 (transfer) **Freshmen** 73% were admitted **Housing** Yes **Expenses** Tuition $4788; Room & Board $6031 **Undergraduates** 48% women, 13% part-time, 11% 25 or older,

OHIO

0.4% Native American, 2% Hispanic American, 8% African American, 5% Asian American/Pacific Islander **The most frequently chosen baccalaureate fields are** business/marketing, home economics/vocational home economics, social sciences and history **Academic program** English as a second language, advanced placement, accelerated degree program, self-designed majors, honors program, summer session, adult/continuing education programs, internships **Contact** Dr. Mabel G. Freeman, Director of Undergraduate Admissions and Vice President for First-Year Experience, The Ohio State University, 3rd Floor, Lincoln Tower, 1800 Cannon Drive, Columbus, OH 43210. Telephone: 614-292-3974. Fax: 614-292-4818. E-mail: askabuckeye@osu.edu. Web site: http://www.osu.edu/.

THE OHIO STATE UNIVERSITY AT LIMA
LIMA, OHIO

General State-supported, 4-year, coed **Entrance** Noncompetitive **Setting** 565-acre small-town campus **Total enrollment** 1,356 **Student-faculty ratio** 13:1 **Application deadline** 7/1 (freshmen), 7/1 (transfer) **Freshmen** 72% were admitted **Housing** No **Expenses** Tuition $3606 **Undergraduates** 59% women, 20% part-time, 25% 25 or older, 0.2% Native American, 0.5% Hispanic American, 2% African American, 1% Asian American/Pacific Islander **Academic program** English as a second language, advanced placement, accelerated degree program, honors program, summer session, adult/continuing education programs **Contact** Ms. Marissa Christoff Snyder, Admissions Counselor, The Ohio State University at Lima, 4240 Campus Drive, Lima, OH 45804. Telephone: 419-995-8220. E-mail: admissions@lima.ohio-state.edu. Web site: http://www.ohio-state.edu/.

THE OHIO STATE UNIVERSITY AT MARION
MARION, OHIO

General State-supported, 4-year, coed **Entrance** Noncompetitive **Setting** 180-acre small-town campus **Total enrollment** 1,390 **Student-faculty ratio** 12:1 **Application deadline** 7/15 (freshmen), 7/1 (transfer) **Freshmen** 98% were admitted **Housing** No **Expenses** Tuition $3606 **Undergraduates** 59% women, 29% part-time, 33% 25 or older, 0.1% Native American, 1% Hispanic American, 2% African American, 1% Asian American/Pacific Islander **Academic program** English as a second language, advanced placement, accelerated degree program, honors program, summer session, adult/continuing education programs **Contact** Mr. Mathrey Moreau, Admissions Coordinator, The Ohio State University at Marion, 1465 Mount Vernon Avenue, Marion, OH 43302-5695. Telephone: 740-389-6786 Ext. 6337. Web site: http://www.ohio-state.edu/.

THE OHIO STATE UNIVERSITY–MANSFIELD CAMPUS
MANSFIELD, OHIO

General State-supported, 4-year, coed **Entrance** Noncompetitive **Setting** 593-acre small-town campus **Total enrollment** 1,495 **Application deadline** 7/1 (freshmen), 7/1 (transfer) **Freshmen** 94% were admitted **Housing** No **Expenses** Tuition $3606 **Undergraduates** 62% women, 29% part-time, 24% 25 or older, 0.4% Native American, 1% Hispanic American, 4% African American, 2% Asian American/Pacific Islander **Academic program** English as a second language, advanced placement, accelerated degree program, honors program, summer session, adult/continuing education programs **Contact** Mr. Henry D. Thomas, Coordinator of Admissions and Financial Aid, The Ohio State University–Mansfield Campus, 1680 University Drive, Mansfield, OH 44906-1599. Telephone: 419-755-4226. Web site: http://www.ohio-state.edu/.

THE OHIO STATE UNIVERSITY–NEWARK CAMPUS
NEWARK, OHIO

General State-supported, 4-year, coed **Entrance** Noncompetitive **Setting** 101-acre small-town campus **Total enrollment** 2,079 **Student-faculty ratio** 23:1 **Application deadline** 7/1 (freshmen), 7/1 (transfer) **Freshmen** 97% were admitted **Housing** No **Expenses** Tuition $3606 **Undergraduates** 58% women, 24% part-time, 24% 25 or older, 1% Native American, 1% Hispanic American, 4% African American, 2% Asian American/Pacific Islander **Academic program** English as a second language, advanced placement, accelerated degree program, honors program, summer session, adult/continuing education programs **Contact** Ms. Ann Donahue, Director of Enrollment, The Ohio State University–Newark Campus, 1179 University Drive, Newark, OH 43055-1797. Telephone: 614-366-9333. Web site: http://www.ohio-state.edu/.

OHIO UNIVERSITY
ATHENS, OHIO

General State-supported, university, coed **Entrance** Moderately difficult **Setting** 1,700-acre small-town campus **Total enrollment** 20,163 **Student-faculty ratio** 21:1 **Application deadline** 2/1 (freshmen), 5/15 (transfer) **Freshmen** 78% were admitted **Housing** Yes **Expenses** Tuition $5493; Room & Board $6276 **Undergraduates** 55% women, 7% part-time, 6% 25 or older, 0.3% Native American, 1% Hispanic American, 3% African American, 1% Asian American/Pacific Islander **The most frequently chosen baccalaureate fields are** business/marketing, communications/communication technologies, education **Academic program** English as a second language, advanced placement, accelerated degree program, self-designed majors, honors program, summer session, adult/continuing education programs, internships **Contact** Mr. N. Kip Howard Jr., Director of Admissions, Ohio University, Athens, OH 45701-2979. Telephone: 740-

OHIO

Ohio University *(continued)*
593-4100. E-mail: admissions.freshmen@ohiou.edu. Web site: http://www.ohio.edu/.

OHIO UNIVERSITY–CHILLICOTHE
CHILLICOTHE, OHIO

General State-supported, 4-year, coed **Entrance** Noncompetitive **Setting** 124-acre small-town campus **Total enrollment** 1,645 **Application deadline** 9/1 (freshmen), 9/1 (transfer) **Housing** No **Expenses** Tuition $3246 **Undergraduates** 35% 25 or older **Academic program** Advanced placement, accelerated degree program, self-designed majors, summer session, adult/continuing education programs, internships **Contact** Mr. Richard R. Whitney, Director of Student Services, Ohio University–Chillicothe, 571 West Fifth Street, Chillicothe, OH 45601. Telephone: 740-774-7200 Ext. 242 or toll-free 877-462-6824 (in-state). Fax: 740-774-7295. Web site: http://www.ohio.edu/chillicothe/.

OHIO UNIVERSITY–EASTERN
ST. CLAIRSVILLE, OHIO

General State-supported, 4-year, coed **Entrance** Noncompetitive **Setting** 300-acre rural campus **Total enrollment** 1,118 **Student-faculty ratio** 23:1 **Application deadline** Rolling (freshmen), rolling (transfer) **Housing** No **Expenses** Tuition $3033 **Undergraduates** 68% women, 27% part-time, 32% 25 or older, 0% Native American, 0.1% Hispanic American, 2% African American, 0.1% Asian American/Pacific Islander **Academic program** Advanced placement, accelerated degree program, self-designed majors, summer session, adult/continuing education programs **Contact** Mr. Kevin Chenoweth, Student Services Manager, Ohio University–Eastern, 45425 National Road, St. Clairsville, OH 43950-9724. Telephone: 614-695-1720 Ext. 209 or toll-free 800-648-3331 (in-state). E-mail: chenowet@ohio.edu.

OHIO UNIVERSITY–LANCASTER
LANCASTER, OHIO

General State-supported, comprehensive, coed **Entrance** Noncompetitive **Setting** 360-acre small-town campus **Total enrollment** 1,664 **Application deadline** Rolling (freshmen), rolling (transfer) **Freshmen** 100% were admitted **Housing** No **Expenses** Tuition $3246 **Undergraduates** 59% women, 42% part-time, 46% 25 or older, 0.5% Native American, 1% Hispanic American, 1% African American, 1% Asian American/Pacific Islander **The most frequently chosen baccalaureate fields are** communications/communication technologies, business/marketing, education **Academic program** Advanced placement, accelerated degree program, self-designed majors, summer session, adult/continuing education programs **Contact** Dr. Scott Shepherd, Director of Student Services, Ohio University–Lancaster, 1570 Granville Pike, Lancaster, OH 43130-1097. Telephone: 740-654-6711 Ext. 209 or toll-free 888-446-4468. E-mail: shepherd@ouvaxa.cats.ohiou.edu.

OHIO UNIVERSITY–SOUTHERN CAMPUS
IRONTON, OHIO

General State-supported, comprehensive, coed **Entrance** Noncompetitive **Setting** 9-acre small-town campus **Total enrollment** 1,891 **Application deadline** Rolling (freshmen), rolling (transfer) **Freshmen** 100% were admitted **Housing** No **Expenses** Tuition $2988 **Undergraduates** 66% women, 40% part-time, 56% 25 or older, 1% Native American, 0.3% Hispanic American, 2% African American, 0.4% Asian American/Pacific Islander **Academic program** Self-designed majors, summer session, adult/continuing education programs **Contact** Dr. Kim K. Lawson, Coordinator of Admissions, Ohio University–Southern Campus, 1804 Liberty Avenue, Ironton, OH 45638-2214. Telephone: 740-533-4612. Web site: http://www.ohiou.edu/.

OHIO UNIVERSITY–ZANESVILLE
ZANESVILLE, OHIO

General State-supported, comprehensive, coed **Entrance** Noncompetitive **Setting** 179-acre rural campus **Total enrollment** 1,630 **Student-faculty ratio** 17:1 **Application deadline** Rolling (freshmen), rolling (transfer) **Freshmen** 100% were admitted **Housing** No **Expenses** Tuition $3246 **Undergraduates** 72% women, 42% part-time, 33% 25 or older **Academic program** Advanced placement, self-designed majors, summer session, adult/continuing education programs **Contact** Mrs. Karen Ragsdale, Student Services Secretary, Ohio University–Zanesville, 1425 Newark Road, Zanesville, OH 43701-2695. Telephone: 740-588-1440. Fax: 740-453-6161. Web site: http://www.zanesvile.ohiou.edu/.

OHIO WESLEYAN UNIVERSITY
DELAWARE, OHIO

General Independent United Methodist, 4-year, coed **Entrance** Very difficult **Setting** 200-acre small-town campus **Total enrollment** 1,886 **Student-faculty ratio** 13:1 **Application deadline** 3/15 (freshmen), 5/15 (transfer) **Freshmen** 78% were admitted **Housing** Yes **Expenses** Tuition $22,860; Room & Board $6810 **Undergraduates** 52% women, 2% part-time, 2% 25 or older, 0.2% Native American, 2% Hispanic American, 5% African American, 2% Asian American/Pacific Islander **The most frequently chosen baccalaureate fields are** business/marketing, biological/life sciences, social sciences and history **Academic program** Advanced placement, self-designed majors, honors program, summer session, internships **Contact** Ms. Margaret L. Drugovich, Vice President of Admission and Financial Aid, Ohio Wesleyan University, 61 South Sandusky Street, Delaware, OH 43015. Telephone: 740-368-3020 or toll-free 800-922-8953. Fax: 740-368-3314. E-mail: owuadmit@owu.edu. Web site: http://web.owu.edu/.

OTTERBEIN COLLEGE
WESTERVILLE, OHIO

General Independent United Methodist, comprehensive, coed **Entrance** Moderately difficult **Setting**

OHIO

140-acre suburban campus **Total enrollment** 2,985 **Student-faculty ratio** 14:1 **Application deadline** 3/1 (freshmen), rolling (transfer) **Freshmen** 85% were admitted **Housing** Yes **Expenses** Tuition $17,928; Room & Board $5511 **Undergraduates** 65% women, 25% part-time, 37% 25 or older, 0.2% Native American, 1% Hispanic American, 7% African American, 1% Asian American/Pacific Islander **The most frequently chosen baccalaureate fields are** business/marketing, education, health professions and related sciences **Academic program** English as a second language, advanced placement, self-designed majors, honors program, summer session, adult/continuing education programs, internships **Contact** Cass Johnson PhD, Director of Admissions, Otterbein College, One Otterbein College, Westerville, OH 43081-9924. Telephone: 614-823-1500 or toll-free 800-488-8144. Fax: 614-823-1200. E-mail: uotterb@otterbein.edu. Web site: http://www.otterbein.edu/.

PONTIFICAL COLLEGE JOSEPHINUM
COLUMBUS, OHIO

General Independent Roman Catholic, comprehensive, coed, primarily men **Entrance** Minimally difficult **Setting** 100-acre suburban campus **Total enrollment** 112 **Student-faculty ratio** 4:1 **Application deadline** Rolling (freshmen), rolling (transfer) **Freshmen** 100% were admitted **Housing** Yes **Expenses** Tuition $8904; Room & Board $5496 **Undergraduates** 16% 25 or older, 2% Hispanic American, 7% Asian American/Pacific Islander **The most frequently chosen baccalaureate fields are** area/ethnic studies, philosophy **Academic program** English as a second language, advanced placement, internships **Contact** Arminda Crawford, Secretary for Admissions, Pontifical College Josephinum, 7625 North High Street, Columbus, OH 43235-1498. Telephone: 614-985-2241 Ext. 436. Web site: http://www.pcj.edu/.

SHAWNEE STATE UNIVERSITY
PORTSMOUTH, OHIO

General State-supported, 4-year, coed **Entrance** Noncompetitive **Setting** small-town campus **Total enrollment** 3,364 **Student-faculty ratio** 17:1 **Application deadline** Rolling (freshmen), rolling (transfer) **Freshmen** 100% were admitted **Housing** Yes **Expenses** Tuition $3402; Room & Board $5232 **Undergraduates** 62% women, 20% part-time, 31% 25 or older, 1% Native American, 1% Hispanic American, 2% African American, 0.2% Asian American/Pacific Islander **The most frequently chosen baccalaureate fields are** business/marketing, liberal arts/general studies, social sciences and history **Academic program** Advanced placement, honors program, summer session, adult/continuing education programs, internships **Contact** Mr. Bob Trusz, Director of Admission, Shawnee State University, 940 Second Street, Commons Building, Portsmouth, OH 45662. Telephone: 740-351-3610 Ext. 610 or toll-free 800-959-2SSU. Fax: 740-351-3111. E-mail: to_ssu@shawnee.edu. Web site: http://www.shawnee.edu/.

TIFFIN UNIVERSITY
TIFFIN, OHIO

General Independent, comprehensive, coed **Entrance** Minimally difficult **Setting** 108-acre small-town campus **Total enrollment** 1,578 **Student-faculty ratio** 21:1 **Application deadline** Rolling (freshmen), rolling (transfer) **Freshmen** 78% were admitted **Housing** Yes **Expenses** Tuition $11,850; Room & Board $5400 **Undergraduates** 54% women, 22% part-time, 36% 25 or older, 2% Hispanic American, 12% African American, 2% Asian American/Pacific Islander **The most frequently chosen baccalaureate fields are** business/marketing, liberal arts/general studies, protective services/public administration **Academic program** Advanced placement, accelerated degree program, summer session, adult/continuing education programs, internships **Contact** Mr. Darby Roggow, Director of Admissions, Tiffin University, 155 Miami Street, Tiffin, OH 44883-2161. Telephone: 419-448-3425 or toll-free 800-968-6446. Fax: 419-443-5006. E-mail: admiss@tiffin.edu. Web site: http://www.tiffin.edu/.

UNION INSTITUTE & UNIVERSITY
CINCINNATI, OHIO

General Independent, university, coed **Entrance** Moderately difficult **Setting** 5-acre urban campus **Total enrollment** 1,769 **Student-faculty ratio** 16:1 **Application deadline** 10/1 (freshmen), 10/1 (transfer) **Freshmen** 85% were admitted **Housing** No **Expenses** Tuition $6912 **Undergraduates** 66% women, 43% part-time, 95% 25 or older, 0.5% Native American, 9% Hispanic American, 36% African American, 1% Asian American/Pacific Islander **The most frequently chosen baccalaureate fields are** education, business/marketing, protective services/public administration **Academic program** Advanced placement, accelerated degree program, self-designed majors, summer session, adult/continuing education programs **Contact** Ms. Lisa Schrenger, Director, Admissions, Union Institute & University, 440 East McMillan Street, Cincinnati, OH 45206-1925. Telephone: 513-861-6400 or toll-free 800-486-3116. E-mail: admissions@tui.edu. Web site: http://www.tui.edu/.

THE UNIVERSITY OF AKRON
AKRON, OHIO

General State-supported, university, coed **Entrance** Noncompetitive **Setting** 170-acre urban campus **Total enrollment** 24,358 **Student-faculty ratio** 15:1 **Application deadline** 8/15 (freshmen), 8/15 (transfer) **Freshmen** 85% were admitted **Housing** Yes **Expenses** Tuition $4930; Room & Board $5600 **Undergraduates** 52% women, 34% part-time, 45% 25 or older, 1% Native American, 1% Hispanic American, 14% African American, 2% Asian American/Pacific Islander **The most frequently chosen baccalaureate fields are** business/marketing, education, protective services/public administration **Academic program** English as a second language, advanced placement, acceler-

OHIO

The University of Akron *(continued)*
ated degree program, self-designed majors, honors program, summer session, adult/continuing education programs, internships **Contact** Ms. Kim Gentile, Interim Director of Admissions, The University of Akron, 381 Buchtel Common, Akron, OH 44325-2001. Telephone: 330-972-6428 or toll-free 800-655-4884. Fax: 330-972-7676. E-mail: admissions@uakron.edu. Web site: http://www.uakron.edu/.

UNIVERSITY OF CINCINNATI
CINCINNATI, OHIO

General State-supported, university, coed **Entrance** Moderately difficult **Setting** 137-acre urban campus **Total enrollment** 27,289 **Student-faculty ratio** 18:1 **Application deadline** Rolling (freshmen), rolling (transfer) **Freshmen** 82% were admitted **Housing** Yes **Expenses** Tuition $5823; Room & Board $6498 **Undergraduates** 49% women, 25% part-time, 16% 25 or older, 0.3% Native American, 1% Hispanic American, 14% African American, 3% Asian American/Pacific Islander **The most frequently chosen baccalaureate fields are** business/marketing, engineering/engineering technologies, social sciences and history **Academic program** English as a second language, advanced placement, accelerated degree program, self-designed majors, honors program, summer session, adult/continuing education programs, internships **Contact** Terry Davis, Director of Admissions, University of Cincinnati, 2624 Clifton Avenue, Cincinnati, OH 45221-0091. Telephone: 513-556-1100. Fax: 513-556-1105. E-mail: admissions@uc.edu. Web site: http://www.uc.edu/.

UNIVERSITY OF DAYTON
DAYTON, OHIO

General Independent Roman Catholic, university, coed **Entrance** Moderately difficult **Setting** 110-acre suburban campus **Total enrollment** 10,253 **Student-faculty ratio** 15:1 **Application deadline** 6/15 (transfer) **Freshmen** 80% were admitted **Housing** Yes **Expenses** Tuition $16,850; Room & Board $5280 **Undergraduates** 51% women, 8% part-time, 4% 25 or older, 0.1% Native American, 2% Hispanic American, 3% African American, 1% Asian American/Pacific Islander **The most frequently chosen baccalaureate fields are** business/marketing, education, engineering/engineering technologies **Academic program** English as a second language, advanced placement, accelerated degree program, honors program, summer session, adult/continuing education programs, internships **Contact** Mr. Robert F. Durkle, Director of Admission, University of Dayton, 300 College Park, Dayton, OH 45469-1300. Telephone: 937-229-4411 or toll-free 800-837-7433. Fax: 937-229-4729. E-mail: admission@udayton.edu. Web site: http://www.udayton.edu/.

THE UNIVERSITY OF FINDLAY
FINDLAY, OHIO

General Independent, comprehensive, coed, affiliated with Church of God **Entrance** Moderately difficult **Setting** 160-acre small-town campus **Total enrollment** 4,585 **Student-faculty ratio** 16:1 **Application deadline** 7/1 (freshmen), 8/1 (transfer) **Freshmen** 84% were admitted **Housing** Yes **Expenses** Tuition $17,528; Room & Board $6434 **Undergraduates** 57% women, 23% part-time, 26% 25 or older, 0.3% Native American, 2% Hispanic American, 4% African American, 4% Asian American/Pacific Islander **The most frequently chosen baccalaureate fields are** business/marketing, education, health professions and related sciences **Academic program** English as a second language, advanced placement, accelerated degree program, self-designed majors, honors program, summer session, adult/continuing education programs, internships **Contact** Curtis Davidson, Director, Undergraduate Admissions, The University of Findlay, 1000 North Main Street, Findlay, OH 45840-3653. Telephone: 419-434-4638 or toll-free 800-548-0932. Fax: 419-434-4898. E-mail: admissions@findlay.edu. Web site: http://www.findlay.edu/.

UNIVERSITY OF PHOENIX–OHIO CAMPUS
INDEPENDENCE, OHIO

General Proprietary, comprehensive, coed **Entrance** Noncompetitive **Total enrollment** 88,730 **Student-faculty ratio** 11:1 **Application deadline** Rolling (freshmen), rolling (transfer) **Housing** No **Expenses** Tuition $10,500 **Undergraduates** 56% women **Academic program** Advanced placement, accelerated degree program, adult/continuing education programs **Contact** Ms. Beth Barilla, Director of Admissions, University of Phoenix–Ohio Campus, 4615 East Elwood Street, Phoenix, AZ 85040-1958. Telephone: 480-927-0099 Ext. 1218. Fax: 480-594-1758. E-mail: beth.barilla@apollogrp.net. Web site: http://www.phoenix.edu/.

UNIVERSITY OF RIO GRANDE
RIO GRANDE, OHIO

General Independent, comprehensive, coed **Entrance** Noncompetitive **Setting** 170-acre rural campus **Total enrollment** 2,076 **Student-faculty ratio** 18:1 **Application deadline** Rolling (freshmen), rolling (transfer) **Freshmen** 100% were admitted **Housing** Yes **Expenses** Tuition $9176; Room & Board $5362 **Undergraduates** 59% women, 20% part-time, 25% 25 or older **The most frequently chosen baccalaureate fields are** business/marketing, communications/communication technologies, education **Academic program** English as a second language, advanced placement, accelerated degree program, self-designed majors, honors program, summer session, adult/continuing education programs, internships **Contact** Mr. Mark F. Abell, Executive Director of Admissions, University of Rio Grande, PO Box 500, Rio Grande, OH 45674. Telephone: 740-245-5353 Ext. 7206 or toll-free 800-288-2746 (in-state); 800-282-7204 (out-of-state). Fax: 740-245-7260. E-mail: mabell@urgrgcc.edu. Web site: http://www.rio.edu/.

OHIO

UNIVERSITY OF TOLEDO
TOLEDO, OHIO

General State-supported, university, coed **Entrance** Noncompetitive **Setting** 407-acre suburban campus **Total enrollment** 20,313 **Student-faculty ratio** 18:1 **Application deadline** Rolling (freshmen), rolling (transfer) **Freshmen** 99% were admitted **Housing** Yes **Expenses** Tuition $5102; Room & Board $6104 **Undergraduates** 52% women, 25% part-time, 19% 25 or older **The most frequently chosen baccalaureate fields are** business/marketing, education, engineering/engineering technologies **Academic program** Advanced placement, self-designed majors, honors program, summer session, adult/continuing education programs, internships **Contact** Ms. Nancy Hintz, Assistant Director, University of Toledo, 2801 West Bancroft, Toledo, OH 43606-3398. Telephone: 419-530-5728 or toll-free 800-5TOLEDO (in-state). Fax: 419-530-5872. E-mail: adm0017@uofT01.utoledo.edu. Web site: http://www.utoledo.edu/.

URBANA UNIVERSITY
URBANA, OHIO

General Independent, comprehensive, coed, affiliated with Church of the New Jerusalem **Entrance** Moderately difficult **Setting** 128-acre small-town campus **Total enrollment** 1,432 **Student-faculty ratio** 18:1 **Application deadline** Rolling (freshmen), rolling (transfer) **Freshmen** 59% were admitted **Housing** Yes **Expenses** Tuition $12,004; Room & Board $5000 **Undergraduates** 55% women, 37% part-time, 53% 25 or older **The most frequently chosen baccalaureate fields are** business/marketing, communications/communication technologies, education **Academic program** English as a second language, advanced placement, accelerated degree program, self-designed majors, summer session, adult/continuing education programs, internships **Contact** Ms. Mona Newcomer, Admissions Office Manager, Urbana University, 579 College Way, Urbana, OH 43078-2091. Telephone: 937-484-1356 or toll-free 800-787-2262 (in-state). Fax: 937-484-1389. E-mail: admiss@urbana.edu. Web site: http://www.urbana.edu/.

URSULINE COLLEGE
PEPPER PIKE, OHIO

General Independent Roman Catholic, comprehensive, coed, primarily women **Entrance** Minimally difficult **Setting** 112-acre suburban campus **Total enrollment** 1,281 **Student-faculty ratio** 9:1 **Application deadline** Rolling (freshmen), rolling (transfer) **Freshmen** 65% were admitted **Housing** Yes **Expenses** Tuition $14,730; Room & Board $5000 **Undergraduates** 92% women, 48% part-time, 59% 25 or older, 0.2% Native American, 3% Hispanic American, 21% African American, 1% Asian American/Pacific Islander **The most frequently chosen baccalaureate fields are** business/marketing, health professions and related sciences, psychology **Academic program** Advanced placement, self-designed majors, summer session, adult/continuing education programs, internships **Contact** Ms. Jill Oakley-Jeppe, Director of Admissions, Ursuline College, 2550 Lander Road, Pepper Pike, OH 44124. Telephone: 440-449-4203 or toll-free 888-URSULINE (in-state). Fax: 440-684-6138. E-mail: admission@ursuline.edu. Web site: http://www.ursuline.edu/.

WALSH UNIVERSITY
NORTH CANTON, OHIO

General Independent Roman Catholic, comprehensive, coed **Entrance** Moderately difficult **Setting** 100-acre small-town campus **Total enrollment** 1,522 **Student-faculty ratio** 12:1 **Application deadline** Rolling (freshmen), rolling (transfer) **Freshmen** 80% were admitted **Housing** Yes **Expenses** Tuition $12,410; Room & Board $5600 **Undergraduates** 59% women, 25% part-time, 0.4% Native American, 1% Hispanic American, 6% African American, 1% Asian American/Pacific Islander **The most frequently chosen baccalaureate fields are** business/marketing, education, health professions and related sciences **Academic program** English as a second language, advanced placement, accelerated degree program, self-designed majors, honors program, summer session, adult/continuing education programs, internships **Contact** Mr. Brett Freshour, Director of Admissions, Walsh University, 2020 Easton Street, NW, North Canton, OH 44720-3396. Telephone: 330-490-7171 or toll-free 800-362-9846 (in-state); 800-362-8846 (out-of-state). Fax: 330-490-7165. E-mail: admissions@alex.walsh.edu. Web site: http://www.walsh.edu/.

WILBERFORCE UNIVERSITY
WILBERFORCE, OHIO

General Independent, 4-year, coed, affiliated with African Methodist Episcopal Church **Entrance** Minimally difficult **Setting** 125-acre rural campus **Total enrollment** 908 **Student-faculty ratio** 12:1 **Application deadline** 7/1 (freshmen), 7/1 (transfer) **Freshmen** 22% were admitted **Housing** Yes **Expenses** Tuition $10,166; Room & Board $5250 **Undergraduates** 59% women, 10% 25 or older, 0.4% Hispanic American, 91% African American, 0.2% Asian American/Pacific Islander **Academic program** Advanced placement, honors program **Contact** Mr. Kenneth C. Christmon, Director of Admissions, Wilberforce University, PO Box 1001, Wilberforce, OH 45384-1001. Telephone: 937-708-5789 or toll-free 800-367-8568. Fax: 937-376-4751. E-mail: kchristm@wilberforce.edu. Web site: http://www.wilberforce.edu/.

WILMINGTON COLLEGE
WILMINGTON, OHIO

General Independent Friends, 4-year, coed **Entrance** Moderately difficult **Setting** 1,465-acre small-town campus **Total enrollment** 1,243 **Student-faculty ratio** 16:1 **Application deadline** Rolling (freshmen), rolling (transfer) **Freshmen** 80% were admitted **Housing** Yes **Expenses** Tuition $16,514; Room & Board $6251 **Undergraduates** 55% women, 1% part-time, 0.1% Native American, 0.3% Hispanic American,

OHIO

Wilmington College *(continued)*

11% African American, 0.2% Asian American/Pacific Islander **The most frequently chosen baccalaureate fields are** business/marketing, agriculture, education **Academic program** Advanced placement, self-designed majors, honors program, summer session, adult/continuing education programs, internships **Contact** Tina Garland, Interim Director of Admission and Financial Aid, Wilmington College, Pyle Center Box 1325, 251 Ludovic Street, Wilmington, OH 45177. Telephone: 937-382-6661 Ext. 260 or toll-free 800-341-9318 Ext. 260. Fax: 937-382-7077. E-mail: admission@wilmington.edu. Web site: http://www.wilmington.edu/.

WITTENBERG UNIVERSITY
SPRINGFIELD, OHIO

General Independent, comprehensive, coed, affiliated with Evangelical Lutheran Church **Entrance** Moderately difficult **Setting** 71-acre suburban campus **Total enrollment** 2,269 **Student-faculty ratio** 14:1 **Application deadline** 3/15 (freshmen), rolling (transfer) **Freshmen** 85% were admitted **Housing** Yes **Expenses** Tuition $22,840; Room & Board $5776 **Undergraduates** 55% women, 7% part-time, 2% 25 or older, 0.1% Native American, 1% Hispanic American, 6% African American, 1% Asian American/Pacific Islander **Academic program** English as a second language, advanced placement, accelerated degree program, self-designed majors, honors program, summer session, adult/continuing education programs, internships **Contact** Mr. Kenneth G. Benne, Dean of Admissions and Financial Aid, Wittenberg University, PO Box 720, Springfield, OH 45501-0720. Telephone: 937-327-6314 Ext. 6366 or toll-free 800-677-7558 Ext. 6314. Fax: 937-327-6379. E-mail: admission@wittenberg.edu. Web site: http://www.wittenberg.edu/.

WRIGHT STATE UNIVERSITY
DAYTON, OHIO

General State-supported, university, coed **Entrance** Minimally difficult **Setting** 557-acre suburban campus **Total enrollment** 15,810 **Student-faculty ratio** 20:1 **Application deadline** Rolling (freshmen), rolling (transfer) **Freshmen** 92% were admitted **Housing** Yes **Expenses** Tuition $4596; Room & Board $5400 **Undergraduates** 56% women, 20% part-time, 21% 25 or older, 0.4% Native American, 1% Hispanic American, 11% African American, 2% Asian American/Pacific Islander **The most frequently chosen baccalaureate fields are** business/marketing, communications/communication technologies, education **Academic program** English as a second language, advanced placement, self-designed majors, honors program, summer session, adult/continuing education programs, internships **Contact** Ms. Cathy Davis, Director of Undergraduate Admissions, Wright State University, 3640 Colonel Glenn Highway, Dayton, OH 45435. Telephone: 937-775-5700 or toll-free 800-247-1770. Fax: 937-775-5795. E-mail: admissions@wright.edu. Web site: http://www.wright.edu/.

XAVIER UNIVERSITY
CINCINNATI, OHIO

General Independent Roman Catholic, comprehensive, coed **Entrance** Moderately difficult **Setting** 100-acre suburban campus **Total enrollment** 6,660 **Student-faculty ratio** 17:1 **Application deadline** 2/1 (freshmen), rolling (transfer) **Freshmen** 83% were admitted **Housing** Yes **Expenses** Tuition $16,780; Room & Board $7230 **Undergraduates** 58% women, 16% part-time, 15% 25 or older, 0.1% Native American, 1% Hispanic American, 9% African American, 2% Asian American/Pacific Islander **The most frequently chosen baccalaureate fields are** business/marketing, communications/communication technologies, liberal arts/general studies **Academic program** English as a second language, advanced placement, honors program, summer session, adult/continuing education programs, internships **Contact** Mr. Marc Camille, Dean of Admission, Xavier University, 3800 Victory Parkway, Cincinnati, OH 45207-5311. Telephone: 513-745-3301 or toll-free 800-344-4698. Fax: 513-745-4319. E-mail: xuadmit@xu.edu. Web site: http://www.xu.edu/.

YOUNGSTOWN STATE UNIVERSITY
YOUNGSTOWN, OHIO

General State-supported, comprehensive, coed **Entrance** Noncompetitive **Setting** 150-acre urban campus **Total enrollment** 12,250 **Student-faculty ratio** 19:1 **Application deadline** 8/15 (freshmen), 8/15 (transfer) **Freshmen** 88% were admitted **Housing** Yes **Expenses** Tuition $4588; Room & Board $4970 **Undergraduates** 53% women, 22% part-time, 26% 25 or older, 0.3% Native American, 2% Hispanic American, 9% African American, 1% Asian American/Pacific Islander **The most frequently chosen baccalaureate fields are** business/marketing, education, protective services/public administration **Academic program** English as a second language, advanced placement, accelerated degree program, self-designed majors, honors program, summer session, adult/continuing education programs, internships **Contact** Ms. Sue Davis, Interim Director of Undergraduate Admissions, Youngstown State University, One University Plaza, Youngstown, OH 44555-0001. Telephone: 330-742-2000 or toll-free 877-468-6978. Fax: 330-742-3674. E-mail: nsrysu@ysub.edu. Web site: http://www.ysu.edu/.

OKLAHOMA

AMERICAN CHRISTIAN COLLEGE AND SEMINARY
OKLAHOMA CITY, OKLAHOMA

General Independent interdenominational, comprehensive, coed **Entrance** Noncompetitive **Setting** 1-acre small-town campus **Total enrollment** 484 **Student-faculty ratio** 8:1 **Housing** No **Expenses**

OKLAHOMA

Tuition $3516 **Undergraduates** 45% women, 62% part-time, 90% 25 or older, 0% Native American, 22% Hispanic American, 36% African American, 10% Asian American/Pacific Islander **The most frequently chosen baccalaureate field is** philosophy **Academic program** Advanced placement, summer session, adult/continuing education programs, internships **Contact** Dr. Mitchel Beville, Director of Admissions, American Christian College and Seminary, 4300 Highline Boulevard #202, Oklahoma City, OK 73108. Telephone: 405-945-0100 Ext. 120 or toll-free 800-488-2528. Fax: 405-945-0311. E-mail: info@accs.edu. Web site: http://www.accs.edu/.

BARTLESVILLE WESLEYAN COLLEGE
See Oklahoma Wesleyan University

CAMERON UNIVERSITY
LAWTON, OKLAHOMA

General State-supported, comprehensive, coed **Entrance** Minimally difficult **Setting** 160-acre suburban campus **Total enrollment** 5,262 **Student-faculty ratio** 20:1 **Application deadline** Rolling (freshmen), rolling (transfer) **Freshmen** 89% were admitted **Housing** Yes **Expenses** Tuition $2090; Room & Board $2746 **Undergraduates** 57% women, 41% part-time, 46% 25 or older, 5% Native American, 7% Hispanic American, 22% African American, 3% Asian American/Pacific Islander **The most frequently chosen baccalaureate fields are** business/marketing, protective services/public administration, social sciences and history **Academic program** Advanced placement, accelerated degree program, honors program, summer session, adult/continuing education programs **Contact** Ms. Brenda Dally, Coordinator of Student Recruitment, Cameron University, Cameron University, Attention: Admissions, 2800 West Gore Boulevard, Lawton, OK 73505. Telephone: 580-581-2837 or toll-free 888-454-7600. Fax: 580-581-5514. E-mail: admiss@cua.cameron.edu. Web site: http://www.cameron.edu/.

EAST CENTRAL UNIVERSITY
ADA, OKLAHOMA

General State-supported, comprehensive, coed **Entrance** Moderately difficult **Setting** 140-acre small-town campus **Total enrollment** 4,195 **Student-faculty ratio** 19:1 **Application deadline** 9/1 (freshmen), 9/1 (transfer) **Housing** Yes **Expenses** Tuition $2172; Room & Board $2452 **Undergraduates** 59% women, 15% part-time, 37% 25 or older, 15% Native American, 2% Hispanic American, 4% African American, 1% Asian American/Pacific Islander **The most frequently chosen baccalaureate field is** law/legal studies **Academic program** Advanced placement, accelerated degree program, honors program, summer session, adult/continuing education programs, internships **Contact** Ms. Pamela Armstrong, Registrar, East Central University, PMBJ8, 1100 East 14th Street, Ada, OK 74820-6999. Telephone: 580-332-8000 Ext. 239. Fax: 580-310-5432. E-mail: parmstro@mailclerk.ecok.edu. Web site: http://www.ecok.edu/.

HILLSDALE FREE WILL BAPTIST COLLEGE
MOORE, OKLAHOMA

General Independent Free Will Baptist, 4-year, coed **Entrance** Noncompetitive **Setting** 40-acre suburban campus **Total enrollment** 287 **Student-faculty ratio** 15:1 **Application deadline** Rolling (freshmen), rolling (transfer) **Housing** Yes **Expenses** Tuition $6290; Room & Board $4040 **Undergraduates** 41% women, 15% part-time, 12% 25 or older, 8% Native American, 3% Hispanic American, 7% African American, 0.4% Asian American/Pacific Islander **The most frequently chosen baccalaureate fields are** philosophy, business/marketing, philosophy, religion, and theology **Academic program** English as a second language, advanced placement, accelerated degree program, summer session, adult/continuing education programs, internships **Contact** Ms. Sue Chaffin, Registrar/Assistant Director of Admissions, Hillsdale Free Will Baptist College, PO Box 7208, Moore, OK 73153-1208. Telephone: 405-912-9005. Fax: 405-912-9050. E-mail: gosaints@flash.net. Web site: http://www.hc.edu.

LANGSTON UNIVERSITY
LANGSTON, OKLAHOMA

General State-supported, comprehensive, coed **Entrance** Minimally difficult **Setting** 40-acre rural campus **Total enrollment** 3,398 **Application deadline** Rolling (freshmen), rolling (transfer) **Freshmen** 18% were admitted **Housing** Yes **Expenses** Tuition $1713; Room & Board $2964 **Undergraduates** 58% women, 39% part-time, 20% 25 or older **The most frequently chosen baccalaureate fields are** education, health professions and related sciences, psychology **Academic program** Advanced placement, accelerated degree program, honors program, summer session, adult/continuing education programs, internships **Contact** Ms. Vickie Alexander, Langston University, Langston, OK 73050. Telephone: 405-466-3231. Fax: 405-466-3381. Web site: http://www.lunet.edu/.

METROPOLITAN COLLEGE
OKLAHOMA CITY, OKLAHOMA

General Proprietary, 4-year, coed, primarily women **Entrance** Minimally difficult **Total enrollment** 140 **Expenses** Tuition $6593 **Undergraduates** 94% women, 45% part-time, 7% Native American, 1% Hispanic American, 34% African American **Contact** Mr. Keith Wells, Admissions Director, Metropolitan College, 2901 North Classen Boulevard, Suite 200, Oklahoma City, OK 73106. Telephone: 405-528-5000. Web site: http://www.metropolitancollege.edu/.

METROPOLITAN COLLEGE
TULSA, OKLAHOMA

General Proprietary, 4-year, coed, primarily women **Entrance** Minimally difficult **Setting** urban campus **Total enrollment** 112 **Student-faculty ratio** 15:1

OKLAHOMA

Metropolitan College *(continued)*
Freshmen 78% were admitted **Housing** No **Expenses** Tuition $6535 **Undergraduates** 96% women, 71% 25 or older, 12% Native American, 1% Hispanic American, 21% African American **Academic program** Accelerated degree program, adult/continuing education programs, internships **Contact** Ms. Lee Griffith, Admission Representative, Metropolitan College, 4528 South Sheridan Road, Suite 105, Tulsa, OK 74145-1011. Telephone: 918-627-9300. Web site: http://www.metropolitancollege.edu/.

MID-AMERICA BIBLE COLLEGE
OKLAHOMA CITY, OKLAHOMA

General Independent, 4-year, coed, affiliated with Church of God **Entrance** Noncompetitive **Setting** 145-acre suburban campus **Total enrollment** 613 **Student-faculty ratio** 19:1 **Application deadline** Rolling (freshmen), rolling (transfer) **Freshmen** 100% were admitted **Housing** Yes **Expenses** Tuition $6244; Room & Board $5266 **Undergraduates** 48% women, 11% part-time, 53% 25 or older, 3% Native American, 4% Hispanic American, 9% African American, 1% Asian American/Pacific Islander **The most frequently chosen baccalaureate fields are** business/marketing, philosophy, religion, and theology, psychology **Academic program** Advanced placement, accelerated degree program, summer session, adult/continuing education programs, internships **Contact** Ms. Dianna Rea, Director of College Relations, Mid-America Bible College, 3500 Southwest 119th Street, Oklahoma City, OK 73170. Telephone: 405-692-3180. Fax: 405-692-3265. E-mail: mbcinfo@mabc.edu. Web site: http://www.mabc.edu/.

NORTHEASTERN STATE UNIVERSITY
TAHLEQUAH, OKLAHOMA

General State-supported, comprehensive, coed **Entrance** Moderately difficult **Setting** 160-acre small-town campus **Total enrollment** 8,603 **Student-faculty ratio** 17:1 **Application deadline** 8/5 (freshmen), 8/5 (transfer) **Freshmen** 97% were admitted **Housing** Yes **Expenses** Tuition $2130; Room & Board $2724 **Undergraduates** 59% women, 24% part-time, 35% 25 or older, 28% Native American, 1% Hispanic American, 5% African American, 1% Asian American/Pacific Islander **The most frequently chosen baccalaureate fields are** business/marketing, education, protective services/public administration **Academic program** Advanced placement, honors program, summer session, adult/continuing education programs, internships **Contact** William E. Nowlin, Registrar, Department of Admissions and Records, Northeastern State University, 601 North Grand, Tahlequah, OK 74464. Telephone: 918-456-5511 Ext. 2200 or toll-free 800-722-9614 (in-state). Fax: 918-458-2342. E-mail: nsuadmis@nsuok.edu. Web site: http://www.nsuok.edu/.

NORTHWESTERN OKLAHOMA STATE UNIVERSITY
ALVA, OKLAHOMA

General State-supported, comprehensive, coed **Entrance** Moderately difficult **Setting** 70-acre small-town campus **Total enrollment** 2,055 **Student-faculty ratio** 14:1 **Application deadline** Rolling (freshmen), rolling (transfer) **Freshmen** 100% were admitted **Housing** Yes **Expenses** Tuition $2032; Room & Board $2550 **Undergraduates** 54% women, 25% part-time, 26% 25 or older, 4% Native American, 2% Hispanic American, 4% African American, 0.3% Asian American/Pacific Islander **The most frequently chosen baccalaureate fields are** business/marketing, education, protective services/public administration **Academic program** Advanced placement, summer session, adult/continuing education programs **Contact** Mrs. Shirley Murrow, Registrar, Northwestern Oklahoma State University, 709 Oklahoma Boulevard, Alva, OK 73717-2799. Telephone: 580-327-8550. Fax: 580-327-8699. E-mail: smmurrow@nwosu.edu. Web site: http://www.nwosu.edu/.

OKLAHOMA BAPTIST UNIVERSITY
SHAWNEE, OKLAHOMA

General Independent Southern Baptist, comprehensive, coed **Entrance** Moderately difficult **Setting** 125-acre small-town campus **Total enrollment** 1,933 **Student-faculty ratio** 14:1 **Application deadline** 8/1 (freshmen), 8/1 (transfer) **Freshmen** 86% were admitted **Housing** Yes **Expenses** Tuition $10,240; Room & Board $3640 **Undergraduates** 56% women, 19% part-time, 18% 25 or older **The most frequently chosen baccalaureate fields are** education, business/marketing, health professions and related sciences **Academic program** Advanced placement, self-designed majors, honors program, summer session, internships **Contact** Mr. Michael Cappo, Dean of Admissions, Oklahoma Baptist University, Box 61174, Shawnee, OK 74804. Telephone: 405-878-2033 or toll-free 800-654-3285. Fax: 405-878-2046. E-mail: admissions@mail.okbu.edu. Web site: http://www.okbu.edu/.

OKLAHOMA CHRISTIAN UNIVERSITY
OKLAHOMA CITY, OKLAHOMA

General Independent, comprehensive, coed, affiliated with Church of Christ **Entrance** Noncompetitive **Setting** 200-acre suburban campus **Total enrollment** 1,811 **Student-faculty ratio** 16:1 **Application deadline** Rolling (freshmen), rolling (transfer) **Freshmen** 82% were admitted **Housing** Yes **Expenses** Tuition $12,100; Room & Board $4400 **Undergraduates** 50% women, 9% part-time, 3% Native American, 3% Hispanic American, 5% African American, 2% Asian American/Pacific Islander **The most frequently chosen baccalaureate fields are** business/marketing, biological/life sciences, education **Academic program** English as a second language, advanced placement, accelerated degree program, honors program, summer session, adult/continuing

OKLAHOMA

education programs, internships **Contact** Mr. Kyle Ray, Director of Admissions, Oklahoma Christian University, Box 11000, Oklahoma City, OK 73136-1100. Telephone: 405-425-5050 or toll-free 800-877-5010 (in-state). Fax: 405-425-5208. E-mail: info@oc.edu. Web site: http://www.oc.edu/.

OKLAHOMA CITY UNIVERSITY
OKLAHOMA CITY, OKLAHOMA

General Independent United Methodist, comprehensive, coed **Entrance** Moderately difficult **Setting** 68-acre urban campus **Total enrollment** 3,705 **Student-faculty ratio** 14:1 **Application deadline** 8/22 (freshmen), rolling (transfer) **Freshmen** 70% were admitted **Housing** Yes **Expenses** Tuition $10,880; Room & Board $4590 **Undergraduates** 59% women, 21% part-time, 22% 25 or older, 4% Native American, 3% Hispanic American, 5% African American, 2% Asian American/Pacific Islander **The most frequently chosen baccalaureate fields are** liberal arts/general studies, business/marketing, visual/performing arts **Academic program** English as a second language, advanced placement, accelerated degree program, self-designed majors, honors program, summer session, adult/continuing education programs, internships **Contact** Ms. Stacy Messinger, Director of Admissions, Oklahoma City University, 2501 North Blackwelder, Oklahoma City, OK 73106. Telephone: 405-521-5050 or toll-free 800-633-7242 (in-state). Fax: 405-521-5916. E-mail: uadmissions@okcu.edu. Web site: http://www.okcu.edu/.

OKLAHOMA PANHANDLE STATE UNIVERSITY
GOODWELL, OKLAHOMA

General State-supported, 4-year, coed **Entrance** Noncompetitive **Setting** 40-acre rural campus **Total enrollment** 1,226 **Student-faculty ratio** 24:1 **Application deadline** Rolling (freshmen), rolling (transfer) **Freshmen** 54% were admitted **Housing** Yes **Expenses** Tuition $1911; Room & Board $2580 **Undergraduates** 54% women, 19% part-time, 23% 25 or older **The most frequently chosen baccalaureate fields are** agriculture, business/marketing, education **Academic program** English as a second language, advanced placement, accelerated degree program, summer session, adult/continuing education programs, internships **Contact** Registrar and Director of Admissions, Oklahoma Panhandle State University, PO Box 430, 323 Eagle Boulevard, Goodwell, OK 73939-0430. Telephone: 580-349-1376 or toll-free 800-664-6778. Fax: 580-349-2302. E-mail: opsu@opsu.edu. Web site: http://www.opsu.edu/.

OKLAHOMA STATE UNIVERSITY
STILLWATER, OKLAHOMA

General State-supported, university, coed **Entrance** Moderately difficult **Setting** 840-acre small-town campus **Total enrollment** 21,872 **Student-faculty ratio** 18:1 **Application deadline** Rolling (freshmen), rolling (transfer) **Freshmen** 91% were admitted **Housing** Yes **Expenses** Tuition $2794; Room & Board $4856 **Undergraduates** 48% women, 10% part-time, 12% 25 or older, 8% Native American, 2% Hispanic American, 3% African American, 2% Asian American/Pacific Islander **The most frequently chosen baccalaureate fields are** business/marketing, agriculture, engineering/engineering technologies **Academic program** English as a second language, advanced placement, accelerated degree program, self-designed majors, honors program, summer session, adult/continuing education programs, internships **Contact** Ms. Paulette Cundiff, Coordinator of Admissions Processing, Oklahoma State University, 324 Student Union, Stillwater, OK 74078. Telephone: 405-744-6858 or toll-free 800-233-5019 (in-state); 800-852-1255 (out-of-state). Fax: 405-744-5285. E-mail: grl6458@okway.okstate.edu. Web site: http://www.okstate.edu/.

OKLAHOMA WESLEYAN UNIVERSITY
BARTLESVILLE, OKLAHOMA

General Independent, comprehensive, coed, affiliated with Wesleyan Church **Entrance** Minimally difficult **Setting** 127-acre small-town campus **Total enrollment** 834 **Student-faculty ratio** 14:1 **Application deadline** Rolling (freshmen), rolling (transfer) **Freshmen** 60% were admitted **Housing** Yes **Expenses** Tuition $9800; Room & Board $4100 **Undergraduates** 37% 25 or older, 7% Native American, 2% Hispanic American, 6% African American, 2% Asian American/Pacific Islander **Academic program** English as a second language, advanced placement, self-designed majors, summer session, adult/continuing education programs, internships **Contact** Mr. Marty Carver, Director of Enrollment Services, Oklahoma Wesleyan University, 2201 Silver Lake Road, Bartlesville, OK 74006-6299. Telephone: 918-335-6219 or toll-free 800-468-6292 (in-state). Fax: 918-335-6229. E-mail: admissions@okwu.edu. Web site: http://www.okwu.edu/.

ORAL ROBERTS UNIVERSITY
TULSA, OKLAHOMA

General Independent interdenominational, comprehensive, coed **Entrance** Moderately difficult **Setting** 263-acre urban campus **Total enrollment** 3,677 **Student-faculty ratio** 17:1 **Application deadline** Rolling (freshmen), rolling (transfer) **Freshmen** 72% were admitted **Housing** Yes **Expenses** Tuition $12,260; Room & Board $5228 **Undergraduates** 58% women, 9% part-time, 11% 25 or older, 2% Native American, 5% Hispanic American, 16% African American, 3% Asian American/Pacific Islander **The most frequently chosen baccalaureate fields are** business/marketing, communications/communication technologies, philosophy **Academic program** English as a second language, advanced placement, self-designed majors, honors program, summer session, adult/continuing education programs, internships **Contact** Chris Miller, Director of Undergraduate Admissions, Oral Roberts University, 7777 South Lewis Avenue, Tulsa, OK 74171. Telephone: 918-495-6518 or toll-

OKLAHOMA

Oral Roberts University (continued)
free 800-678-8876. Fax: 918-495-6222. E-mail: admissions@oru.edu. Web site: http://www.oru.edu/.

ROGERS STATE UNIVERSITY
CLAREMORE, OKLAHOMA

General State-supported, 4-year, coed **Entrance** Noncompetitive **Setting** small-town campus **Total enrollment** 2,852 **Student-faculty ratio** 21:1 **Application deadline** Rolling (freshmen), rolling (transfer) **Freshmen** 79% were admitted **Housing** Yes **Expenses** Tuition $1730; Room only $3070 **Undergraduates** 64% women, 50% part-time, 42% 25 or older, 24% Native American, 2% Hispanic American, 2% African American, 0.5% Asian American/Pacific Islander **Academic program** Advanced placement, summer session, adult/continuing education programs, internships **Contact** Ms. Becky Noah, Director of Enrollment Management, Rogers State University, Roger's State University, Office of Admissions, 1701 West Will Rogers Boulevard, Claremore, OK 74017. Telephone: 918-343-7545 or toll-free 800-256-7511. Fax: 918-343-7595. E-mail: shunter@rsu.edu. Web site: http://www.rsu.edu/.

ST. GREGORY'S UNIVERSITY
SHAWNEE, OKLAHOMA

General Independent Roman Catholic, 4-year, coed **Entrance** Minimally difficult **Setting** 640-acre small-town campus **Total enrollment** 843 **Student-faculty ratio** 18:1 **Application deadline** Rolling (freshmen), rolling (transfer) **Freshmen** 77% were admitted **Housing** Yes **Expenses** Tuition $9502; Room & Board $4478 **Undergraduates** 56% women, 27% part-time, 19% 25 or older, 7% Native American, 5% Hispanic American, 5% African American, 1% Asian American/Pacific Islander **The most frequently chosen baccalaureate fields are** business/marketing, health professions and related sciences, social sciences and history **Academic program** English as a second language, advanced placement, self-designed majors, honors program, summer session, adult/continuing education programs, internships **Contact** Mr. Dan Rutledge, Director of Admissions, St. Gregory's University, 1900 West MacArthur Drive, Shawnee, OK 74804. Telephone: 405-878-5444 Ext. 447 or toll-free 888-STGREGS. Fax: 405-878-5198. E-mail: admissions@sgc.edu. Web site: http://www.sgc.edu/.

SOUTHEASTERN OKLAHOMA STATE UNIVERSITY
DURANT, OKLAHOMA

General State-supported, comprehensive, coed **Entrance** Moderately difficult **Setting** 176-acre small-town campus **Total enrollment** 4,025 **Student-faculty ratio** 18:1 **Application deadline** 8/15 (transfer) **Freshmen** 72% were admitted **Housing** Yes **Expenses** Tuition $1670; Room & Board $1246 **Undergraduates** 53% women, 21% part-time, 29% 25 or older, 30% Native American, 1% Hispanic American, 5% African American, 1% Asian American/Pacific Islander **The most frequently chosen baccalaureate fields are** business/marketing, education, engineering/engineering technologies **Academic program** Advanced placement, accelerated degree program, honors program, summer session, adult/continuing education programs, internships **Contact** Mr. Rudy Manley, Director of Enrollment Management, Southeastern Oklahoma State University, Box 4225, Durant, OK 74701-0609. Telephone: 580-745-2050 or toll-free 800-435-1327 Ext. 2307. Fax: 580-920-7472. Web site: http://www.sosu.edu/.

SOUTHERN NAZARENE UNIVERSITY
BETHANY, OKLAHOMA

General Independent Nazarene, comprehensive, coed **Entrance** Noncompetitive **Setting** 40-acre suburban campus **Total enrollment** 2,086 **Student-faculty ratio** 21:1 **Application deadline** 8/15 (freshmen), 8/15 (transfer) **Freshmen** 100% were admitted **Housing** Yes **Expenses** Tuition $10,086; Room & Board $2314 **Undergraduates** 54% women, 6% part-time, 21% 25 or older, 3% Native American, 3% Hispanic American, 6% African American, 1% Asian American/Pacific Islander **The most frequently chosen baccalaureate fields are** business/marketing, health professions and related sciences, social sciences and history **Academic program** Advanced placement, accelerated degree program, self-designed majors, honors program, summer session, adult/continuing education programs, internships **Contact** Mr. Larry Hess, Director of Admissions, Southern Nazarene University, 6729 Northwest 39th Expressway, Bethany, OK 73008. Telephone: 405-491-6324 or toll-free 800-648-9899. Fax: 405-491-6320. E-mail: admiss@snu.edu.

SOUTHWESTERN CHRISTIAN UNIVERSITY
BETHANY, OKLAHOMA

General Independent, comprehensive, coed, affiliated with Pentecostal Holiness Church **Entrance** Minimally difficult **Setting** 7-acre suburban campus **Total enrollment** 199 **Student-faculty ratio** 15:1 **Application deadline** Rolling (freshmen), rolling (transfer) **Housing** Yes **Expenses** Tuition $4744; Room & Board $3200 **Undergraduates** 45% women, 5% part-time, 20% 25 or older, 5% Native American, 3% Hispanic American, 9% African American, 1% Asian American/Pacific Islander **The most frequently chosen baccalaureate field is** philosophy, religion, and theology **Academic program** Advanced placement, summer session, internships **Contact** Mr. Johnny Lipton, Director of Admissions, Southwestern Christian University, PO Box 340, Bethany, OK 73008-0340. Telephone: 405-789-7661 Ext. 3449. E-mail: admissions@sccm.edu. Web site: http://www.sccm.edu/.

OKLAHOMA

SOUTHWESTERN OKLAHOMA STATE UNIVERSITY
WEATHERFORD, OKLAHOMA

General State-supported, comprehensive, coed Entrance Moderately difficult Setting 73-acre small-town campus Total enrollment 4,468 Student-faculty ratio 19:1 Freshmen 94% were admitted Housing Yes Expenses Tuition $2138; Room & Board $2550 Undergraduates 56% women, 11% part-time, 16% 25 or older, 5% Native American, 3% Hispanic American, 3% African American, 2% Asian American/Pacific Islander The most frequently chosen baccalaureate fields are business/marketing, education, health professions and related sciences Academic program Advanced placement, accelerated degree program, summer session, adult/continuing education programs, internships Contact Ms. Connie Phillips, Admission Counselor, Southwestern Oklahoma State University, 100 Campus Drive, Weatherford, OK 73096. Telephone: 580-774-3009. Fax: 580-774-3795. E-mail: ropers@swosu.edu. Web site: http://www.swosu.edu/.

UNIVERSITY OF CENTRAL OKLAHOMA
EDMOND, OKLAHOMA

General State-supported, comprehensive, coed Entrance Minimally difficult Setting 200-acre suburban campus Total enrollment 14,099 Student-faculty ratio 20:1 Application deadline Rolling (freshmen), rolling (transfer) Freshmen 96% were admitted Housing Yes Expenses Tuition $2067; Room & Board $3138 Undergraduates 57% women, 32% part-time, 36% 25 or older, 4% Native American, 3% Hispanic American, 7% African American, 3% Asian American/Pacific Islander The most frequently chosen baccalaureate fields are business/marketing, (pre)law, education Academic program English as a second language, advanced placement, accelerated degree program, honors program, summer session, adult/continuing education programs, internships Contact Ms. Linda Lofton, Director, Admissions and Records Processing, University of Central Oklahoma, Office of Enrollment Services, 100 North University Drive, Box 151, Edmond, OK 73034. Telephone: 405-974-2338 Ext. 2338 or toll-free 800-254-4215 (in-state). Fax: 405-341-4964. E-mail: admituco@ucok.edu. Web site: http://www.ucok.edu/.

UNIVERSITY OF OKLAHOMA
NORMAN, OKLAHOMA

General State-supported, university, coed Entrance Moderately difficult Setting 3,500-acre suburban campus Total enrollment 22,646 Student-faculty ratio 19:1 Application deadline 6/1 (freshmen), rolling (transfer) Freshmen 93% were admitted Housing Yes Expenses Tuition $2713; Room & Board $4903 Undergraduates 49% women, 14% part-time, 11% 25 or older, 8% Native American, 4% Hispanic American, 7% African American, 5% Asian American/Pacific Islander The most frequently chosen baccalaureate fields are business/marketing, engineering/engineering technologies, social sciences and history Academic program English as a second language, advanced placement, accelerated degree program, self-designed majors, honors program, summer session, adult/continuing education programs, internships Contact Karen Renfroe, Executive Director of Recruitment Services, University of Oklahoma, 1000 Asp Avenue, Norman, OK 73019. Telephone: 405-325-2151 or toll-free 800-234-6868. Fax: 405-325-7124. E-mail: admrec@ou.edu. Web site: http://www.ou.edu/.

UNIVERSITY OF OKLAHOMA HEALTH SCIENCES CENTER
OKLAHOMA CITY, OKLAHOMA

General State-supported, upper-level, coed Entrance Moderately difficult Setting 200-acre urban campus Total enrollment 2,862 Application deadline 10/1 (transfer) First-Year Students 62% were admitted Housing No Expenses Tuition $2978 Undergraduates 89% women, 15% part-time, 32% 25 or older, 9% Native American, 4% Hispanic American, 5% African American, 3% Asian American/Pacific Islander The most frequently chosen baccalaureate field is health professions and related sciences Academic program Advanced placement, honors program, summer session, internships Contact Dr. Willie V. Bryan, Vice Provost for Educational Services and Registrar, University of Oklahoma Health Sciences Center, PO Box 26901, Oklahoma City, OK 73190. Telephone: 405-271-2655. Fax: 405-271-2480. E-mail: sophie-mack@ouhsc.edu. Web site: http://www.ouhsc.edu/.

UNIVERSITY OF PHOENIX–OKLAHOMA CITY CAMPUS
OKLAHOMA CITY, OKLAHOMA

General Proprietary, comprehensive, coed Entrance Noncompetitive Total enrollment 88,730 Student-faculty ratio 14:1 Application deadline Rolling (freshmen), rolling (transfer) Housing No Expenses Tuition $7950 Undergraduates 56% women, 79% 25 or older The most frequently chosen baccalaureate field is business/marketing Academic program Advanced placement, accelerated degree program, adult/continuing education programs Contact Ms. Beth Barilla, Director of Admissions, University of Phoenix–Oklahoma City Campus, 4615 East Elwood Street, Phoenix, AZ 85040-1958. Telephone: 480-927-0099 Ext. 1218 or toll-free 800-228-7240. Fax: 480-594-1758. E-mail: beth.barilla@apollogrp.edu. Web site: http://www.phoenix.edu/.

UNIVERSITY OF PHOENIX–TULSA CAMPUS
TULSA, OKLAHOMA

General Proprietary, comprehensive, coed Entrance Noncompetitive Total enrollment 88,730 Student-faculty ratio 13:1 Application deadline Rolling (freshmen), rolling (transfer) Housing No Expenses

OKLAHOMA

University of Phoenix–Tulsa Campus *(continued)*
Tuition $7950 **Undergraduates** 99.9% women **The most frequently chosen baccalaureate field is** business/marketing **Academic program** Advanced placement, accelerated degree program, adult/continuing education programs **Contact** Ms. Beth Barilla, Director of Admissions, University of Phoenix–Tulsa Campus, 4615 East Elwood Street, Phoenix, AZ 85040-1958. Telephone: 480-927-0099 Ext. 1218 or toll-free 800-228-7240. Fax: 480-594-1758. E-mail: beth.barilla@apollogrp.edu. Web site: http://www.phoenix.edu/.

UNIVERSITY OF SCIENCE AND ARTS OF OKLAHOMA
CHICKASHA, OKLAHOMA

General State-supported, 4-year, coed **Entrance** Moderately difficult **Setting** 75-acre small-town campus **Total enrollment** 1,452 **Student-faculty ratio** 18:1 **Application deadline** 9/10 (freshmen), rolling (transfer) **Freshmen** 84% were admitted **Housing** Yes **Expenses** Tuition $2198; Room & Board $2590 **Undergraduates** 62% women, 28% part-time, 25% 25 or older, 13% Native American, 2% Hispanic American, 5% African American, 1% Asian American/Pacific Islander **The most frequently chosen baccalaureate fields are** business/marketing, education, social sciences and history **Academic program** English as a second language, advanced placement, accelerated degree program, self-designed majors, honors program, summer session, adult/continuing education programs, internships **Contact** Mr. Joseph Evans, Registrar and Director of Admissions and Records, University of Science and Arts of Oklahoma, 1727 West Alabama, Chickasha, OK 73018-5322. Telephone: 405-574-1204 or toll-free 800-933-8726 Ext. 1204. Fax: 405-574-1220. E-mail: jwevans@usao.edu. Web site: http://www.usao.edu/.

UNIVERSITY OF TULSA
TULSA, OKLAHOMA

General Independent, university, coed, affiliated with Presbyterian Church **Entrance** Moderately difficult **Setting** 160-acre urban campus **Total enrollment** 4,119 **Student-faculty ratio** 11:1 **Application deadline** Rolling (transfer) **Freshmen** 67% were admitted **Housing** Yes **Expenses** Tuition $14,280; Room & Board $4810 **Undergraduates** 52% women, 9% part-time, 12% 25 or older, 5% Native American, 3% Hispanic American, 8% African American, 2% Asian American/Pacific Islander **The most frequently chosen baccalaureate fields are** business/marketing, engineering/engineering technologies, visual/performing arts **Academic program** English as a second language, advanced placement, accelerated degree program, self-designed majors, honors program, summer session, adult/continuing education programs, internships **Contact** Mr. John C. Corso, Associate Vice President for Administration/Dean of Admission, University of Tulsa, 600 South College Avenue, Tulsa, OK 74104. Telephone: 918-631-2307 or toll-free 800-331-3050. Fax: 918-631-5003. E-mail: admission@utulsa.edu. Web site: http://www.utulsa.edu/.

OREGON

THE ART INSTITUTE OF PORTLAND
PORTLAND, OREGON

General Proprietary, 4-year, coed **Entrance** Minimally difficult **Setting** 1-acre urban campus **Total enrollment** 903 **Student-faculty ratio** 16:1 **Application deadline** Rolling (freshmen), rolling (transfer) **Freshmen** 98% were admitted **Housing** Yes **Expenses** Tuition $13,725; Room only $5250 **Undergraduates** 53% women, 21% part-time, 39% 25 or older, 1% Native American, 5% Hispanic American, 2% African American, 5% Asian American/Pacific Islander **The most frequently chosen baccalaureate fields are** business/marketing, visual/performing arts **Academic program** Advanced placement, summer session, internships **Contact** Ms. Kelly Alston, Director of Admissions, The Art Institute of Portland, 2000 Southwest Fifth Avenue, Portland, OR 97201-4907. Telephone: 503-228-6528 Ext. 139 or toll-free 888-228-6528. Fax: 503-525-8331. E-mail: aipdadm@aii.edu. Web site: http://www.aipd.artinstitutes.edu/.

CASCADE COLLEGE
PORTLAND, OREGON

General Independent, 4-year, coed, affiliated with Church of Christ **Entrance** Noncompetitive **Setting** 13-acre urban campus **Total enrollment** 330 **Student-faculty ratio** 16:1 **Application deadline** Rolling (freshmen), rolling (transfer) **Freshmen** 100% were admitted **Housing** Yes **Expenses** Tuition $9600; Room & Board $5200 **Undergraduates** 49% women, 8% part-time, 7% 25 or older, 1% Native American, 3% Hispanic American, 8% African American, 2% Asian American/Pacific Islander **The most frequently chosen baccalaureate fields are** liberal arts/general studies, philosophy, philosophy, religion, and theology **Academic program** Advanced placement, accelerated degree program, summer session, internships **Contact** Mr. Clint La Rue, Director of Admissions, Cascade College, 9101 East Burnside, Portland, OR 97216-1515. Telephone: 503-257-1202 or toll-free 800-550-7678. E-mail: admissions@cascade.edu. Web site: http://www.cascade.edu/.

CONCORDIA UNIVERSITY
PORTLAND, OREGON

General Independent, comprehensive, coed, affiliated with Lutheran Church–Missouri Synod **Entrance** Moderately difficult **Setting** 13-acre urban campus **Total enrollment** 1,054 **Student-faculty ratio** 13:1 **Application deadline** Rolling (freshmen), rolling (transfer) **Freshmen** 61% were admitted **Housing** Yes **Expenses** Tuition $16,200; Room & Board $4300 **Undergraduates** 63% women, 15% part-time, 36%

25 or older, 1% Native American, 3% Hispanic American, 5% African American, 3% Asian American/Pacific Islander **The most frequently chosen baccalaureate fields are** business/marketing, education, liberal arts/general studies **Academic program** English as a second language, advanced placement, accelerated degree program, self-designed majors, summer session, adult/continuing education programs, internships **Contact** Mr. Peter D. Johnson, Director of Admission, Concordia University, 2811 Northeast Holman, Portland, OR 97211-6099. Telephone: 503-493-6521 or toll-free 800-321-9371. Fax: 503-280-8531. E-mail: admissions@portland.edu. Web site: http://www.cu-portland.edu/.

▶ **For more information, see page 418.**

EASTERN OREGON UNIVERSITY
LA GRANDE, OREGON

General State-supported, comprehensive, coed **Entrance** Moderately difficult **Setting** 121-acre rural campus **Total enrollment** 3,023 **Student-faculty ratio** 14:1 **Application deadline** 9/27 (freshmen) **Freshmen** 55% were admitted **Housing** Yes **Expenses** Tuition $3621; Room & Board $5151 **Undergraduates** 58% women, 28% part-time, 35% 25 or older, 2% Native American, 3% Hispanic American, 1% African American, 2% Asian American/Pacific Islander **The most frequently chosen baccalaureate fields are** interdisciplinary studies, business/marketing, liberal arts/general studies **Academic program** English as a second language, advanced placement, self-designed majors, summer session, adult/continuing education programs, internships **Contact** Ms. Christian Steinmetz, Director, Admissions, Eastern Oregon University, One University Boulevard, La Grande, OR 97850. Telephone: 541-962-3393 or toll-free 800-452-8639. Fax: 541-962-3418. E-mail: admissions@eou.edu. Web site: http://www.eou.edu/.

EUGENE BIBLE COLLEGE
EUGENE, OREGON

General Independent, 4-year, coed, affiliated with Open Bible Standard Churches **Entrance** Minimally difficult **Setting** 40-acre suburban campus **Total enrollment** 179 **Student-faculty ratio** 15:1 **Application deadline** 9/1 (freshmen), 9/1 (transfer) **Freshmen** 56% were admitted **Housing** Yes **Expenses** Tuition $6630; Room & Board $3945 **Undergraduates** 47% women, 28% part-time, 19% 25 or older, 1% Native American, 1% Hispanic American, 1% African American, 1% Asian American/Pacific Islander **The most frequently chosen baccalaureate fields are** philosophy, interdisciplinary studies, psychology **Academic program** Advanced placement, summer session, internships **Contact** Mr. Trent Combs, Director of Admissions, Eugene Bible College, 2155 Bailey Hill Road, Eugene, OR 97405. Telephone: 541-485-1780 Ext. 135 or toll-free 800-322-2638. Fax: 541-343-5801. E-mail: admissions@ebc.edu. Web site: http://www.ebc.edu/.

GEORGE FOX UNIVERSITY
NEWBERG, OREGON

General Independent Friends, university, coed **Entrance** Moderately difficult **Setting** 73-acre small-town campus **Total enrollment** 2,640 **Student-faculty ratio** 15:1 **Application deadline** 6/1 (freshmen), 6/1 (transfer) **Freshmen** 91% were admitted **Housing** Yes **Expenses** Tuition $18,325; Room & Board $5770 **Undergraduates** 59% women, 21% part-time, 21% 25 or older, 1% Native American, 3% Hispanic American, 1% African American, 2% Asian American/Pacific Islander **The most frequently chosen baccalaureate fields are** business/marketing, education, interdisciplinary studies **Academic program** English as a second language, advanced placement, accelerated degree program, self-designed majors, honors program, adult/continuing education programs, internships **Contact** Mr. Dale Seipp, Director of Admissions, George Fox University, 414 North Meridian, Newberg, CT 97132. Telephone: 503-554-2240 or toll-free 800-765-4369. Fax: 503-554-3110. E-mail: admissions@georgefox.edu. Web site: http://www.georgefox.edu/.

LEWIS & CLARK COLLEGE
PORTLAND, OREGON

General Independent, comprehensive, coed **Entrance** Very difficult **Setting** 115-acre suburban campus **Total enrollment** 2,947 **Student-faculty ratio** 12:1 **Application deadline** 2/1 (freshmen) **Freshmen** 67% were admitted **Housing** Yes **Expenses** Tuition $22,810; Room & Board $6650 **Undergraduates** 60% women, 2% part-time, 1% 25 or older, 1% Native American, 3% Hispanic American, 1% African American, 6% Asian American/Pacific Islander **The most frequently chosen baccalaureate fields are** biological/life sciences, social sciences and history, visual/performing arts **Academic program** English as a second language, advanced placement, accelerated degree program, self-designed majors, honors program, summer session, internships **Contact** Mr. Michael Sexton, Dean of Admissions, Lewis & Clark College, 0615 SW Palatine Hill Road, Portland, OR 97219-7899. Telephone: 503-768-7040 or toll-free 800-444-4111. Fax: 503-768-7055. E-mail: admissions@lclark.edu. Web site: http://www.lclark.edu/.

LINFIELD COLLEGE
MCMINNVILLE, OREGON

General Independent American Baptist Churches in the USA, 4-year, coed **Entrance** Moderately difficult **Setting** 95-acre small-town campus **Total enrollment** 1,602 **Student-faculty ratio** 12:1 **Application deadline** 2/15 (freshmen), 4/15 (transfer) **Freshmen** 80% were admitted **Housing** Yes **Expenses** Tuition $19,550; Room & Board $6290 **Undergraduates** 55% women, 2% part-time, 2% 25 or older, 1% Native American, 3% Hispanic American, 2% African American, 6% Asian American/Pacific Islander **The most frequently chosen baccalaureate fields are** business/marketing, education, social sciences

OREGON

Linfield College *(continued)*
and history **Academic program** English as a second language, advanced placement, accelerated degree program, self-designed majors, honors program, summer session, adult/continuing education programs, internships **Contact** Ms. Lisa Knodle-Bragiel, Director of Admissions, Linfield College, 900 SE Baker Street, McMinnville, OR 97128-6894. Telephone: 503-434-2489 or toll-free 800-640-2287. Fax: 503-434-2472. E-mail: admissions@linfield.edu. Web site: http://www.linfield.edu/.

MARYLHURST UNIVERSITY
MARYLHURST, OREGON

General Independent Roman Catholic, comprehensive, coed **Entrance** Noncompetitive **Setting** 73-acre suburban campus **Total enrollment** 842 **Student-faculty ratio** 7:1 **Application deadline** Rolling (freshmen), rolling (transfer) **Freshmen** 100% were admitted **Housing** Yes **Expenses** Tuition $11,850 **Undergraduates** 78% women, 70% part-time, 72% 25 or older, 0% Native American, 1% Hispanic American, 1% African American, 2% Asian American/Pacific Islander **The most frequently chosen baccalaureate fields are** business/marketing, communications/communication technologies, visual/performing arts **Academic program** English as a second language, advanced placement, accelerated degree program, self-designed majors, summer session, adult/continuing education programs, internships **Contact** Mr. John French, Academic Advising Specialist, Marylhurst University, 17600 Pacific Highway (Hwy 43), PO Box 261, Marylhurst, OR 97036. Telephone: 503-699-6268 Ext. 3325 or toll-free 800-634-9982 Ext. 6268 (out-of-state). Fax: 503-635-6585. E-mail: admissions@marylhurst.edu. Web site: http://www.marylhurst.edu/.

MOUNT ANGEL SEMINARY
SAINT BENEDICT, OREGON

Contact Registrar/Admissions Officer, Mount Angel Seminary, Saint Benedict, OR 97373. Telephone: 503-845-3951 Ext. 14.

MULTNOMAH BIBLE COLLEGE AND BIBLICAL SEMINARY
PORTLAND, OREGON

General Independent interdenominational, comprehensive, coed **Entrance** Moderately difficult **Setting** 22-acre urban campus **Total enrollment** 840 **Student-faculty ratio** 19:1 **Application deadline** 7/15 (freshmen), 7/15 (transfer) **Freshmen** 79% were admitted **Housing** Yes **Expenses** Tuition $9540; Room & Board $4090 **Undergraduates** 48% women, 11% part-time, 17% 25 or older, 0.2% Native American, 2% Hispanic American, 1% African American, 4% Asian American/Pacific Islander **The most frequently chosen baccalaureate fields are** philosophy, philosophy, religion, and theology **Academic program** Advanced placement, summer session, adult/continuing education programs, internships

Contact Ms. Nancy Gerecz, Admissions Assistant, Multnomah Bible College and Biblical Seminary, 8435 Northeast Glisan Street, Portland, OR 97220-5898. Telephone: 503-255-0332 Ext. 373 or toll-free 800-275-4672. Fax: 503-254-1268. E-mail: admiss@multnomah.edu. Web site: http://www.multnomah.edu/.

NORTHWEST CHRISTIAN COLLEGE
EUGENE, OREGON

General Independent interdenominational, comprehensive, coed **Entrance** Moderately difficult **Setting** 8-acre urban campus **Total enrollment** 480 **Student-faculty ratio** 13:1 **Application deadline** Rolling (freshmen), rolling (transfer) **Freshmen** 99% were admitted **Housing** Yes **Expenses** Tuition $14,580; Room & Board $5247 **Undergraduates** 62% women, 7% part-time, 43% 25 or older, 1% Native American, 2% Hispanic American, 4% African American, 1% Asian American/Pacific Islander **The most frequently chosen baccalaureate fields are** business/marketing, education, psychology **Academic program** Advanced placement, accelerated degree program, self-designed majors, adult/continuing education programs, internships **Contact** Mr. Bill Stenberg, Director of Admissions, Northwest Christian College, 828 East 11th Avenue, Eugene, OR 97401-3745. Telephone: 541-684-7209 or toll-free 877-463-6622. Fax: 541-684-7317. E-mail: admissions@nwcc.edu. Web site: http://www.nwcc.edu/.

OREGON COLLEGE OF ART & CRAFT
PORTLAND, OREGON

General Independent, 4-year, coed **Entrance** Minimally difficult **Setting** 7-acre urban campus **Total enrollment** 95 **Student-faculty ratio** 6:1 **Application deadline** Rolling (freshmen), rolling (transfer) **Freshmen** 29% were admitted **Housing** No **Expenses** Tuition $12,642 **Undergraduates** 73% women, 40% part-time, 58% 25 or older, 0% Native American, 1% Hispanic American, 0% African American, 3% Asian American/Pacific Islander **The most frequently chosen baccalaureate field is** visual/performing arts **Academic program** Advanced placement, adult/continuing education programs, internships **Contact** Ms. Sarah Turner, Admissions Officer, Oregon College of Art & Craft, 8245 Southwest Barnes Road, Portland, OR 97225. Telephone: 503-297-5544 Ext. 141 or toll-free 800-390-0632. Fax: 503-297-9651. E-mail: admissions@ocac.edu. Web site: http://www.ocac.edu/.

OREGON HEALTH & SCIENCE UNIVERSITY
PORTLAND, OREGON

General State-related, upper-level, coed **Entrance** Moderately difficult **Setting** 116-acre urban campus **Total enrollment** 1,849 **Housing** Yes **Expenses** Tuition $6005 **Undergraduates** 84% women, 22% part-time, 64% 25 or older, 2% Native American, 3% Hispanic American, 0.3% African American, 5% Asian American/Pacific Islander **Academic pro-**

gram Advanced placement, summer session **Contact** Ms. Cherie Honnell, Registrar and Director of Financial Aid, Oregon Health & Science University, 3181 Southwest Sam Jackson Park Road, Portland, OR 97201-3098. Telephone: 503-494-7800. E-mail: porterts@ohsu.edu. Web site: http://www.ohsu.edu/.

OREGON INSTITUTE OF TECHNOLOGY
KLAMATH FALLS, OREGON

General State-supported, 4-year, coed **Entrance** Moderately difficult **Setting** 173-acre small-town campus **Total enrollment** 3,088 **Student-faculty ratio** 14:1 **Application deadline** 6/1 (freshmen), 6/1 (transfer) **Freshmen** 61% were admitted **Housing** Yes **Expenses** Tuition $3642; Room & Board $5154 **Undergraduates** 45% women, 37% part-time, 38% 25 or older, 2% Native American, 4% Hispanic American, 1% African American, 6% Asian American/Pacific Islander **The most frequently chosen baccalaureate fields are** engineering/engineering technologies, business/marketing, health professions and related sciences **Academic program** English as a second language, advanced placement, summer session, adult/continuing education programs, internships **Contact** Palmer Muntz, Director of Admissions, Oregon Institute of Technology, 3201 Campus Drive, Klamath Falls, OR 97601-8801. Telephone: 541-885-1150 or toll-free 800-422-2017 (in-state); 800-343-6653 (out-of-state). Fax: 541-885-1115. E-mail: oit@oit.edu. Web site: http://www.oit.edu/.

OREGON STATE UNIVERSITY
CORVALLIS, OREGON

General State-supported, university, coed **Entrance** Moderately difficult **Setting** 422-acre small-town campus **Total enrollment** 18,034 **Student-faculty ratio** 12:1 **Application deadline** 3/1 (freshmen), 5/1 (transfer) **Freshmen** 51% were admitted **Housing** Yes **Expenses** Tuition $3987; Room & Board $5425 **Undergraduates** 47% women, 10% part-time, 8% 25 or older, 1% Native American, 3% Hispanic American, 1% African American, 8% Asian American/Pacific Islander **The most frequently chosen baccalaureate fields are** business/marketing, agriculture, engineering/engineering technologies **Academic program** English as a second language, advanced placement, self-designed majors, honors program, summer session, internships **Contact** Ms. Michele Sandlin, Director of Admissions, Oregon State University, Corvallis, OR 97331. Telephone: 541-737-4411 or toll-free 800-291-4192 (in-state). E-mail: osuadmit@ccmail.orst.edu. Web site: http://oregonstate.edu.

PACIFIC NORTHWEST COLLEGE OF ART
PORTLAND, OREGON

General Independent, 4-year, coed **Entrance** Moderately difficult **Setting** urban campus **Total enrollment** 293 **Student-faculty ratio** 11:1 **Application deadline** 8/1 (freshmen), 8/1 (transfer) **Freshmen** 92% were admitted **Housing** Yes **Expenses** Tuition $12,970; Room only $3537 **Undergraduates** 60% women, 10% part-time, 41% 25 or older, 3% Native American, 5% Hispanic American, 2% African American, 4% Asian American/Pacific Islander **The most frequently chosen baccalaureate field is** visual/performing arts **Academic program** Advanced placement, self-designed majors, summer session, adult/continuing education programs, internships **Contact** Mr. Clarence Goodman, Enrollment Counselor, Pacific Northwest College of Art, 1241 NW Johnson Street, Portland, OR 97209. Telephone: 503-821-8975 or toll-free 800-818-PNCA. Fax: 503-821-8978. E-mail: colin@pnca.edu. Web site: http://www.pnca.edu/.

PACIFIC UNIVERSITY
FOREST GROVE, OREGON

General Independent, comprehensive, coed **Entrance** Moderately difficult **Setting** 55-acre small-town campus **Total enrollment** 2,293 **Student-faculty ratio** 11:1 **Application deadline** 8/15 (freshmen), 8/15 (transfer) **Freshmen** 82% were admitted **Housing** Yes **Expenses** Tuition $18,545; Room & Board $5123 **Undergraduates** 63% women, 7% part-time, 6% 25 or older, 2% Native American, 2% Hispanic American, 0.4% African American, 18% Asian American/Pacific Islander **The most frequently chosen baccalaureate fields are** biological/life sciences, business/marketing, physical sciences **Academic program** English as a second language, advanced placement, accelerated degree program, honors program, summer session, internships **Contact** Mr. Ian Symmonds, Executive Director of Admissions, Pacific University, 2043 College Way, Forest Grove, OR 97116-1797. Telephone: 503-359-2218 or toll-free 800-677-6712. Fax: 503-359-2975. E-mail: admissions@pacificu.edu. Web site: http://www.pacificu.edu/.

PORTLAND STATE UNIVERSITY
PORTLAND, OREGON

General State-supported, university, coed **Entrance** Minimally difficult **Setting** 36-acre urban campus **Total enrollment** 20,185 **Student-faculty ratio** 18:1 **Application deadline** Rolling (freshmen), rolling (transfer) **Freshmen** 85% were admitted **Housing** Yes **Expenses** Tuition $3720; Room & Board $7500 **Undergraduates** 55% women, 42% part-time, 37% 25 or older, 1% Native American, 4% Hispanic American, 3% African American, 10% Asian American/Pacific Islander **The most frequently chosen baccalaureate fields are** business/marketing, psychology, social sciences and history **Academic program** English as a second language, advanced placement, accelerated degree program, self-designed majors, honors program, summer session, adult/continuing education programs, internships **Contact** Ms. Agnes A. Hoffman, Director of Admissions and Records, Portland State University, PO Box 751, Portland, OR 97207-0751. Telephone: 503-725-3511 or toll-free 800-547-8887. Fax: 503-725-5525. E-mail: askadm@ess.pdx.edu. Web site: http://www.pdx.edu/.

OREGON

REED COLLEGE
PORTLAND, OREGON

General Independent, comprehensive, coed **Entrance** Very difficult **Setting** 98-acre suburban campus **Total enrollment** 1,420 **Student-faculty ratio** 10:1 **Application deadline** 1/15 (freshmen), 3/1 (transfer) **Freshmen** 71% were admitted **Housing** Yes **Expenses** Tuition $26,160; Room & Board $7090 **Undergraduates** 54% women, 3% part-time, 5% 25 or older, 1% Native American, 3% Hispanic American, 1% African American, 5% Asian American/Pacific Islander **The most frequently chosen baccalaureate fields are** psychology, biological/life sciences, social sciences and history **Academic program** Advanced placement, accelerated degree program, self-designed majors **Contact** Mr. Paul Marthers, Dean of Admission, Reed College, 3203 Southeast Woodstock Boulevard, Portland, OR 97202-8199. Telephone: 503-777-7511 or toll-free 800-547-4750 (out-of-state). Fax: 503-777-7553. E-mail: admission@reed.edu/. Web site: http://www.reed.edu/.

SOUTHERN OREGON UNIVERSITY
ASHLAND, OREGON

General State-supported, comprehensive, coed **Entrance** Moderately difficult **Setting** 175-acre small-town campus **Total enrollment** 5,465 **Student-faculty ratio** 17:1 **Application deadline** Rolling (freshmen), rolling (transfer) **Freshmen** 92% were admitted **Housing** Yes **Expenses** Tuition $3555; Room & Board $5445 **Undergraduates** 56% women, 25% part-time, 24% 25 or older, 2% Native American, 4% Hispanic American, 1% African American, 4% Asian American/Pacific Islander **The most frequently chosen baccalaureate fields are** business/marketing, communications/communication technologies, social sciences and history **Academic program** Advanced placement, accelerated degree program, self-designed majors, honors program, summer session, adult/continuing education programs **Contact** Ms. Mara A. Affre, Director of Admissions, Southern Oregon University, 1250 Siskiyou Boulevard, Ashland, OR 97520. Telephone: 541-552-6411 or toll-free 800-482-7672 (in-state). Fax: 541-552-6614. E-mail: admissions@sou.edu. Web site: http://www.sou.edu/.

UNIVERSITY OF OREGON
EUGENE, OREGON

General State-supported, university, coed **Entrance** Moderately difficult **Setting** 280-acre urban campus **Total enrollment** 18,956 **Student-faculty ratio** 18:1 **Application deadline** 2/1 (freshmen), 5/15 (transfer) **Freshmen** 90% were admitted **Housing** Yes **Expenses** Tuition $4071; Room & Board $5898 **Undergraduates** 53% women, 10% part-time, 2% 25 or older, 1% Native American, 3% Hispanic American, 2% African American, 6% Asian American/Pacific Islander **The most frequently chosen baccalaureate fields are** business/marketing, communications/communication technologies, social sciences and history **Academic program** English as a second language, advanced placement, accelerated degree program, self-designed majors, honors program, summer session, adult/continuing education programs, internships **Contact** Ms. Martha Pitts, Director of Admissions, University of Oregon, Eugene, OR 97403. Telephone: 541-346-3201 or toll-free 800-232-3825 (in-state). Fax: 541-346-5815. E-mail: uoadmit@oregon.uoregon.edu. Web site: http://www.uoregon.edu/.

UNIVERSITY OF PHOENIX–OREGON CAMPUS
PORTLAND, OREGON

General Proprietary, comprehensive, coed **Entrance** Noncompetitive **Total enrollment** 88,730 **Student-faculty ratio** 12:1 **Application deadline** Rolling (freshmen), rolling (transfer) **Housing** No **Expenses** Tuition $8880 **Undergraduates** 42% women, 100% 25 or older **The most frequently chosen baccalaureate field is** business/marketing **Academic program** Advanced placement, accelerated degree program, adult/continuing education programs **Contact** Ms. Beth Barilla, Director of Admissions, University of Phoenix–Oregon Campus, 4615 East Elwood Street, Phoenix, AZ 85040-1958. Telephone: 480-927-0099 Ext. 1218 or toll-free 800-228-7240. Fax: 480-594-1758. E-mail: beth.barilla@apollogrp.edu. Web site: http://www.phoenix.edu/.

UNIVERSITY OF PORTLAND
PORTLAND, OREGON

General Independent Roman Catholic, comprehensive, coed **Entrance** Moderately difficult **Setting** 125-acre suburban campus **Total enrollment** 3,087 **Student-faculty ratio** 13:1 **Application deadline** 6/1 (freshmen), 6/1 (transfer) **Freshmen** 87% were admitted **Housing** Yes **Expenses** Tuition $19,650; Room & Board $5872 **Undergraduates** 58% women, 5% part-time, 5% 25 or older, 1% Native American, 4% Hispanic American, 1% African American, 9% Asian American/Pacific Islander **The most frequently chosen baccalaureate fields are** business/marketing, engineering/engineering technologies, health professions and related sciences **Academic program** English as a second language, advanced placement, accelerated degree program, self-designed majors, honors program, summer session, adult/continuing education programs, internships **Contact** Mr. James C. Lyons, Dean of Admissions, University of Portland, 5000 North Willamette Boulevard, Portland, OR 97203-5798. Telephone: 503-943-7147 or toll-free 888-627-5601 (out-of-state). Fax: 503-943-7315. E-mail: admissio@up.edu. Web site: http://www.up.edu/.

WARNER PACIFIC COLLEGE
PORTLAND, OREGON

General Independent, comprehensive, coed, affiliated with Church of God **Entrance** Moderately difficult **Setting** 15-acre urban campus **Total enrollment** 571 **Student-faculty ratio** 14:1 **Application deadline Rolling (freshmen), rolling (transfer) **Freshmen** 73% were admitted **Housing** Yes **Expenses** Tuition $15,690; Room & Board $4650 **Undergraduates** 63% women, 39% 25 or older, 1% Native American, 2% Hispanic American, 3% African American, 3% Asian American/Pacific Islander **The most frequently chosen baccalaureate fields are** business/marketing, education, social sciences and history **Academic program** Advanced placement, self-designed majors, honors program, summer session, adult/continuing education programs, internships **Contact** Dawna A. Williams, Chief Admissions and Financial Aid Officer, Warner Pacific College, 2219 Southeast 68th Avenue, Portland, OR 97215. Telephone: 503-517-1020 or toll-free 800-582-7885 (in-state); 800-804-1510 (out-of-state). Fax: 503-517-1352. E-mail: admiss@warnerpacific.edu. Web site: http://www.warnerpacific.edu/.

WESTERN BAPTIST COLLEGE
SALEM, OREGON

General Independent religious, 4-year, coed **Entrance** Moderately difficult **Setting** 107-acre suburban campus **Total enrollment** 725 **Student-faculty ratio** 18:1 **Application deadline** 8/1 (freshmen), 8/1 (transfer) **Freshmen** 76% were admitted **Housing** Yes **Expenses** Tuition $14,360; Room & Board $5340 **Undergraduates** 60% women, 9% part-time, 15% 25 or older, 1% Native American, 2% Hispanic American, 1% African American, 1% Asian American/Pacific Islander **The most frequently chosen baccalaureate fields are** business/marketing, education, home economics/vocational home economics **Academic program** Advanced placement, accelerated degree program, honors program, summer session, adult/continuing education programs, internships **Contact** Mr. Marty Ziesemer, Director of Admissions, Western Baptist College, 5000 Deer Park Drive, SE, Salem, OR 97301-9392. Telephone: 503-375-7115 or toll-free 800-845-3005 (out-of-state). E-mail: admissions@wbc.edu. Web site: http://www.wbc.edu/.

WESTERN OREGON UNIVERSITY
MONMOUTH, OREGON

General State-supported, comprehensive, coed **Entrance** Moderately difficult **Setting** 157-acre rural campus **Total enrollment** 4,878 **Student-faculty ratio** 20:1 **Application deadline** Rolling (freshmen), rolling (transfer) **Freshmen** 92% were admitted **Housing** Yes **Expenses** Tuition $3660; Room & Board $5169 **Undergraduates** 60% women, 8% part-time, 15% 25 or older, 1% Native American, 5% Hispanic American, 2% African American, 3% Asian American/Pacific Islander **The most frequently chosen baccalaureate fields are** business/marketing, protective services/public administration, psychology **Academic program** English as a second language, advanced placement, self-designed majors, honors program, summer session, adult/continuing education programs, internships **Contact** Mr. Rob Kvidt, Director of Admissions, Western Oregon University, 345 North Monmouth Avenue, Monmouth, OR 97361. Telephone: 503-838-8211 or toll-free 877-877-1593. Fax: 503-838-8067. E-mail: wolfgram@wou.edu. Web site: http://www.wou.edu/.

WESTERN STATES CHIROPRACTIC COLLEGE
PORTLAND, OREGON

General Independent, upper-level, coed **Entrance** Moderately difficult **Setting** 22-acre suburban campus **Total enrollment** 331 **Student-faculty ratio** 7:1 **Application deadline** Rolling (transfer) **First-Year Students** 53% were admitted **Housing** No **Expenses** Tuition $15,945 **Undergraduates** 95% 25 or older **Academic program** Summer session **Contact** Dr. Lee Smith, Director of Admissions, Western States Chiropractic College, 2900 Northeast 132nd Avenue, Portland, OR 97230-3099. Telephone: 503-251-2812 or toll-free 800-641-5641. Fax: 503-251-5723. Web site: http://www.wschiro.edu/.

WILLAMETTE UNIVERSITY
SALEM, OREGON

General Independent United Methodist, comprehensive, coed **Entrance** Very difficult **Setting** 72-acre urban campus **Total enrollment** 2,466 **Student-faculty ratio** 10:1 **Application deadline** 2/1 (freshmen), 2/1 (transfer) **Freshmen** 84% were admitted **Housing** Yes **Expenses** Tuition $23,272; Room & Board $6150 **Undergraduates** 56% women, 6% part-time, 2% 25 or older, 2% Native American, 5% Hispanic American, 2% African American, 7% Asian American/Pacific Islander **The most frequently chosen baccalaureate fields are** foreign language/literature, biological/life sciences, social sciences and history **Academic program** Advanced placement, accelerated degree program, self-designed majors, honors program, internships **Contact** Dr. Robin Brown, Vice President for Enrollment, Willamette University, 900 State Street, Salem, OR 97301-3931. Telephone: 503-370-6303 or toll-free 877-542-2787. Fax: 503-375-5363. E-mail: undergrad-admission@willamette.edu. Web site: http://www.willamette.edu/.

PENNSYLVANIA

ALBRIGHT COLLEGE
READING, PENNSYLVANIA

General Independent, 4-year, coed, affiliated with United Methodist Church **Entrance** Moderately difficult **Setting** 110-acre suburban campus **Total enrollment** 1,809 **Student-faculty ratio** 14:1 **Application deadline** Rolling (freshmen), 8/15 (transfer) **Freshmen** 73% were admitted **Housing** Yes **Expenses** Tuition $21,300; Room & Board $6342 **Undergraduates** 57% women, 5% part-time, 1% 25 or older, 1% Native American, 3% Hispanic American, 7% African American, 2% Asian American/Pacific Islander **The most frequently chosen baccalaureate fields**

PENNSYLVANIA

Albright College *(continued)*
are business/marketing, psychology, social sciences and history **Academic program** English as a second language, advanced placement, accelerated degree program, self-designed majors, honors program, summer session, internships **Contact** Mr. Gregory E. Eichhorn, Vice President for Enrollment Management, Albright College, P.O. Box 15234, 13th and Bern Streets, Reading, PA 19612-5234. Telephone: 610-921-7260 or toll-free 800-252-1856. Fax: 610-921-7294. E-mail: admission@alb.edu. Web site: http://www.albright.edu/.

ALLEGHENY COLLEGE
MEADVILLE, PENNSYLVANIA

General Independent, 4-year, coed, affiliated with United Methodist Church **Entrance** Very difficult **Setting** 254-acre small-town campus **Total enrollment** 1,879 **Student-faculty ratio** 13:1 **Application deadline** 2/15 (freshmen), 7/1 (transfer) **Freshmen** 79% were admitted **Housing** Yes **Expenses** Tuition $22,490; Room & Board $5290 **Undergraduates** 53% women, 2% part-time, 1% 25 or older, 0.3% Native American, 1% Hispanic American, 2% African American, 2% Asian American/Pacific Islander **The most frequently chosen baccalaureate fields are** biological/life sciences, psychology, social sciences and history **Academic program** Advanced placement, accelerated degree program, self-designed majors, internships **Contact** Ms. Megan K. Murphy, Dean of Admissions and Enrollment Management, Allegheny College, 520 North Main Street, Box 5, Meadville, PA 16335. Telephone: 814-332-4351 or toll-free 800-521-5293. Fax: 814-337-0431. E-mail: admiss@allegheny.edu. Web site: http://www.allegheny.edu/.

▶ For more information, see page 393.

ALVERNIA COLLEGE
READING, PENNSYLVANIA

General Independent Roman Catholic, comprehensive, coed **Entrance** Moderately difficult **Setting** 85-acre suburban campus **Total enrollment** 1,815 **Student-faculty ratio** 14:1 **Application deadline** Rolling (freshmen), rolling (transfer) **Freshmen** 78% were admitted **Housing** Yes **Expenses** Tuition $14,140; Room & Board $6650 **Undergraduates** 66% women, 29% part-time, 40% 25 or older, 0.3% Native American, 3% Hispanic American, 9% African American, 2% Asian American/Pacific Islander **The most frequently chosen baccalaureate fields are** health professions and related sciences, business/marketing, protective services/public administration **Academic program** Advanced placement, accelerated degree program, honors program, summer session, adult/continuing education programs, internships **Contact** Betsy Stiles, Assistant Dean of Enrollment Management, Alvernia College, 400 Saint Bernardine Street, Reading, PA 19607. Telephone: 610-796-8220 or toll-free 888-ALVERNIA (in-state). Fax: 610-796-8336. Web site: http://www.alvernia.edu/.

ARCADIA UNIVERSITY
GLENSIDE, PENNSYLVANIA

General Independent, comprehensive, coed, affiliated with Presbyterian Church (U.S.A.) **Entrance** Moderately difficult **Setting** 60-acre suburban campus **Total enrollment** 2,992 **Student-faculty ratio** 12:1 **Application deadline** Rolling (freshmen), rolling (transfer) **Freshmen** 84% were admitted **Housing** Yes **Expenses** Tuition $18,670; Room & Board $7980 **Undergraduates** 73% women, 19% part-time, 29% 25 or older, 0.1% Native American, 2% Hispanic American, 11% African American, 3% Asian American/Pacific Islander **Academic program** English as a second language, advanced placement, self-designed majors, honors program, summer session, adult/continuing education programs, internships **Contact** Mr. Dennis L. Nostrand, Director of Enrollment Management, Arcadia University, 450 South Easton Road, Glenside, PA 19038. Telephone: 215-572-2910 or toll-free 877-ARCADIA. Fax: 215-572-4049. E-mail: admiss@arcadia.edu. Web site: http://www.arcadia.edu.

BAPTIST BIBLE COLLEGE OF PENNSYLVANIA
CLARKS SUMMIT, PENNSYLVANIA

General Independent Baptist, comprehensive, coed **Entrance** Minimally difficult **Setting** 124-acre suburban campus **Total enrollment** 837 **Student-faculty ratio** 25:1 **Application deadline** 8/15 (freshmen), rolling (transfer) **Freshmen** 87% were admitted **Housing** Yes **Expenses** Tuition $9870; Room & Board $4892 **Undergraduates** 56% women, 7% part-time, 7% 25 or older, 0.4% Native American, 1% Hispanic American, 0.3% African American, 1% Asian American/Pacific Islander **The most frequently chosen baccalaureate fields are** education, business/marketing, philosophy **Academic program** Advanced placement, summer session, internships **Contact** Ms. Chris Hansen, Applications Coordinator, Baptist Bible College of Pennsylvania, PO Box 800, Clarks Summit, PA 18411-1297. Telephone: 570-586-2400 Ext. 9370 or toll-free 800-451-7664. Fax: 570-585-9400. E-mail: gamos@bbc.edu. Web site: http://www.bbc.edu/.

BLOOMSBURG UNIVERSITY OF PENNSYLVANIA
BLOOMSBURG, PENNSYLVANIA

General State-supported, comprehensive, coed **Entrance** Moderately difficult **Setting** 282-acre small-town campus **Total enrollment** 7,914 **Student-faculty ratio** 20:1 **Application deadline** Rolling (freshmen), rolling (transfer) **Freshmen** 79% were admitted **Housing** Yes **Expenses** Tuition $4992; Room & Board $4442 **Undergraduates** 61% women, 8% part-time, 8% 25 or older, 0.2% Native American, 2% Hispanic American, 3% African American, 1% Asian American/Pacific Islander **The most frequently chosen baccalaureate fields are** business/marketing, education, English **Academic program** Advanced placement, honors program, summer ses-

PENNSYLVANIA

sion, adult/continuing education programs, internships **Contact** Mr. Christopher Keller, Director of Admissions, Bloomsburg University of Pennsylvania, 104 Student Services Center, Bloomsburg, PA 17815-1905. Telephone: 570-389-4316. E-mail: buadmiss@bloomu.edu. Web site: http://www.bloomu.edu.

BRYN ATHYN COLLEGE OF THE NEW CHURCH
BRYN ATHYN, PENNSYLVANIA

General Independent Swedenborgian, comprehensive, coed **Entrance** Minimally difficult **Setting** 130-acre small-town campus **Total enrollment** 172 **Student-faculty ratio** 6:1 **Application deadline** 7/1 (freshmen), rolling (transfer) **Freshmen** 99% were admitted **Housing** Yes **Expenses** Tuition $6009; Room & Board $4581 **Undergraduates** 63% women, 6% part-time, 6% 25 or older, 0% Native American, 0% Hispanic American, 1% African American, 2% Asian American/Pacific Islander **The most frequently chosen baccalaureate fields are** biological/life sciences, education, interdisciplinary studies **Academic program** Advanced placement, accelerated degree program, self-designed majors, internships **Contact** Dr. Dan Synnestvedt, Director of Admissions, Bryn Athyn College of the New Church, PO Box 717, Bryn Athyn, PA 19009-0717. Telephone: 215-938-2503. Fax: 215-938-2658. Web site: http://www.newchurch.edu/college/.

BRYN MAWR COLLEGE
BRYN MAWR, PENNSYLVANIA

General Independent, university, women only **Entrance** Most difficult **Setting** 135-acre suburban campus **Total enrollment** 1,756 **Student-faculty ratio** 9:1 **Application deadline** 1/15 (freshmen), 3/15 (transfer) **Freshmen** 60% were admitted **Housing** Yes **Expenses** Tuition $24,990; Room & Board $8590 **Undergraduates** 4% part-time, 5% 25 or older, 0% Native American, 3% Hispanic American, 4% African American, 15% Asian American/Pacific Islander **The most frequently chosen baccalaureate fields are** foreign language/literature, English, social sciences and history **Academic program** Advanced placement, accelerated degree program, self-designed majors, honors program, summer session, adult/continuing education programs **Contact** Ms. Elizabeth Mosier, Acting Director of Admissions, Bryn Mawr College, 101 North Merion Avenue, Bryn Mawr, PA 19010. Telephone: 610-526-5152 or toll-free 800-BMC-1885 (out-of-state). E-mail: admissions@brynmawr.edu. Web site: http://www.brynmawr.edu/.

BUCKNELL UNIVERSITY
LEWISBURG, PENNSYLVANIA

General Independent, comprehensive, coed **Entrance** Very difficult **Setting** 393-acre small-town campus **Total enrollment** 3,587 **Student-faculty ratio** 12:1 **Application deadline** 1/1 (freshmen), 4/1 (transfer) **Freshmen** 39% were admitted **Housing** Yes **Expenses** Tuition $25,335; Room & Board $5761 **Undergraduates** 49% women, 1% part-time, 1% 25 or older, 0.4% Native American, 3% Hispanic American, 3% African American, 5% Asian American/Pacific Islander **The most frequently chosen baccalaureate fields are** engineering/engineering technologies, business/marketing, social sciences and history **Academic program** Advanced placement, self-designed majors, honors program, summer session, internships **Contact** Mr. Mark D. Davies, Dean of Admissions, Bucknell University, Lewisburg, PA 17837. Telephone: 570-577-1101. Fax: 570-577-3538. E-mail: admissions@bucknell.edu. Web site: http://www.bucknell.edu/.

CABRINI COLLEGE
RADNOR, PENNSYLVANIA

General Independent Roman Catholic, comprehensive, coed **Entrance** Minimally difficult **Setting** 112-acre suburban campus **Total enrollment** 2,100 **Student-faculty ratio** 14:1 **Application deadline** Rolling (freshmen), rolling (transfer) **Freshmen** 86% were admitted **Housing** Yes **Expenses** Tuition $18,090; Room & Board $7860 **Undergraduates** 64% women, 20% part-time, 25% 25 or older, 0.3% Native American, 2% Hispanic American, 7% African American, 2% Asian American/Pacific Islander **The most frequently chosen baccalaureate fields are** business/marketing, communications/communication technologies, education **Academic program** Advanced placement, accelerated degree program, self-designed majors, honors program, summer session, adult/continuing education programs, internships **Contact** Mr. Mark Osborn, Director of Admissions, Cabrini College, 610 King of Prussia Road, Radnor, PA 19087-3698. Telephone: 610-902-8552 or toll-free 800-848-1003. Fax: 610-902-8508. E-mail: admit@cabrini.edu. Web site: http://www.cabrini.edu/.

CALIFORNIA UNIVERSITY OF PENNSYLVANIA
CALIFORNIA, PENNSYLVANIA

General State-supported, comprehensive, coed **Entrance** Moderately difficult **Setting** 148-acre small-town campus **Total enrollment** 5,948 **Student-faculty ratio** 19:1 **Application deadline** 7/30 (freshmen), 7/30 (transfer) **Freshmen** 77% were admitted **Housing** Yes **Expenses** Tuition $5204; Room & Board $5134 **Undergraduates** 53% women, 13% part-time, 20% 25 or older, 0.4% Native American, 0.4% Hispanic American, 5% African American, 0.3% Asian American/Pacific Islander **The most frequently chosen baccalaureate fields are** business/marketing, education, social sciences and history **Academic program** Advanced placement, accelerated degree program, honors program, summer session, adult/continuing education programs, internships **Contact** Mr. William A. Edmonds, Dean of Enrollment Management and Academic Services, California University of Pennsylvania, 250 University Avenue, California, PA 15419. Telephone: 724-938-

PENNSYLVANIA

California University of Pennsylvania *(continued)*
4404. Fax: 724-938-4564. E-mail: inquiry@cup.edu. Web site: http://www.cup.edu/.

CARLOW COLLEGE
PITTSBURGH, PENNSYLVANIA

General Independent Roman Catholic, comprehensive, coed, primarily women **Entrance** Moderately difficult **Setting** 13-acre urban campus **Total enrollment** 1,898 **Student-faculty ratio** 12:1 **Application deadline** Rolling (freshmen), rolling (transfer) **Freshmen** 67% were admitted **Housing** Yes **Expenses** Tuition $13,876; Room & Board $5490 **Undergraduates** 94% women, 41% part-time, 54% 25 or older, 1% Native American, 1% Hispanic American, 19% African American, 1% Asian American/Pacific Islander **The most frequently chosen baccalaureate fields are** business/marketing, education, health professions and related sciences **Academic program** English as a second language, advanced placement, accelerated degree program, self-designed majors, honors program, summer session, adult/continuing education programs, internships **Contact** Ms. Susan Winstel, Assistant Director of Admissions, Carlow College, 3333 Fifth Avenue, Pittsburgh, PA 15213. Telephone: 412-578-6330 or toll-free 800-333-CARLOW. Fax: 412-578-6668. E-mail: admissions@carlow.edu. Web site: http://www.carlow.edu/.

CARNEGIE MELLON UNIVERSITY
PITTSBURGH, PENNSYLVANIA

General Independent, university, coed **Entrance** Very difficult **Setting** 103-acre urban campus **Total enrollment** 8,588 **Student-faculty ratio** 10:1 **Application deadline** 1/1 (freshmen), 3/15 (transfer) **Freshmen** 31% were admitted **Housing** Yes **Expenses** Tuition $25,872; Room & Board $7264 **Undergraduates** 38% women, 4% part-time, 1% 25 or older, 0.4% Native American, 5% Hispanic American, 4% African American, 22% Asian American/Pacific Islander **The most frequently chosen baccalaureate fields are** engineering/engineering technologies, computer/information sciences, social sciences and history **Academic program** English as a second language, advanced placement, accelerated degree program, self-designed majors, honors program, summer session, adult/continuing education programs, internships **Contact** Mr. Michael Steidel, Director of Admissions, Carnegie Mellon University, 5000 Forbes Avenue, Warner Hall, Room 101, Pittsburgh, PA 15213. Telephone: 412-268-2082. Fax: 412-268-7838. E-mail: undergraduate-admissions@andrew.cmu.edu. Web site: http://www.cmu.edu/.

CEDAR CREST COLLEGE
ALLENTOWN, PENNSYLVANIA

General Independent, 4-year, women only, affiliated with United Church of Christ **Entrance** Moderately difficult **Setting** 84-acre suburban campus **Total enrollment** 1,619 **Student-faculty ratio** 11:1 **Application deadline** Rolling (freshmen), rolling (transfer) **Freshmen** 76% were admitted **Housing** Yes **Expenses** Tuition $18,680; Room & Board $6465 **Undergraduates** 51% part-time, 62% 25 or older, 0.2% Native American, 5% Hispanic American, 5% African American, 2% Asian American/Pacific Islander **The most frequently chosen baccalaureate fields are** health professions and related sciences, business/marketing, psychology **Academic program** English as a second language, advanced placement, accelerated degree program, self-designed majors, honors program, summer session, adult/continuing education programs, internships **Contact** Ms. Judith A. Neyhart, Vice President for Enrollment and Advancement, Cedar Crest College, 100 College Drive, Allentown, PA 18104-6196. Telephone: 610-740-3780 or toll-free 800-360-1222. Fax: 610-606-4647. E-mail: cccadmis@cedarcrest.edu. Web site: http://www.cedarcrest.edu/.

▶ For more information, see page 408.

CHATHAM COLLEGE
PITTSBURGH, PENNSYLVANIA

General Independent, comprehensive, women only **Entrance** Moderately difficult **Setting** 34-acre urban campus **Total enrollment** 1,065 **Student-faculty ratio** 13:1 **Application deadline** Rolling (freshmen), rolling (transfer) **Freshmen** 78% were admitted **Housing** Yes **Expenses** Tuition $18,960; Room & Board $6494 **Undergraduates** 10% part-time, 14% 25 or older, 1% Native American, 2% Hispanic American, 11% African American, 2% Asian American/Pacific Islander **The most frequently chosen baccalaureate fields are** biological/life sciences, social sciences and history, visual/performing arts **Academic program** English as a second language, advanced placement, accelerated degree program, self-designed majors, summer session, adult/continuing education programs, internships **Contact** Dean of Admissions and Financial Aid, Chatham College, Woodland Road, Pittsburgh, PA 15232. Telephone: 412-365-1290 or toll-free 800-837-1290. Fax: 412-365-1609. E-mail: admissions@chatham.edu. Web site: http://www.chatham.edu/.

CHESTNUT HILL COLLEGE
PHILADELPHIA, PENNSYLVANIA

General Independent Roman Catholic, comprehensive, coed **Entrance** Moderately difficult **Setting** 45-acre suburban campus **Total enrollment** 1,645 **Student-faculty ratio** 10:1 **Application deadline** Rolling (freshmen), rolling (transfer) **Freshmen** 92% were admitted **Housing** Yes **Expenses** Tuition $17,620; Room & Board $7170 **Undergraduates** 86% women, 37% part-time, 30% 25 or older, 0.4% Native American, 5% Hispanic American, 41% African American, 2% Asian American/Pacific Islander **The most frequently chosen baccalaureate fields are** business/marketing, education, social sciences and history **Academic program** English as a second language, advanced placement, self-designed majors, honors program, summer session, adult/continuing educa-

PENNSYLVANIA

tion programs, internships **Contact** Ms. Jodie King, Associate Director of Admissions, Chestnut Hill College, 9601 Germantown Avenue, Philadelphia, PA 19118-2693. Telephone: 215-248-7001 or toll-free 800-248-0052 (out-of-state). Fax: 215-248-7082. E-mail: chcapply@chc.edu. Web site: http://www.chc.edu/.

▶ For more information, see page 411.

CHEYNEY UNIVERSITY OF PENNSYLVANIA
CHEYNEY, PENNSYLVANIA

General State-supported, comprehensive, coed **Entrance** Minimally difficult **Setting** 275-acre suburban campus **Total enrollment** 1,514 **Student-faculty ratio** 11:1 **Application deadline** Rolling (freshmen), rolling (transfer) **Freshmen** 70% were admitted **Housing** Yes **Expenses** Tuition $4671; Room & Board $5322 **Undergraduates** 55% women, 11% part-time, 13% 25 or older, 0.1% Native American, 1% Hispanic American, 97% African American, 0.1% Asian American/Pacific Islander **The most frequently chosen baccalaureate fields are** business/marketing, communications/communication technologies, social sciences and history **Academic program** Summer session, adult/continuing education programs, internships **Contact** Mr. William Bickley, Interim Director of Admissions, Cheyney University of Pennsylvania, Cheyney and Creek Roads, Cheyney, PA 19319. Telephone: 610-399-2275 or toll-free 800-CHEYNEY. Fax: 610-399-2099. Web site: http://www.cheyney.edu/.

CLARION UNIVERSITY OF PENNSYLVANIA
CLARION, PENNSYLVANIA

General State-supported, comprehensive, coed **Entrance** Minimally difficult **Setting** 100-acre rural campus **Total enrollment** 6,271 **Student-faculty ratio** 18:1 **Application deadline** Rolling (freshmen), rolling (transfer) **Freshmen** 81% were admitted **Housing** Yes **Expenses** Tuition $4359; Room & Board $2420 **Undergraduates** 62% women, 10% part-time, 16% 25 or older, 0.2% Native American, 1% Hispanic American, 5% African American, 1% Asian American/Pacific Islander **The most frequently chosen baccalaureate fields are** business/marketing, education, health professions and related sciences **Academic program** Advanced placement, accelerated degree program, honors program, summer session, adult/continuing education programs, internships **Contact** Ms. Sue McMillen, Interim Director of Admissions, Clarion University of Pennsylvania, Clarion, PA 16214. Telephone: 814-393-2306 or toll-free 800-672-7171. Fax: 814-393-2030. E-mail: smcmillen@clarion.edu. Web site: http://www.clarion.edu/.

COLLEGE MISERICORDIA
DALLAS, PENNSYLVANIA

General Independent Roman Catholic, comprehensive, coed **Entrance** Moderately difficult **Setting** 100-acre small-town campus **Total enrollment** 1,765 **Student-faculty ratio** 14:1 **Application deadline** Rolling (freshmen), rolling (transfer) **Freshmen** 84% were admitted **Housing** Yes **Expenses** Tuition $16,650; Room & Board $6730 **Undergraduates** 73% women, 30% part-time **The most frequently chosen baccalaureate fields are** education, business/marketing, health professions and related sciences **Academic program** Advanced placement, accelerated degree program, self-designed majors, honors program, summer session, adult/continuing education programs, internships **Contact** Ms. Jane Dessoye, Executive Director of Admissions and Financial Aid, College Misericordia, 301 Lake Street, Dallas, PA 18612. Telephone: 570-675-4449 Ext. 6168 or toll-free 800-852-7675. Fax: 570-675-2441. E-mail: admiss@miseri.edu. Web site: http://www.miseri.edu/.

THE CURTIS INSTITUTE OF MUSIC
PHILADELPHIA, PENNSYLVANIA

General Independent, comprehensive, coed **Entrance** Most difficult **Setting** urban campus **Total enrollment** 168 **Application deadline** 1/15 (freshmen), 1/15 (transfer) **Freshmen** 7% were admitted **Housing** No **Expenses** Tuition $695 **Academic program** English as a second language, advanced placement, accelerated degree program **Contact** Mr. Christopher Hodges, Admissions Officer, The Curtis Institute of Music, 1726 Locust Street, Philadelphia, PA 19103-6107. Telephone: 215-893-5262. Fax: 215-893-7900.

DELAWARE VALLEY COLLEGE
DOYLESTOWN, PENNSYLVANIA

General Independent, comprehensive, coed **Entrance** Moderately difficult **Setting** 600-acre suburban campus **Total enrollment** 1,982 **Student-faculty ratio** 16:1 **Application deadline** Rolling (freshmen), rolling (transfer) **Freshmen** 86% were admitted **Housing** Yes **Expenses** Tuition $17,374; Room & Board $6544 **Undergraduates** 53% women, 32% part-time, 24% 25 or older, 0.3% Native American, 2% Hispanic American, 3% African American, 1% Asian American/Pacific Islander **The most frequently chosen baccalaureate fields are** agriculture, business/marketing, protective services/public administration **Academic program** Advanced placement, honors program, summer session, adult/continuing education programs, internships **Contact** Mr. Stephen Zenko, Director of Admissions, Delaware Valley College, 700 East Butler Avenue, Doylestown, PA 18901. Telephone: 215-489-2211 Ext. 2211 or toll-free 800-2DELVAL (in-state). Fax: 215-230-2968. E-mail: admitme@devalcol.edu. Web site: http://www.devalcol.edu/.

DESALES UNIVERSITY
CENTER VALLEY, PENNSYLVANIA

General Independent Roman Catholic, comprehensive, coed **Entrance** Moderately difficult **Setting** 300-acre suburban campus **Total enrollment** 2,730 **Student-faculty ratio** 18:1 **Application deadline**

DeSales University *(continued)*
8/1 (freshmen), 8/1 (transfer) **Freshmen** 73% were admitted **Housing** Yes **Expenses** Tuition $16,340; Room & Board $6270 **Undergraduates** 55% women, 24% part-time, 1% 25 or older, 0.2% Native American, 2% Hispanic American, 1% African American, 1% Asian American/Pacific Islander **The most frequently chosen baccalaureate fields are** business/marketing, health professions and related sciences, visual/performing arts **Academic program** Advanced placement, accelerated degree program, summer session, adult/continuing education programs, internships **Contact** Mr. Peter Rautzhan, Director of Admissions and Financial Aid, DeSales University, 2755 Station Avenue, Center Valley, PA 18034-9568. Telephone: 610-282-1100 Ext. 1332 or toll-free 877-433-72537 (in-state); 800-228-5114 (out-of-state). Fax: 610-282-2254. E-mail: admiss@desales.edu. Web site: http://www.desales.edu.

DICKINSON COLLEGE
CARLISLE, PENNSYLVANIA

General Independent, 4-year, coed **Entrance** Very difficult **Setting** 103-acre suburban campus **Total enrollment** 2,208 **Student-faculty ratio** 12:1 **Application deadline** 2/1 (freshmen), 4/1 (transfer) **Freshmen** 64% were admitted **Housing** Yes **Expenses** Tuition $25,485; Room & Board $6725 **Undergraduates** 58% women, 2% part-time, 1% 25 or older, 0.2% Native American, 2% Hispanic American, 2% African American, 2% Asian American/Pacific Islander **The most frequently chosen baccalaureate fields are** foreign language/literature, English, social sciences and history **Academic program** Advanced placement, accelerated degree program, self-designed majors, summer session, adult/continuing education programs, internships **Contact** Mr. Christopher Seth Allen, Director of Admissions, Dickinson College, PO Box 1773, Carlisle, PA 17013-2896. Telephone: 717-245-1231 or toll-free 800-644-1773. Fax: 717-245-1231. E-mail: admit@dickinson.edu. Web site: http://www.dickinson.edu/.

DREXEL UNIVERSITY
PHILADELPHIA, PENNSYLVANIA

General Independent, university, coed **Entrance** Moderately difficult **Setting** 42-acre urban campus **Total enrollment** 13,546 **Student-faculty ratio** 14:1 **Application deadline** 3/1 (freshmen), rolling (transfer) **Freshmen** 73% were admitted **Housing** Yes **Undergraduates** 38% women, 17% part-time, 12% 25 or older, 0.2% Native American, 2% Hispanic American, 8% African American, 14% Asian American/Pacific Islander **The most frequently chosen baccalaureate fields are** business/marketing, computer/information sciences, engineering/engineering technologies **Academic program** English as a second language, advanced placement, accelerated degree program, honors program, summer session, adult/continuing education programs, internships **Contact** Mr. David Eddy, Director of Undergraduate Admissions, Drexel University, 3141 Chestnut Street, Room 220, Philadelphia, PA 19104-2875. Telephone: 215-895-2400 or toll-free 800-2-DREXEL. Fax: 215-895-5939. E-mail: enroll@drexel.edu. Web site: http://www.drexel.edu/.

▶ For more information, see page 420.

DUQUESNE UNIVERSITY
PITTSBURGH, PENNSYLVANIA

General Independent Roman Catholic, university, coed **Entrance** Moderately difficult **Setting** 43-acre urban campus **Total enrollment** 9,451 **Student-faculty ratio** 14:1 **Application deadline** 7/1 (freshmen), 7/1 (transfer) **Freshmen** 96% were admitted **Housing** Yes **Expenses** Tuition $17,478; Room & Board $6764 **Undergraduates** 58% women, 8% part-time, 14% 25 or older, 0.1% Native American, 2% Hispanic American, 4% African American, 1% Asian American/Pacific Islander **The most frequently chosen baccalaureate fields are** business/marketing, education, health professions and related sciences **Academic program** English as a second language, advanced placement, accelerated degree program, self-designed majors, honors program, summer session, adult/continuing education programs, internships **Contact** Office of Admissions, Duquesne University, 600 Forbes Avenue, Pittsburgh, PA 15282-0201. Telephone: 412-396-5000 or toll-free 800-456-0590. Fax: 412-396-5644. E-mail: admissions@duq2.cc.duq.edu. Web site: http://www.duq.edu/.

EASTERN UNIVERSITY
ST. DAVIDS, PENNSYLVANIA

General Independent American Baptist Churches in the USA, comprehensive, coed **Entrance** Moderately difficult **Setting** 107-acre small-town campus **Total enrollment** 3,054 **Student-faculty ratio** 13:1 **Application deadline** Rolling (freshmen), rolling (transfer) **Freshmen** 81% were admitted **Housing** Yes **Expenses** Tuition $15,150; Room & Board $6490 **Undergraduates** 64% women, 14% part-time, 39% 25 or older, 0.1% Native American, 4% Hispanic American, 13% African American, 1% Asian American/Pacific Islander **The most frequently chosen baccalaureate fields are** business/marketing, education, philosophy **Academic program** English as a second language, advanced placement, accelerated degree program, self-designed majors, honors program, summer session, adult/continuing education programs, internships **Contact** Mr. David Urban, Director of Undergraduate Admissions, Eastern University, 1300 Eagle Road, St. Davids, PA 19087-3696. Telephone: 610-225-5005 or toll-free 800-452-0996. Fax: 610-341-1723. E-mail: ugadm@eastern.edu. Web site: http://www.eastern.edu/.

EAST STROUDSBURG UNIVERSITY OF PENNSYLVANIA
EAST STROUDSBURG, PENNSYLVANIA

General State-supported, comprehensive, coed **Entrance** Moderately difficult **Setting** 184-acre small-town campus **Total enrollment** 5,996 **Student-**

PENNSYLVANIA

faculty ratio 19:1 **Application deadline** 4/1 (freshmen), 6/1 (transfer) **Freshmen** 73% were admitted **Housing** Yes **Expenses** Tuition $4984; Room & Board $4224 **Undergraduates** 58% women, 12% part-time, 12% 25 or older, 0.1% Native American, 3% Hispanic American, 4% African American, 1% Asian American/Pacific Islander **The most frequently chosen baccalaureate fields are** business/marketing, biological/life sciences, education **Academic program** Advanced placement, self-designed majors, honors program, summer session, adult/continuing education programs, internships **Contact** Mr. Alan T. Chesterton, Director of Admissions, East Stroudsburg University of Pennsylvania, 200 Prospect Street, East Stroudsburg, PA 18301. Telephone: 570-422-3542 or toll-free 877-230-5547. Fax: 570-422-3933. E-mail: undergrads@po-box.esu.edu. Web site: http://www.esu.edu/.

EDINBORO UNIVERSITY OF PENNSYLVANIA
EDINBORO, PENNSYLVANIA

General State-supported, comprehensive, coed **Entrance** Moderately difficult **Setting** 585-acre small-town campus **Total enrollment** 7,498 **Student-faculty ratio** 18:1 **Application deadline** Rolling (freshmen), rolling (transfer) **Freshmen** 81% were admitted **Housing** Yes **Expenses** Room & Board $4384 **Undergraduates** 57% women, 9% part-time, 16% 25 or older, 0.2% Native American, 1% Hispanic American, 6% African American, 1% Asian American/Pacific Islander **The most frequently chosen baccalaureate fields are** education, protective services/public administration, visual/performing arts **Academic program** Advanced placement, accelerated degree program, self-designed majors, honors program, summer session, adult/continuing education programs, internships **Contact** Mr. Terrence Carlin, Assistant Vice President for Admissions, Edinboro University of Pennsylvania, Biggers House, Edinboro, PA 16444. Telephone: 814-732-2761 or toll-free 888-846-2676 (in-state); 800-626-2203 (out-of-state). Fax: 814-732-2420. E-mail: eup_admissions@edinboro.edu. Web site: http://www.edinboro.edu/.

ELIZABETHTOWN COLLEGE
ELIZABETHTOWN, PENNSYLVANIA

General Independent, comprehensive, coed, affiliated with Church of the Brethren **Entrance** Moderately difficult **Setting** 185-acre small-town campus **Total enrollment** 1,901 **Student-faculty ratio** 12:1 **Application deadline** Rolling (freshmen), rolling (transfer) **Freshmen** 69% were admitted **Housing** Yes **Expenses** Tuition $21,350; Room & Board $6000 **Undergraduates** 62% women, 9% part-time, 0.2% Native American, 1% Hispanic American, 1% African American, 1% Asian American/Pacific Islander **The most frequently chosen baccalaureate fields are** business/marketing, education, health professions and related sciences **Academic program** English as a second language, advanced placement, honors program, summer session, adult/continuing education programs, internships **Contact** W. Kent Barnds, Director of Admissions, Elizabethtown College, 1 Alpha Drive, Elizabethtown, PA 17022-2298. Telephone: 717-361-1400. Fax: 717-361-1365. E-mail: admissions@acad.etown.edu. Web site: http://www.etown.edu/.

FRANKLIN AND MARSHALL COLLEGE
LANCASTER, PENNSYLVANIA

General Independent, 4-year, coed **Entrance** Very difficult **Setting** 125-acre suburban campus **Total enrollment** 1,887 **Student-faculty ratio** 11:1 **Application deadline** 2/1 (freshmen), 5/1 (transfer) **Freshmen** 55% were admitted **Housing** Yes **Expenses** Tuition $26,110; Room & Board $6300 **Undergraduates** 50% women, 2% part-time, 0% 25 or older, 0.1% Native American, 3% Hispanic American, 2% African American, 3% Asian American/Pacific Islander **The most frequently chosen baccalaureate fields are** business/marketing, interdisciplinary studies, social sciences and history **Academic program** Advanced placement, accelerated degree program, self-designed majors, honors program, summer session, internships **Contact** Ms. Penny Johnston, Acting Director of Admissions, Franklin and Marshall College, PO Box 3003, Lancaster, PA 17604-3003. Telephone: 717-291-3953. Fax: 717-291-4389. E-mail: admission@fandm.edu. Web site: http://www.fandm.edu/.

GANNON UNIVERSITY
ERIE, PENNSYLVANIA

General Independent Roman Catholic, comprehensive, coed **Entrance** Moderately difficult **Setting** 13-acre urban campus **Total enrollment** 3,407 **Student-faculty ratio** 14:1 **Application deadline** Rolling (freshmen), rolling (transfer) **Freshmen** 90% were admitted **Housing** Yes **Expenses** Tuition $14,932; Room & Board $5990 **Undergraduates** 58% women, 13% part-time, 15% 25 or older, 0.4% Native American, 1% Hispanic American, 4% African American, 1% Asian American/Pacific Islander **The most frequently chosen baccalaureate fields are** business/marketing, education, health professions and related sciences **Academic program** English as a second language, advanced placement, accelerated degree program, honors program, summer session, adult/continuing education programs, internships **Contact** Ms. Beth Nemenz, Director of Admissions, Gannon University, University Square, Erie, PA 16541. Telephone: 814-871-7240 or toll-free 800-GANNONU. Fax: 814-871-5803. E-mail: admissions@gannon.edu. Web site: http://www.gannon.edu/.

GENEVA COLLEGE
BEAVER FALLS, PENNSYLVANIA

General Independent, comprehensive, coed, affiliated with Reformed Presbyterian Church of North America **Entrance** Moderately difficult **Setting** 55-acre small-town campus **Total enrollment** 2,174 **Student-faculty ratio** 18:1 **Application deadline** Rolling (freshmen), rolling (transfer) **Freshmen** 80%

PENNSYLVANIA

Geneva College *(continued)*
were admitted **Housing** Yes **Expenses** Tuition $14,050; Room & Board $5940 **Undergraduates** 58% women, 15% part-time, 5% 25 or older, 0.1% Native American, 1% Hispanic American, 5% African American, 0.4% Asian American/Pacific Islander **The most frequently chosen baccalaureate fields are** business/marketing, education, philosophy **Academic program** English as a second language, advanced placement, accelerated degree program, self-designed majors, honors program, summer session, adult/continuing education programs, internships **Contact** Mr. David Layton, Director of Admissions, Geneva College, 3200 College Avenue, Beaver Falls, PA 15010. Telephone: 724-847-6500 or toll-free 800-847-8255. Fax: 724-847-6776. E-mail: admissions@geneva.edu. Web site: http://www.geneva.edu/.

GETTYSBURG COLLEGE
GETTYSBURG, PENNSYLVANIA

General Independent, 4-year, coed, affiliated with Evangelical Lutheran Church in America **Entrance** Very difficult **Setting** 200-acre small-town campus **Total enrollment** 2,258 **Student-faculty ratio** 11:1 **Application deadline** 2/15 (freshmen), rolling (transfer) **Freshmen** 53% were admitted **Housing** Yes **Expenses** Tuition $25,748; Room & Board $6322 **Undergraduates** 52% women, 0.4% part-time, 0.2% Native American, 1% Hispanic American, 2% African American, 1% Asian American/Pacific Islander **The most frequently chosen baccalaureate fields are** business/marketing, English, social sciences and history **Academic program** Advanced placement, accelerated degree program, self-designed majors, adult/continuing education programs, internships **Contact** Ms. Gail Sweezey, Director of Admissions, Gettysburg College, 300 North Washington Street, Gettysburg, PA 17325. Telephone: 717-337-6100 or toll-free 800-431-0803. Fax: 717-337-6145. E-mail: admiss@gettysburg.edu. Web site: http://www.gettysburg.edu/.

GRATZ COLLEGE
MELROSE PARK, PENNSYLVANIA

General Independent Jewish, comprehensive, coed **Entrance** Moderately difficult **Setting** 28-acre suburban campus **Total enrollment** 614 **Student-faculty ratio** 12:1 **Application deadline** Rolling (freshmen), rolling (transfer) **Freshmen** 67% were admitted **Housing** No **Expenses** Tuition $7950 **Undergraduates** 90% women, 86% part-time, 90% 25 or older **The most frequently chosen baccalaureate field is** philosophy, religion, and theology **Academic program** Summer session, adult/continuing education programs, internships **Contact** Ms. Adena E. Johnston, Director of Admissions, Gratz College, 7605 Old York Road, Melrose Park, PA 19027. Telephone: 215-635-7300 Ext. 140 or toll-free 800-475-4635 Ext. 140 (out-of-state). Fax: 215-635-7320 Ext. 140. E-mail: admissions@gratz.edu. Web site: http://www.gratzcollege.edu/.

GROVE CITY COLLEGE
GROVE CITY, PENNSYLVANIA

General Independent Presbyterian, 4-year, coed **Entrance** Very difficult **Setting** 150-acre small-town campus **Total enrollment** 2,334 **Student-faculty ratio** 19:1 **Application deadline** 2/15 (freshmen), rolling (transfer) **Freshmen** 43% were admitted **Housing** Yes **Expenses** Tuition $7870; Room & Board $4410 **Undergraduates** 50% women, 2% part-time, 1% 25 or older, 0.2% Native American, 0.2% Hispanic American, 0.3% African American, 1% Asian American/Pacific Islander **The most frequently chosen baccalaureate fields are** business/marketing, biological/life sciences, education **Academic program** Advanced placement, self-designed majors, summer session, internships **Contact** Mr. Jeffrey C. Mincey, Director of Admissions, Grove City College, 100 Campus Drive, Grove City, PA 16127-2104. Telephone: 724-458-2100. Fax: 724-458-3395. E-mail: admissions@gcc.edu. Web site: http://www.gcc.edu/.

▶ For more information, see page 436.

GWYNEDD-MERCY COLLEGE
GWYNEDD VALLEY, PENNSYLVANIA

General Independent Roman Catholic, comprehensive, coed **Entrance** Moderately difficult **Setting** 170-acre suburban campus **Total enrollment** 2,177 **Student-faculty ratio** 19:1 **Application deadline** Rolling (freshmen), 8/1 (transfer) **Freshmen** 70% were admitted **Housing** Yes **Expenses** Tuition $15,350; Room & Board $7000 **Undergraduates** 76% women, 46% part-time, 50% 25 or older, 0.1% Native American, 2% Hispanic American, 11% African American, 3% Asian American/Pacific Islander **The most frequently chosen baccalaureate fields are** education, business/marketing, health professions and related sciences **Academic program** English as a second language, advanced placement, accelerated degree program, honors program, summer session, adult/continuing education programs, internships **Contact** Mr. Dennis Murphy, Vice President of Enrollment Management, Gwynedd-Mercy College, 1325 Sumneytown Pike, Gwynedd Valley, PA 19437-0901. Telephone: 215-646-7300 or toll-free 800-DIAL-GMC (in-state). E-mail: admissions@gmc.edu. Web site: http://www.gmc.edu/.

HAVERFORD COLLEGE
HAVERFORD, PENNSYLVANIA

General Independent, 4-year, coed **Entrance** Most difficult **Setting** 200-acre suburban campus **Total enrollment** 1,138 **Student-faculty ratio** 9:1 **Application deadline** 1/15 (freshmen), 3/31 (transfer) **Freshmen** 33% were admitted **Housing** Yes **Expenses** Tuition $26,070; Room & Board $8230 **Undergraduates** 52% women, 0% 25 or older, 0.4% Native American, 5% Hispanic American, 6% African American, 13% Asian American/Pacific Islander **The most frequently chosen baccalaureate fields are** biological/life sciences, English, social sciences and history **Academic program** Advanced placement, accelerated degree program, self-designed majors, internships **Contact** Ms. Delsie Z. Phillips, Director of Admission, Haverford College, 370 Lancaster Avenue, Haverford, PA 19041-1392. Telephone: 610-896-1350. Fax: 610-896-1338. E-mail: admitme@haverford.edu. Web site: http://www.haverford.edu/.

▶ For more information, see page 437.

HOLY FAMILY COLLEGE
PHILADELPHIA, PENNSYLVANIA

General Independent Roman Catholic, comprehensive, coed **Entrance** Moderately difficult **Setting** 47-acre suburban campus **Total enrollment** 2,665 **Student-faculty ratio** 11:1 **Application deadline** Rolling (freshmen), rolling (transfer) **Freshmen** 84% were admitted **Housing** No **Expenses** Tuition $13,710 **Undergraduates** 77% women, 42% part-time, 38% 25 or older, 0.1% Native American, 2% Hispanic American, 3% African American, 2% Asian American/Pacific Islander **The most frequently chosen baccalaureate fields are** business/marketing, education, health professions and related sciences **Academic program** Advanced placement, accelerated degree program, honors program, summer session, adult/continuing education programs, internships **Contact** Mrs. Roberta Nolan, Director of Admissions, Holy Family College, Grant and Frankford Avenues, Philadelphia, PA 19114-2094. Telephone: 215-637-3050 or toll-free 800-637-1191. Fax: 215-281-1022. E-mail: rnolan@hfc.edu. Web site: http://www.hfc.edu/.

IMMACULATA COLLEGE
IMMACULATA, PENNSYLVANIA

General Independent Roman Catholic, comprehensive, women only **Entrance** Moderately difficult **Setting** 400-acre suburban campus **Total enrollment** 3,170 **Student-faculty ratio** 13:1 **Application deadline** 8/15 (freshmen), rolling (transfer) **Freshmen** 85% were admitted **Housing** Yes **Expenses** Tuition $15,200; Room & Board $7200 **Undergraduates** 73% women, 17% part-time, 70% 25 or older, 0.1% Native American, 2% Hispanic American, 8% African American, 2% Asian American/Pacific Islander **The most frequently chosen baccalaureate fields are** business/marketing, health professions and related sciences, psychology **Academic program** English as a second language, advanced placement, accelerated degree program, self-designed majors, honors program, summer session, adult/continuing education programs, internships **Contact** Ms. Sandra Zerby, Executive Director of Admission, Immaculata College, PO Box 642, Immaculata, PA 19345-0642. Telephone: 610-647-4400 Ext. 3015 or toll-free 877-428-6328. Fax: 610-640-0836. E-mail: admiss@immaculata.edu. Web site: http://www.immaculata.edu/.

INDIANA UNIVERSITY OF PENNSYLVANIA
INDIANA, PENNSYLVANIA

General State-supported, university, coed **Entrance** Moderately difficult **Setting** 350-acre small-town campus **Total enrollment** 13,457 **Student-faculty ratio** 17:1 **Application deadline** Rolling (freshmen), rolling (transfer) **Freshmen** 57% were admitted **Housing** Yes **Expenses** Tuition $4875; Room & Board $4258 **Undergraduates** 56% women, 7% part-time, 8% 25 or older, 0.3% Native American, 1% Hispanic American, 6% African American, 1% Asian American/Pacific Islander **The most frequently chosen baccalaureate fields are** business/marketing, education, social sciences and history **Academic program** English as a second language, advanced placement, accelerated degree program, honors program, summer session, adult/continuing education programs, internships **Contact** Mr. William Nunn, Dean of Admissions, Indiana University of Pennsylvania, 216 Pratt Hall, Indiana, PA 15705. Telephone: 724-357-2230 or toll-free 800-442-6830. E-mail: admissions_inquiry@grove.iup.edu. Web site: http://www.iup.edu/.

JUNIATA COLLEGE
HUNTINGDON, PENNSYLVANIA

General Independent, 4-year, coed, affiliated with Church of the Brethren **Entrance** Moderately difficult **Setting** 110-acre small-town campus **Total enrollment** 1,302 **Student-faculty ratio** 14:1 **Application deadline** 3/15 (freshmen), 6/15 (transfer) **Freshmen** 79% were admitted **Housing** Yes **Expenses** Tuition $19,360; Room & Board $5290 **Undergraduates** 58% women, 3% part-time, 5% 25 or older, 0.1% Native American, 1% Hispanic American, 1% African American, 0.4% Asian American/Pacific Islander **The most frequently chosen baccalaureate fields are** biological/life sciences, business/marketing, social sciences and history **Academic program** English as a second language, advanced placement, self-designed majors, honors program, summer session, adult/continuing education programs, internships **Contact** Terry Bollman, Director of Admissions, Juniata College, 1700 Moore Street, Huntingdon, PA 16652-2119. Telephone: 814-641-3424 or toll-free 877-JUNIATA. Fax: 814-641-3100. E-mail: info@juniata.edu. Web site: http://www.juniata.edu/.

KING'S COLLEGE
WILKES-BARRE, PENNSYLVANIA

General Independent Roman Catholic, comprehensive, coed **Entrance** Moderately difficult **Setting** 48-acre suburban campus **Total enrollment** 2,226 **Student-faculty ratio** 13:1 **Application deadline** Rolling (freshmen), rolling (transfer) **Freshmen** 83% were admitted **Housing** Yes **Expenses** Tuition $17,450; Room & Board $7230 **Undergraduates** 52% women, 17% part-time, 3% 25 or older, 0.3% Native American, 2% Hispanic American, 3% African American, 1% Asian American/Pacific Islander **The most frequently chosen baccalaureate fields are** business/marketing, education, health professions and related sciences **Academic program** English as a second language, advanced placement, accelerated degree program, self-designed majors, honors program, summer session, adult/continuing education programs,

PENNSYLVANIA

King's College *(continued)*
internships **Contact** Ms. Susan McGarry-Hannon, Director of Admissions, King's College, 133 North River Street, Wilkes-Barre, PA 18711-0801. Telephone: 570-208-5858 or toll-free 888-KINGSPA. Fax: 570-208-5971. E-mail: admissions@kings.edu. Web site: http://www.kings.edu/.

KUTZTOWN UNIVERSITY OF PENNSYLVANIA
KUTZTOWN, PENNSYLVANIA

General State-supported, comprehensive, coed **Entrance** Moderately difficult **Setting** 326-acre rural campus **Total enrollment** 8,268 **Student-faculty ratio** 19:1 **Application deadline** Rolling (freshmen), rolling (transfer) **Freshmen** 69% were admitted **Housing** Yes **Expenses** Tuition $4947; Room & Board $4426 **Undergraduates** 60% women, 10% part-time, 10% 25 or older, 0.2% Native American, 2% Hispanic American, 4% African American, 1% Asian American/Pacific Islander **The most frequently chosen baccalaureate fields are** business/marketing, education, visual/performing arts **Academic program** Advanced placement, accelerated degree program, self-designed majors, honors program, summer session, adult/continuing education programs, internships **Contact** Dr. Valerie Reidout, Acting Director of Admissions, Kutztown University of Pennsylvania, 15200 Kutztown Road, Kutztown, PA 19530-0730. Telephone: 610-683-4060 Ext. 4053 or toll-free 877-628-1915. Fax: 610-683-1375. E-mail: admission@kutztown.edu. Web site: http://www.kutztown.edu/.

LAFAYETTE COLLEGE
EASTON, PENNSYLVANIA

General Independent, 4-year, coed, affiliated with Presbyterian Church (U.S.A.) **Entrance** Very difficult **Setting** 110-acre suburban campus **Total enrollment** 2,330 **Student-faculty ratio** 11:1 **Application deadline** 1/1 (freshmen), 6/1 (transfer) **Freshmen** 39% were admitted **Housing** Yes **Expenses** Tuition $23,758; Room & Board $7413 **Undergraduates** 49% women, 5% part-time, 0% 25 or older, 0.3% Native American, 2% Hispanic American, 4% African American, 2% Asian American/Pacific Islander **The most frequently chosen baccalaureate field is** philosophy, religion, and theology **Academic program** Advanced placement, accelerated degree program, self-designed majors, honors program, summer session, adult/continuing education programs, internships **Contact** Ms. Carol Rowlands, Director of Admissions, Lafayette College, Easton, PA 18042-1798. Telephone: 610-330-5100. Fax: 610-330-5355. E-mail: admissions@lafayette.edu. Web site: http://www.lafayette.edu/.

LANCASTER BIBLE COLLEGE
LANCASTER, PENNSYLVANIA

General Independent nondenominational, comprehensive, coed **Entrance** Minimally difficult **Setting** 100-acre suburban campus **Total enrollment** 818 **Student-faculty ratio** 15:1 **Application deadline** Rolling (freshmen), rolling (transfer) **Freshmen** 76% were admitted **Housing** Yes **Expenses** Tuition $10,540; Room & Board $4800 **Undergraduates** 54% women, 24% part-time, 20% 25 or older, 1% Native American, 1% Hispanic American, 3% African American, 1% Asian American/Pacific Islander **The most frequently chosen baccalaureate fields are** philosophy, education, philosophy, religion, and theology **Academic program** Advanced placement, summer session, adult/continuing education programs, internships **Contact** Mrs. Joanne M. Roper, Director of Admissions, Lancaster Bible College, 901 Eden Road, Lancaster, PA 17601-5036. Telephone: 717-560-8271 or toll-free 888-866-LBC-4-YOU. Fax: 717-560-8213. E-mail: admissions@lbc.edu. Web site: http://www.lbc.edu/.

LA ROCHE COLLEGE
PITTSBURGH, PENNSYLVANIA

General Independent, comprehensive, coed, affiliated with Roman Catholic Church **Entrance** Minimally difficult **Setting** 80-acre suburban campus **Total enrollment** 1,908 **Student-faculty ratio** 18:1 **Application deadline** Rolling (freshmen), rolling (transfer) **Freshmen** 79% were admitted **Housing** Yes **Expenses** Tuition $12,380; Room & Board $6474 **Undergraduates** 61% women, 25% part-time, 28% 25 or older, 0.2% Native American, 1% Hispanic American, 4% African American, 1% Asian American/Pacific Islander **The most frequently chosen baccalaureate fields are** business/marketing, health professions and related sciences, visual/performing arts **Academic program** English as a second language, advanced placement, honors program, summer session, adult/continuing education programs, internships **Contact** Ms. Dayna R. McNally, Director of Enrollment Services, La Roche College, 9000 Babcock Boulevard, Pittsburgh, PA 15237. Telephone: 412-536-1049 or toll-free 800-838-4LRC. Fax: 412-536-1048. E-mail: admsns@laroche.edu. Web site: http://www.laroche.edu/.

LA SALLE UNIVERSITY
PHILADELPHIA, PENNSYLVANIA

General Independent Roman Catholic, comprehensive, coed **Entrance** Moderately difficult **Setting** 100-acre urban campus **Total enrollment** 5,428 **Student-faculty ratio** 16:1 **Application deadline** 4/1 (freshmen), 8/1 (transfer) **Freshmen** 80% were admitted **Housing** Yes **Expenses** Tuition $19,890; Room & Board $7010 **Undergraduates** 57% women, 19% part-time, 17% 25 or older, 0.1% Native American, 5% Hispanic American, 11% African American, 3% Asian American/Pacific Islander **The most frequently chosen baccalaureate fields are** business/marketing, communications/communication technologies, education **Academic program** Advanced placement, accelerated degree program, self-designed majors, honors program, summer session, adult/continuing education programs, internships **Contact** Mr. Robert G. Voss, Dean of Admission and Financial Aid, La

Salle University, 1900 West Olney Avenue, Philadelphia, PA 19141-1199. Telephone: 215-951-1500 or toll-free 800-328-1910. Fax: 215-951-1656. E-mail: admiss@lasalle.edu. Web site: http://www.lasalle.edu/.

LEBANON VALLEY COLLEGE
ANNVILLE, PENNSYLVANIA

General Independent United Methodist, comprehensive, coed **Entrance** Moderately difficult **Setting** 275-acre small-town campus **Total enrollment** 2,117 **Student-faculty ratio** 14:1 **Application deadline** Rolling (freshmen), rolling (transfer) **Freshmen** 79% were admitted **Housing** Yes **Expenses** Tuition $19,810; Room & Board $5890 **Undergraduates** 60% women, 21% part-time, 17% 25 or older, 0.1% Native American, 2% Hispanic American, 2% African American, 1% Asian American/Pacific Islander **The most frequently chosen baccalaureate fields are** business/marketing, education, social sciences and history **Academic program** Advanced placement, self-designed majors, summer session, adult/continuing education programs, internships **Contact** William J. Brown Jr., Dean of Admission and Financial Aid, Lebanon Valley College, 101 N. College Avenue, Annville, PA 17003-1400. Telephone: 717-867-6181 or toll-free 866-582-4236 (out-of-state). Fax: 717-867-6026. E-mail: admission@lvc.edu. Web site: http://www.lvc.edu/.

LEHIGH UNIVERSITY
BETHLEHEM, PENNSYLVANIA

General Independent, university, coed **Entrance** Most difficult **Setting** 1,600-acre suburban campus **Total enrollment** 6,479 **Student-faculty ratio** 11:1 **Application deadline** 1/1 (freshmen), 4/1 (transfer) **Freshmen** 47% were admitted **Housing** Yes **Expenses** Tuition $25,140; Room & Board $7150 **Undergraduates** 41% women, 1% part-time, 1% 25 or older, 0.1% Native American, 3% Hispanic American, 3% African American, 6% Asian American/Pacific Islander **The most frequently chosen baccalaureate fields are** business/marketing, engineering/engineering technologies, social sciences and history **Academic program** English as a second language, advanced placement, accelerated degree program, honors program, summer session, adult/continuing education programs, internships **Contact** Mr. J. Bruce Gardiner, Interim Dean of Admissions and Financial Aid, Lehigh University, 27 Memorial Drive West, Bethlehem, PA 18015. Telephone: 610-758-3100. Fax: 610-758-4361. E-mail: admissions@lehigh.edu. Web site: http://www.lehigh.edu/.

LINCOLN UNIVERSITY
LINCOLN UNIVERSITY, PENNSYLVANIA

General State-related, comprehensive, coed **Entrance** Moderately difficult **Setting** 442-acre rural campus **Total enrollment** 1,871 **Student-faculty ratio** 14:1 **Application deadline** Rolling (freshmen), rolling (transfer) **Freshmen** 53% were admitted **Housing** Yes **Expenses** Tuition $5786; Room & Board $5412 **Undergraduates** 60% women, 4% part-time, 2% 25 or older, 0% Native American, 0.2% Hispanic American, 93% African American, 0.1% Asian American/Pacific Islander **The most frequently chosen baccalaureate fields are** business/marketing, education, social sciences and history **Academic program** Advanced placement, accelerated degree program, self-designed majors, honors program, summer session, adult/continuing education programs, internships **Contact** Dr. Robert Laney Jr., Director of Admissions, Lincoln University, MSC 147, Lincoln University, PO Box 179, Lincoln University, PA 19352-0999. Telephone: 610-932-8300 Ext. 3206 or toll-free 800-215-4858. Fax: 610-932-1209. E-mail: admiss@lu.lincoln.edu. Web site: http://www.lincoln.edu/.

LOCK HAVEN UNIVERSITY OF PENNSYLVANIA
LOCK HAVEN, PENNSYLVANIA

General State-supported, comprehensive, coed **Entrance** Moderately difficult **Setting** 165-acre small-town campus **Total enrollment** 4,352 **Student-faculty ratio** 18:1 **Application deadline** Rolling (freshmen), rolling (transfer) **Freshmen** 81% were admitted **Housing** Yes **Expenses** Tuition $4884; Room & Board $4776 **Undergraduates** 59% women, 7% part-time, 10% 25 or older, 0.3% Native American, 1% Hispanic American, 3% African American, 1% Asian American/Pacific Islander **The most frequently chosen baccalaureate fields are** education, health professions and related sciences, parks and recreation **Academic program** Advanced placement, accelerated degree program, self-designed majors, honors program, summer session, adult/continuing education programs, internships **Contact** Mr. Steven Lee, Director of Admissions, Lock Haven University of Pennsylvania, Office of Admission, Akeley Hall, Lock Haven, PA 17745. Telephone: 570-893-2027 or toll-free 800-332-8900 (in-state); 800-233-8978 (out-of-state). Fax: 570-893-2201. E-mail: admissions@lhup.edu. Web site: http://www.lhup.edu/.

LYCOMING COLLEGE
WILLIAMSPORT, PENNSYLVANIA

General Independent United Methodist, 4-year, coed **Entrance** Moderately difficult **Setting** 35-acre small-town campus **Total enrollment** 1,429 **Student-faculty ratio** 13:1 **Application deadline** 4/1 (freshmen), 6/1 (transfer) **Freshmen** 80% were admitted **Housing** Yes **Expenses** Tuition $19,404; Room & Board $5376 **Undergraduates** 55% women, 3% part-time, 6% 25 or older, 0.4% Native American, 1% Hispanic American, 2% African American, 1% Asian American/Pacific Islander **The most frequently chosen baccalaureate fields are** biological/life sciences, business/marketing, psychology **Academic program** Advanced placement, accelerated degree program, self-designed majors, honors program, summer session, internships **Contact** Mr. James Spencer, Dean of Admissions and Financial Aid, Lycoming College, Admissions House, 700 College Place,

Lycoming College *(continued)*
Williamsport, PA 17701. Telephone: 570-321-4026 or toll-free 800-345-3920 Ext. 4026. Fax: 570-321-4317. E-mail: admissions@lycoming.edu. Web site: http://www.lycoming.edu/.

MANSFIELD UNIVERSITY OF PENNSYLVANIA
MANSFIELD, PENNSYLVANIA

General State-supported, comprehensive, coed **Entrance** Moderately difficult **Setting** 205-acre small-town campus **Total enrollment** 3,303 **Student-faculty ratio** 16:1 **Application deadline** Rolling (freshmen), rolling (transfer) **Freshmen** 73% were admitted **Housing** Yes **Expenses** Tuition $5096; Room & Board $4552 **Undergraduates** 59% women, 11% part-time, 16% 25 or older, 1% Native American, 1% Hispanic American, 3% African American, 1% Asian American/Pacific Islander **The most frequently chosen baccalaureate fields are** business/marketing, education, protective services/public administration **Academic program** Advanced placement, accelerated degree program, self-designed majors, honors program, summer session, adult/continuing education programs, internships **Contact** Mr. Brian D. Barden, Director of Admissions, Mansfield University of Pennsylvania, Alumni Hall, Mansfield, PA 16933. Telephone: 570-662-4813 or toll-free 800-577-6826. Fax: 570-662-4121. E-mail: admissions@mnsfld.edu. Web site: http://www.mansfield.edu/.

MARYWOOD UNIVERSITY
SCRANTON, PENNSYLVANIA

General Independent Roman Catholic, comprehensive, coed **Entrance** Moderately difficult **Setting** 115-acre suburban campus **Total enrollment** 2,925 **Student-faculty ratio** 12:1 **Application deadline** Rolling (freshmen), rolling (transfer) **Freshmen** 81% were admitted **Housing** Yes **Expenses** Tuition $17,429; Room & Board $7310 **Undergraduates** 72% women, 14% part-time, 19% 25 or older, 0.2% Native American, 2% Hispanic American, 1% African American, 1% Asian American/Pacific Islander **The most frequently chosen baccalaureate fields are** business/marketing, education, visual/performing arts **Academic program** English as a second language, advanced placement, accelerated degree program, self-designed majors, honors program, summer session, adult/continuing education programs, internships **Contact** Mr. Robert W. Reese, Director of Admissions, Marywood University, 2300 Adams Avenue, Scranton, PA 18509-1598. Telephone: 570-348-6234 or toll-free 800-346-5014. Fax: 570-961-4763. E-mail: ugadm@ac.marywood.edu. Web site: http://www.marywood.edu/.

MCP HAHNEMANN UNIVERSITY
PHILADELPHIA, PENNSYLVANIA

General Independent, university, coed **Entrance** Moderately difficult **Setting** urban campus **Total enrollment** 2,579 **Student-faculty ratio** 9:1 **Application deadline** 6/1 (freshmen), 6/1 (transfer) **Freshmen** 72% were admitted **Housing** Yes **Expenses** Tuition $10,410; Room & Board $8100 **Undergraduates** 66% women, 40% part-time, 74% 25 or older, 1% Native American, 3% Hispanic American, 21% African American, 4% Asian American/Pacific Islander **The most frequently chosen baccalaureate fields are** health professions and related sciences, liberal arts/general studies **Academic program** Summer session, adult/continuing education programs, internships **Contact** Ms. Jarmila H. Force, Associate Director of Enrollment Management, MCP Hahnemann University, 245 North 15th Street, Mail Stop 472, Philadelphia, PA 19102-1192. Telephone: 215-762-4671 or toll-free 800-2-DREXEL Ext. 6333. Fax: 215-762-6194. E-mail: enroll@mcphu.edu. Web site: http://www.mcphu.edu/.

▶ For more information, see page 456.

MERCYHURST COLLEGE
ERIE, PENNSYLVANIA

General Independent Roman Catholic, comprehensive, coed **Entrance** Moderately difficult **Setting** 88-acre suburban campus **Total enrollment** 3,375 **Student-faculty ratio** 19:1 **Application deadline** Rolling (freshmen), rolling (transfer) **Freshmen** 77% were admitted **Housing** Yes **Expenses** Tuition $14,340; Room & Board $5364 **Undergraduates** 62% women, 15% part-time, 19% 25 or older, 0.3% Native American, 1% Hispanic American, 4% African American, 1% Asian American/Pacific Islander **The most frequently chosen baccalaureate fields are** business/marketing, health professions and related sciences, protective services/public administration **Academic program** Advanced placement, accelerated degree program, self-designed majors, honors program, summer session, adult/continuing education programs, internships **Contact** Mr. Robin Engel, Director of Undergraduate Admissions, Mercyhurst College, 501 East 38th Street, Erie, PA 16546-0001. Telephone: 814-824-2573 or toll-free 800-825-1926. Fax: 814-824-2071. E-mail: admug@paradise.mercy.edu. Web site: http://www.mercyhurst.edu/.

MESSIAH COLLEGE
GRANTHAM, PENNSYLVANIA

General Independent interdenominational, 4-year, coed **Entrance** Moderately difficult **Setting** 400-acre small-town campus **Total enrollment** 2,858 **Student-faculty ratio** 13:1 **Application deadline** Rolling (freshmen), rolling (transfer) **Freshmen** 78% were admitted **Housing** Yes **Expenses** Tuition $17,210; Room & Board $5970 **Undergraduates** 61% women, 2% part-time, 3% 25 or older, 0.2% Native American, 2% Hispanic American, 2% African American, 1% Asian American/Pacific Islander **The most frequently chosen baccalaureate fields are** business/marketing, education, home economics/vocational home economics **Academic program** Advanced placement, accelerated degree program, self-designed majors, honors program, summer session, adult/continuing education programs, internships **Contact**

PENNSYLVANIA

Mr. William G. Strausbaugh, Dean for Enrollment Management, Messiah College, One College Avenue, Grantham, PA 17027. Telephone: 717-691-6000 or toll-free 800-382-1349 (in-state); 800-233-4220 (out-of-state). Fax: 717-796-5374. E-mail: admiss@messiah.edu. Web site: http://www.messiah.edu/.

MILLERSVILLE UNIVERSITY OF PENNSYLVANIA
MILLERSVILLE, PENNSYLVANIA

General State-supported, comprehensive, coed **Entrance** Moderately difficult **Setting** 190-acre suburban campus **Total enrollment** 7,556 **Student-faculty ratio** 18:1 **Application deadline** Rolling (freshmen), rolling (transfer) **Freshmen** 67% were admitted **Housing** Yes **Expenses** Tuition $5053; Room & Board $5100 **Undergraduates** 58% women, 13% part-time, 11% 25 or older, 0.2% Native American, 2% Hispanic American, 6% African American, 1% Asian American/Pacific Islander **The most frequently chosen baccalaureate fields are** business/marketing, education, social sciences and history **Academic program** English as a second language, advanced placement, honors program, summer session, adult/continuing education programs, internships **Contact** Mr. Darrell Davis, Director of Admissions, Millersville University of Pennsylvania, PO Box 1002, Millersville, PA 17551-0302. Telephone: 717-872-3371 or toll-free 800-MU-ADMIT (out-of-state). Fax: 717-871-2147. E-mail: admissions@millersville.edu. Web site: http://www.millersville.edu/.

MOORE COLLEGE OF ART AND DESIGN
PHILADELPHIA, PENNSYLVANIA

General Independent, 4-year, women only **Entrance** Moderately difficult **Setting** 3-acre urban campus **Total enrollment** 613 **Student-faculty ratio** 8:1 **Application deadline** 8/15 (freshmen), rolling (transfer) **Freshmen** 54% were admitted **Housing** Yes **Expenses** Tuition $16,795; Room & Board $6330 **Undergraduates** 25% part-time, 16% 25 or older, 1% Native American, 6% Hispanic American, 10% African American, 6% Asian American/Pacific Islander **The most frequently chosen baccalaureate field is** visual/performing arts **Academic program** Advanced placement, accelerated degree program, summer session, adult/continuing education programs, internships **Contact** Wendy Elliott Pyle, Director of Admissions, Moore College of Art and Design, 20th and the Parkway, Philadelphia, PA 19103. Telephone: 215-568-4515 Ext. 1108 or toll-free 800-523-2025. Fax: 215-965-8544. E-mail: admiss@moore.edu. Web site: http://www.moore.edu/.

MORAVIAN COLLEGE
BETHLEHEM, PENNSYLVANIA

General Independent, comprehensive, coed, affiliated with Moravian Church **Entrance** Moderately difficult **Setting** 70-acre suburban campus **Total enrollment** 1,834 **Student-faculty ratio** 13:1 **Application deadline** 3/1 (freshmen), 3/1 (transfer) **Freshmen** 68% were admitted **Housing** Yes **Expenses** Tuition $20,495; Room & Board $6570 **Undergraduates** 60% women, 21% part-time, 4% 25 or older, 0.3% Native American, 2% Hispanic American, 2% African American, 1% Asian American/Pacific Islander **The most frequently chosen baccalaureate fields are** business/marketing, psychology, social sciences and history **Academic program** Advanced placement, accelerated degree program, self-designed majors, honors program, summer session, adult/continuing education programs, internships **Contact** Mr. James P. Mackin, Director of Admission, Moravian College, 1200 Main Street, Bethlehem, PA 18018. Telephone: 610-861-1320 or toll-free 800-441-3191. Fax: 610-625-7930. E-mail: admissions@moravian.edu. Web site: http://www.moravian.edu/.

MOUNT ALOYSIUS COLLEGE
CRESSON, PENNSYLVANIA

General Independent Roman Catholic, 4-year, coed **Entrance** Minimally difficult **Setting** 125-acre rural campus **Total enrollment** 1,153 **Student-faculty ratio** 14:1 **Application deadline** Rolling (freshmen), rolling (transfer) **Freshmen** 48% were admitted **Housing** Yes **Expenses** Tuition $13,936; Room & Board $5190 **Undergraduates** 75% women, 25% part-time, 41% 25 or older **The most frequently chosen baccalaureate fields are** health professions and related sciences, business/marketing, psychology **Academic program** Advanced placement, summer session, adult/continuing education programs, internships **Contact** Mr. Francis Crouse, Dean of Enrollment Management, Mount Aloysius College, 7373 Admiral Peary Highway, Cresson, PA 16630. Telephone: 814-886-6383 or toll-free 888-823-2220. Fax: 814-886-6441. E-mail: admissions@mtaloy.edu. Web site: http://www.mtaloy.edu/.

MUHLENBERG COLLEGE
ALLENTOWN, PENNSYLVANIA

General Independent, 4-year, coed, affiliated with Lutheran Church **Entrance** Very difficult **Setting** 75-acre suburban campus **Total enrollment** 2,629 **Student-faculty ratio** 13:1 **Application deadline** 2/15 (freshmen), 6/1 (transfer) **Freshmen** 35% were admitted **Housing** Yes **Expenses** Tuition $22,210; Room & Board $5960 **Undergraduates** 57% women, 12% part-time, 9% 25 or older, 0.3% Native American, 3% Hispanic American, 2% African American, 3% Asian American/Pacific Islander **The most frequently chosen baccalaureate fields are** business/marketing, communications/communication technologies, social sciences and history **Academic program** Advanced placement, accelerated degree program, self-designed majors, honors program, summer session, adult/continuing education programs, internships **Contact** Mr. Christopher Hooker-Haring, Dean of Admissions, Muhlenberg College, 2400 Chew Street, Allentown, PA 18104-5586. Telephone: 484-664-3245. Fax: 484-664-3234. E-mail: adm@muhlenberg.edu. Web site: http://www.muhlenberg.edu/.

▶ For more information, see page 459.

NEUMANN COLLEGE
ASTON, PENNSYLVANIA

General Independent Roman Catholic, comprehensive, coed **Entrance** Moderately difficult **Setting** 28-acre suburban campus **Total enrollment** 2,014 **Student-faculty ratio** 16:1 **Application deadline** Rolling (freshmen), rolling (transfer) **Freshmen** 97% were admitted **Housing** Yes **Expenses** Tuition $15,030; Room & Board $7010 **Undergraduates** 65% women, 23% part-time, 20% 25 or older, 0.1% Native American, 1% Hispanic American, 12% African American, 1% Asian American/Pacific Islander **The most frequently chosen baccalaureate fields are** business/marketing, health professions and related sciences, liberal arts/general studies **Academic program** Advanced placement, accelerated degree program, self-designed majors, honors program, summer session, adult/continuing education programs, internships **Contact** Mr. Scott Bogard, Director of Admissions, Neumann College, One Neumann Drive, Aston, PA 19014-1298. Telephone: 610-558-5612 or toll-free 800-963-8626. Fax: 610-558-5652. E-mail: neumann@neumann.edu. Web site: http://www.neumann.edu/.

PEIRCE COLLEGE
PHILADELPHIA, PENNSYLVANIA

General Independent, 4-year, coed, primarily women **Entrance** Minimally difficult **Setting** 1-acre urban campus **Total enrollment** 2,837 **Student-faculty ratio** 16:1 **Application deadline** Rolling (freshmen), rolling (transfer) **Freshmen** 57% were admitted **Housing** No **Expenses** Tuition $10,650 **Undergraduates** 77% women, 76% part-time, 72% 25 or older, 0.2% Native American, 4% Hispanic American, 60% African American, 2% Asian American/Pacific Islander **The most frequently chosen baccalaureate fields are** business/marketing, (pre)law, law/legal studies **Academic program** Advanced placement, accelerated degree program, summer session, internships **Contact** Mr. Steve W. Bird, College Representative, Peirce College, 1420 Pine Street, Philadelphia, PA 19102. Telephone: 215-670-9375 or toll-free 877-670-9190 Ext. 9314 (in-state); 877-670-9190 Ext. 9214 (out-of-state). Fax: 215-545-3683. E-mail: info@peirce.edu. Web site: http://www.peirce.edu/.

PENNSYLVANIA COLLEGE OF TECHNOLOGY
WILLIAMSPORT, PENNSYLVANIA

General State-related, 4-year, coed **Entrance** Noncompetitive **Setting** 927-acre small-town campus **Total enrollment** 5,538 **Student-faculty ratio** 18:1 **Application deadline** Rolling (freshmen), rolling (transfer) **Freshmen** 59% were admitted **Housing** Yes **Expenses** Tuition $8610; Room & Board $5000 **Undergraduates** 34% women, 20% part-time, 23% 25 or older, 1% Native American, 1% Hispanic American, 2% African American, 1% Asian American/Pacific Islander **The most frequently chosen baccalaureate field is** law/legal studies **Academic program** English as a second language, advanced placement, self-designed majors, summer session, internships **Contact** Mr. Chester D. Schuman, Director of Admissions, Pennsylvania College of Technology, One College Avenue, DIF #119, Williamsport, PA 17701. Telephone: 570-327-4761 or toll-free 800-367-9222 (in-state). Fax: 570-321-5551. E-mail: cschuman@pct.edu. Web site: http://www.pct.edu/.

PENNSYLVANIA SCHOOL OF ART & DESIGN
LANCASTER, PENNSYLVANIA

General Independent, 4-year, coed **Entrance** Moderately difficult **Total enrollment** 201 **Application deadline** 5/1 (freshmen), 5/1 (transfer) **Freshmen** 60% were admitted **Housing** No **Expenses** Tuition $10,875 **Undergraduates** 53% women, 22% part-time, 1% Native American, 3% Hispanic American, 2% African American, 1% Asian American/Pacific Islander **The most frequently chosen baccalaureate field is** visual/performing arts **Academic program** Advanced placement, internships **Contact** Ms. Wendy Sweigart, Director of Admissions, Pennsylvania School of Art & Design, Admissions Office, PO Box 59, Lancaster, PA 17608-0059. Telephone: 717-396-7833 Ext. 19. Fax: 717-396-1339. E-mail: admissions@psad.edu. Web site: http://www.psad.edu/.

THE PENNSYLVANIA STATE UNIVERSITY ABINGTON COLLEGE
ABINGTON, PENNSYLVANIA

General State-related, 4-year, coed **Entrance** Moderately difficult **Setting** 45-acre small-town campus **Total enrollment** 3,179 **Student-faculty ratio** 20:1 **Application deadline** Rolling (freshmen), rolling (transfer) **Freshmen** 83% were admitted **Housing** No **Expenses** Tuition $7258 **Undergraduates** 50% women, 24% part-time, 15% 25 or older, 0.1% Native American, 4% Hispanic American, 10% African American, 11% Asian American/Pacific Islander **The most frequently chosen baccalaureate fields are** business/marketing, liberal arts/general studies, protective services/public administration **Academic program** English as a second language, advanced placement, self-designed majors, honors program, summer session, adult/continuing education programs, internships **Contact** Undergraduate Admissions Office, The Pennsylvania State University Abington College, 1600 Woodland Road, Abington, PA 19001. Telephone: 814-865-5471. Fax: 215-881-7317. E-mail: admissions@psu.edu. Web site: http://www.psu.edu/.

THE PENNSYLVANIA STATE UNIVERSITY ALTOONA COLLEGE
ALTOONA, PENNSYLVANIA

General State-related, 4-year, coed **Entrance** Moderately difficult **Setting** 115-acre suburban campus **Total enrollment** 3,823 **Student-faculty ratio** 21:1 **Application deadline** Rolling (freshmen), rolling (transfer) **Freshmen** 87% were admitted **Housing**

PENNSYLVANIA

Yes **Expenses** Tuition $7278; Room & Board $5300 **Undergraduates** 50% women, 9% part-time, 12% 25 or older, 0.1% Native American, 2% Hispanic American, 5% African American, 2% Asian American/ Pacific Islander **The most frequently chosen baccalaureate fields are** business/marketing, engineering/ engineering technologies, protective services/public administration **Academic program** English as a second language, advanced placement, self-designed majors, honors program, summer session, adult/ continuing education programs, internships **Contact** Mr. Richard Shaffer, Director of Admissions and Enrollment Services, The Pennsylvania State University Altoona College, E108 Smith Building, 3000 Ivyside Park, Altoona, PA 16601-3760. Telephone: 814-949-5466. Fax: 814-949-5564. E-mail: admissions@ psu.edu. Web site: http://www.psu.edu/.

THE PENNSYLVANIA STATE UNIVERSITY AT ERIE, THE BEHREND COLLEGE
ERIE, PENNSYLVANIA

General State-related, comprehensive, coed **Entrance** Very difficult **Setting** 727-acre suburban campus **Total enrollment** 3,708 **Student-faculty ratio** 16:1 **Application deadline** Rolling (freshmen), rolling (transfer) **Freshmen** 81% were admitted **Housing** Yes **Expenses** Tuition $7396; Room & Board $5300 **Undergraduates** 37% women, 8% part-time, 8% 25 or older, 0.03% Native American, 1% Hispanic American, 3% African American, 2% Asian American/ Pacific Islander **The most frequently chosen baccalaureate fields are** business/marketing, engineering/ engineering technologies, psychology **Academic program** Advanced placement, honors program, summer session, adult/continuing education programs, internships **Contact** Undergraduate Admissions Office, The Pennsylvania State University at Erie, The Behrend College, 5091 Station Road, Erie, PA 16563. Telephone: 814-865-5471. Fax: 814-898-6044. E-mail: behrend.admissions@psu.edu. Web site: http:// www.pserie.psu.edu/.

THE PENNSYLVANIA STATE UNIVERSITY BERKS CAMPUS OF THE BERKS–LEHIGH VALLEY COLLEGE
READING, PENNSYLVANIA

General State-related, 4-year, coed **Entrance** Moderately difficult **Setting** 240-acre suburban campus **Total enrollment** 2,329 **Student-faculty ratio** 20:1 **Application deadline** Rolling (freshmen), rolling (transfer) **Freshmen** 85% were admitted **Housing** Yes **Expenses** Tuition $7278; Room & Board $5300 **Undergraduates** 40% women, 11% part-time, 9% 25 or older, 0.1% Native American, 3% Hispanic American, 6% African American, 4% Asian American/ Pacific Islander **The most frequently chosen baccalaureate fields are** business/marketing, computer/ information sciences, engineering/engineering technologies **Academic program** Advanced placement, honors program, summer session, adult/continuing education programs, internships **Contact** Ms. Jennifer Peters, Admissions Counselor, The Pennsylvania State University Berks Campus of the Berks–Lehigh Valley College, 14 Perkins Student Center, PO Box 7009, Reading, PA 19610-6009. Telephone: 610-396-6066. Fax: 610-396-6077. E-mail: admissions@ psu.edu. Web site: http://www.psu.edu/.

THE PENNSYLVANIA STATE UNIVERSITY HARRISBURG CAMPUS OF THE CAPITAL COLLEGE
MIDDLETOWN, PENNSYLVANIA

General State-related, comprehensive, coed **Entrance** Moderately difficult **Setting** 218-acre small-town campus **Total enrollment** 3,239 **Student-faculty ratio** 10:1 **Application deadline** Rolling (freshmen), rolling (transfer) **Freshmen** 85% were admitted **Housing** Yes **Expenses** Tuition $7376; Room & Board $5980 **Undergraduates** 51% women, 37% part-time, 41% 25 or older, 0.2% Native American, 2% Hispanic American, 5% African American, 5% Asian American/Pacific Islander **The most frequently chosen baccalaureate fields are** business/marketing, education, engineering/engineering technologies **Academic program** Advanced placement, honors program, summer session, adult/continuing education programs, internships **Contact** Undergraduate Admissions Office, The Pennsylvania State University Harrisburg Campus of the Capital College, 777 West Harrisburg Pike, Middletown, PA 17057-4898. Telephone: 814-865-5471. Fax: 717-948-6325. E-mail: admissions@psu.edu. Web site: http://www.psu.edu/.

THE PENNSYLVANIA STATE UNIVERSITY LEHIGH VALLEY CAMPUS OF THE BERKS-LEHIGH VALLEY COLLEGE
FOGELSVILLE, PENNSYLVANIA

General State-related, 4-year, coed **Entrance** Moderately difficult **Setting** 42-acre small-town campus **Total enrollment** 697 **Student-faculty ratio** 16:1 **Application deadline** Rolling (freshmen), rolling (transfer) **Freshmen** 87% were admitted **Housing** No **Expenses** Tuition $7174 **Undergraduates** 38% women, 26% part-time, 20% 25 or older, 0% Native American, 4% Hispanic American, 1% African American, 9% Asian American/Pacific Islander **The most frequently chosen baccalaureate fields are** business/ marketing, psychology **Academic program** Advanced placement, honors program, summer session, adult/ continuing education programs, internships **Contact** Admissions Coordinator, The Pennsylvania State University Lehigh Valley Campus of the Berks-Lehigh Valley College, 8380 Mohr Lane, Fogelsville, PA 18051. Telephone: 610-821-6577. Fax: 610-285-5220. E-mail: admissions@psu.edu. Web site: http:// www.psu.edu/.

THE PENNSYLVANIA STATE UNIVERSITY SCHUYLKILL CAMPUS OF THE CAPITAL COLLEGE
SCHUYLKILL HAVEN, PENNSYLVANIA

General State-related, 4-year, coed **Entrance** Moderately difficult **Setting** 42-acre small-town campus

PENNSYLVANIA

The Pennsylvania State University Schuylkill Campus of the Capital College *(continued)*
Total enrollment 1,092 **Student-faculty ratio** 15:1 **Application deadline** Rolling (freshmen), rolling (transfer) **Freshmen** 88% were admitted **Housing** Yes **Expenses** Tuition $7154; Room & Board $5300 **Undergraduates** 57% women, 20% part-time, 18% 25 or older, 0.1% Native American, 3% Hispanic American, 13% African American, 4% Asian American/Pacific Islander **The most frequently chosen baccalaureate fields are** business/marketing, protective services/public administration, psychology **Academic program** Advanced placement, summer session, adult/continuing education programs, internships **Contact** Undergraduate Admissions Office, The Pennsylvania State University Schuylkill Campus of the Capital College, 200 University Dirve, Schuylkill Haven, PA 17972-2208. Telephone: 814-865-5471. Fax: 570-385-3672. E-mail: admissions@psu.edu. Web site: http://www.psu.edu/.

THE PENNSYLVANIA STATE UNIVERSITY UNIVERSITY PARK CAMPUS
STATE COLLEGE, PENNSYLVANIA

General State-related, university, coed **Entrance** Very difficult **Setting** 5,617-acre small-town campus **Total enrollment** 40,828 **Student-faculty ratio** 18:1 **Application deadline** Rolling (freshmen), rolling (transfer) **Freshmen** 57% were admitted **Housing** Yes **Expenses** Tuition $7396; Room & Board $5310 **Undergraduates** 47% women, 5% part-time, 3% 25 or older, 0.1% Native American, 3% Hispanic American, 4% African American, 5% Asian American/Pacific Islander **The most frequently chosen baccalaureate fields are** business/marketing, education, engineering/engineering technologies **Academic program** English as a second language, advanced placement, self-designed majors, honors program, summer session, adult/continuing education programs, internships **Contact** Undergraduate Admissions Office, The Pennsylvania State University University Park Campus, 201 Old Main, University Park, PA 16802. Telephone: 814-865-5471. Fax: 814-863-7590. E-mail: admissions@psu.edu. Web site: http://www.psu.edu/.

PHILADELPHIA BIBLICAL UNIVERSITY
LANGHORNE, PENNSYLVANIA

General Independent nondenominational, comprehensive, coed **Entrance** Moderately difficult **Setting** 105-acre suburban campus **Total enrollment** 1,444 **Student-faculty ratio** 15:1 **Application deadline** Rolling (freshmen), rolling (transfer) **Freshmen** 95% were admitted **Housing** Yes **Expenses** Tuition $10,355; Room & Board $5073 **Undergraduates** 55% women, 11% part-time, 20% 25 or older, 0.1% Native American, 1% Hispanic American, 10% African American, 2% Asian American/Pacific Islander **The most frequently chosen baccalaureate fields are** philosophy, education, philosophy, religion, and theology **Academic program** Advanced placement, accelerated degree program, honors program, summer session, adult/continuing education programs, internships

Contact Ms. Lisa Fuller, Director of Admissions, Philadelphia Biblical University, 200 Manor Avenue, Langhorne, PA 19047. Telephone: 215-702-4550 or toll-free 800-366-0049 (out-of-state). Fax: 215-752-4248. E-mail: admissions@pbu.edu. Web site: http://www.pbu.edu/.

PHILADELPHIA UNIVERSITY
PHILADELPHIA, PENNSYLVANIA

General Independent, comprehensive, coed **Entrance** Moderately difficult **Setting** 100-acre suburban campus **Total enrollment** 3,204 **Student-faculty ratio** 12:1 **Application deadline** Rolling (freshmen), rolling (transfer) **Freshmen** 75% were admitted **Housing** Yes **Expenses** Tuition $17,600; Room & Board $7122 **Undergraduates** 66% women, 17% part-time, 22% 25 or older, 0% Native American, 3% Hispanic American, 10% African American, 3% Asian American/Pacific Islander **The most frequently chosen baccalaureate fields are** business/marketing, architecture, visual/performing arts **Academic program** English as a second language, advanced placement, accelerated degree program, honors program, summer session, adult/continuing education programs, internships **Contact** Ms. Christine Greb, Acting Director of Admissions, Philadelphia University, School House Lane and Henry Avenue, Philadelphia, PA 19144-5497. Telephone: 215-951-2800. Fax: 215-951-2907. E-mail: admissions@philau.edu. Web site: http://www.philau.edu/.

POINT PARK COLLEGE
PITTSBURGH, PENNSYLVANIA

General Independent, comprehensive, coed **Entrance** Moderately difficult **Setting** urban campus **Total enrollment** 2,969 **Student-faculty ratio** 16:1 **Application deadline** Rolling (freshmen), rolling (transfer) **Freshmen** 77% were admitted **Housing** Yes **Expenses** Tuition $13,686; Room & Board $5948 **Undergraduates** 55% women, 35% part-time, 37% 25 or older, 0.3% Native American, 1% Hispanic American, 12% African American, 1% Asian American/Pacific Islander **The most frequently chosen baccalaureate fields are** business/marketing, engineering/engineering technologies, visual/performing arts **Academic program** English as a second language, advanced placement, accelerated degree program, self-designed majors, summer session, adult/continuing education programs, internships **Contact** Ms. Michelle Lawrence-Schmude, Dean of Enrollment, Point Park College, Point Park College, 201 Wood Street, Pittsburgh, PA 15222. Telephone: 412-392-3430 or toll-free 800-321-0129. Fax: 412-391-1980. E-mail: enroll@ppc.edu. Web site: http://www.ppc.edu/.

ROBERT MORRIS UNIVERSITY
MOON TOWNSHIP, PENNSYLVANIA

General Independent, comprehensive, coed **Entrance** Moderately difficult **Setting** 230-acre suburban campus **Total enrollment** 4,719 **Student-faculty ratio**

19:1 **Application deadline** Rolling (freshmen), rolling (transfer) **Freshmen** 71% were admitted **Housing** Yes **Expenses** Tuition $12,000; Room & Board $6580 **Undergraduates** 49% women, 30% part-time, 31% 25 or older, 0.2% Native American, 1% Hispanic American, 8% African American, 1% Asian American/Pacific Islander **The most frequently chosen baccalaureate fields are** business/marketing, communications/communication technologies, computer/information sciences **Academic program** Advanced placement, accelerated degree program, honors program, summer session, adult/continuing education programs, internships **Contact** Keith A. Paylo, Assistant Dean of Enrollment Services, Robert Morris University, Enrollment Services Department, 881 Narrows Run Road, Moon Township, PA 15108-1189. Telephone: 412-262-8402 or toll-free 800-762-0097. Fax: 412-299-2425. E-mail: enrollmentoffice@rmu.edu. Web site: http://www.rmu.edu/.

ROSEMONT COLLEGE
ROSEMONT, PENNSYLVANIA

General Independent Roman Catholic, comprehensive, women only **Entrance** Moderately difficult **Setting** 56-acre suburban campus **Total enrollment** 1,108 **Student-faculty ratio** 8:1 **Application deadline** Rolling (freshmen), rolling (transfer) **Freshmen** 81% were admitted **Housing** Yes **Expenses** Tuition $16,750; Room & Board $7310 **Undergraduates** 46% part-time, 55% 25 or older, 0% Native American, 3% Hispanic American, 19% African American, 4% Asian American/Pacific Islander **The most frequently chosen baccalaureate fields are** psychology, business/marketing, social sciences and history **Academic program** English as a second language, advanced placement, accelerated degree program, self-designed majors, honors program, summer session, adult/continuing education programs, internships **Contact** Ms. Rennie H. Andrews, Dean of Admissions, Rosemont College, 1400 Montgomery Avenue, Rosemont, PA 19010. Telephone: 610-527-0200 Ext. 2952 or toll-free 800-331-0708. Fax: 610-520-4399. E-mail: rosecoladmit@rosemont.edu. Web site: http://www.rosemont.edu/.

ST. CHARLES BORROMEO SEMINARY, OVERBROOK
WYNNEWOOD, PENNSYLVANIA

General Independent Roman Catholic, comprehensive, men only **Entrance** Moderately difficult **Setting** 77-acre suburban campus **Total enrollment** 482 **Student-faculty ratio** 8:1 **Application deadline** 7/15 (freshmen), 7/15 (transfer) **Freshmen** 100% were admitted **Housing** Yes **Expenses** Tuition $8800; Room & Board $6020 **Undergraduates** 73% part-time, 23% 25 or older, 0% Native American, 6% Hispanic American, 2% African American, 15% Asian American/Pacific Islander **The most frequently chosen baccalaureate fields are** philosophy, philosophy, religion, and theology **Academic program** English as a second language, advanced placement, accelerated degree program, summer session, adult/continuing education programs **Contact** Rev. Christopher J. Schreck, Vice Rector, St. Charles Borromeo Seminary, Overbrook, 100 East Wynnewood Road, Wynnewood, PA 19096. Telephone: 610-785-6271 Ext. 271. E-mail: vicerectorscs@adphila.org.

SAINT FRANCIS UNIVERSITY
LORETTO, PENNSYLVANIA

General Independent Roman Catholic, comprehensive, coed **Entrance** Moderately difficult **Setting** 600-acre rural campus **Total enrollment** 2,027 **Student-faculty ratio** 11:1 **Application deadline** Rolling (freshmen), rolling (transfer) **Freshmen** 86% were admitted **Housing** Yes **Expenses** Tuition $17,512; Room & Board $6974 **Undergraduates** 61% women, 16% part-time, 13% 25 or older, 0.3% Native American, 1% Hispanic American, 5% African American, 0.4% Asian American/Pacific Islander **Academic program** Advanced placement, accelerated degree program, self-designed majors, honors program, summer session, adult/continuing education programs, internships **Contact** Evan E. Lipp, Dean for Enrollment Management, Saint Francis University, PO Box 600, Loretto, PA 15940-0600. Telephone: 814-472-3000 or toll-free 800-342-5732. Fax: 814-472-3335. E-mail: admission@sfcpa.edu. Web site: http://www.sfcpa.edu/.

SAINT JOSEPH'S UNIVERSITY
PHILADELPHIA, PENNSYLVANIA

General Independent Roman Catholic (Jesuit), comprehensive, coed **Entrance** Very difficult **Setting** 60-acre suburban campus **Total enrollment** 7,313 **Student-faculty ratio** 13:1 **Application deadline** 3/1 (transfer) **Freshmen** 57% were admitted **Housing** Yes **Expenses** Tuition $21,270; Room & Board $8445 **Undergraduates** 54% women, 20% part-time, 0.1% Native American, 2% Hispanic American, 7% African American, 2% Asian American/Pacific Islander **The most frequently chosen baccalaureate fields are** business/marketing, education, social sciences and history **Academic program** English as a second language, advanced placement, accelerated degree program, self-designed majors, honors program, summer session, adult/continuing education programs, internships **Contact** Mr. David Conway, Assistant Vice President of Enrollment Management, Saint Joseph's University, 5600 City Avenue, Philadelphia, PA 19131-1395. Telephone: 610-660-1300 or toll-free 888-BEAHAWK (in-state). Fax: 610-660-1314. E-mail: admi@sju.edu. Web site: http://www.sju.edu/.

SAINT VINCENT COLLEGE
LATROBE, PENNSYLVANIA

General Independent Roman Catholic, 4-year, coed **Entrance** Moderately difficult **Setting** 200-acre suburban campus **Total enrollment** 1,222 **Student-faculty ratio** 14:1 **Application deadline** 5/1 (freshmen), 7/1 (transfer) **Freshmen** 84% were admitted **Housing** Yes **Expenses** Tuition $17,380; Room &

PENNSYLVANIA

Saint Vincent College *(continued)*
Board $5434 **Undergraduates** 49% women, 9% part-time, 8% 25 or older, 0.1% Native American, 1% Hispanic American, 3% African American, 1% Asian American/Pacific Islander **The most frequently chosen baccalaureate fields are** business/marketing, psychology, social sciences and history **Academic program** Advanced placement, accelerated degree program, honors program, summer session, adult/continuing education programs, internships **Contact** Mr. David A. Collins, Director of Admission, Saint Vincent College, 300 Fraser Purchase Road, Latrobe, PA 15650. Telephone: 724-532-5089 or toll-free 800-782-5549. Fax: 724-532-5069. E-mail: admission@stvincent.edu. Web site: http://www.stvincent.edu/.

SETON HILL UNIVERSITY
GREENSBURG, PENNSYLVANIA

General Independent Roman Catholic, comprehensive, coed, primarily women **Entrance** Moderately difficult **Setting** 200-acre small-town campus **Total enrollment** 1,370 **Student-faculty ratio** 13:1 **Application deadline** Rolling (freshmen), rolling (transfer) **Freshmen** 78% were admitted **Housing** Yes **Expenses** Tuition $16,425; Room & Board $5450 **Undergraduates** 82% women, 28% part-time, 13% 25 or older, 0.4% Native American, 2% Hispanic American, 7% African American, 1% Asian American/Pacific Islander **The most frequently chosen baccalaureate fields are** business/marketing, health professions and related sciences, psychology **Academic program** English as a second language, advanced placement, accelerated degree program, self-designed majors, honors program, summer session, adult/continuing education programs, internships **Contact** Ms. Mary Kay Cooper, Director of Admissions, Seton Hill University, Seton Hill Drive, Greensburg, PA 15601. Telephone: 724-838-4255 or toll-free 800-826-6234. Fax: 724-830-1294. E-mail: admit@setonhill.edu. Web site: http://www.setonhill.edu/.

▶ For more information, see page 474.

SHIPPENSBURG UNIVERSITY OF PENNSYLVANIA
SHIPPENSBURG, PENNSYLVANIA

General State-supported, comprehensive, coed **Entrance** Moderately difficult **Setting** 200-acre rural campus **Total enrollment** 7,193 **Student-faculty ratio** 19:1 **Application deadline** Rolling (freshmen), rolling (transfer) **Freshmen** 62% were admitted **Housing** Yes **Expenses** Tuition $5004; Room & Board $4864 **Undergraduates** 54% women, 4% part-time, 5% 25 or older, 0.3% Native American, 1% Hispanic American, 4% African American, 1% Asian American/Pacific Islander **The most frequently chosen baccalaureate fields are** business/marketing, education, protective services/public administration **Academic program** Advanced placement, accelerated degree program, honors program, summer session, internships **Contact** Mr. Joseph Cretella, Dean of Undergraduate and Graduate Admissions, Shippensburg University of Pennsylvania, 1871 Old Main Drive, Shippensburg, PA 17257-2299. Telephone: 717-477-1231 or toll-free 800-822-8028 (in-state). Fax: 717-477-4016. E-mail: admiss@ship.edu. Web site: http://www.ship.edu/.

SLIPPERY ROCK UNIVERSITY OF PENNSYLVANIA
SLIPPERY ROCK, PENNSYLVANIA

General State-supported, comprehensive, coed **Entrance** Moderately difficult **Setting** 611-acre rural campus **Total enrollment** 7,197 **Student-faculty ratio** 18:1 **Application deadline** 5/1 (freshmen), 5/1 (transfer) **Freshmen** 81% were admitted **Housing** Yes **Expenses** Tuition $4942; Room & Board $4210 **Undergraduates** 58% women, 9% part-time, 13% 25 or older, 0.2% Native American, 1% Hispanic American, 3% African American, 0.4% Asian American/Pacific Islander **The most frequently chosen baccalaureate fields are** education, business/marketing, parks and recreation **Academic program** Advanced placement, accelerated degree program, honors program, summer session, adult/continuing education programs, internships **Contact** Ms. Marian Hargrave, Director of Undergraduate Admissions, Slippery Rock University of Pennsylvania, Maltby Center, Slippery Rock, PA 16057. Telephone: 724-738-2111 or toll-free 800-SRU-9111. Fax: 724-738-2913. E-mail: apply@sru.edu. Web site: http://www.sru.edu/.

SUSQUEHANNA UNIVERSITY
SELINSGROVE, PENNSYLVANIA

General Independent, 4-year, coed, affiliated with Lutheran Church **Entrance** Moderately difficult **Setting** 210-acre small-town campus **Total enrollment** 1,949 **Student-faculty ratio** 14:1 **Application deadline** 3/1 (freshmen), 7/1 (transfer) **Freshmen** 76% were admitted **Housing** Yes **Expenses** Tuition $21,270; Room & Board $6000 **Undergraduates** 57% women, 6% part-time, 1% 25 or older, 0.3% Native American, 2% Hispanic American, 2% African American, 2% Asian American/Pacific Islander **The most frequently chosen baccalaureate fields are** business/marketing, communications/communication technologies, education **Academic program** Advanced placement, accelerated degree program, self-designed majors, honors program, summer session, adult/continuing education programs, internships **Contact** Mr. Chris Markle, Director of Admissions, Susquehanna University, 514 University Avenue, Selinsgrove, PA 17870-1040. Telephone: 570-372-4260 or toll-free 800-326-9672. Fax: 570-372-2722. E-mail: suadmiss@susqu.edu. Web site: http://www.susqu.edu/.

SWARTHMORE COLLEGE
SWARTHMORE, PENNSYLVANIA

General Independent, 4-year, coed **Entrance** Most difficult **Setting** 330-acre suburban campus **Total enrollment** 1,473 **Student-faculty ratio** 8:1 **Application deadline** 1/1 (freshmen), 4/1 (transfer) **Freshmen** 26% were admitted **Housing** Yes **Expenses**

Tuition $26,376; Room & Board $8162 **Undergraduates** 53% women, 1% part-time, 0% 25 or older, 1% Native American, 8% Hispanic American, 8% African American, 16% Asian American/Pacific Islander **The most frequently chosen baccalaureate fields are** biological/life sciences, English, social sciences and history **Academic program** Advanced placement, self-designed majors, honors program, internships **Contact** Office of Admissions, Swarthmore College, 500 College Avenue, Swarthmore, PA 19081. Telephone: 610-328-8300 or toll-free 800-667-3110. Fax: 610-328-8580. E-mail: admissions@swarthmore.edu. Web site: http://www.swarthmore.edu/.

TALMUDICAL YESHIVA OF PHILADELPHIA
PHILADELPHIA, PENNSYLVANIA

General Independent Jewish, 4-year, men only **Entrance** Moderately difficult **Setting** 3-acre urban campus **Total enrollment** 114 **Student-faculty ratio** 29:1 **Application deadline** 7/15 (freshmen), 7/15 (transfer) **Freshmen** 78% were admitted **Housing** Yes **Expenses** Tuition $5300; Room & Board $4600 **Undergraduates** 0% 25 or older, 0% Native American, 0% Hispanic American, 0% African American, 0% Asian American/Pacific Islander **The most frequently chosen baccalaureate field is** philosophy, religion, and theology **Academic program** Honors program, internships **Contact** Rabbi Shmuel Kamenetsky, Co-Dean, Talmudical Yeshiva of Philadelphia, 6063 Drexel Road, Philadelphia, PA 19131-1296. Telephone: 215-473-1212.

TEMPLE UNIVERSITY
PHILADELPHIA, PENNSYLVANIA

General State-related, university, coed **Entrance** Moderately difficult **Setting** 76-acre urban campus **Total enrollment** 29,872 **Student-faculty ratio** 14:1 **Application deadline** 4/1 (freshmen), 6/15 (transfer) **Freshmen** 65% were admitted **Housing** Yes **Expenses** Tuition $7324; Room & Board $6800 **Undergraduates** 58% women, 18% part-time, 20% 25 or older, 0.3% Native American, 3% Hispanic American, 26% African American, 8% Asian American/Pacific Islander **The most frequently chosen baccalaureate fields are** business/marketing, communications/communication technologies, education **Academic program** English as a second language, advanced placement, self-designed majors, honors program, summer session, adult/continuing education programs, internships **Contact** Dr. Timm Rinehart, Acting Director of Admissions, Temple University, 1801 North Broad Street, Philadelphia, PA 19122-6096. Telephone: 215-204-8556 or toll-free 888-340-2222. Fax: 215-204-5694. E-mail: tuadm@vm.temple.edu. Web site: http://www.temple.edu/.

THIEL COLLEGE
GREENVILLE, PENNSYLVANIA

General Independent, 4-year, coed, affiliated with Evangelical Lutheran Church in America **Entrance** Moderately difficult **Setting** 135-acre rural campus **Total enrollment** 1,189 **Student-faculty ratio** 14:1 **Application deadline** 8/15 (freshmen), rolling (transfer) **Freshmen** 77% were admitted **Housing** Yes **Expenses** Tuition $12,445; Room & Board $5974 **Undergraduates** 50% women, 9% part-time, 6% 25 or older, 0.3% Native American, 1% Hispanic American, 8% African American, 1% Asian American/Pacific Islander **The most frequently chosen baccalaureate fields are** business/marketing, health professions and related sciences, social sciences and history **Academic program** English as a second language, advanced placement, honors program, summer session, adult/continuing education programs, internships **Contact** Mr. Mark Thompson, Director of Admissions, Thiel College, 75 College Avenue, Greenville, PA 16125-2181. Telephone: 724-589-2176 or toll-free 800-24THIEL. Fax: 724-589-2013. E-mail: admission@thiel.edu. Web site: http://www.thiel.edu/.

THOMAS JEFFERSON UNIVERSITY
PHILADELPHIA, PENNSYLVANIA

General Independent, upper-level, coed **Entrance** Moderately difficult **Setting** 13-acre urban campus **Total enrollment** 2,252 **Student-faculty ratio** 11:1 **Application deadline** Rolling (transfer) **Housing** Yes **Expenses** Tuition $18,200; Room & Board $6463 **Undergraduates** 81% women, 54% part-time, 58% 25 or older, 1% Native American, 2% Hispanic American, 14% African American, 10% Asian American/Pacific Islander **Academic program** Advanced placement, adult/continuing education programs **Contact** Assistant Director of Admissions, Thomas Jefferson University, Edison Building, Suite 1610, 130 South Ninth Street, Philadelphia, PA 19107. Telephone: 215-503-8890 or toll-free 877-533-3247. Fax: 215-503-7241. E-mail: chp.admissions@mail.tju.edu. Web site: http://www.tju.edu/jchp.

UNIVERSITY OF PENNSYLVANIA
PHILADELPHIA, PENNSYLVANIA

General Independent, university, coed **Entrance** Most difficult **Setting** 260-acre urban campus **Total enrollment** 20,013 **Student-faculty ratio** 7:1 **Application deadline** 1/1 (freshmen), 4/1 (transfer) **Freshmen** 22% were admitted **Housing** Yes **Expenses** Tuition $26,630; Room & Board $7984 **Undergraduates** 48% women, 4% part-time, 1% 25 or older, 0.2% Native American, 5% Hispanic American, 6% African American, 20% Asian American/Pacific Islander **The most frequently chosen baccalaureate fields are** business/marketing, engineering/engineering technologies, social sciences and history **Academic program** English as a second language, advanced placement, accelerated degree program, self-designed majors, honors program, summer session, adult/continuing education programs, internships **Contact** Mr. Willis J. Stetson Jr., Dean of Admissions, University of Pennsylvania, 1 College Hall, Levy Park, Philadelphia, PA 19104. Telephone: 215-898-7507. Web site: http://www.upenn.edu/.

PENNSYLVANIA

UNIVERSITY OF PHOENIX–PHILADELPHIA CAMPUS
WAYNE, PENNSYLVANIA

General Proprietary, comprehensive, coed **Entrance** Noncompetitive **Total enrollment** 88,730 **Student-faculty ratio** 13:1 **Application deadline** Rolling (freshmen), rolling (transfer) **Housing** No **Expenses** Tuition $10,350 **Undergraduates** 43% women, 82% 25 or older **The most frequently chosen baccalaureate field is** business/marketing **Academic program** Advanced placement, accelerated degree program, adult/continuing education programs **Contact** Ms. Beth Barilla, Director of Admissions, University of Phoenix–Philadelphia Campus, 4615 East Elwood Street, Phoenix, AZ 85040-1958. Telephone: 480-927-0099 Ext. 1218 or toll-free 800-228-7240. Fax: 480-594-1758. E-mail: beth.barilla@apollogrp.edu. Web site: http://www.phoenix.edu/.

UNIVERSITY OF PHOENIX–PITTSBURGH CAMPUS
PITTSBURGH, PENNSYLVANIA

General Proprietary, comprehensive, coed **Entrance** Noncompetitive **Total enrollment** 88,730 **Student-faculty ratio** 10:1 **Application deadline** Rolling (freshmen), rolling (transfer) **Housing** No **Expenses** Tuition $10,350 **Undergraduates** 51% women **Academic program** Accelerated degree program, adult/continuing education programs **Contact** Ms. Beth Barilla, Director of Admissions, University of Phoenix–Pittsburgh Campus, 4615 East Elwood Street, Phoenix, AZ 85040-1958. Telephone: 480-927-0099 Ext. 1218 or toll-free 800-228-7240. Fax: 480-594-1758. E-mail: beth.barilla@apollogrp.edu. Web site: http://www.phoenix.edu/.

UNIVERSITY OF PITTSBURGH
PITTSBURGH, PENNSYLVANIA

General State-related, university, coed **Entrance** Moderately difficult **Setting** 132-acre urban campus **Total enrollment** 26,710 **Student-faculty ratio** 17:1 **Application deadline** Rolling (freshmen), rolling (transfer) **Freshmen** 60% were admitted **Housing** Yes **Expenses** Tuition $7482; Room & Board $6110 **Undergraduates** 53% women, 14% part-time, 14% 25 or older, 0.2% Native American, 1% Hispanic American, 9% African American, 4% Asian American/Pacific Islander **The most frequently chosen baccalaureate fields are** business/marketing, English, social sciences and history **Academic program** English as a second language, advanced placement, self-designed majors, honors program, summer session, adult/continuing education programs, internships **Contact** Dr. Betsy A. Porter, Director of Office of Admissions and Financial Aid, University of Pittsburgh, 4227 Fifth Avenue, First Floor, Masonic Temple, Pittsburgh, PA 15213. Telephone: 412-624-7488. Fax: 412-648-8815. E-mail: oafa+@pitt.edu. Web site: http://www.pitt.edu/.

UNIVERSITY OF PITTSBURGH AT BRADFORD
BRADFORD, PENNSYLVANIA

General State-related, 4-year, coed **Entrance** Moderately difficult **Setting** 145-acre small-town campus **Total enrollment** 1,465 **Student-faculty ratio** 13:1 **Application deadline** Rolling (freshmen), rolling (transfer) **Freshmen** 82% were admitted **Housing** Yes **Expenses** Tuition $7386; Room & Board $5310 **Undergraduates** 61% women, 36% part-time, 27% 25 or older, 1% Native American, 1% Hispanic American, 2% African American, 1% Asian American/Pacific Islander **The most frequently chosen baccalaureate fields are** business/marketing, psychology, social sciences and history **Academic program** Advanced placement, accelerated degree program, summer session, adult/continuing education programs, internships **Contact** Janet Shade, Administrative Secretary, University of Pittsburgh at Bradford, 300 Campus Drive, Bradford, PA 16701. Telephone: 814-362-7555 or toll-free 800-872-1787. E-mail: shade@imap.pitt.edu. Web site: http://www.upb.pitt.edu/.

UNIVERSITY OF PITTSBURGH AT GREENSBURG
GREENSBURG, PENNSYLVANIA

General State-related, 4-year, coed **Entrance** Moderately difficult **Setting** 217-acre small-town campus **Total enrollment** 1,758 **Student-faculty ratio** 18:1 **Application deadline** 8/1 (freshmen), 8/1 (transfer) **Freshmen** 78% were admitted **Housing** Yes **Expenses** Tuition $7442; Room & Board $5930 **Undergraduates** 56% women, 13% part-time, 15% 25 or older, 1% Native American, 1% Hispanic American, 2% African American, 1% Asian American/Pacific Islander **The most frequently chosen baccalaureate fields are** business/marketing, psychology, social sciences and history **Academic program** Advanced placement, accelerated degree program, self-designed majors, summer session, adult/continuing education programs, internships **Contact** Mr. John R. Sparks, Director of Admissions and Financial Aid, University of Pittsburgh at Greensburg, 1150 Mount Pleasant Road, Greensburg, PA 15601-5860. Telephone: 724-836-9880. Fax: 724-836-7160. E-mail: upgadmit@pitt.edu. Web site: http://www.pitt.edu/~upg/.

UNIVERSITY OF PITTSBURGH AT JOHNSTOWN
JOHNSTOWN, PENNSYLVANIA

General State-related, 4-year, coed **Entrance** Moderately difficult **Setting** 650-acre suburban campus **Total enrollment** 3,096 **Student-faculty ratio** 19:1 **Application deadline** Rolling (freshmen), rolling (transfer) **Freshmen** 85% were admitted **Housing** Yes **Expenses** Tuition $7464; Room & Board $5510 **Undergraduates** 53% women, 11% part-time, 0.2% Native American, 0.5% Hispanic American, 1% African American, 1% Asian American/Pacific Islander **The most frequently chosen baccalaureate fields are** business/marketing, education, social sciences

PENNSYLVANIA

and history **Academic program** Advanced placement, accelerated degree program, self-designed majors, summer session, adult/continuing education programs, internships **Contact** Mr. James F. Gyure, Director of Admissions, University of Pittsburgh at Johnstown, 157 Blackington Hall, Johnstown, PA 15904-2990. Telephone: 814-269-7050 or toll-free 800-765-4875. Fax: 814-269-7044. Web site: http://info.pitt.edu/~upjweb/.

THE UNIVERSITY OF SCRANTON
SCRANTON, PENNSYLVANIA

General Independent Roman Catholic (Jesuit), comprehensive, coed **Entrance** Moderately difficult **Setting** 50-acre urban campus **Total enrollment** 4,658 **Student-faculty ratio** 13:1 **Application deadline** 3/1 (freshmen) **Freshmen** 88% were admitted **Housing** Yes **Expenses** Tuition $19,530; Room & Board $8434 **Undergraduates** 57% women, 9% part-time, 8% 25 or older, 0.2% Native American, 2% Hispanic American, 1% African American, 2% Asian American/Pacific Islander **The most frequently chosen baccalaureate fields are** business/marketing, education, health professions and related sciences **Academic program** Advanced placement, self-designed majors, honors program, summer session, adult/continuing education programs, internships **Contact** Mr. Joseph Roback, Director of Admissions, The University of Scranton, Scranton, PA 18510-4622. Telephone: 570-941-7540 or toll-free 888-SCRANTON. Fax: 570-941-4370. E-mail: admissions@uofs.edu. Web site: http://www.scranton.edu/.

THE UNIVERSITY OF THE ARTS
PHILADELPHIA, PENNSYLVANIA

General Independent, comprehensive, coed **Entrance** Moderately difficult **Setting** 18-acre urban campus **Total enrollment** 2,094 **Student-faculty ratio** 10:1 **Application deadline** Rolling (freshmen), rolling (transfer) **Freshmen** 51% were admitted **Housing** Yes **Expenses** Tuition $19,230; Room only $4800 **Undergraduates** 54% women, 3% part-time, 5% 25 or older, 0.2% Native American, 4% Hispanic American, 8% African American, 4% Asian American/Pacific Islander **The most frequently chosen baccalaureate fields are** interdisciplinary studies, communications/communication technologies, visual/performing arts **Academic program** English as a second language, advanced placement, adult/continuing education programs, internships **Contact** Barbara Elliott, Director of Admissions, The University of the Arts, 320 South Broad Street, Philadelphia, PA 19102-4944. Telephone: 215-717-6030 or toll-free 800-616-ARTS. Fax: 215-717-6045. E-mail: admissions@uarts.edu. Web site: http://www.uarts.edu/.

▶ For more information, see page 490.

UNIVERSITY OF THE SCIENCES IN PHILADELPHIA
PHILADELPHIA, PENNSYLVANIA

General Independent, university, coed **Entrance** Moderately difficult **Setting** 35-acre urban campus **Total enrollment** 2,400 **Student-faculty ratio** 15:1 **Application deadline** Rolling (freshmen), rolling (transfer) **Freshmen** 74% were admitted **Housing** Yes **Expenses** Tuition $18,062; Room & Board $7450 **Undergraduates** 69% women, 3% part-time, 7% 25 or older, 0.3% Native American, 3% Hispanic American, 7% African American, 29% Asian American/Pacific Islander **The most frequently chosen baccalaureate fields are** biological/life sciences, health professions and related sciences, physical sciences **Academic program** English as a second language, advanced placement, honors program, summer session, adult/continuing education programs, internships **Contact** Mr. Louis L. Hegyes, Director of Admission, University of the Sciences in Philadelphia, 600 South 43rd Street, Philadelphia, PA 19104-4495. Telephone: 215-596-8810 or toll-free 888-996-8747 (in-state). Fax: 215-596-8821. E-mail: admit@usip.edu. Web site: http://www.usip.edu/.

URSINUS COLLEGE
COLLEGEVILLE, PENNSYLVANIA

General Independent, 4-year, coed, affiliated with United Church of Christ **Entrance** Very difficult **Setting** 140-acre suburban campus **Total enrollment** 1,340 **Student-faculty ratio** 11:1 **Application deadline** 2/15 (freshmen), 8/1 (transfer) **Freshmen** 78% were admitted **Housing** Yes **Expenses** Tuition $24,850; Room & Board $6500 **Undergraduates** 57% women, 1% part-time, 1% 25 or older, 0.1% Native American, 2% Hispanic American, 7% African American, 3% Asian American/Pacific Islander **Academic program** English as a second language, advanced placement, self-designed majors, honors program, adult/continuing education programs, internships **Contact** Mr. Paul M. Cramer, Director of Admissions, Ursinus College, Box 1000, Collegeville, PA 19426. Telephone: 610-409-3200. Fax: 610-409-3662. E-mail: admissions@ursinus.edu. Web site: http://www.ursinus.edu/.

VALLEY FORGE CHRISTIAN COLLEGE
PHOENIXVILLE, PENNSYLVANIA

General Independent, 4-year, coed, affiliated with Assemblies of God **Entrance** Minimally difficult **Setting** 77-acre small-town campus **Total enrollment** 722 **Student-faculty ratio** 19:1 **Application deadline** 8/15 (freshmen), 8/15 (transfer) **Freshmen** 48% were admitted **Housing** Yes **Expenses** Tuition $8261; Room & Board $4400 **Undergraduates** 50% women, 12% part-time, 14% 25 or older, 0.3% Native American, 8% Hispanic American, 4% African American, 2% Asian American/Pacific Islander **The most frequently chosen baccalaureate fields are** education, philosophy **Academic program** English as a second language, advanced placement, summer session, adult/continuing education programs, internships **Contact** Rev. William Chenco, Director of Admissions, Valley Forge Christian College, 1401 Charlestown Road, Phoenixville, PA 19460. Telephone: 610-935-0450 Ext. 1430 or toll-free 800-432-8322. Fax: 610-935-9353. E-mail: admissions@vfcc.edu. Web site: http://www.vfcc.edu/.

PENNSYLVANIA

VILLANOVA UNIVERSITY
VILLANOVA, PENNSYLVANIA

General Independent Roman Catholic, comprehensive, coed **Entrance** Very difficult **Setting** 222-acre suburban campus **Total enrollment** 10,156 **Student-faculty ratio** 13:1 **Application deadline** 1/7 (freshmen), 7/15 (transfer) **Freshmen** 50% were admitted **Housing** Yes **Expenses** Tuition $23,727; Room & Board $8270 **Undergraduates** 51% women, 10% part-time, 4% 25 or older, 0.1% Native American, 5% Hispanic American, 3% African American, 4% Asian American/Pacific Islander **The most frequently chosen baccalaureate fields are** business/marketing, engineering/engineering technologies, social sciences and history **Academic program** English as a second language, advanced placement, accelerated degree program, honors program, summer session, adult/continuing education programs, internships **Contact** Mr. Michael M. Gaynor, Director of University Admission, Villanova University, 800 Lancaster Avenue, Villanova, PA 19085-1672. Telephone: 610-519-4000. Fax: 610-519-6450. E-mail: gotovu@villanova.edu. Web site: http://www.villanova.edu/.

WASHINGTON & JEFFERSON COLLEGE
WASHINGTON, PENNSYLVANIA

General Independent, 4-year, coed **Entrance** Moderately difficult **Setting** 40-acre small-town campus **Total enrollment** 1,240 **Student-faculty ratio** 12:1 **Application deadline** 3/1 (freshmen), rolling (transfer) **Freshmen** 85% were admitted **Housing** Yes **Expenses** Tuition $20,550; Room & Board $5745 **Undergraduates** 49% women, 5% part-time, 1% 25 or older, 0.2% Native American, 1% Hispanic American, 3% African American, 2% Asian American/Pacific Islander **The most frequently chosen baccalaureate fields are** business/marketing, psychology, social sciences and history **Academic program** Advanced placement, accelerated degree program, self-designed majors, honors program, summer session, internships **Contact** Mr. Alton E. Newell, Dean of Enrollment, Washington & Jefferson College, 60 South Lincoln Street, Washington, PA 15301-4601. Telephone: 724-223-6510 or toll-free 888-WANDJAY. Fax: 724-223-6534. E-mail: admission@washjeff.edu. Web site: http://www.washjeff.edu/.

WAYNESBURG COLLEGE
WAYNESBURG, PENNSYLVANIA

General Independent, comprehensive, coed, affiliated with Presbyterian Church (U.S.A.) **Entrance** Moderately difficult **Setting** 30-acre small-town campus **Total enrollment** 1,787 **Student-faculty ratio** 16:1 **Application deadline** Rolling (freshmen), rolling (transfer) **Freshmen** 80% were admitted **Housing** Yes **Expenses** Tuition $12,560; Room & Board $5050 **Undergraduates** 56% women, 10% part-time, 21% 25 or older, 0.1% Native American, 0.4% Hispanic American, 4% African American, 0% Asian American/Pacific Islander **The most frequently chosen baccalaureate fields are** business/marketing, health professions and related sciences, protective services/public administration **Academic program** English as a second language, advanced placement, accelerated degree program, honors program, adult/continuing education programs, internships **Contact** Ms. Robin L. King, Dean of Admissions, Waynesburg College, 51 West College Street, Waynesburg, PA 15070. Telephone: 724-852-3333 or toll-free 800-225-7393. Fax: 724-627-8124. E-mail: admissions@waynesburg.edu. Web site: http://www.waynesburg.edu/.

WEST CHESTER UNIVERSITY OF PENNSYLVANIA
WEST CHESTER, PENNSYLVANIA

General State-supported, comprehensive, coed **Entrance** Moderately difficult **Setting** 547-acre suburban campus **Total enrollment** 12,244 **Student-faculty ratio** 17:1 **Application deadline** Rolling (freshmen), rolling (transfer) **Freshmen** 48% were admitted **Housing** Yes **Expenses** Tuition $4924; Room & Board $4990 **Undergraduates** 60% women, 14% part-time, 13% 25 or older, 0.2% Native American, 2% Hispanic American, 8% African American, 2% Asian American/Pacific Islander **The most frequently chosen baccalaureate fields are** business/marketing, education, English **Academic program** English as a second language, advanced placement, self-designed majors, honors program, summer session, adult/continuing education programs, internships **Contact** Ms. Marsha Haug, Director of Admissions, West Chester University of Pennsylvania, Messikomer Hall, Rosedale Avenue, West Chester, PA 19383. Telephone: 610-436-3411 or toll-free 877-315-2165 (in-state). Fax: 610-436-2907. E-mail: ugadmiss@wcupa.edu. Web site: http://www.wcupa.edu/.

WESTMINSTER COLLEGE
NEW WILMINGTON, PENNSYLVANIA

General Independent, comprehensive, coed, affiliated with Presbyterian Church (U.S.A.) **Entrance** Moderately difficult **Setting** 300-acre small-town campus **Total enrollment** 1,676 **Student-faculty ratio** 13:1 **Application deadline** Rolling (freshmen), rolling (transfer) **Freshmen** 86% were admitted **Housing** Yes **Expenses** Tuition $17,750; Room & Board $5210 **Undergraduates** 61% women, 5% part-time, 1% 25 or older, 0% Native American, 1% Hispanic American, 1% African American, 1% Asian American/Pacific Islander **The most frequently chosen baccalaureate fields are** business/marketing, education, social sciences and history **Academic program** Advanced placement, accelerated degree program, self-designed majors, honors program, summer session, adult/continuing education programs, internships **Contact** Mr. Doug Swartz, Director of Admissions, Westminster College, 319 South Market Street, New Wilmington, PA 16172-0001. Telephone: 724-946-7100 or toll-free 800-942-8033 (in-state). Fax: 724-946-7171. E-mail: swartzdl@westminster.edu. Web site: http://www.westminster.edu/.

WIDENER UNIVERSITY
CHESTER, PENNSYLVANIA

General Independent, comprehensive, coed **Entrance** Moderately difficult **Setting** 110-acre suburban campus **Total enrollment** 5,484 **Student-faculty ratio** 12:1 **Application deadline** Rolling (freshmen), rolling (transfer) **Freshmen** 74% were admitted **Housing** Yes **Expenses** Tuition $19,300; Room & Board $7620 **Undergraduates** 44% women, 6% part-time, 7% 25 or older, 0.3% Native American, 1% Hispanic American, 9% African American, 3% Asian American/Pacific Islander **The most frequently chosen baccalaureate fields are** business/marketing, health professions and related sciences, protective services/public administration **Academic program** English as a second language, advanced placement, accelerated degree program, self-designed majors, honors program, summer session, adult/continuing education programs, internships **Contact** Michael Hendricks, Dean of Admissions, Widener University, One University Place, Chester, PA 19013. Telephone: 610-499-4126 or toll-free 888-WIDENER (in-state). Fax: 610-499-4676. E-mail: admissions.office@widener.edu. Web site: http://www.widener.edu/.

WILKES UNIVERSITY
WILKES-BARRE, PENNSYLVANIA

General Independent, comprehensive, coed **Entrance** Moderately difficult **Setting** 25-acre urban campus **Total enrollment** 3,697 **Student-faculty ratio** 13:1 **Application deadline** Rolling (freshmen), rolling (transfer) **Freshmen** 87% were admitted **Housing** Yes **Expenses** Tuition $18,020; Room & Board $7780 **Undergraduates** 50% women, 15% part-time, 13% 25 or older, 0.3% Native American, 1% Hispanic American, 2% African American, 2% Asian American/Pacific Islander **The most frequently chosen baccalaureate fields are** business/marketing, liberal arts/general studies, psychology **Academic program** Advanced placement, accelerated degree program, self-designed majors, honors program, summer session, adult/continuing education programs, internships **Contact** Michael Frantz, Dean, Enrollment, Wilkes University, PO Box 111, Wilkes-Barre, PA 18766. Telephone: 570-408-4400 or toll-free 800-945-5378 Ext. 4400. Fax: 570-408-4904. E-mail: admissions@wilkes.edu. Web site: http://www.wilkes.edu/.

WILSON COLLEGE
CHAMBERSBURG, PENNSYLVANIA

General Independent, 4-year, women only, affiliated with Presbyterian Church (U.S.A.) **Entrance** Moderately difficult **Setting** 262-acre small-town campus **Total enrollment** 710 **Student-faculty ratio** 10:1 **Application deadline** Rolling (freshmen), rolling (transfer) **Freshmen** 90% were admitted **Housing** Yes **Expenses** Tuition $14,675; Room & Board $6562 **Undergraduates** 51% part-time, 40% 25 or older **The most frequently chosen baccalaureate fields are** biological/life sciences, agriculture, business/marketing **Academic program** English as a second language, advanced placement, accelerated degree program, self-designed majors, summer session, adult/continuing education programs, internships **Contact** Deborah Arthur, Admissions Administrator, Wilson College, 1015 Philadelphia Avenue, Chambersburg, PA 17201. Telephone: 717-262-2002 or toll-free 800-421-8402. Fax: 717-264-1578. E-mail: admissions@wilson.edu. Web site: http://www.wilson.edu/.

YESHIVA BETH MOSHE
SCRANTON, PENNSYLVANIA

Contact Rabbi I. Bressler, Dean, Yeshiva Beth Moshe, 930 Hickory Street, PO Box 1141, Scranton, PA 18505-2124. Telephone: 717-346-1747.

YORK COLLEGE OF PENNSYLVANIA
YORK, PENNSYLVANIA

General Independent, comprehensive, coed **Entrance** Moderately difficult **Setting** 80-acre suburban campus **Total enrollment** 5,293 **Student-faculty ratio** 15:1 **Application deadline** Rolling (freshmen), rolling (transfer) **Freshmen** 71% were admitted **Housing** Yes **Expenses** Tuition $7422; Room & Board $5128 **Undergraduates** 60% women, 22% part-time, 20% 25 or older, 0.2% Native American, 1% Hispanic American, 1% African American, 1% Asian American/Pacific Islander **The most frequently chosen baccalaureate fields are** business/marketing, education, health professions and related sciences **Academic program** Advanced placement, accelerated degree program, self-designed majors, summer session, adult/continuing education programs, internships **Contact** Mrs. Nancy L. Spataro, Director of Admissions, York College of Pennsylvania, York, PA 17405-7199. Telephone: 717-849-1600 or toll-free 800-455-8018. Fax: 717-849-1607. E-mail: admissions@ycp.edu. Web site: http://www.ycp.edu/.

RHODE ISLAND

BROWN UNIVERSITY
PROVIDENCE, RHODE ISLAND

General Independent, university, coed **Entrance** Most difficult **Setting** 140-acre urban campus **Total enrollment** 7,774 **Student-faculty ratio** 8:1 **Application deadline** 1/1 (freshmen), 4/1 (transfer) **Freshmen** 16% were admitted **Housing** Yes **Expenses** Tuition $27,172; Room & Board $7578 **Undergraduates** 54% women, 5% part-time, 1% 25 or older, 1% Native American, 7% Hispanic American, 6% African American, 14% Asian American/Pacific Islander **The most frequently chosen baccalaureate fields are** liberal arts/general studies, biological/life sciences, social sciences and history **Academic program** Advanced placement, accelerated degree program, self-designed majors, honors program, summer session, adult/continuing education programs, internships **Contact** Mr. Michael Goldberger, Director of

RHODE ISLAND

Brown University *(continued)*
Admission, Brown University, Box 1876, Providence, RI 02912. Telephone: 401-863-2378. Fax: 401-863-9300. E-mail: admission_undergraduate@brown.edu. Web site: http://www.brown.edu/.

BRYANT COLLEGE
SMITHFIELD, RHODE ISLAND

General Independent, comprehensive, coed **Entrance** Moderately difficult **Setting** 387-acre suburban campus **Total enrollment** 3,494 **Student-faculty ratio** 19:1 **Application deadline** 3/15 (freshmen), 8/15 (transfer) **Freshmen** 72% were admitted **Housing** Yes **Expenses** Tuition $18,480; Room & Board $7500 **Undergraduates** 39% women, 10% part-time, 7% 25 or older, 0.2% Native American, 3% Hispanic American, 3% African American, 2% Asian American/Pacific Islander **The most frequently chosen baccalaureate fields are** business/marketing, computer/information sciences, English **Academic program** English as a second language, advanced placement, honors program, summer session, adult/continuing education programs, internships **Contact** Ms. Cynthia Bonn, Director of Admission, Bryant College, 1150 Douglas Pike, Smithfield, RI 02917. Telephone: 401-232-6100 or toll-free 800-622-7001. Fax: 401-232-6741. E-mail: admissions@bryant.edu. Web site: http://www.bryant.edu/.

JOHNSON & WALES UNIVERSITY
PROVIDENCE, RHODE ISLAND

General Independent, comprehensive, coed **Entrance** Minimally difficult **Setting** 47-acre urban campus **Total enrollment** 9,261 **Student-faculty ratio** 30:1 **Application deadline** Rolling (freshmen), rolling (transfer) **Freshmen** 82% were admitted **Housing** Yes **Expenses** Tuition $14,340; Room & Board $6150 **Undergraduates** 48% women, 13% part-time, 11% 25 or older, 0.2% Native American, 6% Hispanic American, 12% African American, 3% Asian American/Pacific Islander **Academic program** English as a second language, advanced placement, accelerated degree program, honors program, summer session, adult/continuing education programs, internships **Contact** Ms. Maureen Dumas, Dean of Admissions, Johnson & Wales University, 8 Abbott Park Place, Providence, RI 02903-3703. Telephone: 401-598-2310 or toll-free 800-342-5598 (out-of-state). Fax: 401-598-2948. E-mail: admissions@jwu.edu. Web site: http://www.jwu.edu/.

PROVIDENCE COLLEGE
PROVIDENCE, RHODE ISLAND

General Independent Roman Catholic, comprehensive, coed **Entrance** Very difficult **Setting** 105-acre suburban campus **Total enrollment** 5,308 **Student-faculty ratio** 13:1 **Application deadline** 1/15 (freshmen), 4/15 (transfer) **Freshmen** 57% were admitted **Housing** Yes **Expenses** Tuition $19,695; Room & Board $7925 **Undergraduates** 57% women, 13% part-time, 10% 25 or older, 0.05% Native American, 4% Hispanic American, 2% African American, 1% Asian American/Pacific Islander **The most frequently chosen baccalaureate fields are** business/marketing, education, social sciences and history **Academic program** Advanced placement, self-designed majors, honors program, summer session, adult/continuing education programs, internships **Contact** Mr. Christopher Lydon, Dean of Enrollment Management, Providence College, River Avenue and Eaton Street, Providence, RI 02918. Telephone: 401-865-2535 or toll-free 800-721-6444. Fax: 401-865-2826. E-mail: pcadmiss@providence.edu. Web site: http://www.providence.edu/.

RHODE ISLAND COLLEGE
PROVIDENCE, RHODE ISLAND

General State-supported, comprehensive, coed **Entrance** Moderately difficult **Setting** 170-acre suburban campus **Total enrollment** 8,513 **Student-faculty ratio** 14:1 **Application deadline** 5/1 (freshmen), 6/1 (transfer) **Freshmen** 69% were admitted **Housing** Yes **Expenses** Tuition $3521; Room & Board $5760 **Undergraduates** 68% women, 36% part-time, 30% 25 or older, 0.3% Native American, 4% Hispanic American, 4% African American, 3% Asian American/Pacific Islander **The most frequently chosen baccalaureate fields are** education, health professions and related sciences, psychology **Academic program** Advanced placement, self-designed majors, honors program, summer session, adult/continuing education programs, internships **Contact** Dr. Holly Shadoian, Director of Admissions, Rhode Island College, 600 Mount Pleasant Avenue, Providence, RI 02908-1924. Telephone: 401-456-8234 or toll-free 800-669-5760 (out-of-state). Fax: 401-456-8817. E-mail: admissions@ric.edu. Web site: http://www.ric.edu/.

RHODE ISLAND SCHOOL OF DESIGN
PROVIDENCE, RHODE ISLAND

General Independent, comprehensive, coed **Entrance** Very difficult **Setting** 13-acre urban campus **Total enrollment** 2,119 **Student-faculty ratio** 11:1 **Application deadline** 2/15 (freshmen), 3/31 (transfer) **Freshmen** 41% were admitted **Housing** Yes **Expenses** Tuition $23,397; Room & Board $6830 **Undergraduates** 63% women, 14% 25 or older, 0.2% Native American, 5% Hispanic American, 3% African American, 11% Asian American/Pacific Islander **The most frequently chosen baccalaureate fields are** architecture, visual/performing arts **Academic program** English as a second language, advanced placement, adult/continuing education programs, internships **Contact** Mr. Edward Newhall, Director of Admissions, Rhode Island School of Design, 2 College Street, Providence, RI 02905-2791. Telephone: 401-454-6300 or toll-free 800-364-RISD. Fax: 401-454-6309. E-mail: admissions@risd.edu. Web site: http://www.risd.edu/.

ROGER WILLIAMS UNIVERSITY
BRISTOL, RHODE ISLAND

General Independent, comprehensive, coed **Entrance** Moderately difficult **Setting** 140-acre small-town campus **Total enrollment** 4,663 **Student-faculty ratio** 17:1 **Application deadline** Rolling (freshmen), rolling (transfer) **Freshmen** 90% were admitted **Housing** Yes **Expenses** Tuition $20,075; Room & Board $8935 **Undergraduates** 51% women, 24% part-time, 2% 25 or older, 0.4% Native American, 2% Hispanic American, 2% African American, 1% Asian American/Pacific Islander **The most frequently chosen baccalaureate fields are** (pre)law, business/marketing, engineering/engineering technologies **Academic program** English as a second language, advanced placement, self-designed majors, honors program, summer session, adult/continuing education programs, internships **Contact** Ms. Julie H. Cairns, Director of Freshman Admission, Roger Williams University, 1 Old Ferry Road, Bristol, RI 02809. Telephone: 401-254-3500 or toll-free 800-458-7144 (out-of-state). Fax: 401-254-3557. E-mail: admit@alpha.rwu.edu. Web site: http://www.rwu.edu/.

SALVE REGINA UNIVERSITY
NEWPORT, RHODE ISLAND

General Independent Roman Catholic, comprehensive, coed **Entrance** Moderately difficult **Setting** 65-acre suburban campus **Total enrollment** 2,467 **Student-faculty ratio** 12:1 **Application deadline** 3/1 (freshmen), rolling (transfer) **Freshmen** 65% were admitted **Housing** Yes **Expenses** Tuition $18,360; Room & Board $8100 **Undergraduates** 68% women, 6% part-time, 6% 25 or older, 0.4% Native American, 2% Hispanic American, 1% African American, 1% Asian American/Pacific Islander **The most frequently chosen baccalaureate fields are** business/marketing, education, protective services/public administration **Academic program** English as a second language, advanced placement, accelerated degree program, honors program, summer session, adult/continuing education programs, internships **Contact** Colleen Emerson, Director of Admissions, Salve Regina University, 100 Ochre Point Avenue, Newport, RI 02840-4192. Telephone: 401-341-2109 or toll-free 888-GO SALVE. Fax: 401-848-2823. E-mail: sruadmis@salve.edu. Web site: http://www.salve.edu/.

UNIVERSITY OF RHODE ISLAND
KINGSTON, RHODE ISLAND

General State-supported, university, coed **Entrance** Moderately difficult **Setting** 1,200-acre small-town campus **Total enrollment** 14,264 **Student-faculty ratio** 18:1 **Application deadline** 3/1 (freshmen), 5/1 (transfer) **Freshmen** 67% were admitted **Housing** Yes **Expenses** Tuition $5386; Room & Board $7028 **Undergraduates** 56% women, 17% part-time, 15% 25 or older, 0.4% Native American, 4% Hispanic American, 4% African American, 3% Asian American/Pacific Islander **The most frequently chosen baccalaureate fields are** business/marketing, communications/communication technologies, health professions and related sciences **Academic program** Advanced placement, accelerated degree program, self-designed majors, honors program, summer session, adult/continuing education programs, internships **Contact** Ms. Catherine Zeiser, Assistant Dean of Admissions, University of Rhode Island, 8 Ranger Road, Suite 1, Kingston, RI 02881-2020. Telephone: 401-874-7100. Fax: 401-874-5523. E-mail: uriadmit@riacc.uri.edu. Web site: http://www.uri.edu.

SOUTH CAROLINA

ALLEN UNIVERSITY
COLUMBIA, SOUTH CAROLINA

General Independent African Methodist Episcopal, 4-year, coed **Entrance** Minimally difficult **Setting** suburban campus **Total enrollment** 466 **Student-faculty ratio** 10:1 **Application deadline** Rolling (freshmen) **Freshmen** 81% were admitted **Housing** Yes **Expenses** Tuition $4750; Room & Board $4210 **Undergraduates** 60% women, 2% 25 or older, 92% Native American, 0.2% Hispanic American, 1% Asian American/Pacific Islander **The most frequently chosen baccalaureate fields are** business/marketing, liberal arts/general studies, social sciences and history **Academic program** Honors program, summer session, adult/continuing education programs, internships **Contact** Admissions Office, Allen University, 1530 Harden Street, Columbia, SC 29204-1085. Telephone: 803-254-4165. Fax: 803-376-5731. E-mail: auniv@mindspring.com.

ANDERSON COLLEGE
ANDERSON, SOUTH CAROLINA

General Independent Baptist, 4-year, coed **Entrance** Moderately difficult **Setting** 44-acre suburban campus **Total enrollment** 1,450 **Student-faculty ratio** 14:1 **Application deadline** 6/30 (freshmen), 8/1 (transfer) **Freshmen** 70% were admitted **Housing** Yes **Expenses** Tuition $11,395; Room & Board $5040 **Undergraduates** 64% women, 22% part-time, 19% 25 or older, 0.4% Native American, 1% Hispanic American, 11% African American, 1% Asian American/Pacific Islander **The most frequently chosen baccalaureate fields are** business/marketing, education, visual/performing arts **Academic program** Advanced placement, honors program, summer session, adult/continuing education programs, internships **Contact** Ms. Pam Bryant, Director of Admissions, Anderson College, 316 Boulevard, Anderson, SC 29621. Telephone: 864-231-5607 or toll-free 800-542-3594. Fax: 864-231-3033. E-mail: admissions@ac.edu. Web site: http://www.ac.edu/.

BENEDICT COLLEGE
COLUMBIA, SOUTH CAROLINA

General Independent Baptist, 4-year, coed **Entrance** Noncompetitive **Setting** 20-acre urban campus **Total**

SOUTH CAROLINA

Benedict College *(continued)*
enrollment 2,936 **Student-faculty ratio** 19:1 **Application deadline** Rolling (freshmen), rolling (transfer) **Freshmen** 68% were admitted **Housing** Yes **Expenses** Tuition $9764; Room & Board $5050 **Undergraduates** 50% women, 4% part-time, 0.1% Native American, 0.3% Hispanic American, 99% African American, 0% Asian American/Pacific Islander **The most frequently chosen baccalaureate fields are** business/marketing, (pre)law, education **Academic program** Advanced placement, honors program, summer session, adult/continuing education programs, internships **Contact** Mr. Gary Knight, Interim Vice President, Institutional Effectiveness, Benedict College, PO Box 98, Columbia, SC 29204. Telephone: 803-253-5275 or toll-free 800-868-6598 (in-state). Fax: 803-253-5267. Web site: http://www.benedict.edu/.

CHARLESTON SOUTHERN UNIVERSITY
CHARLESTON, SOUTH CAROLINA

General Independent Baptist, comprehensive, coed **Entrance** Moderately difficult **Setting** 500-acre suburban campus **Total enrollment** 2,682 **Student-faculty ratio** 17:1 **Application deadline** Rolling (freshmen), rolling (transfer) **Freshmen** 77% were admitted **Housing** Yes **Expenses** Tuition $12,368; Room & Board $4754 **Undergraduates** 61% women, 20% part-time, 28% 25 or older, 0.1% Native American, 5% Hispanic American, 27% African American, 1% Asian American/Pacific Islander **The most frequently chosen baccalaureate fields are** biological/life sciences, business/marketing, education **Academic program** Advanced placement, accelerated degree program, summer session, internships **Contact** Ms. Cheryl Burton, Director of Enrollment Management, Charleston Southern University, PO Box 118087, Charleston, SC 29423-8087. Telephone: 843-863-7050 or toll-free 800-947-7474. E-mail: enroll@csuniv.edu. Web site: http://www.charlestonsouthern.edu/.

THE CITADEL, THE MILITARY COLLEGE OF SOUTH CAROLINA
CHARLESTON, SOUTH CAROLINA

General State-supported, comprehensive, coed, primarily men **Entrance** Moderately difficult **Setting** 130-acre urban campus **Total enrollment** 4,001 **Student-faculty ratio** 15:1 **Application deadline** Rolling (freshmen), rolling (transfer) **Freshmen** 83% were admitted **Housing** Yes **Expenses** Tuition $4601; Room & Board $4525 **Undergraduates** 6% women, 4% part-time, 5% 25 or older, 0.3% Native American, 5% Hispanic American, 8% African American, 3% Asian American/Pacific Islander **The most frequently chosen baccalaureate fields are** business/marketing, engineering/engineering technologies, social sciences and history **Academic program** English as a second language, advanced placement, honors program, summer session, adult/continuing education programs, internships **Contact** Lt. Col. John Powell, Acting Dean of Enrollment Management, The Citadel, The Military College of South Carolina, 171 Moultrie Street, Charleston, SC 29409. Telephone: 843-953-5230 or toll-free 800-868-1842. Fax: 843-953-7036. E-mail: admissions@citadel.edu. Web site: http://www.citadel.edu.

CLAFLIN UNIVERSITY
ORANGEBURG, SOUTH CAROLINA

General Independent United Methodist, 4-year, coed **Entrance** Minimally difficult **Setting** 32-acre small-town campus **Total enrollment** 1,460 **Student-faculty ratio** 14:1 **Application deadline** Rolling (freshmen), rolling (transfer) **Freshmen** 45% were admitted **Housing** Yes **Expenses** Tuition $8290; Room & Board $4445 **Undergraduates** 65% women, 8% part-time, 15% 25 or older, 0% Native American, 0.2% Hispanic American, 94% African American, 0% Asian American/Pacific Islander **The most frequently chosen baccalaureate fields are** education, business/marketing, social sciences and history **Academic program** Advanced placement, honors program, summer session, adult/continuing education programs, internships **Contact** Mr. Michael Zeigler, Director of Admissions, Claflin University, 400 Magnolia Street, Orangeburg, SC 29115. Telephone: 803-535-5340 or toll-free 800-922-1276 (in-state). Fax: 803-535-5387. E-mail: glee@claf1.claflin.edu.

CLEMSON UNIVERSITY
CLEMSON, SOUTH CAROLINA

General State-supported, university, coed **Entrance** Moderately difficult **Setting** 1,400-acre small-town campus **Total enrollment** 17,101 **Student-faculty ratio** 16:1 **Application deadline** 5/1 (freshmen), 8/1 (transfer) **Freshmen** 51% were admitted **Housing** Yes **Expenses** Tuition $5090; Room & Board $4532 **Undergraduates** 45% women, 6% part-time, 5% 25 or older, 0.2% Native American, 1% Hispanic American, 8% African American, 2% Asian American/Pacific Islander **The most frequently chosen baccalaureate fields are** business/marketing, education, engineering/engineering technologies **Academic program** Advanced placement, accelerated degree program, honors program, summer session, internships **Contact** Ms. Audrey Bodell, Assistant Director of Undergraduate Admissions, Clemson University, 105 Sikes Hall, PO Box 345124, Clemson, SC 29634. Telephone: 864-656-5460. Fax: 864-656-2464. E-mail: cuadmissions@clemson.edu. Web site: http://www.clemson.edu/.

COASTAL CAROLINA UNIVERSITY
CONWAY, SOUTH CAROLINA

General State-supported, comprehensive, coed **Entrance** Moderately difficult **Setting** 244-acre suburban campus **Total enrollment** 4,965 **Student-faculty ratio** 19:1 **Application deadline** 8/15 (freshmen), 8/15 (transfer) **Freshmen** 74% were admitted **Housing** Yes **Expenses** Tuition $3770; Room & Board $5450 **Undergraduates** 56% women, 16% part-time, 17% 25 or older, 0.4% Native American, 1% Hispanic American, 8% African American, 1%

SOUTH CAROLINA

Asian American/Pacific Islander **The most frequently chosen baccalaureate fields are** business/marketing, biological/life sciences, education **Academic program** Advanced placement, accelerated degree program, self-designed majors, honors program, summer session, adult/continuing education programs, internships **Contact** Dr. Judy Vogt, Associate Vice President, Enrollment Services, Coastal Carolina University, PO Box 261954, Admissions and Financial Aid Offices, Conway, SC 29528. Telephone: 843-349-2037 or toll-free 800-277-7000. Fax: 843-349-2127. E-mail: admis@coastal.edu. Web site: http://www.coastal.edu/.

COKER COLLEGE
HARTSVILLE, SOUTH CAROLINA

General Independent, 4-year, coed **Entrance** Moderately difficult **Setting** 30-acre small-town campus **Total enrollment** 449 **Student-faculty ratio** 8:1 **Application deadline** Rolling (freshmen), rolling (transfer) **Freshmen** 90% were admitted **Housing** Yes **Expenses** Tuition $15,361; Room & Board $4820 **Undergraduates** 63% women, 3% part-time, 7% 25 or older, 0.4% Native American, 2% Hispanic American, 20% African American, 0.4% Asian American/Pacific Islander **The most frequently chosen baccalaureate fields are** business/marketing, education, visual/performing arts **Academic program** English as a second language, advanced placement, accelerated degree program, self-designed majors, honors program, summer session, adult/continuing education programs, internships **Contact** Mr. David Anthony, Director of Admissions and Student Financial Planning, Coker College, 300 East College Avenue, Hartsville, SC 29550. Telephone: 843-383-8050 or toll-free 800-950-1908. Fax: 843-383-8056. E-mail: admissions@coker.edu. Web site: http://www.coker.edu/.

COLLEGE OF CHARLESTON
CHARLESTON, SOUTH CAROLINA

General State-supported, comprehensive, coed **Entrance** Moderately difficult **Setting** 52-acre urban campus **Total enrollment** 11,428 **Student-faculty ratio** 15:1 **Application deadline** 6/1 (freshmen), 6/1 (transfer) **Freshmen** 65% were admitted **Housing** Yes **Expenses** Tuition $3780; Room & Board $4570 **Undergraduates** 63% women, 10% part-time, 11% 25 or older, 0.2% Native American, 1% Hispanic American, 9% African American, 1% Asian American/Pacific Islander **The most frequently chosen baccalaureate fields are** business/marketing, communications/communication technologies, education **Academic program** English as a second language, advanced placement, accelerated degree program, honors program, summer session, adult/continuing education programs, internships **Contact** Mr. Donald Burkard, Dean of Admissions, College of Charleston, 66 George Street, Charleston, SC 29424-0001. Telephone: 843-953-5670. Fax: 843-953-6322. E-mail: admissions@cofc.edu. Web site: http://www.cofc.edu/.

COLUMBIA COLLEGE
COLUMBIA, SOUTH CAROLINA

General Independent United Methodist, comprehensive, women only **Entrance** Moderately difficult **Setting** 33-acre suburban campus **Total enrollment** 1,471 **Student-faculty ratio** 14:1 **Application deadline** Rolling (freshmen), rolling (transfer) **Freshmen** 79% were admitted **Housing** Yes **Expenses** Tuition $15,870; Room & Board $5240 **Undergraduates** 15% part-time, 25% 25 or older, 0.2% Native American, 2% Hispanic American, 43% African American, 1% Asian American/Pacific Islander **The most frequently chosen baccalaureate fields are** business/marketing, education, protective services/public administration **Academic program** Advanced placement, accelerated degree program, self-designed majors, honors program, summer session, adult/continuing education programs, internships **Contact** Ms. Julie King, Director of Enrollment Management, Columbia College, 1301 Columbia College Drive, Columbia, SC 29203. Telephone: 803-786-3871 or toll-free 800-277-1301. Fax: 803-786-3674. E-mail: admissions@colacoll.edu. Web site: http://www.columbiacollegesc.edu/.

COLUMBIA INTERNATIONAL UNIVERSITY
COLUMBIA, SOUTH CAROLINA

General Independent nondenominational, comprehensive, coed **Entrance** Minimally difficult **Setting** 450-acre suburban campus **Total enrollment** 1,025 **Student-faculty ratio** 19:1 **Application deadline** Rolling (freshmen), rolling (transfer) **Freshmen** 59% were admitted **Housing** Yes **Expenses** Tuition $9140; Room & Board $4520 **Undergraduates** 54% women, 14% part-time, 19% 25 or older, 0.2% Native American, 1% Hispanic American, 5% African American, 1% Asian American/Pacific Islander **The most frequently chosen baccalaureate fields are** philosophy, philosophy, religion, and theology **Academic program** Advanced placement, accelerated degree program, summer session, internships **Contact** Miss Kandi A. Mulligan, Director of College Admissions, Columbia International University, P.O. Box 3122, Columbia, SC 29230-3122. Telephone: 803-754-4100 Ext. 3024 or toll-free 800-777-2227 Ext. 3024. Fax: 803-786-4041. E-mail: yesciu@ciu.edu. Web site: http://www.ciu.edu/.

CONVERSE COLLEGE
SPARTANBURG, SOUTH CAROLINA

General Independent, comprehensive, women only **Entrance** Moderately difficult **Setting** 70-acre urban campus **Total enrollment** 1,527 **Student-faculty ratio** 13:1 **Application deadline** 3/1 (freshmen), 7/1 (transfer) **Freshmen** 79% were admitted **Housing** Yes **Expenses** Tuition $16,850; Room & Board $5140 **Undergraduates** 10% part-time, 12% 25 or older, 0% Native American, 1% Hispanic American, 9% African American, 2% Asian American/Pacific Islander **The most frequently chosen baccalaureate fields are** education, business/marketing, visual/performing arts **Academic program** English as a second lan-

SOUTH CAROLINA

Converse College *(continued)*
guage, advanced placement, accelerated degree program, honors program, summer session, adult/continuing education programs, internships **Contact** Ms. Wanda McDowell, Director of Admissions, Converse College, 580 East Main Street, Spartanburg, SC 29302-0006. Telephone: 864-596-9040 Ext. 9746 or toll-free 800-766-1125. Fax: 864-596-9158. E-mail: admissions@converse.edu. Web site: http://www.converse.edu/.

ERSKINE COLLEGE
DUE WEST, SOUTH CAROLINA

General Independent, 4-year, coed, affiliated with Associate Reformed Presbyterian Church **Entrance** Moderately difficult **Setting** 85-acre rural campus **Total enrollment** 948 **Student-faculty ratio** 14:1 **Application deadline** Rolling (freshmen), rolling (transfer) **Freshmen** 72% were admitted **Housing** Yes **Expenses** Tuition $16,153; Room & Board $5246 **Undergraduates** 60% women, 3% part-time, 1% 25 or older, 0.2% Native American, 1% Hispanic American, 5% African American, 0.2% Asian American/Pacific Islander **The most frequently chosen baccalaureate fields are** business/marketing, biological/life sciences, education **Academic program** Advanced placement, accelerated degree program, summer session, internships **Contact** Mr. Jeff Craft, Director of Admissions, Erskine College, PO Box 176, Due West, SC 29639. Telephone: 864-379-8830 or toll-free 800-241-8721. Fax: 864-379-8759. E-mail: admissions@erskine.edu. Web site: http://www.erskine.edu/.

FRANCIS MARION UNIVERSITY
FLORENCE, SOUTH CAROLINA

General State-supported, comprehensive, coed **Entrance** Moderately difficult **Setting** 309-acre rural campus **Total enrollment** 3,513 **Student-faculty ratio** 14:1 **Application deadline** Rolling (freshmen), rolling (transfer) **Freshmen** 77% were admitted **Housing** Yes **Expenses** Tuition $3790; Room & Board $3892 **Undergraduates** 61% women, 8% part-time, 13% 25 or older, 1% Native American, 0.5% Hispanic American, 31% African American, 1% Asian American/Pacific Islander **The most frequently chosen baccalaureate fields are** biological/life sciences, business/marketing, social sciences and history **Academic program** Advanced placement, accelerated degree program, honors program, summer session, adult/continuing education programs, internships **Contact** Ms. Drucilla P. Russell, Director of Admissions, Francis Marion University, Francis Mellon University, PO Box 100547, Florence, SC 29501-0547. Telephone: 843-661-1231 or toll-free 800-368-7551. Fax: 843-661-4635. E-mail: admission@fmarion.edu. Web site: http://www.fmarion.edu/.

FURMAN UNIVERSITY
GREENVILLE, SOUTH CAROLINA

General Independent, comprehensive, coed **Entrance** Very difficult **Setting** 750-acre suburban campus **Total enrollment** 3,183 **Student-faculty ratio** 12:1 **Application deadline** 1/15 (freshmen), 6/1 (transfer) **Freshmen** 61% were admitted **Housing** Yes **Expenses** Tuition $20,076; Room & Board $5416 **Undergraduates** 56% women, 5% part-time, 4% 25 or older, 0.1% Native American, 1% Hispanic American, 6% African American, 1% Asian American/Pacific Islander **The most frequently chosen baccalaureate fields are** interdisciplinary studies, business/marketing, trade and industry **Academic program** Advanced placement, accelerated degree program, self-designed majors, summer session, adult/continuing education programs, internships **Contact** Mr. David R. O'Cain, Director of Admissions, Furman University, 3300 Poinsett Highway, Greenville, SC 29613. Telephone: 864-294-2034. Fax: 864-294-3127. E-mail: admissions@furman.edu. Web site: http://www.furman.edu/.

JOHNSON & WALES UNIVERSITY
CHARLESTON, SOUTH CAROLINA

Contact Ms. Deborah Langenstein, Director of Admissions, Johnson & Wales University, 701 East Bay Street, Charleston, SC 29403. Telephone: 843-727-3000 or toll-free 800-868-1522 (out-of-state). Fax: 843-763-0318. E-mail: admissions@jwu.edu. Web site: http://www.jwu.edu/.

LANDER UNIVERSITY
GREENWOOD, SOUTH CAROLINA

General State-supported, comprehensive, coed **Entrance** Moderately difficult **Setting** 100-acre small-town campus **Total enrollment** 2,710 **Student-faculty ratio** 16:1 **Application deadline** Rolling (freshmen), rolling (transfer) **Freshmen** 87% were admitted **Housing** Yes **Expenses** Tuition $4242; Room & Board $4376 **Undergraduates** 62% women, 12% part-time, 0.1% Native American, 1% Hispanic American, 19% African American, 0.4% Asian American/Pacific Islander **The most frequently chosen baccalaureate fields are** business/marketing, education, social sciences and history **Academic program** Advanced placement, accelerated degree program, self-designed majors, honors program, summer session, adult/continuing education programs, internships **Contact** Mr. Jeffrey A. Constant, Assistant Director of Admissions, Lander University, 320 Stanley Avenue, Greenwood, SC 29649. Telephone: 864-388-8307 or toll-free 888-452-6337. Fax: 864-388-8125. E-mail: wmarceng@lander.edu. Web site: http://www.lander.edu/.

LIMESTONE COLLEGE
GAFFNEY, SOUTH CAROLINA

General Independent, 4-year, coed **Entrance** Minimally difficult **Setting** 115-acre small-town campus **Total enrollment** 516 **Student-faculty ratio** 9:1 **Application deadline** Rolling (freshmen), rolling (transfer) **Freshmen** 66% were admitted **Housing** Yes **Expenses** Tuition $10,800; Room & Board $5100 **Undergraduates** 50% women, 2% part-time, 11% 25 or older, 0.2% Native American, 1% Hispanic

SOUTH CAROLINA

American, 17% African American, 1% Asian American/Pacific Islander **The most frequently chosen baccalaureate fields are** business/marketing, computer/information sciences, social sciences and history **Academic program** English as a second language, advanced placement, accelerated degree program, self-designed majors, honors program, summer session, adult/continuing education programs, internships **Contact** Ms. Debbie Borders, Office Manager of Admissions, Limestone College, Limestone College, 1115 College Drive, Gaffney, SC 29340-3799. Telephone: 864-489-7151 Ext. 554 or toll-free 800-795-7151 Ext. 554 (in-state); 800-795-7151 Ext. 553 (out-of-state). Fax: 864-487-8706. E-mail: cphenicie@limestone.edu. Web site: http://www.limestone.edu.

MEDICAL UNIVERSITY OF SOUTH CAROLINA
CHARLESTON, SOUTH CAROLINA

General State-supported, upper-level, coed **Entrance** Very difficult **Setting** 61-acre urban campus **Total enrollment** 2,297 **Student-faculty ratio** 12:1 **Application deadline** Rolling (transfer) **First-Year Students** 42% were admitted **Housing** No **Expenses** Tuition $5824 **Undergraduates** 83% women, 27% part-time, 59% 25 or older, 1% Native American, 1% Hispanic American, 15% African American, 2% Asian American/Pacific Islander **The most frequently chosen baccalaureate field is** health professions and related sciences **Academic program** Advanced placement, internships **Contact** Mr. James F. Menzel, Executive Director, Office of Enrollment Services, Medical University of South Carolina, 171 Ashley Avenue, Charleston, SC 29425-0002. Telephone: 843-792-5396. Fax: 843-792-3764. E-mail: smithman@musc.edu. Web site: http://www.musc.edu/.

MORRIS COLLEGE
SUMTER, SOUTH CAROLINA

General Independent, 4-year, coed, affiliated with Baptist Educational and Missionary Convention of South Carolina **Entrance** Minimally difficult **Setting** 34-acre small-town campus **Total enrollment** 986 **Student-faculty ratio** 16:1 **Application deadline** Rolling (freshmen), rolling (transfer) **Freshmen** 94% were admitted **Housing** Yes **Expenses** Tuition $6685; Room & Board $3310 **Undergraduates** 64% women, 3% part-time, 14% 25 or older, 0.1% Hispanic American, 99% African American **The most frequently chosen baccalaureate fields are** business/marketing, protective services/public administration, social sciences and history **Academic program** Accelerated degree program, honors program, summer session, adult/continuing education programs, internships **Contact** Ms. Deborah Calhoun, Director of Admissions and Records, Morris College, 100 West College Street, Sumter, SC 29150-3599. Telephone: 803-934-3225 or toll-free 888-853-1345. Fax: 803-773-3687. Web site: http://www.morris.edu/.

NEWBERRY COLLEGE
NEWBERRY, SOUTH CAROLINA

General Independent Lutheran, 4-year, coed **Entrance** Moderately difficult **Setting** 60-acre small-town campus **Total enrollment** 726 **Student-faculty ratio** 12:1 **Application deadline** Rolling (freshmen), rolling (transfer) **Freshmen** 76% were admitted **Housing** Yes **Expenses** Tuition $15,400; Room & Board $4500 **Undergraduates** 46% women, 7% part-time, 5% 25 or older, 0.1% Native American, 1% Hispanic American, 21% African American, 0.3% Asian American/Pacific Islander **The most frequently chosen baccalaureate fields are** business/marketing, education, social sciences and history **Academic program** Advanced placement, self-designed majors, honors program, summer session, adult/continuing education programs, internships **Contact** Mr. Jonathan Reece, Director of Admissions, Newberry College, 2100 College Street, Smeltzer Hall, Newberry, SC 29108. Telephone: 803-321-5127 or toll-free 800-845-4955 Ext. 5127. Fax: 803-321-5138. E-mail: admissions@newberry.edu. Web site: http://www.newberry.edu/.

NORTH GREENVILLE COLLEGE
TIGERVILLE, SOUTH CAROLINA

General Independent Southern Baptist, 4-year, coed **Entrance** Minimally difficult **Setting** 500-acre rural campus **Total enrollment** 1,380 **Student-faculty ratio** 12:1 **Application deadline** 8/21 (freshmen), 8/21 (transfer) **Freshmen** 93% were admitted **Housing** Yes **Expenses** Tuition $8450; Room & Board $4790 **Undergraduates** 48% women, 9% part-time, 13% 25 or older, 0.1% Native American, 1% Hispanic American, 10% African American, 1% Asian American/Pacific Islander **The most frequently chosen baccalaureate fields are** interdisciplinary studies, philosophy, philosophy, religion, and theology **Academic program** English as a second language, advanced placement, accelerated degree program, self-designed majors, honors program, summer session, internships **Contact** Mr. Buddy Freeman, Executive Director of Admissions, North Greenville College, Admissions, PO Box 1872, Tigerville, SC 29688. Telephone: 864-977-7052 or toll-free 800-468-6642 Ext. 7001. Fax: 864-977-7177. E-mail: bfreeman@ngc.edu. Web site: http://www.ngc.edu/.

PRESBYTERIAN COLLEGE
CLINTON, SOUTH CAROLINA

General Independent Presbyterian, 4-year, coed **Entrance** Very difficult **Setting** 215-acre small-town campus **Total enrollment** 1,202 **Student-faculty ratio** 13:1 **Application deadline** 4/1 (freshmen), 7/1 (transfer) **Freshmen** 78% were admitted **Housing** Yes **Expenses** Tuition $18,200; Room & Board $5156 **Undergraduates** 56% women, 4% part-time, 1% 25 or older, 0% Native American, 1% Hispanic American, 5% African American, 1% Asian American/Pacific Islander **The most frequently chosen baccalaureate fields are** biological/life sciences, business/marketing, psychology **Academic program** Advanced

SOUTH CAROLINA

Presbyterian College *(continued)*
placement, honors program, summer session, internships **Contact** Mr. Richard Dana Paul, Vice President of Enrollment and Dean of Admissions, Presbyterian College, South Broad Street, Clinton, SC 29325. Telephone: 864-833-8229 or toll-free 800-476-7272. Fax: 864-833-8481. E-mail: rdpaul@admin.presby.edu. Web site: http://www.presby.edu/.

SOUTH CAROLINA STATE UNIVERSITY
ORANGEBURG, SOUTH CAROLINA

General State-supported, comprehensive, coed **Entrance** Minimally difficult **Setting** 160-acre small-town campus **Total enrollment** 4,467 **Student-faculty ratio** 17:1 **Application deadline** 7/31 (freshmen), 7/31 (transfer) **Freshmen** 53% were admitted **Housing** Yes **Expenses** Tuition $4096; Room & Board $1792 **Undergraduates** 58% women, 10% part-time, 12% 25 or older, 0.1% Native American, 0.2% Hispanic American, 97% African American, 0.2% Asian American/Pacific Islander **The most frequently chosen baccalaureate fields are** business/marketing, education, home economics/vocational home economics **Academic program** Advanced placement, honors program, summer session, adult/continuing education programs, internships **Contact** Ms. Lillian Adderson, Director of Admissions, South Carolina State University, 300 College Street Northeast, Orangeburg, SC 29117-0001. Telephone: 803-536-8408 or toll-free 800-260-5956. Fax: 803-536-8990. E-mail: carolyn-free@scsu.scsu.edu. Web site: http://www.scsu.edu/.

SOUTHERN METHODIST COLLEGE
ORANGEBURG, SOUTH CAROLINA

General Independent religious, 4-year, coed **Entrance** Moderately difficult **Total enrollment** 92 **Housing** Yes **Expenses** Tuition $4500; Room & Board $4220 **Undergraduates** 60% women, 21% part-time, 0% Native American, 2% Hispanic American, 17% African American, 1% Asian American/Pacific Islander **The most frequently chosen baccalaureate field is** philosophy **Contact** Mr. John Hucks, Director of Admissions, Southern Methodist College, 541 Broughton Street, PO Box 1027, Orangeburg, SC 29116-1027. Telephone: 803-534-7826. Web site: http://www.southernmethodistcollege.org.

SOUTHERN WESLEYAN UNIVERSITY
CENTRAL, SOUTH CAROLINA

General Independent, comprehensive, coed, affiliated with Wesleyan Church **Entrance** Minimally difficult **Setting** 230-acre small-town campus **Total enrollment** 2,166 **Student-faculty ratio** 14:1 **Application deadline** 8/10 (freshmen), 8/10 (transfer) **Freshmen** 65% were admitted **Housing** Yes **Expenses** Tuition $12,800; Room & Board $4480 **Undergraduates** 63% women, 6% part-time, 76% 25 or older, 1% Native American, 1% Hispanic American, 26% African American, 0.3% Asian American/Pacific Islander **The most frequently chosen baccalaureate fields are** business/marketing, education, philosophy **Academic program** Advanced placement, accelerated degree program, honors program, summer session, adult/continuing education programs, internships **Contact** Mrs. Joy Bryant, Director of Admissions, Southern Wesleyan University, 907 Wesleyan Drive, PO Box 1020, Central, SC 29630-1020. Telephone: 864-644-5550 or toll-free 800-289-1292. Fax: 864-644-5972. E-mail: admissions@swu.edu. Web site: http://www.swu.edu/.

UNIVERSITY OF SOUTH CAROLINA
COLUMBIA, SOUTH CAROLINA

General State-supported, university, coed **Entrance** Moderately difficult **Setting** 315-acre urban campus **Total enrollment** 23,000 **Student-faculty ratio** 14:1 **Application deadline** 5/15 (freshmen), 5/15 (transfer) **Freshmen** 70% were admitted **Housing** Yes **Expenses** Tuition $4064; Room & Board $4684 **Undergraduates** 54% women, 16% part-time, 10% 25 or older, 0.3% Native American, 1% Hispanic American, 18% African American, 3% Asian American/Pacific Islander **The most frequently chosen baccalaureate fields are** business/marketing, psychology, social sciences and history **Academic program** English as a second language, advanced placement, accelerated degree program, self-designed majors, honors program, summer session, adult/continuing education programs, internships **Contact** Ms. Terry L. Davis, Director of Undergraduate Admissions, University of South Carolina, Columbia, SC 29208. Telephone: 803-777-7700 or toll-free 800-868-5872 (in-state). Fax: 803-777-0101. E-mail: admissions-ugrad@sc.edu. Web site: http://www.sc.edu/.

UNIVERSITY OF SOUTH CAROLINA AIKEN
AIKEN, SOUTH CAROLINA

General State-supported, comprehensive, coed **Entrance** Minimally difficult **Setting** 453-acre suburban campus **Total enrollment** 3,282 **Student-faculty ratio** 16:1 **Application deadline** 8/1 (freshmen), rolling (transfer) **Freshmen** 59% were admitted **Housing** Yes **Expenses** Tuition $3778; Room & Board $4050 **Undergraduates** 66% women, 31% part-time, 25% 25 or older, 0.2% Native American, 1% Hispanic American, 23% African American, 1% Asian American/Pacific Islander **The most frequently chosen baccalaureate fields are** business/marketing, education, health professions and related sciences **Academic program** English as a second language, advanced placement, accelerated degree program, self-designed majors, honors program, summer session, adult/continuing education programs, internships **Contact** Mr. Andrew Hendrix, Director of Admissions, University of South Carolina Aiken, 471 University Parkway, Aiken, SC 29801-6309. Telephone: 803-648-6851 Ext. 3366 or toll-free 888-WOW-USCA. Fax: 803-641-3727. E-mail: admit@sc.edu. Web site: http://www.usca.edu/.

UNIVERSITY OF SOUTH CAROLINA SPARTANBURG
SPARTANBURG, SOUTH CAROLINA

General State-supported, comprehensive, coed **Entrance** Moderately difficult **Setting** 298-acre urban campus **Total enrollment** 3,993 **Student-faculty ratio** 17:1 **Freshmen** 62% were admitted **Housing** Yes **Expenses** Tuition $4014; Room & Board $3360 **Undergraduates** 64% women, 25% part-time, 29% 25 or older, 0.2% Native American, 2% Hispanic American, 25% African American, 2% Asian American/Pacific Islander **The most frequently chosen baccalaureate fields are** business/marketing, education, health professions and related sciences **Academic program** Advanced placement, accelerated degree program, self-designed majors, summer session, adult/continuing education programs, internships **Contact** Ms. Donette Stewart, Director of Admissions, University of South Carolina Spartanburg, 800 University Way, Spartanburg, SC 29303. Telephone: 864-503-5280 or toll-free 800-277-8727. Fax: 864-503-5727. E-mail: dstawart@uscs.edu. Web site: http://www.uscs.edu/.

VOORHEES COLLEGE
DENMARK, SOUTH CAROLINA

General Independent Episcopal, 4-year, coed **Entrance** Minimally difficult **Setting** 350-acre rural campus **Total enrollment** 756 **Student-faculty ratio** 17:1 **Application deadline** Rolling (freshmen), rolling (transfer) **Freshmen** 80% were admitted **Housing** Yes **Expenses** Tuition $6460; Room & Board $3516 **Undergraduates** 10% 25 or older, 0% Native American, 1% Hispanic American, 98% African American, 0% Asian American/Pacific Islander **Academic program** Advanced placement, honors program, summer session, adult/continuing education programs, internships **Contact** Carolyn White, Dean of Enrollment Management, Voorhees College, Massachusetts Hall, PO Box 678, Denmark, SC 29042. Telephone: 800-446-6250 or toll-free 800-446-6250. Fax: 803-793-1117. E-mail: elfphi@voorhees.edu. Web site: http://www.voorhees.edu.

WINTHROP UNIVERSITY
ROCK HILL, SOUTH CAROLINA

General State-supported, comprehensive, coed **Entrance** Moderately difficult **Setting** 418-acre suburban campus **Total enrollment** 6,306 **Student-faculty ratio** 15:1 **Application deadline** 6/1 (freshmen), 7/1 (transfer) **Freshmen** 74% were admitted **Housing** Yes **Expenses** Tuition $4688; Room & Board $4418 **Undergraduates** 69% women, 13% part-time, 11% 25 or older, 0.4% Native American, 1% Hispanic American, 27% African American, 1% Asian American/Pacific Islander **The most frequently chosen baccalaureate fields are** business/marketing, education, visual/performing arts **Academic program** Advanced placement, honors program, summer session, adult/continuing education programs, internships **Contact** Ms. Deborah Barber, Director of Admissions, Winthrop University, Stewart House, Rock Hill, SC 29733. Telephone: 803-323-2191 or toll-free 800-763-0230. Fax: 803-323-2137. E-mail: admissions@winthrop.edu. Web site: http://www.winthrop.edu/.

WOFFORD COLLEGE
SPARTANBURG, SOUTH CAROLINA

General Independent, 4-year, coed, affiliated with United Methodist Church **Entrance** Very difficult **Setting** 140-acre urban campus **Total enrollment** 1,107 **Student-faculty ratio** 13:1 **Application deadline** 2/1 (freshmen), rolling (transfer) **Freshmen** 82% were admitted **Housing** Yes **Expenses** Tuition $18,515; Room & Board $5480 **Undergraduates** 48% women, 1% part-time, 0% 25 or older, 0.2% Native American, 1% Hispanic American, 9% African American, 2% Asian American/Pacific Islander **The most frequently chosen baccalaureate fields are** business/marketing, biological/life sciences, social sciences and history **Academic program** Advanced placement, accelerated degree program, self-designed majors, summer session, internships **Contact** Mr. Brand Stille, Director of Admissions, Wofford College, 429 North Church Street, Spartanburg, SC 29303-3663. Telephone: 864-597-4130. Fax: 864-597-4147. E-mail: admissions@wofford.edu. Web site: http://www.wofford.edu/.

SOUTH DAKOTA

AUGUSTANA COLLEGE
SIOUX FALLS, SOUTH DAKOTA

General Independent, comprehensive, coed, affiliated with Evangelical Lutheran Church in America **Entrance** Moderately difficult **Setting** 100-acre urban campus **Total enrollment** 1,807 **Student-faculty ratio** 12:1 **Application deadline** 8/1 (freshmen), rolling (transfer) **Freshmen** 85% were admitted **Housing** Yes **Expenses** Tuition $15,460; Room & Board $4478 **Undergraduates** 65% women, 7% part-time, 9% 25 or older, 0.3% Native American, 0.3% Hispanic American, 1% African American, 1% Asian American/Pacific Islander **The most frequently chosen baccalaureate fields are** business/marketing, education, health professions and related sciences **Academic program** Advanced placement, accelerated degree program, self-designed majors, honors program, summer session, adult/continuing education programs, internships **Contact** Robert Preloger, Vice President for Enrollment, Augustana College, 2001 South Summit Avenue, Sioux Falls, SD 57197. Telephone: 605-274-5516 Ext. 5504 or toll-free 800-727-2844 Ext. 5516 (in-state); 800-727-2844 (out-of-state). Fax: 605-274-5518. E-mail: info@inst.augie.edu. Web site: http://www.augie.edu/.

SOUTH DAKOTA

BLACK HILLS STATE UNIVERSITY
SPEARFISH, SOUTH DAKOTA

General State-supported, comprehensive, coed **Entrance** Minimally difficult **Setting** 123-acre small-town campus **Total enrollment** 3,921 **Student-faculty ratio** 24:1 **Application deadline** Rolling (freshmen), rolling (transfer) **Freshmen** 94% were admitted **Housing** Yes **Expenses** Tuition $3871; Room & Board $3024 **Undergraduates** 63% women, 26% part-time, 33% 25 or older, 3% Native American, 1% Hispanic American, 1% African American, 0.4% Asian American/Pacific Islander **The most frequently chosen baccalaureate fields are** business/marketing, education, psychology **Academic program** Advanced placement, accelerated degree program, summer session, internships **Contact** Ms. Judy Berry, Assistant Director of Admissions, Black Hills State University, University Street Box 9502, Spearfish, SD 57799-9502. Telephone: 605-642-6343 or toll-free 800-255-2478. E-mail: jberry@mystic.bhsu.edu. Web site: http://www.bhsu.edu/.

COLORADO TECHNICAL UNIVERSITY SIOUX FALLS CAMPUS
SIOUX FALLS, SOUTH DAKOTA

General Proprietary, comprehensive, coed **Entrance** Minimally difficult **Total enrollment** 826 **Student-faculty ratio** 16:1 **Application deadline** Rolling (freshmen), rolling (transfer) **Freshmen** 95% were admitted **Housing** No **Expenses** Tuition $8838 **Undergraduates** 55% women, 59% part-time, 52% 25 or older, 1% Native American, 0.5% Hispanic American, 2% African American, 1% Asian American/Pacific Islander **The most frequently chosen baccalaureate fields are** business/marketing, computer/information sciences, protective services/public administration **Academic program** Accelerated degree program, summer session, adult/continuing education programs, internships **Contact** Ms. Angela Haley, Admissions Advisor/Mentor, Colorado Technical University Sioux Falls Campus, 3901 West 59th Street, Sioux Falls, SD 57108. Telephone: 605-361-0200 Ext. 113. Fax: 605-361-5954. E-mail: callen@sf.coloradotech.edu. Web site: http://www.colotechu.edu/.

DAKOTA STATE UNIVERSITY
MADISON, SOUTH DAKOTA

General State-supported, comprehensive, coed **Entrance** Minimally difficult **Setting** 40-acre rural campus **Total enrollment** 2,015 **Student-faculty ratio** 19:1 **Application deadline** Rolling (freshmen), rolling (transfer) **Housing** Yes **Expenses** Tuition $4026; Room & Board $2924 **Undergraduates** 49% women, 26% part-time, 17% 25 or older, 1% Native American, 1% Hispanic American, 1% African American, 1% Asian American/Pacific Islander **The most frequently chosen baccalaureate fields are** computer/information sciences, business/marketing, engineering/engineering technologies **Academic program** English as a second language, advanced placement, honors program, summer session, adult/continuing education programs, internships **Contact** Ms. Katy O'Hara, Admissions Secretary, Dakota State University, 820 North Washington, Madison, SD 57042-1799. Telephone: 605-256-5139 or toll-free 888-DSU-9988. Fax: 605-256-5316. E-mail: yourfuture@dsu.edu. Web site: http://www.dsu.edu/.

DAKOTA WESLEYAN UNIVERSITY
MITCHELL, SOUTH DAKOTA

General Independent United Methodist, 4-year, coed **Entrance** Moderately difficult **Setting** 40-acre small-town campus **Total enrollment** 687 **Student-faculty ratio** 13:1 **Application deadline** 8/31 (freshmen), 8/31 (transfer) **Freshmen** 84% were admitted **Housing** Yes **Expenses** Tuition $11,654; Room & Board $3858 **Undergraduates** 60% women, 11% part-time, 23% 25 or older, 4% Native American, 2% Hispanic American, 5% African American, 1% Asian American/Pacific Islander **The most frequently chosen baccalaureate fields are** business/marketing, education, protective services/public administration **Academic program** English as a second language, self-designed majors, honors program, summer session, adult/continuing education programs, internships **Contact** Ms. Laura Miller, Director of Admissions Operations and Outreach Programming, Dakota Wesleyan University, 1200 West University Avenue, Mitchell, SD 57301-4398. Telephone: 605-995-2650 or toll-free 800-333-8506. Fax: 605-995-2699. E-mail: admissions@dwu.edu. Web site: http://www.dwu.edu/.

HURON UNIVERSITY
See Si Tanka Huron University

MOUNT MARTY COLLEGE
YANKTON, SOUTH DAKOTA

General Independent Roman Catholic, comprehensive, coed **Entrance** Moderately difficult **Setting** 80-acre small-town campus **Total enrollment** 1,168 **Student-faculty ratio** 14:1 **Application deadline** Rolling (freshmen), rolling (transfer) **Housing** Yes **Expenses** Tuition $11,384; Room & Board $4272 **Undergraduates** 67% women, 36% part-time, 37% 25 or older, 1% Native American, 2% Hispanic American, 1% African American, 1% Asian American/Pacific Islander **The most frequently chosen baccalaureate fields are** business/marketing, education, health professions and related sciences **Academic program** Advanced placement, accelerated degree program, self-designed majors, honors program, summer session, adult/continuing education programs, internships **Contact** Office of Admissions, Mount Marty College, 1105 West 8th Street, Yankton, SD 57078. Telephone: 605-668-1011 or toll-free 800-658-4552. Fax: 605-668-1607. E-mail: mmcadmit@rs1.mtmc.edu. Web site: http://www.mtmc.edu/.

NATIONAL AMERICAN UNIVERSITY
RAPID CITY, SOUTH DAKOTA

General Proprietary, comprehensive, coed **Entrance** Noncompetitive **Setting** 8-acre urban campus **Total**

SOUTH DAKOTA

enrollment 885 **Application deadline** Rolling (freshmen), rolling (transfer) **Housing** Yes **Expenses** Tuition $9600; Room & Board $3675 **Undergraduates** 46% women, 34% part-time, 43% 25 or older **Academic program** English as a second language, advanced placement, accelerated degree program, summer session, adult/continuing education programs, internships **Contact** Mr. Tom Shea, Vice President of Enrollment Management, National American University, 321 Kansas City Street, Rapid City, SD 57701. Telephone: 605-394-4902 or toll-free 800-843-8892. Fax: 605-394-4871. E-mail: apply@server1.natcolrcy.edu. Web site: http://www.national.edu/.

NATIONAL AMERICAN UNIVERSITY–SIOUX FALLS BRANCH
SIOUX FALLS, SOUTH DAKOTA

General Proprietary, 4-year, coed **Entrance** Noncompetitive **Setting** urban campus **Total enrollment** 350 **Application deadline** Rolling (freshmen), rolling (transfer) **Freshmen** 100% were admitted **Housing** No **Expenses** Tuition $8800 **Undergraduates** 76% 25 or older, 1% Native American, 0% Hispanic American, 1% African American, 0% Asian American/Pacific Islander **The most frequently chosen baccalaureate fields are** business/marketing, (pre)law, computer/information sciences **Academic program** English as a second language, advanced placement, accelerated degree program, summer session, adult/continuing education programs, internships **Contact** Ms. Lisa Houtsma, Director of Admissions, National American University–Sioux Falls Branch, 2801 South Kiwanis Avenue, Suite 100, Sioux Falls, SD 57105. Telephone: 605-334-5430. E-mail: lhautsma@national.edu.

NORTHERN STATE UNIVERSITY
ABERDEEN, SOUTH DAKOTA

General State-supported, comprehensive, coed **Entrance** Minimally difficult **Setting** 52-acre small-town campus **Total enrollment** 3,088 **Student-faculty ratio** 21:1 **Application deadline** 9/1 (freshmen), 9/1 (transfer) **Freshmen** 92% were admitted **Housing** Yes **Expenses** Tuition $3539; Room & Board $2740 **Undergraduates** 58% women, 36% part-time, 19% 25 or older **The most frequently chosen baccalaureate fields are** business/marketing, education, social sciences and history **Academic program** English as a second language, advanced placement, accelerated degree program, self-designed majors, honors program, summer session, adult/continuing education programs, internships **Contact** Mr. Mike Mutzinger, Director of Admissions, Northern State University, 1200 South Jay Street, Aberdeen, SD 57401. Telephone: 605-626-2544 or toll-free 800-678-5330. Fax: 605-626-2587. E-mail: admissions1@northern.edu. Web site: http://www.northern.edu/.

OGLALA LAKOTA COLLEGE
KYLE, SOUTH DAKOTA

Contact Miss Billi K. Hornbeck, Registrar, Oglala Lakota College, 490 Piya Wiconi Road, Kyle, SD 57752-0490. Telephone: 605-455-2321 Ext. 236. Web site: http://www.olc.edu/.

PRESENTATION COLLEGE
ABERDEEN, SOUTH DAKOTA

General Independent Roman Catholic, 4-year, coed **Entrance** Noncompetitive **Setting** 100-acre small-town campus **Total enrollment** 615 **Student-faculty ratio** 12:1 **Application deadline** Rolling (freshmen), rolling (transfer) **Freshmen** 100% were admitted **Housing** Yes **Expenses** Tuition $8758; Room & Board $5356 **Undergraduates** 85% women, 39% part-time, 33% 25 or older, 7% Native American, 1% Hispanic American, 2% African American, 0% Asian American/Pacific Islander **The most frequently chosen baccalaureate fields are** business/marketing, health professions and related sciences, protective services/public administration **Academic program** Advanced placement, accelerated degree program, summer session, adult/continuing education programs, internships **Contact** Mr. Joddy Meidinger, Director of Admissions, Presentation College, 1500 North Main Street, Aberdeen, SC 57401. Telephone: 605-229-8493 Ext. 492 or toll-free 800-437-6060. E-mail: admit@presentation.edu. Web site: http://www.presentation.edu/.

SINTE GLESKA UNIVERSITY
ROSEBUD, SOUTH DAKOTA

General Independent, comprehensive, coed **Entrance** Noncompetitive **Setting** 52-acre rural campus **Total enrollment** 1,200 **Application deadline** 8/20 (freshmen), 8/20 (transfer) **Freshmen** 100% were admitted **Housing** No **Expenses** Tuition $2586 **Undergraduates** 73% 25 or older **Academic program** Honors program, summer session, adult/continuing education programs, internships **Contact** Mr. Jack Herman, Registrar and Director of Admissions, Sinte Gleska University, PO Box 490, Rosebud, SD 57570-0490. Telephone: 605-747-2263 Ext. 224. Fax: 605-747-2098. Web site: http://www.sinte.edu/.

SI TANKA HURON UNIVERSITY
HURON, SOUTH DAKOTA

General Proprietary, 4-year, coed **Entrance** Minimally difficult **Setting** 15-acre small-town campus **Total enrollment** 528 **Student-faculty ratio** 15:1 **Application deadline** Rolling (freshmen), rolling (transfer) **Freshmen** 39% were admitted **Housing** Yes **Expenses** Tuition $8750; Room & Board $2950 **Undergraduates** 45% women, 16% part-time, 23% 25 or older, 12% Native American, 9% Hispanic American, 10% African American, 1% Asian American/Pacific Islander **The most frequently chosen baccalaureate field is** law/legal studies **Academic program** Advanced placement, accelerated degree program,

SOUTH DAKOTA

Si Tanka Huron University *(continued)* honors program, summer session, adult/continuing education programs **Contact** Mr. Tyler Fisher, Director of Admissions, Si Tanka Huron University, 333 9th Street Southwest, Huron, SD 57350. Telephone: 605-352-8721 Ext. 41 or toll-free 800-710-7159. Fax: 605-352-7421. Web site: http://www.huron.edu/.

SOUTH DAKOTA SCHOOL OF MINES AND TECHNOLOGY
RAPID CITY, SOUTH DAKOTA

General State-supported, university, coed **Entrance** Moderately difficult **Setting** 120-acre suburban campus **Total enrollment** 2,424 **Student-faculty ratio** 18:1 **Application deadline** Rolling (freshmen), rolling (transfer) **Freshmen** 93% were admitted **Housing** Yes **Expenses** Tuition $3849; Room & Board $3370 **Undergraduates** 32% women, 20% part-time, 17% 25 or older, 2% Native American, 1% Hispanic American, 0.5% African American, 1% Asian American/Pacific Islander **Academic program** English as a second language, advanced placement, summer session, adult/continuing education programs, internships **Contact** Leonard C. Colombe, Director of Admissions-Acting, South Dakota School of Mines and Technology, 501 East Saint Joseph, Rapid City, SD 57701-3995. Telephone: 605-394-2414 Ext. 1266 or toll-free 800-544-8162 Ext. 2414. Fax: 605-394-1268. E-mail: admissions@sdsmt.edu. Web site: http://www.sdsmt.edu/.

SOUTH DAKOTA STATE UNIVERSITY
BROOKINGS, SOUTH DAKOTA

General State-supported, university, coed **Entrance** Moderately difficult **Setting** 260-acre small-town campus **Total enrollment** 9,350 **Student-faculty ratio** 16:1 **Application deadline** Rolling (freshmen), rolling (transfer) **Freshmen** 94% were admitted **Housing** Yes **Expenses** Tuition $3808; Room & Board $3040 **Undergraduates** 52% women, 18% part-time, 1% Native American, 0.4% Hispanic American, 0.4% African American, 1% Asian American/Pacific Islander **The most frequently chosen baccalaureate fields are** agriculture, engineering/engineering technologies, health professions and related sciences **Academic program** English as a second language, advanced placement, accelerated degree program, honors program, summer session, adult/continuing education programs, internships **Contact** Ms. Michelle Kuebler, Assistant Director of Admissions, South Dakota State University, PO Box 2201, Brookings, SD 57007. Telephone: 605-688-4121 or toll-free 800-952-3541. Fax: 605-688-6891. E-mail: sdsuadms@adm.sdstate.edu. Web site: http://www.sdstate.edu/.

UNIVERSITY OF SIOUX FALLS
SIOUX FALLS, SOUTH DAKOTA

General Independent American Baptist Churches in the USA, comprehensive, coed **Entrance** Moderately difficult **Setting** 22-acre suburban campus **Total enrollment** 1,332 **Student-faculty ratio** 17:1 **Application deadline** Rolling (freshmen), rolling (transfer) **Freshmen** 96% were admitted **Housing** Yes **Expenses** Tuition $12,600; Room & Board $3850 **Undergraduates** 54% women, 19% part-time, 21% 25 or older, 1% Native American, 1% Hispanic American, 1% African American, 0.4% Asian American/Pacific Islander **The most frequently chosen baccalaureate fields are** business/marketing, education, psychology **Academic program** Advanced placement, accelerated degree program, self-designed majors, honors program, summer session, adult/continuing education programs, internships **Contact** Mr. Greg A. Fritz, Associate Vice President of Admissions and Marketing, University of Sioux Falls, 1101 West 22nd Street, Sioux Falls, SD 57105. Telephone: 605-331-6600 or toll-free 800-888-1047 Ext. 6 (out-of-state). Fax: 605-331-6615. E-mail: admissions@usiouxfalls.edu. Web site: http://www.usiouxfalls.edu/.

THE UNIVERSITY OF SOUTH DAKOTA
VERMILLION, SOUTH DAKOTA

General State-supported, university, coed **Entrance** Moderately difficult **Setting** 216-acre small-town campus **Total enrollment** 8,232 **Student-faculty ratio** 15:1 **Application deadline** Rolling (freshmen), rolling (transfer) **Freshmen** 56% were admitted **Housing** Yes **Expenses** Tuition $3885; Room & Board $3151 **Undergraduates** 59% women, 25% part-time, 20% 25 or older, 3% Native American, 1% Hispanic American, 1% African American, 1% Asian American/Pacific Islander **The most frequently chosen baccalaureate fields are** business/marketing, education, health professions and related sciences **Academic program** English as a second language, advanced placement, honors program, summer session, internships **Contact** Ms. Paula Tacke, Director of Admissions, The University of South Dakota, 414 East Clark Street, Vermillion, SD 57069. Telephone: 605-677-5434 or toll-free 877-269-6837. Fax: 605-677-6753. E-mail: admiss@usd.edu. Web site: http://www.usd.edu/.

TENNESSEE

AMERICAN BAPTIST COLLEGE OF AMERICAN BAPTIST THEOLOGICAL SEMINARY
NASHVILLE, TENNESSEE

General Independent Baptist, 4-year, coed **Entrance** Noncompetitive **Setting** 52-acre urban campus **Total enrollment** 106 **Student-faculty ratio** 8:1 **Application deadline** 7/1 (freshmen), 7/1 (transfer) **Freshmen** 100% were admitted **Housing** Yes **Expenses** Tuition $3045; Room only $1600 **Undergraduates** 23% women, 18% part-time, 85% 25 or older, 92% African American **The most frequently chosen baccalaureate field is** philosophy **Academic program** English as a second language, accelerated degree program, self-designed majors, summer session, adult/

TENNESSEE

continuing education programs **Contact** Ms. Marcella Lockhart, Director of Enrollment Management, American Baptist College of American Baptist Theological Seminary, 1800 Baptist World Center Drive, Nashville, TN 37207. Telephone: 615-228-7877 Ext. 35. Fax: 615-226-7855. E-mail: mlockhart@abcnash.edu.

AQUINAS COLLEGE
NASHVILLE, TENNESSEE

General Independent Roman Catholic, 4-year, coed **Entrance** Moderately difficult **Setting** 92-acre urban campus **Total enrollment** 635 **Student-faculty ratio** 15:1 **Application deadline** Rolling (freshmen), rolling (transfer) **Freshmen** 13% were admitted **Housing** No **Expenses** Tuition $8330 **Undergraduates** 61% 25 or older **Academic program** Advanced placement, summer session, internships **Contact** Neil J. Devine, Director of Career Planning and Admission, Aquinas College, 4210 Harding Road, Nashville, TN 37205-2005. Telephone: 615-297-7545 Ext. 426. Fax: 615-297-7970 Ext. 460. Web site: http://www.aquinas-tn.edu/.

AUSTIN PEAY STATE UNIVERSITY
CLARKSVILLE, TENNESSEE

General State-supported, comprehensive, coed **Entrance** Moderately difficult **Setting** 200-acre suburban campus **Total enrollment** 7,033 **Student-faculty ratio** 18:1 **Application deadline** 8/15 (freshmen), rolling (transfer) **Freshmen** 48% were admitted **Housing** Yes **Expenses** Tuition $3208; Room & Board $3670 **Undergraduates** 60% women, 27% part-time, 40% 25 or older, 1% Native American, 5% Hispanic American, 20% African American, 3% Asian American/Pacific Islander **The most frequently chosen baccalaureate fields are** business/marketing, health professions and related sciences, interdisciplinary studies **Academic program** English as a second language, advanced placement, honors program, summer session, adult/continuing education programs, internships **Contact** Mr. Charles McCorkle, Director of Admissions, Austin Peay State University, PO Box 4548, Clarksville, TN 37044-4548. Telephone: 931-221-7661 or toll-free 800-844-2778 (out-of-state). Fax: 931-221-6168. E-mail: admissions@apsu01.apsu.edu. Web site: http://www.apsu.edu/.

BAPTIST MEMORIAL COLLEGE OF HEALTH SCIENCES
MEMPHIS, TENNESSEE

Contact Baptist Memorial College of Health Sciences, 1003 Monroe Avenue, Memphis, TN 38104. Telephone: or toll-free 800-796-7171. Web site: http://www.bmhcc.org/bchs/index.asp.

BELMONT UNIVERSITY
NASHVILLE, TENNESSEE

General Independent Baptist, comprehensive, coed **Entrance** Moderately difficult **Setting** 34-acre urban campus **Total enrollment** 3,129 **Student-faculty ratio** 11:1 **Application deadline** 5/1 (freshmen), 5/1 (transfer) **Freshmen** 74% were admitted **Housing** Yes **Expenses** Tuition $13,400; Room & Board $5666 **Undergraduates** 60% women, 11% part-time, 17% 25 or older, 0.2% Native American, 1% Hispanic American, 3% African American, 1% Asian American/Pacific Islander **The most frequently chosen baccalaureate fields are** business/marketing, liberal arts/general studies, visual/performing arts **Academic program** Advanced placement, accelerated degree program, self-designed majors, honors program, summer session, adult/continuing education programs, internships **Contact** Dr. Kathryn Baugher, Dean of Enrollment Services, Belmont University, 1900 Belmont Boulevard, Nashville, TN 37212-3757. Telephone: 615-460-6785 or toll-free 800-56E-NROL. Fax: 615-460-5434. E-mail: buadmission@mail.belmont.edu. Web site: http://www.belmont.edu/.

▶ **For more information, see page 398.**

BETHEL COLLEGE
MCKENZIE, TENNESSEE

General Independent Cumberland Presbyterian, comprehensive, coed **Entrance** Minimally difficult **Setting** 100-acre small-town campus **Total enrollment** 945 **Student-faculty ratio** 14:1 **Application deadline** Rolling (freshmen), rolling (transfer) **Freshmen** 63% were admitted **Housing** Yes **Expenses** Tuition $8430; Room & Board $4550 **Undergraduates** 53% women, 12% part-time, 50% 25 or older, 1% Native American, 1% Hispanic American, 19% African American, 0.3% Asian American/Pacific Islander **The most frequently chosen baccalaureate fields are** business/marketing, biological/life sciences, education **Academic program** Advanced placement, accelerated degree program, self-designed majors, summer session, adult/continuing education programs, internships **Contact** Mrs. Tina Hodges, Director of Admissions and Marketing, Bethel College, 325 Cherry Avenue, McKenzie, TN 38201. Telephone: 731-352-4030. Fax: 731-352-4069. E-mail: admissions@bethel-college.edu. Web site: http://www.bethel-college.edu/.

BRYAN COLLEGE
DAYTON, TENNESSEE

General Independent interdenominational, 4-year, coed **Entrance** Moderately difficult **Setting** 100-acre small-town campus **Total enrollment** 612 **Student-faculty ratio** 14:1 **Application deadline** Rolling (freshmen), rolling (transfer) **Freshmen** 34% were admitted **Housing** Yes **Expenses** Tuition $12,200; Room & Board $4200 **Undergraduates** 1% 25 or older, 0.4% Native American, 1% Hispanic American, 2% African American, 1% Asian American/Pacific Islander **The most frequently chosen baccalaureate fields are** business/marketing, education, psychology **Academic program** Advanced placement, honors program, summer session, adult/continuing education programs, internships **Contact** Mr. Ronald D. Petitte, Registrar, Bryan College, PO Box 7000, Dayton, TN 37321-7000. Telephone: 423-

Bryan College *(continued)*
775-7237 or toll-free 800-277-9522. Fax: 423-775-7330. E-mail: admiss@bryannet.bryan.edu. Web site: http://www.bryan.edu/.

CARSON-NEWMAN COLLEGE
JEFFERSON CITY, TENNESSEE

General Independent Southern Baptist, comprehensive, coed **Entrance** Moderately difficult **Setting** 90-acre small-town campus **Total enrollment** 2,195 **Student-faculty ratio** 13:1 **Application deadline** 8/1 (freshmen), 8/1 (transfer) **Freshmen** 89% were admitted **Housing** Yes **Expenses** Tuition $12,380; Room & Board $4120 **Undergraduates** 58% women, 9% part-time, 13% 25 or older, 0.2% Native American, 0.4% Hispanic American, 8% African American, 0.3% Asian American/Pacific Islander **The most frequently chosen baccalaureate fields are** business/marketing, education, psychology **Academic program** English as a second language, advanced placement, accelerated degree program, self-designed majors, honors program, summer session, adult/continuing education programs, internships **Contact** Mrs. Sheryl M. Gray, Director of Undergraduate Admissions, Carson-Newman College, PO Box 72025, Jefferson City, TN 37760. Telephone: 865-471-3223 or toll-free 800-678-9061. Fax: 865-471-3502. E-mail: cnadmiss@cn.edu. Web site: http://www.cn.edu/.

CHRISTIAN BROTHERS UNIVERSITY
MEMPHIS, TENNESSEE

General Independent Roman Catholic, comprehensive, coed **Entrance** Moderately difficult **Setting** 70-acre urban campus **Total enrollment** 2,123 **Student-faculty ratio** 14:1 **Application deadline** 8/23 (freshmen), 8/23 (transfer) **Freshmen** 82% were admitted **Housing** Yes **Expenses** Tuition $15,300; Room & Board $4520 **Undergraduates** 55% women, 21% part-time, 26% 25 or older, 0.3% Native American, 2% Hispanic American, 28% African American, 4% Asian American/Pacific Islander **The most frequently chosen baccalaureate fields are** business/marketing, engineering/engineering technologies, psychology **Academic program** Advanced placement, accelerated degree program, honors program, summer session, internships **Contact** Ms. Courtney Fee, Dean of Admission, Christian Brothers University, 650 East Parkway South, Memphis, TN 38104. Telephone: 901-321-3205 or toll-free 800-288-7576. Fax: 901-321-3202. E-mail: admissions@bucs.cbu.edu. Web site: http://www.cbu.edu/.

CRICHTON COLLEGE
MEMPHIS, TENNESSEE

General Independent, 4-year, coed **Entrance** Moderately difficult **Setting** 55-acre urban campus **Total enrollment** 1,043 **Student-faculty ratio** 17:1 **Application deadline** 8/31 (freshmen), 8/31 (transfer) **Freshmen** 76% were admitted **Housing** Yes **Expenses** Tuition $9480; Room only $3200 **Undergraduates** 54% women, 18% part-time, 72% 25 or older, 1% Native American, 0.4% Hispanic American, 47% African American, 0.4% Asian American/Pacific Islander **The most frequently chosen baccalaureate fields are** business/marketing, education, philosophy **Academic program** Advanced placement, accelerated degree program, self-designed majors, summer session, adult/continuing education programs, internships **Contact** Mr. David Wilson, Associate Director of Admissions, Crichton College, 6655 Winchester Road, PO Box 757830, Memphis, TN 38175-7830. Telephone: 901-367-3888 or toll-free 800-960-9777. Fax: 901-366-2650. E-mail: info@crichton.edu. Web site: http://www.crichton.edu/.

CUMBERLAND UNIVERSITY
LEBANON, TENNESSEE

General Independent, comprehensive, coed **Entrance** Moderately difficult **Setting** 44-acre small-town campus **Total enrollment** 1,471 **Student-faculty ratio** 13:1 **Application deadline** Rolling (freshmen), rolling (transfer) **Freshmen** 78% were admitted **Housing** Yes **Expenses** Tuition $10,950; Room & Board $4380 **Undergraduates** 52% women, 16% part-time, 20% 25 or older, 0.1% Native American, 3% Hispanic American, 11% African American, 1% Asian American/Pacific Islander **The most frequently chosen baccalaureate fields are** business/marketing, education, health professions and related sciences **Academic program** Advanced placement, honors program, summer session, adult/continuing education programs, internships **Contact** Mr. Edward Freytag, Director of Admissions, Cumberland University, One Cumberland Square, Lebanon, TN 37087. Telephone: 615-444-2562 Ext. 1232 or toll-free 800-467-0562 (out-of-state). Fax: 615-444-2569. E-mail: admissions@cumberland.edu. Web site: http://www.cumberland.edu/.

DAVID LIPSCOMB UNIVERSITY
See Lipscomb University

EAST TENNESSEE STATE UNIVERSITY
JOHNSON CITY, TENNESSEE

General State-supported, university, coed **Entrance** Moderately difficult **Setting** 366-acre small-town campus **Total enrollment** 11,331 **Student-faculty ratio** 18:1 **Application deadline** Rolling (freshmen), rolling (transfer) **Freshmen** 80% were admitted **Housing** Yes **Expenses** Tuition $3119; Room & Board $4008 **Undergraduates** 58% women, 19% part-time, 29% 25 or older, 0.4% Native American, 1% Hispanic American, 5% African American, 1% Asian American/Pacific Islander **The most frequently chosen baccalaureate fields are** business/marketing, health professions and related sciences, protective services/public administration **Academic program** Advanced placement, accelerated degree program, honors program, summer session, adult/continuing education programs, internships **Contact** Mr. Mike Pitts, Director of Admissions, East Tennessee State University, PO Box 70731, Johnson City, TN 37614-0734. Telephone: 423-439-4213 or toll-free 800-462-

TENNESSEE

3878. Fax: 423-439-4270. E-mail: pitts@etsuvax.etsu-tn.edu. Web site: http://www.etsu.edu/.

FISK UNIVERSITY
NASHVILLE, TENNESSEE

General Independent, comprehensive, coed, affiliated with United Church of Christ **Entrance** Moderately difficult **Setting** 40-acre urban campus **Total enrollment** 845 **Student-faculty ratio** 12:1 **Application deadline** 6/15 (freshmen), 6/15 (transfer) **Freshmen** 71% were admitted **Housing** Yes **Expenses** Tuition $10,089; Room & Board $5182 **Undergraduates** 69% women, 2% part-time, 3% 25 or older, 0% Native American, 0% Hispanic American, 94% African American, 0.4% Asian American/Pacific Islander **The most frequently chosen baccalaureate fields are** business/marketing, English, psychology **Academic program** Advanced placement, self-designed majors, honors program, internships **Contact** Director of Admissions, Fisk University, Admissions Office, Fisk University, 1000 17th Avenue North, Nashville, TN 37208. Telephone: 615-329-8666 or toll-free 800-443-FISK. E-mail: admit@fisk.edu. Web site: http://www.fisk.edu/.

FREED-HARDEMAN UNIVERSITY
HENDERSON, TENNESSEE

General Independent, comprehensive, coed, affiliated with Church of Christ **Entrance** Moderately difficult **Setting** 96-acre small-town campus **Total enrollment** 1,870 **Student-faculty ratio** 13:1 **Application deadline** Rolling (freshmen), rolling (transfer) **Freshmen** 56% were admitted **Housing** Yes **Expenses** Tuition $9580; Room & Board $4710 **Undergraduates** 52% women, 7% part-time, 9% 25 or older, 0.4% Native American, 1% Hispanic American, 5% African American, 1% Asian American/Pacific Islander **The most frequently chosen baccalaureate fields are** business/marketing, education, philosophy, religion, and theology **Academic program** Advanced placement, accelerated degree program, self-designed majors, honors program, summer session, internships **Contact** Mr. Jim Brown, Director of Admissions, Freed-Hardeman University, 158 East Main Street, Henderson, TN 38340-2399. Telephone: 731-989-6651 or toll-free 800-630-3480. Fax: 731-989-6047. E-mail: admissions@fhu.edu. Web site: http://www.fhu.edu/.

FREE WILL BAPTIST BIBLE COLLEGE
NASHVILLE, TENNESSEE

General Independent Free Will Baptist, 4-year, coed **Entrance** Noncompetitive **Setting** 10-acre suburban campus **Total enrollment** 318 **Application deadline** Rolling (freshmen) **Housing** Yes **Expenses** Tuition $7112; Room & Board $3788 **Undergraduates** 7% 25 or older, 0.3% Native American, 2% African American, 0.3% Asian American/Pacific Islander **Academic program** English as a second language, advanced placement, self-designed majors, summer session, internships **Contact** Dr. Milton Fields, Academic Dean, Free Will Baptist Bible College, 3606 West End Avenue, Nashville, TN 37205-2498. Telephone: 615-383-1340 or toll-free 800-763-9222. Fax: 615-269-6028. Web site: http://www.fwbbc.edu.

JOHNSON BIBLE COLLEGE
KNOXVILLE, TENNESSEE

General Independent, comprehensive, coed, affiliated with Christian Churches and Churches of Christ **Entrance** Minimally difficult **Setting** 75-acre rural campus **Total enrollment** 678 **Student-faculty ratio** 16:1 **Application deadline** 8/1 (freshmen), 8/1 (transfer) **Freshmen** 87% were admitted **Housing** Yes **Expenses** Tuition $5500; Room & Board $3900 **Undergraduates** 48% women, 2% part-time, 20% 25 or older, 0.2% Native American, 1% Hispanic American, 2% African American, 0.3% Asian American/Pacific Islander **The most frequently chosen baccalaureate fields are** philosophy, education, philosophy, religion, and theology **Academic program** English as a second language, advanced placement, accelerated degree program, summer session, adult/continuing education programs, internships **Contact** Mr. Tim Wingfield, Director of Admissions, Johnson Bible College, 7900 Johnson Drive, Knoxville, TN 37998. Telephone: 865-251-2346 or toll-free 800-827-2122. Fax: 423-251-2336. E-mail: twingfield@jbc.edu. Web site: http://www.jbc.edu/.

KING COLLEGE
BRISTOL, TENNESSEE

General Independent, comprehensive, coed, affiliated with Presbyterian Church (U.S.A.) **Entrance** Moderately difficult **Setting** 135-acre suburban campus **Total enrollment** 670 **Student-faculty ratio** 11:1 **Application deadline** Rolling (freshmen), rolling (transfer) **Freshmen** 64% were admitted **Housing** Yes **Expenses** Tuition $13,340; Room & Board $4460 **Undergraduates** 58% women, 12% part-time, 10% 25 or older, 0% Native American, 1% Hispanic American, 2% African American, 0.4% Asian American/Pacific Islander **The most frequently chosen baccalaureate fields are** business/marketing, biological/life sciences, liberal arts/general studies **Academic program** English as a second language, advanced placement, accelerated degree program, honors program, summer session, internships **Contact** Mr. Micah Crews, Director of Admissions, King College, 1350 King College Road, Bristol, TN 37620-2699. Telephone: 423-652-4773 or toll-free 800-362-0014. Fax: 423-652-4727. E-mail: admissions@king2.king.bristol.tn.us. Web site: http://www.king.edu/.

LAMBUTH UNIVERSITY
JACKSON, TENNESSEE

General Independent United Methodist, 4-year, coed **Entrance** Moderately difficult **Setting** 50-acre urban campus **Total enrollment** 904 **Student-faculty ratio** 14:1 **Application deadline** Rolling (freshmen), rolling (transfer) **Freshmen** 68% were admitted **Hous-

TENNESSEE

Lambuth University *(continued)*
ing Yes **Expenses** Tuition $9548; Room & Board $4706 **Undergraduates** 58% women, 9% part-time, 12% 25 or older, 0.2% Native American, 1% Hispanic American, 16% African American, 0.2% Asian American/Pacific Islander **The most frequently chosen baccalaureate fields are** business/marketing, education, social sciences and history **Academic program** English as a second language, advanced placement, self-designed majors, summer session, adult/continuing education programs, internships **Contact** Ms. Denes Bardos, Director of Admissions, Lambuth University, 705 Lambuth Boulevard, Jackson, TN 38301. Telephone: 731-425-3323 or toll-free 800-526-2884. Fax: 731-425-3496. E-mail: admit@lambuth.edu. Web site: http://www.lambuth.edu/.

LANE COLLEGE
JACKSON, TENNESSEE

General Independent, 4-year, coed, affiliated with Christian Methodist Episcopal Church **Entrance** Minimally difficult **Setting** 25-acre suburban campus **Total enrollment** 702 **Student-faculty ratio** 15:1 **Application deadline** Rolling (freshmen), rolling (transfer) **Freshmen** 55% were admitted **Housing** Yes **Expenses** Tuition $6350; Room & Board $3800 **Undergraduates** 49% women, 2% part-time, 5% 25 or older, 0% Hispanic American, 99% African American **The most frequently chosen baccalaureate fields are** business/marketing, education, protective services/public administration **Academic program** Advanced placement, honors program, summer session, internships **Contact** Ms. E. Brown, Director of Admissions, Lane College, 545 Lane Avenue, Bray Administration Building 2nd Floor, Jackson, TN 38301-4598. Telephone: 901-426-7532 or toll-free 800-960-7533. Fax: 901-426-7559. E-mail: admissions@lanecollege.edu. Web site: http://www.lanecollege.edu/.

LEE UNIVERSITY
CLEVELAND, TENNESSEE

General Independent, comprehensive, coed, affiliated with Church of God **Entrance** Minimally difficult **Setting** 45-acre small-town campus **Total enrollment** 3,511 **Student-faculty ratio** 20:1 **Application deadline** 9/1 (freshmen), rolling (transfer) **Freshmen** 62% were admitted **Housing** Yes **Expenses** Tuition $7496; Room & Board $4550 **Undergraduates** 57% women, 7% part-time, 11% 25 or older, 0.5% Native American, 3% Hispanic American, 3% African American, 1% Asian American/Pacific Islander **The most frequently chosen baccalaureate fields are** education, business/marketing, philosophy, religion, and theology **Academic program** English as a second language, advanced placement, honors program, summer session, adult/continuing education programs, internships **Contact** Admissions Coordinator, Lee University, PO Box 3450, Cleveland, TN 37311. Telephone: 423-614-8500 or toll-free 800-LEE-9930. Fax: 423-614-8533. E-mail: admissions@leeuniversity.edu. Web site: http://www.leeuniversity.edu/.

LEMOYNE-OWEN COLLEGE
MEMPHIS, TENNESSEE

General Independent, 4-year, coed, affiliated with United Church of Christ **Entrance** Minimally difficult **Setting** 15-acre urban campus **Total enrollment** 734 **Student-faculty ratio** 14:1 **Application deadline** 4/1 (freshmen), rolling (transfer) **Freshmen** 100% were admitted **Housing** Yes **Expenses** Tuition $8450; Room & Board $4620 **Undergraduates** 70% women, 15% part-time, 30% 25 or older, 0% Native American, 0% Hispanic American, 95% African American, 0.3% Asian American/Pacific Islander **The most frequently chosen baccalaureate fields are** business/marketing, engineering/engineering technologies, social sciences and history **Academic program** Advanced placement, accelerated degree program, honors program, summer session, adult/continuing education programs, internships **Contact** Mr. Lonnie Morris, Director of Admissions/Recruitment, LeMoyne-Owen College, 807 Walker Avenue, Memphis, TN 38126. Telephone: 901-942-7302 or toll-free 800-737-7778 (in-state). E-mail: admissions@nile.lemoyne-owen.edu. Web site: http://www.lemoyne-owen.edu/.

LINCOLN MEMORIAL UNIVERSITY
HARROGATE, TENNESSEE

General Independent, comprehensive, coed **Entrance** Moderately difficult **Setting** 1,000-acre small-town campus **Total enrollment** 1,773 **Student-faculty ratio** 9:1 **Application deadline** Rolling (freshmen), rolling (transfer) **Freshmen** 72% were admitted **Housing** Yes **Expenses** Tuition $10,800; Room & Board $4150 **Undergraduates** 67% women, 24% part-time, 28% 25 or older, 0.3% Native American, 0.1% Hispanic American, 3% African American, 0.3% Asian American/Pacific Islander **Academic program** English as a second language, advanced placement, accelerated degree program, self-designed majors, honors program, summer session, adult/continuing education programs **Contact** Mr. Conrad Daniels, Dean of Admissions and Recruitment, Lincoln Memorial University, Cumberland Gap Parkway, Harrogate, TN 37752-1901. Telephone: 423-869-6280 or toll-free 800-325-0900. Fax: 423-869-6250. E-mail: admissions@inetlmu.lmunet.edu. Web site: http://www.lmunet.edu/.

LIPSCOMB UNIVERSITY
NASHVILLE, TENNESSEE

General Independent, comprehensive, coed, affiliated with Church of Christ **Entrance** Moderately difficult **Setting** 65-acre urban campus **Total enrollment** 2,661 **Student-faculty ratio** 16:1 **Application deadline** Rolling (freshmen), rolling (transfer) **Freshmen** 85% were admitted **Housing** Yes **Expenses** Tuition $10,828; Room & Board $5420 **Undergraduates** 57% women, 12% part-time, 10% 25 or older **The most frequently chosen baccalaureate field is** philosophy, religion, and theology **Academic program** Advanced placement, accelerated degree program, honors program, summer session, adult/

continuing education programs, internships **Contact** Mr. Scott Gilmer, Director of Admissions, Lipscomb University, 3901 Granny White Pike, Nashville, TN 37204-3951. Telephone: 615-269-1776 or toll-free 800-333-4358. Fax: 615-269-1804. E-mail: admissions@lipscomb.edu. Web site: http://www.lipscomb.edu/.

MARTIN METHODIST COLLEGE
PULASKI, TENNESSEE

General Independent United Methodist, 4-year, coed **Entrance** Minimally difficult **Setting** 6-acre small-town campus **Total enrollment** 631 **Student-faculty ratio** 17:1 **Application deadline** 8/30 (freshmen), 8/30 (transfer) **Freshmen** 97% were admitted **Housing** Yes **Expenses** Tuition $10,840; Room & Board $3700 **Undergraduates** 61% women, 35% part-time, 31% 25 or older, 1% Native American, 1% Hispanic American, 9% African American, 0.3% Asian American/Pacific Islander **The most frequently chosen baccalaureate fields are** business/marketing, education, psychology **Academic program** English as a second language, advanced placement, self-designed majors, summer session, adult/continuing education programs **Contact** Tony Booker, Director of Admissions, Martin Methodist College, 433 West Madison Street, Pulaski, TN 38478-2716. Telephone: 931-363-9804 or toll-free 800-467-1273. Fax: 931-363-9818. E-mail: admissions@martinmethodist.edu. Web site: http://www.martinmethodist.edu/.

MARYVILLE COLLEGE
MARYVILLE, TENNESSEE

General Independent Presbyterian, 4-year, coed **Entrance** Moderately difficult **Setting** 350-acre suburban campus **Total enrollment** 1,026 **Student-faculty ratio** 14:1 **Application deadline** 3/1 (freshmen), rolling (transfer) **Freshmen** 79% were admitted **Housing** Yes **Expenses** Tuition $17,560; Room & Board $5650 **Undergraduates** 58% women, 3% part-time, 8% 25 or older, 1% Native American, 1% Hispanic American, 6% African American, 1% Asian American/Pacific Islander **The most frequently chosen baccalaureate fields are** business/marketing, biological/life sciences, education **Academic program** English as a second language, advanced placement, self-designed majors, honors program, summer session, adult/continuing education programs, internships **Contact** Ms. Linda L. Moore, Administrative Assistant of Admissions, Maryville College, 502 East Lamar Alexander Parkway, Maryville, TN 37804-5907. Telephone: 865-981-8092 or toll-free 800-597-2687. Fax: 865-981-8005. E-mail: admissions@maryvillecollege.edu. Web site: http://www.maryvillecollege.edu/.

MEMPHIS COLLEGE OF ART
MEMPHIS, TENNESSEE

General Independent, comprehensive, coed **Entrance** Moderately difficult **Setting** 200-acre urban campus **Total enrollment** 299 **Student-faculty ratio** 11:1 **Application deadline** Rolling (freshmen), rolling (transfer) **Freshmen** 73% were admitted **Housing** Yes **Expenses** Tuition $12,790; Room & Board $5200 **Undergraduates** 49% women, 9% part-time, 25% 25 or older, 0.4% Native American, 2% Hispanic American, 12% African American, 1% Asian American/Pacific Islander **Academic program** Advanced placement, summer session, adult/continuing education programs, internships **Contact** Ms. Annette Moore, Director of Admission, Memphis College of Art, 1930 Poplar Avenue, Memphis, TN 38104. Telephone: 901-272-5153 or toll-free 800-727-1088. Fax: 901-272-5158. E-mail: info@mca.edu. Web site: http://www.mca.edu/.

MIDDLE TENNESSEE STATE UNIVERSITY
MURFREESBORO, TENNESSEE

General State-supported, university, coed **Entrance** Moderately difficult **Setting** 500-acre urban campus **Total enrollment** 20,073 **Student-faculty ratio** 23:1 **Application deadline** Rolling (freshmen), rolling (transfer) **Freshmen** 78% were admitted **Housing** Yes **Expenses** Tuition $3194; Room & Board $3800 **Undergraduates** 54% women, 17% part-time, 29% 25 or older, 0.5% Native American, 1% Hispanic American, 11% African American, 2% Asian American/Pacific Islander **The most frequently chosen baccalaureate fields are** business/marketing, interdisciplinary studies, visual/performing arts **Academic program** English as a second language, advanced placement, accelerated degree program, self-designed majors, honors program, summer session, adult/continuing education programs, internships **Contact** Ms. Lynn Palmer, Director of Admissions, Middle Tennessee State University, 1301 East Main Street, MTSU-CAB 208, Murfreesboro, TN 37132. Telephone: 615-898-2111 or toll-free 800-331-MTSU (in-state); 800-433-MTSU (out-of-state). Fax: 615-898-5478. E-mail: admissions@mtsu.edu. Web site: http://www.mtsu.edu/.

MILLIGAN COLLEGE
MILLIGAN COLLEGE, TENNESSEE

General Independent Christian, comprehensive, coed **Entrance** Moderately difficult **Setting** 145-acre suburban campus **Total enrollment** 899 **Student-faculty ratio** 11:1 **Application deadline** Rolling (freshmen), rolling (transfer) **Freshmen** 76% were admitted **Housing** Yes **Expenses** Tuition $13,250; Room & Board $4300 **Undergraduates** 60% women, 3% part-time, 13% 25 or older, 0.4% Native American, 1% Hispanic American, 2% African American, 1% Asian American/Pacific Islander **The most frequently chosen baccalaureate fields are** business/marketing, biological/life sciences, education **Academic program** Advanced placement, accelerated degree program, summer session, adult/continuing education programs, internships **Contact** Mr. David Mee, Vice President for Enrollment Management, Milligan College, PO Box 210, Milligan College, TN 37682. Telephone: 423-461-8730 or toll-free 800-262-8337 (in-state). Fax: 423-461-8982. E-mail: admissions@milligan.edu. Web site: http://www.milligan.edu/.

TENNESSEE

O'MORE COLLEGE OF DESIGN
FRANKLIN, TENNESSEE

General Independent, 4-year, coed **Entrance** Moderately difficult **Setting** 6-acre small-town campus **Total enrollment** 132 **Student-faculty ratio** 3:1 **Application deadline** 8/1 (freshmen), 8/1 (transfer) **Freshmen** 72% were admitted **Housing** Yes **Expenses** Tuition $10,270 **Undergraduates** 90% women, 30% part-time, 29% 25 or older, 0% Native American, 2% Hispanic American, 3% African American, 2% Asian American/Pacific Islander **Academic program** Advanced placement, summer session, adult/continuing education programs, internships **Contact** Chris Lee, Director of Enrollment Management, O'More College of Design, 423 South Margin Street, Franklin, TN 37064-2816. Telephone: 615-794-4254 Ext. 32. Fax: 615-790-1662. Web site: http://www.omorecollege.edu/.

RHODES COLLEGE
MEMPHIS, TENNESSEE

General Independent Presbyterian, comprehensive, coed **Entrance** Very difficult **Setting** 100-acre suburban campus **Total enrollment** 1,551 **Student-faculty ratio** 12:1 **Application deadline** 2/1 (freshmen), 2/1 (transfer) **Freshmen** 64% were admitted **Housing** Yes **Expenses** Tuition $20,536; Room & Board $5900 **Undergraduates** 57% women, 2% part-time, 0.1% 25 or older, 0.1% Native American, 2% Hispanic American, 4% African American, 3% Asian American/Pacific Islander **The most frequently chosen baccalaureate fields are** business/marketing, biological/life sciences, social sciences and history **Academic program** Advanced placement, accelerated degree program, self-designed majors, honors program, summer session, internships **Contact** Mr. David J. Wottle, Dean of Admissions and Financial Aid, Rhodes College, 2000 North Parkway, Memphis, TN 38112. Telephone: 901-843-3700 or toll-free 800-844-5969 (out-of-state). Fax: 901-843-3631. E-mail: adminfo@rhodes.edu. Web site: http://www.rhodes.edu/.

SOUTHERN ADVENTIST UNIVERSITY
COLLEGEDALE, TENNESSEE

General Independent Seventh-day Adventist, comprehensive, coed **Entrance** Moderately difficult **Setting** 1,000-acre small-town campus **Total enrollment** 2,200 **Student-faculty ratio** 16:1 **Application deadline** Rolling (freshmen), rolling (transfer) **Freshmen** 77% were admitted **Housing** Yes **Expenses** Tuition $11,610; Room & Board $3990 **Undergraduates** 55% women, 14% part-time, 10% 25 or older, 0.4% Native American, 10% Hispanic American, 7% African American, 4% Asian American/Pacific Islander **The most frequently chosen baccalaureate fields are** business/marketing, health professions and related sciences, philosophy **Academic program** English as a second language, advanced placement, honors program, summer session, internships **Contact** Mr. Victor Czerkasij, Director of Admissions and Recruitment, Southern Adventist University, PO Box 370, Collegedale, TN 37315-0370. Telephone: 423-238-2843 or toll-free 800-768-8437. Fax: 423-238-3005. E-mail: admissions@southern.edu. Web site: http://www.southern.edu/.

TENNESSEE STATE UNIVERSITY
NASHVILLE, TENNESSEE

General State-supported, comprehensive, coed **Entrance** Minimally difficult **Setting** 450-acre urban campus **Total enrollment** 8,666 **Student-faculty ratio** 26:1 **Application deadline** 8/1 (freshmen), 8/1 (transfer) **Freshmen** 48% were admitted **Housing** Yes **Expenses** Tuition $3033; Room & Board $3600 **Undergraduates** 62% women, 15% part-time, 37% 25 or older, 0.01% Native American, 0.5% Hispanic American, 82% African American, 1% Asian American/Pacific Islander **The most frequently chosen baccalaureate fields are** education, health professions and related sciences, liberal arts/general studies **Academic program** Accelerated degree program, honors program, summer session, adult/continuing education programs, internships **Contact** Ms. Vernella Smith, Admissions Coordinator, Tennessee State University, 3500 John A Merritt Boulevard, Nashville, TN 37209-1561. Telephone: 615-963-5104. Fax: 615-963-5108. E-mail: jcade@picard.tnstate.edu. Web site: http://www.tnstate.edu/.

TENNESSEE TECHNOLOGICAL UNIVERSITY
COOKEVILLE, TENNESSEE

General State-supported, university, coed **Entrance** Moderately difficult **Setting** 235-acre small-town campus **Total enrollment** 8,653 **Student-faculty ratio** 18:1 **Application deadline** Rolling (freshmen), rolling (transfer) **Freshmen** 98% were admitted **Housing** Yes **Expenses** Tuition $2822; Room & Board $3880 **Undergraduates** 46% women, 12% part-time, 28% 25 or older, 0.3% Native American, 1% Hispanic American, 4% African American, 1% Asian American/Pacific Islander **The most frequently chosen baccalaureate fields are** business/marketing, education, engineering/engineering technologies **Academic program** English as a second language, advanced placement, accelerated degree program, honors program, summer session, adult/continuing education programs, internships **Contact** Mrs. Rebecca Tolbert, Associate Vice President for Enrollment and Records, Tennessee Technological University, TTU Box 5006, Cookeville, TN 38505. Telephone: 931-372-3888 or toll-free 800-255-8881. Fax: 931-372-6250. E-mail: u_admissions@tntech.edu. Web site: http://www.tntech.edu/.

TENNESSEE TEMPLE UNIVERSITY
CHATTANOOGA, TENNESSEE

General Independent Baptist, comprehensive, coed **Entrance** Minimally difficult **Setting** 55-acre urban campus **Total enrollment** 699 **Student-faculty ratio** 15:1 **Application deadline** 8/20 (freshmen), 8/15 (transfer) **Freshmen** 99% were admitted **Housing**

Yes **Expenses** Tuition $6450; Room & Board $5120 **Undergraduates** 47% women, 3% part-time, 10% 25 or older, 1% Native American, 2% Hispanic American, 5% African American, 1% Asian American/Pacific Islander **The most frequently chosen baccalaureate fields are** education, business/marketing, philosophy **Academic program** Advanced placement, honors program, summer session, adult/continuing education programs, internships **Contact** Mr. Bruce Snavely, Director of Enrollment Services, Tennessee Temple University, 1815 Union Avenue, Chattanooga, TN 37404-3587. Telephone: 423-493-4371 or toll-free 800-553-4050. Fax: 423-493-4497. E-mail: ttuinfo@tntemple.edu.

TENNESSEE WESLEYAN COLLEGE
ATHENS, TENNESSEE

General Independent United Methodist, 4-year, coed **Entrance** Moderately difficult **Setting** 40-acre small-town campus **Total enrollment** 786 **Student-faculty ratio** 17:1 **Application deadline** Rolling (freshmen), rolling (transfer) **Freshmen** 71% were admitted **Housing** Yes **Expenses** Tuition $8050; Room & Board $4150 **Undergraduates** 63% women, 23% part-time, 35% 25 or older, 0% Native American, 0.3% Hispanic American, 3% African American, 0.1% Asian American/Pacific Islander **The most frequently chosen baccalaureate fields are** business/marketing, parks and recreation, psychology **Academic program** English as a second language, advanced placement, accelerated degree program, self-designed majors, honors program, summer session, adult/continuing education programs, internships **Contact** Mrs. Ruthie Cawood, Director of Admission, Tennessee Wesleyan College, PO Box 40, Athens, TN 37371-0040. Telephone: 423-746-5287 or toll-free 800-PICK-TWC. Fax: 423-745-9335. Web site: http://www.twcnet.org/.

TREVECCA NAZARENE UNIVERSITY
NASHVILLE, TENNESSEE

General Independent Nazarene, comprehensive, coed **Entrance** Noncompetitive **Setting** 65-acre urban campus **Total enrollment** 1,819 **Student-faculty ratio** 16:1 **Application deadline** Rolling (freshmen), rolling (transfer) **Freshmen** 79% were admitted **Housing** Yes **Expenses** Tuition $11,390; Room & Board $5150 **Undergraduates** 55% women, 23% part-time, 28% 25 or older, 1% Native American, 2% Hispanic American, 6% African American, 0.5% Asian American/Pacific Islander **The most frequently chosen baccalaureate fields are** business/marketing, education, philosophy **Academic program** Advanced placement, accelerated degree program, summer session, adult/continuing education programs, internships **Contact** Ms. Patricia D. Cook, Director of Admissions, Trevecca Nazarene University, 333 Murfreesboro Road, Nashville, TN 37210-2834. Telephone: 615-248-1320 or toll-free 888-210-4TNU. Fax: 615-248-7406. E-mail: admissions_und@trevecca.edu. Web site: http://www.trevecca.edu/.

TUSCULUM COLLEGE
GREENEVILLE, TENNESSEE

General Independent Presbyterian, comprehensive, coed **Entrance** Moderately difficult **Setting** 140-acre small-town campus **Total enrollment** 1,794 **Student-faculty ratio** 15:1 **Application deadline** Rolling (freshmen), rolling (transfer) **Freshmen** 85% were admitted **Housing** Yes **Expenses** Tuition $13,400; Room & Board $4500 **Undergraduates** 53% women, 0.3% part-time, 60% 25 or older, 0.1% Native American, 1% Hispanic American, 9% African American, 0.3% Asian American/Pacific Islander **The most frequently chosen baccalaureate fields are** business/marketing, education, physical sciences **Academic program** English as a second language, advanced placement, self-designed majors, summer session, adult/continuing education programs, internships **Contact** Mr. George Wolf, Director of Admissions, Tusculum College, PO Box 5047, Greeneville, TN 37743-9997. Telephone: 423-636-7300 Ext. 611 or toll-free 800-729-0256. Fax: 423-638-7166 Ext. 312. E-mail: admissions@tusculum.edu. Web site: http://www.tusculum.edu/.

UNION UNIVERSITY
JACKSON, TENNESSEE

General Independent Southern Baptist, comprehensive, coed **Entrance** Moderately difficult **Setting** 290-acre small-town campus **Total enrollment** 2,544 **Student-faculty ratio** 12:1 **Application deadline** Rolling (freshmen), rolling (transfer) **Freshmen** 86% were admitted **Housing** Yes **Expenses** Tuition $12,670; Room & Board $4110 **Undergraduates** 59% women, 16% part-time, 24% 25 or older, 0.2% Native American, 1% Hispanic American, 6% African American, 1% Asian American/Pacific Islander **The most frequently chosen baccalaureate fields are** business/marketing, education, health professions and related sciences **Academic program** English as a second language, advanced placement, accelerated degree program, honors program, summer session, adult/continuing education programs, internships **Contact** Mr. Robbie Graves, Director of Enrollment Services, Union University, 1050 Union University Drive, Jackson, TN 38305-3697. Telephone: 731-661-5008 or toll-free 800-33-UNION. Fax: 731-661-5017. E-mail: cgriffin@buster.uu.edu. Web site: http://www.uu.edu/.

THE UNIVERSITY OF MEMPHIS
MEMPHIS, TENNESSEE

General State-supported, university, coed **Entrance** Moderately difficult **Setting** 1,100-acre urban campus **Total enrollment** 20,332 **Student-faculty ratio** 18:1 **Application deadline** 8/1 (freshmen), 8/1 (transfer) **Freshmen** 74% were admitted **Housing** Yes **Expenses** Tuition $3470; Room & Board $3801 **Undergraduates** 59% women, 28% part-time, 30% 25 or older, 0.3% Native American, 1% Hispanic American, 34% African American, 2% Asian American/Pacific Islander **The most frequently chosen baccalaureate fields are** business/marketing, interdisci-

The University of Memphis (continued)
plinary studies, visual/performing arts **Academic program** English as a second language, advanced placement, accelerated degree program, self-designed majors, honors program, summer session, adult/continuing education programs, internships **Contact** Mr. David Wallace, Director of Admissions, The University of Memphis, Memphis, TN 38152. Telephone: 901-678-2101. Fax: 901-678-3053. E-mail: dwallace@memphis.edu. Web site: http://www.memphis.edu/.

THE UNIVERSITY OF TENNESSEE
KNOXVILLE, TENNESSEE

General State-supported, university, coed **Entrance** Moderately difficult **Setting** 533-acre urban campus **Total enrollment** 26,033 **Student-faculty ratio** 14:1 **Application deadline** 1/21 (freshmen), 6/1 (transfer) **Freshmen** 69% were admitted **Housing** Yes **Expenses** Tuition $4034; Room & Board $4402 **Undergraduates** 52% women, 10% part-time, 10% 25 or older, 0.3% Native American, 1% Hispanic American, 6% African American, 2% Asian American/Pacific Islander **The most frequently chosen baccalaureate fields are** business/marketing, engineering/engineering technologies, social sciences and history **Academic program** English as a second language, advanced placement, accelerated degree program, self-designed majors, honors program, summer session, adult/continuing education programs, internships **Contact** Mr. Marshall Rose, Acting Director of Admissions, The University of Tennessee, 320 Student Services Building, Knoxville, TN 37996-0230. Telephone: 865-974-2184 or toll-free 800-221-8657 (in-state). Fax: 865-974-6341. E-mail: admissions@tennessee.edu. Web site: http://www.tennessee.edu/.

THE UNIVERSITY OF TENNESSEE AT CHATTANOOGA
CHATTANOOGA, TENNESSEE

General State-supported, comprehensive, coed **Entrance** Moderately difficult **Setting** 102-acre urban campus **Total enrollment** 8,485 **Student-faculty ratio** 16:1 **Application deadline** 8/1 (freshmen), 8/1 (transfer) **Freshmen** 51% were admitted **Housing** Yes **Expenses** Tuition $3236; Room only $2400 **Undergraduates** 58% women, 19% part-time, 22% 25 or older, 0.3% Native American, 1% Hispanic American, 18% African American, 3% Asian American/Pacific Islander **The most frequently chosen baccalaureate fields are** business/marketing, education, psychology **Academic program** English as a second language, advanced placement, honors program, summer session, adult/continuing education programs, internships **Contact** Mr. Yancy Freeman, Director of Student Recruitment, The University of Tennessee at Chattanooga, 131 Hooper Hall, Chattanooga, TN 37403. Telephone: 423-755-4597 or toll-free 800-UTC-6627 (in-state). Fax: 423-755-4157. E-mail: yancy-freeman@utc.edu. Web site: http://www.utc.edu/.

THE UNIVERSITY OF TENNESSEE AT MARTIN
MARTIN, TENNESSEE

General State-supported, comprehensive, coed **Entrance** Moderately difficult **Setting** 250-acre small-town campus **Total enrollment** 5,900 **Student-faculty ratio** 18:1 **Application deadline** Rolling (freshmen), rolling (transfer) **Freshmen** 55% were admitted **Housing** Yes **Expenses** Tuition $4442; Room & Board $3820 **Undergraduates** 56% women, 15% part-time, 18% 25 or older, 0.3% Native American, 1% Hispanic American, 15% African American, 0.5% Asian American/Pacific Islander **The most frequently chosen baccalaureate fields are** business/marketing, agriculture, interdisciplinary studies **Academic program** English as a second language, advanced placement, accelerated degree program, self-designed majors, honors program, summer session, adult/continuing education programs, internships **Contact** Ms. Judy Rayburn, Director of Admission, The University of Tennessee at Martin, 200 Hall-Moody Administration Building, Martin, TN 38238. Telephone: 901-587-7032 or toll-free 800-829-8861. Fax: 731-587-7029. E-mail: admitme@utm.edu. Web site: http://www.utm.edu/.

THE UNIVERSITY OF TENNESSEE HEALTH SCIENCE CENTER
MEMPHIS, TENNESSEE

Contact Ms. June Peoples, Director of Admissions, The University of Tennessee Health Science Center, 800 Madison Avenue, Memphis, TN 38163-0002. Telephone: 901-448-5560. Fax: 901-448-7585. E-mail: jpeoples@utmen1.utmem.edu. Web site: http://www.utmem.edu/.

UNIVERSITY OF THE SOUTH
SEWANEE, TENNESSEE

General Independent Episcopal, comprehensive, coed **Entrance** Very difficult **Setting** 10,000-acre small-town campus **Total enrollment** 1,442 **Student-faculty ratio** 10:1 **Application deadline** 2/1 (freshmen), 4/1 (transfer) **Freshmen** 74% were admitted **Housing** Yes **Expenses** Tuition $21,340; Room & Board $5950 **Undergraduates** 53% women, 2% part-time, 1% 25 or older, 0.2% Native American, 1% Hispanic American, 4% African American, 1% Asian American/Pacific Islander **The most frequently chosen baccalaureate fields are** English, social sciences and history, visual/performing arts **Academic program** Advanced placement, self-designed majors, summer session, internships **Contact** Mr. David Lesesne, Dean of Admission, University of the South, 735 University Avenue, Sewanee, TN 37383. Telephone: 931-598-1238 or toll-free 800-522-2234. Fax: 931-598-3248. E-mail: admiss@sewanee.edu. Web site: http://www.sewanee.edu/.

TEXAS

VANDERBILT UNIVERSITY
NASHVILLE, TENNESSEE

General Independent, university, coed **Entrance** Very difficult **Setting** 330-acre urban campus **Total enrollment** 10,338 **Student-faculty ratio** 9:1 **Application deadline** 1/4 (freshmen) **Freshmen** 46% were admitted **Housing** Yes **Expenses** Tuition $25,847; Room & Board $8635 **Undergraduates** 52% women, 1% part-time, 1% 25 or older, 0.2% Native American, 4% Hispanic American, 6% African American, 6% Asian American/Pacific Islander **The most frequently chosen baccalaureate fields are** engineering/engineering technologies, biological/life sciences, social sciences and history **Academic program** English as a second language, advanced placement, accelerated degree program, self-designed majors, honors program, summer session **Contact** Mr. Bill Shain, Dean of Undergraduate Admissions, Vanderbilt University, Nashville, TN 37240-1001. Telephone: 615-322-2561 or toll-free 800-288-0432. Fax: 615-343-7765. E-mail: admissions@vanderbilt.edu. Web site: http://www.vanderbilt.edu/.

TEXAS

ABILENE CHRISTIAN UNIVERSITY
ABILENE, TEXAS

General Independent, comprehensive, coed, affiliated with Church of Christ **Entrance** Moderately difficult **Setting** 208-acre urban campus **Total enrollment** 4,673 **Student-faculty ratio** 17:1 **Application deadline** 8/1 (freshmen), rolling (transfer) **Freshmen** 66% were admitted **Housing** Yes **Expenses** Tuition $11,650; Room & Board $4650 **Undergraduates** 55% women, 8% part-time, 7% 25 or older, 0.4% Native American, 6% Hispanic American, 6% African American, 1% Asian American/Pacific Islander **The most frequently chosen baccalaureate fields are** business/marketing, education, interdisciplinary studies **Academic program** English as a second language, advanced placement, self-designed majors, honors program, summer session, adult/continuing education programs, internships **Contact** Mr. Tim Johnston, Director of Admissions, Abilene Christian University, ACU Box 29100, Abilene, TX 79699-9100. Telephone: 915-674-2650 or toll-free 800-460-6228 Ext. 2650. E-mail: info@admissions.acu.edu. Web site: http://www.acu.edu/.

AMBERTON UNIVERSITY
GARLAND, TEXAS

General Independent nondenominational, upper-level, coed **Entrance** Minimally difficult **Setting** 5-acre suburban campus **Total enrollment** 1,648 **Student-faculty ratio** 25:1 **Application deadline** Rolling (transfer) **Housing** No **Expenses** Tuition $4050 **Undergraduates** 67% women, 80% part-time, 98% 25 or older, 1% Native American, 6% Hispanic American, 31% African American, 1% Asian American/Pacific Islander **The most frequently chosen baccalaureate field is** interdisciplinary studies **Academic program** Self-designed majors, summer session, adult/continuing education programs, internships **Contact** Dr. Algia Allen, Vice President for Academic Services, Amberton University, 1700 Eastgate Drive, Garland, TX 75041-5595. Telephone: 972-279-6511 Ext. 135. E-mail: webteam@amberu.edu. Web site: http://www.amberton.edu/.

ANGELO STATE UNIVERSITY
SAN ANGELO, TEXAS

General State-supported, comprehensive, coed **Entrance** Moderately difficult **Setting** 268-acre urban campus **Total enrollment** 6,262 **Student-faculty ratio** 22:1 **Application deadline** 8/1 (freshmen), 8/1 (transfer) **Freshmen** 76% were admitted **Housing** Yes **Expenses** Tuition $2722; Room & Board $4810 **Undergraduates** 56% women, 19% part-time, 20% 25 or older, 0.3% Native American, 20% Hispanic American, 5% African American, 1% Asian American/Pacific Islander **The most frequently chosen baccalaureate fields are** business/marketing, interdisciplinary studies, psychology **Academic program** Advanced placement, accelerated degree program, summer session, adult/continuing education programs, internships **Contact** Mrs. Monique Cossich, Director of Admissions, Angelo State University, Box 11014, ASU Station, Hardeman Administration and Journalism Building, San Angelo, TX 76909. Telephone: 915-942-2185 Ext. 231 or toll-free 800-946-8627 (in-state). Fax: 915-942-2078. E-mail: admissions@angelo.edu. Web site: http://www.angelo.edu/.

ARLINGTON BAPTIST COLLEGE
ARLINGTON, TEXAS

General Independent Baptist, 4-year, coed **Entrance** Minimally difficult **Setting** 32-acre urban campus **Total enrollment** 242 **Student-faculty ratio** 18:1 **Application deadline** Rolling (freshmen), rolling (transfer) **Freshmen** 100% were admitted **Housing** Yes **Expenses** Tuition $4700; Room only $1800 **Undergraduates** 38% women, 19% part-time, 22% 25 or older, 0% Native American, 6% Hispanic American, 1% African American, 1% Asian American/Pacific Islander **The most frequently chosen baccalaureate fields are** philosophy, education, philosophy, religion, and theology **Academic program** Advanced placement, accelerated degree program, summer session, internships **Contact** Ms. Janie Hall, Registrar/Admissions, Arlington Baptist College, 3001 West Division, Arlington, TX 76012-3425. Telephone: 817-461-8741 Ext. 105. Fax: 817-274-1138. E-mail: jhall@abconline.edu. Web site: http://www.abconline.edu/.

AUSTIN COLLEGE
SHERMAN, TEXAS

General Independent Presbyterian, comprehensive, coed **Entrance** Very difficult **Setting** 60-acre suburban campus **Total enrollment** 1,261 **Student-faculty**

TEXAS

Austin College *(continued)*
ratio 13:1 **Application deadline** 8/15 (freshmen), 8/15 (transfer) **Freshmen** 80% were admitted **Housing** Yes **Expenses** Tuition $15,963; Room & Board $6187 **Undergraduates** 56% women, 1% part-time, 2% 25 or older, 1% Native American, 7% Hispanic American, 5% African American, 8% Asian American/Pacific Islander **The most frequently chosen baccalaureate fields are** business/marketing, biological/life sciences, social sciences and history **Academic program** Advanced placement, accelerated degree program, self-designed majors, honors program, summer session, adult/continuing education programs, internships **Contact** Ms. Nan Massingill, Vice President for Institutional Enrollment, Austin College, 900 North Grand Avenue, Suite 6N, Sherman, TX 75090-4400. Telephone: 903-813-3000 or toll-free 800-442-5363. Fax: 903-813-3198. E-mail: admission@austinc.edu. Web site: http://www.austinc.edu/.

AUSTIN GRADUATE SCHOOL OF THEOLOGY
AUSTIN, TEXAS

General Independent, upper-level, coed, affiliated with Church of Christ **Entrance** Minimally difficult **Setting** urban campus **Total enrollment** 75 **Student-faculty ratio** 9:1 **Application deadline** Rolling (transfer) **Housing** No **Expenses** Tuition $2400 **Undergraduates** 31% women, 67% part-time, 82% 25 or older, 10% Hispanic American, 23% African American **The most frequently chosen baccalaureate fields are** philosophy, philosophy, religion, and theology **Academic program** Advanced placement, summer session, adult/continuing education programs **Contact** Ms. Laura Najera, Director of Admissions, Austin Graduate School of Theology, 1909 University Avenue, Austin, TX 78705. Telephone: 512-476-2772 Ext. 203 or toll-free 866-AUS-GRAD (in-state). Fax: 512-476-3919. E-mail: registrar@austingrad.edu. Web site: http://www.austingrad.edu/.

BAPTIST MISSIONARY ASSOCIATION THEOLOGICAL SEMINARY
JACKSONVILLE, TEXAS

General Independent Baptist, comprehensive, coed, primarily men **Entrance** Noncompetitive **Setting** 17-acre small-town campus **Total enrollment** 50 **Student-faculty ratio** 14:1 **Application deadline** 7/17 (freshmen), 8/1 (transfer) **Freshmen** 100% were admitted **Housing** Yes **Expenses** Tuition $2220; Room only $3580 **Undergraduates** 7% women, 74% part-time, 80% 25 or older, 7% Native American, 7% Hispanic American, 11% African American, 0% Asian American/Pacific Islander **The most frequently chosen baccalaureate field is** philosophy, religion, and theology **Academic program** Summer session, adult/continuing education programs, internships **Contact** Dr. Philip Attebery, Dean and Registrar, Baptist Missionary Association Theological Seminary, 1530 East Pine Street, Jacksonville, TX 75766-5407. Telephone: 903-586-2501. Fax: 903-586-0378. E-mail: bmatsem@flash.net. Web site: http://www.geocities.com/athens/acropolis/3386/.

BAYLOR UNIVERSITY
WACO, TEXAS

General Independent Baptist, university, coed **Entrance** Moderately difficult **Setting** 432-acre urban campus **Total enrollment** 14,221 **Student-faculty ratio** 18:1 **Application deadline** Rolling (freshmen), rolling (transfer) **Freshmen** 79% were admitted **Housing** Yes **Expenses** Tuition $12,804; Room & Board $5494 **Undergraduates** 58% women, 4% part-time, 3% 25 or older, 1% Native American, 7% Hispanic American, 6% African American, 5% Asian American/Pacific Islander **The most frequently chosen baccalaureate fields are** business/marketing, education, health professions and related sciences **Academic program** English as a second language, advanced placement, accelerated degree program, self-designed majors, honors program, summer session, internships **Contact** Mr. James Steen, Director of Admission Services, Baylor University, PO Box 97056, Waco, TX 76798-7056. Telephone: 254-710-3435 or toll-free 800-BAYLOR U. Fax: 254-710-3436. E-mail: admissions_office@baylor.edu. Web site: http://www.baylor.edu/.

COLLEGE OF BIBLICAL STUDIES–HOUSTON
HOUSTON, TEXAS

Contact College of Biblical Studies–Houston, 6000 Dale Carnegie Drive, Houston, TX 77036. Web site: http://www.cbshouston.edu/.

THE COLLEGE OF SAINT THOMAS MORE
FORT WORTH, TEXAS

General Independent, 4-year, coed, affiliated with Roman Catholic Church **Entrance** Moderately difficult **Setting** urban campus **Total enrollment** 62 **Student-faculty ratio** 4:1 **Application deadline** Rolling (freshmen), rolling (transfer) **Freshmen** 57% were admitted **Housing** Yes **Expenses** Tuition $9366; Room only $2205 **Undergraduates** 47% women, 13% part-time, 20% 25 or older **The most frequently chosen baccalaureate field is** liberal arts/general studies **Academic program** Summer session **Contact** Mrs. Donna Klein, Dean of Students and Registrar, The College of Saint Thomas More, 3013 Lubbock Avenue, Fort Worth, TX 76109-2323. Telephone: 817-921-2728 or toll-free 800-583-6489 (out-of-state). Fax: 817-924-3206. E-mail: more-info@cstm.edu. Web site: http://www.cstm.edu/.

CONCORDIA UNIVERSITY AT AUSTIN
AUSTIN, TEXAS

General Independent, comprehensive, coed, affiliated with Lutheran Church–Missouri Synod **Entrance** Moderately difficult **Setting** 20-acre urban campus **Total enrollment** 806 **Student-faculty ratio** 12:1 **Application deadline** 8/15 (freshmen), 8/1 (transfer)

Freshmen 64% were admitted **Housing** Yes **Expenses** Tuition $12,570; Room & Board $5460 **Undergraduates** 55% women, 36% part-time, 30% 25 or older, 0.5% Native American, 13% Hispanic American, 4% African American, 0.5% Asian American/Pacific Islander **The most frequently chosen baccalaureate fields are** business/marketing, education, psychology **Academic program** English as a second language, advanced placement, accelerated degree program, honors program, summer session, adult/continuing education programs, internships **Contact** Mr. Jay Krause, Vice President for Enrollment Services, Concordia University at Austin, 3400 Interstate 35 North, Austin, TX 78705-2799. Telephone: 512-486-2000 Ext. 1107 or toll-free 800-285-4252. Fax: 512-459-8517. E-mail: ctxadmis@crf.cuis.edu. Web site: http://www.concordia.edu/.

THE CRISWELL COLLEGE
DALLAS, TEXAS

General Independent, comprehensive, coed, affiliated with Southern Baptist Convention **Entrance** Minimally difficult **Setting** 1-acre urban campus **Total enrollment** 451 **Application deadline** 8/15 (freshmen), 8/15 (transfer) **Housing** No **Expenses** Tuition $3900 **Academic program** Advanced placement, summer session, internships **Contact** Mr. Tommy Weir, Vice President for Institutional Advancement, The Criswell College, 4010 Gaston Avenue, Dallas, TX 75246-1537. Telephone: 214-818-1302 or toll-free 800-899-0012. Fax: 214-818-1310. E-mail: tweir@criswell.edu. Web site: http://www.criswell.edu/.

DALLAS BAPTIST UNIVERSITY
DALLAS, TEXAS

General Independent, comprehensive, coed, affiliated with Baptist Church **Entrance** Moderately difficult **Setting** 288-acre urban campus **Total enrollment** 4,302 **Student-faculty ratio** 19:1 **Application deadline** Rolling (freshmen), rolling (transfer) **Freshmen** 93% were admitted **Housing** Yes **Expenses** Tuition $9750; Room & Board $3932 **Undergraduates** 61% women, 54% part-time, 47% 25 or older, 3% Native American, 8% Hispanic American, 20% African American, 1% Asian American/Pacific Islander **The most frequently chosen baccalaureate fields are** business/marketing, liberal arts/general studies, visual/performing arts **Academic program** English as a second language, advanced placement, summer session, adult/continuing education programs, internships **Contact** Dr. Duke Jones, Director of Admissions, Dallas Baptist University, 3000 Mountain Creek Parkway, Dallas, TX 75211-9299. Telephone: 214-333-5360 or toll-free 800-460-1328. Fax: 214-333-5447. E-mail: admiss@dbu.edu. Web site: http://www.dbu.edu/.

DALLAS CHRISTIAN COLLEGE
DALLAS, TEXAS

General Independent, 4-year, coed, affiliated with Christian Churches and Churches of Christ **Entrance** Minimally difficult **Setting** 22-acre urban campus **Total enrollment** 281 **Student-faculty ratio** 13:1 **Application deadline** Rolling (freshmen), rolling (transfer) **Freshmen** 49% were admitted **Housing** Yes **Expenses** Tuition $6580; Room & Board $3900 **Undergraduates** 46% women, 37% part-time, 84% 25 or older, 1% Native American, 7% Hispanic American, 16% African American, 0.4% Asian American/Pacific Islander **The most frequently chosen baccalaureate fields are** philosophy, business/marketing, philosophy, religion, and theology **Academic program** Advanced placement, accelerated degree program, summer session, adult/continuing education programs, internships **Contact** Mr. Marty McKee, Director of Admissions, Dallas Christian College, 2700 Christian Parkway, Dallas, TX 75234-7299. Telephone: 972-241-3371 Ext. 153. Fax: 972-241-8021. E-mail: dcc@dallas.edu. Web site: http://www.dallas.edu/.

DEVRY UNIVERSITY
IRVING, TEXAS

General Proprietary, 4-year, coed **Entrance** Minimally difficult **Setting** 13-acre suburban campus **Total enrollment** 3,569 **Student-faculty ratio** 20:1 **Application deadline** Rolling (freshmen), rolling (transfer) **Freshmen** 86% were admitted **Housing** No **Expenses** Tuition $8740 **Undergraduates** 28% women, 37% part-time, 53% 25 or older, 1% Native American, 16% Hispanic American, 32% African American, 7% Asian American/Pacific Islander **The most frequently chosen baccalaureate fields are** business/marketing, computer/information sciences, engineering/engineering technologies **Academic program** Advanced placement, accelerated degree program, summer session, adult/continuing education programs **Contact** Ms. Vicki Carroll, New Student Coordinator, DeVry University, 4000 Millenia Drive, Orlando, FL 32839. Telephone: 972-929-5777 or toll-free 800-443-3879 (in-state); 800-633-3879 (out-of-state). Web site: http://www.dal.devry.edu/.

EAST TEXAS BAPTIST UNIVERSITY
MARSHALL, TEXAS

General Independent Baptist, 4-year, coed **Entrance** Moderately difficult **Setting** 200-acre small-town campus **Total enrollment** 1,509 **Student-faculty ratio** 16:1 **Application deadline** Rolling (freshmen), rolling (transfer) **Freshmen** 75% were admitted **Housing** Yes **Expenses** Tuition $9050; Room & Board $3299 **Undergraduates** 53% women, 11% part-time, 7% 25 or older, 1% Native American, 4% Hispanic American, 13% African American, 0% Asian American/Pacific Islander **The most frequently chosen baccalaureate fields are** business/marketing, education, philosophy **Academic program** English as a second language, advanced placement, accelerated degree program, honors program, summer session, adult/continuing education programs, internships **Contact** Mr. Vince Blankenship, Director of Admissions, East Texas Baptist University, 1209 North Grove, Marshall, TX 75670-1498. Telephone: 903-

TEXAS

East Texas Baptist University *(continued)*
923-2000 or toll-free 800-804-ETBU. Fax: 903-938-1705. E-mail: admissions@etbu.edu. Web site: http://www.etbu.edu/.

HARDIN-SIMMONS UNIVERSITY
ABILENE, TEXAS

General Independent Baptist, comprehensive, coed **Entrance** Moderately difficult **Setting** 40-acre urban campus **Total enrollment** 2,335 **Student-faculty ratio** 13:1 **Application deadline** Rolling (freshmen), rolling (transfer) **Freshmen** 69% were admitted **Housing** Yes **Expenses** Tuition $11,250; Room & Board $3515 **Undergraduates** 53% women, 12% part-time, 11% 25 or older, 0.4% Native American, 7% Hispanic American, 4% African American, 1% Asian American/Pacific Islander **The most frequently chosen baccalaureate fields are** business/marketing, biological/life sciences, education **Academic program** Advanced placement, accelerated degree program, summer session, adult/continuing education programs, internships **Contact** Mrs. Stacey Martin, Enrollment Services Counselor, Hardin-Simmons University, Box 16050, Abilene, TX 79698-6050. Telephone: 915-670-5813 or toll-free 800-568-2692. Fax: 915-670-1527. E-mail: enroll.services@hsutx.edu. Web site: http://www.hsutx.edu/.

HOUSTON BAPTIST UNIVERSITY
HOUSTON, TEXAS

General Independent Baptist, comprehensive, coed **Entrance** Moderately difficult **Setting** 158-acre urban campus **Total enrollment** 2,829 **Student-faculty ratio** 16:1 **Application deadline** Rolling (freshmen), rolling (transfer) **Freshmen** 76% were admitted **Housing** Yes **Expenses** Tuition $11,142; Room & Board $4080 **Undergraduates** 69% women, 14% part-time, 23% 25 or older **The most frequently chosen baccalaureate fields are** business/marketing, education, health professions and related sciences **Academic program** English as a second language, advanced placement, honors program, summer session, adult/continuing education programs, internships **Contact** Mr. David Melton, Director of Admissions, Houston Baptist University, 7502 Fondren Road, Houston, TX 77074-3298. Telephone: 281-649-3211 Ext. 3208 or toll-free 800-969-3210. Fax: 281-649-3217. E-mail: unadm@hbu.edu. Web site: http://www.hbu.edu/.

HOWARD PAYNE UNIVERSITY
BROWNWOOD, TEXAS

General Independent Southern Baptist, 4-year, coed **Entrance** Minimally difficult **Setting** 30-acre small-town campus **Total enrollment** 1,526 **Student-faculty ratio** 14:1 **Application deadline** Rolling (freshmen), rolling (transfer) **Freshmen** 88% were admitted **Housing** Yes **Expenses** Tuition $10,400; Room & Board $3834 **Undergraduates** 25% 25 or older, 0.2% Native American, 12% Hispanic American, 9% African American, 2% Asian American/Pacific Islander **The most frequently chosen baccalaureate fields are** business/marketing, education, philosophy **Academic program** English as a second language, advanced placement, honors program, summer session, adult/continuing education programs, internships **Contact** Ms. Cheryl Mangrum, Coordinator of Admission Services, Howard Payne University, HPU Station Box 828, 1000 Fisk Avenue, Brownwood, TX 76801. Telephone: 915-649-8027 or toll-free 800-880-4478. Fax: 915-649-8901. E-mail: enroll@hputx.edu. Web site: http://www.hputx.edu/.

HUSTON-TILLOTSON COLLEGE
AUSTIN, TEXAS

General Independent interdenominational, 4-year, coed **Entrance** Moderately difficult **Setting** 23-acre urban campus **Total enrollment** 618 **Student-faculty ratio** 16:1 **Application deadline** 3/1 (freshmen), 3/1 (transfer) **Freshmen** 89% were admitted **Housing** Yes **Expenses** Tuition $7950; Room & Board $5027 **Undergraduates** 55% women, 24% part-time, 32% 25 or older, 7% Hispanic American, 75% African American, 4% Asian American/Pacific Islander **Academic program** English as a second language, advanced placement, accelerated degree program, summer session, internships **Contact** Ms. Bronte D. Jones, Admission and Financial Aid Services, Huston-Tillotson College, 900 Chicon Street, Austin, TX 78702. Telephone: 512-505-3027. Fax: 512-505-3192. E-mail: taglenn@htc.edu. Web site: http://www.htc.edu.

JARVIS CHRISTIAN COLLEGE
HAWKINS, TEXAS

General Independent, 4-year, coed, affiliated with Christian Church (Disciples of Christ) **Entrance** Minimally difficult **Setting** 465-acre rural campus **Total enrollment** 571 **Student-faculty ratio** 14:1 **Application deadline** Rolling (freshmen), rolling (transfer) **Freshmen** 100% were admitted **Housing** Yes **Expenses** Tuition $5550; Room & Board $3985 **Undergraduates** 58% women, 1% part-time, 1% 25 or older, 0% Native American, 2% Hispanic American, 95% African American, 0% Asian American/Pacific Islander **The most frequently chosen baccalaureate fields are** business/marketing, biological/life sciences, social sciences and history **Academic program** Advanced placement, honors program, internships **Contact** Ms. Serena Sentell, Admissions Counselor, Jarvis Christian College, P.O. Box 1970, Hawkins, TX 75765-9989. Telephone: 903-769-0417 or toll-free 800-292-9517. Fax: 903-769-4842. Web site: http://www.jarvis.edu/.

LAMAR UNIVERSITY
BEAUMONT, TEXAS

General State-supported, university, coed **Entrance** Minimally difficult **Setting** 200-acre suburban campus **Total enrollment** 8,969 **Student-faculty ratio** 25:1 **Application deadline** 8/1 (freshmen), 8/1 (transfer) **Freshmen** 69% were admitted **Housing** Yes

TEXAS

Expenses Tuition $2756; Room & Board $4854 **Undergraduates** 60% women, 34% part-time, 39% 25 or older, 0.4% Native American, 5% Hispanic American, 19% African American, 3% Asian American/Pacific Islander **Academic program** English as a second language, advanced placement, accelerated degree program, self-designed majors, honors program, summer session, adult/continuing education programs, internships **Contact** Ms. Melissa Chesser, Director of Recruitment, Lamar University, PO Box 10009, Beaumont, TX 77710. Telephone: 409-880-8888. Fax: 409-880-8463. E-mail: hunterre@hal.lamar.edu. Web site: http://www.lamar.edu/.

LETOURNEAU UNIVERSITY
LONGVIEW, TEXAS

General Independent nondenominational, comprehensive, coed **Entrance** Moderately difficult **Setting** 162-acre suburban campus **Total enrollment** 3,098 **Student-faculty ratio** 15:1 **Application deadline** 8/1 (freshmen), 8/1 (transfer) **Freshmen** 85% were admitted **Housing** Yes **Expenses** Tuition $12,840; Room & Board $5420 **Undergraduates** 50% women, 56% part-time, 9% 25 or older, 1% Native American, 5% Hispanic American, 17% African American, 1% Asian American/Pacific Islander **The most frequently chosen baccalaureate fields are** business/marketing, education, engineering/engineering technologies **Academic program** Advanced placement, honors program, summer session, adult/continuing education programs, internships **Contact** Mr. James Townsend, Director of Admissions, LeTourneau University, PO Box 7001, Longview, TX 75607. Telephone: 903-233-3400 or toll-free 800-759-8811. Fax: 903-233-3411. E-mail: admissions@letu.edu. Web site: http://www.letu.edu/.

LUBBOCK CHRISTIAN UNIVERSITY
LUBBOCK, TEXAS

General Independent, comprehensive, coed, affiliated with Church of Christ **Entrance** Moderately difficult **Setting** 120-acre suburban campus **Total enrollment** 1,823 **Student-faculty ratio** 16:1 **Application deadline** Rolling (freshmen), rolling (transfer) **Freshmen** 77% were admitted **Housing** Yes **Expenses** Tuition $10,994; Room & Board $3900 **Undergraduates** 57% women, 16% part-time, 30% 25 or older, 0.4% Native American, 10% Hispanic American, 5% African American, 0.4% Asian American/Pacific Islander **The most frequently chosen baccalaureate field is** philosophy, religion, and theology **Academic program** Advanced placement, accelerated degree program, self-designed majors, honors program, summer session, adult/continuing education programs, internships **Contact** Mrs. Rhonda Crawford, Director of Admissions, Lubbock Christian University, 5601 19th Street, Lubbock, TX 79407. Telephone: 806-796-8800 Ext. 260 or toll-free 800-933-7601 Ext. 260. Fax: 806-796-8917 Ext. 260. E-mail: admissions@lcu.edu.

MCMURRY UNIVERSITY
ABILENE, TEXAS

General Independent United Methodist, 4-year, coed **Entrance** Moderately difficult **Setting** 41-acre urban campus **Total enrollment** 1,378 **Student-faculty ratio** 15:1 **Application deadline** Rolling (freshmen), rolling (transfer) **Freshmen** 74% were admitted **Housing** Yes **Expenses** Tuition $10,905; Room & Board $4512 **Undergraduates** 51% women, 15% part-time, 19% 25 or older, 2% Native American, 13% Hispanic American, 8% African American, 1% Asian American/Pacific Islander **The most frequently chosen baccalaureate fields are** business/marketing, education, social sciences and history **Academic program** Advanced placement, accelerated degree program, honors program, summer session, internships **Contact** Ms. Amy Weyant, Director of Admissions, McMurry University, Box 947, Abilene, TX 79697. Telephone: 915-793-4705 or toll-free 800-477-0077. Fax: 915-793-4718. E-mail: admissions@mcm.edu. Web site: http://www.mcm.edu/.

MIDWESTERN STATE UNIVERSITY
WICHITA FALLS, TEXAS

General State-supported, comprehensive, coed **Entrance** Minimally difficult **Setting** 172-acre urban campus **Total enrollment** 5,969 **Student-faculty ratio** 19:1 **Application deadline** 8/7 (freshmen), 8/7 (transfer) **Freshmen** 55% were admitted **Housing** Yes **Expenses** Tuition $2576; Room & Board $4392 **Undergraduates** 57% women, 28% part-time, 28% 25 or older, 1% Native American, 9% Hispanic American, 8% African American, 3% Asian American/Pacific Islander **The most frequently chosen baccalaureate fields are** business/marketing, health professions and related sciences, interdisciplinary studies **Academic program** English as a second language, advanced placement, accelerated degree program, honors program, summer session, adult/continuing education programs, internships **Contact** Barbara Merkle, Director of Admissions, Midwestern State University, 3410 Taft Boulevard, Wichita Falls, TX 76308. Telephone: 940-397-4334 or toll-free 800-842-1922 (in-state). E-mail: school.relations@mwsu.edu. Web site: http://www.mwsu.edu/.

NORTHWOOD UNIVERSITY, TEXAS CAMPUS
CEDAR HILL, TEXAS

General Independent, 4-year, coed **Entrance** Moderately difficult **Setting** 360-acre small-town campus **Total enrollment** 1,114 **Student-faculty ratio** 25:1 **Application deadline** 9/1 (freshmen), 9/1 (transfer) **Freshmen** 67% were admitted **Housing** Yes **Expenses** Tuition $12,531; Room & Board $5604 **Undergraduates** 57% women, 25% part-time, 4% 25 or older, 0.1% Native American, 18% Hispanic American, 22% African American, 2% Asian American/Pacific Islander **The most frequently chosen baccalaureate fields are** business/marketing, computer/information sciences **Academic program** Advanced

TEXAS

Northwood University, Texas Campus *(continued)*
placement, honors program, summer session, adult/continuing education programs, internships **Contact** Mr. James R. Hickerson, Director of Admissions, Northwood University, Texas Campus, P.O. Box 58, Cedar Hill, TX 75104. Telephone: 972-293-5400 or toll-free 800-927-9663. Fax: 972-291-3824. E-mail: txadmit@northwood.edu. Web site: http://www.northwood.edu/.

OUR LADY OF THE LAKE UNIVERSITY OF SAN ANTONIO
SAN ANTONIO, TEXAS

General Independent Roman Catholic, comprehensive, coed **Entrance** Moderately difficult **Setting** 75-acre urban campus **Total enrollment** 3,324 **Student-faculty ratio** 15:1 **Application deadline** Rolling (freshmen), rolling (transfer) **Freshmen** 61% were admitted **Housing** Yes **Expenses** Tuition $12,786; Room & Board $4550 **Undergraduates** 78% women, 39% part-time, 43% 25 or older, 0.4% Native American, 67% Hispanic American, 7% African American, 1% Asian American/Pacific Islander **The most frequently chosen baccalaureate fields are** business/marketing, liberal arts/general studies, psychology **Academic program** English as a second language, advanced placement, summer session, adult/continuing education programs, internships **Contact** Mr. Michael Boatner, Acting Director of Admissions, Our Lady of the Lake University of San Antonio, 411 Southwest 24th Street, San Antonio, TX 78207-4689. Telephone: 210-434-6711 Ext. 314 or toll-free 800-436-6558. Fax: 210-431-4036. E-mail: admission@lake.ollusa.edu. Web site: http://www.ollusa.edu/.

PAUL QUINN COLLEGE
DALLAS, TEXAS

Contact Don Robinson, Director of Admissions, Paul Quinn College, 3837 Simpson-Stuart Road, Dallas, TX 75241-4331. Telephone: 214-302-3520 or toll-free 800-237-2648. Fax: 214-302-3559. Web site: http://www.pqc.edu.

PRAIRIE VIEW A&M UNIVERSITY
PRAIRIE VIEW, TEXAS

General State-supported, comprehensive, coed **Entrance** Moderately difficult **Setting** 1,440-acre small-town campus **Total enrollment** 6,747 **Student-faculty ratio** 18:1 **Application deadline** 7/1 (transfer) **Freshmen** 97% were admitted **Housing** Yes **Expenses** Tuition $3172; Room & Board $6191 **Undergraduates** 56% women, 9% part-time, 16% 25 or older, 0.02% Native American, 2% Hispanic American, 94% African American, 1% Asian American/Pacific Islander **The most frequently chosen baccalaureate fields are** business/marketing, engineering/engineering technologies, health professions and related sciences **Academic program** English as a second language, advanced placement, accelerated degree program, honors program, summer session, internships **Contact** Ms. Mary Gooch, Director of Admissions, Prairie View A&M University, PO Box 3089, Prairie View, TX 77446-0188. Telephone: 936-857-2626. Fax: 936-857-2699. E-mail: mary_gooch@pvamu.edu. Web site: http://www.pvamu.edu/.

RICE UNIVERSITY
HOUSTON, TEXAS

General Independent, university, coed **Entrance** Most difficult **Setting** 300-acre urban campus **Total enrollment** 4,534 **Student-faculty ratio** 5:1 **Application deadline** 1/2 (freshmen), 4/1 (transfer) **Freshmen** 23% were admitted **Housing** Yes **Expenses** Tuition $17,135; Room & Board $7200 **Undergraduates** 48% women, 6% part-time, 1% 25 or older, 1% Native American, 10% Hispanic American, 7% African American, 14% Asian American/Pacific Islander **The most frequently chosen baccalaureate fields are** engineering/engineering technologies, biological/life sciences, social sciences and history **Academic program** Advanced placement, accelerated degree program, self-designed majors, honors program, summer session, internships **Contact** Ms. Julie M. Browning, Dean for Undergraduate Admission, Rice University, PO Box 1892, MS 17, Houston, TX 77251-1892. Telephone: 713-348-RICE or toll-free 800-527-OWLS. E-mail: admission@rice.edu. Web site: http://www.rice.edu/.

ST. EDWARD'S UNIVERSITY
AUSTIN, TEXAS

General Independent Roman Catholic, comprehensive, coed **Entrance** Moderately difficult **Setting** 180-acre urban campus **Total enrollment** 4,151 **Student-faculty ratio** 15:1 **Application deadline** 7/1 (freshmen), 7/1 (transfer) **Freshmen** 74% were admitted **Housing** Yes **Expenses** Tuition $12,728; Room & Board $5118 **Undergraduates** 57% women, 31% part-time, 10% 25 or older, 1% Native American, 28% Hispanic American, 5% African American, 2% Asian American/Pacific Islander **The most frequently chosen baccalaureate fields are** business/marketing, liberal arts/general studies, social sciences and history **Academic program** Advanced placement, accelerated degree program, honors program, summer session, adult/continuing education programs, internships **Contact** Ms. Tracy Manier, Director of Admission, St. Edward's University, 3001 South Congress Avenue, Austin, TX 78704-6489. Telephone: 512-448-8602 or toll-free 800-555-0164. Fax: 512-464-8877. E-mail: seu.admit@admin.stedwards.edu. Web site: http://www.stedwards.edu/.

ST. MARY'S UNIVERSITY OF SAN ANTONIO
SAN ANTONIO, TEXAS

General Independent Roman Catholic, comprehensive, coed **Entrance** Moderately difficult **Setting** 135-acre urban campus **Total enrollment** 4,136 **Student-faculty ratio** 15:1 **Application deadline** Rolling (freshmen), rolling (transfer) **Freshmen** 81%

TEXAS

were admitted **Housing** Yes **Expenses** Tuition $13,480; Room & Board $5380 **Undergraduates** 59% women, 10% part-time, 13% 25 or older, 0.4% Native American, 69% Hispanic American, 3% African American, 2% Asian American/Pacific Islander **The most frequently chosen baccalaureate fields are** business/marketing, biological/life sciences, social sciences and history **Academic program** English as a second language, advanced placement, honors program, summer session, adult/continuing education programs, internships **Contact** Mr. Richard Castillo, Director of Admissions, St. Mary's University of San Antonio, 1 Camino Santa Maria, San Antonio, TX 78228-8503. Telephone: 210-436-3126 or toll-free 800-FOR-STMU (out-of-state). Fax: 210-431-6742. E-mail: uadm@stmarytx.edu. Web site: http://www.stmarytx.edu/.

▶ For more information, see page 472.

SAM HOUSTON STATE UNIVERSITY
HUNTSVILLE, TEXAS

General State-supported, comprehensive, coed **Entrance** Moderately difficult **Setting** 2,143-acre small-town campus **Total enrollment** 12,996 **Student-faculty ratio** 21:1 **Application deadline** Rolling (freshmen), rolling (transfer) **Freshmen** 86% were admitted **Housing** Yes **Expenses** Tuition $2818; Room & Board $3672 **Undergraduates** 57% women, 18% part-time, 18% 25 or older, 0.5% Native American, 9% Hispanic American, 15% African American, 1% Asian American/Pacific Islander **The most frequently chosen baccalaureate fields are** business/marketing, interdisciplinary studies, protective services/public administration **Academic program** English as a second language, advanced placement, accelerated degree program, honors program, summer session, adult/continuing education programs, internships **Contact** Ms. Joey Chandler, Director of Admissions and Recruitment, Sam Houston State University, PO Box 2418, Huntsville, TX 77341. Telephone: 936-294-1828. Fax: 936-294-3758. Web site: http://www.shsu.edu/.

SCHREINER UNIVERSITY
KERRVILLE, TEXAS

General Independent Presbyterian, comprehensive, coed **Entrance** Moderately difficult **Setting** 175-acre small-town campus **Total enrollment** 806 **Student-faculty ratio** 11:1 **Application deadline** 8/1 (freshmen), 8/15 (transfer) **Freshmen** 71% were admitted **Housing** Yes **Expenses** Tuition $12,318; Room & Board $6936 **Undergraduates** 62% women, 14% part-time, 23% 25 or older, 1% Native American, 15% Hispanic American, 2% African American, 1% Asian American/Pacific Islander **The most frequently chosen baccalaureate fields are** business/marketing, parks and recreation, psychology **Academic program** English as a second language, advanced placement, self-designed majors, honors program, summer session, internships **Contact** Ms. Peg Lexton, Dean of Admission and Financial Aid, Schreiner University, 2100 Memorial Boulevard, Kerrville, TX 78028. Telephone: 830-792-7227 or toll-free 800-343-4919. Fax: 830-792-7226. E-mail: admissions@schreiner.edu. Web site: http://www.schreiner.edu/.

SOUTHERN METHODIST UNIVERSITY
DALLAS, TEXAS

General Independent, university, coed, affiliated with United Methodist Church **Entrance** Moderately difficult **Setting** 163-acre suburban campus **Total enrollment** 10,266 **Student-faculty ratio** 12:1 **Application deadline** 1/15 (freshmen), 7/1 (transfer) **Freshmen** 75% were admitted **Housing** Yes **Expenses** Tuition $20,796; Room & Board $7553 **Undergraduates** 54% women, 6% part-time, 6% 25 or older, 1% Native American, 8% Hispanic American, 6% African American, 6% Asian American/Pacific Islander **The most frequently chosen baccalaureate fields are** business/marketing, communications/communication technologies, trade and industry **Academic program** English as a second language, advanced placement, accelerated degree program, self-designed majors, honors program, summer session, adult/continuing education programs, internships **Contact** Mr. Ron W. Moss, Director of Admission and Enrollment Management, Southern Methodist University, PO Box 750181, Dallas, TX 75275-0181. Telephone: 214-768-2058 or toll-free 800-323-0672. Fax: 214-768-0103. E-mail: enrol_serv@mail.smu.edu. Web site: http://www.smu.edu/.

SOUTHWESTERN ADVENTIST UNIVERSITY
KEENE, TEXAS

General Independent Seventh-day Adventist, comprehensive, coed **Entrance** Minimally difficult **Setting** 150-acre rural campus **Total enrollment** 1,191 **Student-faculty ratio** 15:1 **Application deadline** 8/31 (freshmen), 8/31 (transfer) **Freshmen** 64% were admitted **Housing** Yes **Expenses** Tuition $10,020; Room & Board $4778 **Undergraduates** 60% women, 29% part-time, 36% 25 or older, 1% Native American, 15% Hispanic American, 14% African American, 6% Asian American/Pacific Islander **The most frequently chosen baccalaureate fields are** business/marketing, education, philosophy, religion, and theology **Academic program** English as a second language, accelerated degree program, self-designed majors, honors program, summer session, internships **Contact** Mrs. Sylvia Peterson, Admissions Counselor, Southwestern Adventist University, PO Box 567, Keene, TX 76059. Telephone: 817-645-3921 Ext. 294 or toll-free 800-433-2240. Fax: 817-556-4744. E-mail: illingworth@vaxine.swac.edu. Web site: http://www.swau.edu/.

SOUTHWESTERN ASSEMBLIES OF GOD UNIVERSITY
WAXAHACHIE, TEXAS

General Independent, comprehensive, coed, affiliated with Assemblies of God **Entrance** Noncompetitive **Setting** 70-acre small-town campus **Total enroll-

Southwestern Assemblies of God University *(continued)*

ment 1,738 **Student-faculty ratio** 20:1 **Application deadline** Rolling (freshmen), rolling (transfer) **Freshmen** 60% were admitted **Housing** Yes **Expenses** Tuition $7850; Room & Board $4470 **Undergraduates** 52% women, 13% part-time, 24% 25 or older, 2% Native American, 15% Hispanic American, 6% African American, 1% Asian American/Pacific Islander **The most frequently chosen baccalaureate fields are** education, liberal arts/general studies, philosophy **Academic program** Advanced placement, summer session, adult/continuing education programs, internships **Contact** Eddie Davis, Enrollment Services, Southwestern Assemblies of God University, 1200 Sycamore Street, Waxahachie, TX 75165-2397. Telephone: 972-937-4010 Ext. 1121 or toll-free 800-262-SAGU. Fax: 972-923-0006. E-mail: edavis@sagu.edu. Web site: http://www.sagu.edu/.

SOUTHWESTERN CHRISTIAN COLLEGE
TERRELL, TEXAS

Contact Admissions Department, Southwestern Christian College, Box 10, 200 Bowser Street, Terrell, TX 75160. Telephone: 214-524-3341. Web site: http://www.swcc.edu/.

SOUTHWESTERN UNIVERSITY
GEORGETOWN, TEXAS

General Independent Methodist, 4-year, coed **Entrance** Very difficult **Setting** 500-acre suburban campus **Total enrollment** 1,320 **Student-faculty ratio** 11:1 **Application deadline** 2/15 (freshmen), 4/1 (transfer) **Freshmen** 59% were admitted **Housing** Yes **Expenses** Tuition $16,650; Room & Board $5900 **Undergraduates** 57% women, 2% part-time, 1% 25 or older, 1% Native American, 12% Hispanic American, 3% African American, 2% Asian American/Pacific Islander **The most frequently chosen baccalaureate field is** philosophy, religion, and theology **Academic program** Advanced placement, accelerated degree program, self-designed majors, honors program, summer session, internships **Contact** Mr. John W. Lind, Vice President for Enrollment Management, Southwestern University, 1001 East University Avenue, Georgetown, TX 78626. Telephone: 512-863-1200 or toll-free 800-252-3166. Fax: 512-863-9601. E-mail: admission@southwestern.edu. Web site: http://www.southwestern.edu/.

SOUTHWEST TEXAS STATE UNIVERSITY
SAN MARCOS, TEXAS

General State-supported, comprehensive, coed **Entrance** Moderately difficult **Setting** 423-acre small-town campus **Total enrollment** 23,517 **Student-faculty ratio** 25:1 **Application deadline** 7/1 (freshmen), 7/1 (transfer) **Freshmen** 58% were admitted **Housing** Yes **Expenses** Tuition $3578; Room & Board $5152 **Undergraduates** 55% women, 20% part-time, 19% 25 or older, 1% Native American, 19% Hispanic American, 5% African American, 2% Asian American/Pacific Islander **The most frequently chosen baccalaureate fields are** business/marketing, interdisciplinary studies, social sciences and history **Academic program** English as a second language, advanced placement, accelerated degree program, honors program, summer session, adult/continuing education programs, internships **Contact** Mrs. Christie Kangas, Director of Admissions, Southwest Texas State University, Admissions and Visitors Center, San Marcos, TX 78666. Telephone: 512-245-2364 Ext. 2803. Fax: 512-245-8044. E-mail: admissions@swt.edu. Web site: http://www.swt.edu/.

▶ **For more information, see page 478.**

STEPHEN F. AUSTIN STATE UNIVERSITY
NACOGDOCHES, TEXAS

General State-supported, comprehensive, coed **Entrance** Moderately difficult **Setting** 400-acre small-town campus **Total enrollment** 11,569 **Student-faculty ratio** 15:1 **Application deadline** Rolling (freshmen), rolling (transfer) **Freshmen** 67% were admitted **Housing** Yes **Expenses** Tuition $2330; Room & Board $4575 **Undergraduates** 58% women, 12% part-time, 20% 25 or older, 0.5% Native American, 6% Hispanic American, 15% African American, 1% Asian American/Pacific Islander **The most frequently chosen baccalaureate fields are** business/marketing, health professions and related sciences, interdisciplinary studies **Academic program** English as a second language, advanced placement, accelerated degree program, self-designed majors, honors program, summer session, adult/continuing education programs, internships **Contact** Ms. Beth Smith, Assistant Director of Admissions, Stephen F. Austin State University, SFA Box 13051, Nacogdoches, TX 75962. Telephone: 936-468-2504 or toll-free 800-259-9SFA. Fax: 936-468-3849. E-mail: admissions@sfasu.edu. Web site: http://www.sfasu.edu/.

SUL ROSS STATE UNIVERSITY
ALPINE, TEXAS

General State-supported, comprehensive, coed **Entrance** Noncompetitive **Setting** 640-acre small-town campus **Total enrollment** 1,992 **Student-faculty ratio** 17:1 **Application deadline** Rolling (freshmen), rolling (transfer) **Housing** Yes **Expenses** Tuition $2792; Room & Board $3790 **Undergraduates** 48% women, 15% part-time, 24% 25 or older, 0.4% Native American, 47% Hispanic American, 5% African American, 1% Asian American/Pacific Islander **The most frequently chosen baccalaureate fields are** agriculture, business/marketing, education **Academic program** Advanced placement, honors program, summer session, internships **Contact** Mr. Robert Cullins, Dean of Admissions and Records, Sul Ross State University, Box C-2, Alpine, TX 79832. Telephone: 915-837-8050. Fax: 915-837-8431. E-mail: rcullins@sulross.edu. Web site: http://www.sulross.edu/.

TEXAS

TARLETON STATE UNIVERSITY
STEPHENVILLE, TEXAS

General State-supported, comprehensive, coed **Entrance** Moderately difficult **Setting** 165-acre small-town campus **Total enrollment** 8,024 **Student-faculty ratio** 18:1 **Application deadline** 8/1 (freshmen), 8/1 (transfer) **Freshmen** 67% were admitted **Housing** Yes **Expenses** Tuition $2920; Room & Board $4486 **Undergraduates** 54% women, 23% part-time, 27% 25 or older, 1% Native American, 7% Hispanic American, 7% African American, 1% Asian American/Pacific Islander **The most frequently chosen baccalaureate fields are** agriculture, business/marketing, interdisciplinary studies **Academic program** Advanced placement, accelerated degree program, honors program, summer session, adult/continuing education programs, internships **Contact** Ms. Denise Siler, Director of Admissions, Tarleton State University, Box T-0030, Tarleton Station, Stephenville, TX 76402. Telephone: 254-968-9125 or toll-free 800-687-4878. Fax: 254-968-9951. Web site: http://www.tarleton.edu/.

TEXAS A&M INTERNATIONAL UNIVERSITY
LAREDO, TEXAS

General State-supported, comprehensive, coed **Entrance** Moderately difficult **Setting** 300-acre urban campus **Total enrollment** 3,373 **Student-faculty ratio** 12:1 **Application deadline** 7/1 (freshmen), 7/1 (transfer) **Freshmen** 92% were admitted **Expenses** Tuition $2533; Room only $3120 **Undergraduates** 64% women, 36% part-time, 37% 25 or older, 0.1% Native American, 94% Hispanic American, 0.4% African American, 0.2% Asian American/Pacific Islander **The most frequently chosen baccalaureate fields are** business/marketing, education, health professions and related sciences **Academic program** English as a second language, advanced placement, honors program, summer session, internships **Contact** Ms. Veronica Gonzalez, Director of Enrollment Management and School Relations, Texas A&M International University, 5201 University Boulevard, Laredo, TX 78041-1900. Telephone: 956-326-2270. Fax: 956-326-2199. E-mail: mchayez@tamiu.edu. Web site: http://www.tamiu.edu/.

TEXAS A&M UNIVERSITY
COLLEGE STATION, TEXAS

General State-supported, university, coed **Entrance** Moderately difficult **Setting** 5,200-acre suburban campus **Total enrollment** 44,618 **Student-faculty ratio** 22:1 **Application deadline** 2/15 (freshmen), 4/1 (transfer) **Freshmen** 69% were admitted **Housing** Yes **Expenses** Tuition $3722; Room & Board $5266 **Undergraduates** 49% women, 8% part-time, 4% 25 or older, 1% Native American, 9% Hispanic American, 2% African American, 3% Asian American/Pacific Islander **The most frequently chosen baccalaureate fields are** business/marketing, agriculture, engineering/engineering technologies **Academic program** English as a second language, advanced placement, honors program, summer session, internships **Contact** Dr. Frank Ashley, Director of Admissions, Texas A&M University, 217 John J. Koldus Building, College Station, TX 77843-1265. Telephone: 979-845-3741. Fax: 979-845-8737. E-mail: adminfo@tamu.edu. Web site: http://www.tamu.edu/.

TEXAS A&M UNIVERSITY AT GALVESTON
GALVESTON, TEXAS

General State-supported, 4-year, coed **Entrance** Moderately difficult **Setting** 100-acre suburban campus **Total enrollment** 1,366 **Student-faculty ratio** 16:1 **Application deadline** Rolling (freshmen), rolling (transfer) **Freshmen** 87% were admitted **Housing** Yes **Expenses** Tuition $3243; Room & Board $3977 **Undergraduates** 51% women, 10% part-time, 10% 25 or older, 1% Native American, 9% Hispanic American, 1% African American, 2% Asian American/Pacific Islander **The most frequently chosen baccalaureate fields are** biological/life sciences, business/marketing, engineering/engineering technologies **Academic program** English as a second language, advanced placement, accelerated degree program, summer session, internships **Contact** Sarah Wilson, Academic Advisor II, Texas A&M University at Galveston, PO Box 1675, Galveston, TX 77553-1675. Telephone: 409-740-4448 or toll-free 87—SEAAGIE. Fax: 409-740-4731. E-mail: seaaggie@tamu.edu. Web site: http://www.tamug.tamu.edu/.

TEXAS A&M UNIVERSITY–COMMERCE
COMMERCE, TEXAS

General State-supported, university, coed **Entrance** Moderately difficult **Setting** 140-acre small-town campus **Total enrollment** 7,934 **Student-faculty ratio** 17:1 **Application deadline** 8/1 (freshmen), rolling (transfer) **Freshmen** 63% were admitted **Housing** Yes **Expenses** Tuition $2776; Room & Board $4800 **Undergraduates** 59% women, 22% part-time, 13% 25 or older, 1% Native American, 5% Hispanic American, 16% African American, 1% Asian American/Pacific Islander **The most frequently chosen baccalaureate fields are** business/marketing, interdisciplinary studies, social sciences and history **Academic program** Advanced placement, honors program, summer session, adult/continuing education programs, internships **Contact** Mr. Randy McDonald, Director of School Relations, Texas A&M University–Commerce, PO Box 3011, Commerce, TX 75429. Telephone: 903-886-5072 or toll-free 800-331-3878. Fax: 903-886-5888. E-mail: cathy_griffin@tamu-commerce.edu. Web site: http://www.tamu-commerce.edu/.

TEXAS A&M UNIVERSITY–CORPUS CHRISTI
CORPUS CHRISTI, TEXAS

General State-supported, comprehensive, coed **Entrance** Moderately difficult **Setting** 240-acre sub-

TEXAS

Texas A&M University–Corpus Christi *(continued)*

urban campus **Total enrollment** 7,369 **Student-faculty ratio** 22:1 **Application deadline** Rolling (freshmen), rolling (transfer) **Freshmen** 89% were admitted **Housing** Yes **Expenses** Tuition $2306; Room & Board $5661 **Undergraduates** 59% women, 23% part-time, 25% 25 or older, 0.4% Native American, 37% Hispanic American, 2% African American, 2% Asian American/Pacific Islander **The most frequently chosen baccalaureate fields are** business/marketing, health professions and related sciences, interdisciplinary studies **Academic program** Advanced placement, summer session, internships **Contact** Ms. Margaret Dechant, Director of Admissions, Texas A&M University–Corpus Christi, 6300 Ocean Drive, Corpus Christi, TX 78412-5503. Telephone: 361-825-2414 or toll-free 800-482-6822. Fax: 361-825-5887. E-mail: judith.perales@mail.tamucc.edu. Web site: http://www.tamucc.edu/.

TEXAS A&M UNIVERSITY–KINGSVILLE
KINGSVILLE, TEXAS

General State-supported, university, coed **Entrance** Moderately difficult **Setting** 255-acre small-town campus **Total enrollment** 6,150 **Student-faculty ratio** 16:1 **Application deadline** Rolling (freshmen), rolling (transfer) **Freshmen** 99% were admitted **Housing** Yes **Expenses** Tuition $2862; Room & Board $3584 **Undergraduates** 49% women, 22% part-time, 28% 25 or older, 0.2% Native American, 66% Hispanic American, 5% African American, 1% Asian American/Pacific Islander **The most frequently chosen baccalaureate fields are** business/marketing, engineering/engineering technologies, interdisciplinary studies **Academic program** English as a second language, advanced placement, summer session, adult/continuing education programs, internships **Contact** Ms. Laura Knippers, Director of Admissions, Texas A&M University–Kingsville, Campus Box 105, Kingsville, TX 78363. Telephone: 361-593-2811 or toll-free 800-687-6000. Fax: 361-593-2195. Web site: http://www.tamuk.edu/.

TEXAS A&M UNIVERSITY SYSTEM HEALTH SCIENCE CENTER
COLLEGE STATION, TEXAS

General State-supported, upper-level, coed **Total enrollment** 490 **Application deadline** Rolling (transfer) **Housing** No **Expenses** Tuition $5030 **Undergraduates** 97% women, 36% 25 or older, 0% Native American, 12% Hispanic American, 3% African American, 3% Asian American/Pacific Islander **The most frequently chosen baccalaureate field is** health professions and related sciences **Contact** Dr. Jack L. Long, Director of Admissions and Records, Texas A&M University System Health Science Center, PO Box 660677, Dallas, TX 75266-0677. Telephone: 214-828-8230. Fax: 214-874-4567. Web site: http://tamushsc.tamu.edu/.

TEXAS A&M UNIVERSITY–TEXARKANA
TEXARKANA, TEXAS

General State-supported, upper-level, coed **Entrance** Noncompetitive **Setting** 1-acre small-town campus **Total enrollment** 1,233 **Student-faculty ratio** 14:1 **Application deadline** Rolling (transfer) **Housing** No **Expenses** Tuition $1896 **The most frequently chosen baccalaureate fields are** business/marketing, interdisciplinary studies, liberal arts/general studies **Academic program** Advanced placement, self-designed majors, summer session, internships **Contact** Mrs. Patricia E. Black, Director of Admissions and Registrar, Texas A&M University–Texarkana, PO Box 5518, Texarkana, TX 75505-5518. Telephone: 903-223-3068. Fax: 903-223-3140. E-mail: admissions@tamut.edu. Web site: http://www.tamut.edu/.

TEXAS CHIROPRACTIC COLLEGE
PASADENA, TEXAS

Contact Mr. Robert Cooper, Director of Admissions, Texas Chiropractic College, 5912 Spencer Highway, Pasadena, TX 77505-1699. Telephone: 281-998-6017 or toll-free 800-468-6839. Web site: http://www.txchiro.edu/.

TEXAS CHRISTIAN UNIVERSITY
FORT WORTH, TEXAS

General Independent, university, coed, affiliated with Christian Church (Disciples of Christ) **Entrance** Moderately difficult **Setting** 237-acre suburban campus **Total enrollment** 8,054 **Student-faculty ratio** 15:1 **Application deadline** 2/15 (freshmen), 6/15 (transfer) **Freshmen** 72% were admitted **Housing** Yes **Expenses** Tuition $15,040; Room & Board $4870 **Undergraduates** 57% women, 8% part-time, 5% 25 or older, 1% Native American, 6% Hispanic American, 4% African American, 2% Asian American/Pacific Islander **The most frequently chosen baccalaureate fields are** business/marketing, communications/communication technologies, education **Academic program** English as a second language, advanced placement, accelerated degree program, self-designed majors, honors program, summer session, adult/continuing education programs, internships **Contact** Mr. Ray Brown, Dean of Admissions, Texas Christian University, TCU Box 297013, Fort Worth, TX 76129-0002. Telephone: 817-257-7490 or toll-free 800-828-3764. Fax: 817-257-7268. E-mail: frogmail@tcu.edu. Web site: http://www.tcu.edu/.

TEXAS COLLEGE
TYLER, TEXAS

General Independent, 4-year, coed, affiliated with Christian Methodist Episcopal Church **Total enrollment** 511 **Student-faculty ratio** 10:1 **Freshmen** 41% were admitted **Expenses** Tuition $8375; Room & Board $5445 **Undergraduates** 62% women, 3% part-time, 0.2% Native American, 2% Hispanic American, 97% African American, 1% Asian American/Pacific Islander **The most frequently chosen baccalaureate fields are biological/life sciences, parks and recreation, social sciences and history **Contact** Anetha Francis, Enrollment Services Director, Texas College, 2404 North Grand Avenue, PO Box 4500, Tyler, TX 75712-4500. Telephone: 903-593-8311 Ext. 2297. Web site: http://168.44.174.253/.

TEXAS LUTHERAN UNIVERSITY
SEGUIN, TEXAS

General Independent, 4-year, coed, affiliated with Evangelical Lutheran Church **Entrance** Moderately difficult **Setting** 196-acre suburban campus **Total enrollment** 1,473 **Student-faculty ratio** 15:1 **Application deadline** Rolling (freshmen), rolling (transfer) **Freshmen** 81% were admitted **Housing** Yes **Expenses** Tuition $13,540; Room & Board $4150 **Undergraduates** 54% women, 14% part-time, 10% 25 or older, 1% Native American, 17% Hispanic American, 6% African American, 2% Asian American/Pacific Islander **The most frequently chosen baccalaureate fields are** biological/life sciences, business/marketing, parks and recreation **Academic program** English as a second language, advanced placement, accelerated degree program, honors program, summer session, adult/continuing education programs, internships **Contact** Mr. E. Norman Jones, Vice President for Enrollment Services, Texas Lutheran University, 1000 West Court Street, Seguin, TX 78155-5999. Telephone: 830-372-8050 or toll-free 800-771-8521. Fax: 830-372-8096. E-mail: admissions@tlu.edu. Web site: http://www.tlu.edu/.

TEXAS SOUTHERN UNIVERSITY
HOUSTON, TEXAS

General State-supported, university, coed **Entrance** Noncompetitive **Setting** 147-acre urban campus **Total enrollment** 8,119 **Student-faculty ratio** 22:1 **Application deadline** 8/10 (freshmen), 8/10 (transfer) **Freshmen** 21% were admitted **Housing** Yes **Expenses** Tuition $2078; Room & Board $4498 **Undergraduates** 55% women, 16% part-time, 30% 25 or older, 0.1% Native American, 2% Hispanic American, 90% African American, 2% Asian American/Pacific Islander **The most frequently chosen baccalaureate fields are** business/marketing, health professions and related sciences, protective services/public administration **Academic program** English as a second language, accelerated degree program, honors program, summer session, adult/continuing education programs, internships **Contact** Mrs. Joyce Waddell, Director of Admissions, Texas Southern University, 3100 Cleburne, Houston, TX 77004-4598. Telephone: 713-313-7472. Web site: http://www.tsu.edu/.

TEXAS TECH UNIVERSITY
LUBBOCK, TEXAS

General State-supported, university, coed **Entrance** Moderately difficult **Setting** 1,839-acre urban campus **Total enrollment** 25,573 **Student-faculty ratio** 20:1 **Application deadline** Rolling (freshmen), rolling (transfer) **Freshmen** 74% were admitted **Hous-** ing Yes **Expenses** Tuition $3489; Room & Board $5337 **Undergraduates** 46% women, 11% part-time, 9% 25 or older, 1% Native American, 10% Hispanic American, 3% African American, 2% Asian American/Pacific Islander **The most frequently chosen baccalaureate fields are** business/marketing, communications/communication technologies, engineering/engineering technologies **Academic program** English as a second language, advanced placement, accelerated degree program, self-designed majors, honors program, summer session, adult/continuing education programs, internships **Contact** Director Admissions and School Relations, Texas Tech University, Box 45005, Lubbock, TX 79409-5005. Telephone: 806-742-1480. Fax: 806-742-0980. E-mail: admissions@ttu.edu. Web site: http://www.ttu.edu/.

▶ **For more information, see page 481.**

TEXAS WESLEYAN UNIVERSITY
FORT WORTH, TEXAS

General Independent United Methodist, comprehensive, coed **Entrance** Moderately difficult **Setting** 74-acre urban campus **Total enrollment** 2,939 **Student-faculty ratio** 15:1 **Application deadline** Rolling (freshmen), rolling (transfer) **Freshmen** 83% were admitted **Housing** Yes **Expenses** Tuition $10,690; Room & Board $3990 **Undergraduates** 65% women, 36% part-time, 33% 25 or older, 1% Native American, 18% Hispanic American, 19% African American, 2% Asian American/Pacific Islander **The most frequently chosen baccalaureate fields are** business/marketing, education, psychology **Academic program** English as a second language, advanced placement, summer session, adult/continuing education programs, internships **Contact** Ms. Stephanie Lewis-Boatner, Director of Freshman Admissions, Texas Wesleyan University, 1201 Wesleyan Street, Fort Worth, TX 76105-1536. Telephone: 817-531-4422 or toll-free 800-580-8980 (in-state). Fax: 817-531-7515. E-mail: freshman@txwesleyan.edu. Web site: http://www.txwesleyan.edu/.

TEXAS WOMAN'S UNIVERSITY
DENTON, TEXAS

General State-supported, university, coed, primarily women **Entrance** Minimally difficult **Setting** 270-acre suburban campus **Total enrollment** 7,928 **Student-faculty ratio** 13:1 **Application deadline** 7/15 (freshmen), 7/15 (transfer) **Freshmen** 70% were admitted **Housing** Yes **Expenses** Tuition $2504; Room & Board $4427 **Undergraduates** 94% women, 28% part-time, 41% 25 or older, 1% Native American, 11% Hispanic American, 21% African American, 5% Asian American/Pacific Islander **The most frequently chosen baccalaureate fields are** health professions and related sciences, home economics/vocational home economics, interdisciplinary studies **Academic program** Advanced placement, accelerated degree program, honors program, summer session, adult/continuing education programs, internships **Contact** Ms. Teresa Mauk, Director of Admissions, Texas Woman's University, PO Box 425589, Denton,

TEXAS

Texas Woman's University *(continued)*
TX 76204-5589. Telephone: 940-898-3040 or toll-free 888-948-9984. Fax: 940-898-3081. E-mail: admissions@twu.edu. Web site: http://www.twu.edu/.

TRINITY UNIVERSITY
SAN ANTONIO, TEXAS

General Independent, comprehensive, coed, affiliated with Presbyterian Church **Entrance** Very difficult **Setting** 113-acre urban campus **Total enrollment** 2,592 **Student-faculty ratio** 11:1 **Application deadline** 2/1 (freshmen), 2/1 (transfer) **Freshmen** 75% were admitted **Housing** Yes **Expenses** Tuition $16,554; Room & Board $6560 **Undergraduates** 51% women, 2% part-time, 1% 25 or older, 1% Native American, 10% Hispanic American, 2% African American, 7% Asian American/Pacific Islander **The most frequently chosen baccalaureate fields are** business/marketing, English, social sciences and history **Academic program** Advanced placement, accelerated degree program, honors program, summer session, internships **Contact** Christopher Ellertson, Dean of Admissions and Financial Aid, Trinity University, 715 Stadium Drive, San Antonio, TX 78212-7200. Telephone: 210-999-7207 or toll-free 800-TRINITY. Fax: 210-999-8164. E-mail: admissions@trinity.edu. Web site: http://www.trinity.edu/.

UNIVERSITY OF DALLAS
IRVING, TEXAS

General Independent Roman Catholic, university, coed **Entrance** Very difficult **Setting** 750-acre suburban campus **Total enrollment** 3,518 **Student-faculty ratio** 11:1 **Application deadline** 2/15 (freshmen), 7/1 (transfer) **Freshmen** 85% were admitted **Housing** Yes **Expenses** Tuition $16,084; Room & Board $5950 **Undergraduates** 58% women, 6% part-time, 7% 25 or older, 1% Native American, 14% Hispanic American, 2% African American, 6% Asian American/Pacific Islander **The most frequently chosen baccalaureate fields are** philosophy, philosophy, religion, and theology, social sciences and history **Academic program** English as a second language, advanced placement, accelerated degree program, self-designed majors, summer session, adult/continuing education programs, internships **Contact** Mr. Larry Webb, Director of Enrollment, University of Dallas, 1845 East Northgate Drive, Irving, TX 75062-4799. Telephone: 972-721-5266 or toll-free 800-628-6999. Fax: 972-721-5017. E-mail: ugadmis@mailadmin.udallas.edu. Web site: http://www.udallas.edu/.

UNIVERSITY OF HOUSTON
HOUSTON, TEXAS

General State-supported, university, coed **Entrance** Moderately difficult **Setting** 550-acre urban campus **Total enrollment** 33,007 **Student-faculty ratio** 18:1 **Application deadline** 5/1 (freshmen), 5/1 (transfer) **Freshmen** 79% were admitted **Housing** Yes **Expenses** Tuition $3168; Room & Board $5242 **Undergraduates** 53% women, 30% part-time, 22% 25 or older, 0.4% Native American, 20% Hispanic American, 15% African American, 20% Asian American/Pacific Islander **The most frequently chosen baccalaureate fields are** business/marketing, engineering/engineering technologies, psychology **Academic program** English as a second language, advanced placement, accelerated degree program, honors program, summer session, adult/continuing education programs, internships **Contact** Mr. Jose Cantu, Co-Assistant Director of Student Outreach Services, University of Houston, 4800 Calhoun, Houston, TX 77204-2161. Telephone: 713-743-9617. Fax: 713-743-9633. E-mail: admissions@uh.edu. Web site: http://www.uh.edu/.

UNIVERSITY OF HOUSTON–CLEAR LAKE
HOUSTON, TEXAS

General State-supported, upper-level, coed **Entrance** Minimally difficult **Setting** 487-acre suburban campus **Total enrollment** 7,738 **Student-faculty ratio** 14:1 **Application deadline** Rolling (transfer) **First-Year Students** 67% were admitted **Housing** No **Expenses** Tuition $3456 **Undergraduates** 64% women, 51% part-time, 61% 25 or older, 0.4% Native American, 15% Hispanic American, 8% African American, 6% Asian American/Pacific Islander **The most frequently chosen baccalaureate fields are** business/marketing, computer/information sciences, interdisciplinary studies **Academic program** English as a second language, accelerated degree program, self-designed majors, summer session, internships **Contact** Mr. John Smith, Executive Director of Enrollment Services, University of Houston–Clear Lake, 2700 Bay Area Boulevard, Box 13, Houston, TX 77058-1098. Telephone: 281-283-2517. Fax: 281-283-2530. E-mail: admissions@cl.uh.edu. Web site: http://www.cl.uh.edu/.

UNIVERSITY OF HOUSTON–DOWNTOWN
HOUSTON, TEXAS

General State-supported, 4-year, coed **Entrance** Noncompetitive **Setting** 20-acre urban campus **Total enrollment** 8,951 **Student-faculty ratio** 25:1 **Application deadline** 8/1 (freshmen), 8/1 (transfer) **Freshmen** 100% were admitted **Housing** No **Expenses** Tuition $2414 **Undergraduates** 59% women, 51% part-time, 49% 25 or older, 0.3% Native American, 32% Hispanic American, 29% African American, 11% Asian American/Pacific Islander **The most frequently chosen baccalaureate fields are** business/marketing, liberal arts/general studies, protective services/public administration **Academic program** English as a second language, advanced placement, accelerated degree program, summer session, adult/continuing education programs, internships **Contact** Mr. Mike Kerrendal, Director, Admissions and Records, University of Houston–Downtown, One Main Street, Houston, TX 77002. Telephone: 713-221-8931. Fax: 713-221-8157. E-mail: uhdadmit@dt.uh.edu. Web site: http://www.uhd.edu/.

TEXAS

UNIVERSITY OF HOUSTON–VICTORIA
VICTORIA, TEXAS

General State-supported, upper-level, coed **Entrance** Minimally difficult **Setting** small-town campus **Total enrollment** 1,927 **Student-faculty ratio** 16:1 **Application deadline** Rolling (transfer) **First-Year Students** 85% were admitted **Housing** No **Expenses** Tuition $2304 **Undergraduates** 72% women, 63% part-time, 65% 25 or older, 0.2% Native American, 18% Hispanic American, 8% African American, 5% Asian American/Pacific Islander **The most frequently chosen baccalaureate fields are** business/marketing, computer/information sciences, interdisciplinary studies **Academic program** Summer session, adult/continuing education programs, internships **Contact** Mr. Richard Phillips, Director of Enrollment Management, University of Houston–Victoria, 3007 North Ben Wilson, Victoria, TX 77901-4450. Telephone: 361-570-4110 or toll-free 877-940-4848. Fax: 361-570-4114. E-mail: urbanom@jade.vic.uh.edu. Web site: http://www.vic.uh.edu/.

UNIVERSITY OF MARY HARDIN-BAYLOR
BELTON, TEXAS

General Independent Southern Baptist, comprehensive, coed **Entrance** Moderately difficult **Setting** 100-acre small-town campus **Total enrollment** 2,628 **Student-faculty ratio** 17:1 **Application deadline** Rolling (freshmen), rolling (transfer) **Freshmen** 90% were admitted **Housing** Yes **Expenses** Tuition $9890; Room & Board $4039 **Undergraduates** 64% women, 15% part-time, 20% 25 or older, 1% Native American, 10% Hispanic American, 10% African American, 2% Asian American/Pacific Islander **The most frequently chosen baccalaureate fields are** business/marketing, education, liberal arts/general studies **Academic program** English as a second language, advanced placement, accelerated degree program, honors program, summer session, adult/continuing education programs, internships **Contact** Ms. Valerie Hampton, Admissions Clerk, University of Mary Hardin-Baylor, UMHB Station Box 8004, 900 College Street, Belton, TX 76513-2599. Telephone: 254-295-4520 or toll-free 800-727-8642. Fax: 254-295-5049. E-mail: admissions@umhb.edu. Web site: http://www.umhb.edu/.

UNIVERSITY OF NORTH TEXAS
DENTON, TEXAS

General State-supported, university, coed **Entrance** Moderately difficult **Setting** 500-acre urban campus **Total enrollment** 27,858 **Student-faculty ratio** 17:1 **Application deadline** 6/15 (freshmen), 6/15 (transfer) **Freshmen** 72% were admitted **Housing** Yes **Expenses** Tuition $3050; Room & Board $4400 **Undergraduates** 55% women, 22% part-time, 15% 25 or older, 1% Native American, 9% Hispanic American, 10% African American, 4% Asian American/Pacific Islander **The most frequently chosen baccalaureate fields are** business/marketing, interdisciplinary studies, visual/performing arts **Academic program** English as a second language, advanced placement, accelerated degree program, self-designed majors, honors program, summer session, internships **Contact** Ms. Janet Trepka, Coordinator or New Student Mentoring Programs and Vice President of Student Development, University of North Texas, Box 311277, Denton, TX 76203-9988. Telephone: 940-565-3190 or toll-free 800-868-8211 (in-state). Fax: 940-565-2408. E-mail: undergrad@abn.unt.edu. Web site: http://www.unt.edu/.

UNIVERSITY OF PHOENIX–DALLAS/FT. WORTH CAMPUS
DALLAS, TEXAS

General Proprietary, comprehensive, coed **Total enrollment** 88,730 **Student-faculty ratio** 17:1 **Application deadline** Rolling (freshmen), rolling (transfer) **Housing** No **Expenses** Tuition $8310 **Undergraduates** 38% women **Contact** Ms. Beth Barilla, Director of Admissions, University of Phoenix–Dallas/Ft. Worth Campus, 4615 East Elwood Street, Phoenix, AZ 85040-1958. Telephone: 480-927-0099 Ext. 1218 or toll-free 800-228-7240. Fax: 480-594-1758. E-mail: beth.barilla@apolloogrp.edu. Web site: http://www.phoenix.edu/.

UNIVERSITY OF PHOENIX–HOUSTON CAMPUS
HOUSTON, TEXAS

General Proprietary, comprehensive, coed **Total enrollment** 88,730 **Student-faculty ratio** 18:1 **Application deadline** Rolling (freshmen), rolling (transfer) **Housing** No **Expenses** Tuition $8310 **Undergraduates** 66% women, 81% 25 or older **Contact** Ms. Beth Barilla, Director of Admissions, University of Phoenix–Houston Campus, 4615 East Elwood Street, Phoenix, AZ 85040-1958. Telephone: 480-927-0099 Ext. 1218 or toll-free 800-228-7240. Fax: 480-594-1758. E-mail: beth.barilla@apollogrp.edu. Web site: http://www.phoenix.edu/.

UNIVERSITY OF ST. THOMAS
HOUSTON, TEXAS

General Independent Roman Catholic, comprehensive, coed **Setting** 20-acre urban campus **Total enrollment** 4,310 **Student-faculty ratio** 14:1 **Application deadline** Rolling (freshmen), rolling (transfer) **Freshmen** 78% were admitted **Housing** Yes **Expenses** Tuition $13,162; Room & Board $5920 **Undergraduates** 65% women, 30% part-time, 33% 25 or older, 1% Native American, 30% Hispanic American, 6% African American, 13% Asian American/Pacific Islander **The most frequently chosen baccalaureate fields are** business/marketing, education, liberal arts/general studies **Academic program** English as a second language, advanced placement, accelerated degree program, self-designed majors, honors program, summer session, adult/continuing education programs, internships **Contact** Mr. Gerald E. Warren, Assistant Director of Admissions, University of St. Thomas, 3800 Montrose Boulevard, Houston, TX

TEXAS

University of St. Thomas *(continued)*
77006-4696. Telephone: 713-525-3500 or toll-free 800-856-8565. Fax: 713-525-3558. E-mail: admissions@stthom.edu. Web site: http://www.stthom.edu/.

THE UNIVERSITY OF TEXAS AT ARLINGTON
ARLINGTON, TEXAS

General State-supported, university, coed **Entrance** Moderately difficult **Setting** 395-acre urban campus **Total enrollment** 21,180 **Student-faculty ratio** 21:1 **Application deadline** Rolling (freshmen), rolling (transfer) **Freshmen** 85% were admitted **Housing** Yes **Expenses** Tuition $3068; Room & Board $4124 **Undergraduates** 53% women, 32% part-time, 32% 25 or older, 1% Native American, 12% Hispanic American, 13% African American, 11% Asian American/Pacific Islander **The most frequently chosen baccalaureate fields are** business/marketing, engineering/engineering technologies, health professions and related sciences **Academic program** English as a second language, advanced placement, self-designed majors, honors program, summer session, adult/continuing education programs, internships **Contact** Mr. George E. Norton, Interim Director of Admissions, The University of Texas at Arlington, PO Box 19111, 701 South Nedderman Drive, Room 110, Davis Hall, Arlington, TX 76019-0088. Telephone: 817-272-3254. Fax: 817-272-3435. E-mail: adm@uta.edu. Web site: http://www.uta.edu/.

THE UNIVERSITY OF TEXAS AT AUSTIN
AUSTIN, TEXAS

General State-supported, university, coed **Entrance** Very difficult **Setting** 350-acre urban campus **Total enrollment** 50,616 **Student-faculty ratio** 19:1 **Application deadline** 2/1 (freshmen), 3/1 (transfer) **Freshmen** 64% were admitted **Housing** Yes **Expenses** Tuition $3766; Room & Board $5671 **Undergraduates** 51% women, 12% part-time, 7% 25 or older, 0.4% Native American, 14% Hispanic American, 4% African American, 16% Asian American/Pacific Islander **The most frequently chosen baccalaureate fields are** business/marketing, communications/communication technologies, social sciences and history **Academic program** English as a second language, advanced placement, accelerated degree program, self-designed majors, honors program, summer session, adult/continuing education programs, internships **Contact** Freshman Admissions Center, The University of Texas at Austin, John Hargis Hall, Campus Mail Code D0700, Austin, TX 78712-1111. Telephone: 512-475-7440. Fax: 512-475-7475. E-mail: adfre@utxdp.dp.utexas.edu. Web site: http://www.utexas.edu/.

THE UNIVERSITY OF TEXAS AT BROWNSVILLE
BROWNSVILLE, TEXAS

General State-supported, upper-level, coed **Entrance** Noncompetitive **Setting** 65-acre urban campus **Total enrollment** 9,373 **Student-faculty ratio** 15:1 **Application deadline** 8/1 (transfer) **First-Year Students** 100% were admitted **Housing** No **Expenses** Tuition $2114 **Undergraduates** 62% women, 54% part-time, 56% 25 or older, 0.1% Native American, 94% Hispanic American, 0.3% African American, 0.2% Asian American/Pacific Islander **The most frequently chosen baccalaureate fields are** business/marketing, foreign language/literature, liberal arts/general studies **Academic program** Advanced placement, summer session **Contact** Carlo Tamayo, New Student Relations Coordinator, The University of Texas at Brownsville, 80 Fort Brown, Brownsville, TX 78520-4991. Telephone: 956-544-8860 or toll-free 800-850-0160 (in-state). Fax: 956-544-8832. E-mail: cata01@utb.edu. Web site: http://www.utb.edu/.

THE UNIVERSITY OF TEXAS AT DALLAS
RICHARDSON, TEXAS

General State-supported, university, coed **Entrance** Very difficult **Setting** 455-acre suburban campus **Total enrollment** 12,455 **Student-faculty ratio** 19:1 **Application deadline** 8/1 (freshmen) **Freshmen** 56% were admitted **Housing** Yes **Expenses** Tuition $3658; Room & Board $5914 **Undergraduates** 48% women, 35% part-time, 37% 25 or older, 1% Native American, 9% Hispanic American, 7% African American, 21% Asian American/Pacific Islander **The most frequently chosen baccalaureate fields are** business/marketing, computer/information sciences, interdisciplinary studies **Academic program** Advanced placement, accelerated degree program, self-designed majors, honors program, summer session, adult/continuing education programs, internships **Contact** Admissions Office, The University of Texas at Dallas, PO Box 830688 Mail Station MC11, Richardson, TX 75083-0688. Telephone: 972-883-2342 or toll-free 800-889-2443. Fax: 972-883-2599. E-mail: ugrad-admissions@utdallas.edu. Web site: http://www.utdallas.edu/.

THE UNIVERSITY OF TEXAS AT EL PASO
EL PASO, TEXAS

General State-supported, university, coed **Entrance** Minimally difficult **Setting** 360-acre urban campus **Total enrollment** 16,220 **Student-faculty ratio** 19:1 **Application deadline** 7/1 (freshmen), 7/31 (transfer) **Freshmen** 94% were admitted **Housing** Yes **Expenses** Tuition $2541; Room & Board $5165 **Undergraduates** 54% women, 27% part-time, 28% 25 or older, 0.3% Native American, 72% Hispanic American, 2% African American, 1% Asian American/Pacific Islander **The most frequently chosen baccalaureate fields are** business/marketing, engineering/engineering technologies, interdisciplinary studies **Academic program** English as a second language, advanced placement, accelerated degree program, honors program, summer session, adult/continuing education programs, internships **Contact** Ms. Diana Guerrero, Director of Admissions, The University of Texas at El Paso, 500 West University Avenue, El Paso, TX 79968-0001. Telephone: 915-747-5588. Fax: 915-747-5122. E-mail: admission@utep.edu. Web site: http://www.utep.edu/.

TEXAS

THE UNIVERSITY OF TEXAS AT SAN ANTONIO
SAN ANTONIO, TEXAS

General State-supported, university, coed **Entrance** Moderately difficult **Setting** 600-acre suburban campus **Total enrollment** 19,883 **Student-faculty ratio** 24:1 **Application deadline** 7/1 (freshmen), 7/1 (transfer) **Freshmen** 99% were admitted **Housing** Yes **Expenses** Tuition $3503; Room & Board $6113 **Undergraduates** 55% women, 31% part-time, 28% 25 or older, 0.5% Native American, 47% Hispanic American, 6% African American, 4% Asian American/Pacific Islander **The most frequently chosen baccalaureate fields are** business/marketing, biological/life sciences, interdisciplinary studies **Academic program** English as a second language, advanced placement, accelerated degree program, honors program, summer session, adult/continuing education programs, internships **Contact** Mr. John Wallace, Interim Director, The University of Texas at San Antonio, 6900 North Loop 1604 West, San Antonio, TX 78249. Telephone: 210-458-4530 or toll-free 800-669-0916 (in-state); 800-669-0919 (out-of-state). E-mail: prospects@utsa.edu. Web site: http://www.utsa.edu/.

THE UNIVERSITY OF TEXAS AT TYLER
TYLER, TEXAS

General State-supported, comprehensive, coed **Setting** 200-acre urban campus **Total enrollment** 3,742 **Student-faculty ratio** 10:1 **Freshmen** 85% were admitted **Housing** Yes **Expenses** Tuition $2460 **Undergraduates** 65% women, 34% part-time, 47% 25 or older, 1% Native American, 4% Hispanic American, 9% African American, 1% Asian American/Pacific Islander **The most frequently chosen baccalaureate fields are** health professions and related sciences, business/marketing, interdisciplinary studies **Academic program** English as a second language, advanced placement, self-designed majors, honors program, summer session, adult/continuing education programs, internships **Contact** Mr. Jim Hutto, Dean of Enrollment Management, The University of Texas at Tyler, 3900 University Boulevard, Tyler, TX 75799-0001. Telephone: 903-566-7195 or toll-free 800-UTTYLER (in-state). Fax: 903-566-7068. Web site: http://www.uttyler.edu/.

THE UNIVERSITY OF TEXAS HEALTH SCIENCE CENTER AT HOUSTON
HOUSTON, TEXAS

General State-supported, upper-level, coed **Entrance** Moderately difficult **Setting** urban campus **Total enrollment** 3,286 **Application deadline** 12/31 (transfer) **First-Year Students** 30% were admitted **Housing** Yes **Expenses** Tuition $3774 **Undergraduates** 90% women, 2% part-time, 0% Native American, 13% Hispanic American, 14% African American, 12% Asian American/Pacific Islander **The most frequently chosen baccalaureate field is** health professions and related sciences **Academic program** Accelerated degree program **Contact** Mr. Robert L. Jenkins, Associate Registrar, The University of Texas Health Science Center at Houston, 7000 Fannin, PO Box 20036, Houston, TX 77225-0036. Telephone: 713-500-3361. Fax: 713-500-3356. E-mail: uthschro@admin4.hsc.uth.tmc.edu. Web site: http://www.uth.tmc.edu/.

THE UNIVERSITY OF TEXAS HEALTH SCIENCE CENTER AT SAN ANTONIO
SAN ANTONIO, TEXAS

Contact Mr. James Peak, Registrar, The University of Texas Health Science Center at San Antonio, 7703 Floyd Curl Drive, San Antonio, TX 78229-3900. Telephone: 210-567-2629. Web site: http://www.uthscsa.edu/.

THE UNIVERSITY OF TEXAS MEDICAL BRANCH
GALVESTON, TEXAS

General State-supported, upper-level, coed **Entrance** Most difficult **Setting** 100-acre small-town campus **Total enrollment** 1,927 **Student-faculty ratio** 7:1 **First-Year Students** 69% were admitted **Housing** Yes **Expenses** Tuition $2219; Room only $2400 **Undergraduates** 85% women, 36% part-time, 63% 25 or older, 1% Native American, 15% Hispanic American, 12% African American, 7% Asian American/Pacific Islander **The most frequently chosen baccalaureate field is** health professions and related sciences **Academic program** Advanced placement, summer session, internships **Contact** Ms. Vicki L. Brewer, Interim Registrar, The University of Texas Medical Branch, 301 University Boulevard, Galveston, TX 77555-1305. Telephone: 409-772-1215. Fax: 409-772-5056. E-mail: student.admissions@utmb.edu. Web site: http://www.utmb.edu/.

THE UNIVERSITY OF TEXAS OF THE PERMIAN BASIN
ODESSA, TEXAS

General State-supported, comprehensive, coed **Entrance** Moderately difficult **Setting** 600-acre urban campus **Total enrollment** 2,409 **Student-faculty ratio** 17:1 **Application deadline** 8/1 (freshmen), rolling (transfer) **Freshmen** 89% were admitted **Housing** Yes **Expenses** Tuition $2434; Room only $1900 **Undergraduates** 66% women, 33% part-time, 75% 25 or older, 1% Native American, 36% Hispanic American, 3% African American, 1% Asian American/Pacific Islander **The most frequently chosen baccalaureate fields are** business/marketing, foreign language/literature, social sciences and history **Academic program** Advanced placement, summer session, internships **Contact** Ms. Vicki Gomez, Assistant Vice President for Admissions, The University of Texas of the Permian Basin, 4901 East University, Odessa, TX 79762-0001. Telephone: 915-552-2605. Fax: 915-552-2374. E-mail: gomez-v@gusher.pb.utexas.edu. Web site: http://www.utpb.edu/.

TEXAS

THE UNIVERSITY OF TEXAS–PAN AMERICAN
EDINBURG, TEXAS

General State-supported, comprehensive, coed **Entrance** Noncompetitive **Setting** 200-acre rural campus **Total enrollment** 13,640 **Student-faculty ratio** 29:1 **Application deadline** 7/10 (freshmen), 7/10 (transfer) **Freshmen** 77% were admitted **Housing** Yes **Expenses** Tuition $2,704; Room & Board $5531 **Undergraduates** 59% women, 34% part-time, 28% 25 or older, 0.2% Native American, 85% Hispanic American, 0.4% African American, 1% Asian American/Pacific Islander **The most frequently chosen baccalaureate fields are** business/marketing, health professions and related sciences, interdisciplinary studies **Academic program** Honors program, summer session, adult/continuing education programs, internships **Contact** Mr. David Zuniga, Director of Admissions, The University of Texas–Pan American, Office of Admissions and Records, 1201 West University Drive, Edinburg, TX 78539. Telephone: 956-381-2201. Fax: 956-381-2212. E-mail: admissions@panam.edu. Web site: http://www.panam.edu/.

THE UNIVERSITY OF TEXAS SOUTHWESTERN MEDICAL CENTER AT DALLAS
DALLAS, TEXAS

General State-supported, upper-level, coed **Entrance** Moderately difficult **Setting** 98-acre urban campus **Total enrollment** 1,554 **Student-faculty ratio** 3:1 **Application deadline** Rolling (transfer) **First-Year Students** 74% were admitted **Housing** No **Expenses** Tuition $2025 **Undergraduates** 73% women, 33% part-time, 76% 25 or older, 1% Native American, 11% Hispanic American, 12% African American, 6% Asian American/Pacific Islander **The most frequently chosen baccalaureate fields are** health professions and related sciences, home economics/vocational home economics **Academic program** Advanced placement, internships **Contact** Dr. Scott Wright, Director of Admissions, The University of Texas Southwestern Medical Center at Dallas, 5323 Harry Hines Boulevard, Dallas, TX 75390-9096. Telephone: 214-648-5617. Fax: 214-648-3289. E-mail: admissions@utsouthwestern.edu. Web site: http://www.utsouthwestern.edu/.

UNIVERSITY OF THE INCARNATE WORD
SAN ANTONIO, TEXAS

General Independent Roman Catholic, comprehensive, coed **Entrance** Moderately difficult **Setting** 200-acre urban campus **Total enrollment** 4,283 **Student-faculty ratio** 14:1 **Application deadline** Rolling (freshmen), rolling (transfer) **Freshmen** 37% were admitted **Housing** Yes **Expenses** Tuition $13,498; Room & Board $5250 **Undergraduates** 66% women, 40% part-time, 17% 25 or older, 1% Native American, 53% Hispanic American, 6% African American, 2% Asian American/Pacific Islander **The most frequently chosen baccalaureate fields are** business/marketing, health professions and related sciences, liberal arts/general studies **Academic program** English as a second language, advanced placement, accelerated degree program, summer session, adult/continuing education programs, internships **Contact** Ms. Andrea Cyterski, Director of Admissions, University of the Incarnate Word, Box 285, San Antonio, TX 78209-6397. Telephone: 210-829-6005 or toll-free 800-749-WORD. Fax: 210-829-3921. E-mail: admis@universe.uiwtx.edu. Web site: http://www.uiw.edu/.

WAYLAND BAPTIST UNIVERSITY
PLAINVIEW, TEXAS

General Independent Baptist, comprehensive, coed **Entrance** Minimally difficult **Setting** 80-acre small-town campus **Total enrollment** 989 **Student-faculty ratio** 12:1 **Application deadline** Rolling (freshmen), rolling (transfer) **Freshmen** 97% were admitted **Housing** Yes **Expenses** Tuition $8150; Room & Board $3121 **Undergraduates** 60% women, 21% part-time, 21% 25 or older, 0.4% Native American, 17% Hispanic American, 3% African American, 0.4% Asian American/Pacific Islander **The most frequently chosen baccalaureate fields are** business/marketing, education, philosophy **Academic program** Advanced placement, accelerated degree program, honors program, summer session, adult/continuing education programs, internships **Contact** Mr. Shawn Thomas, Director of Student Admissions, Wayland Baptist University, 1900 West 7th Street #712, Plainview, TX 79072. Telephone: 806-291-3508 or toll-free 800-588-1-WBU. E-mail: admityou@mail.wbu.edu. Web site: http://www.wbu.edu/.

WEST TEXAS A&M UNIVERSITY
CANYON, TEXAS

General State-supported, comprehensive, coed **Entrance** Moderately difficult **Setting** 128-acre small-town campus **Total enrollment** 6,675 **Student-faculty ratio** 23:1 **Application deadline** Rolling (freshmen), rolling (transfer) **Freshmen** 88% were admitted **Housing** Yes **Expenses** Tuition $2301; Room & Board $3831 **Undergraduates** 56% women, 21% part-time, 24% 25 or older, 1% Native American, 13% Hispanic American, 3% African American, 1% Asian American/Pacific Islander **The most frequently chosen baccalaureate fields are** business/marketing, health professions and related sciences, interdisciplinary studies **Academic program** English as a second language, advanced placement, self-designed majors, honors program, summer session, adult/continuing education programs, internships **Contact** Ms. Lila Vars, Director of Admissions, West Texas A&M University, WT Box 60907, Canyon, TX 79016-0001. Telephone: 806-651-2020 or toll-free 800-99-WTAMU (in-state); 800-99-WTMAU (out-of-state). Fax: 806-651-5268. E-mail: lvars@mail.wtamu.edu. Web site: http://www.wtamu.edu/.

UTAH

WILEY COLLEGE
MARSHALL, TEXAS

General Independent, 4-year, coed, affiliated with United Methodist Church **Entrance** Noncompetitive **Setting** 58-acre small-town campus **Total enrollment** 584 **Student-faculty ratio** 8:1 **Application deadline** 8/1 (freshmen), 8/1 (transfer) **Housing** Yes **Expenses** Tuition $5840; Room & Board $3732 **Undergraduates** 52% women, 5% part-time, 34% 25 or older, 0.3% Native American, 1% Hispanic American, 88% African American **The most frequently chosen baccalaureate fields are** biological/life sciences, business/marketing, education **Academic program** Self-designed majors, summer session, adult/continuing education programs **Contact** Dr. Rory Bedford, Director of Admissions, Wiley College, 711 Wiley Avenue, Marshall, TX 75670. Telephone: 903-927-3356 or toll-free 800-658-6889. E-mail: vvalentine@wileyc.edu. Web site: http://www.wileyc.edu/.

UTAH

BRIGHAM YOUNG UNIVERSITY
PROVO, UTAH

General Independent, university, coed, affiliated with Church of Jesus Christ of Latter-day Saints **Entrance** Moderately difficult **Setting** 638-acre suburban campus **Total enrollment** 32,771 **Student-faculty ratio** 20:1 **Application deadline** 2/15 (freshmen), 3/15 (transfer) **Freshmen** 65% were admitted **Housing** Yes **Expenses** Tuition $3060; Room & Board $4780 **Undergraduates** 51% women, 11% part-time, 9% 25 or older, 1% Native American, 3% Hispanic American, 0.3% African American, 3% Asian American/Pacific Islander **The most frequently chosen baccalaureate fields are** business/marketing, education, social sciences and history **Academic program** English as a second language, advanced placement, accelerated degree program, honors program, summer session, adult/continuing education programs, internships **Contact** Mr. Erlend D. Peterson, Dean of Admissions and Records, Brigham Young University, Provo, UT 84602-1110. Telephone: 801-378-2539. Fax: 801-378-4264. E-mail: admissions@byu.edu. Web site: http://www.byu.edu/.

SOUTHERN UTAH UNIVERSITY
CEDAR CITY, UTAH

General State-supported, comprehensive, coed **Entrance** Moderately difficult **Setting** 113-acre small-town campus **Total enrollment** 6,095 **Student-faculty ratio** 21:1 **Application deadline** 7/1 (freshmen), rolling (transfer) **Freshmen** 84% were admitted **Housing** Yes **Expenses** Tuition $2194; Room & Board $2866 **Undergraduates** 56% women, 22% part-time, 22% 25 or older, 1% Native American, 2% Hispanic American, 0.5% African American, 1% Asian American/Pacific Islander **The most frequently chosen baccalaureate fields are** business/marketing, communications/communication technologies, education **Academic program** English as a second language, advanced placement, honors program, summer session, adult/continuing education programs, internships **Contact** Mr. Dale S. Orton, Director of Admissions, Southern Utah University, 351 West Center Street, Cedar City, UT 84720. Telephone: 801-586-7740. Fax: 435-865-8223. E-mail: adminfo@suu.edu. Web site: http://www.suu.edu/.

UNIVERSITY OF PHOENIX–UTAH CAMPUS
SALT LAKE CITY, UTAH

General Proprietary, comprehensive, coed **Entrance** Noncompetitive **Total enrollment** 88,730 **Student-faculty ratio** 14:1 **Application deadline** Rolling (freshmen), rolling (transfer) **Housing** No **Expenses** Tuition $8220 **Undergraduates** 39% women, 100% 25 or older **The most frequently chosen baccalaureate fields are** business/marketing, health professions and related sciences **Academic program** Advanced placement, accelerated degree program, adult/continuing education programs **Contact** Ms. Beth Barilla, Director of Admissions, University of Phoenix–Utah Campus, 4615 East Elwood Street, Phoenix, AZ 85040-1958. Telephone: 480-927-0099 Ext. 1218 or toll-free 800-224-2844. Fax: 480-594-1758. E-mail: beth.barilla@apollogrp.edu. Web site: http://www.phoenix.edu/.

UNIVERSITY OF UTAH
SALT LAKE CITY, UTAH

General State-supported, university, coed **Entrance** Moderately difficult **Setting** 1,500-acre urban campus **Total enrollment** 27,668 **Student-faculty ratio** 14:1 **Application deadline** 5/1 (freshmen), 5/1 (transfer) **Freshmen** 91% were admitted **Housing** Yes **Expenses** Tuition $3057; Room & Board $4646 **Undergraduates** 46% women, 37% part-time, 30% 25 or older, 1% Native American, 3% Hispanic American, 1% African American, 4% Asian American/Pacific Islander **The most frequently chosen baccalaureate fields are** business/marketing, health professions and related sciences, social sciences and history **Academic program** English as a second language, advanced placement, accelerated degree program, self-designed majors, honors program, summer session, adult/continuing education programs, internships **Contact** Ms. Suzanne Espinoza, Director of High School Services, University of Utah, 250 South Student Services Building, 201 South, 460 E Room 205, Salt Lake City, UT 84112. Telephone: 801-581-8761 or toll-free 800-444-8638. Fax: 801-585-7864. Web site: http://www.utah.edu/.

UTAH STATE UNIVERSITY
LOGAN, UTAH

General State-supported, university, coed **Entrance** Moderately difficult **Setting** 456-acre urban campus

UTAH

Utah State University *(continued)*
Total enrollment 23,001 **Student-faculty ratio** 26:1 **Application deadline** Rolling (transfer) **Freshmen** 97% were admitted **Housing** Yes **Expenses** Tuition $2591; Room & Board $4180 **Undergraduates** 52% women, 34% part-time, 21% 25 or older, 1% Native American, 2% Hispanic American, 1% African American, 1% Asian American/Pacific Islander **The most frequently chosen baccalaureate fields are** business/marketing, education, home economics/vocational home economics **Academic program** English as a second language, advanced placement, accelerated degree program, self-designed majors, honors program, summer session, adult/continuing education programs, internships **Contact** Mr. Lynn Poulsen, Associate Vice President, Student Services, Utah State University, 1600 Old Main Hill, Logan, UT 84322-1600. Telephone: 435-797-1107. Fax: 435-797-4077. E-mail: admit@cc.usu.edu. Web site: http://www.usu.edu/.

WEBER STATE UNIVERSITY
OGDEN, UTAH

General State-supported, comprehensive, coed **Entrance** Noncompetitive **Setting** 526-acre urban campus **Total enrollment** 16,873 **Student-faculty ratio** 22:1 **Application deadline** 8/24 (freshmen), rolling (transfer) **Freshmen** 100% were admitted **Housing** Yes **Expenses** Tuition $2252; Room & Board $4645 **Undergraduates** 51% women, 41% part-time, 35% 25 or older, 1% Native American, 3% Hispanic American, 1% African American, 2% Asian American/Pacific Islander **The most frequently chosen baccalaureate fields are** business/marketing, education, health professions and related sciences **Academic program** English as a second language, advanced placement, accelerated degree program, self-designed majors, honors program, summer session, adult/continuing education programs, internships **Contact** John Allred, Admissions Advisor, Weber State University, 1137 University Circle, 3750 Harrison Boulevard, Ogden, UT 84408-1137. Telephone: 801-626-6050 or toll-free 800-634-6568 (in-state). Fax: 801-626-6744. E-mail: kolsen4@weber.edu. Web site: http://weber.edu/.

WESTERN GOVERNORS UNIVERSITY
SALT LAKE CITY, UTAH

General Independent, comprehensive, coed **Total enrollment** 2,030 **Student-faculty ratio** 49:1 **Freshmen** 30% were admitted **Expenses** Tuition $3250 **Undergraduates** 52% women, 92% 25 or older, 2% Native American, 6% Hispanic American, 5% African American, 2% Asian American/Pacific Islander **Academic program** Accelerated degree program, adult/continuing education programs **Contact** Ms. Wendy Gregory, Enrollment Director, Western Governors University, 2040 East Murray Holladay Road, Suite 106, Salt Lake City, UT 84117. Telephone: 801-274-3280 Ext. 315 or toll-free 877-435-7948. Fax: 801-274-3305. E-mail: info@wgu.edu. Web site: http://www.wgu.edu/.

WESTMINSTER COLLEGE
SALT LAKE CITY, UTAH

General Independent, comprehensive, coed **Entrance** Moderately difficult **Setting** 27-acre suburban campus **Total enrollment** 2,474 **Student-faculty ratio** 11:1 **Application deadline** Rolling (freshmen), rolling (transfer) **Freshmen** 90% were admitted **Housing** Yes **Expenses** Tuition $14,780; Room & Board $4650 **Undergraduates** 59% women, 15% part-time, 24% 25 or older, 1% Native American, 5% Hispanic American, 0.3% African American, 3% Asian American/Pacific Islander **The most frequently chosen baccalaureate fields are** business/marketing, education, health professions and related sciences **Academic program** English as a second language, advanced placement, accelerated degree program, self-designed majors, honors program, summer session, internships **Contact** Mr. Philip J. Alletto, Vice President of Student Development and Enrollment Management, Westminster College, 1840 South 1300 East, Salt Lake City, UT 84105-3697. Telephone: 801-832-2200 or toll-free 800-748-4753. Fax: 801-484-3252. E-mail: admispub@wsclc.edu. Web site: http://www.westminstercollege.edu/.

VERMONT

BENNINGTON COLLEGE
BENNINGTON, VERMONT

General Independent, comprehensive, coed **Entrance** Very difficult **Setting** 550-acre small-town campus **Total enrollment** 673 **Student-faculty ratio** 9:1 **Application deadline** 1/1 (freshmen), 6/1 (transfer) **Freshmen** 65% were admitted **Housing** Yes **Expenses** Tuition $25,000; Room & Board $6350 **Undergraduates** 68% women, 0.2% part-time, 4% 25 or older, 0.2% Native American, 2% Hispanic American, 1% African American, 2% Asian American/Pacific Islander **The most frequently chosen baccalaureate fields are** interdisciplinary studies, social sciences and history, visual/performing arts **Academic program** English as a second language, self-designed majors, internships **Contact** Mr. Deane Bogardus, Director of Admissions, Bennington College, One College Drive, Bennington, VT 05201. Telephone: 802-440-4312 or toll-free 800-833-6845. Fax: 802-440-4320. E-mail: admissions@bennington.edu. Web site: http://www.bennington.edu/.

BURLINGTON COLLEGE
BURLINGTON, VERMONT

General Independent, 4-year, coed **Entrance** Noncompetitive **Setting** 1-acre urban campus **Total enrollment** 267 **Student-faculty ratio** 8:1 **Application deadline** 8/1 (freshmen), 8/1 (transfer) **Freshmen** 95% were admitted **Housing** Yes **Expenses** Tuition $10,640; Room only $5500 **Undergraduates** 63% women, 37% part-time, 66% 25 or older **The**

VERMONT

most frequently chosen baccalaureate fields are English, philosophy, religion, and theology, psychology **Academic program** Accelerated degree program, self-designed majors, summer session, adult/continuing education programs, internships **Contact** Ms. Cathleen Sullivan, Assistant Director of Admissions, Burlington College, 95 North Avenue, Burlington, VT 05401-2998. Telephone: 802-862-9616 Ext. 24 or toll-free 800-862-9616. Fax: 802-660-4331. E-mail: admissions@burlcol.edu. Web site: http://www.burlcol.edu/.

CASTLETON STATE COLLEGE
CASTLETON, VERMONT

General State-supported, comprehensive, coed **Entrance** Moderately difficult **Setting** 130-acre rural campus **Total enrollment** 1,656 **Student-faculty ratio** 13:1 **Application deadline** Rolling (freshmen), rolling (transfer) **Freshmen** 93% were admitted **Housing** Yes **Expenses** Tuition $5392; Room & Board $5530 **Undergraduates** 61% women, 12% part-time, 13% 25 or older, 0.1% Native American, 1% Hispanic American, 0.4% African American, 0.3% Asian American/Pacific Islander **The most frequently chosen baccalaureate fields are** protective services/public administration, business/marketing, social sciences and history **Academic program** Advanced placement, self-designed majors, honors program, summer session, internships **Contact** Ms. Heather Atwell, Director of Undergraduate Admissions, Castleton State College, Seminary Street, Castleton, VT 05735. Telephone: 802-468-1351 or toll-free 800-639-8521. Fax: 802-468-1476. E-mail: info@castleton.edu. Web site: http://www.castleton.edu/.

CHAMPLAIN COLLEGE
BURLINGTON, VERMONT

General Independent, comprehensive, coed **Entrance** Moderately difficult **Setting** 19-acre suburban campus **Total enrollment** 2,523 **Student-faculty ratio** 13:1 **Application deadline** Rolling (freshmen), rolling (transfer) **Freshmen** 64% were admitted **Housing** Yes **Expenses** Tuition $11,605; Room & Board $8075 **Undergraduates** 54% women, 41% part-time, 5% 25 or older, 1% Native American, 1% Hispanic American, 1% African American, 2% Asian American/Pacific Islander **The most frequently chosen baccalaureate fields are** business/marketing, education, liberal arts/general studies **Academic program** Advanced placement, honors program, summer session, adult/continuing education programs, internships **Contact** Ms. Josephine H. Churchill, Director of Admissions, Champlain College, 163 South Willard Street, Burlington, VT 05401. Telephone: 802-860-2727 or toll-free 800-570-5858. Fax: 802-860-2767. E-mail: admission@champlain.edu. Web site: http://www.champlain.edu/.

COLLEGE OF ST. JOSEPH
RUTLAND, VERMONT

General Independent Roman Catholic, comprehensive, coed **Entrance** Minimally difficult **Setting** 90-acre small-town campus **Total enrollment** 482 **Student-faculty ratio** 12:1 **Application deadline** Rolling (freshmen), rolling (transfer) **Freshmen** 89% were admitted **Housing** Yes **Expenses** Tuition $12,200; Room & Board $6300 **Undergraduates** 66% women, 43% part-time, 53% 25 or older **The most frequently chosen baccalaureate fields are** business/marketing, liberal arts/general studies, psychology **Academic program** English as a second language, advanced placement, accelerated degree program, summer session, adult/continuing education programs, internships **Contact** Mr. Maurice Ouimet, Assistant Dean of Admissions, College of St. Joseph, 71 Clement Road, Rutland, VT 05701-3899. Telephone: 802-773-5900 Ext. 217. Fax: 802-773-5900 Ext. 258. E-mail: admissions@csj.edu. Web site: http://www.csj.edu/.

GODDARD COLLEGE
PLAINFIELD, VERMONT

General Independent, comprehensive, coed **Entrance** Moderately difficult **Setting** 250-acre rural campus **Total enrollment** 623 **Student-faculty ratio** 11:1 **Application deadline** Rolling (freshmen), rolling (transfer) **Freshmen** 99% were admitted **Housing** Yes **Expenses** Tuition $17,966; Room & Board $1482 **Undergraduates** 59% women, 34% 25 or older, 1% Native American, 2% Hispanic American, 2% African American, 1% Asian American/Pacific Islander **The most frequently chosen baccalaureate fields are** education, health professions and related sciences, interdisciplinary studies **Academic program** Advanced placement, self-designed majors, adult/continuing education programs, internships **Contact** Mr. Josh Castle, Admissions Counselor, Goddard College, 123 Pitkin Road, Plainfield, VT 05667-9432. Telephone: 802-454-8311 Ext. 322 or toll-free 800-468-4888 Ext. 307. Fax: 802-454-1029. E-mail: admissions@earth.goddard.edu. Web site: http://www.goddard.edu/.

GREEN MOUNTAIN COLLEGE
POULTNEY, VERMONT

General Independent, 4-year, coed, affiliated with United Methodist Church **Entrance** Moderately difficult **Setting** 155-acre small-town campus **Total enrollment** 659 **Student-faculty ratio** 14:1 **Application deadline** Rolling (freshmen), rolling (transfer) **Freshmen** 72% were admitted **Housing** Yes **Expenses** Tuition $18,280; Room & Board $5850 **Undergraduates** 47% women, 4% part-time, 7% 25 or older, 1% Native American, 2% Hispanic American, 2% African American, 0.2% Asian American/Pacific Islander **The most frequently chosen baccalaureate fields are** business/marketing, education, parks and recreation **Academic program** English as a second language, advanced placement, accelerated degree program, self-designed majors, honors program, summer session, adult/continuing education programs, internships **Contact** Ms. Merrilyn Tatarczuch-Koff, Dean of Enrollment Services, Green Mountain College, One College Circle, Poultney, VT 05764.

VERMONT

Green Mountain College *(continued)*
Telephone: 802-287-8000 Ext. 8305 or toll-free 800-776-6675 (out-of-state). Fax: 802-287-8099. E-mail: admiss@greenmtn.edu. Web site: http://www.greenmtn.edu/.

JOHNSON STATE COLLEGE
JOHNSON, VERMONT

General State-supported, comprehensive, coed **Entrance** Moderately difficult **Setting** 350-acre rural campus **Total enrollment** 1,590 **Student-faculty ratio** 16:1 **Application deadline** Rolling (freshmen), rolling (transfer) **Freshmen** 83% were admitted **Housing** Yes **Expenses** Tuition $5252; Room & Board $5520 **Undergraduates** 58% women, 28% part-time, 10% 25 or older, 2% Native American, 1% Hispanic American, 0.5% African American, 0.2% Asian American/Pacific Islander **Academic program** English as a second language, advanced placement, accelerated degree program, honors program, summer session, internships **Contact** Ms. Kellie Rose, Assistant Director of Admissions, Johnson State College, 337 College Hill, Johnson, VT 05656-9405. Telephone: 802-635-1219 or toll-free 800-635-2356. Fax: 802-635-1230. E-mail: jscapply@badger.jsc.vsc.edu. Web site: http://www.jsc.vsc.edu/.

LYNDON STATE COLLEGE
LYNDONVILLE, VERMONT

General State-supported, comprehensive, coed **Entrance** Moderately difficult **Setting** 175-acre rural campus **Total enrollment** 1,138 **Student-faculty ratio** 17:1 **Application deadline** Rolling (freshmen), rolling (transfer) **Freshmen** 96% were admitted **Housing** Yes **Expenses** Tuition $5252; Room & Board $5520 **Undergraduates** 14% 25 or older **Academic program** Advanced placement, self-designed majors, summer session, adult/continuing education programs, internships **Contact** Ms. Michelle McCaffrey, Director of Admissions, Lyndon State College, 1001 College Road, PO Box 919, Lyndonville, VT 05851. Telephone: 802-626-6413 or toll-free 800-225-1998 (in-state). Fax: 802-626-6335. E-mail: admissions@mail.lsc.vsc.edu. Web site: http://www.lsc.vsc.edu/.

MARLBORO COLLEGE
MARLBORO, VERMONT

General Independent, comprehensive, coed **Entrance** Moderately difficult **Setting** 350-acre rural campus **Total enrollment** 411 **Student-faculty ratio** 8:1 **Application deadline** 3/1 (freshmen), 4/1 (transfer) **Freshmen** 87% were admitted **Housing** Yes **Expenses** Tuition $19,660; Room & Board $6750 **Undergraduates** 57% women, 3% part-time, 10% 25 or older, 1% Native American, 2% Hispanic American, 1% African American, 0% Asian American/Pacific Islander **The most frequently chosen baccalaureate fields are** social sciences and history, English, visual/performing arts **Academic program** Advanced placement, accelerated degree program, self-designed majors, internships **Contact** Ms. Julie E. Richardson, Vice President, Enrollment and Financial Aid, Marlboro College, PO Box A, South Road, Marlboro, VT 05344-0300. Telephone: 802-258-9261 or toll-free 800-343-0049. Fax: 802-451-7555. E-mail: admissions@marlboro.edu. Web site: http://www.marlboro.edu/.

MIDDLEBURY COLLEGE
MIDDLEBURY, VERMONT

General Independent, comprehensive, coed **Entrance** Very difficult **Setting** 350-acre small-town campus **Total enrollment** 2,307 **Student-faculty ratio** 11:1 **Application deadline** 12/15 (freshmen), 3/1 (transfer) **Freshmen** 23% were admitted **Housing** Yes **Expenses** Tuition $34,300 **Undergraduates** 52% women, 2% part-time, 0% 25 or older, 1% Native American, 6% Hispanic American, 2% African American, 6% Asian American/Pacific Islander **The most frequently chosen baccalaureate fields are** area/ethnic studies, English, social sciences and history **Academic program** Advanced placement, accelerated degree program, self-designed majors, honors program, summer session, internships **Contact** Mr. John Hanson, Director of Admissions, Middlebury College, Emma Willard House, Middlebury, VT 05753-6002. Telephone: 802-443-3000. Fax: 802-443-2056. E-mail: admissions@middlebury.edu. Web site: http://www.middlebury.edu/.

NORWICH UNIVERSITY
NORTHFIELD, VERMONT

General Independent, comprehensive, coed **Entrance** Moderately difficult **Setting** 1,125-acre small-town campus **Total enrollment** 2,707 **Student-faculty ratio** 12:1 **Application deadline** Rolling (freshmen), rolling (transfer) **Freshmen** 91% were admitted **Housing** Yes **Expenses** Tuition $16,194; Room & Board $6068 **Undergraduates** 23% 25 or older **The most frequently chosen baccalaureate fields are** liberal arts/general studies, protective services/public administration, social sciences and history **Academic program** English as a second language, advanced placement, summer session, adult/continuing education programs, internships **Contact** Ms. Karen McGrath, Dean of Enrollment Management, Norwich University, 158 Harmon Drive, Northfield, VT 05663. Telephone: 802-485-2013 or toll-free 800-468-6679 (in-state). Fax: 802-485-2580. E-mail: nuadm@norwich.edu. Web site: http://www.norwich.edu/.

▶ For more information, see page 463.

SAINT MICHAEL'S COLLEGE
COLCHESTER, VERMONT

General Independent Roman Catholic, comprehensive, coed **Entrance** Moderately difficult **Setting** 440-acre small-town campus **Total enrollment** 2,630 **Student-faculty ratio** 13:1 **Application deadline** 2/1 (freshmen), 2/1 (transfer) **Freshmen** 64% were admitted **Housing** Yes **Expenses** Tuition $19,680; Room & Board $7255 **Undergraduates** 55% women, 4% part-time, 2% 25 or older, 0% Native American, 1% Hispanic American, 1% African American, 1%

VIRGINIA

Asian American/Pacific Islander **The most frequently chosen baccalaureate fields are** business/marketing, psychology, social sciences and history **Academic program** English as a second language, advanced placement, self-designed majors, honors program, summer session, internships **Contact** Ms. Jacqueline Murphy, Director of Admission, Saint Michael's College, One Winooski Park, Colchester, VT 05439. Telephone: 802-654-3000 or toll-free 800-762-8000. Fax: 802-654-2906. E-mail: admission@smcvt.edu. Web site: http://www.smcvt.edu/.

SOUTHERN VERMONT COLLEGE
BENNINGTON, VERMONT

General Independent, 4-year, coed **Entrance** Minimally difficult **Setting** 371-acre small-town campus **Total enrollment** 457 **Student-faculty ratio** 11:1 **Application deadline** Rolling (freshmen), rolling (transfer) **Freshmen** 68% were admitted **Housing** Yes **Expenses** Tuition $11,290; Room & Board $5648 **Undergraduates** 63% women, 33% part-time, 35% 25 or older, 0% Native American, 2% Hispanic American, 5% African American, 0.2% Asian American/Pacific Islander **Academic program** Advanced placement, accelerated degree program, self-designed majors, honors program, summer session, adult/continuing education programs, internships **Contact** Elizabeth Gatti, Director of Admissions, Southern Vermont College, 982 Mansion Drive, Bennington, VT 05201. Telephone: 802-447-6304 or toll-free 800-378-2782 (in-state). Fax: 802-447-4695. E-mail: admis@svc.edu. Web site: http://www.svc.edu/.

STERLING COLLEGE
CRAFTSBURY COMMON, VERMONT

General Independent, 4-year, coed **Entrance** Moderately difficult **Setting** 150-acre rural campus **Total enrollment** 80 **Student-faculty ratio** 10:1 **Application deadline** Rolling (freshmen), rolling (transfer) **Freshmen** 61% were admitted **Housing** Yes **Expenses** Tuition $13,300; Room & Board $5600 **Undergraduates** 39% women, 1% 25 or older, 0% Native American, 0% Hispanic American, 0% African American, 0% Asian American/Pacific Islander **The most frequently chosen baccalaureate field is** natural resources/environmental science **Academic program** Self-designed majors, honors program, summer session, internships **Contact** John Zaber, Director of Admissions, Sterling College, PO Box 72, Craftsbury Common, VT 05827. Telephone: 802-586-7711 Ext. 35 or toll-free 800-648-3591. Fax: 802-586-2596. E-mail: admissions@sterlingcollege.edu. Web site: http://www.sterlingcollege.edu/.

UNIVERSITY OF VERMONT
BURLINGTON, VERMONT

General State-supported, university, coed **Entrance** Moderately difficult **Setting** 425-acre suburban campus **Total enrollment** 10,081 **Student-faculty ratio** 13:1 **Application deadline** 1/15 (freshmen), 4/1 (transfer) **Freshmen** 80% were admitted **Housing** Yes **Expenses** Tuition $8665; Room & Board $6096 **Undergraduates** 56% women, 16% part-time, 5% 25 or older, 0.2% Native American, 2% Hispanic American, 1% African American, 2% Asian American/Pacific Islander **The most frequently chosen baccalaureate fields are** business/marketing, natural resources/environmental science, social sciences and history **Academic program** English as a second language, advanced placement, self-designed majors, honors program, summer session, internships **Contact** Mr. Donald M. Honeman, Director of Admissions, University of Vermont, Office of Admissions, Burlington, VT 05401-3596. Telephone: 802-656-3370. Fax: 802-656-8611. E-mail: admissions@uvm.edu. Web site: http://www.uvm.edu/.

VERMONT TECHNICAL COLLEGE
RANDOLPH CENTER, VERMONT

General State-supported, 4-year, coed **Entrance** Minimally difficult **Setting** 544-acre rural campus **Total enrollment** 1,272 **Student-faculty ratio** 11:1 **Application deadline** Rolling (freshmen), rolling (transfer) **Freshmen** 71% were admitted **Housing** Yes **Expenses** Tuition $5340; Room & Board $5520 **Undergraduates** 31% women, 30% part-time, 22% 25 or older, 0.2% Native American, 1% Hispanic American, 0.2% African American, 1% Asian American/Pacific Islander **The most frequently chosen baccalaureate fields are** architecture, engineering/engineering technologies **Academic program** English as a second language, advanced placement, accelerated degree program, honors program, summer session, internships **Contact** Ms. Rosemary W. Distel, Director of Admissions, Vermont Technical College, PO Box 500, Randolph Center, VT 05061. Telephone: 802-728-1245 or toll-free 800-442-VTC1. Fax: 802-728-1390. E-mail: admissions@vtc.edu. Web site: http://www.vtc.edu.

VIRGINIA

AMERICAN MILITARY UNIVERSITY
MANASSAS, VIRGINIA

General Proprietary, comprehensive, coed, primarily men **Entrance** Noncompetitive **Student-faculty ratio** 11:1 **Application deadline** Rolling (freshmen), rolling (transfer) **Freshmen** 100% were admitted **Housing** No **Expenses** Tuition $9000 **Undergraduates** 92% 25 or older, 1% Native American, 6% Hispanic American, 16% African American, 2% Asian American/Pacific Islander **Academic program** Adult/continuing education programs **Contact** Ms. Nancy Tilton, Director of Admissions, American Military University, 10648 Wakeman Court, Manassas, VA 20110. Telephone: 703-330-5398 Ext. 882 or toll-free 877-468-6268. Fax: 703-330-5109. E-mail: admissions@amunet.edu. Web site: http://www.amunet.edu/.

VIRGINIA

THE ART INSTITUTE OF WASHINGTON
ARLINGTON, VIRGINIA

General Proprietary, 4-year, coed **Student-faculty ratio** 20:1 **Housing** No **Expenses** Tuition $12,000 **Contact** Ms. Ann Marie Drucker, Director of Admissions, The Art Institute of Washington, 1820 North Fort Myer Drive, Arlington, VA 22209. Telephone: 703-358-9550 or toll-free 877-303-3771. Web site: http://www.aiw.artinstitute.edu/.

AVERETT UNIVERSITY
DANVILLE, VIRGINIA

General Independent Baptist, comprehensive, coed **Entrance** Moderately difficult **Setting** 25-acre suburban campus **Total enrollment** 2,396 **Student-faculty ratio** 14:1 **Application deadline** Rolling (freshmen), rolling (transfer) **Freshmen** 89% were admitted **Housing** Yes **Expenses** Tuition $14,990; Room & Board $5000 **Undergraduates** 61% women, 35% part-time, 16% 25 or older, 1% Native American, 1% Hispanic American, 28% African American, 1% Asian American/Pacific Islander **The most frequently chosen baccalaureate fields are** business/marketing, education, social sciences and history **Academic program** Advanced placement, accelerated degree program, self-designed majors, honors program, summer session, adult/continuing education programs, internships **Contact** Mr. Gary Sherman, Vice President of Enrollment Management, Averett University, English Hall, Danville, VA 24541. Telephone: 804-791-5660 or toll-free 800-AVERETT. Fax: 804-797-2784. E-mail: admit@averett.edu. Web site: http://www.averett.edu/.

BLUEFIELD COLLEGE
BLUEFIELD, VIRGINIA

General Independent Southern Baptist, 4-year, coed **Entrance** Moderately difficult **Setting** 85-acre small-town campus **Total enrollment** 841 **Student-faculty ratio** 24:1 **Application deadline** Rolling (freshmen), rolling (transfer) **Freshmen** 76% were admitted **Housing** Yes **Expenses** Tuition $9140; Room & Board $5060 **Undergraduates** 52% women, 4% part-time, 34% 25 or older, 2% Native American, 1% Hispanic American, 13% African American, 1% Asian American/Pacific Islander **The most frequently chosen baccalaureate fields are** business/marketing, protective services/public administration, psychology **Academic program** Advanced placement, accelerated degree program, self-designed majors, honors program, summer session, adult/continuing education programs, internships **Contact** Office of Admissions, Bluefield College, 3000 College Drive, Bluefield, VA 24605-1799. Telephone: 276-326-4214 or toll-free 800-872-0175. Fax: 276-326-4288. E-mail: admissions@mail.bluefield.edu. Web site: http://www.bluefield.edu/.

BRIDGEWATER COLLEGE
BRIDGEWATER, VIRGINIA

General Independent, 4-year, coed, affiliated with Church of the Brethren **Entrance** Moderately difficult **Setting** 190-acre small-town campus **Total enrollment** 1,260 **Student-faculty ratio** 15:1 **Application deadline** Rolling (freshmen), rolling (transfer) **Freshmen** 87% were admitted **Housing** Yes **Expenses** Tuition $15,490; Room & Board $7760 **Undergraduates** 57% women, 2% part-time, 1% 25 or older, 0.5% Native American, 1% Hispanic American, 6% African American, 1% Asian American/Pacific Islander **The most frequently chosen baccalaureate fields are** business/marketing, education, psychology **Academic program** Advanced placement, honors program, summer session, adult/continuing education programs, internships **Contact** Ms. Linda F. Stout, Director of Enrollment Operations, Bridgewater College, 402 East College Street, Bridgewater, VA 22812-1599. Telephone: 540-828-5375 or toll-free 800-759-8328. Fax: 540-828-5481. E-mail: admissions@bridgewater.edu. Web site: http://www.bridgewater.edu/.

CHRISTENDOM COLLEGE
FRONT ROYAL, VIRGINIA

General Independent Roman Catholic, comprehensive, coed **Entrance** Moderately difficult **Setting** 100-acre rural campus **Total enrollment** 407 **Student-faculty ratio** 12:1 **Application deadline** Rolling (freshmen), rolling (transfer) **Freshmen** 81% were admitted **Housing** Yes **Expenses** Tuition $11,980; Room & Board $4700 **Undergraduates** 57% women, 1% part-time, 3% 25 or older, 0.3% Native American, 3% Hispanic American, 1% African American, 2% Asian American/Pacific Islander **The most frequently chosen baccalaureate fields are** philosophy, philosophy, religion, and theology, social sciences and history **Academic program** Advanced placement, accelerated degree program, summer session, internships **Contact** Mr. Paul Heisler, Director of Admissions, Christendom College, 134 Christendom Drive, Front Royal, VA 22630-5103. Telephone: 540-636-2900 Ext. 290 or toll-free 800-877-5456 Ext. 290. Fax: 540-636-1655. E-mail: admissions@christendom.edu. Web site: http://www.christendom.edu/.

CHRISTOPHER NEWPORT UNIVERSITY
NEWPORT NEWS, VIRGINIA

General State-supported, comprehensive, coed **Entrance** Moderately difficult **Setting** 113-acre suburban campus **Total enrollment** 5,388 **Student-faculty ratio** 20:1 **Application deadline** 3/1 (freshmen), 6/1 (transfer) **Freshmen** 48% were admitted **Housing** Yes **Expenses** Tuition $3112; Room & Board $5750 **Undergraduates** 61% women, 22% part-time, 21% 25 or older, 0.4% Native American, 3% Hispanic American, 14% African American, 3% Asian American/Pacific Islander **The most frequently chosen baccalaureate fields are** business/marketing, psychology, social sciences and history **Academic program** Advanced placement, accelerated degree program, self-designed majors, honors program, summer session, adult/continuing education programs, internships **Contact** Ms. Rebecca Ducknuall, Assistant Director of Admissions, Christopher Newport University, 1 University Place, Newport News, VA 23606-2998. Telephone: 757-594-7205 or toll-free 800-333-4CNU. Fax: 757-594-7333. E-mail: admit@cnu.edu. Web site: http://www.cnu.edu/.

THE COLLEGE OF WILLIAM AND MARY
WILLIAMSBURG, VIRGINIA

General State-supported, university, coed **Entrance** Very difficult **Setting** 1,200-acre small-town campus **Total enrollment** 7,489 **Student-faculty ratio** 12:1 **Application deadline** 1/5 (freshmen), 2/15 (transfer) **Freshmen** 37% were admitted **Housing** Yes **Expenses** Tuition $4780; Room & Board $5222 **Undergraduates** 57% women, 1% part-time, 1% 25 or older, 0.3% Native American, 3% Hispanic American, 5% African American, 7% Asian American/Pacific Islander **The most frequently chosen baccalaureate fields are** business/marketing, English, social sciences and history **Academic program** Advanced placement, accelerated degree program, self-designed majors, honors program, summer session **Contact** Dr. Karen R. Cottrell, Associate Provost for Enrollment, The College of William and Mary, PO Box 8795, Williamsburg, VA 23187-8795. Telephone: 757-221-4223. Fax: 757-221-1242. E-mail: admiss@facstaff.wm.edu. Web site: http://www.wm.edu/.

COMMUNITY HOSPITAL OF ROANOKE VALLEY–COLLEGE OF HEALTH SCIENCES
ROANOKE, VIRGINIA

General Independent, 4-year, coed **Entrance** Moderately difficult **Setting** 1-acre urban campus **Total enrollment** 642 **Student-faculty ratio** 11:1 **Application deadline** 7/31 (freshmen) **Freshmen** 95% were admitted **Housing** Yes **Expenses** Tuition $5430; Room only $2000 **Undergraduates** 77% women, 33% part-time, 50% 25 or older, 0.2% Native American, 1% Hispanic American, 10% African American, 2% Asian American/Pacific Islander **The most frequently chosen baccalaureate field is** health professions and related sciences **Academic program** Advanced placement, accelerated degree program, summer session, adult/continuing education programs, internships **Contact** Ms. Connie Cook, Admissions Representative, Community Hospital of Roanoke Valley–College of Health Sciences, PO Box 13186, Roanoke, VA 24031-3186. Telephone: 540-985-8563 or toll-free 888-985-8483. Fax: 540-985-9773. E-mail: rrobertson@health.chs.edu. Web site: http://www.chs.edu/.

DEVRY UNIVERSITY
ARLINGTON, VIRGINIA

General Proprietary, 4-year, coed **Total enrollment** 243 **Student-faculty ratio** 6:1 **Application deadline** Rolling (freshmen), rolling (transfer) **Freshmen** 71% were admitted **Housing** No **Expenses** Tuition $10,000 **Undergraduates** 18% women, 61% part-time, 44% 25 or older, 0.4% Native American, 4% Hispanic American, 54% African American, 5% Asian American/ Pacific Islander **Contact** Mr. Todd Marshburn, Director of Enrollment Services, DeVry University, Century Building I, Suite 200, 2341 Jefferson Davis Highway, Arlington, VA 22202. Telephone: 866-338-7932. Web site: http://www.crys.devry.edu/.

EASTERN MENNONITE UNIVERSITY
HARRISONBURG, VIRGINIA

General Independent Mennonite, comprehensive, coed **Entrance** Moderately difficult **Setting** 92-acre small-town campus **Total enrollment** 1,304 **Student-faculty ratio** 13:1 **Application deadline** 8/1 (freshmen), 8/1 (transfer) **Freshmen** 70% were admitted **Housing** Yes **Expenses** Tuition $15,300; Room & Board $5400 **Undergraduates** 60% women, 5% part-time, 4% 25 or older, 0.4% Native American, 2% Hispanic American, 6% African American, 1% Asian American/Pacific Islander **The most frequently chosen baccalaureate fields are** business/marketing, education, liberal arts/general studies **Academic program** English as a second language, advanced placement, honors program, summer session, adult/continuing education programs, internships **Contact** Ms. Ellen B. Miller, Director of Admissions, Eastern Mennonite University, 1200 Park Road, Harrisonburg, VA 22802-2462. Telephone: 540-432-4118 or toll-free 800-368-2665. Fax: 540-432-4444. E-mail: admiss@emu.edu. Web site: http://www.emu.edu/.

▶ For more information, see page 422.

EMORY & HENRY COLLEGE
EMORY, VIRGINIA

General Independent United Methodist, comprehensive, coed **Entrance** Moderately difficult **Setting** 163-acre rural campus **Total enrollment** 1,079 **Student-faculty ratio** 14:1 **Application deadline** Rolling (freshmen), rolling (transfer) **Freshmen** 78% were admitted **Housing** Yes **Expenses** Tuition $14,100; Room & Board $5362 **Undergraduates** 52% women, 3% part-time, 4% 25 or older, 0.1% Native American, 1% Hispanic American, 6% African American, 1% Asian American/Pacific Islander **The most frequently chosen baccalaureate fields are** business/marketing, interdisciplinary studies, social sciences and history **Academic program** English as a second language, advanced placement, self-designed majors, honors program, summer session, internships **Contact** Ms. Debbie Jones Thompson, Dean of Admissions and Financial Aid, Emory & Henry College, 30479 Armbrister Drive, PO Box 10, Emory, VA 24327. Telephone: 276-944-6133 or toll-free 800-848-5493. Fax: 276-944-6935. E-mail: ehadmiss@ehc.edu. Web site: http://www.ehc.edu/.

▶ For more information, see page 425.

FERRUM COLLEGE
FERRUM, VIRGINIA

General Independent United Methodist, 4-year, coed **Entrance** Minimally difficult **Setting** 720-acre rural campus **Total enrollment** 920 **Student-faculty ratio** 13:1 **Application deadline** Rolling (freshmen), roll-

VIRGINIA

Ferrum College *(continued)*
ing (transfer) **Freshmen** 70% were admitted **Housing** Yes **Expenses** Tuition $12,950; Room & Board $5600 **Undergraduates** 42% women, 4% part-time, 8% 25 or older, 0.3% Native American, 1% Hispanic American, 19% African American, 1% Asian American/Pacific Islander **The most frequently chosen baccalaureate fields are** business/marketing, biological/life sciences, protective services/public administration **Academic program** Advanced placement, self-designed majors, summer session, adult/continuing education programs, internships **Contact** Ms. Gilda Q. Woods, Director of Admissions, Ferrum College, Spilman-Daniel House, PO Box 1000, Ferrum, VA 24088-9001. Telephone: 540-365-4290 or toll-free 800-868-9797. Fax: 540-365-4266. E-mail: admissions@ferrum.edu. Web site: http://www.ferrum.edu/.

▶ For more information, see page 428.

GEORGE MASON UNIVERSITY
FAIRFAX, VIRGINIA

General State-supported, university, coed **Entrance** Moderately difficult **Setting** 677-acre suburban campus **Total enrollment** 24,897 **Student-faculty ratio** 16:1 **Application deadline** 2/1 (freshmen), 3/15 (transfer) **Freshmen** 68% were admitted **Housing** Yes **Expenses** Tuition $3792; Room & Board $5400 **Undergraduates** 56% women, 28% part-time, 32% 25 or older, 0.4% Native American, 7% Hispanic American, 9% African American, 16% Asian American/Pacific Islander **The most frequently chosen baccalaureate fields are** business/marketing, interdisciplinary studies, social sciences and history **Academic program** English as a second language, advanced placement, accelerated degree program, self-designed majors, honors program, summer session, adult/continuing education programs, internships **Contact** Mr. Eddie Tallent, Director of Admissions, George Mason University, 4400 University Drive, MSN 3A4, Fairfax, VA 22030-4444. Telephone: 703-993-2398. Fax: 703-993-2392. E-mail: admissions@gmu.edu. Web site: http://www.gmu.edu/.

HAMPDEN-SYDNEY COLLEGE
HAMPDEN-SYDNEY, VIRGINIA

General Independent Presbyterian, 4-year, men only **Entrance** Moderately difficult **Setting** 660-acre rural campus **Total enrollment** 1,026 **Student-faculty ratio** 10:1 **Application deadline** 3/1 (freshmen), 7/1 (transfer) **Freshmen** 77% were admitted **Housing** Yes **Expenses** Tuition $18,485; Room & Board $6386 **Undergraduates** 0% 25 or older, 0.4% Native American, 1% Hispanic American, 4% African American, 1% Asian American/Pacific Islander **The most frequently chosen baccalaureate fields are** biological/life sciences, philosophy, social sciences and history **Academic program** Advanced placement, accelerated degree program, honors program, summer session, internships **Contact** Ms. Anita H. Garland, Dean of Admissions, Hampden-Sydney College, PO Box 667, Hampden-Sydney, VA 23943-0667. Telephone: 434-223-6120 or toll-free 800-755-0733. Fax: 434-223-6346. E-mail: hsapp@hsc.edu. Web site: http://www.hsc.edu/.

HAMPTON UNIVERSITY
HAMPTON, VIRGINIA

General Independent, university, coed **Entrance** Moderately difficult **Setting** 210-acre urban campus **Total enrollment** 5,793 **Student-faculty ratio** 16:1 **Application deadline** 3/15 (freshmen), 3/15 (transfer) **Freshmen** 57% were admitted **Housing** Yes **Expenses** Tuition $11,666; Room & Board $5446 **Undergraduates** 62% women, 7% part-time, 10% 25 or older, 0.2% Native American, 1% Hispanic American, 96% African American, 0.4% Asian American/Pacific Islander **The most frequently chosen baccalaureate fields are** biological/life sciences, business/marketing, psychology **Academic program** Advanced placement, accelerated degree program, honors program, summer session, adult/continuing education programs, internships **Contact** Mr. Leonard M. Jones Jr., Director of Admissions, Hampton University, Office of Admissions, Hampton, VA 23668. Telephone: 757-727-5328 or toll-free 800-624-3328. Fax: 757-727-5095. E-mail: admit@hamptonu.edu. Web site: http://www.hamptonu.edu/.

HOLLINS UNIVERSITY
ROANOKE, VIRGINIA

General Independent, comprehensive, women only **Entrance** Moderately difficult **Setting** 475-acre suburban campus **Total enrollment** 1,091 **Student-faculty ratio** 9:1 **Application deadline** 2/15 (freshmen), 6/1 (transfer) **Freshmen** 81% were admitted **Housing** Yes **Expenses** Tuition $17,720; Room & Board $6608 **Undergraduates** 5% part-time, 10% 25 or older, 0.1% Native American, 2% Hispanic American, 5% African American, 2% Asian American/Pacific Islander **The most frequently chosen baccalaureate fields are** English, social sciences and history, visual/performing arts **Academic program** Advanced placement, accelerated degree program, self-designed majors, honors program, adult/continuing education programs, internships **Contact** Ms. Celia McCormick, Dean of Admissions, Hollins University, PO Box 9707, Roanoke, VA 24020-1707. Telephone: 540-362-6401 or toll-free 800-456-9595. Fax: 540-362-6218. E-mail: huadm@hollins.edu. Web site: http://www.hollins.edu/.

JAMES MADISON UNIVERSITY
HARRISONBURG, VIRGINIA

General State-supported, comprehensive, coed **Entrance** Very difficult **Setting** 472-acre small-town campus **Total enrollment** 15,562 **Student-faculty ratio** 17:1 **Application deadline** 1/15 (freshmen), 3/1 (transfer) **Freshmen** 64% were admitted **Housing** Yes **Expenses** Tuition $4094; Room & Board $5458 **Undergraduates** 58% women, 6% part-time, 2% 25 or older, 0.2% Native American, 2% Hispanic American, 4% African American, 5% Asian American/

VIRGINIA

Pacific Islander **The most frequently chosen baccalaureate fields are** business/marketing, computer/information sciences, social sciences and history **Academic program** English as a second language, advanced placement, accelerated degree program, honors program, summer session, adult/continuing education programs, internships **Contact** Ms. Laika Tamny, Associate Director of Admissions, James Madison University, Office of Admission, Sonner Hall MSC 0101, Harrisonburg, VA 22807. Telephone: 540-568-6147. Fax: 540-568-3332. E-mail: gotojmu@jmu.edu. Web site: http://www.jmu.edu/.

JOHNSON & WALES UNIVERSITY
NORFOLK, VIRGINIA

General Independent, 4-year, coed **Entrance** Minimally difficult **Setting** urban campus **Total enrollment** 635 **Student-faculty ratio** 18:1 **Application deadline** Rolling (freshmen), rolling (transfer) **Freshmen** 68% were admitted **Housing** Yes **Expenses** Tuition $14,931; Room & Board $6150 **Undergraduates** 45% women, 5% part-time, 37% 25 or older, 0.2% Native American, 5% Hispanic American, 36% African American, 2% Asian American/Pacific Islander **Academic program** Accelerated degree program, summer session, internships **Contact** Ms. Torri Butler, Director of Student Affairs, Johnson & Wales University, 2428 Almeda Avenue, Suite 316, Norfolk, VA 23513. Telephone: 757-853-3508 Ext. 222 or toll-free 800-277-2433. Fax: 757-857-4869. E-mail: admissions@jwu.edu. Web site: http://www.jwu.edu/.

LIBERTY UNIVERSITY
LYNCHBURG, VIRGINIA

General Independent nondenominational, comprehensive, coed **Entrance** Minimally difficult **Setting** 160-acre suburban campus **Total enrollment** 6,162 **Student-faculty ratio** 21:1 **Application deadline** 6/30 (freshmen), 6/30 (transfer) **Freshmen** 58% were admitted **Housing** Yes **Expenses** Tuition $9500; Room & Board $5000 **Undergraduates** 51% women, 16% part-time, 18% 25 or older, 1% Native American, 2% Hispanic American, 8% African American, 2% Asian American/Pacific Islander **The most frequently chosen baccalaureate fields are** business/marketing, philosophy, philosophy, religion, and theology **Academic program** English as a second language, advanced placement, accelerated degree program, self-designed majors, honors program, summer session, internships **Contact** Mr. David Hart, Associate Director of Admissions, Liberty University, 1971 University Boulevard, Lynchburg, VA 24502. Telephone: 434-582-7307 or toll-free 800-543-5317. Fax: 434-582-2421. E-mail: admissions@liberty.edu. Web site: http://www.liberty.edu/.

LONGWOOD COLLEGE
FARMVILLE, VIRGINIA

General State-supported, comprehensive, coed **Entrance** Moderately difficult **Setting** 160-acre small-town campus **Total enrollment** 4,114 **Student-faculty ratio** 19:1 **Application deadline** 3/1 (freshmen), 6/1 (transfer) **Freshmen** 78% were admitted **Housing** Yes **Expenses** Tuition $4226; Room & Board $4724 **Undergraduates** 66% women, 3% part-time, 3% 25 or older, 0.2% Native American, 2% Hispanic American, 8% African American, 2% Asian American/Pacific Islander **The most frequently chosen baccalaureate fields are** business/marketing, education, social sciences and history **Academic program** English as a second language, advanced placement, accelerated degree program, honors program, summer session, adult/continuing education programs, internships **Contact** Mr. Robert J. Chonko, Director of Admissions, Longwood College, 201 High Street, Farmville, VA 23909. Telephone: 434-395-2060 or toll-free 800-281-4677 Ext. 2. Fax: 434-395-2332. E-mail: lcadmit@longwood.edu. Web site: http://www.longwood.edu/.

LYNCHBURG COLLEGE
LYNCHBURG, VIRGINIA

General Independent, comprehensive, coed, affiliated with Christian Church (Disciples of Christ) **Entrance** Moderately difficult **Setting** 214-acre suburban campus **Total enrollment** 1,937 **Student-faculty ratio** 12:1 **Application deadline** Rolling (freshmen), rolling (transfer) **Freshmen** 75% were admitted **Housing** Yes **Expenses** Tuition $19,005; Room & Board $4400 **Undergraduates** 61% women, 8% part-time, 15% 25 or older, 0.5% Native American, 2% Hispanic American, 8% African American, 1% Asian American/Pacific Islander **The most frequently chosen baccalaureate fields are** business/marketing, education, psychology **Academic program** Advanced placement, accelerated degree program, honors program, summer session, adult/continuing education programs, internships **Contact** Ms. Sharon Walters-Bower, Director of Recruitment, Lynchburg College, 1501 Lakeside Drive, Lynchburg, VA 24501-3199. Telephone: 434-544-8300 or toll-free 800-426-8101. Fax: 804-544-8653. E-mail: admissions@lynchburg.edu. Web site: http://www.lynchburg.edu/.

MARY BALDWIN COLLEGE
STAUNTON, VIRGINIA

General Independent, comprehensive, coed, primarily women, affiliated with Presbyterian Church (U.S.A.) **Entrance** Moderately difficult **Setting** 54-acre small-town campus **Total enrollment** 1,564 **Student-faculty ratio** 11:1 **Application deadline** Rolling (freshmen), rolling (transfer) **Freshmen** 82% were admitted **Housing** Yes **Expenses** Tuition $15,990; Room & Board $7450 **Undergraduates** 96% women, 26% part-time, 32% 25 or older, 0.2% Native American, 4% Hispanic American, 18% African American, 2% Asian American/Pacific Islander **The most frequently chosen baccalaureate fields are** business/marketing, psychology, social sciences and history **Academic program** English as a second language, advanced placement, accelerated degree program, self-designed majors, honors program, adult/continuing education programs, internships **Contact**

VIRGINIA

Mary Baldwin College *(continued)*
Ms. Lisa Branson, Assistant Director for Freshmen Services, Mary Baldwin College, Frederick and New Streets, Staunton, VA 24401. Telephone: 540-887-7221 Ext. 7287 or toll-free 800-468-2262. Fax: 540-886-6634. E-mail: admit@mbc.edu. Web site: http://www.mbc.edu/.

MARYMOUNT UNIVERSITY
ARLINGTON, VIRGINIA

General Independent, comprehensive, coed, affiliated with Roman Catholic Church **Entrance** Moderately difficult **Setting** 21-acre suburban campus **Total enrollment** 3,475 **Student-faculty ratio** 13:1 **Application deadline** Rolling (freshmen), rolling (transfer) **Freshmen** 87% were admitted **Housing** Yes **Expenses** Tuition $14,970; Room & Board $6590 **Undergraduates** 71% women, 25% part-time, 29% 25 or older, 0.2% Native American, 8% Hispanic American, 15% African American, 8% Asian American/Pacific Islander **The most frequently chosen baccalaureate fields are** business/marketing, social sciences and history, visual/performing arts **Academic program** English as a second language, advanced placement, self-designed majors, summer session, internships **Contact** Mr. Mike Canfield, Associate Director of Undergraduate Admissions, Marymount University, 2807 North Glebe Road, Arlington, VA 22207-4299. Telephone: 703-284-1500 or toll-free 800-548-7638. Fax: 703-522-0349. E-mail: admissions@marymount.edu. Web site: http://www.marymount.edu/.

▶ For more information, see page 454.

MARY WASHINGTON COLLEGE
FREDERICKSBURG, VIRGINIA

General State-supported, comprehensive, coed **Entrance** Very difficult **Setting** 176-acre small-town campus **Total enrollment** 4,483 **Student-faculty ratio** 17:1 **Application deadline** 2/1 (freshmen), 3/1 (transfer) **Freshmen** 55% were admitted **Housing** Yes **Expenses** Tuition $3340; Room & Board $5692 **Undergraduates** 67% women, 19% part-time, 24% 25 or older, 0.3% Native American, 3% Hispanic American, 4% African American, 4% Asian American/Pacific Islander **The most frequently chosen baccalaureate fields are** business/marketing, liberal arts/general studies, social sciences and history **Academic program** Advanced placement, accelerated degree program, self-designed majors, summer session, adult/continuing education programs, internships **Contact** Dr. Jenifer Blair, Dean of Undergraduate Admissions, Mary Washington College, 1301 College Avenue, Fredericksburg, VA 22401-5358. Telephone: 540-654-2000 or toll-free 800-468-5614. E-mail: admit@mwc.edu. Web site: http://www.mwc.edu/.

NORFOLK STATE UNIVERSITY
NORFOLK, VIRGINIA

General State-supported, comprehensive, coed **Entrance** Moderately difficult **Setting** 130-acre urban campus **Total enrollment** 6,721 **Student-faculty ratio** 15:1 **Application deadline** Rolling (freshmen), rolling (transfer) **Freshmen** 80% were admitted **Housing** Yes **Expenses** Tuition $2916; Room & Board $5466 **Undergraduates** 63% women, 20% part-time, 23% 25 or older, 0.2% Native American, 1% Hispanic American, 92% African American, 1% Asian American/Pacific Islander **The most frequently chosen baccalaureate fields are** business/marketing, interdisciplinary studies, social sciences and history **Academic program** Advanced placement, accelerated degree program, self-designed majors, honors program, summer session, adult/continuing education programs, internships **Contact** Ms. Michelle Marable, Director of Admissions, Norfolk State University, 700 Park Avenue, Norfolk, VA 23504. Telephone: 757-823-8396. Fax: 757-823-2078. E-mail: admissions@nsu.edu. Web site: http://www.nsu.edu/.

OLD DOMINION UNIVERSITY
NORFOLK, VIRGINIA

General State-supported, university, coed **Entrance** Moderately difficult **Setting** 186-acre urban campus **Total enrollment** 19,627 **Student-faculty ratio** 16:1 **Application deadline** 2/15 (freshmen), 6/1 (transfer) **Freshmen** 70% were admitted **Housing** Yes **Expenses** Tuition $4022; Room & Board $5364 **Undergraduates** 57% women, 33% part-time, 32% 25 or older, 1% Native American, 3% Hispanic American, 23% African American, 7% Asian American/Pacific Islander **The most frequently chosen baccalaureate fields are** business/marketing, engineering/engineering technologies, health professions and related sciences **Academic program** English as a second language, advanced placement, accelerated degree program, self-designed majors, honors program, summer session, adult/continuing education programs, internships **Contact** Ms. Alice McAdory, (Acting) Director of Admissions, Old Dominion University, 108 Rollins Hall, Norfolk, VA 23529-0050. Telephone: 757-683-3637 or toll-free 800-348-7926. Fax: 757-683-3255. E-mail: admit@odu.edu. Web site: http://www.odu.edu/.

RADFORD UNIVERSITY
RADFORD, VIRGINIA

General State-supported, comprehensive, coed **Entrance** Moderately difficult **Setting** 177-acre small-town campus **Total enrollment** 9,142 **Student-faculty ratio** 20:1 **Application deadline** 5/1 (freshmen), rolling (transfer) **Freshmen** 75% were admitted **Housing** Yes **Expenses** Tuition $3069; Room & Board $5233 **Undergraduates** 60% women, 7% part-time, 8% 25 or older, 0.3% Native American, 2% Hispanic American, 6% African American, 2% Asian American/Pacific Islander **The most frequently chosen baccalaureate fields are** business/marketing, interdisciplinary studies, protective services/public administration **Academic program** English as a second language, advanced placement, accelerated degree program, self-designed majors, honors program, summer session, adult/continuing education programs, internships **Contact** Dr. David Kraus, Director of Admissions and Records, Radford University, PO

VIRGINIA

Box 6903, RU Station, Radford, VA 24142. Telephone: 540-831-5371 or toll-free 800-890-4265. Fax: 540-831-5038. E-mail: ruadmiss@runet.edu. Web site: http://www.radford.edu/.

RANDOLPH-MACON COLLEGE
ASHLAND, VIRGINIA

General Independent United Methodist, 4-year, coed **Entrance** Moderately difficult **Setting** 110-acre suburban campus **Total enrollment** 1,150 **Student-faculty ratio** 11:1 **Application deadline** 3/1 (freshmen), 3/1 (transfer) **Freshmen** 80% were admitted **Housing** Yes **Expenses** Tuition $19,095; Room & Board $5300 **Undergraduates** 49% women, 3% part-time, 1% 25 or older, 0.1% Native American, 1% Hispanic American, 5% African American, 1% Asian American/Pacific Islander **The most frequently chosen baccalaureate fields are** business/marketing, interdisciplinary studies, social sciences and history **Academic program** Advanced placement, accelerated degree program, honors program, summer session, internships **Contact** Mr. John C. Conkright, Dean of Admissions and Financial Aid, Randolph-Macon College, PO Box 5005, Ashland, VA 23005-5505. Telephone: 804-752-7305 or toll-free 800-888-1762. Fax: 804-752-4707. E-mail: admissions@rmc.edu. Web site: http://www.rmc.edu/.

RANDOLPH-MACON WOMAN'S COLLEGE
LYNCHBURG, VIRGINIA

General Independent Methodist, 4-year, women only **Entrance** Moderately difficult **Setting** 100-acre suburban campus **Total enrollment** 721 **Student-faculty ratio** 9:1 **Application deadline** 3/1 (freshmen), 6/1 (transfer) **Freshmen** 87% were admitted **Housing** Yes **Expenses** Tuition $18,470; Room & Board $7350 **Undergraduates** 5% part-time, 9% 25 or older, 1% Native American, 3% Hispanic American, 7% African American, 3% Asian American/Pacific Islander **The most frequently chosen baccalaureate fields are** biological/life sciences, English, social sciences and history **Academic program** Advanced placement, accelerated degree program, self-designed majors, honors program, adult/continuing education programs, internships **Contact** Pat LeDonne, Director of Admissions, Randolph-Macon Woman's College, 2500 Rivermont Avenue, Lynchburg, VA 24503-1526. Telephone: 434-947-8100 or toll-free 800-745-7692. Fax: 434-947-8986. E-mail: admissions@rmwc.edu. Web site: http://www.rmwc.edu/.

ROANOKE COLLEGE
SALEM, VIRGINIA

General Independent, 4-year, coed, affiliated with Evangelical Lutheran Church in America **Entrance** Moderately difficult **Setting** 68-acre suburban campus **Total enrollment** 1,790 **Student-faculty ratio** 14:1 **Application deadline** 3/1 (freshmen), 8/1 (transfer) **Freshmen** 74% were admitted **Housing** Yes **Expenses** Tuition $18,681; Room & Board $6008 **Undergraduates** 62% women, 7% part-time, 6% 25 or older, 0.3% Native American, 2% Hispanic American, 4% African American, 1% Asian American/Pacific Islander **The most frequently chosen baccalaureate fields are** business/marketing, English, social sciences and history **Academic program** English as a second language, advanced placement, accelerated degree program, honors program, summer session, adult/continuing education programs, internships **Contact** Mr. Michael C. Maxey, Vice President of Admissions, Roanoke College, 221 College Lane, Salem, VA 24153. Telephone: 540-375-2270 or toll-free 800-388-2276. Fax: 540-375-2267. E-mail: admissions@roanoke.edu. Web site: http://www.roanoke.edu/.

SAINT PAUL'S COLLEGE
LAWRENCEVILLE, VIRGINIA

General Independent Episcopal, 4-year, coed **Entrance** Minimally difficult **Setting** 75-acre small-town campus **Total enrollment** 531 **Student-faculty ratio** 17:1 **Freshmen** 88% were admitted **Housing** Yes **Expenses** Tuition $8380; Room & Board $4568 **Undergraduates** 1% 25 or older, 0% Native American, 0% Hispanic American, 97% African American, 0% Asian American/Pacific Islander **Academic program** Honors program, summer session, adult/continuing education programs, internships **Contact** Mr. Michael C. Taylor, Director of Admissions, Saint Paul's College, 115 College Drive, Lawrenceville, VA 23868. Telephone: 804-848-4268 or toll-free 800-678-7071. Fax: 804-848-0229. E-mail: mtaylor@saintpauls.edu. Web site: http://www.saintpauls.edu.

SHENANDOAH UNIVERSITY
WINCHESTER, VIRGINIA

General Independent United Methodist, comprehensive, coed **Entrance** Moderately difficult **Setting** 100-acre small-town campus **Total enrollment** 2,451 **Student-faculty ratio** 10:1 **Application deadline** Rolling (freshmen), rolling (transfer) **Freshmen** 100% were admitted **Housing** Yes **Expenses** Tuition $17,000; Room & Board $6400 **Undergraduates** 57% women, 9% part-time, 14% 25 or older, 0.3% Native American, 2% Hispanic American, 9% African American, 1% Asian American/Pacific Islander **The most frequently chosen baccalaureate fields are** education, health professions and related sciences, visual/performing arts **Academic program** English as a second language, advanced placement, accelerated degree program, summer session, adult/continuing education programs, internships **Contact** Mr. Michael Carpenter, Director of Admissions, Shenandoah University, 1460 University Drive, Winchester, VA 22601-5195. Telephone: 540-665-4581 or toll-free 800-432-2266. Fax: 540-665-4627. E-mail: admit@su.edu. Web site: http://www.su.edu/.

▶ **For more information, see page 475.**

SOUTHERN VIRGINIA UNIVERSITY
BUENA VISTA, VIRGINIA

General Independent, 4-year, coed **Total enrollment** 481 **Student-faculty ratio** 14:1 **Application**

VIRGINIA

Southern Virginia University *(continued)*
deadline 8/15 (freshmen) **Freshmen** 52% were admitted **Housing** Yes **Expenses** Tuition $15,460; Room & Board $4400 **Undergraduates** 67% women, 4% 25 or older, 1% Native American, 2% Hispanic American, 1% African American, 1% Asian American/Pacific Islander **Academic program** Summer session **Contact** Tony Caputo, Dean of Admissions, Southern Virginia University, One University Hill Drive, Buena Vista, VA 24416. Telephone: 540-261-2756 or toll-free 800-229-8420. E-mail: admissions@southernvirginia.edu. Web site: http://www.southernvirginia.edu/.

SWEET BRIAR COLLEGE
SWEET BRIAR, VIRGINIA

General Independent, 4-year, women only **Entrance** Moderately difficult **Setting** 3,300-acre rural campus **Total enrollment** 738 **Student-faculty ratio** 7:1 **Application deadline** 2/1 (freshmen), 7/1 (transfer) **Freshmen** 81% were admitted **Housing** Yes **Expenses** Tuition $18,010; Room & Board $7300 **Undergraduates** 8% part-time, 4% 25 or older, 1% Native American, 3% Hispanic American, 4% African American, 2% Asian American/Pacific Islander **The most frequently chosen baccalaureate fields are** mathematics, psychology, social sciences and history **Academic program** Advanced placement, accelerated degree program, self-designed majors, honors program, summer session, adult/continuing education programs, internships **Contact** Ms. Margaret Williams Blount, Director of Admissions, Sweet Briar College, PO Box B, Sweet Briar, VA 24595. Telephone: 434-381-6142 or toll-free 800-381-6142. Fax: 434-381-6152. E-mail: admissions@sbc.edu. Web site: http://www.sbc.edu/.

UNIVERSITY OF RICHMOND
RICHMOND, VIRGINIA

General Independent, comprehensive, coed **Entrance** Very difficult **Setting** 350-acre suburban campus **Total enrollment** 3,727 **Student-faculty ratio** 10:1 **Application deadline** 1/15 (freshmen), 2/1 (transfer) **Freshmen** 44% were admitted **Housing** Yes **Expenses** Tuition $22,570; Room & Board $4730 **Undergraduates** 52% women, 1% part-time, 0% 25 or older, 0.1% Native American, 2% Hispanic American, 5% African American, 3% Asian American/Pacific Islander **The most frequently chosen baccalaureate fields are** business/marketing, biological/life sciences, social sciences and history **Academic program** English as a second language, advanced placement, accelerated degree program, self-designed majors, honors program, summer session, adult/continuing education programs, internships **Contact** Ms. Pamela Spence, Dean of Admission, University of Richmond, 28 Westhampton Way, University of Richmond, VA 23173. Telephone: 804-289-8640 or toll-free 800-700-1662. Fax: 804-287-6003. E-mail: admissions@urich.edu. Web site: http://www.richmond.edu/.

UNIVERSITY OF VIRGINIA
CHARLOTTESVILLE, VIRGINIA

General State-supported, university, coed **Entrance** Most difficult **Setting** 1,133-acre suburban campus **Total enrollment** 22,739 **Student-faculty ratio** 16:1 **Application deadline** 1/2 (freshmen), 3/1 (transfer) **Freshmen** 38% were admitted **Housing** Yes **Expenses** Tuition $4421; Room & Board $4970 **Undergraduates** 54% women, 7% part-time, 2% 25 or older, 0.4% Native American, 3% Hispanic American, 9% African American, 11% Asian American/Pacific Islander **The most frequently chosen baccalaureate fields are** engineering/engineering technologies, business/marketing, social sciences and history **Academic program** Advanced placement, accelerated degree program, self-designed majors, honors program, summer session, adult/continuing education programs, internships **Contact** Mr. John A. Blackburn, Dean of Admission, University of Virginia, PO Box 400160, Charlottesville, VA 22904-4160. Telephone: 434-982-3200. Fax: 434-924-3587. E-mail: undergradadmission@virginia.edu. Web site: http://www.virginia.edu/.

THE UNIVERSITY OF VIRGINIA'S COLLEGE AT WISE
WISE, VIRGINIA

General State-supported, 4-year, coed **Entrance** Moderately difficult **Setting** 350-acre small-town campus **Total enrollment** 1,480 **Student-faculty ratio** 17:1 **Application deadline** 8/1 (freshmen), 8/15 (transfer) **Freshmen** 77% were admitted **Housing** Yes **Expenses** Tuition $3470; Room & Board $5226 **Undergraduates** 54% women, 18% part-time, 17% 25 or older, 0.3% Native American, 1% Hispanic American, 5% African American, 1% Asian American/Pacific Islander **The most frequently chosen baccalaureate fields are** business/marketing, psychology, social sciences and history **Academic program** Advanced placement, accelerated degree program, self-designed majors, honors program, summer session, adult/continuing education programs, internships **Contact** Mr. Russell Necessary, Director of Admissions and Financial Aid, The University of Virginia's College at Wise, 1 College Avenue, Wise, VA 24293. Telephone: 276-328-0322 or toll-free 888-282-9324. Fax: 540-328-0251. E-mail: admissions@uvawise.edu. Web site: http://www.uvawise.edu/.

VIRGINIA COMMONWEALTH UNIVERSITY
RICHMOND, VIRGINIA

General State-supported, university, coed **Entrance** Moderately difficult **Setting** 126-acre urban campus **Total enrollment** 25,001 **Student-faculty ratio** 13:1 **Application deadline** 2/1 (freshmen), 8/1 (transfer) **Freshmen** 74% were admitted **Housing** Yes **Expenses** Tuition $3675; Room & Board $5355 **Undergraduates** 59% women, 30% part-time, 19% 25 or older, 1% Native American, 3% Hispanic American, 22% African American, 8% Asian American/Pacific Islander **The most frequently chosen baccalaureate fields are** business/marketing, health professions and related

VIRGINIA

sciences, visual/performing arts **Academic program** English as a second language, advanced placement, accelerated degree program, self-designed majors, honors program, summer session, adult/continuing education programs, internships **Contact** Counseling Staff, Virginia Commonwealth University, 821 West Franklin Street, Box 842526, Richmond, VA 23284-9005. Telephone: 804-828-1222 or toll-free 800-841-3638. Fax: 804-828-1899. E-mail: vcuinfo@vcu.edu. Web site: http://www.vcu.edu/.

VIRGINIA INTERMONT COLLEGE
BRISTOL, VIRGINIA

General Independent, 4-year, coed, affiliated with Baptist Church **Entrance** Minimally difficult **Setting** 27-acre small-town campus **Total enrollment** 918 **Student-faculty ratio** 11:1 **Application deadline** Rolling (freshmen), rolling (transfer) **Freshmen** 67% were admitted **Housing** Yes **Expenses** Tuition $12,210; Room & Board $5300 **Undergraduates** 75% women, 13% part-time, 45% 25 or older, 0.3% Native American, 0.3% Hispanic American, 5% African American, 0.3% Asian American/Pacific Islander **The most frequently chosen baccalaureate fields are** business/marketing, education, visual/performing arts **Academic program** Advanced placement, summer session, adult/continuing education programs, internships **Contact** Ms. Robin B. Cozart, Director of Admissions, Virginia Intermont College, 1013 Moore Street, Campus Box D-460, Bristol, VA 24201. Telephone: 540-466-7854 or toll-free 800-451-1842. Fax: 540-466-7855. E-mail: viadmit@vic.edu. Web site: http://www.vic.edu/.

VIRGINIA MILITARY INSTITUTE
LEXINGTON, VIRGINIA

General State-supported, 4-year, coed, primarily men **Entrance** Moderately difficult **Setting** 140-acre small-town campus **Total enrollment** 1,311 **Student-faculty ratio** 11:1 **Application deadline** 3/1 (freshmen), 3/1 (transfer) **Freshmen** 63% were admitted **Housing** Yes **Expenses** Tuition $5130; Room & Board $4838 **Undergraduates** 0.2% 25 or older, 0.5% Native American, 3% Hispanic American, 5% African American, 4% Asian American/Pacific Islander **Academic program** Advanced placement, accelerated degree program, honors program, summer session, internships **Contact** Lt. Col. Tom Mortenson, Associate Director of Admissions, Virginia Military Institute, 309 Letcher Avenue, Lexington, VA 24450. Telephone: 540-464-7211 or toll-free 800-767-4207. Fax: 540-464-7746. E-mail: admissions@vmi.edu. Web site: http://www.vmi.edu/.

VIRGINIA POLYTECHNIC INSTITUTE AND STATE UNIVERSITY
BLACKSBURG, VIRGINIA

General State-supported, university, coed **Entrance** Moderately difficult **Setting** 2,600-acre small-town campus **Total enrollment** 26,490 **Student-faculty ratio** 23:1 **Application deadline** 1/15 (freshmen), 3/1 (transfer) **Freshmen** 66% were admitted **Housing** Yes **Expenses** Tuition $3664; Room & Board $4032 **Undergraduates** 40% women, 3% part-time, 0.2% Native American, 2% Hispanic American, 5% African American, 7% Asian American/Pacific Islander **Academic program** English as a second language, advanced placement, accelerated degree program, honors program, summer session, adult/continuing education programs, internships **Contact** Ms. Mildred Johnson, Associate Director for Freshmen Admissions, Virginia Polytechnic Institute and State University, 201 Burruss Hall, Blacksburg, VA 24061. Telephone: 540-231-6267. Fax: 540-231-3242. E-mail: vtadmiss@vt.edu. Web site: 00.

VIRGINIA STATE UNIVERSITY
PETERSBURG, VIRGINIA

General State-supported, comprehensive, coed **Entrance** Minimally difficult **Setting** 236-acre suburban campus **Total enrollment** 4,638 **Student-faculty ratio** 17:1 **Application deadline** 5/1 (freshmen), 5/1 (transfer) **Freshmen** 87% were admitted **Housing** Yes **Expenses** Tuition $3312; Room & Board $5594 **Undergraduates** 56% women, 9% part-time, 7% 25 or older, 0.1% Native American, 1% Hispanic American, 96% African American, 0.2% Asian American/Pacific Islander **The most frequently chosen baccalaureate fields are** business/marketing, interdisciplinary studies, social sciences and history **Academic program** Advanced placement, self-designed majors, honors program, summer session, adult/continuing education programs, internships **Contact** Mrs. Irene Logan, Director of Admissions (Interim), Virginia State University, PO Box 9018, Petersburg, VA 23806-2096. Telephone: 804-524-5902 or toll-free 800-871-7611. E-mail: lwinn@vsu.edu. Web site: http://www.vsu.edu/.

VIRGINIA UNION UNIVERSITY
RICHMOND, VIRGINIA

General Independent Baptist, comprehensive, coed **Entrance** Moderately difficult **Setting** 72-acre urban campus **Total enrollment** 1,533 **Student-faculty ratio** 11:1 **Application deadline** Rolling (freshmen), rolling (transfer) **Freshmen** 48% were admitted **Housing** Yes **Expenses** Tuition $10,690; Room & Board $4664 **Undergraduates** 59% women, 4% part-time, 0% Native American, 0.1% Hispanic American, 99% African American, 0% Asian American/Pacific Islander **The most frequently chosen baccalaureate fields are** business/marketing, education, social sciences and history **Academic program** English as a second language, advanced placement, honors program, summer session, adult/continuing education programs, internships **Contact** Mr. Gil Powell, Director of Admissions, Virginia Union University, 1500 North Lombardy Street, Richmond, VA 23220-1170. Telephone: 804-257-5881 or toll-free 800-368-3227 (out-of-state). Web site: http://www.vuu.edu/.

VIRGINIA

VIRGINIA WESLEYAN COLLEGE
NORFOLK, VIRGINIA

General Independent United Methodist, 4-year, coed **Entrance** Moderately difficult **Setting** 300-acre urban campus **Total enrollment** 1,408 **Student-faculty ratio** 13:1 **Application deadline** Rolling (freshmen), rolling (transfer) **Freshmen** 80% were admitted **Housing** Yes **Expenses** Tuition $16,500; Room & Board $5850 **Undergraduates** 68% women, 25% part-time, 35% 25 or older, 1% Native American, 3% Hispanic American, 13% African American, 3% Asian American/Pacific Islander **The most frequently chosen baccalaureate fields are** business/marketing, interdisciplinary studies, social sciences and history **Academic program** Advanced placement, self-designed majors, honors program, summer session, adult/continuing education programs, internships **Contact** Mr. Richard T. Hinshaw, Vice President for Enrollment Management, Dean of Admissions, Virginia Wesleyan College, Office of Admissions, Virginia Wesleyan College, 1584 Wesleyan Drive, Norfolk, VA 23502-5599. Telephone: 757-455-3208 or toll-free 800-737-8684. Fax: 757-461-5238. E-mail: admissions@vwc.edu. Web site: http://www.vwc.edu/.

▶ For more information, see page 492.

WASHINGTON AND LEE UNIVERSITY
LEXINGTON, VIRGINIA

General Independent, comprehensive, coed **Entrance** Most difficult **Setting** 322-acre small-town campus **Total enrollment** 2,124 **Student-faculty ratio** 9:1 **Application deadline** 1/15 (freshmen), 4/1 (transfer) **Freshmen** 35% were admitted **Housing** Yes **Expenses** Tuition $19,345; Room & Board $5750 **Undergraduates** 46% women, 0.2% part-time, 0.2% 25 or older, 0.1% Native American, 1% Hispanic American, 3% African American, 2% Asian American/Pacific Islander **The most frequently chosen baccalaureate field is** philosophy, religion, and theology **Academic program** Advanced placement, accelerated degree program, self-designed majors, honors program, internships **Contact** Mr. William M. Hartog, Dean of Admissions and Financial Aid, Washington and Lee University, Lexington, VA 24450-0303. Telephone: 540-463-8710. Fax: 540-463-8062. E-mail: admissions@wlu.edu. Web site: http://www.wlu.edu/.

WORLD COLLEGE
VIRGINIA BEACH, VIRGINIA

General Proprietary, 4-year, coed **Entrance** Noncompetitive **Setting** suburban campus **Total enrollment** 376 **Application deadline** Rolling (freshmen) **Housing** No **Expenses** Tuition $2243 **Undergraduates** 92% 25 or older **The most frequently chosen baccalaureate field is** education **Academic program** Accelerated degree program, adult/continuing education programs **Contact** Michael Smith, Director of Operations and Registrar, World College, 5193 Shore Drive, Suite 105, Virginia Beach, VA 23455. Telephone: 757-464-4600 or toll-free 800-696-7532. Fax: 757-464-3687. E-mail: instruct@cie-wc.edu.

WASHINGTON

ANTIOCH UNIVERSITY SEATTLE
SEATTLE, WASHINGTON

General Independent, upper-level, coed **Entrance** Noncompetitive **Setting** urban campus **Total enrollment** 920 **Student-faculty ratio** 8:1 **Application deadline** 9/15 (transfer) **Housing** No **Expenses** Tuition $12,510 **Undergraduates** 75% women, 86% part-time, 80% 25 or older, 4% Native American, 2% Hispanic American, 21% African American, 9% Asian American/Pacific Islander **Academic program** Advanced placement, accelerated degree program, self-designed majors, summer session, adult/continuing education programs **Contact** Ms. Dianne Larsen, Admissions Director, Antioch University Seattle, 2326 Sixth Avenue, Seattle, WA 98121. Telephone: 206-441-5352 Ext. 5200. E-mail: dawn_rhodes@cloud.seattleantioch.edu. Web site: http://www.antiochsea.edu/.

BASTYR UNIVERSITY
KENMORE, WASHINGTON

General Independent, upper-level, coed **Setting** 50-acre suburban campus **Total enrollment** 968 **Student-faculty ratio** 15:1 **Application deadline** 3/15 (transfer) **First-Year Students** 66% were admitted **Housing** Yes **Expenses** Tuition $10,000; Room only $3500 **Undergraduates** 82% women, 18% part-time, 56% 25 or older, 0% Native American, 2% Hispanic American, 0% African American, 4% Asian American/Pacific Islander **Academic program** Summer session, internships **Contact** Mr. Richard Dent, Director of Student Enrollment, Bastyr University, 14500 Juanita Drive, NE, Kenmore, WA 98028-4966. Telephone: 425-602-3080. Fax: 425-823-6222. Web site: http://www.bastyr.edu/.

CENTRAL WASHINGTON UNIVERSITY
ELLENSBURG, WASHINGTON

General State-supported, comprehensive, coed **Entrance** Moderately difficult **Setting** 380-acre small-town campus **Total enrollment** 8,826 **Student-faculty ratio** 20:1 **Application deadline** Rolling (freshmen), rolling (transfer) **Freshmen** 89% were admitted **Housing** Yes **Expenses** Tuition $3348; Room & Board $5220 **Undergraduates** 53% women, 12% part-time, 20% 25 or older, 2% Native American, 5% Hispanic American, 2% African American, 4% Asian American/Pacific Islander **The most frequently chosen baccalaureate fields are** business/marketing, education, social sciences and history **Academic program** English as a second language, advanced placement, self-designed majors, honors program, summer session, adult/continuing education programs, internships **Contact** Mr. Mike Reilly, Director of Admissions, Central Washington University, 400 East 8th Avenue, Ellensburg, WA 98926-7463. Telephone: 509-963-1211 or toll-free 866-298-

WASHINGTON

4968. Fax: 509-963-3022. E-mail: cwuadmis@cwu.edu. Web site: http://www.cwu.edu/.

CITY UNIVERSITY
BELLEVUE, WASHINGTON

General Independent, comprehensive, coed **Entrance** Noncompetitive **Setting** suburban campus **Total enrollment** 7,124 **Application deadline** Rolling (freshmen), rolling (transfer) **Freshmen** 100% were admitted **Housing** No **Expenses** Tuition $7280 **Undergraduates** 45% women, 90% part-time, 90% 25 or older, 1% Native American, 3% Hispanic American, 6% African American, 9% Asian American/Pacific Islander **The most frequently chosen baccalaureate fields are** business/marketing, computer/information sciences, liberal arts/general studies **Academic program** English as a second language, advanced placement, accelerated degree program, honors program, summer session, adult/continuing education programs, internships **Contact** Mr. Kent Gibson, Interim Vice President, Admissions and Student Services, City University, 11900 NE First Street, Bellevue, WA 98005. Telephone: 800-426-5596 Ext. 4661 or toll-free 800-426-5596. Fax: 425-709-5361. E-mail: info@cityu.edu. Web site: http://www.cityu.edu/.

CORNISH COLLEGE OF THE ARTS
SEATTLE, WASHINGTON

General Independent, 4-year, coed **Entrance** Moderately difficult **Setting** 4-acre urban campus **Total enrollment** 650 **Student-faculty ratio** 9:1 **Application deadline** 8/15 (freshmen), 8/15 (transfer) **Freshmen** 76% were admitted **Housing** No **Expenses** Tuition $16,200 **Undergraduates** 62% women, 6% part-time, 17% 25 or older **Academic program** Advanced placement, summer session, internships **Contact** Ms. Sharron Starling, Associate Director of Admissions, Cornish College of the Arts, 710 East Roy Street, Seattle, WA 98102-4696. Telephone: 206-726-5017 or toll-free 800-726-ARTS. Fax: 206-720-1011. E-mail: admissions@cornish.edu. Web site: http://www.cornish.edu/.

DEVRY UNIVERSITY
FEDERAL WAY, WASHINGTON

General Proprietary, 4-year, coed **Total enrollment** 561 **Student-faculty ratio** 32:1 **Application deadline** Rolling (freshmen), rolling (transfer) **Freshmen** 89% were admitted **Housing** No **Expenses** Tuition $10,000 **Undergraduates** 19% women, 28% part-time, 31% 25 or older, 3% Native American, 9% Hispanic American, 12% African American, 14% Asian American/Pacific Islander **Contact** Ms. Latanya Kibby, Assistant New Student Coordinator, DeVry University, 3600 South 344th Way, Federal Way, WA 98001-2995. Telephone: 253-943-2800. Web site: http://www.sea.devry.edu/.

EASTERN WASHINGTON UNIVERSITY
CHENEY, WASHINGTON

General State-supported, comprehensive, coed **Entrance** Moderately difficult **Setting** 335-acre small-town campus **Total enrollment** 8,932 **Student-faculty ratio** 21:1 **Application deadline** Rolling (freshmen), rolling (transfer) **Freshmen** 84% were admitted **Housing** Yes **Expenses** Tuition $3186; Room & Board $4786 **Undergraduates** 57% women, 11% part-time, 28% 25 or older, 2% Native American, 4% Hispanic American, 2% African American, 3% Asian American/Pacific Islander **The most frequently chosen baccalaureate fields are** business/marketing, education, social sciences and history **Academic program** English as a second language, advanced placement, self-designed majors, honors program, summer session, internships **Contact** Ms. Michelle Whittingham, Director of Admissions, Eastern Washington University, 526 Fifth Street, SUT 101, Cheney, WA 99004-2447. Telephone: 509-359-6582 or toll-free 888-740-1914. Fax: 509-359-6692. E-mail: admissions@mail.ewu.edu. Web site: http://www.ewu.edu/.

THE EVERGREEN STATE COLLEGE
OLYMPIA, WASHINGTON

General State-supported, comprehensive, coed **Entrance** Moderately difficult **Setting** 1,000-acre small-town campus **Total enrollment** 4,227 **Student-faculty ratio** 22:1 **Application deadline** 3/1 (freshmen), 3/1 (transfer) **Freshmen** 82% were admitted **Housing** Yes **Expenses** Tuition $3191; Room & Board $5610 **Undergraduates** 58% women, 13% part-time, 34% 25 or older, 4% Native American, 4% Hispanic American, 4% African American, 4% Asian American/Pacific Islander **The most frequently chosen baccalaureate field is** interdisciplinary studies **Academic program** Advanced placement, self-designed majors, summer session, internships **Contact** Mr. Doug P. Scrima, Director of Admissions, The Evergreen State College, 2700 Evergreen Parkway NW, Olympia, WA 98505. Telephone: 360-867-6170. Fax: 360-867-6576. E-mail: admissions@evergreen.edu. Web site: http://www.evergreen.edu/.

GONZAGA UNIVERSITY
SPOKANE, WASHINGTON

General Independent Roman Catholic, comprehensive, coed **Entrance** Moderately difficult **Setting** 94-acre urban campus **Total enrollment** 5,128 **Student-faculty ratio** 11:1 **Application deadline** 2/1 (freshmen), 6/1 (transfer) **Freshmen** 82% were admitted **Housing** Yes **Expenses** Tuition $18,541; Room & Board $5680 **Undergraduates** 54% women, 5% part-time, 7% 25 or older, 1% Native American, 3% Hispanic American, 1% African American, 5% Asian American/Pacific Islander **The most frequently chosen baccalaureate fields are** business/marketing, communications/communication technologies, social sciences and history **Academic program** English as a second language, advanced placement, self-designed majors, honors program, summer session, adult/continuing education programs, internships **Contact** Ms. Julie McCulloh, Associate Dean of Admission, Gonzaga University, Ad Box 102, Spokane, WA 99258-0102. Telephone: 509-323-

WASHINGTON

Gonzaga University *(continued)*
6591 or toll-free 800-322-2584 Ext. 6572. Fax: 509-323-5780. E-mail: ballinger@gu.gonzaga.edu. Web site: http://www.gonzaga.edu/.

▶ For more information, see page 433.

HENRY COGSWELL COLLEGE
EVERETT, WASHINGTON

General Independent, 4-year, coed, primarily men **Entrance** Noncompetitive **Setting** 1-acre urban campus **Total enrollment** 258 **Student-faculty ratio** 7:1 **Application deadline** Rolling (freshmen), rolling (transfer) **Freshmen** 79% were admitted **Housing** No **Expenses** Tuition $11,880 **Undergraduates** 21% women, 36% part-time, 68% 25 or older, 1% Native American, 3% Hispanic American, 2% African American, 8% Asian American/Pacific Islander **The most frequently chosen baccalaureate fields are** engineering/engineering technologies, computer/information sciences, visual/performing arts **Academic program** Advanced placement, accelerated degree program, summer session, adult/continuing education programs, internships **Contact** Ms. Cristy Null, Director of Admissions, Henry Cogswell College, 3002 Colby Avenue, Everett, WA 98201. Telephone: 425-258-3351 Ext. 116 or toll-free 866-411-HCC1. Fax: 425-257-0405. E-mail: information@henrycogswell.edu. Web site: http://www.henrycogswell.edu/.

HERITAGE COLLEGE
TOPPENISH, WASHINGTON

General Independent, comprehensive, coed **Entrance** Noncompetitive **Setting** 10-acre rural campus **Total enrollment** 1,127 **Student-faculty ratio** 9:1 **Application deadline** Rolling (freshmen), rolling (transfer) **Freshmen** 9% were admitted **Housing** No **Expenses** Tuition $5430 **Undergraduates** 80% women, 62% part-time, 71% 25 or older, 17% Native American, 48% Hispanic American, 1% African American, 2% Asian American/Pacific Islander **The most frequently chosen baccalaureate fields are** education, law/legal studies, protective services/public administration **Academic program** English as a second language, advanced placement, self-designed majors, honors program, summer session, adult/continuing education programs, internships **Contact** Mr. Norberto T. Espindola, Director of Admissions and Recruitment, Heritage College, 3240 Fort Road, Toppenish, WA 98948-9599. Telephone: 509-865-8500 Ext. 2002 or toll-free 509-865-8508. Fax: 509-865-4469. E-mail: espindola_b@heritage.edu. Web site: http://www.heritage.edu/.

THE LEADERSHIP INSTITUTE OF SEATTLE
KENMORE, WASHINGTON

Contact Mr. Don Werner, Coordinator of Undergraduate Admissions, The Leadership Institute of Seattle, 1450 114th Avenue SE, Suite 230, Bellevue, WA 98004-6934. Telephone: 425-635-1187 Ext. 254 or toll-free 800-789-5467. E-mail: lios@lios.org. Web site: http://www.lios.org/.

NORTHWEST COLLEGE
KIRKLAND, WASHINGTON

General Independent, comprehensive, coed, affiliated with Assemblies of God **Entrance** Moderately difficult **Setting** 65-acre suburban campus **Total enrollment** 1,096 **Student-faculty ratio** 18:1 **Application deadline** 8/1 (freshmen), 8/1 (transfer) **Freshmen** 26% were admitted **Housing** Yes **Expenses** Tuition $11,825; Room & Board $5708 **Undergraduates** 56% women, 5% part-time, 27% 25 or older, 1% Native American, 3% Hispanic American, 3% African American, 6% Asian American/Pacific Islander **The most frequently chosen baccalaureate field is** philosophy, religion, and theology **Academic program** English as a second language, advanced placement, accelerated degree program, self-designed majors, summer session, adult/continuing education programs, internships **Contact** Mr. Myles Corrigan, Associate Vice President of Enrollment, Northwest College, PO Box 579, Kirkland, WA 98083-0579. Telephone: 425-889-5209 or toll-free 800-669-3781. Fax: 425-889-5224. E-mail: admissions@ncag.edu. Web site: http://www.nwcollege.edu/.

NORTHWEST COLLEGE OF ART
POULSBO, WASHINGTON

General Proprietary, 4-year, coed **Entrance** Moderately difficult **Setting** 26-acre small-town campus **Total enrollment** 83 **Application deadline** 6/1 (freshmen), 6/1 (transfer) **Housing** No **Expenses** Tuition $9300 **Academic program** Summer session, internships **Contact** Mr. Craig Freeman, President, Northwest College of Art, 16464 State Highway 305, Poulsbo, WA 98370. Telephone: 360-779-9993 or toll-free 800-769-ARTS. Fax: 360-779-9933. E-mail: kimatnca@silverlink.net. Web site: http://www.nca.edu/.

PACIFIC LUTHERAN UNIVERSITY
TACOMA, WASHINGTON

General Independent, comprehensive, coed, affiliated with Evangelical Lutheran Church in America **Entrance** Moderately difficult **Setting** 126-acre suburban campus **Total enrollment** 3,425 **Student-faculty ratio** 13:1 **Application deadline** Rolling (freshmen), rolling (transfer) **Freshmen** 80% were admitted **Housing** Yes **Expenses** Tuition $17,728; Room & Board $5590 **Undergraduates** 61% women, 8% part-time, 15% 25 or older, 1% Native American, 2% Hispanic American, 2% African American, 5% Asian American/Pacific Islander **The most frequently chosen baccalaureate fields are** business/marketing, education, social sciences and history **Academic program** English as a second language, advanced placement, accelerated degree program, self-designed majors, honors program, summer session, adult/continuing education programs, internships **Contact** Office of Admissions, Pacific Lutheran

WASHINGTON

University, Tacoma, WA 98447. Telephone: 253-535-7151 or toll-free 800-274-6758. Fax: 253-536-5136. E-mail: admissions@plu.edu. Web site: http://www.plu.edu/.

PUGET SOUND CHRISTIAN COLLEGE
MOUNTLAKE TERRACE, WASHINGTON

General Independent Christian, 4-year, coed **Entrance** Minimally difficult **Setting** 4-acre suburban campus **Total enrollment** 227 **Application deadline** 7/15 (freshmen), 7/15 (transfer) **Freshmen** 71% were admitted **Housing** Yes **Expenses** Tuition $3850; Room & Board $2350 **Undergraduates** 52% women, 16% part-time, 37% 25 or older **The most frequently chosen baccalaureate field is** philosophy **Academic program** Advanced placement, summer session, adult/continuing education programs, internships **Contact** Mr. Ben Maxson, Admissions Counselor, Puget Sound Christian College, 7011 226th Place, SW, Mountlake Terrace, WA 98043. Telephone: 425-775-8686 Ext. 506 or toll-free 888-775-8699. Fax: 425-775-8688 Ext. 506. E-mail: admissions@pscc.edu. Web site: http://www.pscc.edu/.

SAINT MARTIN'S COLLEGE
LACEY, WASHINGTON

General Independent Roman Catholic, comprehensive, coed **Entrance** Moderately difficult **Setting** 380-acre suburban campus **Total enrollment** 1,474 **Student-faculty ratio** 13:1 **Application deadline** 8/1 (freshmen), 8/1 (transfer) **Freshmen** 98% were admitted **Housing** Yes **Expenses** Tuition $15,740; Room & Board $4926 **Undergraduates** 53% women, 34% part-time, 61% 25 or older, 1% Native American, 5% Hispanic American, 7% African American, 6% Asian American/Pacific Islander **The most frequently chosen baccalaureate fields are** business/marketing, psychology, social sciences and history **Academic program** English as a second language, advanced placement, accelerated degree program, summer session, adult/continuing education programs, internships **Contact** Mr. Todd Abbott, Director of Admission, Saint Martin's College, 5300 Pacific Avenue, SE, Lacey, WA 98503. Telephone: 360-438-4590 or toll-free 800-368-8803. Fax: 37—412-6189. E-mail: admissions@stmartin.edu. Web site: http://www.stmartin.edu/.

SEATTLE PACIFIC UNIVERSITY
SEATTLE, WASHINGTON

General Independent Free Methodist, comprehensive, coed **Entrance** Moderately difficult **Setting** 35-acre urban campus **Total enrollment** 3,615 **Student-faculty ratio** 16:1 **Application deadline** 6/1 (freshmen), 8/1 (transfer) **Freshmen** 83% were admitted **Housing** Yes **Expenses** Tuition $16,425; Room & Board $6249 **Undergraduates** 66% women, 11% part-time, 10% 25 or older, 1% Native American, 2% Hispanic American, 2% African American, 5% Asian American/Pacific Islander **The most frequently chosen baccalaureate fields are** business/marketing, health professions and related sciences, social sciences and history **Academic program** English as a second language, advanced placement, self-designed majors, honors program, summer session, adult/continuing education programs, internships **Contact** Mrs. Jennifer Feddern Kenney, Director of Admissions, Seattle Pacific University, 3307 Third Avenue West, Seattle, WA 98119-1997. Telephone: 206-281-2517 or toll-free 800-366-3344. Fax: 206-281-2669. E-mail: admissions@spu.edu. Web site: http://www.spu.edu/.

SEATTLE UNIVERSITY
SEATTLE, WASHINGTON

General Independent Roman Catholic, comprehensive, coed **Entrance** Moderately difficult **Setting** 46-acre urban campus **Total enrollment** 5,981 **Student-faculty ratio** 12:1 **Application deadline** 7/1 (freshmen), 8/1 (transfer) **Freshmen** 80% were admitted **Housing** Yes **Expenses** Tuition $17,865; Room & Board $6318 **Undergraduates** 61% women, 9% part-time, 14% 25 or older, 1% Native American, 6% Hispanic American, 4% African American, 21% Asian American/Pacific Islander **The most frequently chosen baccalaureate fields are** business/marketing, engineering/engineering technologies, health professions and related sciences **Academic program** English as a second language, advanced placement, accelerated degree program, self-designed majors, honors program, summer session, adult/continuing education programs, internships **Contact** Mr. Michael K. McKeon, Dean of Admissions, Seattle University, 900 Broadway, Seattle, WA 98122-4340. Telephone: 206-296-2000 or toll-free 800-542-0833 (in-state); 800-426-7123 (out-of-state). Fax: 206-296-5656. E-mail: admissions@seattleu.edu. Web site: http://www.seattleu.edu/.

TRINITY LUTHERAN COLLEGE
ISSAQUAH, WASHINGTON

General Independent Lutheran, 4-year, coed **Entrance** Minimally difficult **Setting** 46-acre suburban campus **Total enrollment** 129 **Student-faculty ratio** 9:1 **Application deadline** 8/15 (freshmen), 8/15 (transfer) **Freshmen** 77% were admitted **Housing** Yes **Expenses** Tuition $8240; Room & Board $4600 **Undergraduates** 63% women, 16% part-time, 22% 25 or older, 2% Native American, 1% Hispanic American, 4% African American, 6% Asian American/Pacific Islander **The most frequently chosen baccalaureate field is** philosophy, religion, and theology **Academic program** English as a second language, advanced placement, adult/continuing education programs, internships **Contact** Ms. Sigrid Olsen Cutler, Trinity Lutheran College, 4221 228th Avenue, SE, Issaquah, WA 98029-9299. Telephone: 425-392-0400 or toll-free 800-843-5659. Fax: 425-392-0404. E-mail: admission@tlc.edu. Web site: http://www.tlc.edu/.

WASHINGTON

UNIVERSITY OF PHOENIX–WASHINGTON CAMPUS
SEATTLE, WASHINGTON

General Proprietary, comprehensive, coed **Entrance** Noncompetitive **Total enrollment** 88,730 **Student-faculty ratio** 13:1 **Application deadline** Rolling (freshmen), rolling (transfer) **Housing** No **Expenses** Tuition $8940 **Undergraduates** 57% women **The most frequently chosen baccalaureate field is** business/marketing **Academic program** Advanced placement, accelerated degree program, adult/continuing education programs **Contact** Ms. Beth Barilla, Director of Admissions, University of Phoenix–Washington Campus, 4615 East Elwood Street, Phoenix, AZ 85040-1958. Telephone: 480-927-0099 Ext. 1218 or toll-free 800-228-7240. Fax: 480-894-1758. E-mail: beth.barilla@apollogrp.edu. Web site: http://www.phoenix.edu/.

UNIVERSITY OF PUGET SOUND
TACOMA, WASHINGTON

General Independent, comprehensive, coed **Entrance** Very difficult **Setting** 97-acre suburban campus **Total enrollment** 2,848 **Student-faculty ratio** 11:1 **Application deadline** 2/1 (freshmen), 6/1 (transfer) **Freshmen** 67% were admitted **Housing** Yes **Expenses** Tuition $22,505; Room & Board $5780 **Undergraduates** 61% women, 3% part-time, 3% 25 or older, 1% Native American, 3% Hispanic American, 2% African American, 11% Asian American/Pacific Islander **The most frequently chosen baccalaureate fields are** business/marketing, English, social sciences and history **Academic program** Advanced placement, self-designed majors, honors program, summer session, internships **Contact** Dr. George H. Mills Jr., Vice President for Enrollment, University of Puget Sound, 1500 North Warner Street, Tacoma, WA 98416-0005. Telephone: 253-879-3211 or toll-free 800-396-7191. Fax: 253-879-3993. E-mail: admission@ups.edu. Web site: http://www.ups.edu/.

UNIVERSITY OF WASHINGTON
SEATTLE, WASHINGTON

General State-supported, university, coed **Entrance** Moderately difficult **Setting** 703-acre urban campus **Total enrollment** 37,412 **Student-faculty ratio** 11:1 **Application deadline** 1/15 (freshmen), 4/15 (transfer) **Freshmen** 79% were admitted **Housing** Yes **Expenses** Tuition $3983; Room & Board $6378 **Undergraduates** 51% women, 13% part-time, 16% 25 or older, 1% Native American, 4% Hispanic American, 3% African American, 23% Asian American/Pacific Islander **The most frequently chosen baccalaureate fields are** business/marketing, biological/life sciences, social sciences and history **Academic program** English as a second language, advanced placement, accelerated degree program, self-designed majors, honors program, summer session, adult/continuing education programs, internships **Contact** Ms. Stephanie Preston, Assistant Director of Admissions, University of Washington, Box 355840, Seattle, WA 98195-5840. Telephone: 206-543-9686. E-mail: askuwadm@u.washington.edu. Web site: http://www.washington.edu/.

WALLA WALLA COLLEGE
COLLEGE PLACE, WASHINGTON

General Independent Seventh-day Adventist, comprehensive, coed **Entrance** Moderately difficult **Setting** 77-acre small-town campus **Total enrollment** 1,823 **Student-faculty ratio** 12:1 **Application deadline** Rolling (freshmen), rolling (transfer) **Freshmen** 52% were admitted **Housing** Yes **Expenses** Tuition $15,372; Room & Board $3459 **Undergraduates** 50% women, 13% part-time, 11% 25 or older, 0.2% Native American, 5% Hispanic American, 2% African American, 5% Asian American/Pacific Islander **The most frequently chosen baccalaureate fields are** engineering/engineering technologies, business/marketing, health professions and related sciences **Academic program** English as a second language, advanced placement, honors program, summer session, internships **Contact** Mr. Dallas Weis, Director of Admissions, Walla Walla College, 204 South College Avenue, College Place, WA 99324. Telephone: 509-527-2327 or toll-free 800-541-8900. Fax: 509-527-2397. E-mail: weisda@wwc.edu. Web site: http://www.wwc.edu/.

WASHINGTON STATE UNIVERSITY
PULLMAN, WASHINGTON

General State-supported, university, coed **Entrance** Moderately difficult **Setting** 620-acre rural campus **Total enrollment** 21,078 **Student-faculty ratio** 17:1 **Freshmen** 81% were admitted **Housing** Yes **Expenses** Tuition $4236; Room & Board $5152 **Undergraduates** 52% women, 17% part-time, 20% 25 or older, 1% Native American, 3% Hispanic American, 3% African American, 5% Asian American/Pacific Islander **The most frequently chosen baccalaureate fields are** business/marketing, communications/communication technologies, social sciences and history **Academic program** English as a second language, advanced placement, honors program, summer session, adult/continuing education programs, internships **Contact** Ms. Wendy Peterson, Director of Admissions, Washington State University, Pullman, WA 99164. Telephone: 509-335-5586 or toll-free 888-468-6978. Fax: 509-335-7468. E-mail: ir@wsu.edu. Web site: http://www.wsu.edu/.

WESTERN WASHINGTON UNIVERSITY
BELLINGHAM, WASHINGTON

General State-supported, comprehensive, coed **Entrance** Moderately difficult **Setting** 223-acre small-town campus **Total enrollment** 11,708 **Student-faculty ratio** 21:1 **Application deadline** 3/1 (freshmen), 4/1 (transfer) **Freshmen** 78% were admitted **Housing** Yes **Expenses** Tuition $3288; Room & Board $5700 **Undergraduates** 56% women, 5% part-time, 3% 25 or older, 2% Native American, 3% Hispanic American, 2% African American, 7% Asian

American/Pacific Islander **The most frequently chosen baccalaureate fields are** business/marketing, education, social sciences and history **Academic program** English as a second language, advanced placement, accelerated degree program, self-designed majors, honors program, summer session, adult/continuing education programs, internships **Contact** Ms. Karen Copetas, Director of Admissions, Western Washington University, 516 High Street, Bellingham, WA 98225-9009. Telephone: 360-650-3440 Ext. 3440. Fax: 360-650-7369. E-mail: admit@cc.wwu.edu. Web site: http://www.wwu.edu/.

WHITMAN COLLEGE
WALLA WALLA, WASHINGTON

General Independent, 4-year, coed **Entrance** Very difficult **Setting** 55-acre small-town campus **Total enrollment** 1,439 **Student-faculty ratio** 10:1 **Application deadline** 2/1 (freshmen), 2/1 (transfer) **Freshmen** 54% were admitted **Housing** Yes **Expenses** Tuition $22,796; Room & Board $6290 **Undergraduates** 56% women, 3% part-time, 1% 25 or older, 1% Native American, 3% Hispanic American, 2% African American, 7% Asian American/Pacific Islander **The most frequently chosen baccalaureate fields are** social sciences and history, biological/life sciences, visual/performing arts **Academic program** Advanced placement, self-designed majors, honors program, internships **Contact** Mr. John Bogley, Dean of Admission and Financial Aid, Whitman College, 345 Boyer Avenue, Walla Walla, WA 99362-2083. Telephone: 509-527-5176 or toll-free 877-462-9448. Fax: 509-527-4967. E-mail: admission@whitman.edu. Web site: http://www.whitman.edu/.

WHITWORTH COLLEGE
SPOKANE, WASHINGTON

General Independent Presbyterian, comprehensive, coed **Entrance** Very difficult **Setting** 200-acre suburban campus **Total enrollment** 1,855 **Student-faculty ratio** 15:1 **Application deadline** 3/1 (freshmen), 7/1 (transfer) **Freshmen** 90% were admitted **Housing** Yes **Expenses** Tuition $18,038; Room & Board $5900 **Undergraduates** 15% 25 or older **The most frequently chosen baccalaureate field is** philosophy, religion, and theology **Academic program** English as a second language, advanced placement, self-designed majors, summer session, adult/continuing education programs, internships **Contact** Admissions Office, Whitworth College, 300 West Hawthorne Road, Spokane, WA 99251-0001. Telephone: 800-533-4668 or toll-free 800-533-4668 (out-of-state). Fax: 509-777-3758. E-mail: admission@whitworth.edu. Web site: http://www.whitworth.edu/.

WEST VIRGINIA

ALDERSON-BROADDUS COLLEGE
PHILIPPI, WEST VIRGINIA

General Independent, comprehensive, coed, affiliated with American Baptist Churches in the U.S.A. **Entrance** Moderately difficult **Setting** 170-acre rural campus **Total enrollment** 802 **Student-faculty ratio** 13:1 **Application deadline** Rolling (freshmen), rolling (transfer) **Freshmen** 64% were admitted **Housing** Yes **Expenses** Tuition $14,440; Room & Board $5200 **Undergraduates** 64% women, 9% part-time, 30% 25 or older, 1% Native American, 1% Hispanic American, 3% African American, 2% Asian American/Pacific Islander **The most frequently chosen baccalaureate fields are** biological/life sciences, health professions and related sciences, parks and recreation **Academic program** Advanced placement, self-designed majors, honors program, summer session, internships **Contact** Ms. Kimberly Klaus, Associate Director of Admissions, Alderson-Broaddus College, PO Box 2003, Philippi, WV 26416. Telephone: 304-457-1700 Ext. 6255 or toll-free 800-263-1549. Fax: 304-457-6239. E-mail: admissions@ab.edu. Web site: http://www.ab.edu/.

▶ **For more information, see page 391.**

APPALACHIAN BIBLE COLLEGE
BRADLEY, WEST VIRGINIA

General Independent nondenominational, 4-year, coed **Entrance** Minimally difficult **Setting** 110-acre small-town campus **Total enrollment** 243 **Student-faculty ratio** 17:1 **Application deadline** Rolling (freshmen), rolling (transfer) **Freshmen** 46% were admitted **Housing** Yes **Expenses** Tuition $6710; Room & Board $3450 **Undergraduates** 51% women, 19% part-time **The most frequently chosen baccalaureate field is** philosophy, religion, and theology **Academic program** Advanced placement, summer session, adult/continuing education programs, internships **Contact** Ms. Sara Stout, Admissions Counselor, Appalachian Bible College, PO Box ABC, Bradley, WV 25818. Telephone: 800-678-9ABC Ext. 3213 or toll-free 800-678-9ABC. Fax: 304-877-5082. E-mail: admissions@abc.edu. Web site: http://www.abc.edu/.

BETHANY COLLEGE
BETHANY, WEST VIRGINIA

General Independent, 4-year, coed, affiliated with Christian Church (Disciples of Christ) **Entrance** Moderately difficult **Setting** 1,600-acre rural campus **Total enrollment** 774 **Student-faculty ratio** 12:1 **Application deadline** 8/15 (freshmen), rolling (transfer) **Freshmen** 71% were admitted **Housing** Yes **Expenses** Tuition $21,004; Room & Board $6000 **Undergraduates** 45% women, 2% part-time, 2% 25 or older, 0.3% Native American, 1% Hispanic American, 4% African American, 1% Asian American/Pacific Islander **The most frequently chosen baccalaureate fields are** communications/communication technologies, education, psychology **Academic program** English as a second language, advanced placement, self-designed majors, internships **Contact** Brian Ralph, Vice President for Enrollment Management, Bethany College, Office of Admission, Bethany, WV 26032. Telephone: 304-829-7611 or toll-free 800-922-

WEST VIRGINIA

Bethany College *(continued)*
7611 (out-of-state). Fax: 304-829-7142. E-mail: admission@mail.bethanywv.edu. Web site: http://www.bethanywv.edu/.

BLUEFIELD STATE COLLEGE
BLUEFIELD, WEST VIRGINIA

General State-supported, 4-year, coed **Entrance** Noncompetitive **Setting** 45-acre small-town campus **Total enrollment** 2,768 **Student-faculty ratio** 17:1 **Application deadline** Rolling (freshmen), rolling (transfer) **Freshmen** 99% were admitted **Housing** No **Expenses** Tuition $2288 **Undergraduates** 62% women, 35% part-time, 41% 25 or older **The most frequently chosen baccalaureate fields are** business/marketing, engineering/engineering technologies, liberal arts/general studies **Academic program** Advanced placement, self-designed majors, summer session, adult/continuing education programs, internships **Contact** Mr. John C. Cardwell, Director of Enrollment Management, Bluefield State College, 219 Rock Street, Bluefield, WV 24701-2198. Telephone: 304-327-4567 or toll-free 800-344-8892 Ext. 4065 (in-state); 800-654-7798 Ext. 4065 (out-of-state). Fax: 304-325-7747. E-mail: bscadmit@bluefield.wvnet.edu. Web site: http://www.bluefield.wvnet.edu/.

CONCORD COLLEGE
ATHENS, WEST VIRGINIA

General State-supported, 4-year, coed **Entrance** Minimally difficult **Setting** 100-acre rural campus **Total enrollment** 3,055 **Student-faculty ratio** 24:1 **Application deadline** Rolling (freshmen), rolling (transfer) **Freshmen** 65% were admitted **Housing** Yes **Expenses** Tuition $2724; Room & Board $4358 **Undergraduates** 57% women, 19% part-time, 14% 25 or older, 0.2% Native American, 0.5% Hispanic American, 5% African American, 1% Asian American/Pacific Islander **The most frequently chosen baccalaureate fields are** business/marketing, education, liberal arts/general studies **Academic program** English as a second language, advanced placement, self-designed majors, honors program, summer session **Contact** Mr. Michael Curry, Vice President of Admissions and Financial Aid, Concord College, 1000 Vermillion Street, Athens, WV 24712. Telephone: 304-384-5248 or toll-free 888-384-5249 (out-of-state). Fax: 304-384-9044. E-mail: admissions@concord.edu. Web site: http://www.concord.edu/.

▶ For more information, see page 417.

DAVIS & ELKINS COLLEGE
ELKINS, WEST VIRGINIA

General Independent Presbyterian, 4-year, coed **Entrance** Minimally difficult **Setting** 170-acre small-town campus **Total enrollment** 668 **Student-faculty ratio** 12:1 **Application deadline** Rolling (freshmen), rolling (transfer) **Freshmen** 83% were admitted **Housing** Yes **Expenses** Tuition $13,864; Room & Board $5626 **Undergraduates** 61% women, 11% part-time, 0% Native American, 3% Hispanic American, 4% African American, 1% Asian American/Pacific Islander **Academic program** English as a second language, advanced placement, accelerated degree program, self-designed majors, honors program, summer session, adult/continuing education programs, internships **Contact** Mr. Matt Shiflett, Director of Admissions, Davis & Elkins College, 100 Campus Drive, Elkins, WV 26241. Telephone: 304-637-1332 or toll-free 800-624-3157. Fax: 304-637-1800. E-mail: admis@dne.edu. Web site: http://www.dne.edu/.

FAIRMONT STATE COLLEGE
FAIRMONT, WEST VIRGINIA

General State-supported, comprehensive, coed **Entrance** Minimally difficult **Setting** 80-acre small-town campus **Total enrollment** 6,724 **Student-faculty ratio** 18:1 **Application deadline** 6/15 (freshmen), 6/15 (transfer) **Freshmen** 97% were admitted **Housing** Yes **Expenses** Tuition $2408 **Undergraduates** 55% women, 32% part-time, 26% 25 or older, 0.3% Native American, 1% Hispanic American, 4% African American, 0.4% Asian American/Pacific Islander **Academic program** English as a second language, advanced placement, accelerated degree program, honors program, summer session, adult/continuing education programs, internships **Contact** Mr. Douglas Dobbins, Executive Director of Enrollment Services, Fairmont State College, 1201 Locust Avenue, Fairmont, WV 26554. Telephone: 304-367-4000 or toll-free 800-641-5678. Fax: 304-367-4789. E-mail: admit@mail.fscwv.edu. Web site: http://www.fscwv.edu/.

▶ For more information, see page 426.

GLENVILLE STATE COLLEGE
GLENVILLE, WEST VIRGINIA

General State-supported, 4-year, coed **Entrance** Noncompetitive **Setting** 331-acre rural campus **Total enrollment** 2,144 **Application deadline** 8/1 (freshmen), 6/1 (transfer) **Freshmen** 100% were admitted **Housing** Yes **Expenses** Tuition $2488; Room & Board $4100 **Undergraduates** 59% women, 23% part-time, 0.3% Native American, 0.3% Hispanic American, 3% African American, 1% Asian American/Pacific Islander **The most frequently chosen baccalaureate fields are** business/marketing, education, social sciences and history **Academic program** English as a second language, advanced placement, accelerated degree program, self-designed majors, honors program, summer session, adult/continuing education programs, internships **Contact** Ms. Brenda McCartney, Associate Registrar, Glenville State College, 200 High Street, Glenville, WV 26351-1200. Telephone: 304-462-4117 Ext. 347 or toll-free 800-924-2010 (in-state). Fax: 304-462-8619. E-mail: visitor@glenville.edu. Web site: http://www.glenville.edu/.

MARSHALL UNIVERSITY
HUNTINGTON, WEST VIRGINIA

General State-supported, university, coed **Entrance** Minimally difficult **Setting** 70-acre urban campus

WEST VIRGINIA

Total enrollment 13,827 **Student-faculty ratio** 20:1 **Application deadline** Rolling (freshmen), rolling (transfer) **Freshmen** 91% were admitted **Housing** Yes **Expenses** Tuition $3212; Room & Board $5028 **Undergraduates** 55% women, 16% part-time, 17% 25 or older, 1% Native American, 0.5% Hispanic American, 4% African American, 1% Asian American/Pacific Islander **The most frequently chosen baccalaureate fields are** business/marketing, education, liberal arts/general studies **Academic program** English as a second language, advanced placement, accelerated degree program, honors program, summer session, adult/continuing education programs, internships **Contact** Dr. Barbara J. Tarter, Interim Admissions Director, Marshall University, 1 John Marshall Drive, Huntington, WV 25755. Telephone: 304-696-3160 or toll-free 800-642-3499 (in-state). Fax: 304-696-3135. E-mail: admissions@marshall.edu. Web site: http://www.marshall.edu/.

MOUNTAIN STATE UNIVERSITY
BECKLEY, WEST VIRGINIA

General Independent, comprehensive, coed **Entrance** Noncompetitive **Setting** 7-acre small-town campus **Total enrollment** 2,525 **Student-faculty ratio** 19:1 **Application deadline** Rolling (freshmen), rolling (transfer) **Freshmen** 100% were admitted **Housing** Yes **Expenses** Tuition $4560; Room & Board $3982 **Undergraduates** 65% women, 29% part-time, 51% 25 or older, 1% Native American, 1% Hispanic American, 8% African American, 1% Asian American/Pacific Islander **The most frequently chosen baccalaureate fields are** business/marketing, education, interdisciplinary studies **Academic program** English as a second language, advanced placement, accelerated degree program, self-designed majors, summer session, adult/continuing education programs, internships **Contact** Marketing Department, Mountain State University, P.O. Box 9003, Beckley, WV 25802-9003. Telephone: 304-253-7351 Ext. 1433 or toll-free 800-766-6067. Fax: 304-253-5072. E-mail: gocwv@cwv.edu. Web site: http://www.mountainstate.edu/.

OHIO VALLEY COLLEGE
VIENNA, WEST VIRGINIA

General Independent, 4-year, coed, affiliated with Church of Christ **Entrance** Minimally difficult **Setting** 299-acre small-town campus **Total enrollment** 453 **Student-faculty ratio** 16:1 **Application deadline** Rolling (freshmen), rolling (transfer) **Freshmen** 48% were admitted **Housing** Yes **Expenses** Tuition $9440; Room & Board $4210 **Undergraduates** 53% women, 2% part-time, 21% 25 or older, 0.4% Native American, 1% Hispanic American, 5% African American, 0.2% Asian American/Pacific Islander **The most frequently chosen baccalaureate fields are** business/marketing, education, philosophy **Academic program** English as a second language, advanced placement, honors program, summer session, adult/continuing education programs, internships **Contact** Mr. Denver Lucky, Director of Admissions, Vice President for Enrollment, Ohio Valley College, #1

Campus View Drive, Vienna, WV 26105. Telephone: 304-865-6202 or toll-free 877-446-8668 Ext. 6200 (out-of-state). Fax: 304-865-6001. E-mail: admissions@ovc.edu. Web site: http://www.ovc.edu/.

SALEM INTERNATIONAL UNIVERSITY
SALEM, WEST VIRGINIA

General Independent, comprehensive, coed **Entrance** Minimally difficult **Setting** 300-acre rural campus **Total enrollment** 538 **Student-faculty ratio** 13:1 **Application deadline** Rolling (freshmen), rolling (transfer) **Freshmen** 22% were admitted **Housing** Yes **Expenses** Tuition $13,640; Room & Board $4432 **Undergraduates** 43% women, 2% part-time, 11% 25 or older, 0.4% Native American, 3% Hispanic American, 9% African American, 1% Asian American/Pacific Islander **The most frequently chosen baccalaureate fields are** biological/life sciences, business/marketing, education **Academic program** English as a second language, advanced placement, accelerated degree program, internships **Contact** Director of Admissions, Salem International University, PO Box 500, Salem, WV 26426-0500. Telephone: 304-782-5336 Ext. 336 or toll-free 800-283-4562. E-mail: admis_new@salem.wvnet.edu. Web site: http://www.salemiu.edu/.

SHEPHERD COLLEGE
SHEPHERDSTOWN, WEST VIRGINIA

General State-supported, 4-year, coed **Entrance** Moderately difficult **Setting** 320-acre small-town campus **Total enrollment** 4,391 **Student-faculty ratio** 17:1 **Application deadline** 2/1 (freshmen), 3/15 (transfer) **Freshmen** 94% were admitted **Housing** Yes **Expenses** Tuition $2608; Room & Board $4454 **Undergraduates** 60% women, 33% part-time, 24% 25 or older, 1% Native American, 2% Hispanic American, 5% African American, 1% Asian American/Pacific Islander **The most frequently chosen baccalaureate fields are** education, business/marketing, liberal arts/general studies **Academic program** English as a second language, advanced placement, accelerated degree program, honors program, summer session, adult/continuing education programs, internships **Contact** Mr. Karl L. Wolf, Director of Admissions, Shepherd College, PO Box 3210, Shepherdstown, WV 25443-3210. Telephone: 304-876-5212 or toll-free 800-344-5231. Fax: 304-876-5165. E-mail: admoff@shepherd.edu. Web site: http://www.shepherd.edu/.

UNIVERSITY OF CHARLESTON
CHARLESTON, WEST VIRGINIA

General Independent, comprehensive, coed **Entrance** Moderately difficult **Setting** 40-acre urban campus **Total enrollment** 1,150 **Student-faculty ratio** 15:1 **Application deadline** Rolling (freshmen), rolling (transfer) **Freshmen** 71% were admitted **Housing** Yes **Expenses** Tuition $14,900; Room & Board $5740 **Undergraduates** 69% women, 21% part-time, 29% 25 or older, 0.5% Native American, 1% Hispanic

WEST VIRGINIA

University of Charleston *(continued)*
American, 5% African American, 1% Asian American/Pacific Islander **The most frequently chosen baccalaureate fields are** business/marketing, health professions and related sciences, parks and recreation **Academic program** English as a second language, advanced placement, accelerated degree program, self-designed majors, summer session, adult/continuing education programs, internships **Contact** Ms. Kim Scranage, Associate Director of Admissions, University of Charleston, 2300 MacCorkle Avenue, SE, Charleston, WV 25304. Telephone: 304-357-4750 or toll-free 800-995-GOUC. Fax: 304-357-4781. E-mail: admissions@uchaswv.edu. Web site: http://www.uchaswv.edu/.

WEST LIBERTY STATE COLLEGE
WEST LIBERTY, WEST VIRGINIA

General State-supported, 4-year, coed **Entrance** Minimally difficult **Setting** 290-acre rural campus **Total enrollment** 2,633 **Student-faculty ratio** 19:1 **Freshmen** 97% were admitted **Housing** Yes **Expenses** Tuition $2516; Room & Board $3540 **Undergraduates** 55% women, 10% part-time, 17% 25 or older, 0.1% Native American, 1% Hispanic American, 3% African American, 0.3% Asian American/Pacific Islander **The most frequently chosen baccalaureate fields are** business/marketing, education, protective services/public administration **Academic program** Advanced placement, accelerated degree program, self-designed majors, honors program, summer session, adult/continuing education programs, internships **Contact** Ms. Stephanie North, Admissions Counselor, West Liberty State College, PO Box 295, West Liberty, WV 26074. Telephone: 304-336-8078 or toll-free 800-732-6204 Ext. 8076. Fax: 304-336-8403. E-mail: wladmsn1@wlsvax.wvnet.edu. Web site: http://www.wlsc.wvnet.edu/.

WEST VIRGINIA STATE COLLEGE
INSTITUTE, WEST VIRGINIA

General State-supported, 4-year, coed **Entrance** Minimally difficult **Setting** 90-acre suburban campus **Total enrollment** 4,836 **Student-faculty ratio** 23:1 **Application deadline** 8/11 (freshmen), 8/11 (transfer) **Freshmen** 100% were admitted **Housing** Yes **Expenses** Tuition $2562; Room & Board $4300 **Undergraduates** 59% women, 36% part-time, 29% 25 or older, 0.5% Native American, 0.5% Hispanic American, 15% African American, 1% Asian American/Pacific Islander **Academic program** Advanced placement, accelerated degree program, summer session, adult/continuing education programs, internships **Contact** Ms. Alice Ruhnke, Director of Admissions, West Virginia State College, Campus Box 197, PO Box 1000, Ferrell Hall, Room 106, Institute, WV 25112-1000. Telephone: 304-766-3221 or toll-free 800-987-2112. Fax: 304-766-4158. E-mail: greenrl@ernie.wvsc.wvnet.edu. Web site: http://www.wvsc.edu/.

WEST VIRGINIA UNIVERSITY
MORGANTOWN, WEST VIRGINIA

General State-supported, university, coed **Entrance** Moderately difficult **Setting** 541-acre small-town campus **Total enrollment** 22,774 **Student-faculty ratio** 19:1 **Application deadline** 8/1 (freshmen), 8/1 (transfer) **Freshmen** 94% were admitted **Housing** Yes **Expenses** Tuition $2948; Room & Board $5326 **Undergraduates** 46% women, 6% part-time, 7% 25 or older, 0.4% Native American, 1% Hispanic American, 4% African American, 2% Asian American/Pacific Islander **The most frequently chosen baccalaureate fields are** business/marketing, engineering/engineering technologies, liberal arts/general studies **Academic program** English as a second language, advanced placement, accelerated degree program, self-designed majors, honors program, summer session, adult/continuing education programs, internships **Contact** Mr. Cheng H. Khoo, Director of Admissions and Records, West Virginia University, Box 6009, Morgantown, WV 26506-6009. Telephone: 304-293-2121 Ext. 1511 or toll-free 800-344-9881. Fax: 304-293-3080. E-mail: wvuadmissions@arc.wvu.edu. Web site: http://www.wvu.edu/.

WEST VIRGINIA UNIVERSITY INSTITUTE OF TECHNOLOGY
MONTGOMERY, WEST VIRGINIA

General State-supported, comprehensive, coed **Entrance** Noncompetitive **Setting** 200-acre small-town campus **Total enrollment** 2,374 **Student-faculty ratio** 16:1 **Application deadline** Rolling (freshmen), rolling (transfer) **Freshmen** 100% were admitted **Housing** Yes **Expenses** Tuition $2836; Room & Board $4682 **Undergraduates** 38% women, 30% part-time, 15% 25 or older, 0.4% Native American, 1% Hispanic American, 7% African American, 1% Asian American/Pacific Islander **The most frequently chosen baccalaureate fields are** business/marketing, engineering/engineering technologies, liberal arts/general studies **Academic program** English as a second language, advanced placement, accelerated degree program, self-designed majors, summer session, adult/continuing education programs, internships **Contact** Ms. Donna Varney, Director of Admissions I, West Virginia University Institute of Technology, Box 10, Old Main, Montgomery, WV 25136. Telephone: 304-442-3071 or toll-free 888-554-8324. Fax: 304-442-3097. E-mail: wvutech@wvit.wvnet.edu. Web site: http://www.wvutech.edu.

WEST VIRGINIA WESLEYAN COLLEGE
BUCKHANNON, WEST VIRGINIA

General Independent, comprehensive, coed, affiliated with United Methodist Church **Entrance** Moderately difficult **Setting** 80-acre small-town campus **Total enrollment** 1,592 **Student-faculty ratio** 14:1 **Application deadline** 8/1 (freshmen), rolling (transfer) **Freshmen** 86% were admitted **Housing** Yes **Expenses** Tuition $18,700; Room & Board $4220 **Undergraduates** 54% women, 5% part-time, 5% 25 or older, 0.2% Native American, 1% Hispanic American, 5% African American, 1% Asian American/Pacific Islander **The most frequently chosen baccalaureate fields are** communications/communication technologies, engineering/engineering technologies, social sciences and history **Academic program** English as a second language, advanced placement, accelerated degree program, self-designed majors, honors program, summer session, adult/continuing education programs, internships **Contact** Mr. Robert N. Skinner II, Director of Admission, West Virginia Wesleyan College, 59 College Avenue, Buckhannon, WV 26201. Telephone: 304-473-8510 or toll-free 800-722-9933 (out-of-state). Fax: 304-472-2571. E-mail: admissions@academ.wvwc.edu. Web site: http://www.wvwc.edu/.

WHEELING JESUIT UNIVERSITY
WHEELING, WEST VIRGINIA

General Independent Roman Catholic (Jesuit), comprehensive, coed **Entrance** Moderately difficult **Setting** 70-acre suburban campus **Total enrollment** 1,466 **Student-faculty ratio** 11:1 **Application deadline** Rolling (freshmen), rolling (transfer) **Freshmen** 88% were admitted **Housing** Yes **Expenses** Tuition $17,240; Room & Board $5420 **Undergraduates** 60% women, 17% part-time, 22% 25 or older, 0.1% Native American, 1% Hispanic American, 2% African American, 1% Asian American/Pacific Islander **The most frequently chosen baccalaureate fields are** biological/life sciences, health professions and related sciences, liberal arts/general studies **Academic program** English as a second language, advanced placement, self-designed majors, honors program, summer session, adult/continuing education programs, internships **Contact** Mr. Thomas M. Pie, Director of Admissions, Wheeling Jesuit University, 316 Washington Avenue, Wheeling, WV 26003-6295. Telephone: 304-243-2359 or toll-free 800-624-6992. Fax: 304-243-2397. E-mail: admiss@wju.edu. Web site: http://www.wju.edu/.

WISCONSIN

ALVERNO COLLEGE
MILWAUKEE, WISCONSIN

General Independent Roman Catholic, comprehensive, women only **Entrance** Moderately difficult **Setting** 46-acre suburban campus **Total enrollment** 1,952 **Student-faculty ratio** 14:1 **Application deadline** 8/1 (freshmen), 8/1 (transfer) **Freshmen** 90% were admitted **Housing** Yes **Expenses** Tuition $12,150; Room & Board $4780 **Undergraduates** 44% part-time, 34% 25 or older **The most frequently chosen baccalaureate fields are** business/marketing, communications/communication technologies, health professions and related sciences **Academic program** Advanced placement, summer session, adult/continuing education programs, internships **Contact** Ms. Mary Kay Farrell, Director of Admissions, Alverno College, 3400 South 43 Street, PO Box 343922, Milwaukee, WI 53234-3922. Telephone: 414-382-6113 or toll-free 800-933-3401. Fax: 414-382-6354. E-mail: admissions@alverno.edu. Web site: http://www.alverno.edu/.

BELLIN COLLEGE OF NURSING
GREEN BAY, WISCONSIN

General Independent, 4-year, coed, primarily women **Entrance** Moderately difficult **Setting** urban campus **Total enrollment** 160 **Student-faculty ratio** 10:1 **Application deadline** Rolling (freshmen), rolling (transfer) **Freshmen** 60% were admitted **Housing** No **Expenses** Tuition $10,454 **Undergraduates** 93% women, 15% part-time, 29% 25 or older, 1% Native American, 1% Hispanic American, 1% African American, 3% Asian American/Pacific Islander **The most frequently chosen baccalaureate field is** health professions and related sciences **Academic program** Advanced placement, accelerated degree program, summer session **Contact** Dr. Penny Croghan, Admissions Director, Bellin College of Nursing, 725 South Webster Avenue, Green Bay, WI 54301. Telephone: 920-433-5803 or toll-free 800-236-8707 (in-state). Fax: 920-433-7416. E-mail: admissio@bcon.edu. Web site: http://www.bcon.edu.

BELOIT COLLEGE
BELOIT, WISCONSIN

General Independent, 4-year, coed **Entrance** Very difficult **Setting** 65-acre small-town campus **Total enrollment** 1,273 **Student-faculty ratio** 11:1 **Application deadline** 2/1 (freshmen), rolling (transfer) **Freshmen** 66% were admitted **Housing** Yes **Expenses** Tuition $22,404; Room & Board $5078 **Undergraduates** 59% women, 4% part-time, 4% 25 or older, 0.5% Native American, 4% Hispanic American, 4% African American, 4% Asian American/Pacific Islander **The most frequently chosen baccalaureate fields are** social sciences and history, biological/life sciences, visual/performing arts **Academic program** English as a second language, advanced placement, self-designed majors, summer session, adult/continuing education programs, internships **Contact** Mr. James S. Zielinski, Director of Admissions, Beloit College, 700 College Street, Beloit, WI 53511-5596. Telephone: 608-363-2500 or toll-free 800-356-0751. Fax: 608-363-2075. E-mail: admiss@beloit.edu. Web site: http://www.beloit.edu/.

CARDINAL STRITCH UNIVERSITY
MILWAUKEE, WISCONSIN

General Independent Roman Catholic, comprehensive, coed **Entrance** Moderately difficult **Setting** 40-acre suburban campus **Total enrollment** 5,855 **Student-faculty ratio** 18:1 **Application deadline** Rolling (freshmen), rolling (transfer) **Freshmen** 71% were admitted **Housing** Yes **Expenses** Tuition $12,780; Room & Board $4840 **Undergraduates** 69% women, 7% part-time, 73% 25 or older, 0.5% Native Ameri-

WISCONSIN

Cardinal Strictch University *(continued)*
can, 3% Hispanic American, 16% African American, 2% Asian American/Pacific Islander **The most frequently chosen baccalaureate fields are** business/marketing, education, health professions and related sciences **Academic program** English as a second language, advanced placement, accelerated degree program, self-designed majors, honors program, summer session, adult/continuing education programs, internships **Contact** Mr. David Wegener, Director of Admissions, Cardinal Stritch University, 6801 North Yates Road, Milwaukee, WI 53217-3985. Telephone: 414-410-4040 or toll-free 800-347-8822. Fax: 414-410-4058. E-mail: admityou@stritch.edu. Web site: http://www.stritch.edu/.

CARROLL COLLEGE
WAUKESHA, WISCONSIN

General Independent Presbyterian, comprehensive, coed **Entrance** Moderately difficult **Setting** 52-acre suburban campus **Total enrollment** 2,921 **Student-faculty ratio** 20:1 **Application deadline** Rolling (freshmen), rolling (transfer) **Freshmen** 85% were admitted **Housing** Yes **Expenses** Tuition $16,200; Room & Board $4970 **Undergraduates** 67% women, 29% part-time, 26% 25 or older, 0.4% Native American, 2% Hispanic American, 2% African American, 1% Asian American/Pacific Islander **The most frequently chosen baccalaureate fields are** business/marketing, education, health professions and related sciences **Academic program** Advanced placement, self-designed majors, honors program, summer session, adult/continuing education programs, internships **Contact** Mr. James V. Wiseman III, Vice President of Enrollment, Carroll College, 100 North East Avenue, Waukesha, WI 53186-5593. Telephone: 262-524-7221 or toll-free 800-CARROLL. Fax: 262-524-7139. E-mail: cc.info@ccadmin.edu. Web site: http://www.cc.edu/.

CARTHAGE COLLEGE
KENOSHA, WISCONSIN

General Independent, comprehensive, coed, affiliated with Evangelical Lutheran Church in America **Entrance** Moderately difficult **Setting** 72-acre suburban campus **Total enrollment** 2,345 **Student-faculty ratio** 16:1 **Application deadline** Rolling (freshmen), rolling (transfer) **Freshmen** 88% were admitted **Housing** Yes **Expenses** Tuition $18,205; Room & Board $5465 **Undergraduates** 55% women, 24% part-time, 12% 25 or older, 0.4% Native American, 4% Hispanic American, 6% African American, 1% Asian American/Pacific Islander **The most frequently chosen baccalaureate fields are** business/marketing, education, social sciences and history **Academic program** Advanced placement, accelerated degree program, self-designed majors, honors program, summer session, adult/continuing education programs, internships **Contact** Mr. Tom Augustine, Director of Admission, Carthage College, 2001 Alford Park Drive, Kenosha, WI 53140-1994. Telephone: 262-551-6000 or toll-free 800-351-4058. Fax: 262-551-5762. E-mail: admissions@carthage.edu. Web site: http://www.carthage.edu/.

COLUMBIA COLLEGE OF NURSING
MILWAUKEE, WISCONSIN

General Independent, 4-year, coed, primarily women **Entrance** Moderately difficult **Setting** urban campus **Total enrollment** 190 **Student-faculty ratio** 18:1 **Application deadline** Rolling (freshmen), rolling (transfer) **Housing** Yes **Expenses** Tuition $16,480; Room & Board $3700 **Undergraduates** 96% women, 18% part-time, 26% 25 or older, 0% Native American, 1% Hispanic American, 2% African American, 0% Asian American/Pacific Islander **The most frequently chosen baccalaureate field is** health professions and related sciences **Academic program** Advanced placement, honors program, summer session **Contact** Mr. James Wiseman, Dean of Admissions, Columbia College of Nursing, Carroll College, 100 North East Avenue, Milwaukee, WI 53186. Telephone: 262-524-7220. Fax: 262-524-7646. E-mail: jwiseman@ccadmin.cc.edu. Web site: http://www.ccon.edu/.

CONCORDIA UNIVERSITY WISCONSIN
MEQUON, WISCONSIN

General Independent, comprehensive, coed, affiliated with Lutheran Church–Missouri Synod **Entrance** Moderately difficult **Setting** 155-acre suburban campus **Total enrollment** 4,810 **Student-faculty ratio** 11:1 **Application deadline** 8/15 (freshmen), 8/15 (transfer) **Freshmen** 64% were admitted **Housing** Yes **Expenses** Tuition $13,610; Room & Board $5070 **Undergraduates** 65% women, 23% part-time, 1% Native American, 1% Hispanic American, 16% African American, 1% Asian American/Pacific Islander **The most frequently chosen baccalaureate fields are** business/marketing, health professions and related sciences, interdisciplinary studies **Academic program** English as a second language, advanced placement, accelerated degree program, self-designed majors, honors program, summer session, adult/continuing education programs, internships **Contact** Mr. Ken Gaschk, Director of Admissions, Concordia University Wisconsin, 12800 North Lake Shore Drive, Mequon, WI 53097-2402. Telephone: 262-243-4305 Ext. 4305. E-mail: kgaschk@bach.cuw.edu. Web site: http://www.cuw.edu/.

EDGEWOOD COLLEGE
MADISON, WISCONSIN

General Independent Roman Catholic, comprehensive, coed **Entrance** Moderately difficult **Setting** 55-acre urban campus **Total enrollment** 2,110 **Student-faculty ratio** 13:1 **Application deadline** Rolling (freshmen), rolling (transfer) **Freshmen** 78% were admitted **Housing** Yes **Expenses** Tuition $13,300; Room & Board $5004 **Undergraduates** 72% women, 25% part-time, 22% 25 or older, 0.2% Native American, 1% Hispanic American, 1% African American, 1% Asian American/Pacific Islander **The most fre-

WISCONSIN

quently chosen baccalaureate field is philosophy, religion, and theology **Academic program** Advanced placement, summer session, adult/continuing education programs **Contact** Mr. Scott Flanagan, Dean of Admissions and Financial Aid, Edgewood College, 1000 Edgewood College Drive, Madison, WI 53711-1997. Telephone: 608-663-2254 or toll-free 800-444-4861. Fax: 608-663-3291. E-mail: admissions@edgewood.edu. Web site: http://www.edgewood.edu/.

LAKELAND COLLEGE
SHEBOYGAN, WISCONSIN

General Independent, comprehensive, coed, affiliated with United Church of Christ **Entrance** Moderately difficult **Setting** 240-acre rural campus **Total enrollment** 3,588 **Student-faculty ratio** 19:1 **Application deadline** 7/15 (freshmen), 7/15 (transfer) **Freshmen** 70% were admitted **Housing** Yes **Expenses** Tuition $13,050; Room & Board $5245 **Undergraduates** 60% women, 63% part-time, 18% 25 or older, 1% Native American, 1% Hispanic American, 5% African American, 2% Asian American/Pacific Islander **The most frequently chosen baccalaureate fields are** business/marketing, computer/information sciences, education **Academic program** English as a second language, advanced placement, honors program, summer session, adult/continuing education programs, internships **Contact** Mr. Leo Gavrilos, Director of Admissions, Lakeland College, PO Box 359, Nash Visitors Center, Sheboygan, WI 53082-0359. Telephone: 920-565-1217 or toll-free 800-242-3347 (in-state). E-mail: admissions@lakeland.edu. Web site: http://www.lakeland.edu/.

LAWRENCE UNIVERSITY
APPLETON, WISCONSIN

General Independent, 4-year, coed **Entrance** Very difficult **Setting** 84-acre small-town campus **Total enrollment** 1,323 **Student-faculty ratio** 11:1 **Application deadline** 1/15 (freshmen), rolling (transfer) **Freshmen** 68% were admitted **Housing** Yes **Expenses** Tuition $22,728; Room & Board $4983 **Undergraduates** 54% women, 6% part-time, 1% 25 or older, 0.5% Native American, 2% Hispanic American, 1% African American, 2% Asian American/Pacific Islander **The most frequently chosen baccalaureate fields are** social sciences and history, biological/life sciences, visual/performing arts **Academic program** Advanced placement, self-designed majors, internships **Contact** Mr. Steven T. Syverson, Dean of Admissions and Financial Aid, Lawrence University, PO Box 599, Appleton, WI 54912-0599. Telephone: 920-832-6500 or toll-free 800-227-0982. Fax: 920-832-6782. E-mail: excel@lawrence.edu. Web site: http://www.lawrence.edu.

MARANATHA BAPTIST BIBLE COLLEGE
WATERTOWN, WISCONSIN

General Independent Baptist, comprehensive, coed **Entrance** Noncompetitive **Setting** 60-acre small-town campus **Total enrollment** 775 **Student-faculty ratio** 16:1 **Application deadline** Rolling (freshmen), rolling (transfer) **Freshmen** 79% were admitted **Housing** Yes **Expenses** Room & Board $4050 **Undergraduates** 52% women, 8% 25 or older, 0.1% Native American, 2% Hispanic American, 1% African American, 1% Asian American/Pacific Islander **Academic program** Accelerated degree program, summer session, internships **Contact** Mr. James H. Harrison, Director of Admissions, Maranatha Baptist Bible College, 745 West Main Street, Watertown, WI 53094. Telephone: 920-206-2327 or toll-free 800-622-2947. Fax: 920-261-9109. E-mail: admissions@mbbc.edu. Web site: http://www.mbbc.edu/.

MARIAN COLLEGE OF FOND DU LAC
FOND DU LAC, WISCONSIN

General Independent Roman Catholic, comprehensive, coed **Entrance** Moderately difficult **Setting** 50-acre small-town campus **Total enrollment** 2,558 **Student-faculty ratio** 13:1 **Application deadline** Rolling (freshmen), rolling (transfer) **Freshmen** 76% were admitted **Housing** Yes **Expenses** Tuition $13,545; Room & Board $4390 **Undergraduates** 69% women, 34% part-time, 42% 25 or older, 1% Native American, 2% Hispanic American, 3% African American, 1% Asian American/Pacific Islander **The most frequently chosen baccalaureate fields are** business/marketing, education, health professions and related sciences **Academic program** Advanced placement, accelerated degree program, self-designed majors, honors program, summer session, adult/continuing education programs, internships **Contact** Stacey L. Akey, Dean of Admissions, Marian College of Fond du Lac, 45 South National Avenue, Fond du Lac, WI 54935. Telephone: 920-923-7652 or toll-free 800-2-MARIAN Ext. 7652 (in-state). Fax: 920-923-8755. E-mail: admit@mariancollege.edu. Web site: http://www.mariancollege.edu/.

▶ For more information, see page 452.

MARQUETTE UNIVERSITY
MILWAUKEE, WISCONSIN

General Independent Roman Catholic (Jesuit), university, coed **Entrance** Moderately difficult **Setting** 80-acre urban campus **Total enrollment** 10,832 **Student-faculty ratio** 15:1 **Application deadline** Rolling (freshmen), rolling (transfer) **Freshmen** 84% were admitted **Housing** Yes **Expenses** Tuition $18,482; Room & Board $6362 **Undergraduates** 55% women, 7% part-time, 0.3% Native American, 4% Hispanic American, 5% African American, 4% Asian American/Pacific Islander **The most frequently chosen baccalaureate fields are** business/marketing, communications/communication technologies, engineering/engineering technologies **Academic program** English as a second language, advanced placement, accelerated degree program, honors program, summer session, adult/continuing education programs, internships **Contact** Mr. Robert Blust, Dean of Undergraduate Admissions, Marquette University, PO Box 1881, Milwaukee, WI 53201-1881. Telephone: 414-288-7004 or

Marquette University *(continued)*
toll-free 800-222-6544. Fax: 414-288-3764. E-mail: admissions@marquette.edu. Web site: http://www.marquette.edu/.

MILWAUKEE INSTITUTE OF ART AND DESIGN
MILWAUKEE, WISCONSIN

General Independent, 4-year, coed **Entrance** Moderately difficult **Setting** urban campus **Total enrollment** 650 **Student-faculty ratio** 16:1 **Application deadline** Rolling (freshmen), rolling (transfer) **Freshmen** 66% were admitted **Housing** Yes **Expenses** Tuition $18,030; Room & Board $6459 **Undergraduates** 50% women, 10% part-time, 14% 25 or older, 1% Native American, 6% Hispanic American, 2% African American, 2% Asian American/Pacific Islander **The most frequently chosen baccalaureate field is** visual/performing arts **Academic program** Advanced placement, summer session, adult/continuing education programs, internships **Contact** Ms. Mary Schopp, Vice President of Enrollment Management, Milwaukee Institute of Art and Design, 273 East Erie Street, Milwaukee, WI 53202. Telephone: 414-291-8070 or toll-free 888-749-MIAD. Fax: 414-291-8077. E-mail: miadadm@miad.edu. Web site: http://www.miad.edu/.

MILWAUKEE SCHOOL OF ENGINEERING
MILWAUKEE, WISCONSIN

General Independent, comprehensive, coed, primarily men **Entrance** Moderately difficult **Setting** 12-acre urban campus **Total enrollment** 2,563 **Student-faculty ratio** 11:1 **Application deadline** Rolling (freshmen), rolling (transfer) **Freshmen** 69% were admitted **Housing** Yes **Expenses** Tuition $20,835; Room & Board $4845 **Undergraduates** 15% women, 21% part-time, 12% 25 or older, 0.3% Native American, 2% Hispanic American, 3% African American, 3% Asian American/Pacific Islander **The most frequently chosen baccalaureate fields are** business/marketing, communications/communication technologies, engineering/engineering technologies **Academic program** Advanced placement, accelerated degree program, summer session, adult/continuing education programs, internships **Contact** Mr. Tim A. Valley, Dean of Enrollment Management, Milwaukee School of Engineering, 1025 North Broadway, Milwaukee, WI 53202-3109. Telephone: 414-277-6763 or toll-free 800-332-6763. Fax: 414-277-7475. E-mail: explore@msoe.edu. Web site: http://www.msoe.edu/.

MOUNT MARY COLLEGE
MILWAUKEE, WISCONSIN

General Independent Roman Catholic, comprehensive, women only **Entrance** Moderately difficult **Setting** 80-acre suburban campus **Total enrollment** 1,216 **Student-faculty ratio** 8:1 **Application deadline** Rolling (freshmen), rolling (transfer) **Freshmen** 89% were admitted **Housing** Yes **Expenses** Tuition $13,394; Room & Board $4630 **Undergraduates** 51% part-time, 46% 25 or older, 1% Native American, 4% Hispanic American, 16% African American, 4% Asian American/Pacific Islander **The most frequently chosen baccalaureate fields are** health professions and related sciences, business/marketing, visual/performing arts **Academic program** English as a second language, advanced placement, accelerated degree program, self-designed majors, honors program, summer session, adult/continuing education programs, internships **Contact** Ms. Amy Dobson, Director of Enrollment, Mount Mary College, 2900 North Menomonee River Parkway, Milwaukee, WI 53222-4597. Telephone: 414-258-4810 Ext. 360. Fax: 414-256-1205. E-mail: admiss@mtmary.edu. Web site: http://www.mtmary.edu/.

NORTHLAND COLLEGE
ASHLAND, WISCONSIN

General Independent, 4-year, coed, affiliated with United Church of Christ **Entrance** Moderately difficult **Setting** 130-acre small-town campus **Total enrollment** 797 **Student-faculty ratio** 14:1 **Application deadline** 8/1 (freshmen), 8/1 (transfer) **Freshmen** 89% were admitted **Housing** Yes **Expenses** Tuition $15,820; Room & Board $4610 **Undergraduates** 56% women, 15% 25 or older, 2% Native American, 2% Hispanic American, 1% African American, 1% Asian American/Pacific Islander **The most frequently chosen baccalaureate fields are** education, biological/life sciences, natural resources/environmental science **Academic program** Advanced placement, accelerated degree program, self-designed majors, summer session, adult/continuing education programs, internships **Contact** Mr. Eric Peterson, Director of Admission, Northland College, 1411 Ellis Avenue, Ashland, WI 54806. Telephone: 715-682-1224 or toll-free 800-753-1840 (in-state); 800-753-1040 (out-of-state). Fax: 715-682-1258. E-mail: admit@northland.edu. Web site: http://www.northland.edu/.

RIPON COLLEGE
RIPON, WISCONSIN

General Independent, 4-year, coed **Entrance** Moderately difficult **Setting** 250-acre small-town campus **Total enrollment** 903 **Student-faculty ratio** 15:1 **Application deadline** Rolling (freshmen), rolling (transfer) **Freshmen** 84% were admitted **Housing** Yes **Expenses** Tuition $19,500; Room & Board $4680 **Undergraduates** 53% women, 2% part-time, 1% 25 or older, 0.5% Native American, 4% Hispanic American, 2% African American, 1% Asian American/Pacific Islander **The most frequently chosen baccalaureate fields are** English, education, trade and industry **Academic program** Advanced placement, accelerated degree program, self-designed majors, internships **Contact** Mr. Scott J. Goplin, Vice President and Dean of Admission and Financial Aid, Ripon College, 300 Seward Street, PO Box 248, Ripon, WI 54971. Telephone: 920-748-8185 or toll-free 800-947-4766. Fax: 920-748-8335. E-mail: adminfo@ripon.edu. Web site: http://www.ripon.edu/.

▶ For more information, see page 468.

WISCONSIN

ST. NORBERT COLLEGE
DE PERE, WISCONSIN

General Independent Roman Catholic, comprehensive, coed **Entrance** Moderately difficult **Setting** 84-acre suburban campus **Total enrollment** 2,131 **Student-faculty ratio** 14:1 **Application deadline** Rolling (freshmen), rolling (transfer) **Freshmen** 84% were admitted **Housing** Yes **Expenses** Tuition $18,007; Room & Board $5162 **Undergraduates** 57% women, 4% part-time, 4% 25 or older, 1% Native American, 1% Hispanic American, 1% African American, 2% Asian American/Pacific Islander **The most frequently chosen baccalaureate fields are** business/marketing, communications/communication technologies, social sciences and history **Academic program** English as a second language, advanced placement, accelerated degree program, self-designed majors, honors program, summer session, internships **Contact** Mr. Daniel L. Meyer, Dean of Admission and Enrollment Management, St. Norbert College, 100 Grant Street, De Pere, WI 54115-2099. Telephone: 920-403-3005 or toll-free 800-236-4878. Fax: 920-403-4072. E-mail: admit@mail.snc.edu. Web site: http://www.snc.edu/.

SILVER LAKE COLLEGE
MANITOWOC, WISCONSIN

General Independent Roman Catholic, comprehensive, coed **Entrance** Minimally difficult **Setting** 30-acre rural campus **Total enrollment** 858 **Student-faculty ratio** 8:1 **Application deadline** 8/31 (freshmen), 8/31 (transfer) **Freshmen** 89% were admitted **Housing** Yes **Expenses** Tuition $13,016; Room only $2600 **Undergraduates** 72% women, 60% part-time, 63% 25 or older, 2% Native American, 1% Hispanic American, 0.4% African American, 1% Asian American/Pacific Islander **The most frequently chosen baccalaureate fields are** business/marketing, education, engineering/engineering technologies **Academic program** English as a second language, advanced placement, accelerated degree program, self-designed majors, summer session, adult/continuing education programs, internships **Contact** Ms. Janis Algozine, Vice President, Dean of Students, Silver Lake College, 2406 South Alverno Road, Manitowoc, WI 54220-9319. Telephone: 920-684-5955 Ext. 175 or toll-free 800-236-4752 Ext. 175 (in-state). Fax: 920-684-7082. E-mail: admslc@silver.sl.edu. Web site: http://www.sl.edu/.

UNIVERSITY OF PHOENIX-WISCONSIN CAMPUS
BROOKFIELD, WISCONSIN

General Proprietary, comprehensive, coed **Total enrollment** 88,730 **Student-faculty ratio** 13:1 **Housing** No **Expenses** Tuition $8850 **Contact** University of Phoenix-Wisconsin Campus, 4615 East Elwood Street, Phoenix, AZ 85040-1948. Telephone: or toll-free 800-228-7240. E-mail: beth.barilla@apollogrp.edu. Web site: http://www.phoenix.edu/.

UNIVERSITY OF WISCONSIN-EAU CLAIRE
EAU CLAIRE, WISCONSIN

General State-supported, comprehensive, coed **Entrance** Moderately difficult **Setting** 333-acre urban campus **Total enrollment** 10,634 **Student-faculty ratio** 20:1 **Application deadline** Rolling (freshmen), 7/1 (transfer) **Freshmen** 75% were admitted **Housing** Yes **Expenses** Tuition $3472; Room & Board $3560 **Undergraduates** 60% women, 8% part-time, 8% 25 or older, 1% Native American, 1% Hispanic American, 1% African American, 3% Asian American/Pacific Islander **The most frequently chosen baccalaureate fields are** business/marketing, education, health professions and related sciences **Academic program** English as a second language, advanced placement, honors program, summer session, adult/continuing education programs, internships **Contact** Mr. Robert Lopez, Director of Admissions, University of Wisconsin-Eau Claire, PO Box 4004, Eau Claire, WI 54702-4004. Telephone: 715-836-5415. E-mail: ask-uwec@uwec.edu. Web site: http://www.uwec.edu/.

UNIVERSITY OF WISCONSIN-GREEN BAY
GREEN BAY, WISCONSIN

General State-supported, comprehensive, coed **Entrance** Moderately difficult **Setting** 700-acre suburban campus **Total enrollment** 5,551 **Student-faculty ratio** 23:1 **Application deadline** 2/1 (freshmen), 4/15 (transfer) **Freshmen** 80% were admitted **Housing** Yes **Expenses** Tuition $3648; Room only $2200 **Undergraduates** 66% women, 20% part-time, 21% 25 or older, 2% Native American, 1% Hispanic American, 1% African American, 2% Asian American/Pacific Islander **The most frequently chosen baccalaureate fields are** business/marketing, biological/life sciences, interdisciplinary studies **Academic program** English as a second language, advanced placement, accelerated degree program, self-designed majors, summer session, adult/continuing education programs, internships **Contact** Ms. Pam Harvey-Jacobs, Interim Director of Admissions, University of Wisconsin-Green Bay, 2420 Nicolet Drive, Green Bay, WI 54311-7001. Telephone: 920-465-2111 or toll-free 888-367-8942 (out-of-state). Fax: 920-465-5754. E-mail: admissns@uwgb.edu. Web site: http://www.uwgb.edu/.

UNIVERSITY OF WISCONSIN-LA CROSSE
LA CROSSE, WISCONSIN

General State-supported, comprehensive, coed **Entrance** Moderately difficult **Setting** 121-acre suburban campus **Total enrollment** 9,105 **Student-faculty ratio** 21:1 **Application deadline** Rolling (freshmen), rolling (transfer) **Freshmen** 69% were admitted **Housing** Yes **Expenses** Tuition $3530; Room & Board $3520 **Undergraduates** 58% women, 7% part-time, 5% 25 or older, 1% Native American, 1% Hispanic American, 1% African American, 2% Asian American/Pacific Islander **The most fre-

WISCONSIN

University of Wisconsin–La Crosse *(continued)*
quently chosen baccalaureate fields are business/marketing, parks and recreation, social sciences and history **Academic program** English as a second language, advanced placement, honors program, summer session, adult/continuing education programs, internships **Contact** Mr. Tim Lewis, Director of Admissions, University of Wisconsin–La Crosse, 1725 State Street, LaCrosse, WI 54601. Telephone: 608-785-8939. Fax: 608-785-8940. E-mail: admissions@uwlax.edu. Web site: http://www.uwlax.edu/.

UNIVERSITY OF WISCONSIN–MADISON
MADISON, WISCONSIN

General State-supported, university, coed **Entrance** Very difficult **Setting** 1,050-acre urban campus **Total enrollment** 41,552 **Student-faculty ratio** 14:1 **Application deadline** 2/1 (freshmen), 2/1 (transfer) **Freshmen** 57% were admitted **Housing** Yes **Expenses** Tuition $4086; Room & Board $5700 **Undergraduates** 2% 25 or older, 0.5% Native American, 2% Hispanic American, 2% African American, 4% Asian American/Pacific Islander **Academic program** English as a second language, advanced placement, accelerated degree program, self-designed majors, honors program, summer session, adult/continuing education programs, internships **Contact** Mr. Keith White, Office of Admissions, University of Wisconsin–Madison, 716 Langdon Street, Madison, WI 53706-1400. Telephone: 608-262-3961. Fax: 608-262-7706. E-mail: on.wisconsin@mail.admin.wisc.edu. Web site: http://www.wisc.edu/.

UNIVERSITY OF WISCONSIN–MILWAUKEE
MILWAUKEE, WISCONSIN

General State-supported, university, coed **Entrance** Moderately difficult **Setting** 90-acre urban campus **Total enrollment** 24,223 **Student-faculty ratio** 19:1 **Application deadline** Rolling (freshmen), rolling (transfer) **Freshmen** 79% were admitted **Housing** Yes **Expenses** Tuition $4057; Room only $2700 **Undergraduates** 55% women, 25% part-time, 22% 25 or older, 1% Native American, 4% Hispanic American, 9% African American, 4% Asian American/Pacific Islander **The most frequently chosen baccalaureate fields are** business/marketing, education, health professions and related sciences **Academic program** English as a second language, advanced placement, self-designed majors, honors program, summer session, adult/continuing education programs, internships **Contact** Ms. Jan Ford, Director, Recruitment and Outreach, University of Wisconsin–Milwaukee, PO Box 749, Milwaukee, WI 53201. Telephone: 414-229-4397. Fax: 414-229-6940. E-mail: deswcb@des.uwm.edu. Web site: http://www.uwm.edu/.

UNIVERSITY OF WISCONSIN–OSHKOSH
OSHKOSH, WISCONSIN

General State-supported, comprehensive, coed **Entrance** Moderately difficult **Setting** 192-acre suburban campus **Total enrollment** 10,909 **Student-faculty ratio** 15:1 **Application deadline** 8/1 (freshmen), 8/1 (transfer) **Freshmen** 82% were admitted **Housing** Yes **Expenses** Tuition $3228; Room & Board $3816 **Undergraduates** 59% women, 14% part-time, 14% 25 or older, 1% Native American, 1% Hispanic American, 1% African American, 2% Asian American/Pacific Islander **The most frequently chosen baccalaureate fields are** business/marketing, education, protective services/public administration **Academic program** English as a second language, advanced placement, accelerated degree program, self-designed majors, honors program, summer session, adult/continuing education programs, internships **Contact** Mr. Richard Hillman, Associate Director of Admissions, University of Wisconsin–Oshkosh, 800 Algoma Boulevard, Oshkosh, WI 54901-8602. Telephone: 920-424-0202. Fax: 920-424-1098. E-mail: oshadmuw@uwosh.edu. Web site: http://www.uwosh.edu/.

UNIVERSITY OF WISCONSIN–PARKSIDE
KENOSHA, WISCONSIN

General State-supported, comprehensive, coed **Entrance** Moderately difficult **Setting** 700-acre suburban campus **Total enrollment** 5,068 **Student-faculty ratio** 20:1 **Application deadline** 8/1 (freshmen), 8/1 (transfer) **Freshmen** 76% were admitted **Housing** Yes **Expenses** Tuition $3,298; Room & Board $4960 **Undergraduates** 59% women, 31% part-time, 23% 25 or older, 1% Native American, 7% Hispanic American, 9% African American, 2% Asian American/Pacific Islander **The most frequently chosen baccalaureate fields are** business/marketing, communications/communication technologies, social sciences and history **Academic program** English as a second language, advanced placement, accelerated degree program, honors program, summer session, adult/continuing education programs, internships **Contact** Mr. Matthew Jensen, Director of Admissions, University of Wisconsin–Parkside, 900 Wood Road, PO Box 2000, Kenosha, WI 53141-2000. Telephone: 262-595-2757 or toll-free 877-633-3897 (in-state). Fax: 262-595-2008. E-mail: matthew.jensen@uwp.edu. Web site: http://www.uwp.edu/.

UNIVERSITY OF WISCONSIN–PLATTEVILLE
PLATTEVILLE, WISCONSIN

General State-supported, comprehensive, coed **Entrance** Moderately difficult **Setting** 380-acre small-town campus **Total enrollment** 5,540 **Student-faculty ratio** 22:1 **Application deadline** Rolling (freshmen), rolling (transfer) **Freshmen** 45% were admitted **Housing** Yes **Expenses** Tuition $3473; Room & Board $3799 **Undergraduates** 39% women, 9% part-time, 16% 25 or older, 0.2% Native American, 1% Hispanic American, 1% African American, 1% Asian American/Pacific Islander **The most frequently chosen baccalaureate fields are** business/marketing, agriculture, engineering/engineering technologies **Academic program** English as a second language, advanced placement, accelerated degree program, self-designed majors, honors program, summer session, adult/continuing education programs, internships **Contact** Dr. Richard Schumacher, Dean of Admissions and Enrollment Management, University of Wisconsin–Platteville, 1 University Plaza, Platteville, WI 53818-3099. Telephone: 608-342-1125 or toll-free 800-362-5515 (in-state). E-mail: admit@uwplatt.edu. Web site: http://www.uwplatt.edu/.

UNIVERSITY OF WISCONSIN–RIVER FALLS
RIVER FALLS, WISCONSIN

General State-supported, comprehensive, coed **Entrance** Moderately difficult **Setting** 225-acre suburban campus **Total enrollment** 5,844 **Student-faculty ratio** 19:1 **Application deadline** Rolling (freshmen), rolling (transfer) **Freshmen** 43% were admitted **Housing** Yes **Expenses** Tuition $3990; Room & Board $3582 **Undergraduates** 61% women, 7% part-time, 6% 25 or older **Academic program** Advanced placement, accelerated degree program, self-designed majors, honors program, summer session, adult/continuing education programs, internships **Contact** Mr. Alan Tuchtenhagen, Director of Admissions, University of Wisconsin–River Falls, 410 South Third Street, 112 South Hall, River Falls, WI 54022-5001. Telephone: 715-425-3500. Fax: 715-425-0676. E-mail: admit@uwrf.edu. Web site: http://www.uwrf.edu/.

UNIVERSITY OF WISCONSIN–STEVENS POINT
STEVENS POINT, WISCONSIN

General State-supported, comprehensive, coed **Entrance** Moderately difficult **Setting** 335-acre small-town campus **Total enrollment** 8,944 **Student-faculty ratio** 20:1 **Application deadline** Rolling (freshmen), rolling (transfer) **Freshmen** 77% were admitted **Housing** Yes **Expenses** Tuition $3375; Room & Board $3738 **Undergraduates** 57% women, 10% part-time, 12% 25 or older, 1% Native American, 1% Hispanic American, 1% African American, 1% Asian American/Pacific Islander **The most frequently chosen baccalaureate fields are** business/marketing, biological/life sciences, natural resources/environmental science **Academic program** English as a second language, advanced placement, accelerated degree program, self-designed majors, summer session, adult/continuing education programs, internships **Contact** Dr. David Eckholm, Director of Admissions, University of Wisconsin–Stevens Point, 2100 Main Street, Stevens Point, WI 54481-3897. Telephone: 715-346-2441. Fax: 715-346-3296. E-mail: admiss@uwsp.edu. Web site: http://www.uwsp.edu/.

UNIVERSITY OF WISCONSIN–STOUT
MENOMONIE, WISCONSIN

General State-supported, comprehensive, coed **Entrance** Moderately difficult **Setting** 120-acre small-town campus **Total enrollment** 7,780 **Student-faculty ratio** 20:1 **Application deadline** Rolling (freshmen), rolling (transfer) **Freshmen** 71% were admitted **Housing** Yes **Expenses** Tuition $3502; Room & Board $3690 **Undergraduates** 48% women, 11% part-time, 12% 25 or older, 0.4% Native American, 1% Hispanic American, 1% African American, 1% Asian American/Pacific Islander **The most frequently chosen baccalaureate fields are** business/marketing, education, engineering/engineering technologies **Academic program** English as a second language, advanced placement, accelerated degree program, honors program, summer session, adult/continuing education programs, internships **Contact** Ms. Cynthia Jenkins, Director of Admissions, University of Wisconsin–Stout, Menomonie, WI 54751. Telephone: 715-232-2639 or toll-free 800-HI-STOUT (in-state). Fax: 715-232-1667. E-mail: admissions@uwstout.edu. Web site: http://www.uwstout.edu/.

UNIVERSITY OF WISCONSIN–SUPERIOR
SUPERIOR, WISCONSIN

General State-supported, comprehensive, coed **Entrance** Moderately difficult **Setting** 230-acre small-town campus **Total enrollment** 2,842 **Student-faculty ratio** 16:1 **Application deadline** 5/1 (freshmen), 5/1 (transfer) **Freshmen** 81% were admitted **Housing** Yes **Expenses** Tuition $3233; Room & Board $3818 **Undergraduates** 61% women, 18% part-time, 28% 25 or older, 2% Native American, 1% Hispanic American, 1% African American, 1% Asian American/Pacific Islander **The most frequently chosen baccalaureate fields are** business/marketing, education, social sciences and history **Academic program** English as a second language, advanced placement, self-designed majors, honors program, summer session, adult/continuing education programs, internships **Contact** Ms. Lorraine Washa, Student Application Contact, University of Wisconsin–Superior, Belknap and Catlin, PO Box 2000, Superior, WI 54880-4500. Telephone: 715-394-8230. Fax: 715-394-8407. E-mail: admissions@uwsuper.edu. Web site: http://www.uwsuper.edu/.

UNIVERSITY OF WISCONSIN–WHITEWATER
WHITEWATER, WISCONSIN

General State-supported, comprehensive, coed **Entrance** Moderately difficult **Setting** 385-acre small-town campus **Total enrollment** 10,551 **Student-faculty ratio** 20:1 **Application deadline** Rolling (freshmen), rolling (transfer) **Freshmen** 77% were admitted **Housing** Yes **Expenses** Tuition $3367; Room & Board $3570 **Undergraduates** 53% women, 10% part-time, 10% 25 or older, 0.4% Native American, 2% Hispanic American, 4% African American, 2% Asian American/Pacific Islander **The most frequently chosen baccalaureate fields are** business/marketing, communications/communication technologies, education **Academic program** Advanced placement, accelerated degree program, self-designed majors, honors program, summer session, adult/continuing education programs, internships **Contact** Dr. Tori A.

University of Wisconsin–Whitewater *(continued)*
McGuire, Executive Director of Admissions, University of Wisconsin–Whitewater, 800 West Main Street, Whitewater, WI 53190-1790. Telephone: 262-472-1440 Ext. 1512. Fax: 262-472-1515. E-mail: uwwadmit@uwwvax.uww.edu. Web site: http://www.uww.edu/.

VITERBO UNIVERSITY
LA CROSSE, WISCONSIN

General Independent Roman Catholic, comprehensive, coed **Entrance** Moderately difficult **Setting** 5-acre urban campus **Total enrollment** 2,167 **Student-faculty ratio** 13:1 **Application deadline** Rolling (freshmen), rolling (transfer) **Freshmen** 85% were admitted **Housing** Yes **Expenses** Tuition $13,630; Room & Board $4710 **Undergraduates** 74% women, 17% part-time, 24% 25 or older, 1% Native American, 2% Hispanic American, 1% African American, 1% Asian American/Pacific Islander **The most frequently chosen baccalaureate fields are** business/marketing, education, health professions and related sciences **Academic program** Advanced placement, accelerated degree program, self-designed majors, summer session, adult/continuing education programs, internships **Contact** Mr. Joe Fischer, Admission Counselor, Viterbo University, 815 South 9th Street, LaCrosse, WI 54601. Telephone: 608-796-3016 Ext. 3016 or toll-free 800-VIT-ERBO Ext. 3010. Fax: 608-796-3020. E-mail: admission@viterbo.edu. Web site: http://www.viterbo.edu/.

WISCONSIN LUTHERAN COLLEGE
MILWAUKEE, WISCONSIN

General Independent, 4-year, coed, affiliated with Wisconsin Evangelical Lutheran Synod **Entrance** Moderately difficult **Setting** 16-acre suburban campus **Total enrollment** 716 **Student-faculty ratio** 12:1 **Freshmen** 86% were admitted **Housing** Yes **Expenses** Tuition $14,116; Room & Board $5100 **Undergraduates** 63% women, 9% part-time, 2% 25 or older, 0% Native American, 1% Hispanic American, 1% African American, 1% Asian American/Pacific Islander **The most frequently chosen baccalaureate fields are** communications/communication technologies, education, visual/performing arts **Academic program** Advanced placement, self-designed majors, summer session, internships **Contact** Mr. Craig Swiontek, Director of Admissions, Wisconsin Lutheran College, 8800 West Bluemound Road, Milwaukee, WI 53226-9942. Telephone: 414-443-8713 or toll-free 888-WIS LUTH. Fax: 414-443-8514. E-mail: admissions@wlc.edu. Web site: http://www.wlc.edu/.

WYOMING

UNIVERSITY OF WYOMING
LARAMIE, WYOMING

General State-supported, university, coed **Entrance** Moderately difficult **Setting** small-town campus **Total enrollment** 12,402 **Student-faculty ratio** 14:1 **Application deadline** 8/10 (freshmen), 8/10 (transfer) **Freshmen** 97% were admitted **Housing** Yes **Expenses** Tuition $2,807; Room & Board $4748 **Undergraduates** 19% 25 or older, 1% Native American, 3% Hispanic American, 1% African American, 1% Asian American/Pacific Islander **The most frequently chosen baccalaureate fields are** business/marketing, education, engineering/engineering technologies **Academic program** Advanced placement, accelerated degree program, self-designed majors, honors program, summer session, adult/continuing education programs, internships **Contact** Ms. Sara Axelson, Associate Vice President Enrollment and Director of Admissions, University of Wyoming, Box 3435, Laramie, WY 82071. Telephone: 307-766-5160 or toll-free 800-342-5996. Fax: 307-766-4042. E-mail: why-wyo@uwyo.edu. Web site: http://www.uwyo.edu/.

DESCRIPTIONS

The full-page descriptions in this section provide a broad overview of some of the colleges and universities profiled in the previous section. These descriptions are offered to help give students a better sense of the individuality of each institution, in terms that include mission statements, campus environments, and academic programs. The absence from this section of any college or university does not constitute an editorial decision on the part of Peterson's. In essence, this section is an open forum for colleges and universities, on a voluntary basis, to communicate their particular messages to prospective college students. The descriptions are arranged alphabetically by the official name of the institution.

ALDERSON-BROADDUS COLLEGE

■ **PHILIPPI, WEST VIRGINIA**

THE COLLEGE

Located on a mountaintop overlooking the Tygart River valley in Philippi, West Virginia, Alderson-Broaddus College is a four-year, coeducational, independent liberal arts college with a history of educational excellence and innovation. Affiliated with the American Baptist Churches, U.S.A., the College has been preparing men and women for leadership for more than 130 years. Today, more than 750 men and women from thirty-eight states and eight countries study at Alderson-Broaddus, preparing for the future with quality programs in a variety of fields. Alderson-Broaddus emphasizes an innovative approach to quality liberal arts education. For example, the College pioneered the first undergraduate physician assistant program in the nation. Alderson-Broaddus is accredited by the North Central Association of Colleges and Schools. The baccalaureate program in nursing is accredited by the National League for Nursing. The Physician Assistant Program is accredited by the Commission on Accreditation of Allied Health Programs (CAAHEP). The teacher education programs are accredited by the National Council for Accreditation of Teacher Education (NCATE). More than fifty student organizations and hundreds of activities provide outstanding opportunities for recreation, personal development, and service. The A-B Battlers have a championship tradition in intercollegiate athletics that includes baseball, basketball, cross-country, and soccer for men and basketball, cross-country, softball, and volleyball for women. A wide range of intramural sports involves most of the student body. The attractions of West Virginia's unspoiled state and national parks are nearby. The wooded 170-acre campus offers outstanding facilities, including modern academic facilities, a 7,200-watt FM radio station, an on-campus cafe, an art gallery, a bookstore, a post office, student lounges, and a sports coliseum with a pool, two gyms, a racquetball court, and a fitness center.

> **For additional information, students should contact:**
> Admissions Office
> Alderson-Broaddus College
> P.O. Box 2003
> Philippi, West Virginia 26416
> Telephone: 800-263-1549 (toll-free)
> E-mail: admissions@ab.edu

ACADEMIC PROGRAM

The academic year consists of two 15-week semesters. Students generally take 15 to 18 semester hours each semester. In addition, the College offers a 10-week summer term. Completion of 128 hours of study is required for graduation. Most of the degree requirements are fulfilled through on-campus study, but some majors require off-campus field work and internships for which credit is awarded. With the help of their academic advisers, students select courses to fulfill requirements for liberal studies and a major. Students may choose elective minors in such areas as business, computer science, education, recreation, and technical writing. An honors program offers academically talented students opportunities for independent scholarship and research.

FINANCIAL AID

Alderson-Broaddus College has an excellent program of financial aid that includes merit, performance, and need-based grants and scholarships, loans, and college work-study. Applicants requesting financial aid are required to submit the Free Application for Federal Student Aid (FAFSA). Nearly 99 percent of all students receive some form of financial assistance.

APPLICATION AND INFORMATION

General admission to the College is on a rolling basis. Students seeking freshman admission must submit a completed application form, a $10 nonrefundable application fee, results of the ACT or SAT, and official copies of secondary school transcripts. In addition to these materials, transfer students must submit a transfer clearance form, provided by Alderson-Broaddus College, and official transcripts from all colleges attended. Separate application requirements apply to the physician assistant program. Specific information and applicable deadlines are forwarded with application materials. When requesting information, applicants should specify a major interest area or note that they are undecided.

ALFRED UNIVERSITY

ALFRED, NEW YORK

THE UNIVERSITY

Alfred University is a residential institution of 2,500 graduate and undergraduate students, located 70 miles south of Rochester, between the Finger Lakes region and the Allegheny Mountains in western New York State. Alfred is comprised of the privately endowed Colleges of Business, Liberal Arts and Sciences, and Engineering and Professional Studies, as well as the publicly supported New York State College of Ceramics, which is comprised of the School of Art and Design and the School of Ceramic Engineering and Materials Science. Alfred is noted for its superior academic quality, outstanding faculty, and commitment to student development. The New York State College of Ceramics is regarded as the world leader in the field of ceramic engineering. The state of New York has identified Alfred University as one of its ten centers for advanced technology research.

For more information, students should contact:
Scott C. Hooker
Director of Admissions
Alumni Hall
Alfred University
Saxon Drive
Alfred, New York 14802
Telephone: 607-871-2115
 800-541-9729 (toll-free)
Fax: 607-871-2198
E-mail: admwww@alfred.edu
WWW: http://www.alfred.edu

ACADEMIC PROGRAM

All academic programs require courses in the liberal arts and sciences; however, specific graduation requirements differ for each college and school within the University. All candidates are required to satisfy a physical education requirement through courses or proficiency examinations. To encourage students with strong ability and initiative, the University recognizes both the Advanced Placement and International Baccalaureate programs. In addition, the University offers its own challenge examination program for currently enrolled students. The University Honors Program is open to all majors and requires an additional essay application for admission to the program. Army ROTC is also available.

FINANCIAL AID

During the 2001–02 academic year, University-funded aid sources provided more than $17 million to undergraduate students. For private-sector programs, 90 percent of freshmen received some form of financial assistance. In the New York State College of Ceramics, 88 percent of freshmen received some form of aid. Aid administered by the University usually consists of a combination of scholarships or grants, loans, and part-time work. Students may be eligible for financial assistance under the Federal Pell Grant, Federal Supplemental Educational Opportunity Grant, Federal Perkins Loan, and Federal Work-Study programs. New York State residents may be eligible for aid under the Tuition Assistance Program. The University sponsors National Merit Scholarships; departmental talent awards; Presidential, Southern Tier, and transfer scholarships; and the Johnathan Allen Award for Leadership.

APPLICATION AND INFORMATION

Candidates must submit a completed Alfred University application form or the Common Application form, SAT I or ACT results, a letter of recommendation, and a $40 application fee. Students who visit campus receive an application fee waiver certificate that may be used on that day or at a later time. They must also have their high school guidance office submit an official transcript. Applicants to the School of Art and Design must submit a portfolio of their work, typically fifteen to twenty slides. The application and portfolio deadline under the early decision plan is December 1, with notification by December 15. The application and portfolio deadline for regular admission is February 1, with notification by mid-March. Transfer applicants should file an application by August 1 for September admission or December 1 for January admission. The School of Art and Design has different application and portfolio deadlines for transfer students, dependent upon the student's previous course work in art. Students should contact the Office of Admissions for further information regarding these deadlines.

ALLEGHENY COLLEGE

- **MEADVILLE, PENNSYLVANIA**

THE COLLEGE

Founded on America's western frontier in 1815, Allegheny is a classical, selective college of the liberal arts and sciences. Although highly regarded as a preprofessional school, its impact on students goes well beyond preparation for careers. Allegheny not only develops in its students such essential skills as writing, critical thinking, and problem solving, it also fosters a capacity for lifelong learning, the ability to manage everyday affairs, responsible citizenship, social skills, and values. While nonsectarian in outlook and practice, Allegheny has been affiliated with the United Methodist Church since 1833. The 1,900 students come from thirty-four states and fifteen other countries. Seven percent are members of minority groups and three fourths reside on campus. On-campus residence is required of freshmen and sophomores and optional for other students, but it is guaranteed for all four years for all who seek it. Faculty members describe Allegheny students as active and hardworking. At Allegheny, students sustain more than 100 clubs, committees, and organizations in drama, dance, vocal and instrumental music, publications, radio, religious life, politics, social service, professional and multicultural interest areas, and the governance of student life. Intramural athletics involve three fourths of the students, and the varsity program is one of the best in NCAA Division III.

For more information, students should contact:

Office of Admissions
Allegheny College
Meadville, Pennsylvania 16335-3902
Telephone: 814-332-4351
               800-521-5293 (toll-free)
E-mail: admiss@allegheny.edu
WWW: http://www.allegheny.edu

ACADEMIC PROGRAM

Allegheny ensures that students develop wholeness across the divisions of knowledge (arts and humanities, social sciences, and natural sciences) as well as expertise in one or more fields. Each student must complete 131 semester credit hours; the major may require 32 to 48 semester credit hours, including a junior seminar and the distinctive Senior Comprehensive Project, while the remainder are electives and Liberal Studies Program courses. The innovative Liberal Studies Program includes two freshman seminars, with strong advising, writing, and speaking components; a sophomore writing and speaking course; and some in-depth study in a subject outside the division of the major. Writing proficiency is emphasized throughout the Allegheny years—it is a central objective of the seminars. It is developed further in the sophomore writing course, after students have mastered some college-level material, and it must be demonstrated in all other courses. The Senior Comprehensive Project, a capstone of the Allegheny education, is a research project that concludes with a final written document and an oral defense of the project. The independent study option allows students to pursue an interest not included in the formal College curriculum.

FINANCIAL AID

A large number of merit-based scholarships are awarded annually, making the College more affordable even to families who do not qualify for need-based financial aid. Trustee Scholarships, which award up to $50,000, are guaranteed for four years of study at Allegheny. Also, scholarships, grants, loans, and campus employment are awarded to students who need assistance to meet College expenses. The Free Application for Federal Student Aid (FAFSA), which establishes an applicant's eligibility for virtually all institutional, state, and federal assistance, must be submitted by February 15. Notices about the receipt of financial aid are sent to students shortly after their acceptance by the College.

APPLICATION AND INFORMATION

The application for admission should be submitted by February 15 (January 15 for early decision), and the SAT I or ACT results should be forwarded to the College by each candidate. Applicants for early decision are notified on a rolling basis through January 31. Regular applicants are informed of the admission decision by April 1.

ALMA COLLEGE

■ **ALMA, MICHIGAN**

THE COLLEGE

Regarded as one of the nation's best liberal arts colleges, Alma College is in its third century of superior education and professional distinction. Founded by Presbyterians in 1886, Alma remains a private liberal arts institution committed to a values-oriented style of education. In a time when many professionals find that their technical training is already out of date, Alma's graduates are entering the job market with an education that will always serve them. Alma's academic philosophy, rooted in the liberal arts tradition and providing a broad educational base with flexible, innovative course work, has earned Alma a Phi Beta Kappa chapter. Students enjoy Alma's new Alan J. Stone Center for Recreation that features a climbing wall, fitness center, four courts, and a suspended three-lane track. The outdoor athletic complex features a multipurpose playing field of artificial turf, soccer and softball fields, tennis courts, an eight-lane track, and nearby Klenk Park for baseball. Even as students have fun, they develop valuable skills for their future. The Hamilton Dining Commons and downtown shops are a short walk from the main academic area on campus.

> **For more information, students should contact:**
> Admissions Office
> Alma College
> 614 West Superior Street
> Alma, Michigan 48801-1599
> Telephone: 800-321-ALMA (toll-free)
> E-mail: admissions@alma.edu
> WWW: http://www.alma.edu
> http://www.alma.edu/admissions/application.htm

ACADEMIC PROGRAM

The College operates on a 4-4-1 calendar—two 4-month terms in the fall and winter and one 1-month term in the spring. During the spring term, there are opportunities for international study as well as for on-campus instruction and research. In keeping with Alma's philosophy of educating the whole person, the College requires that all students complete liberal arts courses spanning the humanities, the natural sciences, and the social sciences. The B.A. and B.S. degree programs require the completion of 136 credits; the B.F.A. and B.M. degree programs, 148 credits. Highly qualified students are challenged by Alma's honors program, featuring a specially designed freshman course that explores the methods of communication used in the liberal arts disciplines. The honors concept extends throughout the four years at Alma. Alma accepts credits earned through the Advanced Placement (AP) Program and the International Baccalaureate Diploma (I.B.) program, and examinations designed by Alma's academic departments.

FINANCIAL AID

At Alma, students can achieve scholarship recognition regardless of need on the basis of outstanding scholastic achievement. Several academically competitive scholarship programs provide awards for eligible students, including a full tuition scholarship for National Merit Finalists. The College also offers performance scholarships in recognition of individual talent, as well as grants, loans, and deferred-payment plans. Up to 400 campus and community jobs are filled by Alma students yearly. To apply for aid, students are required only to file the Free Application for Federal Student Aid (FAFSA) in January of the year of prospective enrollment at Alma.

APPLICATION AND INFORMATION

Students may apply at any time after completing their junior year of high school. Freshman applicants should send the completed application for admission along with a $25 nonrefundable application fee, high school transcripts, and ACT or SAT I scores. Students are required to submit a recommendation from their high school guidance counselor. Early action applications are due by November 1. Transfer students should submit transcripts from each institution attended, the completed application for admission, a $25 nonrefundable application fee, a financial aid transcript, and a Transfer Recommendation Form from the last institution attended. Applications are handled on a rolling basis; students should hear about admission decisions within three weeks after sending an application and records.

AQUINAS COLLEGE

- **GRAND RAPIDS, MICHIGAN**

THE COLLEGE

Located on the eastern edge of the city of Grand Rapids, Aquinas enjoys all of the advantages of Michigan's second-largest city and is just a 3-hour drive from Detroit or Chicago. The Aquinas College campus is an interesting blend of early-nineteenth-century architecture coupled with modern-day structures. The campus abounds with natural beauty; it has been called the most beautiful small campus in Michigan. Founded by the Dominican Sisters of Grand Rapids in 1886, Aquinas has a Catholic heritage and a Christian tradition. The Dominican tradition of working and serving remains alive at Aquinas. The College's curriculum, with its more than forty majors and cognates, is designed to provide students with both breadth and depth and to foster a thirst for knowledge and truth and a spirit of intellectual dialogue and inquiry. Coupled with nationally recognized co-op and internship programs, it prepares students to both live and work in the rapidly changing world of today and tomorrow. Arriving from places as near as Grand Rapids, Chicago, and Detroit and as far as India and China, the 2,605 students include 1,445 full-time, 576 part-time, and 584 graduate students. The Insignis program at Aquinas encourages students of exceptional academic ability to participate in social and intellectual activities such as lectures and receptions for visiting scholars and trips to places of cultural interest. Aquinas offers more than thirty student organizations, ranging from intramural teams and departmental clubs to a wide variety of musical groups, student publications, and service organizations. In addition to its undergraduate degrees, Aquinas also offers Master in the Art of Teaching, Master in Education, Master in Science Education, and Master of Management (with concentrations in marketing, organizational development, health-care management, and international business) degrees.

For more information, students should contact:

Paula Meehan
Dean of Admissions
Aquinas College
1607 Robinson Road, SE
Grand Rapids, Michigan 49506
Telephone: 616-732-4460
            800-678-9593 (toll-free)
E-mail: admissions@aquinas.edu
WWW: http://www.aquinas.edu

ACADEMIC PROGRAM

In addition to their major and minor fields of study, students take an integrated skills course called Inquiry and Expression. This course spans the entire freshman year and has an emphasis on writing integrated with reading critically, oral communication skills, critical thinking, library/electronic research methods, computer utilization, and basic quantitative reasoning. The thematic content is American Pluralism: The Individual in a Diverse America. Sophomores take a yearlong course in the humanities. As juniors they are required to take 3 hours in Religious Dimensions of Human Existence, with a choice among three categories: Scripture, Catholic/Christian Thought, or Contemporary Religious Experience. The senior year includes a capstone course called Global Perspective. Students are also required to be proficient in a second language through the 201 level. There also is a distribution plan in the general education plan covering The Individual in a Global Community; Myth, Mind, Body, and Spirit; Natural World; Artistic and Creative Studies; and Quantitative Reasoning and Technology.

FINANCIAL AID

Aquinas College awards both merit-based financial assistance and traditional need-based assistance to qualified students. The Spectrum Scholarship Program was developed to recognize students' achievements in academics, leadership, and service. More than 90 percent of entering freshmen receive some form of financial assistance. The College administers the traditional grant and loan programs, including Federal Stafford Student Loans and Federal PLUS loans. Athletic grants are also available. The College participates in the Facts Tuition Management Plan. This plan assists students in paying costs over a period of time. To apply for financial assistance, students must complete the Free Application for Federal Student Aid (FAFSA).

THE ART INSTITUTE OF PHOENIX

■ **PHOENIX, ARIZONA**

THE INSTITUTE

The Art Institute of Phoenix (AiPX) was established in 1995. There are now more than 1,100 students who attend the school, seeking Bachelor of Arts (B.A.) and Associate of Applied Science (A.A.S.) degrees or diplomas. The Art Institute of Phoenix is an accredited degree-granting institution fulfilling the evolving needs of the marketplace in a variety of creative careers. At the Art Institute of Phoenix, students learn how to use program-specific technology to bring their creative dreams to life. When they graduate, they have the specialized skills and competencies employers need. Their degree puts them in demand today and prepares them for the future. The average class size is 19 students, and the faculty-student ratio is 1:19. The total undergraduate enrollment is 1,113. There are 713 men and 400 women enrolled, of whom 955 are full-time and 158 are part-time students.

For more information, students should contact:

The Art Institute of Phoenix
2233 West Dunlap Avenue
Phoenix, Arizona 85021
Telephone: 602-678-4300
          800-474-2479 (toll-free)
WWW: http://www.aipx.edu

ACADEMIC PROGRAMS

Programs at the Art Institute of Phoenix rely heavily on technology. When students are studying to prepare themselves for the workplace, they must become proficient in the tools of the workplace. At the Art Institute of Phoenix, those tools are provided. Each program of study has its own technology needs. The animation arts and design and media arts and animation programs rely heavily on PC-platform computers and software used to produce 3-D animation, 2-D ink-and-paint, digital paint, and compositing effects. The Institute's newest bachelor's degree program, digital media production, uses emerging technologies to create, develop, and deliver content. Knowing how to combine traditional production techniques with digital tools is the key to success. It is a career where creativity and technology come face to face with the future. Game art and design students use much of the same equipment as animation arts and design and media arts and animation, with additional tools that allow game prototyping and simulations. Graphic design students have access to MacIntoshes as well as PC platforms to produce camera-ready and final copies of design projects. Interior design students work with PC-based computers and high-quality software to produce their design plans and renderings. Multimedia and Web design students concentrate on designing and producing interactive disks that may be educational, commercial, or entertaining in nature. Video production and digital media production students have a full television studio and control room at their command along with editing suites to complete their work.

FINANCIAL AID

Financial assistance is available for those who qualify. The Art Institute of Phoenix participates in federal, state, and other financial aid programs. Financial aid is divided into three general categories: gift aid, loans, and work-study. Gift aid includes grants, scholarships, and other benefits that do not have to be repaid. Loans need to be repaid, but repayment can usually be delayed until several months after the student leaves school. The Art Institute of Phoenix participates in the Federal Work-Study Program and also assists students in finding part-time jobs in the community.

APPLICATION AND INFORMATION

To arrange an interview or obtain more information, prospective students should contact:

ATLANTA COLLEGE OF ART

■ ATLANTA, GEORGIA

THE COLLEGE

The Atlanta College of Art provides an educational environment for the career-minded student with a talent and passion for art or design. Founded in 1928, the College is an accredited institutional member of the National Association of Schools of Art and Design and the Commission on Colleges of the Southern Association of Colleges and Schools. Approximately 400 students from across the U.S. and from abroad compose a highly charged, creative community that nurtures the development of educated, effective, and successful professionals in the visual arts. The Atlanta College of Art is a founding member of the Woodruff Arts Center, the focus of the cultural life of the region. As the only art college in the United States that shares its campus with three other arts organizations—the High Museum of Art, the Alliance Theater, and the Atlanta Symphony Orchestra—the College is able to offer students access to a variety of art forms and resources on a working and thriving campus. Lombardy Hall provides on-campus housing for 120 students. The double-occupancy apartments are furnished, and each is equipped with an efficiency kitchen. The Student Affairs Office provides information about convenient apartment rentals to students who choose not to live in the residence hall. In addition, the Student Affairs Office provides career planning services and coordinates an internship program for students wishing to gain professional work experience to complement their academic and studio training. Recent internship sponsors have included American Museum of Papermaking, CNN Headline News, Coca-Cola, Georgia Pacific Corporation, IBM, Museum of Modern Art, Turner Publishing, and Zoo Atlanta.

> **For an application and more information, students should contact:**
>
> Vice President of Enrollment Management
> Atlanta College of Art
> Woodruff Arts Center
> 1280 Peachtree Street, NE
> Atlanta, Georgia 30309
>
> Telephone: 404-733-5100
> 800-832-2104 (toll-free)
> E-mail: acainfo@woodruffcenter.org
> WWW: http://www.aca.edu

ACADEMIC PROGRAM

Operating on a two-semester academic year with an optional concentrated summer session, the College requires that students complete 120 credit hours for the B.F.A. degree: 78 in studio (12 credits in visual studies, 12 credits in drawing, 30–36 credits in the major, and 18–24 credits in studio electives) and 42 in liberal arts (12 credits in art history, 18 credits in the humanities, 3 credits in natural science, 6 credits in social science, and 3 credits in math).

FINANCIAL AID

The Atlanta College of Art offers extensive financial assistance to students, combining institutional funds with funds from federal and state grant and loan programs. Each year, need-based grants, loans, and work-study jobs are awarded to students who apply for financial assistance using the Free Application of Federal Student Aid and the College's own financial aid form. While the priority deadline for applying for financial aid is March 15, awards are made on a first-come, first-served basis. The College also offers Merit Scholarships to both entering students and returning students. The Presidential Scholarship is awarded on the basis of the excellence of the portfolio and scholastic achievement. The School of Excellence award is given in recognition of the high quality of the student's high school or two-year college art program and the students' achievement in that program. The Dean's Scholarship is awarded on the basis of ACT or SAT I scores. Georgia residents are eligible for the Georgia Tuition Equalization Grant and the Hope Scholarship program.

APPLICATION AND INFORMATION

Students are admitted to the College on a rolling basis, and an admission decision is made as soon as the applicant file is complete. While there is no official deadline for submission of an application, students are encouraged to apply by March 1 for priority consideration for admission, financial aid, and scholarships.

BELMONT UNIVERSITY

■ NASHVILLE, TENNESSEE

THE UNIVERSITY

Nationally recognized programs thrive on the Belmont University campus, which is located in the heart of the state capital, known both as Music City, U.S.A., and the Athens of the South (for its many educational institutions). Nashville offers big-city advantages with small-town charm. Belmont's vision is to be a premier teaching university, bringing together the best of liberal arts and professional education in a Christian community of learning and service. Central to the fulfillment of that vision are faculty members who have a passion for teaching and the belief that premier teaching is interactive, technology-supported, motivational, creative, and exciting. With an enrollment of more than 3,000 students, Belmont is the third-largest of Tennessee's thirty-five colleges and universities. It is affiliated with the Tennessee Baptist Convention. In addition to seven baccalaureate degrees, Belmont University offers nine graduate degrees: the Master of Business Administration, the Master of Accountancy, the Master of English, the Master of Music, the Master of Music Education, the Master of Education, the Master of Science in Nursing, the Master of Science in Occupational Therapy, and the Doctorate in Physical Therapy.

Further information and application materials may be obtained by contacting:
Office of Admissions
Belmont University
1900 Belmont Boulevard
Nashville, Tennessee 37212
Telephone: 615-460-6785
　　　　　800-56ENROLL (toll-free)
Fax: 615-460-5434
E-mail:
　buadmission@mail.belmont.edu
WWW: http://www.belmont.edu

ACADEMIC PROGRAM

Uniquely positioned to provide the best of liberal arts and professional education, Belmont University offers celebrated professional programs structured to provide an academically well-rounded education. Belmont University operates on a two-semester schedule with classes beginning in late August and ending in early May. Two summer sessions are also offered. The academic program is arranged by school: the College of Arts and Sciences, the College of Business Administration, the College of Health Sciences, the College of Visual and Performing Arts, and the School of Religion. In addition to the degrees offered through the schools, Belmont University offers an honors program, which was created to provide an enrichment opportunity for students who have potential for superior academic performance and who seek added challenge and breadth to their studies. Students enrolled in the honors program are led in designing and working through a flexible, individual curriculum and interdisciplinary general education curriculum by a private tutor who is an honors faculty member. The University's advancements in undergraduate research are credited to a faculty committed to helping students practice their disciplines. The annual Belmont Undergraduate Research Symposium puts Belmont at the forefront of this national movement by providing a public forum for in-depth research at the undergraduate level.

FINANCIAL AID

The financial aid program at Belmont combines merit-based assistance with need-based assistance to make the University program affordable. Institutional merit awards range from full tuition Presidential Scholarships to performance scholarships. Also included are many levels of academic merit awards. Belmont University also administers traditional state and federal programs, including the Federal Pell Grant, Federal Stafford Student Loan, Federal Perkins Loan, Federal PLUS loan, and Tennessee Student Assistance Grants and Scholarships. Campus employment is available. Parents may arrange monthly tuition payments through an outside vendor. To apply for assistance, the student must complete the Free Application for Federal Student Aid (FAFSA).

BENEDICTINE UNIVERSITY

LISLE, ILLINOIS

THE UNIVERSITY

Benedictine University was founded in 1887 as St. Procopius College. One hundred fourteen years later, the University remains committed to providing a high-quality, Catholic, liberal education for men and women. The undergraduate enrollment is 2,000 students. The rate of acceptance of Benedictine University graduates to medical (85 percent), dental (100 percent), and professional schools is significantly above regional and national averages. The liberal arts curriculum has helped place the University among some of the finest small private schools in the nation. *U.S. News & World Report's* 2002 rankings listed Benedictine University as one of the top universities in the Midwest. The magazine also ranked the school one of the top ten in the region for campus diversity. Benedictine University is highly competitive in varsity sports. Men's varsity sports are baseball, basketball, cross-country, football, golf, soccer, swimming, and track. Women's varsity sports are basketball, cross-country, golf, soccer, softball, swimming, tennis, track, and volleyball.

> **For further information, students should contact:**
> Undergraduate Admissions
> Benedictine University
> 5700 College Road
> Lisle, Illinois 60532-0900
> Telephone: 630-829-6300
> 888-829-6363 (toll-free oustide Illinois)
> Fax: 630-829-6301
> E-mail: admissions@ben.edu
> WWW: http://www.ben.edu

ACADEMIC PROGRAM

For graduation, a student must earn at least 120 semester hours, at least 55 of which must be completed at a four-year regionally accredited college. At least the final 45 semester hours must be completed at Benedictine University. The University makes selective exceptions to the normal academic residency requirement of 45 semester hours for adults who are eligible for the Degree Completion Program. Eligibility is limited to those who have nearly completed their undergraduate studies but who, for reasons of employment, career change, or family situation, found it necessary to interrupt their studies. The Second Major Program is designed for people who already have a degree in one area and would like to gain expertise in another. This program allows the student to concentrate on courses that fulfill the requirements of a second major. The student receives a certificate upon completion. Each year, a select number of talented and motivated prospective students are invited to participate in the Scholars Program. The program is designed to enhance the college experience by developing students' international awareness and strengthening their leadership ability.

FINANCIAL AID

In 2001–02, Benedictine University freshmen received assistance totaling $2.9 million from sources that included loans, scholarships and grants, tuition remission, and employment opportunities. Nearly 80 percent of the freshman class participated, receiving an average package of $11,905. Benedictine University has dedicated more than $5 million of the annual budget to providing grants and scholarships to students and separate scholarship programs designed to attract and serve members of minority groups. Students who wish to apply for aid must complete the Free Application for Federal Student Aid (FAFSA), the Benedictine University application for financial aid, and the Benedictine University application for admission.

APPLICATION AND INFORMATION

Applications are reviewed on a rolling basis. Students are encouraged to apply for admission at any time after completing their junior year of high school. Transfer students may apply for admission during their last semester or quarter before anticipated transfer to Benedictine University. Earlier applications are encouraged for scholarship and financial aid opportunities.

BETHEL COLLEGE

■ ST. PAUL, MINNESOTA

THE COLLEGE
Bethel College began its four-year Christian liberal arts program in 1945 but traces its roots to Bethel Seminary, founded in 1871. Bethel is a ministry of the churches of the Baptist General Conference. The College encourages growth and learning in a distinctly Christian environment, continually striving to help students discover and develop the skills God has given them. Campus lifestyle expectations have been designed to build unity within diversity. All Bethel students, faculty, and staff members are expected to follow those expectations during their time as members of the Bethel community. Bethel's more than 3,000 students represent a wide range of national and international cultures and more than thirty denominations.

For more information, students should contact:
Office of Admissions
Bethel College
3900 Bethel Drive
St. Paul, Minnesota 55112
Telephone: 651-638-6242
800-255-8706 Ext. 6242 (toll-free)
Fax: 651-635-1490
E-mail: bcoll-admit@bethel.edu
WWW: http://www.bethel.edu

ACADEMIC PROGRAM
Bethel was named among the top Midwestern universities by *U.S. News & World Report* in 2001. Bethel's general education curriculum has become a model for many other liberal arts colleges nationwide. Students are required to take classes that will give them a broad view of the world and their role as Christians. General education classes are grouped around the following themes: Bible and theology, Western heritage, world citizenship, self-understanding, science and technology, and health and wholeness. In addition, in order to graduate, all Bethel students must demonstrate competence in mathematics, writing, speaking, and computing. Bethel College follows an early semester calendar consisting of two 15-week semesters and a three-week Interim in January. A full-time academic load for each semester is 12 to 18 credits. To graduate, a student must complete a minimum of 122 credits with a cumulative grade point average of at least 2.0 and a minimum 2.25 grade point average in his or her major. Also required are 50 credits of general education. Bethel awards advanced placement in recognition of learning that has been achieved apart from a college classroom situation. A maximum of 30 advanced placement credits can be applied toward a degree program. Students may also individualize their academic program through directed studies with faculty members and through academic internships with off-campus institutions.

FINANCIAL AID
Bethel College strives to make it financially possible for every qualified student to attend. Each year, more than 90 percent of the students receive some kind of financial aid, including scholarships, grants, loans, and assistance in the form of on-campus employment. Students who wish to be considered for financial aid must first be admitted to the College and then submit both the Free Application for Federal Student Aid and a Bethel College Financial Aid Application. Bethel's priority deadline is April 15 of each year. Students who have completed and mailed all necessary forms by this date receive first consideration.

APPLICATION AND INFORMATION
Students wishing to apply for admission to Bethel must send the following: a completed Bethel application form with a $25 nonrefundable application fee; test scores from the PSAT, SAT I, or ACT; transcripts of all course work completed at the high school and college levels; and references from a pastor and an adult friend or employer. Students considering Bethel should apply in the fall of their senior year. The Office of Admissions reviews applications twice each year. Early action decisions are made for students who complete applications by December 1. Bethel's final application decision date is March 1. Applications received or completed after March 1 are considered on a space-available basis.

BOWIE STATE UNIVERSITY

■ BOWIE, MARYLAND

THE UNIVERSITY

Bowie State University began as a normal school in the city of Baltimore in 1865, and it has evolved over the years into a four-year, coeducational, liberal arts institution. It is currently situated on a beautiful 312-acre campus in Prince Georges County, Maryland, and offers both graduate and undergraduate programs of study. Its physical plant is valued at more than $37 million, and its current enrollment is 4,700 students, 1,591 of whom are in the Graduate School. The University has twenty-one buildings on campus with the addition of the new $21-million state-of-the-art Center for Learning and Technology (opened in fall 2000). Two of the buildings (the Communication Arts Center and the physical education complex) were completed in 1973, and an administration building opened in 1977. Five residence halls, including Goodloe Hall, the honors students' residence, and Alex Haley Hall, the new (completed in 1994) state-of-the-art residence hall, house approximately 800 students. The $2.6-million physical education complex houses a 3,000-seat basketball arena, an Olympic-size swimming pool with underwater viewing windows and facilities for 200 spectators, an apparatus gymnasium, a dance studio, a wrestling room, a weight-training room, eight handball/squash courts, a therapy room, and offices for instructors and coaches.

For more information, students should contact:
Office of Enrollment, Recruitment and Registration
Bowie State University
Bowie, Maryland 20715-9465
Telephone: 301-860-3422 or 3423
 410-880-4100 Ext. 3422
 or 3423 (from the
 Baltimore-Columbia
 area)
 877-77-BOWIE (toll-free)
Fax: 301-860-3518
E-mail: admissions@bowiestate.edu
WWW: http://www.bowiestate.edu

ACADEMIC PROGRAM

The University operates on a semester calendar. Academic offerings can be divided into four main areas: humanities, science and mathematics, social sciences, and education. To receive a bachelor's degree, a student must earn a minimum of 120 semester hours with a cumulative grade point average of 2.0 or better. Students are provided the opportunity to complete the General Education Program, acquire lifelong learning skills for a competitive world, and make a successful transition into their junior year. General studies requirements include communication skills, 9 hours; humanities, 9 hours; social sciences, 18 hours; science and mathematics, 9 hours; and physical education, 2 hours. The remaining credit hours can be electives or from major and minor areas of interest.

FINANCIAL AID

Federal Pell Grants, Supplemental Grants, Work-Study, Perkins Loans, and Direct Loans are available. University scholarships, tuition waivers, and diversity grants are awarded. Most awards are based on need. Merit scholarships could be offered to students with cumulative grade point averages of at least 3.0 and minimum SAT I scores of 1100. More than 65 percent of all undergraduate students receive some form of financial aid. Scholarships and assistantships are offered through the Model Institutions for Excellence Program for Science, Engineering, and Mathematics. Deadlines are April 1 for the fall semester and November 15 for the spring semester.

BREVARD COLLEGE

■ BREVARD, NORTH CAROLINA

THE COLLEGE
Founded in 1853, Brevard is a church-related, coeducational liberal arts college that offers innovative four-year and two-year curriculums, with specialties in music, art, environmental studies, wilderness leadership, and other interdisciplinary majors, on a beautiful mountain campus near Asheville, North Carolina. The College's low student-faculty ratio of 10:1, a covenant that binds faculty members and students in a nurturing community of learning, rich cultural offerings, numerous opportunities for student leadership, nationally competitive athletic programs, and incomparable access to national parks, forest, wilderness areas, and white-water recreational rivers make Brevard distinctive. [F65]Inspired by its setting among the world's oldest mountains and founded upon the principles of the Christian faith, Brevard College has the purpose of educating students in the tradition of the liberal arts and in the spirit of love and service. The College's faculty and staff, academic and cocurricular programs, financial resources, and support services are devoted to providing an educational climate that fosters respect for learning and beauty, creativity and hard work, tolerance and personal integrity, intellect and love of knowledge, and vigorous activity and spiritual reflection.

For more information, students should contact:
Director of Admissions
Brevard College
400 North Broad Street
Brevard, North Carolina 28712
Telephone: 828-884-8300
             800-527-9090 (toll-free)
Fax: 828-884-3790
E-mail: admissions@brevard.edu
WWW: http://www.brevard.edu

ACADEMIC PROGRAM
Consistent with the philosophy of the College, various courses at Brevard College use service as a learning component to enhance the classroom environment. Coordination of the student's service experience is performed by the Center for Service Learning, which works with students to prepare transcripts detailing their cocurricular accomplishments.

FINANCIAL AID
Opportunities for student financial aid are available to every student who can show financial need, superior academic achievement, or talent in athletics, art, drama, or music. All students desiring financial aid must submit the Free Application for Federal Student Aid (FAFSA). The College annually awards more than $200,000 in merit scholarships to select students who display academic excellence, unselfish character, and leadership potential as Brevard Scholars. These students participate in a variety of enriched intellectual, cultural, and leadership programs and work closely with distinguished professors who serve both as advisers and program directors. The Angier B. Duke Scholarships, awarded only by Brevard College and Duke University, are the premier scholarships among more than forty Brevard Scholars Awards made each year.

APPLICATION AND INFORMATION
Students must submit an application for admission, a recommendation from the guidance counselor on the form provided by the Office of Admissions, official SAT I or ACT scores, and an official high school transcript. Students are advised of the admission decision as soon as all required application materials are received. In addition, Brevard College requires a medical history and a physical examination of each applicant prior to enrollment to the College.

CALIFORNIA COLLEGE OF ARTS AND CRAFTS

■ OAKLAND AND SAN FRANCISCO, CALIFORNIA

THE COLLEGE
The California College of Arts and Crafts (CCAC) was founded in 1907 with a new approach to art education—to offer training in a wide range of disciplines, creating a spirit of collaboration between artists, craftspeople, and designers. In the ensuing years, the College has expanded its commitment by offering an interdisciplinary curriculum that educates students in the full range of fine arts, architecture, and design studies in the context of a small, private four-year college. Today, CCAC's undergraduate enrollment is about 1,300 men and women.

For more information, students should contact:
Office of Enrollment Services
California College of Arts and Crafts
1111 Eighth Street
San Francisco, California 94107-2247
Telephone: 800-447-1ART (toll-free)
WWW: http://www.ccac-art.edu

ACADEMIC PROGRAM
The Bachelor of Fine Arts requires the completion of a minimum of 126 semester units, of which 75 must be in studio work and 51 must be in humanities and sciences. Undergraduates at CCAC begin in a foundation—or core—program. Here, they begin mastering technical problem-solving and critical skills while being exposed to a variety of media, processes, principles, and imaginative strategies. Core courses are also offered in writing, literature, and art history. Students may also choose to enroll in a class with a community service component. Students select a major after completing this program. A diversified program of arts and humanities reflects CCAC's philosophy that a professional art education occurs in the context of the education of the whole person.

FINANCIAL AID
Scholarships, grants, loans, and work-study awards are available for students on the basis of merit and financial need. Students applying for aid in 2002–03 should submit the Free Application for Federal Student Aid (FAFSA) to the Federal Student Aid Processing Agency by March 1 for priority consideration. CCAC continues to fund students after the priority deadline as long as funds remain available. Applications for Federal Pell Grants and Federal Direct Student Loans may be submitted throughout the school year. CCAC is approved for veterans attending under the Veterans Administration Educational Benefits Program. Approximately 70 percent of students attending CCAC during the 2001–02 year received some type of financial aid. CCAC also offers an extended interest-free payment plan.

APPLICATION AND INFORMATION
Individuals interested in applying for CCAC's merit scholarships should complete their applications by February 15. CCAC's priority deadline for all fall semester applications is March 1. The priority deadline for spring applicants is October 1. Students meeting these deadlines will have priority consideration regarding admission, housing, and financial aid. CCAC reviews undergraduate applications on a rolling admission basis; that is, applications are reviewed in the order in which they are received, and students are accepted and awarded financial aid after the priority dates. The application fee is $40. Persons who wish to take one or more individual courses may register as nondegree students on a space-available basis and receive College credit for courses completed.

CALIFORNIA STATE POLYTECHNIC UNIVERSITY, POMONA

■ POMONA, CALIFORNIA

THE UNIVERSITY

California State Polytechnic University, Pomona (Cal Poly Pomona) is located on the eastern edge of Southern California's San Gabriel Valley. Its 1400-acre campus, featuring lush rolling hills, was once the winter ranch of cereal magnate W.K. Kellogg. While the land and its contents were donated to the state in 1949, Kellogg's hilltop home and award-winning Arabian horses remain as lasting reminders of the university's heritage. As one of a few polytechnical universities in the nation, Cal Poly Pomona's mission is to advance learning and knowledge by linking theory and practice and integrating technology, while preparing students for lifelong learning, leadership, and careers. Its learn-by-doing, polytechnic philosophy has created a reputation of producing individuals who make an immediate impact. This is the reason Cal Poly Pomona graduates are among the most sought-after in today's marketplace.

For more information, students should contact:
Office of Admissions & Outreach
Cal Poly Pomona
3801 West Temple Avenue
Pomona, California 91768
Telephone: 909-869-3210

ACADEMIC PROGRAM

Classes are offered in four 11-week quarters. Candidates for Bachelor of Arts degrees must earn at least 186 quarter units. The Bachelor of Science degree requires at least 198 quarter units. A graduation writing requirement exists for all baccalaureate degrees. Currently, Architecture, Computer Information Systems, and Computer Science are open to California residents only. Cal Poly Pomona offers Air Force and Army Reserve Officers' Training Corps, a California Pre-Doctoral Program, an Educational Opportunity Program, a Teacher Aide Path to Teaching, University Equity Programs, and other special programs. The University features special centers and institutes, such as the innovative Lyle Center for Regenerative Studies, the Apparel Technology and Research Center, the Center for Turf, Irrigation and Landscape Technology, the Equine Research Center, the Ocean Studies Institute, and the Institute for Cellular and Molecular Biology, to name a few.

FINANCIAL AID

The University administers extensive financial aid programs, and each year more than 49 percent of Cal Poly Pomona students receive more than $51 million in financial aid. Applications for academic and merit scholarships must be completed by March 2. Applications for financial aid should be completed as early as possible after January 1 and no later than March 2 for the following academic year. Applicants should contact the financial aid office for information and application material.

APPLICATION AND INFORMATION

Applications are accepted for the following fall on October 1 of the preceding year. Undergraduate deadlines for fall, winter, spring, and summer quarters are April 1, September 1, November 15, and March 1, respectively. The application fee is $55, but waivers may be granted. Applications may be requested from California high schools, community colleges, or CSU campuses by contacting the Office of Admissions & Outreach; however, the University encourages students to apply online at http://www.csumentor.edu. Prospective students are also encouraged to fill out an online request card at http://www.csupomona.edu/~enroll/admissions/contact. Students can access Cal Poly Pomona's home page at http://www.csupomona.edu.

CALVIN COLLEGE

■ GRAND RAPIDS, MICHIGAN

THE COLLEGE

Calvin College is an institution that values both intellect and faith; this view affects every area of campus life from the content of each course to volunteer service and life in the residence halls. Calvin is one of the nation's largest and most respected evangelical Christian colleges. The 2001 fall enrollment was 4,267. Calvin maintains a strong affiliation with the Christian Reformed Church, and students from more than fifty other church denominations across North America and the world choose Calvin for its extensive curriculum and Christ-centered mission.

> **For more information about Calvin or about visiting the campus, students should contact:**
> Admissions Office
> Calvin College
> 3201 Burton Street, SE
> Grand Rapids, Michigan 49546
> Telephone: 800-688-0122 (toll-free in North America)
> Fax: 616-957-6777
> E-mail: admissions@calvin.edu
> WWW: http://www.calvin.edu

ACADEMIC PROGRAM

Calvin College maintains a strong commitment to a liberal arts curriculum as an integral avenue to help students understand God's world and their place in it. The College follows a 4-1-4 academic calendar, consisting of two 4-month semesters with a three-week Interim term during January. Typically, students take four or five courses each semester and one course during the Interim. Graduation requires the successful completion of 124 semester hours. Calvin's core curriculum begins with a first-year gateway course, Developing a Christian Mind, and ends with a capstone course in the senior year. Core curriculum requirements include foreign language, history, literature and arts, mathematics, natural sciences, philosophy, physical education, religion, social sciences, and written and spoken rhetoric. Some requirements can be satisfied by advanced high school work in foreign language, literature, and natural sciences. Qualified students can earn course exemption and/or credit by completing college-level work in high school or by examination. Satisfactory scores on Advanced Placement (AP), International Baccalaureate (I.B.), and/or CLEP exams are also accepted. Students with a cumulative grade point average of 3.3 or higher can apply to the Honors Program for advanced-level courses, interdisciplinary courses, and cocurricular opportunities. Students can also benefit from services offered by the Office of Student Academic Services, which provides academic counseling, tutoring, training in study skills, and review courses in key subjects.

FINANCIAL AID

Sixty percent of Calvin students receive need-based financial aid; demonstrated need is the most important criterion in determining eligibility. Students wishing to be considered for financial aid must be admitted to the College and must submit the Free Application for Federal Student Aid (FAFSA) and Calvin's Supplemental Application for Financial Aid. February 15 is the suggested filing deadline for maximum consideration. Financial awards to eligible applicants consist of state and federal grants, loans, Federal Work-Study funds, and institutional grants and scholarships. Part-time employment is available on campus, and placement preference is given to needy students. Calvin also helps students find off-campus employment and runs a job transportation service that drives them to and from their jobs for a fee.

APPLICATION AND INFORMATION

Applicants must submit a completed application form, a high school or college transcript, results of either the ACT or SAT I, and an educational recommendation completed by a teacher or counselor. Admission decisions are made on a rolling basis beginning in mid-October. Applicants for fall admission are urged to complete their file before February 1, although there is no deadline as long as space remains in the entering class. Campus visits are strongly recommended, although not required. Students and parents are welcome to visit at any time that is convenient for them. The "Fridays at Calvin" campus visit program also provides an excellent opportunity to experience life at Calvin firsthand.

CAMPBELL UNIVERSITY

■ BUIES CREEK, NORTH CAROLINA

THE UNIVERSITY

Founded in 1887, Campbell University has had the distinction of being North Carolina's second-largest private undergraduate institution. Graduate programs were established, and in 1979 the name of the institution was changed from Campbell College to Campbell University. Its current enrollment is more than 7,800 students. In an average year, the student body comes from about ninety North Carolina counties, fifty states, and forty-six countries. The University also has campuses offering a variety of undergraduate and graduate courses at Fort Bragg, Raleigh, Rocky Mount, Jacksonville, and Morrisville, North Carolina, and in Kuala Lumpur, Malaysia.

For more information, students should contact:
Office of Admissions
Campbell University
P.O. Box 546
Buies Creek, North Carolina 27506
Telephone: 910-893-1320
　　　　　　910-893-1415
　　　　　　(international)
　　　　　　800-334-4111 (toll-free)
E-mail: adm@mailcenter.campbell.edu
WWW: http://www.campbell.edu/

ACADEMIC PROGRAM

The curriculum of Campbell University is designed to meet individual needs and interests. During the first two years, students follow a general course of study, the General College Curriculum, to broaden their backgrounds in the basic fields of knowledge. By the end of the sophomore year, they should have selected a major subject for specialized study during the final two years. Basic curriculum requirements for the first two years in semester hours are English, 12; social studies, 6; natural science, 8; religion, 6; music, art appreciation, or drama, 3; foreign language, up to 9, depending on high school credits and the program of study; and health and physical education, 3. Candidates for a bachelor's degree must earn a minimum of 128 credits, including the 3 in health and physical education, while maintaining at least a C average in academic course work; must complete a minimum of 32 semester hours in the departmental major at Campbell; and must average C or better in all courses required for the major. Candidates for the Associate in Arts degree must complete 64 semester hours of work and have at least a 2.0 GPA on all work required for graduation and at least a 2.0 GPA on 80 percent of all work attempted. The Fort Bragg campus is primarily a service for military personnel on active duty, but classes are open to civilian students. Campbell offers the nation's first undergraduate program in trust management and since 1968 has been training prospective trust officers for the banks and trust companies of the region. Campbell also sponsors the Southeastern Trust School, a summer institute for trust officers. Academic programs continue to expand at Campbell University. The charter class entered Campbell's School of Pharmacy in 1986. The school helps serve the health-care needs of North Carolina and beyond. Campbell's School of Education was formally established in 1985 in response to the need for fully qualified educators for the educational system of North Carolina and the country. The University licensure passage rate for 2000 was 99 percent. The Military Science Department offers Army ROTC programs for men and women, leading to commissions as officers in the active Army, Army Reserve, or Army National Guard. In 1989 the Campbell ROTC won the Founder's Award and the Governor's Award as the best detachment in ROTC Region I. In 1999, the unit was rated as the "Best ROTC in the Country." In 1995, an Army ROTC Campbell graduate received the Hughes Trophy.

FINANCIAL AID

Campbell University has private and institutional scholarships, federal grants, loans, and Federal Work-Study Program awards. Loans are available through the Federal Stafford Student Loan Program and the Federal Perkins Loan Program. Needs analysis forms (Free Application for Federal Student Aid) are available January 1 and are due in the Financial Aid Office by March 15 if the applicant wishes to be considered for a maximum award. Ninety-one percent of the student body received financial assistance in 2000–01. All assistance is offered without regard to race, creed, or national origin.

THE CATHOLIC UNIVERSITY OF AMERICA

■ WASHINGTON, D.C.

THE UNIVERSITY
The Catholic University of America (CUA) offers an outstanding collegiate experience, with challenging undergraduate programs based in the liberal arts. CUA is the national university of the Catholic Church and the only higher education institution established by the U.S. Catholic bishops. Founded as a graduate institution more than a century ago, CUA introduced undergraduate education in 1904. The University today serves 5,600 students, including 2,400 undergraduates, from all fifty states and more than 100 other countries. Students from all religious traditions are welcome.

For more information, students should contact:
Director of Admissions
The Catholic University of America
Washington, D.C. 20064
Telephone: 202-319-5305
            800-673-2772 (toll-free)
Fax: 202-319-6533
E-mail: cua-admissions@cua.edu
WWW: http://www.cua.edu

ACADEMIC PROGRAM
Engineering, nursing, music, and architecture students follow study courses that provide professional training integrated with a broad range of academic disciplines. Students in the School of Arts and Sciences undertake a major course of study within a liberal arts curriculum that encompasses the humanities, languages and literature, philosophy, the social sciences, mathematics and natural sciences, and religion. Most majors require the satisfactory completion of forty courses that are 3 credits each for graduation. Certain majors under the Bachelor of Science degree may require additional credits. In addition to the major, students may complete a minor course sequence by utilizing the elective courses included in the undergraduate program. CUA maintains small undergraduate classes, even for introductory courses. Faculty members who teach graduate students also teach undergraduates, enabling freshmen to engage in dialogues with teachers and scholars. CUA offers outstanding academic research and library facilities and exposure to graduate and professional-level programs. Also provided is a University-wide honors program for outstanding undergraduates who seek intense intellectual challenges. The program draws from traditional liberal arts disciplines and professional curricula to offer comprehensive academic experiences.

FINANCIAL AID
CUA administers two separate and distinct financial assistance programs: merit scholarships and need-based financial aid. A number of scholarships, awarded on the basis of academic achievement in secondary school, are available. The University offers financial aid to students based on need as demonstrated by the Free Application for Federal Student Aid (FAFSA) and the Institutional Aid Form, which can be found in the CUA admissions application. Loans, work-study, and University grants are available. Candidates who complete the admission application process before February 15 of their senior year of secondary school are considered for academic scholarships and receive priority for financial aid. Candidates apply for financial aid at the same time they apply for admission. CUA has a need-blind admissions policy and makes admission decisions without regard to financial aid status.

APPLICATION AND INFORMATION
Applicants for the Early Decision Program must apply by November 15 or December 15 and will be notified by December 20 or January 25, respectively. Regular decisions will be made shortly after the February 15 deadline. Candidates for freshman admission must submit CUA's secondary school report, high school transcripts, scores on the SAT I or ACT, and a $55 application fee. CUA accepts transfer applicants each semester. Transfer candidates should request applications for transfer admission from the Office of Admissions and Financial Aid. In addition to the high school records and SAT I or ACT scores, transfer students must furnish transcripts from the school the students are attending (a minimum 2.8 GPA is recommended). Transfer applicants are notified of their status on a rolling basis and at least one month prior to the opening of the semester for which they are applying for admission. Financial aid is awarded on the same basis as for freshman students.

CEDAR CREST COLLEGE

■ ALLENTOWN, PENNSYLVANIA

THE COLLEGE
Since its founding in 1867 as an independent liberal arts college for women, Cedar Crest has educated women for leadership in a changing world. Of the approximately 1,700 students who come to the College annually from twenty-six states and twenty other countries. The 11:1 student-faculty ratio provides for small classes, individual advising, and independent work in an environment that emphasizes interdisciplinary, values-oriented education. The Honor Philosophy is the most compelling statement of each student's rights and responsibilities for her own academic and cocurricular performance. Cedar Crest's health science programs, including environmental science, forensic science, genetic engineering, neuroscience, nuclear medicine, nursing, and nutrition, generate the largest student enrollment. Business, communications, psychology, and education generate the next largest enrollments.

> **For more information, students should contact:**
>
> Vice President for Enrollment
> Cedar Crest College
> 100 College Drive
> Allentown, Pennsylvania 18104-6196
> Telephone: 800-360-1222 (toll-free)
> Fax: 610-606-4647
> E-mail: cccadmis@cedarcrest.edu
> WWW: http://www.cedarcrest.edu

ACADEMIC PROGRAM
Self-designed majors, double majors, minors, independent study programs, and individual and group research projects support serious concentration at the undergraduate level. Working with her adviser, each student designs a program of study that meets the 120-credit College (nursing: 126 credits) and major requirements as well as her personal interests and professional goals.

FINANCIAL AID
Cedar Crest offers a generous program of financial aid based on academic achievement and financial need, including scholarships, grants, loans, and employment. Federal funds available are Federal Pell Grants, Federal Supplemental Educational Opportunity Grants, Federal Perkins Loans, Federal Work-Study Program awards, and Nursing Student Loans. The size of an award varies with need. More than 80 percent of the students at Cedar Crest receive aid. Students applying for financial aid should file the Free Application for Federal Student Aid (FAFSA). Outstanding international students may also qualify for financial aid. Applicants who rank in the top 20 percent of their class and score 1150 or higher on the SAT I (24 on the ACT) can qualify for a scholarship of up to one-half tuition per year. Sibling grants are awarded to students when 2 siblings are attending Cedar Crest full-time, concurrently. Recipients of Girl Scout Gold awards, graduates of Governor's School of Excellence programs, and HOBY alumnae are also eligible for scholarship recognition. Trustee Scholarships of full tuition for senior year are awarded to students with a Dean's List cumulative GPA of 3.55 at the end of their junior year at Cedar Crest. Students must be enrolled full time at Cedar Crest for three years prior to receiving this full tuition scholarship, net federal and state grants. Students can receive an early estimate of aid eligibility by completing a Cedar Crest financial aid application/planner.

APPLICATION AND INFORMATION
Students need to submit the application form, an official transcript of the secondary school record, examination results from the SAT I or ACT, and a personal essay. Cedar Crest has a rolling admission policy; applications are reviewed on a continuing basis. Students are encouraged to apply early in their senior year of high school. Admission is awarded for the fall or spring semester. Transfer students applying to Cedar Crest must fulfill all of the requirements stated above. They must also submit official transcripts and a catalog from each college previously attended. International students must complete the international student application form; students educated in non-English-speaking countries must also submit TOEFL examination scores.

CHADRON STATE COLLEGE

■ CHADRON, NEBRASKA

THE COLLEGE
Chadron State College challenges and prepares students to realize academic, personal, and professional success. These successes are developed through experiences in activities on and off campus. Founded in 1911 as Nebraska State Normal School, Chadron State has a proven record of graduates who excel. Chadron State College has six spacious residence halls, a physical activity center with an indoor track, three versatile basketball/tennis/volleyball courts, a weight-training room, five racquetball courts, and specialized classrooms for dance and gymnastics. Chadron State also has a student center, a beautiful fine arts building with two theaters, an educational technology and distance learning center, a three-story library, and a media center. Sixty-nine campus clubs and organizations, numerous intramural leagues, and ten intercollegiate NCAA Division II athletic teams offer opportunities for involvement and entertainment.

For more information, students should contact:
Ms. Tena Cook Gould
Director of Admissions
Chadron State College
1000 Main Street
Chadron, Nebraska 69337-2690
Telephone: 308-432-6263
          800-242-3766 (toll-free)
Fax: 308-432-6229
E-mail: inquire@csc.edu
WWW: http://www.csc.edu

ACADEMIC PROGRAM
Chadron State College has an academic year divided into fall, spring, and summer semesters. Students seeking a baccalaureate degree from Chadron State College must complete the requirements for the program in addition to the general studies requirements. Bachelor of Arts and Bachelor of Science in education degrees are granted upon completion of a minimum total of 125 semester hours—45 of which must be at the 300 or 400 (junior or senior) level. A grade point average of 2.0 (on a 4.0 scale) must be maintained for the Bachelor of Arts programs, and a 2.5 GPA must be maintained for the Bachelor of Science in education programs.

FINANCIAL AID
Students seeking financial aid must complete the application for admission to Chadron State College and submit the $15 required application fee. Undergraduate students should file the Free Application for Federal Student Aid (FAFSA). After receiving the results from the processor, students should forward them to the College Director of Financial Aid. Undergraduate applications for financial assistance provide consideration for the Federal Pell Grant, Federal Work-Study, Federal Perkins Loan, Federal Supplemental Educational Opportunity Grant, Federal PLUS, and Federal Family Education Loan Programs as well as the State Scholarship Award Program and Student Assistance Program. A monthly payment plan is available through the Business Office. CSC provides electronic FAFSA processing.

APPLICATION AND INFORMATION
The freshman applicant should submit a completed application for admission; a $15 application fee; an official high school transcript reflecting a graduation date, class rank, and overall grade point average; and an official ACT or SAT I score report sent from the testing headquarters. The ACT/SAT I is not required for students who graduated from high school five or more years prior to enrollment at Chadron State. All students must show a physician-validated immunization record. The transfer applicant should submit a completed application for admission, a $15 application fee, a physician-validated immunization record, and official transcripts from all colleges or universities previously attended. If the student has completed fewer than 12 semester hours of credit, he or she must also submit an official high school transcript and ACT or SAT I scores. Application forms, financial aid forms, and other information are mailed upon request. Campus visits are encouraged.

CHAMINADE UNIVERSITY OF HONOLULU

■ **HONOLULU, HAWAII**

THE UNIVERSITY
Chaminade University of Honolulu, a private, coeducational institution, was established in 1955 by the Society of Mary (Marianists). Named after Father William Joseph Chaminade, a French Catholic priest who ministered to his people during the late eighteenth and early nineteenth centuries and who founded the Society in 1817, the University today continues the Marianist mission of educating leaders through faith and reason. To achieve this mission, Chaminade forms a community encompassing people from diverse cultural origins, both traditional and nontraditional, who hold a variety of religious beliefs.

For more information, students should contact:
Admission Office
Chaminade University
3140 Waialae Avenue
Honolulu, Hawaii 96816
Telephone: 808-735-4735
          800-735-3733 (toll-free)
Fax: 808-739-4647
E-mail: admissions@chaminade.edu
WWW: http://www.chaminade.edu

ACADEMIC PROGRAM
The core curriculum at Chaminade is in liberal arts. The University is committed to a broad liberal education for its students and believes that such an education provides a basis for long-term personal growth, a foundation for a career that may encounter job changes, and a background that allows students to rise to leadership positions in their chosen fields and communities. Through undergraduate programs based on the liberal arts tradition, Chaminade seeks to heighten cultural awareness. Coupled with understanding diverse methods of inquiry and participation in Chaminade's multicultural interdependent community, cultural awareness prepares all students for lifelong learning—about themselves, each other, and the world in which they live.

FINANCIAL AID
Those with a high school GPA between 3.5 and 4.0 are eligible for a $5000 yearly scholarship; between 3.0 and 3.49, a $4500 yearly scholarship; between 2.5 and 2.99, a $3500 yearly grant; and between 2.25 to 2.49, a $3000 yearly grant. The Hawaii Grant for new full-time day session students from Hawaii is $1500 per semester. Scholarships and grants, available to regular full-time undergraduate students, are renewable for four years and are awarded without regard to financial need. Students may obtain only one of the Chaminade scholarships or grants. A tuition discount of 20 percent is offered to additional family members when one member of the family is paying full-time tuition.

APPLICATION AND INFORMATION
Chaminade University has a rolling admission process. As soon as all required information is received by the Admission Office, the application is reviewed by an application committee. Students are notified of the committee's decision usually within three to four weeks. Applications are accepted throughout the year. A $50 fee is payable upon application. Web site applications are also available for a $25 fee. All students desiring housing must file an application along with a $300 deposit applicable to the total cost per semester. Space and placement are not guaranteed without this deposit. A housing damage deposit of $100 is also required. Evidence of health insurance coverage from a U.S. insurer is required of all dormitory residents and international students. To ensure full consideration for scholarships or grants, students are urged to complete the appropriate application by April 1.

CHESTNUT HILL COLLEGE

■ **PHILADELPHIA, PENNSYLVANIA**

THE COLLEGE

Chestnut Hill College (CHC) is a four-year Catholic liberal arts college. Founded in 1924 by the Sisters of St. Joseph, it is situated on a 45-acre campus overlooking Wissahickon Creek. Students come from fifteen states, thirteen countries, and many cultural heritages. In fall 2003, Chestnut Hill becomes fully coeducational with its first full-time admission of men to the College. Working adults are enrolled in the accelerated evening and weekend undergraduate program. In addition to its undergraduate degrees, Chestnut Hill awards the M.Ed., M.A., and M.S. in six fields, including education, counseling psychology and human services, holistic spirituality, holistic spirituality and health care, applied technology, and administration of human services as well as a doctoral degree in clinical psychology (Psy.D.). When it comes to student activities, students enthusiastically engage in the many clubs and organizations available and participate in everything from aerobics and horseback riding to golf and archery. The College is NCAA Division III and competes in basketball, field hockey, lacrosse, softball, tennis, and volleyball. Soccer will be added in fall 2003. A swimming pool, a gymnasium, a hockey field, a fitness room, and eight tennis courts provide excellent athletic facilities for Chestnut Hill's students.

For more information, students should contact:

Director of Admissions
Chestnut Hill College
9601 Germantown Avenue
Philadelphia, Pennsylvania 19118-2695
Telephone: 215-248-7001
           800-248-0052 (toll-free)
E-mail: chcapply@chc.edu
WWW: http://www.chc.edu

ACADEMIC PROGRAM

The academic year consists of two 15-week semesters. There are also two 6-week summer sessions. As a liberal arts college, CHC offers courses of study that provide the student with a broad background in the fine arts and humanities, a knowledge of science, and a keen awareness of the social problems of the day, as well as intensive, in-depth study in a major field. CHC confers a B.S. or B.A. degree to students who earn 120 semester hours of credit and satisfy specific requirements set by the faculty. Distribution requirements are as follows: 11 semester hours in natural sciences (8 hours of which must be in a laboratory science), 9 semester hours in social sciences, and 21 semester hours in the humanities. In addition to these 41 hours of credit, every student must take 6 semester hours of religious studies, 6 hours beyond the elementary level in a classical or modern foreign language, and 3 hours in a writing course (unless exempted by the English department). As many as 45 of the 120 semester hours may be within the major area. A student with the ability and proper motivation may be permitted to major in two departments.

FINANCIAL AID

Financial aid is available in the form of academic scholarships, guaranteed loans, work-study programs, federal grants, and Chestnut Hill College grants. Most of these are based on financial need and are awarded in financial aid packages that combine various forms of aid and are tailored to each student's need. More than 75 percent of CHC students receive financial aid to meet College costs. All applicants for aid should file a copy of the Free Application for Federal Student Aid (FAFSA). Merit-based scholarships and awards are granted for academic achievement.

CLAREMONT MCKENNA COLLEGE

CLAREMONT, CALIFORNIA

THE COLLEGE

Founded in 1946 as the third undergraduate college in the cluster of the Claremont Colleges, Claremont McKenna College (CMC) occupies a unique place among American colleges. Through a grounding in the traditional liberal arts, CMC's purpose is to educate future leaders in business, the professions, and public affairs. Economics, government, and international relations are the most popular among twenty-three majors offered at CMC. The College is especially appropriate for students seeking to pursue careers in law, politics, government, international relations, business, management, and finance. Claremont McKenna College is one of seven institutions—five undergraduate colleges and two graduate schools—that constitute the Claremont Colleges. The others are Harvey Mudd College, Pitzer College, Pomona College, Scripps College, the Claremont Graduate University, and Keck Graduate Institute of Applied Life Sciences. The current undergraduate enrollment at CMC is 1,044 (558 men and 486 women).

> **Further information is available from:**
> Richard C. Vos, Vice President and Dean of Admission and Financial Aid
> Claremont McKenna College
> 890 Columbia Avenue
> Claremont, California 91711-6425
> Telephone: 909-621-8088
> E-mail: admission@claremontmckenna.edu
> WWW: http://www.claremontmckenna.edu

ACADEMIC PROGRAM

Students must satisfactorily complete thirty-two semester courses, including general education and major requirements, in order to graduate. General education requirements include one course in mathematics, one course in English composition and analysis, two courses in the natural sciences, two courses in the humanities, three courses in the social sciences, and a senior thesis. In addition, students must complete a third semester of a foreign language and a Questions of Civilization course. Depending on the department, credit or advanced placement, or both, may be granted for college courses taken while in high school. Also, CMC may grant credit for scores of 4 or 5 on Advanced Placement (AP) examinations and for scores of 6 or 7 on higher level International Baccalaureate (I.B.) examinations. CMC sponsors a joint science program with two other Claremont Colleges, Pitzer and Scripps. The Keck Science Center houses modern laboratories for teaching and research, and a large biological field station is located adjacent to the campus.

FINANCIAL AID

Financial aid is awarded in the form of grants (nonrepayable gift aid), student loans, and part-time employment. Grants range from $1000 to $29,000 per year and average $18,050; loans for entering freshmen average $3000 per year. The total amount of aid a student is awarded is based on need. The College offers approximately thirty McKenna Achievement Awards to members of each entering freshman class. These awards are valued at $5000 each and are renewable for each of the four years, provided the student earns at least a B average. To be considered for one of these awards, a student usually must rank among the top 5 percent in his or her high school class and earn a score of more than 680 on both the mathematical and verbal portions of the SAT I. Candidates must also have excellent school recommendations and strong extracurricular involvement, including leadership, and must have filed a completed application by December 20.

APPLICATION AND INFORMATION

Application materials must be received by November 15 or January 2 from applicants seeking early decision, November 1 for midyear entrance, and January 2 for those seeking entrance in the fall.

CLARKSON COLLEGE

■ OMAHA, NEBRASKA

THE COLLEGE

Clarkson College is a regionally accredited private institution, with exceptional programs in nursing, radiologic technology, medical imaging, occupational therapy assistant and physical therapist assistant studies, patient information management, and health-related business. The College offers the personal qualities of a small institution and the technological advantages found within a larger educational environment. Founded in 1888, it was the first school of nursing in Nebraska and the thirty-fifth in the nation and was approved to grant academic degrees in 1984. The baccalaureate and master's programs in nursing and the associate programs have professional accreditation.

For additional information, students should contact:
Enrollment Services
Clarkson College
101 South 42nd Street
Omaha, Nebraska 68131-2739
Telephone: 402-552-3100
        800-647-5500 (toll-free)
E-mail: admiss@clarksoncollege.edu
WWW:
    http://www.clarksoncollege.edu

ACADEMIC PROGRAM

The goal of Clarkson College is to prepare individuals to be competent in the technical aspects of their profession and broadly educated in the liberal arts and sciences. The curriculum is supported by courses in the liberal arts and sciences and combines knowledge of course content with the development of intellectual and clinical competencies. Each student's curriculum plan reflects the individual's needs and interest. Although degree requirements remain constant, the scheduling of courses within the curriculum may be individualized. The flexibility of the programs permits full-time or part-time enrollment. The academic year begins with the fall semester in August, is followed by the spring semester in January, and ends with the summer semester. Candidates for the baccalaureate degree must complete 128 semester hours of course work, including 60 hours of general education and support courses. Advanced placement into the curriculum beyond the beginning of the freshman year is accomplished through transfer of credits or credit by examination and other means. The associate degree program requirements also include a general education component. In addition to the on-campus program, Clarkson provides distance education opportunities. Distance education courses are highly interactive and are offered via the World Wide Web. Faculty members and students communicate through a variety of technological methods and may contact the College help desk for assistance with course-related computer questions. Library support is available through online services, e-mail, and faxing. Clinical experience is provided through qualified preceptors in each student's community.

FINANCIAL AID

In 2001–02, the College awarded financial aid to approximately 90 percent of its undergraduate students. Scholarships, grants, loans, and work-study are available to meet the individual financial needs of students who qualify. Scholarships are awarded to outstanding applicants. Students are required to submit the completed Free Application for Federal Student Aid (FAFSA) or the Renewal Application as well as the Clarkson College Financial Aid Information Form for consideration for all forms of aid.

APPLICATION AND INFORMATION

The enrollment policy of Clarkson College allows potential students to apply anytime during the year. A completed application form, accompanied by the application fee, an official high school transcript or certification of successful completion of the GED, and ACT or SAT scores should be submitted when seeking admission. Students with previous postsecondary course work should also submit an official transcript from each institution of higher education attended.

CLEARY COLLEGE

ANN ARBOR AND HOWELL, MICHIGAN

THE COLLEGE

Cleary College, founded in 1883, is a private business college whose mission is to prepare students for a career in business with skills that exceed the expectations of their employers. Cleary College operates from two campuses in Michigan. The Washtenaw Campus, located in Ann Arbor, and the Livingston Campus, located in Howell, feature flexible classroom arrangements and meeting rooms as well as the computer, satellite, and telecommunications technology needed by today's students. Cleary College enrolls approximately 900 commuter students. Cleary students are focused on business careers and most students work while completing their degrees—either on their own or as part of an internship or degree program requirements. Cleary College emphasizes practical application of business theory and enjoys an excellent reputation among area employers for preparing graduates who succeed in the workplace. In addition to the on-campus offerings, Cleary College also offers a one-year bachelor's degree completion program at extension sites throughout southeastern Michigan.

> **For more information, students should contact:**
> Cleary College Admissions Office
> 3750 Cleary College Drive
> Howell, Michigan 48845
> Telephone: 888-5-CLEARY (toll-free)
> E-mail: admissions@cleary.edu
> WWW: http://www.cleary.edu

ACADEMIC PROGRAM

All Cleary College degree programs are presented in a cohort, compressed calendar format that provides a rigorous educational experience. Students in the cohort move to degree completion in less time than traditional programs. Cleary programs are intended for the serious student who has a clear goal—a career in business—and is motivated to apply energy to reach that goal. Emphasis is placed on providing a learning environment that fosters a mastery of current business theory and technology and the application of these skills to real-life business situations. Cleary strives to graduate students who know exactly what to do in their jobs, have the skills to do it well, and as a result are successful and able to make important contributions to their business organizations and communities. Cleary's B.B.A. programs are offered in two formats: BusinessTrack™ and Direct Degree™. Students can select the format and schedule to suit their specific needs.

FINANCIAL AID

More than 60 percent of students receive some form of financial assistance. Cleary College participates in state and federal financial aid programs and accepts the Free Application for Federal Student Aid (FAFSA). Some of the financial aid programs Cleary participates in include: the Federal Pell Grant, Federal SEOG, Federal College Work-Study, Federal Stafford Loan, and Michigan Tuition Grant. In addition, a number of Cleary College scholarships and grants are available to students.

APPLICATION AND INFORMATION

Applications to the undergraduate program are accepted all year and must be submitted with a $25 nonrefundable application fee payable to Cleary College. It is recommended that applications to the BusinessTrack program be submitted at least six weeks prior to the start of the term. BusinessTrack terms begin in September, January, April, and July. It is recommended that applications to the Direct Degree program be submitted at least eight weeks prior to the start of the term. Direct Degree terms begin in September, October, January, February, April, May, and July.

THE COLLEGE OF WOOSTER

■ WOOSTER, OHIO

THE COLLEGE
One of the first coeducational colleges in the country, the College of Wooster was founded in 1866 by Presbyterians who wanted to do "their proper part in the great work of educating those who are to mold society and give shape to all its institutions." Today it is a fully independent, privately endowed liberal arts college with a rich tradition of academic excellence. That tradition defines student life at Wooster, beginning with the First-Year Seminar in Critical Inquiry and culminating in the Independent Study program. The current enrollment is about 1,800 men and women. Almost all students live on campus, selecting from a variety of housing options.

For more information, students should contact:
Director of Admissions
The College of Wooster
Wooster, Ohio 44691
Telephone: 330-263-2000 Ext. 2270
 or 2322
 800-877-9905 (toll-free)
Fax: 330-263-2621
E-mail: admissions@wooster.edu
WWW: http://www.wooster.edu

ACADEMIC PROGRAM
Wooster's academic program is designed to provide a liberal education that prepares undergraduates for a lifetime of inquiry, discovery, and responsible citizenship. In fall 2001, Wooster instituted a new curriculum, which focuses directly on these curricular goals. To be eligible for a Bachelor of Arts degree, a student must successfully complete thirty-two courses, including a First-Year Seminar in Critical Inquiry and three courses of Independent Study. An overall grade point average of at least 2.0 (on a 4.0 scale) is required for graduation. Students may receive credit for work done at other colleges and for scores of 4 or better on the Advanced Placement tests offered by the College Board. Courses are graded A–D or No Credit unless the student exercises an option to take certain courses on a Satisfactory/No Credit basis.

FINANCIAL AID
Almost all financial assistance is awarded on the basis of need, as determined by the Free Application for Federal Student Aid (FAFSA). Aid is allocated when students are admitted to the College. Financial assistance information and forms should be requested at the time of application. Applications for aid should be submitted by February 15. Merit aid is available on a competitive basis. The College Scholar program offers eight awards of $18,000 each per year, based on a competitive examination. Additional awards of $13,000 per year are available. Selected entering students receive academic and achievement awards independent of the College Scholars program. Synod of the Covenant Scholarships for Presbyterian communicants are available, as are Scottish Arts awards. The Clarence B. Allen Scholarship program awards up to five scholarships of $18,000 a year to entering African-American students with a demonstrated record of academic achievement and promise of continued success in college. The Arthur Holly Compton Scholarships are awarded to students who demonstrate unusual aptitude for Wooster's program of Independent Study. Compton Scholarships of $8000 to $16,000 a year are awarded annually. Music scholarships are awarded to entering first-year students based on auditions in voice or on an instrument. A 15-minute performance of works representing several styles of music is required. Theater scholarships are awarded on a competitive basis. An audition is required. Byron E. Morris Scholarships of up to $6000 are awarded to students who have a demonstrated record of achievement in their school or community in the areas of volunteer/community service or leadership.

COLUMBIA UNIVERSITY, SCHOOL OF GENERAL STUDIES

- **NEW YORK, NEW YORK**

THE UNIVERSITY AND THE SCHOOL
One of the best kept secrets in American higher education, the School of General Studies at Columbia University is the nation's premier college for returning college students. One of the four undergraduate colleges that grace Columbia, the School of General Studies is dedicated to those students who have interrupted or postponed their education by at least one academic year. Unlike the division of the University dedicated to continuing education, the School of General Studies is a degree-granting liberal arts college. The School of General Studies is fully integrated into the Columbia undergraduate curriculum and provides an Ivy League education to the widest range of talented students with the demonstrated potential to succeed. General Studies students come from all walks of life and from varied backgrounds, and for that reason may study full- or part- time. Many degree candidates hold jobs as well as study, and many have family responsibilities. Others attend full-time, experiencing Columbia's more traditional college life. The diversity in the student body makes attendance at Columbia highly attractive. The varied personal experience represented in each classroom allows for discussion and debate and, in turn, for the academic rigor and intellectual development that characterize a Columbia education. The School has more than 1,200 undergraduate degree candidates and about 300 postbaccalaureate premedical students.

> **For more information, students should contact:**
> Office of Admissions and Financial Aid
> School of General Studies
> 408 Lewisohn Hall
> 2970 Broadway
> Columbia University, Mail Code 4101
> New York, New York 10027
> Telephone: 212-854-2772
> E-mail: gsdegree@columbia.edu
> World Wide Web:
>   http://www.gs.columbia.edu

ACADEMIC PROGRAM
The School of General Studies offers a traditional liberal arts education designed to provide students with the broad knowledge and intellectual skills that make possible continued education and growth in the years after college and that constitute the soundest possible foundation on which to build competence for positions of responsibility in the professional world. Requirements for the bachelor's degree comprise three elements: (1) core requirements, intended to develop in students the ability to write and communicate clearly; to understand the modes of thought that characterize the humanities, the social sciences, and the sciences; to gain some familiarity with central cultural ideas through literature, fine arts, and music; and to acquire a working proficiency in a foreign language; (2) major requirements, designed to give students sustained and coherent exposure to a particular discipline in an area of strong intellectual interest; and (3) elective courses, in which students pursue particular interests and skills for their own personal growth or for their relationship to future professional or personal objectives. Students are required to complete a minimum of 124 points for the bachelor's degree; 60 of these may be in transfer credit, but at least 64 points (including the last 30 points) must be completed at Columbia.

FINANCIAL AID
The School of General Studies awards financial aid based upon need and academic ability. Approximately 70 percent of General Studies degree candidates receive some form of financial aid, including Federal Pell Grants, New York State TAP Grants, Federal Stafford and unsubsidized Stafford Loans, Federal Perkins Loans, General Studies Scholarships, and Federal Work-Study Program awards. Priority application deadlines for new students are June 1 for the fall 2002 semester and November 1 for the spring 2003 semester.

APPLICATION AND INFORMATION
Application deadlines are June 1 for the fall semester and November 1 for the spring semester. Applicants from countries outside the U.S. are urged to apply by August 15 for the spring semester and April 1 for the fall semester. Applications are reviewed as they are completed, and applicants are notified of decisions shortly thereafter.

CONCORD COLLEGE

■ ATHENS, WEST VIRGINIA

THE COLLEGE
Concord College, a growing state-supported college committed exclusively to undergraduate instruction, was founded 129 years ago. Concord features accredited career-oriented education with a strong liberal arts base and focuses on the needs of the individual student as its fundamental concern. The beautiful 123-acre campus stands on a ridge of the Appalachian Mountains. Four residence halls and adult studio apartments house up to 1,100 students from twenty-eight states, predominantly from the East, South, and Midwest. Concord also has a large international student population, with thirty nations represented. With a total student population of 3,050, Concord serves the needs of active commuter students who join the residential students in following courses of study in the arts and sciences, business administration, teacher education, and such fields as advertising/graphic design and social work. Preparation for advanced and professional study is a Concord hallmark.

> **For further information, students may contact:**
> Michael Curry
> Vice President for Admissions and Financial Aid
> Concord College
> P.O. Box 1000
> Athens, West Virginia 24712
> Telephone: 304-384-5248 or 5249
> 888-384-5249 (toll-free)
> E-mail: admissions@concord.edu
> WWW: http://www.concord.edu
> http://www.concord.edu/admissions/ (to apply on line)

ACADEMIC PROGRAM
All students must complete a minimum of 128 semester hours with a grade point average of 2.0 (C) or better to receive a degree. A program of general studies, required of all students, includes courses in communication and literature, fine arts, social sciences, natural sciences, mathematics, foreign languages (optional in most majors), and physical education. Credit is awarded for satisfactory scores on the College-Level Examination Program (CLEP), Advanced Placement (AP), and International Baccalaureate tests. An outstanding honors program is also available to qualifying students. Honors courses and independent study projects are available in most departments. Semesters begin in late August and mid-January; there are summer terms as well.

FINANCIAL AID
Concord College has the most generous scholarship program in the West Virginia State College System. Merit awards, athletic and talent scholarships, transfer scholarships, and scholarships for nontraditional students are readily available for qualifying students. Federal Pell Grants, Federal Supplemental Educational Opportunity Grants, Federal Perkins Loans, West Virginia Higher Education Grants, Federal PLUS loans, and Federal Stafford Student Loans are available through the College. The State Student Assistance Program and the Federal Work-Study Program offer opportunities for student employment. To receive priority, the Free Application for Federal Student Aid (FAFSA) must be on file by April 15. Concord offers scholarships to international students. The average scholarship covers about 35 percent of the total institutional cost. Incoming freshmen who are willing to perform community service may apply for the Bonner Scholars Program, which pays up to $3050 per year for four years as long as its criteria are met. Funded by the Corella and Bertram F. Bonner Foundation of Princeton, New Jersey, the award is primarily based on need and prior service. Approximately 85 percent of freshman students receive scholarship, financial aid, or both. In addition, 65 percent of the entire student body receive some form of financial aid.

APPLICATION AND INFORMATION
Applications should be submitted by January 15 for early admission consideration and by August 1 for admission for the fall semester, which begins in late August and ends in December.

CONCORDIA UNIVERSITY

■ PORTLAND, OREGON

THE UNIVERSITY

Concordia University, Portland, is a private, four-year Lutheran university dedicated to the intellectual and professional development of the whole student. Founded in 1905 as an academy, Concordia grew from a junior college to a four-year college in the late 1970s, awarding its first bachelor's degrees in 1980 and graduate degrees in 1996. Concordia attained university status in 1995. The institution's mission statement is, "Concordia University is a Christian University preparing leaders for the transformation of society." The University is composed of three academic colleges: the College of Education, the School of Management and the College of Theology, Arts, and Sciences. Programmatic development through the 1980s and 1990s increased the University's commitment to local and regional needs through several academic additions. These include a nationally recognized health-care administration program, a concentration in e-business within the bachelor's in business administration, and a progressive program emphasis in environmental management. Concordia University (CU) further demonstrates its commitment to remain on the cutting edge of program development with its participation in the nationwide Concordia University System. An innovative intercampus partnership of the ten Concordia institutions of The Lutheran Church–Missouri Synod, the system has a combined enrollment of 15,000 students. Opportunities for enrollment in any one of the ten campuses and the benefits of high-tech distance learning and alternative timelines for degree completion are examples of the advantages of a small college within the framework of a nationwide educational system. Through the resource of compressed video, all system campuses are linked to provide academic offerings via a comprehensive telecommunications system. CU's electronic classroom increases educational accessibility and allows students to benefit from the academic expertise at other member institutions.

For more information, students should contact:
Office of Admissions
Concordia University
2811 Northeast Holman Street
Portland, Oregon 97211
Telephone: 503-288-9371
　　　　　 800-321-9371 (toll-free)
Fax: 503-280-8531
E-mail: admissions@cu-portland.edu
WWW: http://www.cu-portland.edu

ACADEMIC PROGRAM

Concordia operates on a semester calendar with two 15-week semesters. A summer session is offered in selected programs. Academic work is measured in semester hours, and courses are assigned from .5 to 5 semester hours each. For a baccalaureate degree, 124 semester hours are required; for the associate degree, 63 hours are required. All degree-seeking students, regardless of their major, must complete the general education requirements, which include courses in communications, fine arts, humanities, physical education, religion, science, math, and social science. In several academic areas, students may earn credit through successful completion of Advanced Placement and College-Level Examination Program (CLEP) tests.

FINANCIAL AID

The Free Application for Federal Student Aid (FAFSA) is used to determine a student's financial need for the awarding of scholarships, grants, work-study programs, and loans. Most awards are made in the spring for the following academic year. Approximately 95 percent of CU's first-year students receive some form of scholarships and grants. Merit-based scholarships are awarded based on academic history.

APPLICATION AND INFORMATION

Candidates for admission must complete a formal Concordia application for admission, submit test scores and/or high school/college transcripts, and furnish one reference. Applicants are encouraged to apply as early in the academic year as possible. Concordia follows a rolling admission procedure, and candidates are notified of a decision shortly after all the necessary credentials have been received.

DAVIDSON COLLEGE

■ DAVIDSON, NORTH CAROLINA

THE COLLEGE

Founded in 1837, Davidson College consistently ranks as one of the most competitive liberal arts and sciences colleges in the United States. Davidson's student body is made up of 1,600 students from forty-seven states and thirty-four other countries, chosen not only for their academic promise but also for their character and leadership. The liberal arts curriculum at Davidson is designed to give students knowledge and skills that they will put to use throughout their lives. Davidson offers more than 850 courses in twenty major fields and in special interdisciplinary programs. Students benefit from the careful attention of 156 full-time faculty members who are dedicated to teaching and guiding undergraduates.

> **For additional information about Davidson, students should contact:**
> Nancy J. Cable, Ph.D.
> Dean of Admission and Financial Aid
> Davidson College
> Box 7156
> Davidson, North Carolina 28035-7156
> Telephone: 704-894-2230
> 800-768-0380 (toll-free)
> WWW: http://www.davidson.edu

ACADEMIC PROGRAM

The liberal arts curriculum at Davidson gives students a broad-based and rich education, exposing them to many different academic areas. Davidson requires a total of thirty-two courses to graduate. Through the required core curriculum, every Davidson student takes courses in six areas: the fine arts, natural sciences and mathematics, philosophy and religion, literature, history, and the social sciences. Additional courses are taken in composition, foreign language, cultural diversity, and physical education. In addition to the core curriculum, students choose a major by the end of their sophomore year. A major normally requires up to twelve courses, including at least five upper-level courses. The academic year at Davidson consists of two 15-week semesters. Notably, 90 percent of those who enroll at Davidson graduate within four academic years.

FINANCIAL AID

Admission decisions are made without regard to a student's financial need. Through a combination of state, federal, and private sources, Davidson administers in excess of $18 million in student financial assistance. The instructions for applying for need-based aid are included with Davidson's application for admission. Students with financial need are assisted through a combination of Davidson scholarships, federal and state grants, loans, and work-study. Davidson awards merit scholarships to approximately 15 percent of each entering first-year class. These awards recognize students' academic promise, special talents, and personal qualities. Recipients are selected based on the strength of their admission application. For some scholarships, selection may also be based on the outcome of an audition, interview, portfolio review, or writing sample. Merit scholarships range from $2500 to the comprehensive fee and include the following top awards: the Thomas S. and Sarah B. Baker Scholarship (four awarded, comprehensive fee), the John Montgomery Belk Scholarship (six to ten awarded to students from the southeastern U.S., comprehensive fee), the William Holt Terry Scholarship (two awarded to students with exceptional leadership qualities, full tuition), the Bryan Scholarship (two awarded to students who contribute in a superlative manner to their sport as well as to the academic and cocurricular life at Davidson), and the Missy and John Kuykendall Scholarship (three awarded to students who provide service leadership).

APPLICATION AND INFORMATION

Early decision—round one—has an application deadline of November 15 with notification by December 15. Early decision—round two—has an application deadline of January 2 with notification by February 1. Regular decision has an application deadline of January 2 with notification by April 1. To be considered for merit scholarships, students must complete their applications by December 15. Students are encouraged to visit Davidson for a campus tour and an information session with a member of the Admission Office staff.

DREXEL UNIVERSITY

■ PHILADELPHIA, PENNSYLVANIA

THE UNIVERSITY
Drexel is a private, nonsectarian, coeducational university that has maintained a reputation for academic excellence since its founding in 1891. Its academic programs offer students practical preparation for graduate school and a variety of careers. Full-time, paid professional experience through Drexel's cooperative education program is a vital part of a Drexel education. Students gain professional experience in jobs related to their career interests by alternating classroom study with periods of employment in business, industry, and government. More than 2,300 employers from twenty-eight states and fourteen other countries participate in this program. Another distinctive element is the University's microcomputer requirement, through which all undergraduates participate in a computer-enhanced education. Drexel University grants bachelor's, master's, and doctoral degrees. The undergraduate enrollment is 8,500 full-time students, who represent forty-two states and numerous other countries. Seven modern coed residential halls house more than 2,600 students on campus. In addition to the challenging academic atmosphere, Drexel offers its students social, cultural, athletic, and community service opportunities.

For more information, students should contact:
Office of Undergraduate Admissions
Drexel University
3141 Chestnut Streets
Philadelphia, Pennsylvania 19104
Telephone: 800-2-DREXEL (toll-free)
WWW: http://www.drexel.edu

ACADEMIC PROGRAM
Drexel's distinguishing feature is Drexel Co-op: "The Ultimate Internship"™. Combined with rigorous academic programs, this feature provides an education that enables students to bridge the gap between academic studies and the working world. The co-op/internship program generates a two-way educational force: academic knowledge finds concrete form in the workplace, while personal growth and experiential learning on the job enrich the academic experience. All undergraduates are prepared for full-time professional internships through Drexel's cooperative education program.

FINANCIAL AID
Approximately 87 percent of all freshmen receive financial aid. The aid package may contain academic, athletic, or performing arts scholarships; grants; or loans; or part-time employment. Federal programs are also included. All students applying for aid must submit the Free Application for Federal Student Aid by May 1. Notification of incoming freshmen and transfer students begins about March 1. Drexel offers a unique achievement-based award, the A. J. Drexel Scholarship, to all qualified incoming freshmen and transfer students. With an annual award value of up to $10,000, the A. J. Drexel Scholarship is renewable on a yearly basis, provided the student maintains a 3.0 grade point average and full-time status. Criteria include a strong academic record and involvement in extracurricular and community service activities.

APPLICATION AND INFORMATION
Application forms with complete instructions for admission and financial aid and the appropriate college prospectus may be obtained by writing to the address given below. Each application must be accompanied by a nonrefundable application fee of $50; however, the fee may be waived in cases of extreme hardship if requested by the secondary school or if the student visits the campus. Students may access Drexel's online application at the Web site listed below. Applications for regular full-time undergraduate status are accepted throughout the senior year. Drexel subscribes to the College Board's Candidates Reply Date of May 1. Transfer students should apply at least three months before the beginning of the term in which they wish to enroll.

EARLHAM COLLEGE

■ **RICHMOND, INDIANA**

THE COLLEGE
Earlham College offers a challenging intellectual environment that attracts a diverse group of students with a variety of motivations—academic, political, social, athletic, ethical, and career-minded—who want to make an impact on the world. The College's 1,078 students—597 women and 481 men—represent forty-eight states and twenty-seven countries. Students of many races, religious backgrounds, economic levels, and ethnic traditions join together on this Midwestern campus to create and experience the Earlham Effect. They share an experience rooted in the Quaker values of tolerance, equality, justice, respect, and collaboration. They explore an unending desire to see the world differently and to bring about change when necessary. Earlham's commitment to engaging students in a changing world is at the heart of its own mission. The College was founded in 1847 by the Religious Society of Friends (Quakers) and to this day believes that a strong liberal arts education is the best intellectual preparation for life. Earlham, an NCAA Division III affiliate, is a member of the North Coast Athletic Conference. The College offers seven intercollegiate sports for men (baseball, basketball, cross-country, football, soccer, tennis, and track) and eight intercollegiate sports for women (basketball, cross-country, field hockey, lacrosse, soccer, tennis, track, and volleyball). Club sports include swimming, Ultimate Frisbee, and men's lacrosse and volleyball. Twenty-eight percent of the students participate in intercollegiate athletics, and many more participate in an extensive intramural program. Earlham athletic facilities include indoor and outdoor tennis courts; football, baseball, soccer, lacrosse, and hockey fields; an all-weather track; and a $13-million athletics and wellness center. Earlham is a residential college. Students live in the seven residence halls and twenty-seven College-owned houses near the campus.

> **For more information, students should contact:**
> Office of Admissions
> Earlham College
> 801 National Road West
> Richmond, Indiana 47374-4095
> Telephone: 765-983-1600
> 800-EARLHAM (toll-free)
> Fax: 765-983-1560
> E-mail: admission@earlham.edu
> WWW: http://www.earlham.edu

ACADEMIC PROGRAM
Earlham aims to educate for depth and breadth, believing that one's success in the twenty-first century will depend heavily on an ability to understand and make well-educated connections across different intellectual and experiential boundaries. Earlham's General Education Program encourages students to develop competencies in language, social science, natural science, philosophy or religion, and fine arts. Students also complete some course work having multicultural and intercultural dimensions.

FINANCIAL AID
Most financial aid is awarded on the basis of demonstrated need; more than 80 percent of Earlham's students receive financial assistance. Earlham usually meets the full need of all accepted students with a combination of Earlham Grants, endowed scholarships, loans, federal and state grants, and campus work. Students must file both the Free Application for Federal Student Aid (FAFSA) and a special Earlham form. Scholarships are awarded without regard to financial need and recognize academic achievement. Earlham also offers scholarships through the National Merit Scholarship Corporation. Special scholarships are available to members of the Religious Society of Friends (Quakers) and students who will enhance the diversity of the student body. Scholarships and limited financial aid are available for international students.

APPLICATION AND INFORMATION
Earlham offers several admission options. The early decision deadline is December 1 (notification by December 15); the early action deadline is January 1 (notification on February 1); the regular decision deadline is February 15 (notification by March 15); and the transfer deadline is April 1. International students (non-U.S. citizens) should apply by February 1. Applications are accepted after these deadlines as long as places remain in the entering class.

EASTERN MENNONITE UNIVERSITY

■ HARRISONBURG, VIRGINIA

THE UNIVERSITY

Eastern Mennonite University (EMU), a private Christian university founded in 1917, provides a high-quality liberal arts education that emphasizes spiritual growth and cross-cultural awareness. The nurturing environment of EMU's student-oriented campus not only prepares students for a wide variety of careers but also challenges students to answer Christ's call to a life of nonviolence, witness, service, and peacebuilding. The undergraduate experience is enriched by graduate programs in business administration, conflict transformation, counseling, and education. The University also has a seminary. EMU is accredited by the Southern Association of Colleges and Schools. In addition, the nursing, teacher education, and social work programs are accredited by their specialty organizations at the national level. Undergraduate students make up about 1,000 of the 1,400 students. Of the undergraduates, 60 percent are women and 9 percent are American multiethnic students. Four percent come from international settings. Students represent thirty-seven states and sixteen other countries. Most students are traditional college age. Religious backgrounds vary widely, with 60 percent representing Mennonites. EMU is a residential community in which students live on campus until age 21 (unless they are married or live at home). Housing options include traditional residence halls, coed buildings, suite arrangements, apartments for upperclass students, and group houses.

For more information, students should contact:
Ellen B. Miller
Director of Admissions
Eastern Mennonite University
Harrisonburg, Virginia 22802
Telephone: 800-368-2665 (toll-free)
Fax: 540-432-4444
E-mail: admiss@emu.edu
WWW: http://www.emu.edu

ACADEMIC PROGRAM

The academic calendar consists of two 15-week semesters from late August to late April. The baccalaureate degree requires 128 semester hours. All students complete a major, the Global Village general education curriculum, and electives. Twelve honors students are selected from each first-year class. Two of the 12 receive full-tuition scholarships, and 10 are awarded half-tuition scholarships. Other special academic opportunities include credit by examination and extension credit for special programs with outside organizations.

FINANCIAL AID

More than 90 percent of EMU students receive financial aid. Scholarships include those given for academic achievement and an award of $1000 given to new first-year students who are children of alumni. Other grant aid, given to meet financial need, includes federal aid and EMU grants. Admission is need-blind. In addition, students with financial need may obtain federal loans or participate in the work-study program. Virginia residents receive the Virginia Tuition Assistance Grant, regardless of need, which amounts to $3000 or more annually. If students receive grants from their churches, EMU matches up to $1000 per year. No application is needed for academic scholarships except for honors awards. Students applying for need-based aid must complete the Free Application for Federal Student Aid (FAFSA). Applications should be completed by February 15.

APPLICATION AND INFORMATION

The freshman application priority filing date is March 1. The final filing date is August 1. The application deadline for transfer applicants is thirty days prior to the start of the term for both fall and spring. Notification of admission is sent on a rolling basis.

ELMIRA COLLEGE

■ ELMIRA, NEW YORK

THE COLLEGE

Elmira College is a small, independent college that is recognized for its emphasis on education of high quality in the liberal arts and preprofessional preparation. One of the oldest colleges in the United States, Elmira was founded in 1855. The College has always produced graduates interested in both community service and successful careers. Friendliness, personal attention, strong college spirit, and support for learning beyond the classroom help to make Elmira a special place. Elmira College is one of only 258 colleges in the nation to be granted a chapter of the prestigious Phi Beta Kappa honor society. The full-time undergraduate enrollment is about 1,200 men and women. The students at Elmira represent more than thirty-five states, primarily those in the Northeast, with the highest representation coming from New York, New Jersey, Massachusetts, Connecticut, Maine, and Pennsylvania. International students from twenty-three countries were enrolled in September 2001. Ninety-five percent of the full-time undergraduates live in College residence halls. The intercollegiate sports program includes men's and women's basketball, golf, ice hockey, lacrosse, soccer, and tennis and women's cheerleading, field hockey, softball, and volleyball. An intramural program is also available. Emerson Hall houses the student fitness center, a pool, and a gym capable of seating 1000, as well as the Gibson Theatre, which has a state-of-the-art sound and lighting system. Professional societies; clubs; music, dance, and drama groups; a student-operated FM radio station; and the student newspaper, yearbook, and literary magazine also provide numerous opportunities for extracurricular activity.

For more information, students should contact:
Dean of Admissions
Elmira College
Elmira, New York 14901
Telephone: 800-935-6472 (toll-free)
E-mail: admissions@elmira.edu
WWW: http://www.elmira.edu

ACADEMIC PROGRAM

The College's calendar is composed of two 12-week terms followed by a 6-week spring term. Students enroll for four subjects during the 12-week terms, completing the first term by mid-December and the second during the first week of April. The 6-week term, from mid-April through May, may be devoted to a particular project involving travel, internship, research, or independent study. Students are required to participate in internships in order to gain practical and meaningful experience related to their program of study. Credit is awarded for these projects. Special opportunities for outstanding students include participation in thirteen national honorary societies on campus and a chance to assist faculty members in teaching and research. The College also offers an accelerated three-year graduation option for outstanding students. Army and Air Force ROTC are available.

FINANCIAL AID

Financial aid is available for both freshmen and transfer students. Awards are based upon the Free Application for Federal Student Aid (FAFSA) as well as the student's academic potential. Types of aid include grants, scholarships, federal loans, Elmira College loans, and work opportunities. In addition, superior students may qualify for non-need Elmira College Honors Scholarships, which are available to both freshmen and transfer students and range from $4000 to full tuition per year. For 2001–02, the average freshman aid package (including all types of aid) amounted to more than $20,000. Transfer students applying for financial aid must submit a financial aid transcript from all colleges previously attended, whether or not they received financial aid. About 80 percent of the full-time undergraduates receive financial aid.

EMERSON COLLEGE

■ BOSTON, MASSACHUSETTS

THE COLLEGE

Founded in 1880, Emerson is one of the premier colleges in the United States for the study of communication and the arts. Students may choose from more than twenty undergraduate majors and twelve graduate programs supported by state-of-the-art facilities and a nationally renowned faculty. The campus is home to WERS 88.9 FM, the oldest noncommercial radio station in New England; the 950-seat Emerson Majestic Theatre; and *Ploughshares*, the award-winning literary journal for new writing. A pioneer in the fields of communication and performing arts, Emerson was one of the first colleges in the nation to establish a program in children's theater (1919) as well as an undergraduate program in broadcasting (1937). Professional-level training in speech pathology and audiology was inaugurated in 1935, educational FM radio in 1949, closed-circuit television in 1955, and a B.F.A. degree program in film as early as 1972. In 1980, the College created the country's first graduate program in professional writing and publishing. Today, Emerson's 2,700 undergraduate and 800 graduate students come from more than sixty countries and forty-five states and territories. Approximately 1,300 students live on campus; some students live on special theme floors, such as the Writer's Block and Wellness and Digital Culture Floors. The campus also has a 10,000-square-foot fitness center, the Health and Wellness Center, the Student Union, a 100-seat cabaret/multifunction room, and Cultural Center.

For more information, students should contact:
Office of Undergraduate Admission
Emerson College
120 Boylston Street
Boston, Massachusetts 02116-4624
Telephone: 617-824-8600
Fax: 617-824-8906
E-mail: admission@emerson.edu
WWW: http://www.emerson.edu

ACADEMIC PROGRAM

Emerson's academic calendar consists of two 15-week semesters, plus two 6-week sessions during the summer months. The requirements for graduation combine general education and liberal arts courses with advanced, specialized classes that are specific to individual departments and majors. Internships for academic credit are available in almost every major and the Institute for Liberal Arts and Interdisciplinary Studies offers exciting first-year seminars, exclusive honors program classes, independent study options, and innovative courses that cut across academic disciplines.

FINANCIAL AID

Last year, more than 71 percent of Emerson students received some form of financial assistance. The College provided more than $38 million in need-based financial support, packaged in awards that typically combined grant and scholarship, loan, and college work-study. Academic scholarships ranging from $5000 to half-tuition are awarded on a limited basis to students who meet high academic standards. Special performance-based scholarships, averaging $4000, are available to exceptional students in the performing arts. In order to apply for financial assistance, students must complete the FAFSA form, CSS PROFILE, and the Emerson College Application for Financial Assistance. Deadlines are March 1 for September admission or November 15 for January admission. More information about financial assistance at Emerson can be found online at http://www.emerson.edu/fin_aid, or by contacting the Office of Student Financial Services (telephone: 617-824-8655; fax: 617-824-8619; e-mail: finaid@emerson.edu).

APPLICATION AND INFORMATION

First-year candidates for Early Action should file their Application for Admission by November 15 (notifications are mailed by December 15). The regular admission deadline for September admission is February 1 (with notifications mailed by April 1) and November 1 for January admission (with notifications mailed by December 15). Transfer students should submit their applications and supporting credentials by March 1 (for September admission) or November 1 (for January admission).

EMORY & HENRY COLLEGE

■ EMORY, VIRGINIA

THE COLLEGE

Since its founding in 1836, Emory & Henry College has instilled a strong sense of values in students and has prepared them for lifelong learning and success. Among the College's alumni have been congressmen, businesspeople, scientists, teachers, artists, ministers, authors, and many public servants. The College's 900 students (almost equally divided between men and women) constitute a diverse group, coming from rural areas of southwestern Virginia as well as from urban centers nationwide. They represent more than twenty states and several countries.

For more information, students should contact:
Office of Admissions and Financial Aid
Emory & Henry College
P.O. Box 10
Emory, Virginia 24327-0947
Telephone: 276-944-6133
　　　　　800-848-5493 (toll-free)
Fax: 276-944-6935
E-mail: ehadmiss@ehc.edu
WWW: http://www.ehc.edu

ACADEMIC PROGRAM

Emory & Henry offers a liberal arts program with emphasis on writing, reasoning, value inquiry, and knowledge of global concerns, as well as a broad introduction to liberal arts subjects. All students complete a core curriculum, which includes a yearlong, interdisciplinary Western Tradition course and a writing course for all first-year students. Sophomores complete an ambitious Great Books program, and upperclass students take courses related to value inquiry and global studies. Along with the core curriculum, each student completes a major and a minor or a combined program referred to as an area of concentration.

FINANCIAL AID

Forms of aid include need-based and non-need-based scholarships, loans, and part-time jobs. A Bonner Scholars program provides substantial scholarships for selected students who do volunteer work in the surrounding region. Virginia residents are eligible for a special grant based on residence. Merit scholarships are awarded based on academic performance, and many can be renewed based on continued academic success. Ninety-six percent of fall 2000 undergraduates received financial aid. The average aided first-year student received an aid package worth $12,803, meeting 91 percent of need. The priority application deadline for financial aid is April 1 and the deadline is August 1.

APPLICATION AND INFORMATION

To apply for admission, students should submit the basic application form, an essay, a copy of the high school transcript, scores from either the SAT I or the ACT, and a nonrefundable $30 application fee. Transfer applicants must submit a transcript from any college previously attended and a statement of good standing. A rolling admission policy allows notification of the admission decision within two weeks after a file has been completed. Students who have thoroughly researched their college options and have determined that Emory & Henry College is their first choice are encouraged to consider applying under the Early Decision Plan. Although these students may file regular applications with other colleges, it is understood that they are applying for Early Decision only at Emory & Henry College and intend to enroll if admitted. To be considered for Early Decision, a student should submit the completed Application for Admission, including the Early Decision Agreement; the secondary school transcript; and a report of either SAT I or ACT test scores by December 1. The College agrees to notify candidates of their admission by December 20. The $200 enrollment deposit deadline for Early Decision is January 20. Under Early Decision, students will either be admitted or deferred to regular admission.

FAIRMONT STATE COLLEGE

■ FAIRMONT, WEST VIRGINIA

THE COLLEGE
Fairmont State College is the largest state-supported four-year college in West Virginia, with an enrollment of approximately 4,200 students. Founded in 1867, the College is located in the north-central portion of the state in the city of Fairmont, West Virginia. Fairmont State Community and Technical College has an enrollment of 2,300 students and was founded in 1974. In addition to the main campus, which includes thirteen major buildings, classes are also offered at the Robert C. Byrd National Aerospace Education Center in Bridgeport as well as at the Gaston Caperton Center, a 36,000-square-foot state-of-the-art facility in Clarksburg. The College also has satellite facilities reaching across the north-central region of West Virginia and at the Center for Workforce Education at the I-79 Technology Park. Fairmont State College has a rich and proud athletic tradition. The College is a member of NCAA Division II and offers men's teams in baseball, basketball, cross-country, football, golf, tennis, and swimming. The College sponsors women's teams in basketball, cross-country, golf, softball, swimming, tennis, and volleyball. Fairmont State's cheerleaders are consistently among the top teams in the state and the nation. Fairmont State also has an extensive and well-organized intramural program and provides other recreational facilities across the campus. Students who live on campus are housed in one of three residence halls and take their meals at a centrally located dining hall or at the food court in the student center. For those students who prefer to live off campus, private accommodations close to the College are available. Parents who are taking classes at the College may find it convenient to enroll their young children in the day-care center located on the main campus. The Newman Center and the Wesley Foundation are available to minister to the spiritual needs of students; both organizations are adjacent to the Fairmont State campus. There are also various student organizations, honor societies, and social fraternities and sororities to enhance extracurricular life at the College.

For more information or to schedule a tour, students should contact:
Office of Admissions
Fairmont State College
1201 Locust Avenue
Fairmont, West Virginia 26554
Telephone: 304-367-4892
　　　　　　800-641-5678 (toll-free)
304-367-4213 (financial aid)
304-367-4216 (housing)
304-367-4000 (campus operator)
304-623-5721 (Caperton Center)
304-842-8300 (Aerospace Education Center)

ACADEMIC PROGRAM
Fairmont State College offers ninety bachelor's degree programs; Fairmont State Community and Technical College offers forty certificate and associate degree programs. These are offered in the Schools of Business and Economics, Education, Fine Arts, Health Careers, Language and Literature, Science and Mathematics, Social Science, and Technology. Special degrees such as the Regents Bachelor of Arts degree offer nontraditional approaches for individual career or personal requirements. Certificate programs are designed to provide basic skills or increased proficiency in specific occupational areas. Preprofessional studies are designed to prepare students for a wide variety of professional programs beyond a four-year degree.

FINANCIAL AID
Sixty-five percent of Fairmont State students receive some form of financial aid. Guidelines and forms for West Virginia and out-of-state residents are available from high school guidance counselors or Fairmont State's Financial Aid Office.

APPLICATION AND INFORMATION
Campus tours are available Monday through Friday at 10 a.m. and 2 p.m. by appointment. Fairmont State also sponsors a Saturday Campus Visitation Day once each fall and spring semester.

FERRIS STATE UNIVERSITY

■ BIG RAPIDS, MICHIGAN

THE UNIVERSITY

Ferris State University is Michigan's foremost professional and technical university, providing career-oriented education to nearly 11,000 students. Accredited by the North Central Association of Colleges and Schools, the University offers more than 120 majors through the Colleges of Allied Health Sciences, Arts and Sciences, Business, Education and Human Services, Pharmacy, and Technology and the Michigan College of Optometry. These offerings lead to bachelor's and associate degrees and certificates; master's degrees in career and technical education, criminal justice administration, curriculum and instruction, and information systems management as well as fine arts, through Kendall College of Art and Design; and doctorates in optometry and pharmacy. One of Michigan's fifteen public universities, Ferris State University is recognized for its career-oriented educational majors that are designed to meet the technology and workforce demands of business and industry, the health-care professions, and society in general through applied research and practical education. Ferris was founded in 1884 by Woodbridge N. Ferris (1853–1928), a distinguished Michigan educator and politician who served two terms as the state's governor and was elected to the United States Senate. Ferris was a private institution until 1950 when it joined the state higher education system. The college obtained university status in 1987.

For more information, students should contact:
Admissions Office
Ferris State University
420 Oak Street, PRK 101
Big Rapids, Michigan 49307-2020
Telephone: 231-591-2100
　　　　　800-4FERRIS (toll-free)
E-mail: admissions@ferris.edu
WWW: http://about.ferris.edu

ACADEMIC PROGRAM

Ferris is dedicated to the ideal of blending career-oriented professional training with a solid base of general education. While major programs of study provide graduates with the skills and knowledge required to enter a chosen career, general education provides graduates with the academic skills, analytic flexibility, and broad base of knowledge required for continued learning, performance, and advancement in their personal and professional lives. Ferris currently is on the semester system, and the minimum requirement for a baccalaureate degree is 120 semester hours. The average major requires between 120 and 130 semester hours. The minimum number of hours required for an associate degree is 60. The University's academic year begins in August and ends in early May.

FINANCIAL AID

Approximately 71 percent of Ferris students receive some type of financial aid through federal, state, and University programs. In 2000–01, student financial aid included more than $45 million in scholarships, grants, loans, work-study, or a combination of these. The Free Application for Federal Student Aid (FAFSA) must be submitted by April 1 to receive priority consideration for need-based financial aid. The University also provides merit-based scholarships in recognition of superior academic performance and residence-based scholarships for students living on campus who maintain high academic grades. The Woodbridge N. Ferris Scholarship Program offers competitive awards ranging from $500 to $6000 per year to those who qualify. The Residential Life Scholarship offers $2000 per year for entering students who live in a residence hall on campus, have a 3.0 or better high school GPA, and have a minimum score of 20 on the ACT. Information and counseling are available from the Office of Scholarships and Financial Aid (telephone: 231-591-2110 or 800-940-4-AID, toll-free).

FERRUM COLLEGE

- **FERRUM, VIRGINIA**

THE COLLEGE
Ferrum College is a four-year, independent, coeducational college situated on a 700-acre wooded campus in the heart of southwest Virginia's Blue Ridge Mountains. Ferrum is a self-contained community; 77 percent of the student body lives on campus, and many faculty members live on or near campus and are closely involved in campus life. Ferrum also provides in-room Dell computers at no extra charge. Founded in 1913 by the United Methodist Church, Ferrum is a comprehensive liberal arts college accredited by the Southern Association of Colleges and Schools. Ferrum's student body of about 950 (58 percent men, 42 percent women) is a diverse group; while the largest contingent comes from Virginia, twenty-six other states and a number of other countries are also represented. Ferrum's curriculum provides solid career preparation that includes rigorous academics, a strong experiential learning component, and a practical, broad-based, "real-life" emphasis.

> **Further information may be obtained by contacting:**
> Director of Admissions
> Spilman-Daniel House
> Ferrum College
> Ferrum, Virginia 24088-9000
> Telephone: 540-365-4290
> 800-868-9797 (toll-free)
> E-mail: admissions@ferrum.edu
> WWW: http://www.ferrum.edu

ACADEMIC PROGRAM
Ferrum College's comprehensive approach to higher education provides the benefits of liberal arts education with solid, practical career preparation. To graduate, students must complete 127 semester hours of academic work, meet the appropriate distribution and major/minor requirements, and achieve a cumulative grade point average of at least 2.0. Faculty members encourage students to take advantage of the wide variety of experiential learning opportunities available. Internships are required for programs such as agriculture, environmental science, outdoor recreation, teacher education, social work, recreation and leisure, sports management, and sports medicine and strongly recommended for all others, reflecting the College's belief in the value of hands-on learning.

FINANCIAL AID
In 2001–02, 95 percent of Ferrum students were offered some form of financial assistance. For the 75 percent of students receiving need-based aid, the average financial aid package totaled $10,700. Ferrum makes every effort to provide financial assistance consistent with the ability of students and their families to meet college expenses. A comprehensive assistance program includes campus jobs, scholarships, grants, and loans. A typical package consists of 58 percent scholarships and grants, 34 percent low-interest loans, and 8 percent campus-based jobs. Ferrum College is one of a small group of colleges nationwide that offers a unique financial aid opportunity known as the Bonner Scholars Program, which gives qualified students a chance to receive scholarship funds and to become involved in various service projects. The Free Application for Federal Student Aid (FAFSA) and forms concerning grants and scholarships are sent to all applicants and should be completed and submitted no later than March 1 for priority consideration. Virginia residents are eligible for grants from the Tuition Assistance Grant (TAG) Program, and some out-of-state students receive a comparable award offered by the College. Students that apply by January 1 receive priority consideration for grant aid and early estimates of packages.

APPLICATION AND INFORMATION
Applicants should submit a completed application (available on request from the Admissions Office or online at the Web address below), a high school transcript (and a college transcript, if applicable), and scores from the SAT I or ACT.

FITCHBURG STATE COLLEGE

- **FITCHBURG, MASSACHUSETTS**

THE COLLEGE

Fitchburg State College, the Leadership College, is a liberal arts institution where career-oriented and professional education programs thrive. Under the leadership of its president, Dr. Michael Riccards, Fitchburg State has undertaken a number of major initiatives. The College now offers more internship opportunities, a substantially increased Merit Scholarship program, and a guarantee that its graduates will be qualified for jobs in their fields. The College is investing in new technologies in every curriculum to assure that Fitchburg State continues to place more than 85 percent of its graduates in their chosen professions. Fitchburg State's excellent academic reputation and graduate placement can be attributed to a nationally recognized faculty and a commitment to teaching that is unparalleled in Massachusetts. The College serves 2,500 students in its day division and another 4,000 students in its evening and graduate programs. The average class size is 22, and the overall student-teacher ratio remains low at 12:1. A number of special interest clubs are open to all students. Several sororities and fraternities contribute to the social and recreational life of the campus. Hundreds of popular and well-attended activities take place during the year, including films, lectures, concerts, seminars, coffeehouses, pub entertainment, recreational tournaments, performing arts series, and visual arts exhibits. In addition to the bachelor's degrees listed below, Fitchburg State confers the Master of Arts in Teaching (M.A.T.), the Master in Business Administration (M.B.A.), the Master of Education (M.Ed.) in several disciplines, and the Master of Science (M.S.) in communications media, computer science, counseling, and management. Several Certificate of Advanced Graduate Studies (C.A.G.S.) programs are available as well.

> **For further information, students should contact:**
> Director of Admissions
> Fitchburg State College
> Fitchburg, Massachusetts 01420
> Telephone: 978-665-3144
> Fax: 978-665-4540
> E-mail: admissions@fsc.edu
> WWW: http://www.fsc.edu

ACADEMIC PROGRAM

The College operates on a two-semester basis. The first semester begins in early September and ends in mid-December, and the second semester begins in mid-January and ends in mid-May. The curriculum has a strong liberal arts and sciences requirement, providing a strong foundation for either further academic study or a career. Students may obtain practical experience through volunteer placement in social agencies, government offices, and businesses related to their interests. Some major programs require an extensive supervised practicum to complete degree requirements. For education majors, a broad spectrum of student-teaching experiences is available. The four-year honors program, for students with excellent high school records, culminates in a senior thesis or project.

FINANCIAL AID

Many sources of financial aid are available to Fitchburg State students. The College participates in federal and state programs, including the Federal Direct Student Loan Program. Packages consisting of grants, loans, work-study awards, and scholarships are given to students demonstrating financial need. Financial aid applications for the fall semester must be completed by the preceding March 1 to be given priority consideration.

APPLICATION AND INFORMATION

Acceptance of qualified applicants begins in January and proceeds on a rolling basis until all available spaces are taken. Students should apply by April 1 for the fall semester and by December 1 for the spring semester.

FIVE TOWNS COLLEGE

■ DIX HILLS, NEW YORK

THE COLLEGE
Nestled in the rolling hills of Long Island's North Shore, Five Towns College offers students the opportunity to study in a suburban environment that is close to New York City. Founded in 1972, Five Towns College is an independent, nonsectarian, coeducational institution that places its emphasis on the student as an individual. Many students are drawn to the College because of its strong reputation in music, media, and the performing arts. The College offers associate, bachelor's, and master's degrees. The College also offers programs leading to the Master of Music (M.M.) degree in jazz/commercial music and in music education. From as far away as England and Japan and from as close as Long Island and New York City, the 900 full-time students reflect a rich cultural diversity. The College's enrollment is 65 percent men and 35 percent women, with a minority population of approximately 34 percent. The College's music programs are contemporary in nature, although classical musicians are also part of this creative community. The most popular programs are audio recording technology, broadcasting, music performance, music business, elementary education, theater, and film/video production.

For further information, students should contact:
Director of Admissions
Five Towns College
305 North Service Road
Dix Hills, New York 11746-5871
Telephone: 631-424-7000 Ext. 110
Fax: 631-424-7008
E-mail: admissions@ftc.edu
WWW: http://www.ftc.edu

ACADEMIC PROGRAM
The music education program is designed for students interested in a career as a teacher of music in a public or private school. The undergraduate program leads to New York State provisional certification, while the graduate program leads to permanent certification. or sound directors, filmmakers, and videographers. The film/video concentration includes extensive technical preparation in videography, filmmaking, linear and nonlinear editing, storyboarding, scriptwriting, producing, and directing. To earn a bachelor's degree, students must accumulate between 120 and 128 credits, depending upon the program of study, with a proper distribution of courses and a GPA of at least 2.0. To earn an associate degree, students must accumulate between 60 and 64 credits.

FINANCIAL AID
The annual tuition at Five Towns College is among the lowest of all the private colleges in the region. Nevertheless, approximately 68 percent of all students receive some form of financial assistance. Need-based and/or merit-based grants, scholarships, loans, and work-study programs are available to qualified recipients, including transfer students. Prospective students are urged to contact the Financial Aid Office as early as possible.

APPLICATION AND INFORMATION
Admission into any music program is contingent upon passing an audition demonstrating skill in performance on a major instrument or vocally. Music students must also take written and aural examinations in harmony, sight singing, and ear training in order to demonstrate talent, well-developed musicianship, and artistic sensibilities. Admission into any theater program is also contingent upon passing an audition. In some cases, the Admissions Committee may request an on-campus interview with an applicant. Music, theater, video arts, and film/video students are encouraged to submit a portfolio tape or reel, if available. Except for applicants applying on an early decision basis, new students are accepted on a rolling basis, with decisions for the fall and spring semesters mailed starting January 15 and September 15, respectively. There is an application fee of $25.

FORDHAM UNIVERSITY

■ NEW YORK, NEW YORK

THE UNIVERSITY
Fordham, New York City's Jesuit University, offers a distinctive educational experience that is rooted in the 450-year-old Jesuit tradition of intellectual rigor and personal respect for the individual. The University enrolls approximately 14,000 students, of whom 7,000 are undergraduates. Fordham has five undergraduate colleges and six graduate schools. In addition to its full-time undergraduate programs, the University offers part-time undergraduate study at Fordham College of Liberal Studies and during two summer sessions. Fordham College at Rose Hill and the College of Business Administration, located on the Rose Hill campus, are adjacent to the New York Botanical Garden and the Bronx Zoo.

> **For more information, students should contact:**
> Fordham University
> Office of Undergraduate Admission
> Thebaud Hall
> 441 East Fordham Road
> New York, New York 10458-9993
> Telephone: 800-FORDHAM (367-3426) (toll-free)
> E-mail: enroll@fordham.edu
> WWW: http://www.fordham.edu

ACADEMIC PROGRAM
Students in all the undergraduate colleges pursue a common core curriculum designed to provide them with the breadth of knowledge necessary for life in the twenty-first century. Drawn from nine disciplines, the common core curriculum includes the study of philosophy, English composition and literature, history, theology, mathematical reasoning, natural science, social sciences, the fine arts, and foreign language. Business students benefit from the common core as well as from additional business core courses.

FINANCIAL AID
More than 80 percent of the entering students enroll with aid from Fordham and from outside sources. Among the major aid programs are the Federal Pell Grants, Federal Supplemental Educational Opportunity Grants, Federal Perkins Loans, work grants sponsored by both the government and the University, and University grants-in-aid. Outside sources of aid include state scholarships (more than 20,000 are awarded to students entering colleges in New York State each year), the New York State Tuition Assistance Program (TAP), privately sponsored scholarships, state government loan programs, and deferred-payment programs. The University also offers academic scholarships ranging from $7500 to the full cost of tuition and room. Applicants for aid must submit the Free Application for Federal Student Aid (FAFSA) and the College Scholarship Service PROFILE. Inquiries should be directed to the Fordham Office of Undergraduate Admission.

APPLICATION AND INFORMATION
Application may be made for either September or January enrollment. The application deadline is February 1 for fall admission. The completed application, the secondary school report, the results of the SAT I or ACT, all financial aid forms, and an application fee of $50 (check or money order made payable to Fordham University) should be submitted by this date. Students are notified beginning March 1. Candidates for early decision should apply by November 1 and receive notification by December 15. Transfer students must apply by December 1 for spring admission or by July 1 for fall admission.

GARDNER-WEBB UNIVERSITY

■ BOILING SPRINGS, NORTH CAROLINA

THE UNIVERSITY

Gardner-Webb University was founded in 1905 as a private high school by a group of Baptist associations. It became a junior college in 1928, was renamed Gardner-Webb College in 1942 in honor of former governor O. Max Gardner, and became a fully accredited senior college in 1971. Gardner-Webb moved to University status in 1993. Gardner-Webb's mission is to provide a high-quality liberal arts education in a Christian environment with the personal touch. The most outstanding characteristics of the University are its Christian environment, sense of community, and proven record of academic distinction. Its origins are obviously deep in Christian tradition, which is exemplified in the lives of staff and faculty members. Because the University is small, students can be well known by a large percentage of the faculty and administration. The cosmopolitan student body (more than 3,564 men and women, of whom nearly 2,700 are undergraduates) represents twenty-eight states and twenty-one other countries and gives an added, valuable dimension to a student's educational experience. Cars are permitted for all. The heritage of the University is reflected in its beautiful landscape and stately brick buildings. However, the University is constantly forging ahead with advanced technology and state-of-the-art facilities.

For further information, students should contact:
Director of Undergraduate Admissions and Enrollment Management
Gardner-Webb University
Boiling Springs, North Carolina 28017
Telephone: 704-406-4GWU
800-253-6472 (toll-free)
WWW:
http://www.gardner-webb.edu

ACADEMIC PROGRAM

The total program is marked by flexibility for the student but encourages, through active faculty advisement, choosing a substantial course of study. Elements of the humanities, the social and physical sciences, and mathematics or related disciplines must be taken.

FINANCIAL AID

Gardner-Webb University makes available to its students a variety of scholarships, loans, grants-in-aid, and work-study awards. Prospective applicants with financial need should contact the financial aid director early in their senior year of high school for a financial need estimate. Applications received after April 1 can be considered only in terms of available funds. An applicant must be accepted for admission before being awarded aid. Students must file the Free Application for Federal Student Aid (FAFSA). Scholarships and other types of aid include academic awards, Christian service awards, endowed scholarships, and annual scholarships. There are several Gardner-Webb loan funds. The University also administers aid from the full range of federal programs: Federal Pell Grants, Federal Work-Study Program awards, Federal Perkins Loans, and federally guaranteed Federal Stafford Student and Federal PLUS loans. North Carolina students have access to state grant funds administered by the University. Scholarships based on academic promise are also granted each year. Of all students, 90 percent receive aid in some form. The two criteria for receiving financial aid are financial need and academic promise.

APPLICATION AND INFORMATION

Applications, together with a nonrefundable $25 application fee, may be submitted for either semester. Early application is advised. Notification of the admission decision is given on a rolling basis upon receipt of all application data. A $150 room deposit for boarding students is due thirty days after acceptance and is refundable until May 1. A $50 deposit is required of commuting students.

GONZAGA UNIVERSITY

■ SPOKANE, WASHINGTON

THE UNIVERSITY

Gonzaga, founded in 1887, is an independent, comprehensive university with a distinguished background in the Catholic, Jesuit, and humanistic tradition. Gonzaga emphasizes the moral and ethical implications of learning, living, and working in today's global society. Through the University Core Curriculum, each student develops a strong liberal arts foundation, which many alumni cite as a most valuable asset. In addition, students specialize in any of more than seventy-five academic areas of study. Gonzaga's 110-acre campus is characterized by sprawling green lawns and majestic evergreen trees. Towering above the campus are the stately spires of St. Aloysius Church, the well-recognized landmark featured in the University logo. Because personal growth is as important as intellectual development, Gonzaga places great emphasis on student life outside of class.

For more information, students should contact:
Dean of Admission
Gonzaga University
Spokane, Washington 99258-0102
Telephone: 800-322-2584 (toll-free)
E-mail: ballinger@gu.gonzaga.edu
WWW: http://www.gonzaga.edu

ACADEMIC PROGRAM

Gonzaga University believes that it is necessary for all students, regardless of their chosen major or profession, to attain an education that goes beyond specialization. Therefore, all students attending Gonzaga receive a strong liberal arts background as well as depth in their major. The Core Curriculum is a very important component of the 128 semester units a student must earn for graduation. The Honors Program challenges special achievers with an integrated curriculum compatible with any major and most double majors. The program requires a separate application. The Hogan Entrepreneurial Leadership Program is for motivated and imaginative student leaders who are interested in creating new ventures and who want to make a difference in the world. A separate application is required. Gonzaga University Summer Term (GUST) offers motivated high school students intensive course work in a variety of academic disciplines. Academic and cocurricular activities are included in the six-week session. Credits earned through the Washington State Running Start Program or International Baccalaureate (I.B.) program are accepted on a class-by-class basis.

FINANCIAL AID

Gonzaga University offers many different types of financial aid to qualified students, including scholarships, Federal Pell Grants, Federal Supplemental Educational Opportunity Grants, work-study jobs, Federal Perkins Loans, Federal Stafford Student Loans, and on- and off-campus employment. In order to apply for financial aid awards, a student must first be accepted by the University and must see that the Free Application for Federal Student Aid (FAFSA) is submitted by February 1. After this date, awards are made on a funds-available basis. Approximately 90 percent of the students at Gonzaga receive financial assistance.

APPLICATION AND INFORMATION

Gonzaga University's priority deadline for admissions applications is March 1. The final deadline is April 1 for freshmen and July 1 for transfer students. The nonbinding early action application deadline is November 15. Students may also apply by using the Common Application, APPLY!, CollegeLink, and the Catholic College Common Application. It is recommended that all students applying for financial aid for the fall semester submit their application materials by March 1.

GOUCHER COLLEGE

■ **BALTIMORE, MARYLAND**

THE COLLEGE

Since its inception in 1885, Goucher College has maintained a reputation for academic excellence and a tradition of high quality combined with flexibility. The past few decades have seen many changes in academic programs and the student population, during which time Goucher has held fast to its commitment to a superior liberal arts education designed to help students achieve their fullest potential. The 1,100 men and women enrolled as undergraduates come from all parts of the United States and many other countries; they represent diverse backgrounds, interests, and points of view. Goucher's strength in the liberal arts comes from its attention to learning both inside and outside the classroom. Academic departments are organized into five divisions: arts, humanities, interdisciplinary studies, natural sciences and mathematics, and social sciences. The Goucher College curriculum encompasses courses from all five divisions; a freshman colloquium; an off-campus learning experience that is satisfied through an internship, study abroad, or an independent research project; and demonstrated proficiency in writing, computers, and a foreign language.

> **For more information, students should contact:**
> Director of Admissions
> Goucher College
> 1021 Dulaney Valley Road
> Baltimore, Maryland 21204-2794
> Telephone: 410-337-6100
> 800-GOUCHER (toll-free)
> E-mail: abooth@goucher.edu
> WWW: http://www.goucher.edu

ACADEMIC PROGRAM

The core curriculum is the foundation for a Goucher education. Recently revised, the core retains Goucher's tradition of academic rigor while becoming more relevant to a changing world. There is a strong emphasis on both interdisciplinary study and the development of a global perspective. Requirements include a demonstrated proficiency in a foreign language, English composition, and computer technology, along with courses in the arts, natural sciences, humanities, social sciences, and mathematics as well as a 3-credit off-campus requirement that reflects the College's belief in balancing classroom theory with real-world experience and that may take the form of an internship, a period of study abroad, or an independent project. All freshmen take the semester-long Freshman Colloquium. Taught in small sections, the course integrates humanities and social sciences perspectives. There is an interdisciplinary honors program in addition to honors courses in each department. The Goucher degree requires 120 semester hours of credit. The departmental major consists of at least 30 credits (about ten courses); the double major requires 60 credits. Goucher's calendar is based on the semester system.

FINANCIAL AID

In an average year, more than half of Goucher's students receive some form of aid; 45 percent are awarded grants, ranging from $400 to the total cost of the education. The average financial aid award is more than $15,000. Goucher participates in the Federal Work-Study Program and helps students benefit from Federal Supplemental Educational Opportunity Grants, Federal Pell Grants, Federal Perkins Loans, Federal Stafford Student Loans, and College loans. Goucher also offers a competitive merit award program.

GRACE COLLEGE

■ WINONA LAKE, INDIANA

THE COLLEGE

Grace College is a Christian undergraduate college of arts and sciences founded in 1948 and affiliated with the Fellowship of Grace Brethren Churches, a conservative evangelical denomination. Grace College attracts students from a variety of conservative evangelical backgrounds and from around the United States and other countries. The College offers an environment and academic program that are conservative in theology and progressive in spirit and that emphasize three qualities for students as they reach adulthood—mature Christian character, academic and career competence, and a heart for service to mankind. Enrollment at Grace College is 1,189, providing an ideal atmosphere in which students can learn, grow, and develop lasting friendships. Grace College has a campus of 165 acres. Approximately 69 percent of the College's students live on campus. The majority of students range in age from 18 to 23 years. More than 44 percent of the students come from Indiana; students also come from thirty-seven other states and seven countries. Approximately one third of the students are affiliated with the Fellowship of Grace Brethren Churches; the other two thirds are from other conservative Christian denominations, particularly Baptist and independent church backgrounds. Grace College's intercollegiate sports are men's baseball, basketball, golf, soccer, and tennis and women's basketball, soccer, softball, tennis, and volleyball as well as cross-country and track and field for both men and women. The men's basketball team won the NAIA Division II national championship in 1992.

For more information, students should contact:
Grace College
200 Seminary Drive
Winona Lake, Indiana 46590
Telephone: 800-54-GRACE (toll-free)
WWW: http://www.grace.edu

ACADEMIC PROGRAM

The Christian liberal arts philosophy of Grace College pervades each program of study and reflects the College's recognition that a broad common core of course work is central to each student's education. When combined with detailed study in a major field, this core establishes the foundation for successful graduate study and for a career.

FINANCIAL AID

The College offers extensive financial assistance to qualified students. Most students receive some sort of financial assistance—in the form of a scholarship, grant, loan, or campus employment—to help pay college costs. The average amount of financial aid awarded to a Grace College student totals $11,119 per year. To be considered for financial assistance at Grace College, students must submit the Free Application for Federal Student Aid (FAFSA). Students may receive Federal Pell Grants, Federal Perkins Loans, and Federal Supplemental Educational Opportunity Grants. In addition, students may be eligible for Federal Work-Study Program awards. The FAFSA should be on file by March 1 for priority consideration. To renew financial aid, students must refile the FAFSA each year.

APPLICATION AND INFORMATION

Students may apply for admission to any semester. Applications are accepted on a rolling basis until January 1 for the spring term and August 1 for the fall term. There is a $20 nonrefundable application fee. Students may also apply on the Grace Web site at no cost. Interested students and their parents are encouraged to visit the campus and to arrange for an interview at that time in order to get a clear picture of Grace College. Arrangements can be made for housing and meals for applicants by contacting the Grace College Visitor's Center.

GROVE CITY COLLEGE

■ **GROVE CITY, PENNSYLVANIA**

THE COLLEGE

The beautifully landscaped campus of Grove City College (GCC) stretches more than 150 acres and includes twenty-seven neo-Gothic buildings valued at more than $100 million. The campus is considered one of the loveliest in the nation. While the College has changed to meet the needs of the society it serves, its basic philosophy has remained unchanged since its founding in 1876. It is a Christian liberal arts and sciences institution of ideal size and dedicated to the principle of providing the highest-quality education at the lowest possible cost. Wishing to remain truly independent and to retain its distinctive qualities as a private school governed by private citizens (trustees), it is one of the very few colleges in the country that does not accept any state or federal monies. Affiliated with the Presbyterian Church (U.S.A.) but not narrowly denominational, the College believes that to be well educated a student should be exposed to the central ideas of the Judeo-Christian tradition. A 20-minute chapel program offered Tuesday and Thursday mornings, along with a Sunday evening worship service, challenge students in their faith. Sixteen chapel services per semester are required out of forty opportunities.

> **For more information, students should contact:**
> Jeffrey C. Mincey
> Director of Admissions
> Grove City College
> 100 Campus Drive
> Grove City, Pennsylvania 16127-2104
> Telephone: 724-458-2100
> Fax: 724-458-3395
> E-mail: admissions@gcc.edu
> WWW: http://www.gcc.edu

ACADEMIC PROGRAM

Grove City College's goal is to assist young men and women in developing as complete individuals—academically, spiritually, and physically. The general education requirements provide all students with a high level of cultural literacy and communication skills.

FINANCIAL AID

Because the College's tuition charges are low, every student, in effect, receives significant financial assistance. Fifty-seven percent of the freshmen receive additional aid from GCC. Students applying for financial assistance must complete Grove City College's financial aid form. Job opportunities are available both on and off campus.

APPLICATION AND INFORMATION

A regular admission applicant should take the SAT I or ACT by October or November of the senior year in high school. The application should include scores on the SAT I (preferred) or the ACT, a high school transcript, references, a recommendation from the student's principal or counselor, and a nonrefundable application fee of $30. An application may be submitted after the eleventh grade. An early decision applicant should take the entrance test in the eleventh grade, visit the College for an interview, and submit the application by November 15; notification of the admission decision is mailed on December 15. Approved early decision applicants must accept by January 15 and submit a nonrefundable deposit of $200. Applicants seeking regular decision must submit the completed application and supporting documents by February 15 of their senior year. Notification of the admission decision is mailed on March 15. Students who are offered admission should reply as soon as possible, but no later than May 1, and include a nonrefundable deposit of $150. Applications received after February 15 will be considered as space permits. The College receives four applications for every freshman vacancy.

HAVERFORD COLLEGE

■ **HAVERFORD, PENNSYLVANIA**

THE COLLEGE
Haverford is the first college established by members of the Society of Friends (Quakers). Founded in 1833, Haverford has chosen to remain small, undergraduate, and residential to carry out its educational philosophy and to maintain a strong sense of community. An Honor Code is created and directed by students and is an important element of the Haverford community. The Honor Code allows students to directly confront academic and social issues in a spirit of cooperation and mutual respect. Haverford's 1,100 students represent forty-five states, Puerto Rico, the District of Columbia, and twenty countries. Twenty-three percent of the students are students of color, while an additional 4 percent are international students. Haverford is a residential campus with 98 percent of the students and 70 percent of the faculty living on campus.

For more information, students should contact:
Office of Admission
Haverford College
370 Lancaster Avenue
Haverford, Pennsylvania 19041-1392
Telephone: 610-896-1350
              610-896-1436 (TTY/TDD)
Fax: 610-896-1338
E-mail: admitme@haverford.edu
        finaid@haverford.edu
WWW: http://www.haverford.edu

ACADEMIC PROGRAM
Students plan their programs using established guidelines and with the help of faculty advisers. They must have at least three courses in each of the divisions of the College: humanities, social science, and natural science. In addition, they must fulfill requirements in foreign language, social justice, writing, and quantitative course work. Flexibility in the curriculum allows opportunities for independent study, foreign study, and noncollegiate academic study. Majors are selected at the end of the sophomore year. Normally, students take four courses per semester and thirty-two courses over four years. Scheduling is flexible, however, and students may arrange programs to meet individual needs, including six-semester, seven-semester, and five-year programs.

FINANCIAL AID
The College has an extensive financial aid program. Approximately 40 percent of Haverford's students receive College grant aid. Candidates for Haverford College funded aid must file the Financial Aid PROFILE with the College Scholarship Service, along with the FAFSA. Applicants may register for the PROFILE by completing a short form, available from their local high school guidance office, and sending it to the College Scholarship Service or by calling the College Scholarship Service at (800) 778-6888. Regular decision students should complete the PROFILE registration process by January 2, so the College Scholarship Service can send the form and have students complete it by the January 31 deadline. The FAFSA is also available from high school guidance offices and must also be filed by January 31. Early decision candidates should complete the PROFILE registration process by October 15 and file the PROFILE form with the College Scholarship Service by November 15.

APPLICATION AND INFORMATION
The application deadlines for admission are November 15 for early decision candidates, January 15 for regular decision candidates, and March 31 for transfer candidates. Haverford also accepts the Common Application, which is available in school guidance offices. The admission office is open from 9 a.m. to 5 p.m. on weekdays (8:30 a.m. to 4:30 p.m. from June to August) and, during the fall, from 9 a.m. to noon on Saturday. Further details are given in the leaflet "Financial Aid at Haverford," which is included in the admission application booklet. Haverford's College Scholarship Service PROFILE code number is 2289, and the FAFSA code number is 003274.

HAWAI'I PACIFIC UNIVERSITY

■ HONOLULU, HAWAI'I

THE UNIVERSITY

Hawai'i Pacific University (HPU) is an independent, coeducational, career-oriented comprehensive university with a foundation in the liberal arts. Undergraduate and graduate degrees are offered in more than fifty areas. Hawai'i Pacific prides itself on maintaining strong academic programs, small class sizes, individual attention to students, an outstanding faculty, and a student population as diverse as the United Nations. HPU is accredited by the Western Association of Schools and Colleges and the National League for Nursing Accrediting Commission. HPU is the largest private university in Hawai'i, with more than 8,000 students from every state in the union and more than 100 countries. The diversity of the student body stimulates learning about other cultures firsthand, both in and out of the classroom. There is no majority population at HPU. Students are encouraged to examine the values, customs, traditions, and principles of others to gain a clearer understanding of their own perspectives. HPU students develop friendships with students from throughout the United States and the world, important connections for success in the global economy of the twenty-first century. In addition to the undergraduate programs, HPU offers several graduate programs: the M.B.A. (with ten concentrations), the Master of Science in Information Systems (M.S.I.S.), the Master of Science in Nursing (M.S.N.), and the Master of Arts (M.A.) in communications, diplomacy and military studies, global leadership, human resource management, organizational change, and teaching English as a second language. HPU has NCAA Division II intercollegiate sports. Men's athletic programs include baseball, basketball, cheerleading, cross-country, soccer, and tennis. Women's athletics include cheerleading, cross-country, soccer, softball, tennis, and volleyball. The housing office at HPU offers many services and options for students. Residence halls with cafeteria service are available on the windward Hawai'i Loa campus, while off-campus apartments are available in the Honolulu and Waikiki areas for those seeking more independent living arrangements.

> **For further information and for application materials, students should contact:**
>
> Office of Admissions
> Hawai'i Pacific University
> 1164 Bishop Street, Suite 200
> Honolulu, Hawai'i 96813
> Telephone: 808-544-0238
> 800-669-4724 (toll-free in U.S. and Canada)
> Fax: 808-544-1136
> E-mail: admissions@hpu.edu
> WWW: http://www.hpu.edu/

ACADEMIC PROGRAM

The baccalaureate student must complete at least 124 semester hours of credit. Forty-five of these credits provide the student with a strong foundation in the liberal arts, with the remaining credits composed of appropriate upper-division classes in the student's major and related areas. The academic year operates on a modified 4-1-4 semester system, featuring a five-week winter intersession. The University also offers extensive summer sessions. A student can earn up to 15 semester hours of credit during the summer. By attending these supplemental sessions, a student may complete the baccalaureate degree program in three years. A five-year B.S.B.A./M.B.A. program is also available.

FINANCIAL AID

The University provides financial aid for qualified students through institutional, state, and federal aid programs. Approximately 40 percent of the University's undergraduate students receive financial aid. Among the forms of aid available are Federal Perkins Loans, Federal Stafford Student Loans, Guaranteed Parental Loans, Federal Pell Grants, and Federal Supplemental Educational Opportunity Grants. To apply for aid, students must submit the Free Application for Federal Student Aid (FAFSA). The FAFSA may be submitted at any time, but the priority deadline is March 1.

APPLICATION AND INFORMATION

Candidates are notified of admission decisions on a rolling basis, usually within two weeks of receipt of application materials. Early entrance and deferred entrance are available.

HIRAM COLLEGE

■ HIRAM, OHIO

THE COLLEGE
Founded in 1850, Hiram College cherishes its heritage as an institution of academic excellence and rare distinction. Hiram's 900 students come from twenty-five states and nineteen countries and represent more than twenty-five different religions. SAT I and ACT scores of Hiram's entering freshmen exceed national norms: in 2001, SAT I medians were 580 (verbal) and 570 (math); the ACT composite median was 24. Between 50 and 60 percent of the College's graduates go on to graduate school or professional school within five years. The College was awarded a Phi Beta Kappa chapter in 1971.

For more information, students should contact:
Director of Admission
Hiram College
Hiram, Ohio 44234
Telephone: 330-569-5169
800-362-5280 (toll-free)
E-mail: admission@hiram.edu
WWW: http://www.hiram.edu

ACADEMIC PROGRAM
Hiram's academic calendar, the Hiram Plan, is unique among colleges and universities. Each fifteen-week semester is divided into a twelve-week and a three-week session. During the three-week session, students take only one intensive course. The plan provides two formats for learning, which increases opportunity for small group study with faculty, study in special topics, hands-on learning through field trips and internships, and study abroad. Hiram College's commitment to the liberal arts is manifested in a core curriculum required of all students. Required courses include the Freshman Colloquium, a small, seminar course on a special topic taught by a student's adviser; First Year Seminar, emphasizing critical thinking, effective writing, and speaking; and a sequence of interdisciplinary courses. The course of study in most areas of major concentration is specified by the departments and divisions. Students generally take ten courses from within a department, as well as two or three courses from related or supporting departments. Alternatively, a student, with the assistance of the adviser, may develop an area of concentration that consists of related courses from different academic areas, crossing departmental lines to focus on particular needs or interests. A student may also submit a proposal for an individually designed program to the Area of Concentration Board.

FINANCIAL AID
More than 75 percent of Hiram's students receive financial aid based on need. All financial aid awards are made on a one-year basis, and each year a new Free Application for Federal Student Aid (FAFSA) must be submitted to determine eligibility. Most financial aid at Hiram is a combination of a loan, a job, and a scholarship or grant-in-aid. Scholarships awarded on the basis of merit are also available and range from $3000 to $12,000 per year. Aid includes Federal Pell Grants, Federal Supplemental Educational Opportunity Grants, Federal Perkins Loans, Federal Stafford Student Loans, state grants, Federal Work-Study awards, and veterans' benefits. Campus employment is available regardless of aid eligibility.

APPLICATION AND INFORMATION
Application materials include the completed application form; a secondary school report, which must be completed and returned to Hiram directly by the high school guidance counselor; the results of the SAT I or ACT; and an essay. Teacher recommendations are also required. The application deadline is February 1. An early decision option is also available. Applicants are encouraged to visit the campus. The Office of Admission, located in Teachout-Price Hall, is open year-round for interviews from 9 a.m. to 4 p.m. on weekdays and from 9 a.m. to noon on Saturday (except during the summer months).

HOFSTRA UNIVERSITY

■ **HEMPSTEAD, NEW YORK**

THE UNIVERSITY
Hofstra University, with more than 100 undergraduate majors and many options within those majors, offers students a first-rate education grounded in the liberal arts. Students attending Hofstra come from forty-four states and sixty-seven countries. The freshman class numbers almost 2,000. The total enrollment at Hofstra is approximately 13,400; there are 8,406 full-time undergraduates and 1,239 part-time undergraduates. Major University divisions are the Hofstra College of Liberal Arts and Sciences, the School of Communication, the Zarb School of Business, the School of Education and Allied Human Services, the Honors College, New College, the School of Law, University Without Walls, the Saturday College, and the University College for Continuing Education. Residential facilities accommodate more than 4,000 students in modern on-campus residence halls. As a result of the Program for the Higher Education of the Disabled, Hofstra is 100 percent accessible to persons with disabilities. Necessary services are provided for wheelchair-bound and other disabled students who meet all academic requirements for admission.

For additional information, students should contact:
Dean of Admissions
Hofstra University
Hempstead, New York 11549
Telephone: 516-463-6700
 800-HOFSTRA (toll-free)
Fax: 516-463-5100
WWW: http://www.hofstra.edu

ACADEMIC PROGRAM
The requirement for the B.A. degree is 124 semester hours, of which 94 must be in liberal arts and 30 in free electives. Successful completion of at least 124 semester hours with a quality point average of 2.0 or better is required for graduation. For the major, each academic department defines the special pattern of required and suggested study that suits its discipline. Beyond this major requirement, five general requirements in humanities, natural sciences, social sciences, English, and foreign languages must be fulfilled. A candidate for graduation with the degree of B.B.A. must successfully complete at least 128 semester hours with a quality point average of 2.0 or better, completing at least 64 hours in liberal arts subjects (humanities, mathematics, natural sciences, and social sciences), 40 hours in general business courses (accounting, business law, finance, general business, international business, management, marketing, and quantitative methods), and all major and additional requirements as listed under the department of specialization. Each of the scientific-technical programs leading to the B.S. degree requires a total of 124 to 134 semester hours, of which approximately half must be in liberal arts courses exclusive of those offered by the academic department of major specialization.

FINANCIAL AID
Financial aid options range from scholarships through assistance grants to loans and part-time jobs. About 81 percent of all students receive financial help. Scholarships average $4100 per year, and loans average $3850 per year. Hofstra subscribes to the principles of the College Scholarship Service in determining the amount of awards. Federal funds include Federal Perkins Loans, Federal Pell and Federal Supplemental Educational Opportunity Grants, and Federal Work-Study Program awards. To be considered for financial aid, completed financial aid applications and credentials (including the Free Application for Federal Student Aid) should be received on or before February 15.

APPLICATION AND INFORMATION
Freshman applicants must submit the application, a $40 application fee, the high school transcript, test scores, and a guidance counselor's recommendation. Transfer students must submit an application, the application fee, high school and college transcripts, and test scores (if fewer than 24 semester hours were attempted at the previous college).

IDAHO STATE UNIVERSITY

◼ POCATELLO, IDAHO

THE UNIVERSITY

Idaho State University (ISU) has existed as an institution since 1901, when it was first established as the Academy of Idaho. It gained university status in 1963. Offering instruction in nearly every area of the arts and sciences, the University also conducts well-rounded programs of training in vocational and technical fields. Bachelor's and master's degrees in a variety of areas are awarded by the College of Arts and Sciences, the College of Business, the College of Education, the College of Engineering, the College of Health Professions, the College of Pharmacy, and the Graduate School. Doctoral degrees offered at ISU include the Doctor of Philosophy, Doctor of Arts, and Doctor of Education. Certificate programs of varying lengths and B.S. and M.S. degrees are included in the curricula of the College of Technology. Because of its location and character, ISU serves a diverse population that includes traditional-age students, nontraditional students, working professionals, and senior citizens. ISU has a total enrollment of nearly 14,000 undergraduate and graduate students; they represent nearly every state in the Union and fifty-seven other countries. U.S. and international students attend the University because of its reputation as an academic and vocational institution of high quality; its relaxed, safe, and rural atmosphere; and its location at the foot of the Rocky Mountains. Through its programs in pharmacy and other health-related professions, ISU is a center for education in the health field. Its programs in education, business, and engineering respond to a variety of current and emerging demands. It serves as a national center for Doctor of Arts degree programs. ISU also has responsibility for Idaho's dental education program.

For additional information and application materials, students should contact:
Office of Enrollment Planning and Academic Services
Campus Box 8054
Idaho State University
Pocatello, Idaho 83209-0009
Telephone: 208-282-3277
Fax: 208-282-4314
E-mail: info@isu.edu
WWW: http://www.isu.edu

ACADEMIC PROGRAM

ISU requires a broad liberal arts education of all candidates for the bachelor's degree. Students are required to complete credits in math, English, speech, the physical and natural sciences, the humanities, and the social sciences before concentrating on their major field. All bachelor's degree candidates must complete a minimum of 128 credit hours. The University operates on the semester system; opportunities are available for receiving credit by examination or tailoring a degree through the Bachelor of University Studies program. Internships are also arranged for students through the Career Development Center and individual departments.

FINANCIAL AID

The goal of the University's financial assistance program is twofold: to reward those students who demonstrate outstanding academic, leadership, or other talents and to aid those students unable to bear the costs of attending the University. ISU provides financial assistance for some 80 percent of its students through grant, loan, work, and scholarship programs. ISU accepts the Free Application for Federal Student Aid (FAFSA). The priority deadline for mailing the FAFSA is March 1. The scholarship application deadline for new and transfer students is February 20. A number of competitive out-of-state-student tuition and reduced fee waivers are also available to domestic and international students, as are campus and off-campus job placement programs.

APPLICATION AND INFORMATION

Deadlines for submission of all application materials are August 1 for the fall semester and December 1 for the spring semester. Notification is made within two weeks of application.

IONA COLLEGE

■ **NEW ROCHELLE, NEW YORK**

THE COLLEGE

Iona College takes its name from the island of Iona in the Inner Hebrides, just off the west coast of Scotland. It was to this tiny island that the Irish monk Columba came in A.D. 563 to establish an abbey from which missionaries went forth to teach and evangelize. The island of Iona became a center of faith and culture that contributed significantly to the civilization of Western Europe. In 1940, the Congregation of Christian Brothers founded Iona College in New Rochelle, New York.

> **For more information, students should contact:**
> Office of Undergraduate Admissions
> Iona College
> New Rochelle, New York 10801
> Telephone: 914-633-2502
>   800-231-IONA (toll-free)
> WWW: http://www.iona.edu

ACADEMIC PROGRAM

For completion, a minimum of 120 credits is required for the majority of B.A. and B.S. degrees, and a minimum of 126 credits is required for all B.B.A. degrees. All students must complete the core curriculum and their school requirements, achieve a scholastic index of at least 2.0, satisfy course requirements in the major field, and secure a satisfactory score on a comprehensive examination or such substitutes as may be specified in the major field of study. The normal course load is five courses per semester. Juniors and seniors usually carry 15–18 credits per semester. A credit corresponds to 1 hour of class work or 2 hours of laboratory work plus 2 hours of supplementary assignments per week for fifteen weeks. Students are considered to be in good academic standing if, in the judgment of the Committee on Academic Standing, they are able to complete their programs of study within four years with a cumulative scholastic index of at least 2.0. An honors program is available for students who want a stimulating learning experience that will permit them to pursue some of their own interests.

FINANCIAL AID

The financial aid program at Iona exists to assist students who would be unable to pursue an education without some form of economic assistance. Scholarships are available for students who have demonstrated strong academic ability throughout high school. Scholarship amounts range from $4000 to full tuition. Nearly 90 percent of Iona students receive some form of financial aid. The average financial aid package is $9500 per year. Financial aid includes Iona scholarships and grants-in-aid, Federal Pell Grants, Federal Supplemental Educational Opportunity Grants, Federal Stafford Student Loans, Federal Perkins Loans, New York State Tuition Assistance Program awards, and on- and off-campus employment through the Federal Work-Study Program. Deferred tuition payment plans are also available. Applicants for financial aid should file the Free Application for Federal Student Aid (FAFSA) as soon after January 1 as possible for the following fall semester.

APPLICATION AND INFORMATION

Iona's rolling admissions policy enables year-round applications. In addition, Iona has an Early Action Plan. Students who apply under this plan must have completed their application by December 1. Decisions will be mailed by December 20. To ensure acceptance into certain academic programs, however, applications should be filed no later than March 15. Completed applications are reviewed immediately upon receipt, and acceptances are mailed in the spring. The Committee on Admissions requires applicants to submit a completed College application form along with an application fee of $25. A student fills in part of the application and gives the form to his or her high school counselor to be completed. The applicant must also request the secondary school to forward to the College a transcript of grades and a recommendation from a high school official. Veterans are required to supply a copy of their Separation Qualification Record, showing service training and schools completed. Transfer students must supply an official transcript of grades from high school and each college attended.

ITHACA COLLEGE

■ **ITHACA, NEW YORK**

THE COLLEGE
Coeducational and nonsectarian since its founding in 1892, Ithaca College enrolls approximately 6,200 students. The College community is a diverse one; virtually every state is represented in the student population, as are more than seventy-five other countries. Students come to Ithaca College to get active, hands-on learning that brings together the best of liberal arts and professional studies. The program is offered in five schools: the School of Humanities and Sciences (2,250 students), School of Business (600 students), Roy H. Park School of Communications (1,250 students), School of Health Sciences and Human Performance (1,300 students), and School of Music (500 students). There are approximately 300 graduate students.

> **For more information, students should contact:**
> Paula J. Mitchell
> Director of Admission
> Office of Admission
> Ithaca College
> 100 Job Hall
> Ithaca, New York 14850-7020
> Telephone: 800-429-4274 (toll-free)
> 607-274-3124
> Fax: 607-274-1900
> E-mail: admission@ithaca.edu
> WWW: http://www.ithaca.edu

ACADEMIC PROGRAM
Undergraduate programs of study address two primary issues: the need for rigorous academic preparation in highly specialized professional fields and the need for students to prepare for the complex demands of society by acquiring an intellectual breadth that extends beyond their chosen profession. Each degree offered requires a minimum of 120 credit hours and a specified number of liberal arts credits. The academic year comprises two 15-week semesters, from late August to mid-December and from mid-January to mid-May. ROTC programs are offered in conjunction with Cornell University.

FINANCIAL AID
Financial aid, which totals more than $80 million from all sources, is extended to approximately 80 percent of Ithaca students. To apply for financial aid, students should check the proper space on the College's admission application, and if seeking federal aid, submit the Free Application for Federal Student Aid (FAFSA) by February 1 with the U.S. Department of Education at the address indicated on the form. Early decision candidates should follow the time line outlined under the Application and Information section below. All accepted applicants are considered for merit aid in recognition of their academic and personal achievement. Programs providing grants and loans include the Federal Work-Study, Federal Pell Grant, Federal Perkins Loan, Federal Stafford Student Loan, and Federal Supplemental Educational Opportunity Grant.

APPLICATION AND INFORMATION
For freshman regular decision, prospective students should apply by March 1; applicants are notified of a decision on a rolling basis no later than April 15 and must confirm their enrollment by May 1. Freshman applicants seeking institutional and federal aid should file the FAFSA by February 1 with the federal processor. For freshman early decision, which is binding, students should apply by November 1; applicants are notified by December 15 and must confirm their enrollment by February 1. Early decision applicants seeking institutional and federal financial aid should submit the Financial Aid PROFILE, available from the College Scholarship Service, by November 1 and the FAFSA by February 1. Students who want to transfer into Ithaca College should apply by March 1 for fall admission and by December 1 for spring admission. Applicants seeking institutional and federal financial aid should file the FAFSA by February 1. All applicants must submit a $55 application fee. Ithaca's application for admission is available on the Web at http://www.ithaca.edu/admission.

KETTERING UNIVERSITY

■ FLINT, MICHIGAN

THE UNIVERSITY
Kettering University (formerly GMI Engineering & Management Institute) offers education for the real world. Nearly 100 percent of Kettering's students receive a job offer or are accepted by graduate schools before receiving their diplomas. Kettering University has a unique partnership that offers students, business, and industry an opportunity found at no other undergraduate college in America. Kettering, a professional cooperative engineering, management, science, and math university, is the only institution that assists incoming freshmen to be selected by companies for cooperative employment, a process initiated for all accepted students. Kettering University successfully integrates the practical aspects of the workplace into the world of higher education through its more than 750 corporate partners, corporations, and agencies located throughout the United States, Canada, and selected countries. Kettering's corporate partners represent most major industrial groups; many are recognized as worldwide leaders in business innovation and manufacturing technology. These corporations share a commitment to "grow their own" engineers and managers by employing exceptionally talented young men and women in one of the ten baccalaureate degree programs.

For more information, students should contact:
Admissions Office
Kettering University
1700 West Third Avenue
Flint, Michigan 48504-4898
Telephone: 810-762-7865
　　　　　800-955-4464 (toll-free in the United States and Canada)
E-mail: admissions@kettering.edu
WWW: http://www.kettering.edu

ACADEMIC PROGRAM
Although each program at Kettering University has its own sequence requirements, 160 credit hours are generally required, including thesis credit hours. The program involves nine academic terms and nine co-op terms, two of which are focused on the capstone thesis project, which is done on behalf of the student's co-op employer. Students alternate between eleven-week periods of academic study on the campus in Flint and twelve-week periods of related work experience with their corporate employer. The academic year consists of two 3–month academic terms on campus and two 3–month terms of paid work experience. A typical Kettering University cooperative student may earn up to $65,000 in co-op wages through the complete program.

FINANCIAL AID
In addition to all traditional sources of aid, all Kettering students benefit from a special resource that is significant and not need based. One of the many advantages of attending Kettering University is the opportunity for students to earn a salary during their co-op work terms. Co-op income is substantial and can help cover part of the cost of a Kettering education by supplementing the family contribution and the standard forms of need-based and merit-based financial aid. Students who live at home during work experience periods are able to contribute a greater proportion of earnings directly to educational expenses. About 70 percent of students are able to live at home during work terms. The typical range of co-op earnings over the five-year program is $40,000 to $65,000. Kettering University offers all the traditional forms of financial aid, both need- and merit-based. The new Kettering Scholarship program, with awards up to $60,000, is available to qualified applicants. Because of their talents, many students win scholarships from agencies and organizations from their local communities. Michigan residents are often recipients of the Michigan Competitive Scholarship/Tuition Grant. More than 92 percent of the 2001 entering class received some form of financial aid, making a private education at Kettering very affordable.

APPLICATION AND INFORMATION
Prospective freshmen are encouraged to file their application early in their senior year. Admission decisions for transfer applicants are based on college record for those who have completed at least 30 credits. Applications are accepted all year long; however, early application greatly increases visibility for early employment possibilities in the co-op search process.

LAGRANGE COLLEGE

■ **LAGRANGE, GEORGIA**

THE COLLEGE
Founded in 1831, LaGrange College is the oldest private college in Georgia. A four-year liberal arts and sciences college affiliated with the United Methodist Church, LaGrange is ranked in the top ten and as the seventh "best value" among Southern comprehensive colleges by *U.S. News & World Report*. The College has an enrollment of approximately 1,000 men and women and a student-faculty ratio of 11:1. With only 11 students in the average classroom, LaGrange College provides a challenging and supportive academic environment.

For additional information, students should contact:
Office of Admission
LaGrange College
601 Broad Street
LaGrange, Georgia 30240
Telephone: 706-880-8005
        800-593-2885 (toll-free)
Fax: 706-880-8010
E-mail: lgcadmis@lgc.edu
WWW: http://www.lgc.edu

MAJORS AND DEGREES
LaGrange College offers the Bachelor of Arts (B.A.) degree in art and design, biochemistry, biology, chemistry, computer science, early childhood education, English, history, human services, mathematics, middle childhood education, political science, psychology, religion, Spanish, and theater arts with concentrations available in Christian education, Latin American studies, women's studies, and youth ministry. Students interested in secondary education careers first pursue a bachelor's degree in their preferred subject area (including art and music), and then enroll in the College's one-year Master of Arts in Teaching program. The Bachelor of Science (B.S.) degree is available in accounting, business administration, chemistry, computer science, and mathematics. The Bachelor of Music (B.M.) degree is available with concentrations in creative music technologies, church music, and performance. The Bachelor of Science in Nursing (B.S.N.) degree is also offered. Preprofessional programs of study, as preparation for graduate and professional study, are available in dentistry, engineering, law, medicine and allied fields, optometry, pharmacy, physical therapy, theology/seminary, and veterinary medicine.

ACADEMIC PROGRAM
Each program of study contains a substantial interdisciplinary core component. Providing a background in the natural and social sciences, arts, and humanities, the core helps students see how subjects interrelate while developing the research and problem-solving skills employers and graduate schools seek most.

FINANCIAL AID
As a private college, LaGrange is committed to helping meet the difference between the funds any student has available and the cost of attending LaGrange College. More than 80 percent of LaGrange students receive some combination of financial awards, with more than $8 million awarded annually.

APPLICATION AND INFORMATION
Applications for admission are evaluated on a rolling basis and should be submitted at least one month prior to the beginning of the semester in which entrance is desired. Applicants can expect to receive notification within two to three weeks of the date that all documents are submitted. Weekday campus visits are encouraged, and appointments can be arranged by contacting the Office of Admission.

LE MOYNE COLLEGE

■ SYRACUSE, NEW YORK

THE COLLEGE
Le Moyne College is a four-year Jesuit college of approximately 2,100 undergraduate students that uniquely balances a comprehensive liberal arts education with preparation for specific career paths or graduate study. Founded by the Society of Jesus in 1946, Le Moyne is the second-youngest of the twenty-eight Jesuit colleges and universities in the United States.

> **For more information, students should contact:**
> Dennis J. Nicholson
> Director of Admission
> Le Moyne College
> Syracuse, New York 13214-1399
> Telephone: 315-445-4300
> 800-333-4733 (toll-free)
> E-mail: admission@lemoyne.edu
> WWW: http://www.lemoyne.edu

ACADEMIC PROGRAM
While each major department has its own sequence requirements for the minimum 120 credit hours needed for the Le Moyne degree, the College is convinced that there is a fundamental intellectual discipline that should characterize the graduate of a superior liberal arts college. Le Moyne's core curriculum provides this foundation by including studies of English language and literature, philosophy, history, religious studies, science, mathematics, and social sciences. For exceptional students, Le Moyne offers an integral honors program that includes an interdisciplinary humanities sequence as well as departmental honors courses. Le Moyne also offers a part-time course of study during evening hours through its Center for Continuous Learning. Le Moyne students may enroll in Army and Air Force ROTC programs at Syracuse University.

FINANCIAL AID
Financial aid is offered to 95 percent of Le Moyne's students through scholarships, grants, loans, and work-study assignments. Le Moyne offers a generous program of merit-based academic and athletic scholarships as well as financial aid based on a student's need and academic promise. Federal funds are available through the Federal Pell Grant, Federal Work-Study, Federal Supplemental Educational Opportunity Grant, and Federal Perkins Loan programs. A student's eligibility for need-based financial aid is determined from both the Free Application for Federal Student Aid (FAFSA) and the Le Moyne Financial Aid Application Form. It is recommended that these forms be mailed by February 1.

APPLICATION AND INFORMATION
The Admission Committee reviews applications and mails decisions on a rolling admission cycle beginning January 1. The priority deadline for applications is March 1; all students who wish to be considered for academic non-need scholarships should have a completed application on file in the Office of Admission before this date. Students who wish to be considered under the early decision program must have a completed application submitted by December 1. Early decision applicants will by notified by December 15. Transfer students are encouraged to apply before May 1 for the fall semester and December 1 for the spring semester. A fun-filled two-day orientation program takes place in mid-summer.

LOYOLA MARYMOUNT UNIVERSITY

■ LOS ANGELES, CALIFORNIA

THE UNIVERSITY

Loyola Marymount University, situated on a picturesque campus, offers competitive students an education of high quality in a friendly and relaxed atmosphere. As successor of the oldest institution of learning in southern California, St. Vincent's College, the University is steeped in a tradition and history of dedication to academic excellence and the total development of its students. Although the emphasis is within the undergraduate school (full-time enrollment is 4,808 and part-time enrollment is 366), 1,424 students attend the Graduate Division, primarily in the evening hours, working toward master's degrees in the fields of arts, arts in teaching, business administration, education, and science (including engineering). The School of Law, situated at a separate campus, has both day and evening divisions and offers the Juris Doctor degree. Law school enrollment is 1,407.

> **For more information about Loyola Marymount University, prospective students should contact:**
>
> Matthew X. Fissinger
> Director of Admissions
> Loyola Marymount University
> One LMU Drive
> Los Angeles, California 90045
> Telephone: 310-338-2750
> 800-LMU-INFO (toll-free)
> Fax: 310-338-2797

ACADEMIC PROGRAM

While premajor and major requirements differ with each area of study, a core curriculum is maintained as a degree requirement in the fields of American cultures, communication skills, fine arts, history, literature/psychology, mathematics/science, philosophy, social science, and theology, thus ensuring each student a balanced education. The maximum requirement in each of the core fields is 6 units of academic work. The interdepartmental honors program provides challenges for the exceptional student. The academic calendar consists of two semesters and a six-week optional summer session.

FINANCIAL AID

Approximately 75 percent of the University's undergraduate students receive some type of financial assistance. The total amount of financial aid awarded to students is approximately $70 million. Students applying for aid must file the Free Application for Student Aid (FAFSA) and the CSS PROFILE. All students are expected to apply for the Federal Pell Grant, and California residents must apply for the California grants. Most aid is awarded on the basis of need, but the University does offer merit scholarships (including full-tuition scholarships). The priority date for financial aid is February 15. Aid is awarded after that date on a funds-available basis.

APPLICATION AND INFORMATION

Applicants must submit official transcripts from the last high school attended and from each college attended, arrange for SAT I or ACT scores to be sent to the Office of Admissions, submit a recommendation form from an official of the last school attended, and file an application with the $45 nonrefundable fee. Applications are considered when all necessary documents have been received prior to the deadline of the semester for which application is made. The deadlines are February 1 for the fall semester and December 1 for the spring semester. International students who are not legal residents of the United States must follow the same admission procedure but are required to submit all completed data before the following deadlines: fall semester, June 1; spring semester, December 1. International students must also submit scores on the Test of English as a Foreign Language (TOEFL), submit a statement of financial responsibility for all obligations covering the full period of time for which the student is making application, be certain all records of previous academic training are original or authentic copies with notarization, and have notarized English translations of all the required records.

LOYOLA UNIVERSITY CHICAGO

■ CHICAGO, ILLINOIS

THE UNIVERSITY
Loyola University Chicago is the most comprehensive Jesuit university in the United States. Founded in 1870 by priests of the Society of Jesus, Loyola continues the Jesuit commitment to education, which is well-grounded in the liberal arts and based on excellence in teaching and research. Loyola attracts students from all fifty states and seventy-four countries to its nine schools and colleges: the Stritch School of Medicine, the School of Law, the College of Arts and Sciences, the School of Business Administration, the Niehoff School of Nursing, the School of Education, the School of Social Work, the Graduate School, and Mundelein College (for adult and lifelong learning). Each year, Loyola enrolls nearly 1,000 freshmen and 400 transfer students.

For more information, students should contact:
Undergraduate Admission Office
Loyola University Chicago
820 North Michigan Avenue
Chicago, Illinois 60611
Telephone: 312-915-6500
             800-262-2373 (toll-free)
E-mail: admission@luc.edu
WWW: http://www.luc.edu/

ACADEMIC PROGRAM
Jesuit educators believe that a solid foundation in the liberal arts and sciences is essential for students entering all professions. Loyola's Core Curriculum is designed to give students this foundation. The core requirements vary by college but usually include courses in literature, expressive arts, history, social sciences, mathematical and natural sciences, philosophy, and theology. The core allows students who are undecided about their majors to explore all possibilities before deciding upon a field of study.

FINANCIAL AID
Loyola attempts to meet the financial need of as many students as possible. Seventy-five percent of Loyola students receive some form of aid, including University-funded scholarships and grants, federal and state grants, work-study, and loans. Students are encouraged to file the Free Application for Federal Student Aid (FAFSA) by mid-February in order to receive consideration for all types of aid. Merit scholarships are awarded to entering freshmen who have outstanding academic records. Presidential, Damen, and Loyola scholarships are awarded to students who rank at the top of their high school graduating class and score well on the ACT or SAT I. Scholarship amounts for these programs are $5000–$10,000 per year. These awards are renewable for up to three years. Other scholarships available include competitive awards for students admitted to the Honors Program and students from Jesuit/BVM/Sisters of Christian Charity high schools, National Merit/National Achievement finalists, theater scholarships (awarded by audition), and debate, leadership, nursing, and public accounting awards. Transfer students who have completed 30 hours of college credit with an outstanding record of academic achievement may receive a Transfer Academic Scholarship. These awards are renewable for up to three years.

APPLICATION AND INFORMATION
Applicants are notified of the admission decision three to four weeks after the application, supporting credentials, secondary school counselor recommendation, and $25 application fee are received. Prospective students are encouraged to visit the campus. The Undergraduate Admission Office encourages students to schedule individual appointments and campus tours or to participate in one of the many campus programs offered throughout the year.

LOYOLA UNIVERSITY NEW ORLEANS

■ NEW ORLEANS, LOUISIANA

THE UNIVERSITY
Founded by the Jesuits in 1912, Loyola University's more than 35,000 graduates have excelled in innumerable professional fields for more than eighty years. Approximately 3,500 undergraduate students enjoy the individual attention of a caring faculty in a university dedicated to creating community and fostering individualism while educating the whole person, not only intellectually, but spiritually, socially, and athletically. Loyola students represent forty-nine states and forty-eight countries. This diversity is found in a setting where the average class size is 22 students. More than 43 percent of the students permanently reside outside Louisiana, and 30 percent belong to minority groups. Loyola's 20-acre main campus and 4-acre Broadway campus are located in the historic uptown area of New Orleans and are hubs of student activity. The University's residence halls, equipped with computer labs, kitchen, laundry, and study facilities, are home to 40 percent of the undergraduate students. The Joseph A. Danna Center, the student center, houses five food venues, including the remodeled Orleans Room, Pizza Hut, N'Awlins Poboys, Smoothie King, and a gourmet coffee shop. Also found in the Danna Center are an art gallery, travel agency, hair salon, concierge desk, and post office. Nationally affiliated fraternities and sororities are among Loyola's more than 120 student organizations. During the fall's Organizational Fair, students can join the award-winning newspaper, the Loyola University Community Action Program (a volunteer community service organization, the largest such club on campus), or one of the many special interest groups. Students can also take this opportunity to sign up for one of Loyola's club sports. Every year students participate in club cheerleading, crew, cycling, dance, men's lacrosse, men's and women's rugby, men's soccer, swimming, and water polo. Loyola participates in the National Association of Intercollegiate Athletics (NAIA) men's baseball, basketball, and cross-country and women's basketball, cross-country, soccer, and volleyball. The Recreational Sports Complex offers six multipurpose courts, an elevated running track, an Olympic-size swimming pool, weight rooms, and aerobics and combat-sports facilities. The career services offered by the Counseling and Career Services Center include career counseling and testing, assistance with choosing a course of study, recommendations about graduate and professional school, and assistance in securing internships and jobs. Career development services include individualized consultation and counseling, with personality and career-interest testing, a career exploration course, career-related speakers, and a career information library. Publications include information on a wide range of career choices, graduate school directories, scholarship and financial aid directories, and field-specific directories of employers. The Joseph A. Butt, S.J., College of Business Administration is fully accredited at both the undergraduate and graduate levels by the AACSB International–The Association to Advance Collegiate Schools of Business and houses the Mildred Soule and Clarence A. Lengendre Chair in Business Ethics. The College of Music, founded in 1932, gives students the opportunity to combine liberal studies with professional music courses in the only college of music conducted by the Jesuit fathers in the United States.

FINANCIAL AID
Loyola University's endowment provides money for financial aid in addition to that provided by federal funding. Assistance in the forms of merit- and talent-based scholarships, loans, work-study program awards, and grants is awarded on the basis of academic achievement and need. More than 450 scholarships are awarded annually to students with competitive grades and test scores. To apply for one of the scholarships, students must have a GPA of at least 3.2 and competitive standardized test scores. Offers of financial aid are not made until after admission. Notifications of awards are sent in early February. Awards of need-based financial aid packages are made on a first-come, first-served basis and are announced in mid-March.

LUTHER COLLEGE

■ DECORAH, IOWA

THE COLLEGE
Luther College, founded in 1861, is a four-year residential liberal arts college of the Evangelical Lutheran Church in America. The College, which was founded by Norwegian immigrants, is an academic community of faith and learning where students of promise from all beliefs and backgrounds have the freedom to learn, to express themselves, to perform, to compete, and to grow. The College, located in Decorah, Iowa, is home to 2,575 students from thirty-five states and thirty-seven countries. Thirty-six percent of the students are from Iowa; 86 percent come from the four-state area of Iowa, Minnesota, Wisconsin, and Illinois. Each year, approximately 150 international students choose to study at Luther.

For more information about Luther, students should contact:
Admissions Office
Luther College
Decorah, Iowa 52101-1042
Telephone: 563-387-1287
　　　　　800-458-8437 (toll-free)
Fax: 563-387-2159
　　 563-387-1060 (international)
E-mail: admissions@luther.edu
　　　 (admissions)
　　　 lutherfa@luther.edu (financial planning)
　　　 lundsony@luther.edu
　　　 (international)
WWW: http://www.luther.edu

ACADEMIC PROGRAM
Luther operates on a 4-1-4 academic calendar. The first semester runs from September to December, followed by a 3-week January Term and the second semester, which runs from February to May. Two four-week summer sessions are offered in June and July. Each candidate is required to complete a total of 128 semester hours of credit with a C average or better. At least 76 of the required 128 semester hours must be earned outside the major discipline. Each senior writes a research paper in his or her major. Students are required to complete the following number of semester hours of credit in designated areas: 12 of Paideia, an interdisciplinary course; 9–12 of religion/philosophy; 7–8 of natural science; 6–8 of social science; 3–9 of foreign language (proficiency based); 3–4 of fine arts; 3–4 of global studies; 3–4 of quantitative or symbolic reasoning; and 2 of physical education. Advanced placement and credit by examination are available. A qualified student may develop an interdisciplinary major with a faculty adviser.

FINANCIAL AID
More than 95 percent of all Luther students receive financial aid in the form of grants, such as the Federal Pell Grant; scholarships from Luther and other sources; loans; and jobs on campus. Luther awards Regent and Presidential Scholarships to those demonstrating superior academic achievement. The amount of aid given is determined by the College's analysis of the Free Application for Federal Student Aid. The priority deadline for a financial aid application is March 1. Students receive notification of financial aid awards after their acceptance for admission.

APPLICATION AND INFORMATION
An application, SAT I or ACT scores, an educator's reference, a transcript of previous academic work, and a $25 application fee are required for admission. On-campus interviews are recommended but not required.

LYNN UNIVERSITY

- BOCA RATON, FLORIDA

THE UNIVERSITY

Founded in 1962, Lynn University is a private, coeducational institution located in Boca Raton, Florida. The University, small by design, provides an environment within and outside the classroom in which a community of learners can pursue academic excellence. Faculty, staff, and students contribute to an atmosphere that nurtures creativity, fosters achievement, and values diversity. Accredited in 1967 by the Southern Association of Colleges and Schools, Lynn University has steadily grown to become a comprehensive university offering undergraduate and graduate programs in more than thirty disciplines. Lynn leads the country in offering majors in many of the world's fastest-growing professions, thus preparing its students to meet the career demands of the twenty-first century.

For additional information about admission, to obtain an application packet, or to arrange for an interview and tour of the campus, prospective students should contact:

Office of Admission
Lynn University
3601 North Military Trail
Boca Raton, Florida 33431-5598
Telephone: 561-237-7900
          800-888-5966 (toll-free)
Fax: 561-237-7100
E-mail: admission@lynn.edu
WWW: http://www.lynn.edu

ACADEMIC PROGRAM

The University is committed to student-centered learning, where faculty and staff members provide personalized attention to students who have varying levels of academic proficiency with a motivation to excel. A full range of academic and support programs is coordinated to serve the increasingly diverse needs of all students. These are enhanced by the favorable 19:1 student-faculty ratio. The Freshman Seminar is the cornerstone to freshman advising at Lynn and provides an introduction to college life for all new students. The course includes academic success strategies, time management, communication skills, study and test-taking techniques, academic advisement, and career development. The course is taught by select members of the faculty and staff who serve as mentors to new students throughout their freshman year. The Honors Program strives to create a dynamic academic environment that will serve to heighten intellectual curiosity, promote free and active inquiry, and stimulate creative discovery among students with particularly strong academic promise. The innovative curriculum, team-taught by faculty members, encompasses the full breadth of the liberal arts and sciences while promoting both an in-depth exploration and a broad intellectual synthesis of the ideas and concepts that have shaped the dilemmas and choices of the past, present, and future. The Freshmen Frontiers Program provides a smooth transition to college life for incoming students.

FINANCIAL AID

The University has a broad program of student financial aid, including scholarships, grants, work-study, and loans. Academic, athletic, and need-based scholarships are awarded. Inquiries may be made to the Office of Student Financial Services.

APPLICATION AND INFORMATION

There is no formal deadline for admission, and applicants are notified on a rolling basis upon receipt of all credentials. The application fee is $25.

MARIAN COLLEGE OF FOND DU LAC

■ FOND DU LAC, WISCONSIN

THE COLLEGE

Marian College is a community of students and faculty and staff members working together toward the pursuit of excellence in education. Founded in 1936 by the Congregation of Sisters of Saint Agnes as a private school for teacher education, Marian now offers more than forty majors and minors in professional and preprofessional programs. A strong liberal arts curriculum, combined with outstanding experiential education opportunities, gives students the reasoning, problem-solving, and communication skills essential for any career choice. An active campus life provides many opportunities for the 1,200 traditional undergraduate students, 600 adult completion students, and 700 students pursuing master's degrees. The Marian community has many social organizations and clubs as well as twelve NCAA Division III athletic programs, including men's baseball, basketball, golf, ice hockey, soccer, and tennis and women's basketball, golf, soccer, tennis, and volleyball. Student life is further enhanced by a variety of programming that brings national entertainers to the Marian campus. Through its programming, Marian shows a continuous commitment to the service of diverse populations.

For additional information regarding the application process or for other information, students may contact:

Stacey Akey
Assistant Vice President and Dean of
 Enrollment Management
Marian College
45 South National Avenue
Fond du Lac, Wisconsin 54935
Telephone: 920-923-7650
 800-2-MARIAN Ext. 7650
 (toll-free)
E-mail: admissions@mariancollege.edu
WWW:
 http://www.mariancollege.edu

ACADEMIC PROGRAM

Six instructional divisions comprise Marian academic programming: the Division of Arts and Humanities, the Division of Business, the Division of Educational Studies, the Division of Mathematics and Natural Sciences, the Division of Nursing, and the Division of Social and Behavioral Science. In addition to classroom learning, more than 90 percent of Marian students receive hands-on work experience through internships, co-ops, and clinical programs prior to graduation. The classroom experience is further enhanced by the Marian Honors Program for exceptional students and the EXCEL Program for freshman students who need additional support for continued success in college. All students, regardless of their specific degree program, must successfully complete 48 credits in the liberal arts general curriculum. Marian students must complete the requirements for at least one major and take at least 128 total hours of credit with a minimum average of 2 grade points for each credit hour. The senior year, or at least the last 32 credit hours, must be completed at Marian College. Credit is awarded for CLEP subject and general examinations according to current Marian criteria and policies. Details may be obtained from the Assistant Dean of Academic Affairs. The College conducts traditional academic programs in two semesters, the first from late August to mid-December and the second from mid-January to mid-May. There is also a two-week Maymester in mid-May and a two-week Winterim in December. Students may also take advantage of extensive summer school sessions.

FINANCIAL AID

The Marian College Financial Aid Office coordinates an active program of financial assistance for students. More than 93 percent of students are recipients of aid, which is based on need and/or academic merit. The principal sources of aid include the Federal Pell Grant Programs, the Federal Work-Study Program, and Marian assistance. Academic scholarships, including the Academic Achievement Award ($7500), the Presidential Scholarship ($5000), the Naber Leadership Award ($3000), the Sister Mary Shelia Burns Award, and numerous other renewable scholarships and awards are available to entering students.

MARYMOUNT COLLEGE OF FORDHAM UNIVERSITY

- **TARRYTOWN, NEW YORK**

THE COLLEGE

Marymount College, founded in 1907, is an independent, four-year liberal arts college in the Catholic tradition that equips and empowers women to achieve their full potential, preparing them for leadership roles in a rapidly changing society. Building upon a long relationship, Marymount College consolidated with Fordham University as of July 1, 2002, to create a new model of a Catholic women's college—one that enjoys the academic and administrative resources of a major university while retaining the character of a small liberal arts college. The new school—with a strengthened religious and intellectual focus—is now known as Marymount College of Fordham University. Founded in 1841, Fordham is New York City's Jesuit University, enrolling approximately 14,000 students among its ten undergraduate, graduate, and professional schools.

For further information, prospective students should contact:

Director of Admission
Marymount College of Fordham
  University
100 Marymount Avenue
Tarrytown, New York 10591
Telephone: 914-332-8295
          800-724-4312 (toll-free)
Fax: 914-332-7442
E-mail: admiss@mmc.marymt.edu
WWW: http://www.marymt.edu

ACADEMIC PROGRAM

Supporting targeted work goals and rewarding intellectual curiosity require a carefully blended curriculum. The core curriculum—common to all majors at Marymount College of Fordham University—is crafted for this purpose, giving special emphasis to critical thinking, communication, and problem-solving skills. The core curriculum is built upon a strong foundation of classic liberal arts courses. To meet the requirements, students complete courses in such areas as literature, philosophy, theology, history, foreign language, social science, natural science, fine arts, math, computer science, and American pluralism. In addition, students also participate in a first semester seminar, which offers students a choice of courses among a range of disciplines that apply feminist theory to discussions and analysis of common readings. The goal of the core is to develop the habits of heart and mind that are the hallmarks of a liberal education. The core curriculum blends reverence for tradition with openness to new challenges and new ways of knowing and engaging the world. It is designed to nurture curiosity, inspire a love of learning, and provide students with the foundation they will need to engage in lifelong learning. Candidates for either the Bachelor of Arts or Bachelor of Science degree must complete 120 semester credits, fulfill the requirements of the core, and complete the requirements of their major program. Students are encouraged to participate in the internship program to earn college credit. Credit is awarded for successful scores on the College-Level Examination Program (CLEP) general and subject examinations. Students may also earn credit through Advanced Placement (AP) tests.

FINANCIAL AID

In 2000–01, Marymount College students received approximately $8.9 million in student financial aid. Of this, $5 million came from federal programs, $982,000 came from state programs, and more than $3 million came from the College. Trustee grants and scholarships are also available. Financial aid applicants are required to file the FAFSA. It is recommended that the form be submitted by February 1. Early applicants can expect to receive their award notifications beginning April 15.

APPLICATION AND INFORMATION

The application, a $30 fee, official high school records, and test scores should be submitted by April 15 for admission to the fall term or by December 1 for the spring term. Notification of the admission decision, given on a rolling basis, begins in late fall. Deferred admission and early admission are available.

MARYMOUNT UNIVERSITY

■ ARLINGTON, VIRGINIA

THE UNIVERSITY
Marymount University is a comprehensive, co-educational Catholic institution, founded in 1950 by the Religious of the Sacred Heart of Mary. Marymount emphasizes excellence in teaching, attention to the individual, and values and ethics across the curriculum. Approximately 2,100 undergraduate and 1,500 graduate students are enrolled, representing thirty-eight states and eighty-two countries. The University offers thirty-seven undergraduate majors and twenty-six graduate degrees through its four schools: Arts and Sciences, Business Administration, Education and Human Services, and Health Professions. The University is accredited by the Commission on Colleges of the Southern Association of Colleges and Schools. Located in Arlington, VA, minutes from the heart of Washington, D.C., Marymount takes full advantage of resources in the nation's capital. Nationally and internationally known speakers frequently visit Marymount's campus, enriching the university experience. In addition, many students have internships with federal departments, international businesses, and technology companies. The State Department, Smithsonian museums, and Congressional offices are popular internship sites.

For more information, students should contact:
Chris Domes, Vice President of Enrollment Management
Marymount University
2807 North Glebe Road
Arlington, Virginia 22207-4299
Telephone: 703-284-1500
          800-548-7638 (toll-free)
E-mail: admissions@marymount.edu
WWW: http://www.marymount.edu

ACADEMIC PROGRAM
Marymount University's goal is to help each student achieve his or her full potential. While students study a liberal arts core curriculum and the required elements of their discipline, they are able to work with their faculty adviser to tailor an academic program that fits their personal and career objectives. Requirements for earning a degree include a cumulative GPA of 2.0 or better and a minimum of 36 credits as a student at Marymount. The total number of credits required to earn a degree varies by program. Marymount operates on a semester system. Small classes and personal attention help ensure student success and a strong sense of community. An honor system guides academic and social conduct. The cultural and educational resources of the nation's capital add to the curriculum through off-campus activities. Excellent academics, ethics across the curriculum, and a focus on service complete the solid foundation Marymount provides students.

FINANCIAL AID
Marymount provides an extensive scholarship and grant program and participates in all federal and state aid programs. To be considered for aid, students must file the Free Application for Federal Student Aid (FAFSA) with the College Scholarship Service. Approximately 45 percent of the fall 2001 full-time, first-year students received need-based aid and 76 percent received some form of financial assistance. The financial compensation is in the form of scholarships, grants, loans, work-study awards, or on-campus employment. The average financial aid package for freshman is $16,057, which includes all forms of financial aid.

APPLICATION AND INFORMATION
High school students seeking admission are advised to apply early during their senior year. They should submit an application, a nonrefundable fee of $35, a high school transcript, SAT I or ACT scores, evidence of expected graduation from an accredited high school, and a recommendation from a high school counselor or an appropriate school official. Those who have attended another college or university must submit the application, $35 fee, test scores, evidence of high school graduation, transcripts of college-level study, and a recommendation from the Dean of Students at the previous institution. The University has a rolling admission policy and notifies applicants soon after the application process is completed and the Admissions Committee has acted on the application.

MCDANIEL COLLEGE

■ **WESTMINSTER, MARYLAND**

THE COLLEGE

McDaniel College (formerly Western Maryland College) provides an ideal location for learning that brings together students from twenty-three states and nineteen countries. Its picturesque campus, including a nine-hole golf course, is situated on a hilltop in historic Westminster, just a short drive from two of the nation's major metropolitan centers, Baltimore and Washington, D.C. McDaniel College was one of the first coeducational colleges in the nation and has been both innovative and independent since its founding in 1867. The tradition of liberal arts studies rests comfortably at McDaniel, which has exemplary teaching, both at the undergraduate and graduate levels, as its central mission. Faculty members are engaged in research and professional writing, are involved at the highest levels of their respective professions, and are sought after as consultants in many spheres, but their primary mission is teaching. The enrollment of 1,600 undergraduates enables McDaniel College to care about students in a personal way, to provide individual guidance, and to be responsive to the needs of students.

For more information, students should contact:
M. Martha O'Connell, Dean of Admissions
McDaniel College
2 College Hill
Westminster, Maryland 21157-4390
Telephone: 410-857-2230
  800-638-5005 (Voice/TDD) (toll-free)
E-mail: admissio@wmdc.edu
WWW: http://www.wmdc.edu

ACADEMIC PROGRAM

McDaniel College's flexible curriculum enables students to acquire a broad base of knowledge in the areas of humanities, natural sciences and mathematics, and social sciences and to pursue in-depth learning in one or more of the sixty fields of study. The program links wide-ranging educational experiences with strong career preparation through an extensive internship program. A total of 128 credit hours is required for graduation. First-year-student seminars provide students with a unique opportunity to become better prepared for many facets of college life. Limited to 15 students, these courses on a variety of topics emphasize important skills—writing, oral presentation, study skills, critical thinking, and time management. Faculty advisers offer guidance across the curriculum and work closely with their advisees as they make decisions about course and major selections and planning strategies. Students may also request help from the Center for Career Services, which offers vocational testing, counseling, and guidance. During the College's January Term, a three-week term between the fall and spring semesters, students and faculty members are encouraged to explore new areas and expand their intellectual horizons.

FINANCIAL AID

McDaniel College supports a program of financial aid to eligible students on the basis of both need and merit. Nearly 80 percent of McDaniel students receive financial assistance. Students who have been accepted by the College and can demonstrate financial need as required by the federal government may be eligible for assistance in the form of scholarships, grants, loans, and opportunities for student employment. Typically an award is a package of these four resources, tailored to the student's needs. Academic scholarships covering partial to full tuition are available for qualified students based on their academic record, SAT I or ACT scores, and extracurricular involvement. First-year students should apply by February 1; transfer scholarships are competitive, and preference is given to students who apply before March 15. The College also offers partial and full ROTC scholarships. To apply, students should file the Free Application for Federal Student Aid (FAFSA) with the federal processor and apply for admission to McDaniel. Students also must submit a McDaniel College financial aid application, which is available upon request.

APPLICATION AND INFORMATION

Deadlines for receiving completed applications are December 1 for early action, February 1 for academic scholarship consideration, and March 15 for regular admission. Applications from transfer students are accepted through the summer.

MCP HAHNEMANN UNIVERSITY
COLLEGE OF NURSING AND HEALTH PROFESSIONS

- **PHILADELPHIA, PENNSYLVANIA**

THE UNIVERSITY AND THE SCHOOL

MCP Hahnemann University (MCPHU) is an academic health center that includes more than 2,700 students in its School of Medicine, College of Nursing and Health Professions, and School of Public Health. The University grants degrees from the associate through the doctorate in more than eighty programs. It has a rich heritage spanning two centuries of health-care education. Hahnemann University was founded in 1848, while Medical College of Pennsylvania was founded in 1850. In 1993 the two schools consolidated into one institution. In the College of Nursing and Health Professions, there are 659 undergraduate students. The student population is not only culturally diverse but also age-diverse, ranging from high school graduates to older adults. The University is also sensitive to the many time constraints placed on today's students, so many programs offer flexible scheduling. MCPHU has adapted to changing health-care and health-system trends via continually updated curricula, leading-edge technology and equipment, and continuing education and development for its faculty members.

For more information, students should contact:
Office of Enrollment
MCP Hahnemann University
245 North 15th Street
Mail Stop 472
Philadelphia, Pennsylvania 19102-1192
Telephone: 215-762-8288
   800-2-DREXEL Ext. 6333
E-mail: enroll@mcphu.edu
WWW: http://www.mcphu.edu

ACADEMIC PROGRAM

Candidates for graduation must have fulfilled all course requirements in the major curriculum prescribed by the program director. Associate degree candidates must have completed course work equivalent to a minimum of 60 semester hours with a minimum cumulative grade point average of 2.0 on a 4.0 scale. In addition, the following distributional requirements must be met: 3 semester hours each of social sciences, humanities, and natural sciences and 6 semester hours of English (6 semester hours in college-level composition, 6 semester hours in combined college-level composition and literature, or 3 semester hours in college-level composition and 3 semester hours in literature). Bachelor's degree candidates must have completed course work equivalent to a minimum of 120 semester hours with a minimum cumulative grade point average of 2.0. In addition, the following distributional requirements must be met: 3 semester hours each of mathematics/statistics and computer science; 6 semester hours each of humanities and natural sciences; 6 semester hours of English (see above); and 12 semester hours of social sciences (3 semester hours of health administration and management may be selected in lieu of 3 semester hours of a social science at the program director's discretion).

FINANCIAL AID

MCPHU awards funds to students from loan programs, work-study, and numerous scholarship and grant programs. Awards are based on financial need, with the neediest students funded first. Some scholarship funds are awarded to students based on both financial need and academic merit. Students must complete the Free Application for Federal Student Aid (FAFSA) form to be considered for any aid from the University.

MILLS COLLEGE

■ OAKLAND, CALIFORNIA

THE COLLEGE

Mills is the only women's college among the many fine educational institutions in the San Francisco Bay Area. Founded in 1852 as the first women's college west of the Rockies, it is committed to remaining a women's college because it believes that such an environment offers women special advantages in preparing for new roles and responsibilities. A small, liberal arts college, Mills enrolls more than 700 undergraduate women and 300 graduate women and men. The faculty is equally divided between women and men, and the ratio of students to faculty is approximately 11:1. The College has remained small because ideas and enthusiasm are more readily transmitted in a community of this size. Classes are normally small; 88 percent have 20 or fewer students. Faculty members observe each person's work closely, encouraging high performance and offering individual instruction when appropriate.

For more information, students should contact:
Avis E. Hinkson
Dean of Admission
Mills College
5000 MacArthur Boulevard
Oakland, California 94613
Telephone: 510-430-2135
            800-87-MILLS (toll-free)
Fax: 510-430-3314
E-mail: admission@mills.edu
WWW: http://www.mills.edu

ACADEMIC PROGRAM

To earn a Mills B.A., students must take thirty-four semester courses (usually four courses each semester). Grading is traditional, and a pass-fail option is available outside the major. First-year students take interdisciplinary seminars on such topics as Science and Pseudoscience, Tribal Cultures in Fact and Fiction, and Music and the Written Word. Students are also expected to choose two courses from each of four areas (natural sciences and mathematics, social sciences, humanities, and fine arts), a one-semester multicultural or cross-cultural course, and one course that heavily stresses writing skills. They also must choose at least half their courses from outside their major field. Students complete their chosen major with a senior project or thesis.

FINANCIAL AID

More than 80 percent of Mills students are awarded a financial aid package that includes a loan, campus work-study, and a scholarship grant from Mills, outside sources, or both. Awards are based on both need and academic merit. Scholarship grants range from $200 to full tuition per year. Mills makes a special effort to provide financial aid to members of minority groups who demonstrate need. Almost 90 percent of Mills undergraduates who apply for financial aid are offered assistance. Financial aid applicants are expected to apply for assistance from appropriate outside sources, such as the National Merit Scholarship, Federal Pell Grant, and California State Grant programs. More than 40 percent of Mills students have some of their determined need offset by such outside awards. Loans may be obtained by most students, and 45 percent of undergraduates are offered campus work opportunities; some students take off-campus jobs. All freshman and transfer candidates who are California residents must file the Free Application for Federal Student Aid (FAFSA) to be considered for all types of government aid and must also file the Cal Grant GPA Verification Form. Students who seek Mills scholarship funds must also file the Mills Financial Aid Form. Priority is given to applicants who meet the published deadlines.

APPLICATION AND INFORMATION

The priority deadline for admission applications is February 1. Applicants are notified by the Admission Committee in late March. All students are encouraged to meet this deadline; however, international students, merit scholarship applicants, and all other financial aid applicants must apply by February 1. Financial aid is awarded on a first-come, first-served basis, starting with those who meet the deadline. Financial aid awards are made after admission decisions.

For admission to the spring term, the deadline is November 1, and admission decisions are mailed in late December. Students who want to be considered for a California State Grant for the spring semester must apply by the previous March 2 deadline.

MINNEAPOLIS COLLEGE OF ART AND DESIGN

■ **MINNEAPOLIS, MINNESOTA**

THE COLLEGE

The 114-year-old Minneapolis College of Art and Design, along with The Minneapolis Institute of Arts and the Children's Theatre Company, occupies three square blocks in a residential neighborhood just south of the downtown district. The three institutions constitute one of the largest art centers in the nation. There are currently 348 men and 250 women enrolled in the B.F.A. program. The College maintains furnished apartments in modern residences, which can accommodate approximately 185 students (35 percent of the entire student population). In addition to its regular academic program, the College offers evening, Saturday, and summer school classes and art-related films, lectures, performances, and conferences through the Continuing Studies Office. The MCAD Gallery hosts exhibitions during the academic year, providing students with an excellent opportunity to view the work of important contemporary artists and designers. As part of a visiting artists program, nationally prominent artists, designers, and critics visit the campus for varying periods of time to teach, lecture, and work with students and faculty members. Although there are a variety of campus social events each year, students who apply to the College should be aware that its standards of professionalism and performance demand a significant commitment. In addition to its undergraduate programs, the Minneapolis College of Art and Design offers the Master of Fine Arts degree in visual studies.

For more information, students should contact:

Admissions Office
Minneapolis College of Art and Design
2501 Stevens Avenue South
Minneapolis, Minnesota 55404
Telephone: 612-874-3760
          800-874-6223 (toll-free)
Fax: 612-874-3701
E-mail: admissions@mcad.edu
WWW: http://www.mcad.edu/

ACADEMIC PROGRAM

In order to be awarded the B.S. degree, students are required to complete 120 semester credits, 36 of which concentrate in courses relating to visualization (e.g., communication theory and marketing: history, strategies, forms and perceptions, media analysis, hypermedia), and 18 credits, which are taken within MCAD's studio offerings. Students are also required to participate in team-based projects, an externship or study abroad program, and a senior project/exhibit. This degree program offers course work in visual persuasion and information techniques applicable to the fields of advertising/marketing, science/technology, entertainment, education, and corporate communications. The B.F.A. program requires students to complete 120 semester credits. Eighteen of these are in the first-year Foundation Studies program, 39 are in the liberal arts area, and 63 are in the studio. To facilitate the growth of the perception and judgment necessary for meaningful creative endeavor, the College has developed a curriculum that stresses critical thinking, artistic inquiry, professional responsibility, and interdisciplinary dialogue. The goals of the first-year Foundation Studies Program are to develop a student's ability to integrate verbal and visual communication skills and enhance personal expression while preparing for the major areas of study. Course work within the various majors provides students with a solid foundation in craftsmanship and offers both technical and conceptual information. All students are encouraged to expand their interests and technical abilities in other disciplines through elective courses. Complementing work in the studio courses, the Liberal Arts Division offers study in history, criticism, literature, philosophy, religion, and the social and behavioral sciences.

FINANCIAL AID

More than 87 percent of the College student body receive financial aid to meet education costs. Financial aid administered by the College comes from federal, state, and private sources and includes Federal Pell Grants, Federal Stafford Student Loans, Federal Supplemental Educational Opportunity Grants, Federal Perkins Loans, and Minnesota State Scholarships and Grants-in-Aid. College-controlled aid includes a variety of College grants, scholarships, and work-study contracts. Aid from private sources is also available. To qualify, applicants must submit the Free Application for Federal Student Aid (FAFSA).

MUHLENBERG COLLEGE

ALLENTOWN, PENNSYLVANIA

THE COLLEGE

Founded in 1848 and affiliated with the Lutheran Church, Muhlenberg College has the primary purpose of helping students develop those capacities of imaginative and critical thinking that make possible humane and responsible living within a free society. A secondary, but related, purpose is to provide students with excellent undergraduate preparation for socially useful and fulfilling occupations. Muhlenberg students achieve the College's goals by assuming strong individual responsibility for intense involvement in vigorous academic work and for personal involvement within the College community. The more than 100 student organizations provide outlets for the diversified cultural, athletic, religious, social, leadership, and service interests of the students. The campus is primarily residential; more than 90 percent of the 2,100 students live on campus. A close sense of community develops naturally, one in which their diversified academic and personal interests enable students to contribute positively to the intellectual and personal growth of their peers. Students are aided by an active Career Planning and Placement Service in relating academic and personal knowledge and skills to appropriate career goals and in obtaining positions upon graduation. More than one third of a typical graduating class proceeds immediately to graduate or professional school.

> **For further information, interested students should contact:**
> Christopher Hooker-Haring
> Dean of Admission and Financial Aid
> Muhlenberg College
> Allentown, Pennsylvania 18104-5586
> Telephone: 484-664-3200
> E-mail: admissions@muhlenberg.edu
> WWW: http://www.muhlenberg.edu

ACADEMIC PROGRAM

The A.B. and B.S. programs emphasize breadth of study in the liberal arts as well as in-depth study of a particular academic major. All students must fulfill requirements in foreign culture, the humanities, social sciences, and natural sciences. Strong achievement on Advanced Placement examinations may enable a student to receive advanced placement, possibly with credit. Scores of 4 or 5 earn automatic credit. Scores of 3 are evaluated by the appropriate department. Students work closely with academic advisers to formulate programs well suited to their individual interests, abilities, needs, and goals. Generally, students are expected to declare their major at the end of the freshman year; however, many students later change their academic major with no difficulty. A double major is possible, and several fields are available as minor programs. These minor fields are accounting, anthropology, business administration, chemistry, computer science, economics, English, French, German, history, Jewish studies, mathematics, music, philosophy, physics, political science, religion, sociology, Spanish, and women's studies. In addition, independent study and research are available. The College also enriches the freshman-year experience through more than thirty special-focus Freshman Seminars.

FINANCIAL AID

Muhlenberg College endeavors to make its educational opportunities available to all qualified students regardless of their financial circumstances. While most financial aid at Muhlenberg is based on financial need as demonstrated by the College Scholarship Service Financial Aid PROFILE, there is also a limited amount of merit aid available. Typically, about 65 percent of Muhlenberg's students qualify for and receive financial aid.

APPLICATION AND INFORMATION

Students who wish to be considered for admission should submit a completed application form as early as possible during their senior year of secondary school and no later than February 15. Candidates receive notice of admission decisions in late March. Early decision and early admission plans and transfer admission are possible.

NEW YORK UNIVERSITY

■ **NEW YORK, NEW YORK**

THE UNIVERSITY

New York University (NYU) was founded in 1831 by Albert Gallatin, Secretary of the Treasury under Thomas Jefferson; he believed that the place for a university was not in "the seclusion of cloistered halls but in the throbbing heart of a great city." NYU draws top students from every state and more than 125 countries. The distinguished academic atmosphere attracts the teachers, and the teachers and the atmosphere together attract the students who are capable of benefiting from both. Within three years of graduation, 80 percent of NYU's students go on to postbaccalaureate work. Of those who apply for admission to medical school, 85 percent are accepted, placing NYU well above the national average. The faculty includes world-famous scholars, researchers, and artists, among them Nobel laureates, winners of the Pulitzer Prize, and members of the National Science Foundation. NYU is a member of the prestigious Association of American Universities. A study sponsored by the National Science Foundation placed NYU among the top four universities in the country in the number of "leading intellectuals" on the faculty. Full professors teach on both the graduate and undergraduate levels. Seven undergraduate divisions provide extensive offerings in a wide range of subjects: more than 2,500 courses in 160 major fields are available to NYU's full-time undergraduates. The average class size is under 30, and the faculty-student ratio is 1:12—benefits generally associated with a much smaller institution. NYU's residence hall program is an important aspect of the total educational experience. Approximately 11,000 undergraduate students live in twenty University residence halls.

For more information, students should contact:
Office of Undergraduate Admissions
New York University
22 Washington Square North
New York, New York 10011
Telephone: 212-998-4500
WWW: http://www.nyu.edu/ugadmissions/

ACADEMIC PROGRAM

Requirements for graduation vary among departments and schools. A liberal arts core curriculum is an integral part of all areas of concentration. The baccalaureate degree requires completion of at least 128 credits. The University calendar is organized on the traditional semester system, including two 6-week summer sessions. Some divisions offer part-time programs during the day and evening and on weekends.

FINANCIAL AID

Financial aid at NYU comes from many sources. All students are encouraged to apply for financial assistance or one of NYU's innovative financing plans. Seventy-three percent of NYU's full-time undergraduates receive financial assistance. Each year more than 1,700 entering freshmen are awarded scholarships based on academic promise and/or financial need. The University may offer a package of aid that includes scholarships or grants, loans, or work-study programs. NYU requires the submission of the Free Application for Federal Student Aid (FAFSA). The deadline for filing this financial aid form is February 15 for the fall semester and November 1 for the spring semester.

APPLICATION AND INFORMATION

For entrance in the fall term, the application for admission—including all supporting credentials—must be received by November 15 (early decision freshman candidates), January 15 (freshmen), or April 1 (transfer students). For entrance in the spring term, the application materials must be received by November 1 for both freshman and transfer candidates. For entrance in the summer, the application materials should be received by April 15 for both freshman and transfer candidates. Applications for admission received after these dates are considered only if space remains. Official notification of fall admission is made on April 1 and on a rolling basis thereafter.

NORTHEASTERN UNIVERSITY

■ BOSTON, MASSACHUSETTS

THE UNIVERSITY
There is a certain energy about Northeastern. It comes from bright, ambitious students with a sense of purpose. In the classroom, in the workplace, in campus activities, and in the city of Boston—the ultimate college town—Northeastern students stimulate their minds, investigate career options, participate in community affairs, and graduate personally and professionally prepared. Northeastern students not only acquire knowledge, they learn how to apply it. Through Northeastern's innovative co-op program and its emphasis on practice-oriented education—internationally recognized among the top cooperative education programs in the world—students alternate classroom learning with periods of full-time, paid work related to their major or interests.

For more information, students should contact:
Office of Undergraduate Admissions
Northeastern University
150 Richards Hall
360 Huntington Avenue
Boston, Massachusetts 02115
Telephone: 617-373-2200 (voice)
617-373-3100 (TTY)
E-mail: admissions@neu.edu
WWW: http://www.neu.edu

ACADEMIC PROGRAM
Northeastern's internationally known cooperative education program enables students to gain practical and lively workplace experience integrated with their academic studies. Students alternate quarters of work and study (after completing their freshman year) and generally spend five years earning their bachelor's degree. A four-year co-op option is available to speech-language pathology and audiology, engineering, business, and computer science students, and a four-year non-co-op schedule is available to students in the College of Arts and Sciences. A University-wide honors program gives students opportunities to participate in enriched educational experiences such as honors equivalents of required academic courses, interdisciplinary colloquia, independent research, and study abroad.

FINANCIAL AID
The University operates a substantial aid program designed to make attendance at Northeastern feasible for all qualified students. By coordinating the resources of the University and various public and private scholarship programs, the Office of Student Financial Services was able to provide more than $100 million to more than 8,600 students last year. Eighty-four percent of the freshman class received some form of financial aid. Financial aid is based on need and academic promise and may consist of a grant, a loan, part-time employment, or any combination of these three. To apply, students must file a Free Application for Federal Student Aid (FAFSA) and a PROFILE form with the College Scholarship Service by February 15. Students who are accepted by March 2 have priority in receiving funds.

APPLICATION AND INFORMATION
Admission to Northeastern University is selective. Each year, the University receives many more applications from students than can be accommodated. As a result, the admissions committee must make fine distinctions between applicants. For best consideration, applicants are encouraged to submit all required materials by the published deadlines. Freshman applicants interested in merit scholarships should apply by January 1. Freshmen who apply for the fall entrance date by February 15 are mailed a decision by April 1. If accepted for fall admission, freshmen are required to send a tuition deposit by May 1 to secure a place in the class. For transfer students, the priority deadline for the fall semester is May 1. Admission decisions for transfer applicants are made on a rolling basis as long as space in a college and program is available. Personal informational interviews are available by appointment only. Campus tours and group information sessions are held daily and are available without an appointment. Open house programs are scheduled throughout the year.

NORTHWOOD UNIVERSITY

- **MIDLAND, MICHIGAN; CEDAR HILL, TEXAS; AND WEST PALM BEACH, FLORIDA**

THE UNIVERSITY

Northwood University was founded in 1959 by Dr. Arthur E. Turner and Dr. R. Gary Stauffer, who had decided that the liberal arts approach to business did not really expose students to the wealth of opportunities the world of work had to offer. Established originally in Alma, Michigan, the school moved to Midland in 1961. The Texas campus was opened in 1966. Other expansions include the Florida campus in West Palm Beach and the Northwood University Margaret Chase Smith Library Center in Skowhegan, Maine. Northwood University also coordinates a nontraditional program, University College, headquartered at the Midland, Michigan, campus; extension centers are located on all three campuses and in Carlsbad, New Mexico; Chicago, Illinois; Fort Worth, Texas; Detroit, Flint, and Lansing, Michigan; Tampa, Florida; Indianapolis, Indiana; Louisville, Kentucky; New Orleans, Louisiana; and Selfridge ANG Base, Michigan.

ACADEMIC PROGRAM

Northwood University's programs have been designed to prepare men and women for specific career goals. The courses for the major (approximately 30 percent of the total requirements) are reinforced by classes in general business (30 percent) and the humanities (40 percent). Northwood believes strongly in the free enterprise system and, accordingly, has designed its curriculum to reflect this belief. All students must satisfactorily complete core courses in accounting, business law, economics, management, and marketing. No matter what the ultimate career goal of a student may be, he or she will have acquired a set of basic skills as preparation for the productive world of work. This academic program, however, does not prohibit students from appreciating the arts. Northwood strongly promotes the interrelationship between the business and art worlds by providing on- and off-campus voluntary programs.

FINANCIAL AID

Students should file the Free Application for Federal Student Aid (FAFSA). Available aid includes Federal Pell Grants, Federal Supplemental Educational Opportunity Grants, state and institutional grants and scholarships, Federal Stafford Student Loans, loans for parents, and Federal Work-Study awards. Approximately 70 percent of students receive some type of financial aid.

For more information, students should contact the appropriate location:

Director of Admissions
Northwood University
4000 Whiting Drive
Midland, Michigan 48640
Telephone: 989-837-4273
           800-457-7878 (toll-free)
WWW: http://www.northwood.edu

Director of Admissions
Northwood University, Florida Campus
2600 North Military Trail
West Palm Beach, Florida 33409
Telephone: 561-478-5500
           800-458-8325 (toll-free)

Director of Admissions
Northwood University, Texas Campus
1114 West FM 1382
P.O. Box 58
Cedar Hill, Texas 75104
Telephone: 972-293-5400
           800-927-9663 (toll-free)

Director of Admissions
University College
4000 Whiting Drive
Midland, Michigan 48640
Telephone: 989-837-4411
           800-445-5873 (toll-free)

NORWICH UNIVERSITY

■ NORTHFIELD, VERMONT

THE UNIVERSITY

Norwich University is unique among institutions of higher education. No other university combines a military tradition of nearly two centuries, a broad range of traditional undergraduate degree programs, and innovative low-residency and nonresidency programs in higher education. Students on the Northfield campus may enroll in the Corps of Cadets and follow a disciplined military regime or join civilian students who lead a more traditional collegiate lifestyle. Both groups are coeducational and attend classes and participate in sports and other activities together.

> **For more information, students should contact:**
>
> Dean of Enrollment Management
> Norwich University
> 27 I.D. White Avenue
> Northfield, Vermont 05663
> Telephone: 800-468-NORWICH (6679) (toll-free)
> E-mail: nuadm@norwich.edu
> WWW: http://www.norwich.edu

There are approximately 1,600 students enrolled on the Northfield campus. In keeping with its mission, the University provides opportunities for all students to develop leadership skills and a strong commitment to community services.

ACADEMIC PROGRAM

To qualify for the baccalaureate degree, students must have a final cumulative quality point average of at least 2.0. Teacher licensure candidates reserve the eighth semester for sixteen weeks of student teaching. Individual departmental requirements are outlined in the Norwich catalog. Approximately 25 percent of entering freshmen have undeclared majors. For military cadets, eight semesters of Army, Air Force, or Naval ROTC are required. Prior to the start of the junior year, a cadet may elect to contract with his or her ROTC program of study for consideration for a commission upon graduation as a second lieutenant in the Army, Air Force, or Marine Corps or as an ensign in the Navy. A cadet not wishing to contract for a commission has no military obligation upon completion of the required four years of ROTC courses. Norwich students entering their junior year may enroll in the nation's first college-based Peace Corps Preparatory Program. Participants in the program take specialized courses designed to prepare them for assignments in Third World countries, perform voluntary community service during the school year, and spend six weeks in a foreign country, during the summer between their junior and senior years, with an established service agency. The curriculum is an acceptable alternative to the Military College requirement for senior year ROTC participation for those students not seeking an officer's commission.

FINANCIAL AID

All applicants for financial aid must submit both the CSS PROFILE form and the Free Application for Federal Student Aid (FAFSA). Financial awards are made on the basis of need, but academic and extracurricular activities are taken into consideration. Most awards consist of an aid package of University scholarships, work-study programs, federal grants, and student loans. Winners of three- and four-year Army, Air Force, and Naval ROTC scholarships are strongly encouraged to consider the Norwich program. ROTC scholarship winners attending Norwich University receive full scholarships for room and board as long as they maintain scholarship status each year. ROTC students receive an annual uniform allowance, and students who are working toward a commission through advanced ROTC receive a monthly subsistence allowance during the school year. Eligible students may also apply for three- and two-year Air Force, Army, and Naval ROTC scholarships while attending Norwich. For further ROTC scholarship information, students should write to the Admissions Office. Norwich offers academic scholarships to students who have demonstrated outstanding academic achievements. These scholarships are offered to students who are placed in the top 10 or 20 percent of their high school class.

APPLICATION AND INFORMATION

There is no deadline for applications. The University uses a rolling admission system; an admission decision is announced as soon as all of an applicant's materials have been received, processed, and reviewed.

PRATT INSTITUTE

■ BROOKLYN, NEW YORK

THE INSTITUTE

Founded in 1887 on its present site in Brooklyn by industrialist and philanthropist Charles Pratt, the Institute educated on nonbaccalaureate levels for its first half-century. As the educational preparation necessary for various professions expanded, Pratt Institute moved with the times. It granted its first baccalaureate degree in 1938 and started its first graduate program in 1950. Pratt continues to add programs at all educational levels, including undergraduate and graduate programs in art history and graduate programs in art education and design management. Although the characteristics and educational requirements of the professions for which Pratt prepares people have changed over the course of a century, the Institute has succeeded in pursuing its abiding purpose—to blend theoretical learning with professional and humanistic development. In educating more than four generations of students to be creative, technically skilled, and adaptable professionals as well as responsible citizens, Pratt has gained a national and international reputation that attracts undergraduate and graduate students from more than forty-six states, the District of Columbia, Puerto Rico, the Virgin Islands, and seventy countries.

> **For more information about Pratt Institute, students should contact:**
>
> Office of Admissions
> Pratt Institute
> 200 Willoughby Avenue
> Brooklyn, New York 11205
> Telephone: 718-636-3669
> 800-331-0834 (toll-free)
> E-mail: admissions@pratt.edu
> WWW: http://www.pratt.edu

ACADEMIC PROGRAM

Educating professionals for productive careers in artistic and technical fields has been the mission of Pratt Institute since it assembled its first group of students in 1887. Within the structure of that professional education, Pratt students are encouraged to acquire the diverse knowledge that is necessary for them to succeed in their chosen fields. In addition to the professional studies, the curriculum in each of Pratt's schools includes a broad range of liberal arts courses. Students from all schools take these courses together and have the opportunity to examine the interrelationships of art, science, technology, and human need. At the time of graduation, students in the associate degree programs have completed 66 credit hours of course work. In the bachelor's programs, credit-hour requirements range from 132 to 135 credits, depending on the particular program. For the Bachelor of Architecture degree, 175 credits are required. With an additional 27 or 49 credits of study, students in the School of Architecture can choose a combined B.Arch./M.S. in urban design or a combined B.Arch./M.S. in city and regional planning degree program. Pratt's academic calendar consists of two semesters plus a winter term that allows students to choose alternative courses or various options usually not offered during the fall or spring semester. A number of summer sessions are offered.

FINANCIAL AID

Pratt Institute offers a large number of grants, scholarships, loans, and awards on the basis of academic achievement, financial need, or both. More than 75 percent of Pratt students receive aid in one or more of these forms. Through funds from the federal and state governments, contributions from Pratt alumni, and industry scholarships, Pratt is able to maintain an effective aid program in a time of escalating costs. Pratt attempts to ensure that no student is prevented by lack of funds from completing his or her education.

APPLICATION AND INFORMATION

Pratt has two admissions deadlines: January 1 and February 1. To receive full consideration, students must submit applications by February 1 for anticipated entrance in the fall semester and by October 15 for anticipated entrance in the spring semester. All applicants must submit transcripts from high schools and any college attended and letters of recommendation. Additional professional requirements are requested by each department.

RENSSELAER POLYTECHNIC INSTITUTE

■ TROY, NEW YORK

THE INSTITUTE

The oldest technological university in the English-speaking world, Rensselaer Polytechnic Institute was founded in 1824 "for the purpose of instructing persons in the application of science to the common purposes of life." Still pursuing that original mission, Rensselaer has become one of the world's premier research universities. More than 100 programs and 1,000 courses lead to bachelor's, master's, and doctoral degrees. Undergraduates pursue their studies in the Schools of Architecture, Engineering, Humanities and Social Sciences, Management and Technology, and Science and in the interdisciplinary program in information technology (IT). Rensselaer's long tradition of cross-disciplinary, real-world, industry-oriented research and education is clearly reflected in cross-school programs, such as product design and innovation, and unusual degree offerings, such as bioinformatics and molecular biology; electronic media, arts, and communication; and information technology. Rensselaer's unique B.S. degree program in information technology requires students to choose an area in which they wish to apply IT from more than thirty second disciplines that are taught by experts from across the University. Rensselaer's more than twenty interdisciplinary research and academic centers have achieved international recognition in such fields as microelectronics, simulation-based engineering, advanced computing, student leadership, multimedia arts, and composite materials. Strong and deep ties to a broad range of firms, from large multinational corporations to fast-growing entrepreneurial ventures, help ensure the relevance of educational and research initiatives and offer rich co-op, internship, and employment opportunities for students. Rensselaer's 5,100 undergraduate and 1,900 graduate students are a bright, ambitious, and technologically savvy group who come from all fifty states, the District of Columbia, Puerto Rico, the Virgin Islands, and seventy-eight other countries. A wide variety of nonacademic activities, virtually all of which are run by the students, are available.

> **For more information, students should contact:**
> Rensselaer Admissions,
>   Undergraduate Programs
> Rensselaer Polytechnic Institute
> Troy, New York 12180
> Telephone: 518-276-6216
> Fax: 518-276-4072
> E-mail: admissions@rpi.edu
> WWW: http://admissions.rpi.edu

ACADEMIC PROGRAM

Rensselaer leads the nation in educational reform with its award-winning, studio-based interactive approach to teaching. Although there are still lectures, more and more classes involve lively discussion, team problem solving, and faculty mentoring as opposed to instructing. In the past two years, faculty members have also renewed the curriculum, replacing the traditional five or six 3-credit-course model with a "4x4" curriculum of four 4-credit-hour courses. All incoming students are required to have a laptop computer that meets Rensselaer's specifications. While each school has its own sequence requirements, the following minimums apply to all students: 124 credit hours and a 1.8 quality point average in total courses; 24 credit hours in physical, life, and engineering sciences; 24 in humanities and social sciences; 30 in a selected discipline; and 24 in electives. Students are strongly encouraged to learn outside of the classroom with independent projects, faculty research, study abroad, and cooperative education. The Undergraduate Research Program offers hands-on experience to students in hundreds of areas where a full-time undergraduate may participate for credit or pay during the academic year or the summer. Co-op assignments give students the opportunity to add practical experience to their academic study. The study-work schedule is such that students graduate in the class with which they matriculated. Air Force, Army, and Naval/Marine ROTC programs are available on an elective basis.

FINANCIAL AID

Nearly all freshmen who have financial need are offered assistance under a comprehensive program of scholarships, loans, and part-time employment that provides annual assistance ranging from $100 up to full tuition, room, and board. Available federal funds include student loans, Federal Work-Study Program awards, and ROTC scholarships.

THE RICHARD STOCKTON COLLEGE OF NEW JERSEY

■ POMONA, NEW JERSEY

THE COLLEGE
The Richard Stockton College of New Jersey is an undergraduate college of arts, sciences, and professional studies within the New Jersey System of Higher Education. Named for Richard Stockton, one of the New Jersey signers of the Declaration of Independence, the College was authorized by the passage of the state's 1968 bond referendum for higher education and accepted its charter class in 1971. More than 6,000 students are enrolled at the College, which provides distinctive traditional and alternative approaches to education. Stockton seeks to develop the analytic and creative capabilities of its students by encouraging them to undertake individually planned courses of study that promote self-reliance and an acceptance of and responsiveness to change. The College's campus provides an excellent natural setting for a wide range of outdoor recreational activities, including sailing, canoeing, hiking, jogging, and fishing. Students and faculty and staff members take part together in an extensive intramural and club sports program that includes aikido, crew, flag football, golf, soccer, softball, street hockey, swimming, and volleyball. At the intercollegiate level, the College fields teams in men's baseball, basketball, lacrosse, and soccer; women's basketball, crew, soccer, softball, tennis, and volleyball; and men's and women's cross-country and track and field.

For more information or application forms, students should contact:
Dean of Enrollment Management
The Richard Stockton College of New Jersey
P.O. Box 195
Pomona, New Jersey 08240-0195
Telephone: 609-652-4261
Fax: 609-748-5541
E-mail: admissions@stockton.edu
WWW: http://www.stockton.edu

ACADEMIC PROGRAM
To earn a baccalaureate degree at Stockton, a student must satisfactorily complete a minimum of 128 semester credits. Degree programs include a combination of general studies and program (major field) studies. The Bachelor of Arts student must earn a total of 64 credits in general studies; the Bachelor of Science student must earn 48. General studies courses are broad cross-disciplinary courses designed to introduce students to all major areas of the curriculum and to the broadly applicable intellectual skills necessary for success in college. Students must select some courses from each major curricular area. The only specifically required courses within general studies are the basic studies courses (up to three), from which students may be exempted on the basis of diagnostic testing. The Bachelor of Arts student must earn a total of 64 credits in program studies; the Bachelor of Science student must earn 80. Program studies (major field) requirements are carefully structured and emphasize sequences of specific courses. Students at Stockton have special opportunities to influence what and how they learn by participating in the major decisions that shape their academic lives. The main avenue of participation is the preceptorial system, which enables students to work, on a personalized basis, with an assigned faculty-staff preceptor in the planning and evaluation of individualized courses of study and in the exploration of various career alternatives. Stockton's academic programs emphasize curricular organization and methods of instruction that promote independent learning and research, cross-disciplinary study, problem solving, and decision making through analysis and synthesis.

FINANCIAL AID
Financial aid is available in the form of scholarships, grants, loans, and jobs. Aid is awarded both on a competitive (merit) basis and according to need. Students seeking financial aid should file the Free Application for Federal Student Aid (FAFSA) by March 1. This form is used by the College in evaluating all applications for financial aid.

RIDER UNIVERSITY

■ LAWRENCEVILLE, NEW JERSEY

THE UNIVERSITY

Founded in 1865, Rider University is an independent, coeducational, nonsectarian institution accredited by the Middle States Association of Colleges and Schools. Rider has two campuses, one in Lawrenceville, New Jersey, and one in Princeton, New Jersey. Rider's four academic units include the College of Business Administration; the College of Liberal Arts, Education, and Sciences; the College of Continuing Studies; and Westminster Choir College, located in Princeton, New Jersey. More than 95 percent of Rider's full-time faculty members hold a doctorate or other appropriate advanced degree. Primarily a teaching institution, Rider University selects instructors who are committed to imparting the knowledge and skills of a particular discipline. Full professors teach at all levels.

> **For more information, students should contact:**
> Director of Admissions
> Rider University
> 2083 Lawrenceville Road
> Lawrenceville, New Jersey 08648-3099
> Telephone: 609-896-5042
>   800-257-9026 (toll-free)
> E-mail: admissions@rider.edu
> WWW: http://www.rider.edu

ACADEMIC PROGRAM

Rider University operates on the semester system. Each College requires a minimum of 120 semester hours of credit for graduation; the last 30 semester hours of credit must be earned at Rider University. The College of Business Administration requires that a student earn at least 45 semester hours, including the last 30, at Rider University. The Baccalaureate Honors Program is available to students in all programs. Rider University recognizes the Advanced Placement (AP) Program and offers credit and placement for scores of 3, 4, or 5 on most AP tests. Credit is awarded for the College-Level Examination Program (CLEP) tests provided that the minimum required score is obtained. The minimum score varies according to the specific area covered by the examination.

FINANCIAL AID

Most financial aid is based upon demonstrated financial need. Students and their parents are required to file the Free Application for Federal Student Aid (FAFSA) prior to March 1 to be considered for financial assistance administered by Rider University. The University maintains a need-blind admission policy and attempts to meet the full financial need of all eligible applicants. Entering students are eligible for consideration for Federal Pell Grants, Federal Supplemental Educational Opportunity Grants, Federal Work-Study awards, Federal Perkins Loans, New Jersey Tuition Aid Grants, New Jersey Distinguished Scholar Scholarships, Rider University grants, Trustee Scholarships, Alumni Scholarships, and other forms of institutional aid. Rider University offers six merit-based scholarship programs for qualified applicants. These scholarships, the Presidential, Diversity, Provost, Dean's, Founders, and Transfer scholarships, are for up to $15,000 and are renewable for up to four years of study if the student maintains the minimum grade point average specified by the Scholarship Committee. Rider also offers two full-tuition actors scholarships.

APPLICATION AND INFORMATION

Rider University works on a rolling admissions basis, but it encourages applications for the fall semester to be submitted by February 15 if the student wishes to obtain housing on the campus. Applications for the spring semester should be submitted by December 15. An early action option is available. Students must submit all necessary documentation by November 15 and are notified of an admissions decision by December 15. The application fee of $40 should be included with the application. Students are notified of the admission decision in approximately three to four weeks, in accordance with the rolling admission policy. Transfer applicants receive the same priority for admission, housing, and financial aid as freshman applicants.

RIPON COLLEGE

■ **RIPON, WISCONSIN**

THE COLLEGE
One key reason why students choose Ripon College from among the more than 3,500 colleges and universities in the country is that Ripon offers an intensely personal undergraduate education. Since 1851, Ripon has provided a personal liberal arts education that makes a remarkable difference in the lives of students. *U.S. News & World Report* recently ranked Ripon among those national liberal arts colleges that offer "high quality education at a reasonable cost." Companies look for college graduates who can adapt to change and who can write, use modern technology with confidence, communicate, and make a contribution to a team. These are the skills that a Ripon education offers students. Ripon's curricular emphasis focuses on Communicating Plus. This program aims to assist students in the development of superior written and oral communication, critical-thinking, and problem-solving skills. Ripon is a residential college; 90 percent of students live on campus, and because students remain on campus after classes have ended, learning occurs around the clock. All students are encouraged to participate in Ripon's numerous extracurricular activities, including the campus radio station and the Student Senate. Ripon College is fully accredited by the North Central Association of Colleges and Schools.

> **For further information, students should contact:**
> Dean of Admission
> Ripon College
> 300 Seward Street
> P.O. Box 248
> Ripon, Wisconsin 54971-0248
> Telephone: 800-94-RIPON (toll-free)
> E-mail: adminfo@ripon.edu
> WWW: http://www.ripon.edu

ACADEMIC PROGRAM
Since its founding, Ripon has been a liberal arts college. Students have the opportunity to study all fields of human knowledge, including the social sciences, the natural sciences, the humanities, and the fine arts. While other colleges have become increasingly specialized, Ripon has remained steadfast in its belief that the liberal arts are the key for a life of both personal and professional success. Ripon operates on a schedule of two 15-week semesters and an optional 3-week "Maymester."

FINANCIAL AID
Ninety percent of Ripon students receive financial assistance that meets 100 percent of their financial need. The average financial aid award equals 78 percent of a student's total costs. Ripon's extensive scholarship program is designed to recognize and reward applicants for their talents and abilities. Currently, seventeen types of scholarships that range from $1000 to full tuition annually are available.

APPLICATION AND INFORMATION
Prospective students who value a challenging liberal arts and sciences education in a small, caring community are invited to visit the campus, sit in on Ripon classes, and see firsthand how Ripon students and professors interact with one another. Students who wish to apply to Ripon College should submit a completed application form, a secondary school transcript, results of standardized tests, and the $30 application fee. Ripon College application forms are available from the admission office and at the College's Web site (address below). Ripon participates in the Common Application Plan and accepts photocopies of the Common Application in place of the Ripon College application form. Common Application forms are available in many secondary school guidance offices. Ripon also accepts applications that are made through the Wisconsin Mentor site (http://www.wisconsinmentor.org/admissionapp). Candidates for fall term consideration are encouraged to apply early. Notification of fall term admission occurs within two weeks of the completion of the student's application. Students applying for spring term consideration should submit applications by December 15. Notification occurs shortly thereafter.

ST. AMBROSE UNIVERSITY

■ DAVENPORT, IOWA

THE UNIVERSITY

St. Ambrose offers all the advantages needed for a successful college experience and a bright future—a great selection of classes, top-of-the-line resources, professors who challenge and encourage, and the kind of people who will be friends for life. The student body comprises more than 3,300 (53 percent women, 47 percent men), all of whom acquire intellectual awareness for lifelong self-education. Professors, staff members, and fellow students challenge each other to be not just as smart as they can be but as good as they can be. St. Ambrose has been providing this style of education, one that nurtures the spirit while training the mind, for nearly 125 years.

> **For more information or to arrange a campus visit, students should contact:**
> Meg Higgins
> Director of Admissions
> St. Ambrose University
> 518 West Locust Street
> Davenport, Iowa 52803
> Telephone: 563-333-6300
>   800-383-2627 (toll-free)
> E-mail: admit@sau.edu
> WWW: http://www.sau.edu

Founded in 1882, the University was named for St. Ambrose, the fourth-century saint and bishop of Milan, who was a doctor, scholar, author, orator, and teacher. Classes first met in two rooms of a diocesan school. Today, the campus comprises more than 40 acres in a residential section of Davenport, with twenty-six buildings, including historic Ambrose Hall. Housing at St. Ambrose, the best in the region, combines the comforts of home with the privileges of independence for the more than 1,100 students who live on campus. Brand-new apartment-style residence halls have kitchen-equipped units for groups of 4 and 6 students, and other halls provide extras such as semiprivate bathrooms and study rooms on each floor. At the graduate level, the University offers master's degrees in accounting, business administration, criminal justice, educational leadership, information technology management, juvenile justice education, occupational therapy, organizational leadership, pastoral studies, postsecondary disability services, social work, and special education. Doctoral degrees are offered in business administration and physical therapy. St. Ambrose has eighteen varsity sports for men and women in a widely varied athletic program. Five hundred undergraduate students, almost half of all campus residents, participate in NAIA Division II sports.

ACADEMIC PROGRAM

The best education combines courses that teach students how to think with those that help them apply that thinking to the real world. St. Ambrose has always emphasized liberal arts studies and career education enriched by a Catholic heritage of social justice and service. Students must complete a minimum of 120 semester credits (usually forty courses). Some bachelor's programs have additional requirements. Ninety-eight percent of graduates are employed or in graduate school within six months of graduation.

FINANCIAL AID

Federal, state, and University financial aid programs, scholarships, loans, grants, work-study and cooperative programs, and University employment opportunities are available. Federal programs include the Federal Pell Grant, Federal Supplemental Educational Opportunity Grant, Federal Work-Study, and Federal Stafford Loan programs. State programs are the Iowa Scholarship, Iowa PLUS Loan, and Iowa Tuition Grant programs. The priority deadline for financial aid applications is March 15 for the next fall semester. In addition to submitting an application for admission, applicants for financial aid must submit the Free Application for Federal Student Aid (FAFSA). This form is available in the offices of high school counselors or in the St. Ambrose University Financial Aid Office, or online at http://fafsa.ed.gov/.

APPLICATION AND INFORMATION

The completed application for admission, high school transcripts or equivalent credentials, and test scores should be sent to the Director of Admissions. Students also may apply online at http://www.sau.edu/admissions.

ST. FRANCIS COLLEGE

■ BROOKLYN HEIGHTS, NEW YORK

THE COLLEGE

Small, urban, friendly, and caring, St. Francis College was established in 1884 by the Franciscan Brothers of Brooklyn. Today St. Francis is an independent Catholic, Franciscan coeducational college that confers degrees in the arts and sciences and preprofessional disciplines. It is chartered by the Board of Regents of the University of the State of New York and accredited by the Middle States Association of Colleges and Schools. Throughout its long history, the College has offered an education of high quality that reflects its willingness to adapt to a constantly changing society and at the same time retain its tradition of liberal education. St. Francis has an average enrollment of 2,300 students, most of whom come from the Greater New York metropolitan area. The College also takes pride in its sizable international student population; almost eighty nations are represented. Young men and women from a variety of backgrounds feel at home and fit in at St. Francis. It is easy to make friends in the warm, trusting atmosphere that characterizes this college community. St. Francis has a full range of extracurricular activities and publications as well as twenty-nine clubs and four fraternities and sororities. Major activities include student government, the yearbook, the campus newspaper, the literary magazine, and professional societies such as the St. Thomas More Pre-Law Society. Athletics are a high priority at St. Francis, and the College is a member of the Northeast Conference and NCAA Division I. St. Francis sponsors eighteen varsity sports, which include championship men's baseball, basketball, and soccer teams; women's basketball, softball, and volleyball teams; and men's and women's cross-country, indoor/outdoor track, swimming, tennis, and water polo teams. In addition, there is an extensive intramural program that includes basketball, billiards, softball, and volleyball.

For more information, students should contact:
Office of Admissions
St. Francis College
180 Remsen Street
Brooklyn Heights, New York 11201
Telephone: 718-489-5200
E-mail: admissions@stfranciscollege.edu
WWW: http://www.stfranciscollege.edu

ACADEMIC PROGRAM

Each candidate for a bachelor's degree must complete a total of 128 credit hours and achieve a cumulative index of at least 2.0. In keeping with its liberal arts framework, the College requires all students to take a core curriculum of 42 credit hours in the humanities, social sciences, and natural sciences. For each major, each department specifies a number of required courses to give depth, unity, and direction to the course of study. After meeting these College and departmental requirements, students may select the remainder of their courses to suit their own needs and special interests. To enhance its degree programs, the College offers minors in a wide variety of subject areas.

FINANCIAL AID

More than 80 percent of the students at St. Francis receive some form of financial aid. A comprehensive financial aid program enables the College to offer eligible students financial aid packages that consist of combinations of scholarships, grants, loans, and student employment. A typical student receives more than $7000 in scholarships, grants, and government support. Financial assistance is available from the TAP, Federal Pell Grant, and Federal Supplemental Educational Opportunity Grant Programs. Merit scholarships provided by the College can enhance government funds, and range from $1500 to full tuition. Students seeking assistance for the academic year must file the appropriate College forms by February 15 in order for their financial aid to be processed.

APPLICATION AND INFORMATION

While applications are accepted on a rolling basis, those received before March 1 receive priority of consideration. More information about St. Francis College is available from the Office of Admissions.

ST. MARY'S COLLEGE OF MARYLAND

ST. MARY'S CITY, MARYLAND

THE COLLEGE

St. Mary's is a public, state-supported, coeducational college dedicated to providing an excellent liberal arts education. There are 605 men and 919 women enrolled full-time, and 1,231 of these students live on campus. Part-time enrollment is 164 students. St. Mary's combines the educational and personal advantages of a small private college with the affordability of a public institution. Active learning and the development of critical thinking are encouraged in the discussion-oriented format made possible by modest class size. Student leadership in academic, cultural, and social spheres is aided by the community atmosphere; opportunities are greater than at larger schools, and involvement is easier.

For more information, students should contact:
Director of Admission
St. Mary's College of Maryland
18952 East Fisher Road
St. Mary's City, Maryland 20686
Telephone: 240-895-5000
            800-492-7181 (toll-free)
Fax: 240-895-5001
E-mail: admissions@smcm.edu
WWW: http://www.smcm.edu

ACADEMIC PROGRAM

The course of study at the College provides both diversity and depth, leading to a broad understanding of the liberal arts and a specific competence in at least one major field. All students must complete requirements for one of the majors cited above and the general education requirements. The general education requirements are designed to develop skills in communication and analysis, acquaint students with the legacy of the modern world, confront students with the forces and insights that are shaping the modern world, and promote the capacity for integration and synthesis of knowledge. History students can take advantage of the College's location on the site of colonial St. Mary's City, Maryland's first state capital. Many experts consider this area to contain the most abundant and earliest undisturbed artifacts of any American seventeenth-century town. St. Mary's College offers several courses in aquatic biology as an option within the major program in biology. The College's location on the St. Mary's River, a tributary of the Potomac near the mouth of the Chesapeake Bay, is ideal for the study of estuarine ecology. A strong music program provides advanced training in composition and piano performance and the impetus for a jazz ensemble, percussion ensemble, choir, chamber vocal group, wind ensemble, and chamber orchestra for classical performances. Students may receive credit for high scores on the Advanced Placement Program examinations. Independent study for credit is possible in every major, allowing students to investigate subjects not covered in normal course offerings. Also available is the opportunity for students to design their own majors.

FINANCIAL AID

The Office of Financial Aid provides advice and assistance to students in need of financial aid and joins other College offices in awarding scholarships and loans and in offering part-time employment under the work-study program. Several full scholarships are awarded to Maryland residents on a merit basis, and other scholarships, loans, and grants for students are awarded on the basis of ability and need as determined by the federal government's Free Application for Federal Student Aid, which should be filed no later than March 1.

ST. MARY'S UNIVERSITY OF SAN ANTONIO

■ SAN ANTONIO, TEXAS

THE UNIVERSITY

St. Mary's University is a 150-year-old, private, coeducational institute of higher education administered by the Society of Mary (Marianists). St. Mary's offers small classes and personal attention while integrating the core curriculum into each student's degree plan. Encompassing course work in the arts, humanities, social sciences, and natural sciences, the core helps develop creativity, analytical skills, and an understanding of the human condition. A St. Mary's education challenges students to academic excellence and personal integrity, preparing them for success in their careers and their lives. Founded in 1852, the University maintains a 135-acre campus in northwest San Antonio, 10 minutes from downtown. Modern and historic buildings combine to provide students with state-of-the-art learning facilities and comfortable living areas. In fall 2001, St. Mary's enrolled 1,519 students in the Graduate School and School of Law, and 2,618 undergraduates in the Schools of Business and Administration; Humanities and Social Sciences; and Science, Engineering and Technology. The undergraduate population is comprised of 41 percent men and 59 percent women; 7 percent are out-of-state residents. There are 208 international students representing forty-one countries.

For application forms and more information, students should contact:

Director of Undergraduate Admissions
St. Mary's University of San Antonio
One Camino Santa Maria
San Antonio, Texas 78228-8503
Telephone: 210-436-3126
            800-FOR-STMU (toll-free)
Fax: 210-431-6742
E-mail: uadm@stmarytx.edu
WWW: http://www.stmarytx.edu

ACADEMIC PROGRAM

The University operates on a semester calendar. Advanced placement and/or credit may be granted to students who have scored 3 or higher on the appropriate College Board Advanced Placement examination. Up to 30 credit hours may be granted through the general examinations of the College-Level Examination Program (CLEP) or specific University-administered departmental exams. Admission into an honors program is available for freshmen demonstrating high ability.

FINANCIAL AID

More than 80 percent of all St. Mary's students receive financial aid funds. A number of academic, music, and athletic scholarships are awarded on a non-need basis. All other financial aid awards are based solely on financial need, as determined by an analysis of the Free Application for Federal Student Aid (FAFSA). Presidential Scholarships may be awarded to incoming freshmen who are in the top 10 percent of their high school class and have an ACT composite score of at least 26 or an SAT I combined score of at least 1150. All students who have applied by March 1 are considered for scholarships. Students should mail the FAFSA by February 15 so that the processed document is on file in the Office of Financial Assistance by April 1, the financial assistance priority deadline. St. Mary's undergraduates may qualify for the federally sponsored Federal Pell Grant, Federal Supplemental Educational Opportunity Grant, Federal Perkins Loan, Federal PLUS loan, Federal Stafford Student Loan, and Federal Work-Study programs. At the state level, students can apply for the Tuition Equalization Grant, State Incentive Grant, College Access Loan, and Texas College Work-Study programs. In addition, students may qualify for the St. Mary's University grants and scholarships.

APPLICATION AND INFORMATION

The application deadline is two weeks prior to registration; however, applicants interested in scholarship consideration must apply by March 1 of the year they intend to enroll. Students applying for financial aid and/or residence hall space on campus are strongly urged to submit all necessary forms and information prior to April 1. When all records are on file, the Admissions Committee will notify the student of its decision.

SAVANNAH COLLEGE OF ART AND DESIGN

■ **SAVANNAH, GEORGIA**

THE COLLEGE

The Savannah College of Art and Design (SCAD) is a private coeducational college preparing students for careers in the visual and performing arts, building arts, design, and the history of art and architecture. The College emphasizes individual attention in a positively oriented environment and offers intellectual diversity that enriches, a learning experience that challenges, and an environment that is creatively centered. A balanced fine arts and liberal arts curriculum has attracted students from every state and from more than seventy-five countries, making SCAD one of the largest art and design colleges in the United States; current enrollment is approximately 5,500 students. In addition to the Bachelor of Arts (B.F.A.) degree, the College awards the Master of Fine Arts (M.F.A.), the Master of Arts (M.A.), and the Master of Architecture (M.Arch.). The College is accredited by the Commission on Colleges of the Southern Association of Colleges and Schools to award bachelor's and master's degrees. The Master of Architecture (M.Arch.) is also accredited by the National Architectural Accrediting Board (NAAB). Among its distinctions, the College has been cited by the National Trust for Historic Preservation, the American Institute of Architects, and the International Downtown Association for adaptive reuse of more than forty historic buildings to create a unique urban campus.

> **For more information, students should contact:**
> Admission Department
> Savannah College of Art and Design
> P.O. Box 2072
> Savannah, Georgia 31402-2072
> Telephone: 912-525-5100
>   800-869-7223 (toll-free)
> Fax: 912-525-5986
> E-mail: admission@scad.edu
> WWW: http://www.scad.edu

ACADEMIC PROGRAM

The College operates on the quarter system. Fall, winter, and spring sessions extend from mid-September through May. Summer sessions in Savannah run from late June through August. Short sessions in New York and abroad are offered throughout the year. Students may earn credits during all sessions. The total course of study for a B.F.A. degree consists of 180 quarter credit hours (thirty-six courses). Of these, a student takes 35 to 50 hours in the foundation studies program, 55 to 65 hours in the liberal arts program (with a concentration on art history classes), 60 to 70 hours in the major area of study, and 10 to 20 hours of electives. The five-year B.F.A./M.Arch. degree requires 225 hours, which include 35 foundation hours, 60 hours of liberal arts study, 95 hours in the major program, and 35 hours of electives. Independent study programs are also available to students wishing to pursue a highly specialized area of study. The College offers professional and academic counseling, with special programs for first-year students and tutors for all students available at no charge. The Writing Assistance Center offers assistance to students at all levels.

FINANCIAL AID

Approximately 54 percent of undergraduates and 45 percent of freshmen receive financial assistance. SCAD has a number of financial aid programs, including scholarships, grants, loans, or any combination of these from federal (including the Federal Direct Student Loan Program), state, and College sources. Students may also help finance educational expenses with jobs secured through the Federal Work-Study Program or the College's Student Placement Service. Many employment opportunities exist in the Savannah area, and the College refers interested students to appropriate part-time or free-lance jobs when available. A detailed listing of the financial aid programs may be obtained from the financial aid office. Scholarships for incoming students are awarded through the Admission Office.

APPLICATION AND INFORMATION

Although there are no application deadlines, students are encouraged to apply as early as possible. Files are reviewed as soon as they are complete, and applicants are notified immediately of their admission status. Only accepted students are eligible for scholarship consideration and financial aid. The nonrefundable application fee is $50.

SETON HILL UNIVERSITY

■ **GREENSBURG, PENNSYLVANIA**

THE UNIVERSITY

In 1918, the Sisters of Charity founded Seton Hill University to help women open new doors through the power of education. Since that time, Seton Hill has been recognized as a leader in liberal arts education. Today, Seton Hill University is ranked by *U.S. News & World Report* as a top institution for its academic reputation among northern liberal arts colleges. Seton Hill University, a liberal arts and sciences, coeducational institution, is situated in the Laurel Highlands, an area of southwestern Pennsylvania known for its beautiful scenery and wealth of outdoor activities such as skiing, cycling, hiking, and white-water rafting. Recreational opportunities include on-campus lectures, theater productions, a fitness center, and aerobics classes, as well as University-sponsored trips to Pittsburgh for cultural and sports events. Seton Hill has varsity teams for women in basketball, cross-country, equestrian competition, golf, soccer, softball, tennis, and volleyball; for men in cross-country, equestrian competition, golf, and tennis; plus a variety of intramural teams. At the graduate level, Seton Hill grants the Master of Arts degree in art therapy, counseling psychology, elementary education, special education, and writing popular fiction, a Master of Science in management, and a Master of Education in technologies-enhanced learning.

For more information, students should contact:
Mary Kay Cooper
Director of Admissions and Adult Student Services
Seton Hill University
Seton Hill Drive
Greensburg, Pennsylvania 15601-1599
Telephone: 724-838-4255
             800-826-6234 (toll-free)
Fax: 724-830-1294
E-mail: admit@setonhill.edu
WWW: http://www.setonhill.edu

ACADEMIC PROGRAM

Seton Hill offers five divisions, with the opportunity to self-design a major, all enhanced by the University's award-winning core curriculum. Special programs are available for students who are undecided about their major. The Seton Hill University Honors Program is available for students who have distinguished themselves academically in high school. Prior to graduation all students complete a portfolio, a four-year compilation of their academic, professional, and personal achievements at Seton Hill. Portfolios allow students to showcase their learning and assist them in documenting their accomplishments as they transition from students to practicing professionals. Students hoping to one day own a business may be interested in Seton Hill University's National Education Center for Women in Business. The center is the first organization of its kind in the United States to offer courses in business ownership and entrepreneurial activities to students in any major.

FINANCIAL AID

Seton Hill University's Financial Aid Office works with each student to develop an aid package from the wide variety of scholarships, grants, loans, and work-study programs available. Seton Hill offers Presidential Scholarships valued annually from $4106 to $8212, which are automatically awarded to students who rank in the top 10 percent, 20 percent, or 30 percent of their high school class and meet the admission criteria. In addition, valedictorian, leadership, community service, art, music, theater, biology, chemistry, math, and athletic scholarships are awarded based on merit.

APPLICATION AND INFORMATION

Seton Hill University has a rolling admissions policy. Decisions of the Admissions Committee are rendered shortly after all application materials have been submitted. The first-time freshman applicant should submit a completed application form, a $30 nonrefundable application fee, an official secondary school transcript that includes the applicant's rank and cumulative grade point average, and official score reports from either the SAT or ACT. Prospective students who do not have SAT or ACT scores may submit two graded written assignments from their junior or senior year for consideration.

SHENANDOAH UNIVERSITY

■ WINCHESTER, VIRGINIA

THE UNIVERSITY

Shenandoah University was founded at Dayton, Virginia, in 1875. Although the institution was established to provide "classical" and music studies, by 1888 an unusual blend of educational opportunities had been formulated that included arts, sciences, music, medical arts, and business management. These programs, on a much more sophisticated basis, are found at Shenandoah today. In 1960, Shenandoah moved to a 62-acre campus in Winchester, Virginia. The main campus is now more than 100 acres with nineteen buildings, including six residence halls.

For more information, students should contact:

Director of Admissions
Shenandoah University
1460 University Drive
Winchester, Virginia 22601
Telephone: 540-665-4581
            800-432-2266 (toll-free)
Fax: 540-665-4627
E-mail: admit@su.edu

Of these six facilities for boarding students, one is for women and five are coeducational. There are five additional buildings at off-campus locations. Shenandoah's historical relationship with the United Methodist Church does not place sectarian obligations on any student. Shenandoah's students have the distinct advantage of being on a small campus near large metropolitan cultural centers. Such student organizations as academic fraternities, service and honor organizations, and various departmental clubs provide opportunities for leadership and recreation. Students come to Shenandoah because they want an educational experience of superior quality and believe that the facilities of a small campus, with a personal atmosphere, are the most conducive to achieving this experience. Fifty-six percent of the 2,459 students are from Virginia; the remaining 44 percent represent forty-five states and thirty-two countries. Graduate study is also available at Shenandoah. Programs are offered in athletic training, business administration, dance, education, music, nursing, occupational therapy, pharmacy, physical therapy, and physician assistant studies. Further information about graduate study may be obtained by writing to the Director of Admissions.

ACADEMIC PROGRAM

Shenandoah's academic calendar is divided into fall and spring semesters. Summer terms, ranging in length from two to eleven weeks, are also available. Each academic division (arts and sciences, business, conservatory, and health professions) offers diversified programs, with specific courses required by the various accreditation agencies. Credit is available through the tests of the College-Level Examination Program (CLEP), Proficiency Examination Program (PEP), and Advanced Placement (AP) Program and through various departmental challenge examinations.

FINANCIAL AID

Shenandoah makes every effort to assist students in finding resources to finance their education. Approximately 91 percent of the University's students receive some type of financial aid. Shenandoah annually awards more than $20 million in aid to students in the form of grants, loans, scholarships, and employment on the campus. Previous financial aid packages have averaged approximately $13,000 per undergraduate student per year. To qualify for scholarships and financial aid, students must submit the Free Application for Federal Student Aid (FAFSA). Aid is awarded on a first-come, first-served basis, as funds are available. A student must be accepted for admission to a degree program before a financial aid offer is made. Specific information regarding financial aid should be requested from the Director of Financial Aid.

APPLICATION AND INFORMATION

To apply, a student must submit an application with a $30 nonrefundable application fee, SAT I or ACT scores, and an official high school transcript. Transfer students must submit an official college transcript for all postsecondary course work in addition to meeting the freshman score and transcript requirements. Applicants are notified of the admission decision after receipt of all credentials.

SIMPSON COLLEGE

■ **INDIANOLA, IOWA**

THE COLLEGE

Simpson College was founded in 1860. The institution was named Simpson College to honor Bishop Matthew Simpson (1811–1884), one of the best-known and most influential religious leaders of his day. The College is coeducational; although it is affiliated with the United Methodist Church, it is nonsectarian in spirit and accepts students without regard to race, color, creed, national origin, religion, sex, age, or disability. For more than a century, Simpson has played a vital role in the educational, cultural, intellectual, political, and religious life of the nation. The College has thirty-two buildings on 73 acres of beautiful campus and enrolls 1,900 students. Extracurricular activities at Simpson are designed to supplement and reinforce the academic program and contribute toward a total learning experience. Students may participate in student government, publications, music, theater, and social groups. Simpson competes in eighteen intercollegiate sports and has an extensive intramural program for both men and women. Men's and women's athletics at Simpson are governed by the NCAA. Simpson also has chapters of three national fraternities, one local fraternity, and four national sororities.

> **For more information, students should contact:**
> Office of Admissions
> Simpson College
> 701 North "C" Street
> Indianola, Iowa 50125
> Telephone: 515-961-1624
> 800-362-2454 (toll-free)
> E-mail: admiss@simpson.edu
> WWW: http://www.simpson.edu

ACADEMIC PROGRAM

Simpson operates on a 4-4-1 academic calendar. The first semester starts in late August and ends in mid-December; the second semester starts in mid-January and ends in late April. A three-week session takes place during the month of May. During this period, students have the opportunity to take one class that focuses on a single subject, to study abroad, or to participate in a field experience or internship. New students are assigned faculty advisers who aid them in constructing academically sound majors. Students must participate in one May Term class or program for each year of full-time study or its equivalent at Simpson College. All students must complete the requirements of the Cornerstone Studies in liberal arts and competencies in foreign language, math, and writing. To earn the Bachelor of Arts degree, students may take no more than 42 hours in the major department, excluding May Term programs, and 84 hours in the division of the major, including May Term programs. Also, at least 128 semester hours of course work must be accumulated with a grade point average of C (2.0) or better. For a Bachelor of Music degree, the same requirements apply, except that 84 hours must be earned in the major, excluding May Terms, and the candidate is limited to 12 additional hours in the division of fine arts. Also, at least 132 hours of course work must be completed with a cumulative grade point average of C (2.0) or better.

FINANCIAL AID

Simpson College seeks to make it financially possible for qualified students to experience the advantages of a college education. Generous gifts from alumni, trustees, and friends of the College, in addition to state and federal programs of student aid, make this opportunity possible. Simpson offers financial aid on both a need and non-need basis. Need is determined by filing the Free Application for Federal Student Aid. Financial aid granted on a non-need basis includes academic scholarships, which are awarded on the basis of prior academic records, and talent scholarships, which are available in theater, music, and art. The talent scholarships are determined by audition/portfolio.

APPLICATION AND INFORMATION

Simpson's rolling admission policy allows flexibility; however, early application is recommended. Transfer and foreign students are welcome. Students are strongly encouraged to visit the campus.

SOUTHERN CONNECTICUT STATE UNIVERSITY

■ NEW HAVEN, CONNECTICUT

THE UNIVERSITY

Southern Connecticut State University creates the kind of rich academic and social environment that encourages students to discover who they are, who they want to be, and how to make their dreams for the future come alive today. Founded in 1893, Southern is a public, multifaceted, coeducational university offering 116 undergraduate and graduate programs in the full range of academic and professional disciplines. It enriches those disciplines with fascinating internships, unique research opportunities, a challenging faculty, and a dynamic campus life. Southern is located in New Haven, the heart of "academic Connecticut," and students take full advantage of the city and its many beautiful communities. Southern comprises seven academic schools: Arts and Sciences; Business; Education; Communication, Information, and Library Sciences; Health and Human Services, which includes programs in nursing, public health, recreation and leisure studies, and social work; Graduate Studies; and Extended Learning. For highly motivated students, Southern offers a number of honors programs, including the Honors College.

> **For more information, students should contact:**
> Sharon Brennan
> Director of Admissions and Enrollment Management
> Admissions House
> Southern Connecticut State University
> 131 Farnham Avenue
> New Haven, Connecticut 06515-1355
> Telephone: 203-392-SCSU
> 888-500-SCSU (toll-free)
> WWW: http://www.Southernct.edu

ACADEMIC PROGRAM

The University operates on a two-semester calendar. The fall semester usually begins the first week in September and ends before Christmas. The spring semester, which includes a one-week spring recess in March, runs from the third week of January to the middle of May. Southern also offers two 5-week sessions during the summer and a three-week intersession program each January. Throughout its history, Southern has held fast to the conviction that the best education stresses the liberal arts and sciences. To ensure all students a chance to acquire such an education, Southern has designed a strong yet flexible program that underscores the basics while encouraging individual choice and self-expression.

FINANCIAL AID

The Financial Aid Office coordinates a number of programs. These programs, which include grants and scholarships, long-term low-interest loans, and part-time student employment, are based on the demonstrated financial need of students and their families. The University offers the Federal Perkins Loan, the Federal Pell Grant, the Federal Supplemental Educational Opportunity Grant, the Federal Stafford Student Loan, the Federal PLUS loan, and the Federal Work-Study Program. Southern also provides assistance through alumni scholarships. More than 40 percent of Southern's undergraduates receive some form of financial aid. Students interested in applying for assistance must complete the Free Application for Federal Student Aid (FAFSA) and send it to the central processor so that it is received by April 16. The Financial Aid Office also requires students to submit additional forms, including a University financial aid application. All required forms have deadlines and are available at the Financial Aid Office.

APPLICATION AND INFORMATION

Candidates for admission should apply by May of their senior year in high school. The Admissions Office mails its first notice of acceptance on December 1, and early applicants have priority for housing and financial aid. Applicants must submit previous academic records, including a complete transcript of high school grades and rank in class; an admission application; a $40 nonrefundable fee; a written recommendation from the high school principal, a teacher, or a guidance counselor; and an official copy of the SAT I report.

SOUTHWEST TEXAS STATE UNIVERSITY

■ SAN MARCOS, TEXAS

THE UNIVERSITY
Southwest Texas State University (SWT) is a comprehensive public university committed to providing an intellectually stimulating and socially diverse climate for its graduate and undergraduate students. Serving approximately 23,500 students, SWT is the sixth-largest public university in the state. Chartered in 1899, SWT's original mission was to prepare Texas public school teachers. It became renowned for carrying out this mission, but today it does far more. The school has grown to become a multipurpose university offering programs in the Colleges of Applied Arts, Business, Fine Arts and Communication, Health Professions, Education, Liberal Arts, and Science and in the Graduate College. Beyond the classroom, SWT promotes self-enrichment and intellectual vigor in a number of affordable ways. Performances in theater, opera, and film, as well as a full range of musical concerts provide students with an assortment of cultural arts events to attend. Other University-sponsored student activities include intramural and club sports; peer mentoring; various bands, including marching, symphonic, and jazz; the student media; a Greek system; and a variety of outdoor recreational activities. The $26.5-million LBJ Student Center is the focal point of most campus activity and also houses SWT's student support offices.

For more information, students should contact:
Undergraduate Admissions Center
Southwest Texas State University
429 North Guadalupe
San Marcos, Texas 78666-5709
Telephone: 512-245-2340
E-mail: admissions@swt.edu
WWW: http://www.swt.edu

ACADEMIC PROGRAM
SWT operates on a two-semester calendar system with the fall semester beginning in late August and the spring semester in mid-January. SWT also offers two 5-week summer sessions. Students may earn college credit hours through the University's credit-by-examination program (AP, CLEP, IB, and departmental exams). The Honors Program offers interdisciplinary courses as part of a five-course requirement, which includes the honors thesis, for graduation in the program. Class size is limited to 17 students. Air Force and Army ROTC programs are also offered. At SWT, all students are required to complete a 46- to 49-hour general studies curriculum that serves as the common foundation for all majors. The requirement for a bachelor's degree is the successful completion of approximately 128 to 136 semester hours, depending on the degree plan.

FINANCIAL AID
Financial aid is provided in the form of grants, loans, work-study, and scholarships. Students should apply early for financial aid. The priority deadline for returning the Free Application for Federal Student Aid (FAFSA) form for the fall semester is April 1. To ensure an early response, students should apply as soon as possible after January 1. For an application or other financial aid materials, students should write to the Office of Student Financial Aid, 601 University Drive, San Marcos, Texas 78666-4602. Scholarships are awarded on a competitive basis and are available at SWT for qualified new and continuing admitted students. They range from $500 to $5000, with a variety of criteria, including academic achievement, proposed major, hometown, economic need, and athletic and performance-based talent. SWT's premier scholarship is the Mitte Foundation Scholarship Program.

SPRINGFIELD COLLEGE

■ SPRINGFIELD, MASSACHUSETTS

THE COLLEGE

Ever since Professor James A. Naismith invented the game of basketball in 1891, Springfield College has enjoyed an international reputation as a pioneer in physical education and wellness. Founded in 1885 to train leaders for the YMCA, Springfield College has grown and expanded upon these fields and is known today for expertise in sports and movement activities, allied health sciences, human and social services, and the arts and sciences. Guiding all aspects of student-life is the distinctive "humanics" philosophy, which emphasizes education of the whole person—spirit, mind and body—for leadership in service to others. Community service is encouraged, and many courses augment classroom learning with fieldwork in community programs that are related to studies. Springfield College is accredited by the New England Association of Schools and Colleges and serves more than 4,000 undergraduate and graduate students at its main campus. Another 1,000 students are enrolled in weekend or evening programs of its School of Human Services at eight satellite campuses around the country. At Springfield, cocurricular activities and athletics form an integral part of the undergraduate experience. There are more than 100 organizations and opportunities for involvement including drama, music, theater, dance, and other clubs. The College offers the largest undergraduate athletics program in the nation for an institution of its size. Ninety percent of undergraduates play intramural sports and more than 30 percent participate in intercollegiate athletics. There are men's and women's teams in basketball, cross-country, gymnastics, lacrosse, soccer, swimming, tennis, track, and volleyball. Women's teams also include field hockey and softball, and there are additional men's teams in baseball, football, golf, and wrestling. Nine campus residence halls provide guaranteed on-campus housing for four years.

> **For more information, students should contact:**
>
> Office of Admissions
> Springfield College
> 263 Alden Street
> Box M
> Springfield, Massachusetts 01109
> Telephone: 413-748-3136
>   800-343-1257 (toll-free)
> E-mail: admissions@spfldcol.edu
> WWW:
>   http://www.springfieldcollege.edu

ACADEMIC PROGRAM

Consistent with Springfield College's humanics philosophy, undergraduate education is designed to promote an understanding of how the spirit, mind and body work together in preparing students for a life of leadership in service to others. This approach combines theory and practice, augmenting classroom learning with extensive fieldwork opportunities. The College has a two-semester academic calendar. To graduate, students must complete 130 credits including required courses for the major field of study, electives, and required courses for all students (English, philosophy, social science, health, history, mathematics, and natural science).

FINANCIAL AID

Students who feel they do not have sufficient funds to pay the costs of their educations are encouraged to apply for financial aid in the form of grants, loans, and student employment. Financial aid offered by Springfield College is based on need, intellectual promise, leadership, and character. The College gives full consideration to students who submit the Free Application for Federal Student Aid (FAFSA) and the College Scholarship Service Financial Aid PROFILE by March 15, 2003 for first-year students and May 1, 2003 for transfer students. Students not eligible for financial aid may still be considered for institutional employment.

APPLICATION AND INFORMATION

Springfield College's Admissions Committee reviews applications upon receiving them. For the 2003-04 academic year, applications are due April 1, 2003 for the first-year students and August 1, 2003 for transfer students. For the 2004 athletic training and physical therapy programs, applications are due December 1, 2003. For the 2004 physician assistant and occupational therapy programs, applications are due January 15, 2004.

TEIKYO POST UNIVERSITY

■ **WATERBURY, CONNECTICUT**

THE UNIVERSITY

Founded in 1890, Teikyo Post University is a globally focused, private, coeducational, residential institution. The University is accredited by the New England Association of Schools and Colleges. In 1990, the former Post College became affiliated with the Teikyo University Group, which resulted in a name change and a dramatically enlarged mission and scope. Teikyo Post University's mission centers around four fundamental themes: globalization, restructuring the economy around information and knowledge, technology, and collaboration. As a small, private university, Teikyo Post has the time and resources to take a personal interest in every student. The University is dedicated to providing a cohesive global environment in which more than 1,200 students from the United States and thirty countries learn to become knowledgeable participants in the global marketplace. While participating in a close and caring University community, students learn to appreciate attitudes and cultures through classes, course offerings, activities, and one-on-one relationships with faculty members and peers.

Further information may be obtained by contacting:
Office of Admission
Teikyo Post University
800 Country Club Road
P.O. Box 2540
Waterbury, Connecticut 06723-2540
Telephone 203-596-4520
          800-345-2762 (toll-free)
Fax: 203-756-5810
E-mail: tpuadmis@teikyopost.edu
WWW: http://www.teikyopost.edu

ACADEMIC PROGRAM

To receive an associate degree from Teikyo Post, students must complete a minimum of 60 credit hours. For the bachelor's degree, students must complete a minimum of 120 credit hours. As an institution offering both four-year and two-year programs, Teikyo Post provides associate degree students with three options upon graduation: pursue a career in their field of study, remain at the University in the Bachelor of Science or Bachelor of Arts degree program, or transfer to another four-year college or university. All programs offer opportunities for internships and cooperative education. For students seeking additional academic challenges, the Teikyo Post University Honors Program offers the opportunity to pursue independent research and special projects under the guidance of a faculty member. The University has a two-semester calendar.

FINANCIAL AID

Teikyo Post offers financial assistance through the Federal Work-Study, Federal Supplemental Educational Opportunity Grant, Federal Stafford Student Loan, and Federal Perkins Loan programs. Aid is awarded upon evidence of financial need, as determined by the Free Application for Federal Student Aid (FAFSA). In addition, the University has its own scholarship and grant-in-aid programs, both academic and athletic, and participates in all state programs that are applicable. In order to apply for financial assistance, a student must apply for admission and be accepted to Teikyo Post and then submit the FAFSA. An institutional application for financial aid must also be submitted. A student may apply for the Federal Pell Grant by submitting the application directly to the federal government or by submitting the FAFSA.

APPLICATION AND INFORMATION

Students should send an application for admission, accompanied by a nonrefundable application fee of $40. Teikyo Post University accommodates candidates by processing applications on a rolling basis. It is advantageous to file an application as early as possible. This allows the Admissions Committee to give an application the attention it deserves and enables the applicant to prepare for college life. An application is reviewed when all the necessary credentials have been received.

TEXAS TECH UNIVERSITY

LUBBOCK, TEXAS

THE UNIVERSITY

Texas Tech University, founded in 1923, is a residential state university with a population of 25,000 students who come from all fifty states and ninety-nine other countries. Students at Texas Tech have the opportunity to study from more than 300 graduate and undergraduate degree programs. Academics are the top priority at Texas Tech, and students find admission standards to be comparable with other state institutions. No other state university in Texas rivals Texas Tech in offering such diverse academic programs on one campus. The University is built around nine colleges: Agricultural Sciences and Natural Resources, Architecture, Arts and Sciences, Business Administration, Education, Engineering, Honors, Human Sciences, and Visual and Performing Arts. A law school, which often boasts the highest number of students passing the bar exam in Texas, is conveniently located on the main campus. Also present is the Texas Tech University Health Sciences Center with its Schools of Medicine, Nursing, Pharmacy, and Allied Health. David J. Schmidly, Ph.D., serves as University president and believes that academic diversity coupled with high educational standards is the key that has placed Texas Tech among the most notable universities in the state. Texas Tech has become a leader in academic programs ranging from pioneering research with the U.S. Department of Agriculture to improving alternative fuel capabilities for the nation's leading auto makers. Wind engineering research has led to the creation of shelters that withstand the nation's most deadly tornadoes. Students also find opportunities to master the arts with instruction from classically trained musicians as well as unique study abroad programs. The creation of the Institute for Environmental and Human Health provides a new addition to the academic program.

For more information, students should contact:
Office of Admissions and School Relations
Texas Tech University
Box 45005
Lubbock, Texas 79409-5005
Telephone: 806-742-1480
Fax: 806-742-0980
E-mail: admissions@ttu.edu
WWW: http://www.ttu.edu
http://www.srel.ttu.edu

ACADEMIC PROGRAM

Texas Tech's undergraduate curriculum provides courses in more than 150 programs of study. Recently, students at Texas Tech have seen an increase in competitive scholarships and the creation of the University's Honor's College. Students accepted into the college find unparalleled undergraduate research opportunities for students in all major disciplines. As a result, Texas Tech students are consistently awarded the prestigious Barry M. Goldwater Scholarship for science, engineering, and mathematics. Since 1995, 19 Texas Tech students have received the Goldwater Scholarship. In 2001, a Texas Tech student was recognized as a Truman Scholar. The latest accomplishment is a Gates–Cambridge scholar awarded in 2002 for study at Cambridge in 2003–04.

FINANCIAL AID

A variety of financial aid is offered in the form of scholarships, grants, and loans. Competitive scholarships are awarded on academic merit, SAT I or ACT scores, and class rank. More than 300 Presidential Endowed Scholarships are awarded to students each year. Need-based assistance is also available in the form of scholarships, government and private loans, grants, and work-study. Students' need for assistance is determined from the Free Application for Federal Student Aid (FAFSA). For a guide to scholarships and deadlines, students should contact the Office of Financial Aid (telephone: 806-742-3681; Web site: http://www.fina.ttu.edu).

APPLICATION AND INFORMATION

All students should submit the *State of Texas Common Application*, a high school transcript, SAT I or ACT test scores, and the $50 application fee. Applications can be found on the Web at http://www.applytexas.org.

TOWSON UNIVERSITY

■ TOWSON, MARYLAND

THE UNIVERSITY

Established in 1866, Towson University (TU) is a regional comprehensive university that offers degree programs in the liberal arts and sciences and preprofessional and professional areas of study. The University's beautiful 328-acre campus is located in the suburban community of Towson, Maryland, just 8 miles north of downtown Baltimore. Towson is nationally recognized for its programs in business, communications, computer information systems, education, fine arts, health professions, and women's studies. The University offers sixty bachelor's degree programs, thirty-five master's degree programs, and three applied doctoral programs and emphasizes excellence in teaching and continued scholarly growth by faculty members. Towson University is composed of eight colleges: the College of Business and Economics, the College of Education, the College of Fine Arts and Communication, the College of Health Professions, the College of Liberal Arts, the College of Science and Mathematics, the College of Graduate Education and Research, and the College of Extended Programs. The University enrolls nearly 17,000 full- and part-time students, including more than 800 international students from 100 countries.

For more information, students should contact:
Office of Admissions
Towson University
8000 York Road
Towson, Maryland 21252-0001
Telephone: 888-4TOWSON (toll-free)
WWW: http://www.towson.edu

ACADEMIC PROGRAM

The University follows the semester system, with spring and fall semesters, an optional January minimester, three 5-week summer sessions, and one 7-week summer session. The University's goal is to enrich lives by providing a strong liberal arts and sciences education for all students. More than 900 courses are offered during the spring and fall semesters and the summer sessions. Students can attend full-time or part-time, and classes are offered during the day, in the evening, and on Saturday.

FINANCIAL AID

Approximately 66 percent of the full-time undergraduates at Towson University receive financial assistance of some kind. Assistance is available to eligible students through loans and grants from major federal and state programs, scholarships, and on- and off-campus employment. In addition, the University offers non-need scholarships based on merit or academic performance.

APPLICATION AND INFORMATION

Towson offers admission to qualified candidates on a continuous (rolling admissions) basis. Applicants should submit all appropriate application materials and required academic credentials by May 1 for fall admission and by December 1 for spring admission. Priority admission is granted beginning October 1 to those freshman applicants whose secondary school record indicates an overall 3.0 or above average in academic courses from grades 9 to 11 and whose combined SAT I score is at least 1100. It is the applicant's responsibility to forward all required forms and credentials (test scores, transcripts, and recommendations) to the Admissions Office in accordance with established deadlines. Incomplete applications or those improperly filled out are subject to cancellation. A nonrefundable $35 application fee or authorized fee-deferment form is required at the time the application is filed. Application forms are available online at the site listed below or by calling or writing to the Office of Admissions.

TULANE UNIVERSITY

■ NEW ORLEANS, LOUISIANA

THE UNIVERSITY

Tulane University in New Orleans is known nationally and internationally for its teaching and research. At Tulane a student can get an international education in a European city without leaving America. One of a handful of national independent universities in the South, Tulane was founded in 1834 as the Medical College of Louisiana and reorganized as Tulane in 1884. The University is comprehensive by nature, with more than 11,000 students enrolled in eleven schools and colleges ranging from the liberal arts and sciences through a full spectrum of professional schools: law, medicine, business, engineering, architecture, social work, and public health and tropical medicine. Tulane's 5,600 full-time undergraduates choose from seventy majors in colleges of liberal arts and sciences, engineering, architecture, and business and may opt for joint-degree programs in Tulane's professional schools to earn undergraduate and graduate degrees in a shorter period of time.

> **For more information, students should contact:**
> Richard Whiteside
> Vice President for Enrollment
>   Management
>   and Institutional Research
> Tulane University
> 210 Gibson Hall
> 6823 St. Charles Avenue
> New Orleans, Louisiana 70118-5680
> Telephone: 504-865-5731
>   800-873-9283 (toll-free)
> Fax: 504-862-8715
> E-mail:
>   undergrad.admission@tulane.edu
> WWW: http://www.tulane.edu/
>   Admission

ACADEMIC PROGRAM

The liberal arts and sciences curriculum has proficiency requirements in English, a foreign language, and mathematics. Each student must also complete courses distributed across the disciplines—humanities and fine arts, social sciences, and sciences—in a nine-course requirement that gives each student a common basis of knowledge. Proficiency in writing is also required. The School of Engineering emphasizes design, research, and laboratory experimentation for its Bachelor of Science degree programs in biomedical, chemical, civil, computer, electrical, environmental, and mechanical engineering as well as computer science. The modern laboratories in the engineering complex, including the $12-million Boggs Center for Energy and Biotechnology, support courses and studies in subjects as varied as robotics, environmental clean-up, the design of artificial joints, laser fabrication, and drug purification. The School of Architecture takes advantage of its location in New Orleans, a fascinating living architecture laboratory, where about 300 students are enrolled in the five-year Bachelor/Master of Architecture program. Students graduate fully prepared to become licensed architects with no further study. The faculty members, nationally known for their scholarship and art as well as their teaching, often involve students in real-world architectural concerns. The A. B. Freeman School of Business offers majors in accounting, business, finance, management, and marketing, leading to the Bachelor of Science in Management degree.

FINANCIAL AID

The University operates a comprehensive aid program; more than half of the students receive some form of financial aid. The average financial aid package (through scholarships, federal grants, loans, and work-study jobs) was nearly $23,000 for 2001–02. Need, determined by family financial information on the Free Application for Federal Student Aid and the PROFILE from the College Scholarship Service, establishes the appropriate amount of assistance. Merit, based on academic record, determines the proportion of Tulane-funded scholarships in the aid package.

APPLICATION AND INFORMATION

Regular decision applications should be submitted by January 15 for admission to the fall semester; admission notification is made no later than April 1, with a May 1 deposit deadline. Deans' Honor Scholarship applicants must apply by December 15 and are notified by February 20. Early decision/early application candidates should have all credentials on file by November 1 for notification by December 15. The application fee is $55.

UNITED STATES MILITARY ACADEMY

■ **WEST POINT, NEW YORK**

THE ACADEMY

The United States Military Academy, the nation's oldest service academy, celebrating its 200th anniversary, offers young men and women one of the premier education and leadership development programs in the nation. West Point advocates the "whole person" concept. The Military Academy has, since its founding in 1802, provided a broadly structured undergraduate curriculum that balances the physical sciences and engineering with the behavioral and social sciences. West Point's mission is to educate, train, and inspire the Corps of Cadets so that each graduate is a commissioned leader of character committed to the values of duty, honor, and country; professional growth throughout a career as an officer in the United States Army; and a lifetime of selfless service to the nation. The Military Academy provides its graduates with a solid foundation for intellectual and moral/ethical growth that is essential for successfully handling high-level responsibilities in national service. When students enter West Point, they are also beginning a profession. Upon graduation, cadets are commissioned as second lieutenants in the U.S. Army and are normally required to serve on active duty for at least five years. There are approximately 4,000 men and women enrolled at West Point. Cadets compete annually for Rhodes, Olmsted, Marshall, and Daedalian scholarships and for National Science Foundation, Truman, and Hertz graduate fellowships. West Pointers who remain in the Army are normally selected to attend civilian graduate schools in the United States or abroad between their fourth and tenth years of service. The Academy develops the nation's future Army leaders by immersing cadets in programs of academic, military, and physical development.

> **For more information, students should contact:**
> Director of Admissions
> United States Military Academy
> 606 Thayer Road
> West Point, New York 10996-1797
> Telephone: 845-938-4041
> E-mail: admissions@www.usma.edu
> WWW: http://www.usma.edu/
>   Admissions

ACADEMIC PROGRAM

The academic program at the United States Military Academy provides cadets with a broad background in the arts and sciences and prepares them for future graduate study. The total curriculum is designed to develop essential character, competence, and intellectual ability in an officer. The core curriculum is the foundation of the academic program and provides a foundation in mathematics, basic sciences, engineering sciences, information technology, humanities, behavior sciences, and social sciences. The core curriculum, ranging in size from twenty-six to thirty courses, depending on the field of study or major, represents the essential broad base of knowledge necessary for success as a commissioned officer while also supporting each cadet's choice of academic specialization. Classes at West Point are small, averaging 12 to 18 cadets per section. Cadets receive individual attention, and tutorial sessions are available upon request. Advanced and honors courses are available to cadets having exceptional ability. All cadets study military science and receive classroom instruction in the principles of small-unit tactics and leadership during a two-week intersession between the first and second semesters. Concentrated summer field training provides each cadet with the opportunity to learn and practice individual military skills and to apply the principles of tactics and leadership studied in the classroom.

FINANCIAL AID

There are no financial aid programs because expenses are paid by the U.S. government. Scholarship awards may be used by candidates to offset the cost of the initial deposit.

APPLICATION AND INFORMATION

Prospective candidates should write to Admissions, stating their interest in the Military Academy. Each applicant will be sent a Precandidate Questionnaire and prospectus, which outlines the West Point entrance requirements. All applicants are encouraged to start a candidate file at West Point at the end of their junior year or as soon thereafter as possible. This allows for early completion of all candidate file requirements.

UNIVERSITY OF MARYLAND, COLLEGE PARK

- **COLLEGE PARK, MARYLAND**

THE UNIVERSITY

Throughout its 145-year history, the University of Maryland has served as a premier public research university while dedicating itself to providing the highest quality undergraduate education. Designated as the state's flagship university, Maryland attracts the best students and faculty members from across the nation and around the world. Students enroll at Maryland for the reputation and quality of its academic programs, the outstanding and diverse opportunities both in and outside the classroom, and the success of its alumni. Choosing from among more than 100 academic programs, 21,951 full-time and 2,687 part-time undergraduates are taught by a faculty of more than 1,900. Approximately 8,551 master's- and doctoral-level students are enrolled in the graduate school. About 75 percent of Maryland's undergraduates are state residents, with the remaining quarter coming from all fifty states, the District of Columbia, three territories, and 110 other countries. Maryland's diversity is one of its strongest assets, with 40 percent of students belonging to minority groups. More than 8,000 undergraduates live on-campus.

> **For application forms and further information about the University of Maryland, students should contact:**
> Office of Undergraduate Admissions
> University of Maryland
> College Park, Maryland 20742-5235
> Telephone: 301-314-8385
>   800-422-5867 (toll-free)
>   301-314-9197 (TTY)
> Fax: 301-314-9693
> E-mail: um-admit@uga.umd.edu
> WWW: http://www.maryland.edu

ACADEMIC PROGRAM

Undergraduate education at Maryland aims to provide students with a sense of identity and purpose, a concern for others, a sense of responsibility for the quality of life around them, a continuing eagerness for knowledge and understanding, and a foundation for a lifetime of personal enrichment and success. Within a research setting such as Maryland's, undergraduate students take strong, interdisciplinary courses taught by renowned researchers and scholars. Every undergraduate completes at least 120 credit hours to earn a degree, 46 of which are general education or CORE courses. The purpose of CORE is to help students achieve the intellectual integration and awareness they need to meet challenges in their personal, social, political, and professional lives. Although each program is unique, generally 30 to 36 credit hours are earned in the major field. Students may earn a double major, earn a certificate in a second area of study, and use AP and IB credit toward a degree.

FINANCIAL AID

An array of financial aid programs, including scholarships, grants, loans, and student employment opportunities, are available to undergraduates. To be considered for maximum need-based financial aid, students must submit the completed FAFSA to the FAFSA processor in time for receipt and acceptance by the University's February 15 priority financial aid deadline. The University proudly offers several merit scholarships for academically and creatively talented students; approximately $4 million per year is awarded. To be considered for most merit scholarships, an application for admission must be submitted by December 1. Last year, 68 percent of full-time students who applied for financial aid received it and were awarded an average of $7300.

APPLICATION AND INFORMATION

Applications for fall freshman admission are due by February 15. Students are encouraged to apply by Maryland's priority application deadline of December 1 for best consideration for admission, merit-based scholarships, and invitation to University Honors or College Park Scholars. The spring freshman application deadline is December 15. Applications for fall transfer admission are due by July 1; for the spring semester, December 1. International students and students with any foreign academic records have earlier deadlines.

UNIVERSITY OF MASSACHUSETTS DARTMOUTH

■ NORTH DARTMOUTH, MASSACHUSETTS

THE UNIVERSITY

The University of Massachusetts Dartmouth traces its roots to 1895 when the Massachusetts legislature chartered the New Bedford Textile School and the Bradford Durfee Textile School in Fall River. As the region's economic base shifted from textiles to more diverse manufacturing and service industries, the program of the colleges changed. Courses were developed to respond to the needs of new generations of students, stimulated by the clear economic and social advantages of a well-educated citizenry. In 1962 Southeastern Massachusetts Technological Institute (SMTI) was created, and in 1969, out of a need and a clear demand for a comprehensive public university, SMTI became Southeastern Massachusetts University. Then, in 1988, the Swain School of Design was merged with the University's College of Visual and Performing Arts. In 1991, a new University of Massachusetts system was created, which combined the Amherst and Boston campuses with the University of Lowell, Southeastern Massachusetts University, and the Medical Center in Worcester. Today, UMass Dartmouth provides educational programs, research, extension, and continuing education and cyber education in the liberal and creative arts and sciences and in the professions. A broad range of bachelor's and master's degrees and one program leading to a doctorate are offered. UMass Dartmouth enrolls approximately 6,500 students; 90 percent are from Massachusetts, with a growing number from other states and countries outside the United States. A residential campus with a variety of student organizations, athletic programs, cultural opportunities, and interest groups, the University fosters personal development, diversity, and responsible citizenship.

> **For more information, students should contact:**
> Office of Admissions
> UMass Dartmouth
> 285 Old Westport Road
> North Dartmouth, Massachusetts 02747-2300
> Telephone: 508-999-8605
> Fax: 508-999-8755
> E-mail: admissions@umassd.edu
> WWW: http://explore.umassd.edu/

ACADEMIC PROGRAMS

The University operates on a two-semester calendar with the fall semester beginning the first week of September and concluding in mid-December and the spring semester beginning in late January and concluding in late May. A five-week intersession is offered between semesters. Summer term courses are offered in June, July, and early August. Undergraduate students usually enroll in four or five courses each semester, and a typical course earns 3 credits. An undergraduate degree requires a minimum of 120 credits (there are a few majors which require 135 credits); a student can complete degree requirements for a specified major within a department or an approved interdepartmental major (30 credits). Students must also complete requirements according to the degree being sought. Special learning opportunities include independent study, contract learning, and directed study; study abroad; study at a nearby university through cross-registration; and credit by examination.

FINANCIAL AID

Nearly all students are eligible for some type of financial aid. UMass Dartmouth awards financial aid based on federal, state, and institutional guidelines; students must submit the Free Application for Federal Student Aid (FAFSA). In determining need, the Financial Aid Services Office considers the total costs of attending the University (tuition, fees, books, room and board, the cost of commuting, and an allowance for living and personal expenses). The difference between total University cost and the estimate of expected family contribution is the amount that the financial aid staff considers to be financial need.

APPLICATION AND INFORMATION

Admissions is rolling except for early decision (freshman). The early decision deadline is November 15, with notification by December 15. All other decisions are made within three weeks of the completion of an application. For application forms and related information, students may call, write, or e-mail the admissions office.

UNIVERSITY OF MINNESOTA, CROOKSTON

■ CROOKSTON, MINNESOTA

THE UNIVERSITY

Nationally recognized as a leader in information technology education, the University of Minnesota, Crookston (UMC), is part of the world-renowned University of Minnesota System. Founded in the late 1800s as a research station and then as a school of agriculture, UMC became a part of the University of Minnesota in 1965. Today, UMC is a four-year, public coeducational institution of 1,650 full- and part-time students. Its focus on polytechnic education, commitment to technology, and overall high-quality programs have captured national attention. UMC earned a ranking in *U.S. News & World Report*'s 2000 listing of America's Best Colleges and received other national notice in publications such as the *Washington Post* and the *Atlanta Journal-Constitution*. UMC is continuing to evolve to meet the educational demands of Minnesota and the world by developing a technology-rich, interactive living and learning community. UMC was one of the first campuses in the nation (1993) to begin issuing notebook computers to all full-time students. The university has become known nationally as the "Thinkpad University" and has emerged as one of the most technologically advanced campuses in the country. UMC's mission of research and discovery, teaching and learning, and outreach and public service encompasses applied undergraduate instruction and research in agriculture; aviation; business; education management; environmental and natural resources; equine industries; health management; hotel, restaurant, and institutional management; information networking management; scientific and technical communication; sport and recreation management; and appropriate interdisciplinary studies.

For more information, students should contact:
Office of Admissions and Financial Aid
170 Owen Hall
University of Minnesota, Crookston
2900 University Avenue
Crookston, Minnesota 56716-5001
Telephone: 218-281-8569
             800-862-6466 (toll-free)
WWW: http://www.crk.umn.edu

ACADEMIC PROGRAM

Students enroll in classes at UMC on a semester calendar system. With UMC's emphasis on technology, teaching methods are dramatically different. Students find a classroom environment that is completely connected to technology, allowing students and instructors to gain access to information and exchange information more effectively. That classroom environment also includes the latest in computer- and video-presentation technology that is available to instructors. Communication between faculty members and students now includes the use of e-mail and the World Wide Web for such tasks as distributing a course syllabus, sending out assignments or worksheets that had previously been distributed as printed handouts, and turning in assignments to faculty members. In addition, students have 24-hour access to UMC's library holdings as well as to all of the information available on the World Wide Web through the personal computer each student is issued.

FINANCIAL AID

Removing financial barriers to students' enrollment and success is the ultimate goal of UMC's financial aid program. UMC wishes to ensure that any qualified student who desires to pursue an education at UMC can obtain sufficient resources to do so. Accordingly, the University's Office of Admissions and Financial Aid administers a number of financial aid programs. A number of need-based funding sources are available for new, incoming freshman students as well as for transfer students—whether part-time or full-time. UMC also offers a variety of merit-based scholarships.

APPLICATION AND INFORMATION

Applying for admission to the University of Minnesota, Crookston, involves some important preliminary steps. Freshman students should send high school transcripts, submit an application fee and a completed application form, and submit results from the ACT. Transfer students must send college transcripts and submit an application fee and completed application form. The application priority deadline is March 1.

UNIVERSITY OF SAN DIEGO

■ **SAN DIEGO, CALIFORNIA**

THE UNIVERSITY

Known for its firm commitment to the liberal arts, the University of San Diego has created academic programs providing students with skills necessary to grow and advance personally and professionally. Beyond the traditional arts, sciences, and humanities, USD has developed some exceptional programs in business, engineering, marine science, international relations, and the health sciences. With a holistic philosophy, USD seeks to foster competence, international and cultural sensitivity, professional responsibility, and a spirit of volunteerism in each student. Both independent and Catholic, the University places a special emphasis on the exploration of human values. The students who share in the life at USD and contribute to its growth are a diverse group representing all fifty states and more than sixty countries. There are currently 4,500 undergraduates out of a total University enrollment of 6,800 students. Fifty percent of USD's undergraduate students reside on campus, many in recently constructed facilities. The residence halls consist of traditional dormitories, suites, and apartment-style buildings. Several meal plans accommodate different schedules and tastes in food. A friendly campus atmosphere, the opportunity for close rapport between faculty and students, and small classes that facilitate personal attention and faculty accessibility characterize the educational environment at the University of San Diego. Numerous campus activities are available to students.

For additional information about the University of San Diego, students should contact:

Director of Undergraduate Admissions
University of San Diego
5998 Alcalá Park
San Diego, California 92110
Telephone: 619-260-4506
           800-248-4873 (toll-free)
Fax: 619-260-6836
WWW: http://www.sandiego.edu

ACADEMIC PROGRAM

All of USD's programs are built solidly on the liberal arts, developing critical thinking skills through an emphasis on fundamental disciplines, written and oral communication, and an understanding of the past. USD gives special attention to the exploration of human and spiritual values, the interrelations of knowledge, and the development of an international perspective. The University operates on a 4-1-4 academic calendar. Normally, the student is in residence for eight semesters and completes approximately forty-four courses, completing a minimum of 124 units.

FINANCIAL AID

The primary purpose of the financial aid program at USD is to provide financial assistance to students who, without such aid, would be unable to attend the University. Each financial aid package is individually designed to meet a student's need, as indicated by the Free Application for Federal Student Aid (FAFSA) and the USD Financial Aid Application (USDFAA). Fifty percent of the students receive aid consisting of scholarships, grants, loans, and campus employment in packages ranging from $200 to $20,350 per academic year.

APPLICATION AND INFORMATION

Application for admission is made through the Undergraduate Admissions Office. Forms should be completed and filed, together with a transcript of credits, as early as possible and no later than January 5 for freshmen and March 1 for transfers. Upon receipt of all necessary materials, each application is reviewed. Candidates are notified of acceptance by April 15. USD observes the Candidates Reply Date (May 1) set by the College Board and requests accepted applicants to notify the University of their intentions by that date.

UNIVERSITY OF SOUTH FLORIDA

■ **TAMPA, FLORIDA**

THE UNIVERSITY

The University of South Florida (USF) is among America's largest and most dynamic national research universities. Founded in 1956, USF opened in 1960 with an enrollment of nearly 2,000 and now has more than 37,000 students in almost 200 degree programs at all levels. As the principal university for the Tampa Bay region, USF serves the community and offers degrees at several campuses: Tampa, St. Petersburg, Lakeland, and Sarasota/Manatee, with additional centers in Pinellas, Pasco, and Hernando counties and downtown Tampa. USF's national stature as an academic institution was acknowledged in 2000 by the Carnegie Foundation for the Advancement of Teaching, which ranked the University in the top tier of American colleges and universities as Doctoral/Research-Extensive. USF is among the top three tier-one universities in the state of Florida. In 2000–01, USF researchers generated more than $186 million in contract and grant funding.

> **For more information, students should contact:**
> Director of Admissions
> Mr. Dewey E. Holleman, Director of Admissions
> University of South Florida
> 4202 East Fowler Avenue, SVC-1036
> Tampa, Florida 33620-9951
> United States
> Telephone: 813-974-3350
> 877-USF-BULL (873-2855, toll-free)
> Fax: 813-974-9689
> E-mail: http://www.usf.edu/askrocky
> WWW: http://usfweb.usf.edu/enroll/admiss/ admiss.htm

ACADEMIC PROGRAM

USF offers students a well-rounded education through a core curriculum of general education and liberal arts requirements. In addition to fulfilling the general education requirements, each student must complete the necessary major and/or minor requirements to reach the minimum of 120 hours for graduation. USF also requires students to complete 9 hours of exit requirements; these courses complement the overall curriculum of all degree programs. University Honors, Learning Communities, and University Experience are programs that help students broaden their horizons and expand their critical thinking skills. The University also offers Army and Air Force ROTC leadership courses and off-campus courses for those students who prefer to study independently.

FINANCIAL AID

The University of South Florida awards $138 million in aid to assist students reach their educational goals. Financial aid is awarded according to each student's need, academic standing, and/or talents in relation to college costs and may include grants, loans, scholarships, and/or part-time employment. The priority application deadline is December 31 for academic scholarships and March 1 for federal and institutional aid. Programs based on need include Federal programs such as Pell Grant, Work-Study, and Stafford and Perkins Loans. State aid includes programs such as the Florida Student Assistance Grant, Florida College Career Work-Study Program, and the Florida Bright Futures Scholarship program. To qualify for federal and state aid, students should submit the Free Application for Federal Student Aid (FAFSA).

APPLICATION AND INFORMATION

Students are encouraged to apply at least two semesters prior to the in which they wish to enter USF. All admitted students are required to attend an orientation program prior to registering for classes. Freshman admissions deadlines are June 1 for the fall semester, October 1 for the spring semester, and March 1 for the summer semester. Students transferring to USF are encouraged to apply by these priority dates as well. Information sessions, student-guided campus tours, and tours of the residence halls are available Monday through Friday at 10 a.m. and 1 p.m., excluding University holidays. USF also hosts First Saturdays each month. Appointments are encouraged.

UNIVERSITY OF THE ARTS

■ PHILADELPHIA, PENNSYLVANIA

THE UNIVERSITY

The only university in the nation devoted exclusively to education and training in design and the visual, media, and performing arts, the University of the Arts (UArts) is located in the heart of Philadelphia's professional arts community. More than 2,000 students from forty states and thirty countries are enrolled in the undergraduate and graduate programs. Composed of the College of Art and Design, the College of Performing Arts, and the newly formed College of Media and Communication, the University offers intensive concentration within a major field as well as creative challenges in multidisciplinary exploration. Founded in 1876, the Philadelphia College of Art and Design is one of the country's leading art colleges, with nationally renowned design, fine arts, and crafts departments. Since its founding in 1870 as the Philadelphia Musical Academy, the Philadelphia College of Performing Arts has expanded to include a School of Dance, with programs in ballet, modern, jazz, and tap, as well as a School of Theater Arts, with acting and musical theater. In 1996, the University inaugurated the College of Media and Communication to prepare students for new careers in emerging interdisciplinary fields, such as multimedia design, electronic communication, information architecture, computer-generated design, electronic arts and performance, and writing for film/TV.

> **For additional information, students should contact:**
> Office of Admission
> University of the Arts
> 320 South Broad Street
> Philadelphia, Pennsylvania 19102
> Telephone: 215-717-6030
> 800-616-ARTS (toll-free)
> Fax: 215-717-6045
> WWW: http://www.uarts.edu

ACADEMIC PROGRAM

Students are attracted to UArts because of its dynamic, creative atmosphere. Whether majoring in dance, sculpture, graphic design or multimedia, they enjoy interacting with their talented peers in other disciplines. A minimum of 123 credits is required for graduation, including 18 credits in the Foundation Program, 42 credits in the major, 42 credits in liberal arts, 15 credits in electives (9 credits of which must be taken in a department other than the major), and 6 credits in other areas outside the major. Students may request credit by examination in liberal arts subjects and by portfolio examination in studio art subjects. In the College of Performing Arts, the School of Music program stresses individualized training, with a performance emphasis. Students undergo intensive training in theory and musicianship. Private lessons are supplemented by master classes and ensemble work. In the School of Dance, two years of ballet, modern, and jazz dance are required before students choose a major in the junior year. Electives include improvisation repertory, partnering, Spanish dance, ethnic dance, character, and mime. The School of Theater Arts concentrates on developing the student's skill as an actor. In addition to the acting studio, requirements include courses in movement, stage combat, mime, and modern dance.

FINANCIAL AID

More than 85 percent of the University's students received more than $22 million in scholarships and other financial aid in 1999–2000. The University funds presidential scholarships based on artistic potential and academic achievement. Financial aid is also available on the basis of the applicant's demonstrated financial need. Applicants must submit the Free Application for Federal Student Aid (FAFSA). March 1 is the suggested filing date.

APPLICATION AND INFORMATION

In addition to submitting a portfolio or auditioning, applicants should submit their high school transcript, SAT I or ACT scores, one letter of recommendation, and a personal statement of purpose. The placement of transfer students is made after an evaluation of their portfolio or audition and a determination of their approved credits. The University of the Arts follows a system of rolling admission. All students are notified within two weeks of the receipt of all required materials. Students are encouraged to submit applications by March 15 for fall admission and December 1 for spring admission.

VALPARAISO UNIVERSITY

■ **VALPARAISO, INDIANA**

THE UNIVERSITY

Valparaiso University was founded in 1859 by citizens of Valparaiso, Indiana, but its recent history dates from 1925, when it was purchased by the Lutheran University Association. Valpo is one of the nation's largest Lutheran-affiliated universities, yet it remains independent and is open to individuals of all faiths. The University's 3,600 students represent most states and more than forty countries; 66 percent come from outside of Indiana. Valparaiso University is a residential community in which activities outside the classroom form an important part of campus life; more than 66 percent of its students live on campus.

> **For more information, students should contact:**
> Office of Admissions
> Valparaiso University
> Valparaiso, Indiana 46383-6493
> Telephone: 219-464-5011
> 888-GO-VALPO (toll-free)
> Fax: 219-464-6898
> E-mail: undergrad_admissions@valpo.edu
> WWW: http://www.valpo.edu

ACADEMIC PROGRAM

Valparaiso University has a long tradition of combining professional colleges with a strong commitment to the values and broadening experiences of the liberal arts. The University helps students of varied interests and objectives to clarify their goals and explore new possibilities. Programs are structured to provide a solid base for exploration in various fields, while offering students the freedom to develop depth in a specific interest. This philosophy is extended through the upper division, where students have three options in completing a degree: an individual plan of study involving the major and complementary courses from related fields of study, the election of a second academic major in addition to the first, or a special minor in connection with the major. Career planning is aided through the professional programs and the University's Career Center. Many students also gain professional work experience in their chosen field before graduation by participating in the cooperative education program and internships. Valparaiso operates on the semester system; the fall semester begins in late August and ends before Christmas, and the spring semester starts in early January and ends during the second week in May. Valpo also has two summer terms that further extend opportunities for study on campus or at various off-campus locations. The University participates in the Advanced Placement Program, the College-Level Examination Program, and the International Baccalaureate Program.

FINANCIAL AID

Eighty-five percent of Valparaiso's students receive financial aid totaling more than $30 million. The University attempts to make up the difference between the cost of attending Valparaiso and the amount a family can afford, as determined by the Free Application for Federal Student Aid (FAFSA). Valpo aid is available in the form of scholarships, grants, loans, and campus employment, and often the aid is a package of these awards. Students are also encouraged to apply for the federal government's Federal Pell Grant, Federal Perkins Loan, and Federal Supplemental Educational Opportunity Grant, state scholarships where applicable, and the various private grants and scholarships that are available. Early application is recommended for Valpo assistance, since the awarding of aid begins in February of the year of enrollment.

APPLICATION AND INFORMATION

An applicant must complete a formal University admission application or the Common Application to be considered for admission. In addition, Valpo requires a high school transcript (complete through the junior year), ACT or SAT I scores, and college transcripts (when applicable). Valpo's nonbinding early action option requires applicants to submit their applications no later than November 1. Regular admission notification begins on a rolling basis after December 1. First priority for scholarship consideration is given to those who apply for admission by the early action deadline; preference is then given to those who apply by January 15.

VIRGINIA WESLEYAN COLLEGE

■ NORFOLK/VIRGINIA BEACH, VIRGINIA

THE COLLEGE
Virginia Wesleyan College is a community of scholars who strongly believe that education is the key to achieving life's goals and that the environment in which learning takes place makes all the difference in reaching these goals. The expansive 300-acre campus of this coeducational four-year college of liberal arts and sciences is designed to provide every opportunity to live and learn in an energetic, value-centered academic climate. Affiliated with the United Methodist Church and accredited by the Commission on Colleges of the Southern Association of Colleges and Schools, the College maintains a diverse student body and a low student-faculty ratio. Students come to Virginia Wesleyan from more than thirty states and twenty countries and indicate that they are attracted to the College primarily because of its size, the high quality of its academic program, its location, and its friendly atmosphere. Virginia Wesleyan seeks to attract students who can take advantage of the College's commitment to innovation, relevance, and involvement. Students who desire a strong, individualized academic program, who want the opportunity to study matters of concern to them in a key East Coast area, who have the ability to assume responsibility for their education, and who want to be involved with their colleagues and professors in creating a vital educational experience find a receptive environment.

> **For more information, students should contact:**
> Office of Admissions and Financial Aid
> Virginia Wesleyan College
> 1584 Wesleyan Drive
> Norfolk/Virginia Beach, Virginia 23502-5599
> Telephone: 757-455-3208
> 800-737-8684 (toll-free)
> Fax: 757-461-5238
> E-mail: admissions@vwc.edu
> WWW: http://www.vwc.edu

ACADEMIC PROGRAM
The College offers a liberal arts curriculum that is designed to allow students considerable freedom in planning their own program yet also ensures that they acquire not only the breadth of knowledge traditionally emphasized in a liberal education but also a sound foundation in a specific field. A challenging honors program, in which students compete for full scholarships, is offered each year. The academic calendar is on the 4-1-4 plan, featuring a one-course term in January when students can take special-topic courses, traditional and interdisciplinary courses, and travel-study courses in the United States and abroad. They can also participate in off-campus internships, field study programs, independent study, and senior projects. The College offers study-abroad programs in a number of countries. A personalized faculty and peer advising system is the cornerstone of the College's transition programs. Freshman Seminar assists students in adjusting to college life, and the Senior Integrative Experience helps students progress to life after graduation. The College also offers services ranging from tutoring to individualized programs for students with special needs through the Learning Resources Center.

FINANCIAL AID
The College believes that no student who wishes to attend Virginia Wesleyan College should be denied the opportunity because of limited financial resources. The director of financial aid is available to counsel students and their families regarding financial planning. In cases of demonstrated financial need, students may qualify for grants, low-interest loans, and work-study. Financial need is determined by an analysis of the Free Application for Federal Student Aid (FAFSA). March 1 is the mailing deadline for applying for financial assistance. The College also offers merit scholarships, without regard to need, to entering students with outstanding academic records. Scholarships ranging from $4000 to full comprehensive fees (over four years) are awarded to students based on their test scores, academic record, interviews, and essays. Leadership Scholarships from $4000 to $24,000 are available to students with demonstrated leadership abilities as evidenced through community service, extracurricular participation, and volunteerism. Special deadlines may apply. Students who think they may qualify should contact the Office of Admissions and Financial Aid.

WARREN WILSON COLLEGE

■ ASHEVILLE, NORTH CAROLINA

THE COLLEGE
Since its founding in 1894, Warren Wilson College has educated students with a unique triad of a strong liberal arts program, work for the College, and service to those in need, which makes Warren Wilson unlike any other college. Its 750 students come from forty-two states and twenty-five countries, creating a diverse and vibrant academic community. The academic program features a first-rate faculty that does all of the teaching and frequently participates in research with students. The average class size is small, and discussion is an important part of teaching. Fifteen majors are offered, with a commitment to quality in each program. Art, English, economics and business administration, education, biology, the nationally recognized environmental studies program, and outdoor leadership are the most popular majors. Students at Warren Wilson are integral to the day-to-day operation of the College. Each student works 15 hours a week at a job that is essential to running the school. This experience helps build student confidence (students learn that there is no job they cannot learn to do) and a strong sense of community at the College. Many juniors and seniors have work assignments that coincide with their major. Students receive a work fellowship in the amount of $2472 each year for the work they do. Service is also integral to the College's way of thinking. Warren Wilson is one of only a few colleges in the country that require student participation in community service for graduation. Service is offered to a wide range of individuals and agencies, nationally and abroad. Students must provide at least 20 hours of service each year to someone off campus. The 1,100-acre campus includes a 300-acre working farm, 600 acres of forest, 25 miles of hiking trails, and a white-water kayaking course. The campus and the area are havens for outdoor activities, such as white-water sports, hiking, camping, mountain biking, and rock climbing. Ninety-three percent of the students and 70 percent of the faculty members live on campus.

For more information, students should contact:

Office of Admission
Warren Wilson College
701 Warren Wilson Road
Asheville, North Carolina 28815-9000
Telephone: 800-934-3536 (toll-free)
E-mail: admit@warren-wilson.edu
WWW:
    http://www.warren-wilson.edu

ACADEMIC PROGRAM
The goal of the degree program at Warren Wilson College is the completion of three well-designed areas of study. First, students are expected to complete a core of required courses based on the theme "ways of knowing." A student earns 4 credits in each of the ten core areas. Second, students must develop a strength in one or more disciplines. A minimum of 128 semester hours is required for the baccalaureate degree, including the core plus major hours. Finally, a student must demonstrate the ability to work effectively with others by participation in a work-and-service program. There is a required freshman seminar designed to provide new students the opportunity to explore various fields. A senior seminar, designed as a capstone experience, is required, as is a senior letter to evaluate the student's college experiences. All Warren Wilson students must demonstrate competence in writing and mathematics either through testing or by completing core courses. Each semester in the academic calendar is broken into two 8-week terms. A student traditionally takes only two courses per term (3 or 4 credit hours per course). There are two honors programs at Warren Wilson. One is in English and the other is in the Division of Natural Sciences, where honors can be earned in biology, chemistry, environmental studies, and mathematics.

FINANCIAL AID
Warren Wilson offers a comprehensive financial aid program that seeks to enroll students from all economic backgrounds. This is accomplished through a combination of work, loans, grants, entitlements, and scholarships to students who complete their file prior to May. Students and their families should file the FAFSA and the Warren Wilson Financial Aid Application to be considered for all possible funds.

WASHINGTON COLLEGE

■ CHESTERTOWN, MARYLAND

THE COLLEGE
Founded in 1782, Washington College is the tenth-oldest college in the United States. George Washington, for whom the College was named, was an early benefactor and member of the College's Board of Visitors and Governors. Today, the College is one of the few nationally recognized selective liberal arts institutions with an enrollment of fewer than 1,200 students. The intimacy of a small-college environment, the tradition of a challenging liberal arts curriculum, and the relaxed informality characteristic of the Chesapeake Bay region continue to exert their influence on the College and all who come to it. The current enrollment is 1,200 men and women.

> **Further information and application forms are available from:**
>
> Office of Admissions
> Washington College
> 300 Washington Avenue
> Chestertown, Maryland 21620-1197
> Telephone: 410-778-7700
> 800-422-1782 (toll-free)
> E-mail: adm.off@washcoll.edu
> WWW: http://www.washcoll.edu

ACADEMIC PROGRAM
The College's four-course plan is intended to broaden and deepen a student's education by providing for the intensive study of a limited number of subjects and by encouraging individual responsibility for learning. General education requirements include two freshman seminars and ten semester courses chosen from the following categories: social science, natural science, humanities, fine arts, quantitative studies, and foreign language. Candidates for a degree must satisfactorily complete thirty-two semester courses and must fulfill the senior obligation (for example, a comprehensive examination or thesis). Washington College offers a nationally renowned creative writing program and awards the prestigious Sophie Kerr Prize every year to the graduating senior who shows the most promise for a career in literary endeavors. Successful scores (4 or 5) on Advanced Placement examinations can provide exemption from distribution requirements. With the aid of a faculty adviser, students can construct their own major fields of study in some areas or pursue independent study for course credit.

FINANCIAL AID
Washington College offers financial assistance to approximately 85 percent of its student body. Awards are based on need and academic performance. Financial aid includes scholarships, grants, loans, and jobs. The College participates in the Federal Perkins Loan Program, the Federal Stafford Student Loan Program, and the Federal Work-Study program. Federal Pell Grants and Federal Supplemental Educational Opportunity Grants are applicable to Washington College. In addition, financial assistance from the Maryland scholarship program and other state programs can be applied to expenses at the College. Members of the National Honor Society and Cum Laude Society who are admitted to Washington College are awarded $40,000 academic scholarships ($10,000 annually for four years). Other academic scholarships ranging in value from $5000 to $17,500 are offered without regard to financial need. To be eligible for financial assistance, applicants should file the FAFSA by February 15. An application for admission, with all supporting credentials, should be received by February 15 to establish eligibility. Students interested in Federal Pell Grant assistance or in-state scholarship programs must apply directly to the program concerned.

APPLICATION AND INFORMATION
The application, a $40 fee, the high school transcript (and college transcript, for transfer applicants), scores on the SAT I or ACT, and two teacher recommendations are required. Applications for early decision must be received by November 15, and candidates are notified of the admission decision by December 15. For regular admission, forms must be submitted prior to February 15. Regular-decision candidates are notified of the admission decision on a rolling basis between January 15 and April 1. Applicants for financial assistance must complete the procedures outlined under Financial Aid.

WEBBER INTERNATIONAL UNIVERSITY

■ BABSON PARK, FLORIDA

THE UNIVERSITY

Webber International University was founded in 1927 by Roger Babson, who was an internationally known economist in the early 1900s. The four-year independent coeducational university is located on a beautiful 110-acre campus along the shoreline of Lake Caloosa, 45 minutes from Disney World, Cypress Gardens, and many other attractions. Webber is accredited by the Southern Association of Colleges and Schools. Built on a strong tradition that sets it apart, the University exemplifies integrity, high standards, and achievement. Webber International University provides an environment that encourages success through academic excellence and hard work. About 275 men and 250 women are enrolled as undergraduates at Webber. Sixty-eight percent of them are from Florida; the other 32 percent represent twenty-one states and twenty-eight different countries.

For application forms, catalogs, and additional information, students should contact:

Webber International University
1201 North Scenic Highway
P.O. Box 96
Babson Park, Florida 33827-9990

Telephone: 863-638-2910
E-mail: admissions@webber.edu
WWW: http://www.webber.edu

ACADEMIC PROGRAM

The school operates on the semester system with two 15-week semesters, a six-week Summer Term A, and a six-week Summer Term B. The University requires the completion of 60 credit hours for the Associate of Science degree and 120 credit hours for the Bachelor of Science degree with a minimum grade point average of 2.0. The average course load is 15 hours per semester. Students in the Bachelor of Science degree program are required to complete approximately 30 hours in the major, 36 hours in the business core, 36 hours in the general education core, and 18 hours of tailored electives. Students in the Associate of Science degree program are required to complete 27 hours in the business core, 18 hours in the general education core, and 15 hours in the major and tailored elective. The Bachelor of Science degree in general business studies requires the completion of 45 hours in the general business studies core, 39 hours in the general education core, and 36 hours of tailored electives. All students must complete 30 of the last 33 hours at Webber International University to receive a degree. Credit is awarded for successful scores on Advanced Placement (AP) and College-Level Examination Program (CLEP) general tests.

FINANCIAL AID

The Student Financial Aid Department offers students its counsel and assistance in meeting their educational expenses. Aid is awarded on the basis of an applicant's need, academic performance, and promise. Approximately 80 percent of the students at Webber International University receive financial assistance. To demonstrate need, applicants are required to file the Free Application for Federal Student Aid (FAFSA). Various types of aid, such as scholarships, grants, loans, and Federal Work-Study awards, are used to meet student needs. A limited number of no-need scholarships are available; these awards are based on academic performance, on community and college service, or on athletic ability in basketball, tennis, volleyball, golf, soccer, softball, cross-country, and track and field. Applicants for aid must reapply each year. Webber participates in the Federal Perkins Loan, Federal Supplemental Educational Opportunity Grant, and Federal Work-Study programs.

APPLICATION AND INFORMATION

An application is ready for consideration by the Admissions Committee when it has been received with a $35 application fee for domestic students and $75 for international students, the required test scores and references, and transcripts from each school attended. The University uses a system of rolling admissions. It is recommended that applications be submitted as early as possible, since on-campus housing is limited. (Freshmen are required to live in the dormitory unless they reside with a parent, guardian, or spouse.)

WELLS COLLEGE

■ AURORA, NEW YORK

THE COLLEGE

Wells College, founded in 1868, is proud to be the second institution in the country to award the baccalaureate degree to women. Its founder, Henry Wells, who built his fortune with the creation of the Wells Fargo Express, believed that women would play a vital role in the future of America. What truly distinguishes Wells from other colleges and universities is that it dares to be small. With an enrollment of 462 students, Wells students do not sit quietly among rows of neatly lined desks; instead, they join their classmates and professors around seminar tables where they are expected to contribute their ideas. Wells faculty members are widely published and respected in their fields, but teaching is their first priority. Academic opportunities include independent and interdisciplinary study, internships, and study-abroad programs. In addition, a campus newspaper, several musical and drama groups, a literary magazine and book arts center, environmental and political organizations, and other organizations provide important opportunities for student involvement. A full program of cultural events, symposia, and lectures enhances the academic and social life of the College.

> **For more information about Wells College or to schedule a campus visit, students should contact:**
>
> Admissions Office
> Wells College
> Aurora, New York 13026
> Telephone: 800-952-9355 (toll-free)
> E-mail: admissions@wells.edu
> WWW: http://www.wells.edu

ACADEMIC PROGRAM

The academic philosophy at Wells is firmly rooted in the liberal arts. The College is organized into four academic divisions: the humanities, natural and mathematical sciences, social sciences, and the arts, but faculty members in all divisions work together to produce a curriculum that recognizes connections between subject areas and fits many pieces together, just as they fit together in life. Students take two multidisciplinary courses during their first year that have an emphasis on the scope and breadth of human inquiry and creative synthesis necessary for leadership in a wide range of areas. Wells 101, Approaches to the Liberal Arts, is a shared experience for first-year students in the fall that incorporates a multidisciplinary approach to familiarize students with the liberal arts. Writing, critical thinking, discussion, collaborative learning, respect for diversity, and attendance at campus cultural events are integral to the course. Wells 102, the first-year seminar, consists of various topics that continue to develop writing and other skills that are important to students in their academic careers. Wells students are traditionally required to complete a thesis or project during the senior year. While the core curriculum provides a shared academic experience for students, the senior thesis provides a student with the opportunity to complete a thoughtful, in-depth analysis of a topic of the student's choosing.

FINANCIAL AID

Approximately 85 percent of Wells students receive financial aid packaged in the form of grants, scholarships, and loans.

APPLICATION AND INFORMATION

Applications should be received early in the senior year of high school and not later than March 1 of the year in which entrance is desired. Applications from early decision and early action candidates must be received by December 15. Transfer applications are reviewed on a rolling basis. Transfer students are eligible for merit scholarships and financial aid. A campus visit is highly recommended for prospective students. Typically, the visit includes a guided tour of the Wells College campus and facilities, overnight accommodations in the residence halls, a personal interview, and the option of attending classes. Appointments with faculty members and financial aid representatives are also available.

WENTWORTH INSTITUTE OF TECHNOLOGY

■ BOSTON, MASSACHUSETTS

THE INSTITUTE

Wentworth Institute of Technology was founded in 1904 to provide education in the mechanical arts. Today, it is one of the nation's leading technical institutes, offering study in a variety of disciplines. Wentworth has a current undergraduate day enrollment of approximately 3,000 men and women (2,400 full-time) and graduates more engineering technicians and technologists each year than any other college in the United States. The technical education acquired at Wentworth enables graduates to assume creative and responsible careers in business and industry. Wentworth is located on a 35-acre campus on Huntington Avenue in Boston.

> **For more information, students should contact:**
> Admissions Office
> Wentworth Institute of Technology
> 550 Huntington Avenue
> Boston, Massachusetts 02115
> Telephone: 617-989-4000
>   800-556-0610 (toll-free)
> Fax: 617-989-4010
> E-mail: admissions@wit.edu
> WWW: http://www.wit.edu

ACADEMIC PROGRAM

At Wentworth Institute of Technology, college-level study in technological fundamentals and principles is combined with appropriate laboratory, field, and studio experience. Students apply theory to practical problems, and they acquire skills and techniques by using, operating, and controlling equipment and instruments particular to their area of specialization. In addition, study in the social sciences and humanities provides a balanced understanding of the world in which graduates work. Wentworth's programs of study are more practical than theoretical in approach, and the Institute's academic requirements demand extensive time and effort. During the first two years of study in a degree program at Wentworth, students lay the foundation for more advanced study in the third and fourth (and fifth, where applicable) years. While nearly all majors allow continuous study from the freshman through the senior year, the architecture major requires a petition for acceptance to the baccalaureate program during the sophomore year. All bachelor's degree programs are conducted as cooperative (co-op) education programs: upon entering their third year, students alternate semesters of academic study at Wentworth with semester-long periods of employment in industry. Two semesters of co-op employment are required.

FINANCIAL AID

Scholarships are available to students who demonstrate need and academic promise. Merit scholarships are also available. Wentworth also provides federal and state financial assistance, such as Federal Pell and Federal Supplemental Educational Opportunity Grants, Federal Perkins Loans, Federal Work-Study awards, Gilbert Matching Grants, and Massachusetts No-Interest Loans to students with financial need in accordance with federal and state guidelines. Wentworth participates in the Federal Direct Lending program. As a result, students are eligible to borrow under the Federal Direct Stafford Loan program and parents may borrow under the Federal Direct PLUS program. Individuals participating in these programs borrow money directly from the federal government rather than through lending institutions. In addition to these need-based programs, Wentworth also participates in the MEFA loan program sponsored by the Massachusetts Educational Financing Authority. Wentworth offers several payment options through payment plans and alternative loan financing. To apply for financial aid, new students should complete the Free Application for Federal Student Aid (FAFSA) by March 1. Applications received after this date will be considered as funds allow.

APPLICATION AND INFORMATION

Students are admitted to Wentworth for September and January enrollment. The priority application deadline for the fall semester is May 1; for the spring, the deadline is December 1. Notification of admission is made on a rolling basis.

WESTERN ILLINOIS UNIVERSITY

■ **MACOMB, ILLINOIS**

THE UNIVERSITY

The campus of Western Illinois University (WIU) extends over 1,464 acres and includes fifty-two buildings. The residence halls on campus provide for a variety of lifestyles and house more than half of the 13,089 students at the University. Single and double rooms, study floors, nonsmoking rooms, and academic major areas are just a few examples of residence options. There are 10,652 undergraduate students currently enrolled. Although the majority of students are from Illinois, forty-five other states and forty-five countries are represented in the student body. Career placement services are offered to graduating students and graduates. Nearly 93 percent of the graduates who register with the job placement office are placed in desirable positions. Health services are available through the Beu Health Center, which is located in the center of the campus and is staffed and in operation at all times when the University is in regular session.

> **For more information, students should contact:**
> Admissions Office
> Sherman Hall 115
> Western Illinois University
> 1 University Circle
> Macomb, Illinois 61455-1390
> Telephone: 309-298-3157
> 877-PICKWIU (toll-free)
> WWW: http://www.wiu.edu

ACADEMIC PROGRAM

It is the philosophy of the University that a broad general education should be an integral part of every degree program. Thus, approximately one third of the degree requirements involve study and the development of fundamental skills in the arts and sciences. The remainder of the program is devoted to either a comprehensive major or a major/minor plus general electives. Credit is awarded for acceptable scores on CLEP general and subject examinations and on the College Board's Advanced Placement examinations in English, foreign languages, history, and mathematics. Proficiency examinations are administered on campus through specific departments. Special educational opportunities for students with high aptitude and superior ability are offered in all colleges at WIU through the honors college. Western Illinois University is on the semester system; the fall semester closes before the Christmas holidays and the spring semester closes in mid-May. Two 4-week summer sessions run concurrently with one 8-week summer session from mid-June to early August. Western offers a four-year and a two-year program in the study of military science through Army ROTC. Successful completion of the program and requirements for the baccalaureate degree leads to a commission as a second lieutenant in the Army.

FINANCIAL AID

During the 2000–01 academic year, 11,197 WIU undergraduate students received financial aid from funds totaling $60 million. Financial aid is available through state and federal programs for full- or part-time WIU students. Students should use the Free Application for Federal Student Aid (FAFSA) to apply for the following state and federal programs: Federal Pell Grant, Federal Supplemental Educational Opportunity Grant, Federal Perkins Loan, Federal Stafford Student Loan, Federal Work-Study Program, and Illinois Monetary Award Program (MAP). Students should begin the process by completing their federal income tax return as early as possible to provide accurate information on the FAFSA and then filing the FAFSA as soon as possible after January 1. Many student jobs are available in areas such as secretarial work, food service, and building and grounds maintenance. WIU also awards talent grants and academic scholarships. Talent grants are offered in men's and women's athletics, music, art, theater, agriculture, student services, and debate. More than 1,000 students annually receive scholarships through the WIU Foundation. The majority of scholarships reward high academic potential and achievement, while others consider hometown, academic interest, or financial need. To receive an application for WIU scholarship opportunities, students should contact the WIU Scholarship Office.

WESTERN MICHIGAN UNIVERSITY

- **KALAMAZOO, MICHIGAN**

THE UNIVERSITY
Western Michigan University is one of the nation's leading midsized universities, making a difference in the world through a commitment to academic excellence and public service. *U.S. News & World Report* has ranked the University "in the major leagues of American higher education" as one of the country's 100 top national universities. WMU is one of only ninety-one public universities in the nation—and only four in Michigan—to have a chapter of Phi Beta Kappa, the nation's premier honor society.

> **For more information, students should contact:**
> Office of Admissions and Orientation
> Western Michigan University
> 1903 West Michigan Avenue
> Kalamazoo, Michigan 49008-5720
> Telephone: 616-387-2000
> 800-400-4WMU (toll-free)
> WWW: http://www.wmich.edu

Founded in 1903, WMU has seven degree-granting colleges—Arts and Sciences, Aviation, the Haworth College of Business, Education, Engineering and Applied Sciences, Fine Arts, and Health and Human Services—as well as the Graduate College and Lee Honors College. The University offers 254 academic programs, more than 160 of them at the undergraduate level. Major factors in WMU's success include promotion of out-of-class learning and creation of cutting-edge instructional facilities. More than $320 million has been spent on new buildings and state-of-the-art equipment over the past decade, including $50 million in modern student recreation facilities.

ACADEMIC PROGRAM
WMU offers undergraduate students a rich blend of academic majors and minors, as well as its general education program. This program assures that students graduate with proficiencies and perspectives they need to succeed in the next century. The University Curriculum Program is for students who are undecided about a major and wish to explore WMU's academic offerings. Last fall, more than 2,100 students enrolled in the University Curriculum Program, which won a national award for outstanding academic advising. The Lee Honors College provides undergraduates with a unique living/learning environment offering the intimacy of a small college with the resources of a major university.

FINANCIAL AID
Last year, more than 18,000 students received financial assistance totaling nearly $123 million. There are three basic types of financial aid: merit-based programs, need-based programs, and student employment. Merit-based programs include the Medallion Scholarship and the Cultural Diversity Scholarship Programs, the University's two most honored scholarships for entering freshmen. Awards range from $4800 to $32,000 over four years. Other scholarships and awards include the Army ROTC awards, Michigan National Guard awards, the Award for National Merit Scholarships, and many other sponsored and departmental scholarships for new and currently enrolled students. Merit-based scholarships also are available to community college transfer students, ranging in value from $1000 to $6000. Need-based loans, grants, college work-study, and other aid options are provided for students who demonstrate particular financial need. To be considered, students should complete the Free Application for Federal Student Aid. The student employment option reflects research indicating that students who work part-time are more likely to graduate than students who do not work at all. About 40 percent of WMU's students work while in school, and more than 1,200 jobs are offered through the college work-study program. WMU provides a tuition payment plan through Academic Management Services (AMS) and Tuition Management Systems. This allows parents and students to pay college costs in monthly installments. No interest is charged for these services, which may be renewed annually for $45. Students should contact AMS at 800-556-6684 or Tuition Management Systems at 800-722-4867 for more information.

WILLIAM PATERSON UNIVERSITY OF NEW JERSEY

- WAYNE, NEW JERSEY

THE UNIVERSITY

Since its founding in 1855, William Paterson University has grown into a comprehensive state institution whose programs reflect the area's need for challenging, affordable educational options. Ideally midsized (the total enrollment is 10,466, of whom 8,862 are degree-seeking undergraduates), William Paterson offers a wider variety of academic programs than smaller universities, yet provides students with a more personalized atmosphere than larger institutions. Once the site of the family estate of Garret Hobart, the twenty-fourth vice president of the United States, William Paterson's 370-acre spacious campus, which has wooded areas and waterfalls, offers an environment in which students may develop both intellectually and socially. Although the majority of the University's students come from the New Jersey and New York vicinity, some international and out-of-state students enroll each year. Twenty-six percent of the undergraduates reside on campus in residence halls or apartment-style facilities, which accommodate 2,292 students. In general, on-campus housing is offered on a first-come, first-served basis.

> For additional information and to apply online, students should go to the undergraduate admissions site at the address listed below or contact:
> Office of Admissions
> William Paterson University of New Jersey
> Wayne, New Jersey 07470
> Telephone: 973-720-2125
> 877-WPU-EXCEL (toll-free)
> WWW: http://www.wpunj.edu

ACADEMIC PROGRAM

Students must complete a minimum of 128 credits to earn a baccalaureate degree. Degree programs include a 60-credit general education requirement, 30–60 credits in a major, and 20–40 in elective courses. (In specialized degree programs, such as the B.F.A. and the B.M., general education and major course requirements may differ.) Students uncertain of which career path to follow may take advantage of advisement and counseling programs. In addition, the general education requirements enable students to take up to 60 credits before declaring a major, so that they can acquire a basic understanding of all major fields of knowledge before having to choose a specific area. Diagnostic testing and career seminars, provided by the Career Development Office, also ensure that students receive the guidance necessary to make wise course selections and career decisions. William Paterson offers a variety of special programs. Honors programs are designed for those ambitious and well-qualified students who want to add a challenging dimension to their major. Currently, there are seven honors programs—in biopsychology, cognitive science, humanities, life science and environmental ethics, music, nursing, and performing arts.

FINANCIAL AID

Financial aid is available through a number of federal and state grant, loan, scholarship, and work-study programs. To apply for need-based aid, students must file the Free Application for Federal Student Aid (FAFSA) with the United States Department of Education by the priority date of April 1. Both the University and the Alumni Association award a number of competitive scholarships, based solely on academic merit, to entering freshmen. They are the Scholarships for Academic Excellence, Scholarships for African-American and Hispanic Students, and Trustee and Presidential Scholarships. Academic Achievement Scholarships are awarded only on a competitive basis to continuing students.

APPLICATION AND INFORMATION

Application forms and transcripts from candidates for freshman status must be received by May 1 for fall admission and November 1 for spring admission. Transfer students, readmitted students, and students seeking a second bachelor's degree must submit their materials by May 1 and November 1 for fall and spring entry, respectively. However, the University closes the application process earlier when the number of new and continuing students strains its ability to provide effective programs and services. A $35 application fee is required. Applications are reviewed on a rolling basis. Campus tours are available during the fall and spring semesters on weekdays by appointment when classes are in session.

INDEX

The index lists the colleges and universities in this almanac alphabetically. Page numbers refer to each college's profile; page numbers in **bold-faced** text refer to full-page descriptions.

INDEX

Abilene Christian University (TX) 343
Academy of Art College (CA) 49
Adams State College (CO) 74
Adelphi University (NY) 234
Adrian College (MI) 182
Agnes Scott College (GA) 100
Alabama Agricultural and Mechanical
    University (AL) 35
Alabama State University (AL) 35
Alaska Bible College (AK) 41
Alaska Pacific University (AK) 41
Albany College of Pharmacy of Union
    University (NY) 234
Albany State University (GA) 101
Albertson College of Idaho (ID) 112
Albertus Magnus College (CT) 80
Albion College (MI) 183
Albright College (PA) 301
Al Collins Graphic Design School (AZ) 42
Alcorn State University (MS) 201
Alderson-Broaddus College (WV) 377, **391**
Alfred University (NY) 234, **392**
Alice Lloyd College (KY) 148
Allegheny College (PA) 302, **393**
Allen College (IA) 137
Allen University (SC) 325
Alliant International University (CA) 50
Alma College (MI) 183, **394**
Alvernia College (PA) 302
Alverno College (WI) 381
Amberton University (TX) 343
American Academy of Art (IL) 113
American Baptist College of American
    Baptist Theological Seminary (TN) 334
American Christian College and Seminary
    (OK) 290
American College of Computer &
    Information Sciences (AL) 35
American College of Prehospital Medicine
    (FL) 88
American Indian College of the Assemblies
    of God, Inc. (AZ) 42
American InterContinental University
    (CA) 50
American InterContinental University
    (FL) 88
American InterContinental University,
    Atlanta (GA) 101
American InterContinental University,
    Atlanta (GA) 101
American InterContinental University
    Online (IL) 114
American International College (MA) 169
American Military University (VA) 363
American University (DC) 86
Amherst College (MA) 169

Anderson College (SC) 325
Anderson University (IN) 129
Andrew Jackson University (AL) 35
Andrews University (MI) 183
Angelo State University (TX) 343
Anna Maria College (MA) 169
Antioch College (OH) 276
Antioch University Los Angeles (CA) 50
Antioch University McGregor (OH) 276
Antioch University Santa Barbara (CA) 50
Antioch University Seattle (WA) 372
Appalachian Bible College (WV) 377
Appalachian State University (NC) 263
Aquinas College (MI) 183, **395**
Aquinas College (TN) 335
Arcadia University (PA) 302
Argosy University-Orange County (CA) 50
Argosy University-Sarasota (FL) 89
Arizona State University (AZ) 42
Arizona State University East (AZ) 43
Arizona State University West (AZ) 43
Arkansas Baptist College (AR) 46
Arkansas State University (AR) 46
Arkansas Tech University (AR) 46
Arlington Baptist College (TX) 343
Armstrong Atlantic State University
    (GA) 101
Armstrong University (CA) 50
Art Academy of Cincinnati (OH) 276
Art Center College of Design (CA) 50
The Art Institute of Boston at Lesley
    University (MA) 169
The Art Institute of California (CA) 51
The Art Institute of California-San
    Francisco (CA) 51
The Art Institute of Colorado (CO) 74
The Art Institute of Fort Lauderdale (FL) 89
The Art Institute of Phoenix (AZ) 43, **396**
The Art Institute of Portland (OR) 296
Art Institute of Southern California (CA) 51
The Art Institute of Washington (VA) 364
Art Institutes International at San Francisco
    (CA) 51
Asbury College (KY) 149
Ashland University (OH) 276
Assumption College (MA) 170
Athens State University (AL) 35
Atlanta Christian College (GA) 101
Atlanta College of Art (GA) 101, **397**
Atlantic Union College (MA) 170
Auburn University (AL) 35
Auburn University Montgomery (AL) 36
Audrey Cohen College (NY) 234
Augsburg College (MN) 194
Augustana College (IL) 114
Augustana College (SD) 331

INDEX

Augusta State University (GA) 102
Aurora University (IL) 114
Austin College (TX) 343
Austin Graduate School of Theology (TX) 344
Austin Peay State University (TN) 335
Ave Maria College (MI) 183
Averett University (VA) 364
Avila College (MO) 205
Azusa Pacific University (CA) 51

Babson College (MA) 170
Baker College of Auburn Hills (MI) 184
Baker College of Cadillac (MI) 184
Baker College of Clinton Township (MI) 184
Baker College of Flint (MI) 184
Baker College of Jackson (MI) 184
Baker College of Muskegon (MI) 184
Baker College of Owosso (MI) 185
Baker College of Port Huron (MI) 185
Baker University (KS) 144
Baldwin-Wallace College (OH) 277
Ball State University (IN) 129
Baltimore Hebrew University (MD) 162
Baltimore International College (MD) 163
Baptist Bible College (MO) 205
Baptist Bible College of Pennsylvania (PA) 302
The Baptist College of Florida (FL) 89
Baptist Memorial College of Health Sciences (TN) 335
Baptist Missionary Association Theological Seminary (TX) 344
Barat College (IL) 114
Barber-Scotia College (NC) 263
Barclay College (KS) 144
Bard College (NY) 235
Barnard College (NY) 235
Barry University (FL) 89
Bartlesville Wesleyan College (OK) 291
Barton College (NC) 264
Bastyr University (WA) 372
Bates College (ME) 159
Baylor University (TX) 344
Bay Path College (MA) 170
Beacon College and Graduate School (GA) 102
Becker College (MA) 170
Belhaven College (MS) 202
Bellarmine University (KY) 149
Bellevue University (NE) 218
Bellin College of Nursing (WI) 381
Belmont Abbey College (NC) 264
Belmont University (TN) 335, **398**
Beloit College (WI) 381

Bemidji State University (MN) 194
Benedict College (SC) 325
Benedictine College (KS) 144
Benedictine University (IL) 114, **399**
Bennett College (NC) 264
Bennington College (VT) 360
Bentley College (MA) 171
Berea College (KY) 149
Berklee College of Music (MA) 171
Bernard M. Baruch College of the City University of New York (NY) 235
Berry College (GA) 102
Bethany College (KS) 144
Bethany College (WV) 377
Bethany College of the Assemblies of God (CA) 51
Beth Benjamin Academy of Connecticut (CT) 80
Bethel College (IN) 129
Bethel College (KS) 144
Bethel College (MN) 194, **400**
Bethel College (TN) 335
Bethesda Christian University (CA) 52
Beth HaMedrash Shaarei Yosher Institute (NY) 235
Beth Hatalmud Rabbinical College (NY) 235
Beth Medrash Govoha (NJ) 226
Bethune-Cookman College (FL) 89
Beulah Heights Bible College (GA) 102
Biola University (CA) 52
Birmingham-Southern College (AL) 36
Blackburn College (IL) 114
Black Hills State University (SD) 332
Blessing-Rieman College of Nursing (IL) 115
Bloomfield College (NJ) 226
Bloomsburg University of Pennsylvania (PA) 302
Bluefield College (VA) 364
Bluefield State College (WV) 378
Blue Mountain College (MS) 202
Bluffton College (OH) 277
Boise Bible College (ID) 112
Boise State University (ID) 112
Boricua College (NY) 235
Boston Architectural Center (MA) 171
Boston College (MA) 171
The Boston Conservatory (MA) 171
Boston University (MA) 171
Bowdoin College (ME) 159
Bowie State University (MD) 163, **401**
Bowling Green State University (OH) 277
Bradley University (IL) 115
Brandeis University (MA) 172
Brenau University (GA) 102

INDEX

Brescia University (KY) 149
Brevard College (NC) 264, **402**
Brewton-Parker College (GA) 103
Briarcliffe College (NY) 235
Briar Cliff University (IA) 137
Bridgewater College (VA) 364
Bridgewater State College (MA) 172
Brigham Young University (UT) 359
Brigham Young University–Hawaii (HI) 110
Brooklyn College of the City University of New York (NY) 236
Brooks Institute of Photography (CA) 52
Brown University (RI) 323
Bryan College (TN) 335
Bryant and Stratton College, Cleveland (OH) 277
Bryant College (RI) 324
Bryn Athyn College of the New Church (PA) 303
Bryn Mawr College (PA) 303
Bucknell University (PA) 303
Buena Vista University (IA) 137
Burlington College (VT) 360
Butler University (IN) 129

Cabrini College (PA) 303
Caldwell College (NJ) 226
California Baptist University (CA) 52
California Christian College (CA) 52
California College for Health Sciences (CA) 52
California College of Arts and Crafts (CA) 53, **403**
California Institute of Integral Studies (CA) 53
California Institute of Technology (CA) 53
California Institute of the Arts (CA) 53
California Lutheran University (CA) 53
California Maritime Academy (CA) 53
California National University for Advanced Studies (CA) 54
California Polytechnic State University, San Luis Obispo (CA) 54
California School of Professional Psychology (CA) 54
California State Polytechnic University, Pomona (CA) 54, **404**
California State University, Bakersfield (CA) 54
California State University, Chico (CA) 54
California State University, Dominguez Hills (CA) 55
California State University, Fresno (CA) 55
California State University, Fullerton (CA) 55

California State University, Hayward (CA) 55
California State University, Long Beach (CA) 55
California State University, Los Angeles (CA) 56
California State University, Monterey Bay (CA) 56
California State University, Northridge (CA) 56
California State University, Sacramento (CA) 56
California State University, San Bernardino (CA) 56
California State University, San Marcos (CA) 57
California State University, Stanislaus (CA) 57
California University of Pennsylvania (PA) 303
Calumet College of Saint Joseph (IN) 129
Calvary Bible College and Theological Seminary (MO) 205
Calvin College (MI) 185, **405**
Cambridge College (MA) 172
Cameron University (OK) 291
Campbellsville University (KY) 149
Campbell University (NC) 264, **406**
Canisius College (NY) 236
Capella University (MN) 195
Capital University (OH) 277
Capitol College (MD) 163
Cardinal Stritch University (WI) 381
Carleton College (MN) 195
Carlos Albizu University, Miami Campus (FL) 89
Carlow College (PA) 304
Carnegie Mellon University (PA) 304
Carroll College (MT) 216
Carroll College (WI) 382
Carson-Newman College (TN) 336
Carthage College (WI) 382
Cascade College (OR) 296
Case Western Reserve University (OH) 278
Castleton State College (VT) 361
Catawba College (NC) 265
The Catholic University of America (DC) 86, **407**
Cazenovia College (NY) 236
Cedar Crest College (PA) 304, **408**
Cedarville University (OH) 278
Centenary College (NJ) 226
Centenary College of Louisiana (LA) 154
Center for Creative Studies-College of Art and Design (MI) 185
Central Baptist College (AR) 46

INDEX

Central Bible College (MO) 205
Central Christian College of Kansas (KS) 145
Central Christian College of the Bible (MO) 205
Central College (IA) 137
Central Connecticut State University (CT) 81
Central Methodist College (MO) 206
Central Michigan University (MI) 185
Central Missouri State University (MO) 206
Central State University (OH) 278
Central Washington University (WA) 372
Central Yeshiva Tomchei Tmimim-Lubavitch (NY) 236
Centre College (KY) 149
Chadron State College (NE) 218, **409**
Chaminade University of Honolulu (HI) 111, **410**
Champlain College (VT) 361
Chapman University (CA) 57
Charles R. Drew University of Medicine and Science (CA) 57
Charleston Southern University (SC) 326
Charter Oak State College (CT) 81
Chatham College (PA) 304
Chestnut Hill College (PA) 304, **411**
Cheyney University of Pennsylvania (PA) 305
Chicago State University (IL) 115
Chowan College (NC) 265
Christendom College (VA) 364
Christian Brothers University (TN) 336
Christian Heritage College (CA) 57
Christian Life College (IL) 115
Christopher Newport University (VA) 364
Cincinnati Bible College and Seminary (OH) 278
Circleville Bible College (OH) 278
The Citadel, The Military College of South Carolina (SC) 326
City College of the City University of New York (NY) 236
City University (WA) 373
Claflin University (SC) 326
Claremont McKenna College (CA) 57, **412**
Clarion University of Pennsylvania (PA) 305
Clark Atlanta University (GA) 103
Clarke College (IA) 138
Clarkson College (NE) 218, **413**
Clarkson University (NY) 236
Clark University (MA) 172
Clayton College & State University (GA) 103
Clear Creek Baptist Bible College (KY) 150

Clearwater Christian College (FL) 90
Cleary University (MI) 185, **414**
Clemson University (SC) 326
Cleveland Chiropractic College-Kansas City Campus (MO) 206
Cleveland Chiropractic College-Los Angeles Campus (CA) 58
Cleveland College of Jewish Studies (OH) 278
The Cleveland Institute of Art (OH) 278
Cleveland Institute of Music (OH) 279
Cleveland State University (OH) 279
Coastal Carolina University (SC) 326
Coe College (IA) 138
Cogswell Polytechnical College (CA) 58
Coker College (SC) 327
Colby College (ME) 159
Colby-Sawyer College (NH) 223
Coleman College (CA) 58
Colgate University (NY) 237
College for Creative Studies (MI) 185
College Misericordia (PA) 305
College of Aeronautics (NY) 237
College of Biblical Studies–Houston (TX) 344
College of Charleston (SC) 327
College of Mount St. Joseph (OH) 279
College of Mount Saint Vincent (NY) 237
The College of New Jersey (NJ) 226
The College of New Rochelle (NY) 237
College of Notre Dame (CA) 58
College of Notre Dame of Maryland (MD) 163
College of Our Lady of the Elms (MA) 172
College of Saint Benedict (MN) 195
College of St. Catherine (MN) 195
College of Saint Elizabeth (NJ) 226
College of St. Joseph (VT) 361
College of Saint Mary (NE) 218
The College of Saint Rose (NY) 237
The College of St. Scholastica (MN) 195
The College of Saint Thomas More (TX) 344
College of Santa Fe (NM) 232
College of Staten Island of the City University of New York (NY) 237
College of the Atlantic (ME) 159
College of the Holy Cross (MA) 172
College of the Ozarks (MO) 206
College of the Southwest (NM) 232
College of Visual Arts (MN) 196
The College of William and Mary (VA) 365
The College of Wooster (OH) 279, **415**
Collins College: A School of Design and Technology (AZ) 43
Colorado Christian University (CO) 74

INDEX

The Colorado College (CO) 75
Colorado School of Mines (CO) 75
Colorado State University (CO) 75
Colorado Technical University (CO) 75
Colorado Technical University Denver
  Campus (CO) 75
Colorado Technical University Sioux Falls
  Campus (SD) 332
Columbia College (MO) 206
Columbia College (NY) 238
Columbia College (SC) 327
Columbia College Chicago (IL) 115
Columbia College-Hollywood (CA) 58
Columbia College of Nursing (WI) 382
Columbia International University (SC) 327
Columbia Southern University (AL) 36
Columbia Union College (MD) 163
Columbia University, School of General
  Studies (NY) 238, **416**
Columbia University, The Fu Foundation
  School of Engineering and Applied
  Science (NY) 238
Columbus College of Art and Design
  (OH) 279
Columbus State University (GA) 103
Community Hospital of Roanoke Valley–
  College of Health Sciences (VA) 365
Conception Seminary College (MO) 207
Concord College (WV) 378, **417**
Concordia College (AL) 36
Concordia College (MN) 196
Concordia College (NY) 238
Concordia University (CA) 58
Concordia University (IL) 115
Concordia University (MI) 186
Concordia University (MN) 196
Concordia University (NE) 218
Concordia University (OR) 296, **418**
Concordia University at Austin (TX) 344
Concordia University Wisconsin (WI) 382
Connecticut College (CT) 81
Converse College (SC) 327
Cooper Union for the Advancement of
  Science and Art (NY) 238
Coppin State College (MD) 163
Corcoran College of Art and Design
  (DC) 86
Cornell College (IA) 138
Cornell University (NY) 239
Cornerstone University (MI) 186
Cornish College of the Arts (WA) 373
Covenant College (GA) 103
Creighton University (NE) 218
Crichton College (TN) 336
The Criswell College (TX) 345
Crossroads Bible College (IN) 129

Crown College (MN) 196
The Culinary Institute of America (NY) 239
Culver-Stockton College (MO) 207
Cumberland College (KY) 150
Cumberland University (TN) 336
Curry College (MA) 173
The Curtis Institute of Music (PA) 305

Daemen College (NY) 239
Dakota State University (SD) 332
Dakota Wesleyan University (SD) 332
Dallas Baptist University (TX) 345
Dallas Christian College (TX) 345
Dalton State College (GA) 103
Dana College (NE) 219
Daniel Webster College (NH) 223
Darkei Noam Rabbinical College (NY) 239
Dartmouth College (NH) 223
Davenport University, Dearborn (MI) 186
Davenport University, Grand Rapids
  (MI) 186
Davenport University, Kalamazoo (MI) 186
Davenport University, Lansing (MI) 187
Davenport University, Warren (MI) 187
David Lipscomb University (TN) 336
David N. Myers University (OH) 280
Davidson College (NC) 265, **419**
Davis & Elkins College (WV) 378
Deaconess College of Nursing (MO) 207
Defiance College (OH) 280
Delaware State University (DE) 85
Delaware Valley College (PA) 305
Delta State University (MS) 202
Denison University (OH) 280
Denver Technical College (CO) 76
Denver Technical College at Colorado
  Springs (CO) 76
DePaul University (IL) 116
DePauw University (IN) 129
DeSales University (PA) 305
Design Institute of San Diego (CA) 58
DeVry College of Technology (NJ) 227
DeVry Institute of Technology (NY) 239
DeVry University (AZ) 43
DeVry University, Fremont (CA) 59
DeVry University, Long Beach (CA) 59
DeVry University, Pomona (CA) 59
DeVry University, West Hills (CA) 59
DeVry University, Colorado Springs
  (CO) 76
DeVry University, Denver (CO) 76
DeVry University (FL) 90
DeVry University, Alpharetta (GA) 104
DeVry University, Decatur (GA) 104
DeVry University, Addison (IL) 116
DeVry University, Chicago (IL) 116

INDEX

DeVry University, Tinley Park (IL) 116
DeVry University (MO) 207
DeVry University (OH) 280
DeVry University (TX) 345
DeVry University (VA) 365
DeVry University (WA) 373
Dickinson College (PA) 306
Dickinson State University (ND) 274
Dillard University (LA) 154
Divine Word College (IA) 138
Doane College (NE) 219
Dominican College (NY) 239
Dominican School of Philosophy and Theology (CA) 59
Dominican University (IL) 116
Dominican University of California (CA) 59
Dordt College (IA) 138
Dowling College (NY) 240
Drake University (IA) 139
Drew University (NJ) 227
Drexel University (PA) 306, **420**
Drury University (MO) 207
Duke University (NC) 265
Duquesne University (PA) 306
D'Youville College (NY) 240

Earlham College (IN) 130, **421**
East Carolina University (NC) 265
East Central University (OK) 291
Eastern Connecticut State University (CT) 81
Eastern Illinois University (IL) 117
Eastern Kentucky University (KY) 150
Eastern Mennonite University (VA) 365, **422**
Eastern Michigan University (MI) 187
Eastern Nazarene College (MA) 173
Eastern New Mexico University (NM) 232
Eastern Oregon University (OR) 297
Eastern University (PA) 306
Eastern Washington University (WA) 373
East Stroudsburg University of Pennsylvania (PA) 306
East Tennessee State University (TN) 336
East Texas Baptist University (TX) 345
East-West University (IL) 117
Eckerd College (FL) 90
Edgewood College (WI) 382
Edinboro University of Pennsylvania (PA) 307
Education America, Colorado Springs Campus (CO) 76
Education America, Denver Campus (CO) 76
Education America, Honolulu Campus (HI) 111

Education America, Southeast College of Technology, Mobile Campus (AL) 36
Education America, Tempe Campus (AZ) 44
Education America University (CA) 60
Edward Waters College (FL) 90
Elizabeth City State University (NC) 266
Elizabethtown College (PA) 307
Elmhurst College (IL) 117
Elmira College (NY) 240, **423**
Elms College (MA) 173
Elon University (NC) 266
Embry-Riddle Aeronautical University (AZ) 44
Embry-Riddle Aeronautical University (FL) 90
Embry-Riddle Aeronautical University, Extended Campus (FL) 90
Emerson College (MA) 173, **424**
Emmanuel Bible College (CA) 60
Emmanuel College (GA) 104
Emmanuel College (MA) 173
Emmaus Bible College (IA) 139
Emory & Henry College (VA) 365, **425**
Emory University (GA) 104
Emporia State University (KS) 145
Endicott College (MA) 174
Erskine College (SC) 328
Eugene Bible College (OR) 297
Eugene Lang College, New School University (NY) 240
Eureka College (IL) 117
Evangel University (MO) 207
Everglades College (FL) 91
The Evergreen State College (WA) 373
Excelsior College (NY) 240

Fairfield University (CT) 81
Fairleigh Dickinson University, College at Florham (NJ) 227
Fairleigh Dickinson University, Metropolitan Campus (NJ) 227
Fairmont State College (WV) 378, **426**
Faith Baptist Bible College and Theological Seminary (IA) 139
Fashion Institute of Technology (NY) 240
Faulkner University (AL) 36
Fayetteville State University (NC) 266
Felician College (NJ) 227
Ferris State University (MI) 187, **427**
Ferrum College (VA) 365, **428**
Finch University of Health Sciences/The Chicago Medical School (IL) 117
Finlandia University (MI) 187
Fisk University (TN) 337
Fitchburg State College (MA) 174, **429**

INDEX

Five Towns College (NY) 241, **430**
Flagler College (FL) 91
Florida Agricultural and Mechanical University (FL) 91
Florida Atlantic University (FL) 91
Florida Baptist Theological College (FL) 91
Florida Christian College (FL) 91
Florida College (FL) 91
Florida Gulf Coast University (FL) 92
Florida Institute of Technology (FL) 92
Florida International University (FL) 92
Florida Memorial College (FL) 92
Florida Metropolitan University-Brandon Campus (FL) 92
Florida Metropolitan University-Fort Lauderdale Campus (FL) 92
Florida Metropolitan University-Jacksonville Campus (FL) 93
Florida Metropolitan University-Lakeland Campus (FL) 93
Florida Metropolitan University-Melbourne Campus (FL) 93
Florida Metropolitan University-North Orlando Campus (FL) 93
Florida Metropolitan University-Pinellas Campus (FL) 93
Florida Metropolitan University-South Orlando Campus (FL) 93
Florida Metropolitan University-Tampa Campus (FL) 93
Florida Southern College (FL) 94
Florida State University (FL) 94
Fontbonne University (MO) 208
Fordham University (NY) 241, **431**
Fort Hays State University (KS) 145
Fort Lewis College (CO) 76
Fort Valley State University (GA) 104
Framingham State College (MA) 174
Franciscan University of Steubenville (OH) 280
Francis Marion University (SC) 328
Franklin and Marshall College (PA) 307
Franklin College of Indiana (IN) 130
Franklin Pierce College (NH) 223
Franklin University (OH) 281
Freed-Hardeman University (TN) 337
Free Will Baptist Bible College (TN) 337
Fresno Pacific University (CA) 60
Friends University (KS) 145
Frostburg State University (MD) 164
Furman University (SC) 328

Gallaudet University (DC) 87
Gannon University (PA) 307
Gardner-Webb University (NC) 266, **432**
Geneva College (PA) 307

George Fox University (OR) 297
George Mason University (VA) 366
Georgetown College (KY) 150
Georgetown University (DC) 87
The George Washington University (DC) 87
Georgia Baptist College of Nursing of Mercer University (GA) 105
Georgia College and State University (GA) 105
Georgia Institute of Technology (GA) 105
Georgian Court College (NJ) 228
Georgia Southern University (GA) 105
Georgia Southwestern State University (GA) 105
Georgia State University (GA) 105
Gettysburg College (PA) 308
Glenville State College (WV) 378
Global University of the Assemblies of God (MO) 208
Globe Institute of Technology (NY) 241
Goddard College (VT) 361
God's Bible School and College (OH) 281
Golden Gate University (CA) 60
Goldey-Beacom College (DE) 85
Gonzaga University (WA) 373, **433**
Gordon College (MA) 174
Goshen College (IN) 130
Goucher College (MD) 164, **434**
Governors State University (IL) 117
Grace Bible College (MI) 188
Grace College (IN) 130, **435**
Graceland University (IA) 139
Grace University (NE) 219
Grambling State University (LA) 155
Grand Canyon University (AZ) 44
Grand Valley State University (MI) 188
Grand View College (IA) 139
Grantham College of Engineering (LA) 155
Gratz College (PA) 308
Great Lakes Christian College (MI) 188
Green Mountain College (VT) 361
Greensboro College (NC) 266
Greenville College (IL) 118
Griggs University (MD) 164
Grinnell College (IA) 140
Grove City College (PA) 308, **436**
Guilford College (NC) 267
Gustavus Adolphus College (MN) 196
Gwynedd-Mercy College (PA) 308

Hamilton College (NY) 241
Hamilton Technical College (IA) 140
Hamline University (MN) 197
Hampden-Sydney College (VA) 366
Hampshire College (MA) 174

INDEX

Hampton University (VA) 366
Hannibal-LaGrange College (MO) 208
Hanover College (IN) 130
Harding University (AR) 46
Hardin-Simmons University (TX) 346
Harrington Institute of Interior Design (IL) 118
Harris-Stowe State College (MO) 208
Hartford College for Women (CT) 81
Hartwick College (NY) 241
Harvard University (MA) 175
Harvey Mudd College (CA) 60
Haskell Indian Nations University (KS) 145
Hastings College (NE) 219
Haverford College (PA) 308, **437**
Hawai'i Pacific University (HI) 111, **438**
Hebrew College (MA) 175
Hebrew Theological College (IL) 118
Heidelberg College (OH) 281
Hellenic College (MA) 175
Henderson State University (AR) 47
Hendrix College (AR) 47
Henry Cogswell College (WA) 374
Heritage Bible College (NC) 267
Heritage Christian University (AL) 37
Heritage College (WA) 374
High Point University (NC) 267
Hilbert College (NY) 242
Hillsdale College (MI) 188
Hillsdale Free Will Baptist College (OK) 291
Hiram College (OH) 281, **439**
Hobart and William Smith Colleges (NY) 242
Hobe Sound Bible College (FL) 94
Hofstra University (NY) 242, **440**
Hollins University (VA) 366
Holy Apostles College and Seminary (CT) 82
Holy Family College (PA) 309
Holy Names College (CA) 60
Holy Trinity Orthodox Seminary (NY) 242
Hood College (MD) 164
Hope College (MI) 188
Hope International University (CA) 61
Houghton College (NY) 242
Houston Baptist University (TX) 346
Howard Payne University (TX) 346
Howard University (DC) 87
Humboldt State University (CA) 61
Humphreys College (CA) 61
Hunter College of the City University of New York (NY) 242
Huntingdon College (AL) 37
Huntington College (IN) 131
Huron University (SD) 332

Husson College (ME) 159
Huston-Tillotson College (TX) 346

Idaho State University (ID) 113, **441**
Illinois College (IL) 118
The Illinois Institute of Art (IL) 118
The Illinois Institute of Art-Schaumburg (IL) 118
Illinois Institute of Technology (IL) 119
Illinois State University (IL) 119
Illinois Wesleyan University (IL) 119
Immaculata College (PA) 309
Indiana Institute of Technology (IN) 131
Indiana State University (IN) 131
Indiana University Bloomington (IN) 131
Indiana University East (IN) 131
Indiana University Kokomo (IN) 132
Indiana University Northwest (IN) 132
Indiana University of Pennsylvania (PA) 309
Indiana University–Purdue University Fort Wayne (IN) 132
Indiana University–Purdue University Indianapolis (IN) 132
Indiana University South Bend (IN) 132
Indiana University Southeast (IN) 133
Indiana Wesleyan University (IN) 133
Institute of Computer Technology (CA) 61
Interior Designers Institute (CA) 61
International Academy of Design & Technology (FL) 94
International Academy of Design & Technology (IL) 119
International Baptist College (AZ) 44
International Bible College (AL) 37
International College (FL) 94
International College and Graduate School (HI) 111
International Fine Arts College (FL) 95
International Technological University (CA) 61
Iona College (NY) 243, **442**
Iowa State University of Science and Technology (IA) 140
Iowa Wesleyan College (IA) 140
Ithaca College (NY) 243, **443**

Jackson State University (MS) 202
Jacksonville State University (AL) 37
Jacksonville University (FL) 95
James Madison University (VA) 366
Jamestown College (ND) 274
Jarvis Christian College (TX) 346
Jewish Hospital College of Nursing and Allied Health (MO) 208

INDEX

Jewish Theological Seminary of America (NY) 243
John Brown University (AR) 47
John Carroll University (OH) 281
John F. Kennedy University (CA) 61
John Jay College of Criminal Justice of the City University of New York (NY) 243
Johns Hopkins University (MD) 164
Johnson & Wales University (CO) 76
Johnson & Wales University (FL) 95
Johnson & Wales University (RI) 324
Johnson & Wales University (SC) 328
Johnson & Wales University (VA) 367
Johnson Bible College (TN) 337
Johnson C. Smith University (NC) 267
Johnson State College (VT) 362
John Wesley College (NC) 267
Jones College (FL) 95
Jones International University (CO) 77
Judson College (AL) 37
Judson College (IL) 119
The Juilliard School (NY) 243
Juniata College (PA) 309

Kalamazoo College (MI) 188
Kansas City Art Institute (MO) 209
Kansas City College of Legal Studies (MO) 209
Kansas State University (KS) 145
Kansas Wesleyan University (KS) 146
Kean University (NJ) 228
Keene State College (NH) 223
Kehilath Yakov Rabbinical Seminary (NY) 244
Kendall College (IL) 119
Kendall College of Art and Design of Ferris State University (MI) 189
Kennesaw State University (GA) 106
Kent State University (OH) 281
Kentucky Christian College (KY) 150
Kentucky Mountain Bible College (KY) 151
Kentucky State University (KY) 151
Kentucky Wesleyan College (KY) 151
Kenyon College (OH) 282
Kettering University (MI) 189, 444
Keuka College (NY) 244
King College (TN) 337
King's College (PA) 309
Knox College (IL) 120
Kol Yaakov Torah Center (NY) 244
Kutztown University of Pennsylvania (PA) 310

ratory Institute of Merchandising
 Y) 244
 College (PA) 310

LaGrange College (GA) 106, **445**
Lake Erie College (OH) 282
Lake Forest College (IL) 120
Lakeland College (WI) 383
Lake Superior State University (MI) 189
Lakeview College of Nursing (IL) 120
Lamar University (TX) 346
Lambuth University (TN) 337
Lancaster Bible College (PA) 310
Lander University (SC) 328
Lane College (TN) 338
Langston University (OK) 291
La Roche College (PA) 310
La Salle University (PA) 310
Lasell College (MA) 175
La Sierra University (CA) 62
Laura and Alvin Siegal College of Judaic Studies (OH) 282
Lawrence Technological University (MI) 189
Lawrence University (WI) 383
The Leadership Institute of Seattle (WA) 374
Lebanon Valley College (PA) 311
Lees-McRae College (NC) 267
Lee University (TN) 338
Lehigh University (PA) 311
Lehman College of the City University of New York (NY) 244
Le Moyne College (NY) 244, **446**
LeMoyne-Owen College (TN) 338
Lenoir-Rhyne College (NC) 268
Lesley University (MA) 175
Lester L. Cox College of Nursing and Health Sciences (MO) 209
LeTourneau University (TX) 347
Lewis & Clark College (OR) 297
Lewis-Clark State College (ID) 113
Lewis University (IL) 120
Liberty University (VA) 367
LIFE Bible College (CA) 62
Life University (GA) 106
Limestone College (SC) 328
Lincoln Christian College (IL) 120
Lincoln Memorial University (TN) 338
Lincoln University (CA) 62
Lincoln University (MO) 209
Lincoln University (PA) 311
Lindenwood University (MO) 209
Lindsey Wilson College (KY) 151
Linfield College (OR) 297
Lipscomb University (TN) 338
Livingstone College (NC) 268
Lock Haven University of Pennsylvania (PA) 311

INDEX

Logan University-College of Chiropractic (MO) 209
Loma Linda University (CA) 62
Long Island University, Brentwood Campus (NY) 245
Long Island University, Brooklyn Campus (NY) 245
Long Island University, C.W. Post Campus (NY) 245
Long Island University, Southampton College (NY) 245
Long Island University, Southampton College, Friends World Program (NY) 245
Longwood College (VA) 367
Loras College (IA) 140
Louisiana College (LA) 155
Louisiana State University and Agricultural and Mechanical College (LA) 155
Louisiana State University Health Sciences Center (LA) 155
Louisiana State University in Shreveport (LA) 155
Louisiana Tech University (LA) 156
Lourdes College (OH) 282
Loyola College in Maryland (MD) 165
Loyola Marymount University (CA) 62, **447**
Loyola University Chicago (IL) 121, **448**
Loyola University New Orleans (LA) 156, **449**
Lubbock Christian University (TX) 347
Luther College (IA) 140, **450**
Luther Rice Bible College and Seminary (GA) 106
Lycoming College (PA) 311
Lyme Academy College of Fine Arts (CT) 82
Lynchburg College (VA) 367
Lyndon State College (VT) 362
Lynn University (FL) 95, **451**
Lyon College (AR) 47

Macalester College (MN) 197
Machzikei Hadath Rabbinical College (NY) 245
MacMurray College (IL) 121
Macon State College (GA) 106
Madonna University (MI) 189
Magdalen College (NH) 223
Magnolia Bible College (MS) 202
Maharishi University of Management (IA) 141
Maine College of Art (ME) 160
Maine Maritime Academy (ME) 160
Malone College (OH) 282
Manchester College (IN) 133

Manhattan Christian College (KS) 146
Manhattan College (NY) 246
Manhattan School of Music (NY) 246
Manhattanville College (NY) 246
Mannes College of Music, New School University (NY) 246
Mansfield University of Pennsylvania (PA) 312
Maple Springs Baptist Bible College and Seminary (MD) 165
Maranatha Baptist Bible College (WI) 383
Marian College (IN) 133
Marian College of Fond du Lac (WI) 383, **452**
Marietta College (OH) 283
Marist College (NY) 246
Marlboro College (VT) 362
Marquette University (WI) 383
Marshall University (WV) 378
Mars Hill College (NC) 268
Martin Luther College (MN) 197
Martin Methodist College (TN) 339
Martin University (IN) 133
Mary Baldwin College (VA) 367
Marygrove College (MI) 190
Maryland Institute, College of Art (MD) 165
Marylhurst University (OR) 298
Marymount College of Fordham University (NY) 247, **453**
Marymount Manhattan College (NY) 247
Marymount University (VA) 368, **454**
Maryville College (TN) 339
Maryville University of Saint Louis (MO) 210
Mary Washington College (VA) 368
Marywood University (PA) 312
Massachusetts College of Art (MA) 175
Massachusetts College of Liberal Arts (MA) 175
Massachusetts College of Pharmacy and Health Sciences (MA) 176
Massachusetts Institute of Technology (MA) 176
Massachusetts Maritime Academy (MA) 176
The Master's College and Seminary (CA) 62
Mayo School of Health Sciences (MN) 197
Mayville State University (ND) 274
McDaniel College (MD) 165, **455**
McKendree College (IL) 121
McMurry University (TX) 347
McNeese State University (LA) 156
MCP Hahnemann University (PA) 312, **456**
McPherson College (KS) 146
Medaille College (NY) 247

INDEX

Medcenter One College of Nursing (ND) 274
Medgar Evers College of the City University of New York (NY) 247
Medical College of Georgia (GA) 106
Medical University of South Carolina (SC) 329
Memphis College of Art (TN) 339
Menlo College (CA) 62
Mercer University (GA) 107
Mercy College (NY) 247
Mercy College of Health Sciences (IA) 141
Mercyhurst College (PA) 312
Meredith College (NC) 268
Merrimack College (MA) 176
Mesa State College (CO) 77
Mesivta of Eastern Parkway Rabbinical Seminary (NY) 247
Mesivta Tifereth Jerusalem of America (NY) 248
Mesivta Torah Vodaath Rabbinical Seminary (NY) 248
Messenger College (MO) 210
Messiah College (PA) 312
Methodist College (NC) 268
Metropolitan College, Oklahoma City (OK) 291
Metropolitan College, Tulsa (OK) 291
Metropolitan College of Court Reporting (AZ) 44
Metropolitan College of Court Reporting (NM) 232
Metropolitan State College of Denver (CO) 77
Metropolitan State University (MN) 197
Miami University (OH) 283
Michigan State University (MI) 190
Michigan Technological University (MI) 190
Mid-America Bible College (OK) 292
MidAmerica Nazarene University (KS) 146
Mid-Continent College (KY) 151
Middlebury College (VT) 362
Middle Tennessee State University (TN) 339
Midland Lutheran College (NE) 219
Midway College (KY) 152
Midwestern State University (TX) 347
Miles College (AL) 37
Millersville University of Pennsylvania (PA) 313
Milligan College (TN) 339
Millikin University (IL) 121
Millsaps College (MS) 202
Mills College (CA) 63, **457**

Milwaukee Institute of Art and Design (WI) 384
Milwaukee School of Engineering (WI) 384
Minneapolis College of Art and Design (MN) 197, **458**
Minnesota Bible College (MN) 198
Minnesota State University, Mankato (MN) 198
Minnesota State University Moorhead (MN) 198
Minot State University (ND) 275
Mirrer Yeshiva (NY) 248
Mississippi College (MS) 203
Mississippi State University (MS) 203
Mississippi University for Women (MS) 203
Mississippi Valley State University (MS) 203
Missouri Baptist College (MO) 210
Missouri Southern State College (MO) 210
Missouri Tech (MO) 210
Missouri Valley College (MO) 210
Missouri Western State College (MO) 211
Molloy College (NY) 248
Monmouth College (IL) 121
Monmouth University (NJ) 228
Montana State University-Billings (MT) 216
Montana State University-Bozeman (MT) 216
Montana State University-Northern (MT) 216
Montana Tech of The University of Montana (MT) 216
Montclair State University (NJ) 228
Montreat College (NC) 269
Montserrat College of Art (MA) 176
Moody Bible Institute (IL) 122
Moore College of Art and Design (PA) 313
Moravian College (PA) 313
Morehead State University (KY) 152
Morehouse College (GA) 107
Morgan State University (MD) 165
Morningside College (IA) 141
Morris Brown College (GA) 107
Morris College (SC) 329
Morrison University (NV) 222
Mountain State University (WV) 379
Mount Aloysius College (PA) 313
Mount Angel Seminary (OR) 298
Mount Carmel College of Nursing (OH) 283
Mount Holyoke College (MA) 177
Mount Ida College (MA) 177
Mount Marty College (SD) 332
Mount Mary College (WI) 384
Mount Mercy College (IA) 141
Mount Olive College (NC) 269
Mount St. Clare College (IA) 141

INDEX

Mount Saint Mary College (NY) 248
Mount St. Mary's College (CA) 63
Mount Saint Mary's College and Seminary (MD) 165
Mt. Sierra College (CA) 63
Mount Union College (OH) 283
Mount Vernon Nazarene University (OH) 283
Muhlenberg College (PA) 313, **459**
Multnomah Bible College and Biblical Seminary (OR) 298
Murray State University (KY) 152
Musicians Institute (CA) 63
Muskingum College (OH) 284

NAES College (IL) 122
Naropa University (CO) 77
National American University, Colorado Springs (CO) 77
National American University, Denver (CO) 77
National American University (MO) 211
National American University (NM) 232
National American University (SD) 332
National American University-St. Paul Campus (MN) 198
National American University-Sioux Falls Branch (SD) 333
The National Hispanic University (CA) 63
National-Louis University (IL) 122
National University (CA) 63
Nazarene Bible College (CO) 77
Nazareth College of Rochester (NY) 248
Nebraska Christian College (NE) 220
Nebraska Methodist College (NE) 220
Nebraska Wesleyan University (NE) 220
Ner Israel Rabbinical College (MD) 166
Neumann College (PA) 314
Newberry College (SC) 329
New College of California (CA) 64
New College of Florida (FL) 95
New England College (NH) 224
New England Conservatory of Music (MA) 177
New England School of Communications (ME) 160
New Hampshire Institute of Art (NH) 224
New Jersey City University (NJ) 228
New Jersey Institute of Technology (NJ) 229
Newman University (KS) 146
New Mexico Highlands University (NM) 233
New Mexico Institute of Mining and Technology (NM) 233
New Mexico State University (NM) 233

New Orleans Baptist Theological Seminary (LA) 156
New School Bachelor of Arts, New School University (NY) 248
Newschool of Architecture & Design (CA) 64
New World School of the Arts (FL) 95
New York Institute of Technology (NY) 248
New York School of Interior Design (NY) 249
New York University (NY) 249, **460**
Niagara University (NY) 249
Nicholls State University (LA) 156
Nichols College (MA) 177
Norfolk State University (VA) 368
North Carolina Agricultural and Technical State University (NC) 269
North Carolina Central University (NC) 269
North Carolina School of the Arts (NC) 269
North Carolina State University (NC) 270
North Carolina Wesleyan College (NC) 270
North Central College (IL) 122
Northcentral University (AZ) 44
North Central University (MN) 198
North Dakota State University (ND) 275
Northeastern Illinois University (IL) 122
Northeastern State University (OK) 292
Northeastern University (MA) 177, **461**
Northern Arizona University (AZ) 44
Northern Illinois University (IL) 123
Northern Kentucky University (KY) 152
Northern Michigan University (MI) 190
Northern State University (SD) 333
North Georgia College & State University (GA) 107
North Greenville College (SC) 329
Northland College (WI) 384
North Park University (IL) 123
Northwest Christian College (OR) 298
Northwest College (WA) 374
Northwest College of Art (WA) 374
Northwestern College (IA) 142
Northwestern College (MN) 199
Northwestern Oklahoma State University (OK) 292
Northwestern Polytechnic University (CA) 64
Northwestern State University of Louisiana (LA) 157
Northwestern University (IL) 123
Northwest Missouri State University (MO) 211
Northwest Nazarene University (ID) 113
Northwood University (MI) 190, **462**

Peterson's ■ College & University Almanac 2003   www.petersons.com   **513**

INDEX

Northwood University, Florida Campus (FL) 96
Northwood University, Texas Campus (TX) 347
Norwich University (VT) 362, **463**
Notre Dame College (OH) 284
Notre Dame de Namur University (CA) 64
Nova Southeastern University (FL) 96
Nyack College (NY) 249

Oak Hills Christian College (MN) 199
Oakland City University (IN) 134
Oakland University (MI) 190
Oakwood College (AL) 37
Oberlin College (OH) 284
Occidental College (CA) 64
Oglala Lakota College (SD) 333
Oglethorpe University (GA) 107
Ohio Dominican College (OH) 284
Ohio Northern University (OH) 284
The Ohio State University (OH) 284
The Ohio State University at Lima (OH) 285
The Ohio State University at Marion (OH) 285
The Ohio State University-Mansfield Campus (OH) 285
The Ohio State University-Newark Campus (OH) 285
Ohio University (OH) 285
Ohio University-Chillicothe (OH) 286
Ohio University-Eastern (OH) 286
Ohio University-Lancaster (OH) 286
Ohio University-Southern Campus (OH) 286
Ohio University-Zanesville (OH) 286
Ohio Valley College (WV) 379
Ohio Wesleyan University (OH) 286
Ohr Hameir Theological Seminary (NY) 249
Ohr Somayach/Joseph Tanenbaum Educational Center (NY) 249
Oklahoma Baptist University (OK) 292
Oklahoma Christian University (OK) 292
Oklahoma City University (OK) 293
Oklahoma Panhandle State University (OK) 293
Oklahoma State University (OK) 293
Oklahoma Wesleyan University (OK) 293
Old Dominion University (VA) 368
Olivet College (MI) 191
Olivet Nazarene University (IL) 123
O'More College of Design (TN) 340
Oral Roberts University (OK) 293
Oregon College of Art & Craft (OR) 298

Oregon Health & Science University (OR) 298
Oregon Institute of Technology (OR) 299
Oregon State University (OR) 299
Otis College of Art and Design (CA) 64
Ottawa University (KS) 147
Otterbein College (OH) 286
Ouachita Baptist University (AR) 47
Our Lady of Holy Cross College (LA) 157
Our Lady of the Lake University of San Antonio (TX) 348
Ozark Christian College (MO) 211

Pace University (NY) 250
Pacific Lutheran University (WA) 374
Pacific Northwest College of Art (OR) 299
Pacific Oaks College (CA) 65
Pacific States University (CA) 65
Pacific Union College (CA) 65
Pacific University (OR) 299
Paier College of Art, Inc. (CT) 82
Paine College (GA) 108
Palm Beach Atlantic College (FL) 96
Palmer College of Chiropractic (IA) 142
Park University (MO) 211
Parsons School of Design, New School University (NY) 250
Patten College (CA) 65
Paul Quinn College (TX) 348
Paul Smith's College of Arts and Sciences (NY) 250
Peabody Conservatory of Music of The Johns Hopkins University (MD) 166
Peace College (NC) 270
Peirce College (PA) 314
Pennsylvania College of Technology (PA) 314
Pennsylvania School of Art & Design (PA) 314
The Pennsylvania State University Abington College (PA) 314
The Pennsylvania State University Altoona College (PA) 314
The Pennsylvania State University at Erie, The Behrend College (PA) 315
The Pennsylvania State University Berks Campus of the Berks-Lehigh Valley College (PA) 315
The Pennsylvania State University Harrisburg Campus of the Capital College (PA) 315
The Pennsylvania State University Lehigh Valley Campus of the Berks-Lehigh Valley College (PA) 315

INDEX

The Pennsylvania State University Schuylkill Campus of the Capital College (PA) 315
The Pennsylvania State University University Park Campus (PA) 316
Pepperdine University, Malibu (CA) 65
Peru State College (NE) 220
Pfeiffer University (NC) 270
Philadelphia Biblical University (PA) 316
Philadelphia University (PA) 316
Philander Smith College (AR) 48
Piedmont Baptist College (NC) 270
Piedmont College (GA) 108
Pikeville College (KY) 152
Pillsbury Baptist Bible College (MN) 199
Pine Manor College (MA) 178
Pittsburg State University (KS) 147
Pitzer College (CA) 65
Plattsburgh State University of New York (NY) 250
Plymouth State College (NH) 224
Point Loma Nazarene University (CA) 66
Point Park College (PA) 316
Polytechnic University, Brooklyn Campus (NY) 250
Pomona College (CA) 66
Pontifical College Josephinum (OH) 287
Portland State University (OR) 299
Potomac College (DC) 87
Practical Bible College (NY) 251
Prairie View A&M University (TX) 348
Pratt Institute (NY) 251, **464**
Presbyterian College (SC) 329
Prescott College (AZ) 44
Presentation College (SD) 333
Princeton University (NJ) 229
Principia College (IL) 123
Providence College (RI) 324
Puget Sound Christian College (WA) 375
Purchase College, State University of New York (NY) 251
Purdue University (IN) 134
Purdue University Calumet (IN) 134
Purdue University North Central (IN) 134

Queens College of the City University of New York (NY) 251
Queens University of Charlotte (NC) 270
Quincy University (IL) 123
Quinnipiac University (CT) 82

Rabbinical Academy Mesivta Rabbi Chaim Berlin (NY) 251
Rabbinical College Beth Shraga (NY) 251
Rabbinical College Bobover Yeshiva B'nei Zion (NY) 252
Rabbinical College Ch'san Sofer (NY) 252
Rabbinical College of America (NJ) 229
Rabbinical College of Long Island (NY) 252
Rabbinical Seminary Adas Yereim (NY) 252
Rabbinical Seminary M'kor Chaim (NY) 252
Rabbinical Seminary of America (NY) 252
Radford University (VA) 368
Ramapo College of New Jersey (NJ) 229
Randolph-Macon College (VA) 369
Randolph-Macon Woman's College (VA) 369
Reed College (OR) 300
Reformed Bible College (MI) 191
Regis College (MA) 178
Regis University (CO) 78
Reinhardt College (GA) 108
Rensselaer Polytechnic Institute (NY) 252, **465**
Research College of Nursing (MO) 212
Rhode Island College (RI) 324
Rhode Island School of Design (RI) 324
Rhodes College (TN) 340
Rice University (TX) 348
The Richard Stockton College of New Jersey (NJ) 229, **466**
Rider University (NJ) 230, **467**
Ringling School of Art and Design (FL) 96
Ripon College (WI) 384, **468**
Rivier College (NH) 224
Roanoke Bible College (NC) 271
Roanoke College (VA) 369
Robert Morris College (IL) 124
Robert Morris University (PA) 316
Roberts Wesleyan College (NY) 252
Rochester College (MI) 191
Rochester Institute of Technology (NY) 252
Rockford College (IL) 124
Rockhurst University (MO) 212
Rocky Mountain College (MT) 217
Rocky Mountain College of Art & Design (CO) 78
Rogers State University (OK) 294
Roger Williams University (RI) 325
Rollins College (FL) 96
Roosevelt University (IL) 124
Rose-Hulman Institute of Technology (IN) 134
Rosemont College (PA) 317
Rowan University (NJ) 230
Rush University (IL) 124
Russell Sage College (NY) 253
Rust College (MS) 203
Rutgers, The State University of New Jersey, Camden (NJ) 230

INDEX

Rutgers, The State University of New Jersey, Newark (NJ) 230
Rutgers, The State University of New Jersey, New Brunswick (NJ) 230

Sacred Heart Major Seminary (MI) 191
Sacred Heart University (CT) 82
Sage College of Albany (NY) 253
Saginaw Valley State University (MI) 191
St. Ambrose University (IA) 142, **469**
St. Andrews Presbyterian College (NC) 271
Saint Anselm College (NH) 224
Saint Anthony College of Nursing (IL) 124
St. Augustine College (IL) 125
Saint Augustine's College (NC) 271
St. Bonaventure University (NY) 253
St. Charles Borromeo Seminary, Overbrook (PA) 317
St. Cloud State University (MN) 199
St. Edward's University (TX) 348
St. Francis College (NY) 253, **470**
Saint Francis Medical Center College of Nursing (IL) 125
Saint Francis University (PA) 317
St. Gregory's University (OK) 294
St. John Fisher College (NY) 253
St. John's College (IL) 125
St. John's College (MD) 166
St. John's College (NM) 233
St. John's Seminary College (CA) 66
Saint John's Seminary College of Liberal Arts (MA) 178
Saint John's University (MN) 199
St. John's University (NY) 253
St. John Vianney College Seminary (FL) 97
Saint Joseph College (CT) 83
Saint Joseph's College (IN) 134
Saint Joseph's College (ME) 160
St. Joseph's College, New York (NY) 254
St. Joseph's College, Suffolk Campus (NY) 254
Saint Joseph Seminary College (LA) 157
Saint Joseph's University (PA) 317
St. Lawrence University (NY) 254
Saint Leo University (FL) 97
St. Louis Christian College (MO) 212
St. Louis College of Pharmacy (MO) 212
Saint Louis University (MO) 212
Saint Luke's College (MO) 213
Saint Martin's College (WA) 375
Saint Mary College (KS) 147
Saint Mary-of-the-Woods College (IN) 135
Saint Mary's College (IN) 135
Saint Mary's College of Ave Maria University (MI) 192
Saint Mary's College of California (CA) 66

St. Mary's College of Maryland (MD) 166, **471**
Saint Mary's University of Minnesota (MN) 200
St. Mary's University of San Antonio (TX) 348, **472**
Saint Michael's College (VT) 362
St. Norbert College (WI) 385
St. Olaf College (MN) 200
Saint Paul's College (VA) 369
Saint Peter's College (NJ) 231
St. Thomas Aquinas College (NY) 254
St. Thomas University (FL) 97
Saint Vincent College (PA) 317
Saint Xavier University (IL) 125
Salem College (NC) 271
Salem International University (WV) 379
Salem State College (MA) 178
Salisbury University (MD) 166
Salve Regina University (RI) 325
Samford University (AL) 38
Sam Houston State University (TX) 349
Samuel Merritt College (CA) 66
San Diego State University (CA) 67
San Francisco Art Institute (CA) 67
San Francisco Conservatory of Music (CA) 67
San Francisco State University (CA) 67
San Jose Christian College (CA) 67
San Jose State University (CA) 67
Santa Clara University (CA) 68
Sarah Lawrence College (NY) 254
Savannah College of Art and Design (GA) 108, **473**
Savannah State University (GA) 108
Schiller International University (FL) 97
Scholl College of Podiatric Medicine at Finch University of Health Sciences/ The Chicago Medical School (IL) 125
School of the Art Institute of Chicago (IL) 125
School of the Museum of Fine Arts (MA) 178
School of Visual Arts (NY) 255
Schreiner University (TX) 349
Scripps College (CA) 68
Seattle Pacific University (WA) 375
Seattle University (WA) 375
Seton Hall University (NJ) 231
Seton Hill University (PA) 318, **474**
Shasta Bible College (CA) 68
Shawnee State University (OH) 287
Shaw University (NC) 271
Sheldon Jackson College (AK) 41
Shenandoah University (VA) 369, **475**
Shepherd College (WV) 379

INDEX

Shimer College (IL) 126
Shippensburg University of Pennsylvania (PA) 318
Shorter College (GA) 108
Sh'or Yoshuv Rabbinical College (NY) 255
Siena College (NY) 255
Siena Heights University (MI) 192
Sierra Nevada College (NV) 222
Silver Lake College (WI) 385
Simmons College (MA) 178
Simon's Rock College of Bard (MA) 179
Simpson College (IA) 142, **476**
Simpson College and Graduate School (CA) 68
Sinte Gleska University (SD) 333
Si Tanka Huron University (SD) 333
Skidmore College (NY) 255
Slippery Rock University of Pennsylvania (PA) 318
Smith College (MA) 179
Sojourner-Douglass College (MD) 167
Sonoma State University (CA) 68
South Carolina State University (SC) 330
South Dakota School of Mines and Technology (SD) 334
South Dakota State University (SD) 334
Southeastern Baptist College (MS) 204
Southeastern Bible College (AL) 38
Southeastern College of the Assemblies of God (FL) 97
Southeastern Louisiana University (LA) 157
Southeastern Oklahoma State University (OK) 294
Southeastern University (DC) 87
Southeast Missouri State University (MO) 213
Southern Adventist University (TN) 340
Southern Arkansas University–Magnolia (AR) 48
Southern Baptist Theological Seminary (KY) 153
Southern California Bible College & Seminary (CA) 69
Southern California Institute of Architecture (CA) 69
Southern Christian University (AL) 38
Southern Connecticut State University (CT) 83, **477**
Southern Illinois University Carbondale (IL) 126
Southern Illinois University Edwardsville (IL) 126
Southern Methodist College (SC) 330
Southern Methodist University (TX) 349
Southern Nazarene University (OK) 294

Southern New Hampshire University (NH) 224
Southern Oregon University (OR) 300
Southern Polytechnic State University (GA) 109
Southern University and Agricultural and Mechanical College (LA) 157
Southern University at New Orleans (LA) 158
Southern Utah University (UT) 359
Southern Vermont College (VT) 363
Southern Virginia University (VA) 369
Southern Wesleyan University (SC) 330
South University (GA) 109
Southwest Baptist University (MO) 213
Southwestern Adventist University (TX) 349
Southwestern Assemblies of God University (TX) 349
Southwestern Christian College (TX) 350
Southwestern Christian University (OK) 294
Southwestern College (AZ) 45
Southwestern College (KS) 147
Southwestern Oklahoma State University (OK) 295
Southwestern University (TX) 350
Southwest Missouri State University (MO) 213
Southwest State University (MN) 200
Southwest Texas State University (TX) 350, **478**
Spalding University (KY) 153
Spelman College (GA) 109
Spring Arbor University (MI) 192
Springfield College (MA) 179, **479**
Spring Hill College (AL) 38
Stanford University (CA) 69
State University of New York at Albany (NY) 255
State University of New York at Binghamton (NY) 255
State University of New York at Buffalo (NY) 256
State University of New York at Farmingdale (NY) 256
State University of New York at New Paltz (NY) 256
State University of New York at Oswego (NY) 256
State University of New York at Stony Brook (NY) 256
State University of New York College at Brockport (NY) 256
State University of New York College at Buffalo (NY) 257

INDEX

State University of New York College at Cortland (NY) 257
State University of New York College at Fredonia (NY) 257
State University of New York College at Geneseo (NY) 257
State University of New York College at Old Westbury (NY) 257
State University of New York College at Oneonta (NY) 258
State University of New York College at Potsdam (NY) 258
State University of New York College of Agriculture and Technology at Cobleskill (NY) 258
State University of New York College of Environmental Science and Forestry (NY) 258
State University of New York Empire State College (NY) 258
State University of New York Health Science Center at Brooklyn (NY) 259
State University of New York Institute of Technology at Utica/Rome (NY) 259
State University of New York Maritime College (NY) 259
State University of New York Upstate Medical University (NY) 259
State University of West Georgia (GA) 109
Stephen F. Austin State University (TX) 350
Stephens College (MO) 213
Sterling College (KS) 147
Sterling College (VT) 363
Stetson University (FL) 97
Stevens Institute of Technology (NJ) 231
Stillman College (AL) 38
Stonehill College (MA) 179
Stony Brook University, State University of New York (NY) 259
Strayer University (DC) 88
Suffolk University (MA) 179
Sullivan University (KY) 153
Sul Ross State University (TX) 350
Susquehanna University (PA) 318
Swarthmore College (PA) 318
Sweet Briar College (VA) 370
Syracuse University (NY) 260

Tabor College (KS) 148
Talladega College (AL) 38
Talmudical Academy of New Jersey (NJ) 231
Talmudical Institute of Upstate New York (NY) 260
Talmudical Seminary Oholei Torah (NY) 260
Talmudical Yeshiva of Philadelphia (PA) 319
Talmudic College of Florida (FL) 98
Tarleton State University (TX) 351
Taylor University (IN) 135
Taylor University, Fort Wayne Campus (IN) 135
Teikyo Loretto Heights University (CO) 78
Teikyo Post University (CT) 83, **480**
Telshe Yeshiva-Chicago (IL) 126
Temple University (PA) 319
Tennessee State University (TN) 340
Tennessee Technological University (TN) 340
Tennessee Temple University (TN) 340
Tennessee Wesleyan College (TN) 341
Texas A&M International University (TX) 351
Texas A&M University (TX) 351
Texas A&M University at Galveston (TX) 351
Texas A&M University-Commerce (TX) 351
Texas A&M University-Corpus Christi (TX) 351
Texas A&M University-Kingsville (TX) 352
Texas A&M University System Health Science Center (TX) 352
Texas A&M University-Texarkana (TX) 352
Texas Chiropractic College (TX) 352
Texas Christian University (TX) 352
Texas College (TX) 352
Texas Lutheran University (TX) 353
Texas Southern University (TX) 353
Texas Tech University (TX) 353, **481**
Texas Wesleyan University (TX) 353
Texas Woman's University (TX) 353
Thiel College (PA) 319
Thomas Aquinas College (CA) 69
Thomas College (ME) 160
Thomas Edison State College (NJ) 231
Thomas Jefferson University (PA) 319
Thomas More College (KY) 153
Thomas More College of Liberal Arts (NH) 225
Thomas University (GA) 109
Tiffin University (OH) 287
Toccoa Falls College (GA) 110
Torah Temimah Talmudical Seminary (NY) 260
Tougaloo College (MS) 204
Touro College (NY) 260
Touro University International (CA) 69
Towson University (MD) 167, **482**
Transylvania University (KY) 153
Trevecca Nazarene University (TN) 341

INDEX

Trinity Baptist College (FL) 98
Trinity Bible College (ND) 275
Trinity Christian College (IL) 126
Trinity College (CT) 83
Trinity College (DC) 88
Trinity College of Florida (FL) 98
Trinity College of Nursing and Health Sciences Schools (IL) 126
Trinity International University (IL) 127
Trinity Lutheran College (WA) 375
Trinity University (TX) 354
Tri-State University (IN) 135
Troy State University (AL) 39
Troy State University Dothan (AL) 39
Troy State University Montgomery (AL) 39
Truman State University (MO) 213
Tufts University (MA) 180
Tulane University (LA) 158, **483**
Tusculum College (TN) 341
Tuskegee University (AL) 39

Union College (KY) 153
Union College (NE) 220
Union College (NY) 260
Union Institute & University (OH) 287
Union University (TN) 341
United States Air Force Academy (CO) 78
United States Coast Guard Academy (CT) 83
United States International University (CA) 69
United States Merchant Marine Academy (NY) 261
United States Military Academy (NY) 261, **484**
United States Naval Academy (MD) 167
United Talmudical Seminary (NY) 261
Unity College (ME) 161
University at Buffalo, The State University of New York (NY) 261
University of Advancing Computer Technology (AZ) 45
The University of Akron (OH) 287
The University of Alabama (AL) 39
The University of Alabama at Birmingham (AL) 40
The University of Alabama in Huntsville (AL) 40
University of Alaska Anchorage (AK) 42
University of Alaska Fairbanks (AK) 42
University of Alaska Southeast (AK) 42
The University of Arizona (AZ) 45
University of Arkansas (AR) 48
University of Arkansas at Little Rock (AR) 48

University of Arkansas at Monticello (AR) 48
University of Arkansas at Pine Bluff (AR) 49
University of Arkansas for Medical Sciences (AR) 49
University of Baltimore (MD) 167
University of Bridgeport (CT) 84
University of California, Berkeley (CA) 69
University of California, Davis (CA) 70
University of California, Irvine (CA) 70
University of California, Los Angeles (CA) 70
University of California, Riverside (CA) 70
University of California, San Diego (CA) 70
University of California, Santa Barbara (CA) 70
University of California, Santa Cruz (CA) 71
University of Central Arkansas (AR) 49
University of Central Florida (FL) 98
University of Central Oklahoma (OK) 295
University of Charleston (WV) 379
University of Chicago (IL) 127
University of Cincinnati (OH) 288
University of Colorado at Boulder (CO) 78
University of Colorado at Colorado Springs (CO) 78
University of Colorado at Denver (CO) 79
University of Colorado Health Sciences Center (CO) 79
University of Connecticut (CT) 84
University of Dallas (TX) 354
University of Dayton (OH) 288
University of Delaware (DE) 85
University of Denver (CO) 79
University of Detroit Mercy (MI) 192
University of Dubuque (IA) 142
University of Evansville (IN) 136
The University of Findlay (OH) 288
University of Florida (FL) 98
University of Georgia (GA) 110
University of Great Falls (MT) 217
University of Hartford (CT) 84
University of Hawaii at Hilo (HI) 111
University of Hawaii at Manoa (HI) 111
University of Hawaii-West Oahu (HI) 112
University of Houston (TX) 354
University of Houston-Clear Lake (TX) 354
University of Houston-Downtown (TX) 354
University of Houston-Victoria (TX) 355
University of Idaho (ID) 113
University of Illinois at Chicago (IL) 127
University of Illinois at Springfield (IL) 127
University of Illinois at Urbana-Champaign (IL) 127

INDEX

University of Indianapolis (IN) 136
The University of Iowa (IA) 142
University of Judaism (CA) 71
University of Kansas (KS) 148
University of Kentucky (KY) 153
University of La Verne (CA) 71
University of Louisiana at Lafayette (LA) 158
University of Louisiana at Monroe (LA) 158
University of Louisville (KY) 154
University of Maine (ME) 161
The University of Maine at Augusta (ME) 161
University of Maine at Farmington (ME) 161
University of Maine at Fort Kent (ME) 161
University of Maine at Machias (ME) 162
University of Maine at Presque Isle (ME) 162
University of Mary (ND) 275
University of Mary Hardin-Baylor (TX) 355
University of Maryland, Baltimore County (MD) 167
University of Maryland, College Park (MD) 167, **485**
University of Maryland Eastern Shore (MD) 168
University of Maryland University College (MD) 168
University of Massachusetts Amherst (MA) 180
University of Massachusetts Boston (MA) 180
University of Massachusetts Dartmouth (MA) 180, **486**
University of Massachusetts Lowell (MA) 180
The University of Memphis (TN) 341
University of Miami (FL) 98
University of Michigan (MI) 192
University of Michigan-Dearborn (MI) 192
University of Michigan-Flint (MI) 193
University of Minnesota, Crookston (MN) 200, **487**
University of Minnesota, Duluth (MN) 200
University of Minnesota, Morris (MN) 201
University of Minnesota, Twin Cities Campus (MN) 201
University of Mississippi (MS) 204
University of Mississippi Medical Center (MS) 204
University of Missouri-Columbia (MO) 214
University of Missouri-Kansas City (MO) 214
University of Missouri-Rolla (MO) 214
University of Missouri-St. Louis (MO) 214

University of Mobile (AL) 40
The University of Montana-Missoula (MT) 217
The University of Montana-Western (MT) 217
University of Montevallo (AL) 40
University of Nebraska at Kearney (NE) 221
University of Nebraska at Omaha (NE) 221
University of Nebraska-Lincoln (NE) 221
University of Nebraska Medical Center (NE) 221
University of Nevada, Las Vegas (NV) 222
University of Nevada, Reno (NV) 222
University of New England (ME) 162
University of New Hampshire (NH) 225
University of New Hampshire at Manchester (NH) 225
University of New Haven (CT) 84
University of New Mexico (NM) 233
University of New Orleans (LA) 158
University of North Alabama (AL) 40
The University of North Carolina at Asheville (NC) 272
The University of North Carolina at Chapel Hill (NC) 272
The University of North Carolina at Charlotte (NC) 272
The University of North Carolina at Greensboro (NC) 272
The University of North Carolina at Pembroke (NC) 272
The University of North Carolina at Wilmington (NC) 273
University of North Dakota (ND) 275
University of Northern Colorado (CO) 79
University of Northern Iowa (IA) 143
University of North Florida (FL) 99
University of North Texas (TX) 355
University of Notre Dame (IN) 136
University of Oklahoma (OK) 295
University of Oklahoma Health Sciences Center (OK) 295
University of Oregon (OR) 300
University of Pennsylvania (PA) 319
University of Phoenix-Atlanta Campus (GA) 110
University of Phoenix-Boston Campus (MA) 181
University of Phoenix-Colorado Campus (CO) 79
University of Phoenix-Dallas/Ft. Worth Campus (TX) 355
University of Phoenix-Fort Lauderdale Campus (FL) 99

INDEX

University of Phoenix-Hawaii Campus (HI) 112
University of Phoenix-Houston Campus (TX) 355
University of Phoenix-Idaho Campus (ID) 113
University of Phoenix-Jacksonville Campus (FL) 99
University of Phoenix-Louisiana Campus (LA) 158
University of Phoenix-Maryland Campus (MD) 168
University of Phoenix-Metro Detroit Campus (MI) 193
University of Phoenix-Nevada Campus (NV) 222
University of Phoenix-New Mexico Campus (NM) 234
University of Phoenix-Northern California Campus (CA) 71
University of Phoenix-Ohio Campus (OH) 288
University of Phoenix-Oklahoma City Campus (OK) 295
University of Phoenix-Oregon Campus (OR) 300
University of Phoenix-Orlando Campus (FL) 99
University of Phoenix-Philadelphia Campus (PA) 320
University of Phoenix-Phoenix Campus (AZ) 45
University of Phoenix-Pittsburgh Campus (PA) 320
University of Phoenix-Sacramento Campus (CA) 71
University of Phoenix-St. Louis Campus (MO) 214
University of Phoenix-San Diego Campus (CA) 72
University of Phoenix-Southern Arizona Campus (AZ) 45
University of Phoenix-Southern California Campus (CA) 72
University of Phoenix-Southern Colorado Campus (CO) 80
University of Phoenix-Tampa Campus (FL) 99
University of Phoenix-Tulsa Campus (OK) 295
University of Phoenix-Utah Campus (UT) 359
University of Phoenix-Washington Campus (WA) 376
University of Phoenix-West Michigan Campus (MI) 193
University of Phoenix-Wisconsin Campus (WI) 385
University of Pittsburgh (PA) 320
University of Pittsburgh at Bradford (PA) 320
University of Pittsburgh at Greensburg (PA) 320
University of Pittsburgh at Johnstown (PA) 320
University of Portland (OR) 300
University of Puget Sound (WA) 376
University of Redlands (CA) 72
University of Rhode Island (RI) 325
University of Richmond (VA) 370
University of Rio Grande (OH) 288
University of Rochester (NY) 261
University of St. Francis (IL) 128
University of Saint Francis (IN) 136
University of St. Thomas (MN) 201
University of St. Thomas (TX) 355
University of San Diego (CA) 72, **488**
University of San Francisco (CA) 72
University of Sarasota (FL) 99
University of Sarasota, California Campus (CA) 72
University of Science and Arts of Oklahoma (OK) 296
The University of Scranton (PA) 321
University of Sioux Falls (SD) 334
University of South Alabama (AL) 41
University of South Carolina (SC) 330
University of South Carolina Aiken (SC) 330
University of South Carolina Spartanburg (SC) 331
The University of South Dakota (SD) 334
University of Southern California (CA) 73
University of Southern Colorado (CO) 80
University of Southern Indiana (IN) 136
University of Southern Maine (ME) 162
University of Southern Mississippi (MS) 204
University of South Florida (FL) 99, **489**
The University of Tampa (FL) 100
The University of Tennessee (TN) 342
The University of Tennessee at Chattanooga (TN) 342
The University of Tennessee at Martin (TN) 342
The University of Tennessee Health Science Center (TN) 342
The University of Texas at Arlington (TX) 356
The University of Texas at Austin (TX) 356
The University of Texas at Brownsville (TX) 356

INDEX

The University of Texas at Dallas (TX) 356
The University of Texas at El Paso (TX) 356
The University of Texas at San Antonio (TX) 357
The University of Texas at Tyler (TX) 357
The University of Texas Health Science Center at Houston (TX) 357
The University of Texas Health Science Center at San Antonio (TX) 357
The University of Texas Medical Branch (TX) 357
The University of Texas of the Permian Basin (TX) 357
The University of Texas-Pan American (TX) 358
The University of Texas Southwestern Medical Center at Dallas (TX) 358
The University of the Arts (PA) 321, **490**
University of the District of Columbia (DC) 88
University of the Incarnate Word (TX) 358
University of the Ozarks (AR) 49
University of the Pacific (CA) 73
University of the Sciences in Philadelphia (PA) 321
University of the South (TN) 342
University of Toledo (OH) 289
University of Tulsa (OK) 296
University of Utah (UT) 359
University of Vermont (VT) 363
University of Virginia (VA) 370
The University of Virginia's College at Wise (VA) 370
University of Washington (WA) 376
The University of West Alabama (AL) 41
University of West Florida (FL) 100
University of West Los Angeles (CA) 73
University of Wisconsin-Eau Claire (WI) 385
University of Wisconsin-Green Bay (WI) 385
University of Wisconsin-La Crosse (WI) 385
University of Wisconsin-Madison (WI) 386
University of Wisconsin-Milwaukee (WI) 386
University of Wisconsin-Oshkosh (WI) 386
University of Wisconsin-Parkside (WI) 386
University of Wisconsin-Platteville (WI) 386
University of Wisconsin-River Falls (WI) 387
University of Wisconsin-Stevens Point (WI) 387
University of Wisconsin-Stout (WI) 387

University of Wisconsin-Superior (WI) 387
University of Wisconsin-Whitewater (WI) 387
University of Wyoming (WY) 388
University System College for Lifelong Learning (NH) 225
Upper Iowa University (IA) 143
Urbana University (OH) 289
Ursinus College (PA) 321
Ursuline College (OH) 289
Utah State University (UT) 359
Utica College of Syracuse University (NY) 261

Valdosta State University (GA) 110
Valley City State University (ND) 276
Valley Forge Christian College (PA) 321
Valparaiso University (IN) 136, **491**
Vanderbilt University (TN) 343
VanderCook College of Music (IL) 128
Vanguard University of Southern California (CA) 73
Vassar College (NY) 261
Vermont Technical College (VT) 363
Villa Julie College (MD) 168
Villanova University (PA) 322
Virginia College at Birmingham (AL) 41
Virginia Commonwealth University (VA) 370
Virginia Intermont College (VA) 371
Virginia Military Institute (VA) 371
Virginia Polytechnic Institute and State University (VA) 371
Virginia State University (VA) 371
Virginia Union University (VA) 371
Virginia Wesleyan College (VA) 372, **492**
Viterbo University (WI) 388
Voorhees College (SC) 331

Wabash College (IN) 137
Wadhams Hall Seminary-College (NY) 262
Wagner College (NY) 262
Wake Forest University (NC) 273
Waldorf College (IA) 143
Walla Walla College (WA) 376
Walsh College of Accountancy and Business Administration (MI) 193
Walsh University (OH) 289
Warner Pacific College (OR) 300
Warner Southern College (FL) 100
Warren Wilson College (NC) 273, **493**
Wartburg College (IA) 143
Washburn University of Topeka (KS) 148
Washington & Jefferson College (PA) 322
Washington and Lee University (VA) 372
Washington Bible College (MD) 168

INDEX

Washington College (MD) 169, **494**
Washington State University (WA) 376
Washington University in St. Louis (MO) 215
Wayland Baptist University (TX) 358
Waynesburg College (PA) 322
Wayne State College (NE) 221
Wayne State University (MI) 193
Webber International University (FL) 100, **495**
Webb Institute (NY) 262
Weber State University (UT) 360
Webster University (MO) 215
Wellesley College (MA) 181
Wells College (NY) 262, **496**
Wentworth Institute of Technology (MA) 181, **497**
Wesleyan College (GA) 110
Wesleyan University (CT) 84
Wesley College (DE) 85
Wesley College (MS) 204
West Chester University of Pennsylvania (PA) 322
Western Baptist College (OR) 301
Western Carolina University (NC) 273
Western Connecticut State University (CT) 85
Western Governors University (UT) 360
Western Illinois University (IL) 128, **498**
Western International University (AZ) 46
Western Kentucky University (KY) 154
Western Maryland College (MD) 169
Western Michigan University (MI) 194, **499**
Western Montana College (MT) 217
Western New England College (MA) 181
Western New Mexico University (NM) 234
Western Oregon University (OR) 301
Western State College of Colorado (CO) 80
Western States Chiropractic College (OR) 301
Western Washington University (WA) 376
Westfield State College (MA) 181
West Liberty State College (WV) 380
Westminster Choir College of Rider University (NJ) 231
Westminster College (MO) 215
Westminster College (PA) 322
Westminster College (UT) 360
Westmont College (CA) 73
West Suburban College of Nursing (IL) 128
West Texas A&M University (TX) 358
West Virginia State College (WV) 380
West Virginia University (WV) 380
West Virginia University Institute of Technology (WV) 380
West Virginia Wesleyan College (WV) 380

Wheaton College (IL) 128
Wheaton College (MA) 181
Wheeling Jesuit University (WV) 381
Wheelock College (MA) 182
White Pines College (NH) 225
Whitman College (WA) 377
Whittier College (CA) 73
Whitworth College (WA) 377
Wichita State University (KS) 148
Widener University (PA) 323
Wilberforce University (OH) 289
Wiley College (TX) 359
Wilkes University (PA) 323
Willamette University (OR) 301
William Carey College (MS) 205
William Jewell College (MO) 215
William Paterson University of New Jersey (NJ) 232, **500**
William Penn University (IA) 143
Williams Baptist College (AR) 49
Williams College (MA) 182
William Tyndale College (MI) 194
William Woods University (MO) 215
Wilmington College (DE) 86
Wilmington College (OH) 289
Wilson College (PA) 323
Wingate University (NC) 273
Winona State University (MN) 201
Winston-Salem State University (NC) 274
Winthrop University (SC) 331
Wisconsin Lutheran College (WI) 388
Wittenberg University (OH) 290
Wofford College (SC) 331
Woodbury University (CA) 74
Worcester Polytechnic Institute (MA) 182
Worcester State College (MA) 182
World College (VA) 372
Wright State University (OH) 290

Xavier University (OH) 290
Xavier University of Louisiana (LA) 159

Yale University (CT) 85
Yeshiva Beth Moshe (PA) 323
Yeshiva Derech Chaim (NY) 262
Yeshiva Geddolah of Greater Detroit Rabbinical College (MI) 194
Yeshiva Karlin Stolin Rabbinical Institute (NY) 262
Yeshiva of Nitra Rabbinical College (NY) 263
Yeshiva Ohr Elchonon Chabad/West Coast Talmudical Seminary (CA) 74
Yeshiva Shaar Hatorah Talmudic Research Institute (NY) 263
Yeshivath Viznitz (NY) 263

INDEX

Yeshivath Zichron Moshe (NY) 263
Yeshivat Mikdash Melech (NY) 263
Yeshiva Toras Chaim Talmudical Seminary (CO) 80
Yeshiva University (NY) 263

York College (NE) 222
York College of Pennsylvania (PA) 323
York College of the City University of New York (NY) 263
Youngstown State University (OH) 290